icp
INTERNATIONAL CENTER OF PHOTOGRAPHY

ENCYCLOPEDIA OF PHOTOGRAPHY

icp

INTERNATIONAL CENTER OF PHOTOGRAPHY

ENCYCLOPEDIA OF PHOTOGRAPHY

A POUND PRESS BOOK

CROWN PUBLISHERS, INC.   NEW YORK

A Pound Press/Crown Publishers, Inc. Book
Published by Crown Publishers, Inc.
One Park Avenue, New York, New York 10016 and simultaneously in Canada by
General Publishing Company Limited.

This book was produced in conjunction with
The Photographic Book Co., a division of
PBC International, Inc.

Library of Congress Cataloging in Publication Data
Main entry under title:

ICP encyclopedia of photography.

   "A Pound Press Book."
   1. Photography—Dictionaries. I. International
Center of Photography. II. Title: I C P encyclopedia
of photography.
TR9.I24   1984   770'.3'21   84-1856
ISBN 0-517-55271-X

10   9   8   7   6   5   4   3   2   1

First Edition

Printed in Hong Kong

STAFF FOR THE ICP ENCYCLOPEDIA OF PHOTOGRAPHY

Editorial Director	**Cornell Capa** **Director, ICP**
Editor-in-Chief	**Jerry Mason**
Editor	**William L. Broecker**
Managing Editor	**Michael Mason**
Editorial Production	**The Photographic Book Co.**

Staff for ICP

Archives and Collections	**Miles Barth**
Director of Special Exhibitions	**William A. Ewing**
Executive Assistant	**Anna Winand**
Research/Cataloger, Archives and Collections	**Gina Medcalf**
International Board of Advisers for Photographer Inclusion	**Ryszard Bobrowski (Poland), Rosellina Burri-Bischof (Switzerland), Lanfranco Colombo (Italy), Robert Delpire (France), James Enyeart (U.S.A.), Anna Farova (Czechoslovakia), Roy Flukinger (U.S.A.), Arthur Goldsmith (U.S.A.), Julia Van Haaften (U.S.A.), Rune Hassner (Sweden), Manfred Heiting (Germany), Boris Kossoy (Brazil), Robert Kirschenbaum (Japan), Jean-Claude Lemagny (France), David Mellor (England)**

Staff for The Photographic Book Company

Executive Director	**Herb Taylor**
Production Director	**Cora Sibal**
Managing Editor	**Linda Z. Weinraub**
Photo Editor	**Christopher Bain**
Art Director	**Richard Liu**
Art Associates	**Charlene Sison** **Erlinda Dintemann**
Contributors	**Jaroslav Andel, Algis Balsys, Peter Bates, Dinah Berland, Ryszard Bobrowski, William L. Broecker, Sally Eauclaire, John Egana, William Ewing, Joan Fontcuberta, Don Garbera, Dorothy Gelatt, Jeremy George, Jeffrey Gilbert, Arthur Goldsmith, Jan Grover, Judith Gutman, Rune Hassner, Manfred Heiting, James Hugunin, Boris Kossoy, Leonard Lessin, Steven Henry Madoff, John McDonald, Gina Medcalf, Nicolas Monti, Kate Nearpass, Chris Philipps, John Phillips, Gerald Pozniak, Martin Silverman, Michael Simon, Georgia Smith, Abigail Solomon-Godeau, Ruth Spencer, Maren Stange, Rosella Stern, William Tyler, David Vestal, Robert Walsh, Wendell White, Leif Wigh, Anna Winand.**

How to Use the Encyclopedia

- Entries are listed alphabetically according to letter sequence in each heading, without regard for spaces, up to a comma. For example:

  > Niépce, Joseph Nicéphore
  > Niépce de Saint-Victor, Claude Félix Abel
  > Niépceotype

  Similarly, abbreviations are entered in alphabetical order according to their letter sequence, not the words for which the letters stand. For example:

  > Annan, Thomas
  > Ansco
  > ANSI
  > Anthony, Edward

- Although there are a few entries for specific products of major importance in the development of photography (e.g., **Kodachrome; Leica**), in general look first for the generic name of a process, material, or piece of equipment, and for the last name of an individual. Some 100-plus headings are "blind" entries that will guide you to the articles where that topic is included in the discussion.

- In the case of individuals for whom there is no separate entry, look for the activity or process with which they are associated.

- The cross-references listed at the end of an article in SMALL CAPITALS direct you to entries where a significant amount of additional or related information will be found. There may also be topics mentioned in an article for which there are entries that are not included in the cross-references. In most cases, photographers mentioned within an article are not included in the cross-references so as to avoid undue repetition; however there may well be entries for them. It is assumed you will look for the names and topics that are of interest to you in addition to those listed.

- Familiarize yourself with the various appendices. They cover books and periodicals; clubs, societies, associations; and photographers not treated in individual entries.

Contents

Editor's Preface

The *ICP Encyclopedia of Photography* is intended to give the general reader a comprehensive view of the medium in a single volume. The view provided by some 1,300 entries describes the current state of the aesthetic, communicative, scientific, technical, and commercial applications of photography; it describes how the medium developed; and it identifies the photographers, scientists, and inventors who have been and are responsible for this development.

Several categories of entries are used to accomplish this purpose. Historical entries describe the invention and development of the equipment, materials, processes, and procedures of photography. For convenient reference, the major entries of this sort are included in summary lists within the articles **History of Photography** and **Color Photography—History.** Many of the articles dealing with the applications of photography (e.g., **Advertising Photography; Architectural Photography**) include sections that trace the historical development of that aspect of the medium.

Entries devoted to processes, techniques, and applications for the most part describe principles and methods. In many cases there is sufficient specific information in an article to permit carrying out a process, but it is expected that the reader especially interested in operational detail will consult the extensive bibliographical appendix to discover the most useful handbooks, manuals, and other instructional publications on the topic of interest. This appendix also lists works of photographic biography, history, criticism and appreciation, aesthetic theory, scientific principles, collecting, business practices, compilations of photographers' pictures, and periodicals.

Some 250 biographical entries deal with photographers whose work has shaped and defined the expressive and communicative uses of the medium; many other photographers are mentioned in entries dealing with the applications and the history of photography. An additional 100-plus biographical entries are devoted to scientists, inventors, and others who have influenced the growth of the medium by achievements other than the production of images. The photographers chosen for biographical treatment were selected by an international board of advisors (listed on page 5). Each advisor was asked to nominate the individuals whose photographs were of major importance in that individual's country or area of activity. Nominations were limited to photographers born before 1940 so that even the youngest persons included are now in mid-career and have had ample time to achieve recognition for significant work, not just youthful promise. The list was reviewed and revised several times in consultation with the advisors, and many painful eliminations were made in order to come within the space limitations of a one-volume, multi-topic work while maintaining an appropriate historical, aesthetic, and international balance. These biographical entries are supplemented by the biographical appendix, which lists more than 2,000 photographers of importance.

A significant number of entries are devoted to aesthetic, expressive, and communicative aspects of photography (e.g., **Art of Photography; Criticism of Photography; Documentary and Social Documentary Photography; Fantasy in Photography; Photojournalism**) so as to discuss the development of content in the medium as well as the development of technical procedures. Other entries (e.g., **Contrast; Exposure; Latent Image**) explain the physical and chemical theory and principles of the medium. Still other entries are devoted to topics such as collecting, books and literature, museums and collections, agencies and picture libraries, copyright, permissions, selling and exhibiting photographs, and many other related subjects. Because photographic societies, organizations, and associations are so numerous, it was not possible to give them individual treatments; instead, they are included in an appendix.

In a one-volume work, the length of individual articles must necessarily be quite limited. Within the allotted space, the contributors have diligently attempted to be simultaneously thorough and concise. The level of discussion is appropriate to the intelligent general reader, as well as the photographic specialist. It is the function of an encyclopedia to explain what has been and what is, not to attempt to describe the future; speculation and prediction are the province of periodicals, not reference works. As with all reference works that attempt to include the contemporary state of things, there is the problem that the contemporary state is evolving and changing even as the book is being prepared. Great effort has been made to include the most current information, and to include only those developments which appear to be truly significant contributions or advances in the medium. There are undoubtedly errors of omission and misplaced emphasis. It is hoped that they are minor, and that the reader will keep in mind that preparing an encyclopedia is a human and therefore fallible enterprise. Fortunately, a book can be revised, corrected, and updated in subsequent editions. Suggestions toward that end from users of the encyclopedia will be welcome.

—WILLIAM L. BROECKER

Introduction

When Jerry Mason of Pound Press approached the International Center of Photography two years ago with the proposal of creating a single-volume encyclopedia of photography, we were intrigued by the idea. We knew that there was a great need for such a book. ICP is involved in photographic exhibitions, collections, and education programming requiring such a resource. We welcomed the opportunity to help ourselves, as well as the world outside, and agreed to collaborate.

All concerned sought to produce a volume light enough to hold in hand, beautiful to look at, and inexpensive enough for wide public use, one that would cover the range from the aesthetic and historical to the technical and practical aspects of the medium. We attempted to obtain a selection of photographs that would appropriately illustrate the work of photographers proposed by our international advisors, work that would demonstrate historical perspective and the beauty, as well as the reality and the unimaginable variety of imagery, inherent in the medium.

The encyclopedia's main function is to document the scope of photography since its invention; to demonstrate in words and images its power and range of artistic expression; to provide a tight list of pioneers of the medium, those who have invented, created, and provided it with something unique of their own. These biographical entries provide some factual detail and insight into the works of each individual selected. This list includes only those born during or just prior to the first 100 years since the beginning of the medium, that is, between 1840 and 1940. Admittedly, this is a limiting decision, but it has the merit of allowing for the test of time and perspective on the work performed.

The additional listing of over 2,000 photographers provides a skeletal reference about the known important practitioners of the medium. The bibliography facilitates the further opportunity to learn more about these important photographers.

You will find in appropriate places credits for the many contributors who made this volume possible. I would like to thank Jerry Mason for his faith and vision, William L. Broecker for the massive writing and editing work he poured forth, and The Photographic Book Co. staff under Herb Taylor's direction for their unflagging production effort. Grateful acknowledgement is extended to our international advisors, to David Eisendrath, Jr., for his many helpful suggestions, and to the staff members of ICP for their candor and generosity of spirit in making their recommendations.

—CORNELL CAPA
Director
International Center of Photography

Abbe, Ernst

German; 1840–1905

A physicist, Ernst Abbe was professor of physics and mathematics and director of the astronomical and meteorological observatories at the University of Jena (now in East Germany). From 1866 he was also a partner and technical director of the Carl Zeiss Optical Works, of which he became owner after the death of Zeiss in 1888. Abbe designed innovative lenses, particularly substage condensers and oil-immersion objectives for microscopes, supervised research, and made scientific investigations in optics and the chemistry of glass. He devised a mathematical method and a practical instrument for measuring the refractive index (light-bending power) of glass, to obtain a quantity known today as the Abbe number assigned to each kind of optical glass. In the mid-1880s, Abbe, Zeiss, and Otto Schott formed a company under Schott's name and direction to develop and manufacture new kinds of glass incorporating borate and phosphate compounds. These new *Jena glasses* had optical properties superior to common crown and flint glasses. They made possible revolutionary lens designs for photography, astronomy, and microscopy, including the first anastigmat, calculated by Abbe and manufactured by Zeiss.

See also: ANASTIGMAT; JENA GLASS; REFRACTION; ZEISS, CARL.

Abbe, James

American; 1883–1973

For two decades in the first half of the 20th c., James Abbe was one of the world's leading photographers of high society and the entertainment world, known for his masterful lighting of studio portraiture. Among his famous sitters were Fred Astaire, the Gish sisters, Charles Chaplin, Rudolph Valentino, Mary Pickford, Noel Coward, and Irving Berlin. Abbe was also a photojournalist in the 1930s who photographed such world leaders as Hitler, Mussolini, Stalin, Franklin Roosevelt, and Franco, and documented Russia under Stalin and the beginnings of Hitler's regime.

Abbe was born in Alfred, Maine and educated at public schools in Newport News, Virginia. He began to photograph at age 12 and worked in his father's bookstore from 1898 to 1910. After photographing sailors and ships for tourist cards, Abbe was a freelance photojournalist in Virginia from 1913 to 1917 when he established a studio in New York City. He was based in New York for the next six years, publishing the first photocover of the *Saturday Evening Post,* and stage photography in the *New York Times,* the *Ladies' Home Journal,* and other popular periodicals.

In 1922–1923 Abbe worked as a still photographer, actor, and writer for film studios in Hollywood, New York, and Italy, collaborating with Mack Sennett and D.W. Griffith. From 1924 to 1932 he operated a studio in Paris but traveled extensively in Europe, Mexico, and U.S.S.R. His work appeared in such journals as *Vu, Vogue, Vanity Fair, Harper's Bazaar,* and *Berliner Illustrirte Zeitung,* and he began writing accompanying text in 1930. Abbe covered the Mexican revolution in 1932 and was the first foreign correspondent to photograph Stalin when the Russian leader gained power.

An important book of Abbe's images, *I Photograph Russia,* was published in 1934. Abbe returned to the United States that year and worked in Larkspur, Colorado as a freelance photojournalist until 1936. His last photographic work was done as a war correspondent for the North American *Alliance* newspapers in 1936–1937, covering the Loyalist side in the Spanish Civil War.

From 1938 until his retirement in 1961, Abbe worked briefly as a rancher, then as a radio broadcaster (at one point, he had his own news show called "James Abbe Observes") and television critic in San Francisco and Oakland, California. He died at the age of 90 in 1973. A major collection of his celebrity portraits, *Stars of the Twenties,* was published in 1975.

Abbe's work was included in group shows at the Victoria and Albert Museum, London, in 1975; George Eastman House, Rochester, N.Y., in 1977; Kunsthaus, Zurich, in 1979; and

the International Center of Photography, New York, in 1979. He was honored by solo exhibitions at the Washburn Gallery, New York, in 1975, 1976, 1978, and 1983; Canon Photo Gallery, Amsterdam, in 1976; and Photographer's Gallery, London, in 1977.

Abbott, Berenice

American; 1898–

Like many other aspiring young artists of her generation, and with no notion of becoming a photographer, Berenice Abbott left New York for Paris in 1918, intending to become a sculptor. For two years she traveled between Paris and Berlin, the world centers of contemporary art, finally settling in Paris and becoming a photographic assistant to Man Ray. By 1925 she was a professional portrait photographer. Her photographs of this period—including many of the ma-

jor art and literary figures of the 1920s (Cocteau, Duchamp, Gide, Joyce, Mauriac, etc.)—are characterized by careful lighting, a natural quality of pose and expression, and the formal clarity and precision that Abbott has always claimed as her goal.

Paris was as rich in émigré photographers as it was in artists, those photographers including Brassaï, Gisèle Freund, André Kertesz, Germaine Krull, and Man Ray. It was, however, the photography of 70-year-old Eugène Atget that struck Abbott with the force of revelation and that seems to have furnished her with a sense of aesthetic ancestry and a clear direction for her future work. Describing Atget's photographs, years later Abbott wrote: "Their impact was immediate and tremendous . . . a sudden flash of recognition—the shock of realism unadorned." After Atget's death in 1927, Abbott purchased (aided by the dealer Julien Levy) the

thousands of negatives and prints from his meager estate. Until their sale in 1968 to the Museum of Modern Art in New York, she functioned as a virtual curator of the Atget material, printing, publishing, and exhibiting it.

While the "realism unadorned" of Atget's work provided Abbott with a formal prototype, the overall subject of Atget's photography—an encyclopedic documentation of Old Paris and its environs—may have suggested to her the value of such a record. Returning to New York in 1929, she embarked upon a similar project, photographing in a systematic, precise, and detailed fashion the rapidly changing face of New York City. Attentive to both the smallest details and the largest architectural configurations, recording individual shop windows or canyons of skyscrapers, Abbott found an inexhaustible subject in the urban landscape. For four years she supported the project herself, working for maga-

Abbott, Berenice. "Exchange Place" (n.d.). Courtesy Berenice Abbott.

zines such as *Fortune* and *Life* and teaching photography at The New School for Social Research in 1934. In 1935 the project, now entitled "Changing New York," became an official documentation supported by the Works Project Administration of the Federal Art Project (WPA). In 1939 a selection of the photographs was published as a book under the same title.

Abbott had occasionally photographed scientific subjects for *Life* magazine; however, by the 1950s her understanding of how scientific principles could be photographically illustrated expanded into a commissioned project for the Physical Science Study Committee. This resulted in an exhibition ("The Image of Physics") and in three secondary school books on physics illustrated with Abbott's photographs.

Abbott's next major project was a photographic documentation of U.S. Route No. 1, running from Maine to Florida. It was in the course of this photographic project that Abbott discovered Maine, to which she subsequently relocated.

An aesthetic of modernist realism has stamped all of Abbott's work, from the early Paris portraits to the massive collective portrait of New York City to the graphic and inventive scientific photography of the 1950s. For Abbott "speed and science" constituted both the essence of photography and the essence of the 20th c.; for all the art inherent in her pictures, it was in a single-minded pursuit of those qualities that Abbott created her impressive body of work.

See also: ATGET, EUGENE; RAY, MAN.

Aberrations of Lenses

Lens aberrations are deviations from perfect image-forming performance. They occur because the refractive index (bending power) of a given kind of optical glass or plastic is not the same for all wavelengths of light, and because the degree of curvature sufficient to focus light striking a given zone of the lens surface from a particular angle may be insufficient (or more than sufficient) for light rays striking the same zone at a different angle. The result may be one or more of the following conditions:

1. Light rays (or the wavelengths constituting the rays) diverging from a given subject point are not converged (focused) to a correspondingly distinct image point, but instead form a minute patch of greater size laterally, in depth, or both.

2. Light rays from points on a flat plane at the focused subject distance are not all imaged on a corresponding flat plane.

3. Light from points at various lateral distances from the lens axis is not imaged at exactly corresponding distances from the axis.

The specific aberrations created by these conditions are described below. Aberrations are corrected in lens design and manufacture by combining lens elements of different kinds of glass with various degrees of surface curvature and spacing so that the performance errors of one element are counteracted by another. "Correction" is a relative term, for aberrations cannot be eliminated completely; in practice it means reducing aberrations to the point at which their effects on image quality are insignificant for the purposes for which a given lens is to be employed. Modern photographic lenses of even quite low cost generally have a degree of correction at least equal to that available in the best lenses of 50–75 years ago. The finest lenses today are so nearly free of fundamental aberrations that their images are of higher optical quality than can be recorded by most contemporary emulsions.

Fundamental Aberrations. There are seven fundamental aberrations of concern in practical photographic optics. They are known as third-order Seidel aberrations, named for the optical mathematician who in 1855 ranked the complexity of various lens anomalies and their correction. The chromatic aberrations vary in degree with the wavelength composition of the light; the other aberrations have essentially equal effects on all wavelengths. The seven aberrations are as follows.

Spherical aberration. Light rays from a given subject point that pass through the outer areas of the lens converge to cross the axis closer to the lens than rays that pass through the central area. The result is a circular patch of light with a bright center, rather than a clearly defined bright point; these patches produce reduced sharpness and lower contrast throughout the image. So-called portrait lenses have purposely uncorrected (or slightly corrected) spherical aberration. Correction of this aberration is accomplished by the use of positive-negative element pairs which have opposite degrees of spherical aberration; by the use of glass with a high refractive index so that minimum surface curvatures are required; or by the use of one or more elements with aspheric surfaces. Reducing the lens aperture also reduces spherical aberration because this blocks the light rays passing through the outer lens zones; however, it is an impractical primary method of control because of its effect on exposure.

Axial or longitudinal chromatic aber-

ration. The wavelengths constituting each ray of light are dispersed as they are refracted and are brought to a focus at different distances behind the lens; the blue wavelengths are focused closest to the lens, the red wavelengths farthest away, and the other wavelengths are ranged between. Wherever the focal plane (film) is placed within this range, there will be sharp points for objects of the wavelength color focused there, surrounded by unsharp circles formed by the other wavelengths; objects of other colors will not be focused as sharply. Reducing the lens aperture improves sharpness because it increases the depth of focus at the image plane. Correction is achieved by the use of glasses with different dispersive characteristics for specific wavelength ranges. A lens corrected for chromatic aberration of two colors—usually yellow and blue-green—is called an *achromat;* one corrected for three colors (red, yellow, and blue-green) is an *apochromat.*

Transverse or lateral chromatic aberration. Dispersion of light rays striking the lens obliquely produces different degrees of magnification of an object or a subject point; the magnification varies according to wavelength. The result is red-green-blue fringing around object edges in color photographs or unsharp edges in black-and-white photographs. Reducing aperture size does not affect this aberration.

Astigmatism. Light rays striking the lens obliquely from a given point are not necessarily dispersed, but they are never converged to a distinct point. At some distance behind the lens the point is imaged as a short, straight line in one direction, and at a greater distance as a short line in a direction at right angles to the first; midway between these two distances there is a circle of least confusion (or elliptical distortion) representing the subject point. If the subject is a wagon wheel, for example, it is possible to obtain a sharp image of the spokes or of the rim, but not of both simultaneously; the midway focal position produces an equal degree of unsharpness in the radial (spoke) and the tangential (rim) elements. Correction of astigmatism requires the use of at least three separate elements of different refractive index and carefully computed differences in surface curvature; a greater number of elements is required if some are to be cemented together.

Coma. Off-axis light rays striking the lens obliquely from a subject point are imaged as a series of overlapping circles of different size according to whether they passed through outer or central zones of the lens. The result is a bright point that blurs at one side into a widening patch of light somewhat like the tail of a comet; the overall effect is reduced image contrast. Correction is similar to that for astigmatism, but more difficult to achieve.

Field curvature. The sharpest image forms a curved (spherical) plane on which each point is the same distance from the optical center of the lens; this condition is a direct consequence of lens elements having spherical surfaces. Since the film plane is flat, the image there is not uniformly sharp because the edges and corners are at a greater distance from the optical center of the lens than is the center of the film. Reducing the lens aperture improves overall sharpness because it increases the depth of focus. Special optical formulas are used in *flat-field lenses* to overcome this aberration. Such lenses are used extensively in graphic arts and copy work and commonly are also apochromats.

Curvilinear distortion. Straight subject lines are imaged as curving lines because the degree of magnification varies continuously outward from the center of the lens. In *pincushion distortion,* lines bow inward toward the center of the field; in *barrel distortion* they bow outward. The location of the aperture in relation to the optical center of the lens generally determines which kind of distortion will occur. In lenses of narrow and moderate coverage angles, the aperture can be placed so that no noticeable distortion is produced. In very-wide-angle lenses barrel distortion is extremely difficult to avoid; in fisheye lenses it is not avoided, but is deliberately designed-in, for reasonable sharpness over the entire field can only be achieved at the expense of pronounced curvilinear distortion.

See also: DISPERSION; DISTORTION; LENSES; OPTICS; REFRACTION.

Abney, Sir William de Wiveleslie

English; 1843–1920

A chemist and major contributor to the early growth of the scientific understanding of photography, Abney was responsible for a number of discoveries and inventions, including: negative intensification with copper bromide and silver nitrate; the first silver chloride gelatin-emulsion printing-out paper; the use of hydroquinone as a developing agent; and the intermittency effect in exposure. He was the first true authority on photography to assume (in 1892) presidency of the Photographic Society of London; in his second year of tenure the Society gained the patronage of Queen Victoria and became the Royal Photographic Society of Great Britain. He served as president in two later terms, for a total of five years service, and twice received the Progress Medal of the Society. His investigations and writings included work on the chemistry of photography, sensitometry, densitometry, photometry, spectral analysis, and solarization.

Abstract Photography

Two major approaches have been common in producing abstract images in photography. In one, a single attribute of the subject—e.g., form, texture, pattern, or color—is exaggerated and emphasized so as to become the major aspect of representation, while all other characteristics are suppressed or deemphasized; however, the subject generally remains recognizable. In the second approach the image is nonrepresentational or nonobjective: shapes, forms, tones, or colors not associated with an identifiable subject are presented for the purpose of evoking aesthetic or emotional response.

The earliest photographic experimentation, at the very beginning of the 19th c., produced unintentional abstraction of form in reverse-tone silhouettes created by placing objects on sensitized material for exposure. However, the abstract character of these rudimentary photograms was not recognized as a mode of expressive representation. The first intentional abstract photographs are generally considered to be the work of Alvin Langdon Coburn, who in 1912 produced a series of pictures entitled "New York from Its Pinnacles." Aiming his camera downward from some of the tallest buildings in the city, he obtained a flattened perspective without a horizon line that emphasized the two-dimensional pattern aspect of the scene below. Coburn's growing interest in the abstraction and manipulation of forms for aesthetic rather than descriptive purposes soon resulted in the first nonobjective images in photography. In 1916 he produced a series of *Vortographs,* created by photographing pebbles, bits of broken glass, and similar material through an improvised kaleidoscope; the content of such images was a random pattern of shapes and tones repeated in two or more segments with mirror-image symmetry. Exploitation of the photogram technique as a mode of producing nonobjective abstract images began with collage records (Schadographs) made by Christian Schad in 1918, and in the work of Laszlo Moholy-Nagy and Man Ray, both of whom developed this method extensively during the 1920s. Moholy-Nagy also created light modulators—plastic sculptural constructions with kinetic illumination—which were photographed to record abstract tonal patterns. Francis Bruguière achieved similar effects by projecting light from various angles onto abstract forms constructed of rolled, folded, and cut paper and photographing the modulations of light and shade. Lotte Jacobi produced images of great tonal complexity and subtle beauty by photographing light projected on flat and curved white surfaces, and by recording the traces of a light source attached to the end of a free-swinging pendulum (physiograms). Many other photographers have explored these and similar techniques. Other methods of producing nonrepresentational patterns and colors include the random treatment of films or papers with splashes of chemical solutions; the creation of "negatives" by treating plastic or glass with ink, paints, crystallizing solutions, heat, engraving, or abrasion; the use of optical distortion materials or liquids in front of lenses or light sources; and the use of manipulatable electronic signals either to expose film or paper directly, or to create a pattern on a cathode-ray tube which is then photographed. This list is only suggestive, not exhaustive.

The distortion of forms which remain essentially recognizable has usually been accomplished by optical means such as unsymmetrical apertures (self-portraits by the futurist Antonio Bragaglia), distorting mirrors (nudes by André Kertész), and extreme-wide-angle lenses (nudes by Bill Brandt). The manipulatable surface of contemporary materials such as Polaroid SX-70 film has been exploited by Lucas Samaras and others to create distortions of form and color while an image is processing. Combinations of elements and images, distorted or undistorted, in the manner of surrealism, expressionism, and similar movements have generally been produced by multiple exposure (Francis Bruguière), montage (Moholy-Nagy), or combination and multiple printing (Jerry N. Uelsmann).

Especially before the 1950s, the imagery of abstract photography largely derived from prior accomplishments in painting, often with a time lag of up to a decade, and this in spite of the freely acknowledged influence of photographic visual revelations on painters—e.g., the derivation of Marcel Duchamp's "Nude Descending a Staircase" from chronophotographs of E. J. Marey. While much of photographic abstraction was blatantly imitative of painting, some

workers achieved a true integration of the aesthetic attitudes of a movement in painting with the unique qualities of the photographic medium. The abstract expressionist close-ups of cracked paint, rusting metal, and other fragments made by Aaron Siskind are examples of this kind of fusion.

Direct, optically undistorted records of natural subjects often have been given an abstract character by means of tonal change: negative images, extreme high contrast, posterization, extreme or "incorrect" filtration, the use of infrared-sensitive or other specialized materials, and similar techniques. Far more subtle and aesthetically complex are images in which the undistorted, realistic representation of which "straight" photography is capable is fully utilized, and the abstract content is a result only of the way in which the subject was viewed. Such images operate simultaneously on the levels of documentary realism and aesthetic abstraction; examples include Edward Weston's photographs of nudes, dune, clouds, shells, and vegetables, and Paul Strand's images of architectural and household or machine details. Many straightforward scientific photographs, such as electron micrographs, have abstract qualities attributed to them because the subject matter is unidentifiable but evokes the same kind of aesthetic response as acknowledged abstractions.

The *equivalents* of Alfred Stieglitz, direct images of clouds, are a kind of aesthetic-philosophical abstraction meant to symbolize inner experience but not by means of stylized representation; the experience derived from the picture depends upon what the viewer brings to it, and the function of the image is simply to serve as an emotionally neutral point of contact between the sensibility of the viewer and that of the photographer. The concept was further explored by Minor White, who insisted that beyond the level of humanistic and aesthetic response, the function of an equivalent was to trigger a religico-mystical experience—perhaps the most abstruse and least visual attitude so far developed toward abstract photography.
See also: Entries for individual photographers cited; EQUIVALENT IMAGE; FANTASY IN PHOTOGRAPHY; MINIMALISM IN PHOTOGRAPHY; PHOTOGRAM; SUBJECTIVE PHOTOGRAPHY; SURREALISM IN PHOTOGRAPHY.
Color photograph: p. C-1.

Achromat

An achromat is a lens corrected for chromatic aberration so as to bring two colors to a common focus: usually blue-

violet because all emulsions have primary sensitivity to those wavelengths, and yellow or yellow-red because those wavelengths are a major portion of the brightest image preferred for focusing. The uncorrected wavelengths constitute the *secondary spectrum,* which has little significant effect in most photography; in fact, virtually all ordinary camera lenses are achromats. A lens corrected for a third color is an apochromat.
See also: ABERRATIONS OF LENSES; APOCHROMAT; LENSES.

Acid

An acid is a compound of hydrogen which yields hydrogen ions in a chemical reaction in order to accept metallic ions and form a compound called a salt. Acids have pH values of less than 7; in concentrated form they are very corrosive and must be handled with care. When being diluted or added to a solution, a concentrated acid must be added slowly to the water, not the reverse, so as to avoid boiling or spattering. The major acid in photography is acetic acid, used in a stop bath to neutralize the alkalinity of developer absorbed in the emulsion, and used in a fixer to improve the efficiency of the solution and to enable a hardener, if one is included, to be effective. Boric acid—one of the few acids in powder or crystalline rather than liquid form—is used as a buffer in fixers to extend the working life by maintaining the required level of acidity. Sulfuric acid is used in reducers, bleach baths, and solutions to remove stains from processing equipment.
See also: pH.

Actinic

The ability of certain wavelengths of the electromagnetic spectrum to cause changes in various substances is called the actinic power of the energy. Ultraviolet and almost all visible wavelengths are actinic for all panchromatic emulsions; they create the change called exposure. Only portions of the visible wavelengths (and ultraviolet) are actinic for orthochromatic and blue-sensitive emulsions. Infrared energy is actinic for specially sensitized emulsions such as false-color film. X-rays, gamma rays, and cosmic rays also have an actinic effect on photographic materials.

Action Photography

Moving subjects can be photographed to render all elements of the picture sharp or to make either the background or the subject blurred. The first technique permits close examination of the subject, while the second provides a visual equivalent of the subjective feeling of movement. Ordinary contemporary cameras offer shutter speeds up to 1/4000 sec., permitting sharp, action-freezing pictures of most human, animal, and vehicular movement if there is sufficient light. Portable electronic flash units typically provide bursts of light 1/750 to 1/25,000 sec. in length, depending upon their power, distance to the subject, and related factors. Such units make it possible to freeze movement regardless of the ambient light level. Specialized equipment and techniques, described in the entry on high-speed photography, can make exposures as short as one picosecond (one million-millionth, or 10^{-12} sec.).

In non-flash photography the shutter speed required to freeze movement of a given speed depends on two factors: the direction of the movement relative to the film plane and the image size of the moving element. Action across the field of view at a constant distance (i.e., parallel to the film plane) requires a faster shutter speed than action diagonally toward or away from the camera, which in turn requires a faster shutter speed than head-on action directly toward or away from the camera. For any given direction of movement, larger image size—whether produced by moving closer to the subject or by using a longer-focal-length lens—requires a faster shutter speed to obtain equal sharpness. For example, the following shutter speeds are the typical maximums required to freeze various movements across the field at a distance of 10–15 feet (3–4.5 meters), using a normal-focal-length lens:

Activity	Shutter Speed
Slow walking; gestures	1/500 sec.
Fast walking; vehicles 10–15 mph (16–24 km/hr)	1/1000 sec.
Sports; running; vehicles 20–40 mph (32–64 km/hr)	1/2000 sec.
Animals racing; birds flying; vehicles to about 65 mph (105 km/hr)	1/4000 sec.

If the movement is diagonally across the field of view, a shutter speed half as fast as those given will usually be sufficient; if the movement is directly toward or away from the camera, a shutter speed one-fourth as fast may be used. Similar-ly, if the image size is reduced, a proportionally slower shutter speed may be used. For example, doubling the distance (or using a lens of half the focal length) reduces the image size by one half, permitting a shutter speed half as fast to be used.

A blurred subject is recorded simply by using a shutter speed too slow for the speed and direction of the action. A blurred background is produced by panning (swinging) the camera to follow the moving subject; a relatively slow shutter speed, such as 1/50 or 1/25 sec., will record most subjects sharply while the background is blurred by the camera movement. Some subject blurring may also occur if the shutter speed or panning is too slow, or if extremities of the subject (such as the hands and feet of a runner) are moving at a greater rate.
See also: HIGH-SPEED PHOTOGRAPHY; MOTION STUDY AND ANALYSIS.

Activator; Accelerator

The alkali in a developing solution is called an activator or accelerator because it enables the developing agent to become chemically active or increases the rate of activity. The great majority of general-purpose film and paper developers use sodium carbonate as an activator. Some fine-grain and low-contrast developers use a very mild alkali such as borax as an activator, while others simply rely on the slight alkalinity of the preservative, sodium sulfite. Strong alkalis such as sodium hydroxide are used for rapid-acting developers which produce high contrast and increased graininess. Vigorous film developers of this sort require a large quantity of preservative to protect the developing agents from rapid oxidation, and a significant amount of restrainer to prevent excessive fog in the emulsion being processed. Some activators require a buffer in the formula to maintain the solution pH at a relatively constant level of alkalinity for a consistent rate of activity with repeated or extended use; other activators—notably sodium and potassium carbonate, and sodium metaborate—are essentially self-buffering.
See also: ALKALI; BUFFER; CONTRAST; FOG; GRAIN; pH; PRESERVATIVE; RESTRAINER.

Acutance

Acutance, or contour sharpness, is the objective measure of edge sharpness in an image; i.e., how distinctly the line at which two areas of different density meet is recorded in the emulsion. Acutance differs from sharpness, which is a subjective evaluation of the clarity of details, and from resolution or resolving power, which is a measure of how closely two details may be spaced while remaining visually distinct.

Acutance is determined by exposing an emulsion with a knife edge laid across it. Diffraction and irradiation cause the light to spread across this border, with the result that microdensitometer readings across the line reveal a gradual density change rather than an abrupt change from the unexposed to the exposed area. Acutance is the value derived from statistical analysis of the density readings of this border gradient. Fine-grain, thin emulsions have high acutance values because they produce the least spreading of the light. So-called acutance developers either develop less of the faintly exposed portions of the line spread, thus reducing the gradient width, or produce an edge effect called the Mackie line, which gives an impression of increased sharpness, although it may not measure out as truly higher acutance.
See also: DIFFRACTION; EDGE EFFECTS; IRRADIATION; MACKIE LINE; RESOLVING POWER; SHARPNESS.

Adams, Ansel

American; 1902-1984
Throughout his long and prolific career, Ansel Adams created a body of work which has come to exemplify not only the purist approach to the medium, but to many people the definitive pictorial statement on the American western landscape. He was also strongly associated with a visionary sense of the redemptive beauty of wilderness and the importance of its preservation. The prestige and popularity of his work has been enhanced by the extraordinary technical perfection of his photography and his insistence on absolute control of the photographic processes.

Born in San Francisco, Adams manifested an early interest in music and the piano, an interest which he initially hoped to develop into a professional career. In 1916 he took his first photographs of the Yosemite Valley, an experience of such intensity that he was to view it as a lifelong inspiration. He studied photography with a photofinisher, producing early work influenced by the then prevalent pictorialist style. Each summer he returned to Yosemite where he developed an interest in conservation. These trips involved exploration, climbing, and photography, and by 1920 he had formed an association with the Sierra Club. In 1927 his first portfolio was

Adams, Ansel. "Moonrise, Hernandez, New Mexico" (1941). Courtesy the Ansel Adams Publishing Rights Trust.

published, *Parmelian Prints of the High Sierras*.

In 1928 he married Virginia Best and began to work as an official photographer for the Sierra Club. His decision to devote his life to photography was influenced by his strong response to the straight photography of Paul Strand, whom he met in 1930. Adams's first important one-man show was held in 1931 at the M. H. de Young Memorial Museum, and in the same year his work was exhibited at the Smithsonian Institution. The following year Adams and several other California-based photographers, notably Edward Weston and Imogen Cunningham, founded Group *f/64*. For Adams and Weston especially, the *f/64* philosophy embodied an approach to perfect realization of photographic vision through technically flawless prints. Despite this, Adams never decried experimentation as such, and he himself used a variety of large-format and miniature cameras.

After meeting with Alfred Stieglitz in 1933, he began a gallery in San Francisco, the Ansel Adams Gallery. The first of his books dealing with the mastery of photographic technique, *Making a Photograph*, was published in 1935. Meanwhile, Adams had impressed Stieglitz so much that an important one-man exhibition of his work was shown at An American Place in 1936.

During the following two years Adams moved into the Yosemite Valley and made trips throughout the Southwest with Weston, Georgia O'Keefe, and David McAlpin. His photographs accompanied the 1938 publication of *Sierra Nevada: The John Muir Trail*. Having met Beaumont and Nancy Newhall in New York in 1939, the following year Adams, along with McAlpin, assisted in the foundation of the Department of Photography at the Museum of Modern Art (MOMA). With the arrival of World War II, Adams went to Washington, D.C., where he worked as

a photomuralist for the Department of the Interior. During this time he began to develop a codification of his approach to exposure, processing, and printing—the *zone system*. In effect, this system aimed at previsualization of the final print from a given set of conditions. Work from a war-time photo essay on the plight of interned Japanese-Americans was exhibited at MOMA in 1944 under the title *Born Free and Equal*. During 1944–1945, Adams lectured and taught courses in photography at the museum. This teaching was followed by the establishment of one of the first departments of photography at the California School of Fine Arts (later the San Francisco Art Institute) in 1946.

Following his award of a Guggenheim Fellowship in 1948 to photograph national park locations and monuments, there were five productive years of important photographic work. The first of numerous portfolios, *Portfolio 1: In Memory of Alfred Stieglitz*, was issued in

1948, and in the same year he began to publish technical volumes in the *Basic Photo Series*. Throughout 1950 he made trips to Hawaii, Alaska, and Maine, and in that year *Portfolio 2: The National Parks and Monuments* was issued.

In 1953 he collaborated with Dorothea Lange on a *Life* commission for a photo essay on the Mormons in Utah, and in 1955 he began a photography workshop in Yosemite. *Portfolio 3: Yosemite Valley* was published by the Sierra Club in 1960.

In each of his images Adams aimed to modulate the range of tones from rich black to whitest white in order to achieve perfect photographic clarity. He also developed a knowledge of the techniques of photographic reproduction to assure that the quality of any reproduced work might approach as closely as possible the standard of the original print.

In 1962 Adams moved to Carmel, California, where in 1967 he was instrumental in the foundation of the Friends of Photography, of which he became president. A retrospective show of his work, 1923–1963, was exhibited at the de Young Museum, and in 1966 he was elected a Fellow of the American Academy of Arts and Sciences. In the late 1970s his prints sold to collectors for prices never equaled by a living American photographer. By that time Adams had given up active photography to devote himself to revising the *Basic Photo Series,* publishing books of his life's work, and preparing prints for a variety of exhibitions.

Adamson, Robert
See: HILL, DAVID OCTAVIUS.

Additive Color Printing
The method of making photographic prints from color negatives or transparencies by using the primary colors of light (red, green, blue) for exposure is called additive or tricolor printing. It differs from the more common method, subtractive color printing, in that only three filters—red, green, and blue—of a single strength (density) are used. Three exposures must be made, one through each filter, or three individually filtered light sources must be used for a single simultaneous exposure. In subtractive printing various densities of secondary color (cyan, magenta, yellow) filtration are combined to adjust the color balance of a single light source during a single exposure. The subtractive method requires stocking an entire range of densities of each filter color, or having equip-

ment with built-in variable filtration; it also requires calculating new filter combinations as well as new exposure times when printing adjustments are made. The filters for additive color printing are of a single density, so exposure time is the only variable.

Although automatic additive color contact printers and enlargers have been used by high-volume mass-production facilities for many years, additive printing in the small, manually operated darkroom has been a somewhat cumbersome operation. The need to make three separate exposures more than triples the time required for one print, as compared to subtractive printing, and the act of twice changing the filter in the enlarger light head or under the lens carries a great risk of moving something with the result that the three exposures will not be in precise register on the print.

Producing a test strip is rather involved. A sheet of paper is given a base exposure (e.g., 10 seconds) through the blue filter; then it receives a series of stepped exposures (e.g., 10, 20, 30, 40 seconds) from top to bottom through the green filter; finally it receives a similar stepped series of exposures from left to right through the red filter. The processed result gives various exposure combinations from which the necessary times can be determined, or from which further tests can be made. Although tedious, this procedure is quite feasible using No. 25 (red), No. 98 (blue), and No. 99 (green) filters.

Recently, additive printing has become far easier and more practical for the individual photographer with the introduction of a small- to medium-format enlarger with a built-in tricolor light head. Three tungsten-halogen lamps are equipped with individual red, green, and blue dichroic filters. A control timer can be set to turn on the three lights simultaneously and to turn them off individually when the proper time for each exposure has elapsed. Test exposures are made by adjusting the timer settings. The results achieved with the additive color method use the same print materials and are indistinguishable from those achieved with the subtractive color method in both negative-positive and reversal printing.
See also: ADDITIVE COLOR SYNTHESIS; COLOR BALANCE; DICHROIC FILTER; SUBTRACTIVE COLOR SYNTHESIS.

Additive Color Synthesis
Additive color synthesis is the method of creating color by mixing various proportions of two or three distinct stimulus

colors of light. These *primary colors* are commonly red, green, and blue, however they may be any wavelengths sufficiently separated in the spectrum to stimulate distinct receptors on the retina of the eye. The CIE color system specifies the stimulus wavelengths to be used for precise colorimetry.

The distinguishing features of additive color synthesis are that it deals with the color effects of light rather than with pigments, dyes, or filters, and that the stimuli come from separate monochromatic sources. (In subtractive color synthesis a complex mixture of wavelengths is obtained from a single source. The most common example of additive color synthesis is the color television screen, which is a mosaic of red, green, and blue phosphor dots; at normal viewing distances the eye does not distinguish the dots, but blends or adds their stimulus effects to obtain a composite color effect. Additive color mixing can be demonstrated by individually equipping three strong, white light sources such as slide projectors with deep red, green, and blue filters and shining their beams in various overlapping patterns on a white surface.

The principles of additive color synthesis are as follows (numerals indicate relative proportions).

(a) Equal stimulus proportions of two primary colors create a *secondary color:*

PRIMARY MIX		SECONDARY
1 Red + 1 Blue	=	Magenta
1 Blue + 1 Green	=	Cyan
1 Green + 1 Red	=	Yellow

(b) Equal stimulus proportions of all three primaries create white: 1 Red + 1 Blue + 1 Green = White.

(c) Unequal proportions of two or three primaries create other colors:

2 Red + 1 Green = Orange
2 Green + 1 Red = Lime (Chartreuse)
1 Blue + 1 Green + 4 Red = Brown

All color sensations can be produced in this way, including those red-blue mixes (purples and magentas) not found at any wavelength band in the spectrum.

In photography, the principles of additive color synthesis underlie making separation negatives for photomechanical reproduction of color images, and dye transfer and similar printing processes; in the darkroom, additive color printing uses red, green, and blue exposures to obtain prints from color negatives and transparencies.

See also: ADDITIVE COLOR PRINTING; CIE COLOR SYSTEM; COLOR; SUBTRACTIVE COLOR SYNTHESIS; VISION.

Advertising Photography

Photographs made for advertising purposes include every kind of subject and thus require every kind of photographic skill. The functions of advertising photographs are to help sell products and services, to communicate information, to build public images, and to attract support for causes and activities. The first task of the photograph is to capture attention; only then can a message be communicated. In some cases the photograph serves as a simple illustration of the idea or message contained in accompanying text. In other cases the photograph is far more important—and usually more effective—because it embodies the main idea; the text, if any, simply reinforces what is communicated visually.

Technical development. Advertising photography is essentially a 20th c. development, primarily because it relies on photomechanical reproduction, which did not achieve sufficient quality at a cost affordable to most advertisers until well into this century. Photographs were used as early as the 1850s to illustrate goods offered for sale—particularly fashionable, custom-made clothing—but they either were distributed as actual prints (usually small cartes-de-visite—a very limited and somewhat expensive practice) or more commonly were reproduced from plates made by hand engraving or lithographic methods. Although slow, the handwork required by the printing technology of the period allowed the image to be corrected and enhanced, a practice continued by retouching when photographic methods came into common use.

Halftone processes suitable for reproducing photographs on the high-speed presses used to print magazines and newspapers were introduced in the 1880s, but advertisers largely ignored them in favor of the better quality, ease of manipulation, and lower cost offered by older methods. In medium- and low-cost periodicals and catalogs, reproduction quality was limited more by the paper used than by any deficiencies of photography or halftone methods from the 1890s on.

Black-and-white photographs began to appear in advertisements just after 1900, but they were not widely used until the 1920s. Even from that time, the growth of photography to its position as the major mode of advertising illustration was relatively slow. Yearly anthologies of commercial illustration, design, and advertising suggest a rapid growth of photographic illustration, but such compilations tend to select the unsual and innovative, and to emphasize work appearing in higher rather than average or lower quality publications. Examination of a wide range of magazines, newspapers, and catalogs, shows that through the 1930s, hand-drawn illustrations were more common in advertisements than were photographs.

Color photography, which now dominates advertising illustration, did not come into widespread use until after the late 1940s, when the large-format films of high color quality developed just before and during World War II became widely available. The first color photographic materials, introduced from about 1905 to 1920, used additive-color screens that could not easily be reproduced without moiré (interference patterns); in addition, color fidelity was uncertain at best and could not readily be corrected by retouching. When an advertisement required a photographic color illustration, the procedure was to photograph the separations (images on separate black-and-white films taken through red, green, and blue filters) directly from the subject. This was a cumbersome method, restricted to still-lifes and other absolutely motionless subjects. One-shot color cameras, invented by F. E. Ives and others, used interior beam-splitters and filters so that all the separations could be obtained in a single exposure, rather than three shots, but the exposure time was usually so long that no subject movement was permissible. The trouble and expense involved limited the use of color photographs to advertisements concerned with projecting an aura of prestige — advertisements for luxury automobiles, fine liquors, elegant yachts, and the like. The introduction of a practical monopack subtractive-color film (Kodachrome) in 1935 made it possible to obtain high-quality transparencies—from which separations could later be made in the engraving studio—with no more difficulty than taking black-and-white pictures. The resulting rapid expansion of color advertising photography was cut short by the restrictions of World War II. Since the 1950s, continuous improvements in films, photographic equipment, and reproduction methods have brought advertising illustration to a level of great technical excellence; at the same time, it has achieved great variety in style.

Stylistic development. At the beginning of the 20th c., almost all photographs used in printed advertisements were straightforward product and user pictures. The realism of the photographic image was intended to validate the claim or message; for example, to prove to the reader: this is the actual satisfied user of our hearing aid, whose testimonial is ". . . . "; or: the gasoline-powered boats we manufacture are exactly like this. In small advertisements, the photograph might be the only illustration, but in half- or full-page ads a photograph of the product was commonly used as a small "spot," while a drawing or painting was used as the major attention-getting or theme-setting illustration. In the late 1910s, nonspecific or open-end situation illustrations also began to appear. A picture of a man and a woman in earnest conversation might be used with any of several headlines: "Let me tell you. . . . ," "Have you heard. . . ? ," "I'm glad I learned. . . ," and many others. The "reality" of photography often led to the use of photographs with themes of insecurity, inadequacy, or fear, while hand-drawn illustrations were more often used with themes of accomplishment, optimism, and self-satisfaction.

Great diversification of style in advertising illustration occured in the 1920s. The dramatic-incident ad, previously a nearly full-page short story text with an incidental illustration, became a large (often full-page bleed) "story" photograph accompanied by an emotional headline (e.g., "Often a bridesmaid; never a bride," "Why didn't he ever call again?" for a breath-cleansing mouthwash) and only one or two paragraphs of text. The then-revolutionary technique of visually advertising a product without actually showing it in an illustration was introduced by a hand-lotion company, using an Edward Steichen photograph of a woman's hands peeling potatoes; subsequent ads in the campaign showed hands washing clothes, scrubbing a floor, and performing other potentially skin-damaging tasks. The 1920s also introduced the practice of borrowing art styles for advertising purposes, both in the overall design of ads and in the illustrations used. Man Ray and Francis Bruguière produced Surrealist images featuring various products; Steichen perfected an Art Deco approach and then went on to a streamline-moderne style; and many others followed suit.

Glamorized, dramatized product photography emerged in the 1930s as Hollywood techniques of creating cream-smooth highlights and shadows, spotlighted emphasis, and satin backgrounds were applied almost indiscriminately to perfume bottles, automobile tires, typewriters, loaves of bread, and anything else offered for sale. Some photographers, such as Victor Keppler, began to build reputations for their versatility; others for their specialties, such as Anton Bruehl, one of the first masters of advertising color photography. During this decade, "advertising photographer" became an established professional category. A documentary style also emerged in the 1930s, especially in advertisements for charitable and social service agencies, whose role during the Depression was of major importance. This approach became the no-nonsense photojournalistic style used in almost all advertising illustration during the war years of the 1940s.

The post-war decades brought photography to dominance in advertising, using a succession of styles appropriate to the cultural changes of the times; expansive luxury, girl-next-door wholesomeness, self-fulfillment, civil equality, space exploration, scientific brilliance, sexual liberation, science-fiction fantasy, and many other themes. Today almost all illustrative styles of the past are used along with the most recent innovations, because there is a greater number of products offered to a greater diversity of specifically identified buying audiences than ever before. Photographers working in the field are essentially anonymous, known only to the art and advertising directors who may hire their services. Only in the specialized field of fashion illustration have any advertising photographers gained a significant public reputation, and these are a very small number.

Current practice. The content, design, and style of an advertising photograph are most often determined by an art director, who engages a photographer to actually make the illustration. The instructions to the photographer may be highly specific and include detailed sketches, or they may be more general requests for pictures that convey a given idea or mood. In the most limited situation, a photographer may tape a tracing of the sketch over the ground glass of the view camera to insure getting exactly what is required; at the other extreme, he or she may be free to experiment with imaginative interpretations of the basic idea. In all cases, the photographer is expected to produce technically excellent photographs. In product illustration and many other kinds of advertising photography, technical excellence means perfect composition and exposure, ex-

treme sharpness, rich colors, and similar characteristics. But in illustrations for disaster relief services or fire insurance advertising, for example, technical excellence may consist of creating a grainy, available-light "grab shot" feeling commonly associated with news photography. The photographer's skill lies in being able to grasp what the art director wants, however it may be expressed, and delivering a picture with the expected qualities.

Depending on the kind of advertisement and its theme, a specific assignment may actually be a problem in close-up or scientific photography, in portraiture, in theatrical or architectural photography, in abstraction or fantasy, or in any of a great number of other areas. Product advertising usually calls for pictures of the product itself, with its visual qualities enhanced, or for pictures of the product being used, with a clear indication that the users are being made happy by the benefits it provides. Benefits are often implied by the mood or the situation of a picture, which says in effect that you can feel or become like this. Services are often advertised by "situation" pictures that show the services being performed or delivered or show the satisfied customer/client who has received them. Before-and-after pictures showing the need for a product or service and the results of obtaining it are also common advertising illustrations. Public-image advertising may show people (the candidate, the board of director, the clerks who serve you), facilities (the extensive factory; the modern classroom), or more general illustrations that project a sense of integrity, friendliness, reliability, or some other quality. Advertisements in support of causes and activities often use photographs that show a condition that ought to be protested or corrected, or the activities of those who ought to be supported; appeals for aid portray the victims to be helped; public service and informational advertisements show where to go, what to do, how to do it.

Because the range of advertising is so great and so varied, photographers tend to become specialists—in food, fashion, or automobile illustrations, for example, or in "mood" pictures or "situation" pictures. Many advertisements use more than one photograph—for example, an attention-getting illustration and one or more close-ups of the specific product being advertised. Commonly these are done by different specialists, and the results are combined by the art director, who prepares the ad for reproduction. The major use of advertising photographs is in magazines and newspapers; other outlets include catalogs,

brochures, promotional literature, point-of-purchase displays, billboards, car cards, posters, instruction manuals, annual reports, direct-mail pieces, product packaging, and television commercials.

Today the vast majority of advertising photographs are made in color. The best color reproduction in printed media is obtained from a transparency rather than a print, and if black-and-white reproduction is also required, it is a simple matter to prepare an appropriate printing plate from the color original. All kinds of cameras and lenses are used, as appropriate to the picture problem. Product photographs are most often made with a large-format view camera because it permits precise composition, the camera movements provide maximum control over distortion and sharpness, and the large original image provides the best reproduction of detail. Medium- and small-format cameras are used when movement and flexibility are of prime importance. The entire range of technical devices and special techniques is also called on as required. Front and rear projection make it possible to place a product or model in any setting throughout the world without leaving the studio. Filters, masks, and special lenses can provide correction and control or can produce unusual visual effects. Duplicators and special darkroom techniques make it possible to combine and alter images with great freedom. Retouching and a variety of procedures in reproduction offer additional ways to obtain the desired final image. The advertising photographer must be familiar with all such techniques and, if he or she does not employ them directly, must be able to recommend or call for their use when required. However, the starting point is to capture in the camera an image that carries the desired message and to present it in a way that will cause a reader to stop, look, and pay attention.

See also: FASHION PHOTOGRAPHY; PRODUCT PHOTOGRAPHY.

Aerial Fog
See: FOG; FOGGING.

Aerial Image
See: FOCUSING; LENSES; OPTICS.

Aerial Perspective
See: PERSPECTIVE.

Aerial Photography
Most aerial photography is concerned with taking air-to-ground views, but the

field includes air-to-air pictures of other craft, cloud formations, and meteorological phenomena. Aerial photographs are made for a variety of civilian and military purposes. Geographical and geological surveying are major applications. In many cases the only practical means of discovering new mineral deposits or identifying likely sites, particularly in rough or climatically harsh terrain, is from the air. Agriculture, forestry, ecology, and related fields make use of aerial views to study the health and distribution of various species of plant and animal life. Aerial photographs of archeological sites can provide records before a location is disturbed by ground investigation and can document stages of progress in overall views of excavation or other work. Subtle differences in soil color or other factors observable only from the air may indicate where structures once stood or are buried. Military applications of aerial photography include surveillance and intelligence-gathering, reconnaissance, and post-strike recording to determine attack accuracy and target damage.

Aerial surveying can be divided into two major areas: qualitative pictures to determine the size, shape, texture, and color of objects on the ground, and photogrammetry for precision mapmaking. Much photogrammetry is done with specialized cameras oriented for views directly perpendicular to the ground below. The photographs obtained primarily show the outlines of objects and areas and their relative positions. Most other types of aerial surveying obtain oblique-angle views that show ground features in relief. To minimize atmospheric effects on exposure and image quality, a great deal of aerial surveying and record photography is done at low altitudes in the 500- to 1500-foot (152- to 457-meter) range. A high-wing monoplane provides maximum camera visibility without interference from the wing or struts. Helicopters are sometimes used for extremely low-altitude work or in areas inaccessible to fixed-wing aircraft, but they are more expensive to operate and generate substantially more vibration, particularly when hovering.

Pictorial, record, and informal surveying aerial photographs can be taken with any good-quality camera and ordinary films. At low altitudes it is common to open the window or remove the door of a small plane for a clearer view. In such cases a bellows-type camera must be protected from vibration or damage from the slipstream of air. Camera and photographer must be equipped with individual safety cables or

belts. A light- or medium-yellow filter is used with black-and-white films to minimize the haze effects of blue wavelengths and ultraviolet scattered by the atmosphere. Ordinary color films require an ultraviolet or skylight filter. Haze problems increase with altitude or as the camera angle of view becomes more horizontal because the subject is seen through an increased depth of atmosphere. Films especially intended for aerial photography (usually designated by the prefix *aero-*) have extended red sensitivity or built-in filtration characteristics to minimize haze effects and improve contrast. Some aerial films are supplied primarily in long rolls 5½ or 9 in. (14 or 23 cm) wide for use in specialized aerial cameras. These cameras have long-focal-length (e.g., 40 in. [102.6 cm] or longer) infinity fixed-focus lenses. They have special pressure plates to ensure film flatness in the focal plane, built-in filtration, automatic/non-automatic and continuous/single-frame modes of operation, and registration and data-recording features.

Military aerial photography in peacetime is now accomplished almost entirely by fixed and orbiting satellites, which transmit digitized images to ground recording stations, and by very high-speed high-altitude airplanes. The SR-71 aircraft, successor to the well-known U-2, is capable of cruising at 80,000 feet (24 kilometers) at multiples of the speed of sound. Extremely sophisticated, secret equipment is used to obtain pictures at visible, infrared, ultraviolet, and other wavelengths. Most such systems are all-electronic. When film is used, it is automatically processed in flight, and the images are electronically transmitted to ground recorders and interpretation facilities. Some military surveillance equipment can provide distinct images of human beings and even smaller subjects from distances or altitudes greater than 100 miles (161 kilometers).

Air-to-ground and air-to-air photography can be accomplished by travelers through the windows of commercial aircraft with almost any kind of camera. Often a pilot will circle or bank past areas of interest near the flight destination to provide passengers with a good view. Photographs can be taken with the lens held as close to the window as possible to avoid reflections of the interior of the plane. No part of the camera should touch the body of the plane, or vibration will be picked up. A yellow or ultraviolet filter—depending on the kind of film used—is desirable, but a polarizing filter should not be used, because it may produce visible interference patterns in interaction with the window material.

Black-and-white films should be processed for extra contrast if possible to further overcome haze effects. Additional exposures at one *f*-stop less than normal are recommended, because visual impressions of brightness are often inaccurate in the air.

Planned air-to-air photography at close range requires experienced pilots and aircraft of matched performance so that neither is forced to fast or slow speeds or maneuvers that are unsafe. The photographer must only be a passenger in the plane, free to concentrate on taking pictures with no responsibility for operating the aircraft.
See also: PHOTOGRAMMETRY; PHOTOGRAPHY.
Color photograph: p. C-2.

Ag; AgX

The chemical symbol for silver is Ag. In general discussions and equations relating to photographic emulsions, the symbol AgX may be used to indicate a silver halide in the reaction without specification; i.e., X may stand for the bromide, chloride, or iodide component.
See also: CHEMISTRY OF PHOTOGRAPHY; HALIDE/HALOGEN.

AGFA

AGFA is the acronym for *Aktiengesellschaft für Anilinfabrikation* (Aniline Manufacturing Corporation), the name adopted in 1873 by a dye manufacturing company which had been established near Berlin seven years earlier. The major role of aniline and related compounds in photographic materials led the company to begin manufacturing films in 1908, followed by camera production in 1928, the year in which it also purchased the Ansco Company in the U.S. It introduced a subtractive color film (Agfacolor) in 1936, the year following the debut of Kodachrome film; produced the first negative-positive color or motion-picture film in 1940; and marketed the first 35mm camera with automatic exposure control, the Optima, in 1959. In 1964 AGFA merged with the Belgian concern Gevaert Photo-Producten, a major manufacturer of film, x-ray, graphic arts, and office copying materials and equipment. Today Agfa-Gevaert is the largest European producer of photographic and related imaging materials and systems.

Agitation

Uniform processing requires agitation of the solutions during use to ensure that chemical byproducts and exhausted solution are flushed away from the emulsion and replaced by fresh solution. Inadequate or improper agitation can produce uneven development—usually evident as streaks or patches of weak tone or color—fixing, and washing. Conversely, overagitation of film during development can produce excessive contrast, graininess, and fog, or streaks of excessive density produced by developer surging through film sprocket holes or the flow holes of sheet-film holders. Constant agitation of films in other solutions and in wash water is harmless, within the limits of physical damage to the emulsion, and constant agitation of prints in all solutions is desirable.

Automatic processing machines and large-volume tanks generally use bursts of an inert gas (nitrogen) from appropriately located jets to create turbulence within solutions. In hand-processing with small, capped tanks, agitation is achieved by inverting the tank with a twisting motion at the intervals recommended in processing instructions. Some tanks have a central rod for rotating the film reel inside. Sheet-film agitation is accomplished by lifting the holders, tilting them to a 45-degree angle to drain off the solution, reimmersing the film, and repeating the process with a tilt in the opposite direction. Prints in open trays are agitated either by seizing one corner of the print and moving it back and forth in the solution, or preferably by raising alternate corners of the tray to wash the solution across the emulsion. Whatever method of agitation is used, it must be repeatable to provide standardized results, but it must create a random flow of solution—regular flow or turbulence patterns can produce streaking.

Albumen Processes

The first photographic materials to have coatings similar to modern emulsions used albumen (egg white) as the coating medium. This transparent liquid protein material adheres firmly to almost any material upon drying. It was first used for photographic purposes in 1848 by Abel Niépce de Saint-Victor to make glass plate negatives. The rendition of tones and details obtained with these plates was far superior to that of the calotype paper negative, but the albumen coating would crack and flake off after a period of time, destroying the image. Introduction of the collodion (wet plate) process three years later eliminated this problem and made Niépce's process obsolete. In 1850 L. D. Blanquart-Evrard introduced albumen paper for making prints; it was immensely successful and remained the standard printing paper until almost the end of the 19th c. The coating kept the image on the surface of the paper, rather than impregnated in the fibers as in prints made by the salt paper process, and it added a gloss or sheen that improved the visual depth of the image.

Albumen plates and paper were prepared in a similar manner. A small amount of ammonium chloride solution was added to liquid egg white, which was then beaten to a froth and allowed to clear and settle at least twice. Glass plates were coated by pouring the liquid evenly over them; papers were floated face down on a shallow tray of the liquid. After drying, coated materials could be kept indefinitely. They were sensitized immediately before use by brushing the surface (or floating the paper) with a silver nitrate solution slightly acidified with nitric acid; greater sensitivity was obtained with a sensitizing solution of silver nitrate, ammonia, and grain alcohol in water. The materials were dried in the dark before exposure; the image was developed in a gallic acid or iron sulfate solution, or was produced by printing-out, without development. Print tones were enhanced by treatment in a gold chloride toning solution.

Albumen prints of the 19th c. exhibit yellowish discoloration and fading; the causes of these changes and safe methods of arresting them are areas of urgent inquiry among photographic conservators today. A few specialists now produce albumen paper chiefly for special editions for collectors, and to produce facsimile prints from 19th c. negatives for museums and institutions with historical photographic collections. Albumen-on-glass lantern slides were called Hyalotypes in the U.S.

See also: BLANQUART-EVRARD, LOUIS D.; CALOTYPE; COLLODION PROCESS; HYALOTYPE; LANTERN SLIDE; SALT PAPER PROCESS.

Alinari, Giuseppe
Italian; 1836–1890

Alinari, Leopoldo
Italian; 1832–1865

Alinari, Romualdo
Italian; 1830–1891

The Alinari brothers, Florentine publishers of postcards and art reproductions sold around the world, were among the most renowned photographic families of the 19th c. Their photographs aspired to the most exactingly faithful documentation of Italian architecture, art treasures, landscapes, as well as portraiture. Praised by contemporaries including Ruskin, Burckhardt, and Martinelli, the photographs made by the Alinaris are today a major body of source and illustrative material for social historians, art critics, and scholars, and were equalled only by the work of their contemporaries, Robert MacPherson and Carlo Ponti.

The Alinari brothers, sons of an engraver, were born in the late 1820s and early 1830s. Leopoldo served as an apprentice to the eminent Florentine engraver Luigi Bardi, and learned the rudiments of photography from him in the late 1840s. In 1852, now using the collodion process, Leopoldo established a photographic studio in the Via Nazionale, Florence. Two years later, he and his brothers entered into partnership. "Fratelli Alinari, Fotografi Editori" soon achieved an international reputation.

In the late 1850s, while Giuseppe and Romualdo managed the business of the studio, Leopoldo traveled and photographed throughout Italy, specializing in photographs of artistic monuments and other works of art in Florence, Rome, Naples, Pompeii, and other cities. In 1860, the Alinaris were commissioned by Prince Albert of England to photograph the drawings of Raphael in Florence, Venice, and Vienna. In the early 1860s, the brothers opened a portrait studio and expanded their publishing firm. Leopoldo died in 1865.

During the next several years, while Florence was the seat of the Italian government, the photographers of the Alinari studio were responsible for portraits of cultural figures and statesmen including Garibaldi and King Victor Emmanuel II. In the 1870s, the Alinari firm expanded further, employing anonymous photographers to record daily life and art treasures throughout the country.

Following the deaths of the two remaining brothers in the 1890s, the Alinari concerns first were managed by Leopoldo's son Vittorio, then, in 1920, sold to an outside group of businessmen. To this day, the firm is a major photographic publisher, with an archive of over 200,000 negatives (some of enormous size, up to 51″ × 35″) of Italian scenes and art treasures, including the work of photographers such as James Anderson, Giacomo Brogi, Fiorentini, and Mannelli.

In recent years, several exhibitions of the work of the Alinaris have been held in Florence, including a major retrospec-

Alinari Brothers. "Piazza Signoria and the Uffizi Gallery, Florence" (ca. 1850). Courtesy Marcuse Pfeifer Gallery, New York.

tive of 700 photographs, *The Alinaris: Photographers in Florence 1852–1920,* at Forte Belvedere.

See also: MACPHERSON, ROBERT; PONTI, CARLO.

Alkali

A base is a metallic oxide or hydroxide that is the opposite of an acid: in chemical reaction with an acid, a base gives up metallic ions to form a salt. An alkali is a base that is soluble in water. In concentrated form these compounds may be extremely corrosive; their values are above 7 on the pH scale. When dissolved in water, a strong alkali such as sodium or potassium hydroxide generates a great amount of heat very quickly. For this reason, cold water in an unbreakable container (stainless steel, hard rubber, plastic) should be used, and the alkali should be slowly sifted in as the water is stirred constantly. To function effectively, virtually all developing agents used today require an alkali as an activator in the solution.

See also: ACTIVATOR/ACCELERATOR; DEVELOPING AGENT; pH.

Allegorical Photographs

The use of allegory in the visual arts typically involves the fashioning of an image to represent or "stand for" some preconceived idea or theme. Thus, in addition to its obvious visual content, the allegorical image refers back to a second level of meaning. In the simplest instances of allegory, such abstract notions as Virtue and Vice may be vividly portrayed in human form. More complex allegories sometimes attempt to find visual equivalents for specific themes drawn from religion or mythology.

One of the earliest and best known attempts at photographic allegory was Oscar J. Rejlander's 1857 masterwork, "The Two Ways of Life." Through the use of multiple negatives and painstaking combination printing, Rejlander composed a moralizing allegory patterned directly after Raphael's painting "The School of Athens." An implied narrative centered on two young men, personifications of Youth, who are poised at the threshold of adulthood and must choose their paths. A dense assembly of allegorical figures represent such opposed concepts as Idleness, Gambling, and Complicity, on the one hand, and Good Works, Industry, and Religion, on

the other. While in some ways clumsy and heavy-handed, "The Two Ways of Life" remains one of the most ambitious attempts at photographic allegory to date.

Because the older art of painting possessed a long tradition of allegorical representation, photographers often relied upon such sources for their motifs. Subjects such as the *memento mori*—the arrangement of a still life of fruits, flowers, or other objects around a human skull, dramatically alluding to the transience of human life—have attracted photographers from the 1850s up to Irving Penn in his most recent work. Considered in this light, Arthur Rothstein's famous FSA photograph of a cow's skull on the drought-parched South Dakota soil might well be conceived as an allegorical image, since its implications extend far beyond the recording of a purely local or immediate situation.

Frequently, however, allegorically in-

tended photographs depend heavily on external factors, especially their titles, to convey their secondary meaning. A Julia Margaret Cameron photograph of three women in classical robes can be understood as an allegory only when its title is revealed—"Faith, Hope, and Charity." In the same way, Gertrude Käsebier's well-known "Blessed Art Thou Among Women" (ca. 1900), which depicts a young girl being guided across a threshold by a long-robed woman, relies almost entirely on its title to make clear its reference to the education of the Virgin Mary.

In some allegorical photographs, emblems rather than figures in a staged tableau serve to convey allegorical meaning. Tina Modotti's 1920s still-life of a gun, a sickle, and ears of corn, for example, serve as an effective allegory of the Mexican Revolution because her choice of objects and their combination charges them with a secondary, rhetorical meaning.

Alpert, Max. "Russian Soldiers Moving West
on Hitler's Troops" (1944). Permanent collection, ICP, New York.

From about 1910 onward, allegory
largely disappeared from photography
and painting as Western culture lost interest in didactic moralism and the view
that symbolically communicated spiritualism provided enlightenment. Part of
the spiritual slack was taken up by symbolic images derived from popularized
concepts of Freudian and Jungian
psychology, and personification turned
to representations of psychoses and
neuroses. Today, allegorical elements
may be found in some of the work of
Duane Michals, Ralph Gibson, Jerry N.
Uelsmann, Frederick Sommer, and similar photographers, but in general,
aspects of Surrealism, psychological abstraction, and fantasy are far more prominent.
See also: ABSTRACT PHOTOGRAPHY;
PICTORIAL PHOTOGRAPHY; FANTASY IN
PHOTOGRAPHY; SURREALISM IN PHO-
TOGRAPHY.

Alpert, Max

Russian; 1899–1980
Max Alpert documented over 50 years of

life in the Soviet Union as a photojournalist and war correspondent. An early
photo-reporter, Alpert specialized in the
photography of industrial building during the Soviet Union's first Five Year
Plan. In 1931, collaborating with the
photographers Shaiket and Tulesa and
the editor Mezhericher, he created the
seminal picture-story *Twenty-Four
Hours in the Life of the Filippov Family*.
These 78 images detailing the life of a
Moscow metalworker were widely published and exhibited. Alpert's war
photographs of German and Russian
soldiers and civilians are noted for their
compassion and telling detail. In the
postwar period, he returned to the documentation of Soviet industrial reconstruction.
Alpert was born in Simferopol, near
Odessa in the Ukraine, where he was
educated at the Jewish School from 1906
to 1910. Self-taught as a photographer,
he worked on a freelance basis in Odessa
from 1914 to 1919. He fought in the Red
Army in Odessa from 1919 to 1921, and
worked for Moscow's Help the Children
Commission from 1921 to 1924.
Alpert was a photo-reporter for the
Moscow *Workers Newspaper*

(Rabochaya Gaseta) from 1924 to 1929,
when he became a correspondent for
Pravda. In 1931 he transferred to *USSR
in Construction (SSSR na Stroike)* magazine, where he remained for ten years.
During World War II, Alpert served
as a war correspondent and photographer on the Russian front for
TASS, the government news agency.
After the war, he was a photographer-
correspondent from 1945 to 1948 with
the Soviet Information Office (Sovin-
formburo), Moscow, for *Soviet Union*
magazine from 1948 to 1951, for *Isogis*
Publishers, Moscow, from 1951 to 1958,
and again for the Soviet Information
Office from 1958 to 1961. From 1961
until his death in Moscow in 1980,
Alpert traveled and photographed in the
Soviet Union and abroad as a correspondent for the APN Press Agency,
Moscow.
Alpert was an early and regular contributor to *AIZ (Arbeiter Illustrirte
Zeitung)* magazine, and was the subject
of several books published in the Soviet
Union, including *Troublesome Profession* (1962) and *Max Alpert* (1974). He
was also the recipient of numerous
awards during his long career.

Alvarez Bravo, Manuel

Mexican; 1902–

Deeply rooted in the culture of the Mexican people, Manuel Alvarez Bravo has created a major body of photographic work the significance of which has gone unrecognized until recent years. He has focused on the subtleties of human interaction, particularly in the lower classes, to make eloquent images of dreams, death, and transient life.

Bravo was born in Mexico City, the son and grandson of painters and photographers. He attended a Catholic grade school, later worked as a copy clerk while studying accounting at night school, and became an office boy for the Mexican Treasury Department. He remained with the Treasury Department in a variety of capacities until 1931. He began serious literary studies in 1917, and music and painting studies at the Academia Nacional de Bellas Artes the following year.

Bravo became interested in photography in 1922 and purchased his first camera two years later. He experimented with abstract images of folded papers in 1926–1927. In 1926 he received First Prize at the Regional Exhibition in Oaxaca. Bravo met Tina Modotti, who had learned photography as a companion of Edward Weston, in 1927. She deeply influenced and encouraged his work. He began his first significant work soon after their meeting and became a major figure in the blossoming Mexican art movement of the 1930s. Bravo taught photography at the Escuela Central de Artes Plasticas under Diego Rivera in 1929–1930. He began to photograph paintings and murals for *Mexican Folkways* magazine at this time.

In 1930–1931 Bravo was cameraman on Sergei Eisenstein's uncompleted film *Que Viva Mexico*. He was given his first one-man show of photographs at Galeria Posada in Mexico City in 1932. Soon after, he met Paul Strand and Henri Cartier-Bresson, both of whom admired his work. He exhibited at the Julien Levy Gallery in New York City with Cartier-Bresson and Walker Evans in 1935 and taught at Hull House in Chicago in 1936.

Bravo met André Breton, founder of Surrealism, in 1938 through Diego Rivera. Although he was never a member of the movement, Bravo developed an interest in Surrealist aesthetics and imagery, as evidenced in his strongest personal work. However, during the 1940s and 1950s Bravo did little personal photography, concentrating his attention on cinematography and teaching at the Sindicato de Trabajadores de la Producción Cinematografica de Mexico. He

was a founder of El Fondo Editorial de la Plastica Mexicana and has been one of its directors and chief photographer since 1959. He resumed a more active photographic career in the 1960s and continues to live and work in Mexico City.

Bravo is an Honorary Member of the Academia de Artes in Mexico. He has been the recipient of numerous awards, including the Sourasky Art Prize (1974) and the National Art Prize (1975). Bravo has been a Guggenheim Fellow and is honored by a permanent room in his name at the Museum of Modern Art in Mexico City. He has exhibited throughout the world, with major shows at the Photo League in New York City, the Philadelphia Museum of Art, the Art Institute of Chicago, the International Museum of Photography in Rochester, New York, the Witkin Gallery in New York City, and the Corcoran Gallery in Washington, D.C.

Amateur Movement

Throughout the world today, non-professional photographers take 80 to 90 percent of the several billion pictures produced every year. Making photographs by and for oneself has become an integral part of the culture of industrialized society, as the ease of operating modern cameras and the reliability of modern photofinishing have brought photography within the reach of everyone. In countries such as Japan and the United States, the activity amounts to a national pastime. The emergence of the amateur as a significant factor in

photography was very slow in the first half century of the medium's development, but enormous growth suddenly occurred between 1890 and 1910, and the pace has seldom slackened since.

From 1840 to 1850 few people other than technically curious experimenters took up photography non-professionally. This was largely because the first processes—the daguerreotype and the calotype—were difficult to master and produced uncertain results. In addition, equipment had to be custom-made, materials—especially the silver-coated copper plates for daguerreotypes—were expensive, and in many locations professionals controlled the rights to use of the processes.

The amateur photographer began to leave a mark on the medium after the introduction of the wet-plate collodion process in 1851. Although complex and cumbersome, it produced excellent results, was relatively inexpensive, and was available to all. Photographic manufacturers and suppliers emerged to provide ready-made equipment and supplies, and the availability of inexpensive, high-quality prints on paper stimulated great interest. Although the number of amateurs attracted to the medium increased slowly, the influx prompted the creation of photographic societies and clubs in rapid profusion. The Photographic Societies of London and of Leeds were founded in 1853. Similar organizations appeared in most cities in England, major centers in continental Europe, and in the U.S. in the following decade. The first American camera club that included amateurs as members was

Amateur Movement. Photograph taken with an early Kodak camera, the Hawkeye (n.d.). Private collection

THE 3½ x 3½ HAWK-EYE.

founded in New York in 1861, by Henry T. Anthony and 20 other photographers. While most such organizations had professional members, amateurs soon came to hold the floor, making their aesthetic values and personal preferences dominant. The success of Henry Peach Robinson's Pictorialist movement was due in large part to the support he received from the amateur members of the London Photographic Society. Amateurs made up a substantial percentage of the ranks of the naturalist and Secessionist movements that followed in Europe and in the U.S. For the most part these were "serious" amateurs, interested in photography as an expressive medium, although their level of achievement frequently was far below their professed standards and aims.

The introduction of the Kodak camera in 1888 marks the start of the greatest expansion photography has ever seen: the rise of the snapshot and family album amateur photographer. The key to this success was the Kodak's simplicity and the freedom from technical considerations it allowed the user. The camera, and its thousands of successors and imitators, had few controls or adjustments; film was easy to load; several pictures (up to 100 with the first Kodak) could be

taken on each roll; and the difficult (to amateurs) procedures of developing and printing were taken care of by commercial establishments that sprang up to supply such services. Every development in equipment and supplies for amateurs since that time has followed the precept of the original Kodak slogan: "You press the button, we do the rest."

By the late 1890s, "serious" amateurs with artistic ambitions lamented the dramatic influx of what they called "button pushers" and "Kodak fiends" into amateur camera clubs. In 1897 Alfred Stieglitz, himself one-time editor of the *American Amateur Photography* magazine, wishfully predicted that "Photography as a fad is well-nigh on its last legs." That, of course, proved to be hardly the case. The steady technological improvements in cameras and photofinishing processes have continued to expand the amateur market; the introduction, especially, of inexpensive color photography in the 1930s, set off a new burst of amateur activity.

Since World War II, the arrival of instant photography and increasingly automatic cameras have opened new realms to the amateur photographer. In 1948 Edwin Land introduced his original Polaroid Land Camera, which delivered

black-and-white prints 60 seconds after exposure. Polaroid's subsequent perfection of an instant color process in 1963 was accompanied by its introduction of a camera with automatic shutter-controlled exposure. Particularly in the last decade, this automatization of cameras has proceeded at a remarkable pace, thanks mainly to advances in the use of microelectronics to regulate focus, exposure, and built-in flash units. By effectively guaranteeing that even the novice can produce clear, sharp, properly exposed photographs, such advances have placed photography within virtually everyone's grasp, and contributed to its near-universal appeal.

Today it is the snapshot amateur who is the foundation of photographic marketing and picture-taking. The amateur movement is sustained by a great number of clubs and societies that variously appeal to amateurs at all levels; by courses offered in schools, colleges, and social organizations; and by an uncountable number of galleries, exhibitions, competitions, and opportunities to display photographs throughout the world.

See also: ART PHOTOGRAPHY; KODAK; SNAPSHOT; SNAPSHOT AESTHETIC.

Ambrotype

An ambrotype is a positive-appearing image on glass made by the collodion process in the same standard sizes and displayed in the same kinds of cases as the daguerreotype. The densities of a collodion negative can be bleached to light gray tones with nitric acid or mercuric chloride. When such an image is placed against a black background, the highlights and middletone areas are lighter than the thinner, dark areas through which the background can be seen; as a result, the image looks positive. This effect was discovered in 1851 by Frederick Scott Archer, inventor of the collodion process, and Peter Fry. In improved form it was patented in the U.S. and England in 1854 as a portrait process by James Ambrose Cutting, a Philadelphia photographer who called it the ambrotype. Primarily because it was so much cheaper, the ambrotype almost immediately eliminated the daguerreotype as a portrait medium. The sizes and mountings were the same, and the public did not seem to care that it was tonally less rich than the daguerreotype, while professional photographers found the collodion process easier and less expensive to use.

Although occasionally dark violet or ruby-black glass was used, most ambrotypes were made on clear glass which was then either lacquered black on the back or placed over black paper or velvet in a mounting case. Today, disintegration of the backing often makes an ambrotype appear severely damaged although the image is in fact intact. It is a relatively simple matter to remove the glass plate, clean it, and renew the backing to restore the image to a near-original appearance. It is also possible to make contact prints or enlargements from the unbacked glass image. The printing characteristics differ from those of modern negatives, but quite good results can be achieved in many cases.

There were two variants of the ambrotype: the melanograph, with the emulsion coated directly on black paper, and the immensely successful ferrotype (tintype), which used a sheet of dark metal, thus eliminating the fragility of the glass and the need for a padded mounting case.

See also: ARCHER, FREDERICK SCOTT; COLLODION PROCESS; CUTTING, JAMES A.; DAGUERREOTYPE; FERROTYPE.

"An American Place"

The gallery operated by Alfred Stieglitz at Room 1710, 509 Madison Avenue, New York City, from December 1929 until his death in 1946, was known as "An American Place." Photogaphic exhibits included the works of Paul Strand, Stieglitz, Ansel Adams, and Eliot Porter. Far more important in the development of American modern art were the many exhibitions of paintings and other works by Georgia O'Keefe, Arthur Dove, Charles Demuth, Marsden Hartley, John Marin, and others.

See also: GALLERIES, PHOTOGRAPH; STIEGLITZ, ALFRED.

Anaglyph

See: STEREOSCOPE.

Anamorphic Image

An anamorphic image has different scales of magnification along the horizontal and vertical axes. The resulting distortion is usually so great that the subject is virtually or actually unidentifiable. Originally, anamorphic paintings and drawings may have been used as a kind of visual encryption because they concealed their content, or certain aspects of their content, which in some cases was political, satirical, or pornographic—or all three. The usual method of producing such images was to copy exactly the image seen in a concave or convex cylindrical mirror. When the anamorphic image was then viewed as

Ambrotype Process. Photographer unknown; unidentified portrait, with half of the black backing removed. (ca. 1860). Private collection.

reflected by a mirror of the same curvature, the normal proportions were restored. Anamorphic images reached a peak of popularity as decorative elements and "visual anagrams" in the 17th and 18th c. In the 19th c. some photographers experimented primarily for the sake of novelty, by photographing the distorted mirror image with a normal lens and then viewing the resultant print in the mirror.

In 1897 Ernst Abbé designed a lens for direct anamorphic photography. However, large-scale photographic use of the principle came only in the mid-20th c. with the use of anamorphic lens or prism elements for wide-screen motion-picture systems such as Cinemascope and Panavision. In these systems the pictures are photographed in a wide format, using a camera lens with a vertical angle of view equal to that of a normal lens, but with a horizontal angle of view

two to three times greater; the lens does not distort the image. When release prints are made from the wide-format negative, anamorphic elements in the optical printer reduce the width of each image to that of a normal 35mm motion-picture frame; the result is extreme vertical distortion because of the horizontal squeezing. The film is shown on a standard projector equipped with a matching anamorphic system in front of the lens to unsqueeze the image and spread it across the screen in its original proportions. The same basic method is used to prepare wide-screen slides within the ordinary 35mm still-picture format. The anamorphic attachment is used first in front of the normal camera lens and then in front of the projection lens. Anamorphic devices are also used to squeeze large amounts of material onto standard film in various document storage and reproduction systems.

Anastigmat

A compound lens with a significant degree of correction for all aberrations, but especially for astigmatism, and based on either a symmetrical or a triplet arrangement of the elements, is called an anastigmat. The first anastigmat was designed by Paul Rudolph and Ernst Abbe and was produced by Zeiss in 1889. Today virtually all camera lenses are anastigmats with two-color achromatic correction of chromatic aberration.
See also: ABERRATIONS OF LENSES; LENSES; ZEISS, CARL.

Angle of View

The angle of view of a camera lens is the measurement in degrees of the angle formed by lines projected from the optical center of the lens to the extremities of the field of view. This angle is determined by the lens focal length and the negative format the lens is designed to cover, and is equal to the angle formed by lines projected back to the extremities of the format when the lens is focused at infinity. The maximum usable angle is determined by the diagonal of the format, the greatest dimension that must be covered; this is the angle usually given in manufacturers' lens specifications. The actual horizontal and vertical angles of view are less than this maximum because the corresponding format dimensions are shorter. Optical designers commonly refer to the half-angle measured between the lens axis and a line projected to one extremity of the format diagonal.

In terms of the maximum angle usually specified, a "normal" lens—one with a focal length about equal to the format diagonal—has an angle of view of about 50 degrees; the perspective produced by such a lens closely corresponds to that seen by the human eye. Lenses of longer focal length have narrower angles of

view and lenses of shorter focal length have wider angles of view as follows:

Lens Category	Angle of View
Telephoto	
Extreme	6°–15°
Medium	16°–25°
Moderate	26°–45°
Normal	46°–56°
Wide-angle	
Moderate	57°–70°
Medium	71°–90°
Extreme	91°–115°
Fisheye	150°–200+°

The term *camera angle of view* refers to the direction from which the subject is viewed in comparison to the head-on eye-level (or center-of-interest-level) line of view that is generally considered normal and emotionally or expressively neutral. The angle of view may be to one side (*e.g.*, three-quarters right, 90 degrees left, etc.) or above or below the normal line. In general, a high angle of view looking down on the subject tends to diminish the importance of a single, central object; alternatively, a high angle may be used to make the planlike layout of elements in a complex scene clearer. A low angle of view looking up at a subject tends to exaggerate its height and therefore its assumed importance. This angle is also a means of eliminating extraneous background details at the subject's level.
See also: COVERING POWER.

Angstrom Unit

The angstrom unit is equal to 1/10,000,000 millimeter; it is named for Anders Angstrom (1814–1874), a Swedish physicist and astronomer who was a founder of spectrography. Today, in place of the Angstrom unit (Å), scientists use the *nanometer* (nm), a unit ten times larger, to measure wavelengths of light. Thus, the visible portion of the electromagnetic spectrum extends from 4000 Å to 7000 Å, or from 400 nm to 700 nm.
See also: SPECTRUM; WAVELENGTH.

Aniline Process

A method of making direct prints from plans, line drawings, and similar originals on translucent paper or cloth, the aniline process was patented in England in 1864 by William Willis. No negative was required, and the process was not suitable for printing continuous tone or halftone images. Paper was sensitized by brushing one surface with a solution of ammonium or potassium bichromate (dichromate) and phosphoric acid in water. When dry, it was exposed by contact through the line original using sunlight.

The image was developed by the action of aniline dye fumes in a closed container; the copy had blue-black lines. Today similar results are obtained with the less hazardous chemicals and prepared materials used in various diazo processes.
See also: DIAZO PROCESSES.

"Animal and Human Locomotion"

This is a general title which encompasses the various editions and abridgements of the major publication of the work of Eadweard Muybridge in motion study and analysis. The original publication, entitled *Animal Locomotion*, was issued in 1887 by J. P. Lippincott, who had advanced money for Muybridge's pioneering work at the University of Pennsylvania in 1884 and 1885. The publication consisted of 781 plates of motion-sequence photographs printed as collotypes on 19″ × 24″ heavy linen paper, and explanatory text. The entire set in portfolio albums cost $500, or $550 if bound into 11 separate volumes. A portfolio of 100 selected plates was also available, and individual plates were sold for $1.00 each.

Each plate contained a sequence of 10 to 48 pictures showing the stages of movements of various animals, birds, and human beings. Domestic as well as exotic animals from the Philadelphia zoo (e.g., a Bactrian camel, a guanaco) were shown walking, running, trotting, galloping, and moving in other characteristic gaits. Humans were shown in athletic activities and in everyday movements as common as picking up a fallen handkerchief or descending a set of steps while carrying a cup and saucer. The movements of crippled and abnormally formed individuals were also shown. The intent was to present an analytical visual catalog of movement for primary use by scientists, physicians and surgeons, and artists. In 1899 Muybridge prepared *Animals in Motion*, a 100-plate selection from the larger work, and in 1901 *The Human Figure in Motion*, a similar selection.
See also: MOTION STUDY AND ANALYSIS; MUYBRIDGE, EADWEARD.

Animation

Animation is the technique of giving apparent movement to drawings or normally inanimate objects by presenting to the eye a rapid series of images in which one or more elements have changed position slightly in each successive image. The effect depends upon the persistence of vision, a phenomenon recognized in the production of "flip books"

Angle of View

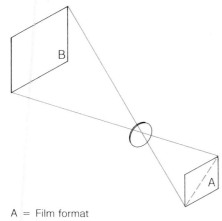

A = Film format
B = Corresponding field covered

Annan, J. Craig. "A Lombardy Ploughing Team" (1894); photogravure. Royal Photographic Society, Bath, England.

in antiquity, and scientifically investigated in the early 19th c., leading to the phenakistiscope, praxinoscope, zoetrope, and similar instruments.

The hand-drawn sequences used at first gave way to photographs in the 1880s when rapid-sequence camera techniques were devised by those engaged in motion study and analysis. The relative crudeness of most early efforts was overcome with the invention of the continuous-projection celluloid-strip motion picture. Interestingly, the earliest animated movies did not rely on drawings, but—as in the films of Georges Méliès in the 1890s—used stop-motion photography to bring objects to life. The first drawn films were white-on-black cartoon faces and stick figures created in the U.S. in 1906 by J. Stuart Blackton and in France in 1908 by Emile Cohl (Emile Courtet). The first cartoon film to receive significant public recognition was *Gertie, the Trained Dinosaur*, created in 1914 by Winsor McCay, famous for his artistically pioneering comic strip *Little Nemo*.

Animated motion pictures are photographed one frame at a time for projection at a rate of 24 frames per second. Many more than 24 drawings are required for one second of projection time, because most frames combine several drawings to accommodate many moving elements. In the earliest films all elements, moving and unmoving, were drawn on a single sheet of paper for each frame. In 1914 Earl Hurd patented the technique of drawing the changing elements on sheets of celluloid (cels) which were laid over a background of the stationary elements. Subsequent improve-

ments included registration pegs to keep a stack of cels with matching edge holes aligned as some were changed and others retained; a transilluminated stage for the cels which could be moved in precise increments horizontally (east-west) and vertically (north-south), and which would allow long-strip backgrounds to be pulled through; and pantograph and automatic (not computer-controlled) controls to move the camera precisely in any pattern over the plane of the drawings, as well as toward and away from the stage. The most famous production facility, Disney Studios, produced two especially notable technical innovations in addition to major classic short and feature-length cartoon films. One was a two-story-high camera incorporating seven separately illuminated stages on which the cells were placed to obtain composite scenes of great visual depth. The second was a method of combining live action and cartoon animation, in which the frames of the live movement, originally photographed against a black background, are projected as aerial images in the same plane as the drawings so both can be compositely recorded by the animation camera.

Production of an animated film begins with a storyboard, which assembles rough sketches of major action and story-line developments in general order. The sound track is recorded first and then animators draw the key illustrations of character positions and expressions. "In-betweeners" draw the many sequential images that represent the stages of movement from one major position to another. These drawings are

done in ink on the front surface of a cel. "Inkers" add color on the back side of the cels so that any edge irregularities are masked under the inked outline on the front. In mass-produced television cartoons, stock figure outlines are used repeatedly, along with stock sequences of movements for limbs and facial features. In feature-length films, virtually every frame is a carefully conceived and individually drawn image.

Modern animated films cover the entire range of drawing styles from photorealism to objective and non-representational abstraction. Some animators build their images from collages of various materials and picture fragments. Others adopt the techniques developed by Canadian Norman McLaren in the 1940s of drawing directly on the film. Some of the most intricate images are now computer-generated either on a high-resolution television screen which is photographed by a synchronized camera, or by controlling a laser beam which exposes each film frame directly. *See also:* MOTION PICTURES; MOTION STUDY AND ANALYSIS; PHENAKISTISCOPE; PRAXINOSCOPE; STOP-MOTION PHOTOGRAPHY; STORYBOARD; VISION; ZOETROPE.

Annan, J. Craig

Scottish; 1864–1946

J. Craig Annan was an important pictorial photographer and exponent of the photogravure process. He was responsible for a renewal of interest in the work of Hill and Adamson when, in approximately 1890, he rediscovered their

Annan, Thomas. "Close No. 46 Saltmarket"
(ca. 1870). Library of Congress.

Stieglitz to head the International Society of Pictorial Photographers in 1900, and he became its first and only president in 1904. Annan exhibited at the Photo-Secession Galleries in 1906 and was well represented at Stieglitz's International Exhibition of Pictorial Photography in Buffalo, New York, in 1910. Annan was referred to in the catalog of that show as "one of the chief forces in the development of pictorial photography."

In 1898 Annan published a limited edition portfolio, *Venice and Lombardy: A Series of Original Photographs.* He exhibited regularly in group and solo shows in London, Europe, and the United States. He was given a retrospective at the Royal Photographic Society in London (1900) and exhibited at the Paris International Exhibition (1900), the Glasgow International Exhibition (1901), the Scottish National Salons (1905 to 1909), and the Salon of the Paris Photo-Club (1906). He was honored with one-man shows at Arbuthnot's Kodak, Ltd. in Liverpool in 1912 and at the A.P. Little Gallery in London in 1913.

Annan became disenchanted with the direction of the Linked Ring and participated in the organization and exhibition of the London Secession in 1911.

He was awarded an Honorary Fellowship of the Royal Photographic Society in 1924 and was elected to the Fellowship of the Royal Society of Arts in 1936. He died near Glasgow in 1946.

Annan, Thomas

Scottish; 1829–1887
Thomas Annan, father of the photographer J. Craig Annan, was a versatile photographer known for his portraiture, architectural and landscape views, reproductions of paintings, and the documentation of the inhabitants and buildings of the slums of Glasgow. The photogravure process was introduced to Great Britain in 1883 by Annan and his son.

Annan was born in Darsie, Fife, Glasgow, the son of a flax spinner and miller. He worked as a copperplate engraver before opening a calotype studio in the Woodlands district of Glasgow in 1855. Annan was an ardent admirer of the work of Henry Fox Talbot and a friend of David Octavius Hill.

In 1857 Annan established another studio in Glasgow and began to specialize in the photographic reproduction of works of art and in architectural photography. He opened a portrait studio and photographic printing works in 1859.

calotype portraits and made photogravures of them. He was an early experimenter with hand-held cameras, and his photographs of Dutch, Spanish, and Italian subjects were highly acclaimed in the photographic journals of the day. In *Camera Work* of 1904 Joseph Keiley wrote that "...the work of J. Craig Annan has stood out in bold relief and marked its creator as one of the foremost artists in photography, not only in England but in the whole world.... He is today the real leader of British Pictorial Photography."

Annan grew up in the midst of the Glasgow and Edinburgh art circles. He studied natural philosophy and chemistry and worked in his father's printing factory and portrait studio (T.R. Annan and Sons) from the late 1870s. He and his father studied in Vienna with the inventor of the Heliogravure/photogravure process, Karel Klíč, in 1883, and

soon thereafter introduced photogravure reproduction in Great Britain.

Annan exhibited in the Salon of the Linked Ring from 1893 to 1909. He became a member of the society in 1894. That same year Alfred Stieglitz acquired the first of some 60 Annan photos he was to collect, and he wrote of Annan: "Here we deal with a true artist, and a decidedly poetic one at that. We have seen but few pictures to equal that called 'Labor-Evening.'... The picture breathes of atmosphere, it is a piece of nature itself. We can give it no higher praise."

Annan and Stieglitz enjoyed a long professional relationship. Annan's images appeared in five issues of *Camera Work* from 1904 to 1914 (the last of these issues was devoted exclusively to his work). In 1899 Annan invited Stieglitz to select American work for the 1901 Glasgow Exhibition. Annan was invited by

Annan was an early experimenter with the latest printing processes including combination printing, carbon printing, dry plate, and photogravure.

Annan became a regular contributor to exhibitions throughout Great Britain, winning first prize at the Exhibition of the Photographic Society of Scotland in 1865. He was elected a member of the Photographic Society of London in 1863.

In 1868 Annan was commissioned by the Glasgow City Improvements Trust to document the streets and buildings of the city. Though his task was to photograph only the buildings in the city center that were to be cleared away as part of a redevelopment program, Annan made images of many of the poor as well. He worked intermittently until 1877 recording the poverty and squalor. *Photographs of Old Closes, Streets, &c., taken 1868-1877*, a book of forty carbon prints of Annan's images, was published in 1878.

Annan and his son studied in Austria with Karel Klič, the inventor of the photogravure process, and returned to Scotland with the rights to its development. Annan had turned over the bulk of his portrait business to his son several years before and now turned his attention solely to his expanding photographic printing works, abandoning photography by the mid-1880s. He died in Glasgow in 1887.

Annan's views of the Glasgow slums were republished by Dover in 1977.
See also: ANNAN, J. CRAIG; KLIČ, KAREL.

Anschutz, Ottomar

German; 1846–1907
Along with Muybridge, Marey, Mach, and others, Anschutz was a pioneer in photographic motion study and analysis. His earliest work, in 1882, dealt with animals on his estate in Prussia (now part of Poland) and at the Breslau zoo. For this he used a folding hand camera of his own design with a focal-plane shutter capable of exposures as short as 1/1000 sec.; patented in 1888 and produced by C. P. Goerz, it was the first press camera. A 120-picture series of the life of nesting storks, in 1884, included detailed pictures of the birds in flight that astonished scientists and photographers. In 1886 Anschutz adopted Muybridge's system of linked batteries of cameras, and achieved much shorter exposures by using a smaller negative size and very short focal-length (hence wider aperture) lenses. To view his sequence studies of animals, birds, and people in motion, he invented the *tachyscope,* a kind of zoe-

trope with a vertical rather than horizontal rotating drum. For public exhibition he invented the *electrotachyscope,* in which glass positives on a revolving disc were illuminated from behind by a diffused, intermittent electric spark tube. Unlike Muybridge's zoopraxiscope, this was not a projection device; the images were viewed directly and could be seen by only a few people at a time. Anschutz also took spark-illuminated pictures of projectiles in flight at the Krupp weapons works, but in this he was preceded in 1887 by Ernst Mach in Prague, and P. Selcher in Fiume (Rijeka), Yugoslavia.
See also: GOERZ, CARL PAUL; MAREY, ETIENNE JULES; MOTION STUDY AND ANALYSIS; PRESS CAMERA; SHUTTER; ZOETROPE; ZOOPRAXISCOPE.
Color photograph: p. C-2.

Ansco

In 1901 the American photographic manufacturing companies of E. and H. T. Anthony and of Scovill and Adams were combined to form the Anthony and Scovill Co. In 1907 the company adopted the corporate name Ansco. Upon its purchase by the major European photographic manufacturer in 1928, it became AGFA Ansco Co. In the reorganization of German overseas holdings after World War II, the company became part of the General Aniline and Film Corp.(now GAF), which subsequently used "Ansco" as a product trademark.
See also: AGFA; ANTHONY, E. & H. T.

ANSI: American National Standards Institute

The American National Standards Institute (ANSI) is an organization which establishes standards for manufacturing, testing, and evaluating all kinds of equipment and materials. The most familiar evidence of an ANSI standard in photography has been the speed rating assigned to every film, and known as an ASA speed, from the organization's previous name, American Standards Association. (The speed prefix is now being changed to ISO, because the standard has been adopted by the International Standards Organization.) The hundreds of ANSI standards in the field of photography cover lens and flash testing, dimensions of films, spacing of sprocket holes, sensitometric procedures, determination of exposure, and a great variety of other matters.
See also: SPEED OF MATERIALS.

Anthony, Edward

American; 1819–1888
Anthony, Henry T.

American; 1814–1884
The Anthony brothers founded the largest American photographic supply and manufacturing business of the 19th c. Edward Anthony learned the daguerreotype process from Samuel F. B. Morse in 1841, and immediately applied it to field photography, first at the Croton (N.Y.) Reservoir, where he and his brother Henry were construction engineers, then at the St. Lawrence border with Canada, to obtain documentary records for use by the U.S. government in a dispute with Great Britain. In 1842 Edward Anthony established a portrait studio in Washington, D.C., in partnership with J. M. Edwards. Over the next two years the partners photographed all the members of Congress and other officials, compiling a unique collection that was almost completely destroyed by fire in 1859. In 1847 Edward Anthony gave up professional photography to establish a photographic supply business; his brother became a partner shortly thereafter.

By 1851 E. and H. T. Anthony and Co. was the largest photographic supplier in the U.S. Beginning by importing high-quality French daguerreotype plates, the brothers had expanded rapidly in several directions. They became agents and importers for the most important manufacturers, they published the major American photographic journal, they issued cartes-de-visite and stereographs from negatives purchased from others as well as from photographers they financed in the field, and they sold every variety of equipment and supplies; their annual catalog was a photographer's reference book. During the Civil War they advanced equipment and supplies to Mathew Brady's organization, and subsequently accepted a set of several thousand duplicate negatives, along with copyright, in settlement of an accumulated $25,000 debt. In response to business demand they took up the manufacturer of many items; eventually, in addition to a four-story store at 591 Broadway in New York, they had two factories in the city and a third in New Jersey.

The Anthony Co. became the first distributor for Eastman gelatin dry plates in 1880, an arrangement that held eventual irony. Disputes and lawsuits arose later in the decade as the Eastman Co. began to grow. After the death of both brothers, the Anthony Co., in 1900, acquired all rights in the Goodwin Film and Camera Co., including a pend-

ing patent to the basic idea of celluloid roll film. Fourteen years later the company, now evolved into Ansco, received a $5 million judgment against the Eastman Kodak Co. for patent infringement.
See also: ANSCO; BRADY, MATHEW; EASTMAN, GEORGE; GOODWIN, REV. HANNIBAL.

Anti-foggant

A chemical added to a developer to supplement the restrainer in controlling fog is called an anti-foggant. The most common anti-foggant is benzotriazole, available in powder and tablet form. It is useful with films and papers used beyond their marked expiration dates, with materials that have been stored in conditions of high temperature and humidity, or in situations in which developer temperatures are unavoidably above normal, as in tropical processing. It, or an equivalent, is also an essential ingredient in developers that use Phenidone in place of metol as a developing agent. The potassium bromide in such formulas is effective with the hydroquinone, but not with the Phenidone. The chemical 6-nitrobenzimidazole nitrate is an effective anti-foggant in prehardening solutions, and in developers subject to significant aeration, such as with constant-agitation tray or open-tank development of films.
See also: DEVELOPING AGENT; FOG/ FOGGING; RESTRAINER.

Anti-halation Layer

An anti-halation layer is light-absorbent material coated on the back of, or incorporated into, a film base to prevent stray exposure by light reflected from the back of the film chamber. In most films with ordinary cellulose triacetate bases, a translucent anti-halation layer is coated on the back of the base; the light-absorbing material dissolves out during processing, causing a slight coloration of the developer or fixer, which does not affect their subsequent working properties. The purplish or pinkish residual tint often visible in the processed film base is uniform throughout and does not affect the printing characteristics of the negative. Films with polyester bases have a built-in gray dye to prevent halation and "light piping" within the structure of the plastic. This dye does not dissolve out during processing and gives the film base a characteristic gray appearance; it does not affect printing. A few films, and notably Kodachrome color film, have an opaque backing layer which is composed of carbon particles and which is totally

removed during controlled machine processing.
See also: FILMS; HALATION; REM-JET BACKING.

Aperture

See: f-STOP; f-NUMBER.

Aperture-preferred; Aperture-priority

These terms identify the mode of automatic exposure control in which the photographer preselects the lens aperture setting. The automatic control system of the camera then selects the shutter speed required to produce a normally acceptable exposure—based on the camera meter's response to the subject brightness and the film speed setting—or indicates that the scene is outside the limits of acceptable exposure.
See also: AUTOMATIC EXPOSURE CONTROL.

Aplanat

One of the first major improvements in lens design after the Petzval portrait lens of 1840 was the aplanat lens. Introduced in 1866 by Steinheil (and as the *Rapid Rectilinear* lens by Dallmeyer in the same year), its symmetrical design placed matched two-element achromats on either side of the diaphragm to obtain a field of at least 50 degrees at f/8 with virtually no curvilinear distortion. This construction formed the basis for most general-purpose and landscape lenses into the early 20th c., and was adapted to produce wide-angle and middle-distance group portrait lenses with apertures on the order of f/6.
See also: ABERRATIONS OF LENSES; ACHROMAT; DALLMEYER, J. H. & T. R.; STEINHEIL, C. A. & H. A.

Apochromat

A lens corrected for chromatic aberration to bring three wavelength color groups (usually red, green, and blue) to a common focus is called an apochromat. More complex and significantly more expensive than the common achromat, this kind of lens is most often used in a process camera for graphic arts photography. The high degree of color correction limits the maximum aperture to about f/9, and is coupled with equally high correction for other aberrations, especially distortion and flatness of field.
See also: ABERRATIONS OF LENSES; ACHROMAT; OPTICS; PROCESS CAMERA/ PROCESS LENS.

Aquatint

The aquatint technique improves the printing characteristics of an etched plate. After the image is etched, but before the resist is removed, the plate is coated with a solution of rosin dissolved in alcohol; when the alcohol evaporates, specks of rosin remain, forming a random dot pattern. Alternatively, the plate is dusted over with dry rosin and heated until each particle melts sufficiently to adhere to the plate. The plate is then re-etched, producing a "grain" which greatly improves the ink-holding capabilities of the image. The randomness of the grain avoids the possibility of moiré with regularly patterned image details and the rigid feeling often produced by a mechanically ruled halftone screen. W. H. F. Talbot incorporated the aquatint procedure in his patent for Photoglyphy for inked reproduction of photographs.
See also: MOIRÉ; SCREEN, HALFTONE.

Arago, Dominique François Jean

French; 1786–1853
A physicist and astronomer, Arago played a major role in introducing the daguerreotype to the world. His scientific achievements included discovery of the chromosphere between the sun's visible surface and its outer atmospheric layer (corona); accurate measurements of the planets; observation of electrically induced magnetism; discovery of selective polarization of various wavelengths (chromatic polarization); formulation (with A. J. Fresnel) of the fundamental laws of the polarization of light; and the invention of a number of instruments to observe and measure the wavelike properties and behavior of light.

Arago was the first to recognize the significance of Daguerre's invention of photography, and foresaw its immense potential for scientific, communicative, and artistic use. He used his considerable influence and power as permanent Secretary of the Academy of Sciences and as a member of the Chamber of Deputies (i.e., the legislature) to see that the French government purchased the process from Daguerre and the heirs of J. N. Niépce and gave it to the world. He was instrumental in preventing Hippolyte Bayard's direct positive paper process from detracting attention from Daguerre's work, and it was Arago who actually made the presentation before the famous joint session of the Academy of Sciences, the Academy of Fine Arts, and the Chamber of Deputies on August 19, 1939, when details of the daguerre-

Arbus, Diane. "Pro War Parade" (1967). Courtesy Doon Arbus; collection, Museum of Modern Art, New York.

otype process were made public for the first time.

See also: BAYARD, HIPPOLYTE; DAGUERRE, L. J. M.; DAGUERREOTYPE; DIRECT POSITIVE.

Arbus, Diane

American; 1923–1971

A pivotal figure in contemporary documentary photography, Diane Arbus produced a substantial body of work before her suicide in 1971. Her unrelentingly direct photographs of peo-

ple who live on the edge of societal acceptance, as well as those photographs depicting supposedly "normal" people in a way that sharply outlines the cracks in their public masks, were controversial at the time of their creation and remain so today.

Arbus was born Diane Nemerov to a wealthy family in New York City. Her father owned a fashionable Fifth Avenue department store. She was educated at the Ethical Culture School, a progressive institution. At age 18 she married Allan Arbus and began to express an interest in photography. Her father asked Diane

and her husband to make advertising photographs for his store. The couple collaborated as photographers from then on, eventually producing fashion pictures for *Harper's Bazaar*.

Between 1955 and 1957 Arbus studied under Lisette Model. Model encouraged Arbus to concentrate on personal pictures and to further develop what Model recognized as a uniquely incisive documentary eye. Soon after Arbus began her studies with Lisette Model, she began to devote herself fully to documenting transvestites, twins, midgets, people on the streets and in

Archaeological Photography. Timothy O'Sullivan, "Inscription Rock," from the Wheeler Expedition (1873). Library of Congress.

their homes, and asylum inmates. Arbus's pictures are almost invariably confrontational: the subjects look directly at the camera and are sharply rendered, lit by direct flash or other frontal lighting. Her subjects appear to be perfectly willing, if not eager, to reveal themselves and their flaws to her lens.

She said of her pictures, "What I'm trying to describe is that it's impossible to get out of your skin into somebody else's. . . . That somebody else's tragedy is not the same as your own." And of her subjects who were physically unusual, she said, "Most people go through life dreading they'll have a traumatic experience. [These people] were born with their trauma. They've already passed their test in life. They're aristocrats."

Arbus's photographs drew immediate attention from the artistic community. She was awarded Guggenheim Fellowships in 1963 and 1966 to continue her work. In 1967 her work was mounted in the *New Documents* show at the Museum of Modern Art, New York, along with the work of two other influential, new photographers: Gary Winogrand and Lee Friedlander. For the most part, the exhibition received extremely good reviews.

In 1970 Arbus made a limited portfolio containing 10 photographs; by then she had established an international reputation as one of the pioneers of the "new" documentary style. Her work was often compared with that of August Sander, whose *Men Without Masks* expressed similar concerns, although in a seemingly less ruthless manner. In July 1971 Diane Arbus took her own life in

Greenwich Village, New York. Her death brought even more attention to her name and photographs. In the following year Arbus became the first American photographer to be represented at the Venice Biennale. A major retrospective at the Museum of Modern Art, New York, in 1972, which traveled throughout the U.S. and Canada, was viewed by over 7.25 million people. The next year, a Japanese retrospective traveled through Western Europe and the Western Pacific. The 1972 Aperture monograph *Diane Arbus*, now in its twelfth edition, has sold more than 100,000 copies.

Archeological Photography

Some 5000 to 6000 years of history are known through surviving written records, but this represents less than one percent of the time human beings have existed on earth. Knowledge of the greatest part of human heritage can only be obtained by the discovery and careful excavation of sites of ancient cultures. Archeological photographs serve as tools of discovery and as scientific records of the process and product of such investigations.

As in all scientific photography, a good archeological picture must be clear, well-detailed, and entirely straightforward. The function of such a picture is to be a record, not an interpretation; consequently, it must accurately represent what an observer on the scene would have noted. In particular, the photograph must maintain normal perspective so that the size, shape, propor-

tions, and relative positions of objects and structures are not misrepresented. This is primarily a matter of proper choice of lens focal length and camera position. In addition, tones and colors should not be misrepresented, except in the case where exaggeration or change is required to achieve differentiation of details that otherwise would be visually confusing or obscured. This is a matter of the choice of film, filters, and exposure.

Much archeological photography is field photography frequently carried out in conditions that are extremely demanding on both personnel and equipment. A complete record of an archeological project involves photography at three major stages: site location or discovery and survey; field work and excavation; and laboratory work. Location and survey photographs most often are taken from the air. Although aerial photography is not inexpensive, it provides substantial savings over ground surveying in expense and effort. Often it is the only practical way to discover the subtle difference in contour or coloration in the covering earth that reveals traces of sites. Infrared and color films are particularly useful for this kind of investigation. Time of year relative to foliage growth and weather conditions, time of day relative to the direction of light, approach angle, and altitude are major considerations in planning aerial site surveys. In general, early morning or late afternoon and oblique camera angles show site features in relief with the greatest clarity, while midday views taken straight down provide the most accurate data for mapping a site. Most archeological aerial photography is done at altitudes of 1500 feet and lower.

In the course of field work, activities such as clearing away undergrowth and excavation alter and may even destroy the site. The photographic record must document the condition of the site at every step so that information revealed by the state or configuration of elements that are subsequently moved or destroyed is not lost. As significant features are discovered or revealed, they must be recorded in overall views that show their orientation within the site, and in closer views that show their condition *in situ*, before they are removed for laboratory work. Each picture should include an identifying number and one or more scale indicators. Numbers are commonly marked on cards placed in the foreground or on tags attached to objects in close shots. Rulers, meter sticks, and surveyor's rods are commonly used to show scale. The scale indicator must be placed at the same distance from the camera as the object or feature for which it may be used as a reference. This is especially important in overall views because of the great change in magnification (scale) from foreground to middle and distant portions of the scene. Scale rods laid at intervals along the axis of view as well as horizontally across the field of view at various distances are extremely useful in later making relative measurements from photographs. Major objects and features should have individual scale indicators placed alongside or just in front parallel to their greatest dimension. Angled light provides the clearest definition of shapes, contours, and textures; electronic flash is commonly used in close shots either as the main light source or to fill in (lighten) the shadows created by the natural light.

On-site processing of black-and-white films is relatively easy to accomplish even under the most difficult field conditions; printing is another matter and is often left until a return to proper facilities. Color films must be protected against heat and humidity until they can be sent for processing. Although they are expensive and bulky to transport, instant-print films often are used to provide immediate working records at a site, while the permanent, more detailed records are made on conventional films.

Picture and object identification during the on-site phase takes on great importance during laboratory work so that accurate matching and comparisons can be made with objects after they have been cleaned, repaired, and otherwise worked on. Photography at this stage relies primarily on the techniques used with scientific specimens and with art objects: plain backgrounds, large-format films, controlled lighting, and often a variety of special techniques such as those used for macrophotography and infrared or ultraviolet photography.

Archer, Frederick Scott

English; 1813–1857
The basic collodion process for making wet plate glass negatives was invented by Archer, as was the related positive-appearing ambrotype, which supplanted the daguerreotype as a portrait medium and from which the ferrotype (tintype) was derived. Apprenticed to a silversmith, he became a designer and sculptor of relief designs for medallions and coins, and then was established in a business sculpting life-size portrait busts. He learned the calotype (paper negative) process in 1847 in order to get photographs of his subjects from which to work. Photography fascinated him, and

soon he was devoting most of his time and meager income to experimentation.

In 1850 Archer published his discovery of the use of pyrogallic acid as a developer. A year later he published the details of a method for making negatives on glass plates with a coating of sensitized collodion. He gave the process free to "brother photographers" without copyright or patent protection, a ruinous act of generosity. His detailed manual of the collodion process, published in 1852, provided a slight income; an alternative process, the ambrotype, did not; and ideas for in-camera processing, a three-element lens, and a lens with a "fluid" (i.e., moving) element were just enough ahead of their time to come to nothing.

Archer died, nearly penniless, at the age of 44; his wife died a year later. By that time the collodion process had revolutionized photography; it remained virtually the only practical way to make pictures until the mid-1880s. After a four-year subscription effort the world photographic community managed to contribute a total of less than $5,000 to a fund for Archer's orphaned children; the British government awarded them a joint pension amounting to about $250 a year. Photographic historians have repeatedly compared the gross injustice of this with the much larger cash payment and handsome pension the French government gave Daguerre, and with the personal wealth and arrogant lawsuits of W. H. F. Talbot, who even sought to claim that the rights to the collodion and all other processes belonged to him by virtue of his patent on the paper negative process. *See also:* AMBROTYPE; COLLODION PROCESS; FERROTYPE.

Architectural Photography

The primary function of architectural photographs is to record some aspect of a structure for the specific needs of a builder, architect, or historian. The pictures may deal with phases of construction as well as with the finished building, and with the entire exterior structure, its interior, or various parts or details. Most architectural photographs are straightforward records in which visual clarity and technical excellence are the primary requirements, but interpretive photographs and those which emphasize dramatic presentation are often required for purposes of publicity and promotion.

Historical development. The tradition of architectural photography begins at the birth of the medium in 1839–1840. Aside from the technical limitation of long exposures that made buildings one

of the few possible subjects for the earliest photographers, architecture was a subject of considerable cultural importance in the 19th c., and thus became one of photographic importance. Interest in civilizations of the past was intense, spurred by such 18th-c. achievements as the discovery of Herculaneum (1709), Troy (1748), and the Rosetta stone (1799). The most enduring evidences of antiquity were buildings and monuments. The developing science of archaeology fascinated the public and attracted great scholarly activity, especially by the British in Greece (the Elgin marbles were transported from Athens to London in 1806) and the biblical countries of the Middle East, and by the French in Egypt. Immediately upon its invention, photography was pressed into service to document discoveries and to attract government and private support for archaeological work. In the 1840s, the use of photography was limited by the small size, expense, and difficulty of the daguerreotype process, and by the relatively poor rendition of tone and detail of the calotype (paper negative) process. These drawbacks disappeared in 1850–1851 with the introduction of the waxed-paper and collodion-on-glass (wet plate) processes.

Interest in architecture was also a product of curiosity about foreign lands (where for both sociological and technical reasons it was far easier to take pictures of architecture than of the people), spurred by consolidation of the international expansion of European industrialized nations—epitomized by the vast spread of the British Empire, especially in India and coastal China. At home, two factors made architecture a subject of attention from the 1830s onward. One was a surge of nationalism, with an attendant concern for investigating and preserving evidence of historical development (Hill and Adamson's documentation of Scottish ruins, and the work of Charles Marville and several others in recording the renovation of Paris and the restoration of French cathedrals under Napoleon III are two examples). The second factor was the attitude characteristic of the Industrial Revolution that human ingenuity could devise the technology to construct anything, and that achievements of the sort ought to be proudly recorded.

One result of these various cultural factors was that photographs of architecture became a staple of the first photographic books and albums published in every major city, and were widely copied as engravings and lithographs for reproduction in periodicals and books.

The architectural application of photography increased enormously in the 1850s. The waxed-paper process produced negatives with tonal quality and resolving power far superior to calotype negatives. It permitted taking large-size pictures at a fraction of the cost of daguerreotypes, and could provide an unlimited number of prints (the daguerreotype produced a single direct positive image). In addition, the paper could be sensitized days ahead of time, was lightweight to carry on location, and could be processed up to several days after exposure. This was a distinct advantage over the collodion process, introduced at the same time, which used heavier, fragile glass plates that had to be prepared, exposed, and processed on the spot, usually within a total working time of about 20 minutes. However, the even finer print quality that could be obtained from glass plate negatives rapidly made the collodion process dominant until the 1880s, when it was replaced by far more convenient gelatin-emulsion dry plates, which in turn gave way to celluloid-base films, each of which gave equally high quality.

Superb technical quality—equal or superior to that of a great part of today's work—is one of the most notable characteristics of much architectural photography from about 1855 to the end of the century. The glass plate held the emulsion precisely in the image focal plane in the camera, so that every bit of sharpness a lens could deliver was recorded. Negatives were fully exposed to record rich shadow detail, and were developed by inspection to keep highlight densities within a printable range. Prints were made by contact exposure, which avoided magnification of grain, loss of sharpness from a poor or dirty lens or misalignment of the printing equipment, and degradation of tone from scattered light (all of these faults plagued enlargements in the early decades of the 20th c.). In addition, most prints were made with printing-out papers so that the progress of the image could be inspected visually and the exposure terminated at the optimal moment. When large prints were required, large glass plates were exposed in the camera. Images of up to 20″ × 24″ (and occasionally larger) produced in this way had exquisite detail and a compelling sense of reality.

Photographers of the mid- to late-19th c. approached architecture objectively, with the intent to record, not interpret the subject. Among those whose work is judged to be outstanding were, in France: Charles Nègre, Henri Le Secq, Edouard-Denis Baldus, Charles Marville, the Bisson *frères*, and Gustave Le Gray; in Italy: Pompeo Pozzi, Carlo Ponti, the Alinaris, Robert Macpherson, and James Anderson; in Greece: Claude-Joseph-Désiré Charnay, James Robertson, and William James Stillman; in Egypt: Aimé Rochas, Maxime Du Camp, Claudius Galen Wheelhouse, Francis Bedford, Francis Frith, and Felice Beato. Many of these photographers worked in other countries as well. The objective clarity of their work was echoed in pictures by August Sander in the 1920s and 1930s, by Berenice Abbott in the 1930s and 1940s, and in the present period by Bernd and Hilla Becher, Lewis Baltz, and Stephen Shore, among others.

The interpretive approach to architectural photography, in which the photographer makes a conscious aesthetic statement as well as a compelling straightforward record, originated in pictures of English and French cathedrals and old houses made by Frederick H. Evans from about 1890 to 1910. In the opinion of many, the subtle evocation of scale and the sense of light-filled volume accompanying the representation of structure and material in his photographs has never been equalled. If there are rivals to his work, they are the photographs of Paris taken by Eugène Atget in the first two decades of the 20th c. Atget's images are more objectively documentary than Evans's, but equally charged with the feeling that the buildings, monuments, and decorative details they show are the products of human spirit, not just the result of the architect's or engineer's calculations and the journeyman's tools. This appreciation of intrinsic style and spirit was continued in the work of Walker Evans in the 1930s, Danny Lyon ("The Destruction of Lower Manhattan") in the 1960s, and Paul Caponigro and Yukio Futagawa in the 1970s and 1980s. Futagawa's extensive studies of traditional wooden folk-houses in Japan and Europe are especially notable achievements in contemporary architectural photography.

The foregoing summary does not touch on two areas. One is the approach in which the intended aesthetic statement is of greater visual importance than the information conveyed about fundamental aspects of architecture—in short, Pictorialism, whether of the painterly turn-of-the-century variety, or the dynamic dramatization created by optical and color manipulation that developed from the 1920s onward and is widely indulged today. The other approach not summarized is that of the commercial illustrative photographer who specializes in architectural subjects. Such work is the mainstay of the great number of general and professional periodicals and books about architecture published each year. It is by far the most common kind of architectural photography today, and performs a necessary function extremely well. The bulk of contemporary commercial architectural photography is technically excellent, the product of high professional competence. It tends to escape critical notice and evaluation precisely because it is a commercial illustrative product rather than a personal statement. Nevertheless, it constitutes a significant practical application of photography.

Techniques. Architectural photography produced specifically for builders and architects often involves a series of photographs taken at intervals from specified locations to document the progress of construction from beginning to end. On more limited assignments the photographer records sections, interiors, or details. In all cases, accuracy and high image quality are important; scale, perspective, and lighting are the main factors to be dealt with.

Proper lighting is essential to produce clearly defined photographs of buildings. In exterior work the ideal situation is a blue sky with a slight cloud cover. Too much direct light produces pronounced shadows that may obscure details and present exposure problems, while completely diffused light from overcast sky eliminates the highlights and shadows that reveal relief in the surface structure. When light strikes architecture from an angle of approximately 45 degrees above and to one side of the camera position, texture and structure are usually revealed with the greatest clarity without significant shadow problems.

In a finished building the interior lighting may be supplemented with tungsten lamps or electronic flash to permit the use of small lens apertures for maximum depth of field. The character and placement of the added light must be balanced with the existing interior lights to maintain the original effect intended by the architect or designer. In color photography the color temperatures of mixed lighting sources also must be balanced, especially if daylight from windows is included in the scene. Combined interior-exterior views may use of electronic flash entirely (in place of the normal interior lighting) because its color temperature matches that of daylight.

Camera position and lens focal length are critical factors for correct rendition of perspective and spatial relationships. The photographs should allow the viewer to experience the space as it is constructed, rather than a fictional space produced by optical exaggeration or distortion. If the camera is too close to the subject, the nearer parts of the building will appear abnormally enlarged, and parallel lines at an angle to the camera will converge very rapidly; a number of other distortions may also result. To avoid such distortions, the architectural photographer uses a variety of lenses and a camera that permits corrective adjustments. Once the camera viewpoint is established for correct visual perspective, a lens focal length is chosen that will provide the desired image size from that distance. Then the movements offered by a view camera are used as necessary to control linear distortion and sharpness. In particular, back movements are commonly used to place the film plane parallel to the major plane of the subject to avoid unwanted convergence of horizontal or vertical lines. Lens movements are used to include more or less at the top (or a side) of the picture without having to angle the camera position, and to ensure that the plane of sharpness coincides with the major subject plane. Some medium- and small-format cameras and lenses have limited built-in movements similar to those of a view camera lens support. Such equipment is especially useful when small transparencies or slides are required.

Filters are used in architectural photography to achieve color adjustments, improve contrast, reduce reflections or glare, and provide visual emphasis or clarification. Filtration to produce rich sky tone or color is common in most overall views of buildings. Unusual or extreme filtration is used for many photographs that attempt to interpret or dramatize a structure. Often extreme camera positions or settings of camera movements are also used for dramatic effect. In such pictures the function of architectural record gives way to that of pictorial presentation.

See also: CAMERA MOVEMENTS; DISTORTION; PERSPECTIVE.

Color photograph: p. C-3.

Archival Processing

Archival processing is processing for permanence; its purpose is to produce photographs with the highest practicable stability and the longest attainable life. Current estimates based on photographic research are that well-processed black-and-white silver halide film and prints on modern materials should last a thousand years, and perhaps for several thousand years, if they are stored properly. Present-day color photographs generally lack the chemical stability to reach archival permanence. If color films

and prints are frozen and stored under conditions of controlled temperature and humidity, in theory they can be preserved indefinitely without deterioration. An alternative method is to make black-and-white separation negatives from color images. The separations can be archivally processed and used to produce color images from fresh materials whenever required.

To achieve a degree of permanence that reasonably can be considered archival (at least 300 years, but there is no general agreement on this minimum), a black-and-white photograph should not contain chemicals that will harm it, and it should have some built-in protection against harmful chemicals in its environment. No one processing method fits all materials and purposes. Prior to research results announced in 1982, the general procedure was to use fresh fixing solution to remove all unused (undeveloped) silver salts from the film or paper without leaving harmful residues that washing would not remove. This was followed by thorough washing to remove all possible fixer ("hypo") compounds and other processing chemicals. Washing efficiency was improved by treating the photograph in a "washing aid"—typically a 2-percent solution of sodium sulfite—which converted fixer compounds to a more readily soluble form. A hypo eliminator solution, composed of hydrogen peroxide and ammonia, was also used to treat the photograph before the final stage of washing. The ideal was to leave absolutely no traces of chemicals in the emulsion or the base material of the photograph. Additional permanence was achieved by subsequently treating the image in a solution of dilute gold chloride or selenium toner. This coated the silver particles of the image with a microscopic layer of a metal that was far more resistant to attack from chemicals in the storage atmosphere or materials or in the photograph itself.

The newest research upsets some of the assumptions upon which the established procedure was based. It shows that black-and-white films and prints containing no residual hypo are more vulnerable to fading and staining caused by oxidizing chemicals in the environment than photographs that do contain some residual hypo. Pure image silver is not stable. In the absence of residual hypo or any protective coating it tends to break down from its normal form, black filamentary silver, to much smaller particles called colloid silver. Areas of colloid silver on photographs are seen as red or orange spots, and sometimes colloid silver takes the form of mirror-

surfaced areas on the negatives or prints. Gold protective treatment and selenium toning offer some protection; the new discovery is that residual hypo does so as well.

It has long been known that fixing photographs in thiosulfate solutions leaves a deposit of silver sulfide—a stable chemical—adsorbed to the surface of image silver. What was not recognized before is that this sulfide layer is not harmful but is helpful; it protects the image silver. The sulfide layer is not formed primarily during processing, but is formed primarily by reaction of residual hypo with image silver long after the negatives or prints are dry. It is a long, slow process.

Presumably, in the mid-1980s these new findings will generate revised standards and procedures for black-and-white archival processing. A logical interim procedure is based on the recognition that most washing methods are not totally efficient, that washing aids perform a helpful function, and that dilute selenium toning provides a greater degree of protection than does treatment with gold chloride solution. Thus, images should be adequately fixed, treated in selenium toner diluted 1:19 or more with working-strength washing-aid solution, and thoroughly washed (at least three times longer than recommended by washing-aid manufacturers). This procedure is suitable for black-and-white films and for prints on fiber-base papers; there is no evidence that resin-coated water-resistant paper bases have archival permanence. After archival processing films and prints must receive proper storage and handling in order to achieve their intended degree of permanence.

See also: FILING AND STORING PHOTOGRAPHS; FIXING; WASHING.

Aristotype

Aristotype was first a trade name for various non-albumen printing papers, and later a general term for a print made on such papers. It first was used for a collodion silver chloride printing-out paper invented by English photographer George W. Simpson in 1868 and marketed by the Munich firm of Obernetter. The name subsequently was applied to the gelatin silver chloride paper invented by Sir W. Abney in 1886 and first marketed by the Paul Liesegang firm in Düsseldorf. Other manufacturers rapidly produced similar papers, which made albumen paper obsolete by the early 1890s.

See also: ABNEY, SIR WM. DE WIVELESLIE; ALBUMEN PROCESSES; PRINTING-OUT PAPER (P.O.P.)

Art, Photography of

Galleries, museums, libraries, and publishing houses make extensive · use of photographs that record works produced by painters, sculptors, and other artists. The photographer's task, and obligation, in making such records is to be as faithful to the appearance of the original as the medium will allow. Successful photography of works of art requires extensive knowledge of photographic materials and techniques and a painstaking, methodical approach.

Historical development. Copying and reproducing works of art was recognized as a potential application of photography from its very beginning. In *The Pencil of Nature* (1844), W. H. F. Talbot, inventor of the negative-positive process, illustrated photography's use in providing copies of artworks to students, painters, sculptors, architects, historians, and other professionals, as well as to the vast public who could never afford originals. He also showed its value in providing records of works that would be impossible to identify or describe with words. Beginning in the daguerreotype era of the 1840s, most portrait studios advertised an expertise in copying paintings, drawings, and statuary. In one of the first major applications of this sort, Nikolaas Henneman, Talbot's assistant, was engaged to document all the works—artistic, scientific, and industrial—included in the Great Exhibition of 1851 in England.

Throughout the 19th c., accurate translation of colors into equivalent shades of black and white (actually brown and white with most printing papers until the end of the century) was impossible. Until the 1870s, emulsions were only blue-sensitive; from then up to the early 20th c. they were blue- and green-sensitive (orthochromatic). Consequently, the most faithful records were of monochromatic works such as sculpture, engravings, and ink-and-pencil drawings. Copies of colored works such as paintings were sometimes toned or hand-colored to mask or compensate for deficiencies in tonal translation. Unenhanced copies of artworks were not necessarily so distorted as might be supposed, however, especially after the advent of orthochromatic plates and films. The range of colors used in a work of art was frequently more limited than in the actual subject, and the colorants in paints, crayons, and other materials often reflected light in ways that were photographically more effective with photographic emulsions of the time than the colors of light reflected by the subject. In addition, and perhaps most important, the brightness range of a painting or drawing was far less extreme than that of the original subject, which greatly eased the problem of differential exposures for various colors. Visualize, for example, the brightness range from forest shadows to bright sky in a painting in comparison to the actual range of the scene.

Whatever the limitations in fidelity, the demand from the public and from publishers for photographs of artworks increased rapidly from the 1860s onward. The exquisite detail and tonal gradation that could be obtained with the glass plate negative of the collodion process, introduced in the preceding decade, was a significant factor in this growth. So, too, were the improvements in other photographic materials and, from 1880, in methods of halftone reproduction, especially photogravure. Some establishments became major archives of photographs of art, monuments, and architecture from all over the world, notably the firm of Alinari in Italy, and the separate concerns of Francis Frith, G. W. Wilson, and Thomas Annan in England. Their pictures were sold as silver prints, carbon prints, photogravures, lantern slides, and stereographs (of sculpture and architecture).

Introduction of panchromatic emulsions and full-color plates and films from about 1905 brought great improvements in fidelity in black-and-white images of art, and slowly evolving improvements in color images. It became feasible to use filters to adjust tonal or color rendition for greater accuracy. Methods of reproduction also improved steadily in quality. In the 1950s and 1960s, technical advances begun during World War II made large-scale publication of high-quality, full-color reproductions economically feasible; the era of the lavishly illustrated art book resulted. Today, lenses and color films of astonishing quality are coupled with laser scanning, computer enhancement, and related techniques to produce photographs and printed reproductions that in many cases are essentially facsimiles, not simply copies, of the originals.

Techniques. Except when 35mm slides are required, flat works such as paintings, drawings, and prints are usually photographed with a view camera of at least 4″ × 5″ format. The large image size is essential for the highest quality reproduction, and the operating adjustments provided by such a camera permit precision alignment with the subject. The film plane must be perfectly parallel with the original work being recorded, and the illumination must be absolutely even across its entire surface. A lens with no linear distortion and a high degree of correction for other aberrations is required. If the photograph is to be in color, an apochromatic lens is preferred to ensure equally sharp focus of all colors. A sturdy tripod, cable release, and bellows-type lens shade (to minimize flare) are essential accessories. A view camera is also preferred for photographing sculptures and other three-dimensional works, not only for image size, but especially because the lens swing-tilt movement makes it possible to place the plane of maximum sharpness as required while keeping the back (film plane) in the position that produces minimum distortion. As in portrait photography, a longer than normal focal length lens is required to obtain sufficient image size from a lens-subject distance that avoids distortion.

Either tungsten or electronic flash illumination may be used. Flash avoids the danger of heat damage to the work of art, and its color balance permits the use of daylight-type color films without the need for conversion filtration. However, it requires on-the-spot test shots (usually taken with instant-print film) to see its effect and to detect glare, unwanted shadows, and other problems. Tungsten bulbs such as photofloods are less expensive and produce less heat than tungsten-halogen lamps (quartz lights), but they have a much shorter life, and the color temperature of their light drops as the bulbs darken with use. All tungsten bulbs in a setup for color photographs should be changed at the same time so that the output from all sources will match as closely as possible. Aged bulbs can be used for black-and-white and other kinds of less critical photography.

Even, glare-free lighting of flat surfaces is achieved by placing light sources on either side of the camera at an angle of at least 45 degrees from the lens axis. If only two lights or flash units are required, they should be at the same height as the lens. If more are required, they should be equally divided on each side and placed directly above one another at equal distances above and below the lens height. Often it is easier to light a long, rectangular work by turning it so the long dimension is vertical; then it can be covered by an appropriate number of lights on a single stand at each side of the camera. The evenness of the lighting can be checked by incident-light meter readings (or reflected-light readings from a gray card) taken at the corners, edges, and center of the area being photographed. There must be no more than a one-third f-stop difference among the readings.

Three-dimensional objects must be lighted to reveal both form and texture without glare or disturbing shadows. Typically, a frontal main (key) light, a fill light, and a backlight are used, but many variations are called for to bring out distinctive features such as patina, relief decoration, or inlays. Appropriate settings or backgrounds for art objects are an important consideration as well.

Because most artworks are unmoving subjects, slow, fine-grain films may be used to take advantage of their high-quality image characteristics. Most black-and-white photography is done with panchromatic films; filters may be required to achieve good contrast and tonal clarity in the translation of subject colors to shades of gray. High-contrast orthochromatic or blue-sensitive films are valuable in recording drawings, engravings, and other line images. A color film that matches the color temperature of the illumination should be chosen; although conversion filters can be used to adjust the light to the film balance, the fewer elements in the image path, the better the image quality will be. In addition, other filtration may be required to make slight adjustments for the greatest color fidelity. Most color photography of artworks is done on transparency films because their images produce the best results in photomechanical reproduction. Color film should be kept refrigerated until a few hours before use and processed immediately or re-refrigerated until processing is possible. It is useful to stock a large quantity of color film of the same emulsion batch so that information gained from test shots with the first few sheets or rolls will be applicable to a substantial amount of work.

Exposures for color records are best determined by an incident-light meter reading, or a reflected-light reading from a standard gray card. Black-and-white exposures should be based on a reflected-light reading from the subject itself. In almost all cases bracketing shots at greater and lesser exposures should be made; it is impossible to predict the precise exposure that will best capture the expressive nuances of the colors and details of a work of art.

Photography of kinetic sculptures, video presentations, "happenings," and other works with movement or performance elements involves technical and expressive problems related to scientific, dance, and theatrical photography. A medium- or small-format camera may be required for its portability or flexibility of use; medium or fast films may be required to achieve adequate exposures. Information appropriate to these subjects will be found in a variety of other entries.

Artigue Process

The Artigue process was a variation of the carbon process which had the advantages of not requiring a transfer operation and of producing tones of exquisite delicacy, but had the disadvantage of being very delicate to handle until the image had been hardened in an alum solution and thoroughly dried. It was invented in France by Victor Artigue in 1892, and the materials were marketed by him as *charbons velours* beginning in the following year. In England and the U.S. the materials were known as Artigue papers and the final image as an Artigueotype. The Artigue process was also one of the earliest bichromate processes. A tissue with a carbon-pigment coating (later colored pigments were offered) was sensitized with a bichromate solution and when dry was exposed by contact to a negative of thinner densities than most other processes required. The image was developed by repeatedly pouring over it a souplike mixture of warm water and very fine sawdust, which acted together to dissolve and abrade away the unhardened pigment in the highlight and middletone areas.

See also: BICHROMATE PROCESSES; CARBON PROCESSES; TRANSFER PROCESSES.

Artists and Photography

As long as photography was considered a purely mechanical process lying outside the realm of the fine arts, most artists were reluctant to admit any connection with the medium. Only recently has it been learned how extensively 19th- and early 20th-c. painters of the stature of Eugène Delacroix, Gustave Courbet, Thomas Eakins, and Edvard Munch made use of photographs as preliminary studies for their canvases. Although Camille Corot, Jean Millet, and a few others experimented with the quasi-photographic *cliché-verre* process in the mid-19th c., Edgar Degas's use of photography as an independent print medium in the 1890s stands as a major exception to the hostility with which most artists regarded the upstart medium. It was only in the present century that artists who are now widely recognized began to explore the possibilities of photography. Painters like Charles Sheeler, Man Ray, Laszlo Moholy-Nagy, and Herbert Bayer seriously investigated the expressive possibilities of the photographic print. The sculptor Constantin Brancusi used the camera to create photographic images of his sculpture that have been hailed as creative works in their own right. In addition, the use of photographs as constituents of collages and montages was widely prac-

ticed by such artists as Hannah Hoch, Raoul Haussman, and John Heartfield.

Especially since the 1960s, a growing number of artists have been attracted to photography, often for reasons that have little to do with photography's own fine art tradition as embodied in the works of Alfred Stieglitz or Edward Weston. As the traditional boundaries of the fine arts have expanded to include such diverse contemporary art forms as cinema, performance, environmental art, and conceptual art, many artists have turned to photography not only for its ability to document short-duration artworks, but also for its capacity to rapidly provide images that can be incorporated into larger assemblages or mixed-media productions.

Among the most important figures who have adopted photography for use in contemporary art is the painter Robert Rauschenberg, who in the 1950s began to incorporate photographic images culled from magazines and newspapers into his large "combine" paintings. Subsequently, he pioneered in the use of the photosilkscreen technique to transfer images drawn from a wide variety of sources to his canvases. Also quick to adopt the silkscreen process was Andy Warhol, one of the originators of Pop Art, who turned photographs of such popular-culture icons as Elizabeth Taylor, Elvis Presley, and Marilyn Monroe into color-saturated serial images. Warhol employed the same serial technique in a series of silkscreened works focusing on photographs of anonymous catastrophes—auto accidents, airplane crashes, executions—which underscored the ubiquity of photography in modern mass-media culture.

Since the 1950s other artists, including members of the Gutai movement in Japan, and Happening and Fluxus in America and Europe, have relied on photography to provide visual records of events they have staged, which (in a tradition begun by the futurists and Dadaists) have combined many communicative elements. In 1963, for example, the French artist Ben Vautier used photography to document his Fluxus performance piece, which consisted of the artist's swimming across the harbor of Nice. Other pieces were far more elaborate. Among the photographers who specialized in recording events staged by such artists are Koro Honjyo, Shunk-Kender, Robert McElroy, Ute Klophaus, and Peter Moore. The use of photography by avant-garde artists developed quickly during the 1960s and 1970s, especially among the conceptualists, in some of whose works the act or the manner of taking the photograph is an integral part of the art piece. During this period artists such as John Baldessari, Vito Acconci, Douglas Heubler, Hamish Fulton, Michael Snow, Joseph Kosuth, William Wegman, and Robert Smithson were among these incorporating photography into their work in increasingly imaginative and complex ways. Acconci's "Lay of the Land" (1969) was produced by the artist's "lying down in a field, camera held at five points on my reclining body, shooting out at landscape." Smithson, in the piece called "Incidents of Mirror Travel in the Yucatan" (1969), photographed a group of mirrors set up in a variety of locations, and published the photographs and a long accompanying text as the completed work. Intermedia artists like Carolee Schneeman used slide projections in performance works; others used them to create environments.

The widespread use of photography by artists in the last few decades has prompted a number of them to investigate the medium's properties and capabilities as an image-making system. In some cases, as in the work of Michael Snow, Jan Dibbets, and Ger Dekkers, this involves an analysis of the working of the perspective system that is automatically produced by the camera apparatus. In other cases, for example in the work of the British artist John Hilliard, the use of selective focusing as a device for subtly altering the meaning of photographs is explored. More recently, artists such as Victor Burgin have sought in exhibitions to unveil the abuses of photographic imagery used in contemporary advertising.

Photography has played an especially important role during the last decade in the development of what is called narrative art or "story art." This involves the examination of different ways of combining words and pictures, or a series of two or more related images, in order to convey the sense of a (sometimes unconventional) story unfolding. The color photographs of Bill Beckley, for example, allude to but never directly illustrate the short, ambiguous written texts that accompany them. In a related manner, the semi-fictionalized series of "Anecdotes" by the French artist Jean Le Gac have been exhibited as typed pages shown with photographs in which Le Gac appears as a character in the situation that is described.

A surprisingly large number of artists in the last years have used themselves as the subject of their art, and photography has been prominently employed as a medium for such work. Lucas Samaras, in a series of extraordinary "Phototransformations," radically altered the Polaroid photographs on which he had recorded his own image. Similarly, the

German artist Arnulf Rainer has applied vivid paint to the surface of his photographic self-portraits. Another German, Klaus Rinke, has photographed himself performing extended series of physical movements, and exhibited the results as strikingly graphic blocks of prints on gallery walls. Perhaps most interestingly of all, the American artist Cindy Sherman has in the last few years undertaken a large number of fictionalized self-portraits in which she appears in the stereotyped roles in which women have been traditionally portrayed by the mass media. Drawing on the earlier artistic currents of performance art, narrative art, and implicit social criticism, Sherman has employed photography as a medium which can successfully bind together all of these concerns in single, powerful images.

The British painter David Hockney offers the case of an artist who has edged closer and closer to photography during the last decade. Long a passionate amateur photographer (he has collected nearly 30,000 of his casual photographs into albums), Hockney in 1982 began to exhibit what he called "camera drawings." These consisted of large mosaics of Polaroid photographs which presented scenes and human sitters in a fragmented manner recalling Picasso's cubist technique.

See also: CLICHÉ-VERRE; PAINTING AND PHOTOGRAPHY and cross-references listed there.

Art Photography

Photography was initially received as a uniquely capable illustrative medium able to render nature with a fidelity never before seen. The remarkable facility and precision with which photography could render detail, perspective, light, and shadow was enough to fascinate most observers; few felt the need to speculate as to its potential artistic applications.

In the main, the earliest uses of photography were for portraiture and landscape. The aim was to produce an accurate "drawing" of the subject, rather than to use the subject as raw material for the photographer's expressive purposes. By the late 1840s, however, narrative illustrations and pictures in the academic painting style of the period began to appear, and artistically inclined photographers showed increasing interest in using photography to make "beautiful" pictures rather than accurate renderings. The Pictorialist movement, headed by H. P. Robinson from 1858, held that photography could be used to produce artistic images, but only by

adhering to established rules of painterly composition. The Pictorialists consciously strove to emulate their Academic contemporaries in the fine arts. Their main theme was idealized Beauty. To that end, a number of artificial devices were employed: models were costumed and posed to illustrate verses from romantic poetry or moralistic subjects such as The Virtues and The Graces; poses and expressions were rehearsed; and elaborate outdoor scenes were reconstructed in the studio. Combination printing and heavy retouching for "artistic effect" were used widely.

In spite of the artifices used by many Pictorialists, some succeeded in producing photographs that have impact to this day. Julia Margaret Cameron's portraits of her literary aquaintances, while occasionally contrived, often have a directness and simplicity that allows the sitter's character to come forward; Lewis Carroll produced a number of evocative children's portraits.

The Pictorialist period was temporarily interrupted by objections from Peter Henry Emerson, who in 1886 assailed the sentimentality and conservatism of the Pictorialists in a speech to the Camera Club in London. Emerson's contention was that the medium of photography was in and of itself an art— no artifice was needed—and that it, like the other arts, was best used to depict scenes from nature as the eye saw them. Emerson's photographs were direct representations of natural scenery and straightforward studies of life in the rural marshlands of England. The naturalist school headed by Emerson laid the foundation for the "straight" or purist approach that continues as the aesthetic basis for much art photography to this day.

The naturalist doctrine maintained some influence over photographic aesthetics for about a decade; it was supplanted by a more painterly style which drew much of its impetus from Manet, James McNeil Whistler, and other painters of what would become known as the "Impressionist" school. The photographic followers of the Impressionist mode banded together as the Linked Ring in England. Similar secessionist movements arose later in Germany and, under Alfred Stieglitz, in the U.S. While less directly photographic than the naturalists, the Secessionist photographers did not revert to the theatrical practices of the Pictorialists; instead they used the gum-bichromate printing method, soft focus, and other techniques to give their pictures a sense of the artist's "hand." The Secessionists in their turn were challenged by the $f/64$

Group which was founded in California in the 1920s. Members of this group included Edward Weston, Ansel Adams, and Imogen Cunningham. Their aim was to counteract the stale, conservative Pictorialism of the Secessionists with a clean, straight approach. The camera was to be used to talk of formalist and realist issues rather than pictorial ones. The subject was to be presented to the viewer, not interpreted for him or her. This "straight" aesthetic remains strong to the present day, although it exerts far less influence than it did two generations ago.

No specific school of thought holds sway over current photographic art trends; contemporary photographers subscribing to illusionist ideals coexist with those whose main concern is with narrative, abstraction, or formalism. Borrowing freely from various movements in the plastic arts, as well as from imagery of the communications media and the cinema, many contemporary photographic artists use an interdisciplinary approach to make their images.

The question as to whether or not photography is an art, and if so what kind of art it should be, is no longer of much concern to many of those using the medium. They subscribe, consciously or not, to the view that it is the worker, not the medium, that determines whether or not something is art, and they proceed accordingly.
See also: Entries for individual photographers cited; f/64, GROUP; NATURALISTIC PHOTOGRAPHY; PHOTO SECESSION; PICTORIAL PHOTOGRAPHY/PICTORIALISM; STYLE.

ASA

ASA is the acronym for the American Standards Association, which in 1969 became the American National Standards Institute (ANSI). The prefix ASA was retained in film-speed designations until photographic manufacturers adopted ISO ratings (identical to ASA speeds) in the early 1980s.
See also: ANSI; SPEED OF MATERIALS.

Aspect Ratio

The ratio between height and width in photographic and video formats is called aspect ratio. It is an important consideration in order to avoid image cutoff when material produced in one format is transferred to or presented in another. Two typical aspect-ratio problems are photographing material for television presentation and preparing material for use in filmstrips. Composition must conform to the proportions of the ultimate aspect ratio, and the material must be photographed with sufficient "safe area" on all sides so that no essential material will be cut off. Wide-screen motion-picture and slide presentations often use anamorphic images to obtain the required aspect ratio. Common ratios are as follows.

Format	Aspect Ratio
Half-frame 35mm still and filmstrip	(3:4 =) 1:1.33
35mm motion picture	1:1.37
Full-frame 35mm still	(2:3 =) 1:1.5
1¾" × 2¼" (4.5 × 6cm)	1:1.33
2¼" × 2¼" (6 × 6cm)	1:1
2¼" × 3¼" (6 × 8cm)	1:1.44
4" × 5"	1:1.25
5" × 7"	1:1.4
8" × 10"	1:1.25
TV; video recording	(3:4 =) 1:1.33
Wide-screen motion pictures and slides	1:2 and greater

See also: ANAMORPHIC IMAGES; FILMSTRIPS; FORMAT.

Aspheric Lens

An optical element, or a compound lens incorporating an element, having at least one surface on which various points do not have a common radius point is aspheric. Most lens surfaces are sections of spheres: all points on a given surface are equidistant from an origin (radius or center point), and the front and rear surfaces of an element are almost always sections of spheres of different radius. This principle of design produces spherical aberration, which can be corrected by including an aspheric element. The aspheric surface may be a single continuous curve such as a section of a paraboloid (the usual case) or hyperboloid, or it may have compound (convex-concave) curvature, as in the corrector plate of a Schmidt camera and similar mirror lens systems.

It is extremely difficult to design and grind an aspheric surface of high optical quality; for this reason aspheric lenses originally were limited to molded glass lenses not used in the image-forming path, such as the condensers in the illumination sections of projectors and enlargers. Today the development of high-ly sophisticated computer programs for optical design and the control of lens grinding machinery, along with the development of easily molded plastics of high optical quality, have made the inclusion of aspheric elements in camera lenses both practical and common.
See also: ABERRATION OF LENSES; LENSES; MIRROR LENS; OPTICS.

Associations
See: APPENDIX.

Astigmatism
See: ABERRATIONS OF LENSES.

Astrophotography

Astrophotography is principally concerned with subjects outside the earth's atmosphere, although some phenomena taking place in the ionosphere (the outermost portion of the atmosphere) or the interface between the ionosphere and space are also commonly included (e.g., aurorae and meteor showers).

Relatively little astronomical investigation is done by actually looking through a telescope. Most often a photographic or quasi-photographic process is employed, because many astronomical objects are much too faint to be studied by direct visual observation. Photography allows weak light intensities to accumulate on the emulsion, and thus, effectively unobservable objects such as very distant stars are rendered visible. Moreover, the image is preserved so that it may be looked at in detail and compared to other photographs. In this way changes taking place over a period of decades or longer may be determined and quantified. Photography also permits images to be recorded outside the visible spectrum; in particular, the ultraviolet and infrared spectral ranges are helpful to astronomers.

Along with specific-area pictures made for star-mapping purposes, highly specialized photographs, notably spectrographs, are produced. These are images which show the separate wavelengths generated by a celestial body. This technique produces information about the physical composition of the body, as well as its velocity relative to the earth.

A wide variety of equipment may be used for astrophotography, ranging from a simple, ordinary camera to sophisticated and expensive camera and telescope combinations. Large scientific telescopes are in fact camera systems; visual observation, if it is used at all, is employed only to aim the equipment at the intended area of observation. Whatever the scale of the equipment, the primary requirement for all astrophotography is a rigid camera support. For simple photographs of the moon, sun, or aurorae a common tripod is sufficient.

Almost any camera is suitable to photograph near and bright objects, especially if it can be fitted with a telephoto lens. The greatest number of astrophotographs, however, are taken with the aid of a reflecting (mirror system) telescope. A camera may be fitted to a telescope in a number of ways. The simplest method is to position the camera lens directly on the axis of the telescope eyepiece. If a tracking device is used on the telescope, the camera must be mounted to move with it; otherwise, a separate tripod is acceptable, if care is taken not to disturb the alignment during use. Aside from being clumsy, this method of combination uses an unnecessary lens. The image is formed by the optical system of the telescope; the camera is merely a recording device, and its lens is not only unnecessary but undesirable as a potential source of image degradation and light loss. Improved results are obtained by fitting the camera body directly to the telescope eyepiece lens. This method has the added advantage of using the telescope as a camera support.

In a third arrangement, the prime-focus method of coupling, the eyepiece lens is also eliminated, and the image from the telescope's objective mirror (or lens) is focused directly onto the film plane. While there is less magnification with this setup, there is also less light loss from optical-element absorption. A variation of prime-focus direct projection is negative lens projection. The image from the objective passes through an intermediate negative lens which magnifies the image projected onto the film.

Magnification is of importance only for relatively near objects—those seen with dimension. Because of their great distances, most celestial objects are effectively point sources and cannot be magnified. Therefore, the focal length of an instrument intended primarily for observation of the stars is relatively unimportant. However, the diameter of the telescope objective lens or mirror is critical because that determines the light-gathering power and thus whether a faint star can be seen or recorded. Large telescopes such as the 200-inch (5.1-meter) instrument on Mount Palomar are identified by mirror size, not focal length. The relative light-gathering power of reflecting telescopes used for stellar observation is measured by the proportional difference between the squares of the mirror diameters, not the

f-numbers or maximum apertures of their optical systems. Therefore, a 100-inch (2.5-meter) diameter instrument is four times as fast as a 50-inch (1.25-meter) instrument, regardless of focal length. For observation or photography of objects with dimension (e.g., the moon), comparisons of maximum aperture f-numbers do give an accurate indication of the relative image brightnesses the instruments produce.

No matter how fast the telescope or how sensitive the emulsion may be, astrophotography of all but the brightest celestial bodies is likely to require an exposure of minutes or even hours. In professional work a number of techniques have been employed to heighten emulsion sensitivity. Baking a film or plate at 140°F (60°C) for a few hours or giving the emulsion a general pre-exposure (flashing) yields modest results. Placing the film in a vacuum chamber and lowering the temperature for exposure sometimes works well, but this method is limited to specialized equipment. Even with such techniques, an emulsion with extended reciprocity characteristics is required. However, the most sensitive emulsion is not necessarily the best. Resolving power is of primary importance, so an emulsion with the finest grain structure consistent with reasonable exposure times is the one of choice. Dimensional stability is also critically important so that accurate measurements may be made directly from the processed image. For this reason glass plates rather than flexible-base films are used for certain kinds of investigation.

Astrophotography has previously been limited by the atmosphere surrounding the earth. What to a casual observer can seem like a clear sky is more like pea soup to the astrophotographer. The era of astrophotography by instruments located in space, above the earth's atmosphere, is just beginning. Astronomers have reported that the first images obtained from this new vantage point have generated more information than decades of earth-bound astrophotographs. Installations that are accessible by means of the space shuttle or similar methods will use instruments with recoverable film as well as electronic imaging systems.

See also: ECLIPSE PHOTOGRAPHY; MOON PHOTOGRAPHY; SUN PHOTOGRAPHY; TELESCOPE.

Atget, Eugène

French; 1857–1927

Jean Eugène Auguste Atget, among the first of photography's social documen-

ters, has come to be regarded as one of the medium's major figures. His images of Paris are perhaps the most vivid record of a city ever made.

Atget was born in Libourne, near Bordeaux, France, and was raised by an uncle from an early age after the deaths of his parents. He became a cabin boy and sailor and traveled widely until 1879 when he entered the National Conservatory of Dramatic Arts in Paris. He studied there for two years and became an actor with minor roles in repertory and touring companies, but although he was talented, he was never successful. During this period a relationship developed between Atget and the actress Valentine Delafosse, with whom he lived for the rest of his life (she eventually became his photographic assistant). Together they were able to make a poor living for a number of years, but it became clear that Atget had no future as an actor. In 1897 he tried his hand as a painter and was again unsuccessful. He started to photograph the next year at the age of 40.

Atget took no portraits per se, but he did photograph street characters: peddlers, garbage collectors, road workers, and so on. His friend André Calmette wrote that Atget set out to photograph "everything in Paris and its environs that was artistic and picturesque."

In recording the daily appearance of a rapidly changing Paris, Atget made methodical surveys of the old quarters of the city. He was to make over 10,000 photographs of this immense subject in the next 30 years using obsolete equipment: an 18 × 24cm bellows camera, rectilinear lenses, a wooden tripod, and a few plate holders.

Atget operated a small commercial photography business called "Documents pour artistes" and sold his carefully cataloged images to stage designers, art craftsmen, interior decorators, and painters (Braque, Derain, and Utrillo, among others), and to official bodies such as the Bibliothèque Nationale, the Bibliothèque de la ville de Paris, the Musée des Arts Décoratifs, and the Musée Carnavalet. However, few of his clients appreciated his artistry.

The quiet, even understated, appreciation of a subject's beauty in Atget's work has led many to consider him naive, a primitive. In truth, his work is marked by a purity of vision, a refusal of painterly rhetoric, and a deceptive simplicity.

One of Atget's earliest admirers was the young Ansel Adams, who wrote in 1931: "The charm of Atget lies not in the mastery of the plates and papers of his time, nor in the quaintness of costume, architecture and humanity as revealed in his pictures, but in his equitable and inti-

Atget, Eugène. "Avenue des Gobelins"
(1907); gold-toned print-out paper. Collection, Museum of Modern Art, New York.

mate point of view. . . . His work is a simple revelation of the simplest aspects of his environment. There is no superimposed symbolic motive, no tortured application of design, no intellectual ax to grind. The Atget prints are direct and emotionally clean records of a rare and subtle perception, and represent perhaps the earliest expression of true photographic art."

In 1920 Atget sold 2500 negatives relating to the history of Paris, a large portion of the work he had been accumulating for two decades, to the Caisse National des Monuments Historiques. He described these photographs as "artistic documents of fine sixteenth- to nineteenth-century architecture in all the ancient streets of old Paris. . . historical and curious houses, fine facades and doors, panellings, door-knockers, old fountains, period stairs (wood and wrought iron), and interiors of all the churches in Paris (overall views and details)." With the help of the considerable sum he received for this body of work, Atget was able to devote more of his time to photographing with increased dedication and historical awareness those subjects to which he felt closest. Many of his most beautiful images were made during his last years.

In 1926 Atget's neighbor Man Ray published (without credit) a few of Atget's photographs in the magazine *La révolution surréaliste*. This marked the beginning of the important surrealist appreciation of his work. Berenice Abbott, a student of Man Ray's, was impressed by Atget's photographs in 1925, and has been responsible for rescuing his work from obscurity and preserving his prints and negatives, which she acquired upon his death in 1927. She has written: "He will be remembered as an urbanist historian, a genuine romanticist, a lover of Paris, a Balzac of the camera, from whose work we can weave a large tapestry of French civilization."

Atget's work was included in the important modernist exhibition "Film und Foto" in Stuttgart in 1929. The first book of his images was published in 1931. The Abbott Collection is now in the Museum of Modern Art, New York. Atget was the subject of a major retrospective at the Museum in 1969 and of a series of retrospectives there in the early 1980s.

Audiovisual

The term *audiovisual* is applied to a wide range of materials and presentational techniques that are incorporated into a program presented "live" directly to an audience. The most common audiovisual materials are slides, filmstrips, video and audio tape recordings, overhead projection images, and motion pictures. Other materials or "aids" include chalk and felt boards, large-scale charts, photographic enlargements, and scale models.

At one time audiovisual presentations were seldom used outside the school classroom or employee training session. Today they also are an important part of business and sales meetings, product-introduction press conferences, professional symposia, social aid and community programs, presentations at museums and similar institutions, and many other activities.

The function of audiovisual aids is to expand the scope and increase the effectiveness of a program. They stimulate interest and attention by adding variety to the presentation; they improve communication by presenting information in a clear, memorable form. In some cases only a few slides integrated into a talk may be required. In other cases a motion-picture, video tape, or multimedia presentation will do the best job. Thus, planning and preparation may be a one-person task, or, in the case of a large-scale presentation, it may involve writers, graphic artists, designers, photographers, performers, and a variety of technical and production personnel. Whatever the scale, audiovisual materials are aids, not programs; they are meant to be integrated into an overall program. The most effective program includes only materials with relevant content. A good program is a scripted, rehearsed presentation that uses audiovisual materials for support, places them in context, and interacts with the information they present by comment, analysis, and further explanation. A poor program is one in which the person making the presentation does little more than say, "Here is a film on the subject," and lets it go at that.

The audiovisual materials used in a program must be clear and understandable to the intended audience. Lettering and diagrams must be uncluttered and sufficiently large to be seen easily. Each visual image should contain a limited amount of information. Projection conditions should not degrade the image, nor should audience arrangements make viewing difficult. Recorded sound as well as live narration should be clear and distinct.

See also: FILMSTRIPS; MOTION PICTURES; MULTI-MEDIA PRESENTATIONS; OVERHEAD PROJECTOR; PROJECTION; SLIDE PRESENTATION; STORYBOARD; TELEVISION.

Autochrome

The first practical single-plate method of color photography, patented by the Lumière brothers in France in 1904, was made possible by the introduction of a true panchromatic emulsion earlier the same year. In 1907 the Lumières began commercial manufacture of Autochrome plates at their factory in Lyons. The Autochrome was a random-dot screen process which created its effect by the additive color synthesis. A glass plate was coated with a double layer of starch grains dyed to act as primary-color (red, green, blue) filters; spaces between grains were filled with carbon dust so that no unfiltered light would degrade the image. The filter layer was coated with a panchromatic emulsion. The plate was exposed through the base (glass) side so that the subject colors were analyzed by the filter layer before exposing the emulsion. Reversal processing developed the emulsion to a black-and-white negative image and then converted it to a positive transparency. When viewed from the emulsion side (to correct for the left-right reversal caused by the camera lens), the filter layer colored the transmitted light while the positive image modulated the intensities; the eye blended the additive color sensations thus received to produce a full-color image. Later versions of the plate used resin globules in place of the starch and carbon particles.

Autochrome plates required 40 to 60 times more exposure than black-and-white plates, but their color was quite beautiful; the color qualities and the visible graininess of the images produced an effect similar to that of impressionist or pointillist paintings. The Autochrome was manufactured into the early 1930s, when it and other major additive color processes (Finlaycolor and Dufaycolor) gave way to subtractive color materials such as Kodachrome film.

See also: ADDITIVE COLOR SYNTHESIS; DUFAYCOLOR; FINLAYCOLOR PROCESS; LUMIÈRE, A. & L.; SCREEN PROCESSES; SUBTRACTIVE COLOR SYNTHESIS.
Color photograph: p. C-4.

Automatic Camera

Today, an automatic camera generally has either automatic exposure control or automatic focusing, or both, or uses self-processing film for instant photography. The term also may mean an unattended camera that operates at a predetermined rate, such as surveillance cameras in banks, or one that operates from an external signal such as a certain ambient pressure for a balloon-carried or remote underwater camera.

The term was first used by Adolphe Bertsch (French: *chambre automatique*) to describe his small camera introduced in 1860. It was a metal box about 4 inches square with a fixed-focus lens and no shutter. It was "automatic" because the only necessary operation was to point the camera at the subject and remove and replace the lens cap. It could be used with wet or dry collodion-process or albumen-process glass plates. This camera was the direct predecessor of the box cameras that became popular in the 1880s after the invention of gelatin-emulsion plates and films.

Automatic Exposure Control

Almost all modern small-format and instant cameras have built-in sensors and associated circuits which can adjust the shutter speed, the lens aperture, or both, in order to automatically provide proper exposure for the speed of the film being used. Lens-shutter assemblies for larger-format and motion-picture cameras may include similar automatic exposure control circuits. Specialized equipment such as process cameras and high-volume continuous-operation photographic printing machines also have automatic exposure controls.

The simplest, and least versatile, cameras provide totally automatic control or offer the photographer a limited ability to lighten or darken the picture. More sophisticated equipment permits both automatic operation, and manual operation in which the photographer determines exposure and sets the shutter and aperture accordingly. All such camera systems are built around a light-sensitive photocell placed alongside the lens to measure subject brightness directly, or inside the camera to read the brightness of the image as reflected off a mirror or—in the most advanced systems—reflected off the surface of the film itself. The latter arrangement also may permit automatic control of a flash unit during exposure: when sufficient light has been received, the flash output is cut off.

The photocell requires battery power; the response time or relative sensitivity of its associated control circuitry is determined by the speed of the film being used. This speed is indicated to the circuits either by an automatic indexing device on the film container loaded into the camera or by a manual setting control on the camera body. When activated, usual-ly simply by cocking the shutter, an automatic exposure control system may offer one or more of three kinds of operation:

Aperture-preferred mode—the photographer manually selects a lens aperture setting, commonly for desired depth of field (zone of sharpness) properties; the control system then selects the shutter speed required for normal exposure.

Shutter-preferred mode—the photographer manually selects a shutter speed, for example to ensure photographing movement sharply; the control system adjusts the lens aperture accordingly.

Programmed mode—the control system selects both shutter speed and lens setting. In some cameras the control system holds a single shutter speed constant (e.g., 1/125 sec.) and attempts to adjust the aperture for normal exposure; if this is not sufficient, it then also adjusts the shutter speed. In other cameras the aperture is first held constant and the shutter is adjusted. Both methods rely on a sense-and-evaluate program built into the control circuitry.

Most single-lens reflex (SLR) cameras that offer any degree of photographer control of exposure provide metering and setting indications in the camera viewfinder. The indications may consist of meter and follower needles which move in response to changes in subject brightness and camera settings, marks which light up alongside shutter-speed or f-stop numbers, or numbers which themselves light up or are otherwise revealed.

The automatic exposure control systems in modern SLR cameras are extremely sophisticated and can be relied upon to provide sufficient, if not optimum, exposures in the great majority of photographic situations. However, such systems are based on reflected-light metering and have two major limitations. First, the metering cell does not know whether it is seeing light reflected from an average subject, from one that is unusually reflective (e.g., a beach or snow scene), or from one that is unusually unreflective (e.g., a person in dark clothes in shadow). The metering circuits are calibrated for subjects of average reflectance. Many cameras allow the photographer to adjust the metering response for up to two f-stops greater or reduced sensitivity by means of an indicator built into the film-speed control. The second limitation of automatic exposure control systems is the area to which the metering cell responds. In some cameras it is the entire picture area, in others it is a general area concentrated in the center of the picture, and in still others it is a small, clearly defined center spot. When background and central subject brightnesses differ significantly, the more specific readings have greater accuracy. However, it is up to the photographer to aim the camera so that the exposure reading is taken off a suitable subject area. Some cameras permit the exposure reading to be locked in so that it may be taken by first pointing the camera to a fringe area of the picture, if appropriate, or by moving in to take an exposure measurement at close range before moving back to the distance for the desired composition.

Process and copy cameras and printing equipment with automatic exposure controls generally depend on an integrating meter system—one that measures the cumulative brightness received during the course of an exposure. Typically, such systems are calibrated or set for the sensitivity of the material to be exposed. They measure the amount of light transmitted or reflected from the exposing image and turn off the illumination when the optimum level has been reached.

See also: AUTOMATIC FLASH; EXPOSURE; EXPOSURE METERS.

Automatic Flash

Automatic electronic flash units are equipped with a light-sensitive cell similar to that found in light meters, but designed to respond to the extremely short burst of illumination the electronic flash unit produces. This light-sensitive cell is coupled to a circuit that cuts off the flash output when the sensor determines that enough light has reached the scene for proper exposure. Usually automatic flash units give their user a choice of two or more working apertures, the wider aperture allowing a further automatic flash-to-subject distance.

Many automatic flash units are equipped with thyristor circuitry, which stores the unused portion of the flash output for the next exposure, thereby shortening recycle times.

A "dedicated" flash unit has electrical contacts in its mounting foot which couple its circuits with those of a particular camera. Depending on the equipment, these interconnections may automatically set the camera shutter to the required flash synchronization speed, adjust the flash unit sensor to the film-speed setting of the camera metering system, control the lens aperture setting, and display correct flash exposure indication and other information in the camera's viewfinder.

See also: FLASH.

Automatic Focusing

Systems that automatically adjust the lens of a camera, projector, or enlarger to achieve a sharp image are of two types: active and passive. An active system emits and receives sensing energy from which focusing signals are derived. A passive system evaluates various image characteristics, or has interlocking mechanisms that maintain a constant relationship between lens position, subject stage, and image stage.

The active auto-focus systems used in some cameras are time-base rangefinding systems. That is, they emit a burst of sensing energy and count the milliseconds until an echo of energy reflected from the subject is received. From the elapsed time factor a signal is generated to activate a servomotor that adjusts the lens focus setting. Action is initiated as the shutter release is pushed, and internal circuitry delays actual shutter firing until focusing is completed, which typically takes less than a half second.

One active system emits a burst, or "chirp," of ultrasonic wavelengths. It has a distinctive mix of frequencies so that there is little chance of the camera sensor being confused by other wavelengths emitted or reflected by the subject. However, the sound spreads outward in a cone. It is possible for a nearer object to be within the cone—although not visually blocking the main subject in the center of the picture area—and to produce an early reflection that will cause the lens to be focused at the wrong distance. A glass door or window between the camera and the subject will reflect the ultrasonic signal too soon; water in the foreground or around the subject can also cause early reflection. In other situations the system works quite well for simple, straightforward pictures such as the majority of snapshots.

A more foolproof technique is to use infrared (IR) energy for rangefinding because it can be confined in a very tight beam with no significant divergence and it is far less susceptible to spurious reflection. In one system a burst of IR is emitted and the time is counted until an echo is received. A more versatile system emits a continuous beam of IR during the focusing period. The reflected echo spreads outward and is received through two ports equally spaced on either side of the beam axis. Mirrors reflect the energy onto a pair of IR detectors. If the lens is not focused at the subject distance, the detectors receive off-center or otherwise unbalanced inputs. This causes them to activate the focus servomotor, which shifts the lens-film distance. The mirrors move with this adjustment; when they reflect maximum balanced inputs to the detectors, the lens is focused at the subject distance and adjustment stops.

A similar method is used in auto-focus slide projectors. A tiny beam of light and IR is aimed from an angle at the front surface of the slide. It reflects off to the opposite side onto a divided detector cell. If the reflecting surface is exactly in the focal plane of the lens, each half of the detector will receive an equal input. However, if the surface is out of position because of a difference in the thickness of slide mounts, or because the film in an open mount expands from the heat of the projection light and bulges ("pops") out of position, the detector will receive unbalanced inputs. The detector then signals a lens shift until the input is balanced (the detector moves with the lens). Such a system must be aligned by manually focusing the first slide. If slides in open and glass mounts are intermixed, those in the same kind of mount as the alignment-focus slide will be most sharply focused, because the sensing beam will reflect off the film of the open-mount slides, but off the front glass surface of the covered slides.

Passive auto-focus systems that use image evaluation have been built into individual lenses—making them bulky, heavy, and individually quite expensive—and into camera bodies where they have the potential of being used with a variety of lenses. Image evaluation is performed by an array of silicon photo cells or by the mosaic surface of a charge-coupled device (CCD). Some systems obtain the image for evaluation through their own viewing ports, but the most versatile systems—those used in single-lens reflex cameras—operate with the image formed by the camera lens. A beam splitter or equivalent device directs the image both to the viewing screen and to the focusing sensors.

Various methods of image evaluation are used. In one, contrast is measured by a single sensor or by a symmetrical set of sensors, which function on the principle that an image has maximum contrast when it is most sharply focused. The auto-focus system shifts the lens focus back and forth (in much the same way as in visual focusing) and stops when the sensors produce a maximum output. In another method duplicate images are projected onto two sets of sensors. The image is fixed on one set, but the center portion on the other set shifts with the movement of a mirror or prism coupled with the lens focusing movement (as in a visual split-image rangefinder). When the output from both images matches, the lens is focused at the subject distance.

In a third method a single image is projected through an oscillating grid onto two sensors. If the image is sharply focused, the grid will block or uncover the sensors simultaneously; if not, one sensor will be blocked completely or partially when the other is exposed. The resulting imbalance in their outputs generates a signal to the focusing servomotor.

Image-evaluation systems for small-format cameras presently are limited by their need for certain minimum levels of subject brightness and contrast in order to function precisely. An off-center or divided subject (e.g., two people at the same distance but separated, or at different distances but close to the center) can confuse such systems. High-contrast elements in the foreground or background of the image area scanned by the system can also cause focusing confusion.

Most auto-focus enlargers, mass-production printing equipment, and single-purpose copy cameras use mechanical methods to maintain sharp focus. They operate on the principle that as the distance between the film and the copyboard or paper easel changes for various degrees of enlargement or reduction, the lens must extend or retract to a specific position. The lens movement is controlled by an adjustment feeler that travels over a cam, by a proportional gear train, or by eccentric or lazy-tong linkages. Each such method is accurate for only one focal-length lens and must be changed or adjusted for others. It is possible to use image-evaluation auto-focus systems in projectors, enlargers, and copy cameras. However, doing so significantly increases the cost of such equipment, so this application is very limited.

Automatic exposure control systems for hand cameras were perfected in the 1970s. Automatic focusing is the most significant development of the 1980s. The ideal system will place the focusing motor as well as the sensors in the camera body, will use through-the-lens image evaluation, will accept lenses of many different focal lengths and maximum apertures, and will operate equally well with subjects in minimal conditions (e.g., dim light, low contrast) and subjects in normal conditions.

See also: AUTOMATIC CAMERA; AUTOMATIC EXPOSURE CONTROL; FOCUSING.

Autotype

Autotype is a carbon process for making prints from photographic negatives. The name derives from the Autotype Printing and Publishing Co., which purchased the English patent rights from the inventor, J. W. Swan, in 1868. He had improved the process of A. L. Poitevin, primarily by working out a practical double-transfer procedure that corrected the left-right reversal produced by the original method. The Autotype Co. produced materials for use by individual photographers, made prints to order from their negatives, and produced high-quality reproductions for sale as portfolios and individual prints, as well as for inclusion in the books of other publishers. Although the rights to Swan's process were sold in other countries, and there were many imitative processes, the high quality of the English firm's materials and prints led to the eventual use of "autotype" to mean any carbon print. The Autotype Co. introduced materials for prints in colors other than black in 1893; the process remained widely used into the early 20th c.

See also: CARBON PROCESSES; POITEVIN, A. L.

Available-Light Photography

Pictures made by the illumination normally existing in a scene without additional light supplied by the photographer are called available-light photographs. Often this term is used to mean photography under conditions of marginal illumination, but bright sunlight is as much available light as that provided by household lamps, streetlights, bright store windows, candles, campfires, or any other sources present at a scene. The advantages of working with available light include authenticity, consideration for the subject, and convenience.

The character of light and shadow produced by available light creates a sense of realism and visual authenticity in a photograph that is difficult to achieve with arranged lighting. By using the available light the photographer minimizes the chance of disturbing or distracting the subject and often can work unnoticed. In addition to courtesy to the subject, this method helps preserve the mood of the situation, a factor that contributes to both the reality and the emotional expressiveness of a picture. Finally, an available-light photographer needs only the simplest equipment and working methods. A camera and lens, and at most a tripod, are all that is required in most cases.

No special techniques are necessary for available-light photography in daylight or for most other fully-lighted situations, but interiors, night, and unusual or mixed sources of light may present problems. Achieving proper exposure is no longer the major difficulty that it once was. Most modern medium- and small-format cameras have built-in meters of great sensitivity, lenses of $f/2$ or greater maximum aperture are common, and both color and black-and-white films with speeds of up to ISO 1000/31° are readily available. Thus, almost anything that can be seen can be photographed directly, in the existing illumination, although optimum image quality is not obtainable under all conditions. The more uneven, or the weaker, the light on the subject, the more important it is to take an exposure reading from the most important subject area. Some camera and accessory hand meters take very narrow area "spot" readings; otherwise it is necessary to approach the subject closely to take a reading specifically from the desired area. When the light is so dim that only a slight meter response is obtained, a reflected-light reading taken from a white card or cloth is often useful. Because the white surface is 5 times more reflective than the average standard to which meters are calibrated, the exposure reading obtained must be increased by $2\frac{1}{3}$ stops for proper exposure. An alternate method is to divide the film speed by five and reset the meter to that speed; then the white-surface reading can be used directly.

Dim light conditions may also be accommodated by arbitrarily assigning a film an exposure index two or four times greater than its usual speed rating. This permits using an aperture one or two f-stops smaller than the meter reading calls for, or an equivalent faster shutter speed setting. The film is then given increased development (push processing) to achieve reasonably normal contrast in spite of what is in effect underexposure. This "pushing" technique is usable with black-and-white films and color transparency (but not negative) films. Whether film is pushed or not, it is common to make additional shots with increased exposure as protection in all uncertain light conditions.

Available light levels often require the use of shutter speeds that are too slow to ensure that the camera can be held absolutely steady by hand. A tripod, monopod, or other support device is very useful, but often it is sufficient to brace the camera against a wall, lamppost, chair back, or other firm support at the scene. The rule of thumb in obtaining sharp pictures is that a camera can be hand-held at a shutter speed no slower than a fraction about equal to 1/focal length of the lens (e.g., 1/60 sec. with a 50mm lens or 1/30 sec. with a 35mm lens).

Strong light sources, especially those located above the subject, may produce unwanted shadows. Often the shadows can be lightened by use of a white card or cloth or other improvised reflector placed just out of camera range to direct some of the existing light into the dark areas. It is also possible to use flash or other illumination as a supplement to "fill in" the shadows, or to adjust the lighting balance by replacing the bulbs of lamps on the scene with stronger (e.g., photoflood) or weaker bulbs as necessary. However, altering the existing light is an intrusive process that risks losing the advantages of available-light photography. In particular, it is a delicate matter to use supplementary light without creating a degree of visibility in secondary areas, or a degree of emphasis in major areas, that works against a feeling of visual authenticity.

Avedon, Richard

American; 1923–

Known primarily for his work in fashion and portraiture, Richard Avedon recognizes that "a photographic portrait is a picture of someone who knows he's being photographed, and what he does with this knowledge is as much a part of the photograph as what he's wearing or how he looks."

Educated in the New York City public school system and at Columbia University, Avedon served in the photographic section of the Merchant Marine. At age 21 he did his first work for *Harper's Bazaar,* where he became the protegé of the art director Alexey Brodovitch. In 1946 he established the Richard Avedon Studio in New York City. A staff photographer for *Harper's Bazaar, Theatre Arts,* and *Vogue,* Avedon also contributed to *Life, Look, Graphis,* and *US Camera Annual.* He has worked as a television consultant, director, and advertising photographer.

Since the late 1940s, fashion photography has been dominated by the work of Avedon and Irving Penn. Stylistic innovation and emotional complexity mark the development of Avedon's work from his initial admiration for the 1930s Hungarian fashion photographer Martin Munkacsi. Avedon's early photographic work was concerned with depicting motion; later, he concerned himself with arresting that movement. Beginning with a fresh, energetic exploitation of locations, from streets to parks to fashionable nightclubs and casinos, Avedon's fashion illustration evolved into masterful use of gesture and expression in plain studio settings. In portraiture, with the sitter isolated in the studio, Avedon's approach has gone from elegant, high-fashion idealization to an uncompromising directness that is simultaneously arresting, stark, and often disquieting.

A member of the American Society of Magazine Photographers, Avedon received both the Art Directors' Highest Achievement Award and *Popular Photography's* One of the World's Ten Greatest Photographers Award in the 1950s. In 1976 he received the National Magazine Visual Excellence Award for the October 21, 1976 issue of *Rolling Stone,* "The Family," and the Dedication to Fashion Photography Citation from Pratt Institute. In 1978 he was named a President's Fellow of the Rhode Island School of Design and in 1980 he was awarded the Chancellor's Citation from the University of California, Berkeley, and a Certificate of Excellence from the American Institute for Graphic Arts. He was named to the Art Directors Club Hall of Fame in 1982. Avedon's work has been exhibited in group and individual exhibitions and is collected internationally. Numerous books, catalogs, and articles have been written on Avedon's work, including those with texts by such notable authors as Truman Capote and James Baldwin. By 1985 Avedon plans to have completed a portraiture project of working people in the Western United States underwritten by the Amon Carter Museum of Art.
See also: FASHION PHOTOGRAPHY; HIRO; PENN, IRVING; PORTRAITURE.
Photograph: p. 10.

Average Gradient

The slope of a straight line which joins a point of minimum printable density on the characteristic curve of an emulsion to a point of assumed maximum, or near-maximum, printable density is called the average gradient. Like the nearly identical contrast index, it is a measure of the contrast of a negative that takes into account the densities on the toe of the curve, and thus is a more accurate indication of the printing characteristics of the negative than is gamma. Average gradient, abbreviated $\overline{G}$ (G-bar), is the method used by Ilford Ltd. The origination point of the gradient is 0.1 above minimum (filmbase-plus-fog) density. The second point is found by projecting horizontally from the origination a distance of 1.5 log units (equivalent to the exposure or brightness range of a five-stop subject), and then vertically to the straight-line portion of the curve.
See also: CHARACTERISTIC CURVE; CONTRAST; CONTRAST INDEX; GAMMA.

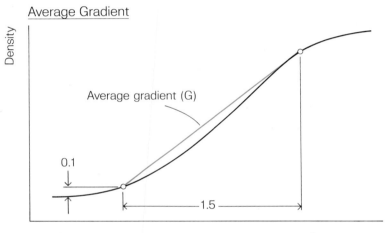

Average Gradient

Bruguière, Francis. "Cut paper abstraction" (1927). Sotheby, New York.

B

Back Focus

The distance, measured along the optical axis, from the rearmost surface of a lens element to the image position (i.e., the film plane in a camera) when the lens is focused at infinity is called back focus (also back focal distance). It is almost never the same as the focal length of a lens, which is measured from the "optical center" (rear nodal point). In wide-angle lenses of reversed telephoto design, the back focus (physical distance) is greater than the focal length (optical distance). This makes it practical to use quite short focal-length lenses on cameras that require space for the movement of a reflex-viewing mirror, or a sizable shutter mechanism, as in motion-picture cameras. In telephoto lenses the back focus is much shorter than the focal length, making their use practical on cameras with fixed body dimensions or limited bellows extension.
See also: FOCAL LENGTH; LENSES; OPTICS.

Backgrounds

The primary function of a background in a photograph is to help clarify the size and shape of the main subject. The color or tone of the background can contribute to the mood of the picture. If the background is not plain, but has detail, it helps create the specific environment or setting in which the subject is seen.

Background colors or tones and details must compliment the subject and not call attention to themselves. The first consideration is to position the camera and subject so that objects in the background do not seem to connect directly with subject. Otherwise, a person may appear to have a flower pot on top of his or her head or tree branches growing from the shoulders. Distracting details or "busy" patterns can be subdued by moving the subject far enough forward or by adjusting the lens depth of field so that these elements are out of focus. Spots of warm, bright colors are a problem in the backgrounds of color photographs, because they tend to advance visually even when out of focus. In some cases background problems can be subdued by burning-in or dodging to make selected elements darker or lighter when making a print.

Outdoors the sky usually offers a plain background, but the low camera angle it requires must be suitable to the subject. Conversely, a higher than normal camera angle can put the subject against a background of grass or other ground cover. In furnished interiors, camera position and lighting are the major background controls available. In studio photography an appropriate background can be constructed. Plain backgrounds are usually provided by sheets of cardboard for small-scale pictures and by rolls of paper up to 9 feet (2.7 meters) wide for larger photographs. The roll can be suspended overhead and the paper pulled down to run behind and forward under the subject, creating a continuous surround without a horizon line. The paper is available in a great variety of shades and colors, and its tone can be adjusted with lighting. Other materials such as fabric and sheet plastic can be used in a similar fashion. Especially when plain backgrounds are used, the lighting on the subject must be adjusted so that distracting shadows do not fall within camera view. Diffused light sources produce softened shadows, and additional light directed onto the background rather than the subject helps to wash out shadows. Scenic and visual backgrounds of all kinds can be created by front or rear projection. These techniques make it possible to show a subject in a setting anywhere in the world without leaving the studio. Although they require special equipment, they eliminate the cost of travel and location shooting and the work involved in building and changing studio settings.
See also: FRONT PROJECTION; REAR PROJECTION.
Color photograph: p. C-5.

Backlight

Backlight is illumination falling on a subject from behind. Its function is to create a highlight on the edges of the subject in order to separate the subject from the background; this is especially helpful when the subject and background have similar tones or colors. The visual effect of backlight is to give a sense of a three-dimensional form standing free in the volume of lighted space in the picture.

To be effective, the intensity of the backlight usually must be at least twice that of the frontal light on the subject (i.e., at least one *f*-stop brighter). In most lighting setups the backlight source is located above the subject either directly behind or slightly off to one side. This creates a highlight on the upper surfaces of the subject, such as on the shoulders and hair of a portrait subject. To avoid flare, the light source must be masked off or the camera lens must have a deep lens shade so that no direct backlight enters the camera. If the backlight source is placed directly behind the subject, it can produce a halo-like glow around the entire form. Dust, smoke, or fog in the air emphasizes the effect. When a subject receives only backlight, with no frontal illumination, a silhouette effect is produced if there is sufficient contrast between the subject and the background. However, a silhouette is usually produced by lighting the background, with no light directed at the subject from the front or the back.
See also: LIGHTING.

Baird, John Logie

Scottish; 1888–1946
Baird was one of the first two men to invent a practical system of television. A radio engineer who turned to experimentation during recovery from a severe breakdown, he first transmitted crude images by wire between two workshop rooms in 1924. His first demonstration of wireless transmission was made in January 1926 in London, and in December he demonstrated wireless television from a completely dark room using infrared rays, a system he called "noctovision." Long-distance cable transmission was achieved in 1927 between London and Glasgow, and wireless transmission was carried out in 1928 from London to New York and to a ship in mid-ocean. The first public broadcast was in 1929 for the BBC, and daily half-hour broadcasts were made in the early 1930s.

Although Baird's work included color, stereoscopic, and large-screen television, his system failed to become the standard method. It relied on a cumbersome and limited mechanical scanning device that produced only ten 30-line pictures a second in its earliest form. Although this was eventually improved to 240-line resolution, it could not pro-

duce quality equal to that of all-electronic television based on the iconoscope camera tube, which was invented by Vladimir Zworykin in 1923 and utilized in all other systems.
See also: TELEVISION; ZWORYKIN, VLADIMIR.

Balance, Color

See: COLOR BALANCE.

Baldus, Edouard-Denis

French; ca. 1813–1882
Like most other mid-19th-c. French photographers, Baldus came to photography from painting. He is best-known for the spare and elegant architectural and landscape views that he made in the 1850s, which are unrivaled in size and clarity. Although he began employing collodion glass-plate negatives by the mid-1850s, he also continued working with paper negatives, which he retouched heavily. Prints from both paper and collodion negatives are deep and richly detailed.

Following service in the Prussian army, Baldus became a naturalized French citizen and painter of portraits and religious subjects. Once interested in photography, however, he rapidly became an eminent practitioner. In 1851, he joined the heliographic (photographic) mission of the Commission des Monuments Historiques and photographed the monuments of Paris and areas south of it—Fontainebleau, Burgundy, the Rhône Valley south to Arles and Nîmes. The next year, the Ministry of the Interior commissioned him to document the Midi. In succession, he

completed commissions in the Auvergne (1854), photographed the sculpture and architectural motifs of the Louvre's new façade (1854–1856), completed a sequence on the French agricultural fair at Champ-de-Mars (1855), documented the building of Baron Rothschild's railroad line (1855) and the flooding of the Rhône (1856), photographed the statues of the Tuileries and Place du Louvre (1858), and made additional views of the newly completed railroad between Paris and Lyons (1859).

Baldus's contributions to photography extend beyond his image-making. In 1852, he began employing a gelatin-coated paper for his negatives, which improved the detail in his calotypes. Like so many photographers of the period, he also explored the possibilities of photomechanical printing methods. In 1851, he became a founding member of the Société Héliographique. In 1857 he became an active member of the Société Française de la Photographie.

Baldus's career in photography lasted only 15 years, from 1849 to 1874. Thereafter he turned his attention to publishing a series of photomechanical reproductions of his views.

Baltermants, Dmitri

Russian; 1912–
Soviet photojournalist Dmitri Baltermants has achieved principal recognition for his coverage of the Russian front during World War II. Born in 1912 in Warsaw, Poland, then a province of the Russian Empire, he moved to Moscow at the age of two. After completing public school, Baltermants worked at var-

Baltermants, Dmitri. "Searching for the Loved Ones at Kerch" (1942). Permanent collection, ICP, New York.

ious jobs including movie projectionist, metal grinder, baker's apprentice, draftsman and finally, apprentice in the printing shop at the newspaper *Izvestia*. In 1923 he entered the University of Moscow to study mathematics and worked part-time arranging photographic window displays. In 1936 he purchased a 35 mm camera, the Fed, a Russian equivalent of the Leica. One of his first photographs, a portrait of a woman aviator, was featured on the cover of *Ogonoik*, the major Soviet picture magazine the same year.

Primarily self-taught, Baltermants studied photography informally with Musinov, an *Izvestiya* reporter, while completing his university studies. Upon graduation in 1938, he began to teach mathematics at the Academy of Soviet Artillery, but in 1939 left teaching to begin his professional career as a photojournalist at *Izvestia*.

When the Soviet Union entered the war in 1941, Baltermants became a war correspondent, first with *Izvestia* and then with the army newspaper *Na Razgrom vraga*. Between 1941 and 1945, he photographed the defeat of the Germans near Moscow, the defense of Sevastopol, the Battle of Leningrad, and the liberation of the U.S.S.R.

One of his most widely published images, "Grief," depicts Russian women keening over the bodies of their husbands and children, slain in a civilian massacre by the Nazis on the muddy plains of the Crimea in 1942. This photograph, included in the 1965 traveling show *World Exhibition of Photography: What is Man?*, prompted one Italian writer to declare Baltermants the "Soviet Robert Capa."

Baltermants considers his best work to be symbolic of larger human issues and to communicate his "concern for the human being." His photographs are also characterized by their strong compositional elements and dramatic use of light and dark.

Since World War II, Baltermants has worked for *Ogoniok*, first as a photojournalist and then as senior editor of the Photography Department. He has served as official photographer for Soviet delegations, including Khruschev's trip to China and Breznev's visit to the United States during the Nixon Administration. Baltermants has been the recipient of several Soviet and European awards and was chosen to participate in a 1983 cultural exchange tour of the United States sponsored by the Citizen Exchange Council, a nonprofit group designed to increase communication between American and Soviet citizens.

Barnack, Oskar

German; 1879–1936

The Leica camera was designed by Oskar Barnack. Apprenticeship to a maker of sextants, orreries, and similar devices changed Barnack's early desire to be a painter into a fascination with technical instruments, astronomy, and photography. After experience as a tool-maker in the precision mechanical and optical industry of Jena, in 1911 he joined the firm of E. Leitz, scientific instrument makers, in Wetzlar. His work in the experimental laboratory was to produce precision machines for intricate manufacturing operations. His original ideas included a revolutionary all-aluminum motion-picture camera (not commercially produced) and a precision stereoscopic camera. In 1905, for his own use as an amateur photographer, he invented a device for taking 15 or 20 pictures in separate rows on a single 5″ × 7″ (13 × 18cm) negative. His fascination with the possibilities of small-format photography were encouraged at Leitz, and in 1914 he handcrafted two all-metal, single-shutter-speed, miniature cameras which used standard 35mm motion-picture film. This was the "Barnack camera" or *Ur*-Leica, the prototype of a photographic revolution. World War I intervened, but after a decade of refinement, Leitz manufactured the first six Leica cameras in December 1924 and introduced the camera publicly the next year. The remainder of Barnack's career was devoted to designing and producing a series of improved Leicas and their hundreds—eventually thousands—of accessory devices.

See also: CAMERA; LEICA.

Barnard, George

American; 1819–1902

George Barnard's best-known photographs were taken during the American Civil War as he followed the route of General William Tecumseh Sherman's campaign through Tennessee, Georgia, and the Carolinas. His elegiac images were used by *Harper's Weekly* and published in *Alexander Gardner's Photographic Sketch Book of the War* and in his own *Photographic Views of Sherman's Campaign* (1866), a book of 61 lavish 10″ × 14″ (25.4 × 35.6cm) prints.

Barnard skillfully photographed the lives of soldiers behind the front lines, but concentrated on the landscapes and city scenes of the aftermath of battle. He worked in a personal style distinguished in its exacting detail and physicality. Upon publication of Barnard's *Photographic Views, Harper's Weekly* stated: "These photographs are views of important places, of noted battlefields, of military works; and, for the care and judgement in selecting the point of view, for the delicacy of execution, for the scope and treatment, and for the fidelity of impression, they surpass any other photographic views which have been

Barnard, George. "View from Confederate Fort on Peachtree Street, Atlanta" (ca. 1862); albumen. Library of Congress.

produced in this country—whether relating to the war or otherwise."

Barnard was born in Connecticut and spent his youth in Nashville, Tennessee. He learned daguerreotypy in 1842 and opened a studio in Oswego, N.Y. the following year. He traveled in the surrounding areas for the next several years. Among his early accomplishments were his 1853 action photographs of burning mills, which were widely reproduced as engravings in the popular press of the day.

Barnard won several prizes for daguerreotypy at exhibitions around the country and served as secretary of the New York State Daguerrian Association. He moved to Syracuse in 1854 to open another studio. By the late 1850s he had switched from daguerreotype to the new collodion process.

In 1860 Barnard worked with the wet-plate process in Cuba, photographing the making of sugar and molasses. Two years later, after assisting Mathew Brady at Lincoln's inauguration, Barnard was among the photographers hired by Brady to document the Civil War. Barnard made views of the battlefields of Bull Run and other sites, but soon broke with Brady, as did Gardner and others, over the issue of byline credit, and went into competition with him.

In 1863 Barnard became the official photographer of the Military Division of the Mississippi, and traveled by mule-drawn covered wagon with Sherman's troops. He documented the devastation of the South until the end of the war,

often returning to the sites of battle after soldiers had withdrawn so that he could achieve the stillness he desired in his images.

Barnard returned to Syracuse in 1866 and moved to Chicago in 1869. Two years later, his gallery and equipment were destroyed in the Great Fire but he was able to document the city's ruins and reconstruction. Barnard published stereographs in Charleston, South Carolina in 1875. Again he lost his business in a fire. He worked briefly with George Eastman in Rochester, N.Y. with the dry-plate process in 1883. From 1884 to 1886 he operated a studio in Plainsville, Ohio. He died in Cedarvale, Onandaga County, N.Y. in 1902.

Barnard's *Photographic Views* was republished in 1977 in conjunction with an exhibition of his work at Helios Gallery, New York.

Barn Doors

Barn doors are a lighting control device. They consist of opaque flaps or blades hinged to a frame that attaches to the front of a spotlight or floodlight instrument. The flaps can be folded into the path of the light to roughly shape the beam and to shadow a portion of the subject to some degree. Thus, extra light can be directed onto the dark clothing of a portrait subject without making the face brighter, or portions of a background or setting can be illuminated without interfering with the main subject lighting.

Bas Relief Images. Andreas Feininger,
"Nude" (ca. 1934). © Andreas Feininger;
Courtesy Daniel Wolf, Inc., New York.

Barn doors are available in two-blade or four-blade forms; in most models the frame can be rotated between horizontal and vertical positions. They are usually painted a non-reflective black, although some are painted white or have a reflective surface so that they can be used in open positions as reflectors.
See also: LIGHTING.

Barrel Distortion

See: DISTORTION; ABERRATIONS OF LENSES.

Bas-Relief Images

Photographs in which objects appear to protrude three-dimensionally from the background in a manner similar to cameos, medallions, and other low-relief sculptures are bas-relief images. The basic technique in creating such images is to contact-print a film image onto another film to obtain a tonal reversal: a positive from a negative, a negative from a positive such as a slide. A sharp second image is obtained by placing the films emulsion-to-emulsion. After processing, the second image is laid over the first on a transilluminated surface such as a light box. The images are moved slightly out of register until the desired degree of bas-relief is seen. Then they are taped

along one edge to maintain their alignment while they are used in an enlarger for printing, are placed in a slide mount for projection, or are placed in a copier to be rephotographed as a composite image.

Several factors in addition to the degree of off-registration affect the results obtained. The original should have objects with clearly defined edges and a relatively plain background. The second film may have a normal or very high-contrast emulsion; graphic arts lith films produce interesting effects in both black-and-white and color bas-reliefs. A positive with greater density and contrast than the negative will produce a negative-looking bas-relief; opposite characteristics will produce a positive effect. Color effects can be added by using filters to expose a black-and-white bas-relief sandwich on color print material.
See also: COMPOSITE PHOTOGRAPHS; LITH FILMS/PAPERS.

Base Fog/Base Density

See: DENSITY; FOG/FOGGING.

Bauhaus

This university-level school of art and architecture was founded by the architect Walter Gropius at Weimar,

Germany, in 1919. Rejecting the 19th c. traditions and beaux-arts classicism that dominated teaching, design, and practice in the arts, the Bauhaus took clean-cut functionalism—expressed in key concepts such as "form follows function" and "less is more"—as a guiding principle. The aim was to marry artistic creativity, skilled craftsmanship, and scientific knowledge to 20th c. methods for the mass production of products and structures. To this end, the faculty (Paul Klee, Lyonel Feininger, Wassily Kandinsky, László Moholy-Nagy, Ludwig Mies van der Rohe, and others) created a revolutionary curriculum in which formal study of pure art and science was coupled with mastery of productive crafts and practical experience in manufacturing and construction. Of particular interest to photographers is Moholy-Nagy's instructional approach to the medium, which began with cameraless experimentation with photographic materials (e.g., with photograms, a technique he devised in the same year as did Man Ray), proceeded to collage and montage images, and finally culminated in camera work. His methods are embodied in his books *The New Vision, Vision in Motion,* and *Painting, Photography, Film.*

Although they eventually revolutionized 20th c. architecture and design, the Bauhaus ideals and methods met great political and academic opposition. The school moved to buildings of Gropius' design in Dessau in 1925. Eventual loss of municipal support there, owing to political developments, led to a move to Berlin in 1932. In 1933 the Nazi government forced the school to close. The faculty dispersed, most fleeing to England and subsequently to the U.S.—notably, Gropius to Harvard, Mies van der Rohe to what is now the College of Architecture, Planning, and Design of the Illinois Institute of Technology, and Moholy-Nagy to the New Bauhaus, which he founded in 1937 in Chicago.
See also: MOHOLY-NAGY, LASZLO; NEW BAUHAUS; PHOTOGRAM.

Bayard, Hippolyte

French; 1801–1887
Working independently and contemporaneously with the other pioneer inventors of photography, by the end of the 1830s Bayard developed a process to produce photographs on paper without a negative—direct positive images that printed during exposure in the camera. Although his haunting and beautifully composed photographs attracted critical acclaim, and although his experimental work was reported and noted, both

aspects of his work were overshadowed in his own time by the success of Daguerre.

The son of a justice of the peace, Bayard was born in Breteuil-sur-Noye in the Département of the Oise. He first became a clerk in a notary's office and later moved to Paris as a minor civil servant in the Ministry of Finance, a position he was to hold for most of his life. From 1837 on, a lively interest in chemistry and the action of light led to his first experiments with photographic processes.

The official notice of Daguerre's achievements communicated to the Academy of Sciences in January 1839 spurred Bayard to perfect his own process for the production of negatives on silver chloride paper, probably in ignorance of William Henry Fox Talbot's similar research in England. He succeeded in this by February. Upon learning that Daguerre's method produced positive images, he set to work and by March had produced direct positives on paper. Bayard submitted examples to Jean-Batiste Biot and Dominique François Arago, members of the Academy. Arago, who by then was committed to furthering Daguerre's invention, dissuaded Bayard from immediate publication of his research in order not to preempt Daguerre's forthcoming success. However, an exhibition of Bayard's photographs was held in auction rooms in Paris, and in June 1839 an award of 600 francs to subsidize Bayard's research was made to him by Duchatel, the Minister of the Interior. After Arago's death, Bayard publicly complained of official procrastination with regard to his early work. This was printed in the photographic revue *La Lumière* in September 1854.

After the public demonstration of Daguerre's method in August 1839 Bayard sought to interest the Academy of Fine Arts in his work. In November of the same year the Academy recommended Bayard's process despite the long exposure required (15-30 minutes), largely because of the comparative portability of the equipment and because the sensitized paper could be stored for as long as a month if it was protected from light. Moreover, they proposed the superiority of Bayard's paper prints because of their usefulness as a starting point for artists' productions. In 1840 Bayard finally made a formal communiqué to the Academy of Sciences, by which time Daguerre had already reaped the rewards of fame. However, Arago and the Academy judged that Bayard had only achieved successes similar to other researchers, notably Jean-Louis Lassaigne and Dr. Andrew Fyfe, although neither of these men had published work concerning direct positives made in the camera.

Embittered by official refusal to acknowledge his precedence, Bayard photographed himself as a suicide, *Le Noyé* (the drowned man) in 1840. He appended a caption which read: "The Government, which has supported M. Daguerre more than is necessary, declared itself unable to do anything for M. Bayard, and the unhappy man threw himself into the water in despair." Despite a renewed appeal by the Academy of Fine Arts there was no immediate reward for Bayard, although in 1842 the sum of 3000 francs was granted to him by the Society for the Encouragement of National Industry.

Notwithstanding the lack of public acknowledgement or recognition, Bayard remained a passionate enthusiast and experimenter in the new medium. By 1842 he was working with the calotype process with considerable success. His calotype images represent a variety of subject matter, all of which exploit the formal possibilities of the medium. His various subjects include still lifes of garden tools, plaster casts in the studio, portraits and self-portraits, views of Montmartre, architecture, and even documentation of the barricades of the Revolution of 1848. Bayard was a member both of the Heliographic Society (founded in 1851) and its offspring, the French Society of Photography (1855). A collection of about 600 of his daguerreotypes, direct positive prints, and albumen-on-glass and collodion photographs is preserved by the latter institution. He also was among the group of select photographers commissioned by the Minister of the Interior's Commission (the Historical Monuments Committee) in 1851 to officially document architecture and monuments throughout France. Bayard worked principally in Normandy for this architectural survey; the work he did then has since been lost. *See also:* ARAGO, FRANÇOIS; DAGUERRE, L. J. M.; DIRECT POSITIVE; TALBOT, WILLIAM HENRY FOX.
Color photograph: p. C-5.

Bayer, Herbert

American; 1900–

Herbert Bayer, an innovative graphic and exhibition designer, worked for many years in photography, photomontage, and "photo-plastics." He is best known for his avant-garde work of the late 1920s and early 1930s, influenced by both surrealist art and Bauhaus design. His photo-plastics, influenced by Lazlo Moholy-Nagy, were constructed still-lifes, including bones and geometrical solids, which emphasized the sculptural aspects of the photographic image.

Bayer was born in Haag, Austria. Between 1919 and 1921, following his service in the Austrian army, he worked as an architect's apprentice and then as a graphic design assistant. In 1921 he enrolled in the Weimar Bauhaus where he studied under Wassily Kandinsky and Moholy-Nagy until 1923.

From 1925 to 1928 Bayer taught advertising layout, visual communications, and typography as a Master Teacher at the Dessau Bauhaus. Although he was familiar with the photographic medium at this time, it was not until he left the Bauhaus in 1928 to work as a graphic designer and exhibition architect in Berlin that he began his intensive involvement with photography. A selection of his work was included in the *Film und Foto* exhibition at Stuttgart in 1929.

Bayer was art director of *Vogue*, Berlin, in 1928–1930. In 1930 he co-designed (with Moholy-Nagy, Walter Gropius, and Marcel Breuer) the *Deutscher Werkbund* exhibition at the Grand Palais, Paris. His work won first prize in a major show of foreign advertising photography that same year. In 1931 he co-designed (with Gropius and Moholy-Nagy) the Berlin *Baugewerkschaften* exhibition.

In 1938 Bayer moved to New York, where he worked in various capacities. He designed and co-edited the exhibition catalog for the Museum of Modern Art's *Bauhaus 1919–1928* show of 1938, and the *Road to Victory* and *Airways to Peace* exhibitions at the Museum of Modern Art in 1942–1943. He was director of art and design for Dorland International in 1945.

Bayer moved to Colorado in 1946 and worked as a design consultant and architect at the Aspen Institute for Humanistic Studies until 1976. During this time he acted as design consultant for such firms as the Container Corporation of America and the Atlantic Richfield Company.

In the late 1960s Bayer designed the *50 Years Bauhaus* touring exhibition which was mounted in London, Tokyo, Chicago, Toronto, and Stuttgart. He was elected a Fellow of the Aspen Institute and named Doctor Honoris Causa by the Technische Hochschule, Graz, Austria, in 1973. He was awarded an honorary Doctorate of Fine Arts by the Philadelphia College of Art in 1974 and was named Honorary Fellow of the Royal Academy of Fine Arts, the Hague, in

1975. Bayer is now retired and lives in Montecito, California.

A show of Bayer's work was held at the Museum of Modern Art in 1977–1978. Other major exhibitions have been mounted at Yale University and at Marlborough Gallery, New York. The Herbert Bayer Archive at the Denver Art Museum was established in 1980.
See also: BAUHAUS.

BCPS: Beam Candlepower Seconds

One measurement of the output of a light source mounted in a reflector is called BCPS—beam candlepower seconds. It is commonly used to express the output of electronic flash units with non-interchangeable reflectors, because exposure information can be derived from it, which is not the case for ratings expressed in watt-seconds or joules. A flash unit which has twice the BCPS rating of another produces enough light for a one-stop difference in exposure. That is, it permits setting the lens aperture one *f*-stop smaller, or using a film with half as great a speed rating, to obtain the same exposure as with the lesser-output unit. An exposure guide number for flash-subject distances measured in feet can be calculated as follows: multiply together the BCPS of the flash unit, the ISO arithmetic speed of the film, and 0.05, and then take the square root of the product. For distances in meters use 0.0045 in place of 0.05.

Since electronic flash bursts last only a fraction of a second, the BCPS measurement expresses the equivalent output that would be generated in one second. For example, a BCPS of 1500, for any particular flash duration, means that the output is equal to the illumination produced by a 1500-candlepower source in one second. Flash-unit output is measured by a meter located on the center axis of the unit (i.e., head-on) at a distance 12 times the diameter of the reflector (or the diagonal of a rectangular reflector). The effective angular coverage of a unit is determined by taking BCPS readings at intervals in a horizontal plane and in a vertical plane, and measuring the angle in each plane between the extremes that are one-half the central-axis reading. This means that subjects located at the fringes of the coverage area receive the equivalent of one *f*/stop less light than subjects in the center of the area, a problem that can be overcome by using a lens with an angle of view less than that of the flash coverage.
See also: GUIDE NUMBER; JOULE.

Beam Splitter

An optical device which divides a single beam of light into two or more beams directed along different paths, or which combines multiple beams into a single path, is called a beam splitter. Divided beams may be identical to the original and to one another (except that the total intensity is divided among them), or they may differ selectively. For example, a dichroic-filter beam splitter in a color television camera directs selected wavelength components of the lens image to the three color-sensitive tubes. Conversely, a combining beam "splitter" unites three colored light beams into a single path to illuminate the negative in some additive color printing devices.

Most beam splitters are mirrors, prisms, or pellicles. Their photographic applications include front projection, holography, and stereoscopic photography. They are a basic component of most rangefinders and of high-intensity, high-volume automatic printing machines in which a half-silvered ("see-through") mirror or equivalent device is permanently mounted in the projected image path to divert part of the light to an exposure control sensor. Some reflex cameras have used a fixed beam splitter in front of the film to divert part of the light to a viewing screen and to permit simultaneous exposure without mirror movement, but the disadvantages of passing an image of reduced brightness to the film have prevented widespread adoption of this arrangement.

See also: DICHROIC FILTER; FRONT PROJECTION; HOLOGRAPHY; MIRROR; PRISMS.

Beard, Richard

English; 1801–1885

A coal merchant who took up photography as a commercial investment, Beard made and lost a fortune in the first decade of the medium. He purchased the rights to the mirror camera of Alexander Wolcott, and opened the first public portrait studio in Europe at the Royal Polytechnic Institute, London, in 1841. Using the speed-improving process developed by J. F. Goddard, Beard's camera operators produced unreversed daguerreotype portraits on plates about $1'' \times 2''$ with exposures of one to four minutes. His immediate commercial success led him to purchase the daguerreotype patent for England, Wales, and the Colonies after only three months. His business grew to four London studios and a branch in Liverpool by 1845.

Changing equipment to the new Petzval portrait lens to obtain larger portraits and shorter exposures, Beard further increased business in 1842 by introducing hand-colored images using a method purchased from its Swiss inventor, J. B. Isenring. Beard's income was more than the equivalent of $125,000 in each of the first years of business, at a time when about $350 a year was considered a good

amount. As sole patent owner, he profited from selling daguerreotype portrait licenses to others throughout England, and he prosecuted patent violators as vigorously as did W. H. F. Talbot in the case of the calotype. Legal action was ruinously expensive however, and the cost of a five-year suit forced him into bankruptcy in 1849. Reduced to a single studio, which he operated with his son Henry, he remained one of London's finest daguerreotypists for several years. His pictures of street tradespeople, taken in the studio, were used as the basis for woodcuts—with street backgrounds added by the engraver—for many illustrations in Henry Mayhew's pioneering sociological work *London Labour and the London Poor* published in 1851.

See also: DAGUERREOTYPE; GODDARD, JOHN F.; MIRROR CAMERA; PETZVAL, J. M.

Beato, Felice A.

British; before 1830–after 1904

Robertson, James

British; active 1852–1865

Felice Beato and James Robertson photographed together in the 1850s in the Mediterranean and the Middle and Far East, producing memorable travel views and war photos with both calotype and wet-collodion processes.

Beato, a naturalized British subject born in Venice, met Robertson in 1850 in Malta. Robertson was the newly appointed superintendent and chief engraver of the British Imperial Mint at Constantinople. The two men photographed in Malta and then traveled to Egypt, Constantinople, and Athens. There is considerable difficulty in attributing individual photographs to either photographer, since most of the images bear the credit "Robertson, Beato and Company." Beato has been described as Robertson's assistant during this time.

In September 1855 Robertson and Beato arrived at Balaclava, following the departure of Roger Fenton. They made over 60 photographs of the fall of Sebastopol, which supplemented Fenton's documentation and were exhibited in London in February 1856. Their photographs were almost exclusively concerned with the aftermath of battle, because of the technical difficulties of working in the midst of the fighting.

Beato and Robertson continued their photography of antiquities and Mediterranean travel sites. They worked together in Palestine in 1857 and documented the aftermath of the Indian Mutiny of 1858. Each continued to make fine photographs separately afterwards.

Beato was responsible for images of

the Siege of Lucknow. He was the first known Western photographer in China, where he traveled in 1860 to report on the major events of the end of the Anglo-French campaign in the Second Opium War. He recorded the destruction of the Imperial Summer Palace near Peking and the capture of Tientsin. He also extensively photographed the people and landscapes of Japan from 1862 on. He made later documentations in China (1870), England, and Egypt, where he worked until 1886 photographing events such as the Sudan Campaign to relieve the British at Khartoum in 1884–1885. Robertson remained the official photographer to the British military forces in India after the Mutiny, working in association with Shepard of Simla.

See also: FENTON, ROGER.

Beaton, Sir Cecil Walter Hardy

British; 1904–1980

A prolific photographer, painter, writer, and theatrical designer, Sir Cecil Beaton's most telling contribution to photography is in the fields of fashion illustration and celebrity portraiture. To both disciplines he brought a flamboyant, inventive use of backgrounds and props often specially constructed by him for the occasion.

Beaton was born into a wealthy London society family in 1904. His father was a leading British timber merchant. The young Cecil attended Harrow, then continued his education at Cambridge. He became interested in photography early on, teaching himself the technical rudiments. His earliest subjects were his sisters, whom he would dress in fancy costumes and place on sets he had designed himself, photographing the result with a simple box camera.

In 1924 Beaton began to work in an office in the city of London, making somewhat offbeat portraits of celebrity aquaintances in his spare time. The pictures led to a contract with *Vogue* magazine in 1928, where he was given the post of cartoonist. While there Beaton began to make occasional fashion and celebrity photographs. This picture-making, at first done on a free-lance basis, evolved into a full-time occupation. Beaton became one of the leading fashion photographers in the 1930s, first for *Vogue* and then for *Harper's Bazaar*. His relationship with these publications lasted for over 25 years, interrupted only by World War II.

During the war Beaton was assigned to the British Ministry of Information as a photographer. His work consisted of documenting the impact of the war on

Beato, Felice. "The Indian Mutiny, Lucknow" (1857); albumen. Victoria and Albert Museum, London.

the people of England and of making records of the British activity along the Near Eastern and Far Eastern fronts. His wartime experience netted him over 30,000 images, all of which are represented in the Imperial War Museum in London.

Beaton resumed his multifaceted career when the war ended, serving as the official photographer of the Royal family, continuing his fashion assignments, and making portraits of notable people. He traveled widely, keeping extensive and profusely illustrated journals from which he produced a number of books. He designed the backdrops, sets, and costumes for many theatrical productions and a number of films. Beaton's numerous awards included two Oscars: one for costume design for the film *Gigi* and the other for the cinema version of

My Fair Lady. Beaton was knighted in 1972 for outstanding cultural achievement.

Beaton's industrious attitude as a photographer was remarkable; using roll-film cameras for the most part, he would produce approximately 30 exposures per hour of shooting. A favorite motif of Beaton's was an arrangement of flowers to set off his model's features, but never at the expense of the garment or accessory that the photograph was supposed to highlight. Beaton's fashion illustrations mark one of the earliest uses of actresses as fashion models. In his writings Beaton displayed an incisive, mischievous wit that showed itself in his descriptions of the people he photographed: he once wrote of Evelyn Waugh that he "... looks like a spoiled cherub with a high temperature"; and of

Marlon Brando "... he seems as unhealthy as a lame duck." One of his last books was *The Magic Image*, written with Gail Buckland and published in 1975. It surveyed "photographic genius" as evidenced in outstanding images from the very beginning of photography, in 1839, to the present day.
Photograph: p. 60.

Becquerel, Alexandre Edmond

French; 1802–1891
A member of a highly respected scientific family, A. E. Becquerel was responsible for many observations and discoveries fundamental to a scientific understanding of photography. His father, Antoine César, was a pioneer in the study of electricity and magnetism;

his son, Antoine Henri, received (along with Pierre and Marie Curie) the 1903 Nobel Prize in Physics for the discovery of radioactivity. In 1839, Edmond Becquerel observed that the action of light on some materials produced detectable magnetic current along with a slight electric current—the photogalvanic effect which was the principle of the first photoelectric exposure meters almost a century later.

The *Becquerel effect*—a latent image is intensified by exposure to wavelengths outside the normal range of sensitivity—was generalized from his discovery that treating an exposed daguerreotype (ultraviolet- and blue-sensitive) to light passing through a red glass plate before development produced a stronger image. Investigating Mungo Ponton's method of sensitizing paper, he discovered that sensitivity increased in proportion to the amount of starch used in the sizing of the paper, a fundamental factor in all subsequent bichromate processes. In the process he called helichromy, he produced natural-color (i.e., without the use of dyes or filters) daguerreotypes of the colors of spectrum, but found no way to make them permanent. His work in 1874 to confirm H. W. Vogel's discoveries of the dye sensitization of emulsions found that incorporating chlorophyll produced greatly improved red sensitivity of the silver halide crystals.
See also: BICHROMATE PROCESSES; DYE SENSITIZATION.

Bede, Cuthbert (Rev. Edward Bradley)

English; 1827–1889

Cuthbert Bede is the pen name of the author of the first humorous book about photography, *Photographic Pleasures—Popularly Portrayed with Pen & Pencil*, published in 1855. Bede revealed a thorough knowledge of the historical development and the processes of photography in 12 chapters that were wittily humorous, gently satirical, and filled with high and low puns on the familiar names and terms of the medium at that time. Many of the 25 illustrations originally appeared as cartoons in *Punch* or *Cruickshank's Weekly;* they were less artistically sophisticated, but also less barbed than the work of illustrators such as Honoré Daumier who came to resent the impact of photography on their field. In a typical passage as a potential portrait customer, he described struggling up five or more flights of stairs to a daguerreotypist's studio located (as were almost all studios) on the top floor in order to have skylight illumination.

Gasping in the apparently thinner air of high altitude, he concluded: "No need now for [a sign] to point out what we have discovered. Ha! ha! We have discovered that Photography is, indeed, High Art."

Beers Formula

The Beers formula was a print developer that produced different contrast on a single grade of paper according to the proportions in which two solutions, each containing a single developing agent, were combined. The "A" solution was a low-contrast developer of 0.8 percent metol and necessary quantities of preservative, activator, and restrainer. The "B" solution contained 0.8 percent hydroquinone plus the other ingredients. Combinations always totaled 16 parts, from 8 parts each of "A" and water for the lowest contrast, to 2 parts "A" and 14 parts "B" for the highest; intermediate mixtures all contained 8 parts water. Most modern papers do not respond with significant variation to the Beers formulation, but it is possible to make a similar variable-contrast developer using stock solutions of two contemporary packaged developers of different characteristics. This provides a more subtle degree of control than a variable-contrast material such as selective-contrast paper, but does not provide as wide an overall range.
See also: VARIABLE-CONTRAST DEVELOPERS.

Bellows

A bellows is a collapsible tube or bag made of flexible leather, plastic, or rubberized cloth which permits moving the lens board closer to or farther from the film plane. Because it provides a continuous range of positions, a bellows is more versatile than fixed-length extension tubes or rings used for the same purpose. However, its lack of rigidity demands a substantial support system to keep the lens properly aligned with the film plane without vibration; this is often a weak point of inexpensive accessory bellows for small-format cameras.

Most bellows are accordion-pleated tubes; they must collapse compactly enough to put the lens a distance equal to its focal length in front of the film in order to focus distant subjects (i.e., those at infinity). A *bag bellows* is not pleated, but is loose enough so that its material can bulge out of the way in order to bring very short focal-length lenses sufficiently close to the film.

The maximum extension of a bellows limits the focal length of the lenses that may be used. Since a lens must be moved farther than one focal length from the film to focus objects closer than infinity, a lens whose focal length is more than about two-thirds of the maximum bellows extension will not be able to be focused over the entire normal range. Extra bellows extension is required for close-up photography. When the extension is twice the lens focal length, the image is life-size (1:1 scale); greater extension is required for macrophotography. In these situations the bellows extension factor has a significant effect on exposure.
See also: BELLOWS EXTENSION FACTOR; CLOSE-UP PHOTOGRAPHY; MACROPHOTOGRAPHY; SCALE.

Bellows Extension Factor

The degree to which exposure must be increased when a lens is located a greater-than-normal distance from the film to obtain greatly enlarged images is called the bellows extension factor; it is also called the *lens extension factor, close-up factor,* and *exposure compensation factor.*

The image the film sees is in effect composed of points of light originating at the lens position. These points of light obey the inverse square law: as the lens-film distance increases, the image brightness decreases. When the lens reaches a distance about 1.3 times its own focal length from the film, increased exposure begins to become necessary to maintain a constant effect on the emulsion. An exposure-meter reading taken through the lens (as with most built-in meters and automatic-exposure-control cameras) responds to the reduced image brightness and provides a compensated exposure indication. However, setups with large-format cameras or unusual combinations of accessories often require that the factor be calculated and applied. A convenient method is based on the image magnification (M), which can be computed by dividing the lens-subject distance into the lens-film distance, both distances being measured from the lens-diaphragm position. Then, the bellows or exposure increase factor equals $(M+1)^2$. The normal exposure time is multiplied by this factor, or the lens aperture is opened to achieve an equivalent increase, based on the principle that each wider *f*-stop doubles the exposure again. That is, opening the lens 1, 2, or 3 *f*-stops increases exposure 2×, 4×, or 8×, respectively. With some lenses, M may need to be adjusted for a

pupil-magnification factor, as explained in the entry on magnification.
See also: CLOSE-UP PHOTOGRAPHY; *f*-NUMBER/*f*-STOP; INVERSE SQUARE LAW; MAGNIFICATION.

Berthon, Rodolphe
French

An astronomical optician, from about 1890 to 1910 Berthon devised the principles embodied in most additive color systems utilizing lenticular screens. Most of his papers and patents were produced jointly with others; presumably the optical contributions were primarily his, and the chemical and color contributions were primarily those of his co-workers. An early patent reveals the idea that a series of tiny lenses behind the prime image-forming lens can dissect the image into discrete, sharply focused elements. This idea was elaborated by Gabriel Lippmann and developed into the lenticular screen. A year later Berthon showed how a filter composed of three primary-color bands placed in front of the lens could be used in combination with a lenticular screen at the film plane to dissect the image into its additive color components in a single exposure. This was the arrangement patented as a practical process by A. Keller-Dorian in 1908 and adapted to produce Kodacolor and Agfacolor, two short-lived additive color movie films, in 1928 and 1931, respectively. Berthon also showed how lenticular film could be produced with the emulsion coated over the ribbed surface rather than placed beneath it, a procedure that made the manufacture of such films considerably easier.
See also: ADDITIVE COLOR SYNTHESIS; KELLER-DORIAN PROCESS; LENTICULAR SYSTEMS; LIPPMANN PROCESS.

Bertsch, Adolphe
French; ?–1871

A microscopist and photographer, Bertsch was one of the first to introduce a matched camera and enlarger system. His *chambre noire automatique,* introduced in 1860, was called an automatic camera because it had a fixed-focus lens. It produced 2¼-inch-square glass plate negatives which were intended to be printed with his megascope enlarger, a device that used reflected sunlight for printing illumination and produced a fixed 10× enlargement. In 1852 Bertsch had patented a spring-driven revolving-disc shutter, a device that was seldom needed in those early days of the collodion period, except occasionally for taking small-format stereographs. It was not used in his "automatic camera."
See also: AUTOMATIC CAMERA; MEGASCOPE.

Bichromate Processes

Bichromate processes are methods of making prints on material coated with a colloid—starch, gum arabic, or gelatin—made light sensitive by treatment with potassium, sodium, or ammonium bichromate (dichromate). When exposed to light, such a coating becomes insoluble in water in direct proportion to the degree of exposure. Thus, when exposed through a negative, the shadow and middletone areas are affected but the highlight areas are not. The image is "developed" by washing with warm water to dissolve away the soluble highlights and parts of the middletones. In the fundamental applications of this principle, the gum bichromate and carbon processes, the emulsion contains a colored or black pigment. Development removes the unnecessary pigment to let the white (or colored) paper base show through in the highlights and middletones; fuller densities of pigment remain in the shadow areas.

A difficulty of this procedure is that the exposure penetrates from the top of the emulsion downward. The fully exposed shadow areas are hardened all the way to the paper base and will adhere securely, but the partially affected middletones have a soluble underlayer and tend to break away from the support, leaving a rather high-contrast image composed primarily of shadows and highlights. Two methods have been adopted to solve this problem. One is to coat the emulsion onto a transparent base (or to render it nearly transparent, as by waxing) and expose the image through the base material; this ensures adhesion of all exposed portions, but degrades sharpness because the negative is separated from the emulsion by the thickness of the base material. The second method is to expose from the front, but to adhere the print face down onto a new support before development. Then the original backing paper is soaked away and the image is developed from what was originally the underside of the emulsion. If the image is left on the new support, this transfer process produces a right-left reversal; some procedures include a second transfer to a final support after development in order to correct the reversal.

Various other bichromate processes use an unpigmented emulsion and add the color at a later stage. The unhardened portions of the emulsion can absorb dyes or dusted-on pigments. Exposure is made through a positive instead of a negative, so the shadow areas remain unhardened; when soaked in a dye, only those areas and the unhardened portions of the middletones are absorptive; the highlights remain colorless. If the exposed emulsion is not dyed but is soaked in cold water, the unhardened portions do not dissolve away, but become receptive to dry pigment dusted on; when the print is dried, the pigment is retained there but not in the hardened highlights. In other dye processes an unpigmented emulsion is exposed through a negative and developed as usual, producing a colorless relief positive; this is then dyed. The dye image may be the final state, or it may be used as a printing master: pressing it against moist paper (*hydrotype* process) transfers the image, as does pressing it against a paper with a special coating of soft gelatin (*pinatype*). The relief master can be redyed repeatedly for multiple printings. Bichromated emulsion has also been used for printing processes similar to collotype and lithography. Exposure is made through a positive and the image soaked in cold water; the highlights swell and become moist enough to reject greasy printing ink applied to the surface. The inked image retained in the shadow areas and middletones is transferred by face-to-face contact under pressure with a suitable paper.

The light sensitivity of potassium bichromate was discovered in 1839 by Mungo Ponton, who succeeded in making crude photograms with paper soaked in a simple bichromate solution. In 1840 Edmond Becquerel discovered that the starch in sized paper greatly increased the sensitivity. W. H. F. Talbot expanded this knowledge by discovering the sensitivity of bichromated albumen, gum arabic, gelatin, and other organic substances. Talbot was the first (in 1852) to patent a bichromate-and-gelatin process, a method of preparing engraving plates he called photoglyphy. The carbon process was invented in 1855 by A. L. Poitevin; it was also the basis of the gum bichromate process. Ready-made carbon printing materials were introduced by J. W. Swan in 1866. Various bichromate and other control processes dominated fine-art photography and pictorialism from the 1870s until about 1920; many are being actively reexplored today.
See also: CARBON PROCESSES; COLLOTYPE; GUM BICHROMATE PROCESS; LITHOGRAPHY; OIL PRINTS; PHOTOGLYPHY; PONTON, MUNGO; SWAN, J. W.; TRANSFER PROCESSES.

Biological Photography

This broad category includes the recording of a wide variety of characteristics of plant and animal life in natural environments and in the laboratory. In many applications it is a branch of medical photography and uses the same techniques to obtain pictures in the photomicrographic, macrographic, close-up, and normal ranges.

As with all scientific applications of photography, biological photographs usually must conform to a relatively inflexible set of criteria. Visual evidence, particularly if used in support of a scientific report, must be entirely straightforward. Substantial easing of this rule may be allowed when the photographs are to be used more generally, but not to the extent of distorting facts. The general guideline is that the picture should show whatever a trained observer would have noticed. Of particular importance is the need for accurate record keeping. Some types of cameras may be equipped with data backs which imprint certain information on the face of the photograph. Nothing, however, is a sufficient substitute for an accurate and complete notebook.

Oftentimes biological photographs of excellent quality are made by professionals in the various relevant specialities who simply find it easier to make their own records rather than employ a photographer. Similarly, photographers specializing in this area commonly are amateur biologists. In either case, the combination of skills helps ensure that useful and accurate photographs will be made.

In general, biological photography can be broken down into two areas: that done in the field and that done in the laboratory. Some subjects involve both kinds of work. For example, photographs of primitive life in fossil form are first made where the fossils are discovered. The initial pictures include enough of the general area to show the context in which the specimen has been found. Additional photographs then are made at closer distances to show the fossil's immediate environment in detail. Care needs to be taken to show, among others things, the kind of soil it was lying in. Subsequently the fossil is gently removed to the laboratory. Details of its infrastructure are recorded on an arrangement similar to a copy stand. The specimen is placed on a germ-free sheet of glass (or other impermeable substance so that one subject does not contaminate another). Lighting is adjusted as necessary to reveal form, color, texture, and other characteristics in various pictures. The camera is mounted on a rigid support to ensure sharp pictures. A ruler or an object of known dimension is included in the picture to provide a scale reference.

Recording the behavior patterns of animals normally takes place in the natural habitat. Often both motion-picture and still cameras are used in tandem. Enlarged prints from motion-picture frames cannot match the quality of those from still-camera negatives. Studies made of a very wide variety of creatures have included their courting rituals, feeding, mating and nesting habits, and births and deaths. A great deal of the scientific information garnered in this way also has considerable educational and entertainment value. The direct sync-sound character of video recording is leading to the widespread use of portable video equipment for such studies.

Among the more visually spectacular uses of the motion-picture camera in biological photography are time-lapse studies of growth. The classic example is of a flower developing from sprout to bud to full bloom. Of equal scientific value are still-picture sequences recording the growth of subjects at different stages. Embryonic development may be recorded by x-ray photography in much the same way as human fetuses are sometimes checked by ultrasound photography.

The ordinary still camera is of primary importance in recording the morphology (form and structure) of animals and plants. Animals are first photographed to show how they appear in their natural state. Then pictures are made periodically during dissection to show accurately the skeletal, muscular, and arterial structures. In addition, pictures are made of any anatomical oddities or anomalies. Choice of subject is the key factor in photographing plants. It is usually critical that a specimen photographed be typical of a species and not a variant. For example, most species exist in dwarf, giant, and sport as well as normal form. When a variant is photographed, it must be labeled as such. All morphological recording is carried out in the laboratory, and much of it is in the close-up range from one-tenth life size (a magnification of $0.1\times$) to life size ($1.0\times$).

Much biological photography at magnifications greater than $1.0\times$ is of elementary cell structures. Nearly all such work represents an application of photomicrography. The specimen is brought to the laboratory and placed on a glass slide which is then positioned on the stage of a compound microscope. The camera is fixed atop the eyepiece, where it records the image. Electronic flash has greatly advanced this branch of biological photography. Unlike continuous light sources, electronic flash seldom generates enough heat to injure or kill microscopic creatures. Moreover, the light pulse is short enough in duration that even the liveliest specimens may be rendered sharply.

See also: CLINICAL PHOTOGRAPHY; MEDICAL PHOTOGRAPHY.

Bischof, Werner
Swiss; 1916–1954

Werner Bischof's photographs, if not his name, were among the world's most famous at the time of his death. For more than a decade he had been one of the foremost journalists, and his photographs had been widely reproduced.

After a brief period of training as a teacher of drawing and physical culture, Bischof attended the Zurich School of the Arts, where he studied graphic art. He thus was one of the handful of postwar European photographers to have received formal photographic training, studying under Hans Finsler.

Bischof spent three years as a graphic artist and freelance photographer, mainly concentrating on studies of light and form, shell and leaf patterns, and some fashion photography. He then moved to Paris in 1939, intending to pursue a career as a painter. However, with the outbreak of war he was drafted. It was during the war years that Bischof's commitment to photography deepened, although he continued to sketch in notebooks throughout his life.

In 1942, Bischof became associated with the picture magazine *Du*, which was to publish many of his most important photographs. Working rapidly, he began to develop in a direction radically different from his earlier work. Instead of concentrating on the purely formal characteristics and possibilities of photography, he began to think of photography as an expression of his ethical and social concerns. Traveling through war-ravaged France, Germany, Italy, and eastern Europe, he came to consider his photography as an instrument of moral witness and an agent of social concern.

In 1949 Bischof joined Henri Cartier-Bresson, David Seymour, Robert Capa, George Rodger, and Ernst Haas as a member of Magnum, the cooperative photo agency. Like them, he shared an enthusiastic belief in the ability of photography to comment on and communicate the dignity and struggles of the world's peoples. He wrote that "only work done in depth, with total commitment, and fought for with the whole heart, can have any value," and later, "I believe we have the obligation to grapple

with the problems around us and to do
so with severe concentration and evaluation, in order to form the image of our
generation." In the following years he
thought intensely about the function of
photography in society, filling notebooks and letters with his reflections.

Bischof's approach to photography is
perhaps exemplified by the work he did
in the famine-stricken region of Bihar,
India, where he was sent by *Life* magazine in 1951. This was followed by a
year in Japan with his wife and young
son and resulted in *Japan,* an important
book over which he exercised careful
control. He expressed a strong desire to
work on extended picture stories which
would then enable him to explore his
subjects in depth. Japan held a special
place in his affections; he evidently
found there something of the refined,
well-ordered world he had long desired
and required as a counterweight to the
harrowing environments he had photographed in previous years.

After a short stay in New York Bischof traveled to Mexico and South
America to photograph Indian life. In
1954 he was killed in an auto accident in
the Andes mountains of Peru.

Since 1955 many exhibitions, including major retrospectives at the Smithsonian Institution and the Louvre, and
traveling shows sponsored by the International Center of Photography, New
York, have confirmed the significance
and lasting import of Bischof's work for
contemporary photojournalism.

Bisson, Louis-Auguste

French; 1814–1876

Bisson, Auguste-Rosalie

French; 1826–1900

The Bisson brothers were hailed for their
outstanding large-scale architectural and
Alpine views in the mid-19th c. They
received many awards at exhibition, including a medal from the Société d'Encouragement pour l'Industrie Natio-

nale (1842), for their early work as
daguerreotypists, and their Paris portrait
studio was successful for many years.
The work for which they are remembered today was produced between 1851
and 1864 using the wet-collodion
process.

The Bisson brothers were born in
Paris, where they spent most of their
lives. Louis-Auguste studied
architecture and chemistry, and worked
as an architect for the city of Paris in the
1830s. He was introduced to photography by Daguerre in 1839. Auguste-
Rosalie worked with their father, a
heraldic painter, and briefly as an inspec-
tor of weights and measures, before
opening a Paris daguerreotype portrait
studio with his brother in 1841. In the
following decade, the brothers made
thousands of portraits, including those
of many artists and statesmen. In 1848
and 1849 alone they made over 900 portraits of members of the Assemblée
Nationale.

Bisson, Auguste and Louis. "Mont Blanc vu de Mont Joli" (1861); albumen from collodion negative. Art Institute of Chicago.

The Bissons turned from daguerreotype to the wet-collodion negative and albumen positive processes in 1851. Three years later they published photographic reproductions of Rembrandt etchings in *L'Oeuvre de Rembrandt reproduit par la photographie, décrit et commenté par M. Charles Blanc*, the first book illustrated with photographs from glass-plate negatives. In 1854 their work appeared in *The Knight, the Devil and Death: Oeuvre d'Albert Durer photographié*.

In 1854 the Bissons were among the founding members of the Société Française de la Photographie. They were active in the field of scientific photography and worked with Achille Deveria and the naturalist Louis Rousseau. Their second studio became a center of the artistic and intellectual life of Paris, and they were appointed official photographers to Napoleon III.

In 1855 the Bissons began a series of superb architectural views and Alpine mountain and glacier photographs. They traveled in France, Belgium, Germany, and Italy, photographing with mammoth wet plates. The brothers made a series of 24 views of the Alps on a climbing expedition accompanying Napoleon III and Empress Eugénie. In the early 1860s, Auguste-Rosalie made the first photographs from the summit of Mont Blanc, a tremendous achievement with the cumbersome collodion process and among almost ceaseless storms.

Between 1853 and 1862 the Bissons' *Reproductions photographiques des plus beaux types d'architecture* appeared in installments. An album of their mountain photography appeared in 1860; in the same year they were named Official Photographers to the Emperor.

The Bisson brothers were forced to sell their Paris business in 1864 as the public demand for large-scale views diminished and that for carte-de-visite views and portraits increased. Louis-Auguste remained as the firm's director under the new owner. Auguste-Rosalie was employed for a time by the firm of Leon et Levy. In 1869 he traveled in the Middle East, photographing in the Nile Valley and at the opening of the Suez Canal.

Black-and-White Images from Color

Full-range black-and-white images can be obtained by photographing a color print or transparency with panchromatic negative film and making prints on a standard black-and-white paper. The tonalities are similar to those obtained by photographing the original subject directly in black and white. They are not identical because of differences between color image dyes and the actual colors of the subject. Full-range prints cannot be obtained by exposing an ordinary black-and-white paper to a color negative (nor a reversal paper to a color transparency), because the paper emulsion lacks red—and usually green—sensitivity. Image areas containing those colors will be translated into dark grays, rather than grays that represent their true equivalent locations on the tonal scale. In addition, the orange or pinkish-tan masking color present in color negatives will further distort the tonal translation. Special papers with panchromatic black-and-white emulsions are manufactured to overcome this problem.

Black-and-White Materials

The materials used in contemporary black-and-white photography fall into four broad categories: conventional films, chromogenic films, printing papers, and processing chemicals.

Conventional black-and-white films have emulsions composed of light-sensitive silver salts suspended in gelatin and coated on a transparent cellulose triacetate or polyester base. Each film emulsion has a specific spectral response within the visible energy range. Blue-sensitive films are sensitive to blue wavelengths only; orthochromatic films are sensitive to all visible wavelengths but red; and panchromatic films are sensitive to wavelengths of all colors. All emulsions are sensitive to ultraviolet, and they may be specially sensitized to infrared. Each film also has a specific sensitivity to light intensity, or "speed." Fast, highly sensitive films are made with larger silver-salt crystals than relatively slow films; all other things being equal, they will produce grainier images than will less sensitive, slow films.

The image produced on conventional black-and-white films is made of metallic silver, which is derived from the silver halides (salts) during development. Chromogenic films also have silver halides in their emulsions, but there is no silver in the final image. Instead, these emulsions also contain special dye-coupler compounds which produce a dark gray-black dye image. Chromogenic films cannot be processed in conventional black-and-white chemicals. Their construction is quite similar to that of color negative films, and they are processed in the same manner and in the same solutions. Chromogenic films are more expensive than conventional types, but they have a wider exposure range. Because of their physical and chemical construction, chromogenic films produce less grainy results when overexposed than conventional films exposed under the same circumstances.

Black-and-white photographic papers are composed of a silver halide gelatin emulsion coated on either a baryta (white-coated) paper or a plastic resin-coated paper base. Most paper emulsions are orthochromatic, allowing the use of amber safelights in the darkroom. A few papers have panchromatic emulsions for making accurate black-and-white tonal translations from color negatives. These papers must be used in total darkness.

Black-and-white papers are available in a variety of contrast grades to accommodate negatives of various density ranges. A number of variable-contrast papers are also available; these have two different emulsion layers combined to respond in a range of contrast renditions. The contrast is controlled with a series of amber (low contrast) and magenta (high contrast) hued filters which are placed in the light path during exposure.

Fiber-base baryta papers have greater longevity and stability and are usually richer in silver than resin-coated papers. The latter have the advantage of shorter processing and washing times and are extremely useful in commercial and other applications where archival image permanence is not necessary.

The commonly used black-and-white chemical processing solutions are: developers, which convert the exposed silver halide crystals to black metallic silver; stop bath (acetic acid), used to neutralize the alkalinity of the developer, thereby effectively stopping its action on the negative or print; and fixer (sodium or ammonium thiosulfate), which makes the unexposed silver halides soluble so that they may be removed. If the unused halides were left in place, the action of light on them (combined with the traces of developer left) would convert them into metallic silver as well, obscuring the original image.

In addition to these fundamental chemicals are fixer neutralizers and eliminators to shorten washing times and render the fixer residue harmless; wetting agents to prevent water spots from forming on the film as it dries; a variety of test solutions to check for any residual chemicals that might be harmful to the longevity of the image; toners to alter the color of the image; and reducers, intensifiers, and bleaches to adjust the contrast or density of the image. Processing procedures and image treatment are discussed in individual entries.

Black-and-White Printing
See: PRINTING, BLACK-AND-WHITE.

Black-and-White Processing
The processing of black-and-white films and prints consists of two basic steps: development to convert the exposed latent image to a visible image, and fixing to preserve the image once it has been produced. Other customary chemical treatments make processing more efficient and help ensure image permanence.

Conventional film processing produces a negative image which represents the light and dark areas of the original scene with opposite tones (densities). This image is transmitted to printing paper by a contact printing or enlarging exposure, and another series of chemical treatments produces a positive print. The processing steps of developing, stop bath, fixing, washing aid, washing and drying, are standard for both films and fiber-base papers. Resin-coated papers do not require the washing-aid step.

Film development is the most crucial part of the procedure, for problems with the negative will become problems in printing. With small-format films the processing steps can be performed with room lights on once the film has been loaded into a daylight-type developing tank. The chemicals are poured in through a lighttight opening in the top.

In the developing solution the exposed silver halides in the film emulsion are reduced to dark metallic silver. The degree of development must be appropriate for the amount of exposure received by the film. Excessive development produces dense and contrasty images with increased graininess and fog. They also may have "blocked" highlights—areas so dense that they are very difficult to print. Underdevelopment produces negatives with thin densities and low contrast.

Development is controlled by time and temperature. For every acceptable working temperature of the developing solution there is a particular length of development (with proper agitation) that will produce a properly developed negative, assuming that the film was exposed correctly. The standard processing temperature is 68°F (20°C), but most films can be developed within a 65–75°F (18–24°C) range by an appropriate adjustment of the developing time. Various developers require different times at a given temperature because they differ in energy, or rate of activity, and different emulsions require different times with a particular developer and temperature. Extremely short developing times reduce the margin of error for over- or underdevelopment and may produce uneven densities. Length of development also can be adjusted to compensate to some extent for exposure errors.

The solution must be properly agitated during processing to ensure an adequate flow of fresh developer over the film surface. Too little agitation can produce uneven development; too much can cause excessive contrast and grain, as well as surge marks on the negative. Agitation is also very important during each subsequent processing step.

The developer action can be stopped at the proper time by a stop bath. The stop-bath solution is acidic, so it neutralizes the alkaline developer. A water rinse is sometimes substituted, but unless the developing time is quite long, a stop bath is best for precise timing of development. Because the stop bath neutralizes the developing solution, any residual developer carried into the fixing bath will be much less likely to reduce the fixer's acidity.

At this point the film emulsion still contains a certain number of unexposed, undeveloped silver halide crystals. These are dissolved in the fixing bath with the result that the film is no longer light sensitive and the image becomes permanent. In standard fixers the active agent is sodium thiosulfate; in rapid fixers it is ammonium thiosulfate. A fixer with a hardening agent should be used to give the film emulsion protection against scratches or other damage.

After the fixing action is complete, the residual fixer must be washed away. This is much easier if the film is first treated with a washing aid or hypo eliminator solution. The washing itself must be thorough if the image is to last. This means that there must be enough complete water changes to effectively eliminate any remaining chemicals.

After washing, the excess water is removed by wiping the film with a sponge or squeegee or by treating it with a wetting agent. The wetting agent causes the water to run off smoothly without leaving water spots. The film can be hung up to dry with the bottom weighted with film clips, or drying can be done with a commercially available film dryer.

The processing of chromogenic black-and-white films is quite different from that of standard films. In fact, they are processed with the same solutions and procedures as color negative films. The final result is a dye image rather than one composed of metallic silver. It is somewhat denser than that of a standard film, but it is used for printing in the same way.

Print development also has time and temperature requirements, but these are not as critical as in film processing. For printing papers the recommended developer temperature is usually 68–70°F (20–21°C), but each paper type has an optimum length of development which is not altered if the temperature is not precisely within the recommended range. Most fiber-base papers require a 2-minute development, but with resin-coated papers the developing times are shorter. It is important that prints be fully developed; a print that is removed from the developer too soon will be mottled or muddy in appearance. Agitation should not be overly vigorous, but it should be continuous throughout development.

The use of an acid stop bath following development is important to neutralize the developer and prolong fixer life. A water rinse should not be used with prints. A rapid fixer is an effective time-saver, but it is not recommended for fiber-base papers if a two-bath fixing procedure is used, because it is so easy to overfix a print to the point of bleaching image highlight detail or making effective washing impossible.

A washing-aid treatment is very important for fiber-base papers because of the difficulty in eliminating chemical residues from these papers. A washing aid should not be used with resin-coated papers. The washing setup must ensure a constant fresh water flow and the continual drainage of chemical-laden water; it is also essential that the prints be kept separated. Resin-coated papers are especially easy to wash because they resist water absorption. A 5-minute wash period is sufficient if it consists of a constant flow of fresh water, while fiber-base papers require at least 20 minutes of washing.

Prints are often treated with diluted selenium toner to enhance the tonality and to provide greater image permanence. The toner can be combined with the washing aid, or it can be used as a separate treatment after washing.

Care also must be taken to prevent the contamination of fiber-base papers during drying. For this reason heated dryers which employ canvas aprons are risky unless the aprons are kept scrupulously clean. Blotting papers and drying racks are slower substitutes, but racks especially provide effective contamination prevention if they are kept clean. Drying is much less of a problem for resin-coated papers. They dry quickly in the open air without curling and thus can be placed on any clean surface.
See also: AGITATION; ARCHIVAL PROCESSING; DEVELOPMENT; DRYING FILMS AND PRINTS; FIXING; STOP BATH; WASHING.

Black Body

A theoretically perfect radiator, one which totally absorbs all energy wavelengths falling upon it and radiates energy only as a consequence of its own temperature, is called a black body. When the radiated energy is within the visible range, the black body provides the basis for the light-temperature correlation known as color temperature. Actual black bodies of high efficiency have been made from blocks of carbon and similar materials. Nearly perfect characteristics for measurements within the visible range are obtained with a hollow chamber (spherical, or nearly so) the interior surface of which is coated with carbon particles and with an opening no larger than 1/100th the interior area. It is heated from the outside, and the small amount of light entering the opening—even directly along the observing axis—is totally absorbed. Consequently, any change in the appearance of the interior is the direct result of a change in temperature.
See also: COLORIMETRY; COLOR TEMPERATURE.

Black Light

Long-wave ultraviolet wavelengths, in the region just beyond the blue end of the visible spectrum, are popularly called black light. Although they are invisible, they can be recorded by film emulsions; in addition, they cause some substances to glow (fluoresce) with unusual colors in the visible range. Incandescent sun lamps, fluorescent and incandescent indoor "plant lights," and BLB (black light blue) fluorescent tubes are all ultraviolet-rich artificial light sources. Electronic flash tubes emit ultraviolet wavelengths, although many portable units have ultraviolet absorbing reflectors or filters to limit this output. Sunlight contains a significant amount of ultraviolet.

To photograph the visible fluorescence produced by black light, the subject should be in a dark room so that stray light cannot wash out the colors. The camera lens should be equipped with a No. 2A filter, which will pass the visible light but will screen out the exposure effects of reflected or stray ultraviolet. Either color or black-and-white film may be used, and exposure may be determined in the normal way with a meter reading from the subject.
See also: ULTRAVIOLET AND FLUORESCENCE PHOTOGRAPHY.

Blanquart-Evrard, Louis-Désiré

French; 1802–1872
An amateur photographer and inventor, Blanquart-Evrard was a major figure in early photographic publishing. He was responsible for important advances in photographic techniques, operated the first major photographic printing and publishing factory, and was the publisher of many volumes illustrated with nature views and art reproductions by amateur and professional photographers.

Blanquart-Evrard was born in Lille, France. A cloth merchant and chemist, he learned the calotype process in 1844 and significantly improved upon the work of Talbot, inventor of the process.

Blanquart-Evrard invented an early process for developing out photographic prints. An early exponent of archival processing, in 1850 he introduced the use of albumen paper for making prints. He opened a printing factory, Imprimerie Photographique, near Lille in 1851. As a pioneer photographic publisher, he was responsible for *Album photographique de l'artiste et de l'amateur* (1851), Maxime DuCamp's *Egypte, Nubie, Palestine et Syrie* (1852), John B. Greene's *Le Nil: Monuments, paysages, explorations photographiques* (1854), Auguste Salzmann's *Jerusalem* (1856), and many other books. With Thomas Sutton, he later opened a second printing operation on the island of Jersey and founded *Pho-*

tographic Notes magazine. Blanquart-Evrard retired from photographic work in 1857. He died in his native Lille at age seventy.

See also: ALBUMEN PROCESSES; BOOKS, PHOTOGRAPHIC.

Bleaching Images

Bleaching is used to reduce a silver image to a colorless state so that it can be redeveloped with different characteristics, or so that other aspects of the image can be made visible. The latter is the case in processing conventional color materials in which a dye image remains when the silver negative or positive image is removed. Various methods of toning and image intensification utilize bleach-redevelop procedures. In reversal processing that uses re-exposure rather than chemical action to render the positive image developable, the negative image first must be completely bleached away. Total image removal is also required in the bleach-out process to produce photo-derived drawings. A bleach containing iodine compounds produces the most effective total image removal; one using potassium ferricyanide tends to leave faint image traces. Partial bleaching is used for reduction of image contrast and density, and as a technique in both black-and-white and color retouching. Bleaching action to produce or reveal an image is the basis of the direct-positive paper process of Hippolyte Bayard, and of the dye destruction process of color printing.

See also: BLEACH-OUT PROCESS; DIRECT POSITIVE; DYE DESTRUCTION PROCESS; INTENSIFICATION; REVERSAL MATERIALS AND PROCESSING; TONER/TONING.

Bleach-Out Process

The bleach-out process is a technique for deriving hand drawings directly from black-and-white prints. A lighter than normal print (to facilitate bleaching) is made on matte-surface paper. When dry, the image is traced or drawn over with a permanent graphite pencil or with waterproof ink of any color. Any amount of direct tracing, departure from the original, shading, cross-hatching, or other drawing techniques may be used. When the handwork is finished, the photographic image is completely bleached away, leaving only the drawing.

A number of bleaching solutions may be used. The most effective for total image removal is a mixture of 0.4 percent iodine and 1.5 percent potassium iodide in water. It produces a brown stain which is easily removed by subsequently

treating the paper in a plain or acid fixer. The drawing is then washed thoroughly and dried. A strong solution of Farmer's reducer may also be used; it has the advantage that its two ingredients—potassium ferricyanide and potassium thiosulfate (hypo)—are readily available photographic chemicals. However, it may produce a yellow tinge that cannot be completely removed. Strong bleaching solutions of any sort may be harmful to the skin. Rubber gloves are a wise precaution, and bleaching should be carried out in a well-ventilated location.

See also: ETCH-BLEACH PROCESS; REDUCER.

Bleed

The term *bleed* is used in photography and the graphic arts to denote an image that runs to the very edge of the print paper or the page, without surrounding borders. A full-bleed image is one that runs to all four edges; a top-, bottom-, left-, or right-bleed image runs to the indicated side (or sides), but has borders on the other sides. A photographic bleed print is usually made in the normal way, with the borders produced by the blades of the paper easel being trimmed off later. When a bleed print is to be mounted, the cleanest results are obtained by mounting it with the borders on and then trimming the borders and mount simultaneously. A vacuum easel or an easel with a tacky coating is required to hold paper flat to produce bleed images to the full paper size without borders to be trimmed. Paper also can be held flat by a sheet of glass, but this may create problems of reflection and flare.

Blocked Highlights

When film is overexposed, or more commonly overdeveloped, the most exposed areas of the negative—those which correspond to the subject highlights—may become so dense that they are effectively opaque and block the light during a printing exposure. This causes those areas to be pure paper-base white in the print, without visible tone or detail. In less extreme cases of blocking some highlight tones may print through, but with inadequate separation and detail. Additional printing exposure to burn-in blocked highlight areas often produces muddy whites or gray tones.

Blocked highlights from known over-exposure can be prevented or minimized by reducing film development accordingly. In general, a 10 to 20 percent reduction in developing time for each *f*-stop of overexposure (up to a maximum of 3 stops) is required. However,

the relationship between overexposure and reduced development varies, depending on the overall contrast range of the scene, the film used, the developer type, and the pictorial result desired. Blocked highlights produced either by overexposure or overdevelopment, or by a combination of the two, can be corrected to some degree by treating the processed negative in a reducer. Different reducer solutions are required according to the cause of the blocking.

See also: BURNING-IN; REDUCER/REDUCTION.

Blocking-out

Painting over details in a black-and-white negative so that they will not register in a subsequent print is called blocking-out. Opaque paint or red dye (paper emulsions are not red-sensitive) is the usual blocking-out medium. The technique is used to change object contours in retouching; to remove traces of support materials in exploded views; to eliminate backgrounds for what is called silhouette photomechanical reproduction of a subject; to cover pinholes and other flaws in graphic arts negatives and positives; and to prepare image elements for composite photographs.

Blossfeldt, Karl

German; 1865–1932

Influenced by the 19th c. German tradition of natural philosophy, Karl Blossfeldt believed that "the plant must be valued as a totally artistic and architectural structure." Combining training as a craftsman with an academic art education, Blossfeldt made thousands of enlargements of details of plant forms in an attempt to reveal the fundamental structures of the natural world and their relation to artistic form. Over a period of 30 years, he photographed leaves, seed pods, stems, and other plant parts, frontally or from above, against neutral white or grey backgrounds in weak daylight, much as though he were photographing architectural details. His black-and-white, sharp-focus descriptions appear semiabstract to the viewer unfamiliar with his subjects, despite his avowed intentions. Blossfeldt's book of 96 enlargements of plant forms, *Urformen der Kunst* (*Archetypes of Art* [1928]), became a landmark of the Neue Sachlichkeit (New Objectivity), as did his *Wundergarten der Natur* (*Magic Garden of Nature* [1932]).

Blossfeldt was born in Schielo, Harz, Germany, and educated in Harzgerode from 1871 to 1881. From 1882 to 1884 he

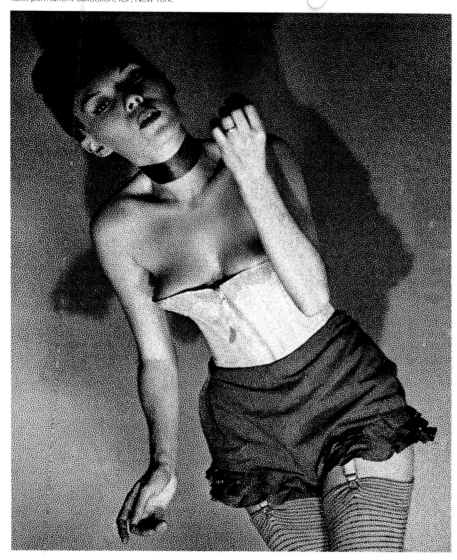

Blumenfeld, Erwin. "Maroua Motherwell, N.Y." (1942). Courtesy Erwin Blumenfeld Estate; permanent collection, ICP, New York.

Blueprint

Photographically, a blueprint is an image in blue tones printed by the cyanotype process. Widespread use of a form of that process to reproduce architectural and construction plans, shop drawings, and similar materials easily and inexpensively established "blueprint" as a name for all such copies; they consisted of white lines on a blue background. The term is retained in professional jargon today, even though the blueprint process is obsolete, and the copies are brown or black lines on a white background produced by the dyeline method or other diazo processes.
See also: CYANOTYPE; DIAZO PROCESSES; DYELINE PROCESS.

Blumenfeld, Erwin

American; 1897–1969
A technical innovator who experimented with reflectors, distorting lenses, solarization and reticulation of negatives, and who specialized in images of the female form, Erwin Blumenfeld became widely known in the 1940s and 1950s for his fashion and commercial photography for American magazines. During many years of work in obscurity in Europe, Blumenfeld developed highly personal imagery: nudes draped in semitransparent materials, urban landscapes, architecture and sculpture informed by the spirit of Dada and Surrealism. His commercial work was responsible for a major revolution in fashion photography.

Blumenfeld was born and educated in Berlin. From 1914 to 1916 he was a dress designer's apprentice. His work in the garment industry prepared him for the fashion photography he would undertake many years later. Drafted into the German Army, Blumenfeld served in the medical corps as an ambulance driver for two years before deserting after his brother's death.

Blumenfeld opened a leather goods shop in Amsterdam where he would live and work for the next 17 years. Already active as an amateur photographer since the age of ten, he displayed his photographs in his shop, wrote verse, painted, and made extensive experiments in collage influenced by his Dadaist friends.

Blumenfeld's first major show of photographs was held in Amsterdam in 1934. His work began to appear at this time in periodicals including *Photographie, arts et métiers*. In 1936 he moved to Paris, where he became friendly with Robert Capa, and started his career as a professional photographer.

In 1937 Blumenfeld shot his first fashion cover, for *Votre Beauté*. His

was a sculptor's apprentice and modeler at the Art Ironworks and Foundry in Magdesprung. He studied painting and sculpture on a scholarship at the School of the Royal Museum of Arts and Crafts in Berlin from 1884 to 1891. On another scholarship from 1891 to 1896, he worked under Professor Meurer in Italy, Greece, and North Africa collecting plant specimens. Blossfeldt began photographing in 1890 and pursued musical studies during these years as well.

Blossfeldt began to photograph plant forms with a camera of his own making in 1899 in Berlin. His systematic documentation commenced the following year. This work was used as part of his teaching at the Kunstgewerbemuseum School where, from 1898 to 1931 he was an instructor, assistant professor, and professor, successively, in the sculpture of living plants. Throughout his career,

Blossfeldt continued to travel, particularly in the Mediterranean, collecting specimens of foreign plants. He retired in 1931. Prints from Blossfeldt's original plates were first published in 1975.

Blossfeldt's work has been included in group exhibitions around the world: *Film und Foto*, Stuttgart, in 1929; *Documenta 6*, West Germany, in 1977; *Paris-Berlin 1900–1933*, Centre Georges Pompidou, Paris, in 1978; and *Avant-Garde Photography in Germany 1919–1939*, San Francisco Museum of Modern Art and ICP, 1980. He was been honored by one-man shows at Zwemmer Gallery, London, in 1929; Galerie Wilde, Cologne, in 1975 and 1978; the Museum of Modern Art, Oxford, in 1978; Arras Gallery, New York, in 1978; and Sonnabend Gallery, New York, in 1979.
See also: NEUE SACHLICHKEIT.

work at this time was noted for its unusual highlights and shadows, and was published in *Verve* magazine along with that of Man Ray, Cartier-Bresson, and Brassai. In 1938 Blumenfeld became a staff photographer with Paris *Vogue*. The following year he traveled to New York where he received immediate acclaim from Alexey Brodovitch and *Life* art director Alexander King, who called Blumenfeld "the greatest living photographer." Blumenfeld signed a contract with *Harper's Bazaar* and did freelance work for *Vogue*.

Having returned to France, Blumenfeld was interned by the Germans as an enemy alien. Released in 1940, he was accused of anti-Nazi propaganda and fled to Martinique. He returned to the United States in 1941, and became a naturalized citizen five years later.

For two years, Blumenfeld shared a studio in New York with Martin Munkacsi. He quickly achieved recognition for his work, and commercial success. From 1944 to 1955 he worked for Condé Nast Publications. Over one hundred of his color photographs were featured as covers for *Look*, *Life*, *Harper's Bazaar*, *Cosmopolitan*, *Vogue*, and *Popular Photography* during these years. Blumenfeld's last decade was spent writing his autobiography. He died in Rome.

Blumenfeld's photographs were exhibited in group shows including *Film und Foto*, Stuttgart, in 1929; *Fashion 1900-1939* at the Victoria and Albert Museum, London, in 1975; *Fashion Photography* at George Eastman House, Rochester, N.Y., in 1977; and the *Photographic Surrealism* traveling exhibition in 1979-1980. One-man shows of Blumenfeld's work have been held at the Witkin Gallery, New York, in 1978; the Sander Gallery, Washington, D.C., in 1980; the Prakapas Gallery, New York, in 1981; the Galerie Zabriskie, Paris, in 1978; the Photographers' Gallery, London, in 1980; and the Centre Georges Pompidou, Paris, in 1982.

Books, Photographic

Photographically illustrated books appeared soon after the invention of photography. Although a few methods were devised to convert the metal plates of daguerreotypes to engraving plates, they were not suitable for book production. Paper prints could be pasted in by hand—a slow, labor-intensive process—but there were no practical processes for direct reproduction until the 1850s, and these were not perfected to make printed reproduction common until the 1880s. Consequently, from 1840 until that time, photographs were routinely copied by hand for reproduction as engravings or lithographs.

However, the first photo-illustrated book did not have copies, but actual pasted-in prints. It was William Henry Fox Talbot's *The Pencil of Nature* (1844-1846), which contained calotype (salt paper print) illustrations. The greater permanence and higher quality of albumen prints, introduced in 1850, led to their more widespread use in the same way. The inclusion of photographic illustrations in books, and the production of books that were essentially picture albums, increased enormously in the 1850s and 1860s following technical improvements and innovations in production by L. D. Blanquart-Evrard and others. The number of such books published has increased in every decade since that time. Today the finest photographic books achieve a level of quality that makes their reproductions virtually indistinguishable from the original prints or transparencies. The following brief account includes books of the past 125 years that represent major achievements in photography as well as in book production; it cannot, of course, be all-inclusive.

After the publication of Talbot's *Pencil of Nature* and such volumes as Mathew Brady's *Gallery of Illustrious Americans* (1850), the most important photographic books were published by Blanquart-Evrard in France in the early 1850s. Frequently these appeared as luxurious, oversize albums containing large photographic prints mounted on heavy cardboard. Most notable were Maxime Du Camp's *Egypte, Nubie, Palestine et Syrie* and Auguste Salzmann's *Jerusalem*, each reflecting the European fascination with the Near East. In addition, Blanquart-Evrard published a number of albums of photographic reproductions of famous artworks and views of classic architecture; these helped revolutionize the way that scholars studied the art of the past.

In the 1850s-1860s, photographically illustrated books mirrored the expanding scope of photography's concerns. The medium's role as the preserver of visual records of the urban past was evident in Thomas Keith's *Old Houses in Edinburgh* (1855). The Englishman Francis Frith's *Views of the Sinai, Palestine, Egypt, Ethiopia . . .* (1860-1863) provided his countrymen with their visual introduction to lands soon to fall under British dominion. In America, Alexander Gardner's *Photographic Sketchbook of the Civil War* (1865-1866) presented a collection of views of the major battlefields of that conflict.

It was during the 1870s that early forms of photomechanical reproduction, such as the autotype and the woodbury-type, came to be widely used. Such processes offered superb fidelity to the original photographs, but proved too expensive to seriously challenge traditional hand-illustration of books. In 1873, John Thomson's *Illustrations of China and Its People* provided an early photographic glimpse of the life and landscape of that country. Thomson's subsequent *Street Life in London*, illustrated with woodburytype reproductions, was the first major work concerning social problems to make use of the testimony of the camera.

Two important new forms of photographic reproduction were introduced during the 1880s. Photogravure, a relatively expensive process which produced exquisite tonal reproduction, was used by the British photographer Peter Henry Emerson in such publications as *Idylls of the Norfolk Broads* (1888), an evocative look at the British marshlands and their inhabitants. The halftone technique, which at last allowed photo-reproductions to be printed on the same presses as type, was employed for the first time in book illustration in Jacob Riis's *How the Other Half Lives* (1890), a vivid account of the hardships endured by New York's immigrant population.

One of the most remarkable publications of the first decades of the 20th c. was Edward S. Curtis's 20-volume *The North American Indian* (1907-1930), which included 1500 gravure reproductions of his own photographs. During the same years, the art photographers of the Photo-Secession movement also made extensive use of the photogravure process, notably in Alvin Langdon Coburn's books *London* (1909), *New York* (1910), and *Men of Mark* (1913).

In the years following World War I, advances in printing technology and the great surge of interest in photography itself spurred the publication of a vastly increased number of photographic books. Germany, especially, produced a number of exceptional works. In *Die Welt ist schön (The World is Beautiful)*, Albert Renger-Patzsch showed the formal beauty of natural and manmade forms seen in close-up. In *Urformen der Kunst (Primordial Forms of Art)*, Karl Blossfeldt displayed microscopic views of plants that resembled ornate sculptural ornaments. And the master portraitist August Sander in 1929 published his *Antlitz der Zeit (Face of the Times)*, the first installment of his never-completed study of the German people.

During the Depression years of the 1930s, books of a documentary nature flourished. Lewis Hine's *Men at Work* (1932) emphasized the dignity of all forms of human labor. Berenice Abbott, inspired by the earlier work of Eugène Atget in Paris, during the 1930s undertook a similar documentary project in her book *Changing New York* (1939). Walker Evans's *American Photographs* (1937) brought together many of the photographs he made for the FSA on the social effects of the Depression. Dorothea Lange and Paul Taylor, in *An American Exodus* (1939), portrayed the plight of migrants forced to flee the Dust Bowl.

In Europe during the same years, important publications included Brassaï's *Paris de Nuit (Paris at Night)*, a look into the nocturnal life of that city, and Bill Brandt's *The English at Home*.

The upheaval brought on by World War II caused a falling-off of the number of photographic books during the 1940s. In 1941, Walker Evans's and James Agee's powerful *Let Us Now Praise Famous Men* provided an intimate glimpse into the lives of Southern sharecroppers. In *Naked City*, the celebrated press photographer Weegee offered his own tour of New York's most sensational and appalling aspects. Wright Morris, in *The Inhabitants*, broke new ground in the format of photographically illustrated books by pairing single evocative images with his own short prose essays.

In the postwar period, interest in photographic books expanded dramatically. During the 1950s several dozen significant volumes appeared, of which the most important include Paul Strand and Nancy Newhall's collaborative *Time in New England* (1950); Ansel Adams's *My Camera in Yosemite Valley* (1950); Henri Cartier-Bresson's *The Decisive Moment* (1952); David Douglas Duncan's Korean War reportage *This Is War*; Richard Avedon's first book, *Observations* (1959); and Aaron Siskind's collection of abstract photographs, titled simply *Photographs* (1959). Undoubtedly the most popular photographic publication of the 1950s was *The Family of Man* (1955), a presentation of the images selected by Edward Steichen for the exhibition of the same name at the Museum of Modern Art. Of greater eventual importance to photographers themselves were Robert Frank's *The Americans* (1959) and William Klein's *Life Is Good for You in New York* (1956), which introduced the off-handed, "snapshot" look to expressive photography.

The dramatic growth of interest in photography during the 1960s and 1970s produced numbers of photographic books. Some were collections of a lifetime of work by veteran photographers, such as Jacques-Henri Lartigue's *Diary of a Century* (1970) or Robert Doisneau's *Three Seconds from Eternity* (1979). Others presented the results of more specifically focused projects by younger photographers, such as Bruce Davidson's Harlem document *East 100th Street* (1970) or Lee Friedlander's ironic *The American Monument* (1976). Finally an increasing number of collections of historical photographs were brought together as interest in photography's past grew. Weston Naef's *Era of Exploration* (1975) revealed the stunning accomplishments of such 19th c. frontier photographers as Timothy H. O'Sullivan and Carleton Watkins. Van Deren Coke's *Avant-Garde Photography in Germany* (1982) took a fresh look at such important figures as Moholy-Nagy. Nancy Hall-Duncan's *History of Fashion Photography* (1979) examined the generally unknown photographers responsible for the world's most famous fashion photographs.

Among the books of the last few decades best suited to provide an introduction to the work of important photographers are Edward Steichen's *A Life in Photography*; Irving Penn's *Moments Preserved*; Berenice Abbott's *The World of Atget*; Robert Capa's *Images of War*; Harry Callahan's *Photographs*; Alfred Eisenstadt's *Witness to Our Time*; Bill Brandt's *Shadow of Light*; Garry Winogrand's *Public Relations*; Dorothea Lange's *Photographs of a Lifetime*; André Kertesz's *Sixty Years of Photography*; Richard Avedon's *Photographs 1947–1977*; W. Eugene Smith's *Minimata*; Ansel Adams's *Yosemite and the Range of Light*; Clarence John Laughlin's *Ghosts Along the Mississippi*; Lee Friedlander's *Self-Portrait*; Duane Michals's *Sequences*; and Joel Meyerowitz's *Cape Light*.

See also: APPENDIX: BIBLIOGRAPHY; BEDE, CUTHBERT; HISTORY OF PHOTOGRAPHY; LITERATURE OF PHOTOGRAPHY; "NATURALISTIC PHOTOGRAPHY"; "PENCIL OF NATURE, THE"; "PICTORIAL EFFECT IN PHOTOGRAPHY."

Bosshard, Walter

Swiss; 1892–1975

Walter Bosshard made his reputation as a pioneer photojournalist and freelance travel photographer in the 1930s. Tim Gidal has written that Bosshard created "the most profound and far-reaching photoreportages of the international political scene throughout the 1930s." His work of three decades, shot with Leica cameras, displays an abiding concern with justice, suffering, and human rights.

During his career, Bosshard published half a dozen books, as well as in-depth photo-essays and accompanying articles in such leading magazines around the world as *The Illustrated London News, Atlantis, Daily Sketch, Berliner Illustrirte Zeitung,* and *Muncher Illustrierte Presse*. A specialist in the documentation of Asian affairs, Bosshard was the first European journalist to interview Mao Zedong at Yenan in 1938, and made incisive portraits of political leaders including Mao Zedong, Chiang Kai-Shek, and Mahatma Gandhi.

Bosshard was born in Richterswil on Lake Zurich. He was educated at schools in Kusnacht, Maennedorf, and Zurich between 1899 and 1910. At the University of Zurich he studied art history and educational theory from 1910 to 1914. He served in the Swiss Army from 1914 to 1918. From 1920 to 1927 he traveled in India, Sumatra, and Siam as a plantation worker and gem agent.

Bosshard began to photograph in 1927, learning basic techniques at Photohaus Ruedi, Lugano, Switzerland. From 1927 to 1929 he served as a photographer and researcher with the German Central Asia Expedition to Tibet and Turkestan under German photographer and explorer Emil Trinkler.

Bosshard worked for the Dephot Agency in Berlin in 1930, and acted as a correspondent and photographer, specializing in Asian topics, for Ullstein Publishers of Berlin between 1930 and 1935.

In 1932 Bosshard accompanied the Graf Zeppelin Arctic expedition. He was associated with the Black Star Agency in New York from 1935 to 1939, and was a correspondent based in Washington, D.C., for the Swiss *Neue Zuricher Zeitung* from 1942 to 1945. During this time he also reported on stories in the Balkans and Near East.

After the war, Bosshard continued to travel, write, and photograph around the world, covering stories including the founding of the United Nations in San Francisco in 1945. Many of his photographs were lost in Peking during the Communist takeover in 1949.

Bosshard was forced to abandon photography in 1953 following an accident in Panmunjon, Korea, but he continued to write and publish until 1960 when he retired to Spain. His archive of 15,000 negatives was donated to Stiftung für die Photographie, Zurich, after his death in 1975.

Bosshard's work was the subject of one-man shows at Kunsthaus, Zurich, in 1977 (a major retrospective), and ICP, New York, in 1978. His photos have also been included in several group shows at Kunsthaus.

Boubat, Edouard

French; 1923–

Edouard Boubat is known chiefly for his humanist approach to photojournalism. His main theme is the idea that there is a common thread linking the everyday life experience of people everywhere; he has documented the way people interact with each other and their environments in France, China, the United States, India, and numerous other parts of the world.

Boubat studied photography at a trade school in France. He began his working life as a technician in a photographic plant, making his own photographs in his spare time. As a young man he met Picasso, who thought Boubat's photographs had promise. Picasso convinced Boubat that he should leave his job and devote all of his time to personal photography. In 1951 Boubat's photographs were exhibited in a group show in Paris, along with the work of Brassai, Izis, and Robert Doisneau. The work was well enough received for the editors of *Réalités* magazine to sign on Boubat as one of their photographers. For the next 15 years or so Boubat traveled to various countries photographing for the magazine.

Boubat continues to photograph people of all social levels at work and play; his pictures appear in various periodicals in France and other countries. A number of books of Boubat's photographs have been published, the most recent being a collection of pictures made in parks and public squares. In 1982 the Witkin gallery in New York City held a major retrospective of Boubat's work.

Bounce Light

Bounce light is produced by aiming a light source at a wall, ceiling, or other reflective surface rather than directly at the subject; the term most often is used to identify reflected light from a flash unit. Bounce light is preferred for many subjects—especially people—because it is less harsh than direct light and produces lighter, more diffuse shadows. It is also used to spread illumination more evenly over an area so that there will be less difference in exposure between nearby and more distant subjects. The light intensity is reduced by this technique.

When used for bounce light, an automatic flash unit will operate properly if the sensor remains aimed at the subject, from the camera position, when the flash head is aimed at the bounce surface. If a guide number is used to determine the lens *f*-stop setting, it must be divided by the total distance the light travels from fllash unit to reflector to subject. The aperture should be opened one additional *f*-stop from the answer arrived at if a clean, white bounce surface is used, or 1½ to 2 *f*-stops if the surface is off-white or a light color. The bounce surface should be white or neutral gray for color pictures; if it is not, the illumination will be tinted upon reflection and will change the subject appearance, especially in flesh tones and white areas.

See also: FLASH; GUIDE NUMBER; LIGHTING; UMBRELLA LIGHTING.

Bourdin, Guy

French; 1933–

Guy Bourdin is one of a very small group of advertising photographers who are given the freedom to invent illustrations rather than having to follow the instructions of an art director. His photography, distinguished for its brilliant coupling of color, design, and emo-

Boubat, Edouard. "Madras, India" (1971).
Courtesy Photo Researchers, New York.

tion, has been exhibited in art galleries and added to museum collections.

Bourdin was born in Paris. Having studied art and design, he began photographing in 1950 while on military service in Africa. Although struggling as a painter, and unsuccessful in applying to be an assistant to Man Ray, he earned the first gallery exhibition of his photographs in 1952. His first fashion illustrations appeared in Paris *Vogue* in 1955, and he was brought to New York to work with the *Vogue* staff in the 1957–1958 season.

Following his return to France, recognition and assignments arrived slowly.

The imaginative audacity of his picture design and the bizarre situations he created for models attracted certain advertisers who wanted to project an image of startlingly elegant contemporaneity for their products. Beginning in 1966, Bourdin was given a sizeable budget and *carte blanche* each year to create visual campaigns for Charles Jourdan shoes. Creators of perfumes, jewelry, and high-fashion gowns became major clients in the 1970s. Bourdin's style was new, and immediately influential. A lingerie catalog, "Sighs and Whispers," that he created in 1976 for the fashionable New York department store, Bloomingdale's,

became a collector's item among photographers, illustrators, and art directors as soon as it was published.

Bourdin acknowledges as his first major photographic influence the intense sensuousness and abstract quality of Edward Weston's photographs of peppers and shells. These qualities pervade Bourdin's work though expressed differently, in some cases through the bold use of vibrant colors contained in dramatic shapes and compositions, in other cases in melodramatic scenes that seem to crackle electrically with projected emotion or sexual tension. There is a posterlike clarity to many of his compositions that reveals a world across the border of the surreal, a totally modern world in which sensuality is ever present but often only glimpsed. His images are uninhibited, occasionally blatant; their sexuality is frequently underscored while the presence of the product is barely acknowledged. As a result, the pictures are seen first as arresting, even startling, images, and second as advertisements. Regarding the quality of aesthetic shock in his photographs Bourdin has said: "It doesn't matter to me if I'm doing art . . . . Photography for me is a way of expressing my surprise before certain objects and certain persons; for singing the poetry of nature or the melancholy of passing time." He has created his own contemporary idiom for accomplishing these things.

See also: ADVERTISING PHOTOGRAPHY; EROTIC PHOTOGRAPHY; FASHION PHOTOGRAPHY; SURREALISM IN PHOTOGRAPHY.

Bourke-White, Margaret

American; 1904–1971

Margaret Bourke-White's career as a photojournalist and industrial photographer spanned three decades from 1927 until the mid-1950s. She became one of the most celebrated photographers of that period, producing notable work throughout the United States, Europe, Russia, and India. She was born in New York City and became interested in photography through a course at Columbia University given by Clarence H. White, dean of American pictorial photographers. Her first published photographs, depicting campus scenes, appeared in the Cornell University newspaper; she graduated from Cornell in 1927.

Bourke-White's professional career began with an assignment to photograph steel-mill activities in Cleveland. Subsequent industrial work brought her to the attention of Henry Robinson Luce, who hired her to do assignments for his new-

ly launched *Fortune* magazine. She produced extensive picture essays on the meat packing plants of Chicago, the upstate New York glass-blowing industry, and the Indiana stone quarries, among other subjects. She also went to the Ruhr valley of Germany, where she documented the steel industry and the rearmament of the German nation.

In 1930 she made the first of several trips to Russia; with official permission she photographed the birth of industrial expansion and the lifestyle of the people. Her pictures appeared in *Fortune*, the *New York Times Magazine*, and in 1931 in her first book, *Eyes on Russia*.

In the U.S. her work during the 1930s established her reputation as a journalist.

Bourne, Samuel. "View over the Ganges River, Varanasi" (1867–1868). Canadian Centre for Architecture, Montreal.

Bourne, Samuel. "View over the Ganges River, Varanasi" (1867–1868). Canadian Centre for Architecture, Montreal.

She wrote and photographed articles about industry, drought in the Texas panhandle, and migrant labor. In 1936 she collaborated with the writer Erskine Caldwell on a project documenting the life of sharecroppers in the southern U.S.; the pictures and text appeared in 1937 in the book *You Have Seen Their Faces*.

In 1936 Bourke-White joined Alfred Eisenstaedt, Peter Stackpole, and Thomas McAvoy to form the photographic staff of Henry Luce's new venture, *Life* magazine. She was sent to Montana to document the construction of Fort Peck Dam. Her pictures were used for the lead article of the first issue, and one photograph of the dam was chosen as the first cover illustration for the magazine.

In the years immediately preceding World War II Bourke-White and Erskine Caldwell traveled to Czechoslovakia, documenting the people as they lived just prior to the Nazi occupation. The couple was married in 1939 and worked for *Life* together through the early years of the war. Both Bourke-White and Caldwell were present during the German attack on Moscow in 1941; Bourke-White was the only western photographer on hand. Bourke-White and Caldwell were divorced in 1942. In that same year Bourke-White was given credentials as an official U.S. Air Force photographer, with use of her pictures to be shared by the Air Force and *Life* magazine. She documented the American campaign in North Africa and then followed Patton's push into Germany. At the close of the war she documented the devastation at Buchenwald.

When the war ended, *Life* sent Bourke-White to India, where she photographed Mohandas Gandhi and re-corded the establishment of the Indian state, and then the riots that preceded and followed the partition of Pakistan from India. Bourke-White was in India interviewing Gandhi a few hours before he was assasinated in 1948.

Bourke-White's association with *Life* continued into the 1950s. In the postwar years she photographed the mines in South Africa, covered the guerilla war in Korea, and did a number of photo essays in the U.S., one of the most notable being a study of the Strategic Air Command. Her photographic output gradually became smaller due to Parkinson's disease, to which she succumbed in 1971.

Bourne, Samuel

British, 1834–1912

The English Victorian photographer Samuel Bourne is best known for his magnificent views of the Himalayas, some made at elevations as high as 18,000 feet (5486 meters) on mammoth collodion plates. Bourne, a landscape photographer in England, arrived in Simla, India, in 1863 and quickly founded a partnership with Charles Shepherd, the owner of the oldest Anglo-Indian photographic company. The firm of Bourne & Shepherd rapidly became the leading provider of Indian landscape and monument views to both visitors and far-off armchair travelers in the British Isles.

An indefatigable traveler, Bourne was the first photographer to document much of the Himalayas; more than half his known negatives were made on his three Himalayan expeditions. Other treks took him through much of India, Burma, and Ceylon, from where he sent entertaining accounts of his adventures to the *British Journal of Photography*.

After relocating from Simla to Calcutta, where he opened a branch of Bourne & Shepherd, Bourne returned to England in 1872, to pursue photography only as a pleasurable hobby.

Boutan, Louis

French; 1859–1934

Louis Boutan was an extraordinary, multi-talented scientist: an entomologist whose research helped save European winemaking from disaster; a marine biologist who became a world authority on pearl oysters and the culture of pearls; and the father of underwater photography.

Boutan was a Doctor of Sciences and a lecturer at the Sorbonne in Paris in the late 1880s. His study of *Phylloxera vastatrix*, an insect that almost destroyed the wine-grape vines of France and the rest of Europe in the 1860s and the 1870s, had gained him a worldwide reputation. About 1890 his interest in marine biology grew and he began research on mollusks at the Arago Marine Laboratory on the Bay of Bayuls in southern France. There he learned to dive with the heavy, hard-helmet, surface-supported equipment that was the state of the art at the time.

In 1892, Boutan realized the need for photographs of the animals he studied in their natural habitat. With the assistance of his brother August, an engineer, he built a watertight case to contain a Delta Detective camera, a newly improved hand camera that used 5″ × 7″ glass plates. The camera had two features especially useful for underwater photography. First, the lens did not have to be focused for subjects more than about 13 ft (4m) away; this eliminated the need for a focus control on the housing. Second, and more important, it accepted a multi-plate magazine that made several exposures possible before reloading was necessary. With this equipment, in the summer of 1893 Boutan made what are regarded as the first successful underwater photographs.

Not totally satisfied with the results, Boutan experimented with a camera that let water enter, flooding the lens and the plate, which was varnished to waterproof the emulsion. Poor results led him to return to constructing watertight boxes to hold larger cameras with lenses that could be focused. Some housings were huge, heavy constructions that were lowered into the water by block-and-tackle and were supported by ropes that ran to buoys floating on the surface.

The slow-speed emulsions available to Boutan required long exposures, especially in deep water where the light was faint. As a result, photographs were often spoiled by water currents or subject movement. To obtain light for short exposures, Boutan devised an underwater flash system. After experimenting with an electrical system that proved to be costly, he developed a device that consisted of a continuous-burning alcohol lamp, an oxygen supply to support combustion, a rubber syringe, and a supply of magnesium. When a flash was wanted, squeezing the syringe bulb blew a burst of powdered magnesium into the flame where it burned in a brief, brilliant flare. This system made it possible to obtain a number of flashes without the need to come to the surface after every picture.

With money provided by the optical industry of France, Boutan continued his experiments and in 1899 produced a photograph made at a depth of 150 ft (about 50m). The photograph was exhibited at the Paris Exposition of 1900. In that same year Boutan published *La photographie Sousmarine*, the first book on underwater photography. It included sections on the construction of watertight housings, available light photography, and artificial light underwater. It was illustrated with his photographs of divers and marine life, and in many ways was quite similar to books on underwater photography published today.
See also: UNDERWATER PHOTOGRAPHY.

Bracketing

Bracketing is the technique of photographing a subject at several different exposure settings for purposes of testing, or to ensure that at least one exposure will be acceptable, or to achieve expressive variations in color saturation, highlight or shadow details, or similar factors. With stationary subjects (e.g., still-lifes, architecture, scenic views) the pictures will be identical except for exposure; with moving subjects content as well as exposure will vary. It is sufficient to change exposure in steps equivalent to one *f*-stop with negative films, and in steps equivalent to one-half stop with transparency (slide) films. This may be done by changing the lens aperture or the shutter-speed setting, or by changing the film-speed setting on the light meter. Many 35mm cameras provide + and − settings at the film-speed control to facilitate bracketing with automatic exposure control. In most cases effective bracketing covers a range from two *f*-stops additional exposure to two *f*-stops

Brady, Mathew. "Abraham Lincoln" (1864); collodion. National Archives.

reduced exposure, in addition to the assumed normal exposure.

The principle of bracketing is used in making a test strip to determine print exposure and in determining the effect of processing changes. The most complex type of bracketing combines exposure and development variations, or changes in exposure and color print filtration, to produce a highly informative ring-around. Methodical procedures, with a consistent degree of change for each variation, are essential to obtain repeatable and therefore useful results.
See also: RING-AROUND; TEST STRIP.

Brady, Mathew

American; 1823–1896
Mathew Brady, an internationally celebrated portrait photographer of the 1840s and 1850s, established a corps of photographers, including Timothy

O'Sullivan and Alexander Gardner, who made a comprehensive documentation of the American Civil War. Brady's photographers recorded the horror of war first hand, making portraits, vistas, and group photographs in close proximity to the fighting, as well as images of the aftermath of battle. These images, reproduced in the popular press of the day in engravings and lithographs, constitute a major contribution to pictorial historical documentation.

Brady was born into a poor Irish family near Lake George, New York. He studied painting under William Page, and learned daguerreotypy from Samuel F.B. Morse and J.W. Draper in New York City.

In 1844 Brady opened a New York studio, the Daguerrean Miniature Gallery, and began an extensive series of portraits of Americans of distinction. Within a few years he was awarded prizes at exhibitions in New York and

Bragaglia, Anton. "The Cellist" (1931).
Sotheby, New York.

London, and he opened other studios in Washington, D.C., and New York. In 1850 Brady published *The Gallery of Illustrious Americans.* Among his sitters were Walt Whitman, Edgar Allan Poe, Jefferson Davis, John Quincy Adams, P.T. Barnum, Dolley Madison, and Mark Twain. Abraham Lincoln is reputed to have credited Brady's photographs of him for his election.

Hampered by failing eyesight, Brady delegated more and more of the portraiture in his studios to assistants such as Alexander Gardner, who worked for him from 1856 to 1863. Brady was, however, the photographer first in the field at the battle of Bull Run. From 1861 to 1865 he and his staff of photographers documented all the major engagements of the War between the North and South. Brady employed 20 teams of photographers, investing over $100,000 in the project. There is great difficulty in the attribution of the 7000 negatives Brady amassed, but it is generally believed that he was directly responsible for few of the photographs of the War, though they were copyrighted under his name and published with the corporate credit line: Photograph by Brady. In 1863 Gardner resigned from Brady's employ to continue photographing on his own and he hired away several of Brady's best men.

After the War, Brady was ruined financially and was forced by his creditors to sell off sets of the Civil War photographs which he had hoped would be in great public demand. He continued to make portraits in a small Washington, D.C., studio until the early 1890s. Destitute and partially blind, Brady died in the poor ward of New York Presbyterian Hospital in 1896 and was buried in Arlington National Cemetery, Virginia. Although many of the Brady glass plate negatives were destroyed, a few thousand have survived; they are in the National Archive in Washington, D.C. *See also:* GARDNER, ALEXANDER.

Bragaglia, Anton Giulio

Italian; 1890–1960
One of the principal protagonists of Italian futurism and a theoretician of "futurist photodynamism," Anton Bragaglia began his artistic activity in 1906 as an assistant director in motion pictures, working in Rome with such directors as Mario Caserini and Enrico Guazzoni.

In collaboration with his brother Arturo, he became interested in photography in 1910 and formulated the first futurist statements in the field, his work paralleling Giacomo Balla's in the pictorial representation of kinetic force.

Bragaglia, accepting the principles of the "Futurist Painting: Technical Manifesto" (1910) proposed a futurist photography, which he called "fotodinamica." From 1911 he elaborated this concept through numerous lectures and communications. In 1913, he opened two one-man exhibitions in Rome of "fotodinamiche" and assembled the texts of his lectures and speeches on the subject in the volume *Futurist Photodynamism,* which was published the same year. "We seek to create the art of Photodynamism," he wrote, "an art special and distinct in its extremely innovative aims and at the same time, we desire to give to Movementalist painting and sculpture the solid basis that today they need most." This declaration aroused the immediate reaction of the futurists who, urged by Umberto Boccioni, denounced Bragaglia and denied any connection between photodynamism (which they felt concerned only the field of photographic innovation) and the "plastic dynamism" of "any dramatic research in the fields of painting, sculpture or architecture."

Bragaglia saw untapped and limitless possibilities in photography as a means of experimentation and thought that only photodynamism could capture the complexity of movement, rhythm, reality, dematerialization. Photodynamism, he claimed, introduces in photography "movementalism and its aim is to record the dynamic sensation of movement and its scientifically true shape, even in dematerialization. . . . We are involved in the area of movement which produces sensation, memory of which still palpitates in our awareness."

Photodynamic images were obtained through long exposures while the subject itself moved, in order to record a "dynamic result, that is the trajectory, synthesis of the whole gesture and meaning of the time we experienced it." The resulting blurred paths were the entire esthetic point of the image, not a technical error. Bragaglia thought there was a substantial difference between this and the instantaneous shot since "there is a gulf between the photograph of a carpenter, exact and still, holding a bucksaw, in the attitude of sawing, and the 'photodynamic' of the same carpenter, in which all movement traces were recorded together with the truly lyric pulsation of the body in action."

In addition to being a photographer, Bragaglia was a writer and art critic; he also founded and directed various art magazines. In 1916–1917 he produced two experimental futurist films: *Thaïs* and *Il perfido incanto.* In 1918 he opened his own art gallery, which was until 1943 a center for avant-garde events, housing some 300 exhibitions and presenting works by Balla, Depero, De Chirico, Boccioni, Klimt, Kandinsky, and other modernists.

Brandel, Konrad. "Theatre in Lazienki Garden, Warsaw" (1875); albumen. Permanent collection, ICP, New York.

In 1919 Bragaglia became interested in theater and directed plays by Rosso di San Secondo and Pirandello. In 1922 he founded the Teatro Sperimentale degli Independenti, which he directed until 1936, and whose activity was fundamental to the development of experimental theater in Italy. He was also a talented set designer and his work in this area was very well known.

From 1926 until his death in 1960, Bragaglia published countless articles and about 30 books, mostly dealing with performing and visual arts, theater, and cinema.

See also: ABSTRACT PHOTOGRAPHY; MOTION STUDY AND ANALYSIS; PAINTING AND PHOTOGRAPHY.

Brandel, Konrad

Polish; 1838–1920

Konrad Brandel was the most interesting Polish photographer working in the great 19th c. tradition. He was born in Warsaw and was the pupil of the "father" of Polish photography, Karol Beyer. In 1865, together with his brother Wladyslaw and M. Olszynski, he opened a studio and a phototype press in Warsaw. A year later he opened his own studio. He was nominated photographer of the University of Warsaw for his *Dermatological Atlas* published in 1875. Brandel received many prizes for works exhibited in Cracow (1869), St. Petersburg (1870), Moscow (1872), Vienna (1873), and Paris (1874).

Brandel took a large number of photographs of Warsaw's architecture. He photographed streets, buildings, monuments, and public parks. In 1872 he published *Nowy album widokow Warszawy (New Album of Warsaw's Views)*. He was an excellent craftsman with great sensitivity to light and a delicate sense of design; his work was both harmonious and lyrical. In 1873, taking advantage of repairs of the Royal Castle tower, he used that vantage point to take pictures for a famous panorama of Warsaw.

In 1881, seven years before the introduction of the No. 1 Kodak Camera, Brandel designed and started to produce a small-size camera (6 × 9cm format) for fast pictures. Known as the "branlowka" or "photorevolver," for its ability to shift plates, some of these cameras were sold abroad and were well received. In 1884, Brandel used the camera to make a full reportage of the meeting of the emperors of Russia, Prussia, and Austria, which took place in Skierniewice, near Warsaw. The Emperor of Austria, Franz Josef, decorated the inventor with a medal. Later on Brandel used the photorevolver for splendid pictures of life in Warsaw. He proved to be a sensitive observer of social life and recorded numerous genre scenes and sights of Warsaw. Brandel collaborated with the press and, in 1894, he started to publish "pictures from nature" in the *Tygodnik Powszechny* weekly, thus becoming the first professional photoreporter in Poland.

Brandel was a Member of the Warsaw Photographic Society, which honored him in 1905. He died in Torun in 1920.

Brandt, Bill. "Parlourmaid and under-par-
lourmaid ready to serve dinner" (1933).
Courtesy Bill Brandt; collection, Museum of
Modern Art, New York.

Brandt, Bill

English; 1904–1983

Born in London of parents who were
both partly of Russian descent, Bill
Brandt spent his early life in Germany in
delicate health. He left a Swiss tuberculosis sanitarium in 1929 to study with the
surrealist Man Ray in Paris. Brandt
worked closely with Man Ray in his studio for three months and continued to
see him regularly for the next two years.
He learned the value of experiment for
its own sake and was profoundly influenced by the surrealist work of Man
Ray and his circle.

After working freelance for *Paris
Magazine* in 1930, Brandt returned to
England where he photographed for
magazines such as *Lilliput, Harper's
Bazaar,* and *News Chronicle* for which
he documented the conditions of England in the depths of the Depression. He
photographed English middle- and

Brassaï (Gyula Halász). "Bijou of Montmartre" (1932 or 1933). Courtesy Brassaï; collection, Museum of Modern Art, New York.

upper-class life both before and during World War II, publishing *The English at Home* (1936), *A Night in London*, (1938), and *The Camera in London* (1948). Working as a photojournalist on assignment, his photography was a singular and idiosyncratic mixture of straight reportage with a consistent, if subtle, streak of strangeness—the legacy of surrealism.

Brandt lost interest in reportage toward the end of the war, and the expressionism and surrealism of his work was accordingly strengthened. He worked extensively with the nude, often with both perspective and figural distortions. Also important in his work were portraits of writers and artists, and ominous brooding landscapes and seashores of the British Isles. Threatening skies at dawn and twilight and shadowed interiors were characteristic subjects. Typical, too, were wide-angle, distorting photographs, often strangely lighted and printed for high contrast with the elimination of middle tones. Highly respected for the intensity and power of his images, Brandt is considered one of the preeminent photographers to have emerged in England. Writing of his work, which runs clearly counter to the dominant post-war style of straight, unmanipulated photography, Brandt has said, "Photography is still a very new medium and everything must be tried and dare. . . photography has no *rules*. It is not a sport. It is the result which counts, no matter how it is achieved."

His later books include *Literary Britain* (1951), *Perspective of Nudes* (1961), *Shadow of Light* (1966), *Bill Brandt Photographs* (1970), and *Bill Brandt: Early Photographs 1930–42* (1975).

Brassaï (Gyula Halász)

French; 1899–

Brassaï is regarded as the photographer whose pictures form the basis upon which many non-Parisians' ideas about Paris are formed. His best known work consists of night scenes of "the City of Lights" in the 1930s, including photographs of the architecture; people in cafes and bars; workers who kept the city going after dark; *clochards* who lived under the bridges; and performers, artists, and writers of the period.

Born Gyula Halász in the (now Rumanian) town of Brasso (whence his adopted name) at the turn of the century, Brassaï's original ambition was to paint. He studied art in Hungary and Germany as a youth, finally coming to Paris in 1924 as a journalist. As a small child he had accompanied his father to that city

and stayed for a year. The city left a lasting impression which became a powerful interest upon his return. Brassaï became fascinated with the nightlife he saw around him, both on the streets and in public gathering places. He claimed that the images he saw haunted him; recording them became something of an obsession. Although he was a skillful painter, he found the medium too time consuming and lacking immediacy.

During this time he befriended a fellow expatriate, André Kertész, who finally convinced Brassaï to try his hand at photography. For the first six years of his life in Paris Brassaï had avoided photography, considering the medium to be too mechanical and impersonal. His opinion changed quickly when he saw the results of his first efforts to record Paris after dark. He immersed himself in his new-found pastime and in 1933 produced a book of night pictures

entitled *Paris de Nuit*, which met with critical acclaim.

Brassaï's wanderings around the cafes and bars of Paris brought him into contact with many of the artists and writers living in the city during that period. He established lifelong ties with Picasso, Giacometti, Sartre, Henry Miller, and many others.

Many of Brassaï's pictures of the city of Paris were used in magazines; others remained unseen and unpublished until later in his career. These pictures depict in a non-judgmental and keenly observed fashion the prostitutes, opium addicts, lovers (both homosexual and heterosexual), street hoodlums, performers, and nighttime revellers of prewar Paris.

Brassaï's reputation as a photographer had reached the United States by the mid-thirties, and some of his work was incuded in an exhibition entitled *Photog-*

Abstract Photography. Rosamond Wolff Purcell, "You Can" [Fred Astaire] (1981); 8″ × 10″ Polacolor. © R.W. Purcell; courtesy Marcuse Pfeifer Gallery, New York.

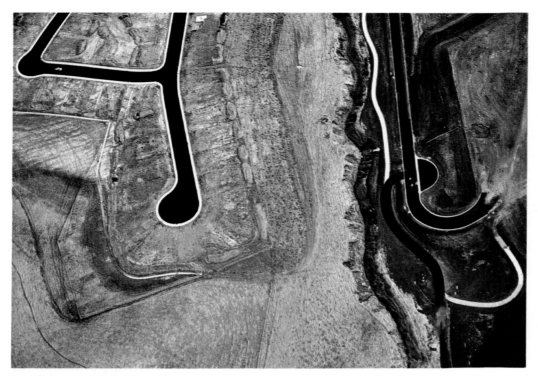

Aerial Photography. Robert Hartman, "Near Pittsburg, Calif." (1982). © Robert Hartman.

Anschutz, Ottomar. "Lissa (Posen)" (1889); albumen. Courtesy Manfred Heiting, Frankfurt-am-Main.

Architecture, Photography of. Don Dubroff,
"Saint Nicholas Ukranian Catholic Cathedral"
(1979). © 1979 Don Dubroff.

Autochrome Process. Arnold Genthe, "Mabel Cramer" (ca. 1910). Library of Congress.

Backgrounds. Hand-painted backgrounds are widely used in commercial photography as well as in television and movies. Background © Sara Oliphant, New York; photo © Larry Robbins.

Bayard, Hippolyte. "Moulins de Montmarte percement de la Rue de Tholozée" (ca. 1842); calotype. Courtesy Société Française de Photographie, Paris.

Burrows, Larry. "A wounded G.I. reaches out
to a stricken comrade, Vietnam" (1966).
Courtesy Vicky Burrows; Time Inc.

Cabinet Print. Design from the back of a typical cabinet print. Private collection.

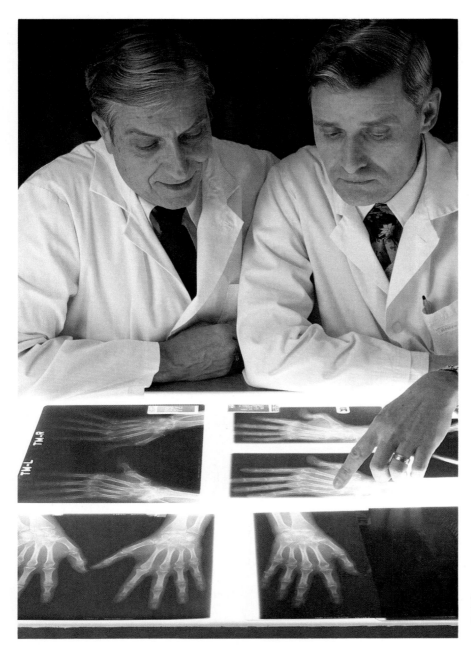

Clinical Photography. Dick Luria, Cover photograph from Warner-Lambert Annual Report. © 1981, Dick Luria.

raphy: *1839–1937* at the Museum of Modern Art. Brassaï continued to document Parisian life and make environmental portraits of his fellow artists until the outbreak of World War II. Unrestricted photography in occupied France being all but impossible, Brassaï turned to his earlier discipline of drawing. At the end of the war a selection of these drawings was published. Brassaï then returned to his camera and at the same time began work on a novel, *Histoire de Marie*, which was published with an introduction by Henry Miller in 1948. Three years later a collection of Brassaï's photographs was published under the title *Camera in Paris*.

In the 1950s Brassaï turned his camera on the graffiti he found in his wanderings through the city streets; he also traveled and photographed in various parts of France and Spain. He continued to work in other media, making drawings, paintings, and sculpture. His friendship with Picasso resulted in a highly acclaimed book on the artist and his contemporaries, *Conversations avec Picasso*, published in 1964.

In 1968 the Museum of Modern Art in New York mounted a one-man show of Brassaï's photographs. Brassaï continued to make photographs and to write a number of books and articles about his contemporaries. In 1975 he published *Henry Miller—Grandeur Nature*, considered to be one of the most telling treatises on Miller's life and works. The following year he produced *The Secret of Paris of the 30's*, a book and a major exhibit seen in the U.S. at the Marlborough Gallery in New York. Brassaï continues to work and live in France, where he has been a naturalized citizen since 1948.

Braun, Adolphe

French; 1811–1877

Artist and entrepreneur, Adolphe Braun was a 19th c. pioneer in the photographic reproduction of artworks on an industrial scale. Born at Besançon, France in 1811, he became a designer of textile patterns for a French cloth-manufacturing house. He began photographing flowers in the early 1850s as a basis for his textile designs. He extended this interest to form "a collection of studies intended for artists who employ flowers as decorative elements." Braun's flower and still-life photographs of the 1850s and 1860s were taken in direct sunlight with a small aperture and long exposure times (up to one-half hour) using collodion negatives that were printed on 20-in. (50.8cm) sheets. They were unique for their time in both size and subject matter

and won critical acclaim for their technical excellence and their resemblance to 17th-c. Dutch still-life painting.

Braun's flower portfolio was followed by a landscape album photographed in Alsace. He also employed a team of photographers to make landscape and architectural views throughout Europe. One of his own landscape studies, "Le Chateau de Chillon" of 1867, was copied seven years later by the painter Gustave Courbet for an oil painting of the same name.

In addition to still-lifes, landscapes, architectural views, and studio portraits, Braun also made group portraits of the court of Napoleon III. In 1864, he composed a photomontage of the Emperor's entourage consisting of dozens of cut-out portraits assembled into a mountainous mass with Napoleon at the peak.

Next, Braun turned to the photographic reproduction of artworks. Paintings and drawings had been reproduced photographically before Braun, but never on the scale or with the same degree of technical success that he achieved. In 1866 he purchased the French and Belgian rights to the carbon printing process perfected by Alphonse Poitevin and built a photographic printing plant at Dornach-Mulhouse in Alsace. He then proceeded to visit all the major galleries and museums of Europe and to photograph their old-master drawings, paintings, and sculptures. He also photographed the frescoes of the Sistine Chapel. By 1868, Braun was producing 1,500 prints a day and had accumulated 4,000 collodion negatives. By 1870, he had amassed a collection of 8,000 plates. The widespread publication of photographic reproductions of artworks pioneered by Braun was to have an important effect on the study of art history as well as on the critical and popular consideration of art objects.
See also: CARBON PROCESSES.

Photograph: p. 82.

Brewster, Sir David

Scottish; 1781–1868

A notable physicist, Brewster published more than 400 books and papers describing his discoveries and inventions in optics and related fields, and was closely associated with the early development of photography, especially as a supporter of W. H. F. Talbot. In 1802 he published an account of the experiments of Thomas Wedgwood and Humphry Davy, the first recorded work in 19th c. progress toward the invention of photography. His own investigations of the nature of light produced a basic law of polarization and in 1816 led to the invention of

the kaleidoscope, an instrument originally intended for studying refraction and polarization. In 1844 he invented the first stereoscope to use separate eyepiece lenses, a design which supplanted the mirror system of Sir Charles Wheatstone. Brewster promoted adoption of the Fresnel dioptric (lens-mirror) system for lighthouse beacons in England, and was one of the earliest proponents of microphotography. An ordained minister of the Scottish Free Church, he became aware of the church-related portrait project of D. O. Hill and introduced him to Robert Adamson, bringing about one of the great collaborations in the history of photography. Interested in the artistic development of the medium, he purchased one of the four copies of O. J. Rejlander's landmark picture "The Two Paths of Life."
See also: FRESNEL LENS; HILL, DAVID OCTAVIUS; MICROPHOTOGRAPHY; STEREOSCOPE; TALBOT, WILLIAM HENRY FOX; WEDGWOOD, THOMAS; WHEATSTONE, SIR CHARLES.

Bright-Field Illumination

The microscope lighting technique called bright-field illumination is also frequently used in close-up and macrophotography of small objects. It creates a plain background that is brighter than the subject, and because the lighting silhouettes the subject, it is particularly valuable for revealing external edge contours, especially with dark-colored subjects. In non-microscopic photography bright-field illumination is usually created by shining light through diffuse background material or by reflecting frontal light off an opaque (usually white) background; in microscopy a condenser system focuses light rays directly into the lens field, as in Kohler illumination. The subject is seldom fully silhouetted; light transmitted through a thin subject may reveal internal structure, or frontal light may be added to reveal surface detail.
See also: DARK-FIELD ILLUMINATION; KOHLER ILLUMINATION; MACROPHOTOGRAPHY.

Brightness Range

The degree of difference between the intensities of the darkest and brightest parts of a subject is called the brightness range, or more properly the luminance range. The brightness of any subject area is the product of how much light falls on the area and how reflective it is. Thus, the brightness range must be measured by reflected-light meter readings taken directly from the subject. Reflected-light

Braun, Adolphe. "Still life" (n.d.). International Museum of Photography at George Eastman House.

readings from a standard gray card, or incident-light readings reveal the lighting (illuminance) range, but do not take into account the effect of differences in reflectivity of various subject areas. The range is expressed as the number of *f*-stops difference between the dark-area and light-area readings, or as an equivalent ratio.

BRIGHTNESS RANGE

No. of Stops	Ratio
1	1:2
2	1:4
3	1:8
4	1:16
5	1:32
6	1:64
7	1:128
8	1:256
9	1:512
10	1:1024

Although panchromatic films can easily record subjects with a 10-stop (1:1024) brightness range, printable detail with ordinary processing is limited to about a 7-stop range. The photographer can choose to favor dark-area or light-area details by adjusting exposure, or can make a mid-range exposure, knowing that some detail at each end may be lost. With subjects of excessive brightness range, black-and-white nega-

tive development can be reduced to compress the image into a printable range of negative densities. Conversely, a negative of a subject with a shorter-than-normal brightness range can be given increased development to expand its printing range. Color films can generally encompass a 7-stop subject range, with a 5-stop range limit on useful detail in the image; processing control of atypical brightness ranges is not practical in color work.

Because flare in the lens and camera interior scatters some light into the dark areas, the brightness range of the image falling on the film is always less than the brightness range of the subject. The brightness range of a print will be even less, because viewing light is scattered by the print paper and is absorbed by the silver or dyes that form the image. A projected image always has a greater brightness range than a print of the same picture, because light travels through the image just once (in a print it must pass through the image to the paper base, then back through the image to the viewer), and because most projection screens have higher reflectivity than print-base materials.

See also: GRAY CARD; EXPOSURE METERS; TONE REPRODUCTION.

Broad Lighting

In portraiture broad lighting is an arrangement in which the main light source is located close to the camera and illuminates the side of the subject's face

that is closest to the lens. The somewhat flat illumination this produces helps to make narrow or thin faces look wider; it also minimizes facial texture such as wrinkles, beard lines, and skin pores. For good modeling and pleasing results the main light placement is balanced with fill light on the shadowed side of the face, backlight, and appropriate background or set lighting. Broad lighting is also commonly used with rectangular, boxy items in product illustration.

See also: LIGHTING; NARROW LIGHTING.

Brodovitch, Alexey

American; 1898–1971
An immigrant of aristocratic Russian background, for more than two decades Alexey Brodovitch exerted an influence that revolutionized magazine design in the U.S. and that directly affected the styles and careers of a great number of photographers. Richard Avedon, Hiro, Lisette Model, and Irving Penn are only a few of those who recognize a debt to his demands, his suggestions and criticisms, and his teaching. The number of illustrators and journalists indirectly formed by his publications and the work of those he trained is uncountable.

In 1934 Brodovitch was brought to *Harper's Bazaar* as art director by Carmel Snow. During the next 24 years in this position he created a new vision for the printed page and inspired photographers to give him the pictures that turned magazine reading into interactive viewing, engaging the audience in dynamic participation in communication. On the pages of *Bazaar* he made distinctive use of white space, bleed photos, and the concept of montage and pacing as in a motion picture. His layouts of photographs, text, and artwork saw the basic design unit to be the large horizontal rectangle of the two-page spread rather than the narrow vertical of the single page. His endless experiments in the use of type and illustrations left their mark on a generation of American designers and image-makers.

Although *Bazaar* was a fashion magazine, Brodovitch did not limit the visual content to the styles of the day; he wanted the magazine to contain the flavor of all of life in that period. Like Diaghilev's charge to Jean Cocteau, "Astonish me!" was Brodovitch's challenge to the photographers who worked for him and who studied in his workshops at the Philadelphia Museum School and New York's New School. The journalistic work of Henri Cartier-Bresson mingled with the images of brilliant new illustrators, surprising readers and causing them to stop, look, attend.

A magazine and book designer of the greatest skill, Brodovitch was also a painter and, when he wished, a fine photographer as well. During his early days there many of the covers for *Bazaar* were taken from paintings by him. In the 1930s he photographed the Ballets Russes de Monte Carlo on stage while it was touring the U.S. These photographs were published in 1945 in a limited edition book, *Ballet*, which is now a milestone in photography. Soft forms, blurred movement and colors, and an uninterrupted visual sense of motion created an effect that revolutionized the then-current concepts of image-making and encouraged photographers to experiment freely.

Brodovitch's other major photographic achievement was a set of forceful images made with a tiny camera concealed in a cigarette pack and taken in a sanatorium where he spent the last years of his life. His greatest legacy, however, is to be seen by comparing the pages of fashion magazines today and the pages of his period at *Bazaar* with those of the 1920s and early 1930s; his ability to get photographers to do their best and the brilliantly effective ways in which he displayed their work is clearly evident.

Broloid Process

In this variation of the carbro process, the silver image of a *bro*mide print is converted to a (carbon) pigment image, with cellu*loid* support material used at an intermediate stage.
See also: CARBRO PROCESS.

Bromide Paper

Black-and-white enlarging paper with an emulsion containing silver bromide and a small amount of silver iodide is called bromide paper; little or no silver chloride is included. It is the fastest (most light-sensitive) printing paper, a characteristic often indicated by "Rapid" or "Speed" in its trade name, along with "Bro-," "-brome," or some similar indication of its emulsion. Bromide paper produces neutral black tones and can achieve higher grades of contrast than chloride or chloro-bromide papers. The emulsion may contain up to twice as much silver as ordinary chloro-bromide emulsions. Paper of this type with a gelatin emulsion was first produced by P. Mawdsley, founder of the Liverpool Dry Plate and Photographic Printing Co., in 1873 (collodion-bromide emulsions had first appeared in the 1850s). A similar paper, which met with better success, was patented by J. W. Swan in 1879.

Bromoil Process

The most widely used method of producing oil prints is the bromoil process, because the use of bromide paper permits making the image exposure by direct enlargement from a small-format negative if desired; it is not necessary to make a final-size negative for a contact printing exposure. The basic procedure was described by Edward J. Wall in 1907, and bromoil was introduced as a practical process in England by C. Welborne Piper in the same year.

The original soft-emulsion bromide paper is no longer manufactured, but a few modern matte-surface enlarging papers may be used; those on water-resistant ("RC") bases work best. Since the process depends on making some portions of the emulsion absorb water and swell, care must be taken to avoid hardening or tanning the gelatin during processing. The paper is exposed to a negative in the normal manner and developed. A full-contrast negative but a somewhat flat print with very open shadow detail and printed-in highlight detail is required; a soft-working (low contrast) developer produces the least hardening action. After a stop bath, the image is treated in a fixer to which no hardener has been added. After washing, the silver image is bleached in a slightly acidified solution of copper sulfate and potassium bromide which contains 0.2 percent potassium bichromate. The bleached print is washed, treated in a plain hypo solution to remove the bleached image compounds, and washed again. At this stage it is ready to be inked or colored.

Thinned lithographic ink, or pigment mixed in a similar oil base, is applied by a stippling action with a moderately soft brush, or by rolling on with an artist's brayer. The color is absorbed by the shadow and middletone portions of the gelatin, but not by the highlight portions. Saturation and contrast are built up by repeated applications. A single color may be used, or a variety of colors may be applied in different areas of the image; a wide range of control is available to the colorist. The final image is allowed to set, or it can be transferred to another support by pressure-contact in a suitable printing press.
See also: TRANSFER PROCESSES.

Brownie Camera

Although other manufacturers had attempted and failed to create a camera with appeal to children as well as adults, the Eastman Kodak Company succeeded with the Brownie box camera, introduced to the public through an extensive

advertising campaign in 1900. Its name was taken from the popular Brownie characters in illustrations of books and verse by Palmer Cox, not from Eastman's chief camera designer, Frank Brownell. The original model cost $1.00 and took 6 pictures 2¼ inches square on paper film at 10¢ a roll or on celluloid film at 15¢ a roll; development, printing, and mounting cost 40¢. Its simplicity and low cost made it immensely popular. Models using various sizes of film appeared in subsequent years, and the last Brownie model was discontinued in 1965.
See also: CAMERA.

Bruguière, Francis Joseph

American; 1879–1945
The work of Francis Bruguière, the American surrealist and abstract photographer, was a major factor in the critical acceptance of photography as a modern art medium.

Born in San Francisco into a wealthy banking family, Bruguière was privately educated and developed an interest in painting and music. In 1905 he came to New York where he met Frank Eugene (Smith) and Alfred Stieglitz. Eugene encouraged Brugière to investigate the aesthetic possibilities of photography, giving him technical advice and indoctrinating him in pictorial photography. Bruguière's early pictures were conventionally pictorial, with softly depicted nudes in the typically allegorical settings of the period. Stieglitz accepted him as a member of the Photo Secession, but Brugière remained on the fringes of the movement.

Returning to San Francisco in 1906 in the wake of the earthquake that wiped out the family fortune, Bruguière decided to devote himself professionally to photography, although he continued to paint in an increasingly modernist mode. He opened a studio where he made photographic portraits and pictorial images that, while competent, showed no particular individuality. In 1910 four of Bruguière's photographs were included in the International Photo Secession exhibition at the Albright-Knox galleries in Buffalo, New York. This was the only time he exhibited with his fellow Secessionists, for he preferred to work in virtual isolation. Although reproductions of his work appeared in Stieglitz's *Camera Work*, he did not exhibit again until 1927.

In 1912 and 1913 photographs made during travels in Europe and Greece began to reflect his dissatisfaction with pictorialism. His pictures became more concerned with the inherent forms of the subject and passed through a period of "straight" photography to experimentation with multiple exposures used to juxtapose several discrete images on one film. He noted that his interest was in exploring psychological responses to imagery that seemed not to be born of reality.

In 1919 Bruguière established a studio in Manhattan and began photographing for *Vanity Fair, Vogue,* and *Harper's Bazaar.* His interest in the theater and in the design possibilities of controlled lighting led him to the Theater Guild, for which he became the official photographer. He was one of the first to record theater productions using no illumination beyond that necessary for production itself. In his personal work he continued to experiment with multiple-exposure images, eventually producing a body of work that was to be the scenario for a film entitled *The Way.* The film was to be a surrealist tour de force. Although never completed, the surviving photographic records of the scenario are considered to be the first examples of surrealist photography in America.

The first major exhibition of Bruguière's work was at the Art Center in New York in 1927. The show consisted of 94 photographs and a number of paintings. Multiple-exposure images, light patterns, and purely abstract images made by arranging and lighting cut paper and other objects in a nonrepresentational fashion made up the majority of the photographs. The fantastic content and modernist execution of these images predated the official introduction of Surrealism to America by four years. Critical acclaim for the exhibition was all but unanimous, and it compared Bruguière's vision and influence to that of Brancusi and Stieglitz.

In 1928 Bruguière moved to London, and in the same year he was elected an honorary member of the German Secession on the basis of photographs he exhibited at Der Sturm galleries in Berlin. In England he started a new series of abstractions and produced the first British abstract film, entitled *Light Rhythm.* Through the illustrator and designer, E. McKnight Kauffer, he met a number of advertising clients who were anxious to promote their products with illustrations as up-to-the-minute as the newest of modern art. Kauffer and Bruguière collaborated on a series of cubist-inspired advertising posters. In 1937 he was commissioned to design the gateway to the British Pavilion at the Paris Exposition.

Bruguière spent the last five years of his life in the English countryside, where he painted, began an unfinished autobiography, and studied the Tao and the works of C. G. Jung. He died of pneumonia on V-E Day in 1945.
See also: SURREALISM IN PHOTOGRAPHY.
·Photograph: p. 50.

"B" Shutter Setting

At the "B" speed setting, a shutter opens when pressure is applied to the shutter release and remains open until the pressure is removed. The "B" is variously taken to stand for "bulb" (after old squeeze-bulb-actuated air-pressure releases) or "brief" (for a short time exposure). It differs from the "T" (time) setting, at which the release must be pressed twice—once to open the shutter and again to close it. Today many small-format cameras have only a "B" setting in addition to the usual speeds; a locking cable release is used to hold the shutter open for long time exposures at this setting. However long the "B" exposure, a tripod or other firm support is necessary to prevent camera movement.

BSI: British Standards Institute

The British Standards Institute (BSI) is equivalent to the American National Standards Institute (ANSI). BSI film speeds were identical to the ASA speeds used in the U.S. Both countries—and most of the rest of the world—now specify ISO speeds, which are the same as the previous speeds except for the prefix letters.
See also: ANSI; SPEED OF MATERIALS.

Bubble-Chamber Photography

Nuclear particles traveling at nearly the speed of light are far too small and fast to be photographed directly, but when they pass through a pressurized chamber of liquid hydrogen or helium, they leave a trail of vapor bubbles which can be photographed. The bubble chamber is lighted from behind with electronic flash to produce dark-field illumination; flash duration is about 1/10,000 sec., but the duration of particle movement is even less. Very-fine-grain blue-sensitive film is used in modified precision high-speed motion-picture cameras. Since the particle paths move through three dimensions, two cameras are used to obtain stereoscopic records in which movement in depth as well as horizontal and vertical movement can be measured.
See also: DARK-FIELD ILLUMINATION.

Bubble Emulsion; Bubble Image

See: VESICULAR IMAGES AND EMULSIONS.

Buffer

A buffer maintains the acidity or alkalinity (pH) of a solution at a relatively constant level as chemical reactions take place. In photography buffers are used to extend the working life of developers, fixers, and various color processing solutions. In development, acidic hydrogen ions are released; the buffer combines with them to keep the solution at the alkalinity required for proper activity of the developing agent. Sodium carbonate, sodium metaborate, and sodium phosphate are common developer buffers; sodium carbonate is often used as a self-buffering activator in a developer. In fixing, increasing alkalinity is counteracted by a buffer which releases hydrogen ions to maintain the acidity at a level which promotes efficient action; boric acid is the most common buffer in fixers.
See also: ACTIVATOR/ACCELERATOR; DEVELOPMENT; FIXING; pH.

Bulhak, Jan

Polish; 1876–1950
Jan Bulhak sought to discover and express the essential character of the Polish spirit and heritage by artistic examination of the landscape, architecture, and eventually the people and daily life, of his native country. His mature work married a Pictorialist aesthetic with a deep, emotional, socially concerned nationalism to produce in the 1930s what he called "motherland photography." The formal qualities of these pictures, and their obvious love and devotion to the subject, had a strong impact on his contemporaries and made Bulhak one of the major figures of the Polish photographic scene.

"Motherland photography," he wrote, "is a pictorial representation of a country with human actions and creations existing in it, that is so truthful and accurate that it can deepen the knowledge of motherland and multiply the joy and pride ensuing from national self-knowledge. Unlike country-loving of old, which contented itself with a narrower scope of the landmarks of nature and folk art, motherland photography broadens the range of concerns to include all the visually perceptible manifestations of human existence; it reproduces not only the relics of the past and natural phenomena but the entirety of the life of man, the earth and the motherland as they are. Motherland photography draws on universal country-loving as its subject."

Born in Ostaszyn, Bulhak studied philosophy at the Jagellonian University in Cracow from 1897 to 1899. He began taking pictures in 1905, and studied photography under Hugo Erfuth in Dresden in 1911 and 1912. Returning to Poland, he entered into close cooperation with a known painter, Ferdynand Ruszczyc. Both were enamored of the beauty of the Polish landscape and architecture. Under Ruszcyzyc's inspiration Bulhak began, in 1912, a photographic inventory of the monuments of architecture in Vilna, the neighboring regions, and finally the whole of Poland, eventually amassing a rich collection of architectural photographs—10,000 items cataloged in 158 albums under the heading *Polska wobrazach fotograficz* (Poland in Photographic Pictures). The remarkably careful composition and high formal quality of these relatively little-known photographs prove Bulhak to have been a photographer extremely sensitive to form, space, and light, an artist capable of articulating both the abstract and the poetic dimensions of the photographic medium.

In 1919 Bulhak assumed the chair of photography at the Stefan Batory University at Vilna and lectured there until 1939. As a teacher and photographer Bulhak approached photography from the aesthetics of painting and classical graphic design. He sought to discover in photography the formal aesthetic values common to the fine arts. "We have to look in the surrounding world," he wrote in one of his numerous books, "for such sections of reality which, owing to their concentration and visual lighting, would be distinct and constitute not only an object in itself but its symbolical notion. In other words, we have to seek a motif and create an image with the help of photography. The photographer's motifs are everywhere and nowhere. Apart from the artist's personality, shrewdness, and sensitivity, they are determined by a single moment of time. . . ." In other writings on the expressive quality of tonal variations—chiaroscuro—in photography, Bulhak revealed an indebtedness to his artistic master and friend, the leading French Pictorialist Constant á Puyo. The handling of motif—the singling out and elaboration of the essential elements of a picture—and the graphic values created by dextrous use of chiaroscuro were the foundation of Bulhak's first major achievements in photography. At first devoted to purely aesthetic—even academic—subjects and images, during the post-World War I period of shaping the renascent independent Polish statehood Bulhak began to become concerned with the ability, and even the obligation, of the artist to communicate with others. "It is not enough to seek oneself in Poland," he wrote, "one has

Bulhak, Jan. "The Clock Tower, Royal Castle, Warsaw" (1930). National Library, Warsaw.

to seek Poland itself." His devotion to this quest eventually produced the masterpieces of motherland photography for which he is now best known.

Jan Bulhak died February 4, 1950 in Gizycko, Poland.

Bullock, Wynn

American; 1902–1975

Wynn Bullock attempted to expand the range and enrich the quality of his awareness through photographic work and philosophical investigation. His evocative, enigmatic images of objects and nudes in natural settings explored and illustrated his ideas about language, space-time, and the relationship of man to nature. His finely printed works heighten our consciousness of natural process. He wrote, "My inner development as a photographer I measure to the degree I am aware of, have developed a sense of, and can symbolize (visually) reality in all of its four dimensions."

Bullock was born Percy Wingfield Bullock in Chicago, Illinois. At the age of five he moved to South Pasadena, California. As a young man he became interested in music, and he studied languages, music, and voice in New York City from 1925 to 1927 in preparation for a career as a concert tenor. He made his livelihood throughout the 1920s as a singer in musical revues.

In 1928 Bullock became acquainted with the work of French Impressionist and Post-Impressionist painters while pursuing his musical studies in Paris. His

interest in the visual arts deepened, and he came to admire the photographs of Man Ray and Moholy-Nagy. He began to photograph as a hobby at this time, but continued his music career in Berlin and Milan.

From 1931 to 1937 Bullock managed his wife's real-estate business in West Virginia. He did not formally study photography until 1938 to 1940, when he developed a close relationship with Edward Kaminski at the Los Angeles Art Center School where he became interested in solarization and other experimental techniques. Between 1940 and 1941 Bullock studied with the semanticist Alfred Koryzbski, whose ideas about symbolization processes influenced Bullock's life's work.

Bullock's experimental photographs (mainly solarized prints) were exhibited in 1941 in the first one-man photography show at the Los Angeles County Museum. He worked as a commercial and portrait photographer before serving

in the United States Army in 1942. He was discharged in 1943 to do photographic work for the aircraft industry, and he did commercial and portrait work again from 1944 to 1946.

From 1946 to 1967 Bullock worked as a commercial photographer in Monterey, California, enjoying a long association with the Fort Ord military base. He met Edward Weston in 1948 and began to take "straight" photographs, abandoning his experimental work for a number of years. In 1957 he was awarded an honor medal for work in the Salon of International Photography and was honored by the Professional Photographers of Northern California in "National Recognition for His Contribution to Professional Photography as a Fine Art." The same year he returned to experimental work, including color light abstractions.

In 1967 Bullock retired from commercial work in order to reevaluate his photography and achieve a fresh per-

spective. In his last years he wrote two important lectures: "The Nude," and "The Concepts and Principles of Wynn Bullock," which summarize his thoughts. He was the subject of two documentary films and explored the philosophical meanings of images until his death in 1975.

During his career Bullock taught and lectured at many institutions, including the Chicago Institute of Design, the University of California at Santa Clara, and San Francisco State College. He was a Trustee and Chairman of the Exhibition Committee of the Friends of Photography, Carmel, California, from 1968 to 1970. Bullock's work was included in group shows throughout the world: in *The Family of Man* and other exhibitions at the Museum of Modern Art in New York City; at the George Eastman House, in Rochester, New York, at the Whitney Museum in New York City; at the Victoria and Albert Museum in London; and at ICP in New York City. He was the subject of one-man shows at UCLA; the Rhode Island School of Design in Providence; the Royal Photographic Society in London; the Metropolitan Museum of Art in New York City, the Art Institute of Chicago; and the San Francisco Museum of Art.

Bunsen, Robert Wilhelm

German; 1811–1899

Bunsen made original discoveries in many areas, including organic chemistry, and did pioneering work with Gustav Kirchoff in using the spectroscope for chemical analysis. His work with Sir Henry Roscoe laid many of the foundations in the field of photochemistry. Bunsen and Roscoe invented the grease-spot photometer, one of the first instruments for measuring the intensity of a light source. A sheet of paper was illuminated from one side with a source of known intensity and from the other side with the source to be measured. The test source was moved closer and farther away until a grease spot in the center of the paper was equally illuminated from both sides, at which point it became almost invisible. The two distances of the light sources made it possible to calculate the unknown intensity using the inverse square law. Bunsen and Roscoe discovered the reciprocity effect in exposure and provided other information that was highly useful in the development of sensitometry by Hurter and Driffield. In 1859 they also reported the potential usefulness of burning magnesium wire as an artificial light source for photography; its intensity and wavelength output were exactly suited to the camera materials of the day. It was first used for practical photography in 1864.

See also: INVERSE SQUARE LAW; PHOTOMETER/PHOTOMETRY; RECIPROCITY; SENSITOMETRY.

Burning-in

The printing technique of burning-in, or printing-in, is used to give additional exposure to selected areas of an image after the main or overall exposure has been given. In making prints from a negative, burning-in serves to darken the selected area or print-in details or tones in highlight areas. When prints are made on reversal paper, from a positive rather than a negative, burning-in lightens the selected area.

In enlarging, burning-in is usually achieved with a piece of cardboard with a hole in the center. The cardboard is held between the lens and the print paper and moved so that the hole lets light fall only on the desired area. The projected image is visible on the upper side of the card to aid in positioning the hole, which is somewhat smaller than the area to be covered on the print; raising or lowering the card controls the size of the projected patch of light. The card is moved continuously during the burning-in exposure so that a sharp outline of the hole will not be recorded. In color printing an appropriate filter can be placed over the hole to affect color balance as well as exposure. Large areas such as sky or foreground can be burned-in by letting light fall past the edge of a card held to shadow the other portion of the print; moving the card during exposure "feathers," or blends, the two areas smoothly.

The amount of additional exposure required can sometimes be determined from the original test strips or prints by examining the sections that received more than the optimum overall exposure. Otherwise additional tests or trial-and-error prints must be made. It is often most convenient and efficient to experiment with burning-in exposure units that are one half the basic exposure. Thus, if the overall exposure is 12 seconds, the first test for burning-in would be 6 seconds more, the second 12 seconds more, and so on. If the area to be covered is small, the proportionately small hole in the cardboard acts as a kind of *f*-stop, reducing the effective light transmission in comparison to the overall exposure; therefore, an extensive burning-in exposure may be required. It is sometimes helpful to open the enlarging lens aperture one or two *f*-stops from the setting used for the main exposure in order to project more light. Care must be taken not to jiggle the alignment or affect the focus when changing the aperture. If several areas must be burned-in, it may be simpler to give the entire print the long exposure these areas require while dodging (shadowing) the areas that require less exposure.

See also: DODGING; VIGNETTE.

Burrows, Larry

British; 1926–1971

Many photographers have photographed war throughout the world, yet none dared to spend nine years of the war in Vietnam putting on film moments of human horror, devastation, and suffering in the manner Larry Burrows did. His photographs from Vietnam permit no escape: looked at once, they compel one to look again and again. There were times Burrows himself wondered whether it was right to focus so intimately on other people's griefs, on their moments of total abandonment. Yet he felt compelled to record these moments, if only to show the total horrors of war to those who remained indifferent or simply could not imagine the agonizing sufferings of the people trapped in it.

To obtain his pictures, Burrows was out in the field with the men he photographed, their dangers and fears becoming his own. He took risks, but always knowing what he was doing, always planning, always aware of his surroundings and his own vulnerability. His deepest wish—to photograph both South and North Vietnam in a time of peace—was not granted: he died in a helicopter crash in Laos in February 1971. He had covered the war in Vietnam since 1962.

Larry Burrows was born in London. After working at the *Daily Express*, he joined the Keystone Agency as a photographer and darkroom technician. He moved on to *Life*, first in London and later in New York and was on the staff of that magazine until his death.

Burrows learned early that perfectionism, patience, and careful planning are often needed to obtain the right image. It was not unusual for him to repeat a long day's work because he was not satisfied with the first results or because the lighting or the composition were not quite right. No job was too small or too big for him, and to each assignment he would bring the same dedication.

This early training allowed Burrows to record the war in Vietnam in a masterly manner. But even in the jungles of Vietnam, nothing was left to chance. He traveled with cases filled with equipment and film carefully selected in advance, and always ready to cover any unforseen event. He himself was loaded down with a battery of cameras dangling from his neck and shoulders. In his pictures taken from the air, he involved the pilots and crews, carefully explaining his ideas with sketches, and flying for several days if necessary to achieve the compositions he visualized.

Vietnam was by no means Burrows's first war: Suez, the U.S. landing in Lebanon, the Congo, Cyprus, were only a few of many arenas of war he recorded. He is remembered as a war photographer, but he covered many other assignments as well, including Churchill, royalty in England and elsewhere, and Billy Graham touring foreign countries.

Larry Burrows was the recipient of numerous awards. They included the Robert Capa Award in 1964 and in 1966, the Magazine Photographer of the Year Award in 1967, the British Press Picture of the Year Award in 1967, and many others. He was also a Fellow of the Royal Photographic Society of Great Britain.

Color photograph: p. C-6.

Cartier-Bresson, Henri. "Behind the Gare St. Lazare, Paris" (1932). Henri Cartier-Bresson/Magnum.

Cabinet Photograph

The cabinet photograph was introduced as a new standard size for studio portraits when waning public enthusiasm for the smaller carte-de-visite began to affect photographers' businesses. It was proposed by G. W. Wilson in 1862 and first became a commercial success in 1866 when offered by the London studio of F. R. Window. At one time three picture sizes were offered: No. 1, 5¼″ × 4″, by far the most widely used; No. 2, 5¾″ × 4″; and Special, 6″ × 4¼″. The embossed or decorated mounting card was the same for all sizes (6½″ × 4¼″) with the photograph placed to provide a deep bottom margin for the photographer's signature or studio logotype. The cabinet size provided far more satisfying individual and group portraits than the carte-de-visite, and the format rapidly became successful throughout the world. Cabinet photographs of celebrities, especially those in government and the theater, were immensely popular and avidly collected by many people; at the peak of the cabinet period, in the 1880s, studios in large cities sold thousands of such pictures each year, in addition to their usual portrait business. In about 1900 the introduction of folding cameras using roll film for "postcard size" (3½″ × 5½″) pictures began to reduce the demand for cabinet portraits; by World War I the style had disappeared almost completely.

See also: CARTE-DE-VISTE.
Color photograph: p. C-7.

Callahan, Harry

American; 1912–

Self-taught in photography, Harry Callahan enjoys a long and influential career which began in 1938. After studying engineering at Michigan State University he worked first for the Chrysler Corporation and then at the General Motors Photographic Laboratories in Detroit. Callahan's early photographic work was influenced by Ansel Adams, whom Callahan heard lecture, and by the life of Alfred Stieglitz. In 1946 he met Moholy-Nagy and joined the faculty of Chicago's Institute of Design, becoming chairman of the photography department in 1949. He left Chicago in 1961 to become chairman of the photography department at the Rhode Island School of Design, serving in that capacity until 1973 and continuing to teach there until 1977.

Callahan's work is personally oriented; many of his pictures artistically interpret his family relationships, especially portraits of his wife, Eleanor, and daughter, Barbara. His early work experimented with representational abstraction; recent work in color includes additional subject matter, both city and landscapes as well as multiple exposures.

Known as a teacher as well as a photographer, Callahan was the recipient of a Diploma and Plaque from the *photokina* Exhibition of 1951 in Cologne, the Graham Foundation Grant in 1956, the Photography Award from the Rhode Island Arts Festival in 1963, and the Rhode Island Governor's Award for Excellence in the Arts in 1969. In 1972 he was awarded the Distinguished Contribution Award from the National Association of Schools and a Guggenheim Fellowship. In 1976 he received the Photographer and Educator Award from the Society for Photographic Education and in 1977 he was named an Honored Photographer of the Rencontres Internationales de la Photographie at Arles, France. In 1978 Callahan was the first photographer to represent the United States with a one-man exhibition of his work at the Venice Biennale. His work in black-and-white and color has been included in international exhibitions and a major monograph with text by John Szarkowski was published in 1976 in connection with his retrospective at the Museum of Modern Art in New York. In 1980 Callahan's latest work was

Callahan, Harry. "Back of Elinor in attic" (1948). Courtesy Harry Callahan.

documented in the books *Water's Edge* and *Harry Callahan: Color.* The Callahan archive, which contains approximately 20,000 prints, 5,000 slides, and 100,000 negatives, plus correspondence and other papers, is at the Center for Creative Photography, Tucson, Arizona.
See also: NEW BAUHAUS.

Callier Effect

Light scattering that increases the effective printing contrast of a negative in a condenser enlarger is called the Callier effect; it was noted in 1909 by André Callier, a Belgian physicist who formulated a method of measuring the basic effect (Q-factor). When the essentially parallel rays of light from a condenser illumination system pass through a negative, the relatively great densities in the highlights scatter some of the light, while little or no scattering takes place in

the nearly transparent shadow areas of the image. As a result, highlights in the projection print (enlargement) receive reduced exposure, as would be the case with a negative of greater density range (higher contrast) in other illumination systems. The Callier effect does not occur in a diffused-light enlarger nor in contact printing. For this reason, negatives for these procedures must be developed to a higher degree of actual contrast in order to have the same effective printing contrast as a negative used in a condenser system.
See also: CONTRAST; Q-FACTOR.

Calotype

The paper negative or calotype process, also called the Talbotype, was invented by W. H. F. Talbot and patented by him in 1841. The name was coined from *kalos,* Greek for "beautiful." It was a significant improvement over the salt-

paper process Talbot called photogenic drawing, because the negative paper was prepared with silver iodide rather than with the less-sensitive silver chloride, and because image formation was completed by development and not simply by a printing-out exposure in the camera. A typical calotype exposure was about 1 minute at $f/11$ (few lenses of the time were faster) in bright sunlight; salt-paper exposures were 20 to 45 minutes or longer.

Good-quality rag paper was prepared for making a negative by brushing over one side with a silver nitrate solution; when dry, this was treated with a potassium iodide solution to form silver iodide in the paper fibers. Now light-sensitive, the paper was dried and stored in the dark. For use, its sensitivity was increased by brushing over the paper with a solution of silver nitrate, gallic acid, and acetic acid (gallo-nitrate of silver, in Talbot's terms); it then was

damp-dried in blotters in the dark. After exposure, the image was developed by a second treatment with gallo-nitrate of silver solution, fixed with hyposulfite of soda—a procedure recommended by Sir John Herschel—washed, and dried. Prints were made by printing-out contact exposure on ordinary salt paper without development; although this took longer, it permitted inspecting the progress of the print in order to accommodate the contrast differences of various negatives.

Calotype positives have coarse detail—a consequence of having to print through the fibers of the paper—and high contrast; they are in no way as tonally rich, finely detailed, or lustrously beautiful as daguerreotypes, with which they could not compete commercially. Only Hill and Adamson achieved pictures of artistic worth with the calotype. This was partly because Talbot vigorously prosecuted those who attempted to make calotypes without purchasing an expensive license. His assistants, Nikolaas Henneman and Thomas Malone, produced good-quality prints at the establishment Talbot financed to produce his book *The Pencil of Nature* and to make illustrations for other publishers, but they had little success with a calotype portrait studio in London. For about two years, A. F. J. Claudet offered calotype portraits along with daguerreotypes at his London studio, but the calotype's comparative lack of quality made it less popular in spite of the larger sizes that could be produced. Outside England, the waxed-paper process, based on the calotype, was more widely used and produced superior images, but all paper negative processes disappeared almost immediately when the collodion process for glass plate negatives was introduced in 1851.

See also: GALLIC ACID; PENCIL OF NATURE, THE; PHOTOGENIC DRAWING; SALT-PAPER PROCESS; TALBOT, WILLIAM HENRY FOX; WAXED-PAPER PROCESS.

Camera

A camera is a lighttight fixed or adjustable box equipped with a film-holding device at one end and an image-forming lens at the other end. Evolved from the camera obscura, the modern camera has a viewing system to aid in composition of the image and a shutter mechanism to expose the film to light transmitted by the lens. An adjustable diaphragm built into the lens controls the intensity of light that passes through. In all but the simplest cameras, the camera or the lens has a focusing adjustment that changes the lens-to-film distance to obtain a sharp image of the objects at various distances.

Modern small and medium-size cameras accept a film roll or cassette pack sufficient for several exposures. A transport mechanism in the camera advances the roll film after each frame has been exposed. Large cameras use individual sheets of film; adapters permit the use of roll and pack films as well. Finally, many modern cameras, from the simple to the most complex, have some form of light metering and exposure control system integrated into the camera body. Efforts throughout the history of the development of the camera have concentrated on simplifying its operation. Today cameras are products of high technology.

The most sophisticated cameras currently incorporate electronic components that control many of the mechanical functions, including exposure, focusing, and film advance. The term *automatic* is often used to describe the camera itself, or the means by which any one function is controlled. One way to classify cameras is by the design of the viewing and focusing system. The simple viewfinder, rangefinder, single-lens reflex (SLR), twin-lens reflex, and view camera are all types of cameras designated in this way. Another way to differentiate cameras is by the film size, or format, they accept. Cameras range in size from the smallest spy cameras to the largest of view cameras. Other examples are the small-format 35mm SLR, and the 2¼-inch medium-format SLR such as the Hasselblad.

The modern large-format view camera is the direct descendant of the portable camera obscura used by pioneers of photography such as Niépce and Daguerre. The early camera of the 1830s and 1840s had a viewing screen at the rear of the camera as the modern view camera does. The camera body was constructed of two telescoping boxes that were adjusted to focus the image. Today's view camera accomplishes the same function with a flexible bellows. In the early camera a large metal or glass plate coated with light-sensitive material replaced the ground glass after focusing. The lens cap served as a simple shutter. Materials and lenses were so slow that long exposure times of several hours were required in bright sunlight. This fact, along with the camera's bulky and heavy construction, necessitated the use of a rigid, heavy camera stand. The first popular roll film box camera revolutionized photography. The Kodak, introduced in 1888 by George Eastman, was simple to operate, portable, and its roll film was commercially processed.

In the years to follow, faster lenses and films were developed to capture life in natural, existing light with short exposure times; these elements permitted major improvements in camera design. As small hand cameras evolved in the succeeding years, cumbersome large-format studio cameras also changed. Photographers who still preferred the high-quality image produced by the large-format negative wanted a portable hand

Camera

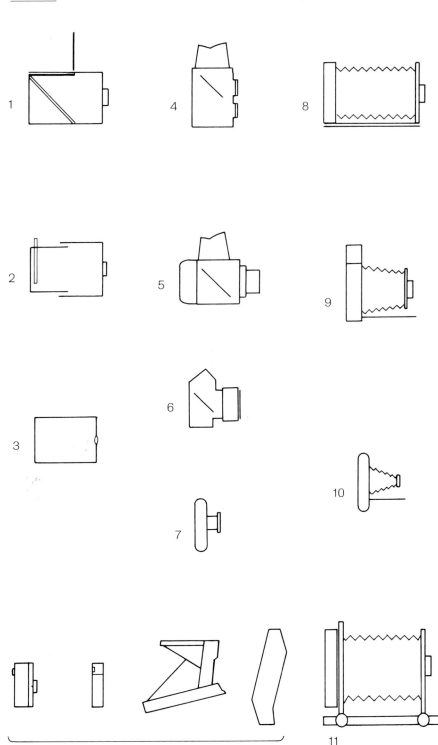

version. The field cameras of the 1890s were certainly lighter and smaller than their predecessors, but a truly hand-holdable press, or technical, camera was developed early in the 20th c., as were innovative medium-format designs. A highly significant development in the evolution of the camera came in 1924 with the small, versatile 35mm Leica. The 1928 Rolleiflex used medium-size roll film and through the 1940s was still considered a compromise in quality when compared to the popular Speed Graphic 4″ × 5″ press camera. Higher resolution lenses and films finally made the 35mm camera popular with photo-journalists in the early 1950s. At that time Japan began to manufacture copies of the favorite German 35mm cameras, and soon thereafter produced original improvements. The wide availability of these models contributed to the ever-increasing popularity of the small 35mm hand camera. The next great change in the evolutionary process came with cameras for instant photography using Polaroid instant materials, introduced by Dr. Edwin Land in 1947. The photographer could now create images without the involved chemical processes of the darkroom.

The needs of photographers and the ever-expanding uses of photography have been driving forces in the development of highly specialized camera designs throughout the history of the medium. Early photographers created unique cameras such as the ''Mammoth,'' which produced 4½′ × 8′ images, to photograph a new luxury train for the Paris Exhibition. The 1900s also saw the ''Skyscraper'' camera, with a perspective-control feature that could faithfully capture the true form of the new-style buildings. Today cameras designed for underwater, aerial, panoramic, and other special photographic applications are common. The modern camera is the product of over 100 years of evolutionary change. Trial and error, genius, and accidental discovery all played roles in developing the current state of the art. Advancements in the application of electronics and improved computer-designed optics are employed in all types of cameras, from the latest instant model to the traditional view camera.

See also: CAMERA OBSCURA; EASTMAN, GEORGE; FORMAT; INSTANT PHOTOGRAPHY; KODAK; LAND, EDWIN H.; LEICA; SHUTTER; SHUTTER RELEASE.

Camera Lucida

A device to assist in drawing accurately from life, the camera lucida was invented in 1807 by W. H. Wollaston. Its name means "lighted room" to indicate that its image could be seen in fully-lighted surroundings, unlike a camera obscura image. A small prism supported by a rod above the drawing paper was aimed at the subject. Looking down, the artist saw the subject reflected in the prism, and his or her hand and the paper below. With practice, the subject could be seen as if projected on the paper so its outline and details could be traced with relative accuracy. It was no substitute for drawing or sketching talent, a fact ruefully noted by W.H.F. Talbot, and which impelled him to invent the first practical negative-positive system of photography. Modern versions of the camera lucida use a half-silvered "magic mirror" prism so that the drawing surface is seen directly through the reflected subject image. Commercial artists refer to the device as a "lucy."

See also: CAMERA OBSCURA; WOLLASTON, W.H.

Camera Movements

Camera movements include adjustments of camera component positions and camera location for control of composition, sharpness, distortion, and other image factors. A view camera permits independent adjustment of the lens position at the front and the film plane at the rear; a press camera offers some lens adjustments, but seldom permits back adjustments. Movements of the lens board and the camera back in a flat plane are used to change the framing, or location of the subject in relation to the rectangle of the format. Left-right movement is called *shift;* up-down movement *rise* and *fall.* A lens rise is often used to bring the top of a subject into view without having to aim the camera upward; a fall of the back would accomplish the same thing (the image being inverted in the camera). When extreme adjustment is needed, both components may be moved in opposite directions. The back may also *rotate* to change from vertical to horizontal framing, or for minor adjustments, such as making the sides of the picture parallel with vertical or horizontal lines in the subject. The lens is pivoted around its axes to make critical adjustments of sharpness; a *tilt* pivots it up or down and a *swing* pivots it right or left. The lens movement chosen for use in a given situation is determined by the fact that the near and far planes of the depth of field around the subject are always parallel to the vertical plane through the lens (*i.e.,* parallel to the lens mounting board). Tilting or swinging the back corrects (or induces) linear distortion of the subject, but cannot increase sharpness. In general, the lens adjustment for maximum sharpness over a given subject plane requires a back position that induces some distortion (the Scheimpflug condition).

The usual sequence of adjusting camera movements is: (1) Move the back and front toward or away from one another to focus the subject. (Moving only the back adjusts focus without changing image magnification, often an important factor in close-up or scientific and technical photography.) (2) Use shift, rise, or fall to position the subject within the frame; rotate the back if necessary. (3) Tilt or swing the back to correct linear distortion. (To remove distortion, move the back so the film plane is parallel to the subject plane.) (4) Tilt or swing the lens to make the plane of sharpness coincide with the most important subject plane. (5) Readjust focus as in the first step, if necessary.

Two pivoting movements may be used with a camera mounted on a tripod: a *pan* to point the camera left or right and a *tilt* to point it up or down. Some tripods also have a telescoping center post to raise or lower the camera position. Motion-picture and television cameras are usually mounted on a dolly, crane, or other wheeled support which permits a variety of movements to change camera location. A *dolly-in* moves the camera toward the subject and a *dolly-out* (or *-back*) moves it away. (Zoom lens movements are often used in place of dolly movements, but their expressive effect is not the same, because although the field of view changes in a similar manner, the perspective in the scene does not.) A *trucking* movement carries the camera past a plane of the subject at a constant distance. *Traveling* moves the camera in unison with subject movement: alongside as in trucking, *leading* by moving backward as the subject advances toward the lens, or *following* after a subject moving away from the lens. Most equipment allows the camera to pan and tilt during these movements and includes a means to *boom* the camera up or down to a different height.

See also: DEPTH OF FIELD; DISTORTION; PERSPECTIVE; SCHEIMPFLUG CONDITION.

Camera Obscura

The camera obscura is a drawing device which projects an image of the subject onto a surface where it may be traced. Originally it was an actual dark room (the literal meaning of its Latin name) with a small hole in one wall or a window blind. Light rays passing through the hole formed an image of the outside scene on the opposite wall or on drawing material placed in the light's path; the same principle underlies pinhole photography today.

The camera obscura was in regular use by artists for accurate rendition of scale and perspective by the time of Leonardo da Vinci; by 1560 it had been improved upon by the addition of a lens for a brighter image and a diaphragm for sharper rendition. The first truly portable, boxlike camera obscuras appeared about 1650; derivations of this design were the cameras which all early inventors of photographic processes used more than a century and a half later. Portable camera obscuras with an internal mirror to reflect the image upward to tracing paper laid over a glass plate in the top are the direct ancestors of modern medium-format single-lens reflex cameras such as the Hasselblad.

See also: CAMERA.

Camera Supports

A firm support to prevent camera movement is essential for sharp photographs during exposures 1/15 sec. and longer, when using long-focal-length lenses, or where vibration from camera operation or external factors may be a problem. Camera supports allow for precise composition and framing and must be used with cameras that are too heavy or bulky to be hand-held conveniently or securely. The most common kind of support is the tripod; it secures the camera with a threaded bolt which screws into the camera base. A good tripod must be large enough and strong enough to provide adequate support; a flimsy or undersized tripod is likely to be a cause of problems rather than a solution. Valuable features in a tripod are a telescoping center post, which permits the camera to be raised or lowered without having to readjust the leg position or extension, and a three-way pan head. This type of head allows the camera to be turned ("panned") right or left, tilted up or down, or swung from a horizontal to a vertical orientation. A simple but popular camera support is the monopod, which is basically a one-legged tripod.

Another device for steadying the camera is the chain-pod, which attaches to the belt or slips under the foot while the camera is pulled upward against its tension. A chest-pod has one or more short legs which brace against the body; a gunstock support is held like a rifle. For unusual circumstances, special clamps and suction cups are used to attach cameras to existing railings, walls, or other features on the scene. Some

photographers use a "soft" support such as a bean bag or a folded sweater to cradle the camera on uneven surfaces. Many long or heavy lenses mount directly to a tripod by means of a socket in a collar around the barrel; this removes the strain of their weight at the point at which they attach to the camera. For lenses without a tripod socket, a "V" support which mounts on a secondary tripod can support the lens while the camera is supported separately. Studio photographers commonly rely on a large camera stand incorporating counterweights to support very large and heavy equipment. Such stands are usually on wheels and have provision for raising and lowering the camera over a greater range than most tripods provide.

"Camera Work"

Generally considered to be the finest American art magazine of the first half of the 20th c., *Camera Work* was edited and published by Alfred Stieglitz. Nominally a quarterly publication, the 50 issues that appeared between 1903 and 1917 were seldom on schedule, largely because all contributions were unpaid, and because money was often lacking. Stieglitz spared no effort or expense, especially in the quality of the reproductions of photographs and later paintings. The major portfolio in each issue was composed of hand-pulled photogravures tipped-in by hand on colored mounts. Stieglitz individually inspected each gravure sheet, hand-spotting dust marks or other imperfections as necessary. Similar care was taken with the gravures, halftones, and four-color machine-press reproductions on other pages. Whenever possible, the gravure plates were made from the photographers' original negatives under their personal supervision. Many felt that the reproductions in the magazine surpassed their original prints.

The work of all the Photo-Secession photographers was published at various times, and the portraits of Julia Margaret Cameron and Hill and Adamson received their first American publication in *Camera Work,* as did paintings by Picasso, Braque, Picabia, Rodin, Marin, Dove, O'Keeffe, and many other modern artists. The criticism, reviews, and articles that comprised the text were of the highest quality. Sadakichi Hartmann, Charles Caffin, and Paul Haviland were among the most frequent writers. The magazine began with 647 subscribers; 1000 copies of every issue were printed, but the subscription list never reached that number. Contributors were paid with extra copies of the issue containing

their work—ample reward, for within a few years they were all collector's items. The final double issue, No. 49/50, featured the photographs of Paul Strand. Changing tastes had reduced the list of paying subscribers to 37, and in 1917 Stieglitz wearily terminated the magazine and his gallery, 291. During its 15 years of publication, *Camera Work* had expressed and helped define the transition from a soft-focus, atmospheric Pictorialism to the beginnings of a "modern" aesthetic based on a hard-edged, powerfully direct realism that came to be called "straight" photography.

See also: STIEGLITZ, ALFRED; PHOTO SECESSION; 291.

Cameron, Julia Margaret

British; 1815–1879

Nothing in Julia Margaret Cameron's family background, class, or personal circumstances serves to explain why at

the age of 48, presented with a camera as a gift from her two daughters, she embraced photography with an avidity that bordered on obsession. Born in Calcutta to a well-to-do British family, she was educated in France and England and in 1824 married the jurist Charles Hay Cameron. They settled in Sri Lanka (Ceylon), where in addition to working on the legal code of that country, Charles Cameron acquired a number of coffee plantations. In 1848 the Camerons returned to England and established themselves in the Isle of Wight.

From the moment of her camera acquisition, Cameron was an indefatigable photographer. Her subject matter consisted exclusively of portraits and fancy-dress tableaux (e.g., quintessentially Victorian photographs made to illustrate Alfred Lord Tennyson's *Idylls of the King*). Working with the wet collodion process, she had her garden greenhouse converted to a darkroom and studio, and in the next ten years she made a steady stream of images. Friends, family, servants, and even passersby were conscripted as models by Cameron. Inasmuch as the Cameron milieu included many of the great figures of Victorian arts, letters, and science, our sense of the faces (and to a certain extent the personalities) of notables such as Sir John Herschel, Thomas Carlyle, Charles Darwin, and Lord Tennyson has often been determined by Cameron's representations of them. In 1875 the Camerons returned to Sri Lanka, where, except for a few photographs of local subjects, Cameron abandoned photography.

Cameron's photographs passed largely into obscurity until they were enthusiastically rediscovered by Alfred Stieglitz and the Photo Secessionists.

Her images were strongly influenced by the English Pre-Raphaelite painters, and nowhere more so than in her costume pieces illustrating religious, literary, poetic, and mythological themes. Although equally romantic in conception, it is principally her portraits that have entered the canon of art photography. Unique among contemporary portrait production, Cameron's photographs are notable for the extreme intimacy and psychological intensity of effect achieved by the use of extreme close-up, suppression of detail (sometimes accompanied by peripheral blurring), and dramatic lighting. The Pictorialist-like effect of Cameron's work in fact was remarkably close in appearance and sensibility to much of the photography championed in Stieglitz's *Camera Work*. This certainly was a crucial factor in her rediscovery at the beginning of the 20th c. Her attempts, and success, at psychological penetration—conveying the inner spirit, in her terms—are recognized today as being decades ahead of their time.

Candid Photography

Candid photographs show people, places, and things as they are naturally, without changes due to the photographer's presence. Snapshots are candid photographs, but so are many of the finest examples of documentary photography, photojournalism, and environmental portraiture. The particular charm of candid photographs is their quality of revelation. The subjects are not posed or directed; they simply remain themselves. In this kind of photography the photographer is the invisible person rather than the center of activity.

Anyone or any place is a potential subject for candid photography. The key to successful pictures is in the timing and judgment exercised by the photographer, who attempts to release the shutter just when a revealing expression, gesture, or moment is displayed. It is these brief moments which visually distinguish one person from another, one situation from another, and which make them memorable.

Possibly the most important factor in getting good candids of people is the photographer's ability not to be obtrusive. Most often subjects take their cue from the photographer's attitude, and one frequently adopted attitude is relaxed confidence. Eventually people become used to the clicking of the shutter and ignore the photographer; that is when the best pictures are made. Other important factors are patience and an absence of furtiveness while subjects become accustomed to the situation. People respond most openly to openness on the part of the photographer. The adjustment period provides a good opportunity for the photographer to study interactions among the subjects and to determine likely vantage points.

As in action photography it is desirable to preset as many controls as possible. Timing is difficult enough without having the additional concern of adjusting dials. In addition, to maintain the proper mood it is virtually mandatory to work by existing light. It is not likely that subjects half blinded by a flash unit will continue to behave normally.

Any small- or medium-format camera is appropriate for candid photography. Among the most useful equipment features are fast interchangeable lenses (or a zoom lens), a large number of exposures possible per roll of film, easily manipulated controls, and a quiet shutter. All of these features must be coupled with smooth operating technique and the familiarity with equipment achieved by constant practice. It then becomes possible to concentrate on the subject and to be ready when candid, revealing moments occur.

See also: AVAILABLE-LIGHT PHOTOGRAPHY.

Candle; Candela; Candlepower

The candle is a unit for measuring the intensity of a light source. Originally, a candle of specified composition and dimensions was used as a standard light source for photometry. Today the standard source is taken as 0.16 sq. in. (1 sq. cm) of a black body glowing at a temperature of 1496K (1769°C; 3216°F; solidification point of platinum). The candle (U.S.) or candela (international usage) is defined as an intensity equal to 1/60 the intensity of this standard source. Candlepower means the same, but it is an obsolete and often misused term.

See also: BLACK BODY; LIGHT UNITS.

Capa, Robert
American; 1913–1954

Robert Capa was the most highly acclaimed war photographer of his time. His classic photograph "Death of a Loyalist Soldier" (1936) was one of his many deeply felt images of heroism and suffering on the front lines and in the war-torn lives of civilians, subjects which he documented extensively during his career.

Capa was born André Friedmann in Budapest, Hungary. He attended Imre Madàcs Gymnasium, Budapest, from 1923 to 1931, and studied political science at Deutsche Hochschule für Politik, Berlin from 1931 to 1932, after being exiled from Hungary for his political activism. Capa began to photograph in 1930 and was first employed as a darkroom assistant at the Deutsche Photodienst (Dephot) Agency, Berlin. His first published photograph was of Leon Trotsky.

In 1933 he left Nazi Germany for Paris, where he developed close friendships with Henri Cartier-Bresson and David ("Chim") Seymour, with whom he shared darkroom space. In 1936, taking the name Robert Capa, he began his career as a freelance photographer specializing in documentation of political movements and war.

Capa covered the activities of the Republican forces in the Spanish Civil War in 1936. He made many of his most memorable images at this time. In 1938 he covered the Japanese invasion of China.

Capa was a war correspondent for *Life* and *Collier's* in North Africa and Europe with the United States Army from 1941 to 1946. In 1947, with Cartier-Bresson, Seymour, George Rodger, and Bill Vandivert, he founded the Magnum Photos cooperative agency of which he was president from 1951 to 1954. He became a naturalized American citizen in 1946. From 1948 to 1950 Capa documented the emergence of the state of Israel. While photographing on a special assignment for *Life* in 1954, Capa was killed by a land mine in Thai-Binh, Indochina.

Capa was awarded the United States Medal of Freedom in 1947 and (posthumously) the French Croix de Guerre with Palm in 1954. He also received the George Polk Memorial Award that year and the American Society of Magazine

Capa, Robert. "Spain" (1936). Permanent collection, ICP, New York.

Photographers Award in 1955. Also in 1955 the Overseas Press Club and *Life* established the Robert Capa Gold Medal Award, which is given annually "for superlative photography requiring exceptional courage and enterprise abroad." The International Fund for Concerned Photography, formerly the Bischof/Capa/Seymour Memorial Fund, was established in 1966, and was the basis for the creation of the International Center of Photography in 1974. Its founding director, Cornell Capa, is the younger brother of Robert Capa. Robert Capa was named to the Hall of Fame of the Photographic Art and Science Foundation in 1976.

Capa's work has been included in many important touring exhibitions throughout the world, including *The Family of Man* (1955), *The World As Seen By Magnum* (1960), *The Concerned Photographer* (1967), and *The Classics of Documentary Photography* (1974). One-man shows of his work were held at the Smithsonian Institution in 1960 and again in 1964. His books include *Death in the Making* (1937), *Slightly Out of Focus* (1947), and *Images of War* (1964).

Caponigro, Paul

American; 1932–

Paul Caponigro is known for his landscapes and subtle images of natural forms. His photographs register with great intensity the enduring, eternal qualities of stones and the most delicate plant life. Lotte Jacobi has called him "a poet among photographers. . . . Through his work that rare thing happens: what the heart feels is revealed in a radiance of outward form." His silver prints are distinguished in their highly controlled gradations and variations of tone.

Caponigro was born in Boston, Massachusetts. He became interested in photography as a high-school student and attended the College of Music at Boston University for one year before his apprenticeship at a Boston commercial photograhy studio in 1952. Caponigro was drafted into the United States Army in 1953 and served as a photographer for the next two years. While stationed in San Francisco he began studies at the California School of Fine Arts under the direction of Minor White and a former student of Ansel Adams, Benjamin Chin. Discharged from the

Army in 1955, Caponigro returned to Boston where he began work as a freelance photographer, doing personal, creative photography in his spare time. He did further study with Chin and Alfred Richter in San Francisco in 1956, and in 1957–1958 with Minor White in Rochester, New York.

Caponigro's first one-man show, *In the Presence of. . . ,* was held at George Eastman House in 1958. He assisted White at several summer workshops the following year. In 1960 he began a long association with the Polaroid Corporation as a consultant in photo-research, architectural photography, and other creative fields.

Caponigro received a Guggenheim Fellowship in 1966 for photographic studies of Ireland's ancient monuments and a second Guggenheim in 1975. He has photographed extensively in England, Ireland, and France. He has been the recipient of numerous other awards, including a First Prize at the Tenth Boston Arts Festival (1961), National Endowment for the Arts Photography Fellowships (1971 and 1974), the Art Directors Club of New York Award

Caponigro, Paul. "Running white deer,
Ireland" (1967). Courtesy Paul Caponigro.

(1974), and a National Endowment for the Arts Grant (1975).

Caponigro has taught and conducted workshops at many colleges throughout the country, including Boston University, New York University, Yale, and Princeton. His work has been included in group shows at the Museum of Modern Art in New York City, the Smithsonian Institution in Washington D.C., and the Whitney Museum in New York City. He has been honored with solo exhibitions at the Museum of Modern Art, the San Francisco Museum of Art, the Art Institute of Chicago, the Friends of Photography in Carmel, California, and the Victoria and Albert Museum in London. He has lived and worked in Santa Fe, New Mexico, since 1973.

Carbon Processes

There have been several methods of making prints from photographic negatives or positives using an emulsion containing particles of carbon or colored non-silver pigment to form the image. They were invented not only to obtain colored images, but also to avoid discoloration and fading, widespread problems with mid-19th c. silver-image prints. The fundamental carbon method is in fact a bichromate process; it was patented in 1855 by A. L. Poitevin in France. Paper with a gum-arabic (later gelatin) and carbon-pigment emulsion was sensitized with potassium bichromate and exposed by contact under a negative. Exposed areas of the emulsion hardened, but unexposed areas remained soluble, and so dissolved away when the image was developed in warm water. The result was a high-contrast image, suitable for line subjects such as plans and ink drawings, but lacking middletones. This was be-

cause the exposure effect occurred from the top down, so soluble emulsion was either trapped beneath, giving those areas full instead of partial density, or was dissolved away, leaving the hardened area above unconnected to the base and therefore free to break away. Exposing the paper from the back avoided this problem, but shadow images of the paper fibers degraded image tones and details. Various methods were proposed to transfer the emulsion face-down onto another support before development so the paper could be stripped away and the image developed from the more soluble side. The early transfer methods were too involved or too delicate to become widely used, but these problems were overcome with gelatin-emulsion carbon tissues and transfer sheets patented by J. W. Swan in 1864 and introduced commercially by him two years later.

The first major project with the new materials was a reproduction of D. O. Hill's painting of the clergy of the Scottish Free Church, based on hundreds of calotype portraits. In the 1890s J. Craig Annan's carbon prints of these forgotten 1843–1844 portraits established recognition of Hill and Adamson as the first artistic masters of photography. Swan's process involved single transfer to a new support, which produced right-left reversal of the image. Workers at the Autotype Co., which had purchased Swan's English patent in 1868, developed a practical double-transfer method to correct the image reversal, and introduced improvements in handling that increased the usefulness and popularity of carbon printing.

Variants of the basic carbon process include the Artigue process, photomezzotint, carbro, and trichrome carbro;

each is described in a separate entry. Poitevin also patented an entirely different process in 1860. Exposed portions of paper coated with ferric chloride and tartaric acid became sticky and retained carbon pigment dusted or brushed on in proportion to the degree of exposure. This image was then sealed with a coating of collodion and transferred to a final support paper.

See also: BICHROMATE PROCESSES; POITEVIN, A. L.; SWAN, J. W.; TRANSFER PROCESSES.

Carbro Process

The most versatile carbon process for obtaining prints in which the image is formed of permanent (i.e., non-fading) pigment rather than silver is the carbro process. It is a development of the ozotype and ozobrome processes patented by Thomas Manly in 1899 and 1905, respectively. The name *carbro* was given to an improved version marketed by the Autotype Co. in 1919 and still in limited use today; it reflects the fact that a *carbon* tissue is used in conjunction with a *bromide* print. In all other carbon processes the tissue must be exposed directly, in contact with a final-size negative or positive transparency, using sunlight or a high-intensity, ultraviolet-rich artificial source. In carbro, the image is formed by chemical action when the tissue is placed face-to-face with a developed and fixed print on bromide paper. This offers the great advantage of making enlargements from small-format negatives if desired; of using ordinary light sources; and of dodging, burning-in, and using other controls, as in ordinary photographic printing. In addition,

Carbro Process. Edward P. McCurty, "On the Elbe" (n.d.). Smithsonian Institution.

the bromide print can be used to make up to six carbon prints before it must be replaced.

The print must be made on a bromide paper that does not have a hardened supercoating (anti-abrasion layer) on the surface, and must be processed in a nonhardening developer and fixer so that the emulsion remains permeable for later chemical action. The carbon tissue is sensitized in a solution of potassium bichromate, which provides the necessary hardening action, and potassium ferricyanide and potassium bromide, which provide a chemical bleaching action; alum or formalin is included in the solution to prevent excessive swelling of the gelatin emulsion. When ready, the tissue is squeegeed emulsion-to-emulsion with the thoroughly washed, wet bromide print. As the silver image in the print is bleached, the carbon emulsion hardens in direct proportion to the amount of bleaching that takes place. Thus, in shadow areas it is completely hardened, in middletones only partly hardened, and in highlights hardened little or not at all. After 15 minutes the carbon tissue is peeled away and placed face-down on a transfer sheet which will be the final image support. It is then developed as in basic carbon printing: the sandwich is soaked until the backing paper of the carbon tissue can be peeled away, then warm water dissolves the unhardened portions of the carbon emulsion, leaving just the hardened, image-forming pigment. The bleached bromide print can be redeveloped in its original developer and used to sensitize another carbon tissue. This can be repeated up to five times.

In an alternate procedure the carbon emulsion is left on the bromide print—the backing paper is peeled away and the carbon image is developed on top of the bromide emulsion. The underlying print may be left in its bleached state, or it may be redeveloped to add its density and detail to the final image. Controlled three-color printing can be achieved by an extension of the basic carbro procedure, called trichrome carbro.

See also: AUTOTYPE; BROMIDE PAPER; CARBON PROCESSES; OZOBROME PROCESS; OZOTYPE; TRICHROME CARBRO PROCESS.

Carbutt, John

English; 1832–1905

Carbutt was a photographer and manufacturer whose career in the U.S. encompassed all aspects of photography. He came to the U.S. in 1853 and built a highly successful portrait business in Chicago, publishing in 1868 the first photographically illustrated biographical dictionary in this country, *Biographical Sketches of the Leading Men of Chicago,* with pasted-in cabinet-size portraits, of which 50,000 were made for the total edition. Two years earlier he had been one of the first photographers to record the westward expansion of the railroads, producing a set of 300 stereographs of construction work, Indians, settlers, and scenic views along the path of the Union Pacific Railway. These ventures convinced him of the potential of photographic publishing, and in 1870 he established the American Photo-Relief Printing Co. in Philadelphia to produce Woodburytypes for book illustrations. Related photographic aspects of the business proved more successful, and he began the manufacture of materials and supplies. In 1879 he introduced the first gelatin-coated glass dry plates in the U.S., *Keystone* plates, and supplied them to Eadweard Muybridge for his work at the University of Pennsylvania. In 1888 he produced the first commercially successful celluloid-base film in the world, *Carbutt's Flexible Negative Film,* and was one of the first suppliers of prepared magnesium powder for early flash photography.

See also: CABINET PHOTOGRAPH; CELLULOID; WOODBURYTYPE.

Carjat, Etienne

French; 1826–1906

Like his friend Nadar, Etienne Carjat was as much a journalist and graphic caricaturist as a photographer. He brought to his photographic portraits an incisive eye honed through making pencil caricatures for *Le Diogène* (1856) and *Le Gaulois* (1857), where the radical simplification of line and gesture became a trademark that transferred to his photographs.

Carjat began photographing about 1855. Six years later, he opened a Paris studio and began receiving recognition for his portraits: an honorable mention in a London salon (1862), awards in Paris (1863–1864), Berlin (1867), and at the Paris Exposition Universelle (1867). Yet he never devoted himself wholeheartedly to photography; instead, he continued to edit journals and to draw caricatures for the popular press.

Few subjects other than portraiture attracted Carjat. He made hundreds of cartes-de-visite, but his were markedly different than those of Disdéri and other photographers, being as stripped-down and spare as theirs were elaborate. Rather than posed with pillars and swags of drapery, Carjat's subjects were shown against plain backdrops to heighten the effect of gesture and expression, elements frequently lost amid the overstuffed and visually aggressive props of most portraits of the day. The same severity of setting and lighting were applied to even greater effect in Carjat's larger-format pictures. In the best portraits, for example those of Charles Baudelaire and Gioacchino Rossini, the dramatic posture and expression alone convey the portraitist's interpretation. Indeed, Carjat's flair for capturing the spirit of his celebrity-subjects frequently equaled or excelled that of his better-known contemporary, Nadar, who de-

Carjat, Etienne. "Charles Baudelaire" (ca. 1863); collodion. Collection, Museum of Modern Art, New York.

pended heavily on dramatic sidelighting for his effects. The two men are generally regarded as the masters of portrait photography in Europe in the third quarter of the 19th c.

See also: CARTE-DE-VISITE; NADAR; PORTRAITURE.

Carlson, Chester

American; 1906–1968

The inventor of modern xerography—the most widespread electrophotographic process for obtaining copies of documents, printed images, and photographs—Chester Carlson was trained in physics at the California Institute of Technology. In the early 1930s he worked in the research and patent departments of Bell Telephone Laboratories, New York. By 1935 he had recognized the need for a dry copy process, and in 1937 he took out his first patent for a static electricity process (electrophotography). A year later he and Otto Kornei, a German physicist, obtained the first image-transfer copy utilizing a dry powder pigment (toner) controlled by static electrical charges. Development of the process took several years and a partnership with the Battelle Memorial Institute in Ohio. The Haloid Company, a photocopier manufacturer in Rochester, New York, purchased the rights to the process in 1947 and began to develop practical copying machines, which were introduced in 1950. Haloid coined the name *xerography* (Greek: dry writing); with the success of the machines the company became Xerox Corporation.

See also: ELECTROPHOTOGRAPHIC PROCESSES; XEROGRAPHY.

Carte-de-visite

French for "visiting card," the name carte-de-visite was used universally for a 2¼″ × 3½″ photograph, usually a full-length portrait, mounted on a 2½″ × 4″ card. The idea of photographic visiting cards, passports, licenses, and similar documents was advanced by Louis Dodero in Marseilles in 1851. The card idea was patented and introduced in Paris in 1854 by André Disderi, but did not catch on until 1859 when Napoleon III had cartes made for public distribution as he left on a military campaign against Italy; the style was an overnight sensation. Similarly, in England it caught on only after a set of cartes of Queen Victoria and the royal family was issued in 1860 by J.J.E. Mayall. The carte-de-visite was the first wildfire fad in photography. Literally millions were made every year in most major countries, and even small studios reported making as many as 6000 negatives and 50,000 prints in the peak year of 1866.

Although never actually used as visiting cards, people exchanged carte portraits, keeping them in albums with special cut-out pages, and avidly collected cartes of celebrities in government, theater, the military, and other walks of life. Cartes were sold as souvenir sets at tourist attractions around the world and were issued as advertising novelties. Abraham Lincoln attributed his first election to his Cooper Union speech and to cartes made at the time, thousands of which were distributed by Mathew Brady in New York and Alexander Hesler in Chicago.

Cartes-de-visite were made by the collodion or wet-plate process. Several exposures were made on a single plate and contact-printed on albumen paper. These exposures were cut apart and mounted on the cards. Disderi had patented a method of taking eight exposures on a full plate (6½″ × 8½″) using a shifting plate holder devised by A. F. J. Claudet. However, the standard equipment quickly became a four-lens camera and a back that shifted the plate just once. The lenses could be uncapped one, two, or four at a time to make the exposures; the pose was changed between exposures to obtain variety. Photographers usually made multiple exposures of the poses they thought the customer would most likely choose in order to reduce the work of printing. Although cartes were made into the 1880s, the craze began to wane in the mid-1860s, and the public came to prefer the larger card-mounted cabinet photograph.

See also: CABINET PHOTOGRAPH; DISDÉRI, ANDRÉ A.E.; WET-PLATE PROCESS.

Cartier-Bresson, Henri

French; 1908–

Henri Cartier-Bresson has long been considered to be among the world's most important photojournalists. His aesthetic of the "decisive moment"—the revelatory instant—and his aversion to "arranged" photographs and contrived settings have influenced photographers since the 1930s.

Cartier-Bresson has moved with ease among three fields of artistic endeavour: painting, film, and photography. Passionate about painting and drawing from an early age, he studied for a number of years with Cottenet and the cubist painter André Lhote. He studied literature as well as painting at Cambridge in 1928. Cartier-Bresson began to photograph with a Brownie box camera as a hobby, but became seriously interested in photography while recuperating from an illness in 1931. In 1933 he discovered the Leica camera, the small size and silent shutter of which helped him to achieve the anonymity and inconspicuousness he desired; he believed that it was necessary for a photographer to blend in with the surroundings so as not to influence the behavior of the subjects. He has considered the work of Kertész, Munkacsi, and Atget as important influences on his own practice. The cinema was also of significance; he has said that "from some of the great early films I learned to look and to see."

Cartier-Bresson's first photography exhibition was held at the Gallery Julien Levy in New York in 1932, and his first reportage appeared in France in *Vu* magazine in the same year. His mastery of the camera was immediately apparent; his mature style was arrived at almost instantly.

Cartier-Bresson traveled to Mexico for ethnographic work in 1934, and to the U.S. where he studied cinematography with Paul Strand in 1935. At this time he exhibited in shows with Manuel Alvarez Bravo and Walker Evans. He assisted film director Jean Renoir on important films in 1936 and 1939, and made his own documentary film concerning hospitals in Republican Spain in 1937. In the same year he began to contribute reportage to various magazines and newspapers on a regular basis.

Cartier-Bresson was drafted into the Film and Photo Unit of the French Army in 1940 and was taken prisoner by the Germans soon after. He escaped from Wuttemberg prison on his third attempt and became active in the clandestine Resistance in 1943. He organized the filming and photography of the German Occupation of Paris and its Liberation and began to make photographic portraits of artists such as Matisse, Braque, and Bonnard. In 1945 he filmed a documentary of homecoming POWs and reported for the U.S. Office of War Information.

Returning to the U.S. in 1946, on a cross-country trip Cartier-Bresson photographed many American writers and artists including William Faulkner, Alfred Stieglitz, and Saul Steinberg. He also assisted in the preparation of a "posthumous" show of his work organized by the Museum of Modern Art in the mistaken belief that he had been killed in the war.

In 1947 he joined with Robert Capa, David ("Chim") Seymour, and others to form the Magnum agency. He traveled extensively for the next 20 years, producing an enormous body of memorable images. He photographed major events including Gandhi's funeral, the Chinese Civil War, and the first few months of existence of the People's Republic of China. He journeyed to the Soviet Union, Cuba, Canada, Japan, and again to Mexico and China, specializing in candid photographs of people in public places. Throughout these years he regularly published both his travel photo-essays and his images of contemporary French life in the world's most important journals. He left Magnum in 1966 and has devoted the last 15 years to drawing, painting, and photography. Since 1979 the International Center of Photography has circulated his major retrospective, *Henri Cartier-Bresson: Photographer*, on three continents, gaining millions of viewers of his work, an unprecedented exhibition audience for a photographer. A book of the same title was published as well.

About his own work Cartier-Bresson has written: "Above all, I craved to seize the whole essence, in the confines of one single photograph, of some situation that was in the process of unfolding itself before my eyes.... To take photographs means to record—simultaneously and within a fraction of a second—both the fact itself and the rigorous organization of visually perceived forms that give it meaning. It is putting one's head, one's eye and one's heart on the same axis."

Photograph: p. 88.

Casasola, Agustin Victor

Mexican; 1874–1938

Agustin Victor Casasola was one of the first photojournalists of the 20th c. in the Western Hemisphere. Born in Mexico City, Casasola went to work there as a journalist at the age of 20 and devoted his life to compiling a photographic documentation of his time. In 1903, he founded the Mexican Association of Journalists; in 1911, the first Society of Press Photographers; and two years later the first Agency of Photographic Information.

Casasola's most important achievement is the photographic record he created of Mexico's national agony, the shattering Revolution that lasted from 1910 to the early 1920s. Like Mathew Brady, he included the work of other photographers along with his own, so that it is not always possible to know whether a given photograph is by Casasola himself or by some other photographer. He had, however, two advantages over Brady. He and his collaborators worked on all sides of the conflict, and had access to faster negative materials which enabled them to capture action shots that eluded Brady and his men.

The Casasola archive ranges from old-fashioned studio portraits with painted backdrops and natural lighting to scenes that were apparently made on the battlefield under fire, although some of these may have been staged for the camera.

Just as the Revolution itself represented an ultimate, cataclysmic break with the past, so too did Casasola's photographic visions of this event. Although he was born and started photographing in the 19th c., photographically he would have nothing to do with idyllic, stereotyped portrayals of Mexico and its people that had characterized all prior visual efforts. Instead, he confronted the disasters of war. His landscapes were of death and violence and destruction; his people were the participants in a nightmare. Quite often Casasola portrayed women in his work, women at the focal point of action.

In the end, Casasola's unflinching confrontation with the war brought home its impact even to would-be bystanders, affecting the entire nation's consciousness even to the present day. His photographs have an unposed spontaneity that suggests the mobility and ease of the 35mm camera. They are all the more remarkable, thus, when one realizes that Casasola worked only with cumbersome large-format equipment, including a tripod and glass plate negatives.

Casasola died in Mexico City on March 30, 1938. Within the past decade, the Mexican government has established a National Historical Photographic Archive of which the Casasola Collection is the cornerstone.

Catadioptric and Catoptric Lenses

Mirror lenses are of two types. A *catoptric* (or catatropic) imaging system consists of only reflecting (mirror) elements, such as the Wolcott daguerreotype camera of 1840, and the Gregorian and Cassegrainian telescopes. This design is potentially very useful in scientific and technical applications because it permits a maximum aperture of $f/1$ or larger, is totally free of chromatic aberration (especially secondary spectrum), and has virtually no absorption of near-ultraviolet and infrared wavelengths. However, there is significant field curvature, so film must be held in a spherical form to record all points with equal sharpness. The *catadioptric* design combines refracting (lens) elements with reflecting elements to obtain flatness of field while retaining most of the advantages of the catoptric system. All photographic mirror lenses, modern reflecting telescopes, and the Schmidt camera are catadioptric systems.

See also: MIRROR LENS; SCHMIDT CAMERA; TELESCOPE; WOLCOTT, ALEXANDER S.

CC Filters

Color-correction (CC) filters are used to make slight changes in the color balance of light by affecting just one or two primary colors. In taking pictures they are most often used with color transparency film. They are too pale to be useful with black-and-white film, and it is easier to make color corrections during printing with color negative film. CC filters are available in the secondary colors, cyan, magenta, and yellow, which individually absorb red, green, and blue, respectively. The filters are also available in primary red, green, and blue, each of which absorbs the other two primaries in equal degree.

CC filters have densities ranging from 0.025 to 0.50, measured in terms of the color(s) they absorb, not the total amount of light. Intermediate or higher densities can be achieved by combining two or more filters of the same color (e.g., 0.025 + 0.025 of any color equals 0.05 of that color). Two different secondary color filters may be used together in order to control two primaries to different degrees; this is common in color printing. All three secondary colors or any two primaries are not used together, because the common amount of density they share is equivalent to neutral density, which reduces light transmission without affecting color balance.

The filters are most commonly available as thin gelatin sheets that must be placed in a suitable holder or frame. They are identified by density (usually without the decimal point) and color initial (e.g., CC30Y, CC025M, CC50B,

etc.). Enlargers for subtractive color printing have built-in CC filtration in the form of continuously adjustable cyan, magenta, and yellow dichroic filters.

See also: COLOR BALANCE; DICHROIC FILTER; NEUTRAL DENSITY; SUBTRACTIVE COLOR SYNTHESIS.

Celluloid

The plastic material now known as celluloid was patented in 1861 as *Parkesine* by its English inventor, Alexander Parkes. It is prepared by dissolving nitrocellulose (guncotton, the same basic material used to produce collodion) with naptha, amyl acetate, fusel oil, and camphor, and pouring it to set in molds or as large flat sheets. It was first used as a substitute for ivory, bone, and tortoise shell in billiard balls, combs, handles, and similar items, and to make detachable shirt collars and cuffs that could be wiped clean with a damp cloth. Although suggested for use in place of glass as a support for photographic emulsions in 1881, the material manufactured then was too thick, streaky, and optically unsuitable. In 1888 J. W. Hyatt—who had coined the name *celluloid* and founded the Celluloid Manufacturing Company in Newark, New Jersey —succeeded in producing optically clear sheets only 0.01″ thick. This material was used by John Carbutt to begin manufacture of the first successful plastic-base sheet films in the same year. The Rev. Hannibal Goodwin applied for a U.S. patent for the idea of celluloid roll film in 1887. The patent was granted in 1898, but the Eastman Co. had already begun manufacturing such film in 1889. The resultant patent infringement suit, which ended in a \$5 million judgment against Eastman in 1914, is a landmark in the history of photography.

Celluloid film base is extremely flammable and will dissolve and disintegrate when kept in closed containers for long periods of time. Early in the 20th c. it was replaced by nonflammable cellulose acetate materials (invented in France in 1901) as a base for still films; these are designated "Safety Films." However, the original nitrate base material continued to be used for some motion-picture negatives as late as 1950, and many early movies have been lost because of its self-destructive properties.

See also: CARBUTT, JOHN; EASTMAN, GEORGE; GOODWIN, REV. HANNIBAL.

Celsius

See: TEMPERATURE SCALES.

Centigrade

See: TEMPERATURE SCALES.

Ceramic Processes

Photographic images can be produced on porcelain, earthenware, enamel, and similar surfaces. The simplest procedure creates unfired images which must be protected with clear varnish. The printing surface is coated with a commercially prepared liquid emulsion, and the image is exposed by contact or projection from a negative. It is processed by swabbing on the solutions or by immersing the object in tanks of solution. Permanent, fired-on images require a method of applying powdered oxides or other glazing materials to the surface in the image pattern and then firing the object in a kiln. One method is to prepare a negative photosilkscreen image to use as a stencil for applying fine-particle liquid glazes to the object. A second method is to coat the surface with a bichromate emulsion in which glaze powders are used in place of pigments. It is exposed by contact under a negative and washed with warm water to dissolve away the unwanted glaze in the highlights and middletones. A third method consists of coating the surface with an emulsion of gelatin, sugar, water, and potassium bichromate. This dries to a tacky state, so it can only be exposed by projection. A positive transparency is used, and emulsion tackiness is destroyed in proportion to the amount of exposure received in each area. When glaze powders are dusted-on, they adhere only in the shadow and middletone areas. In general, slow, low-temperature firings produce the richest images. Results vary according to whether the image is applied to greenware, bisqueware, or a previously glazed surface. It is difficult to avoid image distortion with highly curved or irregular surfaces.

See also: BICHROMATE PROCESSES; ENAMEL PROCESS; GLASS, PHOTOGRAPHS ON; PHOTOSILKSCREEN PROCESS.

cgs System

The centimeter-gram-second system of measurement.

See: METRIC SYSTEM.

Chambi, Martín

Peruvian; 1891–1973
Martín Chambi was a documentary and portrait photographer in Cuzco, Peru, who between 1920 and 1955 recorded the society and inhabitants of Cuzco as well as local events and landscapes. Only

Chambi, Martin. "Campesinos testifying, Palace of Justice, Cuzco, Peru" (ca. 1931). Courtesy Edward Ranney and the Chambi Family.

a regional celebrity during his lifetime, Chambi was given international attention when approximately 14,000 glass plate negatives were discovered in his studio two years after his death.

Born in Coasa, in the district of Carabaya, Puno Province, in 1891, Chambi learned the rudiments of his trade as a boy from the photographer of a British gold mining company. In 1908 he began a nine-year photographic apprenticeship in the portrait studio of Max T. Vargas and Brother in Arequipa. In 1917 he married and moved to Sicuani, where he established his own studio and published the first photographic postcard in Peru. The first one-man exhibition of his work was also held that year at the Centro Artistico in Arequipa.

In 1920 Chambi moved to Cuzco, where he opened a new studio, associating with the painter and photographer Huan Manuel Figueroa Aznar. Here he began to travel in the intellectual and artistic circles of the city. In 1921 his work was included in the Exposición Agropecuario-Industrial in Arequipa. He exhibited periodically during the 1920s and 1930s, and was given one-man shows at the Consejo Provincial of Cuzco (1924), the Consejo Provincial of Puno (1925), and the Gran Hotel Bolívar, Lima (1927). In 1925 he was also awarded a gold medal at the International Artistic Exhibition in La Paz, Bolivia.

In the 1920s Chambi was influenced by the "indigenista" consciousness which was growing in Peru at this time. During this decade he traveled widely, photographing Inca ruins, Indian life, and even the activities and costumes of outlying mountain communities. At his studio in Cuzco he produced portraits of town leaders, bourgeois families, local heroes like the Italian Enrique Rolandi (the first aviator to clear the Cordilleras), and professional groups such as the Guardia Civil and the Supreme Court Justices of Cuzco. Outside of the studio he recorded local celebrations, including weddings, parties, and festivals, as well as other newsworthy events.

Between 1940 and 1970 Chambi stopped traveling so extensively, preferring to record events and sites in and around Cuzco. His photographs of the ruins and monuments at nearby Machu Picchu are among his most highly valued works, although his cityscapes of Cuzco are no less important, for they record a town which was radically altered later by the earthquake of 1950. Chambi's photographs were widely published during his lifetime by the South American press. One image of an Indian flutist sitting next to a llama was used by the Peruvian government as a postage stamp.

Throughout his life Chambi was active in cultural and artistic affairs, helping in 1927 to found the Instituto Americano de Arte in Cuzco. Years later he helped to found and promote the professional photography classes at the Escuela Nacional de Artes Gráficas in Lima (1971). That same year he was a founder and unofficial director of the Academia de Artes Plasticas, now the Escuela de Artes Plasticas. Chambi died in Cuzco in 1973.

Changing Bag

A changing bag is a portable chamber used for lighttight operations when no darkroom is available. Constructed of two layers of lightproof fabric up to about 20″ × 24″ in size, it looks like a shirt with the neck and bottom sewn shut. Zippers at one end permit placing film and equipment inside; elastic cuffs on the sleeves prevent light from entering when the photographer reaches inside to load film holders or perform similar tasks.

Characteristic Curve

The graph showing how much density is produced in a photographic emulsion by increasing amounts of exposure is called a characteristic curve. Since development also affects the formation of density, the information recorded in the curve is valid only for a specified developer, processing time, and temperature. The graph line almost always is S-shaped, beginning with a horizontal portion that represents the density of the base material and the slight fog that accompanies development. The *toe* portion of the curve reveals the first responses, in which the amount of density added increases with each exposure step; this portion represents the darkest shadow areas in a negative or the highlights in a positive image. In the long *straight-line* section, density increases an equal (or nearly equal) amount for each exposure increase; middletones are represented here. The *shoulder* portion reveals a smaller amount of density buildup for each exposure step; these are the highlight densities of a negative or the shadow-area densities of a positive. If exposure is increased after the maximum density has been reached, the curve may turn downward again, showing that density is lost.

Values on the axes of the graph are expressed as logarithms to provide equal units in both dimensions and to keep the graph to a reasonable size. On the horizontal log H or log E axis a change of 0.3 in value is equivalent to a difference of one *f*-stop in exposure; density values on the vertical axis cannot be related directly to equivalent *f*-stop changes. The vertical slant of the curve indicates the relative contrast of the emulsion; a steeper slope indicates greater contrast. This can be expressed as a number derived from the slope of the straight-line portion (gamma) or of a line connecting two significant points on the curve (average gradient; contrast index). The graph of a

CHARACTERISTIC CURVE

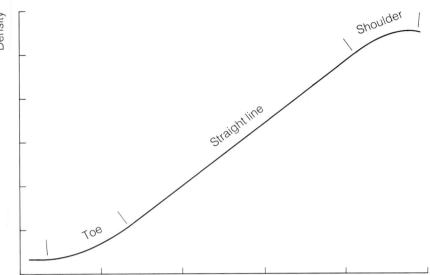

color film or paper has three curves to show the individual response of the red-, green-, and blue-sensitive emulsion layers.

See also: AVERAGE GRADIENT; COLOR MATERIALS; CONTRAST; CONTRAST INDEX; DENSITOMETRY; DENSITY; DEVELOPMENT; FOG/FOGGING; GAMMA; SOLARIZATION.

Chemical Focus

The point at which ultraviolet wavelengths (originally called "chemical rays" before their nature was known) and blue wavelengths come to focus behind a lens is called the chemical focus. If the lens is uncorrected for chromatic aberration, longer wavelengths (green, red, infrared) will come to focus at points farther behind the lens. In the early days of photography when materials had only blue sensitivity, this was of little importance; it became significant when orthochromatic and panchromatic materials were invented.

Chemical Fog

See: FOG, FOGGING.

Chemistry of Photography

The physical aspect of photography—as distinguished from the communicative or expressive aspect—is a series of chemical processes and reactions. Only the key process of exposure is not a "wet" process—one that utilizes solution-borne chemicals to accomplish

the required action. Exposure is the photochemical reaction that occurs when energy (light, infrared, ultraviolet, x-rays, etc.) causes silver compounds to break down sufficiently to form a latent image. Virtually all other chemical processes in photography depend upon solutions; they can be placed in three functional groups:

1. Those which produce light-sensitive materials—emulsion chemistry;
2. Those which produce the visible image—standard processing;
3. Those which modify the visible image—aftertreatment such as reduction or toning.

Some fundamentals of standard processing are outlined here in very simplified form; the cross-references lead to additional explanations of specific processes.

Basic reactions. Emulsions require silver nitrate, prepared by dissolving metallic silver in hot nitric acid:

$$Ag + HNO_3 \rightarrow AgNO_3 + H_2O$$
Silver / Nitric Acid / Silver Nitrate / Water

The hydrogen released in the reaction both forms water, which boils off as steam, and escapes as a gas.

Light-sensitive silver halide crystals are produced by reaction of silver nitrate and a suitable halogen compound—potassium bromide in the great majority of emulsions—in a gelatin solution:

$$AgNO_3 + KBr \rightarrow AgBr + KNO_3$$
Silver Nitrate / Potassium Bromide / Silver Bromide / Potassium Nitrate

Some emulsions include potassium chloride and potassium iodide, which form corresponding silver halides. The potassium nitrate dissolves out of the emulsion during washing stages in manufacture; the precipitated halide crystals are held in suspension by the gelatin. They are modified by further reaction with sulfur, which forms silver sulfide sensitivity specks, and by various dye sensitizers which extend the halide sensitivity to the blue and red portions of the visible spectrum. Other compounds added to the emulsion do not become active until later stages of the photographic process. These compounds include developing agents in self-processing, activation, and stabilization emulsions; color-forming dye couplers in color materials; and substances that prevent excessive swelling of the gelatin in the processing solutions.

The silver halide crystals are composed of positive silver ions and negative halogen ions. They are essentially insoluble in water, but those which are affected by exposure (i.e., those which hold the latent image) ionize slightly in water, separating some of the ions:

$$AgBr \rightarrow Ag^+ + Br^-$$
Silver Bromide / Silver ion / Bromine ion

This makes development possible. Development is an oxidation-reduction reaction. Developing agents are compounds that give up electrons (oxidize) which in turn combine with silver ions to form metallic atoms (reduction):

$$Ag^+ + e^- \rightarrow Ag$$
Silver ion / Electron from Developing Agent / Metallic Silver

Developers. Developing agents are organic compounds, most of which are benzene-related; these include ortho- and para- forms of dihydroxybenzenes, aminophenols, and phenyldiamines (meta- forms generally do not function as developers). Modern developing agents require an alkaline solution to become active and other chemicals to maintain or improve their effectiveness. Thus, a developer is chemically complex. A typical developer contains the following functional ingredients:

Solvent—water; liquid concentrates may also include an organic solvent to help keep various compounds in solution.

Developing agents—a great many developers use two agents to take advantage of their *superadditive* effect, a complex interaction that greatly improves the working characteristics of both compounds.

Akali—to activate the developing agents or to accelerate their activity.

Preservative—to protect the developing agents from non-functional (non-image-forming) oxidation; usually sodium sulfite.

Restrainer—to prevent development of unexposed silver halides; usually potassium bromide. Some developers also require an *anti-foggant* to supplement the restrainer.

The image characteristics produced by development depend largely on the choice of developing agents and the alkalinity of the solution. In broad terms, slow, soft-working developers have an alkaline pH of 8.5 to 9.0; the great majority of moderate-activity developers have a pH of 9.5 to 10; and energetic, high-contrast developers have a pH of 10.2 to 12.0.

Developers for color emulsions are far more complex than those for black-and-white emulsions. Whereas oxidation by-products are kept to a minimum in black-and-white development, they are an important and active factor in color development. They react with the color couplers to enable the formation of image dyes along with the silver image. Highly complex developing agents are used to produce the necessary kind and quantity of oxidation compounds. The developing agents are made very active by high alkalinity and elevated operating temperature; the amount of preservative is kept to a minimum so as not to suppress oxidation during development. Developer penetration through the multiple emulsion layers of color materials is assisted by an organic solvent such as benzyl alcohol so that image formation occurs essentially simultaneously at all depths. A secondary restrainer and a silver solvent are used to avoid fog from the high level of activity. However, the second developer in reversal processing includes an efficient fogging agent to render the unexposed (i.e., positive image) halides developable without the need for re-exposure of the emulsion. Color developers also include various compounds that increase the efficiency of dye coupling and improve color contrast.

Other solutions. The subsequent steps in processing are much less complex

than development. An acidic stop bath neutralizes the alkali in the developer, bringing image-forming chemical activity to a halt in 10 to 20 seconds. A stop bath is usually a solution of acetic acid—less commonly of potassium metabisulfite—with a pH of about 3.5. A plain water rinse will also stop development, but far less efficiently, by diluting the developer and flushing it out of the emulsion.

In color processing the metallic silver image must be converted to compounds that can be dissolved out of the emulsion to leave only the composite dye image. This is achieved by a bleaching solution that converts the silver to colorless halides; these halides can then be taken care of by the fixing and washing steps required to dispose of any other halides that were originally unexposed and undeveloped.

The fixer is commonly a solution of the pentahydrated, prismatic crystalline form of sodium thiosulfate ($Na_2S_2O_3 \cdot H_2O$) or the equivalent compound, ammonium thiosulfate, which is more rapid acting and has greater capacity. The fixing agent provides high ionic activity, combining with silver ions as the halides dissociate in the water solution to form silver complexes such as sodium monoargentodithiosulfate ($Na_3[Ag(S_2O_3)_2] \cdot 2H_2O$). Rapid capture of the silver ions allows the halides to continue breaking down so that within a relatively short time no light-sensitive, insoluble crystals remain. The argentothiosulfates are readily soluble in water and are removed in the subsequent washing process. A plain solution of fixer in water soon becomes inactive; more effective solutions include a slight amount of acid, a preservative to combat breakdown of the fixing agent, a buffer to maintain the working pH of the solution, and, especially in film-fixing solutions, compounds that harden the emulsion upon drying.

See also: ACTIVATOR/ACCELERATOR; BUFFER; COUPLERS, COLOR; DEVELOPING AGENT; DEVELOPMENT; EMULSION; FIXING; HARDENER; LATENT IMAGE; M-Q DEVELOPER; P-Q DEVELOPER; MIXING PHOTOGRAPHIC SOLUTIONS; OXIDATION-REDUCTION; pH; PRESERVATIVE; REDUCER/REDUCTION; RESTRAINER; STOP BATH; SUPERADDITIVITY.

Chevalier, Charles Louis

French; 1804–1859
Opticians and instrument makers in Paris, Charles Chevalier and his brother Vincent produced the telescoping-box camera obscuras that Niépce and Daguerre used in their early experi-

ments, and were responsible for the two men becoming aware of one another's work. Charles Chevalier designed the first doublet (two elements cemented together) achromatic meniscus lens in 1830, and later supplied it for the "official" Daguerre cameras manufactured by Giroux; it had a maximum aperture of about $f/12$. In 1840 he introduced a primitive iris diaphragm to improve image sharpness in the camera, produced a wooden camera that folded flat when the end pieces were removed, and took some of the earliest photomicrographs. In the same year he designed the first convertible lens—a triplet with two interchangeable front elements: one for landscapes the other for portraits. This lens was produced until about 1859, but most photographers chose the faster Petzval lens, also introduced in 1840, for portrait work.

See also: ACHROMAT; CAMERA OBSCURA.

Chevreul, Michel Eugène

French; 1786–1889
A chemist who made important investigations of the nature of dyes and coloring materials, organic compounds, and wine fermentation, near the end of his life Chevreul became the subject of the world's first photo-interview. He was president of the Academy of Sciences in 1839 when Daguerre's process was made public at a joint session with the Academy of Fine Arts, and served again as president in 1867. His color research led to his becoming head of the Gobelin tapestry works. He evolved original theories of color and discovered the laws of simultaneous contrast of colors—the phenomenon that causes a color to vary according to the adjacent colors seen at the same time, and that causes the eye to produce a composite single color when it views a whirling disc with two or more distinct color segments. This work influenced the Neo-Impressionist painters, especially Seurat and Signac. In 1886 he was interviewed by Nadar on "The Art of Living to be 100 Years Old." Nadar's son Paul photographed the interview using the new Eastman paper-base roll film to take more than 100 pictures while a stenographer recorded the conversation. A selection of these were published with quotes from Chevreul as captions in September of that year—the first photo-illustrated interview.

See also: DAGUERRE, L. J. M.; NADAR.

Chiaroscuro

Chiaroscuro (Italian for "light-dark") is the representation of various degrees of lightness and darkness in a monochrome image; the expressive quality of the graduated middletones, as opposed to the posterlike impact of solid areas of white and black; and the characteristic that distinguishes a continuous-tone image from a line (white-black) image.

"Chim"

See: SEYMOUR, DAVID.

Chloride Paper

The light-sensitive halide in the emulsion of chloride paper is silver chloride. It is slower (less sensitive) than bromide and chloro-bromide papers and thus is suitable only for contact printing. It produces a blue-black image tone. The earliest print material, salt paper used for calotype prints, was a chloride paper with the silver halides absorbed into the fibers of the paper surface. The first silver chloride gelatin emulsion was invented by J. M. Eder and G. Pizzighelli and was used on a developing-out paper in 1882. That same year Sir William Abney invented a printing-out paper with a similar emulsion. Improved chloride papers are still used today for contact printing.
See also: GASLIGHT PAPER.

Chloro-bromide Paper

The emulsion of chloro-bromide photographic printing paper contains both silver chloride and silver bromide crystals; its printing speed (light sensitivity) is intermediate between chloride and bromide papers, and it can be used for both contact printing and enlarging. Its usual image tone is warm brown-black, but the tone and speed vary with the proportions of the two silver halides. As the silver bromide content increases, the image tone becomes more neutral black and the printing speed increases. The first chloro-bromide gelatin emulsion was invented in 1883 by J. M. Eder; it was offered on a commercially produced paper a year later.

Chrétien, Gilles-Louis

French; 1754–1811
In 1786 Chrétien invented the *physionotrace*, a pre-photographic device for obtaining multiple copies of a portrait. The equipment consisted of a kind of pantograph with a sight at the end of the movable arm and a pen at the moved or "slave" point of the device. The operator looked through the sight and moved it to trace the subject's profile and other details; the pen made an ink tracing of the movements at a reduced scale on a copper plate. The plate was engraved, other details being added by hand in the process, and used to print the portrait; under the best conditions, upward of 300 copies could be printed before the plate became unusuable.
See also: PANTOGRAPH.

Chromatic Aberration

See: ABERRATIONS OF LENSES.

Chromogenic Development

In chromogenic development a dye image is produced in an emulsion as a silver halide image is developed there simultaneously; the silver image is subsequently bleached away so that only the dye image remains. Almost all color materials use chromogenic development to produce cyan, magenta, and yellow dyes in their three-layer emulsions; a few black-and-white negative films also use chromogenic development to produce various densities of black dye. The dyes are formed by color couplers which are colorless until their associated silver halide cystals are reduced by a developer. The principles of producing a color image derived from oxidation products of the developing agent—primary color development—were discovered by R. E. Liesegang in 1895 and B. Homolka in 1907. The use of color couplers—secondary color development—was patented in 1912 and 1914 by Rudolph Fischer, who coined the term *chromogenic*. The opposite method of producing a color image is the dye destruction process, in which full-strength dyes are present in the emulsion at the beginning and are removed selectively during processing.
See also: COLOR MATERIALS; COUPLERS, COLOR; DYE DESTRUCTION PROCESS.

Chronophotography

See: MAREY, ETIENNE JULIES; MOTION STUDY AND ANALYSIS.

Cibachrome Process

See: DYE DESTRUCTION PROCESS.

CIE Color System

The worldwide standard system for scientific color measurement is that recommended by the International Commission on Illumination (Commission Internationale de l'Eclairage—CIE). It is the only genuinely psycho-physical method of describing color available today. A particular shade of red, for example, may be said to appear vermilion, rust, scarlet, etc., depending upon the color sense or psychological response of the observer. The CIE System expresses nearly any color in mathematical terms. The value of this method is that a color may be described accurately to someone not physically present (e.g., a printer in Europe) without depending on physical samples.

Two features in particular separate the CIE System from purely psychological methods. First, the color of each wavelength in the visible range of the spectrum is defined in terms of the amount of red, green, and blue from standard light sources required to match it visually. The defined matches are the result of averaging the judgments of a large number of observers into what is now called the "standard observer." The second major feature is the exact definition of the color temperature of a few standard light sources to be used when describing a color. Standard A illuminant (2856K) is intended to be the equivalent of a high-wattage tungsten lamp; standard D65 (6500K) is currently replacing Standard C as the source equivalent to daylight. In certain limited circumstances other standard illuminants may be used.

In perceptual terms color has three principal attributes: hue, saturation, and brightness. The CIE System expresses these characteristics as dominant wavelength, excitation purity, and luminous transmittance (or reflectance), respectively. By the use of the standard observer tables, the mixture of the primaries for any sample can be translated into a single dominant wavelength. Excitation purity, expressed in percentage, represents how much of spectrally pure color is in a sample. Luminous transmittance is calculated on a scale of 1.00 (transparent) to 0.00 (opaque).

In order to place a sample clearly within the context of all possible colors, a chromaticity diagram is often used. This consists of a horseshoe-shaped curve drawn within one quadrant of a common x-y graph. The visible wavelengths from 400 to 700nm are marked off along the curved diagram, representing the spectrally pure colors. A straight line connecting the ends of the curve represents the artificial or dual colors such as magenta and purple. To avoid negative identification numbers, the dual colors are designated in terms of their complementary spectral colors located directly opposite on the graph. Depending on the light source, pure white (a mixture of all colors) is located at some point near the center of the horseshoe; this is the illuminant point. By mathematical interpolation, each mixed-color sample can be located within the horseshoe from the x- and y-axis coordinates. A line drawn from the the illuminant point through the color position is extended to the boundary to identify the dominant wavelength of the color. The position of the color on that line relative to the pure-white point indicates its excitation purity. A 50 percent pure color, for example, is halfway between the boundary and the illuminant point. Since only two variables may be plotted on a graph, the luminous transmittance is usually recorded near the color's position.

Although primarily intended to define colors of light, the CIE System can be adapted to describe the color of reflective surfaces, and in that way it is useful for pigments, dyes, and other colorants.
See also: COLOR; COLORIMETRY.

Cinematography

See: MOTION PICTURES.

Circle of Confusion

The circle of confusion is the size of the largest circle (open center) which the eye cannot distinguish from a dot (filled-in center). It is the primary objective factor in the sharpness of an image, and the limiting factor of depth of field. At the average close-focusing limit of 10 in. (25cm), the human eye cannot distinguish between a dot and a circle 0.01 in. (0.25mm) in diameter; this is the maximum possible size of the circle of confusion. A lens makes image points only of subject points exactly at the focused distance; subject points nearer or farther away are imaged as tiny circles at the focal plane (film position). As long as these tiny circles are 0.01 inch in diameter or smaller, those subject details will appear as sharp *in a contact print* as the details exactly at the focused distance. However, most photographs are not contact prints, but are enlargements in which these circles are also enlarged. For that reason, the circle of confusion for acceptable sharpness in each format must be smaller than the maximum possible size. In computing depth-of-field tables, the limiting size of the circle of confusion can be related to the focal length of the standard, or "normal," lens. In medium formats it is taken by many manufacturers as 1/1500 of the focal length, and in small formats it is taken as 1/2000 of the focal length. For example, in 35mm photography the normal lens focal length is 2 in. (50mm), and the circle of confusion is 0.001 in. (0.025mm).
See also: DEPTH OF FIELD; DEPTH OF FOCUS; SHARPNESS.

Claudet, Antoine-François-Jean

French; 1797–1867

French scientist Claudet was the first professional daguerreotypist to work in Great Britain and one of the art's most significant improvers. He introduced the sensitization of silver plates with chlorine vapor in 1841 and made important accelerations in daguerreotype exposure-time. Claudet took out several patents in the early 1840s covering the use of red "safe" light in the darkroom, artificial lighting, and painted backdrops for portraiture. He was the inventor of the focimeter, photographometer, and stereo-daguerreotypy. Claudet pioneered the use of hand-colored daguerreotypes and invented an early motion-reproduction device, the Phenakistiscope, in 1851.

Claudet was born in Lyons, France. He worked as a glass merchant in Great Britain for more than a decade before learning the daguerreotype process from Daguerre himself in 1839. He purchased the first license to operate a photographic business in England the same year and established a supply house for daguerreotype materials.

Claudet opened his first London portrait studio, the Adelaide Gallery, in 1841 and began to use the daguerreotype and calotype processes and, later, wet-collodion. He earned a reputation as one of the most artistic daguerreotypists and became official photographer to Queen Victoria in 1853. Claudet was named Chevalier of the Légion d'Honneur by the Emperor of France in 1863. He died in London in 1867, one month after his Regent Street studio, the Temple of Photography, and its contents were destroyed in a fire.

Clergue, Lucien

French; 1934–

Lucien Clergue, well known as a photographer, is also the founder of the *Rencontres Internationales de la Photographie*. This summer-long festival, held in Arles, France, features internationally recognized photographers presenting their work. The workshops that are also part of the festival led to the establishment in 1982 of the *Ecole Internationale de la Photographie*, a full-time graduate program.

Clergue teaches at the University of Marseilles and at the New School in New York City. His first book, *Corps Mémorable*, with poems by Paul Eluard, was published in 1957; a number of others have followed, on subjects including nudes, bullfighting, the Camargue, and the poet St. John Perse. Clergue has been the cinematographer of several films. His work appears in major

periodicals, and is in numerous collections. He won the Lumiere Prize in 1966.
Photograph: p. C-36 (Nude Photography).

Clerk Maxwell, James

See: MAXWELL, JAMES CLERK.

Cliché-verre

This method of making direct photographic reproductions of drawings or paintings on glass was invented by W. H. F. Talbot in about 1835, but has been rediscovered many times by a variety of artists and photographers. A sheet of glass is coated with an opaque varnish or paint; when the coating is dry, a drawing is made with an engraving needle or similar instrument, scratching through the coating to the glass. The glass is then used as a negative to make a contact print or enlargement on photographic print paper. A sheet of hard or flexible plastic, or a sheet of film that has been exposed to white light and developed to maximum density, may be used in place of glass. Scratching through a photographic emulsion gives a more ragged-edge line than that obtained with coated glass. An alternate technique is to make the drawing on a clear base material with opaque or translucent inks; this produces white or light-tone lines in the print, whereas the coated-glass method produces black lines.
See also: FLORENCE, A.H.R.; HYALOTYPE.

Clinical Photography

Clinical photography is that branch of medical photography devoted to living patients rather than to samples or specimens. It provides records for diagnosis, progress reports, and similar information. It is distinct from biomedical imaging areas which record tissue specimens, bacteriological cultures, and related subjects. Biomedical photography often employs a microscope or other specialized equipment; clinical photography is commonly done with an ordinary camera, lens, and lighting equipment.

Like other kinds of scientific photographs, a good clinical photograph is a straightforward representation of what is directly observable; accurate in tone or color, size, and proportion; and shown without expressive interpretation. Two aspects in particular require special attention: perspective and orientation. Improper perspective resulting from too close a camera location will distort the proportions of the body. This is unacceptable when the photographs are to be used for surgical reference (especially reconstructive or plastic surgery), for before-after comparison, or for diagnosis. Conversely, too great a camera distance may flatten the body unnaturally. In general, a lens of about twice normal focal length permits full-format images from a distance that does not create distortion. Orientation refers to identification of the location of the photographed area on the body. A good clinical photograph will be specific enough to show clearly and in detail the area in question, yet will include sufficient surrounding area for the spot to be located on the body. In some instances, such as a lesion on the hand, this is relatively easy. In other cases, as in a rash on the back, it may be more difficult. When necessary, a second locator picture taking in a wider area of view may be made.

Probably the most common type of clinical photography is a picture series that records progress during treatment. A photograph is made of the diseased area when the physician first sees the patient and periodically thereafter. Both the doctor and the patient may benefit from this series of pictures. For the doctor it can be an invaluable memory aid when treatment takes places over a prolonged period. The physician can see precisely the value of his or her methods and better determine whether medication or therapy ought to be continued or changed. In some situations it is extremely discouraging to the patient to persist in what may seem to be therapy without results. Photographs can provide evidence that change is occurring and that treatment is beneficial. Similarly, before-and-after pictures of others are helpful in convincing patients of the potential benefits of corrective or reconstructive surgery; after such surgery photographs are used to show patients improvements in their own conditions.

While serial pictures are most common, single images can be equally as important, particularly as an aid in diagnosis. There may be relatively few doctors competent in certain specialities. When a problem develops and a relevant specialist cannot physically attend the patient, pictures can be sent to the specialist to supplement other data.

Sometimes the clinical photographer will be asked to make a kind of picture story of a medical procedure such as a particular surgical technique. In this case, he or she will be expected to be able to function as part of a surgical team and be aware of operating theater procedures and requirements.

Clinical photography is most often carried out in two locations: in a studio or photo-facility room set aside for the purpose, and at the bedside or in the treatment room of the clinic or hospital. A studio is usually provided with a view camera (most often 4" × 5") and smaller

format equipment, and suitable lighting and background equipment. In general, electronic flash is widely used to reduce the discomfort of the heat and glare produced by continuous light sources. Background material is chosen with a consideration for its effect on the clarity and accuracy of the picture. A black background causes the subject to seem lighter than it really is; color backgrounds may reflect a color cast on the subject or influence color perception when the picture is examined. The greatest accuracy is achieved with a background that is a gray tone close to but not exactly the same tone as the color of the subject that will be recorded; in most cases this is a matter of choosing a tone in terms of light- or dark-colored skin. Other aspects of clarity in black-and-white photography may require the use of orthochromatic (red-blind) film or appropriate filters to make certain conditions, such as a reddish rash, more clearly visible. When such a technique is used, it must be carefully noted.

A location kit for bedside or treatment-room photography usually consists of a small-format camera and a portable (or built-in) flash unit. The kit is frequently kept as simple as possible so that non-photographers may use it as well with only minimal instruction. An experienced photographer may include close-up accessories, a few filters, or other basic devices in the location kit.

An important aspect of clinical photography is the interaction between the photographer and the patient. Patients are apprehensive, even frightened, of the unfamiliar activity centering around them. A gentle, reassuring professional manner helps to make the photographic task easier and more productive. Good organization and careful preparation of the materials and equipment likely to be needed for a session limit the demands placed on the patient and helps free the photographer to devote some time to the psychological aspects of the situation. *See also:* BIOLOGICAL PHOTOGRAPHY. Color photograph: p. C-8.

Close-up Photography

Close-ups are magnified images obtained at subject-to-lens working distances shorter than those normally permitted with ordinary equipment. The relative size, or scale, of close-up images on the film is from one tenth the actual size of the subject to the same size (1:1 or life size). The term *extreme close-up* is often used to designate the range of images from one-half to life size. Macrophotography produces images from life size up to about 50×, while photomicrography produces greater magnifications.

(The dividing line between the two is not fixed, but occurs at whatever point it becomes more convenient or necessary to use a microscope.)

Close-ups reveal characteristics and details not readily perceptible to the eye either in examining the subject or a normal-range photograph of the subject. Close-ups are essential sources of information in scientific, technical, and medical photography; they are a source of visual fascination and beauty in more ordinary applications.

To obtain close-up images it must be possible to focus sharply on the subject at much closer than normal distances. (The minimum focusing distance of a normal lens is typically about 10 times its focal length.) Some small-format camera lenses have a built-in capacity to focus down to a distance that produces an image one-half life size; this is often indicated by the (inaccurate) designation "macro-" in the lens name. With other lenses it is necessary to shorten the effective focal length of the lens, or to mount the lens at a greater distance from the film; both methods permit closer focusing.

A positive supplementary lens or so-called close-up attachment placed in front of a camera lens reduces its effective focal length. This is a simple method that requires no special accessories—the supplementary lens attaches like a filter—but is limited in flexibility and in the quality of the image obtained. The entry on supplementary lenses explains their capabilities and basic use.

A lens can be mounted farther from the film by inserting a rigid extension ring or tube or an adjustable bellows between the camera body and the lens. Extension rings and tubes differ only in their relative lengths. Two or more lengths may be combined for increased extension as necessary, but except in the case of a telescoping tube, each length provides essentially only one degree of magnification with a given lens. A slight range is obtainable by means of the lens focusing adjustment; however, the best results are usually produced with the lens focus set at infinity. An accessory bellows permits a continuous range of extensions; as long as it has a firm supporting track, it is the preferred choice when a variety of image sizes is required.

The size of the image depends on the focal length of the lens and the distance from the lens to the subject. As this distance decreases, the lens-film distance must increase. The lens-subject distance is greater than the lens-film distance for images up to life size. At that point the two distances are the same; each is equal to twice the focal length of the lens. As

Coburn, Alvin Langdon. "St. Paul's, from Ludgate Circus" (ca. 1907); Hand-pulled gravure. Permanent collection, ICP, New York.

magnification increases into the macrophotographic range, the lens-film distance becomes the greater of the two. Formulas for computing these distances—useful in planning setups and selecting extension accessories—are given in the entry on optics. Methods of calculating image size are given in the entries on magnification and scale.

The increased extension necessary for close-ups requires additional exposure of the film to obtain normal negatives or transparencies. An exposure metering system that takes readings from the image inside the camera—a so-called through-the-lens meter—indicates the compensated exposure. If it is part of an automatic control system, it will provide the correct exposure in the normal manner as long as the reading is taken from an appropriate part of the subject and the image brightness is within the range of the meter/control system. When a through-the-lens meter reading is not available, the required exposure increase factor can be calculated from the image magnification (M), or from the lens-film distance (v) and the lens focal length (F) as follows:

Factor = $(M + 1)^2$ or Factor = $v^2 \div F^2$

(The first calculation applies to normal focal-length and symmetrical lenses. With other lenses, the pupil magnification may have to be taken into account, as explained in the entry on magnification.) The exposure time indicated by a normal meter reading of the subject must be multiplied by the factor, or the indicated lens aperture setting must be increased by an equivalent number of f-stops. The lens-film distance is measured from the lens diaphragm, or from the rear nodal point, as explained in the entry on optics. Close-ups obtained with supplementary lenses do not require exposure compensation because the lens remains a normal distance from the film.

Accurate, well-composed close-ups require a camera with through-the-lens viewing. This avoids misframing because of parallax—the difference between the lines of view when the lens and viewing system are separate—and permits precise focusing. Single-lens reflex cameras and view cameras provide this kind of viewing. Sharpness is a particularly difficult problem in close-ups because even when the focus is precisely set on a desired point, the depth of field is very shallow. In close-ups whatever depth of field is available is almost equally divided in front of and behind the point focused on. Sharpness is enhanced by the use of a small lens aperture to increase depth of field; by the use of a rigid support for camera and lens; by releasing a reflex viewing mirror before releasing the shut-

ter, if possible, to avoid vibration during the exposure; and by shielding the camera and subject from breezes or other potential causes of movement.
See also: BELLOWS; DEPTH OF FIELD; MACROPHOTOGRAPHY; MAGNIFICATION; OPTICS; PHOTOMICROGRAPHY; PUPIL MAGNIFICATION; SCALE; SUPPLEMENTARY LENS.

Clubs, Photographic

See: APPENDIX.

Coburn, Alvin Langdon

British; 1882–1966

Alvin Langdon Coburn's major contribution to the development of the photographic art came midway through his career, when he began to make the first known examples of purely abstract photographs, which he dubbed *Vorto-*

raphs. These were inspired by the English vorticist movement in painting, an offshoot of cubism.

Coburn was born in Boston. He became interested in photography as a child, making his first attempts at age eight. The photographer F. Holland Day, a distant relative, met Coburn in 1898 and convinced him to take up photography full time. A year later Day took Coburn to England to assist in organizing the New American School Exhibition. During a two-year stay Coburn became acquainted with the most prominent pictorial photographers of the day.

Coburn returned to the U.S. in 1901, making pictures both in New York and across the country. He established a studio on Fifth Avenue in New York, where he exhibited his own work. Influenced by Tonalism, his work of this period owed much in its mood to the paintings of James McNeil Whistler. Coburn found that often the photographic process gave him results that were too hard-edged for his liking. As a result he began to experiment with a variety of soft-focus techniques, occasionally dispensing with the camera lens altogether, substituting in its place a card with a pinhole in it.

In 1903 Coburn was elected to the Linked Ring Brotherhood and became a founding associate of the Photo-Secession at the behest of Alfred Stieglitz, with whom he had begun corresponding the year before. A one-man show of Coburn's photographs was mounted at the New York Camera Club, and he began working at Gertrude Käsebier's studio. Up to this time, most of Coburn's photographs had been made using platinum; he now began to manipulate the surface by adding a gumbichromate coating over the platinum.

In 1904 *Metropolitan* magazine commissioned Coburn to produce a series of portraits depicting Britain's leading artists and literati. His photographs of G. B. Shaw, H. G. Wells, G. K. Chesterton, and others soon established Coburn as one of the leading portraitists of the era. Two years later he toured the cities of Europe in order to illustrate a comprehensive anthology of Henry James's writings, the first of several such projects.

In 1910 and 1911 Coburn traveled through the western U.S. making pictures of the Grand Canyon and other natural scenes. He returned to New York in 1912 to make his last photographs in America, a series of pictures from the tops of skyscrapers. Pointing his camera straight down, he eliminated the horizon line and created a flattened perspective and abstracted view that was all but unknown in photographic work up to then. A one-man show in London in 1913 contained these pictures, entitled *New York from Its Pinnacles*.

The concern with abstraction soon became a primary one for Coburn. In 1917 he showed his first Vortographs—pictures made with the aid of a kaleidoscope-like mirror attachment in front of the lens. This device broke up the subject into a series of nonrepresentational planes, producing the first examples of purely abstract photographic images. During this period Coburn continued with portraiture. *Men of Mark*, a book of 33 portraits of famous writers and intellectuals, was published in 1913, followed by *More Men of Mark* in 1922. By the 1920s Coburn also had become involved in Freemasonry and mysticism; he remained fascinated with mystical pursuits for the rest of his life.

After a solo exhibition at the Royal Photographic Society in 1924, Coburn's photographic output began to wane. In 1930 he donated his extensive collection of photographs by his predecessors and contemporaries to the Society, and he all but ceased photographing. His correspondence with Stieglitz ended in 1931. He became a naturalized British subject in that year and settled in Wales. He did not reappear on the photographic scene until the middle 1950s, when he again began to make rather quiet pictures of nature scenes and other subjects. Coburn died in 1966 at the age of 84.

Coherent Light
Light of a single wavelength in which all waves are vibrating in phase, are of the same amplitude, and are traveling in the same direction.
See: LASER; LIGHT; WAVELENGTH.

Collage
A collage is a visual image produced by pasting together cut or torn pieces of one or more images, often in combination with three-dimensional objects or fragments; it is also the technique of creating such an image. There is no attempt to conceal the fact of assemblage; instead, the pattern of edges and shapes may be exploited for its expressive quality, along with or in place of the objective visual content of the elements. Even when a single image is cut in uniform shapes and assembled in a regular pattern, the effect is to add an abstract quality to the image. Montage, a related technique, may use any of a number of procedures, of which collage is one.
See also: ABSTRACT PHOTOGRAPHY; MONTAGE.

Collecting Photographica
Since the 1960s the value of photographic images, equipment, accessories, and books as collectors' items has risen sharply. The rapid increase in art collecting and the phenomenal increase in prices for paintings that occurred during this period gave rise to an increased interest in collecting photographs for investment purposes. With that interest came a parallel interest in other photographica as collectible commodities. The trend was accelerated when major art auction houses began to hold sales of historical cameras, photographs, and various kinds of photographic ephemera.

The professional collector's interest in things photographic rose at about the same time that photography as a pastime experienced its greatest expansion. As more people became interested in making pictures, more also became interested in the historical development of the tools used for picture-making. Thus, on an amateur level there has been a tremendous increase in the numbers who collect photographic equipment as well as use it. Prices for used equipment of all kinds soared until the recession of the late 1970s and early 1980s dampened the collecting fervor somewhat, and the price spiral slowed significantly. In spite of this, the supply of antiquities is limited, so many items that were once plentiful and inexpensive are now more difficult to locate and consequently command increasingly higher prices.

Few people consciously begin to collect photographic equipment as a hobby. Most of those who are not involved with collecting as a speculative investment begin with an interest in the creative or technological aspects of photography. They may find themselves in possession of three or four cameras or other photographic tools that they keep more for nostalgic or historical reasons than for pragmatic ones. Others discover old cameras, posing chairs, tintypes, or the like in attics or while hunting for other antiques, and become intrigued by the possibilities of building a collection purely for pleasure. In most cases modest private collections are somewhat haphazard, having been assembled more on the basis of attraction to each individual piece than on a systematic attempt to build a comprehensive representation of specific equipment or a particular period of photographic history. While collections of this sort have personal value to their owners, their overall intrinsic value is limited by a lack of completeness or direction. A planned approach to collecting usually will provide a greater sense of gratification along with an increase in monetary and historical value.

Aside from photographs themselves, by far the most popular items for collection are cameras, lenses, and accessories. Some collectors concentrate on a specific make and model of a camera of historical significance; others expand their collections to include as many examples as they can find of the products of a particular manufacturer. Still other collectors have a fondness for a certain camera type and concentrate their efforts in that direction. The box camera, for example, used to be relegated to musty attics or to the back shelves of thrift shops and could be had for a dollar or so. A recent surge of interest in this item among collectors on a budget has driven up the price of certain models more than ten times. Even so, there are so many different makes and models of box cameras in existence that anyone interested in collecting all but the very earliest Kodaks, Kodak Brownies, and Bulls-Eyes has a very fertile field for exploration without the need to invest large amounts of money. In addition, many box cameras were made in the 120 and 620 roll-film formats. Both types of film are still available, so the collector can enjoy using these remarkably capable, simple cameras as well as looking at them.

Certain camera makes have a mystique all their own. The Leica, for example, is probably the most collected camera in existence. Introduced in the 1920s by Ernst Leitz, GMBH of Wetzlar, Germany, the Leica was the first commercially successful 35mm camera and helped establish a new way of photographing. Leica collecting societies exist throughout the world, and the camera system is so extensive that some people collect just the accessories offered for the various models.

Other cameras prized by amateur collectors include the twin-lens Rolleiflex (whose used prices were surprisingly moderate until the company discontinued the camera, causing a rise in the item's collector status); the Zeiss Super Ikonta, a folding roll-film camera of excellent precision and design; the Kodak Retina, a German-made folding, rangefinder-type 35mm camera; and numerous other models from Germany, England, Italy, France, Japan, and the United States. Collectors with specific interests frequently attend auctions or collectors' gatherings to seek out items too rare to be found among the used equipment stores.

The collecting of cameras does not have to be historically or technically oriented. Some collectors have disdain for a serious approach and choose to collect cameras noted for their novelty. Some specialize in designs that never quite worked properly; others concentrate on cameras made as promotional items—cameras shaped like cartoon characters, radios, bars of soap, and the like.

Whatever the collector's field of interest, he or she should do all the research possible about the period in which the sought-after cameras or other items were made, their manufacturers, and their availability and current worth. Such information can be obtained from books on antique and collectible cameras, from articles on collecting in photographic and antiques magazines, and from fellow collectors, especially through membership in a collecting society.

One of the most fertile areas for camera collecting is currently made or recently discontinued equipment. Some of the items available for a pittance now are bound to be prized collector's items in the future. Almost all items connected with photography have the potential of being collectibles. Instruction manuals and advertising pamphlets, original packages, long-discontinued film rolls, and interestingly designed developing tanks are all collected by some for their own sake. Other collectibles include lenses, light meters, film holders, shutters, projectors, enlargers, and the like. The frames and cases made for daguerreotypes, ambrotypes, and tintypes are collected for their own qualities, as are advertising cards many early photographers attached to their work. Photographic campaign buttons and jewelry are popular novelties with some collectors. Other novelty items include cigarette and cigar holders specially designed to produce a photographic image "by the action of smoke" on a small slip of preexposed paper placed in the holder before use. Stanhopes—microphotographs set into tourist trinkets, watch fobs, and costume jewelry, and equipped with their own built-in viewing system—are also prized.

In spite of the swelling ranks of collectors, many items of interest can still be found in thrift shops, attics, and flea markets. Anyone interested in starting a collection should inform friends and relatives, telling them of this interest. A notice on a local bulletin board may produce information and contacts. Many communities host periodic swapmeets and photographica fairs where items can be bought or exchanged; these are usually advertised in local newspapers. Above all, the best starting point is membership in a photographic collecting society. Telephone directories, photographic dealers, and historical societies are good sources for locating collectors' organizations.

See also: BOOKS, PHOTOGRAPHIC; HISTORY OF PHOTOGRAPHY; LITERATURE OF PHOTOGRAPHY.

Collections, Photographic

See: COLLECTING PHOTOGRAPHICA; CONSERVATION OF PHOTOGRAPHS; MUSEUMS AND COLLECTIONS; PICTURE AGENCIES AND LIBRARIES.

Collimated Light; Collimator

Collimated light is composed of visible wavelengths traveling parallel paths. Sunlight, and light from a source effectively at infinity, is collimated.

A collimator is a lens and lamp device that produces collimated light; it is used to inspect and adjust optical systems. *See also:* LIGHT.

Collodion Processes

The various methods of obtaining photographic images on materials having a light-sensitive coating of collodion all stem from the original method published in 1851 by Frederick Scott Archer. The basic ingredient of collodion is guncotton (nitrocellulose; pyroxylin), which is obtained by treating cotton (cellulose) fibers with nitric and sulfuric acids; it was invented in 1846 in Basel by C. F. Schoenbein. The following year Menard and Domonte discovered that although insoluble in water, guncotton dissolved in a mixture of alcohol and ether to form a sticky, viscous liquid they named collodion. When flowed or painted onto a surface, the solvents evaporate, leaving a tough, transparent flexible film impervious to air and water. Collodion was first used in 1848 in place of gauze and tape as a protective covering over surgical incisions and wounds. As "spirit gum" it was used in the theater up to the mid-20th c. as an adhesive for false beards and similar elements of makeup.

Several photographers suggested the possible use of collodion in place of albumen on printing paper, but Archer was the first to devise a practical process. His early efforts with collodion-coated paper were unsuccessful, as were his efforts with coated glass plates, until he discovered that the problem arose from letting the collodion dry before the plate was used. When dry, the pores of the coating closed so that processing solutions could not penetrate to the exposed silver halide crystals. In addition, the halides lost sensitivity when dried in the presence of the excess silver nitrate used in their formation, and the silver nitrate dried to a crystalline surface pattern that interfered with details in the image. These problems could be overcome by exposing and processing the plate while the collodion was still tacky, giving rise to the popular name *wet-plate process* for Archer's glass plate negative procedure. Derivative processes included the ambrotype and ferrotype (tintype) for obtaining positive images; various procedures for printing photographs on glass, ceramics, or any other surface which would accept a coating of collodion; and stripping films and plates which continued to be used for photomechanical reproduction well into the 20th c., long after gelatin had replaced collodion in all other photographic applications. Unsensitized collodion was also used to add a high-gloss surface coating to prints made on albumen paper.

A number of methods of making dry plates with collodion emulsions were introduced in the 1860s. Most involved adding syrup, sugar solution, or some other soluble substance to keep the collodion pores open when the plate dried; others used a top coating of sensitized albumen or gelatin. Most such materials were not commercially successful, largely because they required at least six times more exposure than the wet collodion processes. In spite of the effort and inconvenience involved in making wet plate negatives, most photographers chose to carry a darkroom box or tent and all the necessary processing chemicals and equipment with them in the field rather than work with long exposures.

See also: ALBUMEN PROCESSES; AMBROTYPE; ARCHER, FREDERICK SCOTT; DRY PLATES; FERROTYPE; STRIPPING FILM; WET-PLATE PROCESS.

Collotype

Collotype is a bichromate process for obtaining high-quality ink reproductions of photographic images; it is based upon reticulation of a colloid—albumen or gelatin—coating on the printing plate. The process was invented in 1855 by A. L. Poitevin, who used an albumen coating on lithographic stone and called the process photolithography. Perfected gelatin-coating processes were introduced in 1868 by Josef Albert (*Albertype*), and by Husnik, Gemoser, and Obernetter (*Lichtdruck*), and in 1869 by Ernest Edwards (*Heliotype*). The process was widely used commercially for book illustrations and fine print reproductions that were almost indistinguishable from photographic prints. It was equally as exquisite as the Woodburytype, but required far less equipment and was less expensive to produce. The collotype finally gave way to photogravure, but is used as an art medium today and for specialized purposes such as reproduction of intricate graded-color works and fine-art facsimile images.

To make a collotype, a sheet of plate glass is given a base coating of adhesive gelatin which is then overcoated with a layer of gelatin sensitized with potassium bichromate. This is exposed by contact with a negative so that the shadow and middletone areas harden. The plate is soaked in cold water, causing the gelatin in the unhardened areas to swell considerably. When dried with controlled heating, these areas dry smooth, but the shadows and middletones reticulate in a network of tiny cracks or valleys. For printing, the emulsion is dampened, and then rolled over with a greasy lithographic ink; the highlight areas have absorbed water and do not accept the ink, but the ink is retained in the reticulations in the other areas. The plate is then covered with a sheet of paper and the image transferred by pressure in a hand press or by burnishing the back of the paper. Inks of different strengths or colors can be used in various parts of the image. The random pattern of the reticulations avoids moiré, making this an especially useful way to make reproductions from halftone or other screened images.

See also: BICHROMATE PROCESSES; HELIOTYPE; MOIRÉ; POITEVIN, A. L.; SCREENED NEGATIVES/PRINTS; WOODBURYTYPE.

Color

Color is a phenomenon of perception, not an objective component or characteristic of a substance. Color is an aspect of vision; it is a psychophysical response consisting of the physical reaction of the eye and the automatic interpretive response of the brain to wavelength characteristics of light above a certain brightness level (at lower levels the eye senses brightness differences but is unable to make color discriminations). The methods of colorimetry describe certain characteristics of color by comparison and matching (Munsell, Ostwald systems), and measure certain factors (CIE system), but no overall quantification of a unique characteristic identifiable as "color" is possible.

A convenient reference point for discussing color is white light, which is composed of all visible wavelengths in equal stimulus proportions—i.e., causing equal degrees of eye response. When its wavelengths are separated by a prism or diffraction grating, white light reveals a visible sequence of the elementary colors: red, orange, yellow, green, blue, indigo, and violet. The eye perceives these colors when presented with their individual wavelengths or with mixtures of various wavelengths. It can also see colors not present in dispersed white light—notably red-blue mixes such as purple and magenta.

In addition to dispersion by a prism or diffraction, color is produced in a number of ways:

Selective emission of wavelengths by a light source.

Selective reflection of wavelengths by opaque substances (e.g., dyes, pigments) that absorb some wavelengths and reflect others.

Color

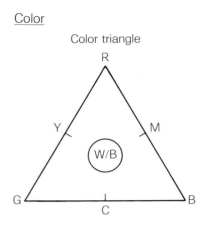

Color triangle

Selective transmission of wavelengths by translucent and transparent materials (e.g., transmission filters, colored liquids).

Interference which selectively cancels some wavelengths, as caused by dichroic thin-film coatings.

The production of color by polarization, scattering, fluorescence, and other causes can be related to those above, although these are sometimes considered separately.

Aside from monochromatic (single-wavelength) light, all colors are a mixture of wavelengths. The mixture required to create any color sensation can be produced in two ways—by adding together wavelengths from separate sources of colored light, or by subtracting the unnecessary wavelengths from white light. The Young-Helmholtz three-color theory of color vision explains both actions in terms of receptor cells (cones) in the retina that are individually sensitive to red, green, or blue wavelengths; all color sensations result from the various proportions in which these receptors are stimulated. Additive color synthesis combines various proportions of red, green, and blue light—the primary, or building, colors. Subtractive color synthesis uses colorants (dyes, inks, pigments) of the opposite or complementary colors to remove various proportions of the primaries. The Maxwell color triangle, originally created to demonstrate additive color mixing, shows the relationship of both methods. The primary colors of light (R, G, B) are at the points. Colors produced by adding two primaries lie along the leg between them. The complementary colors—cyan, magenta, and yellow (C, M, Y)—are midway on the legs, because each is a mixture of equal proportions of the primaries at either end. Mixtures of the three primaries lie inside the triangle. An equal mixture of all three colors of light produces white, located at the center. The complementary colors are so named because, when combined with the primary color directly opposite, each completes the set of three primaries. Thus, each complementary pair (red-cyan, green-magenta, blue-yellow) in proper proportions adds up to white.

In subtractive color synthesis with dyes, pigments, filters, etc., the key colors are cyan, magenta, and yellow, because in acting on white light each absorbs or otherwise blocks its opposite primary color. When any two complementaries are combined, they block two primaries and transmit or reflect the third—the primary they both contain, located at the point between them on the color triangle. When three complementaries are combined, their resultant color lies inside the triangle and is increasingly darker as the proportions approach the center, because an increasing number of wavelengths is being subtracted. At the center, in equal proportions, the subtractive colors produce black.

White, black, and grays are achromatic colors—sensations without hue. Grays are simply degrees of white-black lightness (or darkness). *Hue* is that aspect related to the color name; it is what is commonly meant by the word "color." The objective equivalent of hue is the dominant wavelength—the wavelength present in the greatest proportion among all those contributing to the color sensation; it can be determined by physical examination and measurement of the light. *Saturation*, or *chroma*, is the richness of a color—the degree to which it is free of black or gray; a desaturated hue looks "grayed-out." The objective measurement of saturation is called purity. *Value, brightness*, or *lightness* relates the color impression to a corresponding scale of grays from white to black; it is the aspect that makes a color seem a light or dark example of a hue. "Brightness" is applied to additively produced colors; "lightness" to subtractively produced colors. The objective measurement of value is called *luminance*. The *chrominance* of a color is the combination of hue and saturation (chroma) characteristics without regard for brightness. The objective equivalent is chromaticity—the combination of dominant wavelength and purity.

See also: ADDITIVE COLOR SYNTHESIS; COLORIMETRY; DIFFRACTION; DISPERSION; INTERFERENCE; LIGHT; SPECTRUM; SUBTRACTIVE COLOR SYNTHESIS; VISION; WAVELENGTH.
Color photograph: p. C-9.

Color Balance

The relationship of the colors in an image to one another and, especially, to the colors of the original subject is called color balance; it is commonly evaluated in terms of the apparent fidelity of the colors, and the purity (freedom from color tinges) of neutrals (white and grays) and areas of major importance such as skin tones. Color balance can be adjusted by the choice of emulsion and by the use of filters when making the film or print exposure. As applied to illumination, color balance means the relative proportions of the wavelengths constituting the light. The color balance of an emulsion refers to the kind of illumination with which it will give "true" color reproduction without the need for corrective filtration; it is usually identified by a general term such as "daylight" or "tungsten," or by a specific color temperature (e.g., 3200K).
See also: COLOR MATERIALS; COLOR TEMPERATURE.

Colorimetry

Colorimetry is the science of measuring color. Because color is a psychophysical phenomenon, no single system of measurement has been devised to encompass all its aspects. However, various systems have been developed that provide data by which colors can be produced and reproduced with great accuracy and repeatability. Subjective methods such as the Munsell and Ostwald color systems define color in terms of *hue* (color name), *value* (lightness, brightness), and *chroma* (saturation; richness or intensity). These aspects vary with the physical characteristics of the color agents as they are perceived by a viewer. Thus, they vary with the viewing conditions—the color composition of the illumination, its intensity, the presence of other colors (simultaneous contrast effect), and psychological factors in the viewer. In these systems the specifications of a test color are determined by comparing it with sample colors in an atlas. The atlas provides objective standards for comparison in the form of color patches, but the apparently equal steps by which the patches vary in each of the three dimensions have been subjectively established, and the comparison itself is a subjective judgment.

Objective colorimetric systems measure the spectral composition of the color, or the proportions of three key colors required to produce a match to the test color. Spectral composition is determined by measuring the amount of each wavelength in the spectrum that is reflected from a colored surface (or transmitted by a transparent or translucent material) in comparison to the spectral output of a standard source of illumination. The CIE color system determines the proportions of three stimulus wavelengths—essentially red, green, and blue light—required to match the test color by means of additive color synthesis. A colorimeter composed of two white surfaces joined at a right angle faces an observer like an arrow. The test color is projected or displayed on one side; the stimulus colors are projected on the other side. The observer adjusts the intensities of the three stimuli until the color mixture they produce matches the test color. By repeating the procedure with many different observers, individual differences in vision and reaction can be cancelled out, and an "average observer" match can be established. The proportionate stimulus values are then plotted on a color graph (chromaticity diagram) to indicate the *dominant wavelength* (objective equivalent of hue), *purity* (freedom from white; equivalent of saturation or chroma), and *luminance* (equivalent of value or lightness) of the test color. A system which makes measurements in terms of subtractive color synthesis uses a Lovibond tintometer. In this device a white surface is viewed through overlapping optical wedges colored cyan, magenta, and yellow. These are adjusted until the surface appears to match the test color. The proportionate densities of the wedges can be plotted directly, or can be converted to CIE coordinates. Other systems of colorimetry are essentially variations of the subjective and objective methods described here.
See also: ADDITIVE COLOR SYNTHESIS; CIE COLOR SYSTEM; COLOR; MUNSELL SYSTEM; OSTWALD COLOR SYSTEM; SPECTRUM; SUBTRACTIVE COLOR SYNTHESIS; VISION.

Coloring Prints and Slides
See: OIL COLORING; PAINTING ON PHOTOGRAPHS; TONER/TONING.

Color Materials
Films and printing papers for color photography create images by means of subtractive synthesis of color using cyan, magenta, and yellow dyes. Almost all materials produce these dyes by means of chromogenic development, which activates color couplers in the emulsion or in the developer; a few materials begin with a full complement of dyes and produce the image by dye destruction processing. The dyes are located in a three-layer emulsion; each layer has ordinary silver halide crystals, but is able to respond only to light of a

single color: red, green, or blue. This allows the emulsion to analyze the subject (or the image in printing) in terms of its primary color content in a single exposure, and that makes it possible to photograph moving as well as stationary subjects. The relative sensitivity of each layer is adjusted so that the overall color balance of the emulsion will produce "true" (normal looking) colors when exposed by illumination of a particular color temperature. "Daylight" emulsions are balanced for use with light having a 5500K color temperature; "Type A" emulsions are balanced for 3400K light; "Tungsten" or "Type B" emulsions are balanced for 3200K light. Films have either daylight or tungsten emulsions (there is only one Type A film) and almost all printing papers have Type B emulsions. If the illumination and the emulsion do not match in color balance, filters can be used to change the color composition of the light passing through the lens.

In negative films and ordinary (positive) printing papers the dye image is produced as the silver image is developed; in reversal films and papers the dye image is produced during the second development along with the positive silver image. Each dye is located in the layer that was exposed by its complementary color: cyan in the red-sensitive layer, magenta in the green-sensitive layer, and yellow in the blue-sensitive layer. Processed color negatives also contain residual dye densities to balance the printing effect of the cyan and magenta dyes, which do not have perfect absorption or transmission characteristics. The residual dyes give color negatives an overall pinkish-tan or orange-brown appearance. In all chromogenic materials the silver image in each layer is bleached away in a final step of processing, leaving only the corresponding composite dye image. Self-processing films for instant photography have similar three-layer emulsions, but the processing involves diffusion transfer of the dyes to a final image-forming layer. A few color printing materials also produce image by diffusion transfer.

See also: CHROMOGENIC DEVELOPMENT; COLOR BALANCE; COLOR TEMPERATURE; DIFFUSION TRANSFER PROCESS; DYE DESTRUCTION PROCESS; FILTERS; KODACHROME; KODACOLOR; REVERSAL MATERIALS AND PROCESSING; SUBTRACTIVE COLOR SYNTHESIS.

Color Photography— History

At its birth, the fact that photography could not record and reproduce the actual colors of a subject was mitigated by the exquisite detail and tonal quality of the first practical process, the daguerreotype. However, the desire for full-color images—or some approximation to realistic color—occupied many photographers and experimenters throughout the 19th c., and indeed has continued to do so. A great number of substitute methods have been devised to add colors to an image either by hand or by chemical processes, or by printing black-and-white negatives on single-color materials. Such approaches are discussed in the entries *Painting on Photographs, Toners and Toning, Pigment Processes*, and the related topics indicated there; they are outside the scope of this entry, which briefly outlines the development of various methods to produce color photographs more directly. In the following chronology, key words in SMALL CAPITALS indicate entries where additional information may be found.

1802 Thomas YOUNG advances the idea that colors are sensations, not physical properties of objects, and that they can be created by ADDITIVE COLOR SYNTHESIS: stimulation of the eye with various proportions of three primary colors. The idea is elaborated in the 1840s to 1860s by von HELMHOLTZ in the three-color theory of VISION.

1810 Johann Seebeck notes that silver plates with partial sensitization with silver chloride duplicate the colors of light falling on them. In the late 1840s this becomes the basis of heliochromy: direct color images recorded on daguerreotype plates, investigated independently by Edmond BECQUEREL and NIÉPCE DE SAINT-VICTOR. It is also the basis of the Hillotype hoax of Rev. Levi HILL in the early 1850s.

1855 James Clerk MAXWELL suggests the use of filters to obtain primary-color records by photographic means for use in creating color images according to the Young-Helmholtz theory.

1861 Using black-and-white slides photographed through primary-color filters by Thomas Sutton, Maxwell demonstrates additive color synthesis. The results are imperfect, and the method works by a fluke not explained for almost 100 years, but the basis of modern color photography has been laid.

1862 Louis DUCOS DU HAURON patents a camera with internal beam splitters to divide the image from a single lens into three images. This is the basis of the one-shot color

camera and related devices perfected by Frederick Eugene IVES in the 1890s and after, notably the KROMSKOP for integrated viewing of three-color black-and-white images as a single full-color image.

1868–1869 Ducos Du Hauron publishes *Les Couleurs en Photographie* setting forth the theoretical bases of almost all ADDITIVE and SUBTRACTIVE COLOR SYNTHESIS processes subsequently developed by others, including MOSAIC SYSTEMS and SCREEN PROCESSES in which tiny primary-color elements at the film plane perform the fundamental color analysis of the image. At the same time, Charles Cros independently demonstrates image synthesis based on three-color SEPARATION NEGATIVES AND POSITIVES. Both men take red, blue, and yellow (instead of green) as primary colors, but because of the green component of yellow light their various demonstrations are reasonably successful.

1891 The LIPPMANN PROCESS is invented to produce full-color images by interference among wavelengths of light, without the use of dyes, pigments, or other colorants. It is a scientifically elegant method, but impractical for general use.

1894 John JOLY patents the first line-screen process for additive color images; it is introduced commercially in 1896.

1899 R. W. Wood patents a method of producing full-color DIFFRACTION PHOTOGRAPHS: black-and-white color separations are viewed by primary-color light produced by diffraction gratings in a viewer invented by F. E. Ives.

1904 The LUMIERE brothers obtain patents for an additive-color plate with an integral mosaic; introduced in 1907 as the AUTOCHROME plate, it is the first truly successful process for general photography in color.

1906 The FINLAYCOLOR PROCESS for producing additive color images using improved regular screens (rather than random mosaics) is patented; the process is applied in the separate Thames Colour Screen (1908) and the integral Thames Colour Plate (1909).

1909 The first practical LENTICULAR SYSTEM for additive-color images is patented by Rodolphe Berthon; an improved version for motion pictures in the early 1920s is commonly called the KELLER-DORIAN PROCESS.

1910 The Dioptichrome plate, a regular-screen additive color process that became more popular than the Lumière Autochrome process is patented; an improved version in the 1920s is introduced as DUFAY-COLOR.

1912 Rudolph FISCHER and H. Siegrist patent a subtractive color film composed of three layers, each effectively sensitive to one primary color, and incorporating COLOR COUPLERS to produce dye images by CHROMOGENIC DEVELOPMENT as the silver positive image is produced in the course of reversal processing. Their work draws on prior dye-development discoveries by Liesegang (1895) and Homolka (1905), and forms the basis for all subsequent monopack subtractive color films, a priority that is seldom acknowledged.

1914 The Fischer-Siegrist method is introduced in an amateur movie film for TWO-COLOR PHOTOGRAPHY, rather than three-color.

1925 The Jos Pé Company introduces a dye imbibition process in which RELIEF IMAGES from color separations are dyed in subtractive colors (cyan, magenta, yellow) and the dye images are assembled by a TRANSFER PROCESS in register on a single gelatin film; it is the basis of the subsequent TECHNICOLOR, WASH-OFF RELIEF, and DYE TRANSFER processes.

1934 Gasparcolor materials introduce the first commercial DYE DESTRUCTION PROCESS, in which a subtractive color image is formed by removing unnecessary dyes rather than forming the required amounts of dye in the emulsion of a print material. The process is an improvement of the Utocolor process of 1910, and builds on patents obtained by J. H. Christensen from 1918 on; its is the forerunner of the Cibachrome process introduced after World War II.

1935 Leopold GODOWSKY and Leopold MANNES, working with the Kodak Research Laboratories, produce KODACHROME film, the first successful monopack, subtractive color reversal film. It solves the problem of color couplers migrating between emulsion layers by including them in separate developers rather than in the emulsion.

1936 Agfa produces a subtractive color reversal film with color couplers fixed in place in the emulsion layers and using a single developer to produce the positive image.

1939 The Agfacolor process introduces a monopack color negative film and a monopack-emulsion paper for negative-positive printing.

1942 KODACOLOR film, the first negative film with completely anchored color couplers in each emulsion layer is introduced.

1950 Kodacolor negative film is produced with residual colored couplers to produce a self-masking feature that compensates for the printing deficiencies of the cyan and magenta image dyes.

1963 Polacolor, a DIFFUSION TRANSFER peel-apart color print film for camera use is introduced.

1972 A self contained, single-sheet color diffusion transfer film is introduced, Polaroid SX-70 film.

1981 Agfa and Ilford introduce films that produce black-and-white negatives by chromogenic action with a standard color negative developer.

1982 Kodak introduces diffusion transfer materials for color printing in the darkroom from negatives or transparencies.

1983 Kodak introduces a one-sheet diffusion transfer color camera film in which the positive image can be peeled away after processing so that the bulky base material and negative layers can be discarded.

1983 Polaroid Corp. introduces a diffusion transfer 35mm color slide film incorporating an additive-color screen.

See also: COLOR; COLORIMETRY; COLOR MATERIALS; HISTORY OF PHOTOGRAPHY; LITERATURE OF PHOTOGRAPHY.

Color Printing

See: PRINTING, COLOR.

Color Sensitometry

See: DENSITOMETRY; SENSITOMETRY.

Color Temperature

Color temperature is a means of specifying the color of light produced by an incandescent (tungsten filament) source, or by a continuous radiator such as the sun. Light is said to have a particular color temperature if its color matches that of the light emitted by a black body heated to that temperature as measured in Kelvins on the absolute scale. Thus, 3200K light looks the same as light from a black body heated to 3200K. The wavelength composition of the light from the incandescent source will not be exactly the same as that radiated by the black body, but there is sufficient correspondence so that film response can be adjusted and controlled for predictable results. That is not the case with light from fluorescent tubes and other sources such as mercury- and sodium-vapor streetlights, which produce a noncontinuous spectrum. Although such light may be assigned an *equivalent color temperature* on the basis of visual matching, the response of photographic emulsions will be quite different and essentially unpredictable.

Light of low color temperature is red-yellow; as the temperature rises, the proportion of blue wavelengths increases and the light looks increasingly white. The color temperature of light can be raised or lowered by the use of filters, which can be rated in terms of the number of mireds they shift the light. A mired is a reciprocal unit of measurement derived from the color temperature. The color temperatures of some common light sources are as follows:

SOURCE	COLOR TEMPERATURE
Open blue sky	12000–18000K
Overcast sky	7000K
Average noon daylight; electronic flash (daylight emulsion balance)	5500K
500-watt 3400K photolamp (Type A emulsion balance)	3400K
500-watt 3200K tungsten lamp (tungsten, Type B emulsion balance)	3200K
75–300-watt household lamps	2800–3000K

See also: BLACK BODY; COLORIMETRY; FILTERS; KELVIN; MIRED.

Color Vision

See: VISION.

Coma

See: ABERRATIONS OF LENSES.

Combat Photography

See: WAR PHOTOGRAPHY.

Combination Images

See: COLLAGE; COMPOSITE PHOTOGRAPHS; MONTAGE; MULTI-IMAGE TECHNIQUES; MULTIPLE EXPOSURES, MULTIPLE PRINTING.

Commercial Photography

See: ADVERTISING PHOTOGRAPHY; FREELANCE PHOTOGRAPHY; MODELS; PORTRAITURE; PRODUCT PHOTOGRAPHY; PROFESSIONAL PHOTOGRAPHY; STUDIO PHOTOGRAPHY; SELLING PHOTOGRAPHS.

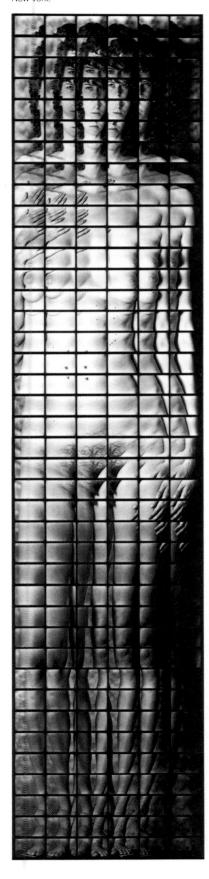

Composite Photographs. Mark Berghash, "Parts XXVI, Birgit" (1980); 35mm contact prints, actual size 18″ × 52″. © Mark Berghash; courtesy Marcuse Pfeifer Gallery, New York.

Compensating Developer

A compensating developer retards formation of highlight densities without affecting gradation in the shadow densities of a negative; the result is to compress a subject of extreme brightness range into a more easily printable density range. A typical compensating developer contains metol as the developing agent and has low alkalinity, a formulation that favors the production of potassium bromide during development. Metol is sensitive to the restraining action of bromide. Because the greatest amount of silver is reduced in the highlight areas, the greatest amount of bromide is formed there and development is significantly retarded. Little silver is reduced in the shadow areas, so there is little bromide and development proceeds at a normal rate. Agitation must be limited so as not to wash the bromides out of the highlights, which would eliminate the differential in the restraining action in various parts of the image. A two-bath developer also produces compensating action, because the developing agent is exhausted in the highlight areas sooner than in the shadow areas. Compensating development is not effective with thin-emulsion films, because they can retain only a limited amount of bromide in any given area.
See also: CONTRAST; DEVELOPMENT; TWO-BATH DEVELOPMENT.

Complementary Colors
See: COLOR.

Composite Photographs

Composite photographs combine two or more different images to form another, single picture. The resulting image may be, according to the photographer's intent, realistic or fantastic. There are three basic methods of construction, which may be used individually or in combination: (1) several elements are recorded on a single piece or frame of film (multiple exposure); (2) portions of various negatives or slides are registered on a single print (multiple printing or combination printing); and (3) elements from various photographs are cut out, pasted together on a common support, and rephotographed—this last step distinguishing the process from montage. Composite images may also be created by sandwiching negatives or slides together for printing or projection.

Composite techniques arose as a means of circumventing the limitations of the first photographic processes. Early landscape photographers, for example, discovered that wet collodion negatives were unusually sensitive to blue light, and yielded greatly overexposed sky tones. To attain a realistic image, they commonly masked the sky portion of their negative when printing, and then carefully printed-in a properly exposed sky from a separate negative.

A similar difficulty involved the long exposure times required by early photographic materials, which rendered it virtually impossible to execute a large group composition. In the 1850s, ingenious British photographers like Oscar Rejlander and Henry Peach Robinson began to employ combination printing to bring together a great many individual negatives in a single complex composition. Rejlander's famous 1857 work "The Two Ways of Life" utilized over 30 negatives in a meticulously planned composition, and achieved a remarkably realistic overall effect.

Photography's technical progress eventually rendered such stratagems unnecessary. But in the 1920s and 1930s, European artists and photographers such as John Heartfield, Raoul Haussman, and Herbert Bayer began to revive composite techniques to create startling images unobtainable by ordinary means. While still frequently encountered in advertising, the techniques of composite photography have been kept alive most notably in the work of Jerry N. Uelsmann. A master of the complex process of multiple printing, Uelsmann has fashioned uncanny, paradoxical images of astonishing technical perfection.

When composites are produced, an effort may be made to conceal the fact that more than one photograph is used in the final image, or it may be left apparent (with the success of the picture depending upon its graphic effect). If the effort is to make the composite appear to be a single photograph, then key elements—perspective, quality and direction of lighting, exposure—must have matching characteristics among the images being combined. Matching perspective is most easily accomplished by using lenses of similar focal length (assuming the same format in each case), and printing with similar degrees of enlargement. In making paste-up composites, care must be taken to match types and weights of paper; cuts should be made in areas of the image that will help conceal the join, such as object edges, dark-featured objects, and out-of-focus areas; and the edges of joins must be cleanly cut, the backs of the edges thinned and smoothed with fine sandpaper if necessary. After the paste-up is assembled (with any non-staining adhesive), the edges can be retouched before rephotographing.
See also: COLLAGE; MONTAGE; MULTIPLE EXPOSURE/MULTIPLE PRINTING.

Composition

Photographers have entertained a remarkable variety of contradictory opinions about the role of composition in photography. Edward Weston, for example, working with a tripod-mounted 8″ × 10″ view camera in whose ground glass he could carefully inspect the image formed by his lens, recommended the practice of previsualizing the final print before the exposure was even made. Henri Cartier-Bresson's early photographs, on the other hand, were at first derided as "anti-photographic" because they broke so completely with the conventional pictorial devices of the 1930s. Using a handheld 35mm camera and intuitively seeking the "decisive moment" when a host of objects and events would come fleetingly into balance, he produced images whose undeniable coherence could never, all the same, be precisely predicted. Still later, the Surrealist photographer Man Ray sought to dispense with the idea of composition entirely, when he loaded a Polaroid camera and made exposures while swinging it randomly around a room. Ray called the resulting images "unconcerned photographs," and delighted in the unplanned, aleatory look of photographs made without the photographer's active intervention. Three distinct methods, embodying three distinct attitudes toward the process of picture-making—yet all unquestionably successful for the photographers who practiced them.

Considered as one of the latest offsprings of the centuries-old Western pictorial tradition, it should not seem surprising that historically, photography has assimilated and put to regular use many of the pictorial conventions associated with older media such as painting. From the medium's first days, photographers attempted to reproduce the characteristic visual devices of the masterworks of painting. But these attempts were seldom successful except on a trivial level. Photography, inescapably tied to the particulars of the world before the lens, could rarely attain the calculated perfections of placement, proportion, lighting, and line found in the greatest achievements of painting.

Yet from the medium's earliest decades, well-intentioned writers have sought to provide beginning and amateur photographers with rules and recipes guaranteed to assure successful pictures. These might involve such strategies as mentally dividing the picture space into a grid and carefully distributing "points of interest," symmetric and asymmetric elements, restful curves, and dynamic diagonals. Then, as now, such artificial guidelines typically neglect the particular strengths and weaknesses of different photographic processes, an understanding of which is an essential part of successful photography. The daguerreotype, for instance, recorded an astonishing wealth of microscopic detail on its polished silver plates, and reproduced an extraordinary range of delicate tonal gradations; it lent itself to subjects that demanded painstaking description. Its rival process during the 1840s, the calotype, employed a paper negative which tended to disperse detail and reduce all subjects to simplified patterns of darks and lights. As was recognized by the best photographers of that era, the dutifully precise daguerreotype and the romantic, atmospheric calotype demanded very different forms of pictorial organization to accentuate the strengths, and not the weaknesses, of each. The same lesson holds today for those photographers who rely on the precision and detail provided by view-camera negatives, and for those who prefer the speed and graphic economy characteristic of the best small-format work.

While various ostensible rules for composition are still dangled before every beginning photographer, it has been observed that the most artfully composed photographs do not always yield the most expressive, satisfying photographs. For the photographer who wishes to fully understand and exploit the possibilities of photographic picture-making, the idea of composition must be expanded beyond its usual reference to the arrangement of figures and forms within the picture space. Instead that notion should be broadened to include an awareness of the key variables that stamp the photographic image with its special visual structures. By carefully considering how these various factors affect the overall visual composition of the photographic image, the serious photographer becomes better equipped to employ photography as a flexible medium, one adapted to a vast range of pictorial applications.

The relation of pictorial forms to the picture frame. According to John Szarkowski of the Museum of Modern Art, the relation of figure to ground, and of each to the picture frame, represents the essential problem of photographic design. The 19th c. expeditionary photographer Timothy H. O'Sullivan, for example, in photographing the geological landforms of the American Southwest, consciously framed his photographs to take advantage of the jagged mountain ridges where the land met the sky. By playing off these jagged lines against the picture frame, O'Sullivan transformed the intermediary sky portion of his photographs into a dynamic shape pictorially significant in its own right.

The relation of forms within the picture frame. Depending on the photographer's intention, a significant object may be isolated within the picture space—as with Edward Weston's well-known photographs of vegetable forms; or, alternatively, the picture may be packed with a superabundance of detail of seemingly equal value—as with Garry Winogrand's photographs of large political gatherings where coherence is achieved by means of sophisticated repetitions or "rhyming" of visual shapes throughout the photograph.

Point of view. The seemingly simple question of where to place the camera in relation to the subject is often one of the most crucial decisions faced by the photographer, and one which plays a large part in determining a photographer's particular style. Walker Evans, for instance, consistently sought to locate his camera at eye level, squarely in front of his architectural subjects; such a stance, he felt, helped contribute to the tone of plain-spoken, unvarnished observation that he sought. For a photographer like Margaret Bourke-White, on the other hand, the search for unorthodox perspectives was an important concern, in keeping with the photojournalist's need to constantly rediscover the world from fresh viewpoints.

Length of exposure. Historically, the ever-diminishing duration of photographic exposures has dramatically altered the way in which photographs represent the world. The first daguerreotypes, whose exposure times ranged up to half an hour, rendered bustling city streets as utterly devoid of people. By the 1880s, the advent of stop-action photographs overthrew centuries of artistic convention, when it was revealed for the first time how a bird's wings looked in flight, or a horse's legs at a gallop. With the introduction of electronic flash after the 1930s, the problem for photographers became how to envision and contend with a technique that made it possible to form an image in the smallest fraction of a second. As practiced by such disparate photographers as Dr. Harold Edgerton, Gjon Mili, and Mark Cohen, flash photography has dramatically demonstrated that the most exciting and original photographs are frequently those which could not be anticipated by any preexisting conventions of composition.

On the other hand, the use of long exposures to deliberately produce blurred images of moving objects has been ingeniously exploited by artists such as Alexey Brodovitch, Richard Avedon, Irving Penn, and Ernst Haas. Brodovitch's photographs of ballet dancers, taken at shutter speeds of ½-sec. or longer, and Haas's famous images of the swirling motion of a bullfight, provide startling visual evocations of the dynamism of their subjects.

Focus. The use of selective focus can serve to emphasize certain objects and deemphasize others. In many of the photographs of Diane Arbus, for example, the subjects of her portraits are dramatically isolated in the foreground of the picture while the background is thrown out of focus and rendered indistinct.

Depth of field. By the use of a relatively wide-angle lens, or by stopping down the aperture of his lens, the photographer can create images that are sharply in focus from foreground to background. Characteristic of the best work of 19th c. American landscape photographers, this reproduction of the entire visual field in crisp focus presents the world as the eye never sees it. The masterful use of depth of field by members of the *f*/64 Group such as Edward Weston and Ansel Adams contributes to the feeling of heightened reality achieved by their photographs.

Conceptual Photography

This school of photography, which emerged from the conceptualist movement in painting in the 1960s, questions and explores the very nature of photographic expression. Although conceptualist photographs show real objects in the real world, they are not made to capitalize on the unquestioned acceptance of the realistic representation (mimetic veracity, in formal terms) that is a fundamental property of the medium, and is the foundation of the straight or purist approach to photographic expression. Rather, conceptualist photographs ask or force the viewer to become consciously aware of the artificial character of that reality; in so doing, they pose the question: What is the concept "a photograph"?

Two aspects of the question itself are especially revealing, even explanatory, of the concerns of conceptualism. First, the question does not ask what is the concept of (story, meaning, aesthetic/philosophic idea behind) *this* photograph; it asks what is the concept "photograph" itself. The second aspect is implicit in the first: the assumption that the fundamental "meaning" of a photograph is not carried in the object—the photograph—but in the minds of viewers, and that although each viewer may have a different idea (concept) of what a photograph is—of "what 'a photograph' means to me"—there is a fundamental concept "photograph" that subsumes all of these. This theory is distantly descended from the 12th c. foundations of conceptualism in philosophy, which held that universals exist only in the mind, not independently, and that they are patterns to which externals correspond. It follows from the second aspect that the photograph as unique object has no intrinsic value, and indeed many conceptualist photographers work only with the idea of mass reproduction in mind. This is, of course, the direct opposite of the purist "fine print" attitude that a significant part of the true meaning (or expressiveness) of a photograph is inherent in its being a finely crafted object, the individual print.

Conceptual photographs are reflexive in being "about" their own medium, and self-referential in asking about the nature of their own meanings. It was conceptual art that gave impetus to the succeeding, more specific trend, conceptual photography. The foremost early practitioners of conceptual photography were disgruntled painters and sculptors trying to dematerialize the art object. Perhaps photographers were too close to their own medium to be able to initiate the self-referential gesture, although Kenneth Josephson's pioneering work with photographs-within-photographs matched similar concerns seen in the photographic work of Canadian filmmaker Michael Snow, and New York artists Victor Burgin and Les Levine. Vanguard conceptual artist Joseph Kosuth stressed the movement's concern with reflexivity in his dictum *Art as Idea as Idea,* while Douglas Huebler's deceptively simple photograph-text juxtapositions and John Baldessari's more convoluted use of words and photograph suggested the importance of social and verbal context in the production of photographic meaning.

Conceptual photography might be more clearly referred to as "meta-photography," literally after- or beyond-photography. Meta-photography is photography-as-a-medium becoming self-aware, and self-conscious about its own nature. Its subject matter is the "axioms" and variables of photography itself, the very basis of photographic rhetoric. In order to examine the how and why of photographic meaning, its images manipulate such aspects unique to the medium as:

1. The capacity to isolate a phenomenon;

2. The mimetic veracity of sharply focused, continous-tone (or color) representation;

3. The paradox of tense: a present image records that which has been;

4. The apparent rationality of the optically formed image.

Conceptualist photographs may make consideration of the medium inescapable by a forceful reminder of its materials, or by relating a representation to what is represented, or by comparing "realities." For example:

A photograph showing two-and-a-half frames on a strip of 35mm film running at an angle across the rectangle of the picture area, with the sprocket holes, frame lines, and edge markings as clearly visible as the images on the film.

A photograph of a white-bordered, snapshot-size photograph of sand plunged part-way into (or emerging from) the center of a bed of sand.

A photograph of a landscape showing a hand holding a white-bordered photograph of a portion of the same landscape, positioned so that the image is visually continuous from the "real" landscape to the photographed photograph and back to "reality."

In much the same way that the analytic philosophers (Wittgenstein, Russell, Ayer, and Quine) went back to analyze simple propositions and declarative sentences in an attempt to rethink philosophy, some conceptual photographers have looked to the naive snapshot, "analyzing" its visual rhetoric, playing with its capacity to signify veracity and literalness. Influential in this vein were the small self-published books by Ed Ruscha. *Twenty-Six Gasoline Stations, Every Building on Sunset Strip,* and *Various Small Fire and Milk* (to name a few) were mid-to-late 1960s productions that laid the base for other forays into using the rhetoric of popular imagery within the context of Fine Art. Hence, the "dumb snapshot" was used to great effect by Douglas Huebler, John Baldessari, Mike Mandel, and Larry Sultan in their book *Evidence* (1977) and, about the same time, by Tony De Lappa in his faked photo-album study of a couple's courting, marriage, and eventual divorce, *Portraits of Violet and Al.* Common to all these artworks was a concern for the vernacular image over the esoterics of the photographic "equivalent," that ambiguous visual cipher standing in for the intuitional relationships between photographer and the "thing-itself," and between photographic print and a sensitive viewer. Robert Heinecken's work makes the point. He culls his imagery from the glut of pornography, fashion photography, and other visual detritus cluttering our image-oriented society. Mixing and matching, Heinecken's sexualized alchemy turns trash into visual gems. Although his earlier works are more correctly seen as "photoconceptualist," his later works are overtly conceptual.

A more objective conceptual approach was used by the late Italian photographer Ugo Mulas in his *Verifications* series and by West Coast photographer-theorist Lew Thomas in his "structuralist trilogy" of books: *Photography and Language, Structural(ism) and Photography, and Photography: the Problematic Model.*

Although conceptual art's heyday was on the wane by 1970, as late as the mid-1970s the academic photographic community was only becoming aware of its impact on younger photographers. One critic, Joseph Czarnecki, writing in 1975 on an installation of found photographs assembled by Larry Sultan and Mike Mandel, quipped: "One might ask . . . it's Art, but is it Photography?" His rebuke echoed the thoughts of many more traditional photographic practitioners.

In the early stages of the conceptual photography trend, geography played an important role. The West Coast, especially the San Francisco Bay Area, nurtured the aspirations of first- and second-generation conceptualists. By the early 1980s, however, the trend had become widespread as an attitude within the academic photographic community, an attitude that has lost some of its "monastic" rigor and become more hedonistic as increasing numbers of photographers load their cameras with color film. A case in point would be John Divola's *Zuma* series. Exploiting the photographic gray zone between fact and fiction, Divola explores the nature of the photographic paradox and still manages to delight the eyes with his large color prints. Recent work by Barbara Jo Revelle plays with the ambiguity between family snapshot and documentary photography, anchoring her imagery within a suggestive verbal context. But unlike her earlier work, color replaces the black-and-white print.

The most recent conceptualist productions have been labeled post-structuralist by many critics. The name change indicates the shift in emphasis from exploring photographic rhetoric in itself to studying how ideologies are implicit in that visual rhetoric.

Given the manipulative potential offered by increasing interaction of electronic and conventional photographic imaging, and the impact of work in artificial intelligence on formulations of "meaning," it is inescapable that the conceptualist attitude will continue to affect photographic endeavors.

See also: ARTISTS AND PHOTOGRAPHY; ART OF PHOTOGRAPHY; PAINTING AND PHOTOGRAPHY; SNAPSHOT AESTHETIC.

Condenser

A single lens or group of lenses called a condenser system may be used between the light source and the image-forming lens of an enlarger or projector to achieve even illumination and maximum brightness. Condensers are also used in spotlights to form a beam of illumination. The most common projection/enlarging condenser systems are composed of two plano-convex lenses mounted with their curved surfaces facing one another. Their combined focal length is chosen so as to focus an image of the light source at the position of the image-forming lens; this ensures that little or no light falls outside the coverage of the image system. The negative or slide is positioned so that a maximum amount of light passes through it, with as little spillage around the edges as the shape of the format permits. (A square format fits the circular illumination path more efficiently than the long rectangle of the 35mm format, for example. In any case, the negative holder or slide mount should be opaque to mask off light outside the image area.) Since the lens-to-film distance varies when different formats are used or different size enlargements are made, it should be possible to reposition the light source or the condenser to maintain maximum efficiency. Some enlargers accomplish this by having one movable and one stationary condenser lens to change the effective focal length of the condenser system as necessary. Spotlights usually permit moving the bulb position and use a single, modified condenser called a Fresnel lens.

See also: FRESNEL LENS; LENSES.

Conservation of Photographs

Photographic conservation is specifically concerned with the physical preservation of both antique and contemporary images produced by the great variety of processes that the medium encompasses. The materials and the complex chemical nature of photographic images pose unique problems. Unlike the conservation of paintings, artworks on paper, books, and physical objects—for which successful treatment techniques have been developed in the course of at least three centuries of experience and research—photographic conservation is a new and experimental field. However,

concern about the problems of conservation is not new. Since the beginnings of photography there has been serious concern about image impermanence, as it was early evident that the inherent physical and chemical instability of photographic materials can cause fading, staining, and dimensional change. A reflection of this concern was the appointment in 1855 of the "Fading Committee" of the London Photographic Society. In a series of technically accurate recommendations, the committee suggested that photographs should receive proper processing and that they should be stored in an environment free of excessive relative humidity and airborne contaminants. Despite this advice, relatively few photographs have been prepared or cared for in this manner. Over the years, collections have accumulated images produced by a considerable variety of processes, but only in the last two decades has there been significant recognition of the value of photographs as historical documents and as fine art coupled with a growing understanding of their essential fragility. And although some causes of deterioration have long been identified, only recently has there been accurate determination of some of the actual processes of deterioration—the kind of information that is essential in order to devise effective countermeasures.

It is important that all persons who administer a collection—from file clerks to curators and directors—be aware of safe procedures for the care and handling, storage, and display of photographs. At least one member of the staff should have specific training in conservation practices, or a specialist should be consulted to establish procedures that will be adhered to by all. (The services of a specialist are essential in extraordinary circumstances such as damage from fire and smoke, flooding, a storm, or other disaster.) In the U.S., the Graphic Arts Research Center at the Rochester (New York) Institute of Technology serves as a major coordinator of information and research from all over the world; the Center also conducts workshops and seminars in photographic conservancy. Two organizations that can assist in contacting qualified conservators are the Photographic Materials Group of the American Institute for the Conservation of Historic and Artistic Works, Washington, D.C., and the International Institute for Conservation of Historic and Artistic Works, London, England.

As detailed more fully in the entry on filing and storing photographs, the best means to prevent deterioration is to handle photographs with great care and to store them in a carefully controlled environment. Chemical activity is accelerated in the presence of moisture, heat, and light. High relative humidity, especially in combination with high temperature or light, contamination from poor processing, improper storage enclosures, and air pollution will all promote damage. Optimum storage conditions are a dark, relatively dry (30–40 percent relative humidity), cool (60°F [18°C] or less), clean (air-filtered) environment. The handling of images and the duration of display should be minimized, and light levels during display should be kept low—10 footcandles or less. Color images in particular should not be displayed where daylight—either direct sun or open skylight—can fall on them. Products used for storage (e.g., envelopes, boxes, folders) and for display (mounting boards, mats, etc.) must be chosen with care; some materials that are safe for use in conservation of paper works may not be appropriate for photographic images. Professional advice is particularly valuable in these areas.

Attention to and treatment of specific images is an important but delicate matter. The first step is to record the present condition with written and perhaps photographic documentation. Positive identification of the photographic process and the components of the object is necessary before determining a safe course of treatment. In a general sense, the components of a photographic object include the final image material (metallic silver, platinum or other metals, organic or inorganic dyes, pigments, etc.), a binder (gelatin, albumen, collodion), and a support (paper, metal, glass, plastic). One or more of these components may be in a deteriorated condition. Treatment options are quite limited and may include cleaning, mending tears or breaks, and remounting or recasing. For some problematic objects, even washing in pure water may not be advisable. Although there are procedures for restoring some kinds of images, as described in the entry on that topic, the variety and complexity of photographic materials and the ways in which they deteriorate make most attempts at direct restoration of the original unadvisable—they are likely to be unsuccessful, or even destructive. Any recommendations for treatment must be considered with caution; a good conservator will not promise the impossible. A second opinion regarding treatment of very valuable objects is a wise precaution.

Much more basic research is needed in order to understand the problems that conservancy must solve and to provide the information for safe restorative treatment. The care and treatment of albumen prints—the major output of 19th c. photography throughout the world—is an area of intense current investigation. As explained in the entry on archival processing, fixing and washing procedures for long-term permanence also are a subject of new research and are quite likely to be revised from past practices. New information will suggest improved procedures in many areas, but in any case, optimum processing, thoughtful handling and storage, and the use of environmental controls are the best preventive measures to insure the longevity of photographs.

See also: ARCHIVAL PROCESSING; FILING AND STORING PHOTOGRAPHS; RESTORING PHOTOGRAPHS.

Contact Paper

Some printing papers are suitable only for contact-printing exposures; their emulsions are too slow (insensitive to light) to respond to the intensity of enlarging images. A contact paper is usually a chloride-emulsion paper.

See also: CHLORIDE PAPER; CONTACT PRINTING.

Contact Printing

Contact printing provides a positive that is the same size as the negative image. A contact print is made by positioning the negative directly against the printing paper rather than by projecting the image as in enlarging.

Contact printing has two major purposes. The most common, because of the wide use of roll films, is to make a proof sheet of an entire roll cut into strips of convenient lengths. The other is to make prints from large-format sheet films. This is usually done only with 8″ × 10″ and larger films, since even 5″ × 7″ film is commonly enlarged.

Proof sheets and prints can be made with a printing frame. Several types are available, but they all have the function of holding the negatives in place and firmly pressed emulsion-to-emulsion against the printing paper. One side of the frame is a sheet of clear glass or plastic; it is hinged to an opaque base side and locks shut against it after the frame is loaded. Some frames have grooves into which the negatives are inserted. The frame is loaded with the paper emulsion facing the glass side, and the negatives above the paper with their base side toward the glass.

Loading is done under a safelight. The frame then is exposed to white light to make the print. Frequently the frame is placed on the baseboard of an enlarger which has been adjusted so that its light adequately covers the glass area; the enlarger timer is used to control the length of exposure. Correct exposure can be found by means of test strips or prints, but a little experimentation will establish an enlarger position and the requisite exposure for most negatives, especially when making proofs. After exposure the print paper is processed.

Prints and proof sheets may also be made with a *contact printer*. This is a box with a hinged pressure lid over a glass stage; the interior contains a diffused white light source for printing and a safelight for loading. As with the printing frame, the negative and paper are pressed together emulsion to emulsion facing the light source for exposure. In sophisticated printers the amount of light reaching each area of the negative can be controlled with switches, and the overall exposure can be controlled with a built-in timer.

See also: PROOF PRINTS.

Contact Sheet

See: PROOF PRINTS.

Continuous-Tone Image

In a continuous-tone image modulations from light to dark are produced by variations in the density of the image-forming substance: silver in conventional black-and-white photographic images, and dyes in color and chromogenic black-and-white images. In continuous-tone photographic emulsions the image-forming densities are directly dependent upon the amount of exposure received in each area; tone variations occur in a smooth, continuous manner without gaps or jumps in the tonal scale other than those created by the characteristics of the subject itself.

A *half-tone* image attempts to imitate continuous tones by means of small dots or lines of an ink (or other substance) of various sizes and spacing but of a single density. Where the dots touch and blend, the maximum black or color tone is produced. Intermediate tones are produced when the dots are spaced so that some percentage of the background (usually white paper) is visible between them. The dots are so small that they cannot individually be distinguished in most cases, and the eye blends the ink and paper colors to form a composite impression of a tone. The smaller, and thus more widely spaced, the dots are, the lighter the tone appears.

A *posterized* image simplifies the continuous-tone scale into only a few densities, each of which represents a number of tones immediately lighter and darker than itself. It is as if a 15-step stairway were simplified into a 3-step stair spanning the same distance. Posterized images can be produced by manipulation of continuous-tone materials or by half-tone methods of reproduction. In general, posterization is limited to four or five density steps; the eye tends to perceive a greater number of steps as half-tone representation of continuous tone.

A *line* image is composed of only two tones: the background color and a single, maximum density of silver, dye, or ink. The image has no sense of tone because it is not broken up into dots, but consists only of solid areas of maximum tone. High-contrast "lith" films and papers that only record subject brightnesses as no exposure or maximum exposure are used to obtain photographic line images. *See also:* PHOTOMECHANICAL REPRODUCTION; POSTERIZATION; SCREENED NEGATIVES AND PRINTS.

Contrast

Contrast is the subjective impression of how tones differ in relative lightness and darkness within a subject or a photograph. The more tones differ, the higher the contrast; the less they differ, the lower the contrast. Contrast also can be measured in terms of the amount of light transmitted or reflected by various areas of the image.

The perception of contrast in a picture is affected to some extent by psychological factors. A print of a sad or depressing subject is likely to be seen as having lower contrast than a print of a happy, appealing subject, even though actual measurements show the contrasts to be equal. The degree to which psychological factors are significant is difficult to estimate and impossible to measure in any meaningful way. The fact that they do operate is evidenced in the different reactions and perceptions evoked by prints of the same subject made with different contrasts, and in the practice of choosing a particular contrast range in order to reinforce or add a certain emotional character to an image.

The objective contrast characteristics of a black-and-white image can be seen and evaluated with comparative accuracy. Contrast in a color image is affected by the fact that color perception is an extremely complex psychophysical process. Colors that have identical measured brightnesses may appear to be different because certain hues are perceived as brighter than others (yellows, for example, appear brighter than blues). This is partly a matter of the psychological associations of certain colors, associations which vary from culture to culture. Color contrast is also a matter of objective differences in hue. The contrast between a red and a blue or a green of the same brightness is greater than the contrast between the same red and an equally bright yellow or orange (both of which contain red).

Most black-and-white photographs have moderate, or "normal" contrast, with tones that range from white paper or clear film through a series of grays to solid black or opaque. The highest possible contrast reduces all tones to the extremes—black against white with no grays. The lowest possible contrast reduces all variations to a single tone—light, dark, or in between; it is no contrast at all.

Contrast is experienced differently in looking at subjects, negatives, and transparencies, and in looking at prints. In subjects, negatives, and transparencies, overall contrast is largely the difference between whatever extremes happen to be present—the lightest and darkest values. These may be white and black; black and dark gray in the case of a dark subject in poor light; white and light gray in the case of a high-key subject and surroundings; or two middle grays such as those which might translate the color extremes of a tanned blonde lying on sand in full sunlight. The degree of difference between intermediate tones is also an indication of contrast in these situations, but it is of less importance than the impression given by the difference between the extremes.

In black-and-white prints, where the overall range is essentially the same—paper white to maximum silver black—whether the subject contrast is high or low, the abrupt or gradual nature of changes between the intermediate tones is the main element of contrast. The higher the contrast, the more abrupt the change, and as a consequence, the fewer the tonal steps from one extreme to the other.

Besides overall contrast, there is local contrast: the contrast among tones in a particular area of the photograph. Often different degrees of local contrast occur within a given picture. For example, shadow or dark-tone areas commonly show less local contrast than middle-tone areas in a negative. This is because they are recorded on the toe of the characteristic curve of the film's response, where the density differences produced by various exposures are less than on the straight-line portion of the curve, where middle tones are recorded. Printing papers are designed to accommodate these differences and produce contrasts that seem to be equal in all areas, although they may not be the same according to objective measurements. Both the physiology and the psychology of vision have an effect here.

The contrast of a subject is measured by reflected-light meter readings taken from the darkest and lightest significant areas. The difference between the two, expressed in *f*-stops or as a ratio, is the brightness range or luminance range of the subject. As explained further in the entry on brightness range, an average subject has a contrast or range of about 7 stops, or exposure steps, which is equivalent to a 1:128 ratio.

The contrast of negatives, transparencies, and prints is measured with a densitometer, an instrument that compares the amount of light transmitted or reflected by a portion of the image with the amount of light directed onto it. Film contrast is measured with a transmission densitometer; print contrast is measured with a reflection densitometer. When the fundamental or characteristic contrast of an emulsion is to be measured, it is exposed to a step wedge—a gray scale with steps that differ in exactly equal degrees of transmission or reflectivity. Each step thus produces a known amount of exposure. After the emulsion is processed, a density reading is taken from each step reproduced in the image, and the result is plotted against its exposure on a graph. The result is a *characteristic curve* of the emulsion response for a particular degree of development. Contrast can be measured from the characteristic curve in a number of ways. The most common is the slope or degree of upward slant of the straight-line portion of the curve (gamma) or of a line drawn between two significant densities on the curve (average gradient; contrast index).

All photographic emulsions have a characteristic degree of contrast defined by the response to normal exposure (i.e., to an average subject) and optimum processing. In general terms, slow, fine-grain emulsions have higher inherent contrast than faster, larger-grain emulsions. The contrast of continuous-tone black-and-white films can be significantly varied by development: increased development produces increased contrast. However, development cannot significantly affect the response of high-contrast lith films. Because color processing is essentially invariable for best results, little contrast control by means of development is possible with color negative or transparency films, although limited push processing (extended development) has some effect with transparency films. Prints normally are given

Contrast Index

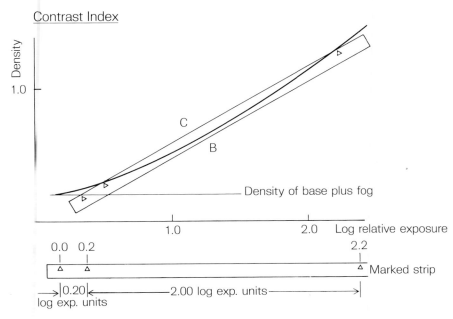

Contrast index = the slope of line C = $\dfrac{\text{rise}}{\text{run}}$ = $\dfrac{0.8 \text{ density units}}{1.8 \text{ log exp. units}}$ = 0.44

maximum (infinity) development. In black-and-white printing a slight amount of contrast control is possible by choice of developer, but not by varying development time. Black-and-white papers are supplied in various grades of contrast, from 0 (lowest contrast) to 5 (highest contrast), or with a variable- or selective-contrast emulsion that varies in response according to whether it is exposed through a yellow or a magenta filter. Color print papers are supplied in a single contrast grade; contrast is controlled by filtration to adjust the color balance of the negative image and by exposure. Masking, a procedure of adjusting the relative printing densities of some portions of the image, also provides contrast control in color printing. *See also:* AVERAGE GRADIENT; BRIGHTNESS RANGE; CHARACTERISTIC CURVE; COLOR; CONTRAST INDEX; DENSITOMETRY; GAMMA; GRAY SCALE; MASKING; SENSITOMETRY; STEP WEDGE; VARIABLE-CONTRAST DEVELOPERS; VARIABLE-CONTRAST MATERIALS; VISION.

Contrast Index

Contrast index is the method devised by Eastman Kodak Co. to indicate the relative printing contrast of negatives. In most black-and-white photography optimum exposure produces shadow-area densities that lie on the toe of the characteristic curve of the film. Using gamma as a measure of contrast ignores these shadow values; in fact, two negatives with different gammas may have

the same effective printing contrast and require the same contrast-grade paper. Like the nearly identical Ilford average gradient method, contrast index takes the shadow values into account; the two negatives described would have the same contrast index. Stated another way, all negatives developed to the same contrast index will print best on the same contrast-grade paper, regardless of the differences in their gammas. Kodak publishes contrast-index development data for its films. The general relationship between contrast index and paper grade is as follows; note that contact printing and enlarging with a diffused light source require higher negative contrast to obtain the same results as with a condenser enlarger.

CONTRAST INDEX		PAPER
Condenser	Diffusion; Contact	Contrast Grade
0.53	0.70	1
0.43	0.57	2
0.35	0.48	3
0.29	0.39	4
0.23	0.31	5

The contrast index of a given characteristic curve can be determined in the following manner. A small reference ruler is prepared with three marked points: zero, the point 0.2 log units greater than zero, and the point 2.2 log units greater than zero. A reference line is drawn across the graph at the level of the base-plus-fog density. The ruler is moved

over the graph, keeping the zero point on the base-density reference line until the position is found at which the 0.2 mark intersects with the toe of the curve and the 2.2 mark simultaneously intersects with the straight-line portion. These two points are marked and a line is drawn connecting them. The points represent the minimum and maximum useful, or printable, densities; the *slope* of the line connecting them is the contrast index of the curve. The slope is calculated by dividing the difference between the densities of the two points (the rise) by the difference between their log exposure values (the run). For example, if the densities are 0.3 and 1.1, rise equals 0.8; and if the log exposure values are 0.9 and 2.7, run equals 1.8. Then:

Contrast index = 0.8 ÷ 1.8 = 0.44
See also: AVERAGE GRADIENT; CHARACTERISTIC CURVE; GAMMA.

Cookie; Cucaloris

A cucaloris—"cookie" in lighting jargon—is a device used to create light patterns on the background of a photographic, television, or motion-picture set. It is an opaque card in which cutouts of various shapes and patterns have been made. The pattern may be abstract, or representational of a window frame, branches and leaves, or other elements appropriate to the setting. The cookie is placed in front of the principal background light source, which is positioned so that the light and shadow pattern falls on the background but not on the main subject or foreground objects. The purpose is to provide visual variety in an otherwise plain setting, or to suggest certain aspects of a scene or setting without actually having to construct them.
See also: LIGHTING.

Copying Photographs

Photographs are commonly copied because the original negative or transparency is lost, fragile, especially valuable, or unobtainable. Both black-and-white and color pictures can readily be duplicated with good results by amateurs, and many photographic studios find this work a lucrative sideline.

The primary considerations in copying prints are flat, even lighting, and absolute parallelism between the camera back (film plane) and the surface of the print being copied to avoid keystoning distortion. Light from both sides of the print should be adjusted until exposure readings at the corners match a reading at the center. Alternatively, a pencil or ruler can be held perpendicular to the print center and the lighting adjusted until the shadows cast on each side are equal in tone. The angle from each light to the lens-subject axis must be at least 45° or direct glare will be photographed on the print surface. This is a problem especially with glossy prints and images on metal, such as daguerreotypes; through-the-lens viewing makes it easy to see and correct this situation. A tripod or other camera support is essential to ensure a parallel setup and to hold the camera steady during exposure, which may be relatively long. Equal measurements from each camera corner to the corresponding print corners indicate head-on alignment.

Color photographs must be illuminated with light that matches the color balance of the film used for the copy. Slides and larger-format color transparencies must be illuminated from behind with diffused light. If filters are required to adjust the light source or to create special color effects, they are best placed behind the slide being copied rather than directly in front of the camera lens. Single-tube copiers, extension tubes, or accessory bellows are available for most 35mm cameras to permit same-size (1:1) copying of slides. A flat-field macro lens produces better sharpness than an ordinary camera lens at such close distances.

Excessive contrast in the duplicate is the most common exposure/processing problem in copying. With black-and-white films full exposure—based on an incident-light reading or a reflected-light reading from a standard gray card—and reduced development are required to ensure that the highlight portions of the image are easily printable. A good copy negative looks flat compared to the original negative; the desired copy print contrast can be achieved by choice of paper grade. Best results with color transparencies are achieved with duplicating films, which are manufactured with reduced contrast characteristics. Otherwise, a medium or high-speed emulsion will produce less contrast than a slow film, and therefore is to be preferred. *See also:* GRAY CARD; KEYSTONING.

Copyright

Copyright is the legal right to control the publication, sale, display, or other use of an original written work, musical composition, photograph or other visual image, and other kinds of works that can be reproduced or performed. The U.S. Copyright Act of January 1, 1978 extends federal copyright protection to all such works at the time of their creation. It is not necessary for the work to bear a copyright notice or be registered with the Copyright Office; however, these things must be done before legal action

can be undertaken against anyone who has misused the work or infringed the copyright.

The person who creates an original work is automatically the copyright owner. However, copyright for work produced in the course of employment generally belongs to the employer. This is true for a photographer in a paid position of regular employment. One undertaking a freelance, one-time, or casual assignment on a "work for hire" basis can transfer ownership of the copyright to the employer by signing a written agreement (sometimes stamped on the back of the paycheck); in the absence of such an agreement, the photographer retains the copyright. If a photographer is commissioned to create photographs to supplement a larger copyrightable work (illustrations for a textbook, for example) the copyright for these may belong to the employer; however a written agreement embodying the terms of the commission is a necessity in order to legally establish that the work was, in fact, a commissioned one.

Copyright extends for the life of the originator plus 50 years. In the case of work done for hire, copyright extends for 75 years from first publication or 100 years from creation, whichever is shorter. The copyright owner can sell, lease, assign, or otherwise transfer copyright to another, but this must be stated specifically in transactions regarding a particular work. When a work is sold or reproduced, copyright is retained by the original owner unless otherwise specified. To protect a work such as a photograph, it should be marked: © *[date] John Photographer*, and the same legend should appear with the photograph when it is published or otherwise reproduced. The word *Copyright* may be used in place of the symbol ©; the date should be the year of creation or first publication. This notice should be on any publicly distributed copies of a photograph, since such distribution legally constitutes publication. Legal damages may not be recoverable if infringement was accidental or unintentional because a work was not properly marked.

For legal reasons (an infringement action; to correct publication with bad notice within the past five years); or simply to clearly establish copyright, photographs can be registered with the Copyright Office. Forms, instructions, and full details of the provisions of the Copyright Act can be obtained by mail from the Register of Copyright, Library of Congress, Washington, D.C., and from some U.S. government offices in major cities. The preceding details are

only a brief summary of some provisions of the Act.

The doctrine of fair use, recognized by the Act, permits some limited uses of a work without infringement. These uses include criticism, comment, news reporting, teaching, scholarship, and research. Information available from the Copyright Office explains fair-use limits in detail.

Cosindas, Marie
American; 1925-

A graduate of the Modern School of Fashion Design, Marie Consindas attended evening classes in painting, drawing, and graphics at the Boston Museum School. In the late 1950s and early 1960s she began to use the camera as a creative rather than a recording instrument, and for the next five years she worked mostly in black and white. In 1961 several of her photographs were purchased by the Museum of Modern Art in New York. In 1962 she attended the Ansel Adams Workshop in California where Adams urged her to explore color photography. He believed that even in her black-and-white work she actually thought in color. During this period of experimentation she began working with Polaroid color films.

A one-woman exhibition at the Museum of Modern Art in 1966 established Cosindas' reputation nationally as a superb colorist and artist. Later that year the Boston Museum of Fine Arts honored her with the first one-person exhibition given to a living Boston photographer. The following year the Art Institute of Chicago presented her work in a one-woman exhibition and the Metropolitan Museum of Art included her photographs in a group show entitled *Photography in the Fine Arts, Exhibition V*, which traveled around the country. As a result of these three major exhibitions, her work appeared in *Life, Saturday Review, Newsweek, Vogue,* and *Esquire.* In addition, she participated in important group shows in Canada, Mexico, and Italy, and her work was reproduced in virtually every country in Europe. An exhibit of her work appeared at I C P in 1978.

Cosindas was one of the first photographers to use instant film to advantage, making experiments for each print, and then deepening the color to its lushest potential. Her portraits and still lifes successfully challenge paintings in the same genre, and her style is so recognizable that her prints have assumed the status of a trademark both in her personal and commercial work. Edwin Land has written of her: "Once in a long while one has an experience of overpowering

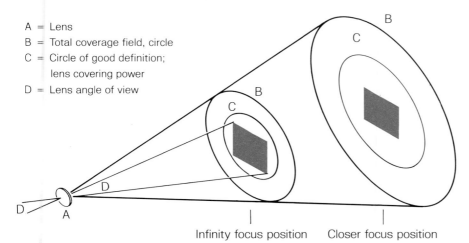

A = Lens
B = Total coverage field, circle
C = Circle of good definition;
    lens covering power
D = Lens angle of view

Infinity focus position   Closer focus position

clarity in suddenly seeing through a new face to the person within. Marie Cosindas has learned how to use photography reliably for this kind of penetration; when we look at her pictures we are almost embarrassed by the intimate revelation of a stranger. It is clear that she could not work without beauty as one of her tools. What else she uses will remain as mysterious as art itself."
Color photograph: p. C-10.

Couplers, Color

Organic compounds which form dyes during chromogenic development of photographic materials and in diazo processes are called color couplers. Almost all color photographic materials have *substantive* couplers incorporated in their three emulsion layers, making it possible to use a single developer to produce the composite dye image. Kodachrome film is unique in not having incorporated couplers; instead, each emulsion layer is developed in a separate processing step by a developer which contains the appropriate *non-substantive* couplers. Image-forming couplers in photographic materials are colorless until a silver halide image is developed; then they couple with by-products of the chemical reduction to form cyan, magenta, and yellow dyes in proportion to the silver density developed in each emulsion layer. Most color negative films also contain color couplers which form an integral mask to correct the printing deficiencies of the cyan and magenta dye images. These are destroyed in proportion to the silver and dye image produced in these layers, so their masking action affects only the other areas of the image layer. A few negative films use colorless couplers to form the corrective mask during development. In either case, it is these masking dyes which give a color negative

an overall pinkish-tan or orange-brown appearance.
See also: CHROMOGENIC DEVELOPMENT; DIAZO PROCESSES; KODACHROME.

Covering Power

The area of good definition that a lens provides at the image plane is its covering power. The term also refers to a measure of the light-stopping effect of the silver in a negative.

A lens has a circular field of view and projects a circular cone of light rays to the image plane. The circle at the image plane falls off severely in illumination and definition of details at the edges (vignetting); the useful area is a smaller diameter circle of good definition. This smaller circle defines the covering power of the lens. It must be large enough to take in the largest dimension—the diagonal—of the film format to be used when the image is at its closest position to the lens—i.e., when the lens is focused at infinity. (When focused at closer distances, the image is farther behind the lens, well within the widening cone of good definition). A lens that will allow the use of camera movements must have greater covering power than a lens for a nonadjustable camera so that the image may be shifted without moving outside the area of good definition. The angle formed by projecting lines from the edges of the coverage circle through the center of the lens defines the lens angle of view.

The covering power of silver in a negative is determined by the mass (weight per square area) of silver required to produce one unit of density. A number of factors affect covering power (for example, it varies according to whether the image receives chemical, physical, or diffusion transfer development), but grain size and shape and

emulsion thickness are of major importance. In general, large grains such as those in the relatively thick emulsions of some fast films are roughly spherical. A large grain particle that blocks light over a given area is thicker and therefore heavier than the total mass of tiny, flat, thin grains that would cover the same area. Since covering power is the ratio between silver mass and the light stopped, the tiny grains typical of slow, thin-emulsion films have greater covering power. Recent advances in emulsion science have made it possible to produce large grains (T or tablet grains) that are comparatively flat and thin; the result is a fast film with high covering power. There is an economic advantage because less silver is required in the emulsion, and an image advantage because a thin emulsion has higher resolving power than a thick emulsion.
See also: DENSITY; RESOLVING POWER; VIGNETTING.

Crayon Pictures

In a "crayon picture" daguerreotype portrait the subject is a vignette image—the body fades out below the shoulders, and the surroundings are featureless white or black, as in an informal crayon or charcoal portrait sketched by hand. The technique was invented by J. A. Whipple of Boston and patented by him or by Marcus Root in 1849. It was used to great effect by Southworth and Hawes in Boston, and by J. J. E. Mayall, who introduced it in England in 1850–1851. The vignette was created by holding a card with an oval cutout several inches in front of the lens and moving it during the exposure (commonly 20–40 seconds long) so that the edges would not register. The card was the same color as the background, and if not black, it had to be illuminated to the same degree to produce the effect of undefined space around the subject.

Crime Photography

Photographs are used in law enforcement to aid in investigations and to provide legally acceptable evidence, records, and identification. Crime photographs are also utilized by private-detective and security agencies, insurance companies, and some large businesses to guard against theft.
Early use. The first crime-related applications of photography were made in the mid-1850s and dealt with identification. The Swiss Department of Justice and Police ordered that all vagrants (assumed to be likely criminals) be photographed; the French police initiated the use of photographically illus-

trated "Wanted" notices soon thereafter. In 1870 it became mandatory to photograph all persons imprisoned in Great Britain, a practice that some wardens had initiated independently as much as 15 years earlier. Copies of the photographs were sent to Scotland Yard to form the first major master file for the identification of criminals and repeat offenders. Most other countries followed suit in the next two decades, as did the police departments of many major cities throughout the world. The formal exchange of photographs along with other information developed early in the 20th c. The kinds of pictures taken for these "rogues' galleries" began to be standardized after 1882, when Alphonse Bertillon patented a system of identification based on measurements of the head, left fingers and forearm, left foot, and height of an individual, taken directly or from photographs made to standard specifications. The method was soon supplemented—and supplanted after the turn of the century—by fingerprinting. Such photography then was simplified to the full-face and profile "mug shots" that are the standard supplement to fingerprint records today.

Techniques for making fingerprints visible on articles of evidence, and of photographing them, originated in forensic laboratories after about 1910, and began to be used regularly in the field in the 1920s. Photographic records of the scenes of crimes were made occasionally in the latter part of the 19th c., but coverage by a police photographer did not become a widespread standard procedure until after 1929, when introduction of the self-contained flashbulb made it practical to use hand cameras and panchromatic films under any conditions. Investigation of evidence by means of ultraviolet illumination became possible in 1893 with the development of specially prepared emulsions; far more practical UV-sensitive materials were introduced in 1921, two years after the first infrared-sensitive emulsions were produced. Infrared was used primarily for analytical crime photography at first; its usefulness in surveillance photography began to be explored in the 1930s and was developed extensively during World War II. Advances in scientific and technical photography are now applied in crime photography as soon as they appear, but the development of this specialized area was quite slow from 1900 to about 1945. This was a matter of legal procedures rather than technical limitations: standards for the admissibility and interpretation of photographic records and evidence had to be evolved and tested in each legal system throughout the world.

Criteria. To be useful, especially if they are to be presented in court as evidence, crime photographs are required to conform to a relatively rigid set of criteria. They must be natural and straightforward, foregoing any tendency toward creative interpretation. Not only must they show what an observer to the scene would have viewed, they must also be undistorted in any sense. Prints which have obviously been burned or dodged may be rejected in a court of law on the grounds that they do not accurately represent what the camera saw. Further, unlike most areas of photography, the whole process, including the negative, is liable to question and ought to be handled and accounted for meticulously to avoid challenge.

One of the most important elements in a presentation is natural perspective—the size relationships in a photograph of objects that exist in three dimensions. Three factors influence perspective: focal length of the camera lens, degree of enlargement, and the viewing distance, which commonly is taken to be about reading distance, or 15 inches (380mm). The formula to determine the proper enlargement is: degree of enlargement equals viewing distance divided by focal length of the camera lens. If a 50mm lens is used, then 380mm ÷ 50mm = 7.5× enlargement, or roughly an 8″ × 10″ print from a 35mm negative.

Different crimes require varying techniques to aid in investigation. In general, pictures show the area around the crime scene, personal injuries in close-up, signs of struggle, evidence of activity just prior to commission of the crime (e.g., a dangling telephone receiver), and anything out of the ordinary which might be pertinent. Careful records must be kept so that each picture can be accurately identified and labeled.

The choice of equipment varies widely depending on the size, activity, and preference of an agency. Long telephoto lenses in conjunction with 35mm systems are favored for surveillance, while crime-scene search units may favor a 2¼-inch format for higher technical quality. Instant-picture processes are frequently used for accident investigations. Special ID cameras have sliding backs so that both front and side views may be put on a single negative. In special circumstances infrared, ultraviolet, x-ray, and other processes sometimes are used. Color film is used increasingly because judges and juries respond more to the apparent reality of color images than to black-and-white images. In some cases, such as an arson investigation, color is mandatory.

See also: FORENSIC PHOTOGRAPHY.

Criticism of Photography

Contemporary criticism of photography addresses a range of distinct questions. (1) At the most basic level, photography criticism asks whether an individual photograph is good or bad, successful or unsuccessful. Is it well-made, stimulating, beautiful? Like art criticism of a similar kind, the aim is to produce a greater appreciation for the qualities of the single picture, as well as a greater awareness of the different ways of responding to a visual image. Among the most successful examples of this kind of criticism are the short, illuminating essays found in John Szarkowski's *Looking at Photographs* (1973). (2) A second approach to photography criticism examines a larger body of photographic work—the lifetime work of a single photographer, for instance, or perhaps the photographs from a single documentary project—and attempts to assess its value or importance in the broadest sense. A book such as Ben Maddow's *Edward Weston: Fifty Years* (1973) looks at the themes which reappear in Weston's photographs throughout his career, and discusses them in relation to Weston's development as an artist. A critical examination of the 1930s social documentary photographs of the FSA group, on the other hand, might consider why they were so effective as a form of social communication in Depression-era America. (3) Finally, a third variety of photography criticism seeks to understand how photography works as a system of visual communication in modern culture. Here the insights and methods of such specialized disciplines as *semiotics* (the study of the way that signs convey complex cultural meanings) and *information theory* (the analysis of the process by which information is coded and transmitted) are called into play, along with those of sociology and psychology.

Historically, the criticism of photography is as old as the medium itself. Until recently, however, photography has had few regularly practicing critics. The most significant body of photography criticism has been the work of talented outsiders, critics-at-large who have written only occasionally about photographic images and their place in the arts and society. Few general newspapers or magazines in any country have published photography criticism on a regular basis. And until recently, the major photographic journals have been specialty publications for photographers rather than the general public.

During most of the 19th c., photography criticism sought to weigh the medium's claims as both an art and a science. Was photography a mechanical medium that simply recorded reality with only the slightest assistance from the photographer? Or could photography—like the traditional art media—respond to the photographer's personal vision? A heated debate took place around just this question, with writers like the Frenchman Francis Wey, one of the most important early photography critics, arguing that photography offered ample scope and flexibility to be considered an artistic medium. The poet and art critic Charles Baudelaire, however, in a scathing attack on the medium in 1859, dismissed photography as the product of a lifeless and mechanical instrument, and as a corrupter of both popular taste and the fine arts.

By the turn of the century, this dispute had given way to another. Among the growing number of critics who had finally accepted photography as an art, there broke out an aesthetic debate as to what kind of art photography ought to try to be. Should photographers imitate the earlier traditions of painting and seek to make their pictures look like precious, handcrafted objects—as did the Pictorialist photographers in Europe and America? Or should photography attempt instead to develop its own standards and traditions—as argued critics like Sadakichi Hartmann in the Photo-Secession journal *Camera Work?* It was out of this critical debate that there emerged the idea of "straight," unmanipulated, sharp-focus photography that attracted Alfred Stieglitz, Edward Weston, and Ansel Adams so powerfully after World War I.

During the social and economic upheaval in 1930s Depression America, a number of critics such as Elizabeth McCausland maintained that photographers should not confine themselves to producing fine art, but should turn their talents to examining the society in which they lived. The social documentary photographs of groups such as the FSA photographic team and the Photo League proved a revelation to many critics, confirming that socially concerned photographers could also produce images of the highest accomplishment.

In the 1960s, as university-trained art historians began to turn in large numbers to the study of photography, the formal techniques of modern art criticism were more frequently applied to photography. The most important formalist approach to analyzing photographs was that presented in John Szarkowski's 1964 book *The Photographer's Eye.* In it he argued that any photograph could be described in terms of five

variables—which he called detail, frame, vantage point, time, and the thing itself—and their interrelation. This kind of analysis was thought to provide the key to understanding the visual language of photography, and how it differed from that of painting.

During the 1970s the widespread acceptance of photography as a legitimate artistic medium gave rise to a burst of new critical activity, as art magazines and major newspapers began to turn to photography with new interest. But while a significant portion of photography criticism still continues to occupy itself with formal analysis and criticism of fine art photographs, the most recent wave of young photography critics has adopted a different perspective altogether. Influenced by earlier writers such as Walter Benjamin and Roland Barthes, they tend to see photography not simply as a fine-arts medium, but as an essential part of the image environment created by modern culture via journalistic photography, advertising photography, celebrity portraiture, publicity photography, and so on. This newest criticism seeks better to understand the ways in which photography, considered in its broadest sense, functions in today's society.

The most important critics and critic-historians have included:

(1839–1900): Francis Wey, Charles Baudelaire, O.G. Rejlander, H.P. Robinson, P.H. Emerson, Oliver Wendell Holmes.
(1900–1930): George Bernard Shaw, Sadakichi Hartmann, Alfred Stieglitz, Charles Caffin.
(1930–1960): Walter Benjamin, Lincoln Kirstein, Roger Fry, László Moholy-Nagy, Paul Strand, James Agee, Elizabeth McCausland, Ansel Adams, Beaumont and Nancy Newhall, Helmut and Alison Gernsheim, André Bazin, Siegfried Kracauer, Minor White, Ralph Hattersley, Jacob Deschin, Irving Desfor.
(1960–   ): John Szarkowski, William Ivins, Nathan Lyons, Weston Naef, Roland Barthes, Gene Thornton, Vicki Goldberg, Max Kozloff, Michael Lesy, Robert Adams, A.D. Coleman, Andy Grundberg, Colin Westerbeck, Jr., Susan Sontag, Janet Malcolm, John Berger, Rosalind Krauss, Abigail Solomon-Godeau, Alan Sekula, Ben Lifson, Victor Burgin, Alan Trachtenberg, Hubert Damisch, Martha Rosler, James Huginin.

See also: APPENDIX: BIBLIOGRAPHY.

Cropping

Cropping is the technique of using only a portion of a negative or slide, rather than the full image, to make a print. Cropping customarily is accomplished by adjusting the enlarger head and the masking blades of the printing easel until only the desired portion of the picture will be exposed on the paper. Cropping is necessary whenever an image of a particular format is printed to the full area of a printing paper with a different length-to-width ratio. For example, both 35mm and 2¼″ × 2¼″ images must be cropped to fill the area of 5″ × 7″ or 8″ × 10″ paper.

Cropping is also a means of improving a photograph. Often too much visual information is included in the picture, reducing the impact of the image. This may be due to a lack of care when the picture was composed, or to the need to work too rapidly to compose carefully, as in trying to capture children at play or follow sports action. In some cameras the viewfinder does not show exactly what the image area on the film will include, with the result that the composition may not be precisely what it seemed or as it was intended. In such cases cropping can eliminate unnecessary material outside the center of interest and can "tighten" the picture organization to increase its effectiveness.

Cropping can also provide an opportunity to rethink a picture to some degree. A landscape composition with a broad vista may look right through the viewfinder, but in a sample print it may not seem sufficiently unified. Reducing the picture to a more tightly focused central area or shifting the edges to adjust the visual balance may result in a stronger image. The possible improvements that cropping might give can be explored with two L-shaped pieces of cardboard fitted together to make a rectangular frame and laid over the print. The open center area can be made wider or narrower and the rectangle shifted over the image to try out various compositions.

Cropping is not only a corrective technique. As a tool for picture analysis it can strengthen a photographer's ability to visualize the final image while viewing the subject through the camera.
See also: COMPOSITION.

Cunningham, Imogen
American; 1883–1976
Imogen Cunningham began photographing in 1901 after being inspired by the work of Gertrude Käsebier. Born in Portland, Oregon, she graduated from the University of Washington in Seattle

with a major in chemistry and went to work in the studio of Edward S. Curtis, where she learned the process of platinum printing. In 1909 she continued her education in photographic chemistry at the Technische Hochschule in Dresden. After meeting with Käsebier and Alfred Stieglitz in New York on her return trip from Europe, Cunningham settled in Seattle around 1910 and opened a portrait studio which was an immediate success. In 1915 she married the etcher Roi Partridge. Her best known work, floral studies from her garden, was produced during the 1920s and 1930s.

One of the pioneers of modernism on the West Coast, Cunningham was among the founding members of Group *f*/64. She excelled in portraiture and after her picture of the dancer Martha Graham was published in *Vanity Fair* in 1932, she worked for the publication in New York and Hollywood until 1934. Her worked gained greater recognition after 1950; she was awarded a Guggenheim Fellowship in 1970 and in the decade that followed had exhibitions at numerous institutions, including the San Francisco Museum of Art, the Art Institute of Chicago, and the Metropolitan Museum of Art. At age 92 she began her last project, *After Ninety*, a book of portraits cut short by her death in 1976. Through her last interview, Cunningham advocated self-education in photography.

Curtis, Edward Sheriff

American; 1868–1952

Edward Curtis's well-known Indian photographs grew almost incidentally from his concerns as a turn-of-the-century Pictorialist photographer. A partner in a Seattle photography and photoengraving firm, Curtis had become an adept at Pictorialist landscape and portrait conventions. In 1896 he won a bronze medal from the Photographers' Association of America, a Pictorialist group, for his romantic images. A year later, he went into business alone as a full-time commercial Pictorialist. It was at this point that he first photographed Indians.

In his earliest pictures, Indians were merely elements in a romantic landscape. But when Curtis sailed to Alaska in 1899 as a member of the E. H. Harriman Expedition, he recognized the important role that photography could play in ethnography. The scientists on that expedition pointed out the importance of documenting the vanishing ways of Alaska's tribes, and Curtis saw how vital photography could be to that enterprise.

After his return to Seattle and a visit at the Crow Indian reservation in Montana (1900), Curtis decided to devote himself to the monumental task of documenting the dress, habits, and appearance of the North American Indians before white culture could totally destroy or assimilate them.

Between 1900 and 1906, with the eventual support of President Theodore Roosevelt and the patronage of J. Pierpont Morgan, Curtis and his large team of assistants photographed Indian tribes in the Southwest, the Great Plains, and the Pacific Northwest. The first volume of *The North American Indian* was published in 1907; the final, 20th volume was published 27 years later.

Though hailed throughout their publication years for their value as documents of American Indian culture, Curtis's photographs are probably of greater importance as evidence of the way in which those cultures were filtered through a romantic Caucasian "noble savage" sensibility and a Pictorial technique. Curtis's view of the Indian could not broach evidences that Indian culture was changing. Thus details of automobiles and manufactured goods and apparel were scratched out of his negatives when they appeared among his subjects. Skies were darkened or lightened for romantic effect. Props and costumes were hauled from Indian group to Indian group, there to be photographed on new subjects for picturesque, "timeless" effect.

Only in the last photographs made in Oklahoma and Alaska did Curtis produce relatively straight documentary images. He died in 1952, unremembered. The rarity of his 20-volume life's work (only about 250 sets were produced) has made *The North American Indian* a highly priced commodity on the photographic sales market since Curtis's rediscovery in the late 1960s.
Color photograph: p. C-11.

Curvature of Field

See: ABERRATIONS OF LENSES.

Cut

A cut is the instantaneous change from one picture to the next in motion pictures and television. It is the primary editing device to link images, because as an element of visual syntax it is essentially invisible and therefore interferes least with the viewer's subjective involvement in the content of the presentation. The other transitional devices are significantly more intrusive because they involve a measurable amount of time during which a perceptible change occurs in image intensity (fade-out, fade-in), clarity (dissolve), or sharpness (defocus, refocus).
See also: DISSOLVE; EDITING; FADE-IN/FADE-OUT.

Cutaway

The cutaway is an editing device used in developing the visual narrative in motion pictures and television. It is a cut to a

different subject or action than that of the preceding shot or the main line of development. A cutaway to an element or character directly related to the main subject, and in the same scene, may serve three basic purposes: to show the object of attention, to show a response or reaction, or to cover a gap in the action. This last use may be to accelerate the narrative development—so that the time required for a character to rise and walk to the door, for example, need not be shown—or to avoid the disturbance of a jump cut. A cutaway may also change the narrative to a different location and action occurring simultaneously with that of the first scene. Repeated cutaways and *cutbacks* between two separate lines of action constitute the narrative technique called *parallel editing*.
See also: CUT; EDITING; JUMP CUT.

Cutting, James Ambrose

American; 1814–1867
A Philadelphia photographer who was memorialized in the name Ambrotype, James Ambrose Cutting attempted to monopolize photography in America as vigorously as did W. H. F. Talbot in England. Having learned the daguerreotype and collodion processes of photography, in 1854 Cutting patented a method of presenting or packaging collodion positives on glass. The positive process itself had been invented by Frederick Scott Archer, inventor of the basic collodion process; Cutting's innovation was to cement a protective cover glass over the processed image using balsam cement around the edges, a technique already used to hold lens elements in place. The common procedure up to that time had been to cover the image with a clear varnish. In any event, protection was little needed with the collodion positive, for it was in no way as delicate as the surface of a daguerreotype, which it attempted to mimic. Cutting did not name the process, but a year later fellow Philadelphian Marcus A. Root coined the name *Ambrotype* for all

such images, and it has remained the identifying term.

Cutting, along with Isaac Rehn, also took out several other patents in 1854. The most important of these covered the idea of using bromine compounds—specifically, potassium bromide—in collodion to obtain silver bromide (the most light sensitive of the silver halides) when the plate was sensitized. Exposures of practical length were hardly obtainable without the use of bromide, but the idea was not original. As early as 1840, J. F. Goddard had discovered the use of bromine crystals to increase the sensitivity of daguerreotype plates, and Dr. C. M. Cresson had mentioned his use of bromine to Cutting a year before the patent was filed. Nevertheless, the patent gave him the right to sell licenses for any collodion photography and to sue those who operated without a license; Cutting's agents proceeded against unlicensed photographers in several areas of the U.S. In 1858 Cutting also obtained the first patent in the U.S. for a method of photolithography. He died in a mental institution in 1867, a year before the same examiner who had awarded him the bromine-collodion patent reversed himself and refused to extend the patent on the grounds that it incorporated nothing new or unknown at the time and should not have been granted in the first place.
See also: AMBROTYPE; ARCHER, FREDERICK SCOTT; GODDARD, JOHN F.; TALBOT, WILLIAM HENRY FOX.

Cyanotype

The cyanotype is the most widely used of the many iron printing processes derived from Sir John Herschel's discovery in 1841-1842 that a number of iron compounds were light sensitive. The cyanotype is also called the ferroprussiate (iron-Prussian blue) process, and most commonly the blueprint process. It has enjoyed wide popularity from time to time because its chemistry and handling are simple and it is versatile. The basic process produces a white image

with blue middletone and shadow areas; other colors can be produced, including a blue image on a white background, and prints can be made from either negatives or positive transparencies on paper or cloth sized with starch, or other materials.

Two stock percentage solutions are required for the basic cyanotype: a 20 percent solution of ferric ammonium citrate and a 10 percent solution of potassium ferricyanide. (Green citrate crystals produce greater sensitivity than brown crystals.) Equal quantities are mixed together and brushed onto the paper to coat it completely; the paper is dried in the dark. Exposure is by contact under a contrasty negative; the image prints-out, typically in about 15 minutes in direct sun, or 30 minutes under a 275-watt sunlamp. The image must be overprinted, especially in the shadows, because it will lighten during washing. No development is required; the print is simply washed for 5 to 10 minutes. A final rinse in a 1 percent hydrochloric or acetic acid solution deepens the blue tone somewhat, but a 10 percent solution of hydrogen peroxide (3 percent strength) in water is better and more permanent. To make a direct positive print from a positive transparency rather than a negative, the paper is coated only with the citrate solution; after exposure the ferricyanide solution is used as a developer and the print is washed. Formulas for producing other image colors are given in a number of works on alternative and historic printing processes.

A variation which produces a blue image on a white background was invented by H. Pellet in 1878. The paper is coated with a mixture of a 50 percent ferric chloride solution (1 part), 50 percent ferric ammonium citrate solution (1½ parts), and 20 percent gum arabic solution (4 parts). After being dried in the dark, it is exposed under a positive until a faint yellow image has printed-out; the final blue image is developed with a 20 percent potassium ferricyanide solution, and the print is washed.
See also: IRON PRINTING PROCESSES.
Color photograph: p. C-12.

Doisneau, Robert. "The Innocent" (1979). Courtesy Photo Researchers; permanent collection, ICP, New York.

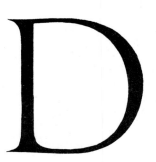

Dagor Lens

A six-element symmetrical lens noted for its high-quality image-forming capability, the original Dagor lens design was created by Emil von Hoegh of C. P. Goerz, A. G. in 1893. The first version was called the Dagor Double Anastigmat. Derived from other forms of symmetrical designs, the Dagor was a great improvement over rapid rectilinear styles. New optical glasses developed at the turn of the century (Jena glass) allowed Goerz to construct the Dagor with two symmetrical groups of three cemented elements. This greatly improved lens performance, particularly in eliminating coma and distortion. The von Hoegh calculations created a unique lens with a wide field coverage of 70 degrees at f/6.8, relatively fast for the time. Although the lens design itself was exceptional, the famous Goerz quality standards made it a notable optic and sustained its popularity over the years.

The symmetrical design allowed the front and rear lens elements to be used separately as well as together, resulting in three different focal lengths. As with other convertible lenses, image quality decreased somewhat when a single group was used. The lens was then more suitable for portraiture because of reduced sharpness and increased focal length.

Dagor-design lenses were produced by C. P. Goerz in Germany and Switzerland, and in the U.S. by Goerz American Optical. The names Golden Dagor, Dagor, and Gold Dot Dagor refer to the same design. Lenses were produced in focal lengths ranging from 40mm to 302mm. Goerz was absorbed by Schneider Corporation of America in the 1970s, and the Dagor is no longer in production.

See also: ANASTIGMAT; GOERZ, CARL PAUL; HOEGH, EMIL VON; JENA GLASS.

Daguerre, Louis Jacques Mandé

French, 1787–1851

L. J. M. Daguerre is considered the inventor of photography because he was the first to perfect a widely applicable photographic process. Daguerre's method produced a unique direct positive image on a silver-coated copper plate; it was introduced as the daguerreotype in 1839.

At the age of thirteen Daguerre was apprenticed to an architect, but in 1803 he became a pupil of Degotti, a scenic designer with the Paris Opera. Later Daguerre began work as a painter and designer for Parisian theaters, and by the 1820s he had achieved a measure of fame through his association with Prévost on a popular entertainment of the time, the panorama. His work in this field of illusionistic spectacle, a combination of painting and theater, led to his establishment of the Diorama with Charles Marie Bouton, described in a separate entry.

Daguerre's interest in the possibility of photographic representation stems from the early 1820s. By 1824 he was seriously attempting to determine a method of fixing the image projected by the camera obscura. In this he was aided by the Parisian opticians and lensmakers Charles and Vincent Chevalier, who informed him that Joseph Nicéphore Niépce was involved in similar research. After over a decade of experimentation Niépce was prepared to publish a photographic process which he termed *heliography.* Returning from a trip to London in 1827, he met Daguerre in Paris, where he was impressed by the Diorama and was persuaded not to publish his as yet imperfect research. Niépce later asked Daguerre to help in the development of heliography, and in December 1829 a joint 10-year partnership was contracted.

Prior to 1829 Daguerre had produced no significant photographic image, but under the impetus of the new partnership he began to experiment with silvered copper plates made sensitive by exposure to iodine. For five years his investigations went unrewarded, until in 1835 he left an exposed plate inside a cupboard of chemicals. Later an image appeared upon the plate, and by a process of trial and error Daguerre was able to isolate mercury vapor (from a broken thermometer) as the key to development of the latent image.

In 1833, following the death of Niépce, Daguerre renegociated his contract with his late partner's heir, Isidore,

and the firm's name was changed from Niépce-Daguerre to Daguerre and Isidore Niépce. Having developed the latent image of the exposed plate, Daguerre then attempted to make the image permanent. The fixing process was finally achieved in 1837 by washing the plate in a warm salt solution. Daguerre was then able to present one of his first successful plates to Cailleux, Curator of the Louvre, in the same year. The plate, a still life taken in Daguerre's studio, is now in the collection of the Société Française de la Photographie in Paris. During 1838 Daguerre offered Niépce's heliographic process and his own daguerreotype method for sale by subscription or outright sale at 200,000 francs. Not surprisingly, there was little response at that price, and Daguerre turned to the French government. François Dominique Arago—Deputy (senator) physicist, and astronomer—agreed that Daguerre should receive a substantial annuity and that the government should publish the process openly and without restraint.

On January 7, 1839 Arago announced Daguerre's discovery to the Académie des Sciences. A report of this communication appeared in English less than two weeks later in the *Literary Gazette*, which caused William Henry Fox Talbot to submit to Arago and Biot a report of his own negative-positive process and a claim for priority in the fixing and preservation of the image from a camera obscura in 1834. Talbot's efforts in England were announced to the Royal Institution and the Royal Society on January 25 and were made public in February.

On March 8 of the same year, the Diorama was destroyed by fire, and due to the urgent requests of Arago a bill was prepared for acceptance of the daguerreotype process by the French government. The bill proposed that for information regarding the Diorama, daguerreotype, and any future developments, Daguerre was to be granted a pension of 6,000 francs, with 4,000 francs for Isidore Niépce.

At a crowded joint meeting of both the Académie des Sciences and the Institut de France on August 19, 1839, the details of the daguerreotype process were publically described by Arago. The daguerreotype created an immediate sensation, was widely reported, and was followed later in the month by the publication of Daguerre's *Histoire et description des procédé du Daguerreotype et du Diorama*. The handbook contained technical information and illustrations of daguerreotypy and heliography, as well as a record of Arago's report to the Deputies and the action of the government.

Many awards were bestowed on Daguerre, adding to his fame. He was promoted from Chevalier d'Honneur to Officer of the Legion of Honour by Louis Philippe and was admitted as an honorary member of the Academies of Edinburgh, Munich, Vienna, and the American National Academy of Design. In 1840 Daguerre retired with his wife to an estate at Bry-sur-Marne. He seems to have been involved little in the development of photography after this time. *See also:* ARAGO, FRANCOIS; DAGUERRE-OTYPE; NIÉPCE, JOSEPH NICÉPHORE.

Daguerreotype

The first practical process of photography, invented by L. J. M. Daguerre, was presented free to the world through the

Daguerreotype. John Plumbe, "First Daguerreotype of U.S. Capitol" (1846). Library of Congress.

efforts of Francois Arago on August 19, 1839. Formed on a silver plate, the daguerreotype has the most exquisite image qualities in photography: a range of lustrous, silvery tones unattainable by any other process and a complete freedom from grain. However, the image is exceedingly delicate (it can be damaged by just a light touch of a finger), the silver plate is highly susceptible to tarnishing, and the image is a unique direct positive; it cannot generate multiple identical copies as can a negative.

Daguerreotype plates were copper, plated with silver on one side. Standard "whole plate" size was 6½″ × 8½″; smaller sizes were equal divisions of the whole plate, the most popular being quarter plate (3¼″ × 4¼″) and sixth plate (2¾″ × 3¼″). The smaller sizes were less expensive, and because they could be covered by a shorter-focal-length lens used closer to the plate, they required shorter exposures. Whole-plate exposures were typically two to three times longer than quarter-plate exposures, and at least ten times longer than sixth-plate exposures. Most photographers improved their plates by *galvanizing* (electroplating) an additional thin layer of silver on the surface. This was done by connecting the plate and a piece of silver (a coin, for example) to a wet-cell battery and suspending them in an electrolytic bath. The actual steps in making a daguerreotype were as follows.

First the corners of the plate were bent backward so it could be gripped in a holder with the face exposed for *buffing* with pumice and jeweler's rouge and a series of paddles covered with kid leather or buckskin, fine flannel, or silk. A well-buffed plate looked almost black because of the way light was scattered by the almost microscopic parallel scratches buffing produced.

The plate then was placed face down at the top of a chimneylike box about 10 in. tall for *coating*, or sensitizing. Fumes rising from a heated dish of potassium iodide cyrstals at the bottom of the box reacted with the plate to form light-sensitive silver iodide on the surface. Exposures with such a plate were typicallly 20 to 40 minutes. In 1840 J. F. Goddard discovered that a second treatment with bromine fumes greatly increased the sensitivity. Most daguerreotypists evolved their own formulas—various proportions of potassium bromide and potassium chloride crystals—for the "quickstuff" used for the second coating.

Next the plate was placed in a holder and inserted in the camera for *exposure*, made by taking the cap off the lens and replacing it after sufficient time. Using quickstuff in the sensitizing process, and the *f/3.6* Petzval lens (introduced in 1840), quarter-plate exposures of about 20 seconds were possible, making it feasible to take portraits. The mirrorlike plate produced an image reversed left-for-right unless a correcting prism or mirror was used in front of the lens.

The plate then was placed face down at a 45-degree angle in a box like the coating boxes for *mercurializing* to develop the image. Fumes of heated mercury, diffused by a piece of gauze stretched across the interior of the box,

reacted with the exposed portions of the plate to form whitish deposits of a mercury-silver amalgam. In this way the highlights and middletones of the image were brought out.

In the next step the plate was rinsed in a solution of hyposulfite of soda to destroy the light sensitivity of the unexposed, undeveloped portions of the surface. This method of *fixing* had been suggested by Sir John Herschel in 1839. Image tones were made deeper and warmer (browner) in appearance by *gilding*—treatment in a gold chloride solution, introduced in 1840 by Hippolyte Fizeau. Finally the plate was rinsed in distilled water and dried over a gentle flame.

The delicate image was protected by a cover glass sealed to the plate at the edges with gummed paper. A stamped brass mat with an oval, rectangular, or fancywork opening was placed over the glass and held with a brass binding frame pressed by hand around the edges. The entire packet was then wedged into a velvet-lined case with a padded, hinged cover; cases were made of leather-covered wood or a thermoplastically-molded compound of sawdust and shellac (called a Union case). The cost of a portrait ranged from about $2.00 for a sixth plate to more than $30.00 for a whole plate, prices that in the 1840s and 1850s were beyond most people, except for special occasions. Hand-coloring increased the price, for it was a delicate operation. Individual dots of paint could be applied to represent the beads in a necklace or gold buttons, for example, but larger areas could not safely be touched; they were treated by a stencil method invented in 1840 by a Swiss daguerreotypist, J. B. Isenring. Finely sifted dry pigment and gum arabic were mixed and sprinkled over a paper mask with openings cut for the areas, such as a face, to be tinted. Breathing by mouth on the plate provided enough warmth and moisture to make the gum arabic adhere to the surface. Apparently some direct-color daguerreotypes were made by accident at various times, but none was permanent, and the claim of Rev. Levi Hill to have invented a permanent method evidently was fraudulent.

The daguerreotype was an instant success when introduced, but it was not easily mastered. The first daguerreotype in the U.S. was made within eight weeks of the Paris demonstration in 1839, and in European countries even sooner. Daguerre's manual of instruction was translated into every major language and went through 21 editions in two years. W. H. F. Talbot's calotype process, invented at the same time, could not match

the quality of the daguerreotype, which dominated photography until the introduction of the collodion process in 1851. The daguerreotype lasted a few more years and then virtually disappeared, but it had established photography as a major medium of art and communication in the world.
See also: CALOTYPE; COLLODION PROCESS; DAGUERRE, L. J. M.

Dahl-Wolfe, Louise

American; 1895–

Louise Dahl-Wolfe worked for most of her career as a portraitist, still-life and fashion photographer for *Harper's Bazaar.* She was one of the first fashion photographers to pioneer the use of color and to shoot in faraway locations. She is known for her careful attention to composition and lighting, and for her insistence on the highest reproduction standards.

Louis Dahl was born and raised in San Francisco, California. She studied design and color with Rudolph Schaeffer and painting with Frank Van Sloan at the California School of Fine Arts (later named the San Francisco Institute of Art) from 1914 to 1917, and again in 1921–1922. She became interested in photography upon meeting and seeing the pictorial work of Annie Brigman in 1921. Her early artistic influences included Impressionist and Post-Impressionist paintings, which she encountered at the San Francisco World's Fair in 1915, and the ballets of Diagheliv and Nijinsky, which she saw performed in 1916.

Dahl worked as a sign designer for the Federal Electric Co., San Francisco from 1920 to 1922. She studied design and decoration, and architecture at Columbia University, New York in 1923. In 1924 she was employed as an assistant to decorator Beth Armstrong in San Francisco, and from 1925 to 1927 she worked for Armstrong, Carter and Kenyon, a fashion wholesale company.

In 1927–1928 Dahl traveled with photographer/journalist Consuela Kanaga in Europe. She met painter and sculptor Meyer (Mike) Wolfe in Tunisia and married him soon after. In 1929 she worked for New York decorators Hofstater and Co.

Dahl-Wolfe began to concentrate on photography in San Francisco and Tennessee in the early 1930s. Her first published photograph, "Tennessee Mountain Woman," appeared in *Vanity Fair* in 1933 and was included in the first photography show at the Museum of Modern Art, New York in 1937.

Dahl-Wolfe, Louise. "Colette" (1951). Courtesy Louise Dahl-Wolfe; permanent collection, ICP, New York.

From 1933 to 1960, Dahl-Wolfe operated a New York photographic studio that did freelance advertising and fashion photography for such stores as Bonwit Teller and Saks Fifth Avenue. From 1936 to 1958 she was a staff fashion photographer at *Harper's Bazaar* where she worked closely with editors Carmel Snow and Diana Vreeland. From 1958 until her retirement in 1960, she again worked as a freelance photographer for *Vogue, Sports Illustrated,* and other periodicals.

In addition to her fashion photography, Dahl-Wolfe made memorable portraits of people in the arts, including Colette, Edward Hopper, Bette Davis, Paul Robeson, and Cecil Beaton.

During her career she traveled widely throughout South American and Europe, to North Africa and Hawaii. In 1939 Dahl-Wolfe received the Art Directors Club of New York Medal, and two years later, she received a second award from that body. She has exhibited with her husband at the Southern Vermont Art Center, Manchester (1955), and the Country Art Gallery, Old Westbury, New York (1965).

Dahl-Wolfe's work has appeared in group shows, including *Photography 1839–1937* at the Museum of Modern Art, New York (1937); *Women of Photography: An Historical Survey* at the San Francisco Museum of Modern Art and Sidney Janis Gallery, New York (1975–1976), and *Recollections: Ten Women of Photography* at ICP, New York (1979). A major traveling show, organized by the Smithsonian Institu-

tion, Washington, D.C., circulated in 1982. A large body of Dahl-Wolfe's photographs is in the collection of the Fashion Institute of Technology, New York.

Dallmeyer, John Henry

German; 1830–1883

Dallmeyer, Thomas Ross

English; 1859–1906

The Dallmeyers, father and son, were opticians and lens manufacturers in England who produced a number of important developments in photographic lenses. J. H. Dallmeyer's first lenses were based on the Petzval lens, but had softer definition, a wider angle of view, and greater speed. The *pistolgraphe* of Thomas Skaife used a Dallmeyer portrait lens of $f/1.1$ maximum aperture. In 1866 Dallmeyer used a similar lens in a camera he patented for taking four 3″ × 4″ pictures on a single whole plate (6½″ × 8½″) which was shifted between exposures. In 1861 he had introduced a triple achromat, the first non-distorting lens, and one unequalled, until about 1890, for flatness of field and freedom from astigmatism. The Dallmeyer Rapid Rectilinear lens of 1866 (like the Steinheil Aplanat of the same year) was the first design free of barrel and pincushion distortion, and was the most famous symmetrical doublet lens—two cemented elements of equivalent optical design were located on either side of the diaphragm, facing in opposite directions, to form a convertible lens in which the components could be used individually or in combination for a total of three different focal lengths.

In 1887 T. R. Dallmeyer and F. Beauchamp patented the first between-the-lens shutter, constructed like an iris diaphragm with overlapping leaves that opened outward while maintaining a circular opening. In 1891 T. R. Dallmeyer patented the first telephoto lens design, placing an element group of negative power behind a front group of positive power. The same principle was independently introduced in Germany that same year by Dr. Adolf Miethe and C. & H. Steinheil. It permitted achieving great image magnification with as little as one-quarter of the bellows extension required with long-focus lenses. Dallmeyer's soft-focus Bergheim Portrait Lens of 1896 was one of the first varifocal lenses, with a focal-length range from 35 to 55 inches.

Other Dallmeyer innovations included the first single wide-angle lens, improvements in telescope design, and a number of advanced convertible and varifocal designs. T. R. Dallmeyer received the Progress Medal of the Royal Photographic Society and served as its president from 1900 to 1903.

See also: ACHROMAT; GUN CAMERAS; LENSES; PETZVAL, J.; STEINHEIL, C. A. & H. A.; VARIFOCAL LENS.

Dance Photography
See: THEATRICAL AND DANCE PHOTOGRAPHY.

Dancer, John Benjamin
English; 1812–1887
Dancer was an optician, microscopist, and instrument maker. He first took daguerreotypes in 1840 with a camera of his own design, and made the first daguerreotype through a microscope, using a gas-illuminated instrument. (Others made calotypes in the same year using solar microscopes.) In 1853 he reversed the idea and made the first reduced-size copies which were so small they could only be viewed in a microscope. Such images were later a popular novelty known as Stanhopes. In 1853 he also produced the first version of a stereoscopic camera, which he patented and began to manufacture in 1856. It was based on Sir David Brewster's suggestion for a twin-lens design. In final form it had matched lenses, each covered by a revolving plate with four different apertures, and shutters of Dancer's own design. The lens board moved on geared tracks for focusing. A plate-holding box below the camera body also moved on tracks so that 12 glass plates could be lifted individually into picture-taking position by means of a slot in the bottom of the camera and a hooked rod that engaged a loop on the top of a wooden frame holding each plate.

See also: MICROPHOTOGRAPHY; PHOTOMICROGRAPHY; STANHOPE; STEREOSCOPE.

Dark-Field Illumination
The dark-field lighting technique is used in microscopy, close-up photography, and macrophotography. The subject is illuminated, but the surrounding area (background) is not and thus appears black. Dark-field illumination is especially valuable for revealing the internal structure of translucent subjects by means of light shone through from behind, and for revealing delicate edge detail by backlighting. In microscopes it is created by an opaque center stop between the light source and the substage condenser. This blocks the central rays directed toward the lens and permits only the outer rays to reach the subject. The outer rays are passing at cross-angles that would miss the lens, but when they strike the subject many are diffused toward the lens, with the result that the subject has a transilluminated glow. With opaque subjects in non-microscope setups, frontal light is used in combination with a highly light-absorbent background (e.g., black velvet) preferably placed some distance behind the subject.

See also: BRIGHT-FIELD ILLUMINATION.

Darkroom
A lighttight room is required for processing film and for making contact prints and enlargements. The working space in a darkroom is customarily divided into "wet" and "dry" areas. The wet area is where the processing is done. It contains the trays or tanks for chemical solutions and preferably a sink and running water. The dry area is where the enlarger is used and where printing accessories are kept.

A darkroom must provide complete darkness for certain procedures. These include loading roll film into a developing tank, developing sheet film in trays or deep tanks, and some aspects of color printing. With black-and-white printing papers, and with some color papers, a properly filtered safelight can be used for working illumination.

Ideally, a darkroom will contain sufficient working space and facilities to provide for all the requirements of film and print processing. In an amateur's home darkroom, however, compromises usually will have to be made. Both storage space and a wash area may have to be located outside the darkroom, for example. Such limitations need not compromise print quality for a skillful and careful worker.

All darkrooms, whether professional or temporary, must be adequately ventilated for protection against chemical dust and fumes. They also must be kept scrupulously clean to prevent contamination of solutions and other photographic materials, and in some cases to protect other household members.

A darkroom is absolutely necessary only for processing sheet film and for print-making. Roll film can be loaded into a lightproof (daylight type) tank in any area that can be made completely dark, or in a changing bag, and then processed anywhere that is convenient.

Davidson, Bruce
American, 1933–
Bruce Davidson has been a noted personal documentary photo-essayist since the late 1950s. Capturing quiet moments of privacy and loneliness, his unembellished, extended portraits of the ways of life of outsiders and the disenfranchised in contemporary America have been widely influential among younger photographers.

Born in Oak Park, Illinois, Davidson was actively interested in photography from the age of ten. He assisted a commercial photographer in Chicago during his teens. From 1953 to 1956 he studied photography with Ralph Hattersley at the Rochester Institute of Technology. He did photographic illustration for Eastman Kodak Chemical Products briefly before studying philosophy and graphic arts at the Yale University School of Design with Josef Albers in 1957. A photostory of Davidson's football locker-room images was published in *Life* while Davidson was improving his technical skills as a darkroom technician and photographer in the United States Army.

Davidson began freelancing in New York and Paris, where he photographed his famous "Widow of Montmartre" series. His early influences were Henri Cartier-Bresson and W. Eugene Smith. He joined Magnum as an associate photographer in 1958 and became a full member the following year. Working for Magnum allowed Davidson the freedom to pursue stories of his own conception as well as assignments. From 1959 to 1969 he published photo-essays on a

Davidson, Bruce. "Circus Clown Midget" (1958). Bruce Davidson/Magnum.

not a compound; the presence of hydrogen in acids; the electrical nature of chemical reactions; the principles of electrolysis; and the isolation of pure potassium, sodium, calcium, barium, boron, magnesium, and strontium. His most famous invention was a safety lamp for miners in which a tube of metal mesh around the open flame of an oil lamp transmitted light, but dissipated the heat so rapidly that the flame could not ignite the explosive gases prevalent in mines. Davy's role in the first documented experiments to record images on materials made sensitive to light, which occurred in about 1799, is described in the entry for his fellow investigator, Thomas Wedgwood.

Day, Frederick Holland
American, 1864–1933
F. Holland Day was a literary aesthete among the first proponents of photography as a fine art, and an early leader of the Pictorialist movement whose ideas and images were influential at the turn of the century. Day was a superb portraitist, a fine printer, and the bearer of high standards regarding framing, mounting, and reproduction of photographs, but his career included little more than a decade of real artistic achievement. The almost total neglect of his work until recent years was due to a number of factors. Day's "decadent" aestheticism has not worn well. The scandals which greeted the appearance of his mythological nudes and Crucifixion images, as well as those created by his publishing works by Oscar Wilde and Aubrey Beardsley, seemed somewhat trivial to later generations, suggesting that he too was trivial.

Today he appears even more eccentric perhaps than he did to his contemporaries. He fought a losing battle with Alfred Stieglitz for leadership of the American photographic art community, so his work was not firmly linked to that of a movement such as, the Photo-Secession (which he declined to join). Finally, a fire in his studio destroyed much of his work in 1904, making the evidence for evaluation fragmentary.

Day was born to great wealth in Norwood, Massachusetts, and was educated privately. Before beginning to photograph in about 1887, Day was a confirmed bibliophile, one of the earliest admirers of Keats, whose imagery was a lasting influence on his photography. In 1885 Day and the Catholic poet Louise Imogen Guiney, with whom he was to share a lifelong relationship, began a search for Keatsiana which was to result in significant discoveries of letters and

variety of subjects in magazines such as *Realities, Du, Look, Life, Esquire,* and *Vogue.*

Davidson was a Guggenheim Fellow in 1962. He taught at the School of Visual Arts in New York City in 1964 and later in private workshops. He photographed Los Angeles ghettos during 1966, and began a two-year project of controversial photographs of New York's Spanish Harlem (East 100th Street) in 1968. He received a grant from the National Endowment for the Arts for this work in 1969 and published a selection of the images in 1970.

In the next decade Davidson turned to film-making, including adaptations from the work of Novel Laureate I.B. Singer. His color essay, *Subway,* was exhibited at the International Center of Photography in 1983, with a book planned for publication in 1984.

Davy, Sir Humphry
English; 1778–1829
Humphry Davy was a brilliant chemist and physicist whose discoveries included the properties of nitrous oxide (laughing gas); the fact that chlorine is an element,

Day, Frederick Holland. "Christ with Mary and Saint" (1898). Library of Congress.

manuscripts. Day was also obsessed with the work of writers such as Balzac and Maeterlinck.

Day joined the Boston Camera Club in 1891, and by 1896 he had become only the third American to be elected to the Linked Ring Brotherhood. In 1895 George Davison wrote to Stieglitz to call his attention to Day's talent. In 1897 day was invited by Stieglitz to be represented in *Camera Notes,* and he soon became a regular contributor of photographs and texts including articles on art and the camera, which evidenced his wide knowledge of painting from Rembrandt to Whistler. At this time Day began lasting friendships with Clarence White and Gertrude Käsebier. He exhibited 100 prints at the New York Camera Club and started a series of sacred images concerning the last days of Christ. Day began to compete with Stieglitz for the

attention of European photographers as a spokesman for pictorialism and an organizer of exhibitions. The two men never resolved their conflicts despite repeated overtures from both sides.

In 1899 Day was a member of the jury for the Philadelphia Photographic Salon with Käsebier, White, Johnston, and Troth. He gave up the publishing firm he had owned with Herbert Copeland for the previous six years and undertook projects such as the hanging of White's one-man show at the Boston Camera Club. The next year he traveled to England with the young Alvin Coburn, a distant cousin, to organize the controversial *New School of American Photography* exhibition at the Royal Photographic Society.

Day exhibited many important works at his Boston studio as well, including photographs by Frederick Evans,

Coburn, and Käsebier, and the drawings of Kahlil Gibran. In 1904 a fire in the studio destroyed thousands of prints, negatives, paintings, and drawings. Day made very few photographs after the catastrophe, but he did occasionally exhibit, perhaps most notably at the London Photographic Salon after a ten-year absence. He was bedridden in 1917 and lived in seclusion for many years, pursuing genealogical and horticultural studies and continuing his explorations of the work of Keats. He died in his family home in 1933.

See also: LINKED RING BROTHERHOOD; PHOTO SECESSION; PICTORIAL PHOTOGRAPHY; PICTORIALISM.

Dayal, Lalla Deen

Indian; 1844–1910

Lalla Deen Dayal, as gregarious as he was able, was one of the first Indian photographers to be successful and to be respectfully recognized by the British Government in India as well as by an Indian elite. Born in Sardhana, he moved to Indore about 1865 where, after being educated as a civil engineer, he worked as a draftsman in the Indore Public Works Department and at some point apparently began to teach himself photography; in 1874 he started to study photography in a formal way. Two years later he took a leave of absence from his job to travel through India and build up a catalog of photographs of monuments, sites, and people that he hoped would become the foundation of a photographic business. His choice of subjects reflected a double world, for he photographed the scenes he thought the British would want and those, like the Jain temples in Rajasthan (he was a Jain), that were close to his heart.

Dayal opened his first studio, in Indore, about 1878 and soon was noted for his capacity to make photographs in both an indigenous style—with many points of interest and a tendency toward representing a flattened space—and in a traditional Western style using one-point perspective. In the 1880s he photographed various army camps, providing highly charged pictures of troops on maneuvers at Delhi, Secunderabad, Meerut, and Poona. Many of these were printed in various books and were highly regarded for their "instantaneous" character, although most were in fact posed situations. Dayal also took formal portraits of viceroys, commanding officers, and a range of British civil and military leaders with their families. His group portraits of this period were printed in deep, meticulous albumen tones that glowed with a gold-intesification finish he developed. His work was much admired by both the British and Indian worlds, and Sir Lepel Griffin included 89 of his photographs in *Famous Monuments of Central India* (London, 1888), a volume with close to 500 pictures of India and an explanatory text.

Dayal opened a second studio, the first of a succession in Bombay, about 1888. His third location in that city, established in 1896, became the most fashionable in India, a gathering place for Bombay's elite. Such notables as J. J. Tata, India's first major industrialist, and the Nizam of Hyderabad continuously made their way there. Having become an official photographer to the Nizam in 1884, Dayal moved to Secunderabad, close to Hyderabad, and established a studio there, leaving the Indore and Bombay operations in the charge of his sons. Under the eventual management of his second son, Gyan Chandra, these studios developed a broader and deeper reach into the Indian community. In the first decade of the 20th c., nobles, merchants, and community leaders—a middle range of successful Indian notables—became the foundation of the Dayal studio clientele.

In 1894 Deen Dayal was honored by the Nizam and given the honorary title of Raja. Following custom, at the age of 50, he went into semiretirement to photograph only for the Nizam, leaving virtually all other activities to his studios. At the height of their activities, at the turn of the century, the studios provided a full range of services—black-and-white photographs; painted photographs done in the Indian style (many on ivory or porcelain); reprints of earlier photographs; enlargements (usually retouched and charcoalled for artistic effect); studio portraits; oil transfer prints; and portraits painted as copies from studio photographs. In addition, photographs were distributed through various commercial agents throughout India.

At the height of this activity, Dayal employed as many as 50 people, including a woman, who photographed Muslim women (who were not to be seen by men); an Englishman, who was most expert at making photographs in the Western style; retouching and refinishing experts; a specialist in coloring ivory and porcelain images; and an Italian artist/photographer who was expert in producing enlarged oil portraits. Others were field photographers, sent to photograph road building and other projects instituted by the Nizam to provide work and food in periods of drought and famine.

Near the end of his life, Deen Dayal recalled his photographic career in a

hand-penned autobiographical statement; with loving remembrance, he looked back upon the days when he was first an amateur. He died in 1910.

Daylight

Daylight is natural illumination which varies widely in color composition, intensity, and character. The light for which daylight-type color films are balanced is considered to have a color temperature of 5500K. (Most electronic flash illumination has a similar color temperature, so the two kinds of light can be mixed freely without problems of color balance.) This "photographic daylight" is equivalent to an average mixture of direct sun and open blue-sky illumination as found in the U.S. on a clear day between about 10 A.M. and 4 P.M. Earlier and later in the day, daylight has a lower color temperature and is considerably warmer (redder) in appearance. This is because when the sun is at a low angle its light has to travel a greater distance through the earth's atmosphere, and the blue wavelengths are scattered to a greater degree than the green and red wavelengths. For properly balanced color photography with such light, a bluish filter is required. Conversely, the light from the open sky without direct sun has a very high color temperature (as much as 12,000 to 18,000K) and is very blue. This kind of light falls on a subject in an area shaded from the direct sun but open to the sky; a reddish or yellowish filter is required to adjust the light to the color balance of daylight-type film. Various degrees of overcast tend to screen out red rays, making the light bluer than normal as well as reducing its intensity. Direct sunlight is extremely intense; in highly reflective situations such as snow, sand, or a body of open water, the light is even more intense.

Proper daylight exposure can be estimated from the sky condition and the ISO (ASA) arithmetic film speed. For a subject lighted from the front by direct sun, average exposure is $f/16$ at a shutter speed of $1/$film speed (e.g., a shutter speed of $1/125$, with an ISO 125 film). In beach or snow conditions, one stop less exposure ($f/22$) is required. Cloudy bright-sky illumination with no distinct subject shadows requires about two stops more exposure ($f/8$), and heavy-overcast or open-shade illumination requires about three stops more ($f/5.6$). Most photographers rely on bracketing for good results when estimating exposure.

The character of daylight varies from the harshness of direct sun, which creates bright highlights and casts deep, hard-edged shadows, to the soft, directionless quality of heavy overcast, which provides no modelling or shadows and tends to reduce forms to flat shapes. In general, somewhat diffuse daylight, as on a bright overcast day, provides a brightness range and degree of modelling that produce the most pleasing results with color film.

See also: BRACKETING; COLOR BALANCE; COLOR TEMPERATURE.

De Carava, Roy. "Man coming up subway stairs" (1953). Courtesy Roy De Carava.

Decamired

The decamired is a unit of value used to rate the effect of filters on the color temperature of light; it is related to the *mired*. The decamired value of light is equal to 100,000 divided by the color temperature of the light, or equal to the mired value of the light divided by 10. Some manufacturers identify their color control filters as R (reddish, warming) or B (bluish, cooling) plus the shift in decamireds the filter can produce. Thus, an R10 (or R10DM, or +10DM) filter produces a 10-decamired shift that warms (reddens, lowers the color temperature of) the light. A B5 (B5DM; −5DM) filter cools the light (raises the color temperature, makes it bluer) the equivalent of 5 decamireds. Some color-temperature light meters give readings in decamireds, or directly in R and B filter values.

See also: COLOR TEMPERATURE; MIRED.

DeCarava, Roy

American, 1919–

Roy DeCarava first won acclaim in 1955 for his collaboration with writer Langston Hughes on *The Sweet Flypaper of Life,* a classic book about everyday life in Harlem. DeCarava has photographed black life over three decades with tenderness and an acute sense of harsh political realities. His subjects have included jazz musicians (John Coltrane, Billie Holiday, and Lester Young), children, and New York City street life.

James Hinton has praised DeCarava as "the first black man who chose by intent to document the black and human experience in America . . . . He has never wavered from that commitment. He was the first to devote serious attention to the black aesthetic as it relates to photography and the black experience in America."

DeCarava was born in New York City and grew up in Harlem. He graduated from Textile High School and studied painting at Cooper Union from 1938 to 1940. From 1940 to 1942 he studied painting and print-making at the Harlem Art Center, and he attended the George Washington Carver Art School in 1944.

DeCarava started photographing in 1946 to document his paintings. The following year a one-man exhibition of his serigraphs was held at Serigraph Gallery in New York. He gave up painting to devote himself to photography. His first solo exhibition of photographs was held at the Forty-Fourth Street Gallery in New York in 1950.

In 1952 DeCarava became the first black artist to receive a Guggenheim Fellowship. The photographs he made during his Fellowship year included many which appeared in *Sweet Flypaper.* . . . From 1954 to 1956 DeCarava operated A Photographer's Gallery in New York, one of the first galleries devoted to photography as a fine art. Among the photographers he exhibited were Ralph Eugene Meatyard, Harry Callahan, and Ruth Bernhard. DeCarava's own work appeared in the *Family of Man* exhibition of 1955 and was particularly admired by Edward Steichen.

DeCarava worked as a commercial artist, photographing in his spare time, until 1958 when he began to freelance as a photographer. From 1963 to 1966 he ran the Kamoinge Workshop for young black photographers. He worked in the late 1960s as a contract photographer for *Sports Illustrated.*

In 1972 DeCarava received the Benin Award for his contributions to the black community as a photographer. In 1975 he was appointed Associate Professor of Art at Hunter College in New York, where he continues to teach. He was commissioned by the Corcoran Gallery in Washington, D.C., to photograph that city as a Bicentennial project.

DeCarava has had over 15 one-man shows, including major retrospectives at the Museum of Fine Arts in Houston (1975), the Witkin Gallery in New York (1980), and the Studio Museum in Harlem (1983). He lives and works in Brooklyn, New York.

Deckel, Friedrich
German; 1871–1948
Deckel was an engineer and manufacturer of precision instruments. His Compound shutter, introduced in 1902, raised the diaphragm shutter—invented in 1887 by T. R. Dallmeyer and F. Beauchamp—to a new level of precision. It was "compound" because it had two mechanisms: a spring-driven clockwork system for speeds from 1/25 to 1/200 sec., and a pneumatic-retard air cylinder to control speeds from 1 sec. to 1/10 sec. In 1912 Deckel produced a much improved design, the Compur shutter, which is still the basic design used in many view camera lenses. It replaced the air cylinder, which had proved troublesome in field work, with a precision gear train for the slow speeds; the clockwork mechanism for the higher speeds was redesigned as well. The shutter was cocked with a lever, and speeds were selected in early models by turning a small dial mounted at the top of the rim. This dial was later replaced by a milled edge by which the entire rim was turned to change speed settings; it was easier to grip and less likely to be accidentally moved out of position. Further refinements increased the maximum speed to 1/500 sec. Deckel's company eventually became part of Zeiss-Ikon; today Compur shutters are manufactured by Prontor-Werke.

Definition
Definition is the relative clarity of details, shapes, tones, and colors in an image. It is the composite result of resolving power, acutance, sharpness, edge effects, graininess, and contrast, each of which is discussed in a separate entry. The starting point for the highest possible definition is a slow, fine-grain, thin-emulsion film; an apochromatic (three-color corrected) lens; and a camera or film holder that will keep the film absolutely flat. In precision work glass or metal plates are used instead of film to ensure flatness. Factors that limit or degrade definition with any lens-film-camera combination include unclean lens surfaces, flare, vibration, diffraction, overexposure, and overdevelopment. These factors are as important when a print is made, particularly an enlargement, as when the film is exposed in the camera.

Demachy, Robert. "Unidentified woman" (1899). The Gernsheim Collection, Humanities Research Center, University of Texas at Austin.

Demachy, Robert
French; 1859–1937
Robert Demachy, a central figure of the Pictorial movement in Paris, is best known for his mastery of the gum bichromate process, which he used to create some of the masterpieces of turn-of-the-century Impressionistic photography. These ranged in subject matter from portraits and landscapes to urban views, nudes, studies of dancers, and pictures of the then new phenomenon of the automobile. Demachy was a vocal and prolific defender of Pictorial photography, writing extensively on the aesthetic aspects of print manipulation and

on the technical processes he used to create his images.

Throughout his photographic life, Demachy was a staunch and unrelenting proponent of the painterly image. His criticism of "straight" photography often bordered on disdain; he claimed that an unmanipulated photograph taken directly from nature was not artistic per se, being little more than a mediocre representation of a theme to which the true artist brought his own hand. This view is well expressed in Demachy's gum prints, which often echo the techniques and style of Degas and other Impressionist painters.

The son of a wealthy banker, Demachy was born in the Paris suburb of St. Germain-en-Laye. As a young man, Demachy worked as a banker himself, indulging in painting and music as hobbies. In 1880 he became seriously interested in photography; his early platinum prints were received well enough for him to be elected to the Société Française de la Photographie in 1882. His artistry grew, and a decade later his photographs were included in the first international photographic exhibition held at the Palais des Beaux Arts in Paris.

In 1894, Demachy found a newly improved version of the gum bichromate process so much to his liking that he began to use it immediately. He capitalized on the manipulation of color and texture the process offered to produce images with prominent brushstrokes and suppressed background details for the next 12 years.

In 1894 Demachy also founded the *Photo Club de Paris*, along with C. Puyo, Maurice Buquet, and other Pictorialists. The group's first exhibition, the French Salon, was held in the same year. Demachy served as a member of the editorial board of a publication containing reproductions of pictures from the exhibition. It was through this folio of pictures that Alfred Stieglitz first became aware of Demachy's work. On the basis of the exhibition and this publication, Demachy was elected to the ranks of the Linked Ring in 1895. One of the founders of the Linked Ring, Alfred Maskell, also had become deeply interested in the gum bichromate process, and collaborated with Demachy on a book that became the classic text on methods and materials: *Photo Aquatint, or The Gum Bichromate Process* (London, 1897).

By 1899, Stieglitz had acquired original prints made by Demachy, and had communicated his appreciation of Demachy's efforts to Clarence H. White, who included examples of the work in group shows held at the Newark (Ohio) Camera Club. Stieglitz published reproductions of Demachy's work, first in *Camera Notes* and, in the years that followed, several times in *Camera Work*.

In 1905 Demachy was given honorary membership in the Royal Photographic Society, and was awarded the French Legion of Honor for outstanding contribution to French culture. With Puyo as collaborator, Demachy selected the French entries, which included a number of his own photographs, to the 1905 London Photo Salon.

In this same period, Demachy began to experiment with the Rawlings oil process. The results pleased him enough to make him stop using gum bichromate completely by 1906. Together with Puyo, Demachy published a treatise, entitled *Les Procédés d'Art et Photographie* (Paris, 1906), outlining his aesthetic views. By now, Demachy had become the prominent spokesperson for the French Pictorialists. By virtue of his ongoing association with Stieglitz, he was given the task of selecting France's entries to the Photo-Secession galleries show of 1906.

Five years later, after much experimentation, Demachy introduced the oil transfer printing method, examples of which he exhibited in 1910 at the Society of Amateur Artists in Paris. Another exhibition of his work in oil transfer was given the same year in his Paris studio. Demachy continued to use the oil transfer method until the outbreak of the Great War in 1914, when he dropped photography altogether and began to sketch. The last major exhibition of his photographic work while he was still living took place in 1931 at the Studio St. Jacques, Paris; the show consisted of a retrospective of Demachy's gum prints, along with work of his friend Puyo. Demachy died in 1937.

See also: GUM BICHROMATE PROCESS; OIL PRINTS; PICTORIAL PHOTOGRAPHY/ PICTORIALISM.

de Meyer, Baron Adolf (Gayne)

French; 1868–1946

Baron de Meyer is best remembered for his stylish photographs of socialites, actresses, and fashion models in *Vogue* and *Vanity Fair* in the decades 1910–1930, but his first celebrity was as an English Pictorialist before World War I.

De Meyer, who made his home in London before the War, first exhibited in a Linked Ring salon in 1898. He became a member of the Ring in 1906 and later exhibited at Alfred Stieglitz's New York gallery, 291. Along with his serious Pictorialist work, de Meyer also photographed the wealthy and fashionable circle surrounding the Prince of Wales (later Edward VII). In fact, his baronetcy was created by the King of Saxony specifically so that de Meyer and his stylish wife, Olga (reputedly the illegitimate daughter of Edward VII), could attend the coronation as members of the peerage. As a patron of Diaghilev and the Ballets Russes, de Meyer helped sponsor that troupe's first London appearance in 1911 and there photographed Nijinsky.

When World War I broke out, de Meyer's title meant repatriation to the land of his title or internment in an English prisoner-of-war camp; he elected instead a third course: life in America, where Condé Nast had offered him a post as photographer on his fashionable journals, *Vogue* and *Vanity Fair*. De Meyer's high-key, soft-focus images of American celebrities won him fame throughout the 1910s and 1920s. His ornate style with dazzling rim light and elegant settings, was perfect for that period, but was ill-suited to the hard-edged, tough-minded realism of 1930s fashion photography; his work fell from favor. De Meyer moved to Los Angeles after his wife's death in 1929; he died there in 1946, his supremely glamorous and idealized photography a relic of a more innocent age.

Photograph: p. 140.

Densitometry

Photographic densitometry is the part of sensitometry that deals with measuring the results of exposure and processing. Specifically, densitometry measures the opacity of silver or dye images in films and prints; in order to plot the measurements on a linear graph, they are expressed as the logarithms of opacity, called densities. Density measurements are used to determine film speed, evaluate exposure and processing, measure contrast, examine color response, measure granularity, and investigate a number of other factors.

Measurements are made with a densitometer, a specialized photometer that compares the amount of light directed at the image with the amount of light that passes through or is reflected. In an optical densitometer the comparison is made by eye: the brightness of a reference patch of light is adjusted to match the brightness of the area being measured. In a photoelectric or electronic densitometer the comparison is made by a photocell and associated circuitry. Negatives and transparencies are measured with a transmission densitometer, which shines light through the image. Prints are measured with a reflection densitometer, which shines light onto the

is accomplished by taking the readings through primary color filters: a red filter for the cyan layer, a green filter for the magenta layer, and a blue filter for the yellow layer. The resulting characteristic curve thus has three plot lines. In evaluating color exposure, filtration, or processing, it is common to use material exposed to a neutral gray test card, which reflects all wavelengths equally. For general purposes, color density readings can be taken through a set of standard filters, Nos. 92 (red), 93 (green), and 94 (blue). For precise color sensitometry, special filter sets are used: Status A filters for transparencies and projection images; Status M filters for negatives; and Status D filters for prints.

See also: CHARACTERISTIC CURVE; COLOR MATERIALS; DENSITY; EDGE EFFECTS; GRAIN/GRAININESS AND GRANULARITY; PHOTOMETER; PHOTOMETRY; SENSITOMETRY; SPEED OF MATERIALS; STEP WEDGE.

Density

Density is a measure of the light-blocking (or light-absorbing) power of a silver or dye deposit in a photographic emulsion; it is also the logarithm of the opacity of the deposit. Density measurements are plotted against the logarithms of the exposures received by various parts of an emulsion to produce the characteristic curve of its response. Even unexposed portions of films have measurable density composed of the slight light absorption of the base material and the trace of fog produced by development. The first printable density (i.e., that can produce a tone just perceptibly lighter than maximum black in a print) is about 0.1 above the filmbase-plus-fog density of most films. The density range of a negative, measured from the minimum printable density to the density of a diffuse highlight, is an indication of the overall contrast of the image (but not necessarily of the local contrast between distinguishable tones).

In general, a density range of 0.80 is required to produce a full-range black-and-white print on No. 2 contrast-grade paper using a condenser enlarger; a density range of 1.05 is required with a diffusion enlarger, or to make a contact print. Shorter density ranges require higher grades of contrast to make equivalent prints. In the moderately and heavily exposed portions of an emulsion, the amount of density formed varies with the degree of development; in the least-exposed areas even brief development produces all the density that can be formed. Excess density caused by over-

surface from a 45-degree angle; the reading is taken at a 90-degree angle to the area illuminated. The area measured is quite small—typically a circle no more than ⅛-in. (3mm) in diameter. A microdensitometer, used to measure granularity and examine edge effects, may read an area only 0.0004 in. (0.01mm) wide. Measurements are made directly in logarithmic density units and displayed on a dial, a scale with an indicator needle, or a digital readout panel. The scale range for continuous-tone films is 0–3.0 and for graphic arts (lith) films 0–6.0; reflection densitometers commonly have a range of 0–4.0. In each case the scale limit is higher than the maximum density that kind of material can produce.

Density measurements of an image may be compared to one another, for example to determine the range between shadows and highlights, or they may be plotted against distance as they are taken step-by-step across a particular area; this is commonly the procedure in microdensitometry. Most often, densities are plotted against the logarithm of exposure received in each area; the result is a graph of the emulsion response for the stated processing, called a *characteristic curve*. In sensitometry, an emulsion is given a series of increasing exposures, usually by means of a *step wedge*, to provide a known base against which to plot the densities. A single reading of each area is sufficient with black-and-white images. However, with a visual densitometer it is common to take at least three separate readings of an area and average them to cancel out variations in visual judgment. Because color images are formed in three emulsion layers, a separate reading must be made for each layer in the area measured. This

development is a primary source of graininess in an image.
See also: CHARACTERISTIC CURVE; CONTRAST; DENSITOMETRY; FOG/FOGGING; GRAIN/GRAININESS AND GRANULARITY; SENSITOMETRY.

Depth of Field

The range in front of and behind a sharply focused subject in which details also look sharp in the final image is called depth of field. It occurs because the eye cannot distinguish between a circle smaller than a particular limiting size and a sharply-focused point in the image. Thus, although cones of light rays from subject points at various distances do not converge exactly at the image plane, if they form circles sufficiently small as they cross the plane, they will appear equally sharp. Anything that causes the cone angles to be smaller at the image plane increases the depth of field at the subject. In operative terms, this is accomplished by setting the lens aperture to a smaller f-stop, by moving farther away from the subject, or by changing to a shorter-focal-length lens; a combination of two or all three procedures will further increase depth of field. Conversely, depth of field is decreased by using a larger f-stop, a longer-focal-length lens, or a position closer to the subject.

Depth of field is primarily related to image size. When used at the same f-stop, and at distances which produce equal image sizes, all lenses—regardless of focal length—produce the same depth of field. The depth-of-field scales on lens barrels and the tables in manufacturers' literature are based on a circle of confusion small enough to permit the usual degree of enlargement required to make prints from a particular film size. A reasonably accurate calculation can be made from the hyperfocal distance of the lens for the f-stop to be used in a given situation as follows. Divide the hyperfocal distance, H, by the focused lens-to-subject distance, u, to get the quantity n:

$$n = H \div u$$

Then the near limit, N_L (distance from the camera to where the depth of field begins), and the far limit, F_L (distance to the end of the depth of field), can be determined from H and n:

$$N_L = H \div (n + 1) \text{ and } F_L = H \div (n - 1)$$

At subject distances within the normal focusing range of a lens, the total depth of field lies about one third in front of the subject and two thirds behind. In

Depth of Field

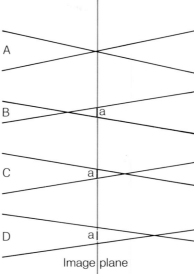

A = Cone of light rays from subject point at focused distance

B = Cone of light rays from a more distant subject point

C = Cone of light rays from a closer subject point

D = Cone of light rays from a subject point closer than C

a = Limiting size of circle of confusion

Depth of Field. Subject points corresponding to A, B, and C are within the depth of field and will look sharp in the final image. Subject point corresponding to D is closer than the near limit of depth of field and will not look sharp.

close-up and macrophotography, it is essentially equally divided on either side of the subject plane.
See also: CIRCLE OF CONFUSION; HYPERFOCAL DISTANCE.

Depth of Focus

The zone of sharpness on either side of the image plane of a lens is called depth of focus. In a sense, inside the camera at the film plane it corresponds to depth of field outside the camera at the focused subject plane. Depth of focus begins in front of the image plane, at the plane where converging cones of light reach the limiting size of the circle of confusion; it ends behind the image plane where diverging cones of light reach that diameter. At most it is a few hundredths of an inch deep; it varies with the same factors that change depth of field because their effect is to increase or decrease the angle of the light cones, caus-

Depth of Focus

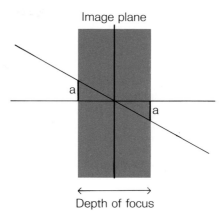

a = Limiting size of circle of confusion

ing the limiting planes to occur farther from or closer to the image plane. Depth of focus provides some focusing latitude; as long as the film is within this zone, the image will have the same degree of sharpness. If portions of the film should buckle or bulge outside the depth-of-focus limits, the image in those areas will no longer appear sharp. It is the function of pressure plates and other film-holding features in cameras to keep the film within these limits. In very large-format cameras (8″ × 10″ and larger), film held only at the extreme edges may easily sag enough in the center to create this problem, especially if the camera is aimed at a downward angle. In precise work such as graphic arts photography and photofabrication the problem is overcome by the use of a vacuum back to hold the film or by the use of glass, plastic, or metal plates instead of film.
See also: CIRCLE OF CONFUSION; DEPTH OF FIELD.

Desensitizing

Desensitizing is a chemical treatment to reduce the light sensitivity of an exposed emulsion, usually to permit processing such as inspection development under brighter than normal safelight conditions. Desensitizers are dye compounds; the most widely used are phenosafranine, pinakryptol green, and pinakryptol yellow. They can be used as a prebath, before development, or (except pinakryptol yellow) they can be added to a developer. However, their performance with modern films of high color sensitivity and emulsion speed and contemporary developers is not easily predictable.

More satisfactory results may be obtained by the use of a commercially prepared desensitizer, most of which are based on these or related compounds. *See also:* LATENSIFICATION; REDUCTION.

Developing Agent

A developing agent is any of a number of chemicals that can convert the latent image of a film or print to a visible state. The most common developing agents are metol, hydroquinone, Phenidone, pyro, glycin, para-aminophenol, and para-phenylene diamine. Virtually all contemporary developers work principally by oxidation-reduction of light-sensitive crystals in the emulsion. During exposure a minute part of an exposed silver halide crystal is reduced to metallic silver by the photoelectric effect of the light; the remainder of the crystal is unaffected. The developing agent completes reduction of exposed crystals to metallic silver.

Although many developing agents are at least slightly active in a chemically neutral solution, the time required for development is impractically long. To increase their activity and effectiveness, most agents are used in an alkaline solution; the higher the pH, the faster working the developer. The activity of the agent also varies with the solution temperature—as the temperature rises, activity increases—but the useful range is limited. Temperatures below 65°F (18°C) may require excessively long developing times. Below 55°F (13°C), hydroquinone—one of the most widely used developing agents—is completely inactive. Over 100°F (38°C) there is risk of emulsion damage, and emulsion fog is produced. Black-and-white developers are commonly used at 68°F (20°C). In color processing greater activity is required to limit the length of time the emulsion is immersed in the solutions; consequently, temperatures in the range of 85–100°F (29–38°C) are used.

The effects various developing agents have on image characteristics differ according to their chemical properties. Some agents produce very fine grain, while others yield maximum emulsion speed. Hydroquinone, for example, produces excellent contrast and highlight density, but has relatively little effect in shadow areas; metol performs in the opposite way. Many developers include more than one developing agent in order to obtain a combination of characteristics and more efficient action. *See also:* DEVELOPMENT; OXIDATION-REDUCTION; pH; SUPERADDITIVITY.

Developing-Out Materials

Almost all films and papers have emulsions that require only brief exposure to form a latent image which is subsequently converted to a visible image by the chemical action of development. These developing-out materials are the opposite of printing-out materials in which the image is produced only by the action of the exposing light on the emulsion.

For a large part of the 19th c. plates and films were developed (although some could be used in a printing-out mode), but printing-out was used to obtain prints. With the introduction of gelatin-emulsion papers in the 1880s print development became easier and more reliable; it also increased the number of prints that could be produced in any given amount of time. Today very few printing-out materials are available. *See also:* DEVELOPMENT; PRINTING-OUT PAPER.

Development

Development is the process by which a photographic latent image is converted to a visible image. The chemical aspects of development in various materials are covered in some of the entries listed as cross-references; certain practical aspects of development procedure are discussed here.

Film development is the most sensitive step in the photographic process; a small variation in formula, time, temperature, or handling can have a significant effect on the quality of the image. Color print development is also very sensitive, but black-and-white print development offers some leeway for variation without adverse effect. Within limits, black-and-white film development can be varied in order to control image characteristics, particularly contrast. Color film and print processing is essentially invariable.

Development control begins with a properly mixed solution. Liquid concentrates must be accurately measured and diluted. Prepackaged powder mixes must be used entirely, and completely dissolved in the specified amount of water. It is not possible to measure out only a portion of the powder because the particles of the various ingredients are not likely to be evenly distributed. In developers compounded from formula, accurate measurement of developing agents, alkali (activator), and restrainer is especially important. To prevent rapid breakdown of developing agents or the formation of unwanted compounds, water temperature should be no higher than 125°F (50°C) and ingredients should be mixed in the specified order. The type of developer should be appropriate to the emulsion. There is little point in using a fine-grain developer with a fast film, which forms large grains, or in using an energetic, contrasty developer with a slow film, which has inherently high contrast. In print developing a "mismatch" is sometimes useful for expressive control—e.g., using a neutral-tone developer to limit the effect of a warm-tone paper.

Virtually all film development is based on time and temperature recommendations rather than on direct inspection of the image. Consequently, these factors must be accurately measured; an error of two degrees Fahrenheit, or a half-minute in a planned ten-minute development, can noticeably change black-and-white contrast. The recommendations must be examined carefully; some manufacturers provide data that produce negatives suitable for use in diffusion enlargers. If a condenser enlarger is to be used, less development is required.

Efficient development requires proper agitation to flush by-products away from the emulsion surface. Agitation to dislodge air bubbles from the emulsion surface and to ensure thorough wetting during the first 15 to 30 seconds of film development is especially important. Insufficient agitation produces uneven development, while overagitation increases contrast significantly and may cause streaks of overdevelopment where solution has surged through film sprocket holes or around the edges of reels or film holders. Prints generally benefit from constant agitation because they are processed individually and are developed to maximum obtainable density, whereas film development is stopped well before the maximum is obtained (except in the case of high-contrast lith films). Prewetting a film for tank development is sometimes suggested, but seldom required. However, sheet films that are to be developed together by rotation through a tray of solution should be individually prewetted to prevent their sticking together. Tray development in this manner is a delicate operation because of the danger of scratching an emulsion against the corners of the other films. Contact of film emulsions with the air must be minimized during development to avoid aerial fog; this is especially a consideration in tray development and in lifting sheet-film hangers out of tanks during agitation.

Consistent development from film to film is most easily achieved by diluting a quantity of developer for one-time use and then discarding it. This is feasible with small-film tank development, which uses a minimum quantity of solution, but not with large tanks. In the latter case, accurate replenishment of the developer after each use will provide consistency. Paper developer cannot be replenished. It is used for maximum development with each print, and has its surface exposed to the air for an extended time, which promotes oxidation; it should be replaced with fresh developer at regular intervals during a printing session.

The degree of development directly influences negative contrast; increased development—whether by time, temperature, agitation, or some combination of these—produces increased contrast. Overdevelopment is recognizable by dense middletones and extremely dense highlights with normal shadow densities; frequently there will be noticeably increased fogging in the thin areas. In general, it can be distinguished from overexposure, which produces excess density in all areas without exaggerated local contrast. Development techniques to limit contrast include reduced development, use of a compensating developer, division of a formulated developer into two solutions, and alternate immersions in developer and in a water bath. Print images are far less susceptible to control by development than film images. Too little development produces weak tones. Prolonged print development—four to ten times longer than normal—can add a trace of tone or a sense of detail in the highlight areas on some papers; on others it produces fog before it adds to the image.

See also: AGITATION; CHEMISTRY OF PHOTOGRAPHY; COLOR MATERIALS; COMPENSATING DEVELOPER; CONTRAST; DIFFUSION TRANSFER PROCESS; FOG/ FOGGING; INSPECTION DEVELOPMENT; LATENT IMAGE; MIXING PHOTOGRAPHIC SOLUTIONS; REPLENISHER; TWO-BATH DEVELOPMENT; WATER-BATH DEVELOPMENT.

Diaphragm

In photographic equipment, a diaphragm is a light-control device composed of overlapping opaque leaves that open outward from the center, usually forming a circular opening. Most lenses have a built-in iris diaphragm to control the effective aperture through which image-forming light can pass; various size openings are indicated by the *f*-stop markings on the iris control. Many lenses also have a diaphragm shutter of similar construction which opens outward completely at all speeds so that light will be transmitted through the full area at whatever aperture the iris has been set. This also makes possible flash synchronization at all speeds. Projectors

and lighting instruments may incorporate an iris diaphragm to adjust light intensity or the size of the light beam.
See also: f-STOP/*f*-NUMBER.

Diapositive

Diapositive is chiefly a European term for a slide or transparency. It is a positive image viewed by transmitted rather than reflected light. The name is formed from the Greek *dia-* (through).

Diazo Process

In diazo processes color images are produced by the action of light on material containing diazonium compounds. These compounds decompose upon exposure to blue and ultraviolet wavelengths, losing their ability to react with couplers to form azo dyes. In positive-to-positive printing, exposure destroys the dye-forming property in the highlights and (partially) in the middletones so that dyes are produced in areas in which the original also had densities. In negative-to-positive printing, compounds are used that have their dye-forming ability made permanent by exposure; it is the unexposed portions of middletones and highlights that do not react during processing. Development is achieved with an alkali—commonly ammonia. The exposed material is simply placed in a container filled with ammonia fumes, or the surface is wiped over with a weak solution. Heat can also develop some diazo compounds, as in certain vesicular emulsions. Diazo materials require contact printing exposures under photographic negatives or positives, or other images on translucent or transparent material. The *Dyeline* process, which has completely supplanted the blueprint, produces dark-line/white-background copies of plans, drawings, and documents. Ozalid and related copying materials are diazo-based, and diazo emulsions on transparent bases are used for color proofs in photomechanical reproduction. Cyan, magenta, and yellow diazo materials are exposed under appropriate separation negatives or positives and are assembled in register to obtain the proof. The first practical diazo process, the primuline process, was introduced in 1890.
See also: OZALID PROCESS; PRIMULINE PROCESS; VESICULAR IMAGES, EMULSIONS.

Dichroic Filter

Dichroic filters affect light by reflecting some wavelengths and transmitting others, in contrast to conventional

filters, which absorb the wavelengths they do not transmit. These filters consist of glass with multiple thin-layer coatings on one or both surfaces. The coating—similar to those used to reduce flare on lens elements—creates interference reflections with certain wavelengths; the coating can be chosen to provide much greater selectivity and narrow-band, sharp-cut transmission than dyes and other absorptive agents. Because heat-resistant glass can be used and the coatings have an extremely long life, dichroic filters are employed in the light heads of color enlargers and similar equipment in which conventional filters would melt or fade very quickly. Factors of weight and cost limit camera use of dichroic filters to special-purpose applications.
See also: FILTERS, INTERFERENCE.

Dichroic Fog

See: FOG, FOGGING.

Dichromate Processes

See: BICHROMATE PROCESSES.

Diffraction

Diffraction is the apparent bending of the path of light rays passing an obstruction having a thin, sharply defined edge. Visually, it creates a band of lighter tone just inside the shadow area of the obstruction or, when looking toward the obstruction, a halo of light spreading into the object outline. Diffraction is a result of the wavelike properties of light. As a wavefront encounters the edge, secondary waves are generated which spread into the shadow area. The same phenomenon produces secondary ripples when a wave of water flows past a sharp edge.

Diffraction occurs at the edges of the diaphragm as light passes through a lens. At large apertures the effect is lost in the overall brightness of the image and in the combined effects of various lens aberrations. Reducing the aperture size reduces the aberration effects and provides increased sharpness by increasing the depth of field. However, at very small apertures diffraction becomes more noticeable than the aberrations, primarily as a loss of sharpness in image details. In small- and medium-format photography the smallest lens aperture is unlikely to reach the critical size. But in larger formats, in which the lens coverage is extremely large compared to aperture diameters, diffraction can become a significant factor. At the point that diffraction produces a discernible effect, a lens is

said to be *diffraction limited.* Using apertures beyond the diffraction limit may be productive when factors other than resolution are of primary importance in the image. Even in a lensless system it is not possible to reduce aperture size sufficiently to obtain a uniformly bright image of a point of light; diffraction causes alternating light and dark rings around the central bright spot, a phenomenon known as the *Airy disc.* Diffraction may be purposely created, as with a diffraction grating, for purposes of observing the wavelength composition of light.
See also: DIFFRACTION GRATING; RESOLVING POWER.

Diffraction Grating

A diffraction grating is a wavelength-separating device used to reveal the color components of light. The grating is a pattern of very fine opaque lines on a transparent or reflective surface. The lines are parallel and number 1000 or more per inch (395-plus per centimeter). When light passes through or is reflected from the grating, diffraction bends each wavelength to a different degree, with the result that white light is spread into the full color spectrum. Mixed-color light reveals the colors of its composition, while monochromatic light produces a pattern of alternating light and dark bands. Transmission diffraction gratings are used in instruments for spectrography because they separate the light into bands of equal width, whereas a prism produces a spectrum with bands of decreasing width from the violet end to the red end.
See also: DIFFRACTION; SPECTROGRAPHY.

Diffraction Photographs

Images produced in natural color (i.e., without using dyes or filters in the final positive) by means of diffraction gratings are called diffraction photographs. The method was patented in the U.S. by R. W. Wood in 1899. Like most processes that required precise registration of two or more images, it achieved no commercial success. The convenience of using a single plate—even if the results were of poorer color quality—was far more important to most photographers. Three color separation negatives were made and contact printed onto glass plates to obtain black-and-white positive transparencies of the red-, green-, and blue-record exposures. Each positive was placed in contact with a wavelength-selective diffraction grating, and the three images were bound together in reg-

ister. When viewed in a Diffraction Chromoscope (Kromskop)—a device invented by Frederick Eugene Ives in 1900—the gratings produced red, green, and blue light modulated by the densities of their associated positives, and a full-color image was seen.
See also: DIFFRACTION GRATING; KROMSKOP; SEPARATION NEGATIVES.

Diffusion

The scattering of light from a more or less uniform path into many different directions is called diffusion. It occurs with light reflected from an unpolished or matte surface and with light transmitted through a translucent material. Photographers diffuse light in order to "soften" its quality. This reduces the light intensity; spreads the illumination over a larger area; produces lighter, less distinct shadows; renders details less harshly or sharply; and reduces the intensity of highlights. Aside from placing a diffuser in front of a light source, the most common techniques of diffusion are bounce lighting, tent lighting, and umbrella lighting.

Diffusion also refers to the movement of molecules or ions through a medium, as in the diffusion transfer process.
See also: BOUNCE LIGHT; DIFFUSION TRANSFER PROCESS; TENT LIGHTING; UMBRELLA LIGHTING.

Diffusion Transfer Process

When an exposed negative image is developed in an emulsion, the undeveloped portion corresponds to the opposite aspect of the image, the positive. Almost all self-processing instant-photography materials operate by causing the positive-aspect silver or dye-formers to transfer by diffusion out of the negative emulsion layer(s) to a receiving layer where the visible positive image forms. The three phases—negative development, transfer, and positive development—occur simultaneously, so that positive image formation begins immediately. With black-and-white materials the positive may be completed in ten seconds; with color materials it may take one to five minutes or longer.

The basic phenomenon of silver in solution diffusing from one emulsion to another was first noted in the 1850s, but no practical use of this action was made until 1939–1940. At that time A. Rott of Gevaert and E. Weyde of Agfa independently invented almost identical processes for the reflex copying of documents. A negative sheet reflex-exposed to the original document was dampened with a developer and pressed face-to-face with

a receiving sheet similarly dampened; in a short time the negative image had developed and the positive image had transferred to the receiving sheet, where it developed. The process was suitable only for high-contrast line copy. The true photographic use of diffusion transfer—to produce normal contrast continuous-tone images—was actively investigated from the early 1940s by Edwin Land and his associates at the Polaroid Corporation. A practical in-camera process was demonstrated in 1947 and marketed beginning in 1948.

Two emulsions or, in color materials, sets of emulsion layers are required—negative and positive. In peel-apart materials these are on separate sheets that are pressed together for processing and later separated. In single-sheet or integral films the negative layers are below the positive layers; they are hidden from view at the end of the process by an opaque white layer that forms a background for the positive image. The negative emulsion is essentially a conventional film emulsion except that molecules of developing agent are included with the silver halide crystals. The receiving emulsion is a gelatin layer that contains nuclei of compounds on which the positive image can form; this emulsion is not light sensitive.

The fundamentals of photographic diffusion transfer are simplest in a black-and-white peel-apart film. The negative sheet is exposed in the camera in the normal way. Then it is pulled out of the camera, or film-pack holder, by a paper tab. It passes through a set of rollers that presses it face to face with a sheet of receiving material included in the film pack. At the same time, the rollers rupture a pod of viscous developing reagent and spread it evenly between the two emulsions in a layer about 0.0001 in. (.0025mm) thick. The reagent contains a strong alkali and a silver halide solvent, both of which diffuse into the negative emulsion. There the alkali activates the developing agent, which immediately reduces the exposed halides to a negative image. Simultaneously, the solvent dissolves the unexposed halides. Although fixed in place as crystals, in a dissolved state they can diffuse to the nuclei in the receiving emulsion, which exert an attraction for them. There the silver in the dissolved halides collects on the nuclei, forming the positive image. When the two sheets are peeled apart, the surface reagent clings to the negative, which is discarded or, if on a transparent base, can be neutralized and washed for subsequent use in conventional printing operations. In some films the positive image has to be protected with a coating

Color. Sheila Metzner, "Audrey—Empress"
(1980); freson process. © Sheila
Metzner; courtesy Daniel Wolf Inc., New
York.

Cosindas, Marie. "Richard Merkin" (1967);
polaroid. Courtesy Marie Cosindas.

Curtis, Edward. "Princess Angelina" (ca.
1910); photogravure. Library of Congress.

Cyanotype. Photographer unknown, untitled
(n.d.). Private collection.

Eggleston, William. "Outskirts of Morton,
Mississippi, Halloween" (1971). Courtesy
Middendorf Gallery, Washington, D.C.

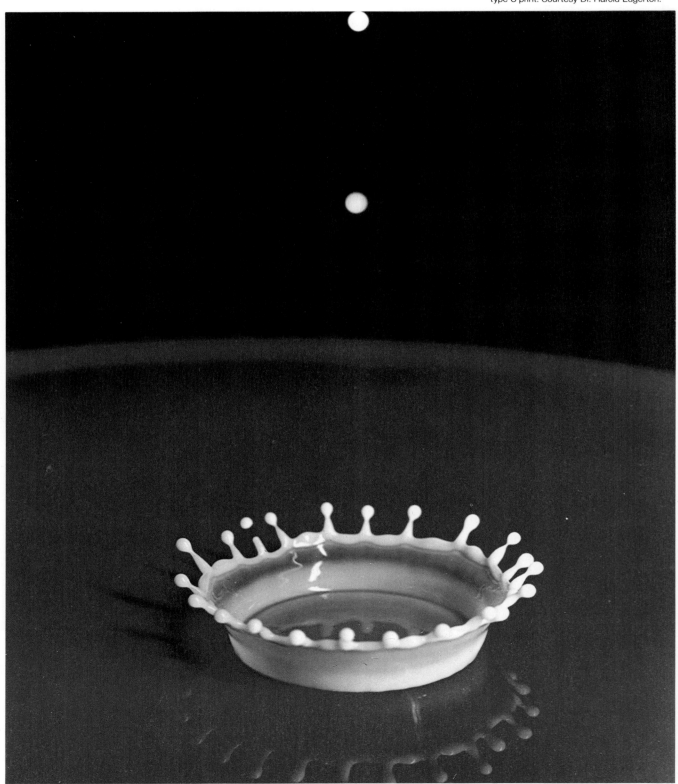

Erotic Photography. Robert J. Steinberg,
"N & L II" (1982). © Robert Steinberg; courtesy Marcuse Pfeifer Gallery, New York.

Expedition Photography. Bradford Washburn, "Ama Dablam; 22,516 ft. in the Nepal Himalayas. 8″ × 10″ color, from 20,000 ft. with the airplane door off, on oxygen (a first)." Courtesy Bradford Washburn.

wiped on with an impregnated swab. This coating has chemicals that neutralize the emulsion and a plasticizer that dries to form a protective top layer. In other films neutralizing compounds are contained in the positive emulsion, and no coating is required. The image is grainless—no structure can be seen even with a microscope—because it is formed by physical development; as a result it has high resolving power. Contrast depends upon the emulsion characteristics, and in some films can be varied somewhat by changes in processing time.

Diffusion transfer color films have three silver halide negative layers individually sensitive to red, green, or blue light, and associated cyan, magenta, and yellow dye-developer or dye-releaser layers. In a peel-apart color film, dye-forming compounds are locked in place wherever the negative image is developed; in other areas they are released to diffuse to the receiving sheet to produce a positive color image. Similar action occurs in diffusion transfer darkroom materials for color printing. The chemical action is also essentially the same in single-sheet Polaroid SX-70 films, but some physical details differ. The receiving layers are on top of the negative layers; they are completely transparent, so they do not interfere with the image during exposure. The lens image is reflected onto the face of the film by a mirror so that the final image will have proper left-right orientation. As the film emerges from the camera, reagent is forced between the upper group of receiving layers and the lower group of negative layers. The reagent contains an opaque material to protect the negative layers from further exposure. The image processes below, and the positive dye-formers diffuse up through the reagent to the top. As the process completes itself, the black reagent layer bleaches to a clean, white background for the color image.

Kodak Instant Print films function in a completely unique way. The receiving layers are separated from the negative layers by a white background and a protective opaque layer. The film is exposed from the base side, so no mirror-reversal of the lens image is required. Exposure is trapped within each affected halide crystal; in effect, the latent image is hidden from the developer. As the film emerges from the camera an opaque developer is spread within the very back layer. It diffuses upward to develop the unexposed halides, producing a direct positive silver image. Wherever that image forms, the corresponding dyes are released to diffuse upward to the top receiving layers where they form the visible positive image. With some films the positive image can be removed after processing, and the negative layers and their thick base material discarded. This provides the convenience of one-piece films in the camera, but eliminates unnecessary weight and thickness in the final print.

Polachrome 35mm Autoprocess color slide film is also unique. It is an additive color screen film composed of a panchromatic emulsion covered with a screen of 3000 parallel red, green, and blue lines running lengthwise in the frame. Exposure is made through the screen, which analyzes the image in terms of its primary color proportions. For processing, the emulsion is wound in contact with an auxiliary strip that carries an activator. Diffusion transfer produces a black-and-white positive image in the exposed emulsion. The negative image, undeveloped halides, and processing by-products are removed when the auxiliary strip is peeled away. When the slide is projected, the positive silver densities in the image modulate the light intensities in each area while the color screen gives them the appropriate primary hues. The result is a re-creation of the original subject colors. Two panchromatic black-and-white slide films that process in a similar manner are also available. One has a continuous-tone emulsion, the other a very high-contrast emulsion; no color screen is required.

See also: ACTIVATOR; ADDITIVE COLOR SYNTHESIS; COLOR MATERIALS; LAND, E. H.; SCREEN PROCESSES.

Digital Images

Digital images are reproductions derived from the dissection of an optical image, or the image in a photographic negative or positive, into electronically encoded picture elements (pixels). An optical image can be dissected by focusing it onto a charge-coupled device (CCD), a silicon chip composed of thousands of individual light-sensitive pixels. Each pixel emits an electrical signal in proportion to the strength of the light falling on it. A color image is analyzed by three dissections in which the image is focused in succession through red, green, and blue filters onto the CCD. The analysis of photographic images is commonly performed by a scanner which directs a laser or electron beam across the original and takes a reading at each pixel position. Reflected-energy readings are taken from prints, and transmitted-energy readings from negatives and transparencies; with color images three primary-color readings are made simultaneously.

The size of the pixel depends upon system design and the importance of resolution of details in the image. If 0.01 in.—the limit of the circle of confusion at normal viewing distance—were taken as a standard, an 8″ × 10″ image would be divided into 800,000 pixels. Most systems have much greater resolving power, ranging from patterns of 1024 horizontal by 1024 vertical lines (1,048,576 pixels) to 4096 × 4096 lines (16,777,216 pixels) or higher. The pixel array is square to accommodate horizontal and vertical formats equally. The CCD or scanner output represents brightness or density at each point. This information is immediately converted to binary numbers—digits—equivalent to the densities. In that form the data can magnetically be recorded and stored, can be computer processed for image enhancement, can be transmitted at very high speed over vast distances (e.g., from outer space), or can be used to control simultaneous (real-time) reproduction systems.

The major advantage of digital encoding is that the information is represented by a series of pulses and spaces (no pulses). This system is inherently error- and distortion-free because although the signal level may decrease or vary greatly or be masked by noise (static, spurious signals), as long as it is possible to distinguish electronically between pulse and no-pulse, the data can be translated accurately and the image reproduced without significant loss or change. Analog encoding, which converts information into a modulated continuous signal such as a varying voltage, is much more susceptible to interference and distortion. Digital images are reproduced in three major ways: on a television screen the scanning electron beam of which is varied according to the digital signals, on photographic prints or films which are exposed by a scanning laser beam of varying intensity, or by ink-jet printers which deposit points of ink in a replication of the pixel scanning pattern.

Digital data of any sort can be recorded on a photographic emulsion, using the medium for information storage rather than image creation. The photographic equivalent of pulse-no pulse to represent each data bit is density-no density. Only tiny points of density, with no gradation, are required, so an extremely fine-grain, thin, high-contrast emulsion can be used to obtain maximum resolving power. Techniques of microphotography permit recording a pattern of more than 150 million bits per square cm (0.16 square in.) of emulsion. Holography, Lippmann-process emulsions, and other specialized photographic techniques and materials can achieve even higher storage capacities. A major advantage of photographic information storage is that the data are not endangered by electronic failure or stray electronic or magnetic currents, as are data stored on magnetic disks and tapes. *See also:* IMAGE DISSECTION; IMAGE ENHANCEMENT; MICROPHOTOGRAPHY; SPACE PHOTOGRAPHY.

Dimmer

An electrical dimmer is a device used to control the output of a continuous light source such as an incandedscent bulb. Dimmers are also available for use with fluorescent tubes, but fluorescent lighting is seldom purposely used for photography. The most common kind of dimmer is a rheostat or a solid-state (thyristor) device that controls current flow. A variable, or dimming, transformer controls voltage flow to a light source. As the current or voltage flow is reduced, the light output drops. The dimmer setting is usually adjusted by a rotating dial control or a sliding switch lever; in most dimmers the change is smoothly continuous from full off to full on.

In black-and-white photography dimmers are used in studio setups to adjust lighting intensity and in the darkroom as a means of exposure control (in addition to time) so that an optimum aperture setting of an enlarger lens need not be changed. Dimmers are seldom used to adjust light intensity in color photography because voltage or current changes produce changes in the color temperature of the light. However, variable transformers are used to ensure that bulbs receive their full rated voltage so that they will produce illumination of the rated color temperature. This is necessary because the nominal 110 or 120 volts of domestic electricity may vary by several volts according to demands within the overall system. In the studio a variable transformer may be used to operate lights at reduced voltage during setup and adjustment, and then at full voltage only when pictures are actually being taken. This procedure greatly extends the working life of high-output bulbs. In the darkroom a constant-voltage transformer in the printing light circuit guards against color temperature changes regardless of supply-line voltage fluctuations during color exposures. *See also:* SERIES-PARALLEL CIRCUIT.

DIN

DIN is the acronym for Deutsche Industrie Norm, the German organization equivalent to the American National Standards Institute (ANSI). DIN speeds for films are detemined by the same sensitometric methods as ASA and ISO (International Standards Organization) speeds, but are expressed on a logarithmic scale. In ISO speed markings, the number following the slant line and marked with a ° symbol is a logarithmic scale speed identical to the DIN speed and equivalent to the arithmetic speed preceding the slant line. For example, ISO 400/27° = DIN 27. *See also:* SPEED OF MATERIALS.

Diopter

The optical power of a lens to affect the path of light rays is measured in diopters. Lens power is the reciprocal of the focal length of the lens measured in meters (i.e., 1/focal length in meters, or the equivalent, 1000/focal length in millimeters). A lens that increases the convergence of light rays passing through has a positive (+) power—e.g., +5 diopters. A lens that increases the divergence (decreases the convergence) of light rays has a negative (−) power. The number by which a supplementary lens is commonly identified in photography is its power in diopters. The focal length of a lens, in millimeters, is equal to 1000 divided by its power in diopters. *See also:* FOCAL LENGTH; SUPPLEMENTARY LENS.

Diorama

In general, a diorama is a detailed, realistic representation of a scene incorporating painted or photographic backgrounds, models, taxidermic specimens, and similar elements, as in museum displays. Originally dioramas were miniature scale models, often of an entire section of a city or an equally extensive and complex subject. In 1822 L. J. M. Daguerre and Charles Marie Bouton opened a new kind of diorama in Paris: larger-than-life "living paintings" exhibited in a theater to an audience of up to 350 people. The paintings, 71½ ft. long and 45½ ft. high (21.5m long and 13.8m high), were composed of elements on the front surface of thin linen painted in transparent colors and elements on the rear surface painted in opaque colors. They were illuminated by windows and skylights equipped with roller shades, shutters, and color diffusers so that the lighting could be adjusted to reveal the front painting by direct light, the rear painting by transmitted light, or various blendings of the two images. Smooth, gradual changes in the lighting made it appear that the scene depicted was growing and changing, much like the effect produced by a series of dissolves in motion pictures and television today. Dramatic visual presentations such as the destruction of an Alpine village by avalanche or the inauguration of Solomon's temple, and depictions of Mont Blanc and other scenic views fascinated audiences because the realism of the painting—supplemented by some foreground objects on stage and offstage sound effects—was compellingly illusionistic; spectators would occasionally throw coins or paper balls to convince themselves that what they were seeing was actually painted on a flat surface and was not a huge, ingenious scale model.

Daguerre often used a camera obscura to make drawings that were accurate in scale and perspective as reference studies for the diorama paintings. His desire to reduce the immense amount of preliminary work each painting required led him to experiment with ways to record the camera obscura image automatically, without drawings by hand. The ultimate result of these experiments was the daguerreotype, the first practical photographic process. The original Diorama was destroyed by fire in 1839 and was never rebuilt. Similar dioramas constructed in London by Bouton, and in a number of other European cities by imitators, survived until the mid-19th c., but none achieved the immense popularity of the Parisian theater. *See also:* CAMERA OBSCURA; DAGUERRE, L. J. M.

Direct Positive

Direct positive materials produce a positive image (from exposure to a subject or a positive image) in one step without an intermediate negative stage. The term is also commonly used as a synonym for reversal materials and processes because the material exposed in the camera carries the final positive image; there is no printing or copying step, although a negative image is produced in the course of processing. True direct positive materials include those used in some diazo processes; one-step and some peel-apart diffusion transfer films; and some special-purpose films which are preexposed in manufacture so that image exposure produces a kind of solarization that yields positive tones directly upon development. Direct positive reversal materials include slide and transparency films, and papers used to make prints from them; papers used in coin-operated photo booths and similar unattended equipment; and a variety of dye destruction, document copying, and special-purpose films and papers.

Disdéri, André Adolphe. "Ballerina," probably Martha Muravieva, Paris Opera Dancer (ca. 1864). International Museum of Photography at George Eastman House.

The first practical photographic process, the daguerreotype, was a true direct positive process. The ambrotype and the ferrotype (tintype) were the major direct positive processes during the collodion period in the mid-19th c. One of the most ingenious procedures was that of Hippolyte Bayard, who invented a direct positive paper process at the same time the daguerreotype was invented. Bayard prepared salt paper and exposed it to sunlight until it printed-out to a uniform black. To take a picture, he brushed over the paper with a solution of potassium iodide and exposed it in the camera while damp. The action of the light liberated iodine, which bleached the black surface in the highlight and middletone areas in proportion to the amount of exposure received. The process was completed with conventional fixing and washing.
See also: AMBROTYPE; DAGUERREOTYPE; DIAZO PROCESSES; DIFFUSION TRANSFER PROCESS; FERROTYPE; REVERSAL MATERIALS AND PROCESSING; SALTPAPER PROCESS; SOLARIZATION.

Disdéri, André-Adolphe-Eugène
French; 1819–1889
At the height of his fame and fortune in the 1860s, Disdéri produced thousands of carte-de-visite portraits each month. His studios (a branch was opened in London in 1865) were patronized by the wealthy and powerful, including Napoleon III and his family, and were described by his contemporary, Ernest Lacan, as the "biggest in Paris."

Disdéri has been frequently dismissed as a mere technician whose mass-production of carte portraits cheapened the artisanal quality of the photographic product, but this is too simple and censorious a view. For while Disdéri's contribution to photography is indeed most visible in his cartes and later cabinet portraits, he also contributed a number of practical inventions and innovations to his profession. In 1852, he perfected a formula for "instantaneous" exposures on collodion glass-plates; in 1858 he patented a method for preparing printing papers without the costly addition of gold salts to the fixer; in 1861 he invented a developing box for use in "instantaneous" photography; and in 1867 he patented a photomechanical printing process similar to and derived from Woodbury's.

Disdéri also published four practical and aesthetic manuals on photography: one on collodion technique (1853), one on photographic methods (1853), another on photographic reproduction of works of art (1861), and *L'Art de la photographie* (1862).

Before beginning his profitable Parisian portrait business, Disdéri had photographed genre scenes and made a series on childhood pleasures in Nîmes, where he had moved after leaving his family and daguerreotype studio in Brest. After photographing the same agricultural fair that Baldus had documented at the Champ-de-Mars in 1854, Disdéri moved to Paris and filed for a patent on his carte-de-visite plate-

holder. This invention divided the collodion plate into ten smaller negative areas, thus allowing the operator to make ten separate exposures on a single plate. Despite an early bankruptcy (1856) in pursuing his carte portrait business, Disdéri's skills as a photographer, organizer, and self-promoter led to his great success in the late 1850s and the 1860s.

His documentation of the devastated French landscape following the Franco-Prussian war in the 1870s was his last fine work. By 1875, Disdéri was selling his negatives to raise cash. He closed his Paris studios and reappeared in 1877 in Nice, where he worked at the humble trade of oceanfront photographer. In 1899, he returned to Paris penniless and ill and died at the Hôspital Ste.-Anne, a charitable institution.
See also: CARTE-DE-VISITE.

Disk Cameras
Cameras using a circular film or glass plate on which several pictures are taken around the periphery are called disk cameras. The disk idea was a pre-roll-film solution to the problem of securing multiple exposures with a single loading of a relatively compact, easy-to-carry camera. Other heavier and more cumbersome solutions involved multiple lenses in front of a fixed rectangular plate, or a shifting back behind a single lens, both used for carte-de-visite photographs, or a magazine containing a stack of rectangular plates which were shifted by various mechanical means. The disk permits rotating a film or plate around a single axis, an arrangement that has mechanical simplicity, can achieve high operational speeds, and allows a camera body of minimal depth since there is no need to accommodate the thickness of spools or cassettes; however, the height and width must allow for the diameter of the disk, which is somewhat greater than the vertical dimension of two frames. The disk also makes it easier to keep the emulsion flat in the focal plane of the lens, especially as compared to the problems encountered with roll and cassette-load films on very small-diameter spindles.

The first disk camera was one of several gun cameras based on this principle: Thompson's Revolver Camera, invented in England but introduced in France as the Revolver Photographique in 1862. It took four exposures 7/8 in. (2.2cm) in diameter on a 2 15/16 in. (7.7cm) diameter glass wet plate. One of the most sophisticated early disk cameras was the Fusil Photographique—photo rifle—of E. J. Marey, used for high-speed motion study and analysis. His first model, in

1882, had 12 glass dry plates mounted on a flat disk; it could operate at a rate of 12 pictures per second with effective exposures of almost 1/1000 sec.; an improved model in 1888 used a disk of celluloid-base film that accommodated 48 exposures at higher rates of operation. In the U.S., R. D. Gray introduced his Vest Camera in 1886—in Europe it was known as Stirn's Vest Camera—which was less than an inch thick, but 5¾ in. (14.6cm) in diameter. Hidden beneath the vest, the lens protruded through a buttonhole to make 6 exposures 1⅝ in. (4.13cm) in diameter on a 5½ in. (14.0cm) circular glass dry plate. Several disk cameras have imitated watches: notably the "pocket watch" Photoret of 1893; a 1939 wristwatch design by Steiner and Heckelmann of Munich, which used a mirror to reflect the lens image onto the film; the 1948 Steineck A-B-C wrist camera with an *f*/2.5 lens; the Petal, a pocketwatch design, from Sakura of Japan in 1948; and a large, plastic wristwatch camera, the Wristamatic, in the U.S. in 1981. By far the most successful disk camera is the Kodak *Disc*, introduced in 1982. Less than ¾ in (1.9cm) thick, it takes 15 pictures each 5/16" × ⅜" (0.8 × 0.9cm) on individual frames of celluloid-base color film mounted around a 2½ in (6.4cm) diameter disk. *See also:* CARTE-DE-VISITE; GUN CAMERA; MAREY, ETIENNE JULES.

Dispersion

The separation of the wavelengths which constitute a beam of light is called dispersion. It is the result of refraction rather than diffraction or interference, which also may cause separation. Dispersion occurs only with light that strikes a transparent medium at an angle, and only with a medium, such as glass, that has a different refractive index (bending power) for each wavelength. The most familiar example of dispersion is the spectrum produced when white light is transmitted by a prism. Lens elements produce dispersion because their curved surfaces ensure that almost all light strikes at an angle; the result is chromatic aberration. It is corrected by using additional elements of opposite curvature, or by employing refractive indices which counteract the dispersion. *See also:* DIFFRACTION; INTERFERENCE; REFRACTION.

Disposal of Photographic Wastes

In general, limited quantities of photographic waste products are not highly damaging to the environment and so are not of great importance. Most non-commercial consumers of photographic material use relatively small amounts. Consequently, there is little danger of large quantities of chemicals being dumped and overloading a disposal system. The highly toxic or dangerous chemicals such as chromium, cyanide, and strong acids are normally used in such small amounts and are so diluted that they fall within environmentally acceptable limits.

There are some exceptions to the above, most notably the high concentration of silver and the large demand for oxygen of many developing solutions. Whether it is necessary to pretreat darkroom waste prior to releasing it into a community sewer system, either for environmental concern or in conformance with local statutes, depends in large part on the volume of the discharge. Most individuals, processing only a few rolls of film or prints at a time, need have no concern. Large laboratories, especially those using the more corrosive color chemistry, use a variety of arrangements. A common method is the holding tank. Waste from a processing run is funneled into a large tank and bled off slowly. This avoids large, sporadic infusions of potentially harmful chemicals. Further dilution of the waste is sometimes achieved by adding more water as the effluent is discharged. An approximation of this idea can be used by the individual for small amounts of corrosive chemicals to safeguard household plumbing. The sink or other container is filled two-thirds full with water, the waste is added, and the dilute mixture is then discharged through the pipes. Additional protection is achieved by chemically neutralizing solutions before disposal (e.g., by mixing used stop bath and developer, or washing aid/hypo eliminator and fixer). The largest processors maintain commercial treatment facilities or contract to have the sludge removed by a professional disposal service. Consumers with home septic-tank systems should note that a few photographic by-products, especially sodium or potassium dichromate, may seriously injure the bacteria essential to the tank's effective functioning. Further, the ratio of photographic waste to total waste should never exceed 10 percent. Personnel of local water and sewage departments can provide pertinent information and guidance. *See also:* SILVER RECOVERY.

Dissolve

A dissolve is a visual transition between two pictures used in editing motion-picture and television presentations. As the first picture is fading out (losing intensity), the second is simultaneously fading in; there is no change in overall screen brightness, so one picture seems to melt or dissolve into the other. The dissolve provides a sense of continuity while joining two scenes with significant differences in time or location or both. Thus, it may be used to carry the narrative line to an earlier time (flashback), or to concurrent action in another place. It is not as abrupt or energetic as a cut, and does not mark a major pause in development as does a fade-out, fade-in transition. Particularly in television, the dissolve also is used between two shots of the same subject and action to preserve mood—for example, the flow of music or dance. *See also:* CUT; FADE IN/FADE-OUT.

Distortion

A deviation in an image from the size, shape, proportions, tones, or colors of the original subject is a distortion. Some distortions are inherent in the photographic process and are accepted as being normal. The translation of colors into shades of gray is a basic distortion, and relative brightnesses (contrasts) within shadow and highlight portions of an image must be exaggerated in comparison to those in middletone portions for the image to seem accurate, or "real." Similarly, the individual colors in a color image that has an overall feeling of accuracy will not necessarily be exact matches with the actual subject colors. In some cases altered tones, colors, or shapes—e.g., as produced by filters, or irregular glass or mirrors—are deliberately created for expressive purposes. Other distortions are unintended and unwanted.

A focal plane shutter used at speeds which produce a narrow slit for exposure may distort the shape of a moving subject. The moving image is exposed in stages as the shutter slit moves across the film, so that a continuous displacement of position is recorded. If the shutter movement is at right angles to the image movement, a leaning or diagonally stretched shape is recorded. A typical example is a leaning automobile with oval wheels, resulting from vertical shutter movement while the vehicle moved rapidly across the field of view. Shutter movement in the same direction as image movement produces elongation; shutter movement in the opposite direction to image movement produces a compressed or squashed image.

The lens aberration called distortion is an off-axis fault that causes tangential straight lines in the image (i.e., those not crossing the axis) to curve either inward

Distortion

Film-plane distortion

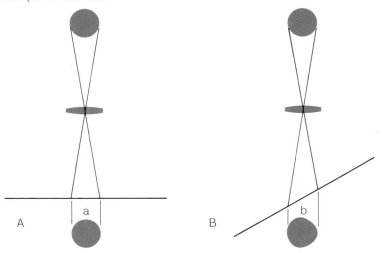

A = Film plane parallel to subject plane registers details at subject distance in true proportions

B = Angled film plane stretches image over greater area, distorting shape and proportions

Wide-angle distortion

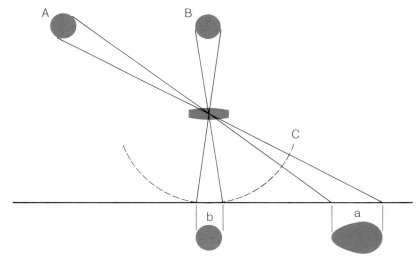

Distortion. A wide-angle lens sees equal widths of solid objects A and B, but image *a* is wider than *b* and distorted because of extreme angular projection onto the film plane. Only a curved film plane, C, would register images of equal size.

(pincushion distortion) or outward (barrel distortion). It is a noticeable problem primarily in wide-angle lenses. Extreme barrel distortion is common, and intended, in fisheye lenses; it is unavoidable if the plane at the focused distance is to be imaged as a flat plane (i.e., on the film). Few lenses are entirely free of distortion, but in most its effect is undetectable.

The distortion of solid object shapes at the edges of a wide-angle field occurs because the images of the shapes are projected obliquely onto the film plane, as shown in the diagram. Similar distortion occurs when the film plane is not parallel to the subject, as shown. This problem (explained further in the entry on keystoning) and related plane distortions can be corrected through the use of camera movements to bring the film plane parallel with the subject plane, or by tilting the paper or the negative (or both) in enlarging to achieve a similar result.

Distortion of object proportions is caused by differences in image magnification because some parts of the object are significantly farther from the lens than others. This is in fact a special problem of perspective, not true distortion, and the effect disappears if the image is viewed from the proper distance, as explained in the entry on perspective. However, viewing distance tends to remain constant, not to be adjusted for the special requirements of each image, so images with unusual perspective characteristics appear distorted. Proportions may purposely be distorted for expressive effect—e.g., to exaggerate the height of a basketball player—but in portraiture, medical and scientific photography, and most other kinds of objective photography the effect is unacceptable. The fundamental problem in portraiture is as follows; it is the same in other kinds of pictures, as is the solution.

The tip of the nose is about 6 in. in front of the ears in an average person. At a camera (lens) distance of 3 ft, the nose is closer by $\frac{1}{7}$ of the distance (6 in. out of a total 42 in. to the ears) and is magnified to a proportionately greater degree. Although mathematically small, the difference is quite noticeable in a photographic image. Those parts of the face and head between the nose and ears are various other distances from the lens and so are magnified in corresponding various degrees. Because they are all part of the same object, the differences blend in a continuous change that makes the nose and lips look stretched forward. If the camera is moved to 9 ft, no distortion is detectable, because the nose is now only $\frac{1}{19}$ (6 in./114 in.) of the distance closer and the difference in magnification is insignificant. In order to obtain the same overall image size at the greater distance, the lens can be changed for one of proportionately longer focal length (i.e., 3× longer for a change from 3 to 9 ft).

Tone and color distortions are caused by errors in matching the color balance of the illumination and the emulsion in exposure, in filtration, and in processing. Distortions of this sort are far more noticeable in color images than in black-and-white images.

See also: ABERRATIONS OF LENSES; CAMERA MOVEMENTS; KEYSTONING; MAGNIFICATION; PERSPECTIVE.

D-Log E, D-Log H Curve

The characteristic curve of a processed emulsion is a graph that plots density (the logarithm of opacity) versus the logarithm of exposure. It is sometimes identified as the D-Log E curve because the symbol E was originally used for exposure (= light intensity × time). D stands for density. International scientific usage now defines E as illuminance, measured in lumens per square meter (lux). The international symbol for exposure is H (= E × time), so the graph is more properly identified as the D-Log H curve. In the past this kind of graph was also called the *H & D Curve* after Hurter and Driffield, who originated it in the course of their pioneering work in sensitometry.

See also: CHARACTERISTIC CURVE; DENSITY; EXPOSURE; OPACITY; SENSITOMETRY.

Dmitri, Ivan (Levon West)

American; 1900–1968

An etcher of international renown, Levon West changed his name and his medium in mid-career when he took up photography. He became an important illustrative color photographer in the 1940s and 1950s, working primarily for the *Saturday Evening Post,* then retired as a professional photographer to found the project Photography in the Fine Arts. The first PFA exhibition was held at the Metropolitan Museum of Art, New York, in 1959, and went on to appear in museums around the world in the next decade. Four more PFA exhibitions were mounted during that period, and a special show was organized by PFA at the New York World's Fair in 1965.

Born in Centerville, South Dakota, Levon West studied at the University of Minnesota, and after graduation in 1924 enjoyed a successful career as an etcher and watercolorist. In 1937 he became Ivan Dmitri, photographer. In the next 22 years he completed more than 200 assignments for the *Saturday Evening Post, Fortune, Vogue, U.S. Camera, Collier's,* and *Popular Photography,* working in India, Greenland, Chile, and throughout the U.S. He was the author of *Kodachrome and How to Use It* (1940) and *Flight to Everywhere,* a book of his work as a war correspondent-photographer in 1943 and 1944.

Dmitri founded Photography in the Fine Arts in 1958. As an impresario of photographic exhibitions he was a controversial figure. He was both praised and criticized for his use of experts in painting and the other fine arts to judge the PFA exhibitions, and for including works that had originally been produced as commercial illustrations. However, the PFA exhibitions were extremely popular, and they helped introduce photography as an expressive medium to the rapidly expanding museum-going public of the post-World War II years. The PFA project ended shortly after Dmitri's death in 1968, in New York City.

Documentary and Social Documentary Photography

The term "documentary photography" really has two meanings, one containing the other. In the very broadest sense, every photograph is documentary: it stands as evidence after an event that the event did in fact occur; even fictional or manipulated photographs document the artistic taste of the time. In general, though, documentary photographs are thought of as those in which the events in front of the lens (or in the print) have been altered as little as possible from what they would have been had the photographer not been there. To this end, successful documentary photographers have developed various approaches and personal styles of behavior while working that permit them to be present on the scene they are photographing while influencing it minimally.

The second meaning of documentary photography is often distinguished from the first by the word "social." Social documentary describes a kind of photography that attempts to document (and perhaps to influence) social conditions. In this sense it is quite distinct from those kinds of documentation—news photography for example—which are typically concerned with recording events rather than ongoing conditions. This is not to say that a social documentary photograph or essay may not be inspired by an out-of-the-ordinary event (an earthquake or a bombing, for example), but that the focus of the report will be on how that event affects, or reveals, the ongoing conditions of peoples' lives. Particularly since World War II, as the Western world has become more aware of the ecological interrelationships of all things on this planet, social documentary lenses have also been turned towards subjects outside of the narrowly defined human sphere, with an awareness of their great and immediate significance for human life.

From the photographic medium's inception in 1839, its ability to provide accurate, impartial transcriptions of the visual world was called upon to satisfy the public's growing curiosity about the look of distant lands and their inhabitants, as well as to supply visual records of important contemporary events. In 1849–1850, for example, the French photographer Maxime du Camp collected photographic views of ancient sites in the Near East, which he published in a sumptuous book that was hailed not only by archeologists but by the popular press as well. The British photographer Roger Fenton, in 1855, compiled a famous series of 360 images detailing the closing phases of the Crimean War; his prints were sold to an avid public by booksellers, and reproduced as wood engravings in the *Illustrated London News.* During the American Civil War of 1861–1865, the celebrated Mathew Brady assembled a group of nearly 20 photographers to produce a visual record of that conflict, eventually gathering a historically invaluable collection of 10,000 negatives. Following the Civil War, expeditionary photographers such as Timothy H. O'Sullivan, Carleton Watkins, and William Henry Jackson overcame great physical obstacles to transport their unwieldy wet-plate apparatus to the farthest reaches of the unexplored Western territories, and delighted not only geologists but a wide public with astonishing views of natural wonders such as California's Yosemite Valley.

Photography's documentary value was further extended by its ability to produce a series of detailed images at short intervals; thus it became possible to reproduce in photographs the stages of complex operations as they unfolded in time. An early example of such a documentary sequence can be found in Robert Howlett's remarkable photographs of the construction of the British steamship *The Great Eastern* in 1857. An equally fascinating sequence, by the French photographers Delmaet and Durandelle, follows step-by-step the construction of the magnificent Paris Opera in the late 1860s.

Such applications of photography confirmed what the French writer Ernst Lacan had maintained in 1856: "Photography is everywhere. One by one it registers the memorable facts of our collective life . . . our glories, our celebrations, our calamities, and bequeathes them to the archives of history."

The rapidly changing face of the 19th-c. city also provided a role for photography to play: the recording of those relics of the urban past that seemed doomed to disappear irrevocably. In the early 1860s Charles Marville began an official photographic survey of the old quarters of Paris that were being demolished to make way for the new system of boulevards. Marville's evocative images—like those of Eugène Atget at the turn of the century—not only reproduced precise architectural detail; they captured a moving sense of the city's vanishing past as well. A similar commission was undertaken by the Scottish photographer Thomas Annan in 1868 in Glasgow. Annan was engaged to compile a documentary record of that city's notorious slum district—one of the worst in Europe—which had been slated for eradication as part of an urban renewal scheme. Annan's photographs, published in an album called *Old Closes and Streets of Glasgow,* revealed the squalor of the narrow, dirty streets inhabited by the city's poor and disenfranchised.

While not intended as an exercise in social criticism, photographs like Annan's suggested that photography might be successfully employed to bring before the public eye striking evidence of social injustice, and thus to awaken the viewer's conscience as well. An important forerunner of the social documentary approach is John Thomson's series *Street Life in London,* published in monthly installments in 1877. Thomson took his camera into the city's streets, and, with the writer Adolphe Smith, produced vivid pictures of the daily lives of London's working-class population and street merchants. This sympathetic presentation of the "dangerous" classes was a bold step in Victorian England, and the reproduction of Thomson's images by the superb Woodburytype process guaranteed that they would convey the maximum emotional force.

In the late 1880s, the Danish-born immigrant Jacob Riis began an important photographic documentation of the sordid living conditions suffered by America's urban poor. A newspaper reporter by profession, Riis was quick to recognize the value of hard-hitting images; using magnesium flash, he succeeded in obtaining interior photographs of immigrant families packed into wretched tenements. In books like *How the Other Half Lives* (1890) and *The Children of the Poor* (1898), Riis used reproductions of his photographs to lend urgency to his indictment of the living conditions forced upon these urban dwellers.

Following in Riis's footsteps, the American sociologist Lewis Hine found in photography a superb means to drive home his own critique of the ills visited upon immigrants, the laboring classes, and the destitute. Hine's 1905 picture series of the arrival of European immigrants at New York's Ellis Island remains a classic of humanitarian social documentary, as do his later photographs revealing conditions in textile mills, sweat shops, and mines. Hine called his approach "social photography," and insisted that the camera should be directed by a social conscience. Far from being stridently critical, however, Hine also depicted the dignity of working people and the comforts of family life. He insisted, "I wanted to show the things that had to be corrected. I wanted to show the things that had to be appreciated."

In the United States, the 1930s emerged as the heroic age of social documentary photography, in part as a response to the social and economic havoc wrought by the Depression. The work of the photographic section of the Farm Security Administration stands as the high-water mark of social documentary in this country. Organized in 1935 by Roy Stryker, a former economics instructor at Columbia University, the FSA group eventually included such figures as Walker Evans, Dorothea Lange, Russell Lee, Arthur Rothstein, Marion Post Wolcott, and Jack Delano. Their photographs of Dust Bowl refugees, Alabama sharecroppers and their shanties, the uprooted and the homeless, helped awaken Americans to the plight of their fellow citizens. Eventually numbering over 270,000 negatives, the work of the FSA photographers helped define the essentials of the American approach to social documentary.

But the FSA photographers were by no means the only group working in this direction in the 1930s. From 1936 to 1951, New York's Photo League served as a magnet for socially concerned photographers. Its members included exceptionally talented photographers such as Sid Grossman, Sol Libsohn, Aaron Siskind, and Jerome Liebling, and its projects included such important ventures as the Harlem Document (1938–1940).

After World War II, many of the essential concerns of the social documentary tradition were passed on to a group of socially committed photojournalists who sought, through their pictures, to contribute to human understanding in the fragile postwar world. Numbered among these "concerned photographers" were Robert Capa, W. Eugene Smith, Dan Weiner, David Seymour ("Chim"), and Werner Bischof.

In 1962 the revival of the FSA Depression-era photographs in the Museum of Modern Art's exhibition *The Bitter Years* triggered a renewal of the social documentary approach in America. Especially in its evocation of the struggle of black Americans in the civil rights movement, social documentary could boast such powerful accomplishments as Danny Lyon's photographs for the Student Non-Violent Coordinating Committee published in *The Movement* (1964), and Leonard Freed's *Black in White America* (1968).

The emergence of a new generation of socially concerned photographers in the 1960s coincided with the decline of the mass-circulation picture magazines in the United States. (In Europe, where there has been less competition from commercial television for advertising revenues, similar magazines have remained successful.) In 1972 the two largest-circulation picture magazines in the U.S., *Look* and the weekly *Life,* ceased publication (*Life* has since been revived as a monthly). The role played by these magazines in presenting in-depth visual reportage was to a great extent assumed by such television programs as "60 Minutes" (CBS), "20/20" (ABC), and "First Camera" (NBC).

For documentary still photography, the single-topic photographic book has become an important medium. Published in increasing numbers since the 1950s, these books have offered the social documentary photographer two important advantages over the mass-circulation magazine format: the opportunity of covering a story more extensively and in greater depth, doing full justice to its complexity; and far greater control over the selection and arrangement of the pictures and the content of the accompanying text.

Paralleling, and sometimes in conjunction with, the growth in numbers of social documentary books, an increasing number of museums and galleries have presented exhibitions of the work of socially concerned photographers.

Concerned with the preservation and continuing evolution of the social documentary tradition, photographer Cornell Capa in 1967 organized the first of two exhibitions under the title *The Concerned Photographer,* both subsequently published in book form. The first exhibition was made up of work by Werner Bischof, Robert Capa, Henri Cartier-Bresson, Dan Weiner, André Kertész, and Leonard Freed; the second exhibited the work of Bruce Davidson, Ernst Haas, Hiroshi Hamaya, Donald McCullin, Gordon Parks, Marc Riboud, W. Eugene Smith, and Roman Vishniac. These exhibitions, which showed the continuum of work by concerned documentary photographers over four decades, reflected Cornell Capa's adoption of Lewis Hine's goal: to show the things that had to be corrected, and the things that had to be appreciated. Following the first of these exhibits, Capa established the International Fund for Concerned Photography, which sought to encourage and assist photographers of all nationalities who were concerned with their world and times. The purpose of this fund was to discover and help new talent, and also to preserve valuable and forgotten archives and to present such work to the public. The second exhibition, *The Concerned Photographer 2,* opened in 1973, and was shown in the U.S., Europe, and Asia; the term *"concerned photographer"* became well

Documentary Photography. John Thomson,
"Street Doctor," from *Street Life in London*
(1877). Library of Congress.

known in the field of photography for linking humanistic concerns to the medium. The aims of the International Fund for Concerned Photography were incorporated into the charter of the International Center of Photography (New York), founded by Capa in 1974, a major photographic institution with archival, exhibition, educational, and publishing functions.

In 1956, *Life* magazine and the Overseas Press Club established the Robert Capa Gold Medal Award which recognized "superlative photography requiring exceptional courage and enterprise abroad." The winners of this award since 1970 have been Kyoichi Sawada (1970); Larry Burrows (1971); Clive W. Limpkin (1972); David Burnett, Raymond Depardon, and Charles Gerretsen (1973); W. Eugene Smith (1974); Dirck Halstead (1975); Catherine Leroy (1976); Eddie Adams (1977); Susan Meiselas (1978); Kaveh Golestan (1979); Steve McCurry (1980); Rudy Frey (1981); Harry Mattison (1982); James Nachwey (1983).

In 1980, the W. Eugene Smith Memorial Fund was formed to award a $10,000 to $15,000 Fellowship to support work "in the humanistic tradition." Recipients of the award to date are Jane Evelyn Atwood, who photographed blind children; Eugene Richards, who photographed the emergency room of a Denver hospital; Sebastio Salgado, who explored the "other Americans" in Latin America; and Milton Rogovin, who is photographing mine workers in the United States and Germany.
See also: Individual photographers cited; FARM SECURITY ADMINISTRATION (FSA); FILM AND PHOTO LEAGUE; PHOTOJOURNALISM; SOCIAL LANDSCAPE.

Dodging

Dodging is a technique for reducing the amount of exposure to a portion of the print area during the enlargement of a negative. This technique prevents the shaded image area from being too dark in the print. Dodging thus is useful for correcting the overall tonal balance of a print and for preserving shadow detail that would otherwise be obscured. With color reversal papers dodging *darkens* the affected area rather than lightening it.

Dodging tools consist of small pieces of opaque plastic or cardboard attached to the end of a thin stick or rigid wire. They are easily homemade with cardboard and lengths of coat-hanger wire. If the print area to be dodged has an unusual shape, a corresponding shape can be cut out of the cardboard.

Dodging is accomplished by holding the dodging tool under the enlarger lens during exposure of the printing paper. The tool is held so that exposure is blocked only to the desired image area. The tool must be kept moving slightly but continuously to prevent a sharp outline from forming around the dodged area.
See also: BURNING-IN.

Doisneau, Robert

French; 1912–
Robert Doisneau, one of France's most popular and prolific reportage photographers, is known for his modest, playful, and ironic images of amusing juxtapositions, mingling social classes, and eccentrics in contemporary Paris streets and cafes. Influenced by the work of Kertész, Atget, and Cartier-Bresson, in over 20 books Doisneau has presented a charming vision of human frailty and life

as a series of quiet, incongruous moments. He has written: "The marvels of daily life are exciting; no movie director can arrange the unexpected that you find in the street."

Doisneau was born in Gentilly in the Val-de-Marne, France. He studied engraving at the Ecole Estienne in Chantilly, but found his training antiquated and useless upon graduation. He learned photography in the advertising department of a pharmaceutical firm. He began photographing details of objects in 1930. He sold his first photo-story to the *Excelsior* newspaper in 1932. He was a camera assistant to the sculptor Andrei Vigneaux and did military service prior to taking a job as an industrial and advertising photographer for the Renault auto factory at Billancourt in 1934. Fired in 1939, he took up freelance advertising and postcard photography to earn his living.

Domon, Ken. Untitled (n.d.). Courtesy Ken
Domon; Pacific Press.

Doisneau worked for the Rapho photo agency for several months until he was drafted in 1939. He was a member of the Resistance both as a soldier and as a photographer, using his engraving skills to forge passports and identification papers. He photographed the Occupation and Liberation of Paris.

Immediately after the war he returned to freelance work for *Life* and other leading international magazines. He joined the Alliance photo agency for a short time and has worked for Rapho since 1946. Against his inclinations, Doisneau did high-society and fashion photography for *Paris Vogue* from 1948 to 1951. In addition to his reportage, he has photographed many French artists including Giacometti, Cocteau, Leger, Braque, and Picasso.

Doisneau won the Prix Kodak in 1947. He was awarded the Prix Niépce in 1956 and acted as a consultant to Expo '67, Canada. A short film, *Le Paris de Robert Doisneau*, was made in 1973.

Doisneau has been the subject of major retrospectives at the Bibliotecque Nationale in Paris, the Art Institute of Chicago, George Eastman House in Rochester, New York, and the Witkin Gallery in New York City. A shy and unassuming man, Doisneau lives in the Paris suburb of Montrouge.

Photograph: p. 129.

Domon, Ken

Japanese; 1909–

Ken Domon has been one of Japan's most influential documentary photographers since the mid-1930s. His work, in opposition to the pictorial tradition of Japanese photography, helped to create a new realism. Domon is considered the leading systematic documentor of ancient Japanese architecture and sculpture, having created an extensive series of photographs of ancient temples. He has also done significant photoreportage concerning Japanese children and the victims of the Hiroshima bombing.

Domon was born in the port town of Sakata City, Yamagata Prefecture. He was raised in Tokyo from the age of eight. His first desire was to become a painter. Domon studied briefly at Tokyo University but was expelled for radical political activities in 1932. He served as an apprentice to Kotaro Miyauchi, of the Tokyo Fine Arts School, from 1933 to 1935. From 1935 to 1945 he was a staff photographer with Nihon Kobo Studios, Tokyo, and began his career as a freelance photographer soon after. He has published seven volumes of photographs and his work has appeared in magazines around the world.

Domon was the founder of the Shudan Photo group in 1950 and was responsible for exhibitions of the work of Western photographers including Margaret Bourke-White, Henri Cartier-Bresson, Bill Brandt, Irving Penn, and W. Eugene Smith. He served as vice-president of the Japan Photographers Society in 1959.

Domon has been the recipient of numerous awards, including the Photographic Culture Prize (1942), Photographer of the Year Award of the Japan Photo Critics Association (1958), the Mainichi Photo Prize (1958), the Minister of Education Award of the Arts (1959), the Photographic Society of Japan Award (1960), the Japan Journalists Congress Award (1960), the Mainichi Art Award (1961), the Grand Prix at the International Exhibition of News Photographs, The Hague (1960), and the Kan Kikuchi Award (1971).

Domon's work has been exhibited in group shows including *New Japanese Photography* at the Museum of Modern Art, New York, in 1974, and *Japanese Photography Today and Its Origins,* a European traveling exhibition in 1979. One-man shows honoring him in Tokyo include two displays of his images of children (1955 and 1960), Hiroshima victims (1968), ancient temples (1972), and the Bunraku puppet theater (1973).

Though paralyzed on his right side several years ago by a stroke, Domon continues to live and work in Tokyo.

Double Exposure

See: MULTIPLE EXPOSURES/MULTIPLE PRINTING.

Draper, John William

English; 1811–1882
As a university professor, M.D., and pioneer of photography, Draper's career in the U.S., from 1833 on, embraced university teaching in chemistry and physiology, active practice as a physician, and both theoretical and practical investigations of photography. His earliest studies in radiant energy were preliminary steps to what would become the field of spectrum analysis (spectrography); they also provoked his immediate interest in photography when the daguerreotype process was made public.

He took his first pictures in September 1839 and began experimenting to improve the process. The following March he made the first photograph of the moon, and in June or July took the earliest surviving portrait in photography. The subject was his sister, Dorothy Catherine Draper, who sat with her eyes closed and white powder on her face (for greater reflectivity) for a 30-minute exposure in direct sun. At that time he and Samuel F. B. Morse established the world's first photographic portrait studio, a glass-topped structure on the roof of the building of New York University, where they were both professors. Daguerreotypes were made for $4.00, with exposures of 20 seconds to 2 minutes, depending upon conditions. He proposed the idea of taking extremely miniature photographs which would be greatly enlarged for viewing, the procedure known as microphotography, of which he became one of the first successful practitioners.

Draper's research in 1840 noted the regression of the latent image: the fact that it begins to deteriorate immediately after exposure, and after a certain time becomes undevelopable. It was a common problem with all early photographic processes, but is virtually insignificant for most kinds of photography with modern materials.

In 1841 Draper rediscovered and elaborated on the law of photochemical absorption, first noted by T. F. Grotthuss in 1817 and now known as the Grotthuss-Draper law: only those wavelengths of light that are absorbed

can cause chemical change or reaction; the other wavelengths have no effect. It is the principle underlying the discoveries of H. W. Vogel and others of the dye sensitization of emulsions to make them responsive to wavelengths other than ultraviolet and blue. In 1842 Draper took the first photograph of the spectrum of the sun, a daguerreotype which he sent to Sir John Herschel. His subsequent career included further research in radiant energy and photochemistry and writing the standard text on human physiology used in the mid-19th c.
See also: DYE SENSITIZATION; MORSE, SAMUEL F. B.; SPECTROGRAPHY/ SPECTROSCOPE.

Driffield, Vero Charles

English; 1848–1915
A chemist and amateur photographer, Driffield's collaboration with Ferdinand Hurter established the first scientific method to determine the speed of materials used in photography. Their results, published in 1890, created the field of sensitometry, which embraced their original methods of photometry and densitometry.
See also: DENSITOMETRY; HURTER, FERDINAND; PHOTOMETER/PHOTOMETRY; SENSITOMETRY; SPEED OF MATERIALS.

Drtikol, František

Czechoslovak; 1883–1961
František Drtikol was first acclaimed in the decade prior to World War I as Czechoslovakia's premier photographer of artists and writers. He worked at that time in a soft-focus, pictorial style that he abandoned after 1917. His later work consisted primarily of female nude studies, influenced by the art nouveau studies of his youth, that became increasingly abstract and harshly lit. Drtikol is often credited with influencing the photographic practice of the Bauhaus artists. The work of his last active years as a photographer employed figurines and plywood cutouts rather than live models, in settings influenced by the forms of cubist painting.

Drtikol started his career in photography as an apprentice at the studio of Antonín Matas in 1898. From 1901 to 1903 he studied at the Teaching and Research Institute for Photography in Munich, where he became acquainted with the artistic ideals of Jugendstil and symbolism. Before founding a portrait studio of his own, Drtikol spent several years as a journeyman at different photographic studios in Central Europe. His studio, opened in Prague in 1910, was for a quarter-century a famous place

where celebrities and foreign visitors came to have their portraits taken. Apart from commissions, Drtikol devoted himself to photographing still life, landscapes, and above all, the nude. He participated in many exhibitions at home and abroad, including the U.S. where an exhibition of his work traveled in the 1920s. His works were published in numerous magazines and yearbooks, and won many awards. Drtikol also organized courses for amateur photographers, and by his work and teaching influenced young Czech photographers, among others Josef Sudek and Jaromír Funke. His work achieved its peak in the 1920s. In the following decade he became increasingly preoccupied with orientalism, the occult sciences, and painting. These interests led him to give up his photographic activity: he sold his equipment and closed the studio in 1935.

Drtikol is well known for his nudes, which represent perhaps the best example of the art deco style in photography. In these pictures he succeeded in combining the human body with a geometrical decoration. However, his work is characterized by symbolic and expressive as well as decorative elements, all of which derive from the early influence of Jugendstil and symbolism. During the late 1910s and early 1920s he integrated motifs and themes of symbolism, expressionism, and cubism into an original personal style.

In various works Drtikol combined visual elements with different degrees of emphasis and emotional weight. For example, in the portfolio *Z pražských dvorů a dvorečku* (From Prague's Courtyards and Backyards), published together with Augustin Skarda in 1911, he stressed expressionistic elements, anticipating a similar trend in literature and film. The expressive use of cast shadows and tonal contrasts—also explicit in some Drtikol's nudes and portraits—has a symbolic as well as compositional meaning. Reflecting this interrelationship, Drtikol wrote: "The [cast] shadow plays an independent role, especially as far as the flat picture surface is concerned; it gives life, it draws attention, it is equally important as the object itself."

While in Drtikol's work of the 1920s the decorative, expressive, and symbolic elements were equally balanced, in the 1930s symbolism came to the fore. This shift led Drtikol to the end of his photographic career. As described in his statement *Ars una, species mille:* ". . . a great break took place in my outlook on the world and its events in the thirties . . . [resulting in an] inclination away from the materialist way of thinking and com-

Drtikol, Frantisek. Untitled (1907). Courtesy Manfred Heiting, Frankfurt-am-Main.

plete submersion in my own inner feelings; my former method of work sufficed to express my artistic visions. And so I arrived at the idea of replacing a live body [i.e., the model before the camera], which I could not locate in space in the manner in which I would have liked, with figures which I composed, cut out and painted plastically myself."

After closing his photographic studio, Drtikol devoted himself to painting and studies in oriental philosophy. He was made a member of the Union of Creative Artists in 1948. His work as a photographer was forgotten by the time of his death in 1961 but began to receive deserved attention following a major retrospective at the Museum of Decorative Arts, Prague, in 1972.

Drtikol was the recipient of many prizes at exhibitions around the world including a Bronze Medal in 1903 at the Internationale Austellung für Photographie und Graphische Kunst in Mainz, Germany. Solo exhibitions of his photographs have been held at S.I.C.O.F., Milan, in 1973; Photographers' Gallery, London, in 1974; and at the Royal Photographic Society, London, in 1974. His work has also been exhibited in group shows including *Photography into Art*, in London, in 1973, and *Photographic Surrealism*, an American touring exhibition, in 1979. Drtikol's archive of over 20,000 prints, negatives, and personal documents is in the Museum of Decorative Arts, Prague.

Drum and Tube Processing

Photographic prints may be processed using a drum or tubelike container in place of trays for reasons of convenience, economy, and consistency. This kind of processing is most often used for color prints, but it is equally suitable for black-and-white prints. A typical drum processor consists of a motorized revolving drum oriented horizontally so that its lower third passes through a trough that holds the processing solutions. The print is placed emulsion-side-out (in most cases) around the circumference of the drum. It is held in place by a wide-mesh plastic webbing that is loose enough for processing solution to reach all parts of the emulsion as the drum rotates continuously. The trough permits quick draining and filling so solutions can be changed. Some drums have temperature-controlled troughs and lighttight covers. A processing tube is an opaque plastic cylinder with a removable cap at one end. The print is placed inside curved against the wall of the tube with its emulsion facing inward. A small amount of processing solution is poured in, the end cap replaced, and the tube laid horizontally for use. It is agitated by hand, rolling it back and forth, or by a motorized cradle that rotates it continuously. Some tubes have a light-trapped quick-empty/refill end cap for changing solutions.

A single drum or tube replaces a number of processing trays; particularly in the case of large-format prints this pro-

vides a great saving in work space. A much smaller amount of each solution is required than is the case with tray processing. This offers a savings in the cost of chemicals. Less solution surface is exposed to the air, reducing oxidation effects, and the solution is confined to a smaller space, making temperature control easier. Especially with motor-driven equipment, the agitation is always uniform and it is easier to time each processing step accurately, with the result that consistent, repeatable print quality can be obtained more easily.

Drum and tube processors have two disadvantages: capacity and cost. Most processors accept a maximum of four prints at a time, depending upon their surface area and the size of the prints. Their original cost is generally greater than that of trays, especially in the case of motorized equipment. The expense eventually may be recovered from savings in chemical costs, but working convenience and efficiency are usually the most important factors.

See also: STABILIZATION PROCESS.

Drying Films and Prints

Proper drying restores photographic materials to a condition in which they can be handled safely for printing and other uses. The most common evidences of improper drying are splotches of uneven density in films, caused by water drops on the emulsion, and wavy edges or bulging center portions in prints, caused by uneven shrinkage from excessive heat during drying. Removal of excess surface water is the first step. Films may be wiped gently with a photographic-quality sponge or chamois, or immersed for a minute in a final rinse of a few drops of wetting agent in water, and then hung to dry. The wetting agent permits the water to flow freely off the film and to break into tiny droplets of similar size which evaporate at a relatively uniform rate. Films treated this way should not be wiped down, or the effect of the treatment will be negated. Prints may be wiped on both sides with a rubber-bladed squeegee or placed between dry blotters for about five minutes before being transferred to a dryer or fresh blotters. Forced-air drying, with or without heating, is advisable for films only if the air supply is filtered; otherwise, dust particles may be driven into the soft emulsion, from which they cannot be removed later without damage. Hanging film in a dust-free enclosure—with a weight at the bottom of roll and 35mm films—is the best procedure.

Prints may be placed between blotters, laid on open mesh screens, or

Du Camp, Maxime. "Mosque de Sultan Kansou-El-Gouri" (ca. 1851); calotype. Collection, Museum of Modern Art, New York.

placed in a heated dryer. Prints on water-resistant papers must be laid face up in a dryer to prevent emulsion damage; air-drying is best with such papers, which dry rapidly in any case. A blower-type hair dryer set at medium or low temperature can be used to accelerate drying; this is particularly useful with color test prints which must be dry before the color can be evaluated. Fast drying of films and prints can be achieved by bathing them for 2 minutes in ethyl or isopropyl (*not* methyl) alcohol diluted with 20 percent water. The alcohol displaces most of the water in the material and will evaporate in 4 or 5 minutes when the print or film is hung to dry at a temperature of no more than 80.5°F (27°C). Prints may also be dried quickly in a microwave oven, but cautious experimentation is required to establish the time and power setting.

Dry Mounting

Prints may be fastened to a mounting board by means of a dry adhesive tissue; there are two types of such tissue, one activated by heat and the other by pressure. Thermal dry-mounting tissue is impregnated with a shellac that melts at 180-210°F (82-99°C). When it melts, it is partially absorbed into both the paper backing of the print and the surface of the mounting board; when it cools a permanent bond is formed. It is simple to use and forms a chemically inert barrier that helps protect the print from substances in the mounting board. In practice the tissue is first tacked to the back of the print with a heated iron. After both are trimmed to size, the tissue is tacked to the mounting board, the print face is covered with a protective piece of scrap paper, and the sandwich is placed in a heated mounting press. With care, dry mounting also can be accomplished with a household electric flat iron.

"Cold-mount" tissue requires only pressure, which is supplied by a set of rollers or by a hand burnisher. The absence of heat makes it particularly safe for use with color prints and those made on resin-coated papers or for plastic-coated mounting materials. Cold-mount tissue also permits relatively easy removal or repositioning of a print, procedures that are difficult to do with heat-activated tissue without damaging the print.

Dry Plates

Glass or metal plates coated with a light-sensitive emulsion which is dry when used are called dry plates. All plates and films now have dry emulsions, but the wet-plate process dominated the first period of great growth in photography from 1850 to about 1885. The daguerreotype was a dry metal plate, but in the sense of photography as a negative-positive medium, the first true dry plate was an adaptation of the albumen process to glass. Several types of collodion dry plates were introduced after 1860, but they were not particularly successful because they were so much less light sensitive than wet plates. Practical dry plates became available in the late 1870s, after improvement of the gelatin silver halide emulsion first described in practical form by R. L. Maddox in 1871.

See also: ALBUMEN PROCESSES; MADDOX, RICHARD LEACH; SWAN, J. W.; WET-PLATE PROCESS.

DuCamp, Maxime

French; 1822–1894

The only known photographs by the Parisian journalist and man of letters Maxime DuCamp are a series of 220 waxed-paper negatives taken on a trip with the writer Gustave Flaubert in Greece, the Middle East, and Asia Minor between 1849 and 1851. In preparation for this trip, DuCamp learned the rudiments of the calotype process from Gustave Le Gray in 1849. Flaubert was commissioned to make reports to the Chambers of Commerce, DuCamp was commissioned by the French Ministry of Education. It was DuCamp's task to make an exhaustive documentation of various ancient monuments and sites, many of which he had visited previously during the late 1840s. DuCamp often included a human figure within the frame in his photographs in order to indicate the scale of his subjects. His intuitive sense of expressive composition and his choice of the time of day when the sunlight was most revealing of form or carved surface decoration, produced many outstanding images in spite of the primitive process by which the photographs were taken.

DuCamp's work was published in several volumes by Blanquart-Evrard. Among the earliest and most lavishly photographically illustrated books of the 19th c., DuCamp's *Egypte, Nubie, Palestine et Syrie. Dessins photographiques recueillis pendant les années 1849, 1850 et 1851* (Paris: Gide et J. Baudry, 1852) included 125 images of such subjects as the Sphinx, the Colossus of Abu Simbel, and the Great Pyramids. A second volume, *Le Nil, Egypte et Nubie*, was published two years later.

Immediately upon publication, DuCamp's photographs were acclaimed around the world, but DuCamp abandoned photography upon his return to France and devoted himself to literature, founding the journal *Revue de Paris* in which Flaubert's *Madame Bovary* appeared.

DuCamp served with the French National Guard during the Revolution of 1848 and was awarded the Cross of the Legion of Honor in 1853. He published his memoirs, *Souvenirs littéraires,* in 1883, and died in Paris in 1894. An account of the journey made by DuCamp and Flaubert, *Flaubert in Egypt,* by Francis Steegmuller, was published in 1972.

See also: BLANQUART-EVRARD, L. D.; LE GRAY, GUSTAVE; WAXED-PAPER PROCESS.

Ducos du Hauron, Louis

French; 1837–1920

French pianist Louis Ducos du Hauron became a pioneer scientist in the field of color photography. His work *Les Couleurs en Photographie* (1869) was an important theoretical exploration of additive and subtractive methods of color reproduction, many of which were impracticable for years after his discoveries because of the limited color sensitivity of contemporary plates.

Ducos du Hauron investigated the possibilities of silver bromide collodion, colored light filters, and bleaching processes. He was the inventor of an early cinematograph in 1859. With his brother Alcide, he published a second pamphlet, *Photographie des Couleurs,* in 1870. Ducos's view of Angoulême (1877) is one of the earliest surviving color photographs. His work was exhibited regularly at the Paris Photographic Society from 1869 on. In 1891 Ducos patented the anaglyph three-dimensional photographic process. He was awarded the Progress Medal of the British Royal Photographic Society for his work in three-color heliochromy in 1900.

See also: ANAGLYPH; COLOR PHOTOGRAPHY—HISTORY.

Dufaycolor

The most successful screen process for producing transparencies by additive color synthesis was invented in France in 1910 by Louis D. Dufay. Called the Dioptichrome plate, it became more popular than the Lumière autochrome plates largely because the size of its color elements permitted use of faster emulsions. The plate consisted of a mosaic of alternating green and blue dye squares crossed at right angles by a pattern of parallel red dye lines, each element measuring only 0.002 in. (0.05mm) in width. This filter screen was coated over with a panchromatic emulsion. Exposure was through the base, so the emulsion behind each color element was exposed only if there was light of the corresponding primary color at that point in the image. The plate was reversal processed so that a black-and-white positive image remained. When viewed by transmitted light, the transparency and the color screen worked together to produce a full-color image. An improved version of the process was given the name Dufaycolor in the 1920s, and a method of developing a negative image and printing positive copies was introduced. The only major rival was the Finlaycolor process, which used a separate rather than an integral color screen. Although Dufaycolor materials were available up to the mid-1940s, the process and all other additive processes had given way a decade earlier to materials in which chromogenic development produced dyes which formed the image by subtractive synthesis of color (most notably, Kodachrome film).

See also: ADDITIVE COLOR SYNTHESIS; AUTOCHROME; COLOR PHOTOGRAPHY—HISTORY; FINLAYCOLOR PROCESS; MOSAIC SYSTEMS; SCREEN PROCESSES.

Duncan, David Douglas

American; 1916–

David Douglas Duncan is an internationally acclaimed photographer and writer whose work has appeared in over a dozen books and countless periodicals in the past 40 years. He is known for work in three categories: combat photography, photo-essays on Picasso, and underwater nature photography. He received the Robert Capa Gold Medal from the Overseas Press Club in 1968 and has twice been named Photographer of the Year by the American Society of Magazine Photographers. He was the first photographer to be given a one-man show by the Whitney Museum in New York City.

Duncan was born in Kansas City, Missouri. He studied archaeology at the University of Arizona and marine zoology and deep-sea diving at the University of Miami. His first professional photographs were undersea images. He began to travel the world as a photographer, foreign correspondent, and art historian in 1938. He was the official camera person for the Michael Lerner Chile-Peru expedition of the American Museum of Natural History, and worked for Nelson Rockefeller's Office of Inter-American Affairs photographing in Mexico and Central America.

As a highly decorated Marine in the South Pacific during the World War II, Duncan shot combat photographs which won him immediate recognition. For his intimate portraits of soldiers in the midst of battle he became known as "the Legendary Lensman."

Duncan became a *Life* staff photographer after the war and, for the next ten years he photographed major stories in Palestine, Iran, Greece, Korea, and Indo-China. He was sent wherever there was trouble in the world.

In 1956 Duncan left *Life* to join *Collier's* and traveled with writer John Gunther to Russia, where he began extensive documentation of Kremlin art treasures. Later that year he met Picasso, with whom he established a close friendship. In the next several years Duncan took over 50,000 photographs of the artist and his work, including the official estate photos taken for the French government. Duncan's work with Picasso has resulted in the publication of four books. Of this collaboration Duncan has said: "As a photographer, I found it was more exhausting to be with Picasso for a day than to be in combat. When I was photographing Picasso, I was constantly under the full tension of waiting for what he would do next, and you don't have that complete, unrelieved tension even in combat."

During the late 1960s, Duncan covered the Vietnam War for *Life* and ABC-TV. He published his autobiography, *Yankee Nomad,* in 1966, and a book, *I Protest,* in 1968, in which he denounced the American action in Vietnam. In recent years his color photographs of underwater plant and animal life have garnered much attention. Duncan's work in each of his specialties continues to be published and exhibited throughout the world.

Duplicate Images

Photographic prints, transparencies, and negatives are duplicated to protect a valuable original from excessive handling or use, and to obtain multiple copies of the image for widespread distribution or use. Large numbers of duplicates are often required for publicity and promotional purposes, for educational and training presentations, and for use in libraries and picture agencies. A print is duplicated by photographing it to obtain a copy negative from which subsequent prints can be made. A negative is duplicated by contact-printing it onto film to obtain a positive transparency, and then repeating the process to obtain a negative. A more efficient method, which produces better quality, is to use a direct-duplicating film, one that produces a negative from exposure to a negative with normal processing; no intermediate stage is necessary. Color transparencies are duplicated either by photographing them directly on transparency (reversal) film, or by making an intermediate negative (interneg) which is then used to make positives on an appropriate print film.

There are several ways to copy a negative or positive film image onto another piece of film. The simplest way is to put the original in a slide projector and photograph the image from the surface of the screen; this, however, offers the least quality. Most 35mm and medium-format cameras accept a bellows or rigid-tube copying accessory that fits in front of the lens. The original image is placed in front of a light diffuser in the device, and the diffuser is lighted from the other side with daylight, electronic flash, or another suitable source. High-volume duplicating is done most efficiently with a specialized copying stand that has a stage designed to hold the original and illuminate it from behind with diffused electronic flash. Commercial duplicating laboratories use similar equipment with a modified 35mm motion-picture camera that accepts long rolls of film and makes single-frame exposures. Contact printing, with the original placed emulsion to emulsion with the duplicating film, requires the least equipment, but is often affected with problems of dust, alignment, and uniform contact between the films. Direct projection, using an enlarger, onto the duplicate film offers the choice of same-size, enlarged, or reduced duplicates. It also provides the greatest opportunity for corrective filtration, burning-in or dodging, and similar techniques. Of course, such alterations do not provide a duplicate in the sense of a facsimile, but they do provide an improved copy; in most cases the distinction is not important.
See also: COPYING PHOTOGRAPHS; DIRECT POSITIVE.

Dye Destruction Process

Dye destruction is a method of producing color prints from positive transparencies or negatives which depends on bleaching unnecessary dyes out of the emulsion, rather than using chromogenic development to produce dyes in the emulsion; it is also called the silver-dye bleach process. Dye destruction print materials consist of three silver halide emulsion layers, each sensitized to one primary color of light, as in conventional color materials. However, each layer also contains a full density of a complementary color dye; yellow in the blue-sensitive layer, magenta in the green-sensitive layer, cyan in the red-sensitive layer. In modern materials these are azo dyes, which are far more permanent and resistant to fading from

the effects of light than the dyes used in other print materials. However, the dyes do become susceptible to bleaching when a silver halide image is developed.

In direct positive printing from a slide, exposure records a negative image in the emulsion; when this is developed, the associated dye densities can be bleached away, leaving only dye deposits which correspond to the positive aspects of the image. In a final step, the negative silver image is bleached and removed along with the unexposed, undeveloped silver halides in the positive image. The result is a subtractive color positive dye image. In negative-positive printing, the silver image is reversal processed, and the dyes are bleached after the second development step. Because subject colors were reversed in the negative, this procedure produces a positive print image.

Early in the 20th c. the dye destruction principle attracted great interest, but met with little commercial success. The Utocolor process introduced in 1910 relied on the bleaching action of the light on dyes exposed beneath a color transparency; it was only partly successful because the dyes did not fade (bleach) at a uniform rate and because of color differences between the additive color autochrome transparency and the subtractive color dyes in the print material. The Gasparcolor process of 1934 used dye destruction to form color images in motion-picture film. Dye destruction became successful after World War II with the introduction of Cibachrome materials, which are unique in photography today. They are available with opaque white bases for making prints, and transparent bases for making duplicate transparencies; only direct positive materials are produced.
See also: ETCH-BLEACH PROCESS; REVERSAL MATERIALS AND PROCESSING; SUBTRACTIVE COLOR SYNTHESIS.

Dyeline Process

See: DIAZO PROCESS.

Dye Sensitization

Dye sensitization is the technique by which the color sensitivity of silver halides is extended to various wavelengths. It is an application of the Grotthuss-Draper law, which states that only the absorbed portion of light can cause a chemical reaction. Silver halides are inherently sensitive to ultraviolet and blue, but not to longer wavelengths (green and red). However, certain dyes can absorb longer wavelengths and in the process affect halides as if they had been directly exposed. In emulsion manufac-

ture the halide crystals are treated with these compounds to produce orthochromatic, panchromatic, and infrared-sensitive materials. The discovery of dye compounds suitable for use with photographic materials was made by H. W. Vogel in 1873.
See also; ORTHOCHROMATIC; PANCHROMATIC; VOGEL, HERMANN WILHELM.

Dye Toning

The conversion of a black and gray-tone silver image directly to a color image by the absorption of dyes is based on the fact that a number of silver compounds can act as mordants for various dyes, the most effective being silver iodide. The silver image is developed normally, then chemically converted to silver iodide. Depending upon the degree of toning desired, the iodide conversion may be partial or complete. The image is then immersed in a dye bath and after a suitable time washed in water. The dye rinses out of the clear portions of the emulsion, but is held in the image areas in proportion to the amount of mordant there. The partial silver image may be left to add its density to the total image, or it may subsequently be bleached away.

In the Uvachrome process introduced by A. Traube and G. Miethe in 1906, dye toning was used to produce full-color images. Low-contrast separation positives were prepared on stripping film, converted to silver iodide, and dye-toned cyan, magenta, and yellow. The dyed emulsions were removed from their original bases and assembled in register on a final base which was either opaque white to produce a print, or transparent for viewing by transmitted light. A great number of alternate processes were invented, differing primarily in the particular mordanting compound to which the silver image was converted, and the chemical composition of the dyes used.

Although dye toning offers great versatility and the opportunity to use dyes that are much more permanent than those in most photographic materials, it is little used today, largely because the process is involved and lengthy and the materials are expensive. Films and papers with integral color couplers that are processed by chromogenic development are much easier to use, especially to produce full-color images.

Dye Transfer Process

The dye transfer printing process creates a color image in an emulsion that absorbs dyes from a series of gelatin relief images; it is the most versatile and successful of the transfer and assembly processes.

Based on various earlier dye imbibition and wash-off relief techniques, the dye transfer process was introduced as a unified system of procedures and materials in the mid-1930s by Eastman Kodak Co.; it was known as the wash-off relief process. An improved process brought out by Kodak in 1946 is the basis of the system used today by custom-work laboratories and individual photographers for the highest quality color prints. The process offers unequalled control over contrast and color balance in the print, including changing colors completely (e.g., blue mashed potatoes, scarlet bananas) if desired. This feature is responsible for the wide use of the dye transfer process in advertising and fine art illustration to produce the most subtly corrected and enhanced illustrations. The dyes that constitute the final image are far less susceptible to fading than those of conventional color photographic materials, making dye transfer prints a preferred choice for long-term display and for collecting. Although no color image can itself achieve the permanence of an archivally processed black-and-white image, the separation negatives used in the process are on black-and-white film. These can be archivally processed and used to produce new dye transfer prints at any time in the future, even if the original color image and all other prints have deteriorated or perished.

Separation negatives are obtained by photographing the original print or transparency on black-and-white film through red, green, and blue filters. The negatives then are used to expose special matrix films which in turn are used to transfer the dyes in printing. A special panchromatic matrix film permits making the printing matrices directly from a color negative without need for an in-termediate positive print or transparency. The matrix film has a gelatin emulsion that is hardened by the effect of exposure; it is exposed through the base so that hardened gelatin will adhere in middletone areas where the exposure does not completely penetrate the emulsion. The film is developed in a special tanning developer, or in a conventional film developer followed by a bleach-hardening solution of potassium dichromate and sulfuric acid. In either case, the gelatin is further hardened in proportion to the amount of exposure received in each area.

Each matrix film then is washed in warm water until all the unexposed, unhardened gelatin dissolves, leaving a colorless gelatin relief positive image. The image is reversed left-for-right because each film was exposed through the base, but this is corrected when the matrix is pressed face-down against the final printing sheet. The matrices can be used immediately or dried for use at a later time. When used, they are all first lightly dyed with a single color for registration of their images; this dye is then rinsed out, and the matrices are dyed for printing. Dyes of any color may be used, but for normal full-color reproduction the usual colors for subtractive synthesis of color are used. The matrix made from the blue separation negative is dyed yellow; the matrix from the green separation negative is dyed magenta; and the matrix from the red separation negative is dyed cyan. Dyeing is simply a matter of placing the matrix in an appropriate color solution for about five minutes; in that time the gelatin absorbs as much dye as it can hold. The matrix is then rinsed to remove excess dye from the surface and used for printing. The concentration of dye in the color bath determines the depth of the color; the relative acidity of the color bath and the rinse affect contrast (increased acidity produces increased contrast).

The print is made on special receiving paper, which has a clear gelatin emulsion, or on ordinary, unexposed black-and-white photographic paper which has been thoroughly fixed and washed to remove all silver halides. The print paper is soaked in a mordant solution so the emulsion will accept the dyes readily, without fringing or bleeding at the edges of dyed areas. The print paper is fastened face up on a smooth surface; each matrix in turn is squeegeed face down against it and allowed to remain until the dye is absorbed by the mordanted emulsion. The dyes are transferred in the order cyan, magenta, yellow. In addition to color control at the dyeing stage, further control is available in printing by re-dyeing any matrix for two or more transfers. It is at this stage that accurate registration of the images is essential, otherwise blurred outlines and color fringes will be produced.

Careful attention to temperatures and drying conditions, and the use of plastic- rather than celluloid-based films are essential throughout the process to ensure that no image shrinks or expands in relation to the others. After the final transfer, the image sheet is squeegeed on both sides to remove excess liquid and is hung to dry. The matrices can be cleaned and redyed to make additional prints, or they can be washed and dried for use at a later time. Although the process is involved and requires careful attention to details—especially to the sequence of dyeing and rinsing one matrix while the previous matrix is transferring its color—it is possible to achieve color quality unattainable with any other process.

See also: DYE TONING; MORDANT; REGISTRATION OF IMAGES; SEPARATION NEGATIVES; SUBTRACTIVE COLOR SYNTHESIS; TRANSFER PROCESSES.

Evans, Frederick H. "Sea of Steps" (1898);
platinum. Philadelphia Museum of Art.

E

Eastman, George

American; 1854–1932

Self-supporting from his mid-teens, George Eastman took up photography with the wet plate process in 1877. His experiments in the next two years with the newly introduced do-it-yourself gelatin emulsions produced improvements that led to formation of the Eastman Dry Plate Co. in 1880. The Eastman-Walker roll holder for use on standard view cameras, introduced in 1884, used a roll of paper coated with a gelatin emulsion; after processing, the paper was oiled to make it nearly transparent for printing. The following year Eastman American film was offered. It was a roll stripping film in which the processed gelatin emulsion was removed from the paper backing and transferred to a glass or thick gelatin support for printing. The No. 1 Kodak camera of 1888 used American Film; 1889 and subsequent models used Eastman celluloid roll film. Although Eastman was the first to produce celluloid-base roll films commercially, a patent for the idea had been applied for in 1887 by Rev. Hannibal Goodwin. A patent infringement suit was finally decided in 1914 with a $5 million judgement against the Eastman Co.; it was paid to the Ansco Co., which had become owners of Goodwin's rights.

The rapid growth of Eastman Kodak Co. included materials for professionals, an expanding line of cameras and films for amateurs, and chemical and paper production. The Edison Kinetoscope of 1899 used the first celluloid motion-picture film in the U.S., from Kodak. In 1923, 16mm reversal film on daylight-loading spools for amateur moviemaking was introduced. Several color processes culminated in Kodachrome film, introduced in 1935, and Ektachrome film, developed during World War II and offered publicly in 1946. Drop-in 126- and 110-size film cartridges, self-processing instant films, diffusion transfer color printing materials, and a disk-format camera were among the popular-market products introduced in the following decades.

During his lifetime Eastman gave more than $100 million to support health clinics, medical education, colleges for black Americans, symphony orchestras and other cultural institutions, and a great number of scientific and social research organizations. He took his own life in 1932, at the age of 78, leaving the message, "My work is done; why wait?"
See also: DISK CAMERAS; GOODWIN, REV. HANNIBAL; KODACHROME; KODAK; STRIPPING FILM.

Eclipse Photography

Various techniques are used to take pictures of celestial bodies when they are partly or totally blocked from view or shadowed by another body. The sun and the moon are large enough to be satisfactorily photographed with or without the aid of a telescope; other celestial bodies are so distant that a telescope is required. The moon is eclipsed by the shadow of the earth passing between it and the sun. The sun is eclipsed for an observer on earth by the body of the moon crossing the line of view. On some occasions, the moon is close enough to the earth to totally block the body of the sun for some observers; only the glowing outer atmosphere, or corona, around the sun can be seen. At other times, the moon is so distant that the sun is only partially blocked from view from all possible observation points on earth. Although the sun and moon differ greatly in size, their distances from the earth are proportionally different so that they have essentially the same visual diameter. This makes it possible to use the same method to calculate the image size either body will have on film:

Focal length of camera lens ÷ 110

If the camera is used in conjunction with a telescope, the calculated image size is multiplied by the power of the telescope.

Lunar eclipse photography is both safe and easy, requiring only high-speed film, a tripod for the camera, and a lens of as long focal length as possible. With an ISO 400/27° film, exposures range from 1/250 sec. at $f/22$ for the full, unclouded moon, to about 1 sec. at $f/2.8$ during the time of maximum eclipse. Solar-eclipse photography is more difficult and is potentially dangerous, especially for amateurs. It is difficult because direct sunlight is 600,000 or more times brighter than direct moonlight. Slow-speed films are useful, and the intensity of the light must be reduced 10,000 to 100,000 times to come within the exposure range of most films. These reductions can be obtained, respectively, with 4.0 and 5.0 neutral density filters. Exposure during partial eclipse phases can be calculated as follows:

$$\text{Exposure time (in sec.)} = (f/\text{number})^2 \div \\ (\text{arithmetic film speed} \times 10^{7-D})$$

where D = the density of the neutral density filter. Exposures during totality will be 10 to 100 times longer at the same f-stop, but without the neutral density filter. Exposure bracketing is almost essential because atmospheric conditions also affect results.

With a camera mounted on a tripod, a sequence of the progress of an eclipse can be taken on a single frame with an exposure about once every 10 minutes; this is enough time so that the images will not overlap. This procedure requires a means of taking multiple exposures without advancing the film, and eliminates the possibility of bracketing exposures.

Problems and solutions. The major problem of solar eclipse photography is the possibility of serious injury to the photographer's eyes or to equipment from ultraviolet and infrared wavelengths as well as the intense visible portion of direct sunlight. Ordinary color filters, polarizers, and neutral density filters offer no protection to the eyes, even in through-the-lens viewing systems, whether direct (as in view cameras) or indirect (as in mirror/prism reflex cameras). The sun may be viewed safely through a sandwich of two layers of black-and-white film that has been completely exposed to light and developed to maximum density. Color films and chromogenic black-and-white films offer no protection. The protective sandwich should be placed in front of the eyes before looking at the sun, or in front of the lens before looking into the viewing system. To avoid damage from focused rays inside the camera, the lens should not be left uncapped while pointed at the sun except during the time of actual exposure.

See also: MOON PHOTOGRAPHY; NEUTRAL DENSITY; SUN PHOTOGRAPHY; TELESCOPE.

ECPS : Effective Candlepower Seconds

The output of a light source in a reflector is measured in effective candlepower seconds (ECPS), a measurement essentially the same as beam candlepower seconds (BCPS). The fundamental difference is that BCPS is measured directly on the central axis of the light source, whereas ECPS is the average of readings taken at specified positions around the central axis. The resultant figures differ by less than 10 percent in almost all cases, and may be used interchangeably in comparing electronic flash units or computing exposure.

See also: BCPS; ELECTRONIC FLASH.

Eder, Josef Maria

Austrian; 1855–1944

The discoveries and publications of J. M. Eder were fundamental contributions to the science and chemistry of photography and photomechanical reproduction from about 1875 to 1925. Eder was the author of one of the most comprehensive histories of photographic technology, which comprised two massive volumes in the final (fourth) edition, published in 1932. His earliest research discovered that cadmium salts increased the speed of collodion plates. In 1879 he invented a process of image intensification using lead compounds, and discovered the processes of coloring silver images by first converting them to silver ferrocyanide; this was the basis of almost all subsequent dye toning procedures.

In 1880 Eder discovered the powers of pyrocatechin as a developing agent; it was used for the next 50 years in a great number of standard developer formulas. He produced the first silver chloride emulsion that responded to alkaline development; although such papers did not become commercially successful until the 1890s, alkaline development rapidly became the standard procedure—as it remains today—largely by virtue of its speed and ease of controlled variation. In 1884, the same year in which H. W. Vogel produced an orthochromatic collodion emulsion, Eder discovered the use of erythrosin, a far more effective dye sensitization compound, for the same purpose in gelatin emulsion; it is still used today. He founded the Graphic Arts Institute of Austria in 1888, one of the earliest university-level institutions for education and training as well as scientific research in photography and related reproduction methods.

In 1889 Eder introduced the use of sodium bisulfite to maintain the acidity of fixing baths in order to prevent exces-sive swelling of gelatin emulsions and subsequent reticulation. In 1898 he promoted the use of a new sensitometer to standardize industrial and scientific practices, and in 1919 he invented an improved optical wedge for sensitometry. His numerous technical publications included a monumental *Comprehensive Handbook of Photography* first published in 1884 and kept in print for 50 years.

See also: DYE SENSITIZATION; DYE TONING; INTENSIFICATION; ORTHOCHROMATIC; RETICULATION; VOGEL, HERMANN WILHELM; WEDGE, OPTICAL.

Edge Effects

Certain distortions of density that occur in an image as a result of local chemical interaction during processing are called edge effects; they are also called, or related to, adjacency, border, and neighborhood effects. The effects occur at the boundary between areas that have received significantly different degrees of exposure and that therefore generate different degrees of chemical activity during development. In general, they are caused by a reduction of activity when exhausted developer or restraining by-products diffuse into an area, or by an increase in activity when unexhausted developer diffuses into an area. Increased development just within the edge of the more exposed of two areas produces an emphasis of density called the *Mackie line*. The *Eberhard effect* results when the Mackie lines at each edge of a very narrow common area—or the line around the inner edge of a very small spot—merge to produce an overall density greater than that produced in a wider area that received the same exposure. The *Kostinsky effect* produces reduced development between the edges of two areas of essentially equal exposure. The result is an apparent displacement of the two images away from one another, or a narrowing of the image widths of a series of closely spaced elements such as parallel lines.

See also: DENSITY; KOSTINSKY EFFECT; MACKIE LINE.

Edge Light

See: BACK LIGHT; RIM LIGHT; SIDELIGHT.

Edgerton, Dr. Harold E.

American; 1903–

Edgerton is an electrical engineer, an Institute Professor Emeritus at the Massachusetts Institute of Technology, inventor of the high-speed gas discharge tube, and a leading innovator in high-speed and remote-control photography. His work investigating the operation of electric motors by means of stroboscopic photography led to the invention of stroboscopes utilizing improved light-emitting gas discharge tubes triggered by high-voltage pulses. A major factor in this work was his discovery in the early 1930s that tubes filled with xenon or other rare gases have greatly increased light output. Such tubes are the basis of all electronic flash units, which were first manufactured for general photographic use in the early 1940s. His inventions for control of very high-speed motion-picture and still photography include a number of devices and methods for triggering a flash unit or stroboscope at the right instant to illuminate the particular phase of the phenomenon being investigated.

Edgerton has designed underwater camera and electronic flash equipment for use by Jacques Yves Cousteau, the U.S. Navy, and a number of scientific expeditions; has served as consultant on high-speed, remote-area, and space photography problems; and has developed integrated radar-television-photographic systems for use in attended and unattended explorations. His photographs include a number of milestones in high-speed image recording, especially color pictures of bullets in flight and similar phenomena.

See also: ELECTRONIC FLASH; HIGH-SPEED PHOTOGRAPHY; MOTION STUDY AND ANALYSIS; STROBOSCOPIC PHOTOGRAPHY.

Color photograph: p. C-14.

Editing

Visual editing consists of reviewing a group of pictures in order to select the most useful images and place them in an order that makes an effective presentation. It is a process as important with still photographs as with motion-picture and television footage. Implicit in the procedure is the understanding that a variety of information and details are to be communicated, and that the sequence in which they are seen determines the kind of communication that takes place.

In movies and television, editing determines not only the order of the images but also how long each image is seen. In a slide presentation editing establishes the sequence, but the person making the presentation controls the time factor and can choose to go back to earlier images if desired. In a book, magazine, or portfolio presentation editing determines the sizes of the images and the juxtapositions on a page or a spread (facing pages), but

the reader/viewer can start at any point, go forward or backward, repeat, and decide how much time to spend with each image. Although these various kinds of presentations are quite different, certain editing principles apply to them all.

The purpose of the presentation must be clearly identified. It may be informal entertainment (vacation slides to be shown to friends), selling one's work or services (a portfolio to be shown to an art director or editor), reporting (news pictures), commenting or informing (a documentary essay), or creating (a fictional story, a "mood" piece). Without a clear purpose, editing has no organizational spine. Only pictures directly related to that purpose and appropriate to the intended audience should be selected. If a portfolio is meant to show an ability as a documentary photographer, landscapes and formal portraits have no place in it, no matter how good they are. If work is being submitted to a fashion magazine, pictures of sports action are not likely to be appropriate.

Only technically excellent pictures should be selected. Substandard quality calls attention to itself, interrupts the flow of the presentation, and raises doubts about the photographer's standards or ability. Technically weak or flawed pictures may be used if their quality is part of the point to be made (e.g., during the sandstorm this was the best that could be obtained).

Pictures should be grouped to create separate scenes or short sequences within the overall presentation. For example, in a commercial photographer's portfolio food pictures, product pictures, and fashion pictures should be grouped accordingly, not intermingled. The pictures in each short sequence then should be arranged in the most effective order. In a visual narrative (picture story, motion picture) this often takes the following form: *long shot,* or overall view, to orient the viewer to the situation; *medium shot* to direct attention to the major area or group of interest; and *close-up* to single out a particularly significant person or detail. Often it is effective to begin with a close-up to capture attention and provoke interest and then to proceed to more generally informative pictures. In a non-narrative presentation such as a portfolio of commercial illustrations, effective sequences are built in terms of the relation of colors, tones, and shapes as well as the subject matter of the pictures.

The flow of the presentation should vary in rhythm and pace, and these should match the mood of the sequence. With still photographs size and place-

ment on the page, as well as the flow from page to page, determine these factors. Composition, color, tonality, and the pace of change all affect the mood of a sequence. In motion pictures and television changes in the size of the shots (long shot, close-up, etc.) and the length of time they are kept on the screen provide variety. In these media pace is also controlled with various transition devices. These include the cut, cutaway, dissolve, and fade (out and in).

In many presentations editing also involves the material that accompanies the images: dialogue or narration, music, sound effects, captions, text. A portfolio may have only visual content to be organized, or a news story may have only captions, while a motion picture has a complex accompaniment to be prepared. Just as the interactions between pictures affect what the viewer sees, so do these additional factors. The purpose of accompaniment is to help the picture speak more clearly, not to speak for the picture. The most effective accompaniment reinforces or expands on what the picture is saying without repeating it.

See also: CUT; DISSOLVE; FADE-IN/FADE-OUT.

Education, Photographic

In photography's first years, the most reliable method of learning the difficult daguerreotype and calotype processes was to study with a photographer who had already mastered the necessary chemical manipulations. Accounts from the 1850s, for example, describe the noted French photographer Gustave Le Gray as surrounded by a circle of eager students drawn from all walks of life. The rapid growth of interest in the new medium soon led to the establishment of more formal programs of instruction, as with the introduction of photography into the University of London's course of study in 1856. As a rule, such instruction was entrusted to professors of chemistry or physics, who diligently schooled their students in the scientific principles underlying the photographic process, rather than in pictorial principles. The photographer Alfred Stieglitz, for instance, received his only formal instruction from the eminent German photochemist Hermann Vogel in the mid-1880s.

In this century, photography's growing importance as a professional vocation, as a vehicle of mass communication, and as a medium of personal expression has contributed to a steady diversification of photographic education. The Photo League, which emerged from the 1936 split-up of the New York

Film and Photo League, taught with emphasis on the social documentary tradition. One of the key moments in the development of modern American photographic education came in 1937, when the influential Bauhaus teacher Laszlo Moholy-Nagy established the New Bauhaus in Chicago. Better known today as the Institute of Design at the Illinois Institute of Technology, its program emphasized the original Bauhaus ideal of integrating the fine and applied arts. In the years just after World War II, the photography department of the Institute attracted a large number of G.I. Bill students, who studied under teachers such as Harry Callahan, Arthur Siegel, and Aaron Siskind. Subsequently, during the 1950s and 1960s, many of the photographer-teachers trained at the Institute went on to establish similar programs—stressing the mastery of photographic craft and its application to problems of formal design—at major American universities and art schools.

In addition to such academic programs, the 1950s and 1960s also saw the birth of a strong photographic "workshop" movement. Organized by teacher-photographers like Minor White and Nathan Lyons, such classes concentrated on the creative and expressive aspects of photography, and offered informal, "anti-classroom" environments. Typical workshops featured intensive instruction and discussion in periods ranging from a few days to several weeks. By 1969 this approach found a more permanent home in the Visual Studies Workshop founded by Lyons in Rochester, N.Y.

In 1963 a national professional organization, the Society for Photographic Education, grew out of the efforts of teachers like Lyons, White, and Siskind.

The great increase over the past two decades in the number of people using photography as more than a casual hobby has given rise to a significant increase in the number and types of photographic educational facilities in the United States and abroad. Most colleges and universities currently offer some courses in photography. Many have full-fledged departments of photography, offering undergraduate and graduate degrees in a variety of disciplines, including photographic history, photographic education and art therapy, photojournalism, fine-arts photography, and photographic science and technology.

The typical undergraduate degree curriculum in photographic art is a four-year program; the degree given is a Bachelor of Fine Arts in photography. Required courses include a survey of the history of photography; various courses in studio and darkroom skills; a study of the fundamental chemical and physical aspects of the medium; and courses in which the student's personal or applied work is critiqued by instructors and discussed by fellow students. Elective courses commonly include workshops in early or experimental photographic processes; philosophy; criticism; and studies in related fields such as film, television, graphic arts, and painting. In an accredited institution a student in search of a bachelor's degree will also be required to undertake a number of courses in English, history or international relations, psychology and anthropology, and other subjects associated with the liberal arts. The aim of the college or university granting an undergraduate degree in photographic art is to provide an environment in which the student can deepen his or her involvement in the medium while at the same time developing a knowledge of and curiosity about the world culture in which it exists and will be used. Degree programs in photographic science and technology emphasize courses in theory and in chemical and physical principles rather than courses in applications and communication or artistic expression.

Graduate degrees are given for more specialized study. Most master's degree programs in the U.S. focus on study and research in the technological or historical aspects of photography, but an increasing number of schools offer a Master of Fine Arts degree for creative work. The International Center of Photography in New York City is distinguished for its particularly comprehensive educational program in the field of photography, including a photojournalism program for advanced journalists, a full-time studies program, a Master of Arts program in conjunction with New York University, and many lectures, workshops, weekly courses, seminars, and symposia.

For those less interested in a degree and more attracted to the field of applied photography, there are vocational schools and technical institutes offering certificate programs in studio skills, commercial portraiture, retouching, and other trade-related topics. Generally speaking, these institutions are much less concerned with the aesthetics of photography than their academic counterparts, but many give the student in search of marketable skills a firm grounding in the most commercially popular modes and styles of photographing.

Both types of institutions often give extension and night courses, some of which may carry degree credit. Such courses are useful to the beginner who wants to expand his or her understanding of the medium's technical aspects, and to the more advanced student who would like access to studio or darkroom space and professional advice. Some museums, camera clubs, and community centers offer courses in photography for modest fees. A recent addition to the field of photographic education is the "network" learning program found in some major cities. The network offers a number of courses in various subjects taught by private individuals who advertise their services in the local network newspaper.

Certain photographic manufacturers offer courses in fundamental techniques and camera handling for the interested public. The courses are usually one- or two-day lecture and workshop programs. While these ventures are acknowledged public-relations exercises given by the manufacturer, many are well planned to provide genuinely useful information and training to the beginner or intermediate amateur in a limited time. A more leisurely and usually more comprehensive approach to short-time study can be found in numerous annual workshops offered throughout the United States and Europe. The more prestigious workshops attract well-known photographers as guest teachers and lecturers. Most workshops are given in the summertime, allowing students to combine a vacation with a specialized learning experience.

Edwards, Hugh

American; 1904–

As Curator of Photography at the Art Institute of Chicago (AIC) from 1959 to 1970, Hugh Edwards was an influential proponent of photography's place in the art museum, with a personal preference for the realistic photographic image.

Edwards was born in Paducah, Kentucky. He became associated with the AIC in 1929 as a library assistant. During the 1930s he worked in the department of prints and drawings, and was impressed early on by Walker Evans's *American Photographs*. Edwards was assistant to Carl O. Schniewind, Curator of Prints and Drawings, who inaugurated photography shows at the AIC in 1940. He also acted as assistant to Curator of Photography Peter Pollack until 1957.

Edwards was named Curator of Photography at the AIC in 1959. He soon began a series of important exhibitions of contemporary photographers and historical masters. In the first five years of his tenure as curator, Edwards was responsible for shows by Robert

Frank, Ray Metzker, Minor White, Dennis Stock, Edward Weston, George Platt Lynes, Clarence John Laughlin, Dorothea Lange, Art Sinsabaugh, Henry Fox Talbot, David Octavius Hill, Roger Fenton, Alexander Gardner, and Peter Henry Emerson.

Edwards was a contributor to the Encyclopaedia Britannica and to a number of other books on photographic subjects. He lives in Hyde Park, Illinois.

Eggleston, William

American; 1937–

The color photographs of William Eggleston first came to public attention in the mid-1970s, most forcefully in the 1975 exhibition *William Eggleston's Guide,* which originated at the Museum of Modern Art, New York City, and traveled to five other U.S. museums. Color photography offered for exhibition up to that time had remained within the conventions of art photography, modern painting, and commercial illustration. Eggleston's work startled audiences by intensifying the banality of the color snapshot to a level that demanded aesthetic response, something that many viewers were unprepared to give, responding instead with outrage that "this" should be offered as art. The problem was that they were forced to confront the emptiness, even the visual insipidness, of typically American scenes. His pictures showed nondescript interiors and exteriors typical of modern American blindness to style or taste—quintessentially bland rooms, garage doors, houses, intersections. The photographs were dye-transfer prints that translated well-composed snapshot views into large-size images of saturated color and heightened contrast. Andy Warhol forced attention on the formal aspects of soup cans, cleanser boxes, and similar mundane objects by physically enlarging them to enormous proportions. Eggleston forced attention by exaggerating the ungraceful seeing and falsely "real" color of amateur 35mm slide photography. In effect, visual shouting made audiences confront the lack of beauty or style in the snapshots and the contemporary environment that they were accustomed to accepting without notice. It was the snapshot aesthetic used with a nonviolent vengeance, and the echoes of the attack have not died.

William Eggleston was born in Memphis, Tennessee, in 1937. Educated at Vanderbilt University, Delta State College, and the University of Mississippi, he makes a living as a freelance photographer in the Mississippi-Tennessee region and in Washington, D.C. He has been a lecturer in Visual and Environmental Studies at Harvard University (1974), a researcher in color video at the Massachusetts Institute of Technology (1978–1979), and recipient of grants from the Guggenheim Foundation, the National Endowment for the Arts, and the Arts Survey. His personal work is done primarily in the rural southeastern United States where he currently uses large-format equipment and color negative materials to photograph land- and skyscapes with a romantic vision well beyond that of snapshots.

See also: SNAPSHOT AESTHETIC.

Color photograph: p. C-13.

Eisendrath, David B.

American; 1914–

Beginning his career as a stringer for various newspapers and magazines, David Eisendrath progressed from being an accomplished photojournalist and an outstanding industrial and technical photographer to the position he has occupied for more than two decades as one of the most sought-after and most highly respected consultants in scientific and functional photography. A true polymath, whose advice is based on years of experience as well as research and a great breadth and depth of knowledge, Eisendrath is unique in his ability to provide direct, practical solutions to complex problems for nontechnical illustrative photographers and for engineers and scientists alike. His services are also highly valued for his acquaintanceship with technical experts and skilled professionals in a great variety of fields outside photography. He not only can supply answers, when necessary or helpful he can place clients in contact with specialists who can accomplish whatever is required.

Born in Chicago to a family of industrial chemists and manufacturers, David Eisendrath became seriously interested in photography and science in high school. At the University of Chicago from 1932 to 1937, he photographed virtually all campus activities for student publications and sold freelance submissions to local newspapers while taking a degree in literature and doing graduate work in anthropology. After graduation he joined the staff of the Chicago *Times* and acted as a stringer photographing Chicago-area celebrities and events for *Time* and *Life* magazines. Among his accomplishments at the *Times* was a nationwide scoop in getting the first pictures of the gangster Al Capone after his release from the federal penitentary.

Eisendrath moved to New York in 1940 as a charter member of the innovative newspaper *PM.* During World War II he worked for the U.S. Department of State and the Office of War Information as a photographer, war correspondent, and editor.

After the war, Eisendrath established himself as a freelance industrial and technical photographer in New York. Pioneering work in using electronic flash and all kinds of equipment for practical photography, his talent as a photographer, and his ability to understand the most difficult industrial and scientific subjects soon built his reputation as the man who could photograph anything. His willingness to share his knowledge and experience in a constant stream of articles, columns, and technical papers made it inevitable that photographers, technicians, managers, and others would begin to bring their problems to him in person. By the mid-1960s his activities as a consultant occupied at least as much time as his work as a photographer. Today, consultancy and writing constitute almost all of his professional work.

For many years, while photographing assignments for major U.S. corporations, Eisendrath wrote hundreds of featured columns that were noted for their clarity and liveliness as well as their informativeness in *Industrial Photography, Photo Methods for Industry (PMI),* and *Popular Photography* magazines. At the same time he created illustrated feature articles for *True* magazine and produced papers for specialized scientific publications. Currently he is a contributing and consulting editor for *Modern Photography* and serves as a consultant to the New York *Times;* his technical writing continues as well.

Eisendrath is a member of the ASMP, the National Press Photographers Association, the Society of Photographic Scientists and Engineers, the Professional Photographers of America, and the Industrial Photographers Association of New York. He is a Fellow of the Photographic Society of America, and a member of many other technical and journalistic organizations. He has served on committees for photographic standards for the American National Standards Association (ANSI, formerly ASA) since 1949. From 1977 to 1979 he worked for the U.S. Congressional Select Committee on Assassinations as a member of the Photographic Evidence Panel. More than 100 awards and citations from photographic, journalistic, and scientific organizations have acknowledged his contributions and achievements as a most universally respected expert in his field.

Eisenstaedt, Alfred. "V.J. Day" (1945). Alfred Eisenstaedt, LIFE Magazine, © 1945 Time Inc.

Eisenstaedt, Alfred

American; 1898–

Alfred Eisenstaedt frequently has been described as the father of photojournalism. In fact, he was one of a handful of pioneers who developed photo-reportage in the late 1920s and early 1930s, coincident with the emergence of the high-speed 35mm camera.

Eisenstaedt was born in Dirschau, West Prussia, in 1898. His father, a retired department-store owner, moved the family to Berlin in 1906, and the Eisenstaedts remained there for the next 29 years. Eisenstaedt served in the German Army in World War I and suffered shrapnel wounds during the German offensive in Dieppe. He became a professional photographer in 1929, and his first assignment was to cover the Nobel Prize ceremony in Stockholm, at which Thomas Mann became Nobel Laureate for literature. Thereafter Eisenstaedt

traveled widely to the Swiss resorts where the wealthy and titled gathered; to the capitals of Europe, where he photographed leaders and great events (among them, the first meeting of Hitler and Mussolini); and to Ethiopia on the eve of war with Italy.

After leaving Hitler's Germany in 1935, Eisenstaedt helped to introduce photojournalism to the United States. He became, along with Margaret Bourke-White, one of *Life*'s original four photographers and remained with the magazine for the next 40 years. During that time he had some 2000 assignments and more than 90 *Life* covers. As a working photographer Eisenstaedt was an editor's dream. When he was sent out to do a story, he always came back with usable photographs—photographs that did not betray a personal or political position. His work had what became known as "Eisie's Eye."

Still active in his career in his eighties, in 1979 Eisenstaedt returned to his native country after an absence of 44 years to photograph contemporary Germany as he had photographed it a half-century earlier.

Eisenstaedt's photographs have appeared in almost every major photography magazine and in many photo anthologies. Among the books devoted to his photographs are *Witness to Our Time, The Eye of Eisenstaedt,* and *People*. He has received numerous honors, and his work has been exhibited widely in galleries and was on view in 1981 at the International Center of Photography in an exhibit entitled *Eisenstaedt: Germany*.

Electronic Flash

Electronic flash is illumination of very high intensity and extremely short duration. The major components of an electronic flash unit or system are a gas-discharge tube, a power source, a power-storage capacitor, and a trigger circuit. When the trigger circuit releases the high voltage stored in the capacitor, a brilliant electrical discharge is instantaneously generated through the gas between two electrodes inside the flash tube. The typical flash duration is about 1/1000 sec., but it can be many times shorter. Unlike the filling of a flash cube or bulb, the gas is not consumed when a flash of light is produced, so the tube can be reused thousands of times.

The power-storage capacitor of an electronic flash unit can store only direct current (DC) voltage to provide the high voltage required to activate the flash tube. In addition to accepting power from batteries and other DC sources, most flash units have adapters or built-in circuits to convert alternating current (AC) to direct current. The storage capacitor can build up a charge equivalent to several thousand volts from a low-voltage supply in only a few seconds; thus, 110- or 220-volt domestic AC, low-voltage AC from a transformer, and alkaline or rechargeable nickel-cadmium batteries which produce only a few volts of DC are all suitable for powering electronic flash systems.

Some modern cameras are equipped with built-in flash systems powered by batteries in the camera or the film pack. Many 35mm and medium-format cameras use independent flash units that carry their own power sources. These flash units are connected to the camera by means of a synchronizing (sync) cord or by means of contacts in the "hot" accessory shoe of the camera and the matching mounting foot of the flash unit. A flash unit that interconnects with the metering and exposure-control system of a particular camera is called a *dedicated* flash unit.

The power units for studio electronic flash systems use 110- or 220-volt AC and can operate a number of flash heads (flash tubes mounted in a variety of reflective and directional housings) simultaneously. These heads often include a continuous-output bulb to provide light during set-up that will show the direction and general effect of the flash. Many studio and portable flash units have a variable power control which can be set to use only a portion of the energy available in the capacitor. Lower power settings reduce the light output. This provides reduced exposure without the need to change the lens *f*-stop setting or the flash-to-subject distance; it also permits using a unit for fill light or some other supplementary purpose that requires less intensity than the key light.

The output of a flash unit in a fixed (self-contained) reflector is commonly measured in beam candlepower seconds (BCPS), or expressed as a guide number (GN) from which exposure can be calculated. Flash tubes, which may be used in a variety of reflectors, are rated in terms of their power requirements in joules or watt seconds. Because the flash duration is so short, shutter speed is not the major factor in electronic flash exposure, no matter what the light output is. The shutter must be completely open at the time the flash fires (X synchronization). This can be achieved at any speed with a between-the-lens shutter, but it requires a setting of 1/60 or 1/125 sec. (depending on the camera) or slower with a focal-plane shutter; the maximum speed is usually marked in color or with a lightning-bolt symbol. Exposure is determined by the flash-to-subject distance and the *f*-stop setting of the lens. The basic exposure computation using a guide number is:

$$\text{Lens } f\text{-stop} = \text{GN} \div \text{flash-to-subject distance}$$

Most flash units have a table or dial to perform the exposure calculation. An automatic flash unit incorporates a light sensor that shuts off the light output for proper exposure when the lens is set to a suitable *f*-stop and the subject is anywhere within a specified distance range.

When the flash fires, the capacitor must build up a new power charge for the next flash. The time it takes to do this is called recycle time. At low-power settings, or at close subject distances with an automatic flash unit, recycle time may

be 1 second or less; under other conditions it may range from 5 to 15 seconds. The color temperature of the illumination from most electronic flash units is 5600 to 6000K; this is equivalent to "photographic daylight," so electronic flash can be used with daylight-type color films without the need for corrective filtration.

See also: AUTOMATIC FLASH; BCPS; BOUNCE LIGHT; FLASH; FLASH FILL; GUIDE NUMBER; MODELING LIGHT; MULTIPLE FLASH; SYNCHRONIZATION.

Electron Imaging

The field of electron imaging encompasses a wide variety of systems that use controlled electron energy to produce images on a screen that can be photographed, or to expose photographic materials directly. The most common system is television, in which the optical image focused onto the camera tube is translated into a varying signal that in a receiver varies the intensity of an electron beam that "paints" a corresponding image on the phosphor coating of the picture tube. The displays of other cathode-ray tube devices such as oscilloscopes and radar scopes are similarly created by an electron beam. These screen displays can be photographed with ordinary cameras and films. Alternatively, in equipment that permits, the film can be exposed directly by the electron beam. This provides higher quality images with greatly increased resolving power.

Very high-quality photographs from satellites are obtained by means of an electronic camera. A signal derived from its pictures is transmitted to earth, where it is used for direct exposure of film by a scanning electron beam. Direct beam exposure is also used to obtain photographic records of computer-generated or computer-processed images; the computer output controls the beam intensity and path across the emulsion.

Electron imaging produces extremely high resolving power because a typical electron beam is from 40 to 200 times narrower than the shortest wavelength of light. In electron microscopes this makes it possible to obtain micrographs at magnifications up to 6,000,000× by photographing a screen display, or up to more than 100,000× by direct electron exposure.

The small dimension of an electron beam makes it possible to permanently record much more digital data in a given area of film emulsion than is possible by light exposure. Similarly, an electron beam permits precision direct exposure of photoresist materials at scales many times smaller than can be achieved with

light. The photoresist is not light sensitive, but is hardened by electron exposure. This technique is used in the production of computer microchips, which may have large numbers of elements less than one light wavelength in size or spacing.

See also: DIGITAL IMAGES; ELECTRON MICROGRAPHY; MICROPHOTOGRAPHY; PHOTORESIST; SPACE PHOTOGRAPHY; TELEVISION.

Electron Micrography

Images photographed by means of an electron microscope can show some details magnified as much as six million times. In comparison, compound optical microscopes can attain maximum useful magnifications of about 2000× with light as the illuminant, or 5000× with ultraviolet. (Greater magnifications are obtainable, but they are "empty" because no finer details are revealed.) This difference in performance is primarily a function of resolving power—the ability to make tiny, closely spaced details visually distinct—and maximum resolving power is primarily a function of the size of the energy that illuminates the subject. The shortest wavelength of light is about 400nm long (1 nanometer [nm] = 0.000,000,039 inch), and the shortest wavelength of ultraviolet energy sometimes used for optical micrographs is about 365nm. The limit of resolution with such energy is a particle size or spacing of about 130nm. The energy beam in an electron microscope is typically from 10 to 1.5nm in diameter, and the limit of resolution is about 0.2nm. Consequently, the image can be magnified up to 3000 times more than an optical microscope image without reaching the point of empty magnification. In addition, the image formed in an electron microscope has much greater depth of field than that of an optical microscope, which increases the amount of useful information that can be recorded in a micrograph (microscope photograph).

The electron microscope was invented in the 1930s. Today two types of microscope, transmission and scanning, are used for a great variety of scientific and industrial investigations. They are large, heavy, and very expensive instruments consisting of the microscope chamber, very-high-voltage power supplies, and electronic control units. The microscope itself is a hollow vertical column with an electron gun at one end. The filament of the gun emits a stream of electrons through the center of a series of circular magnetic "lenses" which direct and focus the beam onto the specimen at the

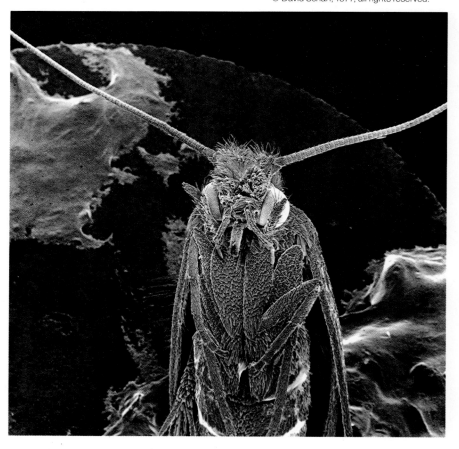

other end of the column. Air must be pumped out of the column to create a vacuum before operation begins.

A transmission electron microscope (TEM) is used to investigate internal structure. The specimen can be no more than about 2.5mm in diameter, and typically only 0.00005 to 0.0001mm (50 to 100nm) thick, although the beam in a very high-voltage TEM can penetrate specimens of up to 0.001mm (1000nm) thickness or more. The more dense portions of the specimen absorb a greater amount of the illuminating energy, so the image formed by the penetrating beam varies in intensity with variations in the specimen structure. The image is projected onto a fluorescent screen for visual examination. To make a micrograph, the screen is moved out of the way so that the image can fall on a photographic film or plate inserted in the chamber below. Special fine-grain emulsions are used to obtain optimum image quality. A TEM is commonly used for magnifications of 500× to 300,000×, with a resolution of about 1nm, but resolution of better than 0.2nm is possible at a magnification of about 6,000,000×; that is sufficient to produce images of individual atoms.

In a scanning electron microscope (SEM) the electron beam does not penetrate the specimen. Instead it is focused onto one point and scanned over the surface in a rectangular pattern much like that of a television screen (other scanning patterns may be used). The specimen emits secondary electrons in response, the emission varying with the surface structure. (Non-metallic specimens are prepared with a gold or gold alloy coating a few molecules thick to make the specimen electron-emissive.) The emitted electrons are collected and focused onto a fluoroscope screen for viewing. A micrograph is made by photographing the screen with an ordinary film emulsion. SEM micrographs reveal surface detail with striking three-dimensional lighting and extreme depth of field because the image is produced by scanning the subject on a point-by-point basis. The range of magnification is a remarkable 10× to 100,000× with a resolution of 20nm.

Electron micrography is used to investigate crystal structure, surface composition and wear, metallic composition, oxide growth, particle size, smoke and pollution analysis, bacteria structure and growth, cell and tissue composition, and a great variety of phenomena and characteristics at near- or even sub-molecular scale.

See also: FLUOROGRAPHY; PHOTOMICROGRAPHY.

Electrophotographic Processes

Since the 1930s, a number of processes have been developed that rely on a pattern of electrical charges to form or record an image that is subsequently made permanently visible. These electrophotographic processes are distinguished by the fact that the final image is formed on or in the material that receives the charges. Thus they differ from processes in which the image is held as a charge pattern and made temporarily visible with supplementary equipment (videotape, videodisk), and from processes in which the charge pattern is used to form an image that is then recorded by photographic exposure. They are also distinct from processes such as Kirlian photography, in which light accompanying electrical currents is recorded.

By far the most widely used electrophotographic process is *xerography,* the method used in most office document-copying equipment. In this process an overall pattern of static electrical charges representing the entire image is transferred to paper or other base material. There it attracts a pigment that is fused to the base to form the permanent image. Other processes, used to make enlarged prints from microfilms and in photofabrication, use charge patterns to attract pigment particles carried in liquid (electrophoresis) or to electroplate metal onto a base in an image-revealing pattern (electrolytic electrophotography). Such processes are under active investigation because they show the ability to amplify a small exposing charge into a much greater image effect, much as silver halides do.

See also: KIRLIAN PHOTOGRAPHY; XEROGRAPHY.

Electrotype

The electrotype is a process by which duplicate printing surfaces can be obtained for the photomechanical reproduction of relief or intaglio images. A plastic mold (matrix) is made from the master letterpress (raised relief) or engraved (intaglio) plate, and the surface electroplated with copper. When sufficiently thick, the copper form is removed from the matrix and filled with supporting metal to strengthen it for use as a printing plate. In this way many identical plates can be obtained from a single matrix for high-volume printing on several presses simultaneously, or to maintain quality by replacing a plate at the first signs of deterioration. The first electrotype process in photography was

Emerson, Peter Henry. "Gathering Water-lilies" (1886); platinum. Art Institute of Chicago.

invented for use with daguerreotypes by Hippolyte Fizeau in 1841. Photogalvanography, invented by Paul Pretsch in 1854, produced an electrotype plate from a bichromate process relief image. J. W. Swan's photomezzotint process of 1865 was similar but used a carbon process print as a master image. Modern electrotypy descends from improvements of the photomezzotint.

See also: FIZEAU, HIPPOLYTE; PHOTO-GALVANOGRAPHY; PHOTOMEZZOTINT.

Emerson, Peter Henry

British; 1856–1936

Peter Henry Emerson, aesthetician of the "naturalistic," was a major force in late 19th c. art photography. His photographs and books were widely influential and posed questions of photographic theory—especially as to the status of photography as a fine art and its relationship to painting—that are still debated today. He believed that it was the photographer's task to discover the camera's own rules. He attacked the popular painting-derived photography of his day (the "high art" photography of H. P. Robinson and O. G. Rejlander) and was an early admirer of many photographers now regarded as major figures. His own platinum and photogravure prints featured landscapes, seascapes, and genre scenes of rural life in East Anglia.

Emerson, a distant relative of American philosopher Ralph Waldo Emerson, was born in Cuba of a British mother and an American father who were wealthy plantation owners. He spent his early youth in the northeastern United States and moved to England in 1869. He attended Cranleigh School, King's College Hospital, and Clare College, Cambridge, pursuing medical and scientific studies and acquiring several degrees. He came to photography by way of ornithology.

Emerson bought his first camera and received instruction from E. Griffiths in 1881–1882. He joined the Royal Photographic Society and had his first exhibition in 1882 at Pall Mall. In 1885 he entered the "Amateur Photographers at Home" competition and was awarded a first medal at the Bond Street Amateur Photographers exhibition.

Emerson abandoned his medical career in 1886, devoting himself to descriptive writing and photography at the Norfolk Broads. His river scenes and pictures of fishermen, farmers, and others, were influenced by the painting of Turner, Whistler, and the French Impressionists. He was elected to the council of the Royal Photographic Society in the same year.

In 1889 Emerson published his book *Naturalistic Photography*, in which he defended photography as an independent art. Viewing photography as a merging of art and science, he believed that through choice of subject, lighting, framing, and selective focusing, fine photographs could be made. The key to true art, he felt, was to photograph natural subjects in their natural surroundings, without artificial techniques and manipulations.

The following year, after the second edition of his immensely influential book had appeared, his views changed. In a pamphlet, *The Death of Naturalistic Photography: A Renunciation,* he disclaimed his earlier opinions, doubting the validity of photography as an art form and consenting to the notion of the photographer's freedom to manipulate the image. He withdrew the remaining copies of his book for revision.

In 1892 Emerson was a founding member of the Linked Ring Brotherhood. He received the Royal Photographic Society Progress Medal for artistic photography in 1895. Between 1886 and 1895 he published eight sets of photographs in portfolios and books. In 1899 he published an expanded and expurgated third edition of *Naturalistic Photography;* the original final chapter, "Photography—A Pictorial Art," became "Photography—Not Art."

Although Emerson continued to photograph, he neither exhibited nor published after 1900. He was honored that year with a retrospective at the Royal Photographic Society. In 1925 he personally issued medals for high achievement in photography to Hill and Adamson, Bayard, J. Craig Annan, J. M. Cameron, Nadar, and Brassai. He was working on a history of pictorial photography when he died at Falmouth in 1936.

See also: NATURALISTIC PHOTOGRAPHY; PICTORIAL PHOTOGRAPHY; ROBINSON, HENRY PEACH.

Emulsion

A suspension of light-sensitive silver halide crystals in gelatin coated on the surface of photographic films, papers, and plates is called an emulsion. Emulsions differ in speed (light sensitivity), granularity (grain), spectral (wavelength) sensitivity, and contrast. Speed, granularity, and contrast are all related to the size of the halide crystals. In general, a fast emulsion contains a predominance of large crystals, has relatively low contrast, and is applied in a thick coating to obtain sufficient covering power of silver in the processed image. The crystal size and emulsion thickness produce high granularity (graininess in the image). A slow emulsion contains primarily tiny halide crystals, has high contrast, and is applied in a thin coating. The crystal size and thin coating produce very low granularity, while the crystal size and contrast characteristics produce very high resolving power.

All emulsions are sensitive to ultraviolet and blue wavelengths. Spectral sensitivity is extended by the addition of various dye compounds (dye sensitization) during manufacture. *Ordinary emulsions* (an obsolescent term) have only blue (and UV) sensitivity; *orthochromatic* emulsions are "red blind" but sensitive to other colors of light; *panchromatic* emulsions are sensitive to all colors of light. Sensitivity may also be extended to invisible wavelengths other than ultraviolet; e.g., infrared and x-rays. Most emulsions for color materials have dye-forming couplers added; those for dye destruction processing have full-strength dyes added.

The emulsions of stabilization and activation (rapid processing) papers and of self-processing films for instant photography and other diffusion transfer processes all include molecules of developing agents along with the silver halides. Film emulsions contain silver bromide, the most light-sensitive of the silver halides. Paper emulsions contain various proportions of silver bromide and silver chloride (contact-printing paper emulsions have only silver chloride). All emulsions contain a small percentage of silver iodide. Many materials have more than one emulsion layer. Films with extended exposure range have a high-speed and a low-speed layer; variable contrast papers have a blue-sensitive high-contrast layer and a lower-contrast green-sensitive layer; color films have three layers of effective individual color sensitivity (red, green, blue), but one or more of these may be divided into high- and low-speed layers.

Formation of emulsions. Emulsions are manufactured by dissolving a basic halide such as potassium bromide in a solution of gelatin and water, then adding silver nitrate. During a "ripening" period of several hours at a warm temperature, tiny silver nitrate crystals form and grow in size as some dissolve and are redeposited on others. One square inch of emulsion contains several billion halide crystals. The crystals are essentially insensitive to light until traces of sulfur and other compounds are added late in the ripening process. These "impurities" create *sensitivity specks* in the crystals that serve as points for the formation of a latent image during exposure and as development centers during processing. The ripened emulsion is cooled to a jelly, cut into noodles, and washed to remove excess chemicals and byproducts. The noodled emulsion is reheated to the melting point and held at temperature for after-ripening or "digestion" during which the speed increases and the contrast changes; couplers, preservatives, and other substances are added during this process. Finally, the emulsion is coated onto a continuously moving roll of suitable base material. The emulsion is set by chilling and allowed to dry; then the material is cut into standard sizes and is packaged.

See also: COLOR MATERIALS; CONTRAST; COUPLERS, COLOR; COVERING POWER; DEVELOPING AGENT; DIFFUSION TRANSFER PROCESS; DYE DESTRUCTION PROCESS; DYE SENSITIZATION; GELATIN; GRAIN; RAPID PROCESSING; RESOLVING POWER; SILVER HALIDE; SPECTRAL SENSITIVITY; SPEED OF MATERIALS; STABILIZATION PROCESS; VARIABLE CONTRAST MATERIALS.

Enamel Processes

There are several processes for forming photographic images on enameled metal plates, or for forming images in enamel on uncoated plates. The basic procedures are much the same as those of various ceramic processes, differing primarily in the glaze materials and the firing temperature. The first enamel method, invented in the mid-1860s, was to transfer a collodion positive, stripped from its glass plate, to the enameled surface. When fired, the silver fused to the enamel while the collodion burned away; the image could be strengthened by adding various metallic compounds to the firing. A later process involved preparing a carbon process positive with enamel oxides instead of pigments in the emulsion that was transferred to the plate for firing. The American *Enameline* process used a bichromated coating on a metal plate that was exposed under a halftone (screened) negative. The unexposed emulsion was washed away, the remaining positive image was fired over a direct gas flame to enamelize it, and the plate was then etched in acid to throw the image into greater contrast and relief.

Today a silver image for direct burn-in is most easily produced by coating the plate with a liquid emulsion that is exposed to a negative and processed before firing. Various preparations can be made for dusting on powdered enamels. One procedure is to coat the plate with a bichromated solution that remains tacky in shadow and middletone areas after exposure under a positive, so as to retain the oxides that form the image during firing. Another procedure is to transfer an image from the relief surface of a photoetched metal plate. The plate is coated with silkscreen squeegee oil and the image portions are picked up by pressure with waxed paper that is used to transfer them to the enameled plate; during dusting-on, the oxides will adhere only to the image portions. To form only the image in enamel, selected portions of an uncoated photoetched plate can be prepared for enameling by the same techniques used to give a flat plate an overall coating. Firing produces an enamel image against a plain metal background.

See also: CERAMIC PROCESS; GLASS, PHOTOGRAPHS ON.

Endoscope

An endoscope is a long, thin, tubular device for viewing or, with a camera at the eyepiece, photographing inside cavities through openings too small or otherwise restricted for direct viewing. Some special-purpose (*bore* or *cavity*) cameras have an endoscopic optical system in place of a conventional lens. In most cases a prism or other device at the tip provides a view at an angle to one side of the body of the instrument. Light is provided by a miniature bulb at the tip or by a variety of methods of directing illumination along the viewing axis into the cavity. Originally made of hollow tubing and miniature optical elements, endoscopes today largely rely on very high quality fiber optic systems which are both compact and flexible. Some fibers in a tubelike bundle carry illumination, others transmit the image. Endoscopes are inserted through natural openings or incisions to make medical examinations inside the body. They are also widely used to examine the insides of machines, opaque containers, and similar locations, and to take apparent eye-level on-the-spot still photographs and motion pictures in miniature scale-model constructions.

See also: FIBER OPTICS.

Enlarger

Projection devices used to print photographic images in sizes larger or smaller than the original negative or slide, enlargers are most commonly used to magnify the original image from two to ten times. Modern enlargers use a variety of light sources: tungsten, quartz-halogen, or fluorescent. The lamp is contained in a lamphouse and projects its light through a condenser lens or diffusion screen onto the negative. The light image then enters a bellows and lens assembly, where it is focused onto light-sensitive materials held in an easel on the baseboard of the enlarger. The head of the enlarger consists of the lamphouse, negative carrier, bellows, and lens. It is supported above the baseboard by a vertical column or girder assembly. Raising or lowering the head enlarges or reduces the size of the projected image on the baseboard.

There are two types of enlargers: condenser and diffusion. The condenser type employs one or more condenser lenses to direct the light from the lamphouse in essentially parallel rays through the negative. In a diffusion enlarger the light passes through frosted glass or a diffusing screen, or is reflected from a diffusing surface, and thus is traveling in many directions as it reaches the negative.

Diffusion enlargers commonly are used for color images of all kinds and for black-and-white portraits. The diffused light makes negative blemishes less apparent on the print, softens image details in a flattering way, and generally provides a suitable contrast for color printing. If corrective filtration is accomplished in the lamphouse, diffusion ensures thorough mixing of the filtered light. Most black-and-white printing is done with condenser enlargers. These produce greater apparent sharpness in a print from a given film size and produce an image that most readily matches the standard contrast grades (or contrast filters) of black-and-white printing papers. Some enlargers have interchangeable heads for the two kinds of printing.

The lens of the enlarger is specially designed to work best at close range and on a flat field, but otherwise it is similar to a camera lens. With the use of an external timer and the f-stops provided on the enlarger lens, close control of the print exposure is possible. The standard lens for 35mm film is 50mm; for 6 × 6cm film, 100mm; and for 4″ × 5″ film, 150mm. Shorter-focal-length lenses can be employed to obtain larger magnifications.

Enlargers are generally designed to work best with specific film formats. Small enlargers handle subminiature, 110, and 35mm film; medium-format enlargers handle roll-film negatives up to 6 × 7cm; large models are best suited for 4″ × 5″ and larger film. The negative is sandwiched in a negative carrier, which can be made of solid plates of glass, or of metal or plastic plates with cutouts appropriately sized for the film in use.

Color Enlarging. Color printing requires color adjustment of the exposing light. A simple condenser enlarger can be used for subtractive color printing if it can accommodate magenta, yellow, and cyan acetate filters between the condenser and the negative carrier. More advanced color enlargers feature lamphouses that permit dialing in the color and density combinations through built-in gelatin or dichroic filters. These are usually diffusion-type enlargers. A small number of color enlargers use the additive color method with three separate light sources, each making a separate exposure of different intensity in red, blue, and green light.

Like sophisticated cameras, enlargers can be designed with automatic features such as exposure control, color correction, auto focus, automatic film transport in the negative carrier, and power-lift for the enlarger head.

See also: ENLARGING; PRINTING, BLACK-AND-WHITE; PRINTING, COLOR.

Enlarging

Enlarging is the process of making a print in which the image is larger than the image on the original negative or transparency. This is accomplished by using an enlarger to project the film image onto the printing paper. Film can be used in place of the printing paper to obtain an enlarged copy negative or transparency.

Enlarging papers have chlorobromide or bromide emulsions that are relatively fast (light sensitive). The chloride emulsions of contact printing papers are too slow to respond to the light levels produced by most enlargers. Papers may have fiber or resin-coated bases, and emulsions that produce different degrees of contrast and have various textures and surfaces (e.g., glossy, matte, "silk"). Black-and-white papers are available in numbered contrast grades (No. 2 is considered normal contrast) or with an emulsion the contrast of which can be varied with yellow and magenta printing filters. Color papers, almost all of which have resin-coated bases, are supplied in a single, normal contrast grade. Different kinds of emulsions are available to make color prints from negatives and from transparencies. Most enlarging papers are processed in a series of solutions essentially the same as those used for film processing. A few special papers use activation, stabilization, or diffusion transfer processing. Black-and-white papers may be handled under appropriate safelight illumination; most color papers must be handled in complete darkness.

Once a picture has been chosen by examining a contract sheet or a set of proof prints made from negatives or by viewing a group of transparencies, the steps in making an enlargement are: test strips, trial or work prints, final print. The selected image is inserted in the film carrier of the enlarger, and with the enlarger light turned on, the head is raised or lowered to obtain the desired picture size. The image must be focused carefully on a piece of scrap paper placed in the printing easel on the enlarger baseboard. A specialized magnifier ("grain focuser") makes precise focusing easy. Most easels have adjustable blades that are moved to mask off a chosen area if the entire image is not to be printed.

Test strips are sample exposures; they are made on individual strips of paper laid across the image area, or on a partial sheet of paper that is covered in steps to provide a series of exposures. When processed, test strips are examined to determine what overall exposure is best, and what additional or reduced exposures may be required in specific areas of the picture. If the contrast or color balance of the image is not correct, additional test strips may be made in which these factors are varied, or experimental adjustments may be made in the first few work prints.

While test strips may cover only key portions of the picture, work prints include the entire image area. The first print is made at the best exposure determined from the tests. It is examined for overall exposure, contrast, color balance, and the need for printing controls. Subsequent test prints incorporate changes and adjustments in these factors, including procedures such as burning-in and dodging to control exposure in local areas. Each successive work print gets closer to the desired result, until the best possible print is obtained. The procedures used to produce that print then are repeated to make one or more final prints that are processed fully (work prints are often examined after only partial fixing) and taken through all the stages of final finishing, such as trimming, spotting, and mounting.

Color enlarging differs from black-and-white enlarging primarily in the need to adjust the color balance of the printing light. This is achieved by placing appropriate filters in the lamphouse or under the lens or by changing the settings of built-in filters. Various films and papers have different basic filter requirements, and the balance of the image being printed may require special adjustment (the procedures are described in the entries on color printing).

There are several accessories that can make enlarging easier and more efficient. In addition to a focusing magnifier and an adjustable-blade paper easel, the most useful item is a timer switch that controls exposure by turning the enlarger on and off at any preset interval from one second to several minutes. Both spring-powered and all-electronic timers are available; the latter type is generally more accurate and more versatile. An enlarging exposure meter and a color analyzer, both of which make readings from the projected image, are useful when a high volume of enlarging is done from a great variety of images and film types. However, these devices must be calibrated by test printing for each grade of paper and must be recalibrated when a different type of paper is used.

Equivalent Image. Alfred Steiglitz, "Equivalent F" (1921–38). Courtesy Georgia O'Keeffe; Collection, Museum of Modern Art, New York.

See also: ADDITIVE COLOR PRINTING; BURNING-IN; CONTACT PRINTING; DIFFUSION TRANSFER PROCESS; DODGING; DRYING FILMS AND PRINTS; DRY MOUNTING; ENLARGER; MOUNTING PHOTOGRAPHS; PRINT FINISHING; PRINTING, BLACK-AND-WHITE; PRINTING, COLOR; RAPID PROCESSING; STABILIZATION PROCESS; TEST STRIP; VARIABLE-CONTRAST MATERIALS.

Episcope; Epidiascope

These are technical names for projection machines of the design called overhead projectors–so called because the reflex optical system is located above a horizontal subject stage and projects the image at a right angle onto a vertical screen. An episcope (Greek *epi* = on, onto) accommodates only opaque materials and illuminates them from above. An epidiascope (Greek *dia* = through) has a transparent stage and a second illumination system below to permit the use of transparent and translucent as well as opaque materials.
See also: PROJECTORS.

Equivalent Image

The term *equivalent* was applied by Alfred Stieglitz to a kind of photograph whose intent is to evoke in the viewer an emotional state as intense as—equivalent, though not necessarily identical to—that of the photographer at the time the picture was made. An equivalent image is a *straight* photograph; i.e., one in which representation is realistic, and technique is used directly, without manipulation and without the stylistic devices or concern for conventional prettiness that characterize pictorial photography. The source of the viewer's response is not the objective subject matter of the photograph—any more than melody or lyrics are the true source of response to great music; rather, it is the experience of seeing, or listening, that evokes the response. Stieglitz's first photographs in this vein were of clouds—the most emotionally neutral subject matter he could find—and were variously titled "Songs of the Sky" and "Clouds, Music." The term *equivalent* arose from the effort to put into words the concept that only direct experience provides valid understanding or emotion, that only feelings obtained in this way can be true feelings, and that "all true things are equal to one another";

thus to communicate true feeling one must work without artifice only in response to direct experience. The concept of the equivalent image became central to the work of a number of photographers, most notably that of Minor White in the 1960s and 1970s, who enveloped it in an aura of philosophical and spiritual mysticism.
See also: PICTORIAL PHOTOGRAPHY; STIEGLITZ, ALFRED; SUBJECTIVE PHOTOGRAPHY.

Erfurth, Hugo

German; 1874–1948
Hugo Erfurth has been called "the most significant (European) portrait photographer of the twenties." Trained in the Pictorial school, Erfurth displayed an interest in the avant-garde art worlds of Weimar Germany, and he became known as the foremost documentor of the post–World War I German intelligentsia. His portrait studios in Dresden and Cologne were among the main gathering places for people in the arts.

Erfurth's important sitters included Walter Gropius, Marc Chagall, Richard Strauss, Kathe Kollwitz, Mies van der Rohe, Oskar Kokoschka and Vassily Kandinsky. His later work was influenced by the sharp focus, frontality, and odd-angle views of the New Vision and the New Objectivity movements, but he continued to work with antiquated oil-pigment printing techniques. The frequent result was a modernist composition recorded in a pictorialist manner.

Born in Halle, Germany, Erfurth studied art at the Academy of Arts in Dresden and photography with a leading portraitist and pictorial photographer of Dresden from 1892 to 1896. Within a few years he took over the studio of the Dresden court photographer. Erfurth designed a special photography section for the 1904 Great Dresden Exhibition. He taught photography for several years until the outbreak of World War I.

Erfurth operated his own portrait studio in Dresden from 1896 to 1934, and in Gaienhofen am Bodensee from 1943 to 1948. He was a founding member and Chairman of the Jury of the Society of German Photographers for nearly three decades, during which he exerted powerful influences on the standards of German photographic work. His own photographs were included in countless exhibitions of the day, including the 1929 Film und Foto exhibition at Stuttgart. His work in areas other than portraiture was destroyed in a bombing raid in 1943, but Erfurth worked steadily until his death in 1948.

Erfurth was the recipient of numerous awards throughout his career, including a Silver Medal at the International Amateur Photography Exhibition, Erfurt, Germany (1894), the Weimar German Photographers Association Award (1903), the State Medal of the German Reich, Frankfurt, Germany (1926), and the Achievement Award for

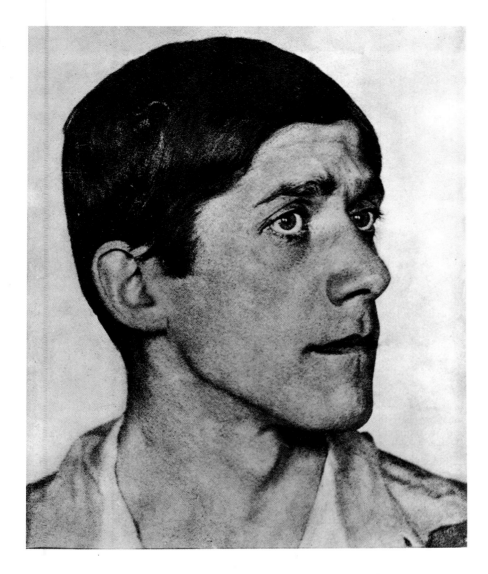

Erfurth, Hugo. "Oskar Kokoschka" (1919); oil pigment print. Collection, Museum of Modern Art, New York.

German Handicrafts, Frankfurt (1939). A major exhibition of his work was held at Photokina in Cologne in 1951, and the first one-man show of his photographs in the United States, *Hugo Erfurth: Between Tradition and the Avant-Garde*, was mounted at ICP in New York in 1982.

Erotic Photography

Erotic photographs are those which depict the human form in a manner intended to create a sexual response in the viewer. Erotic photographs are distinguished from pornography by the fact that while the latter both shows and intends to provoke explicit sexual activity, an erotic photograph need contain neither nudity nor direct sexual suggestion; many current advertising pictures, for a wide range of products, have strong erotic overtones. The boundary of the acceptability of the erotic (in art, litera-

ture, and the performing arts as well as in photography) has shifted back and forth in various times and places.

Erotic photographs began to appear in France (and to a lesser extent in England) in 1840–1841, almost immediately after the appearance of the first photographic processes. By the 1850s an underground market in erotic photography was flourishing, fed by the sexually repressive, paternalistic mores of the recently industrialized French and English societies. In both countries, photographic depiction of the nude was illegal and punishable by imprisonment (though in most cases only public display or sale of such pictures was prosecuted). As public moral standards relaxed somewhat in the 1860s and 1870s, nude photographs began to surface, although suggestive images met with societal resistance.

An extensive underground market for erotic—and pornographic—imagery de-

veloped with the growth of the photographic medium. As new formats and technologies appeared—the *carte-de-visite*, stereoscopic photographs, photographic postcards, instantaneous photographs, and the various photomechanical processes that adapted photography to the printed page—erotic subjects were disseminated ever more widely. By the 1880s "spicy" or "frisky" French postcards, showing women in various coy and suggestive costumes and poses, were sold relatively openly and became quite successful in the United States. The narrative sequences of stereographic cards, with titles like "The French Maid," remained popular well into this century.

By the end of the 19th c., the widespread commercialization of blatantly erotic photography led photographers with serious artistic aims to avoid erotic themes. Eager to confirm the artistic possibilities of the medium, the Pictorialists, and to some degree the Secessionists, concerned themselves with the idealization of the human form in nude studies, turning back to classical painting and sculpture for inspiration.

In the first decades of the 20th c. photographs of an erotic nature began to surface more frequently. "Art" photographers used the cloak of apparent classicism to deal with sexual subjects in an indirect way, and wildly erotic advertising illustration began to be done photographically as well as by hand. E.J. Bellocq's portraits of prostitutes in the Storyville section of New Orleans were frequently tinged with eroticism.

A remarkable resurgence of erotic themes in art photography took place after World War I, spurred by the Dada artists' determination to upset the conventions of middle-class life, and by the Surrealists' infatuation with the theories of Freud. In France, for example, Surrealist painters such as Man Ray and Hans Bellmer sought to suggest the erotic components of dream states, fantasies, and private obsessions. Many of Brassaï's pictures documenting Paris night life in the early 1930s show women, often fully clothed, in an erotic light. In America in the same decade, Paul Outerbridge, Jr., produced a provocative series of color photographs of anonymous, fetishized nudes; and Imogen Cunningham's suggestions of sexual forms in her delicate plant and flower studies displayed an allusive eroticism, as did the writhing green peppers and in-

Erotic Photography. Ralph Gibson, untitled, from *Days at Sea* (1974). Courtesy Ralph Gibson.

timately nested shells in Edward Weston's famous photographs.

Today, the ubiquity of erotica in the mass media—ranging from *Playboy* centerfolds and the gauzy confections of David Hamilton to the more deliberately perverse fashion imagery of Helmut Newton and Guy Bourdin—has again devalued the notion of the erotic as a subject for most serious art photographers. Those who have continued to explore erotic themes have often tended to push at the boundaries separating the erotic from the pornographic. Robert Heinecken, in the late 1960s, investigated the shock value of pornographic imagery incorporated into his complex assemblages; his more recent *He and She* series combines sometimes explicit SX-70 images and written dialogue. Les Krims has revived the format of the composed studio tableau to set forth elaborate, often outrageous erotic fantasies. And in the last decade, in particular, homosexual erotic themes have begun to

be publicly explored in photography, most notably in the work of Robert Mapplethorpe and Arthur Tress. *See also:* FANTASY IN PHOTOGRAPHY; SURREALISM IN PHOTOGRAPHY. Color photograph: p. C-15.

Erwitt, Elliott

American; 1928–

Born of Russian parents in Paris, Elliott Erwitt came to the U.S. at the age of ten. He graduated from Hollywood High School and attended Los Angeles City College, drifting into photography as a teenager. "It seemed like a pretty good way to make a living," he says, ". . . less painful than other ways. Since then I have wondered whether I could have made it any other way."

In 1948, at the age of 20, Erwitt came to New York, and within 6 years—2 of which he spent in the army—he was near the top in the highly competitive field of magazine photography. The quality of

Erwitt's work won quick recognition from editors and from mentors such as Edward Steichen, Roy Stryker, and Robert Capa. Erwitt has been a member of Magnum Photos since 1953.

Erwitt moved from documentary projects to spot news stories, including the Moscow trip during which he made the classic picture of the "kitchen debate" between Richard Nixon and Premier Khruschev. A series of assignments, visual accounts of people and places, for *Holiday* and other magazines have taken him all over the world; his advertising and commercial photographs have appeared in most of the popular magazines both here and abroad. In recent years he has turned to motion pictures and has filmed a number of stunning documentaries with a strong ironic tone.

Throughout his career Erwitt has been able to maintain a personal point of view. In the introduction to Erwitt's book *Photographs and Anti-Photographs* (1972), John Szarkowski, Director of the

Department of Photography at the Museum of Modern Art, wrote: "His simple snapshots are no more heroic than the hapless and untidy lives of individual men. They deal with the empty spaces between happenings—with the anticlimactic non-event. His subjects seem the patient victims of unspecified misunderstandings, awaiting the prompter's cue on a stage designed for a different play. Over their inactivity hangs the premonition of a pratfall. From these unmemorable occasions Erwitt has distilled, with wit and clarity and grace, the indecisive moment."

Escher, Karoly

Hungarian; 1890–1966

The Hungarian photojournalist and documentary photographer Karoly Escher produced his most powerful images during the Depression years leading up to World War II. His most significant images echo Lartigue's humor and, to a

slightly lesser extent, the work of André Kertész. Two major themes imbue his work: the coming storm of World War II (excruciatingly imminent in Hungary, precariously balanced between Germany to the west and Russia to the east), and the dispossessed working people of the Depression era. Escher's pictures reflect a deep emotional commitment to humanity; they speak to a broad audience and cut across differences of experience and social classification.

Hungarian photojournalism in the early 1930s was heavily influenced by that of the German working-class photographers whose photographs appeared in such leftist publications as *Die Arbeiter Illustrierte Zeitung* and *Der Arbeiter Fotograf*. Between 1929 and 1931, this movement had a strong echo in Hungary, where the effects of the Depression on the lower classes were no less than in Germany, the most economically devastated country in Europe. By 1932, however, government-directed police censorship brought to a halt the

publication of such heavily politicized material, and the task of social documentation fell to the few middle-class photographers who had not emigrated. Escher's work, equally powerful but less politically biased than that of most of his contemporaries, continued to be published and to appeal to a broader audience.

Escher continued to work as a photojournalist after the war, but only "Return from Auschwitz" conveys the same intensity as his earlier work.

Photograph: p. 176.

Erwitt, Elliott. "New Haven" (1955). Elliott Erwitt/Magnum.

Escher, Karoly. "The Horse of the Apocalypse" (n.d.). Courtesy Michael Simon, Beloit, Wisconsin.

Etch-Bleach Process

High-contrast images can be converted to very fine-line images that have the appearance of delicate photo-drawings, but without the need for hand work, by the etch-bleach process. The image may be on film or paper, and may be dyed to a single color. The process may also be used for reversal processing of images on high-contrast film.

Either a positive or a negative image may be converted to a fine-line representation, but a positive produces results that are easiest to read. The image should be on high-contrast lith film, fully exposed and developed, or printed from a lith film negative; resin-coated paper provides the easiest handling for prints. After thorough fixing and washing, the image is placed in the etch-bleach solution; this may be done in white light. The solution consists of 1 percent each of citric acid and cupric chloride in water, to which an equal volume of 3 percent hydrogen peroxide solution is added just before use. After soaking five minutes or more, the image can be removed by gentle swabbing with a piece of cotton. Both the silver image and the gelatin in the image areas is removed, down to the film or paper base. This leaves a fine line of silver outlining the highlight areas of the image, which remain as a clear gelatin relief (the process

can also be extended to remove all traces of silver). A combined tone and line image can be obtained by painting over selected areas with a rubber cement solution (frisket) to protect them during the etch-bleach action. This can subsequently be peeled away, or removed with a rubber eraser. After washing, the image can be dried as is, or can be dyed immediately or at some later time. Soaking the image in a plain acetic acid stop bath for a minute or two makes the gelatin relief more receptive to many dyes. Watercolors, food dyes, dye-transfer dyes, color retouching dyes, and similar materials may be used.

Reversal processing of lith film can be carried out under a suitable safelight. After the image is fully developed, it is rinsed and placed directly in the etch-bleach solution. When all silver has been dissolved away, it is rinsed again and then exposed to white light so that all remaining halides in the emulsion are affected. Then the image is developed and washed in the normal manner; no fixing is necessary.

See also: BLEACH-OUT PROCESS; HIGH-CONTRAST MATERIALS; LITH FILMS, PAPERS; RELIEF IMAGES; REVERSAL MATERIALS AND PROCESSING; TONE-LINE PROCESS.

Eugene, Frank

American; 1865–1936

Frank Eugene enjoyed a prominent position within Alfred Stieglitz's Photo-Secession for his heavily manipulated portrait and figure images, which he worked over with pencils, etching needles, and pen-and-ink. In many pictures he attempted to make the photographic image appear to emerge from a hand-etched surroundings, much as a sculptor may leave unfinished stone around a polished figure.

Sadakichi Hartmann, the Photo-Secession's chief critical supporter, disapproved of Eugene's manipulations but considered them as evidence, at least, of photography's plastic powers in the hands of an artist. Overall, however, Hartmann's judgment was that Eugene's work was "reflective, not original," an assessment that still stands.

Eugene's interest in controlling and altering straight photographs arose from his training in painting and etching. He attended City College of New York and the Royal Bavarian Academic of Fine Arts in Munich, afterward returning to New York to become a portrait painter. At this point, his interest in photography brought him into contact with the Stieglitz circle, where he became a founding member of the Photo-Secession.

Eugene, Frank. "Alfred Steiglitz" (1900); photogravure. Collection, Museum of Modern Art, New York.

In 1906, Eugene moved to Germany, where he became well known for his paintings in the then-fashionable Jugendstil manner. In 1913, he received one of the first important non-scientific or technical academic appointments in photography: Royal Professor of Pictorial Photography at the Royal Academy of Graphic Arts in Leipzig.

Evans, Frederick H.
British; 1853-1943

Frederick Evans, an advocate of purist photography, came to prominence at the turn of the century, making his reputation in architectural photography. Little is known of his early life. In the 1870s he was employed as a bank clerk, and he visited the U.S. in 1873. He opened a bookshop in London in the early 1880s and began to photograph at that time. In 1887 he received his first recognition: a medal from the Royal Photographic Society for his exhibit of photographs of natural forms seen through a microscope. As a bookseller Evans encountered the young Aubrey Beardsley, whose work he encouraged, helping to arrange the publication of Beardsley's illustrations for *Le Morte d'Arthur*. Evans exhibited a series, *At Home Portraits*, in 1891, of which he wrote: "I think portraiture by the camera can give a far greater, more intimate sense of identity than any save the work of the very greatest painters."

Around 1890 Evans began to photograph English and French medieval cathedrals, a series which would gain him great attention. Deeply impressed by the architectural watercolor drawings of Turner, he sought to capture similar feelings of light and space. In 1897, 120 of his photographs were shown at the Architectural Club of Boston. A year later he retired from his bookshop and devoted himself entirely to photographic work. A large one-man exhibition at the Royal Photographic Society in London firmly established his reputation in 1900. In the same year he was elected to the prestigious Linked Ring Brotherhood, whose Salon exhibits he would design and hang for the next several years.

An issue of *Camera Work* was devoted to Evans's photographs in 1903, accompanied by an appreciation by George Bernard Shaw. Evans was the first British contributor to the journal. The editor, Alfred Stieglitz, called him "the greatest exponent of architectural photography."

A prolific writer until the time of World War I, Evans's publications included a series of controversial articles in *Amateur Photographer* explaining his philosophy of "pure" photography in 1903–1904. He later became involved in a critical exchange with the leading pictorialist Robert Demachy over the status of photography as an art form.

Professional assignments for *Country Life* magazine in 1905–1906 enabled Evans to photograph chateaus throughout France. Many of these images were displayed soon after in an exhibit at the Photo-Secession Galleries in New York City.

After battling Steichen and Coburn over the selection of photographs for the Photography Salon of 1908, Evans joined the "Salon des Réfusés." Despite this controversy Stieglitz included 11 Evans prints in the International Exhibit of Pictorial Photography in Buffalo, New York, perhaps the most important show of art photography in America up to that time.

During the war years Evans confined his photographic output to platinotype editions of drawings by Blake, Holbein, and Beardsley which he published privately. He was thwarted by the scarcity and soaring price of platinum caused by the war, and he had little interest in the rising movements of modern art. He

gave up photography shortly thereafter, when platinum paper was taken off the market.

It was not until 1928 that Evans was elected Honorary Fellow of the Royal Photographic Society. He died in London two days before his 90th birthday. In the next two years there was a revival of interest in his work when the Royal Photographic Society held a Memorial Exhibition and Symposium. In 1964 a show of 84 original prints was mounted at George Eastman House in Rochester, New York. The curator, Beaumont Newhall, called Evans "one of the great pictorial photographers," and wrote further: "Evans sought to make pictures that would be as timeless as the buildings and landscapes they portrayed. . . . It can be no exaggeration to write that his architectural photographs are the greatest of their kind, because he was able to combine precision of definition with a softness and delicacy of gradation

and because he had an extraordinary sense of scale and of light."

See also: ARCHITECTURAL PHOTOGRAPHY; CAMERA WORK; LINKED RING BROTHERHOOD; PICTORIAL PHOTOGRAPHY; STIEGLITZ, ALFRED.

Photograph: p. 160.

Evans, Walker

American; 1903–1975

Walker Evans was an important contributor to the development of American documentary photography in the 1930s. His precisely detailed, frontal depictions of people and artifacts of American life (crammed store interiors, display windows, billboards, etc.) have influenced each succeeding generation of photographers.

Abandoning his early ambitions to write and paint, Evans turned to photography and arrived at a dry, economical, unpretentious style which attempted to

lay bare before the viewer the most literal facts. He was critical from the start of what he termed the "artsicraftsiness" of art photographers such as Alfred Stieglitz and the "commercialism" of those such as Edward Steichen.

Although primarily a photographer of environments rather than people, Evans's social concerns brought him face to face with the victims of the Depression. He tried to capture their stoicism in unflinchingly direct portraits. He believed with Baudelaire that the artist's task was to face head-on the harshest realities and to report them to the larger world. He said: "The real thing that I'm talking about has purity and a certain severity, rigor, or simplicity, directness, clarity, and it is without artistic pretension in a self-conscious sense of the word."

Evans was born in St. Louis, Missouri, and was raised in Kenilworth, Illinois. He attended the Loomis School, Phillips

Academy, and Williams College. After a short time working at the New York Public Library, he traveled to Paris, where he audited courses at the Sorbonne and immersed himself in the writings of Flaubert and Baudelaire. He returned to New York in 1927 and began to photograph seriously the following year. His photographs were used to illustrate an edition of his friend Hart Crane's *The Bridge* in 1930. The same year, at the suggestion of Lincoln Kirstein, he began to document early Victorian houses in New England and New York. These photographs were exhibited at the Museum of Modern Art in New York in 1933. Kirstein and Evans collaborated on three books in the following years, and many early Evans images were published in Kirstein's journal *Hound & Horn*.

Evans's first exhibition was held at the Julien Levy Gallery in 1932. That same year he provided illustrations for Carleton Beals's book *The Crime of Cuba*. In 1935 Evans made photographs of African art exhibited at the Museum of Modern Art for distribution to colleges and libraries by the General Education Board. Evans was hired by Roy Stryker of the Farm Security Administration at this time. He took part in the FSA's photographic survey of rural America at various times during the next four years, reporting primarily on southern states. At the same time he photographed pre–Civil War architecture for his own interests.

In the summer of 1936 Evans took a leave of absence from the FSA in order to work on a *Fortune* magazine project with the writer James Agee. The team lived with Alabama sharecropper families for two months. Their work was rejected by *Fortune* but was published as a book, *Let Us Now Praise Famous Men*, in 1941. The photographs Evans took for the FSA and this volume represents some of his most important and influential work.

In 1938 Evans began to take candid shots of subway riders and people in the streets. In this work he relinquished control of framing and lighting in order to achieve the purest record of the moment. From 1943 to 1945 he was a staff writer for *Time*. He became a staff writer and the sole staff photographer at *Fortune* in 1945. He worked at *Fortune* for the next 20 years in these roles and as an independent associate editor. *Fortune* published many of Evans's photo-essays with his own texts. He was Professor of Graphic Design at Yale University from 1965 until his death in New Haven 10 years later.

During his lifetime Evans was the recipient of many awards. He was a Guggenheim Fellow in 1940 and received an honorary degree from Williams College in 1968. His photographs were exhibited all over the world, including several major shows at the Museum of Modern Art.

See also: FARM SECURITY ADMINISTRATION.

Evidence Photography
See: FORENSIC PHOTOGRAPHY.

EV (Exposure Value) System

The exposure value system is a mechanical-linkage system for semiautomatic control of exposure settings. Used on lenses with built-in shutters, it is primarily for small-format cameras and is now largely replaced by electronic methods of automatic exposure control.

The basis of the EV system is a scale of numbers, each representing a series of equivalent exposure settings. For example, EV 10 represents an exposure of 1/500 sec. at $f/1.4$ and all other shutter and f-stop combinations (within the limitations of the lens) that give the same exposure. When an EV system lens is set to a particular EV number, it physically interconnects the aperture and speed controls at an appropriate combination of settings. Thereafter, whenever one control is moved to a different setting, the other control changes its setting to maintain the same relative exposure. A different exposure is obtained by setting the lens to a different EV number; each number produces a halving or doubling of the exposure—i.e., a one-stop change. The EV number required for a given situation is determined by reference to a simple exposure estimating chart, or by using an exposure meter that provides EV as well as f-number and shutter-speed readings.

See also: AUTOMATIC EXPOSURE CONTROL.

Exhibitions

The rapid growth since the 1960s of public interest in photography as an art has generated a parallel growth in the number of places and opportunities for individuals to exhibit their work. From the 1850s through the first two decades of this century, photographic art exhibitions were restricted to a relatively small number of salons and galleries, all of which showed to an initiated few the efforts of their more talented members. Present-day descendants of the salons, including the Royal Photographic Society (RPS) in England and the Photo-

graphic Society of America (PSA), still restrict the vast majority of their exhibitions to members' photographs, as do many of the better-known photographic galleries in large cities. Art museums, such as the Georges Pompidou Centre des Arts in Paris or the Museum of Modern Art in New York City, usually give exhibitions only of those photographers who have already established a national or international reputation. Major photographic institutions largely divide their schedules between historic material and the work of significant contemporary photographers.

Photographic societies, such as the RPS or PSA, have specific guidelines governing the size and number of prints each prospective exhibitor is allowed to submit. The submissions received by the society generally are judged for aesthetic and technical merit by a selection committee made up of senior members or established critics and photographers. In some cases the shows are "open"—i.e., not restricted in subject matter. At other times thematic shows are given, the entrants being asked to submit only landscapes, portraits, nature studies, and so on.

Cooperative galleries, made up of dues-paying members, follow much the same procedure for their exhibitions, although they are not as likely to restrict the size or content of the exhibitor's work. The selection committees of co-op galleries usually are made up of members who are elected annually for this task. The annual changeover of the committee helps assure members that they have an influence on the kind of work shown. Most exhibitions mounted by co-op galleries come about not by general invitation, but at the request of specific members with a body of work and funds to help defray the cost of the exhibition. If the work meets with the selection committee's approval, the photographer is given a date for the exhibition and is asked to assume a percentage of the cost, ranging from 25 percent to the total amount required to frame the show, publicize it, and meet related expenses. Those galleries requiring a substantial outlay of funds on the part of the exhibitor therefore function as "vanity galleries" to some extent, providing little more than a space for those members who can afford the cost of showing their own work. Most cooperative galleries function on a more democratic basis, however, mounting group shows and setting aside substantial amounts of membership money for exhibition purposes.

In recent years private business concerns have become increasingly involved in the exhibition of photographic art.

Banks, large stores, and corporations often provide exhibition space and require little or no financial outlay from the photographer. This may be done as a public service or for promotional purposes on the part of the sponsor. Municipal institutions and social and fraternal organizations similarly may provide exhibition space for photographers.

Most museums with photographic collections and most major photographic galleries reserve at least one day a week to accept photographers' portfolios for consideration. In the case of organizations with international reputations and schedules planned two or three years in advance, such review is not for the purpose of discovering exhibition material, but rather is to see work by new photographers and to keep abreast of recent developments in the medium.

Many galleries will take time to acknowledge work they feel is promising, even if they cannot find an immediate use for it. The photographer may be asked to submit more work in the future or, more rarely, he or she may be invited to join the gallery. In the latter case the photographer is usually required to produce a number of photographs for the gallery to keep on hand and to prepare material for a show (usually with other photographers at first). In most cases the gallery assumes publicity and hanging costs, taking from 25 to 50 percent of sales to cover expenses and make some profit. Many galleries require that a photographer sign an exclusive contract, thereby making the gallery the sole agent for exhibition, sale, and publication of the photographer's pictures.

At whatever level it is mounted, an exhibition is a public assertion that the work shown is of sufficient expressive merit (and technical competence) to warrant attention. It is the expectation of those attending an exhibition that this will be the case. That expectation puts a heavy burden of responsibility on the photographer and the sponsoring organization. It is a mark of the growth of the medium that the responsibility has been met with a continual increase in quality in the last two decades.

See also: AN AMERICAN PLACE; ART OF PHOTOGRAPHY; LITTLE GALLERIES OF THE PHOTO-SECESSION; LINKED RING BROTHERHOOD; MUSEUMS AND COLLECTIONS; SALON PHOTOGRAPHY.

Existing-Light Photography

Existing-light photography is the making of photographs using only the light that normally illuminates the subject.
See: AVAILABLE-LIGHT PHOTOGRAPHY.

Expedition Photography

From the 1850s photography has been an important part of expeditions made for archaeological, geological, geographic and geodesic, biological, cultural and anthropological, and many other purposes. Whereas expeditions of the past were concerned primarily with discovery, those of today are mainly for purposes of investigation. The places and features of the face of the earth have been recorded; most expeditions now go where known phenomena or life forms that are of interest exist. The frontiers of discovery are now beneath the oceans and in space, where photography is accomplished by remotely controlled or automatically operating equipment.

Whatever the nature of the project, expedition photography has two major purposes: to record the preparations, personnel, and activities of the project, and to gather information and data for later analysis. Photographs taken for the latter purpose may provide supporting information (e.g., this is the overall formation from which the samples were taken; this is the artifact in place, before it was completely unearthed and removed for examination) or may provide the primary evidence to be evaluated (e.g., this is how the people dress; this is the way they stand and gesture in formal conversation). All kinds of expeditions can use still photography to advantage for these purposes; those concerned with living or changing subjects (e.g., biological or anthropological projects; investigations of volcanic activity or ocean dynamics) often find motion-picture records of even greater value.

Depending on the size of the field team, the scope of the investigations to be made, and the available funds, photography may be carried out as an additional duty by one or more of the team specialists, or by a full-time photographer who is included as one of the team members. Even if he or she is a specialist in some aspect of the expedition activity, the photographer must become as familiar as possible with all other aspects so as to understand the special requirements that, when met, will make pictures especially useful and informative. Similarly, the photographer must be familiar with a wide range of techniques. In the course of a single day it may be necessary, for example, to take overall orientation views, telephoto records of birds and animals, and macrorange closeups of details.

The first step in planning expedition photography is to establish what is expected and who will own the rights to the pictures. The first concern is important in deciding what photographic

equipment and supplies to take; the second can be of major importance for many years after the project has been completed. Copyright in work done for hire belongs to the person or organization doing the hiring. In some cases the photographer can arrange to retain various rights, often as part payment for the work to be done. Then it is important to specify what those rights are—exhibition; book or magazine publication; commercial exploitation, as through a picture agency; etc.—and what credits or acknowledgements must appear with the pictures, however they may be used. It is also wise to have a written agreement as to the right of other expedition members to take pictures and sell them.

The nature of the expedition will impose limitations on equipment and supplies. A single 35mm camera and lens and a few cartridges of film may be the maximum on a mountain-climbing project, while an extended archaeological dig may permit a great variety of equipment. Seldom is it possible to take everything that might be helpful, so most choices are a compromise between the irreducible minimum and the ideally complete. The basic rule is to avoid specialized items where more versatile ones can be adapted for multiple uses. A comprehensive list must be revised several times, with the true value of each item being questioned and justified each time. Once an "A" list of essential items has been prepared, a "B" list can be made to include in order of priority the supplementary equipment that would be helpful. If space or other factors permit, the "B" list provides a guide for expansion.

It is important to include chemicals and equipment to process film in the field in order to make checks of exposure and proper equipment operation. Containers are required to protect both exposed and unexposed films, and supplies must be included to package and ship films for processing if, as is usually the case, field processing is to be kept to a minimum. It is a wise precaution to ship film to an individual who has the responsibility of having it processed, reporting any problems, and shipping additional supplies or replacement equipment as necessary.

Logistical details such as passports and visas, inoculations, travel arrangements, and customs and import/export forms may be partially the responsibility of each team member or may be in the hands of a single coordinator. The photographer has the special responsibility of having equipment prepared for use under whatever conditions may be encountered. Special precautions and operating procedures for various conditions are discussed in other entries.

See also: ARCHEOLOGICAL PHOTOGRAPHY; TROPICAL PHOTOGRAPHY; WINTER PHOTOGRAPHY.

Color photograph: p. C-16.

Exploded Views

Diagrammatic photographs that show the exact relative placement and assembly order of parts in a machine or instrument are called exploded views. Photographs of this type are used in technical manuals, texts and instruction books, and service guides. Exploded views are accomplished under photographic studio conditions, where maximum control of lighting and exact positioning of the parts are possible. The components of the machine or instrument are laid out in exact assembly order, but separated sufficiently for each part to be seen clearly. The parts are mounted on glass or white-painted supports, suspended with fine thread, or supported by concealed rods and stiff wires from behind; often a combination of methods is used. The whole assembly is photographed against a plain, usually white, background for clarity and separation of the parts. A large-format view camera is used for precise alignment and maximum image detail. Broad, flat, diffused light sources are used to cut down on specular highlights, eliminate shadows, and mask the method of suspension.

Exploded views can be photographed in color or black-and-white; the final image is usually retouched to remove all traces of how the parts were suspended. The final result shows the parts of the machine "floating" in their exact assembly order.

See also: PHANTOM VIEW.

Exposure

Exposure is the effect of radiant energy, especially light, on a photographic emulsion. Exposure is significant only when it is sufficient to initiate the reduction of silver halide crystals to metallic silver (or an equivalent breakdown of other compounds, as in diazo emulsions), causing the formation of an invisible latent image. Some (printing-out) emulsions can be reduced directly to a visible image by exposure, but this is a slow, very limited procedure.

The amount of exposure (E) received by an emulsion is the product of the intensity (I) of the radiation and the length of time (t) it strikes the emulsion, classically expressed:

$$E = I \times t.$$

In the modern symbols of the International Standard system, exposure is H and illuminance is E, making the formula for photographic exposure

$$H = E \times t.$$

In either formulation it is obvious that many different values for illuminance and time can produce the same exposure; such pairings have reciprocal relationships as represented in practice by the various combinations of f-stop and shutter-speed settings that give equal exposures. However, when t becomes large and E (or I) becomes correspondingly small, as in a time exposure, this reciprocity fails, with the consequence that the exposure must be increased in order to produce the expected effect on the emulsion.

Controlling exposure. Exposure is controlled by varying intensity and time. The first is accomplished by adjusting the lens aperture setting and perhaps by the use of filters, the second by adjusting the shutter speed (or the timer setting in printing). The practical problem is determining what exposure is required to produce expected results. The starting point is an accurate sensitivity or speed rating of the emulsion to be used. That may be the manufacturer's assigned ISO/ASA film speed, or it may be an effective or working film speed determined by practical tests; this is usually called an *exposure index* (EI). Film exposure can be estimated on the basis that an average subject front-lighted by sun and open sky will be adequately recorded at $f/16$ with a shutter speed equivalent to 1/Film speed (ISO or EI). Other conditions (e.g., sidelight; clouds; shade) require more exposure. An exposure meter can provide more accurate indications with a great variety of subjects under greatly differing conditions.

A reflected-light meter is calibrated on the assumption that an average subject reflects 18–20 percent of the light falling on it. (The $f/16$ rule, above, is based on the same assumption.) In terms of a 10-step, black-to-white gray scale, an 18 percent reflectance gray is in the middle, the fifth step above maximum black. When the meter is used to measure the brightness of a given subject area, it responds on the basis of 18 percent reflectance whether or not that is actually the case, and indicates an exposure that will reproduce the tone as the equivalent mid-scale gray. Recognition of this fundamental fact is the key to determining exposure for controlled results in black-and-white photography. If it is appropriate and desirable to have the metered subject tone represented by

middle gray, the meter-indicated exposure may be used. But if that subject tone ought to be a different gray shade, a different exposure is required. Each exposure change that is equivalent to a difference of one f-stop produces a one-step shift of the gray scale rendition of the measured tone. (The actual change can be accomplished by adjusting the f-stop or the shutter speed, or in auto-exposure cameras by changing the film speed setting.) Less exposure results in a darker gray shade, more exposure in a lighter gray shade in the final positive image (print). For example, the average light-skinned person reflects 35–40 percent of the light, twice as much as the meter's standard. A portrait exposed according to the meter reading would render the skin unnaturally dark; one exposed one f-stop more would render the skin one gray shade lighter, which corresponds more closely to its true relative brightness. However, a dark-skinned person reflects about 20 percent of the light, so that a meter-indicated exposure would produce a natural-looking rendition.

A greater degree of exposure control in black-and-white photography is achieved by considering the brightness range of the subject. This technique is the foundation of the *zone system;* it takes into account the fact that tonal rendition of the dark subject areas is determined only by exposure, but that rendition of the brighter areas can be adjusted to some degree by development. The brightness range is measured by reflected-light readings of the darkest and brightest areas in which there is detail that must be visible in the print. Exposure is determined from the dark-area meter reading. In order to make that area an appropriate dark tone, the actual exposure must be the equivalent of two or three f-stops less than the meter indication. Additional steps in zone system procedures calculate where that exposure will register the highlights and whether or not development adjustment is therefore necessary.

Color film. Exposure of color film, especially transparency film, is commonly based on an incident light meter reading, or the equivalent: a reflected-light reading from an 18 percent gray card. This procedure assumes a fully lighted subject of normal brightness and color range. Alternatively, exposure can be based on a reflected-light reading from the most important area of the subject. If that is a light area, such as light colored skin, exposure should be increased one f-stop from the meter reading. It is difficult to predict what exposure will look best with transparency film because the intensity of the projector or other transmitted viewing light is an important variable. Many photographers find that giving about one-half *f*-stop less than calculated exposure produces pleasing color saturation in most cases. It is common to bracket (make additional exposures) in color photography, especially on the side of reduced exposure, to insure good results.

Black-and-white printing exposures are rapidly and easily determined by test strips or other sample exposures because processing is rapid. This procedure also makes it possible to evaluate contrast at the same time. Color printing exposures can also be made by tests, while simultaneously testing for proper filtration. Enlarging exposure meters or other exposure estimating devices are widely used because color print processing is relatively lengthy, making the test strip method too slow.

See also: EXPOSURE METERS; GRAY CARD; GRAY SCALE; RECIPROCITY; SPEED OF MATERIALS; ZONE SYSTEM.

Exposure Automation

Modern cameras and shutters use a variety of techniques and mechanisms for automatically controlling either the amount of exposure given a film or print, or the moment at which an exposure is made, or both. Systems for automatic exposure control built into cameras may provide one or more of three operational modes: aperture priority, in which shutter speed is automatically determined; shutter priority, in which lens aperture setting is automatically controlled; and programmed operation in which both factors are automatically controlled. High-volume printing machines, process cameras, and similar equipment incorporate devices that measure cumulative exposure from pulsed or continuous light sources and cut off exposure based on the density characteristics of the original image and the sensitivity of the emulsion being exposed. Moment-of-exposure automation extends from the delayed release "self-timer" built into many cameras, to remote control devices of all kinds and degrees of sophistication.

See also: AUTOMATIC EXPOSURE CONTROL; REMOTE CONTROL.

Exposure Meters

A photographic exposure meter consists of a photometer (light-intensity meter) and associated circuits or devices which translate the light data into specific exposure adjustments or recommendations. The earliest exposure meters used visual evaluation (extinction meter; visual photometer) or sample strips of sensitized paper. In the latter device the amount of time required for the sample to darken to a particular tint, when exposed to the light falling on the subject, was related by a chart or table to equivalent camera settings for films of various speeds. The photoelectric meter first appeared in the 1920s. In its most common form it employed a selenium-coated sensor (cell) that generated a small amount of voltage in proportion to the amount of light striking it. The voltage caused an indicator needle to move across a scale of light-value numbers. The indicated value was set by hand on a rotating-dial calculator marked with *f*-numbers and shutter speeds so that a range of equivalent exposure settings was displayed. The cell had to be about 1½ in. (40mm) in diameter in order to have sufficient surface area to generate the voltage required to move the indicator. This was suitable for hand-held and pocket-size meters, but was too large for meters to be built into many cameras.

Almost all meters today use photoconductive (rather than photovoltaic) cells. The first such meters, introduced in the 1960s, used cadmium sulfide (CdS) cells; now cells based on silicon, germanium, and gallium compounds are also used. These cells require battery power to supply voltage in the meter circuit; they control the current flow in the circuit because their conductivity varies in proportion to the intensity of the light striking them. They are much more sensitive to light than selenium cells, and their meter function does not depend upon their size. That makes them usable for built-in meters in medium- and small-format cameras, as well as for hand-held meters. The battery power in the meter circuit can be used to power an indicator needle or motorized calculator dials, or to energize liquid crystal (LC) or light-emitting diode (LED) displays of *f*-stops and shutter speeds or various exposure-indication symbols. In automatic exposure control systems associated circuits actually adjust the *f*-stop or shutter speed, or both, in response to the meter's electrical output.

To provide accurate exposure data, a meter must be preset for the sensitivity (speed) of the film to be used. This is accomplished with a control variously marked ISO, ASA, or DIN (initials of the standard speed systems). The speed setting either adjusts the relationship between calculator scales or the response of electronic circuits. Accuracy also depends on the kind of reading the meter makes and the area that the reading includes.

A *reflected-light* reading measures the intensity of light coming from the subject; it is taken by pointing the meter cell at the subject. All built-in camera meters and most hand-held meters make reflected-light readings. An *incident-light* reading measures the intensity of light falling onto the subject; it is taken by holding the meter at the subject position with the cell pointed toward the intended camera position. A white diffusing cover in front of the cell collects light coming toward the subject from all frontal directions. Some hand-held meters take only this kind of reading; others have a removable diffuser so they can be used for either kind of reading. An accessory diffuser is available for taking incident-light readings with some built-in camera meters; it is placed in front of the lens like a filter. The particular advantages of each kind of reading are discussed in the entries on exposure and brightness range.

Meter coverage is an important factor whenever the main subject and the surroundings have significant differences in brightness. When the entire scene is of the same general brightness, an overall or wide-area reading is suitable. Incident-light meters and reflected-light *averaging* meters (which typically have a 30-degree or larger cone of acceptance) have this kind of coverage. Built-in averaging meters read the entire image area and give all parts equal weight. A *center-weighted* camera meter gives more importance to the brightness level in the middle of the picture, typically about the center third of the area. A *spot* meter reads an area of only 1 to 2 degrees in diameter, although the camera or meter viewer shows a much larger area for convenience in aiming.

A meter cell cannot tell whether it is being used for an incident-light or a reflected-light reading, nor whether the subject is dark- or light-colored, a uniform tone or a variegated pattern. Meters are calibrated on the assumption that the subject is reflecting about 18 percent of the light falling on it; this is the reflectance of an average subject or scene illuminated by frontal sunlight. If that is not the case, a reading must be taken from a selected important area of the subject, or an overall reading must be adjusted in terms of the subject's nonaverage reflectance. This is discussed in the entry on exposure.

Specialized Meters. An *electronic flash* meter is an incident-light meter that can respond to the brief flash of light and hold the peak reading; in most such meters the reading is directly in *f*-stops. An *integrating* meter adds together the effect of repeated flashes or pulses of light and indicates the cumulative reading. A printing or *enlarging* meter determines darkroom exposures; some models read the reflected brightness of the projected negative image, while others take an incident-light reading from a diffuser temporarily placed under the lens to integrate all the image brightnesses. Printing meters must be calibrated for specific grades of paper. A *color temperature* meter does not provide exposure data, but indicates the relative red-green-blue content of the light; it may indicate the filtration required to match the light to a given type of color film emulsion. *See also:* AUTOMATIC EXPOSURE CONTROL; BRIGHTNESS RANGE; EXPOSURE; EXTINCTION METER; INTEGRATING METER; PHOTOMETER/PHOTOMETRY; SPEED OF MATERIALS.

Extension

The distance between the lens and the film plane of a camera is called the lens extension; the term is also used to mean the distance between a given lens position and its normal infinity focus position—e.g., the lens mount on a rigid-body camera. Extension is measured from the "optical center" of a lens. With lenses of normal focal length or symmetrical design, it is sufficient to measure from the iris diaphragm in the lens. With telephoto and wide-angle lenses, extension must be measured from the rear nodal point. This point can be determined by setting the lens at its infinity focus position and measuring forward from the film plane a distance equal to the focal length of the lens. The nodal point will fall behind the diaphragm of most wide-angle lenses, and in front of the diaphragm of most telephoto lenses; in either case it may even fall outside the physical body of the lens.

To focus objects at infinity, the lens-to-film extension must be equal to the focal length of the lens; greater extension is required to focus objects at closer distances. Lenses in self-focusing mounts have sufficient built-in adjustable extension to focus down to about 10 times their focal length; some can focus closer, but with most lenses closer focusing is achieved by inserting extension tubes, rings, or an accessory bellows between the lens and the camera body. Lenses without focusing mounts—such as those for large-format cameras—must be used with a bellows or other adjustable mounting system. The total extension required for any degree of image magnification (M) can be determined as follows:

$$\text{Extension} = \text{Focal length of lens} \times (M + 1).$$

In the case of a rigid-body camera, the body thickness provides one focal length of extension, so the additional extension required is simply:

$$\text{Focal length} \times M.$$

As extension increases, the brightness of the image on the film decreases in obedience to the inverse square law. When the total extension is greater than about 1.3 focal lengths, exposure compensation is required. Through-the-lens meters or automatic exposure control systems provide the necessary compensation. In other cases, exposure correction can be determined from the bellows extension factor. *See also:* BELLOWS EXTENSION FACTOR; INVERSE SQUARE LAW; MAGNIFICATION; OPTICS.

Extinction Meter

One of the earliest exposure-determination devices, an extinction meter relies on visual evaluation of the subject viewed through a neutral density filter or screen. The simplest extinction meter is a step wedge of numbered, increasing densities. The subject is viewed through successive steps until the last visible number is found. A reference table relates the step numbers to film speeds and exposure settings. A more sophisticated meter uses an optical wedge of continuous densities. The wedge is moved across the eyepiece, progressively extinguishing image brightness until subject details disappear. The wedge control incorporates an exposure scale or has numbered settings used in conjunction with a reference table. An iris diaphragm may be used in place of the wedge; it is slowly closed to the point at which subject details are no longer visible.

The difficulty with extinction meters is the involuntary adaptation of the eye to changes in brightness. The visual evaluation must be made quickly, or only after a standard delay time at each setting; otherwise the eye will adjust to the reduced brightness and see details that were previously indistinguishable. Meters of this sort are obsolete for photographic work, but similar devices are used to estimate the temperature of incandescent subjects such as pottery inside a kiln, or molten metal. *See also:* NEUTRAL DENSITY; STEP WEDGE; WEDGE, OPTICAL.

Eye
See: VISION.

F

Fabric Prints

Photographic images on cloth can be produced by ink or dye transfer through a stencil, by exposure of an emulsion coated on the cloth, or by exposure of cloth that has absorbed a sensitizer in its fibers. The transfer method requires preparation of a photosilkscreen stencil from a suitable image. Then a variety of inks, dyes, or paints may be used to print the image, depending upon the nature of the cloth. Some colorants are suitable only for natural fibers, others for synthetics; some are absorbed by the fibers, others require heat, ultraviolet exposure, or chemical treatment to bond permanently. Craft and hobby shops, art stores, and manufacturers of dyes and inks supply a wide range of such materials suitable for specific kinds of fabrics.

Presensitized fabrics are offered for certain diazo processes, primarily for making copies of plans and drawings. These can be exposed by contact under a suitably high-contrast positive or negative. Some photographic suppliers offer so-called photosilk or photolinen coated with a silver halide emulsion for exposure to a continuous-tone negative. Most such material is heavy and stiff, intended for hand coloring and display as an imitation painting, but it can be toned, used uncolored, or treated in other ways as well. A liquid emulsion is also available for coating fabric; it is exposed and developed by ordinary photographic procedures.

Fabrics can be directly sensitized with the solutions used for the cyanotype, kallitype, or vandyke processes. These are all based on the light sensitivity of iron compounds, which are slow enough to require contact-printing exposures by sunlight or ultraviolet. Although best results are obtained with fabric that has been sized, the sensitizers are to some degree absorbed by the fibers, with the result that the final image seems more integral to the fabric than with other processes. The cyanotype produces images in blue tones; the vandyke process in brown tones; and the kallitype in black, purplish-brown, or sepia tones, depending upon the developer used.
See also: CYANOTYPE; DIAZO PROCESSES; KALLITYPE; PHOTOSILKSCREEN PROCESS; VANDYKE PROCESS.

Fade-In; Fade-Out

In motion pictures and television, when a picture fades in, it grows from a dark screen (TV "black") to full brightness; when it fades out, it dims from full brightness to black. The two devices are commonly used together to form a visual transition that marks off major sections in the narrative development of a presentation. The fade-out/fade-in transition may take less than a second, or may be prolonged for up to several seconds, according to the degree of pause considered most effective in terms of audience reaction. The transition is equivalent to lowering and raising the curtain between acts of a theatrical presentation or to the division of a book into parts set off by intervening section-title pages.

Seldom is either kind of fade combined with some other element of editing syntax. For example, it is unusual for a presentation to cut to black and then fade in the next picture, or to fade out and then cut to the following scene. When a fade-out and fade-in overlap, the effect is that one picture dissolves into the next. A related technique fades to or from "white"—a screen of maximum, imageless brightness. Because this is so unconventional, it calls attention to itself much more than "black" fades. It addition, the brightness may dazzle the viewers, affecting their perception of the following scene until their eyes have readjusted.
See also: CUT; DISSOLVE; EDITING.

Fading

Under certain conditions photographic images are subject to fading and related visible changes over a period of time. The problem is more severe and much more difficult to combat with color images than with those in black-and-white. This is because the image-forming dyes in most color materials are inherently unstable, whereas the cause in black-and-white is primarily a matter of processing procedures.

The fading of silver-image prints has been a problem since the very beginnings of photography on paper, the calotype process of 1840. The major causes were identified in 1855 by the Fading Committee of the London Photographic Society, the first investigatory body appointed by the society. Then, as now, the primary cause of fading is chemical compounds—especially sulfur and fixer (hypo) compounds—retained in the base material. Additional causes are retained moisture and the penetration of contaminants from mounting cements and materials. Silver images on nonabsorbent materials such as metal and glass have shown far less tendency to fade or discolor than those on paper bases. Current procedures and recommendations for achieving long-term permanence of black-and-white images are discussed in the entry on archival processing.

It should be noted that images on resin-coated papers are apparently more susceptible to atmospheric attack than those on fiber-based papers, and that both print and negative images are given a significant measure of protection from such attack by treatment in a very dilute (1:20 or more) selenium toning solution. Fading can also result from storage in contact with chemically impure envelopes, folders, and plastic sleeves. Sulfur compounds from rubber cement and similar adhesives will penetrate paper bases and attack images, as will impurities in mounting boards. A layer of heat-activated dry-mounting tissue is apparently safe in itself and provides a barrier against other attack through the base.

Only color images formed in metallic dyes, such as those used in current dye-destruction materials (e.g., Cibachrome), show virtually no fading. The dyes used in the dye transfer process are somewhat less fade-resistant, but are far more stable than the organic dyes used in virtually all other color films and papers. Heat, moisture, and sunlight all promote rapid fading of conventional color photographic images. The rate of fading varies with the material and the conditions. In some cases noticeable change occurs within a few months; in other cases images remain visually unchanged for years. In general, a color print displayed on a shaded wall will last far longer than one in the direct path of window light; a print kept in an air-conditioned, low-humidity environment will last longer than one kept in a steam-heated room, hung near a fountain or aquarium, or similarly displayed.

Color fading can be prevented by storing images in lighttight, moisture-proof packages at temperatures near or below freezing. Another procedure is to make separation negatives of the original image on black-and-white film, which can be archivally processed. This permits making a new color print from fresh materials whenever required, using the dye transfer or similar processes. Thus, although the original may fade, it can, in essence, perpetually be recreated.
See also: ARCHIVAL PROCESSING; FILING AND STORING PHOTOGRAPHS.

Fahrenheit
See: TEMPERATURE SCALES.

False-Color Film
In a false-color film the usual color sensitivity and dye production characteristics have been altered in order to obtain distinctive visual records of otherwise indistinguishable or invisible subject characteristics. The most common type of false-color film is infrared-sensitive color film. Normal three-layer color film has the following response characteristics, from the top layer down: blue sensitivity (yellow dye image), green sensitivity (magenta dye image), red sensitivity (cyan dye image). The altered response of infrared false-color film is: infrared sensitivity (cyan dye), green sensitivity (yellow dye), red sensitivity (magenta dye). This film is normally used with a yellow filter so that no blue light exposure is recorded. Blue can appear in an image because of the way the subtractive color dyes interact, but it does not correspond to the blue content of the original subject. In terms of basic color rendition, a positive image from false-color film shows green objects as blue, red objects as green, and objects emitting or reflecting only infrared as red. In fact most subject colors are mixtures of several wavelengths, and many objects reflect some infrared as well as visible colors, with the result that the colors in the final image are quite varied and complex. Nevertheless, the principle remains that infrared-rich objects are made visually distinctive.
See also: INFRARED PHOTOGRAPHY; SUBTRACTIVE COLOR SYNTHESIS.

Fantasy in Photography
For a medium commonly thought to be inherently objective and realistic, photography has produced a rich body of work in the fantasy vein. While fantasy is usually considered to flow from a vivid imagination, photography must by its very nature begin with the visual materials of reality. A painter may convincingly depict a castle in the sky, a creature from another world, or an apparition from beyond the grave, for a painting may spring as easily from a mental image as from physical reality. But because photography must begin from something real set before the lens, it is much more difficult for a photograph to succeed in entering the realm of fantasy. The viewer can hardly avoid the impulse to search out the stagecraft, so to speak.

The most commonplace examples of the use of fantasy in photography—so commonplace they are seldom considered fantasy—are those found in fashion, glamour, and advertising images. Here the photograph's reputed believability serves to lend credence to images which resemble nothing likely to be encountered in real life. These manufactured visions of the perfect woman, the gleaming sports car, or the ideal vacation spot have become the elements of our most widely shared collective fantasies. Magazine images of models and performers—in large degree the products of the combined skills of the make-up artist, the photographer, and the retoucher—become the standards by which real-life women are judged. The long, lean automobile—made to seem even longer and leaner by the use of the wide-angle lens—becomes a universal symbol of excitement and power. The glistening white sands of a tropical resort—whose sheen is enhanced by carefully selected photographic filters—serve as an ideal of dazzlement with which few real coastlines can compete.

The incorporation of fantasy into photography might be said to begin with one of the inventors of the medium, Hippolyte Bayard. In 1840 Bayard staged a photograph presenting himself as a corpse—an imaginative protest against what he felt was the French government's neglect of his invention. But this image is something of an anomaly. Only with the introduction of combination printing (the use of several separate negatives to make one picture) in the next decade did photographers begin to fully explore the possibilities of fantasy images. One of the masters of combination, Oscar G. Rejlander, also was among the first to use a deliberate double exposure to produce an expressive effect. In "Hard Times" (1860), Rejlander portrayed an unemployed carpenter brooding by the bedside of his   wife and child who, by means of double exposure, appear also as "ghost" images—the object of the carpenter's thoughts, or perhaps a premonition of their demise. A decade later he displayed a more humorous photograph in the fantasy vein, "O.G.R. the Artist Introduces

Fantasy in Photography. Les Krims, "Dumping Leaves Nothing," from *Idiosyncratic Pictures* (1979). Les Krims; courtesy Freidus/Ordover Gallery, New York.

Fantasy in Photography. Les Krims, "Dumping Leaves Nothing," from *Idiosyncratic Pictures* (1979). Les Krims; courtesy Freidus/Ordover Gallery, New York.

O.G.R. the Volunteer," in which, thanks to combination printing, Rejlander the frock-coated painter gestures toward a second Rejlander attired as a hardy military man.

In the 19th c. such photographs were seldom taken seriously, and were usually judged to be merely "trick photography." A similar reaction on the part of most viewers greeted the "spirit photographs" that enjoyed a certain popularity in the 1880s; these employed obvious double-exposure techniques to supply photographs supposedly showing the shimmering image of departed friends or relatives. Most everyday photographers, and certainly most art photographers of the time, showed little interest in such imagery.

Since the 1920s, however, when Surrealist artists and photographers began seeking to unlock the powers of the unconscious and the imagination, fantasy has become a major photographic mode. For surrealists like Man Ray, Hans Bellmer, and Brassaï, photography's reputation for realism served, paradoxically, to attract them to it. The seeming factuality of the photographic image lent an air of credibility to even the most fantastic scenes, whether staged especially for the camera or created in the darkroom. The flood of fantastic imagery unleashed by the surrealists has remained an important influence not only on art photographers continuing to work in the fantasy mode, but on fashion and advertising photography as well.

Images which convey the impression of a dream state have attracted a number of photographers. In the 1930s and 1940s Clarence John Laughlin, best known for his eerie evocations of decaying mansions and cemeteries in Louisiana, began to incorporate models and masks and to employ double exposures in order to hint at a coexistence of the actual and the imagined. In the 1960s Ralph Eugene Meatyard, a Kentucky optician and weekend photographer, became widely known for somewhat similar photographs showing children and other figures in grotesque masks in deserted rooms. During the same years Duane Michals, in his well-known photo-sequences, attempted to convey the fractured visual logic of the dream; in addition, his innovative use of photographs within photographs served to throw into utter confusion the images' scale of reference. A much more personal effect was attempted in the work of Edmund Teske, who incorporated pictures of his family and friends into multiple-image photographs that transformed the events of his daily life into mythic terms.

In addition to the glossy, air-brushed productions which adorn the pages of *Playboy, Penthouse,* and similar magazines, photographs involving various degrees of sexual fantasy have occupied many photographers of great originality. In the 1950s, Bill Brandt utilized extremely wide-angle lenses and high-contrast printing to depict unearthly female nudes in empty, cavernous apartments. In his series titled "Plastic Love Dream" (1968), Roger Mertin photographed nude figures wrapped in plastic and other reflective materials in settings both indoors and outdoors. The Japanese photographer Eikoh Hosoe, in his book *Killed by Roses* (1963), staged compositions of startling intensity to suggest the complex emotional and sexual attitudes of the poet Yukio Mishima. And Arthur Tress, in such books as *The Dream Collector* (1972) and *Theater of the Mind* (1976), has gone to extravagant lengths to present visual evocations of the fantasy life of the male homosexual.

An acknowledged master of the outrageous or grotesque photographic fantasy is Les Krims, who has insisted that "it is possible to create any image one thinks of." In his hand-manipulated Polaroid photographs with titles such as "Nude with Vegetables between Her Breasts" and "White Bi-plane Tropical Cityscape Nude," Krims has shown that he will not be deterred by the conventions of art photography or good taste.

In one of his most recent series, "Begging in Buffalo," he photographs his own aging mother, clad in a bikini and wearing dark glasses as if she were blind, at different locations in Buffalo, imploringly begging the viewer for a handout. Another well-known practitioner of the "grotesque" mode of fantasy photography is Paul Diamond, who has staged "self-operation" photographs which seem to show him performing surgery on his own body.

In recent years humor has emerged as a major component of photographic fantasy, as young photographers have realized that certain aspects of life are accessible only through laughter. William Wegman has been responsible for a series of photographs featuring his own dog, a weimaraner he named Man Ray, in a variety of comic roles. Outlandishly disguised as an elephant or a bat, Man Ray casts mournful eyes at the viewer as if to acknowledge the inadequacy of his impersonations. By convincing us that the dog is more intelligent and self-aware than his master, Wegman uses what is essentially a fantasy situation to make a point about social role-playing. Another recent attempt to combine humor and photographic fantasy is that of Sandy Skoglund, who creates elaborate fantasy scenes specifically to be photographed. Her "Radioactive Cats" of 1981 depicts a swarm of artificial green felines glowing in a claustrophobic green interior.

Many photographers who began as adherents of the purist "straight" approach found that viewpoint too confining, and unable to express the complexity of the world of the imagination. By turning to the fantasy mode, they have testified to their belief that the world of the imagination has as much importance in photography as the external world before the lens.

See also: ARTISTS AND PHOTOGRAPHY; EROTIC PHOTOGRAPHY; PAINTING AND PHOTOGRAPHY; SURREALISM IN PHOTOGRAPHY.

Farmer, Ernest Howard

English; 1860–1944

In 1894 E. H. Farmer, a photographic chemist, discovered the interaction of potassium bichromate with gelatin in which an image had been formed by exposure and development of silver bromide. This discovery formed the basis of the ozotype and ozobrome processes (and a subsequent improvement, the carbro process) of Thomas Manly, and the bromoil process of E. J. Wall and C. W. Piper. Farmer is best known for the reducer formula which bears his name and which is composed of potassium ferricyanide and sodium thiosulfate (hypo). Invented in 1884, it is still the most widely used reducer today. He also invented a process of intensification in which the image was bleached in a silver bromide and hypo solution and redeveloped in a physical developer. While highly effective with materials of the 1890s, it now has little use.

See also: BROMOIL PROCESS; CARBRO PROCESS; INTENSIFICATION; OZOBROME PROCESS; OZOTYPE; PHYSICAL DEVELOPMENT; REDUCER/REDUCTION.

Farm Security Administration (FSA)

During the depression of the 1930s, the U.S. Government established many social assistance programs and agencies. In 1935 Rexford Guy Tugwell, who was to become one of Franklin D. Roosevelt's close advisors, set up the Resettlement Administration to extend aid to farmers being wiped out by the accumulated effects of drought and erosion, agricultural mechanization and overproduction, and plunging prices caused by the nationwide economic disaster. In 1937

Farm Security Administration. Theo Jung, "Sunday Dinner. Jackson, Ohio" (1936). Library of Congress.

Farm Security Administration. Russell Lee, "Kitchen of Tenant Purchase Client, Hidalgo, Texas" (1939). Library of Congress.

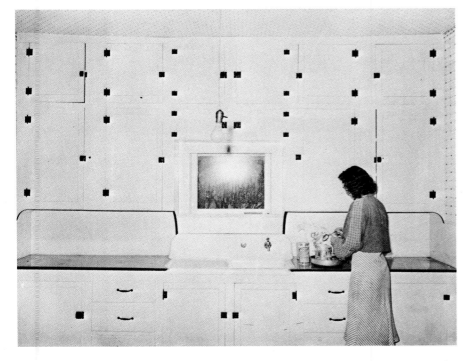

the agency was absorbed by the Department of Agriculture and renamed the Farm Security Administration (FSA).

Tugwell hired Roy Stryker to form the Historical Section, which would record the agency's activities. Although not conceived as a photographic branch, the section's primary activity soon came to be documentary photography. At Columbia University Stryker had used photographs to bring life to his sociological studies. Once at the Resettlement Administration he hired a few young photographers to record America's rural problems and what the agency was doing

about them. His photographers, who were later to become famous, included Dorothea Lange, Ben Shahn, Walker Evans, Carl Mydans, Arthur Rothstein, Russell Lee, and Jack Delano. Later additions included Marion Post Wolcott, John Vachon, John Collier, and Gordon Parks. They moved on and off the very modest FSA payroll according to erratic federal budget allocations.

FSA photography typically was done on individual trips to stricken areas. Before the FSA was formed, Dorothea Lange had begun to photograph migrant workers in California, working with her

sociologist husband, Harold Taylor. This work helped establish the style of FSA photography as a compassionate factual record of people suffering hardship and the conditions they endured. FSA photographers were told to look for the significant detail and to furnish detailed, informative captions.

Stryker's photographers did their homework. Before going to cotton country in the South, they read all they could find about cotton and the South. They carried with them Stryker's detailed, thorough, thoughtful shooting scripts. Whenever anything important turned up, they were encouraged to depart from the script and use their best judgment.

FSA photographers were spread thin and worked hard. There were fewer than a dozen of them to cover a nation. There was consant pressure to keep sending in exposed film for processing at the FSA's lab. The more than 250,000 negatives made in 8 years comprise not only a factual record, but a unique body of works of art. However, art was not the intent of the FSA; it was a by-product of the talents of the photographers and the realities that confronted them. There is nothing precious or self-conscious in most good FSA pictures.

The budget was cut in 1938. Along with others, Walker Evans and Dorothea Lange were let go. Each had taken many of the great FSA pictures for which both they and the project are now remembered. By mid-1942 the FSA had little to do. Wartime demands on agricultural production had quickly reversed rural hardship. People who might have been in migrant labor camps were in the army, in war factories, or back on the farm. There was much pressure on the FSA to now record America's beauty and richness; this became Marion Post Wolcott's specialty. But recording hard times was the FSA photographic project's true work and contribution. The agency expired in 1943, and the photographic activities of the Historical Section were absorbed into the Office of War Information.

See also: Photographers cited; DOCUMENTARY PHOTOGRAPHY.

Fashion Photography

Although closely related to glamour and beauty photography, fashion photography concentrates on illustrating the styles and qualities of clothing and of accessories worn on the person. Glamour photography emphasizes the desirable physical appearance of the subject with only secondary attention paid to what is being worn. In glamour photographs clothing shows off the model; in fashion photographs the model shows off clothing. Beauty photography deals with hair styles, cosmetics, and other direct physical treatments of the body. So-called fashion and beauty magazines use all three kinds of photographs in great number.

Historical development. The first fashion photographs—pictures taken for the purpose of showing costume design, materials, and style—were made in the 1850s and 1860s. In a few instances, albums of actual prints were created for showing to royalty and members of the wealthy classes in France and England. Some fashionable tailors and couturiers who dealt with a less affluent clientele used small carte-de-visite images to show their seasonal offerings; the pictures were distributed at the counter or sent to selected customers. But far more commonly, the photographs were used as source material by the wood engravers and lithographers who illustrated new publications directed at middle-class families: *Godey's Ladies' Book, Harper's Bazaar* (initiated in November, 1867), and many others. A few photographic studios became identified with this kind of work, especially after the mid-1880s, when improvements in the halftone process made good-quality direct-printed reproduction of photographs possible and encouraged the appearance of publications such as *La Mode Pratique, Les Modes, Art et Décoration, Vogue* (first published in 1892), and others devoted to design, decoration, and fashion. Parisian studios led the way in early fashion photography, including the establishments of Mayer and Pierson, Félix, Reutlinger, and Talbot. The pictures showed elegant women posed before painted studio backgrounds or amid standard props and set dressings, but they functioned simply to show the dress or gown with clarity. They are not mood, situation, or romantic-story images; they are essentially straightforward illustrations, however ornate the subject and setting may be.

At about the time of World War I, fashion photographs in the leading magazines began to become elegant illustrations in themselves—pictures with apparent aesthetic pretensions of their own—as well as illustrations of garments. Photographic styles changed in succeeding decades, but this self-conscious striving has remained dominant in much of so-called high fashion illustration, often with the result that the picture idea or treatment becomes more memorable than the fashion being

shown. Picture style first became a noticeable factor in work by Adolph de Meyer for *Vogue* from about 1918, and work by Edward Steichen for *Art et Décoration* from about 1911, and later for *Vanity Fair* and *Vogue*. Both brought the soft-focus, romantic idealization, and other mannerisms of turn-of-the-century Pictorialism to fashion photography. Steichen's work evolved with contemporary changes in taste, first to Art Deco, and then to elegant fantasies of modernism of the sort symbolized in the 1930s by penthouse apartments, satin pajamas, and white telephones. The traditions of lush Pictorialism and aloof elegance were continued in the work of Cecil Beaton in the 1930s and 1940s, and even into the 1950s by John Rawlings, Louise Dahl-Wolfe, and Irving Penn.

Modern painting, most notably Surrealism, stimulated stylistic imitations in fashion photography from the late 1920s. Man Ray and Francis Bruguière were among the first to produce surrealistic fashion illustrations. As the 1930s progressed the style became increasingly commercialized and slick, with a kind of Hollywood superficiality, but some photographers produced memorable pictures in this vein, including Horst P. Horst, George Hoyningen-Huene, Erwin Blumenfeld, and George Platt Lynes.

The most significant development in fashion photography between the two World Wars was an approach that reduced the psychological distance between viewer and model. The freeing of women's lifestyles that began in the 1920s was reflected in pictures of women who were less aloof and elegant, more natural in pose and activity, more attractively "ordinary" in appearance and expression. This was, in fact, a revolution of attitude and technique, one which originated primarily in work done for *Harper's Bazaar* in the 1930s by Martin Munkasci, and carried through the 1940s by Toni Prissell and Herman Landshoff. It was a naturalism perfectly suited to the austerities of design and materials of the World War II era and—after a period of opulent, aloof elegance that reflected the lifting of restrictions and self-control in the immediate post-war years—appeared with fresh life and wit in the work of Richard Avedon in the early 1950s.

The 1960s saw the transition of fashion photography from predominantly black-and-white to at least three-quarters in full color. Major photographers who emerged were Hiro, a master of color and boldly intricate design, and a number of photographers

who brought attitudes not formed by the traditions of the field, including David Bailey, Bert Stern, Art Kane, William Klein, and Jeanloup Sieff. The 1970s and the 1980s have seen the emergence of two additional themes: aggressive sexuality, menace, and implied perversion in the pictures of Helmut Newton, Rebecca Blake, Chris von Wagenheim, Guy Bourdin, and others; and a dreamlike ambiguity of emotion, place, and situation in pictures by Deborah Turbeville, Sarah Moon, and their imitators.

Contemporary characteristics and practice. Fashion photography has evolved from a concern primarily with the tastes and aspirations of the wealthiest readers to an appeal aimed at a young, much more broadly based group. Even though fashion pictures are more egalitarian than before, they still present a romantic ideal. They intend to persuade viewers that they too can become beautiful by adorning themselves with the currently popular style.

Fashion photographs are of two major types: editorial and advertising. Many photographers produce both kinds of pictures. Editorial photographs are used with the articles and other noncommercial informational content of a magazine. They are concerned with showing new styles rather than promoting an individual designer's or manufacturer's product. However, editorial content in fashion magazines is largely determined by what is being offered for sale each season, so a good deal of overlap occurs between the noncommercial and commercial illustration. In general, an editorial fashion photographer has relatively great freedom to experiment and attempt the unusual, whereas the advertising photographer is more closely bound by layout demands and the need to depict the product in a clear, commercially effective way. Editorial photography pays less well than advertising photography, but it offers credit lines and the opportunity to develop an individual style and a professional reputation. These are often the factors that attract advertising assignments which, although the pictures are seldom credited, are financially much more rewarding.

Whichever kind of work a fashion photographer does, the picture idea and layout most often come from an editorial and design group or a supervisor at the magazine or advertising agency. Only the most well-established photographers with top reputations for originality receive carte blanche assignments, the sort that essentially say, "This is the feeling or general idea we want; it's up to you." This is especially true in advertising photography, where the illustration must function not only as part of an individual advertisement, but as an element of a broad or extended campaign that may involve many other ads and illustrations in a number of other media. A key decision in any assignment is which model or models to use. The choice usually belongs to the designer, editor, or client, who may welcome suggestions from the photographer, or who may have definite tastes that must be accommodated. Models are hired from agencies, some of which specialize in glamourous, sophisticated, "high fashion" types, others of which concentrate on providing "ordinary" and unusual-looking people.

A fashion photographer generally has much higher overhead costs than many other kinds of photographers. He or she must maintain a studio equipped with versatile photographic and lighting equipment. A certain degree of style and elegance in location and physical conditions is often considered necessary to attract and suitably impress clients. In addition, the photographer commonly employs a number of specialists on a regular or an assignment-by-assignment basis. A studio/darkroom assistant is often a young photographer trying to break into the business. A receptionist/secretary is essential for scheduling the flow of people in a busy studio. A hair and makeup stylist is usually hired for each assignment. A clothing or accessory stylist may be required (although often supplied by the client). In a successful studio a business support team is also necessary. At a minimum, this includes the photographer's agent—who is responsible for making contacts, showing sample work, and negotiating contracts—and an accountant/tax advisor. A business manager may also be required.

Whether a studio is an extensive business organization or consists only of a photographer and part-time assistants, the key factor is the ability of the fashion photographer. Fashion illustration for mail-order catalogs generally demands "needle-and-thread" pictures that show material, style, pattern or color, and workmanship in a straightforward manner. Editorial or advertising illustration for the most fashionable magazines may require images produced with great imagination and complex technical expertise or with skillful manipulation of the mood and attitude of a model. Few photographers excel in all areas of fashion illustration, although they may be fully competent in many. Those who are most successful have accurately identified the kind of work they do best, have established a recognizable style

or approach, and have repeatedly demonstrated enthusiastic adaptability to the changes of design and style that constitute what fashion magazines and advertisers call fashion.
See also: ADVERTISING PHOTOGRAPHY; GLAMOUR PHOTOGRAPHY; MODELS.
Color photograph: p. C-17.

Feininger, Andreas

American; 1906–
One of the world's most prolific photographers, Andreas Feininger has excelled in several fields, including photography of architecture, sculpture, cityscapes; nature photography; photojournalism; microscopic and telescopic views. In all of his work a concern for precise composition and structural form is evident. Feininger's work has appeared regularly in *Life* magazine and other popular periodicals throughout the world, and he is the author of many influential books on photographic techniques.

Feininger was born in Paris, the son of American artist and composer Lyonel Feininger. He was educated at public schools in Germany. From 1922 to 1925 he studied cabinet-making under Walter Gropius at the Weimar Bauhaus and architecture at the Weimar Bauschule. He did further studies in architecture from 1926 to 1928 and became interested in photography at that time. Feininger first worked as an architect and photojournalist in Dessau and Hamburg, and then in 1932–1933 he was an assistant in the office of Le Corbusier in Paris. He worked as a freelance photographer in Stockholm, specializing in architectural and industrial photography from 1933 to 1939, when he moved to New York.

In 1940–1941 Feininger was employed as a freelance photographer with the Black Star Photo Agency in New York, and it was then that he made the first of his contributions to *Life*. The following year he served as a war correspondent and photographer with the United States Office of War Information.

Feininger became a Staff Photographer with *Life* in 1943. He contributed nearly 350 assignments to its pages during the next 19 years. Since 1962 he has worked as a freelance photographer based in New York and Connecticut.

Feininger has published dozens of books in a dozen languages. He has been the recipient of numerous awards, including a Bronze Medal from the Fotografiska Foreningen, Stockholm (1938 and 1939), a Gold Medal from the Art Directors Club of Metropolitan Washington (1965), and the Robert Leavitt Award of the American Society of Magazine Photographers (1966). His work has been included in group shows

at the Museum of Modern Art in New York City, George Eastman House in Rochester, New York, the Metropolitan Museum of Art in New York City, the San Francisco Museum of Modern Art, and ICP. Solo exhibitions of his work have been held at the Smithsonian Institution in Washington, D.C., the American Museum of Natural History in New York City, and ICP. Feininger's photographic archive will be donated to the Center for Creative Photography in Tucson, Arizona.
See also: BAUHAUS.
Photograph: p. 184.

Fellig, Arthur

See: WEEGEE.

Fenton, Roger

English; 1819–1869
Roger Fenton's reputation as the first war photographer is based on the fact that in 1855 he was the first to achieve extensive coverage related to a prolonged conflict: the Crimean War. In the preceding decade others had photographed battle sites in various places throughout the world, but none had undertaken extended projects.

The son of a wealthy member of Parliament, Fenton earned a Master of Arts degree, studied in the studio of the English painter Charles Lucy, and then in 1841 or 1842 in the atelier of Paul Delaroche in Paris. Three of Fenton's fellow students in France were to emerge as major photographers by the beginning of the 1850s: Gustave Le Gray, Charles Nègre, and Henri Le Secq. Fenton returned to England in 1844 to study law and practice as a solicitor. He continued to paint, submitting works to the Royal Academy, and to pursue his interest in photography. By 1847 he and several other amateur calotype photographers (including Frederick Scott Archer, who later invented the wet collodion process) had formed the Photographic Club, which in 1853 became the Photographic Society, and in which he served as secretary until 1856.

A major figure in promoting the photographic medium, in 1852 Fenton helped organize the first exhibition in Great Britain devoted to photography at the Society of Arts. The exhibition included over 800 pictures representing a variety of processes, but excluded daguerreotypes, which were produced primarily by commercial portraitists. The following year he was active in presenting the first exhibition of the Photographic Society, which featured 1500 images.

Fenton, Roger. "Valley of the Shadow of Death" (1855). Library of Congress.

Fenton was instrumental in having copyright protection extended to include photographs by an Act of Parliament in 1858, and in convincing W. H. F. Talbot to relax his patent restrictions on the calotype—restrictions that had seriously hindered the development of British photography prior to 1852.

Fenton undertook the first of his photographic commissions abroad in 1852, traveling to Russia to document the construction of a suspension bridge over the Dnieper at Kiev and photographing architecture in St. Petersburg and Moscow; he used the waxed paper negative process invented by Le Gray. His Crimean War undertaking was financed by a Manchester publisher, William Agnew, who retained the rights to the photographs. Fenton outfitted a horse-drawn van extensively for wet-plate photography and departed for the Crimea in 1855 in the same month in which the British government resigned

in the face of public outrage over the increasing cost, mismanagement, and loss of life in the war. Fenton's mission received royal patronage as well as the assistance of the Duke of Newcastle, the Secretary of State for War. This official support may have tempered his coverage, for none of the approximately 360 photographs he took before the end of the siege of Sebastopol deal with the devastation, loss of life, hardship, and almost total lack of medical care reported so vividly in newspaper dispatches to England. It is also true that the limitations of the wet plate process and unreliable support from British officials in the Crimea helped force Fenton to concentrate on portraits of officers, groupings of soldiers, general views of the port and fortifications, and scenes of camp life. The photographs that Fenton sent to England were copied as wood engravings and printed in the *Illustrated London News*. After falling ill, Fenton

returned to England shortly before the fall of Sebastopol and the Russian retreat. He was received by the Queen, who bought 20 of his pictures to present to Napoleon III, whose forces had fought along with the British. The Crimean photographs were exhibited and then published by subscription throughout 1855–1856, but the public was bitterly tired of the war, and the project fared far less well than had been hoped.

For the next seven years Fenton occupied himself with a variety of photographic enterprises. Then, in 1862 he abruptly announced his retirement from photography, auctioned off all his equipment, and for the remainder of his life worked as a solicitor, never taking another photograph.

See also: LE GRAY, GUSTAVE; LE SECQ, HENRI; NÈGRE, CHARLES; TALBOT, WILLIAM HENRY FOX.

Ferrez, Marc. "Negro woman from Bahia" (ca. 1880); albumen. Courtesy Marcos Suplicy.

Ferrez, Marc

Brazilian; 1843–1923

The author of some of Brazil's most representative 19th c. photography, Ferrez was the son of the French sculptor and medal-engraver Zepherin Ferrez, who arrived in Brazil in 1816 as part of the French Artistic Mission.

Born in Rio de Janeiro, Ferrez lost both his parents to illness when he was seven. Sent to Paris for schooling, he returned to Brazil in 1859 and took a position with a firm in Rio that dealt in typography, paper sales, bookbinding, imported prints, and related items. In the early 1860s he set up a photography studio directed by the German engineer Franz Keller, from whom he apparently learned photography; the two collaborated in producing views of Rio and landscapes of surrounding areas for sale to foreign tourists.

In 1867 Ferrez went into business for himself, working exclusively with Brazilian themes. He took photos for the Imperial Navy, specializing in panoramic views. When his studio was completely destroyed by a fire in 1873, he went to Paris for new equipment; on his return in 1875 he began documentary work for the Imperial Geographic and Geologic Commission. He took part in an expedition through eastern Brazil headed by the Commission's director, the Canadian scientist Charles Frederick Hartt, photographing various regions as well as the Botocudos Indians of Bahia.

In 1878, Ferrez opened a new studio in Rio from which he continued his documentary activities on various themes: architecture, naval subjects, rail-roads, urban views, monuments, coffee plantation scenes, etc. His anthropological interests are evident in his portraits of blacks, indians, and even the street vendors of Rio. Of special interest among his urban studies is a series (requested by the Rio municipal government) known as the "Central Avenue Album," a turn-of-the-century collection of building fronts on the new major thoroughfare intended to modernize the appearance of the capital city, then overrun with dilapidated houses. This well-planned series is a valuable source for the study of architecture and urbanism in Rio of that period.

Ferrez commercialized his large collection of Brazilian scenes with the sale of postcards, stereographs, and copies of his photographs in various formats and in portfolios and albums. His shop also handled the sale of cameras and other photographic and moving-picture equipment. When movies were introduced to Brazil, Ferrez won distribution rights of Pathé products, and in 1907 opened a Pathé movie theater. He exhibited his panoramic photographs at various international expositions in Philadelphia, Paris, Amsterdam, St. Louis, and elsewhere, often winning prizes and other forms of recognition.

Ferro-cupric, Ferro-gallic Processes

These two iron processes were invented by A. L. Poitevin in 1861 for making prints from very high-contrast negatives or line drawings. In both, sensitized paper was printed-out to a faint image, then developed to produce a strongly colored image; a darkroom was not necessary for processing. In the ferro-cupric process, paper was brushed directly or floated on a slightly acidified solution of copper chloride and iron (ferric) chloride. Development and toning produced a range of colors from red to greenish-black or purple. The ferro-gallic or ferro-tannic process was a substitute for the blueprint process that provided dark-line images. It was more complex to prepare because the paper was coated with a gelatin or gum arabic solution of ferric chloride and ferric sulfate. It could be dusted with gallic acid or tannic acid powder just before exposure and developed in water, or exposed without dusting and developed in a solution of either acid. Gallic acid produced purple-black lines, tannic acid produced brown lines.

See also: BLUEPRINT; IRON PRINTING PROCESSES; POITEVIN, A. L.

Ferrotype

The generic name of the direct positive on metal popularly called the *tintype*, is ferrotype. It was essentially an ambrotype made on a piece of thin sheet iron that had been enameled black or brown-black. The plate was coated with collodion and sensitized just before use, as in the wet plate process. The most common size was about the same as the carte-de-visite, 2¼″ × 3½″, but both larger and smaller ferrotypes were made. The smallest were "Little Gem" tintypes, postage-stamp size, made simultaneously on a single plate in a camera with 12 or 16 lenses, and clipped apart with tin snips to be pasted on the back of small cards with cutouts for the image. The basic process was described by A. A. Martin in France, in 1853; it was patented in 1856 by William Kloen and Daniel Jones in England, and by Hamilton Smith in the U.S. The name *ferrotype* was supplied by the U.S. plate manufacturer; Peter Neff called the process *melaino-type* in commercializing Smith's patent; *tintype* was coined by the public.

Tintype tones are somewhat drab, compared to other processes. The pictures were produced by unskilled operators, many of whom worked on the streets with cameras that had a slotted bottom for dropping the plate into canisters of developer and fixer. The plate was doused in a bucket of water for a quick rinse, and dried by waving in the air, for on-the-spot delivery to the customer. Although it lacked quality, the tintype has social significance because it brought photography within reach of the working class and the poor. A single carte-de-visite size plate or a dozen Little Gems cost twenty-five cents or less. Consequently, the common person began to appear with frequency for the first time in photographs. The low price and immediacy of the tintype made having a photograph taken no longer a special occasion. Spur-of-the-moment pictures became common; many people played, mugged, and generally behaved without restraint or formality in front of the camera. The resulting record is rich in detail and in the revelation of attitudes.

The tintype was immensely popular in the U.S. from about 1860; it was the primary medium by which soldiers and families shared images of one another during the Civil War. In Europe the fad began about a decade later and was never so pervasive as in America. Collodion tintypes gave way to gelatin emulsion dry metal plates in the 1880s. The genre survived with street photographers until almost the mid-20th c. in some parts of the world. It was inevitably replaced by 35mm and instant photography cameras.

The name *ferrotype* had first been used in the mid-1840s by Robert Hunt for a paper negative process in which an iron-compound developer was used. It had no practical or commercial success.
See also: AMBROTYPE; CARTE-DE-VISITE.

Ferrotyping

The procedure for producing a glossy or glazed surface on a photographic print by drying it with the emulsion in contact with a highly polished surface is commonly called ferrotyping. The name reflects the fact that originally plates of enameled sheet iron were used. Today ferrotyping "tins" are chrome-plated metal, stainless steel or, occasionally, scratch-free glass or polished plastic. Only smooth (glossy) emulsion, fiber-base papers can be ferrotyped. Textured emulsions will not take a uniform glaze; the emulsions of resin-coated (RC, waterproof, or water-resistant) papers are likely to adhere to the plate. Successful ferrotyping requires a blemish-free plate surface that has been cleaned of all dust, grease, and other substances that would interfere with uniform contact with every part of the emulsion. The print must be fixed in a fresh hardening fixer, thoroughly washed, and squeegeed face-down onto the plate in a way that prevents air bubbles from being trapped underneath. Best results are obtained with air-drying at a temperature no higher than 75°F (24°C); heated, rotating drum dryers can be used up to 180°F (82°C). Too-rapid drying will cause the print to peel off in stages, producing a ridged surface called "oyster shelling."

Extreme temperatures may also cause uneven shrinkage, producing center bulges or edge fluting.
See also: DRYING FILMS AND PRINTS.

Fiber Optics

The general term *fiber optics* identifies a medium that transmits light by means of strands of optical-quality glass or plastic. Although they are solid, not hollow, the fibers act as "pipes" that guide light along straight, curved, or even spiral paths. Light entering one end of a fiber is reflected back into the fiber each time it encounters the outer wall or border. In traveling 1 inch (2.6cm) of fiber, a light ray may be reflected several hundred times. It is a unique property of refractive materials that within certain limitations on the angle of incidence, almost total internal reflection is achieved. Light loss through the fiber walls is reduced to a negligible amount by "cladding," a coating of low refractive index on the outer surface. (If a non-refractive device such as a metal pipe with the most highly mirrorlike internal wall surface were used, the light would be totally absorbed in the course of only a relatively few reflections.)

Optical fibers are not used individually, but are grouped in bundles or arrays which may be incoherent or coherent. The fibers in an incoherent bundle cross and intertwine so that light is transmitted randomly; such bundles are most useful as sources of illumination. A coherent bundle is arranged so that each fiber's position in relation to all others is maintained from end to end: if a light ray enters a bundle at the lower left, it also exits at the lower left. Because this preserves the pattern of light intensities, coherent bundles are capable of transmitting images.

The limit of the resolving power of a bundle is determined by the diameter of each fiber. Widths may be as little as about ten times the wavelength of the light being transmitted. In practice, this translates to diameters of only a few ten-thousandths of an inch. More elaborate internal fiber structures are being developed that allow fiber-optic bundles to transmit images of photographic quality. One system employing fiber optics produces an instant picture directly from a conventional 35mm camera.

Other applications of fiber optics are in various forms of endoscopes, cathode-ray tube traces, image dissectors and intensifiers, and telephone transmission.
See also: ENDOSCOPE; IMAGE DISSECTION; INCIDENCE, ANGLE OF.

Field Camera

A field camera is a kind of view camera designed to accept sheet film, and portable and sturdy enough to be used on location. The term is primarily British, the American equivalent being simply *view camera*. A field camera generally is of flat-bed rather than monorail design. That is, a solid baseboard rather than a tube or rail carries the tracks along which the lens/bellows support standard moves. The construction is often of wood, with the back forming a kind of shallow box into which the bellows and lens board retract. The baseboard folds upward to close the box for packing and travel. The camera movements, especially of the back, generally are more limited than those of a monorail studio or technical view camera, but sturdiness and portability are more important, and extreme movements are seldom required in its most common applications: architectural, landscape, and some kinds of industrial photography.
See also: CAMERA; CAMERA MOVEMENTS; VIEW CAMERA.

Field Curvature

See: ABERRATIONS OF LENSES.

Field Lens

A field lens is an element added to an optical system to aid in viewing the image by providing wider viewing coverage, more even illumination, or a brighter image in the eyepiece; it does not play a part in primary image formation. The most common field lens is the fresnel lens placed against the ground-glass or matte-surface screen of a view camera or reflex camera. The field lens redirects diverging light rays at the edges and corners of the screen toward the viewing position so that the image appears uniformly bright, without a "hot spot" on the viewing axis and rapid falloff in brightness to the peripheral areas. A similar arrangement provides uniform brightness in slide and transparency viewers that project the image onto the rear of a built-in screen. The condenser lenses of some enlargers function as field lenses to provide even illumination of the image to be projected onto the easel. Field lenses are also essential for full-image viewing in microscopes and refracting telescopes. In the compound eyepieces of such instruments, the field lens is the element farthest from the eye; the other element is the *eye lens*.
See also: FRESNEL LENS.

Filing and Storing Photographs

The filing and storage of photographs impose different but complementary requirements. Filing needs will vary with the person or institution and with the photographs that are to be put in order. Maximum quality storage conditions for conventional black-and-white and color photographs on modern films and papers are required only for archives, museum holdings, and other collections of considerable value. Reasonable storage conditions and practices—avoiding destructive storage materials and excessive heat, humidity, and dirt—generally will go a long way toward keeping photographs safe if they are well processed and on stable films or papers.

Filing. Filing is the system that identifies the photographs and places them in order in the storage space so any negative, slide, or print can be found and brought out easily and quickly. An important part of a file is a catalog that records everything in the collection and shows where to find it. The catalog may be a notebook, a set of index cards, or a computer data file. It must permit easy addition of new listings at all points and must provide easy use. It is organized according to some regular system of picture classification and identification.

For pictures that generally fit well-defined and separate subject categories, a library classification system such as the Dewey Decimal System or the Universal Decimal System offers a simple and flexible way to organize images of most imaginable subjects in a definite and logical order. For large collections such number-keyed systems are necessary to take advantage of the speed and complex cross-referencing that computer filing offers.

Photographers who work in terms of projects or for a number of clients commonly use job or project numbers or the clients' names as the main filing classifiers. For photographers who work in unstructured, random ways, the most useful filing may be by chronology (when the pictures were taken), by place (where they were taken), or by subject (what or whom the pictures show). It is often most efficient to use different criteria for distinct parts of the collection—for example, negatives filed by chronology (using identifying numbers that combine year, month, and day or roll number), and prints by place and subject, with chronology secondary.

Whatever system is adopted, it will be useful only if every item is marked with an identifier and if the catalog is kept up to date. A print generally requires two identifiers: one showing its own file location so it can be refiled accurately, and the other identifying the negative from which it was made.

Storage. Storage involves providing the place and conditions that can best keep the photographs safe. It imposes some additional categories. The size and nature of each item must be considered and provided for. In a collection that includes black-and-white negatives and prints, color negatives, slides and prints, and motion-picture footage in black-and-white and color, it is best to store each kind of item separately in the most suitable conditions and containers. Storage should leave ample room for additions; this calls for good guesswork and flexibility.

Safe storage calls for a clean, well-ventilated space that does not change much in temperature or humidity, and that is free from airborne grit and harmful gases, excessive heat, light and ultraviolet radiation, mold spores, insects, mice, and vandals. Metal shelves and cabinets are recommended.

The list of materials to avoid is long. It has been found that fresh latex paint—dry one or two weeks—does no apparent harm to nearby photographs, while alkyd oil-base points consistently caused stains in prints exposed to their fumes. Detailed recommendations for storage materials and conditions can be found in Kodak Publication No. F-30, *Preservation of Photographs*, and in a number of ANSI photographic (PH1-series) standards published by the American National Standards Institute, 1430 Broadway, New York, N.Y. 10018.

Three factors are of special importance in storing photographs: the acidity or alkalinity of materials in contact with the images, and the humidity and temperature of the storage location. Black-and-white prints generally are best kept in acid-free containers of inert, neutral, pH 7 materials (metal, plastic, and paper), and in some cases, in alkaline-buffered paper or fiberboard with an initial pH of 8 or higher, which becomes lower with age. Albumen prints and modern color prints should not be mounted on or stored in alkaline-buffered papers (although these are considered much less harmful than acid papers, such as most ordinary envelopes, mounting boards, and cardboard boxes). For these media neutral-pH mounting boards and containers are preferred.

In general, uncoated cellulose acetate and polyester, preferably with a smooth matte finish, are good materials for envelopes and interleaving sheets, as are acid-free high-alpha-cellulose papers. Polypropylene storage sheets for color slides are preferred over polyvinyl-chloride (PVC) ones, which can give off harmful gases.

Humidity is very important. Relative humidity (RH) above 60 percent favors fungus growth and can cause gelatin to become sticky. Humidity below 30 percent RH can make prints brittle and tends to curl them. Repeated large changes in humidity can crack emulsions and make them flake or peel, especially at the edges. The consensus of all recommendations points to 30 percent RH as the most suitable condition. However, humidity is a highly variable factor: it changes drastically with temperature. For black-and-white film a steady temperature of 70°F (21°C) or lower is recommended and for color film 35°F (2°C) or lower is suggested. A number of institutions have cold storage rooms for color photographs; these typically maintain a steady temperature of 0°F (−18°C) at relative humidities of 25 to 30 percent. It is believed that color transparencies so kept should long outlast black-and-white photographs kept at normal room temperatures.

Air purity is also an important factor. If possible, photographs should not be stored in areas with high air pollution, and the air should be filtered and treated to remove any harmful gases.

See also: ARCHIVAL PROCESSING; CONSERVATION OF PHOTOGRAPHS; WRITING ON FILMS AND PRINTS.

Fill Light

Fill light is illumination from a second source used to supplement the illumination from the main or key light source. Its purpose is to lower the lighting (contrast) ratio by increasing the relative brightness of the shadow areas of a subject. Fill light is usually diffused light of lower intensity than the key light. If it were of the same intensity, modeling and a sense of three-dimensional form would be lost, and symmetrical-pair "butterfly" shadows might be created. The fill light source is directed at the subject from a 45- to about 170-degree angle away from the key light-to-subject axis. Often fill light is provided by a reflector placed to pick up spill light from the key source. When the main light is direct sun, an electronic flash unit can be used as a fill light source.

See also: BRIGHTNESS RANGE; FLASH FILL.

Film and Photo League

When the Photo League was established at the beginning of the Depression, it was a political organization that thought of photography as a tool for class struggle. At its end in 1951 it was an organization committed to photography, although still with social-activist overtones.

In 1930 the Workers' International Relief, a strikers' aid group in Berlin, started and funded Workers' Camera Leagues in several European and American cities. They were to help publicize the W.I.R. by supplying photographs to the left-wing press—in New York, for instance, to the *Daily Worker* and *New Masses*. In the United States the New York League was the principal branch. It became the Workers' Film and Photo League very soon, shifting its emphasis to propaganda movies. Its members made silent newsreels on social-injustice themes such as hunger and unemployment and showed them to whoever would look, largely in union halls. There was no commercial outlet for such films.

By 1934 the New York Film and Photo League had begun to teach documentary filmmaking, and disagreements about film and its uses surfaced. Most members wanted to go on shooting and showing rough "daily-struggle" footage as fast as possible; a small group calling itself Nykino (for New York cinema) wanted to slow down and learn to use film effectively. Nykino called for a serious study of the medium as well as the message; this was considered bourgeois elitism by the others.

In 1936 the organization split up. The daily-struggle majority moved to new quarters as the New York Film and Photo League; their last film appeared in 1937. The Nykino group left to form their own company, Frontier Films. The still photographers, almost overlooked before, inherited the old quarters and became the Photo League—part photo club, part gallery, part school, and self-supporting. Sid Grossman and Sol Libsohn are credited with bringing the Photo League back to life. They were talented, dedicated photographers who worked hard to help others. Those active in the Photo League also included Eliot Elisofon, Aaron Siskind, Lou Stoumen, Jack Manning, Max Yavno, Dan Weiner, Walter Rosenblum, Morris Engel, Bernard Cole, Rosalie Gwathmey, Paul Strand, and W. Eugene Smith, among many others. Lewis Hine joined in 1940, and after his death Grossman and Libsohn were among the League members who rescued his negatives and prints from the basement of his house. The Photo League cared for Hine's work, issuing two portfolios of well-made prints, exhibiting his photographs, and making them available for publication. When the League folded, Walter Rosenblum rescued the Hine Collection

again and found a new home for it at the George Eastman House in Rochester, New York.

The Photo League held important exhibitions long before most art museums would show photographs. Among these were first one-man shows for Weegee and Lisette Model; others shown include Cartier-Bresson, Alvarez-Bravo, Moholy-Nagy, John Heartfield, Berenice Abbott, Eugene Atget, and the FSA photographers. By the late 1940s the Photo League was attracting distinguished photographers who had no interest in its politics. Ansel Adams, Edward Weston, Barbara Morgan, Helen Levitt, Consuelo Kanaga, and Lisette Model were members, as were Beaumont and Nancy Newhall. Richard Avedon joined in time to exhibit with 95 others in a 1948 show *This is the Photo League*.

In December 1947 the U.S. Attorney General included the Photo League in a list of "Totalitarian, Fascist, Communist and Subversive Organizations." Many years earlier when the Film and Photo League was serious about Marxism this might have had some basis, although probably not in law. In 1947 it had no foundation in the League's activities. Blacklisting had the short-term effect of stimulating people to join and support the Photo League, and the long-term effect, as the threat to people's jobs became clear, of pointlessly killing a useful organization. It disbanded in 1951.

See also: DOCUMENTARY PHOTOGRAPHY; FARM SECURITY ADMINISTRATION.

Films

Photographic films consist of a flexible transparent base material coated with one or more layers of radiation-sensitive emulsion. Photographic plates are similarly coated inflexible materials, usually glass, rigid plastic, or metal. Self-processing "films" for instant photography are of two types. Peel-apart materials consist of a base sheet (usually paper) coated with a filmlike emulsion and a separate receiving or print sheet. Self-contained, one-piece instance "print films" consist of an opaque plastic base coated with both film (negative) and print (positive) emulsions.

Conventional (i.e., non-self-processing) film bases are either a form of cellulose triacetate ("safety base") or polyester plastic. The base material may be dyed or be coated on the back with a light-absorbing substance to prevent halation. The back coating on roll films also serves to resist curling. The face of the base material has a very thin clear gelatin coating called a sub- or subbing

layer, that serves as an adhesive for the emulsion. The emulsion consists of silver halide crystals suspended in gelatin. A black-and-white film may have a single emulsion layer, or two layers of different speed (light sensitivity) to increase its useful exposure range. A color film has at least three silver halide layers, each effectively sensitive to one primary color of light. Some color films have two layers sensitive to one or more of the colors to extend their exposure response. Most color films also have a temporary yellow filter layer between the top and middle emulsion layers to prevent blue-exposure in the green- and red-sensitive emulsions; the yellow color is removed during processing. The top emulsion layer of most films is coated with a colorless supercoating that protects against abrasion. The supercoating and the back of films especially intended for portraiture or some kinds of illustrative photography may have a slight texture or "tooth" to more readily accept retouching.

Films are supplied as narrow, continuous strips in spools, cassettes, or cartridges (35mm and roll films); as individual sheets; or as chips mounted on special supports (e.g., disk films). They are variously classified according to: spectral sensitivity (blue-sensitive, orthochromatic, panchromatic, infrared, daylight or tungsten color, etc.); light sensitivity or speed; relative contrast; and major functional application (portrait, aerial, x-ray, graphic arts, etc.). Most films are intended for used in a camera, for direct exposure to the subject. However, some films (e.g., duplicating, internegative, motion picture print) are intended for exposure to another film image in special copying or printing equipment. Exposure causes a film emulsion to record an invisible latent image; the image is subsequently made visible by the chemical process called development. Negative films produce images in which the tones/brightnesses/colors are the opposite of those to which they were exposed. Direct positive and reversal films produce images that correspond directly to these aspects of the subject. The following entries contain additional information about film characteristics and specialized kinds of films.

See also: ANTI-HALATION LAYER; BLACK-AND-WHITE MATERIALS; CELLULOID; COLOR MATERIALS; DIFFUSION TRANSFER PROCESS; DIRECT POSITIVE; DRY PLATES; EMULSION; FALSE-COLOR FILM; FINEGRAIN FILMS AND PROCESSING; FORMAT; HIGH CONTRAST MATERIALS; INFRARED PHOTOGRAPHY; INTERNEGATIVE; LITH FILMS; NEGATIVE

MATERIALS; NOTCH CODE; PERFORA-
TIONS; REVERSAL MATERIALS AND
PROCESSING; ROLL FILM; SAFETY FILM;
SIZES OF MATERIALS; SPECTRAL SENSITIV-
ITY; SPEED OF MATERIALS; STRIPPING
FILM; TRANSPARENCY MATERIALS;
VESICULAR IMAGES AND EMULSIONS;
X-RAY FILMS, PLATES.

Filmstrips

A filmstrip or slide-film consists of a
sequence of positive still images on a
continuous strip of 35mm film that are
projected one frame at a time. A
filmstrip provides the same kind of presentation as a series of slides but has the
advantage of fixed order and orientation.
There is no chance for individual images
to be turned upside down, placed out of
sequence, or lost. This error-free quality
makes filmstrips popular for business and
educational audio-visual presentations.
From a production standpoint, it is
easier to produce large numbers of
duplicate presentations from a single
master-strip negative than from a collection of individual slides. Most filmstrips
use a 35mm half-frame format (18
× 24mm) with the long dimension as the
width of the picture area. This permits
the film to travel vertically through the
projector. In some strips a double (standard 35mm still) frame size is used with
horizontal film feed, and in either format
the projector gate may need to be rotated
between vertical and horizontal positions.

The primary concerns in preparing a
master-strip negative are to prepare
artwork to a uniform scale so that there
are no major changes in image size from
frame to frame; to center and orient all
material in the same way so that no images are on their sides or upside-down;
and to balance exposure so that image
brightness on the screen is relatively
constant. There are special filmstrip projectors, and some slide projectors accept
adapter gates and lenses. As with slide-
sound presentations, a filmstrip can be
synchronized with a prerecorded tape,
and frame advance can be triggered automatically by audible or inaudible cues.
See also: AUDIOVISUAL.

Filters

A photographic filter is a transparent,
light-altering device used in front of a
camera or enlarger lens or in the path of
light falling on the subject. Filters used
in front of a lens must be of optical
quality so as not to degrade the image;
they are made of glass, plastic, or sheet
gelatin. Filters used in front of a light
source or in the light head of an enlarger
need not be of optical quality, but must
withstand high heat without becoming
distorted or faded; they are made of
heat-resistant glass or cellulose acetate.

Most filters are colored and act subtractively; that is, they absorb from light
wavelengths of the opposite (complementary) color and transmit
wavelengths of their own color. They
differ in color strength (density), but
each filter is uniformly colored throughout. A special class of filters, dichroic
filters, act by interference: thin-layer
coatings on the filter surface cause
selected wavelengths to be reflected and
cancelled, while all others are transmitted. Special-effect filters variously use
unusual or variegated colors, nonuni-
form coloring, and construction or surfaces that create diffraction, refraction,
and other phenomena that alter image-
forming light in visually interesting
ways.

While most filters are used to change
the color balance (wavelength proportions) of the transmitted light, two kinds
act on all wavelengths of light. *Neutral
density* filters are used to reduce the intensity of light by absorbing the same
amount of all colors; they have a gray
appearance and are supplied in several
strengths. *Polarizing* filters act on all
wavelengths vibrating in a particular
plane; they are used to control reflections from non-metallic surfaces and to
improve color saturation by screening
out the polarized component of glare
light.

Filters are identified and described in
various ways. The Kodak Wratten number system is the most widely used
means of identification. When a filter is
designated simply as a No. 8, No. 25,
etc., it can be assumed that this system is
being used. A few manufacturers use
other numbering systems, most of which
include letters (e.g., 15G). Special identification is used with neutral density
filters to indicate strength (e.g., 0.5ND),
with color compensating (CC) filters to
indicate strength and color (e.g.,
CC25Y), and with decamired filters to
indicate the relative degree or color of
the change produced (e.g., −15DM or
B15DM).

In black-and-white photography
filters are used to control contrast by
increasing or decreasing the gray tone
differences between various colors. This
occurs because a filter absorbs its opposite color, so those subject areas expose
the negative less and consequently
appear darker in the print. The degree of
change depends on the filter strength and
its color. A secondary color filter (cyan,
magenta, yellow) has less effect than a
primary color filter (red, green, blue) because the latter transmits only one color
of light.

The relative effects of filter
transmission/absoption can be visualized by considering a scene composed of
a red barn, green grass and foliage, and a
blue sky with white clouds. A yellow
filter transmits red and green, but
absorbs blue. Thus, in a print the sky
will be darker (the degree of change will
depend on the filter strength) and the
white clouds more clearly defined, but
the grass, foliage, and barn will be unchanged in comparison to a print from
an unfiltered negative. A red filter
absorbs blue and green. It will render the
sky darker than in the yellow-filter version (because there are green as well as
blue wavelengths in sky light), so the
clouds will be even more distinct. The
grass will also be darker, but the barn
will be unchanged. A green filter absorbs
blue and red. It will have an effect
on the sky similar to that of the red
filter and will darken the barn, but it
will leave the grass and foliage unchanged.

In color photography filters are used
to adjust the color balance of the image-
forming light. The filters are much less
strongly colored than those used with
black-and-white films. There are three
general kinds. *Conversion* filters make a
gross change in color balance so as to
correct a mismatch of film type and illumination. A filter in the No. 80 series is
used to convert tungsten light with a
color temperature in a range of 3200K to
4200K for use with a daylight-type color
film. A filter in the No. 85 series is used
to convert 5500K daylight or electronic
flash illumination for use with a
tungsten-type film emulsion.

Light balancing filters make smaller
overall changes in color balance. They
are used to match artificial light with a
tungsten-type film. Filters in the No. 82
series have a bluish color and raise the
color temperature of the light; those in
the No. 81 series have a yellowish or
amber color and lower the color temperature. Such filters may also be identified
by mired or decamired (DM) + and −
shift values, as referred to earlier. A few
unnumbered filters are available to make
a general adjustment of light from
fluorescent tubes.

Color compensating filters make quite
small adjustments in just one or two colors of light. They are used to counteract
slight color tinges and to correct minor
color shifts. They are also used to
achieve proper balance in color printing.

There are many special-purpose
filters; the following are some of the major types. *Ultraviolet* filters are of two

types: those which absorb ultraviolet to reduce unwanted exposure in natural light (haze and skylight filters), and those which transmit ultraviolet while absorbing visible wavelengths. *Infrared* filters transmit infrared wavelengths. Those which also transmit some visible wavelengths have a dark red color; those which are totally absorptive in the visible range look black. A *viewing* or preview filter is used to show approximately what a color subject will look like when photographed on panchromatic film. It is dark brown-amber and absorbs enough across the spectrum to eliminate color and show relative brightnesses. It is used in front of the photographer's eye, not in front of the camera lens. *Variable-contrast* filters are used in the darkroom in conjunction with variable-contrast paper; by coloring the exposing light, they vary the contrast response of the paper emulsion.

Physical filters are also used in the darkroom to strain out particles and other impurities in the water supply and in chemical solutions.

See also: CC FILTERS; COLOR BALANCE; COLOR TEMPERATURE; DECAMIRED; DICHROIC FILTER; FLUORESCENT-LIGHT PHOTOGRAPHY; INFRARED PHOTOGRAPHY; NEUTRAL DENSITY; POLARIZER; SUBTRACTIVE COLOR SYNTHESIS; ULTRAVIOLET AND FLUORESCENCE PHOTOGRAPHY; VARIABLE-CONTRAST MATERIALS.

Fine-Grain Films and Processing

By far the great majority of photographs are made by enlarging images recorded on small-format films. Enlargement not only makes the image bigger and thus more visible, but it does the same for the structural characteristic called grain or graininess. Although the greatest degree of enlargement is commonly that of a slide projected on a screen, graininess is often a barely noticeable factor because the viewing distance is relatively great. Graininess is potentially far more noticeable in prints, largely as a consequence of the much closer viewing distance. Photographers who want maximum image quality and resolving power are concerned with keeping grain to a minimum in the negative so that it will have the least possible visibility in a print.

Graininess in a film image is a product of emulsion structure and processing. The processing of color films is essentially invariable, so achieving minimum graininess is almost entirely a matter of selecting a film with a desired characteristic and giving it optimum exposure. Black-and-white processing is quite variable. All general-purpose films can pro-

duce good results when used with any of a great number of developers. Thus, it is possible to select a film for its grain characteristics and then choose a developer that will take maximum advantage of those characteristics.

As explained in the entry on grain/graininess/granularity, the visible "grains" in an image are really clumps of microscopic bits of silver. However, the apparent size of these grains is directly related to the original size of the silver halide crystals in the emulsion before exposure and processing. Films with the smallest halide crystals are slow, thin-emulsion films. Major advances in emulsion design, announced in 1982 and 1983, have reduced the halide crystal size in medium- and high-speed films, so the images they produce have significantly reduced graininess. Nevertheless, the finest grain is produced by slow films, and especially those with a speed of ISO 32/16° or less.

With many subjects normal processing of a slow-speed film will not result in visible graininess in enlargements up to about 8× or 10× (e.g., an 11″ × 14″ print from a full 35mm negative). However, there are three kinds of alternate processing that can reduce the normal grain characteristics of medium- and slow-speed films. All require that the film receive additional exposure (i.e., be rated at a slower speed), so there is no point in using them with high-speed films and losing the primary advantage of such films. Fast films with newly improved emulsions produce their best images with the minimum necessary exposure and normal processing.

Physical development, described in a separate entry, is not feasible with conventional films because it is extremely slow and requires an exposure increase of six times normal or greater. Self-processing instant films utilize physical development in their diffusion transfer processing without loss of speed. Some films produce a usable negative, as well as a print, with an essentially grainless image, but they are not available in small formats.

Low-activity development is the method of most so-called fine-grain developers. Energetic (high-activity) development promotes the particle clumping that is visible as graininess; slow development avoids this problem, and produces no fog, which, like excess density from any cause, would contribute to graininess. Low activity is most effectively achieved by reducing the amount of activator (or using a milder activator) in the developer formula, not simply by diluting the normal formula. The classic developer of this sort is the Kodak D-23 formula,

which contains only a developing agent and a preservative. A low-activity developer produces less contrast in a given period of time than a normal developer; this is seldom a problem, because slow-speed films have inherently higher contrast than faster films.

Solvent development involves a developer ingredient that dissolves some of the developed silver during the course of processing. This proceeds at a slower rate than the development of the image. Its effect is to limit the size of the grain clumps and to erase all traces of fog in slow films. When the Kodak D-23 formula is converted to the D-25 formula by the addition of sodium bisulfite, it becomes a solvent fine-grain developer. Many solvent developers include potassium or sodium thiocyanate, which has a strong solvent action on silver. The standard medium-grain developer known as Kodak D-76 or Ilford ID-11 can be converted to a very fine-grain solvent developer by the addition of ammonium chloride. Solvent developers require from two-thirds to two stops extra exposure of the film, depending on the emulsion and the developer formula. They are not suitable for use with fast films because the relatively great amount of silver in such emulsions increases the production of image fog and the likelihood of dichroic fog.

See also: DEVELOPMENT; FOG/FOGGING; GRAIN/GRAININESS/GRANULARITY; PHYSICAL DEVELOPMENT.

Fingerprint Photography

Police and investigatory agencies use photographs of fingerprints to establish the presence of an individual at a particular place. Since each person's fingerprints are unique, courts readily accept such photographs as evidence. Fingerprints, however, are easily destroyed and investigators carefully and promptly photograph them. As with other types of crime photography, rigid standards of objective technique and presentation must be followed to ensure that the pictures are legally acceptable.

Four types of impressions are encountered. Fingerprints produced by ink on record or identification cards are the simplest to photocopy using high-contrast film. Impressions left by substances on the fingertips, molded impressions imbedded in a soft or liquid substance, or latent fingerprints are more difficult. Often these impressions must be prepared before being photographed, usually by dusting. Knowing the best choice of powder or spraying technique in a particular situation is the result of professional training and experience.

If possible, the fingerprint should be photographed life-size on the negative. Otherwise, a ruler or other scale reference must be included in the picture to indicate the actual size of the fingerprint. A small-enough aperture should be used to assure that all relevant detail is as sharp as possible, particularly on curved surfaces. Care must be taken and, when appropriate, filters used to be certain that the fingerprint shows in sufficient contrast from the supporting material. The final photographic print should show the ridges as a dark pattern against a white background for easy comparison. It may be necessary to make an intermediate film positive in order to make a "negative" print with this tonal relationship.

Any medium- or high-speed panchromatic black-and white film is suitable for clear fingerprints. Weak prints may require a lith film or other very-high-contrast emulsion. For pictures taken in the field, a 35mm single-lens reflex camera fitted with a macro-focusing lens or other close-up capability is a common choice. The light sources which provide the most repeatable results without damage to the evidence are electronic flash and portable ultraviolet units, commonly referred to as black lights. For most fingerprints the light sources are positioned at an oblique angle to reduce glare and accentuate three-dimensional relief.

See also: CRIME PHOTOGRAPHY; FORENSIC PHOTOGRAPHY.

Finlaycolor Process

Finlaycolor was a screen process for the production of full-color images by the additive synthesis of color. The basic idea was patented in England in 1906 by Clare L. Finlay who had perfected a method of producing a color screen of precisely spaced elements, rather than the random mosaic used in the Lumiere autochrome and similar processes. In 1908 it was introduced as the Thames Colour Screen—a separate screen that could be used with any panchromatic film or plate—and a year later as the Thames Colour Plate in which the screen and emulsion were integral in each plate. Both processes languished and essentially died after World War I, but were reintroduced in 1929 and 1931, respectively, in much improved form. The Finlaycolor separate screen process of 1929 was quite successful and rivaled Dufaycolor until the introduction of subtractive color materials in the mid-1930s.

The advantage of a separate screen was that it could be used with any pan-chromatic film—giving the photographer a choice of speed and contrast characteristics—and that duplicates could be made by contact printing on any black-and-white film. Integral screen processes were limited to the emulsion applied in manufacture and were extremely difficult to duplicate without loss of detail and color quality. The Finlaycolor process used a glass screen in the camera composed of a checkerboard arrangement of red, green, and blue filter elements numbering 30,625 per square inch. The film emulsion was pressed in contact with the colored side of the plate for exposure; registration marks on the plate were exposed onto the film outside the image area. Although the film could be reversal processed to produce a positive image, most often it was developed as a negative and then contact printed on another piece of film to obtain a positive transparency in which the densities represented the primary-color analysis of the subject made by the camera screen. For viewing, the positive was bound in contact with an exactly matching color screen on celluloid; registration marks on this screen corresponded to those recorded from the camera plate. When viewed by transmitted light, or projected, the result was a full-color image.

The process was successful because it maintained superior color saturation, and because extreme care in manufacture insured an exact match between camera and viewing screens; the slightest irregularities would have caused color fringing. The major limitation of the process was that duplicates could not be enlarged because that would enlarge the size of the color-analysis elements and they would no longer match the viewing screen. Also—as with all screen color processes—enlargement made the screen pattern obtrusively evident.

See also: ADDITIVE COLOR SYNTHESIS; AUTOCHROME PROCESS; COLOR PHOTOGRAPHY—HISTORY; DUFAYCOLOR; PANCHROMATIC; SCREEN PROCESSES; SUBTRACTIVE COLOR SYNTHESIS.

Finsler, Hans

Swiss; 1891–1972
Hans Finsler was an exceptionally gifted teacher, and notable also as one of the avant-garde photographers who came to prominence in Germany during the late 1920s and early 1930s.

Born in Zurich in 1891, Finsler studied architecture in Munich and there became acquainted with modern art. Although most of the photographers of the period enlisted or were drafted into service during World War I, Finsler was from a neutral country and so was able to spend the war years studying art history with the great scholar Heinrich Wölfflin. He later claimed that Wölfflin's analytical methods and the discipline that had been demanded of him as an architecture student served him well as he taught himself photography.

In 1922 Finsler became an art history teacher and librarian at the Werkstätten Burg Giebichenstein Kunstgewerbeschule (School of Arts and Crafts) near Halle, Germany. From the outset his classes were considered innovative. Indeed, Finsler's course and Max Burchartz's Folkwang classes in Essen offered serious competition to the famous classes of Hans Peterhans at the Bauhaus.

Finsler taught basic photography with full knowledge of the aesthetic approach that came to be called "the new vision," an approach characterized by sharp details, pronounced patterns, closeups of natural and, especially, man-made objects, and arrangements emphasizing geometric and, often, repeating forms. He soon drew the attention of advertising agencies serving imaginative companies who wished to market their merchandise through strikingly illustrated catalogs. Because comparatively few photographers of the 1920s and early 1930s were capable of producing pictures with this bold new look, Finsler was overbooked with commercial assignments and teaching.

In 1932, he returned to Zurich and became head of the photography department at the Kunstgewerbeschule, a position he held until 1958. There he either taught or had some connection with the development of some of the best known post-World War II Swiss photographers, including Werner Bischof, René Burri, Robert Frank, and Emil Schulthess. Fondly remembered by his students, he is said to have been reserved by nature and immune to market or fashion trends. He quietly encouraged each student's self-discovery, prodded each to develop confidence to grow and change. Finsler's own work remained largely unseen for some time after his retirement; when it was seen, the full measure of his artistic achievement as a photographer became known. His book *My Way to Photography* was published in 1972.
Photograph: p. 200.

Fire and Arson Photography

Press photographers photograph fires and their aftermaths as news events. Insurance and arson investigators photograph the same things in an effort to determine the cause of the fire and to

Finsler, Hans. "Light bulb" (1927). Courtesy Stiftung für die Photographie, Kunsthaus, Zurich.

evaluate the damage. Journalistic and legal standards demand straightforward, accurate pictures in these cases. Those photographing fires for nonprofessional reasons are free to interpret the event and to look for striking, dramatic images. But fire is a disaster; there are property and lives—including the photographer's—in danger. Taking trivial pictures in such a situation is indefensible; activities that interfere with fire-fighting efforts are criminal.

Fire photographs are similar to other types of crime photographs. Pictures should be made showing the entire site, particularly in relationship to nearby structures. They should be made from a number of angles to overcome the effects of partially obscured views and deceiving perspective that are inevitable from some locations. While the fire is active, pictures should be made specifically of its most intensive activity. This may help determine areas where accelerants were used. Pictures also should be made of the positioning of the apparatus, of the fire-fighters' activity, and even of curious bystanders who might be arson suspects.

Possibly only war photographers work under conditions as poor as those of the fire photographer. In all circumstances he or she should be concerned first for personal safety; no picture is worth a life. Where conditions warrant, he or she should don gear similar to that of the firefighters themselves. The arson photographer will be expected to accompany the post mortem team as it sifts the ashes inside the building's remains. That, too, can be extremely dangerous.

Fire photography differs somewhat from other branches of crime photography in that it virtually exclusively utilizes daylight-type color film. The color of the flames during the active phase and even that of the ashes may help pinpoint a fire's cause. Due to the harsh circumstances, the basic equipment list must include the sturdiest cameras and accessories. Often cameras designed principally for underwater use are appropriate. The controls are large and easy to manipulate, and the instrument is not liable to damage from the water used to fight the fire. Some form of artificial light is commonly carried—usually one or more electronic flash units—to illuminate shadowed and smoke-filled areas. It should be noted that flash units generate a small spark which could be disastrous in an explosive atmosphere.

See also: CRIME PHOTOGRAPHY; FORENSIC PHOTOGRAPHY.

Fireworks

Firework displays can be photographed in either color or black-and-white; color is more effective because of the brilliant colors produced by the bursts. Since firework displays take place at night, when they are most visible, a tripod is usually helpful. The camera is aimed toward the general area of the display, and the lens is focused at infinity. The shutter is held open with a cable release, using either the "B" or "T" speed setting. It is possible to photograph one display or many on the same frame, depending on the number of bursts during the exposure and the desired effect. If the lens is left open between bursts, it must be covered to prevent stray light from entering the camera and fogging the film.

There is no correct aperture setting, but large lens openings will produce bright, thick light traces with reduced color saturation. Smaller apertures will produce darker, thinner, more colorful lines. If no tripod is available, it is possible to photograph fireworks displays with a hand-held camera at a shutter speed of 1/30 sec. The lens should be at its widest aperture, and the shutter should be tripped when the display is at its most brilliant point.

Fischer, Rudolf
German; 1881–1957
German chemist Rudolf Fischer investi-

gated the properties of chromogenic developers in the early years of this century. Working closely with H. Siegrist, between 1911 and 1914, he made experiments with color dye-coupler plates and three-color films which laid the groundwork for many of today's color technical processes.

Fischer attended the Steglitz Gymnasium, Berlin, and studied chemistry at Strasbourg and the University of Berlin. He was employed as a chemist by several firms including the Chemical Institute, the Pharmaceutical Institute of Berlin, the Neue Photographische Gesellschaft, and the Schering concern before establishing his own company in 1927. Fischer was the author of many books and articles on technical photographic subjects. He was awarded the Prussian Academy of Science Leibnitz Medal for outstanding achievement in 1944.

See also: CHROMOGENIC DEVELOPMENT; COLOR PHOTOGRAPHY—HISTORY; COUPLERS, COLOR.

Fisheye Lens

A fisheye lens has an extremely wide angle of view, from about 140° to 200° or more, and thus extremely short focal length—typically 7.5 to 16mm. The front element has a very large diameter and bulges excessively, like the eye of a fish. The design derives from the Hill Sky Lens, introduced in the mid-1920s to take horizon-to-horizon pictures of cloud formations and other atmospheric phenomena. A fisheye lens produces extreme barrel (outward curving) distortion and exposure vignetting in the outer areas of its field, and exaggerated foreshortening in the center. The distortion can be counteracted to some degree by projecting the processed image through a lens of similar design, or by masking down to the central area. Most such lenses have a maximum aperture of about $f/8$; they are not supplied in focusing mounts because the depth of field extends from a few inches in front of the lens to infinity. Most fisheye adapters or accessories for standard lenses produce a circular, distorted wide field of view but have less angular coverage than a true fisheye lens.

Color photograph: p. C-18.

Fixing

Fixing is the chemical process of removing unused light-sensitive materials from photographs to make them stable against the further action of light, which would otherwise blacken them, destroying the pictures. Fixing is achieved by treating the film or print emulsion in a chemical solution that dissolves the unexposed and undeveloped silver halide crystals.

A number of chemical compounds (among them sodium sulfite, potassium iodide, thiourea, ammonia, and potassium cyanide) will dissolve silver halides, but few of them meet all the requirements for a practical fixer. Today sodium thiosulfate ("hypo") and ammonium thiosulfate are almost universally used. The reaction between the thiosulfate and the unused silver halides in the film or paper is complex. A variety of silver thiosulfate compounds, not all identified, are formed, and these plus hypo must be removed.

Fixing takes place in two main stages. In the first stage the unexposed silver halides are dissolved, so the film becomes clear rather than milky. The same thing happens with paper, but not visibly because of the white background. Paper clearing time can only be determined by test. At the end of the clearing time fixing is still incomplete; the products of the reaction largely are insoluble, so they cannot be washed out. In the second stage of fixing these insoluble chemicals are converted into soluble ones that will wash out. In practical terms the optimum fixing time is generally twice the clearing time. Nothing is gained by fixing longer; with fiber-base prints overfixing is as bad as incomplete fixing, since hypo and fixing products become too deeply embedded in the paper to wash out. Hypo must be washed out of photographs because any considerable amount of residual hypo tends to combine with the silver that forms the image, changing it into yellow or brown silver sulfide, which we see as fading and stains. Until 1982 photographic chemists believed that all possible hypo should be removed from films and prints for the sake of permanence. However, pure silver is not very stable. New experiments show that some residual hypo helps preserve photographs by reacting to coat the particles of image silver with a protective layer of silver sulfide, far more stable than the metal. This is explained more fully in the entry on archival processing.

A plain solution of sodium or ammonium thiosulfate can be used for fixing, but it is quickly ruined by chemicals carried in from the developer. Most fixers contain other ingredients—typically an acid, a preservative, a hardener, and a buffer. The acid prolongs the fixer's life by neutralizing alkalis from the developer. However, the acid itself can break thiosulfate down, releasing harmful sulfur into the fixer. A weak solution of acetic acid is often used. The preservative is usually sodium sulfite, which combines with sulfur to form sodium thiosulfate, thus undoing any harm caused by the acid. The hardener is usually potassium alum. It toughens the gelatin that supports the image. Alum in the fixer strongly retards the washing-out of hypo, especially from fiber-base prints; the alum acts as a mordant, binding the hypo to sizing in the emulsion and paper. In film, alum's wash-retarding effect is minimized when the fixer's pH (acidity) is near the isoelectric point of gelatin (pH 4.9).

Washing aids such as a 2-percent sodium sulfite solution or products sold as "hypo neutralizers" or "hypo clearing agents" go far to make the hypo in alum-hardened prints wash out. They also help with film washing.

A buffer gives the fixer a reserve of acidity and prolongs its working life. A balanced combination of alum and sodium sulfite has a useful buffering effect, and some formulas use additional buffering with boric acid.

A fixer is exhausted when its silver content becomes too high for the accumulated silver thiosulfate complexes to be removed by washing. A film fixer should contain no more than 6 grams of silver per liter; for prints, a fixer should have no more than 1.5 to 2 grams per liter. On reaching those levels, the fixers should be discarded and replaced by fresh fixer. There are simple tests to show silver content. Ammonium thiosulfate "rapid" fixers are widely used. Their working capacity is greater than that of sodium thiosulfate fixers because a larger proportion of the complexes formed in ammonium thiosulfate fixers are soluble and can be washed out. It is now common for a photographer to use a hardening ammonium thiosulfate fixer for film, a non-hardening ammonium thiosulfate fixer for prints on resin-coated (RC) papers, and two baths of a hardening sodium thiosulfate fixer for prints on fiber-base papers.

In two-bath fixing the first bath, used for half the fixing time, removes almost all silver halides, while the second bath, which stays very fresh, mostly converts the fixing by-products into soluble form. This system greatly increases the fixer's working capacity. The first bath is used nearly to exhaustion (its highest acceptable silver content) and is then discarded and replaced by the used second fixer, which now becomes the first fixer, while new second fixer is started. For archival prints the working capacity of a standard acid hardening sodium thiosulfate fixer such as Kodak F-5, used as a single bath, is given as thirty 8″ × 10″ prints per gallon. When used in two baths, its working capacity is given as one-hundred 8″ × 10″ prints per gallon of each of the two baths.

In 1978 Ilford devised a new fixing method for archival fiber-base prints. Relatively concentrated ammonium thiosulfate fixer with no hardener is used for a total fixing time of 30 seconds. Then the prints are washed for 5 minutes, treated in washing aid for 10 minutes, and washed again for a final 5 minutes. This removes almost all hypo in much less than the usual washing time. The short fixing time does not let hypo penetrate far into the paper, so it readily washes out. Such prints may contain so little residual hypo as to need selenium toning for protection.

Fixing is a highly critical stage of normal photographic processing. Effective agitation, accurate time, and the use of fresh solutions are as important in fixing as in development. Unfortunately this importance is often overlooked, probably because while the defects caused by poor development are seen at once, the defects caused by poor fixing, which are just as demanding, often are not seen until years later, too late for repair. Poorly fixed photographs can also destroy well-processed ones stored together with them. Care and thoroughness in fixing are thus imperative for all photographs worth keeping.
See also: ARCHIVAL PROCESSING; HYPO; WASHING.

Fizeau, Armand Hippolyte Louis
French, 1819–1896
A physicist, A. H. L. Fizeau was responsible for significant improvements and unique applications of the daguerreotype process. His technique of "gilding" a daguerreotype with a gold chloride solution after fixing created warmer (brown) image tones with improved contrast. The gold coating also helped protect the image from abrasion and, because gold is chemically much less active than silver, helped protect the plate from oxidation and tarnishing. Gilding was introduced in 1840 and immediately became a standard part of the daguerreotype process throughout the world.

Fizeau apparently discovered the use of bromine fumes to increase the speed of daguerreotype plates shortly after J. F. Goddard. In 1841 he invented the most successful method of engraving daguerreotypes for printing. A gilded image was etched with acid; the gold toning protected the image highlights and middle tones so that only the bare silver was affected; the copper backing plate was varnished on the back to protect it. The image was then electroplated with copper to form a more durable printing surface; aquatint graining was added in large single-tone areas as re-

quired. Finally, the plate was mounted on a wood block to strengthen it for inking and printing in a hand press. Several hundred reproductions—many times the number possible with other processes—could be obtained because the image could be re-electroplated when the copper surface began to show signs of wear.

With the brilliant physicist J. B. L. Foucault, Fizeau investigated the exposure effects of various light sources and of the separated colors of the spectrum on the daguerreotype in 1844. In the following year they took the first detailed photograph of the sun's surface. Working independently, Fizeau recorded new details regarding polarized light and the expansion of crystals under the impact of various kinds of energy. In 1849 he made the first reasonably accurate measurement of the speed of light—a finding refined by Foucault in 1862 to within 1 percent of present-day measurements using a mirror procedure first proposed by François Arago. Fizeau was also the first to suggest that the Doppler effect of frequency change resulting from the movement of the source or the observer applied to light as well as to sound; this principle is the basis of much astronomical information.

See also: ARAGO, FRANÇOIS; AQUATINT; DAGUERREOTYPE; ELECTROTYPE; GODDARD, JOHN F.

Flare
Stray, non-image-forming light that degrades the image in a camera, enlarger, or projector is called flare. Flare is created by light scattered or dispersed within the image system, whereas glare is direct light from a source within the picture area, or a hot-spot reflection of a light source aimed at the scene. Modern camera lens elements have multiple coatings that reduce internal flare to less than 3 percent—compared with 10 percent or more in early uncoated lenses. Nevertheless, internal camera flare can arise from light leaks such as a pinhole in a bellows or a distorted lens mount; from light in the brightest parts of the image reflected by unpainted metal or plastic in the camera; and from using a lens with extra wide covering power. The last problem often arises when a reducing back is used to adapt a large-format camera for a smaller film size. Flare in enlargers and projectors is most often produced by light leaks in the lamp housing, and by light from the easel or screen being reflected from nearby surfaces back into the image area.

The effect of flare in a positive-image

system (camera, projector) is to scatter light into the dark areas, thus reducing the overall contrast or brightness range. For example, a moderate degree of flare (less than 4.5 percent) can reduce a subject brightness range of 160:1 (7⅓ stops) to an image brightness range of 80:1 (6⅓ stops) in the camera. In the negative image projected by an enlarger for printing, light from the most transparent portions—the shadow areas—is scattered into the middletones, creating some reduction of local contrast (the effect in the highlights is unnoticeable except with extreme printing flare).

Control of Flare. The most effective flare control is masking, variously provided by a deep lens shade; by blocking off areas just outside the field of view with light-absorbent flats or material (especially in copy and product photography where fine details and tonal gradations are important); by closing leaks in light sources; and by painting reflective surfaces in the vicinity of the printing area in a darkroom a dark color.

See also: BRIGHTNESS RANGE; COVERING POWER; GLARE AND REFLECTIONS.

Flash
The light of flash illumination can come from two substantially different flash sources: the disposable flashbulb and the reusable electronic flash. They both create similar, instantaneous high-intensity light.

The disposable flashbulb contains loosely spun metal filaments or crumpled foil and gas which are primed and ready to start a combustion process that creates the light. A very-low-energy spark from a 1.5-volt battery or a piezoelectric device is all that is required to ignite the bulb. After a single firing the flashbulb is completely spent and must be replaced. For convenience, several small flashbulbs are mounted in a rotating cube or on a strip or bar that plugs directly into some small-format cameras.

The electronic flash operates by creating a veritable bolt of lightning between two electrodes housed in a rugged quartz-crystal flash tube. The tube is filled with xenon gas. A rapid discharge of high-voltage direct current from the system's capacitor excites the atomic structure of the gas and light energy is emitted. The process is repeatable thousands of times as long as the capacitor is kept ready for another power discharge. This requires batteries or some other dc power source. The duration of an electronic flash burst is much shorter than that of a flashbulb; this makes it

Flash Harry Ellis, untitled, Paris (ca. 1910), an early example of the use of flash in photography. Courtesy Stephen White Gallery, Los Angeles.

much more suitable for obtaining sharp images of fast-moving subjects.
See also: AUTOMATIC FLASH; ELECTRONIC FLASH; GUIDE NUMBER.

Flash Fill

Electronic flash can be used to illuminate shadow areas of a subject when the main (key) light comes from a continuous source. This technique, called flash fill, is particularly useful in outdoor color photography when the sun is the main light source, because electronic flash illumination has essentially the same color balance as sunlight. Therefore, the flash does not require filtration to maintain good color rendition.

The procedure is first to set the camera for proper exposure with the main light using a shutter speed that provides electronic flash synchronization. (That is a maximum of 1/60 sec. on most 35mm cameras with focal-plane shutters, but 1/90 or 1/125 sec. on some; most between-the-lens shutters synchronize at all speeds.) The lens *f*-stop required for this exposure is noted. The flash unit must be adjusted or positioned to produce light equivalent to one or two stops less exposure, depending on the amount of fill desired. (If the flash produced an equal amount of light, the shadow areas would be as bright as the main-lighted areas, and modeling would be lost.)

The effective flash output can be controlled on the basis of the flash-to-subject distance required for normal full exposure. This normal distance can be determined by relating the lens *f*-stop to the data on the chart or distance/exposure scale on most units, or by calculation from the guide number (GN) of the unit, as follows:

Normal distance = GN ÷ *f*-number

If the unit has a variable power control, it is placed at the normal distance and the control set for half- or quarter-power to produce one or two *f*-stops less light, respectively. If the unit does not have variable power settings, output can be reduced by putting a diffuser in front of the light head. Some units have accessory diffusers or neutral density filters that reduce the output one or more stops. The same effect can be improvised by placing a piece of white cloth such as a pocket handkerchief in front of the light head; each layer of cloth reduces the output about one *f*-stop.

Flash illumination can also be controlled by using the unit at full power and changing the distance to the subject as follows:

Normal Distance Multiplied by	=	Light/Exposure Change, in *f*-Stops
2.0		−2
1.4		−1
0.7		+1
0.5		+2

An automatic flash unit should be set for manual operation when used for flash fill by any of the above methods.
See also: BRIGHTNESS RANGE; FILL LIGHT.

Flashing

A flashing exposure is an additional white-light exposure given to an emulsion after the image exposure to reduce contrast, increase the effective speed, or insure proper halftone dot formation. Flashing is also local exposure given to a print to darken the edges, produce a dark-surround vignette image, or suppress details.

One of the most useful applications of flashing in ordinary photography is to reduce image contrast when using color slide film. When the subject brightness range from darkness area to diffuse highlight is greater than the equivalent of five *f*-stops (i.e., 1:32), a normal exposure followed by about 1/200 as much flashing exposure to white light will help record dark area tone and detail without overexposing the highlights. The flashing exposure can be accomplished by holding a white card or paper in the same light as the subject, filling the lens field of view, and making an exposure through a 3.0 neutral density filter at the same *f*-stop and shutter speed used for the normal exposure. (Automatic exposure control cameras must be set for manual operation for this exposure.) Alternatively an 18 percent reflectance gray card can be used with a 2.0 neutral density filter in the same manner. This technique is essentially the same as that used in graphic arts photography when making a negative through a halftone screen. The flashing ("bump" or highlight) exposure insures that a tiny center of density will form in the very light area dots, so that the printing plate in turn will have dots to deposit the slight amounts of ink required to produce tones or tints there.

An exposed film given a flashing exposure by green safelight illumination and push processed may produce the equivalent of a two-stop speed increase; the flashing exposure provides a kind of latensification. The contrast of a single grade of printing paper can be lowered by giving it a diffused white light flashing exposure after the image has been exposed. The limiting factor is how much flashing exposure can be given before highlight areas are fogged. The effect of the exposure is to cause light middletones and highlights to print darker, while dark tones are little affected. Black or very dark print edges are produced by shadowing the central area of the paper during a white light exposure with a flashlight or other directed source. Similarly, the flashing exposure can be worked outward from the center to leave the subject vignetted. Close-range exposure of local areas with a well-masked light source can darken details and blend them into shadow areas to increase the emphasis on the main subject. These local printing operations are made easier by turning the enlarger on with a safelight filter over the lens so that the image can be seen during flashing.

See also: FOG/FOGGING; LATENSIFICATION; PUSHING/PUSH PROCESSING; VIGNETTE IMAGE.

Flat Lighting

Flat lighting is the term for subject illumination that casts no significant visible shadows. Flat lighting minimizes or effectively erases the textures and contours of a subject, reducing its solid form to a flat, two-dimensional shape. Strongly diffused frontlight produces flat lighting. Daylight is considered flat on heavily overcast days when no shadows are cast. Camera-mounted flash units generally produce flat lighting because they equally illuminate all parts of the subject. In studio situations flat lighting is achieved by placing the light source directly on the lens-subject axis, or by placing frontlight sources of equal intensity at equal angles and distances on each side of the lens axis. Flat lighting is required for even illumination when the subject is two-dimensional, as in photographing paintings or copying manuscripts or prints. *See also:* FRONTLIGHTING.

Flexichrome Process

The Flexichrome method of hand-coloring a photographically produced image was introduced by J. Crawford in the U.S. in 1940. A gelatin-relief positive was produced by exposing a matrix film through an ordinary negative and processing it in a tanning developer, which hardened the exposed portions. Washing in warm water removed the soft gelatin in the highlights and middletones, and bleaching removed the silver image. The remaining relief positive was dyed gray to make it visible for working purposes. Special dyes were applied by brush, displacing the gray dye. The artist selected and mixed colors as desired. The extent and depth of the gelatin in each area controlled where and how much dye was absorbed. This interaction between hand and photographic factors permitted great selection and control without the loss of photographic realism. The image was transferred to a final support when coloring was completed. Flexichrome materials are no longer manufactured, but the results can be approximated using matrix films and dyes supplied for the dye transfer process.

Flexography

Flexography is a method of ink-printing an image onto an irregular or nonabsorbent surface. A negative relief image of hardened gelatin is prepared from the original photograph. A mold taken from the relief is used to make a printing sheet of a porous rubber material; shadow areas and middletones stand in relief above the surface of the printing sheet to receive the ink. The printing sheet is backed with compressible material on a roller or platen so that it will conform to all the variations of the surface that receives the image. The ink contains adhesive or binding compounds suitable for the plastic, foil, ceramic, or other surface to be imprinted, and a solvent which evaporates as the image dries. The process is also called *aniline printing,* because aniline dye-based inks originally were used.

Florence, Antoine Hercules Romuald

Brazilian; 1804–1879
Antoine Hercules Romuald Florence is credited with beginning photographic experiments in Brazil in the early 1830s. Evidence suggests that he was an early independent inventor of a photographic process.

Florence was born in Nice, France, where he attended school and showed early talent as a draftsman. Attracted by the sea, he made an around-the-world voyage, stopping at Rio de Janeiro in 1824, although with no intention of remaining. Between 1825 and 1829 he took part in an inland expedition headed by the naturalist Baron von Langsdorff (1774–1852), Russia's Consul General to Brazil. Shortly afterward he married and settled in the village of São Carlos (now Campinas), in São Paulo Province.

Interested in publishing a study of animal sounds (*Zöophonie*) observed in the jungle, Florence was surprised at the almost total absence of printing shops. In 1830 he began to experiment with graphic reproduction, developing a process (*Polygraphie*) on which he made constant improvements. In January, 1833, he made his first photographic experiment, based on information from a young pharmacist, Joaquim Correa de Mello (1816–1877), about the properties of silver nitrate, and on his own knowledge of the camera obscura. Using homemade apparatus and paper sensitized with silver nitrate, he obtained a negative of the view from his window; washed only with water to dissolve the silver nitrate unaffected by light, the image was not permanent. In notes and letters, Florence refers to other images obtained with a camera obscura, but these have not been found.

The dearth of printing facilities in Brazil motivated Florence to continue his photographic experiments, the focus of his interest being the possibility of making copies. His next step: the use of glass plates prepared with a mixture of soot and arabic glue, as for *cliché verre.* With a burin he drew and wrote on the glass and produced contact copies on paper sensitized with silver chloride or gold chloride, obtaining printout images. Attempting to render the images permanent, he was successful with urine and water on gold chloride copies, and with caustic ammonia on silver chloride copies; both worked well as fixers. Florence described his experiments and the use of other photosensitive compounds in various diaries, in French, dating from January 1833. He called his invention *photographie,* using the term in a sentence for the first time in a January 1834 diary entry, five years before Herschel and Mädler, who are usually credited with coining the word. Photographic copies of pharmacy labels, a Mason's di-

Florence, Hercules. "Pharmaceutical labels" (ca. 1833). Courtesy Boris Kossoy, São Paolo.

ploma, and other items still exist to attest to his results.

Florence's research was independent and isolated, carried out in a social and economic context characterized by colonialism and slavery, in a country at the edge of the industrialization process and therefore unable to absorb inventions and technical innovations. He abandoned his work in photography on learning of the European discovery, making no claims in a communication to the press: ". . . I will not dispute my discovery with anyone because two people can have the same idea. . . ." Somewhat ironically, the first demonstrations of daguerreotypy were made in Brazil some few months later.

Florence had a lifetime interest in the arts and applied arts, whether in graphics or in pictorial representation of human types and aspects of Brazil. In 1836 he introduced typesetting in Campinas; in 1842 he published the first newspaper in the interior of São Paulo Province. His iconographic work is priceless for anthropological and ethnographical studies, especially his drawings of Brazilian Indians, which have served as sources of information for scientific research into these areas, both in Brazil and overseas. His accomplishments as an independent inventor of photography remained, until recently, practically unknown.

Detailed, well-documented studies relating to the discovery of this pioneer of photography in Brazil and the Americas can be found in Boris Kossoy's *Hercules Florence 1833: a descoberta isolada da fotografia no Brasil* (1980), and in several English-language articles by the same author in *Image* (March 1977), *Camera* (October 1978), and *Photo History III*, published by the Photographic Historical Society, Rochester (1979).
See also: HISTORY OF PHOTOGRAPHY.

Flow Photography

The techniques of flow photography are used to record phenomena of development or change that are either too brief or progress too slowly to be discernible by the eye, or that are normally invisible—e.g., heat currents in the air, the flow of colorless gases, or the dispersion of one colorless liquid within another. Flow may be the movement and interaction of a continuous medium such as a liquid or gas with regard to external bodies (wind eddies around the corner of a building; the erosion of a river bank) or within itself (below-surface waves in the ocean). It may be the movement of a body transported by a medium (a wood chip floating on a lake) or moving through the medium by means of another force (an aircraft flying against a headwind). Flow may also be the progressive, continuous change of a body (emergence of a plant shoot, its growth, flowering, seeding, withering). The common factor is that all flow phenomena occur through time. Therefore, many techniques of flow photography deal with stretching or compressing the real time of an event to a viewing time that makes details of interest perceptible. High-speed photography makes a sequence of a large number of pictures in a

very short time, typically several hundred or thousand images in less than a second. These images may be examined as individual still photographs, or they may be projected at a normal motion-picture rate to obtain a slow-motion re-creation of the event, such as a bullet passing through a liquid. Time-lapse photography makes a sequence of a relatively few pictures at greater than normal intervals to record stages of very slow change such as plant growth or mud oozing at a rate of an inch an hour. These pictures, too, may be examined individually or projected at a normal rate to produce a speeded-up re-creation.

The patterns and paths of flow may be revealed by a continuous recording made on a single frame or strip of film. Photofinish and streak cameras utilize this principle. If the continuous-flow record is interrupted at regular intervals, velocity and duration can be determined directly from the image. In the single-plate motion-study and analysis records of Jules Marey and Thomas Eakins, these factors could be measured from successive positions of the subject itself; in the multiple-plate records of Eadweard Muybridge a background grid provided the reference for such measurements. The problem of making flow visible in a transparent medium is commonly solved by the use of tracers or by exploiting optical differences that the event creates in a surrounding medium. Tracers include dyes or colored smoke injected into the medium; particles or lights that float on the surface or at various depths; yarn or cloth streamers; light beams shone through the medium at an angle; and similar devices. Optical change is seen in the distortion produced by rising heat waves. Schlieren photography is a highly sophisticated optical differentiation technique based on the fact that gas (e.g., air) waves moving at different velocities have different powers of refraction and can be lighted to reveal their wave shapes.
See also: HIGH-SPEED PHOTOGRAPHY; MOTION STUDY AND ANALYSIS; PHOTO-FINISH PHOTOGRAPHY; SCHLIEREN PHOTOGRAPHY; SLOW-MOTION PHOTOGRAPHY; TIME-LAPSE PHOTOGRAPHY.

Fluorescence

See: ULTRAVIOLET AND FLUORESCENCE PHOTOGRAPHY.

Fluorescent-Light Photography

Fluorescent tubes are the primary source of illumination in most commercial locations; they are also widely used in homes. Although the light they emit looks essentially the same as that from other artificial sources, it is not. The difference becomes apparent in color photographs, where fluorescent light causes a yellow-green or blue-green color cast.

All light sources (with the exception of lasers) produce a mixture of visible wavelengths. Most color films are designed for use with one of two sources, daylight or tungsten, each of which emits energy continuously from blue to red. Fluorescent tubes have discontinuous spectral (wavelength) outputs. They are especially deficient in red output, have "spikes" or peaks of output at various parts of the green and blue regions of the spectrum, and have gaps in between. The problem is made more complex by the number of different kinds of fluorescent tubes available, each with different output characteristics, and thus each producing a different cast on color film. The most common types are daylight, deluxe cool white, cool white, deluxe warm white, and warm white. "Deluxe" tubes emit more red than standard ones, and "cool" tubes produce more blue than warm ones. The deluxe warm white most nearly matches tungsten light.

The primary means of obtaining reasonably well-balanced color photographs with fluorescent illumination is to place one or more corrective filters in front of the camera lens. For optimum results different filtration is needed for each kind of tube with various films. Some film manufacturers publish specific filter recommendations for a variety of tube-and-film combinations. These represent average corrections and are best used as starting points for a series of test exposures. When different types of tubes are used together, or when the tube type cannot be identified, testing is the best procedure. If this is not possible, a certain amount of basic correction can be achieved with a color compensating (CC) filter: a CC30M (magenta) filter for daylight-type color films, and a CC50R (red) filter for tungsten-type color films.

Some filter manufacturers offer a general-purpose fluorescent correction filter for each of the two film types. The filter for daylight-type film is commonly designated FL-D, and that for Type B tungsten film is FL-B or FL-T. Whatever filtration is used, any imbalance should be on the warm side. Slightly reddish skin tones in photographs of people are more acceptable than a greenish or bluish pallor.

A second method of correction is to overwhelm the fluorescent light with stronger illumination from another source. This is accomplished most easily with electronic flash and a lens aperture setting at least one f-stop smaller than would be required for the ambient fluorescent light.

See also: CC FILTERS; FILTERS.

Fluorography

Photography that records the image on a screen which fluoresces (emits visible wavelengths) when illuminated with x-rays is called fluorography. The subject is placed between the x-ray source and the screen; the shadow image, seen from the other side of the screen, varies in intensity according to the transparency of various parts of the subject to the illuminating radiation. The image may be recorded by placing suitable film directly in contact with the screen, or more commonly by using a camera and conventional film. The image may be so faint as to require use of an image amplifier or a very wide-aperture system such as a Schmidt camera. Fluorography is distinct from fluorescence photography, in which the subject itself is caused to fluoresce so it can be photographed directly.

See also: IMAGE AMPLIFIER; SCHMIDT CAMERA; ULTRAVIOLET AND FLUORESCENCE PHOTOGRAPHY; X-RAY PHOTOGRAPHY.

f-Number; f-Stop

The aperture settings of a lens are called f-numbers or f-stops. The term *stop* derives from the early practice of using metal plates with holes of various sizes to block or stop part of the light entering a lens (waterhouse stop). Today an adjustable iris diaphragm or equivalent device is built into almost all lenses or cameras. A variety of numbering systems (e.g., U.S. numbers) came into use along with the first diaphragms, but a system related to the focal length of the lens—as indicated by f—is now universally used. The advantage of this system is that when set to the same f-number, all lenses pass the same amount of light regardless of their focal lengths. This permits standardized, universally useful exposure meters, automatic control systems, and similar devices.

An f-number represents a ratio between lens focal length and the effective diameter of a given aperture. Because it is related to focal length, the f-number is also called the *relative aperture*. The effective diameter of an aperture is the diameter of the bundle of light rays striking the front element that can actually pass through the iris opening inside the lens. Because the effect of lens elements is to cause light rays to converge or diverge, the true or physical diameter of the iris opening may be larger or smaller than the effective diameter. However, the *visual* diameter of the opening, as seen by looking through the front of the lens (a light-colored surface behind the lens aids in making this observation) is the effective diameter from which the f-number is calculated. This diameter is also called the *entrance pupil*. The f-number equals the focal length of the lens divided by the entrance pupil of the aperture. For example, at an aperture with an effective diameter or entrance pupil of ½" (12.5mm), a 2" (50mm) focal-length lens is set to an f-number of 4, commonly written f/4 or F:4. Similarly, a 3" (75mm) lens with an entrance pupil of ¾" (18.75mm) is set to f/4. Although the focal lengths and effective diameters of these two lenses differ, they pass the same amount of light at this setting because they have identical diameter-to-focal length ratios.

Aperture settings are marked so that each position changes the amount of light passing through the lens by a factor of 2: the light is either doubled, or reduced to one-half. Because the light passes through the *area*, not simply the diameter, of the effective aperture, the f-numbers themselves do not double or halve at each step, but change by a factor of 1.4 ($\sqrt{2}$). The international series of f-numbers is: 1; 1.4; 2; 2.8; 4; 5.6; 8; 11; 16; 22; 32; 45; 64; 90; and so on. Each higher number is 1.4× the preceding number (with occasional rounding-off, e.g. 11.3 to 11) and represents a ratio that passes half as much light. That is, a higher number represents a smaller aperture, one that stops twice as much light as the previous aperture. The f-numbers double at every other step in the series, in accordance with the principle that they represent proportional changes in area, not in diameter. The *speed* of a lens is the f-number of its maximum effective diameter—i.e., when the aperture is wide open. In some lenses this number is between two f-numbers in the standard series because the maximum diameter of the lens is the limiting factor. In that case the next marked aperture setting on the lens is that of the nearest full f-number and the standard series progresses from there.

See also: DIAPHRAGM; FOCAL LENGTH; U.S.: UNIFORM SYSTEM; WATERHOUSE STOP.

Focal Length

The fundamental optical characteristic of a lens that determines its angle of view and power of magnification; the distance, measured along the optical axis, from the rear nodal point of the lens to the plane at which the image of an object at infinity is sharply focused.

See also: ANGLE OF VIEW; COVERING POWER; INFINITY; LENSES; MAGNIFICATION; OPTICS.

Focal-Plane Shutter

See SHUTTER.

Focusing

A photographic lens collects light rays originating at various subject distances in front of the lens and causes them to converge on corresponding image points at various distances behind the lens. For the vertical plane at each subject distance, there is a matching plane of image points at a particular image distance. In most photographic equipment there is also a required image location: the film (focal) plane in a camera, the paper surface under an enlarger, and the screen surface in front of a projector. Focusing is the procedure of adjusting the distance between the lens and the required image location until the desired plane of image points falls on that location. Because of the conditions called depth of field and depth of focus, image points lying on other planes may also appear sharply focused, but in fact the sharpest points are those on the image plane corresponding to just one subject plane, the plane at the focused distance. With a camera it is possible to focus over a great range of subject distances. With an enlarger or a projector there is only one subject distance for any particular degree of magnification; it is the distance from the lens to the negative or slide that is being projected.

The movement required for focusing is achieved in two ways. Either the lens has a barrel with integral threads that allow it to extend or retract from a fixed mounting position, or it is mounted on a standard that extends or retracts by means of a bellows. In some large-format cameras the bellows also allows the camera back to be moved while the lens standard remains stationary. This permits focusing without changing the image magnification, which is determined by the lens-to-subject distance. Only a small amount of movement is required to focus over a great range. For example, to focus from infinity down to a near limit of six times its focal length (i.e., to 12-in. or 300mm with a 2-in. or 50mm lens), a lens needs to move only one-fifth of its focal length. In medium- and small-format cameras it is practical and even necessary to have a rigid camera body and to use lenses with barrel focusing. In larger format equipment it is more practical and versatile to use bellows focusing with lenses in non-focusing or "short" mounts.

Some very simple cameras provide no focusing capability. The lens is permanently set to provide a reasonably sharp image of a subject located at any distance from about 4 feet (1.2 meters) to infinity. At the other extreme, there are cameras and lenses that have a built-in capability to measure the subject distance or to evaluate the image and then self-adjust to produce a sharp image (these are discussed in the entry on automatic focusing). With most equipment, focusing is done by the photographer, who makes a visual evaluation of the subject distance or an image and then adjusts the lens-image distance appropriately. There are various ways to do this.

Focusing methods. The simplest, and least accurate, method of focusing is a scale marked with distances or with symbols representing various image magnifications or lens fields of view. A typical set of symbols is a stylized mountain and trees, a group of three human figures, and a head and shoulders. The photographer estimates the distance or chooses a field of view and sets the focusing control to the appropriate point on the scale.

Much greater focusing accuracy is possible with systems that provide an image of the subject for direct visual evaluation. These systems also show the field of view of the lens, either directly or by means of masks or reference lines within the maximum field area. Thus it is possible to evaluate framing or composition and focus at the same time. One such system is a range-viewfinder coupled to the lens. The rangefinder component shows a portion of the subject either divided in half (split-image rangefinder) or as a superimposed double image (coincident-image rangefinder). Adjusting the lens focus control causes the image portions to move in the rangefinder; when they are exactly aligned, the lens is focused on the subject.

A second system is used in twin-lens reflex cameras. A viewing lens that matches the focal length of the camera lens provides an image that is reflected by a mirror onto a screen at the top of the camera. The two lenses are mounted on the same standard; as the focus control is adjusted to obtain a sharp viewing image, the camera lens is moved so it will produce an equally sharp image at the focal plane.

View cameras and single-lens reflex (SLR) cameras permit viewing of the image formed by the camera lens. In a view camera the image is formed directly on a ground glass or equivalent screen at the rear of the camera. In an SLR camera the image is reflected up to a screen by an internal mirror where it can be viewed directly from above, or more commonly by means of a prism and magnifying eyepiece from behind the camera. A fresnel field lens is usually combined with the viewing screen to provide a brighter image in general, but especially to provide uniform brightness over the screen area. The image in a view camera may be examined through an accessory magnifying eyepiece placed directly against the screen to inspect critical focus.

Various kinds of screens and focusing aids are used in SLR cameras to achieve sharp focus adjustments. The most common aid is a center circle containing a split-wedge rangefinder which shows a division or break in the subject when the lens is not precisely focused; this is most useful if there are clearly defined lines or edges in the subject. Often the rangefinder circle is surrounded by a ring or collar area of extremely fine ground-glass texture. This permits critical focusing on fine details that cannot be seen as clearly in the coarser texture of the major part of the screen. Instead of a ground-glass surface, the screen may be composed of thousands of microprisms. These cause an out-of-focus image to look "shattered" into tiny, discontinuous bits or to appear to shimmer as the camera or eye is moved slightly. In some screens the central area is composed of microprisms and the outer area of a ground texture. The viewing hoods of medium-format SLR and twin-lens cameras usually include a pop-up magnifier to help in inspecting image sharpness.

Focusing techniques. Accurate focusing is easy to accomplish with most cameras and subjects of normal brightness. Through-the-lens focusing should be done with the lens set at its largest aperture. This provides the brightest image and the least depth of field so that the difference between in- and out-of-focus conditions can be seen most clearly. A view camera should be focused with a magnifier placed about halfway between the center and one edge of the screen. This will minimize the chances of noticeable differences in center and edge sharpness with a lens that has curvature of field. Focus should be rechecked with a magnifier after a view camera lens is closed to its working aperture; some lenses exhibit a slight focus shift with *f*-stop changes. A zoom lens should be focused at its maximum focal length setting to obtain the greatest magnification and least depth of field; then it can be zoomed to the desired focal length to take a picture. The lens swing and tilt movements of view cameras permit placing the plane of sharp focus on any subject plane; the Scheimpflug condition provides the maximum adjustment of this sort.

Maximum depth of field at any f-stop is achieved by focusing at the hyperfocal distance of that aperture. In large-field views such as landscapes, the best overall sharpness often results from focusing at a distance about one-third into the depth of the picture area. For fast action and unpredictable situations, presetting the focused distance so the depth of field covers a convenient zone permits shooting without delay. In dim light or very low contrast conditions, a pencil flashlight held at the subject position can provide a bright point on which to focus. However sharp focus is achieved, it is useless if the camera moves during the exposure. A fast shutter speed or a firm camera support is essential to recording a sharply focused image.

See also: AUTOMATIC FOCUSING; BELLOWS; CAMERA MOVEMENT; DEPTH OF FIELD; DEPTH OF FOCUS; FRESNEL LENS; HYPERFOCAL DISTANCE; RANGEFINDER; SCHEIMPFLUG CONDITION; SHARPNESS; ZONE FOCUSING.

Fog; Fogging

There are two kinds of fog of concern in photography: atmospheric fog in a scene, and excess, non-image density in an emulsion. Atmospheric fog is composed of suspended drops of moisture often in combination with smoke or dust. It scatters and absorbs light, reducing contrast and color saturation, and limiting visibility. Slight to moderate fog density visually softens a scene and simplifies the background by blending shapes and tones or colors; as density increases, the effective background limit approaches the camera. Objects in fog often are most clearly revealed by sidelight or backlight. Front light, especially from directly at the camera position, is scattered into object-obscuring glare; in low-density fog the glare effect may not be objectionable, but the intensity of the light is rapidly absorbed. Exposure meter readings and flash calculations have slight accuracy in fog. At best they serve as a starting point for a series of increasing exposures. Although some filters provide increased visual penetration of atmospheric haze, they do not have the same effect in fog.

Emulsion fogging is caused by stray, non-image-forming light or by unwanted chemical action. The usual effect is to add a uniform amount of density over all affected areas; it is first noticeable in the areas of least image density. Thus, in negatives it causes a loss of shadow contrast and detail; the effect may not be noticeable in the highlights because the amount of density added there is only a fraction of the total amount. In reversal films and print materials fogging is first noticeable in the highlights, making them muddy or gray. Optical or light fogging has a number of possible causes: flare from a dirty or unshaded lens, light leaks in the camera, careless handling when loading or unloading film, light leaks in the darkroom, flare or leaks in an enlarger, and unsafe safelighting. In-camera optical fogging is confined to the image area; fogging at other times also affects the margins of film.

Chemical fogging of an emulsion most often results from the development of unexposed halides. A slight amount of such development occurs in all cases; it contributes to the fundamental base-plus-fog density of films, but its effect is insignificant, just as it is in print materials. Greater amounts of fog degrade the image. Out-of-date and improperly stored films and papers are likely to have a high fog level because halides become developable with age. Fogging is also produced by excessive developer temperature, agitation, or chemical activity. Adding a restrainer (usually potassium bromide) or an anti-foggant to the solution helps prevent development fog. Other kinds of fogging, and stains that act like fog, may result from using a solvent (fine-grain) developer with fast films; using nearly exhausted developer or fixer, or a fixer that is insufficiently acid (use of an acid stop bath helps avoid this problem); and letting the emulsion contact the air excessively during development, producing an oxidation effect called *aerial fog.* Chemical dust in a darkroom can settle on an emulsion at almost any stage of processing, producing fog or other image effects the source of which is almost impossible to identify.

A special kind of fog is produced by excess silver being deposited on already developed areas of an image. This is *dichroic fog,* so named because the thin metallic surface layer produces interference between wavelengths of transmitted or reflected light. It looks reddish by transmitted light and greenish by reflected light. In old warm-tone prints it often creates a purplish metallic sheen over dark areas of the image. Overworked developers and fixers are the primary source of dichroic fog. Overall chemical fog can sometimes be removed with a subtractive reducer. Dichroic fog is a more difficult problem because it is in the dense areas of the image; chemical treatment to remove it will affect detail in the thinner areas first. The best precautions against fogging are fresh materials and solutions, proper operating temperatures and procedures, and scrupulously clean working conditions.

See also: DICHROIC FILTER; FLARE; REDUCER/REDUCTION.

Footcandle

See: LIGHT UNITS.

Forensic Photography

Forensic photography is concerned with taking pictures that are acceptable as evidence in a court of law. Forensic photography is chiefly the province of law enforcement agencies, but it is also used by private investigation agencies and insurance companies. While individuals may use pictures, as in a small-claims case, legal requirements for their use in court are sufficiently strict that such is not normally the case.

Pictorial evidence, both still and motion, is a powerful, persuasive tool that must conform to a rigid set of requirements in order to be admissible. The single most important requirement for a forensic photograph is that it appear entirely natural. Judges will not admit a picture that seems to have been tampered with or that distorts any aspect of the scene. In particular, a lens and subject-to-camera distance must be selected that will render a normal perspective. That is, the size relationships of objects in the photograph should be equivalent to what they actually are. Thus, telephoto and wide-angle lenses must be employed cautiously. In addition, the print ought to be made with a minimum of burning and dodging. Forensic photographs are not judged on their aesthetic qualities, but on their straightforward clarity.

Although each type of crime requires a specific approach, there are some ground rules common to most. At the scene the photographer must make a series of establishing shots which clearly depict the environment in which the crime took place. The extent of the relevant area may be determined by a detective. In all cases the photographer should follow the suggestions of the investigative professional. Another series of pictures showing the immediate crime scene should be made. Close attention must be paid to signs of personal injury, forced entry, activity immediately prior to the crime, or anything obviously out of place or damaged. A good rule of thumb is when in doubt, photograph it. After leaving the scene the photographer is responsible for documenting the negatives and the subsequent prints as to their authenticity. He or she must be prepared to swear in court that the pictures being presented are the ones that were made at the crime scene. Any irregularity will invalidate the photographs as evidence. The photographer also may be required to present credentials as an expert, especially when he or she is called upon to interpret a picture and explain the procedures used in making the photograph.

In the course of many assignments a wide variety of equipment is likely to be required. The most complex and exotic equipment is used in a laboratory with evidence gathered from the field. For photography at the scene 35mm and medium-format cameras are most common both because they are easily portable and because they accept a variety of accessories. Electronic flash units are used for auxiliary illumination. Occasionally pictures must be made with existing light, so high-speed or other special-purpose films may be required. Because small pieces of evidence may require close-up or macrophotographs, the standard equipment kit should include appropriate lenses or accessories. The following entries include information on procedures and techniques of special value in forensic photography.
See also: FINGERPRINT PHOTOGRAPHY; FIRE AND ARSON PHOTOGRAPHY; INFRARED PHOTOGRAPHY; SURVEILLANCE PHOTOGRAPHY; ULTRAVIOLET AND FLUORESCENCE PHOTOGRAPHY.

Format

The dimensions of standard negative, print, and transparency sizes are called formats. In general, the nominal dimensions of the picture area (e.g., 2¼ inches square) are used for roll, cassette, and cartridge films, while the actual outer dimensions of the material are used for sheet films and print papers. There is a growing trend in the U.S. to identify some formats by their metric sizes—for example, 6 × 6cm rather than 2¼″ × 2¼″—and certain very popular formats are commonly referred to by film size (e.g., 35mm, 110) rather than dimensions. The proportion between the long and short sides of a rectangular format is called the *aspect ratio*. *Small-format* films are 35mm and smaller; *medium-format* films are 120/220 and 70mm roll sizes and sheet films up to 3¼″ × 4¼″; *large-format* films are 4″ × 5″ and larger. The most common format designations are shown in the table below.

Formulas

Preparation of photographic processing solutions from formulas rather than from prepackaged mixes is economically advantageous when large amounts of solutions are being used. It is a necessary procedure to obtain many special-purpose solutions not available as commercial preparations. A solution formula specifies the ingredients, their amounts and forms (e.g., crystal, granular, anhydrous, etc.), and the mixing temperature. Precise measurements are essential in preparing solutions that help form or alter the image (developers, reducers, intensifiers, toners). Small errors in measurement are acceptable in other solutions, such as stop baths and fixers. If the formula does not begin with a stated amount of the solvent (almost always water), about two thirds of the final volume is taken. Ingredients must be dissolved completely, one at a time, in the order stated in the formula. This is extremely important, because various chemical reactions occur at each stage of mixing and a change in the order may produce a weakened or useless solution. As an example, in mixing a developer it is preferable to dissolve the preservative (sodium sulfite) first to protect the developing agents which follow from oxidation. However, metol does not dissolve in the presence of sodium sulfite, so formulas using metol list it as the first ingredient. The use of percentage solutions makes accurate measurement of very small quantities of chemicals easy to accomplish.
See also: MIXING PHOTOGRAPHIC SOLUTIONS; PERCENTAGE SOLUTIONS.

Framing

The term *framing* refers to two different procedures in photography, one used at the time a picture is taken, and the other used when a picture is prepared for presentation.

As a part of camera work, framing is the process of adjusting the camera distance and angle of view to the subject so that the edges of the format mark off or "frame" the desired area. This aspect of picture composition is sometimes described as "cropping in the camera." It is most accurately accomplished using the camera's viewing system. However, with large-format equipment or in physically difficult locations, it is often more efficient to use an auxiliary viewer or a viewing frame for preliminary work to choose the camera position and lens focal length. Then, after the equipment is set up, camera viewing is used to adjust the final framing.

Auxiliary viewers for medium- and large-format cameras are hand-held devices that have a simple zoom optical system or a set of interchangeable masks to show the field of view taken in by various focal-length lenses. A viewing frame is simply a piece of cardboard with a hole in the center cut to the proportions of the film format to be used. If the hole is the same size as the image area recorded on film, it will show a given lens field of view reasonably accurately when held in front of the eye a distance equal to the focal length of the lens.
Framing for Presentation. Placing a photograph in a picture frame gives it protection as well as some degree of formal presentation. It is possible to construct a frame from bulk lengths of molding, but precut wood and metal moldings are available in a great range of styles, finishes, and standard lengths.

COMMON FILM FORMATS

Common Name	Film Size/Name	Image Area
Disc	Disc film	8 ×10mm
110	110	13 ×17mm
126	126	28 ×28mm
Half-frame	35mm	18 ×24mm
35mm (full frame)	35mm	24 ×36mm
645; 6 × 4.5(cm)	120/220; 70mm	2¼″ ×1¾″
6 × 6(cm); 2¼″ square	120/220; 70mm	2¼″ ×2¼″
6 × 9(cm)	120/220; 70mm	2¼″ ×2¼″
9 × 12(cm); 3¼″ × 4¼″	Sheet*	*
4″ × 5″	Sheet*	*
5″ × 7″	Sheet*	*
8″ × 10″	Sheet*	*

*Sheet film sizes are the same as the common name; the image area is about ¼ inch less in each dimension.

Frank, Robert. "London, child running on street" (1952). Courtesy Robert Frank; Collection, Museum of Modern Art, New York.

They have a variety of depths and internal grooves to retain glass, mounting-board, and backing-board components. These precut materials are supplied with special corner fasteners that permit assembly of a frame of almost any size and proportions without the need for carpentry skill. The choice of a frame color and style, like the choice of the color and border size of an overmat, is a matter of taste and aesthetic intent. In general, frames that show a narrow face edge, have a simple contour, and are a plain, neutral color help to direct attention to the image. Frames that are especially wide, ornate, or of striking color call attention to themselves.

Open framing—without a covering piece of glass or plastic—avoids reflections and provides edge protection and a means of hanging the picture on a wall or standing it on a flat surface; it does not protect the image itself. Covering glass or plastic should be colorless and smooth on both surfaces. Inexpensive window glass often has a greenish tint. Non-glare or non-reflection materials have a finely etched pattern on one surface that scatters light enough to gray tones or colors perceptibly and to reduce image contrast as much as the equivalent of one grade of paper. Some smooth

plastics are susceptible to surface scratching with repeated cleaning.

A print to be framed behind glass or Plastic should first be mounted on a good quality board. The board must fit into the frame grooves snugly, but without bending, and the print surface must not touch the face covering. Contact between the emulsion and the glass or plastic may cause spotty glazing (ferro-typing) over a period of time, or the emulsion may adhere, making the print unremovable without damage. This latter problem is particularly a danger with color prints and those prints on resin-coated papers. Some frames have separate grooves to ensure separation between the print mount and the cover. With other frames a paper or cardboard separator is used. This may be concealed by the edge of the frame, or may be a window mat with borders of appropriate width placed over the face of the print. The mounting board supports the print from behind, but a dust seal should also be provided by a separate backing board taped in place all around its edges, or by a piece of paper pasted to the back of the frame. Only chemically safe materials should be used.

See also: MOUNTING PHOTOGRAPHS.

Frank, Robert

American; 1924–

Robert Frank's photoessay *The Americans* is perhaps the most influential book of photographs published in the last 25 years. These images, taken in 1955–1956 on a cross-country trip, although influenced by the work of Bill Brandt, Walker Evans, and André Kertész, created a new idiom of documentary photography. Objective yet intensely personal, shot in an elementary, even haphazard style, Frank's photographs of alienated, lonely Americans engaged in the most banal activities in the most ordinary public settings were glimpses of an American sadness and disenchantment which had never been represented before. Rudolph Wurlitzer has called them "images from the backroads of the culture, the sad-eyed margins where the process of life is most exposed." John Szarkowski wrote that "the book challenged the way Americans were supposed to look. . . . It was about whole segments of life that nobody had thought the proper concern of art."

Frank was born and raised in Zurich, Switzerland. He began to photograph seriously in 1942, and apprenticed with Hermann Eidenbenz (Basel) and

Michael Wolgensinger (Zurich) in the use of large-format cameras and studio lighting. He worked as a photographer at Gloria Films, Zurich, in 1943–1944 and started to develop his mature style of photographing in the streets of Zurich in 1945.

Frank emigrated to the United States in 1947. Encouraged by the art director of *Harper's Bazaar*, Alexey Brodovitch, he began fashion and advertising photography for *Harper's Bazaar* and other periodicals including *Life, Look, Fortune, McCall's,* and *The New York Times*. In addition to his commercial work Frank traveled on assignments in Europe and South America. He published photostories on Welsh miners, London street scenes, and Peruvian Indians. These last appeared in a book together with photographs by Werner Bischof and Pierre Verger. Frank was using a 35mm camera almost exclusively by this time. His later work is inconceivable in any other format.

In 1953 Frank worked with Edward Steichen collecting and selecting photographs for the *Post-War European Photographers* exhibition at the Museum of Modern Art in New York City. In 1955 Frank became the first European-born photographer to receive a Guggenheim Fellowship. For the next two years he traveled throughout the United States creating the images for which he became famous. His selection of 83 photographs (from the over 28,000 frames) was published as *Les Americains* in France in 1958. The following year the first American edition appeared with an introduction by Frank's friend Jack Kerouac.

Frank began making films in 1958. The first, *Pull My Daisy*, made in collaboration with the painter Alfred Leslie and narrated by Kerouac, is considered a classic of the American independent cinema. Frank became more and more devoted to film, giving up still photography by the mid-1960s. He has made his living in recent years as a teacher of cinematography. He lives and works in Nova Scotia, Canada.

Frank's photographs have appeared in a half dozen shows at the Museum of Modern Art in New York, including *The Family of Man* exhibition. He has exhibited at the Art Institute of Chicago, the International Museum of Photography in Rochester, New York, the Kunsthaus in Zurich, and many other galleries and museums.

Freelance Photography

A freelance photographer is one who markets his or her photographic services to a number of different clients rather than working exclusively for one client or through a specific organization. Most freelance photographers begin by taking pictures on speculation (i.e., without a specific assignment or an agreement with a potential client) and submitting them to publications, agencies, and other markets in the hope of making a sale. If the work is of good quality, repeat sales are possible, and these eventually lead to requests and assignments for pictures of particular subjects or events. The successful freelance photographer is one who has established a sufficient number of clients so that work "on spec" is not necessary. Instead, there are enough assignments for which advance payment to cover expenses is available to keep him or her busy.

Freelance markets. The variety of sources for freelance photographic work is broad, encompassing local businesses; trade publications; picture agencies; certain advertising agencies; publishing companies; and major magazines, most of which now use a great deal of freelance photography to avoid the expense of maintaining a large photographic staff. Many of these sources are listed in publications such as *Photographer's Marketplace*, a compilation of concerns and publications that purchase photographs.

Stock picture agencies. "Stock houses" function almost completely with pictures obtained from freelance photographers. These agencies act as repositories and clearing houses for photographs made of specific subjects. Photographs are usually submitted to the stock agency on a consignment basis; the agency keeps a percentage of the fee it charges clients for use of the pictures. Most stock agencies require that the freelance photographer supply them with a large number of pictures of each of several subjects: sunsets, hands, machinery, elderly people, for example. This gives clients a variety of images from which to choose. The procedure is of great benefit to freelance photographers who concentrate on one or two subject areas. Because the need for color photographs is usually far greater than for black-and-white pictures, most stock agencies now deal almost exclusively with color transparencies. A client can easily have an image converted to black and white in reproduction if that is desired.

Magazines and trade publications. Few major magazines now retain full-time photographic staffs. The competition for free-lance assignments from these magazines is quite keen, and the level of work they demand is quite of a very high order. Prospective freelancers interested in working for a major publication must first have a thorough understanding of its picture requirements and must be able to produce work that is at least equal in quality to that currently used. With few exceptions, the major picture and general-interest magazines will review the portfolios of photographers looking for freelance work. However, the number of those seeking assignments is so high that the unestablished freelance photographer should be prepared for rejection, at least at the outset. In most cases, the picture editor or researcher reviewing the portfolio will indicate whether or not the work shown is of potential interest to the publication, and whether or not the photographer should return at some future date with more examples.

Trade publications and special-interest magazines abound, and they are constantly in search of new picture sources and photographers. The freelancer with knowledge or experience in the magazine's specialty area has an advantage when seeking work from such publications. Writing skills are also a great asset; there is an increasing need for photographers who can provide text as well as pictures.

Business markets. Local businesses are a potentially good source of work for the beginning freelance photographer. Realty firms, small architectural concerns, tree and flower nurseries, and other such businesses all make use of photographs for sales, public relations, and other purposes. Local musicians and actors need publicity pictures; the community theater is often a good source of photographic clients.

Advertising agencies rarely use unproven freelance work, relying instead on established photographers who often work on a retainer basis. There is one exception to this: camera advertisers often buy pictures from talented freelancers who use the equipment being advertised.

Associations and legal matters. One of the major disadvantages of freelance photography lies in the lack of legal coverage. Staff photographers are usually protected by their employers from legal action for invasion of privacy, libel, and similar problems. The freelance photographer must make his or her own arrangements for model releases and other permissions. While the contract between a staff or retained photographer and the employer is specific about ownership of the photographs made, a freelance photographer must establish ownership and usage rights with each separate client before taking on the assignments offered. Insurance of equipment and film is another concern for the freelancer.

Certain organizations exist to aid the freelance photographer in these matters. The most notable of these is the American Society of Photographers in Communications, better known as ASMP (from its earlier name, the American Society of Magazine Photographers). This organization offers its members health insurance plans, and insurance specifically tailored to a photographer's requirements, covering equipment damage, prop and clothing damage, and film/negative insurance, among other things. The organization also publishes a pricing guideline of fee ranges for various kinds of editorial and other freelance/commercial photography. It must be noted that the guidelines are just that; actual fees vary widely with market needs and geographic location, and often have little in common with those suggested in the guide. The freelance photographer must function in a buyer's market, especially at the outset or on the local level.

See also: COPYRIGHT; PICTURE LIBRARIES/AGENCIES; RIGHTS AND PERMISSIONS.

Fresnel Lens

The Fresnel lens is a condenser of concentric rings, each equivalent to a section of the curved surface of a plano-convex lens. The Fresnel design eliminates unnecessary thickness between the two surfaces, reducing the weight and making the lens much less susceptible to cracking from rapid expansion when used close to a light source. This principle of lens construction was originated by A. J. Fresnel in the early 19th c. for use in a catadioptric system for increasing the output of lighthouse beacons. Today, basic Fresnel lenses molded from heat-resistant glass are widely used in beam-focusing spotlights. A very closely

Freund, Gisèle. "Eva Peron. General Peron, looking at her with a critical eye, (said) 'Your adversaries will say you look like a chorus girl.'" (ca. 1950). Courtesy Gisèle Freund.

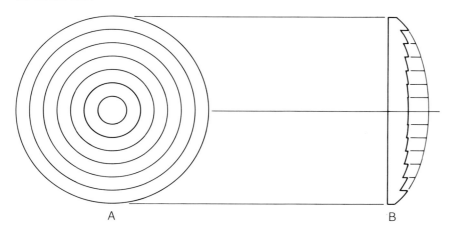

spaced Fresnel pattern embossed in plastic is used as a field lens to produce uniform image brightness in camera viewing systems and self-contained rear projection devices.

See also: CATADIOPTRIC AND CATOPTRIC LENSES; FIELD LENS.

A = Front view
B = Side view and derivation from equivalent plano-convex lens

Freund, Gisèle

French; 1912–

Gisèle Freund's reputation rests largely but not exclusively on her sensitive portraits, some in color, of the greatest literary and artistic figures of this century, among them James Joyce, Samuel Beckett, George Bernard Shaw, H.G. Wells, Virginia and Leonard Woolf, André Malraux, André Gide, Jean Cocteau, Marcel Duchamp, and Henri Matisse. That we have so firm a visual image of the writers and artists who have profoundly shaped our thinking is in some measure due to Freund. But her photoessays on English slums, Buenos Aires, and the revelatory photographs of Evita Peron (1950) evince a high degree of political sensitivity and concern as well.

Born in Berlin-Schöneberg, Germany, Gisele Freund received her first camera

Fresnel Lens

A

B

Friedlander, Lee. "Self portrait" (n.d.). Courtesy Lee Friedlander.

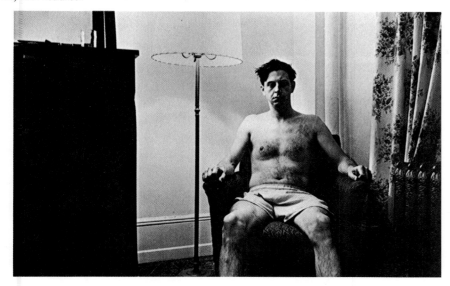

from her father, an art collector, in 1927 at the age of 15. She fled Nazi Germany for Paris in 1933 and enrolled at the Sorbonne, where she received her doctorate for a study of French 19th c. photography. While following her academic interests, Freund established herself as a photographer with her views from Notre Dame (1933) and her first photoessay, published in *Life* (1936).

That same year saw the publication of her dissertation by Adrienne Monnier, the proprietress of La Maison des Amis des Livres bookshop. The two had met in the spring of 1935, beginning a fruitful association that provided Freund access to the literary lights of Paris. Her significant commissions included the dust jacket photographs for Malraux's *Man's Fate* (1935) and Joyce's *Finnegan's Wake* (1939), as well as a color portrait of Joyce for the cover of *Time* (1939).

Although a naturalized French citizen, Freund fled occupied Paris in 1940 and resided for two years at Lot in the French countryside. At the invitation of Victoria Ocampo, editor of the Latin-American literary magazine *Sur,* Freund journeyed to Buenos Aires in 1942. She remained in South America throughout the war, completing assignments in Patagonia, Argentina, and Mexico for American, English, and Latin-American magazines. She also lectured extensively on French literature and arranged to sell at auction the manuscripts of many of her French friends. With the proceeds from these sales, Freund purchased typewriters, ribbons, and food, all of which were shipped back to France after the signing of the armistice.

From 1948 until 1954 Freund was associated with Magnum, the photographers' collaborative set up by Robert Capa. Her portraits of Matisse and Evita Peron date from this period.

Freund's work has been shown in a large number of group and one-person exhibitions. Her first private showing was held at the Peggy Guggenheim Gallery in London (1939) and her New York debut was at the Robert Schoelkopf Gallery (1975). An exhibition of her work was mounted by the Museum of Modern Art in Paris (1968). She was awarded the *photokina* Kulturpreis (1978) and was the first woman to receive the Grand Prix National des Arts (1980). Her numerous publications include the autobiographical *The World in My Camera* (1974), *James Joyce in Paris: His Final Years* (1965), and *Photography and Society* (1980).

Friedlander, Lee

American; 1934–

Lee Friedlander emerged in the early 1960s as a significant photographer of the contemporary American environment. His is a witty, multilayered vision which emphasizes the two-dimensional confines of the picture plane, challenging photography's formal conventions and making familiar objects and people enigmatic through near-surrealist juxtaposition. His images involving reflective and semi-transparent surfaces create playful ambiguities of space and meaning. The awkward, offhanded "snapshot" quality of his work disguises its considerable sophistication.

Friedlander was born in Aberdeen, Washington, and was introduced to photography at age 14. He studied under Edward Kaminski at the Art Center in Los Angeles from 1953 to 1955. He shot portraits of jazz musicians in New York

and New Orleans for album covers in the late 1950s and has made his livelihood as a freelance commercial photographer and as a teacher at UCLA, the University of Minnesota, and Rice University. His work has appeared in *Esquire, Art in America, McCall's, Seventeen, Sports Illustrated,* and other pediodicals.

Friedlander's early work was influenced by Eugene Atget, Walker Evans, and Robert Frank. He was awarded a Guggenheim Fellowship in 1960 and again in 1962 for photographic studies of the changing American scene. His images often featured undramatic views from automobiles and a variety of reflections and images within images. An extensive series of self-portraits is marked by the presence of the photographer's reflection or shadow.

Friedlander was given a one-man show at George Eastman House in Rochester, New York, in 1963. His work was included with that of Garry Winogrand, Duane Michals, Bruce Davidson, and Danny Lyon in the *Toward a Social Landscape* exhibition at George Eastman House is 1966. The following year he exhibited with Winogrand and Diane Arbus in the show *New Documents* at the Museum of Modern Art in New York City.

Friedlander was responsible for the discovery and preservation of the work of E. J. Bellocq in 1968. His prints from Bellocq's glass plates were published as *Storyville Portraits* in 1970. He also collaborated with the artist Jim Dine on a number of projects in the late 1960s. From 1968 to 1971 Friedlander concentrated on a series of party photographs taken with harsh flash. Slides of this work were exhibited at the Museum of Modern Art in 1972. In the same year he was awarded an individual fellowship in photography by the National Endowment for the Arts. During the 1970s Friedlander worked on series of trees, flowers, and bushes, as well as a major project concerning American monuments.

Friedlander photographed the Sculpture Garden of the Hirshhorn Museum in Washington, D. C. in 1975–1976. A major retrospective of his work was held at the Hudson River Museum in Yonkers, New York, in 1978. He received a Friends of Photography award in 1980 and lives and works in New City, New York.

Frith, Francis

English; 1822–1898

A leading topographical and archaeological photographer, and owner of one of

the earliest and largest publishing houses of photographic views, Francis Frith was both successful and influential in the development of photography as a multiple and marketable medium.

At the age of 16 Frith was apprenticed to a cutlery firm in Sheffield, which he abandoned in 1843. After traveling throughout England, Scotland, and Wales, he entered into partnership in a wholesale grocery business in Liverpool. By 1850 he was able to dissolve the enterprise and open an independent printing firm. His serious interest in photography—a medium which must have seemed attractive to a young entrepreneur and printer—dates from the early years of the 1850s. In March 1853 he became one of the founding members of the Liverpool Photographic Society. Although there is little documented work from this period, there are a number of 16″ × 20″ collodion glass plates which are signed and dated 1856 and are of ruined cathedrals and railroad bridges in England. By that year Frith was successful enough to sell his printing business and embark on a photographic expedition to the Middle East.

Following the 19th c. interest in Egypt and Asia Minor, Frith set out to provide accurate topographical records of the Holy Land and the monuments of antiquity. His systematic approach produced work which was remarkable in its clarity, comprehensiveness, and technical finesse. In September of 1856 he sailed for the first time to Egypt. During the following four years Frith was able to make three additional trips, returning periodically to England, where his photographs began to be published and marketed.

Frith employed the wet collodion method, a process that was especially difficult to use in the intense heat, dust, and flies of the Middle East. For a darkroom, Frith constructed a wickerwork, four-wheel carriage with an overhead awning, but occasionally he used the tombs he photographed as improvised darkrooms. Each monument was photographed in three formats: an 8″ × 10″ glass plate negative, a 16″ × 20″ plate, and a stereoscopic negative pair. In many sites more than one exposure in each size was made to reduce the possibility of failure. Frith also often photographed a subject from a distant vantage point, and again from one or more different angles at closer positions. His sets of such views reveal a sensitivity to shadow, form, and surface, and permit the viewer to imaginatively reconstruct the site.

From the spring of 1857 lantern slides produced from stereoscopic views sent back by Frith and published by Negretti and Zambra met with the acclaim of the press and the public. Frith himself returned in July of the same year to arrange publication of a selection of prints from the larger plates.

In November 1857 he returned to Cairo and went on to photograph the Holy Land, Lebanon, and Syria. Before Frith's return to England, James S. Vertue began to issue by subscription a 25-part publication entitled *Egypt and Palestine Photographed and Described by Francis Frith* (January 1858 to spring 1860), including 76 albumen print views. The project was extremely successful and ran to an edition of 2000. Frith returned to England in May 1858, but the resounding success of his enterprises encouraged him to revisit Egypt in the summer of 1859. On this occasion he penetrated further along the Nile than any previous photographer, recording the Temple of Soleb, 1300 miles (2097 kilometers) from Cairo. Nine publications eventually resulted from the combined voyages, among them *Cairo, Sinai, Jerusalem, and the Pyramids of Egypt* (1860) published by Vertue and including 60 albumen prints with an accompanying text by the Egyptologists Mrs. Sophia Poole and her son Reginald Stuart Poole.

From these successes Frith was able to establish the photographic printing and publishing firm F. Frith & Co. at Reigate, Surrey. The largest of such firms in England, it specialized in photographic views and postcards of landscapes and architecture.

After 1861 Frith began to develop the business interests of the firm. Photographers were hired to provide views of Europe, America, and Great Britain. Frith's own photographic travels turned to Europe, where a trip along the Rhine yielded illustrations for Longfellow's *Hyperion*. In addition to hired and contract work, Frith & Co. published the work of the other photographers, notably that of Roger Fenton, the company having purchased the negatives after Fenton's retirement in 1862.

After Frith's death at his winter home in Cannes, the firm continued in business until its liquidation in 1968.

Frontlighting

Frontlighting is illumination that strikes the subject on the side facing the camera. Outdoors it is obtained when the sun is behind the camera position. The same effect is achieved indoors by placing the main light source as close to the camera position as possible, or by using an electronic flash unit mounted on the camera and pointed at the subject.

Frontlight aimed directly along the lens-subject axis is even but flat, producing little modeling of subject features. In most cases the result is unpleasant, and it can be harsh, especially if the light is not diffused. Better results are obtained when the frontlight comes from an angle somewhat to one side and above the lens axis so that shadows are produced which add dimension to the subject. The classic frontlight position is 45 degrees to one side and 45 degrees above the lens axis—so-called architectural lighting. The

depth of the shadows produced depends on the angle of the light and its degree of diffusion; undiffused light produces the darkest, sharpest shadows. Weaker fill light is often added from an opposing direction to "soften" the shadows.
See also: FILL LIGHT.

Front Projection

Front projection is a highly efficient and versatile method of combining projected backgrounds with three-dimensional objects and live subjects in the foreground. It is superior to rear projection because it does not require extra projection space behind the screen; it produces a much brighter and more evenly illuminated image without a hot spot on the projection axis; and it permits much greater freedom in foreground lighting and subject movement.

Projection is accomplished by means of a right-angle beam splitter in front of the camera. The image from a slide projector is reflected to the background screen exactly along the axis of the camera lens, which views the scene through the beam splitter. Although foreground objects block the image from

some parts of the screen, this is not visible in the camera because of the shared optical axis of the system. The size of each object exactly blocks its shadow on the screen, no matter where it is located within the field of view. The screen has a special lenticular surface that reflects light directly back toward its source within an angle of no more than 4 degrees. This provides a background image more than 800 times brighter than the image reflected from an ordinary matte-surface, white screen. The highly directional reflection characteristics also permit lighting the subject fully to wash out traces of the projected image and match the background brightness. As long as the frontal light sources are about 10 degrees or more off the lens-subject axis, light spilling onto the screen is not reflected toward the lens and thus does not affect the background brightness or color. If the projection system is mounted on a common platform with the camera, the setup can easily be moved to a variety of viewpoints without the need for realignment or extensive lighting adjustments.
See also: BEAM SPLITTER; LENTICULAR SYSTEMS; REAR PROJECTION.

Front Projection

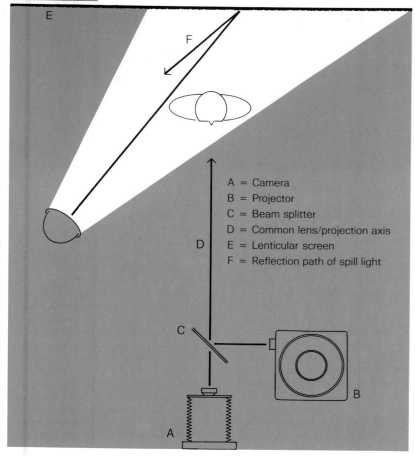

A = Camera
B = Projector
C = Beam splitter
D = Common lens/projection axis
E = Lenticular screen
F = Reflection path of spill light

FSA
See: FARM SECURITY ADMINISTRATION.

f/64, Group

From 1932 to 1935 a small number of California photographers composed an informal organization they called Group f/64. The members included Edward Weston, Ansel Adams, Willard Van Dyke, Imogen Cunningham, Sonya Noskowiak, Henry P. Swift, and John Paul Edwards. The photographers shared a common approach to the medium, perhaps at that time best exemplified in Weston's work: realistic presentation of the subject based on pre-visualization of the final image and arrived at by "straight" (i.e., unmanipulated) technique. This put them in direct opposition to the organized Pictorialism of the period, and their work was bitterly attacked by the leading West Coast pictorialist, William Mortensen.

The first exhibition of Group f/64 was at the de Young Museum in San Francisco in November 1932. It included work by four non-members as well: Consuela Kanaga, Alma Lavenson, Preston Holder, and Brett Weston. Subsequent group shows were held at the Ansel Adams Gallery and the Willard Van Dyke Gallery in San Francisco. Hardly an organization in any meaningful sense—there were no officers, no meetings, no dues—the expressive style championed by the group became the dominant mode of intense realism in American photography often referred to as the West Coast School.
See also: ADAMS, ANSEL; CUNNINGHAM, IMOGEN; PICTORIAL PHOTOGRAPHY; PREVISUALIZATION; WESTON, EDWARD.

Fuhrmann, Ernst

German; 1886–1956
The masterworks of Ernst Fuhrmann comprise some of the most precisely detailed and fascinatingly beautiful studies of plants ever recorded. The pervasive theme of these photographs is the essential likeness of plant and animal. They are a visual illustration of the way he saw the world: as a unit, a series of stages within which, at any given stage, each creature belonging to a higher order embodies all of its previous stages. This series of stages presents itself in two ways: on the one hand as a development over a period of millions of years, and on the other as the present state of all revelations and changes in organic life in the endless cycle of concentration, decomposition, and new concentration. He expressed his attitude: "Scent and color

Fuhrmann, Ernst. Untitled (n.d.). Courtesy
Manfred Heiting Collection, Frankfurt-am-
Main.

are without doubt the beautiful thing about a plant; but the essential point, the interesting and biologically important point, is the structure, and just as the external beauty is kept separate from the color and scent, so too photography keeps this structure separate and thus allows the observer to concentrate his attentions on the essence of the plant."

According to statements from his family and friends, Fuhrmann purposely obscured many details of his life and career in the belief that his pictures alone should speak, that the person of the photographer had no relevance to what they conveyed. Nevertheless, an outline of his career can be reconstructed with some accuracy. He was born in Hamburg in 1886. As a commercial apprentice he was employed partly in his father's business, and partly in the overseas branch of a Hamburg firm until 1914. During this period he published several volumes of poetry, and he decided to follow that vocation. However, a major change apparently occurred when he was called to Hagen by Karl Ernst Osthaus at the Folkwang Museum in 1920. Whether Fuhrmann had begun photographing with serious intent before this is unclear, but in any case photography became a major activity at this time. When the museum was bought by the town of Essen from the Osthaus estate, Furhmann took over the associated publishing operation on his own account and renamed it Folkwang Auriga Publishers. Most of his photographic work was produced between 1929 and 1938. His best known book, *The Plant as a Living Creature*, was published in 1930. It is uncertain whether all of the photographs in the book, credited to the "Folkwang Auriga archives," were taken by him, for Fuhrmann described the work as a joint effort, while claiming for himself authorship of the book.

A restless series of shifts of location occurred in the mid-1930s for which only inaccurate details have been passed on. Fuhrmann emigrated to the U.S. in 1938, and died in New York in 1956.

Funke, Jaromír

Czechoslovak; 1896–1945

As the only son of a well-established lawyer, Jaromír Funke was supposed to pursue the career of his father; he became instead a leader of the modernist movement in Czech photography. Interested in photography from his teens, Funke contributed to the growth of European modern photography during the highly productive period of the 1920s and 1930s. His activity ranged from photographic practice to critical and theoretical writing, to organizing and teaching. He was a founding member of the Photo-Club of Prague in 1923. A year later he, Josef Sudek, Adolf Schneeberger, and several other photographers founded the Czech Photographic Society. In the 1920s Funke collaborated with members of the Czech avant-garde artistic group *Devetsil* and published his work in its magazines and anthologies. In 1931 he became a teacher of photography at the School of Applied Arts in Bratislava, and from 1935 he taught at the State School of Graphic Arts in Prague. He was a member of the Czech film and photo league called the "Film and Photo Group of the Left Front," and one of the founding members of the photographic section of the Mánes Arts Society. Funke published numerous articles that rank among the most important contributions to Czech photographic theory and criticism.

Funke's work recapitulates the development of European photography during its formative years. Starting as an amateur photographer, he shifted from soft-focus Pictorialism to modernist ideals and strategies. At the very beginning of the 1920s he was influenced by two Czech photographers, František Drtikol and Drahomír Josef Ružička. However, at the same time he developed a new approach based on the modernist belief in objectivity and authenticity. In 1923 he made several semi-abstract

Funke, Jaromir. Untitled (ca. 1927). San Francisco Museum of Modern Art, Mrs. Ferdinand C. Smith Fund Purchase.

works anticipating the Neue Sachlichkeit trend.

Funke's light abstractions of the second half of the 1920s parallel similar efforts of László Moholy-Nagy and Francis Bruguiere. In the late 1920s he introduced real objects into his abstract works, thereby approaching assemblage and surrealism. Funke was among the first photographers to be inspired by Atget's work and the surrealist movement. However, his teaching was based on the ideas of functionalism, as expressed in the guidelines for his courses at the Bratislava School of Applied Arts: "We photograph structures, we discover a photogeny of objects, we combine objects in space. Documentary, Advertising and Portrait Photography. The purity of the photographic expression is a matter of principle."

During the years of the Great Depression Funke made a series of documentary photographs devoted to bad housing conditions. Thus, he came to terms with three main movements in art and photography of the 1930s: surrealism, functionalism, and documentary social criticism. He tried to integrate them, and so to create a universally valid model of modern photography. Summing up his concept of modern photography labeled by the term "emotional photography," Funke wrote in 1940: ". . . emotional photography combines together former experience—the composition comes from Pictorialism, the imagination from abstract photography, the structure from Neue Sachlichkeit, the life from reportage photography. These trends supplement, combine and mix with each other. Sometimes one is not able to recognize a particular trend. However, what always matters is: a clear and precise program, and the work."

Funke died in Czechoslovakia in 1945. *See also:* NEUE SACHLICHKEIT.

Garnett, William. "Sand dune #1, Death Valley, California" (1954). Courtesy William Garnett © 1954.

Gabor, Dennis

English; 1900–1979

A physicist, Gabor's accomplishments include major improvements in optical systems for astronomical and microscopical use, and in the design and use of the electron microscope. His work to improve the resolving power of the electron microscope produced the theoretical basis for recording interference images by the technique now known as holography. Although proposed in 1947, the first holograms were not made until 1960, when the required source of coherent light—the laser—was invented.

See also: HOLOGRAPHY; INTERFERENCE; LASER.

Galleries, Photograph

Independent galleries devoted to the exhibition and sale of photographs, and galleries associated with institutions such as museums and art institutes, are a 20th-c. development, although there were certain predecessors in the 19th c. In the 1840s, many major daguerreotype portrait studios included a gallery. This was the only way work could be seen by the public, for each daguerreotype was a unique image and could be duplicated only by rephotographing it, a technically difficult task. The novelty of photography attracted significant numbers of visitors and, as the studio proprietors intended, some would decide to have

portraits made, others to buy copies of the pictures of notables on display. There is no question that these galleries were maintained for their direct commercial value in attracting customers, and their indirect value in building the prestige of the photographer. It was common for studio operators to offer celebrities free sittings in return for being allowed to take additional daguerreotypes which could be exhibited and sold. The galleries Mathew Brady established with his studios in New York and Washington City (D.C.), were particularly successful, largely because of the great number of public figures Brady managed to attract for sittings, but Jeremiah Gurney in New York, Marcus Root in Philadelphia, Southworth and Hawes in Boston, Richard Beard and A. F. J. Claudet in London, and photographers in every major city had similar galleries.

When, after 1850, the collodion wet plate established the paper print as the major kind of photographic image, sales of photographs of other subjects, as well as portraits, increased enormously. In addition to studio galleries, prints were sold by stationers, booksellers, and print dealers. For example, the pictures of Julia Margaret Cameron were handled by the London print sellers P. & D. Colnaghi, who had opened a photographic print department in 1857, while Thomas Agnew of Manchester represented Roger Fenton's views of England and his still-lifes. Most major photog-

raphers had an arrangement with some such establishment to act as sales agents for their prints and stereographs; many were in partnership with a dealer. New pictures were displayed in the shop window or in exhibition space within the store. At the peak of the carte-de-visite fad, in the 1860s, print dealers and shops devoted exclusively to these small card images stocked literally thousands of pictures, arranged by subject category in table-top bins, much as record albums are offered today. Stereographs were similarly presented from the 1870s on.

None of these various commercial establishments was a gallery in the modern sense. The independent gallery—one not connected with a photographer's studio or some other business—emerged from a marriage of the salon exhibition attitude (which developed in the late 19th c.) with the practices of dealers in paintings; it was part of the movement to secure recognition of photography as a fine art. The first, and most famous, such gallery was the Little Galleries of the Photo-Secession, established by Alfred Stieglitz in 1905. Called "291" from 1908 on, this was the gallery of an idealist: photographs were shown only on the basis of their artistic worth; the idea of selling was not even secondary (Stieglitz's attitude, expressed about one of his later galleries, originated here: "Yes, you can buy pictures here, but we do not sell them. There is a difference."). Almost all proceeds from the meager sales went to the artists (making the gallery unique in the 20th c.); expenses were met primarily by private contributions. From 1907 drawings and etchings—and later paintings and sculpture—were also shown, but they were included for artistic reasons, not for the commercial necessity that has motivated most other galleries to follow suit. At Stieglitz's later galleries—The Intimate Gallery (1925–1929), and An American Place (1929–1946) — photographs were exhibited only a small portion of the time.

The first art dealer who attempted to find a market in photographs was Julien Levy, perhaps best known for his representation of surrealist painters. In 1931, the Levy Gallery was inaugurated in New York with a retrospective of American photography. Shows of the work of Berenice Abbott, Eugène Atget, Henri Cartier-Bresson, Walker Evans, George Platt Lynes, Man Ray, Moholy-Nagy, Nadar, and Paul Outerbridge followed. Although the gallery continued to exist until 1949, by 1933 Levy had recognized there was insufficient support, financial or otherwise, to continue dealing only in photographs, and so the range was broadened. In the 1930s and 1940s, a few other individuals attempted to establish galleries for photography in other cities in the U.S. and Europe—for example, Willard Van Dyke and Ansel Adams, in San Francisco—but their success was slight; none was self-sustaining.

After World War II, a number of art galleries began to show photographs occasionally, but there was too little interest and too few buyers to make a reasonable profit for a dealer. The exhibition and sale of photographs was always subsidized by a bookstore, photographic workshop, artists' cooperative, or by the sale of paintings and graphic arts prints. The major pioneering effort was made by Helen Gee, who established and directed the Limelight gallery in New York from 1954 to 1961. Her adjoining coffeehouse supported the gallery financially and provided a congenial atmosphere for the photographic community. The 60 shows Gee mounted at the Limelight included the works of such photographers as Ansel Adams, Eugène Atget, Bill Brandt, Harry Callahan, Paul Caponigro, Robert Frank, Lisette Model, Moholy-Nagy, Aaron Siskind, W. Eugene Smith, Paul Strand, Minor White, and Edward Weston. Encouraged by her example, a few others pioneered as well, making a significant artistic contribution but seldom a profit. Roy DeCarava's gallery, A Photographer's Place (1955–1957), and Norbert Kleeber's Underground Gallery, both in New York, and Carl Siembab's gallery in Boston led the way for what was to take place a decade later.

The late 1960s and early 1970s saw a great expansion in the art market in general, and the first major development of interest in collecting photographs for both artistic and investment motives. A few galleries established at the beginning of this period were able, for the first time, to deal exclusively in photographs and to experience the kind of market and prices that only painting and graphics had previously commanded. The Witkin Gallery, opened in New York by Lee Witkin in 1969, showed photographs from all eras. The Light Gallery, established in New York in 1971 by Tennyson Schad, with Harold Jones as director, showed contemporary photographers. In Washington, D.C., Harry Lunn founded a gallery in 1968 for graphic prints and a parallel publishing and investment company, Graphics International. Photographs, and in particular limited-edition portfolios by leading photographers, proved very profitable for Lunn and the others, who worked carefully to establish a market and build photographers' reputations. When their galleries were founded, prints by Ansel Adams were selling for $50, those by Imogen Cunningham for $15 and $25, and work by Harry Callahan for $100–$150. By 1980 the average prices for vintage prints by these photographers at auction were: Adams, $5000; Cunningham, $500; Callahan, $800. The work of other photographers increased in value as well—not so spectacularly as these examples in most cases, but sufficiently to encourage the opening of galleries throughout the U.S. and in major European cities during the 1970s. Like independent art galleries, these were commercial establishments, devoted to promoting the art of photography because that increased the value of what they were selling. A tightening world economic situation in the early 1980s produced a shaking-out, and many marginal photographic galleries closed, broadened their range, or merged with established painting and print galleries. However, the photograph gallery had established itself as a significant and continuing presence in the world art market.

Non-commercial photograph galleries associated with museums and other institutions were established only very slowly in the 20th c., most after 1950. Stieglitz had succeeded in getting a few institutions to accept photographs for their print collections in earlier decades: the Boston Museum of Fine Arts, the Chicago Art Institute, and—eventually—the Metropolitan Museum of Art in New York. Museum and institutional collections are discussed in a separate entry.

See also: COLLECTING PHOTOGRAPHICA; EXHIBITIONS; MUSEUMS AND COLLECTIONS; PICTURE LIBRARIES AND AGENCIES; 291.

Gallic Acid; Gallo-Nitrate of Silver

Gallic acid was the first developing agent and gallo-nitrate of silver the first developer solution used in photography. Although development of daguerreotype images by mercury fumes preceded use of these solutions in the first negative-positive process, the action was chemically very different and was unique to the daguerreotype. Gallic acid—a vegetable compound like tannic and related acids—was obtained by infusion (soaking in hot water) of gall nuts. Its photographic use was discovered in March or April 1839 by Rev. J. B. Reade, who brushed it over paper sensitized with silver chloride to speed the production of a negative image from light projected by a solar microscope. Reade did not recognize that development was taking place, but regarded the gallic acid as an accelerator. He described its action to W. H. F. Talbot, who then used gallic acid and silver-nitrate solutions to increase the sensitivity of silver-iodide paper prepared for exposure in the camera obscura. Talbot soon discovered that he could combine the two solutions into one, which he called gallo-nitrate of silver. He discovered the development action of this solution in September 1840 when he used it to treat paper that had been exposed in the camera but had produced no visible image by the printing-out action he relied on. Instead of increasing the sensitivity of the paper, the solution brought out a visible image of the previous exposure. Talbot correctly analyzed the overall process as the production of a latent image by exposure, followed by chemical action to produce—develop—a corresponding visual image. He included the use of gallo-nitrate of silver as a pre-exposure sensitizer and as a post-exposure developer in his calotype patent of 1841.
See also: CALOTYPE; DEVELOPING AGENT; SOLAR MICROSCOPE; TALBOT, WILLIAM HENRY FOX.

Gamma

A measurement of contrast, gamma is derived from the straight-line portion of the characteristic curve of a processed emulsion. The procedure was originated by Hurter and Driffield in their pioneering work in sensitometry. Gamma is the

Gardner, Alexander and James. "President Lincoln on Battlefield of Antietam" (1862); albumen. National Archives.

slope (degree of rise or slant) of the straight-line portion of the curve; this is the same as the tangent of the acute angle formed when the straight line is projected to the base line (log of exposure axis) of the graph. It can be determined by dividing the *run* (difference in log exposure values) of two points on the straight line into the *rise* (difference in densities) of the same two points. Gamma is a useful indication of contrast when no subject values fall on the toe or shoulder of the characteristic curve. This is the case with duplicating and x-ray films, and film for aerial photography, which must be exposed and processed to overcome the shadow-erasing effects of atmospheric haze and flare. In most ordinary photography important dark values lie on the toe of the curve. These are ignored by gamma, but are taken into account by the average-gradient and contrast-index methods of measuring contrast.

See also: AVERAGE GRADIENT; CHARACTERISTIC CURVE; CONTRAST; CONTRAST INDEX.

Gardner, Alexander

American; 1821–1882

The classic two-volume *Gardner's Photographic Sketchbook of the War* contains 100 hand-mounted original photographs of many of the most graphic and memorable Civil War images that have come down to us. Like the Brady photographic documentation which engendered Gardner's, uninvolved civilians could now be brought to see the face of war, the look of battlefields littered with dead, the destruction of cities. The camera could now authenticate events. Gardner observed in the *Sketchbook* that "photographic representation of them [the sites of war] will be accepted by posterity with an undoubting faith."

Gardner was born in Paisley, Scotland, of middle-class parents. At the age of 14 he was apprenticed to a jeweler, for whom he worked for seven or eight years. His interests, however, were in literature, science, and social welfare. After moving to Glasgow, he worked as a reporter for the *Sentinel*, one of Scotland's largest newspapers, eventually rising to the position of editor. He spent evenings studying astronomy, optics, and experimental chemistry. He dreamed of founding a utopian community in the U.S. and wrote pamphlets on the subject; in 1856 he sailed to New York where he had accepted a job working for Matthew Brady's gallery. Two years later, he was appointed manager of Brady's Washington branch. Gardner's

obituarist claimed that Gardner had been the one to introduce "imperials"—life-sized photographs, often hand tinted—into this country.

From 1861 to 1862, Gardner headed the group of photographers that Brady organized to accompany the Union armies and make a photographic record of the American Civil War. Then he abruptly left Brady's employ, apparently in a dispute over copyright, inasmuch as Brady published most of the work of his photographers under the Brady name. Gardner took his glass plate negatives with him (perhaps in lieu of back pay), and was joined by his son James and some of Brady's best photographers who continued to photograph under him. Gardner established a Washington studio around the corner from Brady's. He was named an official photographer for the Army of the Potomac, and seems also to have been associated with the Secret Service.

The *Sketchbook* was published in 1866 with text and prints by Gardner. The photographs were individually credited to various photographers, including 45 by Timothy O'Sullivan and 16 by Gardner and by his son. Like Brady, Gardner was not successful in marketing photographs of the war. The *Sketchbook* appeared at a time when the public was anxious to forget the conflict and not even Congress was interested in purchasing his collection.

Gardner's work included not only battlefield scenes and ruins, but many portraits of Lincoln, prison studies of

Lincoln's assassination conspirators, their subsequent hanging, Lincoln's funeral, and portraits of President Johnson and other figures of the Reconstruction. In 1867, Gardner became an official photographer for the Union Pacific Railroad, and documented the landscape and life along the Chisolm Trail running from Kansas to Texas and California. He also photographed the Indians of the Great Plains, the Indian delegates to Congress, and a rogue's gallery for the Washington, D.C., Police in 1873.

Upon his return to Washington, Gardner contracted tuberculosis, a condition perhaps aggravated by his diminishing circumstances. He died in 1882.

Garnett, William A.

American; 1916–

William Garnett has created complex and striking aerial images of the earth's surface, in black-and-white and color, for over three decades. His series of aerial photographs of the United States from Death Valley to the Berkshires, which transform the landscape into abstract patterns of color and texture, was the largest project by a single photographer ever published in *Life*. Garnett has made an art of aerial survey photography.

Garnett was born in Chicago, Illinois. He studied photography at John Muir High School in Pasadena, California, and attended the Art Center School in Los Angeles. In the late 1930s he worked as an architectural photographer. From

1940 to 1944 he was head of photographic and physical evidence laboratories for the Pasadena Police Department and in 1944–1945 served as a Signal Corps motion picture cameraman. His first transcontinental flight, at the war's end, inspired him to begin aerial photography.

Garnett's first aerial photographs were made for commercial clients. He quickly began to develop as an artist in his field, learning to fly his own plane in order to gain full control over his images.From 1945 to 1958 he worked as an advertising and freelance photographer in southern California.

Garnett's aerial photos appeared regularly in *Fortune* from 1954 to 1964 as well as in numerous other journals. His work was included in the *Family of Man, Diogenes IV,* and *100 Master Photographers* exhibitions at the Museum of Modern Art, New York. He was given the first one-man show of aerial photography at George Eastman House, Rochester, N.Y., in 1955 and exhibited at the Brussels World's Fair in 1958. He was awarded Guggenheim Fellowships in 1953, 1956, and 1975. He was a Fellow in Advanced Visual Studies at Massachusetts Institute of Technology in 1967 and has taught photography as a Professor of Design at the College of Environmental Design, University of California at Berkeley, since 1968. In recent years he has contributed to the revitalized *Life,* including photo-essays on volcanoes and earthquakes.

Photograph: p. 218.

Gaslight Paper

Gaslight paper was a contact-printing, developing-out paper with a gelatin–silver chloride emulsion that was slow enough to permit handling under weak artificial light—from gas fixtures—but sensitive enough to be exposed by stronger artificial light. It freed the photographer from having to use sunlight for printing-out exposures—the common practice—and from the difficulties of obtaining a properly ventilated gas safe-light, required with the equally new and more sensitive bromide papers. It was only necessary to keep the ordinary gas jet turned low during set-up, turn it up to full intensity for exposure, and turn it down again during processing. This convenience first made the paper a favorite among amateurs, but it subsequently came into wide professional use as well. The first such emulsion was invented in 1881 by J. M. Eder and G. Pizzighelli, and a paper was manufactured the following year in Vienna by E. Just. The success of gaslight paper really began

with the paper produced in London by Leon Warnerke in 1889 and especially with the introduction of Velox paper in 1893 by the Nepera Chemical Co. of Yonkers, New York.

Gauss, Karl Friederich

German; 1777–1855

As a mathematician, physicist, and astronomer, K.F. Gauss was of such range and stature as had been equaled only by Archimedes and Newton before him. His mathematical work revolutionized higher arithmetic and the theory of numbers, and introduced theories and areas of investigation (e.g., topology) that began to be actively explored only in the 20th c. His unpublished papers revealed his early discovery of principles and systems for which others were credited and upon which they built major reputations in the 19th c. His theoretical work in astronomy led in 1801 to a precise prediction of the time and location that the recently discovered but subsequently lost (from view) asteroid Ceres would reappear. From this he in turn produced major refinements in the theory of celestial motion.

Gauss's concern with the practical applications of science and with the precision of associated instruments resulted in a new understanding of how light is refracted by lenses, and in a new configuration for symmetrical lenses that designers utilized into the 20th c. Gaussian lenses have included some of the best known in photography. This work also produced a system of mathematical and geometrical procedures for determining focal length, image and object distances, image size, magnification, and similar factors, enabling lens designers to work with pencil and paper rather than having to shape pieces of glass in a basically trial-and-error way. A feature of this system is the definition of the *nodal points* (Gauss, or principal points) of a lens and the associated principal planes from which most first-order optical measurements are made.

Gauss's study of electromagnetism produced new information on the wave nature of light; it also produced a practical electrical telegraph—put into limited use—some years before Samuel F. B. Morse perfected his system. The Gauss methods of analysis in geodesy (measurement and mapping of earth areas large enough for surface curvature to be a significant factor) brought precision to what had been a rule-of-thumb branch of surveying. These same methods provide the basis for accuracy in very high altitude aerial photography of the earth, and in surveying and map-

ping of the earth and planets from satellites and space vehicles.

See also: LENSES; OPTICS.

Gelatin

A complex protein substance, gelatin is prepared (by chemical neutralization, shredding, and boiling in distilled water) from tissues found in animal horns, hoofs, bones, tendons, sinew, cartilage, and organ linings. Its two major uses are as a foodstuff and as the binding medium in photographic emulsions, although it has many additional scientific and industrial uses. Photographic gelatin is chemically much purer and physically more highly refined than the food-quality product. It is carefully and extensively blended so that differences arising from widely varying sources of supply are intermixed and distributed to produce a uniform substance with qualities that are uniquely suitable for photographic use.

Gelatin is transparent and colorless, so it does not physically interfere with exposure or image formation. In addition it can absorb the halogen ions liberated during exposure, insuring that a latent image can form. In a liquid state it can be applied in a smooth, uniform coating as thin as a human hair or many times thicker, in one or more layers. Although not physically strong, it is flexible and adheres readily to a great number of supports (e.g., glass, plastic, paper, metal) that can provide the requisite strength. Gelatin holds crystals such as silver halides and particles such as the silver grains or dye compounds that constitute an image, in a colloidal suspension that is uniformly (although randomly) distributed before processing, and that does not permit displacement during or after processing. It absorbs cool water readily and swells without dissolving (it does not dissolve in hot water); it readily gives up water as it dries and shrinks to its original size and shape. This makes it easy to process the colloidally suspended material by chemical action with water-based solutions, and subsequently to wash chemicals out of the emulsion. It can be hardened (made insoluble) by chemical action related to exposure or to development of an image—this is the basis of most bichromate, transfer, and relief processes in photography. And it can be treated with a mordant to fix absorbed dyes in place, as in the dye transfer process. A major disadvantage of gelatin is its susceptibility to physical damage (abrasion, scratching) and the ease with which foreign particles (dust, dirt) can become embedded in it when wet. If

Genre Photography. Peter Henry Emerson,
"Taking up the Eel Net" (1886); platinum.
Copyright © Sotheby Parke Bernet Inc. 1983.

subjected to a sudden temperature change while wet and swollen, it can develop a permanent pattern of irregularities known as *reticulation*. When dry, it becomes brittle at very cold temperatures and will melt at high temperatures.

The first photographic emulsion using gelatin was described in 1871 by Richard Leach Maddox, and manufacture of gelatin-coated materials began a few years later. However, the first major advance—the gelatin dry plate for negatives—did not become established until after 1875, and gelatin-coated papers came into use only in the 1880s.
See also: EMULSION; MADDOX, RICHARD LEACH; RETICULATION.

Genre Photography

Genre photography derives from the French and English genre painting of the 18th and 19th centuries. In the work of such 18th c. painters as Jean-Baptiste Greuze, Jean-Baptiste-Siméon Chardin, Joseph Wright, and George Stubbs, we can see the qualities that would later characterize genre photography: concentration upon tableaux of everyday, middle-class or working-class life; the idealization of hearth and home; childhood, married love, rural life.

Given the popularity of genre painting and prints in the 1840s–1870s, it is not surprising that photographers speedily fell to arranging genre tableaux to vie with work in other mediums. Not only were such photographs popular in their own right; they also proved to their makers and to critics that photography could compete as an art against far more established mediums.

Oscar G. Rejlander (1813–1875) and Henry Peach Robinson (1830–1901) were England's chief practitioners of genre photography, as well as its theoreticians. Rejlander's "The Carpenter and his Family" (1860), for example, depicts an out-of-work carpenter seated despondently beside his sleeping wife and child. Robinson's "Fading Away" (1858), made from five separate negatives, illustrates the consumptive death of a young girl as her family looks on helplessly. Though less cheerful than the vast number of bucolic idylls genre photographers created, both these images share with the rest of their kind the sentimental values of the period.

Genre photographs were made throughout the second half of the 19th c. in Germany, Austria, France, and America. They became a cliché of Pictorialist salons. Even much of Alfred Stieglitz's

very early work could be termed genre, if only because of its emphasis upon the positive aspects of everyday peasant life. Stieglitz's "A Good Joke" (1887) and "The Net Mender" (1894), for example, are premised on the same idealization of working folk that animates the genre scenes of Robinson or Nègre. The same could be said for as varied a group of early 20th-c. Pictorialists as Gertrude Käsebier, Guido Rey, and Clarence White, and, three decades later, William Mortensen.

Genre photography fell out of favor as photographers moved toward exploring their medium's formal properties in the 1910s and 1920s. Recently, surrealistically inflected genre scenes have made an appearance in the works of a number of photographers, for example, Eileen Cowin and Sandy Skoglund. In this post-modernist work, the conventions of earlier genre photographs and paintings are deliberately parodied or inverted to ironic effect.
See also: PICTORIAL PHOTOGRAPHY; SALON PHOTOGRAPHY; SATIRE IN PHOTOGRAPHY.

Genthe, Arnold

American; 1869–1942

Arnold Genthe was active as a photographer for nearly 50 years. His fame rests mainly on his images of turn-of-the-century San Francisco Chinatown and the aftermath of the San Francisco earthquake of 1906. He was a pioneer in dance photography, capturing Pavlova and Isadora Duncan. In later life, he became an acclaimed portrait photographer of celebrities and political figures in Hollywood and on the East coast.

Born in Berlin, Germany, Genthe studied philology and linguistics at the University of Berlin, received a doctorate in philology from the University of Jena in 1894, and did further study at the Sorbonne, Paris.

Genthe came to the United States as a tutor in 1895 and began to photograph as a self-taught hobbyist the following year. He opened a portrait studio in 1897

in San Francisco, where he worked until 1911. He was awarded a *Camera Craft* gold medal in 1901. At the Chicago Society of Amateur Photographers he was called "the king of portrait work on the coast." Of his portrait work Genthe wrote: "I was determined to show people a new kind of photography: there would be no stilted poses; as a matter of fact, no poses at all. I would try to take my sitters unawares, at a moment when they would not realize that the camera was ready. I would show them prints in which a uniform sharpness would be avoided and emphasis laid on portraying a person's character instead of making a commonplace record of clothes and a photographic mask."

From 1896 to 1906, Genthe, a lover of the Orient and Oriental art, used a concealed camera to photograph unobserved the street life and traditions of San Francisco's anonymous Chinese merchants,

opium addicts, children, and other residents. These photographs, which escaped the destruction, in 1906, of Genthe's studio, library, photographic equipment, and collection of Chinese porcelain in the earthquake and fire are now in the archives of the Library of Congress. Using a borrowed camera, Genthe documented the disaster's devastation and survivors.

In 1907–1908, Genthe traveled in Germany, Japan, and South America, shooting Rhineland landscapes, Kyoto architecture, and nudes. His experiments with autochromes were among the first to appear in American magazines. He exhibited in the *International Exhibition of Pictorial Photography* at Buffalo, N.Y., organized by Alfred Stieglitz, who acquired a number of Genthe prints soon afterward.

Genthe moved to New York City in 1911. Working in a soft-focus, romantic

Fashion Photography. Rebecca Blake,
"Celebration at New Year's" (1983).
© Rebecca Blake.

Fisheye Lenses. Photographer unknown,
"The Library of Congress, Washington, D.C."
Library of Congress

Geological Photography. Dane A. Penland,
"Malachite" (1978). Smithsonian Institution.

Glamour. Skrebneski, Untitled (1983).
© Skrebneski; courtesy *Town and Country Magazine*.

Glass, Photographing. Dane A. Penland, "Glass sculpture" (1981). Smithsonian Institution.

Gum Bichromate Process. Harry B. Shaw, "Ann Katrina" (n.d.); gum bichromate. Smithsonian Institution.

Gum Bichromate Process. Daniel Kazimierski, Untitled (1979); four-color gum print. Courtesy Daniel Kazimierski.

Haas, Ernst. "Norway Fjord" (1959). Courtesy
Ernst Haas.

Hamaya, Hiroshi. "Landscape" (n.d.). Courtesy Hiroshi Hamaya.

Hanfstaengl, Franz. Unidentified portrait
(n.d.); albumen. Courtesy Manfred Heiting,
Frankfurt-am-Main.

High Speed Photography. Nobu Arakawa,
"Bursting water balloon at 1/4000 second"
(1983). © Nobu Arakawa.

style, he became a popular photographer of political figures and celebrities.

Genthe became an American citizen in 1918. He wrote an autobiography, *As I Remember,* which was published in 1936. He died in Connecticut in 1942. A retrospective exhibition of his work was presented at the International Center of Photography in 1984.

Geological Photography

Geology is an extremely broad science devoted to investigation of the earth's structure: its composition, its configurations and the dynamics of change, and its formation and nature in the distant history of the planet. There are more than a dozen distinct areas of special investigation within geology, and many more that are combined with such disciplines as biology, geography, hydrogaphy, and astronomy. All of these specialities use photography, some as a major means of investigation, others as one of many tools for making records and performing analysis. There are three major areas of geological photography: aerial survey and satellite photography; field work on the surface and below, as in caves, tunnels, and excavations; and laboratory work. The equipment, materials, and techniques employed cover the entire range of scientific and technical photography. Only some of the major applications can be mentioned.

Both large-area and specific-site aerial photographs are used in geomorphology to study the formation and dynamic changes in land forms. Continental forms are revealed with previously unattainable detail and accuracy by mosaics of satellite photographs. Mountain shapes, fault lines, volcanic activity, the structure of deserts, plains and cliffs, and many other specific subjects are investigated by conventional aerial photography from various altitudes. Economic geology uses aerial photography to help survey and explore for natural resources such as ore and petroleum deposits. Aerial records are used in geological mapping, which superimposes geologic data over topographic maps and views to show the relationship between surface features and life forms and the underlying structure.

Aerial and on-site field photographs are used in structural geology to study the forces that deform rocks, and to record and map deformations and displacements such as upthrusts, faults, and intrusions. Field photography records data on sedimentation, the destruction of rocks by erosive forces, and the formation of new rock beds by deposition of sediment. This work is related to stratigraphy (the area of historical geology that investigates interrelationships between rock layers) and paleontology (which deals with fossil records of ancient life forms). Engineering geology uses photography in investigating the interaction of manmade structures such as buildings, tunnels, and bridges with adjacent rock formations.

Many areas of geology use photography in the field to show the natural situation of specimens of interest, and again in the laboratory to analyze specific samples. Mineralogy and crystallography make wide use of closeups and photomicrographs made by reflected and transmitted ultraviolet, infrared, and polarized illumination as well as ordinary white light. The sample is commonly cut and polished or sliced and ground to a very thin section for such photographs. Photomicrographs are a major tool of micropaleontology, especially in discovering fossils of tiny organisms associated with oil-bearing strata. Similar techniques, and spectrography, are employed in petrology, which studies the composition and origin of rocks; in geochemistry, which investigates the chemical composition and changes brought about by chemical action; and in geophysics, which studies the behavior of geologic materials under various physical stresses. X-ray, fluorescence, and laser photography are also applied in geological analysis. These and many of the specialized procedures mentioned previously are described in separate entries.

Color photograph: p. C-18.

Gernsheim, Helmut Erich Robert

British; 1913–

Both a photographer and a photohistorian, Helmut Gernsheim was born in Munich, Germany. He studied art history at the University of Munich and photography at the Ausburg State School and at Uvachrome Corp. Emigrating to England in 1937, Gernsheim became a British subject in 1946. During World War II he made photographic surveys of architecture for the Warburg Institute, London. In 1942 he married Alison Eames (d. 1969), who played an important collaborative role in his work in the history of photography. Their publications include many classic works, among them *Creative Photography: Aesthetic Trends, 1839–1960,* biographies of L.J.M. Daguerre and Julia Margaret Cameron, and *The History of Photography, from the camera obscura to the beginning of the modern era (1685–1914).* The latter was first issued in 1955 and revised in 1969 and 1982. In 1982 Gernsheim published *The Origins of Photography.*

With Beaumont Newhall and Josef Eder, Gernsheim is one of the most important historians of photography. His own photographs have been widely exhibited and collected in England, Germany, and America. Beginning his own collection of photographs in 1945 at the instigation of Newhall, Gernsheim is credited with rediscovering the world's first photograph, taken in 1826 by Nicéphore Niépce. The Gernsheims donated their collection to the University of Texas at Austin in 1964. The director of Photo-Graphic Editions and a Trustee of the Swiss Foundation for Photography, Gernsheim is an Honorary Fellow of the Club Daguerre, the recipient of the first German Culture Prize for Photography, and of the Gold Medal from the Accademia Italia in 1980. He now resides in Switzerland.

See also: HISTORY OF PHOTOGRAPHY.

Ghosting

Ghosting is a double-image condition that may occur when electronic flash is used as the main light source and the ambient light is fairly bright. The shutter must open fully before the flash unit fires; in the brief instant that the shutter is still open after the flash, strong ambient light may expose a secondary image on the film. The "ghost" image will be fainter than the main exposure and will be visible only if the subject was moving. If the subject were stationary, the two exposures would be in exact register and the ghost or trace image could not be seen; however, it would add slightly to the main exposure.

Ghosting most often occurs when wide *f*-stops or slow shutter speeds are used with flash. It can be avoided by using as small an *f*-stop as the situation allows and the fastest shutter speed that provides flash synchronization.

In some cases ghosting is desired in a picture; it emphasizes the feeling of motion and may soften subject outlines and blur colors in a pleasing way. A dark background will make the ghost image most visible, and a slow shutter speed can be used without significantly affecting the main exposure. A neutral density filter or diffuser in front of the flash will reduce its intensity, permitting use of a larger *f*-stop as well.

See also: SYNCHRONIZATION.

Ghost Photographs

See: PHANTOM VIEW; SPIRIT PHOTOGRAPHY.

Giacomelli, Mario. "Death shall come and it shall have your eyes" (1982). Courtesy Mario Giacomelli.

Giacomelli, Mario

Italian; 1925–

For nearly 30 years, Mario Giacomelli has photographed the landscapes and lives of Italian peasants. Influenced by the poet Leopardi and the painter Giorgio Morandi, Giacomelli (a poet and painter himself) has worked slowly and obsessively, steeping himself in the environments of his subjects, to create images of passionate immediacy. He has printed his photographs on high-contrast paper and emphasized the coarsest grain in order to heighten the harsh yet poetic impact of his documentary images of the old and crippled (in nursing homes and at Lourdes), slaughtered animals, and less disturbing subjects such as seminarians, gypsies, and farmers. Giacomelli's landscapes (the most recent, aerial views) appear as painted or sculpted abstract patches of black and white. His work has focused primarily on Italian subjects, but he has made striking images on trips to Ethiopia and Tibet as well. All his work is held together by a melancholy, sensitive point of view.

Giacomelli was born, educated, and has spent most of his life in Senigallia, an Italian agricultural village on the Adriatic Sea. He learned typography as a boy of 13 and began landscape painting two years later. He served in the Italian Army in 1944 and has operated a typography shop in his native town since that time. Giacomelli began to write poetry in 1948 and has been a photographer since 1954. He studied with Giuseppe Cavalli and has been associated through his teacher with the "la Bussola" and "Misa" photography groups.

Giacomelli's first exhibition of photographs was held at Centro d'Arte in Pescara, Abruzzi, in 1957. The following year he worked briefly on a series of nude studies but soon abandoned staged photography. He has not, however, been averse to the most radical darkroom manipulation of his prints.

Giacomelli has provided photographic illustrations for a story from Edgar Lee Masters' *Spoon River Anthology,* and, for Italian television, has illustrated Leopardi's "To Sylvia." His work has been the subject of a film by M. Gandin and a monograph published by the University of Parma. His work has appeared in *Popular Photography, Camera, Magnum, U.S. Camera Annual, Photographers' Eye,* and other periodicals.

Giacomelli has been honored with one-man shows of his photographs at George Eastman House, Rochester, N.Y., in 1968; the American Academy, Rome, in 1978; Rhode Island School of Design, Providence, in 1980 (a major retrospective); Light Gallery, New York, in 1980; Contrasts/Visions Gallery, London, in 1981; and Photography Gallery, Philadelphia, in 1982. His work has been exhibited in group shows including *Photography in the Twentieth Century* at the National Gallery of Canada, Ottawa; *The Land: Twentieth Century Landscape Photographs Selected by Bill Brandt* at the Victoria and Albert Museum, London; *Contemporary Photography Since 1950* at George Eastman House, Rochester, N.Y.; and *Venice '79.*

Gibson, Ralph

American; 1939–

Ralph Gibson's poetic allegory, *The Somnambulist* (1970), established him as

Gibson, Ralph. Untitled (n.d.). Courtesy
Ralph Gibson.

one his generation's significant photographers. The enigmatic image fragments were ordered according to a sequential logic which required a book format for its full impact, so that the viewer could easily control the pace of response, lingering or moving on quickly to create associative links.

Gibson was born in Los Angeles, California, and he attended high school there. He was a photographer's mate in the U.S. Navy from 1956 to 1960, studied painting and photography at the San Francisco Art Institute in 1960–1961, and worked for a year and a half as a printing assistant to Dorothea Lange. In 1963 he moved to Los Angeles where he became a successful commercial photographer.

Gibson's early black-and-white work was in a street documentary style influenced by Henri Cartier-Bresson, Robert Frank, and William Klein. It emphasized graininess and abstraction of subjects from their surroundings. His first books in this mode attracted little attention.

Between 1967 and 1969, Gibson assisted Robert Frank on the film *Me and My Brother*. In 1969 he moved to New York, where he formed Lustrum Press in order to exert control over the reproduction of his work. Lustrum has published the work of Neil Slavin, Mary Ellen Mark, Larry Clark, Danny Seymour, and Robert Frank as well as Gibson's trilogy of dreamlike photonovels (*The Somnambulist*, *Déjà-Vu*, and *Days at Sea*). Lustrum has also published the successful volumes *Darkroom*, *Darkroom II*, *SX-70*, and *Nude: Theory*. In addition to his books, Gibson's work has appeared in various journals including *Camera*, *Creative Camera*, *Camera 35*, *Popular Photography*, and *Modern Photography*.

In 1975 Gibson's interest in the contexts of image-presentation shifted from books to exhibitions. He joined Leo Castelli graphics that year, exhibiting a series of 16″ × 20″ prints of details of architecture and people all photographed from the same distance at the same camera settings. He worked briefly in color before returning to black-and-white photography in 1979. His work has been exhibited in over 40 one-man shows at the Visual Studies Workshop and George Eastman House, Rochester, N.Y.; the San Francisco Art Institute; and in New York City at Pratt Institute of Art, Cooper Union, Castelli Graphics, and the Museum of Modern Art.

Gibson received fellowships from the National Endowment for the Arts in 1973 and 1975, a CAPS grant from the New York State Council on the Arts in 1977, and the Deutscher Akademischer Austauschdienst award in Berlin in 1979. He lives and works in New York City.

Gilpin, Laura

American; 1891–1979

Born in Colorado Springs, Colorado, Laura Gilpin studied photography under Max Weber and Paul Anderson at the Clarence H. White School from 1916–1918 and did further work in photogravure with Anton Bruehl, Bernard Horn, and Clarence White. After working professionally for the Central City Opera House Association of the University of Denver and the Boeing Aircraft Company in Wichita, Kansas, Gilpin moved her base to Santa Fe, New Mexico, to concentrate on two photographic projects: the Navaho Indian and the Canyon de Chelly. Her technique was expert, especially in platinum printing, and her work serves to document the places and people of the American Southwest.

Primarily a landscape and portrait photographer, Gilpin was the recipient

of an Award of Merit in 1947 from the Photographic Society of America, an Appreciation Award from the Indian Arts and Crafts Board of the Department of the Interior in 1967, the Governor's Award from the State of New Mexico in 1974, and a Guggenheim Fellowship in 1975. Her numerous publications include *The Pueblos: A Camera Chronicle* (1941), *The Rio Grande: River of Destiny* (1949), and *The Enduring Navaho* (1968); the latter won the Western Heritage Center's award for nonfiction in 1969. Her work has been widely exhibited; Gilpin's estate, containing over 26,000 negatives, 20,000 photographs, and her library and personal papers, was given to the Amon Carter Museum in Fort Worth, Texas.

Giroux, Alphonse
French
An instrument maker, Giroux became the exclusive manufacturer of the world's first commercially produced camera (designed for L. J. M. Daguerre's pioneering process) and publisher of the original manual of instruction for taking daguerreotypes. First produced in 1839, each camera had an oval brass plate on the left side that was engraved with Daguerre's signature and the seal of Giroux et Cie. as proof of its genuineness. The camera consisted of two telescoping wooden boxes; it was about 12 inches high and 14 inches wide and extended from 10½ to 20 inches for focusing. Viewing was by means of a ground glass in a frame that attached to the rear. A mirror hinged to the bottom outside edge of this frame lowered to a 45-degree angle to provide reflex viewing from above of a vertically correct image on the ground glass. To take a picture, the frame was replaced by a plate holder with double doors which could be opened from outside the camera to uncover the sensitized face of the plate within. The holder accommodated a plate 6½″ × 8½″, which became established as *whole-plate* size. Although it is no longer used, some subdivisions of this size—e.g., the 2¼″ × 3¼″ quarter plate—remain standard formats today.

The original lens was a single-element meniscus or plano-convex lens with a 16 inch focal length and a maximum aperture of about *f*/14. However, a fixed aperture in the lens mounting reduced the speed to about *f*/17. The lens moved back and forth in a smooth brass tube for a limited degree of fine focusing. A pivoted cover plate at the front was swung out of the way for viewing or to make an exposure. After 1841 the much faster Petzval lens was supplied, and the camera was made in smaller sizes as well. The design was not patented, and it was widely imitated throughout the world.

Giroux's wife was the first woman photographer. Daguerreotypes taken by her were supplied to some dealers in other countries for display along with the cameras as examples of what the equipment could accomplish.
See also: CAMERA; DAGUERREOTYPE; PETZVAL, J.

Glamour Photography
Glamour pictures stress the physically appealing qualities of a subject. This kind of photography uses many of the same techniques as portrait, fashion, and beauty photography, but is distinct from them. While the main subject of both portrait and glamour photography is the person depicted, the portrait attempts to show aspects of individual character or personality while the glamour photograph idealizes physical attractiveness; the intent of the glamour photograph is not to show who a person is, but rather that the person is irresistably desirable. On the other hand, while beauty and fashion photographs may show a person, the real subject is what has been done in the way of makeup, hair styling, or costuming to enhance his or her appearance.

Glamour photographs are descendants of the carte-de-visite portraits first distributed and sold for publicity purposes by theatrical and variety performers in the 1860s. Idealization of the subject became a major characteristic of turn-of-the-century portraiture done in

Glamour Photography. Gary Bernstein, "Sisters" (1977). © Gary Bernstein.

the pictorialist mode. Glamour photography in the contemporary sense emerged as a distinct genre in the 1920s. It was a significant part of campaigns to create and market movie stars, and drew directly on the makeup, lighting, and photographic techniques of romantic motion pictures of the period.

Styles in glamour photography have changed many times with changes in the cultural image of what constitutes a beautiful person. The interaction has been complex, with glamour photographs functioning as both the cause of and the response to shifts in taste. Major glamour stereotypes of women have included the aloof, sleek woman of high society; the mysterious, exotic woman with a porcelain doll perfection; the sultry, sensuous temptress; the exuberant cheesecake or pin-up "girl next door" in sweater or bathing suit; the sophisticated, engaged metropolitan woman; and the sexually active, and available, companion featured in the centerfolds of mens' magazines. Glamour images of men have been equally diverse: the wealthy, worldly sophisticate; the athlete; the rugged outdoorsman; the virile intellectual; and the stalwart iconoclast or socially admirable renegade. There have been many other male and female stereotypes. Changes in the image of what constitutes glamour are also re-

vealed by the physical emphasis of pictures at various periods. This is especially true in photographs of women, in which attention has shifted many times from facial beauty to legs, to bust, to hips, to a full, rounded figure, to a slim, sleek figure.

A photographer may intend to produce glamour photographs as a commercial product, in which case he or she seeks models with the desired physical attributes and the ability to project an appropriate mood or emotion. Or, a photographer may wish to apply the "glamour treatment" in pictures of a particular individual. (This latter aim is also common in commercial illustration, where idealized presentations of products as mundane as toothpaste and automobile tires are sometimes called "glamour shots.") In either case, the task is to create a fictional image, not to achieve a sense of documentary realism. Thus, the picture session has much in common with creating a theatrical scene: careful attention to makeup, costume, setting, and props. A great deal of coaching, coaxing, and emotional encouragement—and even manipulation—may be required to obtain the pose and expression that project the desired mood. The interaction between photographer and subject in attaining this end is perhaps the most

important factor in glamour photography. Maintaining the subject's self-image of beauty, preventing distractions that break the mood, and avoiding model fatigue are major concerns.

The photographic techniques called for are those that flatter and idealize. They include carefully arranged lighting, usually with soft (diffused or reflected) light; soft-focus lenses; filters for tone or color control; special-effect filters; negative or transparency retouching; and a variety of printing techniques. Cameras of all kinds are used for glamour photography; the choice of a format is primarily a matter of the photographer's preference and the standards of quality in the final image, especially if the photograph is to be reproduced. The aim at each step is to conceal irregularities and imperfections so as to depict apparent perfection. *See also:* EROTIC PHOTOGRAPHY; FASHION PHOTOGRAPHY; PORTRAITURE. Color photograph: p. C-19.

Glare and Reflections

Glare is strong, image-degrading light reflected from or emitted by various parts of a subject. Extreme glare obliterates image details; lesser degrees of glare cause colors or gray tones in the affected areas to be too light in the image. Glare is produced by light within the lens field of view, whereas flare is caused by direct light striking the lens from outside the field of view. Glare light may spread outside the image path and cause flare by reflection within the lens or the camera body.

Glare from light sources in the picture can be controlled only by blocking the sources from the direct view of the lens or by reducing the intensity of the light. Filtration at the lens is seldom effective because it affects all other parts of the image as well. Most glare is reflected light and can be controlled to some degree according to the principle that the angle of reflection is equal to the angle of incidence of the light on the surface. Often glare can be reduced by moving the light source or the camera so that the path along the angle of reflection is not aimed directly at the lens. An example of this technique is the practice of photographing at a slight angle, rather than head-on, to a glass, polished wood, or other highly reflective surface when the light source is located at the camera position. The incidence-reflection principle is also embodied in the practice of lighting flat surfaces (as in copy photography) with sources at least 45 degrees off the lens-to-subject axis.

The size of a reflected glare spot and its intensity depends on the character and intensity of the incident light and the nature of the reflecting surface. Direct, specific light, as from a spotlight, causes more intense glare than light that is diffused or that comes from a broad-area source such as a floodlight. A matte or other non-glossy surface creates the largest glare spot because the light is diffused in many directions. Because of this scattering, its intensity is lower than specific-light glare, but also because of the scattering it remains visible (although reduced) when the camera is moved out of the angle-of-reflection path. Smooth, polished and glossy surfaces produce the smallest but most intense spots of reflected glare. If the surface is not flat but has varied contours, it may not be possible to find a light or camera position that eliminates all glare. In that case, glare points may be covered with a dulling spray, an easily removed wax liquid that produces a matte surface.

Reflections are images of objects outside the field of view; they can be seen only on very smooth surfaces such as glass, water, metal, and highly polished wood. Reflections on metallic surfaces can be controlled only by changing the angle of reflection to the lens, or by blocking off the path of the incident light so that only a neutral or black surface is seen in the reflection area. Reflections on non-metallic surfaces can often be reduced or eliminated by using a polarizer in front of the camera lens. Polarizers used over light sources or the camera lens, or both, are also effective in preventing glare.
See also: FLARE; INCIDENCE, ANGLE OF; POLARIZER; REFLECTANCE/REFLECTION.

Glass, Photographing

The physical nature of glass presents a number of photographic problems: it can be opaque, translucent, or transparent, and it usually has a glossy, highly reflective surface that readily reveals not only reflections, but scratches, fingerprints, and other evidences of handling. Direct frontal lighting is difficult to use because of the specular highlights it creates on the surface of the glass. Colorless glass presents the greatest problems because, in essence, it is not meant to be seen; it is meant to be looked through, as in a window or a protective covering over a picture, or it is meant to reveal what it contains, as in a jar or a goblet.

In spite of these difficulties, it is possible to photograph glass in ways that reveal its inherent qualities as well as those of the object that it forms. The easiest way to photograph a transparent container is to fill it with a colored liquid, sand, or other substance that will con-

form to the variations in its shape. Alternate techniques are to leave the transparent object essentially unlighted in front of a brightly lighted background, or to use a dark background and adjust the lighting to create highlights on the edges and major contours of the object. Colored and translucent glass are best revealed by shining light through from behind, below, or above so that the color and texture glow with transmitted illumination. If the surface does not have a matte texture, diffused light produces the best results. The surface contours of a glass object can be made apparent by reflections of material strategically placed out of lens view; these may be strips of light or dark paper, crumpled pieces of foil, or similar materials.

Opaque glass objects present the fundamental problem of a highly reflective surface; often tent lighting will provide the necessary illumination without producing distracting highlights and reflections. A polarizer can be used to reduce or eliminate image reflections on glass surfaces in many cases, but it will not affect specular highlights. Those must be controlled by adjusting the lighting and camera angles so that the highlights fall where they are most effective or least obtrusive. Seldom is it desirable to eliminate such highlights entirely because the result is a lack of the visual brilliance associated with the appearance of glass.
See also: POLARIZER; TENT LIGHTING.
Color photograph: p. C-19.

Glass, Photographs on

There are four fundamental ways to produce a positive photographic—or photographically derived—image on or in glass.
Emulsion on glass. The ambrotype and various lantern slide processes were 19th c. glass positive techniques. Today glass plates precoated with gelatin emulsions are used with reversal processing after direct exposure to the subject (or printing exposure to a positive transparency), or with normal processing after exposure to a negative. Alternatively, a liquid emulsion is applied to a glass surface by the photographer for similar use.

Image transfer. The emulsion of a positive image on a stripping film or paper is adhered to a glass surface and the original backing support stripped away. Or, glass paints, inks, staining colors, or glazelike compounds are deposited in the image pattern on the glass by means of a temporary relief emulsion or by a photosilkscreen or other photo stencil. The image is made permanent by

chemical action or by firing, as in similar ceramic and enamel processes.
Surface alteration. Resist is applied to the glass, usually through a photo stencil, and then the unprotected surface areas are etched with acid, sandblasted, or otherwise abraded to form the image. Alternatively, a glass-etch compound is applied by stencil or transfer and activated chemically or by heat to attack the areas it covers. The thin, colored glass coating of *flashed glass* can be etched away in resist-unprotected areas to form an image of the clear base glass and the coating color. The backing of a mirror can similarly be selectively removed by chemical or physical action.
Internal alteration. Specially sensitized glass contains ultraviolet-sensitive compounds that produce metallic or crystalline-colored images within the glass itself after exposure under a negative and development by heat. Similar glass alters its structure in the developed image areas so that they will etch much more rapidly than non-image areas; this provides etched-in-depth relief images.

Once an image is formed, further treatment is possible. For example, glass with a heat-proof image can be shaped by heating it in a kiln to the point at which it will slump over a form mold. Etched or abraded surfaces are very receptive to many kinds of colorants, which can be applied selectively by hand or by large-area techniques such as spraying.
See also: CERAMIC PROCESS; ENAMEL PROCESSES; HYALOGRAPH; SILKSCREEN PRINTING; STRIPPING FILM.

Glazing

Ferrotyping, the process of drying a gelatin-emulsion printing paper so that it has a glass-smooth surface, is known as *glazing* in Great Britain. This term can also refer to the process of coating a photographic image with clear varnish, liquid plastic, or some other substance that imitates the effect of ferrotyping. In ceramic and enamel processes, the image is fused to the support during one of the glaze firings.
See also: FERROTYPING.

Glossy

Photographic printing papers have various surface textures. A glossy surface is completely smooth, with no discernible texture. Thus, the informal term "a glossy" means a print made on such a paper. Glossy-surface resin-coated papers dry to a very high gloss without special treatment. Glossy-surface fiber-base papers air-dry to a smooth, somewhat less reflective gloss. However, fiber-base papers can be ferrotyped—dried with the emulsion in contact with a polished metal or plastic surface—to a glasslike finish. Because the surface does not scatter light, glossy papers produce the longest tonal scale and deepest blacks or most saturated colors of any printing papers. Glossy prints reveal fingerprints, surface scratches and abrasions, print retouching, and some negative defects that textured-surface (e.g., silk, matte) papers can sometimes hide.

See also: FERROTYPING; RESIN-COATED PAPERS.

Glycerin Development

In platinum printing, glycerin is sometimes used in a process of controlled development. The most versatile technique was worked out by Alfred Stieglitz and Joseph T. Keiley in the first decade of the 20th c. A heavily exposed print is attached to a glycerin-coated sheet of glass or similar smooth working surface and is coated with pure glycerin; the excess is blotted away. Developer is applied with a brush, area by area. The glycerin retards the rate of development so that the photographer can slowly bring a given area up to a desired strength, and it prevents the developer from flowing into adjacent areas. Two solutions may be used—one of straight developer to work on areas where the greatest tone or contrast is desired, and one of equal parts of glycerin and developer for use where subtle control is required. Careful brushwork is necessary to blend the various areas together for a visually unified result. Warm tones and variations of image color can be produced by also using straight and glycerin-diluted developers to which mercuric chloride has been added.

See also: PLATINOTYPE.

Goddard, John Frederick

English; 1795–1866

A science lecturer in London, J.F. Goddard was employed in 1840 by Richard Beard to improve the daguerreotype process by obtaining exposures short enough to make portraiture a practical—and commercially feasible—undertaking. Goddard discovered that using bromine fumes as well as iodine fumes to sensitize the plate increased its speed 5 to 10 times, reducing 20-minute exposures to as little as 2 minutes, for example. He was the first to publish this

procedure (in December 1840) and thus generally is credited with the discovery. However, Dr. Paul Beck Goddard (no relation) and Dr. Martin Boye of the University of Pennsylvania had devised a similar technique almost a year earlier, but apparently only had communicated it to a few Philadelphia photographers. Franz Kratochwila also discovered the value of combined bromine and chlorine fumes as a sensitizer in 1840, and published his results in Vienna just five weeks after Goddard. Working from this new information, photographers throughout the world devised improvements in the formula that brought exposures down to 20 to 40 seconds in the next year; the introduction of the Petzval lens brought a further reduction to less than 10 seconds.

See also: BEARD, RICHARD; DAGUERREOTYPE; PETZVAL, J.

Godowsky, Leopold

American; 1902–1983

Leopold Godowsky and Leopold Mannes together invented Kodachrome film and processing. A classical musician, as was Mannes, Godowsky held chairs as a violinist in two symphony orchestras while studying physics and chemistry at the University of California. At the same time he and Mannes, who was at Harvard, collaborated on research and invention in color photography. They pursued joint careers in music and independent research in New York City, inventing a color motion-picture-film process and a two-layer color still film. In 1930 they were invited to continue their work at Kodak Research Laboratories. They invented two- and three-layer integral (monopack) color films, developed unique methods of color processing, and produced innovations in the use of color couplers in emulsions. Although also active in music, Godowsky maintained a primary career in photographic research with Kodak and later as an independent consultant until his retirement.

See also: COUPLERS, COLOR; KODACHROME.

Goerz, Carl Paul

German; 1854-1923

An optician, Goerz established C. P. Goerz Optical Works in 1886 in a Berlin suburb to manufacture lenses, microscopes, telescopes, and precision optical instruments. In 1888 Goerz produced the revolutionary Anschutz folding press camera, the first camera with a self-

contained (focal plane) shutter capable of speeds as short as 1/1000 sec. In addition to conventional cameras, Goerz subsequently produced novelty designs (a binocular camera in 1908) and special-purpose equipment such as aerial cameras and very long focal-length lenses during World War I, and the first photofinish racing photographic systems in 1922.

Goerz's premier lens designer was Emil von Hoegh, who in 1893 produced the famous Double Anastigmat, later known as the Dagor lens. In 1900 von Hoegh designed the Hypergon lens for Goerz, the first high-quality wide-angle lens, and one that remained unequalled for several decades. The firm introduced many other instruments, including the first optical (extinction) exposure meter. In 1928 C. P. Goerz, Berlin, was absorbed by the Zeiss-Ikon organization. A subsidiary—and later independent company—Goerz Optical Company, New York, produced the famous "Red Dot" (trademark) Artar process lens and other lenses. In 1972 Goerz Optical Company became part of Schneider Optics of America.

See also: ANSCHUTZ, OTTOMAR; DAGOR LENS; EXTINCTION METER; HOEGH, EMIL VON.

Gold Toning

After fixing and washing, photographic silver images can be treated with a dilute gold chloride solution to adjust image tone and to protect the silver from atmospheric pollution. This treatment coats each silver particle with a fine layer of gold, which is impervious to chemical attack.

Gold toning originated in the daguerreotype era, when it was called gilding. It was used to strengthen image contrast and to warm the image tones. In the period of gelatin-emulsion printing-out papers, gold toning was used to neutralize the somewhat unpleasant maroon or purple tones of the image. In modern times gold toning has been used primarily to provide image protection. However, as explained in the entry on archival processing, the most recent research suggests that a dilute selenium toning solution produces a greater degree of protection; it is also considerably less expensive.

The most widely used gold toning solution is the Kodak GP-1 solution, which is prepared from two stock solutions, A and B. The A solution consists of 0.3 oz (10 ml) of 1 percent gold chloride solution mixed into 25 oz (750 ml) of distilled water. The B solution consists of 0.4 oz (10 gm) of sodium or potassium thiocyanate dissolved in 4 oz (125 ml) of distilled water. For use, B is stirred into A until thoroughly mixed, then distilled water is added to total 34 oz (1 liter).

A black-and-white print to be toned must be completely fixed and thoroughly washed free of fixing agents. It is immersed in the toning solution for 10 minutes, with gentle agitation. The image tones will become somewhat cooler; a cold-tone image will develop slightly blue-black shadow areas. After toning, the print must be washed 10 minutes or more in constantly changing water, then squeegeed and dried normally. One quart (or liter) working solution will provide protective toning for seven or eight 8″ × 10″ prints.
See also: ARCHIVAL PROCESSING; TONER/TONING.

Goodwin, Rev. Hannibal

American; 1822–1900
Goodwin was the first person to patent a method of manufacturing celluloid-base film in long, continuous strips that were subsequently cut to finished sizes. Goodwin apparently took up photography to prepare lantern slides for programs and lectures at the House of Prayer in Newark, New Jersey, where he was pastor. He experimented for about ten years before filing for a patent in 1887. The following year John Carbutt and John Wesley Hyatt, who had founded the Celluloid Manufacturing Co., began producing celluloid-base sheet films by a somewhat different method, which they did not patent. Goodwin's application had to be revised seven times before the patent was granted in 1898. In the meantime, Henry M. Reichenbach, working for George Eastman, developed a similar procedure for which he received a patent in 1899, a few months after Eastman actually began to manufacture celluloid roll film.

Goodwin formed the Goodwin Film and Camera Co. in 1900 to manufacture his film, but he was injured in an accident and died later that year. In 1902 Goodwin's company was acquired by E. and H. T. Anthony Co. (which later that year merged with Scovill and Adams to become Ansco), and production of the film began. At the same time, Ansco brought suit against Eastman Kodak Co. on the grounds that although they owned the Reichenbach method, Kodak was actually using key steps in Goodwin's process to manufacture film. Previous suits between Eastman and the Anthonys had been settled out of court; this suit was not. The case continued for several years, culminating in 1914 in a $5 million cash judgment against Kodak. Payment was made both to Ansco and to Goodwin's heirs.
See also: ANSCO; CARBUTT, JOHN; CELLULOID.

Goodwin, Henry B.

Swedish; 1878–1931
Goodwin, born Heinrich Karl Hugo Goodwin Bürgel in Munich, Germany, became the foremost Swedish photographer of his age. He had studied philology, eventually specializing in ancient Nordic languages, especially Icelandic; by 1905 Goodwin also had taught himself photography. He received his PhD from Leipzig University, and in Leipzig he was befriended by the portrait photographer Nicola Perscheid (1864–1930), a strong artist who shaped Goodwin's technical approach to photography and became a father figure to the young philologist.

In 1909 Goodwin settled in Stockholm. Until 1915, he worked as a lexicographer with the publishers Nordstedt & Soner, but also pursued photography. He wrote for *Fotografisk Tidskrift* and *Svenska Fotografen* and published photographs in these Swedish periodicals where Pictorialist ideas were argued. In 1913, through the help of the Swedish Photographers' Association, he brought his mentor Perscheid to Stockholm to teach a week-long course in portrait photography. So convincing were Perscheid's lectures and examples that his style characterized Swedish portrait photography until World War II.

Goodwin himself flourished. He addressed the Swedish Photographers' Association at its summer meeting in 1914 and exhibited with its members in Malmö, and he became the Nordic correspondent of the English bible of Pictorialism, *Photograms of the Year*, a position he held into the early 1920s. In 1915 he exhibited at the Varia Art Gallery in Stockholm and inaugurated his own studio, which he called "Kamerabilden" (Camera Pictures), on Strandvägen, then as now one of the elegant boulevards of the capital. The Swedish upper classes and intelligentsia, and members of the theater and cinema communities, crowded into his studio to have their portraits made. Stockholm photographers were enraged by the popularity of the new studio and spread rumors about the foreigners who had suddenly turned professional and stolen their customers. With the outbreak of World War I, Heinrich Goodwin Bürgel took the anglicized name Henry B. Goodwin.

A vital personal style distinguished Goodwin's photography. He rejected the stock formats of his competitors and chose to print in larger dimensions and with the advanced techniques of bromoil, pigment, gum bichromate, and platinum. The soft-focus lens that he adopted from Perscheid emphasized the central areas of his picture and diffused the sides, and he revived the calotype (paper negative) method of the 1840s; all of these techniques enhanced the romanticism of his portraits. Goodwin also mastered the use of electric light in his studio, and while the incomes of his colleagues plummeted in the long northern winter, when their skylights were useful only a few hours a day, he could work into the dark with artificial illumination.

Goodwin's skill and activity led to important exhibitions abroad. In 1917 his photographs were displayed in London, and the following year in Copenhagen. In 1921 he and his wife and colleague, Ida, visited New York and met Frank Crowninshield, the editor of *Vanity Fair*, who made him a correspondent for the magazine. Crowninshield introduced him to New York socialites and theater personalities whom Goodwin photographed in his hotel suite. An exhibition of these pictures was arranged in Manhattan and it proved a great success. These were the years of Goodwin's best work.

In 1925 Goodwin moved to a studio on Biblioteksgatan in central Stockholm. The income level of Swedish photographers was falling, and possibly Goodwin had tired of trying to convince the cultural establishment that photography was an art that should be shown in museums. He turned to botany, and became a horticulturist of some note. Now he photographed flowers with the passion he had previously directed to female portraits. By the end of the 1920s he became aware of the cool, sharp-edged style of the New Objectivity, but he never completely abandoned his pictorialist ideas. In his book, *Kamerabilden* (1929), he published studies of workers by the German Albert Renger-Patzsch, and in a 1930 article on plant photography, Goodwin recommended the Rolleiflex—a far cry from his old, large-format portrait apparatus.

His most enduring images are of women taken in the first quarter of the 20th c. In sumptuously printed photographs he lingered over the long curves of nude shoulders, confronted the archetypal beauty of a full young torso, or held the intelligent gaze of a social lioness. His painstakingly composed images of women retain their rare sensual freshness today. Their faces and bodies are emotionally vibrant, revealing their responsiveness to his undoubted charm and his deep psychological insight.

Goro, Fritz

American; 1901–

Fritz Goro, a pioneer of science photography since the late 1930s, is highly accomplished in a number of fields from microphotography to radio astronomy. His photo-stories, most of which have appeared in *Life* magazine, include investigations of marine biology, nuclear physics, genetics, and the Arctic environment. His work is an attempt to intensify vision to the greatest precision while retaining the beauty which renders his subjects accessible.

Goro was born in Bremen, Germany. He studied design and sculpture at the Berlin State School of Applied Arts from 1919 to 1921 and at the Weimar Bauhaus from 1921 to 1923. From 1924 to 1928 he was employed as a writer, editor, designer, and art director for Ullstein Publishers, Berlin. He worked as an assistant to the Managing Director of the journal *Müncher Illustrierte* from 1928 to 1933, when he fled Germany.

Goro was a freelance photographer from 1933 to 1936 in Paris, where his work was published in *Vue* and *Vogue*. He then moved to New York, again working as a freelance photographer until 1944, the year he became a naturalized U.S. citizen. Goro began a long association with *Life* at this time, becoming Staff Science Photographer, a position he held until 1966. He continued to work for *Life* on a regular basis between 1966 and 1971, when he again made his living as a freelance photographer for publications such as *Scientific American* and for the Polaroid Corporation Research Division.

Goro was Regents Professor at the University of California at San Diego in 1969 and a Visiting Fellow at Yale University in 1969–1970. He has been a Fellow of the Biological Photographic Association and the New York Microscopical Society. He is the recipient of numerous awards, including the American Medical Association Award (1948), the Art Directors Club of New York/American Institute of Graphic Arts Awards (1974–1975), the New York Microscopical Society Award (1977), and the Life Achievement Award from the American Society of Magazine Photographers (1978).

Goro's work has been included in group shows such as *The Family of Man* and *Photographs from Life* at the Museum of Modern Art in New York City, and at the Grey Art Gallery of New York University. He has been honored with solo exhibitions at the University of Miami in 1969, and at the Polaroid Corporation Headquarters, Cambridge, Massachusetts, in 1981.
Color photograph: p. C-20.

GOST

A prefix used with Russian film-speed designations, GOST is an acronym for Gosudarstvenny J. Standart, an organization similar to the American National Standards Institute (ANSI). Although the method used to derive GOST film speeds is somewhat different from that used for ISO (ASA/ANSI) arithmetic speeds, the results are so similar that either rating may be used in exposure calculations and meter settings. The practical conversion between systems is: 1.1 GOST = ISO, and 0.9 ISO = GOST.
See also: ANSI; SPEED OF MATERIALS.

Grain; Graininess; Granularity

These terms refer to the visible and measurable characteristics of a particular aspect of emulsion structure.

Grain may refer either to the silver-halide crystals in an undeveloped emulsion or to the specks of metallic silver that constitute a developed image. These particles of silver are in fact tiny filamentary strands, not solid bodies like grains of sand, but that is apparent only on the microscopic level.

Granularity is a measurement of the number of grains per unit area in a processed image. It is a statistical average, calculated by averaging microdensitometer readings taken over a given area—on the assumption that the many different grain sizes produce as many different densities—and dividing by the square root of the area. It is an objective factor.

Graininess is a subjective factor; it is the visual impression of texture in image areas that ought to have none, or to have texture of a different character. In terms of subject matter, these are areas of continuous tone such as clear sky, a plaster wall, or smooth skin. Graininess has a sandlike or salt-and-pepper appearance. It is often obscured in areas where the subject has a stronger local texture—e.g., dappled foliage, tweed cloth, or the speckling in granite.

Graininess is not the perception of the actual microscopic grains, but of the combined light-blocking effects of clumps of grains aligned in depth through points in the emulsion. The graininess of a color image is less sharp than that of a black-and-white image because the effect is produced by translucent dye deposits on three different levels in the emulsion; rather than grains, they are dye clouds. The graininess visible in a print is not a function of the paper emulsion, for even the greatest degree of clumping there never reaches visible size; rather, it is the enlarged pattern of the film graininess projected onto the paper along with the image. In general, fast films produce more graininess than slow films because they form larger grains and have thicker emulsions in which vertical clumping can occur. Image graininess is increased by excess density in the negative; this is produced by overexposure, overdevelopment, or especially by a combination of the two. The visibility of graininess also increases as the contrast of the print increases.

Graphic Arts

The term graphic arts encompasses the skills and media used to design and produce printed reproductions of images and text material. It includes those media which, unlike painting or drawing, involve the production of a master image from which reproductions are made. Thus, etching, lithography, gravure, letterpress, xerography, photography, silkscreen, and similar media are all graphic arts. The term now also includes computer-generated images in which the master image is stored in data form for display on a cathode-ray tube (viewing screen) or for reproduction as "hard copy" by means of special printing equipment or direct electron-beam-exposure of photographic material.
See also: ELECTRON IMAGING; GRAPHIC ARTS PHOTOGRAPHY; PHOTOMECHANICAL REPRODUCTION.

Graphic Arts Photography

Photography is used in direct support of all photomechanical reproduction processes, including offset lithography, letterpress, flexography, gravure, and serigraphy. In almost all printing processes the material to be reproduced is photographed on high-contrast black-and-white film in preparation for making a printing plate, stencil, or other reproduction master. Special "lith" films of very high contrast are used so as to separate the image into discrete elements that will carry or transmit ink in the reproduction master. Line art, graphs, diagrams, type, and other single-tone material is photographed directly. Continuous-tone originals such as photographs and paintings are photo-

graphed through a halftone screen. The screen breaks the image into a pattern of dots or lines that vary in size and spacing according to the strength of the various tones. Multi-color originals are photographed through red, green, and blue filters in combination with the halftone screen, to obtain a set of "separations" from which individual color printing plates are made. Graphic arts photography is usually accomplished with specialized "process" cameras and lenses. However, especially for limited reproduction processes, ordinary equipment is suitable if used with precision.
See also: Individual process entries; HALFTONE PROCESSES; LITH FILMS/PAPERS: PHOTOMECHANICAL REPRODUCTION; SCREEN, HALFTONE; SEPARATION NEGATIVES/POSITIVES.

Gray Card

A gray card is a reference standard used to determine exposure of a subject and to evaluate color balance in a processed negative or positive image. Usually about 8″ × 10″ in size, it reflects all visible wavelengths equally (i.e., is neutral in color) and reflects 18–20 percent of the light striking it. This reflectance is about the same as that of the average photographic scene—one with a "normal" distribution of light and dark areas and colors—frontlighted by sunlight. It is also the reflectance factor used to calibrate most exposure meters. Thus, a reflected-light meter reading from a gray card held in the same light as that falling on a subject will indicate essentially the same exposure as an overall reflected-light reading from the subject itself. It will also be the same as the exposure indicated by an incident-light reading taken from the subject position. The *lighting ratio* on the subject can be determined from two gray-card readings—one in which both the key and fill lights illuminate the card, and one in which only the fill light illuminates it. (This will not necessarily be the same as the *brightness ratio* of the subject because reflectance as well as illumination may differ between the lightest and darkest subject areas.) The reverse side of most gray cards is a white surface with a reflectance of 90 percent, five times (2¼ *f*-stops) greater than the gray side. This is a convenience in taking readings under low-level illumination in which the subject or the gray side may not reflect enough light to give a significant meter indication. The meter should be set to a film speed one-fifth of normal to compensate for the extra reflectance of the white surface, or the reading obtained at a normal

film-speed setting should be adjusted proportionately.

In color photography, a gray card photographed in the same light as the subject—either included at the edge of the frame, or photographed on a separate frame—provides a standard neutral reference for color densitometer readings, or for visual evaluation of filtration requirements in printing or further photography. To obtain true-color reproduction, any color cast evident in the gray card must be eliminated. This gray card reference is also an important aid in the photomechanical reproduction of color images.

Gray Scale

The range of tones (shades of gray) from black to white in a photographic print, or the equivalent range of densities in a negative, comprise a gray scale. Although photographic emulsions reproduce a continuous range of tones, for test and reference purposes it is convenient to divide the gray scale into a series of steps, each a single (rather than graduated) tone. In a gray scale for visual comparison to evaluate tone reproduction in a photographic print or halftone image, the steps have equal visual intervals. That is, the degree of difference in tone or lightness between any two adjacent steps looks the same as that between any other two adjacent steps. However the *measured* difference in density from step to step is not equal in a visual scale. Because of the response characteristics of the human eye, the darkest tones in the scale must have greater density differences than the middle and lighter tones in order to have equal visual intervals. A gray scale useful for exposure testing does have equal density increases between its steps. Usually the difference is 0.3—which produces a difference of one *f*-stop of exposure at each step—or 0.15, which produces half-stop exposure differences. When photographed, or when exposed by contact or projection onto film or paper, the densities in the resulting image can easily be plotted against the gray-scale step differences—which now represent logarithms of exposure—to obtain a characteristic curve of the emulsion being investigated.

A *reflectance gray scale* is a positive image on photographic print paper. Such a scale is often photographed in the same light and with the same exposure as used for a subject, to serve as a guide in processing and in photomechanical reproduction. In color photography a gray card and a scale of standard color reference patches are also often included.

A *transmission gray scale* is on a trans-

parent film base. It can be contact-printed, or projected in an enlarger. One use of such a scale is to determine the negative density range suitable for a particular contrast grade of paper. The paper is exposed to the scale by whatever printing method is normally used. When processed and dry, the number of visible steps—from the first tone just lighter than maximum black to the last tone just darker than paper-base white—is counted and multiplied by the density interval between steps. The result is the maximum negative density range that can be printed without the need for burning-in, dodging, or other local exposure controls. For example, if six steps of the image of a half-stop (0.15-step interval) gray scale are visible, the paper can accommodate a negative density range of 0.80; that is the range usable with a No. 2 contrast paper when exposure is made by the average condenser-type enlarger.
See also: CHARACTERISTIC CURVE; TONE REPRODUCTION; WEDGE, OPTICAL; VISION.

Grossman, Sid(ney)

American; 1913–1955
As a photographer and teacher, Sid Grossman exercised a unique influence from the mid-1930s until his death in 1955. Grossman and Sol Libsohn are often credited with bringing the still-photography part of the moribund Film and Photo League back to life as the Photo League in 1936; certainly Grossman was in charge of the Photo League School from 1938 to 1949. A dominant figure by force of pesonality, ability, and commitment, Grossman numbered among his students at the League Walter Rosenblum, Dan Weiner, and Leon Levinstein. Lewis Hine, wanting to improve his printing skills, took a course with Grossman in 1940. After World War II, Grossman persuaded Paul Strand to teach at the school and Edward Weston, Ansel Adams, W. Eugene Smith, and Beaumont and Nancy Newhall to become members. In a much publicized trial of alleged Communists in 1949, Grossman was named as a Communist in testimony that suggested that the Photo League was a subversive organization. In fact, Grossman had never hidden his membership in the Communist Party, and the League, while left-wing, was devoted to photography, not subversion. As a result of the trial, Grossman was, in effect, blacklisted and broke his ties with the League.

Like other members of the Photo League, Grossman and Libsohn believed photography should serve a social purpose. They were also dedicated to collec-

Grossman, Sid. "Labor Day" (1947). Courtesy Mrs. Sid Grossman.

photographers. The Museum of Fine Arts in Houston, Texas houses 6000 Grossman negatives, 4000 contact prints, and 2000 prints. A major exhibition of his work was held there in 1981.

Ground Glass

The viewing and focusing screen in a camera with a through-the-lens viewing system is called the ground glass, although plastic is often used today. The screen has a textured surface that intercepts the aerial image projected by the camera lens. The screen must be translucent, rather than transparent, so that the image-forming light is diffused on a definite plane on which the eye can focus. This also permits the image to be seen from a variety of viewing angles. Glass is textured and rendered translucent by acid etching, grinding with an abrasive, or sand blasting; plastic is molded with an appropriate surface, or is ground with an abrasive. To permit accurate focusing, the textured surface of the screen must be exactly the same optical distance from the lens as the film plane. In a view camera the ground glass corners are commonly cut off to allow air flow in the camera interior as the bellows is extended or retracted, and to permit direct visual inspection of vignetting.

See also: FOCUSING; VIEWING AND FOCUSING SYSTEMS; VIGNETTING.

Gruber, Fritz

German; 1908–

Fritz Gruber has for many years been the organizer of Photokina, a yearly international photographic event held in Cologne, Germany, with which he has been associated since 1949. In 1954 he was the recipient of the Photokina Golden Needle Award.

In the early 1930s Gruber interrupted his philosophy, theater, and journalism studies at the University of Cologne for political reasons (an anti-Nazi weekly he co-founded was suppressed), and in 1933 he emigrated to England, where he worked as an advertising and photography expert. In post-war Germany he founded a photocopying and microcopying business, and became Deputy Chairman of the Society of Photocopying and Reproduction.

Gruber is the founder of the German Society for Photography, a juror of the annual *The German Photoimage*, a juror and advisor of the European Committee for Photo and Film, an executive member and the only German Fellow of the Royal Photographic Society of Great Britain, and an Honorary Excellence of the Fédération Internationale de la Photographie.

tive group effort and worked together on the series Chelsea Document (1938–1939). Grossman's street pictures from the Depression era typically show spirited or dejected people enduring hard times: blacks in Harlem (for the WPA) in 1939, farmers in Oklahoma and Arkansas in 1940. These photographs were taken on large-negative film with a tripod-mounted camera; the prints were highly detailed and grainless. Later, on leave from his army post in Central America (1943–1946), he used a hand-held press camera for photographs taken in Panama, Guatemala, and the Galapagos Islands. He used flash for his series on the Black Christ Festival in Portobello, Panama (1945). After the war Grossman photographed the folksingers Woody Guthrie, Big Bill Broonzy, Leadbelly, and Pete Seeger, using a twin-lens reflex camera (1947). In his well-known Coney Island series (1947) he used the reflex-camera at eye-level

and at close range, like a 35mm camera. To photograph the San Gennaro Festival in New York (1948), he used a borrowed 35mm Contax. Grossman photographed no more New York street scenes after 1949.

After his break with the League, Grossman spent much of his time in Provincetown, on Cape Cod; he studied painting with Hans Hofmann on the GI Bill, taught photography privately, photographed, and learned to fish. His photography moved away from a socially motivated approach to a purely personal visual style which showed a strong concern for content, integrated with a lively and sophisticated sense of form. In New York winters, between Provincetown summers, in the early 1950s, he photographed the New York City Ballet in rehearsal and backstage. He died of a heart attack in 1955. Grossman received little popular recognition in his lifetime despite his considerable influence among

Fritz Gruber has written for many international photographic publications, and is a prolific editor and publisher of photographic books. He is the writer of television programs about or featuring photography. His photographic collection is now held by the Cologne Art Museum.

Guide Number

A guide number is a reference number used to calculate exposure with non-automatic flash. Four factors determine electronic flash exposure: film speed, flash unit light output, flash-to-subject distance, and lens f-stop setting. The guide number (GN) relates film speed and flash output; when either of the remaining factors is known, the other can be calculated as follows:

$$f\text{-number} = \text{GN} \div \text{Flash-subject distance}$$

$$\text{Required flash-subject distance} = \text{GN} \div f\text{-number}$$

The guide number for a given flash unit is different for each film speed. When film speed doubles, the guide number changes by a factor of $1.4\times$; when film speed is halved, the guide number changes by a factor of $0.7\times$. Some flash units have a guide number chart on their housings as well as in their instruction manuals.

Guide numbers differ according to whether the distance is to be measured in feet or in meters. Conversions between a guide number for feet (GN_ft) and a guide number for meters (GN_m) are:

$$\text{GN}_\text{m} = \text{GN}_\text{ft} \times 0.3$$

$$\text{GN}_\text{ft} = \text{GN}_\text{m} \times 3.3$$

An unknown guide number can be determined for a particular film speed by calculation from the BCPS (or ECPS) rating of a flash unit, or by practical test. The calculation is:

$$\text{GN}_\text{ft} = \sqrt{0.05 \times \text{BCPS} \times \text{Film speed}}$$

The film speed to be used is the arithmetic, not the logarithmic speed (i.e., 400 with an ISO 400/27° film). If a film has different ratings for daylight and tungsten illumination, the daylight speed should be used.

A guide number test is made by placing the light unit a convenient distance from a subject and making a series of exposures at various f-stops. When the best exposure is selected from the processed film, the guide number can be calculated from the distance and the f-stop used:

$$\text{GN} = f\text{-number} \times \text{Flash-subject distance}$$

Using color reversal (slide or transparency) film provides results that are the easiest to evaluate.

Guide numbers are especially useful for calculating exposure with bounce flash; for calculating fill-in flash; and for determining the flash-subject distances required for various lighting ratios in multiple-flash set-ups.

See also: BCPS; BOUNCE LIGHT; FLASH FILL; MULTIPLE FLASH.

Gum-Bichromate Process

This non-silver printing method uses paper coated with a gum-arabic solution containing potassium or ammonium bichromate (dichromate) to make it light sensitive, and a pigment to provide image tones. The photographer prepares the coating, including any desired pigment color, and coats a suitable paper, which may be white or a color that contrasts with the pigment for additional effect. When dry, exposure is by contact under a final-size negative to sunlight or an artificial source of ultraviolet light (e.g., sunlamp). As in all bichromate processes, exposed portions (shadow areas) become hardened but unexposed portions remain soluble and dissolve away when the image is developed in warm water. As a result, the pigment gives color to the dark and middletone areas, and the paper color forms the highlights and lightens the middletones. A great deal of control is possible in the choice of pigment and paper, degree of development in local areas, recoating with the same or another color for one or more additional exposures, and a number of other techniques. Gum-bichromate printing was widely used for pictorial photography from the 1880s to about 1920. The acknowledged masters of the expressive use of the process at the time were Robert Demachy and Emile Puyo in France, and several members of the Photo-Secession in the U.S. It is popular with many artists today because the materials are relatively inexpensive and because it permits manipulation of image characteristics with greater freedom and versatility than conventional photographic print processes.

See also: BICHROMATE PROCESSES.
Color photographs: p. C-21.

Gum Print

Any print made by a process using a material coated with sensitized gum arabic (rather than gelatin), and by extension almost all bichromate processes, is referred to as a *gum print*. At the turn of the century the term also referred specifically to a print made by the *gum-platinum process*. A light platinotype was first made from a negative. This was then coated with a gum-bichromate emulsion and reprinted under the same negative. The procedure combined the fine detail and delicate tonal scale of the platinum image with the color and manipulative effects obtainable with gum-bichromate development.

See also: BICHROMATE PROCESSES; GUM-BICHROMATE PROCESS; PLATINOTYPE.

Gun Camera

Cameras shaped like a pistol or a rifle, as well as those used to record the aiming and firing of a weapon, are called *gun cameras.* Aside from novelty toys, gun-shaped and gun-named cameras were almost entirely 19th c. products. The first was invented in England by Thomas Skaife in 1856 and produced as the *Pistolgraph* in 1858. It took a $1\frac{1}{8}''$ circular picture on a single wet plate. It looks today more like a magic lantern (slide projector) than a pistol, but seemed menacing enough at the time for Skaife to be arrested for aiming it at Queen Victoria. Thompson's *Revolver Photographique* of 1862 looked like an antique pistol with a large, flat cylinder between a pistol grip and a tubular lens barrel. Introduced in France, it was the first disk camera, producing four small exposures on a circular wet plate. The camera with the most realistic pistol appearance was Enjalbert's *Photo-Revolver de Poche* (pocket photo-revolver), produced in France in 1883. Its cylinder held 10 dry plates about $\frac{3}{4}'' \times \frac{3}{4}''$ (2 × 2cm) and revolved to change plates each time the hammer was pulled back to cock the shutter; the trigger was the shutter release. The *L'Escopette Pistolet* (carbine pistol) produced in Switzerland in 1889 was a large box with a pistol grip below and a "barrel" like a rounded funnel. It is especially interesting because it was the first non-Eastman camera designed to use Eastman Roll Film manufactured for the No. 1 Kodak. It took 110 exposures about $2\frac{1}{2}'' \times 2\frac{3}{4}''$ (6.35 × 7cm) on a single roll. *Le Photo-Revolver* manufactured in France by Krauss in 1921 looked somewhat like a modern square-edge automatic. Its rectangular handle either offered push-pull plate changing or accepted small-format roll film.

A long-barrel, cannonlike camera was invented in 1874 by P. J. C. Janssen, an outstanding pioneer of modern astronomical photography. He used its revolving plate and shutter chamber to record a

Gun Camera. Gun camera designed by S.P. Langley (ca. 1900). Smithsonian Institution.

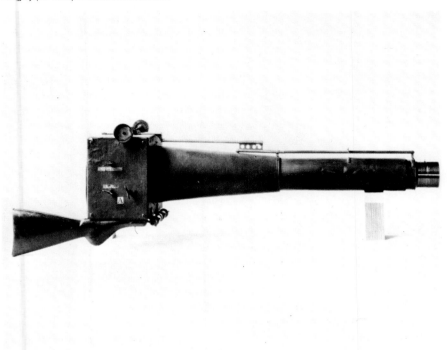

48-image sequence of the transit of Venus across the sun at the rate of one exposure every 1.5 seconds. This mechanism was perfected by E. J. Marey in the 1880s in the *fusil photographique* (photo rifle) he used for high-speed motion study and analysis sequences of subjects such as birds in flight. A rifle design was also used in the Sands and Hunter *Photographic Gun* of 1885, which took pictures on glass plates that were shifted by a revolving cylinder one at a time from a supply chamber to the exposure position behind the lens barrel, and then to a storage chamber. Today, riflestock camera supports are used to hand-hold medium- and small-format cameras fitted with very long-barrel lenses for sports, wildlife, and similar kinds of photography.

Gun-monitoring cameras developed during World War II used 16mm motion-picture film. They were first mounted under the wings of fighter aircraft and in the gun turrets of bombers. They operated in bursts, synchronized with the weapon trigger, and had GSAP (gunsight aiming-point) orientation in order to record the effect of fire under combat conditions. Such cameras were also mounted to record—by means of a beam splitter—the actual gunsight-target image; they were used for both dry-fire and live-ammunition training. Similar combat and training configurations were used with anti-aircraft, artillery, and tank weapons, and are used today with missile and rocket launchers.

The term *gun camera* is also sometimes used in ordnance work to mean a *bore camera*—one used to examine and record the inner surface of weapon barrels. With small-calibre barrels a kind of endoscope is used as a bore camera.

See also: DISK CAMERAS; ENDOSCOPE; MAREY, ETIENNE JULES; MOTION STUDY AND ANALYSIS.

Gurney-Mott Theory

The generally accepted theory explaining latent image formation in a gelatin-silver halide emulsion exposed to electromagnetic energy was advanced by R.W. Gurney and N. F. Mott in 1938. It has subsequently been refined by them and by other investigators. A silver-halide crystal is a lattice configuration of ions—positively charged silver cations and negatively charged halide anions (bromide ions in a film emulsion); there are also one or more silver-sulfide molecules. When a charged particle or quantum of energy—a *photon* of light—strikes a crystal, an electron is displaced from a halide ion. The electron moves through the lattice until it is trapped by a structural defect or by a *sensitivity speck* of silver sulfide. The electron in turn neutralizes a migrating silver cation, forming an atom of metallic silver. The affected halide ion has been converted to a halogen atom (e.g., bromine) by loss of its negative charge (the electron). It moves to the surface of the crystal where it is absorbed by the surrounding gelatin or by various sensitizing compounds. The crystal must be affected this way by at least four separate photons in order to form a latent image that can subsequently be developed. Energy from up to several hundred photons can be absorbed by a single crystal; the maximum depends upon crystal size and the wavelength of the exposing energy. Beyond that point the latent image begins to be destroyed by the process called *solarization*.

See also: EMULSION; LATENT IMAGE; SOLARIZATION.

H

Haas, Ernst

Austrian; 1921–

When Robert Capa saw Ernst Haas's photographs of returning Austrian prisoners of war in 1947, he invited Haas to Paris to join the newly formed Magnum Photo Agency. It was a very fruitful beginning for the career of Haas, who went on to be one of the most influential photographers of his generation.

His first one-man show in Vienna drew prime attention from capital cities everywhere, and since he came to the United States in 1951 there have been many others, including major exhibits in New York City at the Museum of Modern Art (where he was the first photographer to have an exhibit of color work), Asia House, and the International Center of Photography. His photoessays have appeared in such leading magazines as *Life, Holiday, National Geographic, Heute, Du, Paris-Match,* and *Geo.* Assigned as the still photographer on several films including *The Misfits, West Side Story* and *Hello, Dolly,* he was a special consultant to John Houston on the first segment of *The Bible.*

As a young man, Haas had dreamed of going to New York to live. Once there, his first significant work was for *Life*—a pioneering color photo-essay on New York that established him as an immensely talented, innovative photographer. At the time (1953), color photography was a secondary medium

to black-and-white, but it was in color that Haas felt he could best capture the nuances and excitement of the city. *Life* gave Haas a 24-page spread for his "Magic Images of New York," a milestone for color, for Haas, for the magazine.

Although Haas originally worked in a straight reportage style, he gradually became more and more involved with the interpretive possibilities of photography. This was a natural progression for a man who was also intensely interested in poetry. One of his most successful books (now translated in six languages) is his photographic interpretation of the Book of Genesis, *The Creation* (Viking, 1971). Here again he used color to create the mood—the feel of a thought, of a presence.

From there he went on to photograph in color the city of Venice, Germany, the Himalayas, the bullfight, all the while continuing to indulge his fascination with America. His work of this period is characterized by soft, muted tones or by deep, violent shades as the mood dictates, as well as experiments with colors in motion.

Haas is not solely interested in the visual; he is a humorous raconteur, a lover of words as well as music. He derives great pleasure in creating "audiovisuals" where he is able to join the image to music, and in producing books in which he can interweave poetry and image. He has said that he is not seeking a consensus but rather the "interrelationship of all the senses and the arts."

Color photograph: p. C-22.

Halász, Gyula

See: BRASSAÏ.

Halation

Excess exposure caused by reflection of light off the film base back into the emulsion can produce an effect called *halation.* Direct-light sources in the picture and highly reflective surfaces such as a white shirt in direct sun produce enough light to penetrate an emulsion completely. In the blackness of the camera interior, the smooth surface of the film-base material can act as a mirror to this light. The light spreads outward upon reflection, creating a diffuse, halolike glow in the positive image. The degree of spreading may be increased by irradiation within the emulsion. Most modern films either have a highly efficient anti-halation later coated onto the film base or incorporate a light-absorbent substance in the base material for the same purpose, making in-camera halation a relatively rare occurrence today; however, it is quite common in photographs made in earlier periods. In the darkroom halation can occur when a film is exposed by contact or projection to another image, as when making a positive transparency or duplicate negative.

Placing a piece of black paper behind the film to absorb the light passing through the most transparent portion of the exposing image will prevent halation.
See also: ANTI-HALATION LAYER.

Half-Frame Format

In still photography, an image area on 35mm film measuring 18 × 24mm, with the long dimension running across the width of the film, is known as the half-frame format. The full frame of 35mm still photography measures 24 × 36mm, with the long dimension running parallel to the film edges. This was originally called a *double-frame* format because it took up the area of two standard (18 × 24mm) motion-picture frames, for which 35mm film had been originated. The term *half-frame* arose when still cameras for the smaller format were produced. It is also the standard format for most filmstrips.

Halftone Processes

The halftone processes are methods of reproducing images with tonal gradations, such as photographs and paintings, in ink, which has a single tone strength. All halftone processes divide the image into tiny elements—dots or lines—that deposit more or less ink in proportion to the strength of the original image tones in the areas they represent. These ink elements are small enough not to be noticeable to the eye, which blends the ink image with the white paper showing through the spaces between the elements to form a composite impression of tones. The lightness of a tone in any particular area is determined by how much white is seen in proportion to the amount of ink present. In areas of solid black or maximum color saturation, the ink elements merge to cover the paper entirely.

In photomechanical reproduction, the dots or lines commonly are formed in a regular pattern by rephotographing the original image through a screen. The screening exposure may be made directly onto an etching resist on the surface of a printing plate, or onto a high-contrast (lith) film which is subsequently used to prepare the plate for etching. For some kinds of images a screen with a random grain pattern may be used to avoid moiré.

An alternative method of plate preparation is direct engraving. The image is scanned electronically and the resultant signal is used to control a stylus that engraves an appropriate line or dot pattern in the plate surface. The system may operate in real time, with scanning and engraving proceeding simultaneously, or from scanning signals recorded magnetically or stored in a computer. Stylus engraving is faster than screen-photography, but it does not permit retouching or correction of the engraving image, and it cannot achieve as fine a pattern as the screen methods. Superior quality can be achieved by using a laser beam to expose the patterned image on a resist-coated plate.

In the halftone pattern formed on a plate for letterpress (relief) or offset lithographic (planographic) printing, the dots or lines vary in size so that ink is laid down over a greater or lesser area. In a plate for gravure (intaglio) reproduction, the "dots" are pits or cells that are all the same size but that vary in depth. Thus, the amount of ink they can hold varies, and they lay down different densities of ink in printing. This process provides the most faithful approximation of the tonal variations of the original image.

Two specialized methods of halftone reproduction utilize random patterns of printing elements. In *aquatint,* a random dot pattern is produced by particles of powdered resin dusted on the plate surface to form a resist before etching. In *collotype,* a pattern of short, irregular line elements is formed by reticulation of a gelatin coating on the plate. These processes are suitable for short runs and hand-operated presses; they are used primarily for art reproductions or artistic effect.
See also: AQUATINT; COLLOTYPE; CONTINUOUS TONE; SCREEN, HALFTONE.

Halide; Halogen

Halogens are the chemical elements iodine, bromine, chlorine, and fluorine. A halide is a two-element crystalline compound of a halogen and a metal; it is named by the metal and the stem of the halogen plus-*ide* (e.g., gold chloride, potassium bromide). The silver halides are unique in the degree to which they respond to the photochemical (actinic) effects of light and shorter wavelengths of electromagnetic energy, and the degree to which they can be sensitized to other wavelengths.

Halsman, Philippe

American; 1906–1979
Philippe Halsman was internationally famous for his celebrity portraits. He photographed 101 covers for *Life* magazine over a thirty-year period, his first appearing in 1942. He regularly published work in the world's most popular magazines: *Time, Look, Saturday Evening Post, Paris Match,* and *Stern,* among others. Many of the indelible images of celebrities we remember are Halsman's.

Halsman was born in Riga, Latvia, and was a self-taught professional photographer in Paris during the 1930s. He emigrated to the United States with an emergency visa acquired through the influence of Albert Einstein in 1940 and began the work for which he is known.

Halsman's success was due to the incisiveness of his portraits, his ability to reveal something unique about each of his subjects. In this regard, he felt himself in debt to literary psychologists such as Tolstoy and Dostoyevsky. He believed that psychology and conversation were more important for the portraitist than technical expertise.

Of his own work, Halsman wrote: "My main goal in portraiture is neither composition, nor play of light, nor showing the subject in front of a meaningful background, nor creation of a new visual image. All these elements can make an empty picture a visually interesting image, but in order to be a portrait the photograph must capture the essence of its subject.... The photographer probes for the innermost. The lens sees only the surface."

Halsman's method often involved an element of playfulness and obvious humor. For instance, he photographed a series of celebrities jumping in the air. He hoped in this way to peel away social masks and capture unguarded expressions. His photographs are marked by an absence of intimidation even when their subjects are forbidding or imposing figures. Owen Edwards has said of Halsman: "In a portrait, he retains the feeling that at any minute the profound or melancholy face may be totally rearranged into a miraculous smile."

Halsman was the recipient of countless awards and honors. He was the first president of the American Society of Magazine Photographers in 1944, and received a Lifetime Achievement in Photography Award from that body in 1975. He was awarded the Newhouse Citation for journalistic achievement in 1963.

Halsman's work has been exhibited throughout the world, with major shows in Tokyo in 1973 and at the International Center of Photography in 1979. Some of his most familiar portraits include those of Marilyn Monroe, Salvador Dali, Picasso, John F. Kennedy, and J. Robert Oppenheimer. His portraits of Adlai Stevenson, Albert Einstein, and John Steinbeck appeared on U.S. stamps. He shot more *Life* covers than any other photographer.

Halsman, Philippe. "Dali Atomicus" (1949).
Courtesy Yvonne Halsman.

Hamaya, Hiroshi

Japanese; 1915–

Hiroshi Hamaya is one of Japan's most eminent documentary and nature photographers. During his career of over 50 years, working in black and white and in color, he has explored the subtle relationships between people and their physical environments.

Hamaya was born in Tokyo. He became interested in photography at age 15, and following high school he worked for several years as a photographer for a commercial aeronautical research institute and for the Oriental Photo Industry Company. With a Leica he acquired in 1935, he documented life in downtown Tokyo. His first published photographs appeared in *Home Life* magazine in 1936.

Hamaya was a freelance photographer in Tokyo from 1937 to 1945; in Takada City, Niigata Prefecture, from 1945 to 1952; and for the past 30 years in Oiso,

Kanagawa Prefecture. He has been a contributing photographer to Magnum Photo Agency since 1960.

Hamaya has photographed throughout the world: in the Far East, the United States and Western Europe, Mexico, Turkey, and Australia. He has made an extensive documentation of the lives and customs of the people of Japan's "back coast" and "snow country," and a major series of Japanese landscapes. After a brief period in the early 1960s in which he documented Japanese political activities, Hamaya concentrated primarily on color landscape images, often shot from the air.

Hamaya is a member of the Japanese Photographers Society. He is the recipient of numerous Japanese and international photography awards and has published more than a dozen books. He has exhibited widely in group shows in Venice, New York City, Tokyo, and Washington, D.C., including *The Fami-*

ly of Man exhibition. He has been the subject of one-man shows in New York City and Cologne, and the focus of several exhibitions in Tokyo, including *Document of the Heavy Snowfall in 1945 in Takada, Niigata-Ken; The Red China I Saw; Hamaya's Japan* and a major retrospective, *Hiroshi Hamaya: 50 Years of Photography.*
Color photograph: p. C-23.

Hanfstaengl, Franz

German; 1804–1877

Franz Hanfstaengl, who was the leading German portrait lithographer of the mid-19th c. and who founded a world-famous art publishing company, is also recognized as the first master portrait photographer in Germany. Born in Bavaria, Hanfstaengl studied at the Polytechnic Institute and at the Academy of Arts in Munich. He learned the technique of lithography and became so expert that he was able to draw directly on the stone, rather than having to resort to the much more common technique of drawing on paper or parchment for later transfer to the stone. In the decade from 1824 to 1834 the quality of his work gained him a major reputation. His drawings of the famous innovators in the circle around King Ludwig I and Maximilian II were widely acclaimed for their precise resemblance to the real person. During this period he produced his most famous work, the *Corpus Imaginum,* an album of portraits of the leading personalities, nobility, and men of science in Germany.

In 1834 Hanfstaengl established his own firm to publish lithographic portraits, reproductions of art works, and original illustrations. The following year he was commissioned to draw the most important works of art in the State Gallery in Dresden and subsequently moved to that city. The work was completed only in 1852. However, in 1845 Hanfstaengl turned over operation of the Dresden studio to his brothers in order to return to his establishment in Munich. With the introduction of the wet collodion process for making glass plate negatives, he foresaw that photographic reproduction would surpass the quality and detail of lithography. He soon converted his firm's operations to the newest techniques available, and in 1866 purchased the German rights to Joseph Swan's carbon printing process. The quality of the work produced assured the company's position as one of the two or three finest art publishers in Europe well into the 20th c.

At the same time, about 1853, Hanfstaengl turned to photography as a personal medium and opened a portrait studio, working at first with the calotype (paper negative) process and later with the wet plate process. His clients were famous personalities, and although his output of major portraits was limited—some 80 subjects in 15 years—his skill in capturing character and personality brought him fame equal to that of his lithographic period. He was technically innovative, and is credited with originating the technique of retouching negatives. He showed before-and-after prints from retouched negatives at the Universal Exhibition in Paris, in 1855; the innovation attracted great interest and attention from professional photographers and was universally adopted almost immediately.

Other members of Hanfstaengl's family also became successful photographers in the 1860s: Erwin as Court photographer in Paris, and Teich as Court photographer in Dresden. Franz

Hanfstaengl retired completely from all business and professional activity upon the sudden death of his wife and daughter; he died in 1877.
See also: CALOTYPE; CARBON PROCESSES; COLLODION PROCESSES; LITHOGRAPHY; PHOTOLITHOGRAPHY.
Color photograph: p. C-24.

H & D Speed

In the 1880s, Hurter and Driffield, the pioneers of modern sensitometry, devised a method of rating the light sensitivity of a photographic emulsion. This rating, known as the *H & D Speed,* was calculated from the exposure value—in meter-candle-seconds—of the *inertia point.* This point was located by projecting the straight-line portion of the characteristic curve to meet the horizontal projection of the filmbase-plus-fog line. The calculation was: *H & D Speed = 34 ÷ inertia point exposure.* Because the slope (upward slant) of the straight line increased as contrast increased with prolonged development, a speed rating applied only to a specific degree of development. The impractical consequence of this was that a single emulsion could have several different speed ratings. One solution was to develop emulsion samples to several specified degrees of contrast and determine an average inertia from the different curves they generated. Although more useful than any other system of the time, the H & D system has long since been replaced by other methods of determining the speed of materials.
See also: CHARACTERISTIC CURVE; DRIFFIELD, VERO CHAS.; HURTER, FERDINAND; SPEED OF MATERIALS.

Hardener

A hardener is a chemical that reduces the swelling, and consequent softening, of a gelatin emulsion immersed in water solutions such as processing baths. It also helps an emulsion to dry to a denser, tougher state than before treatment. The most common hardeners are ammonium, chrome, or potassium alum (respectively: ammonium aluminum sulfate; potassium chromium sulfate; and potassium aluminum sulfate), or formalin—a 40-percent solution of formaldehyde in water. An alum hardener is a common component of fixing baths, especially those used in film processing. A separate hardening solution may be used as a developer prebath, or as an acidified stop bath in high temperature or tropical processing. Hardening is also recommended before treatment of a fixed negative, as in intensification or reduction.

Some packaged liquid fixers are supplied with a separate hardening solution that may be added as desired. In general, film emulsions should be hardened to protect them against abrasion and other handling damage. Hardening is less important with print emulsions. It may lengthen washing times or interfere with toning, and it makes spotting or retouching more difficult because it makes the emulsion less receptive to corrective dyes. When used, a hardener shortens emulsion drying times.
See also: FIXING.

Hawes, Josiah Johnson

One of the most notable American daguerreotypists; active in Boston as a partner of A. S. Southworth from 1843 to 1862.
See also: SOUTHWORTH, ALBERT SANDS.

Heat Filter

A heat filter separates visible and heat (primarily infrared) wavelengths, transmitting one and absorbing or reflecting the other; it is used to protect delicate specimens, close-up subjects, and film in projectors. Certain kinds of glass transmit more than 80 percent of all light while absorbing 90 percent or more of the accompanying heat. Sheets of such glass are used to protect the condensers as well as the film in projectors, and are used in front of close-up light sources. A half-inch layer of water in a glass-sided tank can screen a subject from some of the heat effects of a light source. Adding a small amount of copper sulfate to the solution increases the heat absorption, but decreases red-wavelength transmission somewhat. The most widely used heat filters are diathermic or "cold" mirrors. These have dichroic surface coatings that reflect the visible wavelengths falling on them but transmit the heat to the underlying glass where it is radiated in other directions. Reflectors in projection lamps and high-output spotlights are now usually cold-mirror devices. Many slide projectors also use an indirect light path for additional protection: a flat-surface cold mirror set at a 45-degree angle reflects light from the lamp to the film and lens, but transmits heat on a different path.
See also: DICHROIC FILTER.

Heat Recording

Various methods are used to obtain a photographic record of the temperature patterns in energy emitted or reflected by a subject. Heat cannot be directly focused into an image nor recorded

Heinecken, Robert. "Photo sculpture" (n.d.). Courtesy Robert Heinecken; collection, Center for Creative Photography, University of Arizona.

directly on photographic materials. However, it may be accompanied by focusable, recordable wavelengths, may produce photographable changes in other substances, or may be converted to a photographable equivalent. Objects with a temperature of about 1022°F (550°C) or higher emit visible wavelengths in an incandescent glow, which can be photographed directly with conventional black-and-white or color film. Below this temperature, down to approximately 482°F (250°C), an object emits infrared wavelengths that can be photographed directly on infrared-sensitive film, using a filter that excludes all visible wavelengths. Recordings of this kind are called *infrared thermal photographs*. The actual temperature variations that can be recorded in a single exposure range from 108°F to 302°F (60°–150°C), depending upon the median temperature of the object and the latitude of the film. With an infrared image converter, recordings in this range can also be made on conventional films.

Thermography is the recording of heat patterns of objects below 482°F. One technique in this range uses a parabolic heat-concentrating mirror system to scan the object surface. The concentrated temperature difference output is passed to associated electronic equipment that generates an electron beam with corresponding variations. The beam, driven in synchronism with the scanner, may expose an emulsion directly or, more commonly, may create a display on a cathode-ray tube which can be photographed as desired. Another thermographic technique uses substances that glow with varying intensity or change color in proportion to differences in temperature. These are applied directly to the surface of the heated object or are used on a thin sheet of support material that is laid on the object or held in close proximity to it. The visible pattern produced can be photographed directly.

See also: IMAGE CONVERTER.

Heinecken, Robert

American; 1931–

Robert Heinecken's work employs unconventional materials, surfaces, and subject matter to explore and confuse the boundaries of photography and sculpture. Since the mid-1960s his work as an artist and teacher has been widely influential on younger American photographers using mixed media techniques. The explicit sexual content of his work has also opened up new areas for photographic exploration.

Heinecken was born in Denver, Colorado, and later moved with his family to Iowa and then to California. He studied at the University of California at Los Angeles from 1951 to 1953 before becoming a U.S. Naval Cadet. From 1954 to 1957 he was a U.S. Marine Corps fighter pilot and flight instructor. In 1957 he returned to UCLA where, as an art major, he received B.A. and M.A. degrees.

Heinecken was appointed Instructor in the Department of Art at UCLA in 1960. He taught design, drawing, and printmaking for two years and was made Assistant Professor in 1962. He was responsible for introducing photography into the fine arts curriculum soon after and began his personal photographic work and intensive study of photographic aesthetics.

In 1963 Heinecken met Nathan Lyons, Van Deren Coke, and Minor White, whom he considers important influences. Two years later he met other influential photographers including Jerry Uelsmann, Ray Metzker, Aaron Siskind, and Harry Callahan.

Heinecken began in the mid-1960s to explore the sculptural possibilities of the photographic medium, using images on three-dimensional surfaces and collage techniques, and experimenting with the manipulation and configuration of found images. He has said of his works: "They are conceived not as a *picture of* something, but as an *object about* something."

In 1967 Heinecken was an instructor at the Advanced Studies Workshop at George Eastman House, Rochester, N.Y., where his work was included in the *Persistence of Vision* exhibition. He has taught at the Ansel Adams Workshops in Yosemite, the State University of New York at Buffalo, the Art Institute of Chicago, and Howard University, in addition to continuing on the faculty of UCLA where he was named Professor of Art in 1974.

Heinecken was Chairman of the Board of the Society for Photographic Education from 1970 to 1972 and a Trustee of the Friends of Photography, Carmel, California, in 1974–1975. In 1976 Heinecken's studio and its contents were destroyed in a fire. His recent work includes images made with a Polaroid SX-70 and the incorporation of written materials.

Heinecken has been the recipient of a Guggenheim Fellowship in 1975 and a National Endowment for the Arts Photography Fellowship in 1977. He has exhibited in group shows at the National Gallery of Canada in Ottawa and in New York City at the Museum of Modern Art and the Whitney Museum. He has been honored with solo exhibitions at Witkin Gallery and Light Gallery, New York; the Pasadena Art Museum; George Eastman House; and the San Francisco Museum of Modern Art.

Heliochromy

The process of recording colors directly on a daguerreotype plate, without the use of filters, dyes, or other color-mediating elements; no helichromes produced permanent recordings.
See: BECQUEREL, ALEXANDRE EDMOND; HILL, REV. LEVI L.; NIÉPCE DE SAINT-VICTOR, CLAUDE FÉLIX ABEL.

Heliography

Nicéphore Niépce used the term *heliography* to identify the process by which he obtained the first permanent images on glass (1822) and on metal (1826) by the action of sunlight (Greek: *helios* = sun; *graphein* = writing, drawing). Niépce coated his materials with a solution of bitumen of Judea, an asphalt compound used as a resist in engraving methods coupled with lithography. He discovered that not only was the bitumen bleached to a light gray color by sunlight, but it also was hardened against the action of its solvent, oil of lavender. In 1822 he coated a glass plate with bitumen and exposed it by contact under an engraving of Pope Pius VII. The engraving had been oiled to make the paper nearly transparent. Sunlight passing through the clear portions hardened the coating on the glass, but those portions shadowed by the lines of the engraving remained soluble. "Development" in oil of lavender dissolved away the unhardened elements, leaving an image in clear lines. When viewed by transmitted light the image was composed of bright lines in the darker field of the remaining opaque coating on the glass. When held against a dark surface and lighted from the front, the image looked black in the surrounding light gray field. Niépce used the same process in 1826 with a $6\frac{1}{2}'' \times 8''$ (16.5 × 20.3 cm) sheet of pewter in place of the glass. After coating, it was exposed for eight hours in a camera obscura focused on the sunlighted scene visible from an upper story window of his home. The brightest parts of the scene bleached and hardened the bitumen. When developed, some coating in the partly exposed middletone, and all coating in the unexposed shadow areas dissolved away, revealing the dark gray metal beneath. The result was a direct positive image, the world's first permanent photograph.
See also: NIÉPCE, JOSEPH NICÉPHORE.

Heliogravure

Based on Nicéphore Niépce's method of heliography, heliogravure was a photo-engraving process invented in 1855 by C. F. Abel Niépce de Saint-Victor, a cousin of Nicéphore, and Claude Lemaître, an engraver. Their method used a steel plate first grained by the aquatint process, then coated with bitumen, exposed under the image to be reproduced, processed, and etched in acid. In some cases a second aquatint step was added after the bitumen exposure. Usually hand engraving was also added to correct and enhance details. The results were high-quality halftone ink reproductions of photographic images. At the same time, Edouard Baldus and Charles Nègre developed a similar bitumen-on-steel process for reproducing line engravings as well as photographs; it did not require hand work for excellent results. W. H. F. Talbot achieved similar results, although of lesser quality at first, using a gelatin-bichromate coating instead of bitumen in the process he patented as photoglyphy in 1858. All of these processes were forerunners of the highest-quality process, photogravure, invented by Karel Klič in 1879.
See also: AQUATINT; PHOTOENGRAVING; PHOTOGRAVURE; PHOTOGLYPHY.

Heliotype

Invented in 1869 by Ernest Edwards and R. L. Kidd, heliotype was an improved collotype process widely used in England to print photographic illustrations in periodicals and books. The gelatin emulsion contained alum to prevent swelling. It was first formed on a glass plate for smoothness and uniformity, then transferred to a metal plate for exposure and processing to a relief image, which was subsequently inked and printed directly. The gelatin received a separate hardening exposure during the process; this and the metal support made it possible to print many times the number of copies obtainable from an ordinary collotype relief. O. G. Rejlander provided many of the negatives—and had posed for several of the pictures, as well—for the first book illustrated with heliotypes, Charles Darwin's *The Expression of the Emotions in Man and Animals,* published in 1872.
See also: COLLOTYPE.

Helmholtz, Hermann Ludwig Ferdinand von

German; 1821–1894
One of the most versatile and accomplished of 19th c. scientists, Helmholtz was a physicist, physician, biologist, mathematician, and philosopher. His major achievements were in physiological optics (the study of the organs and processes of human vision) and acoustics, the two areas in which he could draw upon all his talents and diverse knowledge. He extended the three-color theory of vision first put forth by Thomas Young; invented the ophthalmoscope for the visual examination of the retina, and other instruments; determined the structure and action of the eye and especially its relation to associated nerve networks; expanded J. C. Maxwell's work on reflection and refraction; photographed the solar spectrum; and in literally hundreds of other achievements established the science of physiological optics. His work in mechanical and physiological acoustics was almost equally as extensive. Helmholtz is renowned for major advances in theoretical as well as practical physics; he was also a highly effective and popular writer and lecturer with both scientific and lay audiences.
See also: MAXWELL, JAMES CLERK; YOUNG, THOMAS; VISION.

Henneman, Nikolaas

Dutch; 1813–1875
First valet and then photographic assistant to W. H. F. Talbot—who invented the first negative-positive process, the calotype—Henneman was one of the few to be trained in the process during Talbot's years of experimentation. In 1843, after the calotype had been introduced, Talbot established a photographic studio and printing laboratory at Reading, between London and Talbot's estate, Lacock Abbey, with Henneman in charge. One task of the establishment was to produce the several hundred calotypes required to illustrate Talbot's book *The Pencil of Nature.* Other book illustrations, copies of drawings and paintings, and commissioned works of architectural photography were also undertaken, and equipment and supplies for the calotype process were sold to amateurs, along with the necessary license to carry out the process.

In 1847 the Reading studio was closed, and Talbot established Henneman and Thomas Malone in a portrait studio in London. They eventually bought the business themselves, but did not prosper in spite of a large assignment to print illustrations for the official reports of the Great Exhibition of 1851. Henneman offered lessons in the calotype, gave a one-afternoon short course in photography to O. G. Rejlander—certainly one of the most cursory beginnings for a significant photographer—and apparently ended his career working as an assistant to photographers in the English provinces, notably Oliver Sarony, whose younger brother Napoleon Sarony was

Henri, Florence. "Composition #76" (1929). Courtesy Galleria Martini & Ronchetti, Genoa; collection, Museum of Modern Art, New York.

to become one of the best-known portrait photographers in the U.S.
See also: CALOTYPE; PENCIL OF NATURE, THE; REJLANDER, OSCAR; TALBOT, WILLIAM HENRY FOX.

Henri, Florence

French/American; 1895–
Born of a French father and German mother in New York City, Florence Henri became associated with the European avant-garde of the 1920s and 1930s. She began her education in the United States, then traveled to Germany to study music and art. She continued her art education in Paris in 1924 with Ferdinand Leger, and with Amédée Ozenfant, cofounder with Le Corbusier of an abstract school of painting known as Purism. In 1927, Henri enrolled in the Bauhaus at Dessau. There she was strongly influenced by the ideas and work of Laszlo Moholy-Nagy and Joseph Albers and began to experiment seriously with photography. In 1929 she returned to Paris and rented a studio on Rue Froideveaux.

At first, Henri concentrated on portraiture, but also accepted commissions for advertising, fashion, and illustration. By 1931, she was a well-known portrait photographer with her own studio on Rue de Varennes. She made portraits of many avant-garde artists working in Europe at that time including Hans Arp, Wassily Kandinsky, and Alberto Giaciometti. Simultaneously, Henri continued using photography in an experimental and abstract manner.

Many of Henri's portraits as well as her self-portraits, still lifes, and abstractions are characterized by the use of multiple mirrors and geometric objects. Her compositions with reflecting surfaces, geometric planes, beams, rods, steel balls, and scaffolding are in the constructivist tradition and are often considered reminiscent of Moholy-Nagy's experiments with planes. They are also precursors of the Neo-constructivist work of the 1980s, both in process and attitude. Henri set up her compositions with an interest in the spatial illusion of three-dimensional objects as they are abstractly represented in the two-dimensional space of the photograph—a distinctly contemporary concern.

In 1963, Henri moved from Paris to Bellival in Picardy, France, where she has devoted her later years to abstract painting.
See also: BAUHAUS.

Herschel, Sir John Frederick William

English; 1792–1871
A fundamental contributor to the invention and early growth of photography, Herschel was an astronomer, physicist, and chemist. His interest in photography was largely theoretical, although he made practical discoveries and suggestions; it stemmed from his concern with lenses and the problems of recording observations in astronomy, and from his studies of the chemical and physical action of light and invisible energy (called "chemical rays" at that time) on various

substances. The greatest part of Herschel's career was spent as successor to his father—who had discovered the planet Uranus and the existence of infrared energy, among hundreds of other accomplishements—in the position of private astronomer to the king. This involved completing his father's work on the vast map of the stars in both hemispheres, for which Herschel at times used photographic methods. The map remained unequaled in scope and accuracy until well into the 20th c. Given the immensity of this undertaking, it is astonishing that he made notable contributions in a number of other fields. The following summary lists only a portion of his achievements in photography, none of which he attempted to patent or exploit commercially, to the great benefit of W. H. F. Talbot, among others, who did.

1819—Discovers that the hyposulfites (modern: thiosulfates) dissolve silver salts.

1839—Learns that Daguerre has recorded an image with light-sensitive material, invents a way to sensitize paper, and records an image (negative) through the telescope; makes it permanent by the use of hypo; recommends the use of hypo to Daguerre, Bayard, Talbot, and others.

1839—Suggests to Talbot the benefit of waxing a paper negative after processing to make it more nearly transparent for printing. Is the first in England to adopt the terms "photography" and "to photograph" (first used by German astronomer J. H. von Madler) in place of "heliography" (Niépce) and "photogenic drawing" (Talbot).

1839—Invents a way to coat a glass plate with silver halides; photographs his father's telescope (largest in the world), producing the world's first glass-plate negative; makes prints on paper from the plate.

1840—Introduces the terms "negative," "positive," and "emulsion" in describing his experiments to the Royal Society. Invents a method of making direct positive images on paper before announcement of Bayard's method. Demonstrates that a glass negative backed with black looks positive, anticipating the ambrotype by 11 years. Discovers and communicates—perhaps to J. F. Goddard—that silver bromide is the most light-sensitive of the silver halides. Records a natural color (i.e., without dyes or colorants) image of the spectrum on silver chloride material; fails to make it permanent, but asserts that it someday will be done.

1842—Invents the *anthotype*, an impractical but theoretically interesting bleach-out process using paper sensitized with juices from plants. Invents the *chrysotype*, an iron-sensitized process using gold chloride as a developer; a very slow process. Invents the *cyanotype;* uses it to make prints from glass negatives and to make accurate direct copies of scientific notes and sketches. It becomes universally used as a copying process (the blueprint) for the next century.

1853—Suggests the use of images reduced to microscopic size to store and preserve documents and similar materials.

1860—Suggests the possibility of a rapid-changing glass-plate hand camera capable of taking a "snap shot" in a tenth of a second. Twenty years later the first such cameras are manufactured and the term comes into common use.

1867—Sits for the last time for Julia Margaret Cameron for the portrait generally considered to be her towering masterpiece.

See also: BAYARD, HIPPOLYTE; CYANOTYPE; DAGUERRE, L. J. M.; FIXING; GODDARD, JOHN F.; HISTORY OF PHOTOGRAPHY; HYPO/HYPOSULFITE OF SODA; IRON PRINTING PROCESSES; NIÉPCE, JOSEPH NICÉPHORE; TALBOT, WILLIAM HENRY FOX; WAXED PAPER PROCESS.

Hertz

Hertz is the international standard (SI) unit for the measurement of frequency—the number of times per second a repetitive phenomenon occurs. It is especially applied to the time measurement of electromagnetic energy and is equivalent to the previous term, *cycles per second;* thus, 1 Hertz (Hz) = 1 cycle per second (cps). The unit is named for Heinrich Rudolph Hertz, the 19th c. German physicist who confirmed the electromagnetic theories of James Clerk Maxwell and established the fundamental similarity between electric waves and light waves. Hertz and wavelength—the dimensional measurement of distance between identical points, such as positive peaks, in successive cycles of a phenomenon—are related in the following way. In conceptual terms, Hertz is a count of how many wavelengths pass a reference point in one second. Given the fact that all electromagnetic energy travels at the speed of light (approximately 186,000 miles or 300,000 kilometers per second), fewer long wavelengths can pass the reference point in one second than short wavelengths. Thus, long-wavelength energy has a lower frequency (fewer Hz) than short-wavelength energy.

See also: WAVELENGTH.

Hicks, Wilson

American; 1897–1970

Hicks began his journalistic career in the 1920s on the staff of the Kansas City *Star.* He early learned the craft of picture journalism as editor of the paper's Sunday magazine and of its rotogravure section. Joining the Associated Press in New York in 1928, Hicks served as executive editor and eventually took charge of the AP's feature service and of its newly founded newsphoto service. Moving to *Life* as photographic editor in March, 1937, just three months after the magazine's founding, Hicks was one of the small group of talented editors who developed the magazine's pioneering techniques of photojournalism. Named executive editor just as World War II broke out, Hicks remained with the magazine until 1950, recruiting and directing the stellar group of photographers who covered the war and its aftermath, and continuing to develop and perfect the photo-essay form which found its fullest expression in *Life* during those important years.

As photographic editor, it was Hick's responsibility not only to decide on stories to be assigned to photographers, but also to select from the staff's diverse talents the best photographer for each assignment. Directly in charge of hiring as well, Hicks built the photographic staff from four to more than forty during his thirteen-year tenure. Among those he worked with were Robert Capa, Margaret Bourke-White, Leonard McCombe, David Douglas Duncan, Alfred Eisenstaedt, Gordon Parks, and W. Eugene Smith.

Continuing his contributions to the field after leaving *Life,* Hicks wrote *Words and Pictures: An Introduction to Photojournalism* (1952). Intended as a major statement of photojournalistic principles and theory, the book is equally an account of editorial practices in the glory days of *Life.* An issue of the magazine was "a design which reflects the world's week in sight and echoes it in sound," Hicks wrote, and the thoughtful examples he provided, drawn not only from his own work practice but also from his close observation of others eminent in the field, showed how that reflection was constructed each week.

In 1955, Hicks joined the faculty and administration of the University of Miami in Coral Gables, where he remained until shortly before his death. Beginning in 1957, Hicks co-directed with Morris Gordon an annual Photojournalism Conference at the university which brought together photographers, writers, editors, and art directors for lectures and discussion on the history,

theory, and practice of visual communication. An ample and careful selection of contributions representing the conference's fifteen-year life span is available in *Photographic Communication: Principles, Problems and Challenges of Photojournalism* (1972), edited by R. Smith Schuneman.

High Contrast

The contrast range of a black-and-white image is described by the number of steps (tones) on a scale of equal-interval grays from black to white. A high contrast image is one with very few or no intermediate tones between the extremes. Such an image has a bold, posterlike appearance. It can be produced from a high-contrast subject using normal-contrast photographic materials, or from a normal-range subject using high-contrast materials. Maximum high contrast is produced by "lith" or graphic arts films and papers, which produce only black and white, with no intermediate tones. High-contrast images are frequently employed as an intermediate stage in creating photographic special effects or in photomechanical reproduction.

See also: CONTRAST; LITH FILMS/PAPERS; POSTERIZATION.

High-Contrast Materials

Although conventional slow-speed emulsions have inherently higher contrast response characteristics than fast emulsions, materials that are specifically designated "high contrast" have special emulsions that produce only white and black or a limited scale of gray tones between these extremes. The most common high-contrast materials are black-and-white copy films, and very-high-contrast lith films and papers. The latter are used in the graphic arts and photomechanical reproduction, in creating special effects such as posterization and tone-line images, and in processes such as photosilkscreening. Most of these materials have very slow-speed, orthochromatic emulsions that can be handled under red safelight. However, some "rapid" lith papers have projection (enlarging) speed emulsions, and some films have panchromatic sensitivity. The panchromatic materials are used to make separations from colored subjects or images. Special high-speed (up to ISO 20,000), high-contrast materials are used for phototypesetting, to record oscilloscope and other cathode-ray tube displays, and in a number of scientific and technical applications. A few very-high-contrast materials utilize diffusion trans-

High Key. Lilo Raymond, "Two Pillows" (1976). © Lilo Raymond; courtesy Marcuse Pfeifer Gallery, New York.

fer processing, but most are processed in conventional fashion with a very energetic, high-contrast developer. Lith film development time for maximum contrast is typically 2 to 3 minutes. High-contrast copy films (used to obtain copy negatives for making duplicate prints) are processed in more conventional high-contrast developers in order to retain a full range of well-separated tones.

The purpose of using a very-high-contrast material is to achieve bold, graphic images or clean, distinct halftone patterns by eliminating middle tones. When a full-range subject or image is photographed or printed on a very-high-contrast material, a certain number of tones at the maximum exposure end of the scale will be recorded as black; all others will fail to register and will be represented by white (or clear film). The number of tones that will be recorded, and the boundary or "break point" with those that will not be recorded, is determined by exposure (with some lith papers development can also affect the break point to some degree); increased exposure causes more tones to be recorded as black. The location of the break point can be determined by photographing or printing through a step-ped gray scale (step tablet) with various exposures. Because the steps are merged into all-black and all-white segments, it is easier to see the relative position of the break point by using opposed gray scales—matching scales placed side by side, but with the steps proceeding in opposite directions. The effect of processing on the break point can be determined by developing a series of identical gray-scale exposures for different lengths of time.

See also: CONTRAST; LITH FILMS/PAPERS.

High Key

The term high key describes a subject or an image in which white and light grays or pastel tints are predominant. The light tones are visible in all areas and create an effect of overall lightness or brightness. Small accents of dark tones heighten the high-key effect and help to emphasize differences among the light tones. An effective high-key photograph, with rich light tones, can only be produced with a fully lighted high-key subject. Soft, diffuse light minimizes shadow problems. Attempts to achieve a high-key rendition of a normal-range subject by overexposure of the film or underexposure of the print will only produce weak or muddy tones. However, exposure-meter readings from a high-key subject are deceptive because of the atypical brightness of the subject. An incident-light reading, or a reflected-light reading from a gray card will indicate proper exposure. If a reflected-light reading is taken directly from the subject, the indicated exposure should be increased by the equivalent of one to two *f*-stops for proper results.

See also: BRIGHTNESS RANGE; CONTRAST; EXPOSURE; EXPOSURE METERS; GRAY CARD; LOW KEY.

Highlights

The brightest areas of a subject or an image are called the highlights. An area may be light because of the color of the subject matter, such as pale skin or light-colored clothing, or it may be inherently bright, as with lamps, or fire. Often the brightness of an area derives from reflected light; this is often the case with sand, snow, or water in direct sunlight.

When films and prints are properly exposed and processed, highlights will show detail and traces of color or tone;

they will not be glaring, blank white areas. Indeed, most expressive photographs contain highlights that are detailed and crisp, and which fall within an overall tonal range that is not too contrasty. In some cases subject areas are so bright that they cause unavoidable overexposure. With black-and-white films this can be counteracted by reduced development. Even when highlights are overexposed or overdeveloped in a negative, their intensity in a print often can be reduced by techniques such as burning-in. Highlights in a negative are said to be "blocked" if they are too dense to be printed successfully.

See also: BLOCKED HIGHLIGHTS; BURNING-IN; GLARE.

High-Speed Photography

The definition of high-speed photography must continually be revised. Today some unspecialized 35mm cameras have focal-plane shutters with a nominal maximum speed of 1/4000 sec., and portable electronic flash units that produce light bursts only 1/10,000 sec. to 1/25,000 sec. long are readily available. What now constitutes high-speed photography lies beyond these ordinary capabilities of photography. The limit of the shortest exposure also must continually be redefined. A decade ago it was a few hundred millionths of a second, now it is a few trillionths (picoseconds) or less. And sequence rates of up to 600 million pictures per second (pps) are obtainable.

There are two approaches to securing high-speed images. One is to make a single exposure at the exact instant the event of interest occurs. That instant is sometimes difficult or even impossible to determine or predict—especially as the duration of the entire event grows shorter—and synchronizing the exposure with the instant is at least equally as difficult. The second approach is to take a series of exposures at a very high rate on a continuous strip or a single sheet of film. This increases the chance that whenever the peak instant occurs an exposure will be made. It also records the stages of development immediately before and after the instant. The images can be examined individually or, if taken with the proper equipment, can be projected as a motion picture with an extremely high slow-motion factor.

High-speed photography is often carried out with shutterless cameras because mechanical shutters can only reach top speeds of a few thousandths of a second. Electro-optical shutters such as a Kerr cell can produce exposures of near-nanosecond length, but are extremely limited in application. Capping shutters that open the image path and close it at the beginning and end of an exposure series are used, but the individual exposures are most often controlled by optical manipulation or by turning the light source on and off in a fraction of a second.

The first high-speed photograph, taken by W. H. F. Talbot in 1851, used the flash of a high-intensity electric spark as the exposure control. The camera shutter was open continuously in a darkened room; the brief flash froze the movement of a wagon wheel spinning on a support axle, and the print on a newspaper page attached to the wheel was sharp and readable in the processed image. Spark illumination was used in the 1880s by Ernst Mach and others to obtain pictures of bullets emerging from the muzzles of guns and in flight. Electric-spark illumination is still used for ballistic shadowgraphs, with exposures on the order of 10 nanoseconds. More widely used techniques of exposure control by light duration include electronic flash units that produce a light burst as short as one-millionth of a second, stroboscopes that pulse 10,000 or more times per second, and pulsed lasers that produce light bursts in the picosecond range. At these durations the speed of light itself becomes a significant factor. Light travels just over $11\frac{3}{4}$ in. in one nanosecond (billionth of a second). The timing of a light burst must allow for travel time so that the illumination reaches the subject at the required instant. This is especially a problem in recording very high-speed motion pictures.

In high-speed sequence photography images must be physically separated on the film in order to be clearly visible. At comparatively slow speeds of up to a few hundred exposures per second, motion-picture camera mechanisms and intermittent film movement can be used. At higher rates of speed the strain on the film can tear sprocket holes, and the time required to overcome inertia and get up to speed is too long. Various methods are used to increase the pictures-per-second rate. A smaller frame size is used so that the film has to move less distance between exposures. Continuous pull-through of the film, eliminating intermittent movement, is combined with film loading in festoons or loops rather than on spools or reels.

As the speed of film travel increases, even images created by pulsed light or with pulsed (electro-optical) shutters begin to be blurred by the film movement. This can be overcome by a rotating prism or mirror arrangement that moves the image at the same speed as the film, keeping it sharply focused on one point. Such devices have many facets so that separate images can be tracked in more rapid succession than waiting for one full revolution would permit. Although image or exposure rates are commonly specified as so many pictures per second, this is usually an equivalent rate because the entire recording takes less than a second. In many cases it simply is not possible to load or move enough film for a longer recording. If images are spaced only one-half in. apart, center to center, on the film, a rate of 50,000 pps would require about 2100 ft. of film. Few standard high-speed cameras accept film loads longer than 400 ft.

One solution to this problem is not to make separate images, but to record one long continuous image of a tiny portion of the subject seen through a slit aperture; this technique is described in the entry on streak photography.

A second solution, one which does provide separate images at higher pps rates, is not to move the film. Instead the images are optically formed in rapid succession at various points on the emulsion of a stationary sheet of film. In one method the film is covered with a mosaic of small lenses each of which momentarily forms an image as a rotating mirror or prism sweeps a view of the subject across them. Each image records a different instant of subject movement or change. In another method, optical fibers, each acting as a separate image cable from the camera lens to the face of the film, are made transmissive in succession by an electrical signal.

High-speed videography has been limited by maximum framing rates in the range of 60-2000fps. Without the capability of higher framing rates, greater action-stopping ability within the individual frame is achieved by using shuttered video (1/10,000 sec.) and/or synchronized strobe (1/100,000 sec.). Reduced picture area also helps achieve higher rates. Recent state-of-the-art high-speed video uses photo-capacitance solid state devices to achieve full frame speeds of 2000fps and up to 12,000 partial fps with synchronized strobe, further increasing the action-stopping ability to microseconds within the frame.

See also: FLOW PHOTOGRAPHY; IMAGE DISSECTION; KERR CELL; MIRROR CAMERA; MOTION STUDY AND ANALYSIS; SCHLIEREN PHOTOGRAPHY; STREAK CAMERA; STROBOSCOPIC PHOTOGRAPHY; TELEVISION.
Color photograph: p. C-24.

Hill, David Octavius

Scottish; 1802–1870

Adamson, Robert

Scottish; 1821–1848

The famous partnership and collaboration between the artist D. O. Hill and the photographer Robert Adamson came into being originally in order to produce photographic portraits to assist Hill as a painter. The team, however, produced a wide range of superb, independently valuable work and they were among the first to consistently and successfully employ W. H. F. Talbot's calotype process in Great Britain.

Robert Adamson was the younger brother of Dr. John Adamson, a chemist and academic at the University of St. Andrews, who produced the first calotype portrait in Scotland. Robert Adamson was instructed in photography by his brother, and during late 1842 he began to make calotype images. He apparently opened a professional portrait studio—the first in Scotland—in early 1843 in Edinburgh.

David Octavius Hill was the eighth child of a bookseller and publisher in Perth. He attended the School of Design in Edinburgh and employed his artistic talent learning the new printmaking method of lithography. In the 1820s he began a career as a landscape painter and illustrator. During 1831–1832 he illustrated the works of authors such as Sir Walter Scott and in 1840 prepared engravings to accompany the text of a *Life of Burns*. He was a founding member and secretary of the Royal Scottish Academy (1830) and was active in the formation of the National Academy of Scotland (1850). His paintings were exhibited at the Royal Scottish Academy, the Institution for the Encouragement of the Fine Arts, and the Royal Academy in London.

In May, 1843, 150 ministers took part in a group resignation at a meeting of 500 dignitaries and clergymen of the established Church of Scotland. They assembled at the Free Church of Scotland at Tanfield, Edinburgh, to oppose the appointment of ministers by Royal or landed authority. Hill was inspired by this rebellion to conceive a monumental commemorative painting of the event. Sir David Brewster, aware of the utility and inexpensiveness of the calotype, recommended its use as an aid in amassing the individual portraits required to depict the large assembly. Hill was introduced to Robert Adamson and in the summer of 1843 they began to collaborate on the production of calotype portraits as reference images for the painting.

Essentially, Hill posed and arranged the individual sitters or groups while Adamson attended to the technical aspects of the exposure, processing, and printing. Exposure with the calotype process at that period took one to two minutes and required that subjects be posed outdoors, although the impression of an interior might be simulated by the inclusion of tables, draperies, busts, pedestals, or books within the frame. Hill's painting, "The Signing of the Deed of Demission," (which measured 11 feet, 4 inches by 5 feet [3.45 by 1.5 meters]), was not completed until 1866. This tableau represents the 474 dignitaries, nearly all based on the photographic portraits, but as a consequence having somewhat the appearance of a montage.

From 1843 on, while involved in the calotype portraits, Hill and Adamson expanded their subject matter. Their reputation led to portrait commissions of eminent figures in both the arts and sciences of Victorian society. Some of their most powerful images, however, were made in Scottish seashore villages and depict fishermen and women. They also photographed the architecture and monuments of Scotland, and made calotypes of their friends posed in medieval armor or costumes in tableaux vivants.

Hill's instinctive feeling for bold, simple composition, natural posing, and strong chiaroscuro was well suited to the technical and formal attributes of the calotype. Since images had to be taken in direct sunlight and because the calotype did not reproduce an even range of tones (it tended to extremes of dark and light), the effect achieved often prompted comparison with precedents in British portraiture and even with Dutch masters such as Rembrandt. Sitters were typically posed against dark backgrounds with their features strongly lighted. On occasion light was reflected by means of mirrors, which were manipulated to produce broad, strong lighting effects designed to bring out the personality and highlight the physiognomy of the sitter. Hill commented that the technical imperfections of the calotype, with its generalized rendering of forms, made it artistically superior to the daguerreotype. The final prints were also subject to manipulation by hand. Hill and Adamson's prints were sold bound in albums or as single images, and their calotypes were exhibited at the Royal Scottish Academy from 1844 to 1846.

By the time of Adamson's death in 1848, the short-lived partnership had produced some 1500 images. Hill continued to be involved with photography, becoming a council member of the Photographic Society of Scotland in 1858 and working with another Scottish photographer, Alexander MacGlashon, during the 1860s. As a testament to the joint success and individual qualities of Hill and Adamson, however, neither produced independent work equal to their collaborative efforts.

Their work remained largely forgotten until the 1890s, when James Craig Annan made carbon prints of their work after rephotographing the original prints. Exhibition of these prints in England, and publication in Alfred Stieglitz's *Camera Work*, marked the beginning of the modern recognition of their portraits as a major achievement in the earliest years of photography, one that embodied a style and intuitive understanding of the expressive qualities of the medium that was far in advance of its time.

Photograph: p. 238.

Hill, Rev. Levi L.

American; 1816–1865

Hill was the "inventor" of the apparently fictitious *Hillotype*, which he claimed was a method for making full-color daguerreotypes. His announcement in 1851 of a direct full-color process excited the photographic world. Although there were some theories about how to obtain color photographs, only a few impermanent images of the spectrum had been obtained. The first demonstration of photography using the additive synthesis of color, by James Clerk Maxwell, was a decade in the future. In 1851 colored photographs were hand-colored images.

Hill offered to sell his secret for $10,000 or more, but avoided all opportunities to give a convincing demonstration to the few making serious offers. Most photographers who attempted to visit him in Westkill, New York, found that he was "out," or "too ill" to receive visitors. He next announced a comprehensive manual of the process to be published at $5.00 a copy and obtained a subscription list totalling upward of $15,000. The result was a poorly printed book that described the steps in making a daguerreotype and some added procedures. These apparently were based on the ability of silver chloride to temporarily retain a color image of the spectrum, as individually accomplished in the 1840s by Sir John Herschel and Edmond Becquerel, and later by C. F. Abel Niépce de Saint-Victor in a process he called *heliochromy*.

In 1851 a delegation of New York City professionals judged samples they saw to be hand-colored images applied to a daguerreotype by some transfer

process, or other imitations. Marcus Root, one of a delegation of Boston photographers the following year, reported that what he had seen was a daguerreotype hand-colored by techniques common in most portrait studios and not well done at that. In 1853 a committee investigating the controversy for Congress filed an inconclusive report. The most charitable explanation is that Hill stumbled upon or otherwise achieved a silver chloride image of the spectrum, but was not able to duplicate his results or extend the procedure to ordinary subjects. In an effort to keep interest—and investment—alive while he tried to solve the problem, he prepared faked images to fool the credulous and stall the more perceptive. The generally accepted explanation is that the Hillotype was a complete hoax.

See also: DAGUERREOTYPE; MAXWELL, JAMES CLERK.

Hine, Lewis Wickes

American; 1874–1940
Although Lewis Hine was neither the first—nor certainly the last—photographer to employ his camera in the cause

of social reform, the quality of his best work has rarely been equaled. Even more importantly, Hine's documentation of child labor was instrumental in effecting the reforms for which he struggled. Allied with many of the important figures of the Progressive and Reform movements, Hine was able to use his photographs to mobilize public concern and to generate corrective legislation.

Born in Wisconsin, Hine attended the University of Chicago for a year. In 1901 he came to New York, where his friend Frank A. Manny, Superintendent of the Ethical Culture School, engaged him to teach nature study and geography. In 1904 he began a photographic documentation of immigrants arriving and being processed on Ellis Island, a project he worked on for the next five years. Using magnesium powder flash, he photographed families, individuals, the facilities on the island. Shortly after meeting with Arthur Kellogg, the editor of the reformist social work journal *Charity and the Commons,* Hine was engaged as a freelance photographer for the National Child Labor Committee. Under the aegis of the NCLC, Hine traveled wide-

ly, photographing (often surreptitiously) children working in the mines, factories, and sweatshops of the northeast, the southeast, and the mid-Atlantic states. These photographs were reproduced in newspapers, within NCLC publications, and rented out in stereopticon slide format with accompanying lectures. During this same period, Hine photographed slum conditions in Washington, D.C., conditions in various industries, and street trades in Connecticut.

By the beginning of World War I, Hine had achieved considerable fame as a photographer, social worker, and reformer.

Traveling constantly, photographing, recording, gathering information, Hine considered his activities as a form of evidence for the present and history for the future. In 1918 he joined the American Red Cross. Sent to Europe, he photographed the living conditions of French and Belgian civilians reeling from the ravages of the war. Upon returning to New York, Hine made the photographs available to *The Survey* magazine with the hope of publicizing the devastation he had witnessed.

From 1922 to 1929, Hine was compelled to diversify his photographic activities. These included the acceptance of commercial assignments as well as some experimentation with art photography. Nonetheless, he was able to return to Ellis Island in 1926 to make a new series of photographs of immigrants, and also to continue an ongoing series of photographs of working people and craftsmen. In 1930, Hine photographed the construction of the Empire State Building; a selection of these images appeared two years later as a picture book intended for adolescents entitled *Men at Work*. In 1931, Hine received an assignment from the American Red Cross to photograph the drought-ridden rural communities of Arkansas and Kentucky. A portfolio of mill workers entitled *Through the Loom* produced in 1933 was exhibited at the World's Fair and brought Hine to the attention of TVA officials, who commissioned him to photograph construction activities at two dam sites. In the mid-1930s, Hine tried in vain to work for Roy Stryker's FSA photography project. His financial circumstances seem to have worsened considerably through the 1930s, and he was unable to secure grants from either the Carnegie Corporation or the Guggenheim Foundation. In 1938, however, Berenice Abbott and Elizabeth McCausland became interested in his work and arranged for several articles and retrospective exhibitions.

The magnitude of Hine's accomplishment is now undisputed. From the earliest photographs of newly arrived immigrants, through the relentless "documents" of child labor, to the heroic images of workers constructing the newly rising skyscrapers, Hine's work has a coherence and unity that reflects his principled belief in pictures as communication and his unwavering support and sympathy for the young, the poor, the immigrant, and the worker. As Alan Trachtenberg has written, "To be 'straight' for Hine meant more than purity of photographic means; it meant also a responsibility to the truth of his vision."
See also: DOCUMENTARY PHOTOGRAPHY; FILM AND PHOTO LEAGUE.

Hiro (Yasuhiro Wakabayashi)

Japanese; 1930–
For more than 20 years Hiro has been one of America's premier photographers in the areas of fashion, accessory, and product illustration. The clean, contemporary elegance and graphic power of his images has been imitated by many but rarely equaled, for he brings to his work a unique mix of cultural background, creative imagination, technical expertise, and personal perfectionism.

Hiro was born in Shanghai where his father, a linguist, was working on a Japanese–Chinese dictionary. His family moved to Peking after that city was captured by the Japanese in the late 1930s, and returned to Japan just after the end of World War II. Impressed by the functional design and technical superiority of American military equipment and of goods imported from the U.S. and by the elegance of Western fashion magazines, Hiro studied and apprenticed in photography in Tokyo with the intention of going to the U.S. to work for Irving Penn or Richard Avedon. He arrived in New York in January 1954, but no work was available with either of his idols. Instead, he studied briefly at a vocational photography school and became an assistant to two established commercial photographers. He persisted and finally got a job as an assistant to Avedon in 1956. His talent was immediately apparent and his skill grew so rapidly that in 1958 Avedon encouraged Hiro to become a freelance photographer and to share his studio. At the same time, Avedon brought Hiro's newest work to the attention of Alexey Brodovitch, art director of *Harper's Bazaar*. After an exacting tryout assignment, Hiro was hired to create still lifes for *Bazaar*, and from 1965 to 1975 the magazine had an exclusive contract for his services.

During his early period as a freelance photographer, Hiro also attended the Brodovitch seminars at the New School for Social Research in New York and subsequently was Brodovitch's personal assistant in his American Institute of Graphic Arts Design Laboratory. Both Brodovitch and Avedon were extremely important influences on Hiro, not in directing the development of his style, but in encouraging and responding only to images that were technically impeccable and completely fresh and unimitative in their vision and design. Such standards reinforced Hiro's own instinct never to stop short of perfection or to be satisfied with images that were not unique. His ability to work to these standards took him to the top of his profession almost immediately.

Hiro's illustrations are marked by an integration of color and design that is simultaneously elegant, bold, and subtle. Such a description is not self-contradictory, for the manner in which Hiro achieves startling clarity or intriguing complexity relies on the faultless use of nuances of color, line, and form. Much of his approach obviously derives from the oriental traditions of color, design, and decoration that he absorbed as a youth, but it would be most inaccurate to ascribe his style to those early influences alone. He has also absorbed Western traditions of graphic design and modern functionalism. The result is a style that continually produces the most contemporary statements by finding new ways to use the established elements of both Eastern and Western visual communication.

Hiro lives and works in New York City. He is preparing a book that includes his little-known portraits, landscapes, reportage, and casual pictures as well as the illustrations for which he is world famous.
See also: ADVERTISING PHOTOGRAPHY; AVEDON, RICHARD; BRODOVITCH, ALEXEY.

History of Photography

Like almost all other inventions of the 19th c. and early 20th c., photography was the result of accumulated technical knowledge or information finally being integrated in response to unspoken cultural demand and even necessity. The fundamental piece of equipment, the camera obscura, had existed for more than three centuries. The basic chemical information, the light sensitivity of silver compounds, had been known for almost 100 years. The idea of capturing images from nature with some sort of magic mirror had arisen in literature and fable. And by the beginning of the 19th c. the attitude was well established that with science and mechanics, human ingenuity could accomplish anything it wished. In fact, photography was an idea whose time had come, and so it is not surprising that when it was finally invented, it was invented by several people independently and simultaneously.

The first, unsuccessful experiments in the direction of photography were undertaken by Thomas Wedgwood about 1800. Impermanent images were actually obtained on material inserted in a camera obscura in 1822 by J. Nicéphore Niépce, who recorded the earliest extant permanent image in 1826. Photography in the modern sense—the recording of an image focused by a lens onto light-sensitive silver compounds—arrived, in 1839, into a world that had been primed with advance hints and allusions, in the form of L. J. M. Daguerre's method for making direct positive images on silver-coated metal plates. The development of this method was followed immediately by a method, invented by Hippolyte Bayard, for making direct positives on paper and a paper negative process, invented by W. H. F. Talbot, by which positive prints were made on paper. The *daguerreotype* immediately captured the public imagination and firmly established photography as a new visual medium, because although its procedures were difficult and cumbersome, its results were exquisite. The talbotype, or *calotype*, was technically less perfect, but of far greater long-range importance, for the negative-positive technique is the foundation of virtually all subsequent developments in the medium.

Those developments constitute a great part of the content of this encyclopedia. The accompanying list groups key entries that include significant historical material into three areas of interest: the origins and invention of photography; photographic processes and related technical developments; applications, and the communicative and expressive uses of photography. Most entries also include cross-references that will lead to further information. In addition, this encyclopedia contains more than 200 biographical entries devoted to individual photographers, and more than 150 entries devoted to other persons important in the growth of the medium. Some of these entries are included in the accompanying list, but many more also contain information bearing on the history of photography. The development of color photography is covered in the article COLOR PHOTOGRAPHY — HISTORY.

HISTORY OF PHOTOGRAPHY—KEY ENTRIES

A. Origins and Invention

Arago, F.
Bayard, H.
Calotype
Camera Lucida
Camera Obscura
Chevalier, C. L.
Chretien, G. L.
Daguerre, L. J. M.
Daguerreotype
Draper, J. W.
Giroux, A.
Goddard, J. F.
Herschel, J.
Niépce, J. N.
"Pencil of Nature, The"
Petzval, J. M.
Scheele, C. W.
Schulze, J. H.
Talbot, W. H. F.
Wedgwood, T.
Wolcott, A. S.
Wollaston, W. H.
Young, T.

B. Processes and Technical Developments

Abbe, E.
Agfa
Albumen Processes
Ambrotype
Aniline Process
ANSCO
Anthony, E. & H. T.
Archer, F. S.
Autochrome
Baird, J. L.
Barnack, O.
Bichromate Processes
Brewster, D.
Bromoil Process
Brownie Camera
Cabinet Photograph
Carbon Processes
Carbutt, J.
Carlson, C.
Carte-de-visite
Celluloid
Collodion Processes
Cutting, J.
Dry Plates
Dufaycolor
Dye Sensitization
Eastman, G.
Edgerton, H. E.
Ferrotype
Finlaycolor
Fizeau, H.
Gabor, D.
Gauss, K. F.
Goodwin, Rev. H.
Hill, Rev. L. L.
Hurter, F., & Driffield, V. C.
Ilford
Iron Printing Processes
Jena Glass
Kallitype
Keller-Dorian Process
Kinetoscope
Kodachrome
Kodak
Land, E. H.
Leica
Lumiere, A. & L.
Maddox, R. L.
Mannes, L., & Godowski, L.
Maxwell, J. C.
Mosaic Systems
Mutoscope
Photogravure
Platinotype
Vogel, H. W.
Waxed Paper Process
Wet Plate Process
Woodburytype
Zoopraxiscope
Zworykin, V.

C. Applications, Communicative and Expressive Growth

Abstract Photography
Allegorical Photographs
"Animal and Human Locomotion"
Artists and Photography
Art of Photography
Atget, E.
Bauhaus
Beard, R.
Bischof, W.
Blanquart-Evrard, L. D.
Books, Photographic
Brady, M.
Brassaï
"Camera Work"
Cameron, J. M.
Capa, R.
Cartier-Bresson, H.
Claudet, A. F. J.
Coburn, A. L.
Collecting Photographica
Conceptual Photography
Demachy, R.
Disderi, A.
Documentary Photography
Ducamp, M.
Ducos du Hauron, L.
Emerson, P. H.
Equivalent Image
Farm Security Administration
Fenton, R.
Film and Photo League
Frank, R.
Genre Photography
Hill, D. O., & Adamson, R.
Impressionistic Photography
Kertész, A.
Linked Ring Brotherhood
Marey, E. J.
Motion Study & Analysis
Muybridge, E.
Naturalistic Photography
Neue Sachlichkeit
Painting and Photography
Photogram
Photorealism
Photo Secession
"Pictorial Effect in Photography"
Pictorial Photography
Postvisualization
Previsualization
Rejlander, O. G.
Robinson, H. P.
Sander, A.
Satire in Photography
Smith, W. E.
Social Landscape
Stieglitz, A.
Surrealism in Photography
Thompson, J.
Uelsmann, J. N.

See also: BOOKS, PHOTOGRAPHIC; LITERATURE OF PHOTOGRAPHY.

Hoegh, Emil von
German; 1865–1915

A lens designer for C. P. Goerz Optical Works, Berlin, Hoegh's innovative designs were among the first to exploit the potentials of the newly developed (1890) Jena glass variants of standard crown and flint glasses. His designs, like those of Paul Rudolph, established principles that have been imitated and elaborated upon to the present day. His first major lens was the double anastigmat of 1892, subsequently known as the Dagor lens.

See also: APLANAT; DAGOR LENS; GOERZ, CARL PAUL; JENA GLASS.

Holography

Holography is a unique method of three-dimensional photography. A holographic recording, or hologram (Greek: *holos* = entire; *gram* = message), presents a virtual image of the subject in three dimensions that changes in parallax and perspective as the viewing angle changes. That is, objects in depth visually cover and uncover one another as the viewing angle shifts from side to side, just as they would when seen while walking past the actual objects. Similarly, the distances between objects (depth perspective) change as the viewpoint moves toward or away from the hologram. In a conventional stereoscopic photograph, these changes do not occur as the viewpoint shifts.

Holograms are recorded by means of coherent light—light of essentially a single wavelength in which all waves are precisely in phase (vibrating in unison), are of the same amplitude (size), and are traveling in the same direction. Such light is produced by a laser. Ordinary photographs are made with incoherent light, which is composed of mixed wavelengths with random phase relationships. The image recorded in conventional photography is a lens-focused pattern of the brightness and color differences in the incoherent light reflected or emitted by the subject. The image is directly visible when the negative or transparency is examined.

A hologram records the standing wave pattern created by interference between two beams of light. The recorded pattern does not form a visible image until specially illuminated. Otherwise, the film shows only a pattern of ripples or whorls, indecipherable by eye.

In making a hologram, a beam of coherent light from a laser is passed through a beam splitter. Lenses and mirrors guide one portion of the light to the emulsion; this is the reference beam. The other portion of the light is guided to the subject, where it is reflected toward the emulsion as the object beam. The reference beam is coherent, but the object beam is incoherent because differences in object shapes, textures, and locations cause various portions of the reflected light to travel different distances. The incoherence, or phase differences in the object beam represent spatial information; the amount of light at each point in the beam represents the brightness reflectivity of the subject at that point. The variations in the object beam combine (interfere) with the constant phase and intensity of the reference beam at the film plane, adding or subtracting according to phase and amplitude differences, producing patterns called *interference fringes*. The image recorded on the hologram differs from conventional photographic images in two ways. First, the information it contains is encoded, as in interference fringes. Second, the image contains two kinds of information: the reflected brightness of various points on the subject (recorded as contrast variations in the interference fringes); and the distance of various points on the subject (recorded as spacing variations in the interference fringes). Exposure is controlled by a shutter at the laser's output.

A unique quality of a (single-image) hologram is that the characteristics of the interference pattern are recorded everywhere on the plate. Thus, an entire image can be reconstructed from any portion of the plate—a small fragment of a broken plate, for example. However, the fragment will reproduce perspective and parallax only as seen from a proportionately more restricted viewpoint. Further, the smaller the piece used for reconstruction, the dimmer the image.

The variations in the wave pattern are so finely spaced that an emulsion with a resolving power some 30 times greater than that of ordinary films must be used to obtain sharp holograms. The emulsion must be absolutely flat; coated glass plates are used, or sheet films are adhered to glass. The entire set-up must be absolutely free of vibration; spurious interference that destroys the image pattern can result from as little as a quarter-wavelength vibration in any component, in the subject, or in air currents in the optical path. Most holographic set-ups

are made on isolation tables with massive concrete or metal bases weighing several hundred pounds, or on heavy sand tables supported on pneumatic cushions.

There are two basic kinds of holograms, transmission and reflection. A transmission hologram is made with both the object and reference beams striking the emulsion side of the plate. It is viewed by shining laser light through it and observing the transmitted image from the other side. A reflection hologram is made with two beams striking opposite sides of the plate. It is viewed by reflecting white light, rather than laser light, off the emulsion and observing the image from the illuminated side. No special optical device is required for viewing. The image exists in space; it can be seen and photographed just as if the actual objects were there. Depending on the original set-up and the viewing arrangement, there are limits to the angles from which the image is visible. Although the image can be projected onto a screen, like a conventional slide, this destroys its three-dimensional quality.

A number of variations are possible. Greater fidelity of detail is achieved by splitting the object light into two beams before it encounters the object, each from a different direction. A full-color hologram can be created by using red, green, and blue lasers, each from a different angle, and using matching beams for viewing, or by various single-layer techniques. In a multi-channel hologram, up to several hundred separate images can be recorded on one plate by turning the plate so that the reference beam strikes it at a different angle with each exposure. Shifting the plate angle during viewing makes the successive images visible. Short, limited-parallax motion picture holograms (like 3-D zoetropes) are also possible. A moving subject is photographed under controlled lighting conditions on ordinary movie film. The film is projected frame by frame through a slit-aperture set-up that records each frame as a strip interference pattern on the plate. During viewing the plate or viewing system components move continuously to image each frame in succession.

Holography was described as a theoretical possibility in 1947 by Dennis Gabor, who was working on ways to improve the resolution of images obtained in the electron microscope. Practical application of the idea was not possible until after invention of the laser in 1960. The first two-beam interference image recordings were made shortly thereafter by Emmett Leith and Juris Upatnieks.

At present holography is primarily a scientific and technical tool. It has been used in limited ways for advertising displays and as an art medium, but its applications have been restricted by the cumbersome recording and viewing set-ups required. It has great potential for illustrating texts and magazines with three-dimensional images and for storing entire libraries on a single plate, if the process can be simplified to an extent that makes it commercially feasible. Full-length motion picture holograms have the potential of being the ultimate in three-dimensional movies. Experimental attempts have so far been able to achieve a viewing area no more than four to six seats wide.

See also: INTERFERENCE; LASER; LIGHT; WAVELENGTH.

Hoppé, Emil Otto

British; 1878–1972

E.O. Hoppé was one of the best-known, prolific, and most successful portrait photographers of London high society in the first decades of the 20th c. He made several series of portraits of famous dancers, including members of Diaghilev's Ballet Russe, as well as a considerable body of influential fashion and theatre photography. Hoppé's portraits were acclaimed for their tastefulness, rich tones and textures, and for the unconventional, informal poses of his aristocratic sitters such as Einstein, George V and Queen Mary, Richard Strauss, Mussolini, and a gallery of writers including Henry James, Ezra Pound, Thomas Hardy, Somerset Maugham, George Bernard Shaw, and Sinclair Lewis.

After 1925 Hoppé created another large body of distinguished travel photography, rural and urban landscapes, shooting subjects around the world. In his final years, he was working as a photojournalist and in abstract nature photography.

Emil Otto Hoppé was born in Munich, Germany, and educated in Paris and Vienna. He studied painting under watercolorist Hans von Bartels but was persuaded to enter his family's banking business. Hoppé served in the German Army from 1895 to 1897. He emigrated to England in 1900 and worked there as a clerk for Deutsche Bank until 1907.

Soon after his arrival in London, Hoppé was introduced to photography by J.C. Warburg. He became a photographic hobbyist and joined the Royal Photographic Society as an amateur in 1903. He became friendly with Alvin Langdon Coburn at this time

Hoppe, E.O. "Alice Meynall" (1908). The Gernsheim Collection, Humanities Research Center, University of Texas at Austin.

and was awarded several prizes at exhibitions between 1905 and 1907.

Between 1907 and 1939, Hoppé was a professional photographer and operated a succession of London portrait studios in Barons Court, Baker Street, and South Kensington. He received a Royal Photographic Society Fellowship in 1907 and was given his first one-man show of photographs at the Society's salon in 1910. He had been a founding member of the London Salon of Photography in 1909 and served as art editor and contributor to *Colour* magazine beginning in 1913.

Hoppé began to do fashion photography in 1916, and worked as a freelance photographer specializing in theatre, portrait, and fashion work between 1919 and 1939. He operated a studio in New York during part of the year from 1919 to 1921, and again in 1926. He began to concentrate on travel and landscape images in Britain and Ireland in 1925, and made portraits at Ufa Film Studios in Berlin in 1927. In the next decade he traveled and photographed around the world. Hoppé was director of the Doreign Leigh photo and illustration agency in London beginning in 1939. He continued to publish and exhibit until his death in 1972 at the age of 94.

Throughout his career, Hoppé published photographs and drawings in popular periodicals, including *Vanity Fair*, British *Vogue*, *Lilliput*, *Picture Post*, *The Illustrated London News*, *The Tatler*, and *The Graphic*. He published a dozen books, including his autobiography, *One Hundred Thousand Exposures* (1945).

Hoppé was honored with solo exhibitions at Goupil Galleries, London, in 1913 and 1922 (the latter a major portrait retrospective of 221 prints that solidified Hoppé's reputation); the National Portrait Gallery, London, in 1978; Sonnabend Gallery, New York, in 1979; and Photo Center Gallery, New York University, in 1982. His work was exhibited in group shows including the International Exhibition of Photography, Dresden, in 1909 (at which he was an official British representative); *Fashion 1900–1939* at the Victoria and Albert Museum, London, in 1975; *Fashion Photography* at George Eastman House, Rochester, N.Y., in 1975; and *Old and Modern Masters of Photography* at the Victoria and Albert Museum in 1980.

Horst, Horst P.

American; 1906–

Horst is among the most important fashion photographers of the 20th c. His work for the Condé Nast Corporation spans almost 60 years. As a young photographer he developed a unique style, which has remained consistent to this day, marked by an easy elegance, theatricality, humor, dramatic and inventive composition, and refined and subtle color sensibilities. Technically, complex lighting arrangements underlie his arresting images.

Horst is also well known for his portraits of famous men and women, and his elegant studies of home interiors. He is less well known for his dramatic nudes and delicate still-lifes. He has also employed photography to chronicle his personal travels around the world.

Born in Weissenfels, Germany, Horst first studied art in Hamburg. Finding art school mundane, he made arrangements to work with Le Corbusier in Paris, where he became interested in photography. He was invited by *Vogue's* art director to try his hand in the studio, where he demonstrated a natural talent for the medium. During this period he also developed a close friendship with the fashion photographer George Hoyningen-Huene, posing for him and assisting him in his work. While living in Paris Horst developed close friendships with notables of the worlds of art, literature, and fashion such as Janet Flanner, Gertrude Stein, and Coco Chanel.

Between 1935 and 1940 Horst divided

Horst, Horst P. "Jewelry" (1930). Courtesy
Horst; permanent collection, ICP, New York.

Hosoe, Eikoh. "Ordeal by Roses #6" (1962).
Courtesy Eikoh Hosoe.

his time between New York and Paris, moving permanently to New York in 1940. During the war he served in the United States Army, afterward returning to work on Condé Nast publications. In 1946 he published his first book, *Photographs of a Decade,* which was followed in the same year by *Patterns of Nature.* In 1971 Horst's work was published alongside that of his friend Huene in *Salute to the Thirties.* Horst's work has been exhibited in numerous group shows and on several occasions in private galleries as solo exhibitions. In 1984 a full-scale traveling retrospective of his work in all fields was prepared by the International Center of Photography in New York and a biography by Valentine Lawford was published (Knopf).

Hosoe, Eikoh

Japanese; 1933–
One of Japan's most intriguing photographers, Eikoh Hosoe has elaborated

upon a private, poetic world in several series of stylized, high-contrast photographs made over the last 25 years. His dreamlike nudes and figure studies enact mysterious and erotically suggestive narratives. His major series include "Man and Woman" (1961) and its extension "Embrace" (1971), "Kamaitachi" (1969), and "Ordeal by Roses" (1963 and 1971). The latter two employed the acclaimed dancer Tatsumi Hijikata and the late writer Yukio Mishima as stand-ins for the photographer in landscapes of memory, dreams, death, and desire. Recent work includes photographs of architecture by Gaudi.

Hosoe, the son of a Shinto priest, was born Toshihiro Hosoe in Yonezawa, Yamagata Prefecture, Japan. He began to photograph as a young boy and attended the Tokyo College of Photography from 1951 to 1954, after which he began his career as a freelance photographer. His first one-man show, *An American Girl in Tokyo,* was mounted in 1956 at Konishiroku Gallery, Ginza, Tokyo.

Hosoe has done little commercial work, relying on teaching assignments for his livelihood. He has taught at the Tokyo College of Photography and the Tokyo Institute of Polytechnics for the last decade, and has taught numerous workshops, including the Ansel Adams Workshop at Yosemite. Hosoe has worked as a film director and has published six volumes of his photographic work as well as collaborations with the American writer Betty Jean Lifton.

Hosoe is the recipient of many awards, including the Newcomers Award in 1961 and the Photographer of the Year Award in 1964 both from the Japan Photo Critics Association. In 1970 he received the Art Award of the Japanese Ministry of Education.

Hosoe's work has been exhibited in *Photography in the 20th Century* at the National Gallery of Canada in Ottawa (1967), *New Japanese Photography* at the Museum of Modern Art in New York City (1974), and other group shows around the world. He has been honored with solo exhibitions at several Tokyo galleries and at the Smithsonian Institution in Washington, D.C., the Light Gallery in New York City, George Eastman House in Rochester, New York, the Focus Gallery in San Francisco, and the Friends of Photography in Carmel, California. He continues to live and work in Tokyo.

Hoyningen-Huene, George

American; 1900–1968

George Hoyningen-Huene was an innovative fashion photographer for *Vogue* and *Harper's Bazaar* from 1925 to 1945. His work was characterized by wit and classical composition in highly theatrical studio settings. Huene combined the conventional high-fashion iconography with motifs taken from the avant-garde art movements of his day. He photographed the fashions of all the top designers including Schiaparelli, Grès and Vionnet. Influenced by the fashion photography of Edward Steichen, Huene in turn was a significant influence on photographers such as Horst and Irving Penn. On the occasion of a retrospective of Huene's work at the International Center of Photography in 1980, Richard Avedon wrote, "Huene stands alone. There would be no Fashion Photography as we know it without him."

In addition to his fashion work, Huene made travel and architectural views in the Middle East, Greece, and Africa, as well as portraits of such celebrities as Igor Stravinsky, Jean Cocteau, Greta Garbo, Katherine Hepburn, G. W. Pabst, Marlene Dietrich, and Sophia Loren.

Born into a family of minor Russian nobility in St. Petersburg, Huene later attended the Lutheran Preparatory School and the Imperial Gymnasium in that city. Fleeing Russia during the Revolution, he lived briefly in Sweden before settling in Paris, where he studied art at the Académie de la Grande Chaumière in 1919–1920, and at the studio of the cubist painter André Lhote from 1922 to 1924. During the latter years he also worked as a freelance sketch artist for *Harper's Bazaar* and *Jardin des Modes*, becoming a staff illustrator and studio decorator for Paris *Vogue* in 1924. He began to photograph in 1925.

From 1926 to 1931, Huene was Chief Photographer for *Vogue*, first in Paris, then in New York. After a short period in 1931–1932 with Condé Nast Publications in Hollywood and Berlin, he be-

Hoyningen-Huene, George. "Friends" (Horst and model, Fashion: Izod, from *Vogue*— 1930). Courtesy Condé-Nast Publications Inc.

came a staff fashion photographer for *Harper's Bazaar* in New York, where he worked under the editor Carmel Snow and the designer Alexey Brodovitch from 1935 to 1945.

Huene returned to Hollywood in 1946 to work as a consultant and color designer to George Cukor and other directors. He became a naturalized American citizen the same year. He remained in California where he was an Instructor of Photography at the Art Center School, Los Angeles, until his death in 1968.

Huene received many awards for his fashion photography and was honored with the Photokina Photographic Award in 1963. His images have appeared in major surveys of fashion photography in London, Paris, Los Angeles, and New York, and his work was included in the 1929 *Film und Foto* exhibition, Stuttgart, and in a group exhibit presented jointly by Hofstra University and the Museum of Modern Art, New York. Solo exhibitions of Huene's photographs have been held at the Los Angeles County Museum and in New York at the Sonnabend Gallery. ICP has mounted a comprehensive retrospective of his work.

Hurter, Ferdinand

Swiss; 1844–1898

A chemist, from 1867 on in England, Hurter was a co-worker and fellow amateur photographer of Vero C. Driffield. Together they brought scientific method to the study of exposure, development, and the speed of materials. In evolving the field of study now called sensitometry, they first devised an *actinograph* to measure light intensity and relate it to exposure requirements. Next they created a sensitometer to give a repeatable, uniform set of exposures to an emulsion, and a densitometer (based on the grease-spot photometer of Robert Bunsen) to measure the effect of each exposure after development. To relate the factors in their experiments in terms of measured data, they originated the definition and measurement of density, the graphing method which produces the characteristic curve (at one time commonly called, from their initials, the H & D curve), and the concepts and methods for deriving from the graph the development or contrast factor gamma, and a rating of sensitivity expressed as an H & D speed. Their researches, published beginning in 1890, also covered latent-image theory, the mechanism of negative and positive image development, enlarging, and a number of other topics.

See also: CHARACTERISTIC CURVE; DENSITY; DRIFFIELD, VERO CHARLES; GAMMA; H & D SPEED; LATENT IMAGE; PHOTOMETER/PHOTOMETRY; SENSITOMETRY; SPEED OF MATERIALS.

Hyalograph

A hyalograph is an etched photographic image on glass (Greek: *hualos* = glass; *graphein* = writing, drawing). In its production, a sheet of paper is coated with a gum-bichromate emulsion to which a 10 percent sugar solution or thinned honey has been added. When dry, the paper is exposed by contact under a positive transparency to sunlight or an artificial light source. The image is "developed" by breathing warm moist air on it by mouth, or by very lightly misting it with warm water from an atomizer. The unexposed (shadow) areas and partially exposed middletones become tacky and retain a powdered resist, which is dusted on next; the highlights, hardened by exposure, do not hold the resist. Bitumen powder was used originally; today aquatint resin is used. The face of the emulsion is now pressed in contact with the glass, which has been heated so that it slightly melts the resist, causing it to adhere. When dry, the paper backing and the emulsion are washed away, leaving only a negative resist image on the glass. All non-image areas, including the edges and back of the glass, must be completely covered with varnish or tape to protect them from etching, which is accomplished by suspending the glass face-down over the fumes arising from a hydrofluoric-acid solution in a plastic or hard-rubber container (the acid attacks glass and metal). Good ventilation, rubber gloves, a respirator mask, and goggles are essential for personal protection. When the etching has reached a satisfactory state, the plate is washed, the resist and masking material are removed, and the plate is washed again. The etched glass is meant for viewing against a dark background. The unetched shadow areas let the background color show through; the etched areas block the background and scatter light striking their surfaces so that they look brighter, forming middletones and highlights.

See also: AQUATINT; GLASS, PHOTOGRAPHS ON.

Hyalotype

A hyalotype was a positive transparency on an albumen-coated glass plate (Greek: *hualos* = glass). It was introduced as a method for making lantern slides by Frederick and William Langenheim in 1849. The process was also used for larger glass transparencies placed in windows as decorative images to be viewed by transmitted daylight. It was replaced by the superior method of using collodion-coated glass plates after 1851. The term *hyalotypie* had previously been used for a cliché-verre technique introduced in Germany in 1840 by F. A. W. Netto.

See also: ALBUMEN PROCESSES; CLICHÉ-VERRE; COLLODION PROCESSES; LANGENHEIM, F. & W.; LANTERN SLIDE.

Hyperfocal Distance

The near limit (starting distance, measured from the camera) of the depth of field of a lens focused at infinity is the hyperfocal distance. It is different for each *f*-stop setting of the lens aperture. When a lens is focused at the hyperfocal distance for the *f*-stop in use, depth of field extends from one-half that distance to infinity. Many fixed-focus cameras have the lens set for the hyperfocal distance of the maximum aperture to take advantage of this condition. The hyperfocal distance, H, for any *f*-stop can be calculated from the lens focal length, F, and the circle of confusion, c, for the format in use, as follows:

$$H = F^2 \div (f\text{-no.} \times c)$$

(A useful value for the circle of confusion is 1/1500 of the normal lens focal length; e.g., in 35mm photography, 1/1500 of 50mm, or 0.03mm.) Using the hyperfocal distance simplifies depth-of-field calculations.

See also: CIRCLE OF CONFUSION; DEPTH OF FIELD.

Hypersensitizing

Hypersensitizing is a treatment to increase the speed of a film emulsion before exposure. It is distinct from latensification, in which the film is treated after exposure but before development, and from intensification, in which the developed image is strengthened after the fixing bath. Hypersensitized films should be exposed and processed as soon as possible after treatment because the effect begins to diminish almost immediately. The procedure is of little use for most ordinary photography, but can be of value in astronomical and other kinds of photography in which long exposures at very low light levels are required. The simplest method of hypersensitization is a flashing pre-exposure; it can be applied on a frame-by-frame basis as required, and it involves no chemicals or unusual film handling. An exposure about 1/200 of normal minimum exposure is required. This can be achieved by determining the exposure that produces the first printable tone (i.e., a density about 0.1 above filmbase-plus-fog) and lighting a neutral gray or white surface to that level. Then, an exposure at the indicated shutter speed and *f*-stop through a 2.0 neutral density (ND) filter with an 18 percent gray card—or a 3.0 ND filter with a white surface—will produce the necessary pre-exposure. Chemical hypersensitizing involves soaking the film for about five minutes in distilled water or, for a greater speed increase, a solution of 3 percent 0.880 ammonia and 24 percent pure alcohol in water. The film must be treated and dried quickly in total darkness, and used immediately. This treatment removes soluble restrainer from the emulsion, so that an anti-foggant must be added to the developer to avoid loss of contrast and shadow-area detail. A film can also be hypersensitized by suspending it in a closed location for a few hours with an open container of 20–30 percent potassium metabisulfite solution; fumes from the solution create the chemical reaction. Older methods involving mercury fumes are too poisonous to be attempted today except in the most rigorously controlled and expertly supervised conditions. The amount of speed increase obtained by any method varies with the kind of emulsion and the specific procedures used; it can only be determined by making controlled tests. *See also:* INTENSIFICATION; LATENSIFICATION.

Hyperstereoscopy
See: STEREOSCOPIC PHOTOGRAPHY.

Hypo; Hyposulfite of Soda
The photographic fixing agent now known as *sodium thiosulfate* was originally called hyposulphite of soda. Its property of making silver salts water-soluble, which they normally are not,

was discovered by Sir John Herschel in 1819. He drew on this knowledge to wash the silver halides out of a negative he produced in January 1839, thereby making the image permanent. He suggested this procedure to others, and it was immediately adopted for the daguerreotype process. Strangely, W. H. F. Talbot resisted using it for his calotype process for at least a year, using instead a salt-water solution or potassium bromide, neither of which prevented image fading for long. The term hypo—used even today to mean both the chemical and the fixing bath—derives from the original name of the compound. During the wet plate period (approximately

1850–1875) hypo was generally replaced by potassium or sodium cyanide, which provided more rapid fixing with collodion processes and their acidic developers. Hypo came back into use with the introduction of gelatin-silver halide emulsions and alkaline developers. It has been the universal fixing agent ever since, rivaled only in some applications by the more rapid-acting but less stable related compound, ammonium thiosulfate.
See also: FIXING.

Hypo Eliminator
See: ARCHIVAL PROCESSING; WASHING.

Jacobi, Lotte. "Lotte Lenya" (1930). Courtesy Lotte Jacobi.

I.C.I.

I.C.I. stands for International Commission on Illumination, more properly known as C.I.E. from its title in French: Commission Internationale de l'Eclairage.
See: CIE COLOR SYSTEM.

Identification Photographs

Photographs are widely used to provide descriptions of individuals, or of objects that cannot be described accurately by other methods. The value of photographs to catalog objects and to provide identification in the event of their damage, destruction, or theft was suggested by W. H. F. Talbot in 1844, in his book *The Pencil of Nature*. The use of photographs for insurance purposes is an area of significant growth today. Louis Dodero, a Marseilles photographer, in 1851 suggested the use of photographs as a means for an individual to establish identity (as on passports) or rights (as on permits and licenses). This procedure was first instituted with season tickets issued in 1861 by the Chicago and Milwaukee Railroad. Photographic identification of individuals for purposes of government administration and social control began in Switzerland in 1852 with a policy of photographing all vagrants and beggars. Public-notice identification began the same year in France, with the first photographic "Wanted" notice circulated by the police. Photo records of prisoners and persons arrested for crimes were instituted in England and the U.S. about 1860.

Today personal identity photographs are by far the largest area of identification photography. Almost all are made with instant photography films and cameras that produce two or more identical images in a single exposure. Photographic identification cards, bearer licenses, and the like are commonly laminated in plastic to make them tamperproof. Although not infallible—individuals can change their appearance or photographs can be altered—photography is the most widely used mode of identification because it requires only an immediate visual comparison for verification. All other methods, such as fingerprinting or blood typing, require special equipment, records, and training to make verification.

Ilford

An English company, Ilford is a leading manufacturer of photographic materials. The firm was founded in the London suburb of Ilford in 1879 by A. H. Harman to produce gelatin dry plates—the Ilford Plate—which by the mid-1890s were the largest selling in the world outside the U.S. Originally called the Brittania Works Co., it became a public corporation under new ownership in 1898 and was renamed Ilford, Limited in 1900. The line of plates and papers (added in 1884) was expanded to include cameras, early color materials, and in 1912 roll film and motion picture film. It absorbed several British photographic companies in the 1920s and 1930s, began manufacture of scientific plates and films in 1932, and introduced the developing agent *Phenidone*, a powerful substitute for metol, in 1942. Experience with color processes in the 1930s and following World War II led to an association with CIBA AG of Switzerland in 1963 and introduction of a dye destruction process called Cilchrome, later *Cibachrome*. Ilford became part of CIBA in 1969 and is the managing organization of an international group that includes Lumière (now Ilford) SA of France and CIBA-Geigy Photochemie AG of Switzerland. *See also:* DYE DESTRUCTION PROCESS; P-Q DEVELOPER.

Image Amplifier

An image amplifier is an electronic device or system that multiplies the effect of light in a faint image as much as 15,000 times or more to produce an image that can be seen or photographed easily. Such devices are used for observation and photography in surveillance, astronomy, military operations, underwater investigations, study of high-speed phenomena, and many kinds of night and low-light activities. A powerful image amplifier can make objects on the earth illuminated only by starlight clearly visible.

There are several kinds of image amplifiers. Originally bulky devices that required large, heavy power supplies, modern image amplifiers have been miniaturized to the point that they can be built directly into reasonably compact lenses. An image converter is one kind of image amplifier, although the terms are often used interchangeably, along with "image intensifier." As a broad distinction, an image amplifier or intensifier operates from an original image in the visible range, while an image converter operates from an image formed by invisible wavelengths such as ultraviolet or infrared. An image amplifier may be used as a component of an image converter system.

The basic configuration of an image amplifier consists of an optical lens, a collector screen, amplifier/multiplier stages, and a viewing screen. The optical lens focuses a faint image on the collector screen, which may have an electron-emissive coating or may be a mosaic of charge-coupled device (CCD) elements. The screen emits several hundred or thousand electrons for each photon of light it receives at each point of the image. The electron streams may fall on a succession of such screens, with cascaded increases at each stage, or they may be processed by photomultipliers that achieve an equivalent effect. The output of the final stage of amplification falls on the coating of the viewing screen, which fluoresces with a brightness proportional to the increased electron intensity at each point of the image. The screen image can be viewed directly, or photographed with ordinary films and equipment.

Because amplification deals with electron energy, not electromagnetic wavelengths, the final image has brightness but not color differences. Thus, direct photography produces only black-and-white images. However, successive images obtained through red, green, and blue filters or other wavelength-discriminating devices can be amplified and the resultant output converted to digital form for computer processing or storage. These signals can then be used for electron-beam exposure of a color emulsion to obtain a color-differentiated image or, in some cases, a good approximation of the original subject colors.

See also: ELECTRON IMAGING; IMAGE CONVERTER; IMAGE ENHANCEMENT.

Image Converter

An image converter is a device or system that transforms an image composed of invisible energy (e.g., infrared; ultraviolet; x-ray) into a visible image. It has a typical configuration of cathode, lens, and viewing screen. The invisible image is focused onto a screen (cathode) which emits electrons in proportion to the energy at each point of the image. An electron lens focuses the emitted electrons onto a fluorescent viewing screen which emits proportional amounts of visible wavelengths. An image amplifier may be used in place of the electron lens to obtain a brighter image. A fluoroscope is a simple image converter used to make the shadow image created by x-rays visible. In high-speed photography, the image converter type of camera achieves extremely high picture frequencies. As it is an electronic device, the exposure can be controlled down to about 0.001 microseconds, making possible equivalent recording rates of 50,000 to 6 million pictures per second. The high degree of light amplification also makes it possible to study events of low brightness.

See also: FLUOROGRAPHY; IMAGE AMPLIFIER.

Image Dissection

Instead of being recorded as a unified, integrated visual pattern, an image can be divided into a large number of separated points for recording on a single frame of film. This technique, called *image dissection,* is used to record several hundred documents in each frame at normal operating speeds for copiers. As a technique of high-speed photography, image dissection makes it possible to record several exposures on one frame at an equivalent rate of up to 100 million frames per second. The principle is to reduce movement in the system to a minimum, because movement takes time, and that limits the potential recording rate. The film is motionless; the necessary movement is achieved by optically deflecting the image points. If the points in a dissected image are separated by a distance equal to the width of 25 points, then it is only necessary to deflect one point width—$\frac{1}{25}$ the distance required for ordinary full frame, integrated-point recording—in order to place the points of the next image alongside those of the first.

The original image from the camera lens may be dissected by a multiple-lens screen (lenticular ridges, crossed-lenticular grid, or fly's-eye array of spherical lenslets) in front of the film, or by a fiber optics bundle with the fibers separated the required amount at the film end. Image deflection commonly is achieved by moving the lens screen, by using a rotating (Nipkow) disk with a spiral array of scanning holes behind the camera lens (which reduces image brightness significantly), or by using a rotating mirror similar to that of a streak camera. The recorded images are viewed by projecting them back through a matched system (often the camera itself) so that the points of each image are integrated through the single camera/projector lens. When combined with electronic image tubes, image dissection can produce recording rates of more than one billion frames per second.

Images can also be dissected by means of scanners or charge-coupled devices into analog or digital electrical signals corresponding to each image point. These signals can be transmitted, stored, and manipulated by computer; digital systems are by far the more versatile and sophisticated.

See also: DIGITAL IMAGES; FIBER OPTICS; HIGH-SPEED PHOTOGRAPHY; LENTICULAR SYSTEMS.

Image Enhancement

A photographic image carries information encoded as various densities of silver, or various colors and densities of dyes. At one time the clarity of the information in an image could be altered or improved only by optical and chemical procedures such as copying, intensification, reduction, and toning. Today a wide range of image modifications that previously were difficult or impossible to achieve are accomplished by computer processing techniques that comprise the procedure called image enhancement. The possible modifications include increased brightness, contrast, or sharpness; improved tone or color density and saturation; suppression or elimination of visual noise (spurious non-image elements, like "snow" in a television picture); increased separation or complete isolation of selected image elements from surrounding material; extreme magnification of details; reconstruction of near-original color values from faded images; and reconstruction of images with tears, stains, or other physical damage. Many other modifications are also possible.

Digital translation. Computer image enhancement begins with the translation of the image into digital data. Then modification can be achieved by mathematical rather than optical or chemical means. As described in the entry on digital images, the image is divided into a number of points (*pixels:* picture elements), and each point is expressed as a binary number that represents its relative density, brightness, color (wavelength composition), or some other characteristic. The number of pixels is determined by how many readings are taken, and at what intervals, by a microdensitomer, laser beam, flying spot scanner, charge-coupled device, or some other means. A quantizer translates the output signal from each pixel into a binary number equivalent to its place or value on a reference scale.

For example, image brightnesses or densities might be coded with reference to a scale of 1 to 64. (This is equivalent to a 6 f-stop exposure range, the limit of information-bearing areas recorded from many subjects.) When the contrast (density) range of an image is considerably less than the maximum 1:64 reference range, it can be processed to expand its range by operating on each pixel value separately, without regard for the values of surrounding pixels. If the image has values only from 7 to 20 (as might be the case with a reasonably well lighted but quite low contrast subject), its contrast range is only 1:2.9. A typical contrast-enhancing computer program operates by subtracting a constant from all values and multiplying by another constant. If the constants are 6 and 4, the range expansion is:

$$(7 - 6) \times 4 = 4$$
$$(20 - 6) \times 4 = 64$$

These new minimum and maximum values are a range of 1:16, almost five times greater contrast than the original 1:2.9 range. A point-to-point contrast enhancement program does not add any values or tones, it simply increases the separation between existing values. For example, two mid-range values in the above image, 13 and 14, are originally only one value step different. After processing, they are four value steps different:

$$(13 - 6) \times 4 = 28$$
$$(14 - 6) \times 4 = 32$$

Thus they can be more easily distinguished from one another. All other values undergo similar separation from their adjacent values.

The enhanced image may be displayed on a high-resolution cathode-ray tube (video screen), or the new values can be used to control the intensity of a laser beam or electron beam that exposes photographic material to produce a "hard copy" enhanced print or film image.

Pseudocoloring. Another technique of making image differences visibly clearer is pseudocoloring. The reference scale contains fewer values than a contrast program scale, but each value translates into a particular color. Thus, all image brightnesses within a range represented as value 1 may be reproduced as red, all those in the value 2 brightness range as green, those in the value 3 range as yellow, and so on. The colors are arbitrarily assigned and are not usually intended to correspond to original subject colors (although that is possible if desired).

Pseudocoloring is most often performed with black-and-white images, such as those transmitted from satellites, in which there is no objective indication of original colors. Working with a color video display, it is a simple matter to shift the colors assigned to the various image values to obtain maximum emphasis or clarity of selected image elements before making a photographic hard copy.

Color enhancement. A full-color enhancement program begins with a reading from a maximum density black area such as the border of a color transparency film. This is compared to a computer-stored standard of an ideal reading from the particular type of film being considered. If there are any differences—as might result from misprocessing, fading, or other other causes—the computer derives correction factors for each of the three image dye layers (cyan, magenta, and yellow) and applies them to the color-analysis reading of each pixel. The correction factors can also be adjusted arbitrarily by the system operator. Such programs are used to color-correct images for photographic printing or photomechanical reproduction, to correct or restore substandard images, and to create special effects.

Sharpness enhancement. More complex programs compare adjacent pixel values rather than treating each pixel as an independent point. A principal application of such programs is to enhance image sharpness. A major aspect of sharpness is how distinctly the edges of elements are differentiated from adjoining material (commonly called background). A sharply focused edge is represented by an abrupt shift at the boundary between the element tone or density and that of the background. For example, the edge of a piece of white paper laid on a black background would be indicated by a sudden change in a line of pixel readings that crossed the border. If imaged out of focus, the boundary would be blurred, mixing white and black together. Pixel readings would show a gradual degree of value change from one area to another, representing the light-dark modulation across the border. A sharpness-enhancement program compares the maximum readings from each area and cross-compares the readings in the modulated (blurred) area

with one another and with the maximums. It analyzes the modulation in terms of a series of sine and cosine components (much as a complex musical tone can be resolved into simple constituent waveforms), a process known as taking the Fourier transform of the modulation. Processing can then adjust the waveform data to sharper gradients, so that the reproduced image changes more abruptly along a mathematically determined line within the original area of modulation. The process is extremely complex in practice because few subjects have simple white-black contrasts, and a distinction must be made between blurred edges and surface areas of an element within which brightness is modulated by topographical rather than boundary factors.

Image enhancement is widely used in space and satellite photography, surveillance and scientific photography, and photomechanical reproduction. At the present time it is beyond the reach of the photographer who does his or her own processing and printing. However, the pace at which photography is being integrated with electronics, especially the use of domestic television sets to display images from negative and slide films, makes it probable that some image enhancement programs will be available for use with personal computers within a decade.

See also: BRIGHTNESS RANGE; DIGITAL IMAGES.
Color photograph: p. C-25.

Imperial Prints

The term *Imperial* designated one of several mounting formats introduced in the late 1870s to meet the growing public taste for displaying at home pictures larger than the popular cabinet size. The Imperial mount was 7″ × 10″ (17.8 × 25.4cm), large enough to accommodate a contact print from a full plate (6½″ × 8½″ [16.5 × 21.6cm]) negative; it was almost exclusively used for portraits.

See also: CABINET PHOTOGRAPH.

Impressionistic Photography

The Impressionist movement in painting flourished in France from the mid-1860s to the 1880s, and called up a belated but important echo in photography. Artistically ambitious amateur photographers of the 1890s, seeking to free their medium from its lowly status as "handmaiden of the arts," turned for inspiration to the Impressionists' earlier struggles against the restrictive conventions of painting. If Impressionist painters like Monet and Renoir could renounce realistic representation, and vow to be true to their own fleeting perceptions of the transient face of nature, then why not photographers? The Impressionist aim was not to paint objects, but to render the colors in light-filled air that convey the visual impressions of objects. What especially attracted photographers was the idea that light and its effects in the eye was the real subject.

The most important step towards ushering in an Impressionistic attitude in photography was the publication in Britain of Peter Henry Emerson's book *Naturalistic Photography* (1889). Emerson argued that the human eye focuses sharply on only a tiny portion of the visual field; consequently, he advised photographers that if they wished their images to be true to their perceptions, they should focus sharply only on their central subject, and throw both foreground and background slightly out of focus. Emerson's advocacy of this kind of "differential focusing" immediately touched off a heated row with partisans of the older school of British Pictorial photography, whose members remained convinced that a good photograph must be crisply focused throughout.

But while Emerson never dreamed of suggesting that a photograph should ever be thrown totally out of focus, one of his younger amateur followers soon proposed just such a radical notion. George Davison, in an 1890 lecture on "Impressionism in Photography," maintained that while sharpness and clarity were essential for some pictures, in other cases they could be dispensed with altogether. The deciding factor, he thought, should be the photographer's artistic intent.

To illustrate his point, Davison exhibited a photograph of his own, "The Onion Field," a landscape made not with a lens but with a pinhole in a piece of sheet metal. The photograph, which appeared uniformly, "impressionistically" unfocused, created a sensation and was alternately applauded and condemned. Davison's bold example promptly convinced a great many young photographers to begin working in a similar direction. They imparted a diffused look to their photographs with the aid of pinhole lenses and special soft-focus lenses, used diffusion filters in printing, and even began to dramatically retouch their negatives. The introduction of gum-bichromate printing in 1894 allowed them to manipulate their prints even more expressively—to add multiple colors, for example, or to work directly on the print surface with a painter's brush.

Although Emerson denounced Davison and his followers as extremists, dur-

ing the next decade many "secession" groups sprang up in Europe and the United States, all sharing a belief in the Impressionistic "truth to the ideal." The leading members of these groups included such figures as Robert Demachy in France, Heinrich Kuehn in Austria, and Alfred Stieglitz, Edward Steichen, and Clarence White in the U.S. Acclaim was by no means universal, however. Critics mercilessly lampooned what they called the "Photo-Wooly-Graphic School," and even a writer as sympathetic to photography as George Bernard Shaw confessed to a keen dislike of the new "fuzzographers."

In 1900, a London showing of the work by the "New School of American Pictorial Photography" allowed the British to see how Impressionism in photography had been interpreted on the other side of the Atlantic. Unlike the British, who applied Impressionistic techniques primarily to landscapes and portraiture, Americans like Steichen and Alvin Langdon Coburn touched upon, and transformed, a whole range of subjects drawn from everyday life. Concentrating on unorthodox pictorial effects rather than simply graceful arrangements of form and tone, the Americans demonstrated that they were now to be counted among the most imaginative and innovative photographers in the world.

Nevertheless, only a few years later a rapid turn-around of ideas led many Impressionist photographers to abandon that style, and to begin to reexplore the possibilities of unmanipulated, "straight" photography. The ideas associated with Impressionism had, in the beginning, allowed photographers to realize that their medium, too, could convey non-realistic visions of the world and express the photographer's personal feelings. But by 1910, a growing number of photographers felt it better to rely on ways of seeing that were not so obviously borrowed from painting. When avant-garde photographers like Stieglitz and Coburn began to show what could be accomplished by combining "straight" photography with the compositional devices of cubism, the misty diffusion of Impressionistic photography rapidly lost its hold on ambitious photographers. Today it survives above all in advertising and fashion photography (as in the recent work of Sarah Moon), where it is called upon to supply an atmosphere of nostalgia, romance, and idealization.
See also: ART OF PHOTOGRAPHY; NATURALISTIC PHOTOGRAPHY; PAINTING AND PHOTOGRAPHY; PICTORIAL PHOTOGRAPHY/PICTORIALISM; SALON PHOTOGRAPHY.
Color photograph: p. C-25.

Incidence, Angle of

The angle of incidence is the angle at which a light path, or ray, strikes a surface; it is measured with reference to a perpendicular (the *normal*) to the surface at the point of incidence. On a smooth, reflective surface, the path continues along the *angle of reflectance*, which is exactly equal to the angle of incidence and in the same plane, but on the opposite side of the normal. On a matte surface, light is scattered in several directions, but (except for a theoretically perfectly diffuse surface) a greater proportion travels along the angle of reflectance than in any other direction. This produces a "hot spot" of greater intensity that is most noticeable when the surface is viewed along the angle of reflectance. If the light is traveling through a dense medium toward a less dense medium, there is a transmission-limiting angle of incidence at the border. At this *critical angle* (about 41° in the case of glass-to-air travel) the light is refracted as it emerges to travel exactly parallel with the border; visually, no light is transmitted. At greater angles (i.e., interior incidence paths more nearly parallel with the surface) the light is reflected at the border back into the denser medium. This is the principle of in-line inverting prisms, and of light transmission within the strands of fiber optics materials. The phenomenon of total internal reflection can be frustrated by placing a second layer of dense material parallel with and very close to the first to produce an air gap only a few light wavelengths wide. Then some light will

Angle of Incidence

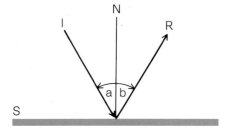

S: Surface
I: Incident ray
N: Normal
R: Reflected ray
a: Angle of Incidence
b: Angle of Reflectance
a = b

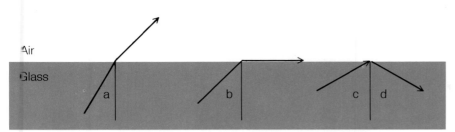

Incidence, Angle of: At less than critical angle, a, light emerges. At critical angle, b, it travels parallel to border. At greater than critical angle, c, it is reflected internally along equal angle, d.

be reflected and the remainder will be transmitted. Certain special purpose beam splitters and dichroic filters are constructed in this way.

See also: FIBER OPTICS; PRISMS; REFRACTION.

Incident Light

Illumination falling on a surface is called incident light. Depending on the nature of the material and its surface, the incident light may be reflected, absorbed, transmitted, or some combination of these. Incident light is measured by holding an appropriate meter at the illuminated surface (subject position), with its collector (usually a translucent white dome or flat disk) pointed toward the intended observer or camera position. Measured incident light is called illuminance; it is measured in footcandles (lumens per square foot) or lux (lumens per square meter), but most incident-light photographic exposure meters provide readings in *f*-numbers and exposure times (shutter speeds).

Incident-light readings are most often used to determine exposure with color films, especially transparency still films, and with motion-picture films. Incident-light readings are also used to determine the lighting ratio or lighting contrast (illuminance range). This is done by comparing a reading of only the light falling on the least-illuminated part of the subject to a reading taken at its most-illuminated point. In terms of arranged lighting, the two readings are of the fill light only and the key-plus-fill light; only light coming from directions that permit it to be reflected toward the camera is included in the readings (e.g., backlight is excluded). This measurement of the illuminance range seldom matches the measured brightness (luminance) range of the subject, because it does not take into account the various

reflectivities of different areas of the subject.

The ratio between the amount of light incident on a surface and the amount reflected or transmitted is used to determine the reflectance, transmittance, absorptance, opacity, and density of a material or a photographic image.

See also: BRIGHTNESS RANGE; EXPOSURE; EXPOSURE METERS; LIGHTING.

Indicator Chemical

A chemical which changes color at a certain level of acidity or alkalinity in a solution, or in the presence of a certain percentage of a particular compound, is referred to as an indicator chemical. A typical indicator stop bath is a standard acetic acid solution to which a small amount of bromcresol purple has been added. It looks yellow (colorless under darkroom safelight) when fresh, but immediately turns a highly visible deep purple when the acidity has been neutralized by developer to nearly the point at which it will no longer be effective.

Some test solutions and papers incorporate indicator chemicals, notably those that test for silver buildup in a fixing bath, and that test for the presence of hypo in film and print wash water. Strips of litmus-impregnated paper are the best known indicator chemical device. The litmus turns blue in alkaline solutions, red in acid solutions, with the change occuring very close to the level of neutrality, pH 7.

Industrial Photography

Industrial photography is concerned with taking pictures in support of manufacturing. It includes in-plant photography of manufacturing processes, laboratory photography to investigate and

analyze materials and products, studio photography of products, and location photography to show preliminary procedures such as mining raw materials and subsequent procedures such as product testing and field use. The pictures produced by the industrial photographer are used in research and development; procedure analysis; employee training; operating, maintenance, and repair publications; advertising and sales materials; catalogs, exhibits, annual reports, and public relations materials; and in a variety of other ways.

While some kinds of industrial photography are done by freelance photographers, most work is done by staff members of a fully equipped photographic department. In general, the in-house department concentrates on the informational and technical photographs that are directly related to the production and operation or use of the product. Pictures for consumer advertising are most often done by an outside specialist in illustration, although in-house pictures may also be used. As in many non-manufacturing companies, the industrial photographic department may also be expected to take care of things such as reproduction of plans, drawings, and documents other than correspondence and financial records; employee identification photographs; visual aids to talks and demonstrations; illustrations for an in-house newsletter; executive portraits; and records of company business and social events.

The well-equipped industrial photographic department commonly uses both still and motion-picture or video cameras of conventional design, as well as highly specialized equipment. Such a department commonly has four kinds of capabilities or facilities in support of its primary work: (1) equipment for on-the-spot photography along the production line and on location; (2) a studio for photography of developmental models and finished products; (3) a laboratory for analytical photography; and (4) a darkroom and associated facilities.

Equipment and procedures differ with the kind of industry. The problems of photographing the manufacture of earthmoving machines are quite different from those of photographing the production of transistor radios or pharmaceutical products, for example. Similarly, the problems of analysis and performance photography in plastics manufacture are different from those in firearms manufacture.

Industrial photographers are versatile and inventive. In addition to producing relatively common photographs such as exploded views and shadowless pictures, they must cope with taking high-speed sequences of production equipment in operation, recording changes in materials inside a furnace or immersed in an acid bath, and similar "impossible" situations. For the most part, industrial photographers are specialists in one or more areas of technical photography; most also have training or special knowledge in some area of engineering, physics, or chemistry. The technical specialties most widely applied in industrial photography are very-high-speed photography; infrared, ultraviolet, fluorescence, and polarized-light photography; close-up and macrophotography; photomicrography; and stroboscopic photography. Other scientific and technical specialties of particular usefulness include thermography, electron micrography, schlieren photography, spectrography, and x-ray photography. All of the above specialties are discussed in separate entries.

While the primary function of industrial photographs is to provide information, many technical images have visual qualities that allow them to be appreciated on an aesthetic level. And, many pictures of plant facilities and work in progress are photographed to be both striking illustrations and informative records. These factors help make industrial photography an imaginative as well as a technical challenge.

Color photograph: p. C-26.

Infinity

The lens focus setting for objects at the greatest possible distance, infinity, is marked ∞ on focusing scales. At this setting the image is located behind the lens at a distance exactly equal to the lens focal length. It is the position of minimum extension: if the film is placed any closer to the lens, nothing will be sharply focused. Because of factors in depth of field and the limitations of the circle of confusion, for all practical photographic purposes objects 1000 yards (915 meters) or more from the lens are effectively at infinity. Most depth-of-field scales and tables are rounded off on this basis. *Infinity development,* or development to gamma infinity, is development of an emulsion to the maximum contrast it can produce; i.e., further development produces no greater slope in the straight line portion of the characteristic curve.

See also: DEPTH OF FIELD; FOCUSING.

Infrared Photography

Infrared (IR) energy occupies a wavelength range in the electromagnetic

Industrial Photography. Cheryl Rossum, "Preflight check of F-18 prototype" (1979). © Cheryl Rossum.

spectrum beginning just beyond the visible red wavelengths, at about 700nm, extending to about 0.1 cm. Practical infrared photography with ordinary cameras and infrared-sensitized films extends from about 700nm to 900nm; highly specialized films and plates are used for scientific photography to about 1200nm. Silver-halide emulsions do not have inherent infrared sensitivity, but can be treated during manufacture to become sensitive in the ranges indicated. In a color film, the normally blue-sensitive layer is made infrared sensitive, and a yellow filter is commonly used to block blue exposure. The relationship of layer sensitivity and the dye color formed is different from that of conventional color film, as explained in the entry on false-color film. This insures that subject areas emitting or reflecting infrared are recorded with significant color distinction from other areas. When only the infrared is to be recorded it is common to use an IR-sensitive black-and-white film and a No. 87, 88, or 89 filter, which blocks visible light and transmits only infrared. Such filters look black. Black-and-white IR films can also be exposed to record visible wavelengths along with the infrared. Usually an orange or a 25A red filter is used to block portions of the visible light so that the effect of the infrared exposure will be a more significant part of the total. Areas that reflect or transmit infrared register more strongly on the negative and thus appear lighter in a black-and-white print. The effect in combination with some visible-light exposure is one of a luminous glow

with softly defined edges because infrared rays do not focus at the same distance behind a lens that the visible light does. Many lenses have an infrared reference mark on the focusing scale; its distance from the infinity symbol indicates an average amount of correction. After the lens is focused visually, it is adjusted just that much to focus the IR rays more sharply.

Sunlight, electronic flash, and photoflood bulbs are IR-rich light sources; household tungsten bulbs emit a smaller proportion of infrared, so greater wattage is required to achieve the same degree of IR exposure as with other sources. Electronic flash is preferred for indoor photography with infrared color film. For IR photography in the dark that does not disturb the subject a flash unit can be fitted with a No. 87 or 87C filter. The No. 87 filter emits a slight red glow that is visible only if looked at directly; the No. 87C filter blocks all visible light but requires greater exposure.

Exposures that record visible as well as IR wavelengths can be based on an exposure meter reading as a starting point; film instruction sheets include recommendations for typical subjects and light sources. It is not possible to predict how much infrared a subject will reflect or emit, so all exposures are based on estimates, or on practical tests under specific conditions. Film is processed normally, but it must be handled in total darkness—with no safelighting—until it has been fixed; most safelights emit infrared to some degree.

Infrared Photography. Minor White, "Cobblestone House, Avon, N.Y." (1958). The Art Museum, Princeton University.

Objects heated above about 480°F (250°C) emit infrared wavelengths in the range to which films are sensitized; see the article on heat recording. Most objects are photographed in IR by the energy they reflect or transmit from an external source. Medical photography; agricultural, ecological, geological, and geographic photography; and many kinds of scientific and technical photography have found important applications for IR-sensitive films.
See also: FALSE-COLOR FILM; HEAT RECORDING; SPECTRUM; ULTRAVIOLET AND FLUORESCENCE PHOTOGRAPHY.

Insert

An element of one picture incorporated into another without show-through of the background picture is called an insert. Double-exposure, superimposure, or sandwiching images creates show-through. An insert is created by photographing one picture through a mask with the required area blocked out, and the second picture through a corresponding mask with that area visible but the other portion blocked out. This can be done on one piece of film (the best method with transparency film), or on separate pieces of film which can be sandwiched or used individually for printing.

In motion pictures the element to be inserted is photographed separately against a plain, light-blue background. From this an opaque, high-contrast mask of the element shape is made on film. The mask is sandwiched with the background negative to block that area during a first printing. Then the element negative is printed into the resulting space. In television the insert element is also placed in front of a blue background. The element's shape serves as an electronic key to blank out the background picture signal and insert its own signal as the two are broadcast or recorded simultaneously.
See also: MULTIPLE EXPOSURE/PRINTING; SUPERIMPOSURE.

Inspection Development

In some cases a film may be examined by safelight during development to evaluate image density and contrast. Early plates and films were routinely developed by inspection because their limited color sensitivity permitted free handling under relatively bright red or orange light; this is also true of many graphic arts films and other orthochromatic materials today. Panchromatic emulsions are most safely and accurately developed in total darkness (e.g., inside a lighttight tank) by time-and-temperature control methods. They can be inspected if necessary, but only for a total of 15 seconds (less for fast films) under very dim (15-watt bulb) dark green safelight kept at least 4 feet (1.2 meters) from the emulsion.

Considerable experience is necessary to judge an image quickly under these conditions. The film is inspected only after at least half the normal developing time has passed. It is held so that light reflects off the emulsion side; nothing can be seen by attempting to look through the milky gray emulsion. Only highlight and the strongest middletone densities will be discernible. If these appear too strong, development may be cut short; if too weak, it can be extended for up to 50 percent longer than normal. Only a very experienced worker can make more of a judgement than this. The dangers of fogging the film or producing solarization in some parts of the image by overexposure to the safelight make inspection development a high-risk technique.
See also: FOG/FOGGING; SOLARIZATION.

Instant Photography

The technology of instant photography makes it possible to secure a positive image from a material immediately after it has been exposed, without intermediate darkroom work. The first successful near-instant photographic process was the ferrotype (tintype), used by street —and bargain-price studio—photographers from the 1850s until well into the 20th c. to give customers a finished image in less than five minutes. Modern instant photography dates from 1946, when a camera using integrated rolls of film and print paper was introduced by Dr. Edwin Land. Today it utilizes single sheets of self-processing film/print material (Polaroid SX-70 and Kodak Instant Print films). Instant transparency films have also been introduced. All such materials utilize diffusion transfer processing.

Coin-operated photo booths provide instant prints by camera exposure of direct positive paper which passes immediately to automatic equipment for reversal processing. Specialized printing-out papers are used for immediate-access records of instrument readouts such as cathode ray tube (e.g., oscilloscope) displays. These are very high contrast materials, not suitable for continuous tone images. Various electrophotographic processes provide instant images, but the equipment is not portable in the hand camera sense, special lighting is required, and the limited tone and color range of the prints does not approach that of silver halide emulsions. Rapid processing procedures for films and prints are not in fact instant photography because they require equipment and procedures in addition to the camera and basic exposure.
See also: DIFFUSION TRANSFER PROCESS.
Color photograph: p. C-27.

Intaglio Processes

Methods of reproduction in which the elements are cut into a material so that the image is below the surface are called intaglio processes. (Latin: *intaliare* = to cut into.) In various processes for photoetching or photoengraving glass or metal, the image may be apparent only because of the differences in depth and texture, or because it has been differently toned, colored, or coated as well. In the intaglio methods of photomechanical reproduction, ink is held in lines or dots below the surface for transfer to the printing paper. In most photoengraving processes the strength of each element depends on the width or size of the intaglio dot or line; in photogravure these elements only vary in depth so that the densities but not the areas of the ink deposits vary in the printed image. The methods of ink reproduction other than intaglio are *planographic* processes, such as lithography, in which the ink is on the plate surface, and *relief* printing, in which the inked areas rise above the supporting plate.
See also: GLASS, PHOTOGRAPHING ON; PHOTOENGRAVING; PHOTOGRAVURE.

Integrating Meter

An integrating meter is a kind of photometer that measures the total (i.e., cumulative) luminance received over a continuous period of time or from a series of discontinuous inputs. A continuous integration meter is often used as an exposure control device in process cameras, automatic printing equipment, and individual darkroom enlargers using continuous light sources. An intermittent integration meter is used to determine exposure with light sources such as pulsed xenon lamps, stroboscopes, and repeat-flash setups. In many kinds of equipment an integrating meter is connected to a switch circuit so that it can automatically turn off the light source when a predetermined exposure level has been reached.

"Integrating meter" is also used, imprecisely, to mean (1) a the kind of reflected-light exposure meter that averages together the brightness variations in a single, overall reading of the scene, or (2) incident-light exposure meters in general, because they have a diffusing screen in front of the light sensitive cell that integrates light from all directions within the acceptance angle of the meter.
See also: EXPOSURE METER; PHOTOMETER/PHOTOMETRY.

Intensification

Intensification is the process of adding density to various areas of a developed and fixed black-and-white negative or print in order to change the contrast of the image. It is accomplished by overall chemical treatment (as distinct from hand retouching of local areas), commonly with a solution that deposits additional metal (usually silver, chromium, or selenium) onto the existing image silver. Negatives can also be intensified with a treatment that adds a stain to the gelatin in the image areas. The stain reduces printing light as effectively as physical density. Another technique with either negatives or prints is to bleach the image to a colorless state and redevelop it to the desired contrast in a conventional or a staining developer.

There are three classes of intensifiers. A *proportional* intensifier adds density in equal proportions (not amounts) throughout the image; this results in a moderate increase of contrast and an overall increase in density, both of which are helpful with a negative that has been somewhat underexposed and underdeveloped. A *super-proportional* intensifier adds much more to the dense (highlight) areas than to the less dense (shadow) areas of the image; it produces a marked increase of contrast that corrects underdevelopment of a properly exposed negative. A *sub-proportional* intensifier adds to the thin densities, but has little effect on the highlights; the result is some degree of correction for underexposure, but primarily a reduction in overall contrast.

Although prints and negatives can be intensified by similar chemical methods, the degree of change obtainable in prints is quite limited. The principal print intensifiers are selenium and gold chloride solutions. Various toners—particularly those that use the bleach-and-redevelop method—provide some intensification along with a change of image color. Like its opposite procedure, *reduction,* intensification can be carried out in full light so that the effect produced can be judged visually. However, because of eye adaptation it is seldom possible to judge a change accurately by watching the image continuously. It is more effective to look at the image only occasionally, so that progressive differences will be more readily apparent. In the case of prints, it is also helpful to have a duplicate untreated image at hand for comparison.
See also: REDUCER/REDUCTION; TONER/TONING.

Interference

Interference is the interaction between wavelengths of energy that causes them to reinforce one another (add together) the more nearly they are in phase (reach a peak simultaneously), or cancel one another (subtract) as they are out of phase. The antireflection coatings of lens elements and those of dichroic filters operate by means of interference effects. They are made a half-wavelength thick for selected wavelengths, with the result that waves reflected from the surface of the glass are 180° (totally) out of phase with those reflected from the surface of the coating, and they cancel one another. In the case of lens coatings, so small an amount of energy is destroyed that the loss in image brightness is more than balanced by the increase in contrast.

The spurious concentric light-and-dark or rainbow-colored shapes in prints, called Newton's rings, are the result of interference effects between wavelengths reflected from the smooth surface of the film base and those reflected from the glass of a negative carrier. The color effects of a Lippmann process image are created by interference effects between the emulsion surface and a mirrorlike surface of mercury. A hologram is a record of the interference patterns between wavelengths coming directly from a coherent light source and wavelengths from the same source reflected by the object being recorded.
See also: DICHROIC FILTERS; HOLOGRAM; LIPPMANN PROCESS; NEWTON'S RINGS; WAVELENGTH.

Intermittency Effect

The intermittency effect is a kind of reciprocity effect in which a number of very short exposures to a given subject produce less effect than a single exposure of equal total length. Its occurence depends on the speed of the emulsion, the intensity of the light, and the length and frequency of the exposures. It is seldom encountered except with stroboscopes and other special-purpose, pulsed light sources or rapid-interruption shutters. In general, it is not significant when the number of brief exposures constituting an image is on the order of 100 or more.
See also: RECIPROCITY.

Internegative

An intermediate negative may be made from a positive transparency or print (or by reversal from an original negative) for use in printing copies. Such an internegative is the preferred way to make duplicates of color transparencies because it permits correction of contrast and color balance first in making the negative, and again in making the duplicate positives. Multiple internegatives from a single original, black-and-white or color, are essential for producing great numbers of

prints for public relations or advertising distribution and similar purposes. Motion-picture release (projection) prints are made from internegatives to protect the original camera negative and the master positive from damage.
See also: COPYING PHOTOGRAPHS; DUPLICATE IMAGES.

Inverse Square Law

The effect of radiant energy such as light varies with the distance between the source and the subject. The mathematical expression of the variation is the *inverse square law.* In photographic lighting, the law applies to bare bulbs, direct electronic flash, and other direct sources whose greatest dimension is one-tenth or less than that of the area of the subject being illuminated.

The basis of the law is the fact that when light radiates equally in all directions from a small-area source, the amount falling on any given area—such as one square foot of surface—is spread over a greater area as the surface is moved farther from the source. As a result, the intensity of the light on any part of the surface decreases as the distance increases—an inverse relationship. The degree of decrease is equal not to how many times the distance increases, but to how many times *squared.*

For example, if the distance changes from 4 ft to 12 ft (1.2 to 3.6m), it is $3\times$ greater, and $3^2 = 9$. Since the effect of light decreases as the distance increases, its intensity is reduced by a factor of nine; i.e., it is one-ninth as intense as at the closer distance. If the distance had decreased, from 12 ft to 4 ft, the intensity would have become nine times brighter.

The inverse square law can also be used to compare the relative illumination from two sources of equal output placed at different distances from a subject. In the above example, the source at 12 ft is one-ninth as bright, at the subject, as the source at 4 ft. Operations with the inverse square law can be simplified by finding the intensity factor, F, from the smaller light-subject distance, S, and the larger distance, L, as follows:

$$F = (L \div S)^2$$

Use F as a multiplier (e.g., $9\times$) in relation to the smaller distance, or as a reciprocal (a fraction beneath 1, e.g., $\frac{1}{9}$) in relation to the larger distance.

The inverse square law also applies to the gravitational attractions of the sun and the planets for one another. Aside from its role in holding the solar system together, this has been of little practical concern to most photographers.

Inverted Telephoto Lens

A short-focal-length, usually wide-angle, lens produced by reversing the sequence of elements in the basic telephoto design; also called a retrofocus lens.
See: LENSES.

Iris

See: DIAPHRAGM.

Iron Printing Processes

Several contact-printing processes are based on the light sensitivity of various iron compounds. The best known are the cyanotype, kallitype, Vandyke process, and platinotype. All rely on the action of light to reduce a ferric (Fe^{3+}) salt to a ferrous (Fe^{2+}) state. Ferrous salts can either combine with another compound (e.g., dye-forming elements in gallic or tannic acid), or can reduce metallic compounds (e.g., of gold, silver, platinum) to pure metal to form an image. The ferric-ferrous photochemical reaction was discovered in 1841–42 by Sir John Herschel, who utilized it in his cyanotype and chrysotype processes. The latter used paper sensitized with ferric ammonium citrate; the developer was gold chloride, which was reduced to a purplish-black metal by the exposed, now ferrous, citrate. Other methods include the ferro-cupric and ferro-gallic processes. During the collodion wet plate period, a solution of iron (ferrous) sulfate was widely used as a developer to reduce the exposed silver halides to a metallic silver image.
See also: CYANOTYPE; FERRO-CUPRIC/FERRO-GALLIC PROCESS; KALLITYPE; PLATINOTYPE; VANDYKE PROCESS.

Irradiation

When light strikes silver halide crystals in an emulsion, the unabsorbed portion is deflected along multiple new paths. This action, called irradiation, produces that part of the spread function attributable to emulsion characteristics. Its practical effect is to reduce resolving power, and to lower contrast as the spacing between image elements decreases—as revealed in measuring the modulation transfer function (MTF) of the emulsion. The amount of irradiation produced by a given intensity of light is proportional to the size of the halide crystals and the thickness of the emulsion. As a result, high-speed films—which have large crystals and thick emulsions—generally have the lowest contrast and resolution characteristics. When halation occurs, irradiation may increase its effect by scattering the reflected light over a larger area.
See also: CONTRAST; HALATION; RESOLVING POWER; SPREAD FUNCTION.

"I" Shutter Setting

In the past, many simple cameras had only two marked shutter settings: *T,* for time exposure, and *I,* for "instantaneous." The *I* setting was a speed of 1/25 sec. in the late 19th and early 20th c., but later often was 1/30 or 1/40 sec. as faster films and lenses tempted amateurs to make snapshots of moving subjects. The actual speed made little exposure difference because of the latitude of the black-and-white films used in such cameras and the more than ample development provided by most commercial photofinishers. It is a speed marking seldom seen today because most of even the simplest cameras have some degree of automatic exposure control.

Isochromatic

Early synonym for orthochromatic.
See: ORTHOCHROMATIC; SPECTRAL SENSITIVITY.

Ives, Frederic Eugene

American; 1856–1937
A pioneer of practical three-color (additive synthesis) photography and photomechanical reproduction in black-and-white and color, F. E. Ives was trained as a printer in Ithaca, New York. He moved to Philadelphia, where by 1884 he was producing very high quality isochromatic (orthochromatic) plates for photomechanical applications. He had already invented various methods to produce halftone dot translations of continuous tone images. In 1886 he invented the first cross-line halftone screen, composed of two plates with finely ruled parallel lines cemented face-to-face, with the rule patterns running at right angles to one another. The resulting dot pattern could capture finer image details than the inks, papers, and especially the printing pressures of the day could reproduce.

Ives entered into partnership to exploit the capabilities of his inventions and by 1890 his company's reproductions were considered at least the equal of the best quality European work. His practical investigations of photoengraving resulted in the discovery of the critical effect on dot size of the distance between the halftone screen and the plate being exposed, and the optimum angle to which a screen must be rotated to expose each plate in three- or four-color work in order to avoid moiré in the final reproduction.

In 1892 Ives introduced the first of a series of three-color cameras, the Photochromoscope. It made separation negatives on a single glass plate in three exposures. These were contact-printed on other plates to obtain positive transparencies. They were viewed in the Chromoscope, which used mirrors and prisms to superimpose the images, each coupled with a filter of the same color used for its corresponding negative. The next year a stereoscopic version, the Kromskop, was introduced followed in 1895 by a (nonstereoscopic) three-color magic lantern, the Projection Kromskop. Subsequent developments included various "one-shot" cameras in which beam splitters and filters were arranged to produce three separation negatives from a single exposure.

In the 1920s, Ives patented a number of basic ideas for materials using dyes for the subtractive synthesis of color, which was to become the dominant method with the introduction of Kodachrome film in 1935. During the 1930s, Ives experimented with two-color photography and printing processes, but the results could not equal those achieved with three-color photographic materials or four-color photomechanical reproduction. Ives' son, Herbert, was a pioneer of the phototransmission of images.

See also: ADDITIVE COLOR SYNTHESIS; PHOTOMECHANICAL REPRODUCTION; SCREEN, HALFTONE; SEPARATION NEGATIVES; SUBTRACTIVE COLOR SYNTHESIS.

Ivorytype

The ivorytype was a positive image apparently printed on ivory; it was an imitation effect. The process was patented by J. J. E. Mayall in 1865. A plain (i.e., uncoated or salt paper) print was laid face up on a glass sheet and hand tinted. Then the glass was heated from beneath to melt white wax rubbed over the face of the print. When sufficiently impregnated, the print was transferred face down to a final size sheet of glass which was also heated to cause the wax to penetrate the paper completely, making it transparent. Upon cooling, the wax kept the print adhered to the glass. It was backed with an ivory-tone card and perhaps covered with a decorative mat on the front. This packet was sealed at the edges and framed. Mayall also described the possibility of coating artificial ivory (e.g., ivory-tone ceramic or, after 1861, celluloid) with an albumen or collodion emulsion and printing on it from a suitable negative.

A second imitation ivory process, the *Eburneum* process (Latin: *ebur* = ivory), was introduced in 1865 by J. M. Burgess. A sheet of glass was waxed (to permit later release of the image) and coated with collodion. This was exposed under a negative to get a positive transparency. An alternative procedure was to transfer a carbon process image to the glass. In either case the image had to be reversed left-for-right in order to be properly oriented for final viewing. After processing, the image was completely covered with an ivory-colored coating of zinc oxide in gelatin. When dry, it was slit around the edges and stripped from the glass plate to be mounted on a support card and viewed from what was originally the back. The image was usually protected by a mat, cover glass, and frame.

Izis (Israel Bidermanas)

French; 1911–1980

Israel Bidermanas, who took the professional name Izis, was born in Mariampole, Lithuania (now Mariampol'ye, U.S.S.R.). At the age of 13 he was apprenticed to a portrait photographer. Learning soft-focus, retouching, and other techniques of commercial flattery led him to resolve that in his personal work he would always respect the truth. In 1930 he traveled to Paris, eventually becoming a French citizen in 1946.

In 1934 Izis opened his first Paris studio and produced portraits, wedding pictures, and similar work. During the German Occupation he was active in the French Resistance, where he served as a photo researcher and recorded numerous pictures of his comrades in the underground.

At the end of the war, Izis freelanced in Paris before joining the staff of *Paris-Match* in 1949. He specialized in photographs of painters, poets, writers, circus people, and similar individualists, but also photographed derelicts, street people, and the urban poor on occasion. Like his contemporary Brassaï, his true subject was the city of Paris itself, which had dazzled him when he arrived as an immigrant and which never failed to hold him enthralled. After 20 years at *Paris-Match*, Izis returned to freelancing, which he pursued until his death in 1980.

Throughout his career Izis shunned equipment or methods that would disturb the subject. He used neither flash nor a light meter, and worked instinctively, taking few shots, always alert, as he expressed it, "like a fisherman waiting for a nibble."

Izis published eight books: *Paris des Reves* (1950), with text by Jacques Prévert and foreword by Jean Cocteau (published in English as *Paris Enchanted*); *Grand Bal du Printemps* (1951), with text by Jacques Prévert; *Charmes de Londres* (1952), with text by Jacques Prévert (published in English as *Gala Day: London*); *Paradis Terrestre* (1953), with text by Colette; *People of the Queen* (1954); *Israel* (1956), with a foreword by André Malraux; *Le Cirque d' Izis* (1965), with text by Jacques Prévert; *Paris des Pòetes* (1967), with text by Jacques Prévert; and *Le Monde de Chagall* (1969), with text by Roy McMullen.

Jackson, William Henry

American; 1843–1942

William Henry Jackson became one of 19th c. America's best-known Western landscape and Indian portrait photographers. A man of enormous energy and stamina, Jackson was a pencil and brush artist, a writer, an explorer, and a prolific photographer who produced tens of thousands of negatives during his long career.

For 25 years Jackson traveled throughout the West with his wet plates and portable darkroom creating a pictorial record of natural wonders. His photographs of the Yellowstone region were instrumental in the creation of America's first national park in 1872. Although some of his contemporaries were responsible for more dramatic views, Jackson's photographs of western mountain regions include many which remain indelible in the public mind.

Born in Keesville, New York, Jackson, whose father was an amateur daguerreotypist, learned photography as a boy and later worked as a photographer's retoucher and colorist. After serving as a military staff artist in the Civil War, Jackson left employment in a Vermont studio to travel west as a bullwhacker. He established a photography concern in Omaha, Nebraska, in 1868. Leaving the day-to-day portraiture to his brother, Jackson photographed the surrounding countryside. He documented the building of the Union Pacific Railroad and made many striking portraits of native Americans.

In 1870 Dr. Ferdinand Vandiveer Hayden invited Jackson to become the official photographer of the United States Geological and Geographical Survey of the Territories. Jackson remained with the Survey until 1878, working closely with the artist Thomas Moran and others. The official report of the Survey for 1875 stated of Jackson's photographs: "They have done very much, in the first place, to secure truth-

Jackson, William Henry. "Mammoth Hot Springs, Lower Basin, looking up, with man" (ca. 1870s). Library of Congress.

Jackson, William Henry. "Mammoth Hot Springs, Lower Basin, looking up, with man" (ca. 1870s). Library of Congress.

fulness in the representation of mountain and other scenery. . . in ethnography, it gives us portraits of the varied families of our great Indian population, representing with unquestioned accuracy the peculiar types of each; their manners of living, dressing, occupations and mythical inscriptions." Jackson's work was exhibited in 1876 at the Centennial Exposition in Philadelphia.

In 1879 Jackson opened a studio in Denver, Colorado, where he sold stereoscopic-card views of his work. He continued to travel and photograph throughout the country. In 1894–1895 he photographed a trip around the world for *Harper's Weekly*. He was part owner of the Detroit Publishing Company from 1898 to 1902, and for many years was Research Assistant to the Oregon Trail Commission.

In the 1930s Jackson, then in his early 90s, executed murals of the Old West for the Department of the Interior. He acted as an advisor to the film *Gone With The Wind* in 1938 and published his autobiography, *Time Exposure*, in 1940.

Jackson's work was included in *Photographs of the Civil War and the American Frontier* at the Museum of Modern Art in New York City in 1942. He died the same year at age 99. His negatives and prints are in the archives of the Edison Institute in Dearborn, Michigan. In 1974 a major exhibition and monograph of Jackson's work was organized by the Amon Carter Center of Western Art in Fort Worth, Texas.

Jacobi, Lotte

American; 1896–

Lotte Jacobi was one of Weimar Germany's most successful and sophisticated portraitists. Her lyrical photographs of the men and women of Berlin's cultural communities combine to form one of our best portraits of the immediate pre-Nazi era. She continued her portrait work in the United States after fleeing Hitler's Germany, and has done significant work with light abstractions since the 1950s.

Jacobi was born into a family of photographers in Thorn, Germany. Her father, grandfather, and great-grandfather were all photographers (her great-grandfather had studied with Daguerre himself). Jacobi took her first photograph with a pinhole camera in 1908. She studied literature and art history at the Academy of Posen from 1912 to 1916. Married in 1917, she had one son, and was eventually divorced in 1924 after years of estrangement.

Jacobi attended the University of Munich and the Bavarian State Academy of Photography from 1925 to 1927, working with the photographer Hanna Seewald and making four films. Her career in photography began at her family's Berlin studio in 1927.

The family business supplied celebrity photos to a variety of newspapers. From 1927 to 1935 Jacobi specialized in portraits of German artists, theater people, musicians, dancers, and film stars. Her sitters included Thomas Mann, Bertolt Brecht, Kurt Weill, Lotte Lenya, Laszlo Moholy-Nagy, and many others. Her work was influenced by that of Alfred Stieglitz, Otto Steinert, and Albert Renger-Patzsch.

Jacobi received a Silver Medal at the Royal Photography Salon, Tokyo in 1931. In 1932–1933 she traveled and photographed in Russia and Central Asia.

When Jacobi fled Nazi Germany for the United States in 1935, much of her work from the preceding decade was lost or destroyed. She operated a New York studio with her sister Ruth for the next 20 years. She continued to do portrait work of such figures as Eleanor Roosevelt, W. H. Auden, Robert Frost, and photographers Stieglitz, Edward Steichen, and Paul Strand.

Her first solo exhibition in America was held in 1937 at Directions Gallery, New York, and her work was included in *Twentieth Century Portraits* at the Museum of Modern Art, New York, in 1942.

During the 1950s Jacobi concentrated on a long series of cameraless photographs or "photogenics." In 1955 she moved to New Hampshire where she established a gallery, Lotte Jacobi Place, in 1963. She studied in 1961–1962 at the University of New Hampshire, and in 1963 at the Atélier 7 in Paris. She has been awarded honorary degrees by the University of New Hampshire and New England College, and was the recipient in 1977 of a National Endowment for the Arts grant to photograph other photographers. Her work appeared in the exhibition *Recollections: Ten Women in Photography* at ICP in 1979.
Photograph: p. 260.

Jammes, André

French

From a family of rare book dealers in Paris, André Jammes's interest in photographs evolved from his study of the history of books and print making. To achieve an understanding of the history of photography, Jammes and his wife, Marie-Thérèse, began to assemble what was to become an important library of documents and a large collection of early photographs. Started after World War II, the Jammes archive now includes the largest and most important collection of the work of Charles Nègre, together with numerous selections of photographs by Blanquart-Evrard, Petiot-Groffier, Nadar, Nicolas, Atget, and many negatives by Benjamin Bracknell Turner and Etienne Carjat. Jammes's book (for which he relied on his archive), *Charles Nègre, photographe, 1820–1880*, was published in Paris in 1963. This was prior to the exhibition of his Nègre photographs at the Munich Stadtmuseum in 1964.

In his catalog for the exhibition *French Primitive Photography* at the Philadelphia Museum of Art in 1969, Jammes again drew on the material from the archive, as he did for *The First Century of Photography: Niépce to Atget* at the Art Institute of Chicago in 1977. In his essay "On Collecting Photographs," Jammes acknowledges his immediate predecessors, the first generation of photograph collectors of the period between the two world wars. He admires their remarkable intuition, curiosity, and "sincere feeling of tenderness for the fragile pictures." Among these collectors were the booksellers E.P. Goldschmidt and Ernst Weil of London, Nicolas Rauch of Geneva, and Pierre Lambert of Paris. In the 1930s, each had tried to interest the public in photography but without commercial success. The Jammes eventually acquired their large stocks of photographs.

The Jammes collection was intended for study. André and Marie Thérèse Jammes and their daughter Isabelle have used the archive to contribute writings, lend photographs, and promote exhibitions. *Die Kalotypie in Frankreich, Beispiele der Landschafts, Architektur und Reisedokumentationsfotografie* at the Folkwang Museum, Essen, in 1966 included photographs from the Jammes collection. More recently, the collection provided material for *Masterpieces of the French Calotype* at the Art Museum, Princeton University, 1983. This exhibition coincided with the publication of Jammes's and Eugenia Parry Janis's book, *The Art of French Calotype with a Critical Dictionary of Photographers 1845–1870* (Princeton, 1983).

See also: BOOKS, PHOTOGRAPHIC; COLLECTING PHOTOGRAPHICA.

Jena Glass

The term Jena glass refers to any of hundreds of varieties derived from the improved optical glasses first produced by Otto Schott, Ernst Abbe, and Carl Zeiss in Jena, Germany, in the 1880s. Up to that time lens makers were largely restricted to using basic crown (high-quality pure silica plate) glass and flint (lead-added) glass, because glasses with higher bending (refractive) powers had such increased dispersion that the resulting chromatic aberration made lenses optically and photographically useless. Beginning in 1881 Schott experimented with adding barium, zinc, boracic acid, and other compounds to crowns and flints, finally achieving varieties with much higher refractive powers but little increase in dispersion. This made it possible to design individual lens element surface curvatures, and combinations of elements, that produced greater correction of geometrical aberrations, wider angles of view, and longer focal lengths without unduly increased size or weight, and especially without increased chromatic aberration. The first lens to utilize Jena glass elements was the anastigmat designed for Zeiss by Paul

Johnston, Frances Benjamin. "Daughters of the American Revolution" (1903). Library of Congress.

Rudolph and introduced in 1889. Further development of Jena glass formulas has produced the rare-earth glasses of today in which lanthanum and other elements have made it possible to greatly reduce the percentage of silica. The result is very high optical quality coupled with very high refractive indices.

See also: ABBE, ERNST; ABERRATIONS OF LENSES; ANASTIGMAT; DISPERSION; REFRACTION.

Johnston, Frances Benjamin

American; 1864–1952

Frances Benjamin Johnston, whose working career spanned over fifty years, was the first woman press photographer in America, if not the world. Born to a well-to-do and well-connected family, she was given her first camera (a Kodak), by its inventor, George Eastman, a family friend. Her family having established itself in Washington, D.C., she apprenticed with Dr. T. W. Smillie at the photographic laboratory of the Smithsonian Institution. Although she had earlier studied painting and drawing, she made increasing use of photography to accompany the articles she wrote for popular magazines. Her first published photographs appeared as illustrations to her article on the U.S. Mint.

In the early 1890s, Johnston opened her own photographic studio in Washington, D.C. It was quite successful and Johnston came to be considered the "photographer of the American Court." She photographed much of of-

ficial Washington: portraits of presidents from Cleveland to Taft, government officials, Cabinet members, as well as their wives and families.

A woman of enormous energy and drive, Johnston did much to encourage women to consider careers in photography, as much by example as by her various proselytizing activities. These included arranging for the exhibition and the publication of photographs by women. After years of "straight" photography both on assignment for magazines and in her portrait commissions, Johnston began to experiment with pictorialism, in a vein similar to that of her close friend Gertrude Käsebier. She was as successful as an art photographer as she had been a photojournalist, to the extent of becoming an associate member of the Photo-Secession in 1904. Among her best work done in the pre-World War I period were a painstaking documentation of the Washington school system and a series of photographs on the Hampton Institute; the latter were much admired and utilized by the Institute's founder, Booker T. Washington.

In the 1920s Johnston became perhaps the first woman photographer to specialize in color processing. She also began an extensive body of work which was to occupy her for the rest of her active career: documenting historic buildings and gardens of the South. For this work she received four consecutive Carnegie Foundation grants in the 1930s, and in 1945 she was made an honorary member of the American Institute of Architects.

At the age of 75, Johnston retired to a less demanding life in New Orleans and took few photographs thereafter. Most of her enormous archive of negatives, prints, and correspondence she donated to the Library of Congress in 1948.

Joly, John

Irish; 1857–1933

A physicist, Joly was the inventor of the first line-screen process for additive color images. The basic idea of his process had been proposed—along with many other basic color ideas—in 1868–1869 by Ducos du Hauron. In 1894, Joly patented a process for making a screen of transparent red, green, and blue lines precisely ruled side by side, 200 to the inch, on a glass plate. The Joly Color Process, introduced in 1896, used such a screen placed against the emulsion of an orthochromatic plate in the camera; after exposure the screen was removed. The plate was processed and contact-printed on another plate to produce a positive black-and-white transparency. This transparency was placed in exact register with the color screen and viewed by transmitted light to see a full-color image. The process had brief success, but was hampered by the deficient red sensitivity of the plates and by the light absorption of the color screen, which reduced the brightness of the viewing image considerably. An identical process using a more finely ruled screen was invented independently at the same time by J. W. McDonough of Chicago. Such systems were immediately outmoded by the single-plate autochrome process when it was introduced in 1907. The separate-screen technique was revived after the introduction of panchromatic emulsions early in the 20th c. and was brought to a high level of quality in the Dufaycolor and Finlaycolor processes.

See also: ADDITIVE COLOR SYNTHESIS; AUTOCHROME; COLOR PHOTOGRAPHY—HISTORY; DUCOS DU HAURON, L.; DUFAYCOLOR; FINLAYCOLOR PROCESS; SCREEN PROCESSES.

Jones, Lloyd Ancile

American; 1884–1954

Jones was a member of the Kodak Research Laboratories staff from its establishment by C. E. K. Mees in 1912 to the end of his career; for much of that time he was head of the Physics Division of the Laboratories. His major research was in sensitometry and the characteristics of emulsions. Among his numerous original contributions, one of the most widely used is the quadrant diagram method of relating subject, negative, and print paper characteristics to analyze tone reproduction in the final image.

See also: QUADRANT DIAGRAM; TONE REPRODUCTION.

Joule

The joule is the international scientific unit of energy. When applied to electromagnetic energy such as electricity, one joule is the work done in one second by a current of one ampere flowing through a resistance of one ohm. This can also be stated as the consumption of one watt of power in one second. In photography the equivalent term *watt-second* (WS) is commonly used to rate the power requirements of high-output electronic flash tubes. Unlike a BCPS rating, a watt-second or joule rating does not describe relative light output and therefore cannot be used directly to calculate exposure. One joule is equivalent to a light output of about 40 lumen-seconds, but the effective output for exposure purposes will vary according to the size and shape of the flash tube and the size, shape, and surface of the reflector (if any) used behind it. Joule or watt-second ratings are primarily useful in determining the maximum load that can be connected to a power unit in studio electronic flash set-ups.

See also: BCPS; LIGHT UNITS.

Jump Cut

In motion-picture and television editing, a cut between two shots of the same subject that eliminates part of the continuous action is a jump cut. The abrupt change that results may be used purposely for surprise or comic effect, especially as a repeated stylistic technique. When done accidentally it interrupts the narrative flow and can cause a break in the viewer's attention or involvement. In a jump cut between shots from the same camera position and with no change in image size, the gap in the action makes elements in the scene seem to jump; e.g., a person from standing to sitting, or a door from open to closed. If the image size also changes—because the camera has moved closer or farther away or the lens focal length has changed—the effect is more disturbing because in addition to the subject jump, the viewer subjectively feels that he or she has been thrown from one viewpoint to the other. The gap can be covered by use of a cutaway shot; the editing sequence is: (1) first shot of subject, (2) cutaway shot of a different subject or detail, (3) second shot of original subject. This technique allows apparently continuous time and action to be telescoped because the time actually occupied by the cutaway shot can be considerably less than that of the eliminated action without causing the viewer to lose a sense of real-time continuity.

See also: CUT; CUTAWAY; EDITING.

Kertész, André. "Mondrian Studio" (1926). Courtesy André Kertész; Susan Harder Gallery, New York.

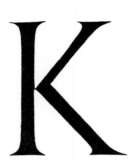

Kallitype

An iron printing process that produces images similar to platinotype images, kallitype is easier and much less expensive to use, and is suitable for printing on fabric as well as paper. It was invented in England by W. W. J. Nichol in 1899, and is a descendant of the iron-silver reduction process Sir John Herschel called chrysotype. Paper is sensitized by brushing it with a solution of ferric oxalate and silver nitrate with a trace of oxalic acid; it may be prepared in artificial light but, once sensitized, must be stored in the dark. Exposure is by sunlight or ultraviolet in contact with a long-scale negative. The various developer formulas, which produce black, brown, or sepia tones, use different proportions of borax and sodium potassium tartrate (Rochelle salts); some sources also give formulas for purple and maroon tones. The image is cleared of chemical discoloration in a potassium-oxalate solution, then fixed with hypo and ammonia, and washed. Because the image is silver, it can be toned by a number of standard methods. The simplest kallitype procedure is the Van Dyke, or brownprint, process; it is more limited in tonal range and image quality.
See also: IRON PRINTING PROCESSES; VAN DYKE PROCESS.

Kalvar Process

Kalvar is a proprietary vesicular emulsion process used with microfilm or other negatives to obtain positive images suitable for direct projection, or for printing on positive-image dyeline (diazo) paper. When exposed by ultraviolet wavelengths, in contact with a negative, heat-activated dry processing produces an image in which minute bubbles trapped in the emulsion act like silver density to modulate the projection light. The process is primarily suitable for high-contrast images such as microfilm records of text pages. The processed image has a density range of about 1.0.
See also: DIAZO PROCESSES; VESICULAR IMAGES/EMULSIONS.

Karsh, Yousuf

Canadian; 1908–

Yousuf Karsh came to international prominence with a 1941 *Life* cover: the famous "English bulldog" portrait of Winston Churchill. Karsh has photographed many thousands of subjects in the last 50 years, principally portraits of distinguished men and women in every field of endeavor: statesmanship, the arts, and the sciences. Karsh prefers to take his portraits in the subject's own environment. His meticulous lighting characteristically emphasizes dramatic highlights and shadows, clarity and rich textures. In his portraits he attempts to convey to the viewer a fusion of the subject's personality with his or her public image and to reveal the sitter's "inward power." Although Karsh's subjects are mainly the achievers of the world, he himself has said that he likes to photograph "the great in spirit, whether they be famous or humble."

Karsh was born in Mardin, Armenia, of Christian-Armenian parents. Fleeing Turkish persecution, his family left Armenia in 1922, and in 1924 Karsh was brought to Canada by his uncle Nakash, a photographer. Financial considerations forced him to abandon his original desire to become a physician. Having shown aptitude for photography, Karsh was sent by his uncle to Boston to study under the eminent portrait photographer John H. Garo. In the stimulating humanistic atmosphere of Garo's studio, Karsh became acquainted with Garo's international circle of artistically accomplished friends. It was there that he decided to photograph those who have influenced our era.

After three years in Boston, Karsh returned to Ottawa in 1932 to open his own studio. It was during this period, at the Ottawa Little Theatre, that he was introduced to the use of incandescent lighting (his previous training in Boston having been with available light). After the appearance of his Churchill portrait in *Life,* which symbolized the indomitable wartime spirit of the British people, Karsh's work was in constant demand and he began to travel throughout the world on portrait assignments, a practice he continues to this day.

In 1943 Karsh extensively photographed British royalty, statesmen, and

Karsh, Yousuf

Karsh, Yousuf. "Churchill" (1941). Courtesy
Yousuf Karsh; © Karsh, Ottawa.

Käsebier, Gertrude. "Blessed art thou amongst women" (ca. 1898); photogravure. Library of Congress.

ized, for the heart and the mind are the true lens of the camera."

Karsh was awarded the Medal of Service of the Order of Canada in 1968 and was made an Honorary Fellow of the Royal Photographic Society, London, in 1970. He has been a Trustee of the Photographic Arts and Sciences Foundation and was named Master of Photographic Arts by the Professional Photographers Association of Canada. In 1971 he was awarded a Presidential Citation (U.S.A.) for meritorious service on behalf of the handicapped; for the last 20 years he has contributed poignant portraits of the poster children of the Muscular Dystrophy Association. Karsh's photographs have been used on the stamps of 15 countries. He has received numerous honorary degrees and published many books including his autobiography, *In Search of Greatness.* His most recent book, *Karsh: A Fifty-Year Retrospective,* contains hitherto unpublished photographs of many of his most famous subjects. He has had major exhibitions at the National Gallery of Canada, George Eastman House, Expo '67, the Corcoran Gallery, the Museum of Modern Art, New York, and many others. In June 1983, his exhibition of 80 portraits inaugurated the opening of the Museum of Photography, Film, and Television in Bradford, England. In September 1983, the International Center of Photography tendered him a 50-year retrospective.

Käsebier, Gertrude

American; 1852–1934

In the catalogue of an exhibition organized by Clarence White in 1910, Gertrude Käsebier was called "the foremost professional photographer in the United States." An early advocate of natural (though often romatic, sentimental) poses in commercial portraiture, she was famous for her unconventional scenes of mother–child relations and portraits of figures such as Rodin and Alfred Stieglitz. Photographing in an impressionistic style influenced by the paintings of Whistler, reworking her prints to eliminate detail, Käsebier was concerned less with composition than with tonal values. Her work was regularly published in the journals of the day. She did much to encourage women in careers in photography.

Käsebier was born Gertrude Stanton in Des Moines, Iowa, and raised in Colorado. She attended the Moravian College for Women, Bethlehem, Pennsylvania, and married Edward Käsebier in 1874. She took amateur photos of her

celebrities. He made portraits of political figures in Washington, D.C., and at the founding of the United Nations in San Francisco in 1945.

Among the illustrious figures Karsh has photographed are a succession of royalty, Popes, and presidents (among them John F. Kennedy); and such other celebrities as Albert Schweitzer, Albert Einstein, Helen Keller, Pablo Casals, Ernest Hemingway, and Georgia O'Keefe. In regard to his working methods, Karsh has emphasized the photographer's need for rapport: "In a successful portrait sitting the photographer must prepare by learning as much as he can about his subject so that immediate rapport will hopefully be real-

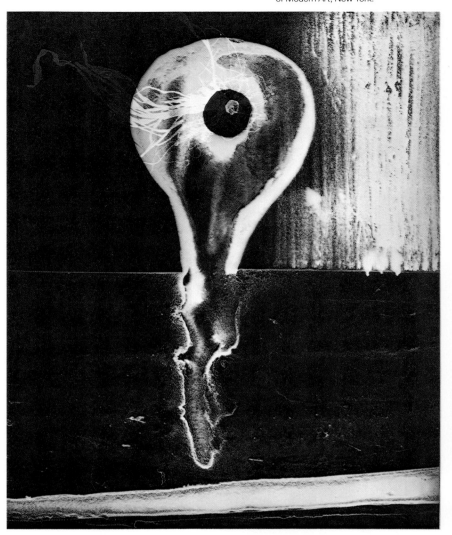

family early in married life. After raising a family, at the age of 36 she began to study painting in New York. By 1893 she was concentrating on photographic work. She apprenticed herself to a chemist in Germany in 1894 in order to learn the technical aspects of photography. In 1897 she worked for a Brooklyn photographer in order to learn the portrait photography business. She opened her own portrait studio in New York City the same year.

Käsebier began exhibiting with 150 portrait studies shown at the Boston Camera Club (1896) and at the Pratt Institute in New York (1897). Ten of her images were included in the first Philadelphia Salon of 1898. The following year, she was a juror for the second Salon with Clarence White and F. Holland Day, and opened a studio in Newport, Rhode Island, where she shot many of her best-known pictorial photographs.

Käsebier was given a solo exhibition at the New York Camera Club in 1899. She became the first American woman member of London's Linked Ring in 1900, and exhibited in Day's *New School of American Pictorial Photography* show at the Royal Photographic Society, London, and in Paris. She was a founding member of the Photo-Secession in 1902.

An ardent admirer of Käsebier's work, Alfred Stieglitz published several gravures of her images in the first issue of *Camera Work* and many more in later issues. She was given a joint exhibition with White at the Photo-Secession Galleries in 1906, and 22 of her prints were included in Stieglitz's *International Exhibition of Pictorial Photography* in Buffalo in 1910. But she and Stieglitz eventually broke contact over the issue of "straight" photography. Käsebier resigned from the Photo-Secession in 1912 and became a founding member, with White and Alvin Langdon Coburn, of the Pictorial Photographers of America four years later.

Käsebier received many honors during her career. She was president of the Women's Federation of the Professional Photographers Association of America in 1910, and was the subject of a major exhibition at the Department of Photography, Brooklyn Institute of Arts and Sciences in 1929.

Käsebier retired from professional photography in 1927 and died five years later at age 82.

Keller-Dorian Process

The Keller-Dorian process was an additive color system that used a panchromatic film with lenticular ribbing on the base. The film was exposed in a camera with the ribbed base facing the lens. A three-band (red, green, blue) filter in front of the lens produced the necessary primary color analysis of the subject. Each lenticule focused its portion of the color-banded image onto the emulsion; there were 550 lenticules to the inch. The film was reversal processed to obtain a positive black-and-white transparency and was projected through a matching filter, which produced a full-color image. The process was introduced in France by Rodolphe Berthon in 1909. Various methods of forming the lenticular base were perfected by Albert Keller-Dorian, an engraver and manufacturer of embossed (relief) printing rollers. The K-D-B process for motion pictures was demonstrated in 1923. It had very limited success because the film base tended to change size slightly, and inconsistently, during processing, which affected sharpness and color registration in pro-

jection; in addition, it was not possible to make additional prints of suitable quality. The system was purchased and improved by Eastman Kodak, and sold as Kodacolor—a 16mm reversal film for amateur movies—from 1928 to 1937. It had no relation to the later color negative film also called Kodacolor.
See also: ADDITIVE COLOR SYNTHESIS; LENTICULAR SYSTEMS.

Kelvin

The Kelvin is used to measure the absolute thermodynamic state of substances. It is the unit of temperature used in the system named for William Thompson, who became Lord Kelvin, a 19th c. English physicist. Thompson devised the absolute temperature system during the course of pioneering work in thermodynamics. The Kelvin is the same as one degree on the Celsius (centigrade) scale, but the starting points are not the same.

Keppler, Victor. "Spectacles" (n.d.). Courtesy Victor Keppler.

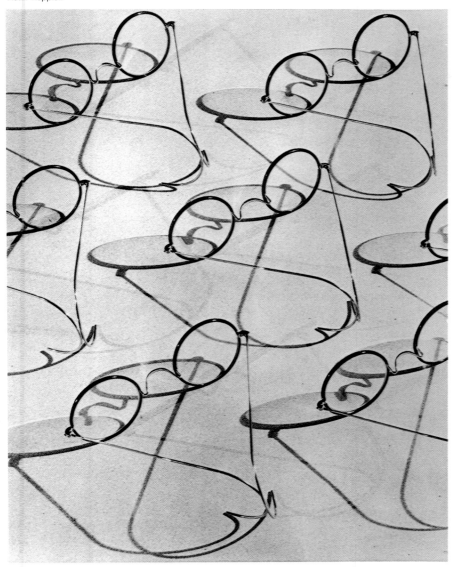

Keppler, Victor

American; 1905–

A pioneer in the use of color in advertising photography and one of that medium's most successful practitioners during the 1930s, 1940s, and 1950s, Victor Keppler was born in 1905 in Manhattan. He became interested in photography as a boy, acquiring his first camera, a used 3¼″ × 4¼″ plate-back instrument for which he paid $1.25, in 1926. Keppler attended the College of the City of New York and apprenticed himself during his summer vacations with Robert Waida, a commercial photographer and graduate of the Clarence H. White School in Philadelphia. A photograph of a bowl of spinach—a significant problem in black-and-white at the time—made on a challenge from an art director at the prestigious advertising agency of Batten Barton Durstine & Osborn, established Keppler's reputation as a man who could handle difficult assignments and launched his professional career.

During the Depression years, when great efforts were made to increase sales in a sagging economy, photography began to revolutionize advertising, and Keppler was in the forefront of this trend. During the 1930s his advertising work included campaigns for such major clients as General Electric, Lever Brothers, American Tobacco Company, DuPont, U.S. Steel, and the Schaefer Brewing Company. Often going to elaborate lengths to create settings, situations, and special effects, Keppler developed a sharply focused, dramatically lit style that attracted wide attention from the advertising and magazine community of the day.

During World War II Keppler was appointed as a dollar-a-year consultant to the War Savings Staff for the Office of the U.S. Treasury and produced a notable series of posters for the war effort.

He continued to maintain a large and active studio during the 1950s, doing more and more commercial and editorial illustration in color, and continuing to win top awards from the New York Art Directors Club. His approach to color photography is best expressed in his book, *The Eighth Art.*

In 1961 Keppler sold his studio and became head of the newly organized Famous Photographers School (FPS), a branch of the highly successful Famous Artists School, a home-study operation founded by artist Albert Dorne in 1947. Guiding faculty members included Richard Avedon, Richard Beattie, Joseph Costa, Arthur d'Arazien, Alfred Eisenstaedt, Harry Garfield, Philippe Halsman, Irving Penn, Bert Stern, and Ezra Stoller. Keppler continued as

Zero Kelvin (0K; the degree symbol ° is not used) is absolute zero, the temperature at which all molecular motion theoretically ceases; this is equal to −273.15°C (commonly rounded off to −273°C). The basic relationship with the common temperature scales is: 273K = 0°C = 32°F. The color temperature of light sources is expressed in Kelvins.
See also: COLOR TEMPERATURE; TEMPERATURE SCALES.

Kepes, Gyorgy

American; 1906–

A painter, designer, and teacher, soon after graduation from art school in Budapest, Kepes became associated with L. Moholy-Nagy in Berlin, where his experiments with photograms under Moholy's influence developed into a concern with abstract photography. He went with Moholy to England, and then to the U.S. as a member of the founding faculty of the New Bauhaus. There he taught two-dimensional design and conducted the light and color workshop. His knowledge of color and pattern produced innovative camouflage designs during World War II. In the post-war period he became Professor of Visual Design at the Massachusetts Institute of Technology. His book *The New Landscape* (1965) was the first significant examination of how revelations of the invisible by scientific and technical photography have expanded and reshaped our composite visual image of the world.
See also: MOHOLY-NAGY, LASZLO; NEW BAUHAUS; PHOTOGRAM.

Founder and Director of FPS until he retired in 1969. A comprehensive selection of his advertising, editorial, and personal work can be found in his autobiography *Man + Camera.*

See also: ADVERTISING PHOTOGRAPHY.

Kerr Cell

The Kerr cell is a type of electro-optic shutter used in high-speed photography and in the control of lasers. It consists of a glass cell filled with nitrobenzene or a similar liquid, placed between polarizers at each end. The polarizers are set in opposition: for example, light entering one end is polarized horizontally and so cannot exit through the vertically oriented polarizer at the other end. Electrodes from a high-voltage power source extend into the liquid. When power is applied, the charged liquid rotates the plane of polarization of light passing through, with the result that the light can exit the cell. Exposures as short as 100-millionth sec. are possible, at rates of up to the equivalent of 50 million per second. Even shorter exposures are possible with a Kerr cell optically triggered by a laser. Because nitrobenzene is yellow, the shutter filters out some blue and ultraviolet. A similar device, the *Kappa cell,* uses water, which has no filtering action and thus is suitable for color photography; however, its response is slower. The *Faraday shutter* uses a glass block wrapped with a high-voltage magnetic coil in place of the liquid-filled cell. Its operation is essentially the same; however, it passes a smaller percentage of the light (i.e., has a smaller working aperture) than a Kerr cell or Kappa cell.

See also: HIGH-SPEED PHOTOGRAPHY.

Kertész, André

American; 1894–

André Kertész is recognized as one of the world's leading photographers. During a career spanning more than 70 years, he has created images of ordinary life, in a style without pretension, using small-format cameras almost exclusively. As his instinctive formal sense has become more assured, he has retained the vital curiosity which first prompted him, at age 18, to make a visual record of his daily life.

Working in a variety of modes, from portraits to still-lifes to nude distortions to photo-reportage, Kertész has consistently captured the telling moment and the overlooked but expressive details of his subjects. He has had an enduring influence upon world photography, particularly in France where he was a mentor to photographers such as Henri Cartier-Bresson, Robert Capa, and Brassaï. Cartier-Bresson has acknowledged this achievement: "Whatever we have done, Kertész did first."

Acclaimed a master by his peers, critics, and curators by the late 1930s, Kertész's reputation suffered during the 1940s and 1950s as his commercial work in America distracted viewers from his European achievements. Since 1963, however, the full range of his mastery—fragile, intimate and gently ironic—has been undeniable. Exhibitions and a stream of books and monographs during the past 20 years of his creative life have reestablished Kertész in his rightful place in the photographic pantheon.

Kertész was born in Budapest, Hungary, where he graduated from the Academy of Commerce in 1912. He became a photographer of street and genre scenes at that time, and worked as a clerk at the Budapest Stock Exchange from 1912 to 1914. During service with the Austro-Hungarian Army in the Balkans and Central Europe in 1914–1915, Kertész photographed his comrades and their activities until he was severely wounded in battle. Many of the images he made were lost during the Hungarian Revolution of 1918.

Kertész's first published photographs appeared in *Erkedes Ujsag* (Interesting Newspaper) in 1917. He returned to work at the Budapest Stock Exchange until 1925, when he moved to Paris. For 10 years, Kertész worked as a freelance photographer in Paris for European magazines including *Vu, Art et Médécine,* the London *Sunday Times, Berliner Illustrirte Zeitung,* and *UHU.* His work as a photojournalist was highly acclaimed at this time, and he made many sympathetic portraits of Paris artists including Léger, Mondrian, Chagall, Brancusi, and Colette. His first one-man show was held at the Sacre du Printemps Gallery, Paris, in 1927.

Kertész was employed by Keystone Studios, New York, in 1936–1937. He intended to remain in America for a short period only, but was unable to return to Europe because of the war. From 1937 to 1949 he worked as a freelance fashion and interiors photographer for such magazines as *Look, Harper's Bazaar, Vogue, Collier's,* and *Town and Country.* He became an American citizen in 1944. From 1949 to 1962 he worked exclusively under contract with Condé Nast Publications. Since 1963 he has devoted himself to personal creative photography and the exhibition and publication of his life's work. He continues to live and work in New York's Greenwich Village.

Kertész has been the recipient of many honors. He has received a Silver Medal at the Exposition Coloniale, Paris in 1930, a Gold Medal at the Venice Biennale in 1962, and the Mayor's Award, New York, in 1977. He was awarded a Guggenheim Fellowship in 1975, is an Honorary Member of the American Society of Magazine Photographers (1965), and was named Commander, Order of Arts and Letters, by the French Government in 1976.

Kertész's work has been exhibited in group shows including: *Film und Foto,* Stuttgart, in 1929; *Photography 1848–1937* at the Museum of Modern Art, New York, in 1937; *The Concerned Photographer* traveling exhibition in 1967; *Documenta 6,* West Germany, in 1977, and *La Photographie Française 1925–1940* at Zabriskie Galleries, Paris and New York, in 1979. He has been the subject of one-man exhibitions at the Art Institute of Chicago (1946), the Bibliothèque Nationale, Paris (1963), the Museum of Modern Art, New York (1964), Light Gallery, New York (1973), Centre Beaubourg, Paris (1977), and Galerie Wilde, Cologne (1981).

Photograph: p. 274.

Kessel, Dmitri

American; 1902–

For almost a quarter of a century, Dmitri Kessel was a member of the illustrious staff of *Life* photographers who traveled the world to find pictures that recorded what life and the world is all about. That staff position was preceded by freelance photojournalism, industrial and advertising photography, work for *Fortune,* and assignment as a World War II correspondent for *Life;* it was followed by more freelance work.

Kessel was born in the Ukraine, Russia, into a family of landowners, and first used a camera as a child. He served as a cavalry officer in the Ukrainian Army, got into difficulty trying to photograph some of the upheavals of the Russian Revolution, and in 1921 went back to school in Moscow to study industrial chemistry and leather tanning. His subsequent wish to enter the Moscow Military Academy was never realized: his family had decided to emigrate from Russia and Kessel was arrested, first in Poland and shortly afterwards in Rumania as well, for lack of identity papers. But friends came to his rescue and, with passport in hand, he arrived in the United States in October 1923.

In New York City, Kessel worked at various jobs and as a correspondent for Russian language newspapers and magazines. At night he attended classes at

City College. His interest in photography began to grow again and he took a course at the Rabinovitch School of Photography in New York. At that time, Kessel began photographing the streets of New York and the people of the city as well. Gradually, however, he drifted into industrial photography, essentially because it paid well. This, and advertising work, led to assignments from *Fortune, Life, Collier's,* the *Saturday Evening Post,* and other publications.

In 1942, Kessel became a war correspondent for *Life.* He photographed scenes of violence and horror in the Congo, in Greece, in Spain, and during the German retreat from occupied territories. His life was at risk more than once, but he always felt that he had to photograph the action around him so others could be informed.

It was after 1944, while still on the staff of *Life,* that Kessel started to take his astonishingly beautiful photographs of churches and of works of art. With a keen eye for beauty and a personal interest in the arts, he experimented with color film and exposures until he could obtain results that satisfied him. His sweeping reportages on the Greek islands, on China, on Rome, the Vatican, and the Sistine Chapel, on St. Mark's in Venice, and on the Hermitage in Leningrad, and many other of the world's fabulous repositories of art, were all published in issues of *Life* or in some of the *Time-Life* book series. In between these great reportages, he found time to photograph many of the famous people in the worlds of politics and the arts. Kessel probably made the last photographs of the great Impressionist Matisse, shortly before the artist's death in the south of France.

For many years Kessel and his American-born wife Shirley have lived in Paris, from which he "commutes" to New York or elsewhere to complete freelance assignments for illustrated books.

Color photograph: p. C-28.

Key Light

The brightest front light falling on a subject is called the main or key light. Its angle, intensity, and relative harshness determine how the three-dimensional form of the subject is modeled, where the major shadows fall, and how sharply the shadows are defined. The key light also largely determines the degree to which surface texture is revealed or emphasized. In most lighting arrangements the key light is supplemented by fill light from another direction which reduces contrast by illuminating the

shadow areas to some degree. The key light is commonly two to six times brighter than the fill light.
See also: LIGHTING.

Keystoning

Keystoning is a kind of linear distortion in which one end of a rectangle is imaged larger than the other. With a vertical rectangle, the resulting wedge shape is like that of the keystone of an arch. The effect can also occur between the ends of a horizontal rectangle. It can be corrected by tilting or swinging the camera to make the film (image) plane parallel with the subject plane.

See also: CAMERA MOVEMENTS; DISTORTION.

Kinetoscope

In 1891 W. K. L. Dickson invented the Kinetoscope—the first continuous-film motion-picture viewing machine—for Thomas Edison, who patented the device. A 50-foot endless loop of positive motion-picture images was permanently threaded on a series of rollers in the machine. A diffused light behind the film illuminated the frame in position at the viewing hood. When a crank was turned the film advanced and an intermittent shutter interrupted the light as each frame changed. In commercial installations—where its competitor was the flip-book Mutoscope—a coin-operated control unblocked and blocked the light at the beginning of the brief presentation. Films were photographed for the Kinetoscope in the *Kinetograph,* the first celluloid-film motion-picture camera, invented by Dickson for Edison in 1888. To obtain enough film for 1½ minutes of operation at 46 frames per second, Dickson had slit a 2¾-inch-wide length of film supplied by John Carbutt. This produced two 25-foot strips, each 35mm wide, which Dickson spliced end-to-end. To insure that the film advanced without slipping, he perforated the film along the edges and used toothed sprocket wheels to impart regular motion. The same devices were used in the viewing machine. Edison contracted for George Eastman to manufacture film to these specifications before the machines went into commercial production, and thus the 35mm motion-picture film standards were established. Edison's Vitascope projector, produced a few years later, used the same film.

See also: LUMIERE, A. & L.; MOTION PICTURES; MUTOSCOPE; VITASCOPE.

Kingslake, Rudolf

American; 1903–
An optical scientist and lens designer Rudolf Kingslake was born and educated in England. Virtually his entire career was spent as head of lens design for Eastman Kodak Co. in Rochester, New York. His achievements include rare-earth optical glasses made with lanthanum oxide; precision optical instruments for military use, especially in World War II; innovative lens designs for mass market, industrial, and scientific cameras; and the first major U.S. program of computer-assisted lens design and evaluation. He has been president of the American Optical Society, a professor at the Rochester Institute of Technology, and editor and author of a great number of the standard reference works in his field.

Kirlian Photography

Kirlian photography is a form of electrophotography first reported in the 1950s. It is named for a Soviet hospital technician, Semyon Kirlian, and his wife, Valentina, who noticed unexplained sparks in their work with diathermy machines and used photographic materials to explore the phenomenon.

The Kirlian process commonly places film directly in contact with the subject, such as a leaf, or someone's fingertips. In one method, the subject rests directly on the film, which is laid emulsion side up on a thin sheet of insulating material. The insulator is placed on top of a sheet of electroconductive metal which is connected to a high-voltage, high-frequency power source. When the power is activated, current passes through the metal electrode. The insulation prevents the main portion of the energy from reaching the film; however, a corona in the ultraviolet and blue wavelengths does pass through the insulator. The surface conduction characteristics of the subject affect the corona energy flow, and the film records the pattern of the discharge. With a transparent object, the discharge may be seen visually and photographed with a camera and lens. In other methods, an air gap is used instead of insulating material between the film and the electrode, or the subject is placed between the film and the electrode, with suitable insulation.

Although some enthusiasts have claimed that the energy flow patterns are auras that reveal psychic states or mystical forces, there is no basis for such interpretations. The basic phenomenon is "skin flow," the passage of very high voltage, high frequency electricity over the surface rather than through the body of a conductor. Considerable variation in image patterns can be created by altering the voltage, waveform, or frequency of the power; by using various electrode and insulating materials; and by adjusting the subject-film-electrode spacing. Atmospheric conditions such as the amount of moisture in or near the subject also seem to affect image patterns.

Few practical applications of Kirlian photography have been discovered. Small internal fissures in metals can be detected without injury to the sample being investigated. It may be possible to develop methods of detecting abnormal biological conditions such as subcutaneous skin problems or agricultural leaf and stem blights. At the present time, however, Kirlian photography remains largely a curiosity.

It should be noted that while the equipment for this process is relatively simple to assemble, it is not without risk. The high voltages required are potentially dangerous. Experimentation should be carried out only by or with someone thoroughly familiar with electricity and electrical safety procedures.

See also: ELECTROPHOTOGRAPHIC PROCESSES.

Kitsch Photography

Kitsch refers to vulgar or over-sentimentalized works that pander to the basest popular taste, yet insist on being taken seriously as works of art. The word kitsch, in German, means both to slap together—as in a slapped-together work of art—and, more pointedly, to scrape up mud from the street. This modern, derogatory use of the term has become widespread only in the 20th c., and usually represents the judgment of the present on self-proclaimed pretensions of artistic worth in works of the past. According to today's prevailing taste, a certain proportion of the "serious" art photography of the 19th c. has come to be considered as unredeemable kitsch.

Works nowadays described as kitsch in photography are said to possess one or all of the following qualities. (1) A hyperabundance of technical sophistication brought to bear on illustrating impoverished ideas. In Oscar J. Rejlander's elaborate composite photograph "The Two Ways of Life" (1857), immense technical virtuosity is put to the task of conveying a moralistic message that was both trivial and contrived even in its own day. (2) Coyness or pretense in presentation. In Lejaren à Hiller's 1930s photographs illustrating "Surgery Through the Ages," for example, disease seems to strike down only nubile, half-dressed young women. The elevated theme serves mainly as a pretext for decorous erotic fantasy. (3) Excessive sentimentality, as in the 19th c. photographer Julia Margaret Cameron's representation of impossibly angelic children or wistful maidens. (4) Inappropriateness of the subject to the photographic medium. The turn-of-the-century Pictorialist photographer F. Holland Day, in a classic example, unabashedly photographed himself as Christ on the Cross. (5) In general, theatrical overproduction of insignificant or clichéd content.

Kitsch is a seriously intended effort that is blind to its own bad taste and feeble content. In contrast, "camp" is a conscious, often affectionate exaggeration of an outdated style or mannerism for humorous effect.

See also: ART OF PHOTOGRAPHY; EROTIC PHOTOGRAPHY; GENRE PHOTOGRAPHY; PICTORIAL PHOTOGRAPHY/PICTORIALISM.

Klein, William

American; 1928–

An international jury at *Photokina 1963* voted William Klein one of the 30 most important photographers in the medium's history. He became famous in Europe immediately upon publication of his strikingly intense book of photographs, *Life Is Good for You in New York—William Klein Trance Witness Revels,* for which he won the Prix Nadar in 1956. Klein's visual language made an asset out of accident, graininess, blur, and distortion. He has described his work as "a crash course in what was not to be done in photography." Klein employed a wide-angle lens, fast film, and novel framing and printing procedures to make images in a fragmented, anarchic mode that emphasized raw immediacy and highlighted the photographer's presence in the scene.

Among Klein's other books (for which he did the design, typography, covers, and texts) are expressive portraits of Rome, Moscow, and Tokyo. His influence upon other photographers since the late 1950s has been underground but pervasive.

Born and raised in New York, Klein graduated from high school at age 14 and subsequently studied sociology at City College of the City of New York. After two years in the United States Army, where he worked as an army newspaper cartoonist, he attended the Sorbonne, Paris, on the G. I. Bill. He studied painting briefly with Fernand Léger and has lived in Paris since 1948, working as a

Klein, William. "Moscow, Girl smiling, old man and woman seated" (1959). Courtesy William Klein; collection, Museum of Modern Art, New York.

painter, graphic designer, photographer, and filmmaker.

Klein exhibited throughout Europe as a painter, producing abstract murals for French and Italian architects. He first photographed his murals in motion in 1952 and began experimenting with the medium. He was very much influenced at this time by the work of Man Ray, Alexander Rodchenko, the Dadaists, and the Bauhaus.

Klein revisited New York in 1954 and began his documentation of the city, hurling himself into the urban chaos. He worked in direct opposition to the model of elegance and discretion he saw in the images of Henri Cartier-Bresson. From 1955 to 1965, Klein produced bizarrely original fashion photography for *Vogue* and other publications. His employer at *Vogue*, Alexander Liberman, wrote, "In the fashion pictures of the fifties, nothing like Klein had happened before. He went to extremes, which took a combination of great ego and courage. He pioneered the telephoto and wide-angle lenses, giving us a new perspective. He took fashion out of the studio and into the streets . . . ."

Klein first took up filmmaking in 1958. In 1965, he abandoned still photography to concentrate on films for the cinema and television. His best known works in this medium are *Cassius the Great* (a film on Muhammad Ali) and *Loin du Vietnam,* on which he collaborated with directors Alain Resnais, Jean-Luc Godard, and others. He has completed over 20 films in the last 25 years.

Klein has exhibited throughout the world at Fuji Gallery, Tokyo; Stedelijk Museum, Amsterdam; Photokina, Cologne; and The International Center of Photography and the Witkin Gallery, New York. He was honored in 1978 at the Arles Festival International. An exhibition of his early work was held at the Museum of Modern Art, New York, in 1980–1981, at which time John Szarkowski wrote: "Klein's photographs of twenty years ago were perhaps the most uncompromising of their time. They were the boldest and superficially the most scrofulous—the most distanced from the accepted standards of formal quality . . . . They really extend what life can look like in pictures. They enlarge the vocabulary."

Klein was the subject of an Aperture monograph in 1981. He returned to still photography part-time in 1978 and continues to live and work in Paris.

Klič, Karel (Karl Klietsch)

Czech; 1841–1926

A painter, illustrator, and printer, Klič was the inventor of the photogravure process of photomechanical reproduction in Vienna in 1879. His method is used even today (in modified form) to get the highest quality ink reproductions of photographs in large numbers. In the original method a copper plate was dusted with resin and heated in preparation for producing aquatint grain. A carbon-process negative tissue was transferred onto the plate, over the resin, and the unhardened gelatin in the shadows and middletones was dissolved with warm water. The plate was then etched in a series of iron chloride baths of different strengths. The varying thickness of the gelatin controlled the depth of etching, the aquatint resin produced a random dot pattern. When the plate surface was cleaned, the image was represented by intaglio dots that varied in depth as well as size. Thus, the density of the ink in the dots varied in the reproduction, much as the density of the silver varied in the original photograph. All other methods produced varied dot size, but only one ink density. Klič attempted to keep the process secret in order to build a more profitable business, but it was published without patent protection by a partner and was rapidly adopted throughout the world.

Much the same thing occurred in England in 1895 to Klič's other major invention: the first practical method of mak-
ing gravure plates for use on high-speed presses with rotating cylinders. High quality had to be achieved in very short impression times (less than one second each) and maintained over long runs; it was impossible to stop the presses to change plates frequently. In this process the necessary dot pattern was produced by a halftone screen rather than the aquatint resin, and a harder metal plate was used with a different degree of etching. Within a few years of the unauthorized disclosure of the process, newspapers throughout Europe and the U.S. were featuring rotogravure, or simply "roto," sections as weekly illustrated supplements.

See also: AQUATINT; CARBON PROCESSES; HALFTONE PROCESSES; INTAGLIO PROCESS; PHOTOGRAVURE.

Kodachrome

Originally, the name Kodachrome identified a two-color process involving separate plates that were reversal processed, dyed, and bound in register for viewing as a transparency. This process was introduced in the U.S. in 1915 and offered until the mid-1920s. The familiar Kodachrome film of today was invented by Mannes and Godowsky in collaboration with personnel of the Kodak Research Laboratories. It was introduced as a 16mm amateur movie film in 1935, and a year later in 8mm, 35mm, and 828 sizes. It was the world's first monopack (integral tripack, or three-layer emulsion) subtractive color film; today it remains the standard to which other color transparency films are compared.

The Kodachrome emulsion is constructed, from top to bottom, of blue-, green-, and red-sensitive layers of silver halides. A temporary yellow filter deposit just below the blue-sensitive layer prevents blue light from affecting the halides below; the filter deposit dissolves out during processing. The unique feature of the Kodachrome emulsion is that it contains no dye-forming color couplers. All other color emulsions do incorporate couplers; in Kodachrome they are contained in the developers. Processing is complex, includes many separate steps, and requires critical control of time and temperature at each step; for this reason it can only be carried out by laboratories equipped with automatic processors devoted only to this purpose.

The original process involved delicate dyeing and bleaching steps; an improved process introduced in 1938 forms the basis of the method used today. After the rem-jet anti-halation backing layer is removed, the silver-halide negative image in all layers is developed and bleached to a colorless state. Then the positive image is produced in each layer separately. First the base of the film is exposed to red light—the reversal exposure for the red-sensitive layer—and processed in a developer that produces the positive silver image and the cyan dye image, formed by couplers in the developer. Next the top layer is reversal-exposed to blue light and developed to a positive silver-and-yellow dye image. The middle (green-sensitive) layer is now obscured to light from both sides, so a fogging developer with magenta color couplers is used. Finally the positive silver images are bleached and the entire emulsion is fixed and washed, leaving only the positive color image formed of subtractive color dyes.

Kodachrome Professional film in sheet film sizes was offered in 1938, but was replaced in the late 1940s by Ektachrome film, which used processing that was far more practical for individual sheets and that could be carried out in any darkroom. Today Kodachrome film is produced as a 35mm still film, and in amateur movie sizes. The contrast, grain, and other image qualities of the basic Kodachrome 25 film are unmatched by any other.

See also: COLOR MATERIALS; COLOR PHOTOGRAPHY—HISTORY; COUPLERS, COLOR; GODOWSKY, LEOPOLD; MANNES, L. D.; REM-JET BACKING; REVERSAL MATERIALS AND PROCESSING; SUBTRACTIVE COLOR SYNTHESIS.

Kodacolor

Originally, the name Kodacolor identified an improved version of the Keller-Dorian lenticular film process. The color negative film now known as Kodacolor was introduced in 1942. It was the first subtractive-color negative film that solved the problem of color couplers migrating from one layer to another. The idea of incorporating couplers (dye-forming) compounds in a multiple-layer film had been patented by Rudolph Fischer in 1912. Efforts to do this were not entirely successful because some coupler molecules wandered when the emulsion was soft and wet with developer, with the result that the wrong dye was produced along with the correct dye in some areas of the image; this grayed the image or created spurious colors. The Kodacolor emulsion kept the couplers anchored in their own layers.

The processing method devised for Kodacolor is, with significant improvements, that used for all color negative films today. A single developer produces the negative silver image in all three layers simultaneously. The couplers are activated by the effect of the silver development, and the corresponding dye images form at the same time. The silver image is bleached and the emulsion fixed and washed to complete processing.

The method of controlling the couplers introduced with Kodacolor was soon duplicated in all other color films (except Kodachrome, which does not use integral couplers), as was a major improvement invented by Wallace T. Hanson and introduced in 1949. This was the coloring of the cyan and magenta couplers so that those not activated to form dyes remained as a mask (printing filter) that corrected the deficiencies of the dye absorption and transmission in these layers. This integral color masking is what produces the overall orange-brown or pinkish-tan coloring seen in all processed color negative films. In 1983 a family of improved Kodacolor emulsions was introduced. These have significantly improved grain and sharpness characteristics, and range in speed from ISO 100/21° to ISO 1000/31°.
See also: COLOR MATERIALS; COLOR PHOTOGRAPHY—HISTORY; COUPLERS, COLOR; KELLER-DORIAN PROCESS; SUBTRACTIVE COLOR SYNTHESIS.

Kodak

Introduced by the Eastman Company in 1888, the Kodak was the first successful roll-film camera. The simple operation of the Kodak and all its successors made picture-taking popular with the general public and created a mass market of

amateurs throughout the world. The original camera, loaded with film for 100 circular pictures 2 in. in diameter, cost $25. The instructions listed only four steps: (1) *Point the camera* (at a subject six feet or more from the fixed-focus lens). (2) *Pull the string* (to cock the spring-driven shutter). (3) *Press the button* (to make the exposure at the single speed of 1/25 sec.). (4) *Turn the key* (to advance the film). When the entire roll was exposed the camera was mailed to the Eastman factory where, for $10, the

pictures were developed, printed, and mounted on cards, and the camera reloaded with fresh film. Advertising stressed the two features that appealed most to amateurs—simplicity and no work—with the slogan, "You press the button, we do the rest." George Eastman chose the name Kodak from a list of many possibilities because it was short, memorable, and would be pronounced the same in almost all languages. The name was first used for a series of box and folding cameras derived from the

Koudelka, Josef. "The Gypsies." (1961).
Josef Koudelka/Magnum.

original design; then it was incorporated into the company name and has since been used in various forms as a trademark for the great majority of Eastman products, e.g., Kodak Brownie camera; Kodachrome film.
See also: BROWNIE CAMERA; EASTMAN, GEORGE.

Kohler Illumination

A standard technique of bright-field illumination used with microscopes, Kohler illumination focuses an image of the light source on the substage condenser. This condenser in turn focuses an image of the field or collector lens of the lamp onto the plane of the specimen. The result is a field of uniform brightness at the specimen even with light sources that are not uniform, such as coiled filament lamps, or that are of very small area and might otherwise create a hot spot of brightness. Kohler illumination is widely used in photomicrography because it permits using a variety of light sources according to the exposure and color balance requirements of the situation, and because it provides higher resolving power and better image quality than other techniques.
See also: BRIGHT-FIELD ILLUMINATION; PHOTOMICROGRAPHY.

Kostinsky Effect

The apparent displacement of two closely spaced point images of essentially equal density is known as the Kostinsky effect. The bromide given off as the images develop becomes much more concentrated in the overlapping diffusion area between them than elsewhere. This restrains development of their neighboring edges to a significant degree, reducing their size and increasing the space between them. In astronomical work—where the effect was first noticed in 1906—the result can be an inaccurate measurement of the separation between two point images of stars. The effect can also cause inaccuracies in photomicrography and can create distortions in optical sound tracks, master patterns for miniaturized printed circuits, and other applications in which high resolving power with precise spacing is essential.
See also: EDGE EFFECTS; RESOLVING POWER.

Koudelka, Josef

Czech; 1938–
Josef Koudelka is known for his highly formalized, sensitive images of the vestiges of gypsy life. Since 1962 he has traveled and extensively documented gypsies in Eastern Europe, England, Ireland, France, and Spain. Entirely independent, constantly on the move like the people he photographs, Koudelka has never accepted magazine or commercial assignments. He has worked for many years without a permanent darkroom, amassing a large backlog of images he has yet to print. His work has focused consistently on the community rituals of everyday life, birth, marriage, and death.

Koudelka was born in Boskovice, Moravia (Czechoslovakia). He received a degree in aeronautical engineering from the Technical University, Prague, in 1961, and worked as an engineer from 1961 to 1967. His first exhibition was held in Prague in 1961. He began to photograph his series on gypsy life soon after.

From 1962 to 1970 Koudelka was a freelance photographer specializing in theater photography. He worked for the Divaldo Theatre, Prague, and was the official photographer of Theatre zu Branou from 1965 to 1970. His later work is clearly rooted in this theatrical training ground. Not only has he been concerned with gypsy social life and cultural rituals (especially musical performances), but he has photographed the same activities many times as though he were still shooting dramatic performances.

Koudelka made his first trip to England in 1961. Leaving Czechoslovakia permanently in 1970, he lived in England from 1970 to 1980. He joined Magnum in 1971 and has enjoyed a close working relationship with Henri Cartier-Bresson.

Koudelka was a member of the Czechoslovakian Union of Artists from 1965 to 1970, and was the recipient of their Annual Award for Theatre Photography in 1967. He received the Robert Capa Memorial Award in 1970, the Prix Nadar in 1978, and a United States National Endowment for the Arts Photography Grant in 1980. In 1976 he was awarded a grant by the British Arts Council to document the disappearing gypsy life in England. In recent years he has photographed religious and other festivities and everyday life in Great Britain and Europe. He has lived in France for the last several years.

Koudelka's work has appeared in magazines including *Look*, *Camera*, and *The New York Times Sunday Magazine*. He has exhibited throughout the world, with major shows in Prague; Bergamo, Italy; Great Britain; Camera Obscura, Stockholm; the Museum of Modern Art, New York; and the Carpenter Center for the Visual Arts at Harvard University.

Kraszna-Krausz, Andor

British; 1904–
Andor Kraszna-Krausz is a renowned editor and publisher who has been professionally active since the 1920s. Born and educated in Hungary, in 1923 he left Budapest University to explore cinematography and photography in Munich. In 1925 he moved to Berlin and joined the oldest established publishing house specializing in these subjects. He edited the professional journal *Filmtechnik* and expanded it into *Filmkunst;* founded the first European periodical for amateur and independent movie-makers, *Film für Alle;* initiated a wide range of books on motion pictures and still photography;

Krull, Germaine. Untitled, from Metal Portfolio, (1922–27). Courtesy Galerie Wilde, Cologne; International Museum of Photography at George Eastman House.

and wrote about movies for his own journals and for *Closeup* in London. He left Germany for England in 1937, and in 1938 established the Focal Press to publish books on the science and techniques of motion pictures and still photography. In a long and distinguished career, Kraszna-Krausz introduced generations of new authors, including many of the most respected authorities and experienced technicians in their fields, and published over 1200 titles, a good number of them translated into as many as 20 languages. The current Focal Press book list includes nearly 300 titles on photography, cinematography, and television, with emphasis on the craft, technology, and science of these media. The *Focal Encyclopedia of Photography* and other works of the imprint have become standard sources of reference in their fields.

See also: APPENDIX: BIBLIOGRAPHY.

Kromskop

The Kromskop was a viewer that produced additive color images from black-and-white separation positives made in the Photochromoscope (Kromskop Camera) of F. E. Ives. Monocular, stereoscopic, and projection models of the viewer were produced for about a decade, beginning in 1895. A special version for viewing diffraction photographs in color was produced in 1906.

See also: ADDITIVE COLOR SYNTHESIS; DIFFRACTION PHOTOGRAPHS; IVES, FREDERICK EUGENE.

Krone, Hermann

German; 1827–1916

Hermann Krone was one of the first persons in the Silesian region of Germany to investigate photography soon after its invention in 1839. Self-taught in photography, he achieved fame for portrait and landscape work and for achievements in scientific photography.

Krone was born in Breslau (now Wroclaw, Poland) and studied natural science at the university there. In 1843, at age 15, he constructed a box camera of his own design equipped with a biconvex achromatic lens and began experimenting with the calotype (paper negative) process. Within a year he also was getting tentative results with his own approximation of the daguerreotype process; by 1847 he had achieved respectable competence in photography without outside aid or instruction.

In 1849 Krone moved to Dresden, where he continued experimentation in photography while making a living as a lithographer by day and as an astronomy lecturer at night. In 1851 he felt master

enough of the medium to open a portrait studio in Leipzig, which met with almost immediate success, as did his efforts in landscape photography. At the same time he continued scientific investigations of phenomena such as multiple solarization. In July of that year he successfully photographed an eclipse of the sun. Although his studio attracted a visit from the King of Saxony, influential local competition forced him to leave Leipzig. He returned to Dresden and opened a new studio. As a landscape photographer he traveled throughout the eastern German states; his best known images of this period were made in certain areas of Saxony.

In 1869, Krone closed his studio to become a professor of scientific photography at the Dresden Polytechnic Institute and to devote himself to astronomical photography. In 1874 he joined an expedition to the Auckland Islands to witness the eclipse of Venus and to make an astonishingly perfect 115-picture record of the event. In the same period, P.J.C. Janssen used a unique gun camera to make sequence pictures of the transit of Venus.

Returning to Europe, Krone continued his research and teaching. He experimented with the Lippmann interference process for color photography in the late 1890s and retired in 1907. He died in 1916 at the age of 90.

See also: GUN CAMERA; LIPPMANN PROCESS.

Color photograph: p. C-29.

Krull, Germaine

French; 1897–

Polish-born Germaine Krull, perhaps the most expressive of the photographers linked to the New Photography or New Objectivity (Neue Sachlichkeit), made her reputation working in Paris in the late 1920s and early 1930s. Krull specialized in the documentation of industrial architecture and machinery: cranes, the Eiffel Tower, Métro stations, etc. She was also responsible for sensitive portraits of her friends including Colette, Jean Cocteau, André Gide, and Henri Malraux. Her photographs were praised by critic and aesthetician Walter Benjamin along with those of Atget, Blossfeldt, and Sander, but it is only since a retrospective organized by Malraux in 1967 that her work has begun to receive proper attention.

Of German descent, Krull was born in Wilda, Poznan, Poland. She was educated in Paris until 1909 and later studied photography and received her M.A. at the Bavarian State Photographic Institute in Munich in 1918. Between 1919

and 1921 Krull operated her own studio and worked as a freelance photographer in Munich and Berlin. She worked as a freelance architectural and industrial photographer in Amsterdam and Rotterdam between 1921 and 1924, publishing in magazines such as *Das Kunstblatt*, *Variétés*, and *Die Dame*, and associating with Man Ray and André Kertész on her trips to paris.

Krull worked in Paris from 1924 to 1932 doing fashion, portrait, advertising, and industrial photography on a freelance basis. She became associated with such members of French artistic circles as Berenice Abbott. Her seminal book, *Métal*, was published in 1927. Krull's work at this time appeared in *Vu*, *Arts et Métiers Graphiques*, *L'Art et Médicine*, and other periodicals, and she was employed by such clients as Peugeot, Citroën, and Columbia Records.

From 1932 to 1940 Krull traveled and photographed in the south of France and throughout Europe. She was married for several years to the Dutch documentary filmmaker Joris Ivens. From 1941 to 1944 she acted in Africa as director of the photographic propaganda division of the French Free Army in Brazzaville and Algiers. She was a war correspondent and photographer for Resistance newspapers in Germany and Italy from 1943 to 1945. All of Krull's early photographic work was lost during the war years.

From 1946 to 1965 Krull traveled and photographed throughout Europe and in Asia, concentrating on the documentation of Buddhist art treasures. For many years she was director of the Oriental Hotel in Bangkok. Krull retired in 1965 to the north of India where she lives with the exiled followers of the Dalai Lama of Tibet.

During her long career, Krull published over 20 volumes of her images. Her work has been exhibited in group shows including: *Abbott/Krull/Kertész/Lotar/Man Ray* at Galérie de l'Escalier in Paris, in 1925; *Film und Foto* in Stuttgart, in 1929; *Documenta 6* in Kassel, West Germany, in 1977; *Paris-Berlin 1900–1933* at the Centre Georges Pompidou, Paris, in 1978; *New Sachlichkeit and German Realism of the "20s"* at the Hayward Gallery, London, in 1979; and *La Photographie Française 1925–1940* at Zabriskie Galleries in Paris and New York, in 1979. Solo exhibitions of her photographs have been held at the Musée du Cinéma, Paris, in 1967; Rheinisches Landesmuseum, Bonn, in 1977; Galerie Wilde, Cologne, in 1980; and Stedelijk Museum, Amsterdam, in 1980.

See also: NEUE SACHLICHKEIT.

Kuehn, Heinrich (Carl Christian Kuhn)

Kühn, Heinrich. "The Toilette" (ca. 1890);
Gum Print. Smithsonian Institution.

Kuehn, Heinrich (Carl Christian Kühn)

Austrian; 1866–1944

Heinrich Kuehn, a Pictorialist photographer who is known for impressionistic prints made in the multiple gum-bichromate process, was the most important member of the Vienna Kamera-Club as well as a member of the Linked Ring in England. The son of a merchant, Kuehn was born in Dresden, Germany, and initially studied medicine and the natural sciences in Leipzig, Berlin, and Freiberg. Shortly after experimenting with microscopic photography in 1887–1888 at the Institute for Pathological Anatomy at Innsbruck and publishing research on cell particles in 1888, he turned his efforts completely to photography.

In 1891 Kuehn was inspired by an exhibition organized by the Vienna Kamera-Club, where he saw photographs by the members of the Linked Ring. He took up freelance photography in Vienna, working primarily in portraiture. In 1894 he joined the Vienna Kamera-Club, where he became friends with the photographer Hans Watzek. The same year, he also exhibited his work at the Photo-Club de Paris and at the Milan International United Exhibitions, where his work was first noticed by Alfred Stieglitz.

Two years later Kuehn was elected a member of the Linked Ring, and during that year was introduced to the gum bichromate process by Hugo Henneberg. With Henneberg and Hans Watzek, he began working more and more with this process. In April 1896, he was the first to exhibit gum-bichromate prints in the Austellung für Amateur-photographie in Berlin, and in October and December of that year published articles on his experiments with the process, using his own prints as illustrations. Also in 1896, Kuehn received a medal for artistic photography from the Vienna Kamera-Club, and exhibited at the London Salon of the Linked Ring. Kuehn, Watzek, and Henneberg became known as the "Trifolium" of the Vienna Kamera-Club, a threesome who far surpassed the photographic efforts of their fellow club members. The Trifolium reached its zenith around 1902.

After Watzek died in May 1903, and Henneberg turned to painting and etching, Kuehn carried on alone with both his own photographic work and his writing and experimenting in the field. In the spring of 1905 he organized a major international exhibition for the Kamera-Club, held at the Galerie Miethke in Vienna, for which he received attention in the U.S. and Europe. The following year he was included in a group exhibition at Alfred Stieglitz's Little Galleries of the Photo-Secession in New York.

Although Kuehn's photographs evolved very little after about 1912, he remained active as a photographer, writer, and inventor. He came to know and associate with Frank Eugene, Edward Steichen, Baron Adolphe de Meyer, and Alfred Stieglitz, with whom he corresponded between 1904 and 1931. Stieglitz also featured his photographs in a 1911 issue of *Camera Work* (#33).

Throughout the 1920s Kuehn experimented with technical innovations in cameras and film materials. During the same decade he also worked as a commercial photographer, primarily for magazines. Kuehn was a contributing editor to the *Photographische Rundschau* during the 1910s and he contributed frequently to *Das Deutsche Lichtbild* and other journals during the late 1920s and 1930s. He died in Birgitz, Austria, on October 9, 1944.

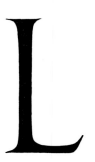

Lambert

See: LIGHT UNITS.

Laminated Images

Laminated photographs are images heat-sealed between sheets of plastic, or images constructed of elements on various layers of material that are assembled and sealed together. Lamination in plastic is widely used to protect identification photographs and make them tamper-proof. It is also used to protect prints and transparencies that are subjected to extensive handling, for example at sales counters or in a sample book or portfolio. Images assembled on various layers of film or other transparent material to which photographs have been transferred may be laminated layer by layer, or in a single outer envelope of plastic. The major concern in lamination is keeping the sealing temperature to a minimum. Black-and-white prints on most fiber-base papers may withstand temperatures of up to 200°F (93°C) for 2 or 3 minutes without negative effect. Prints on resin-coated papers, all color images, and images on film-base material are susceptible to change or damage at much lower temperatures. A test with an expendable sample image is essential with any unfamiliar laminating material or process. Processes that use cements or solvents rather than heat to fuse the plastic are generally not suitable for photographic materials.

Land, Edwin Herbert

American; 1909 –

Inventor, with co-workers, of modern instant photography, Land's first important research was into the nature and behavior of polarized light and materials that cause polarization. Having worked out the theory of an artificial polarizer while a student, after graduation from Harvard Land hired the chemist Joseph Friedman to develop a way to align anisotropic crystals within plastic. They patented the method in 1929, and Land established the Polaroid Corporation to produce it and derivative materials used for sunglasses, gunsights, glare-free lights, and other applications.

Land devoted himself primarily to research related to light and vision, and materials that affect them; this inevitably led to involvement with photography. His young daughter's asking "Why can't I see it now?" during a snapshot session focused his attention on the problem of self-processing, instant-access photographic materials. After several years of research and improvement in the basic diffusion transfer process, he demonstrated a practical camera and film in 1947; they were introduced commercially the following year as the Polaroid Land process. The original materials were separate rolls of film and print paper that took 60 seconds or more to produce a brown-tone print that had to be coated with a liquid plasticizer to prevent fading. Improvements brought neutral black-and-gray image tones; ISO 3000 speed, 10-second films; peel-apart sheet films; negative-plus-positive materials; coating-free films; black-and-white transparency films; an ISO 10,000 speed film for instrument display recording; peel-apart color films; and the first single-sheet instant color material, the SX-70 film. A self-processing 35mm color slide film with a built-in additive color line screen, and black-and-white slide films were introduced in 1983.

Land has also investigated human color vision and demonstrated that classic three-color recording and stimulus, as proposed in the Young-Helmholtz theory, is not required to create full color photographs. This is discussed in the entries on color, vision, and two-color photography.

See also: DIFFUSION TRANSFER PROCESS; POLARIZED LIGHT; POLARIZER.

Landscape Photography

Although the term *landscape* classically refers to the natural, unpeopled scene, photographs of this sort may well include people, buildings, and other elements that provide interest or a sense of scale. The earliest photographic processes required long exposure times, so photographers had essentially only two subjects: landscape and architecture. Although the imperfect translation of colors into photographic shades was an expressive limitation, photography not only increased the popularity of landscape as a subject, but also affected the style of painting. In the 1840s and 1850s, artists such as Camille Corot were greatly influenced by the soft, pictorial quality of the calotype. In the second half of the 19th c., the wet collodion process brought shorter exposure times and a clarity of detail that allowed photographers a choice of treating a landscape as a pictorial exercise or as a compelling, direct experience of nature. Photographers such as the Bisson *frères,* Timothy H. O'Sullivan, Carleton E. Watkins, and William Henry Jackson became acknowledged masters of landscape. In the 20th c., the direct approach was raised to unequalled heights of effectiveness by Edward Weston and Ansel Adams in the U.S. The advent of full-color photography in this century gave additional impetus to landscape photography, largely in a pictorial mode in the hands of most amateurs, but in images of outstanding beauty and realism in the work of photographers such as Eliot Porter.

Like human subjects, the landscape changes appearance and expression, but at the slower rate of weather, light, and seasonal variations. Landscape photographers may need to wait only for a cloud to pass or for the sun to shift position in the sky, or may return to an area on several occasions in search of variety. In the landscape, natural lighting is most dramatic in early morning and late afternoon. Both textural details such as grass, stone, and tree bark, and the larger scale factors of topography, object size, and element massing are clearly revealed by this angular light. The color of light at those times of day also may enhance the scene. Direct summer sun,

especially at midday, creates high contrast and deep, sharply defined shadows that may do more to camouflage than to reveal major aspects of the scene. The quality and color of the light and subject change with the season and the weather. Obviously, the blossoming of spring and the leaf changes of autumn present the most colorful landscape opportunities in many areas with substantial natural vegetation. The seasonal changes are very different, or may not even occur, in more tropical regions, and they have little effect on desert scenes or those above the timberline in the mountains. Winter or overcast days produce diffused sky light that presents problems of excess bluishness and a lack of modelling. Ultraviolet scattered in the atmosphere creates bluishness or a graying of distant tones unless counteracted with proper filtration: a No. 1A (Skylight) filter with color film; a light- or medium-yellow filter with black-and-white film.

Filters also are used frequently in landscape photography to control tonal rendition. In black-and-white photographs green foliage may appear dark and lifeless. A green or yellow filter can correct this problem by lightening the gray tone of green objects. If the sky is prominent, an orange or red filter may be employed to dramatize the contrast between sky, clouds, and ground. With color films a polarizing filter can darken the blue sky without affecting other colors in the scene. Filters must be used carefully to avoid exaggerated effects, especially when a lake or other large body of water is included in the landscape. Just as the blue sky is darkened by various filters, similar changes occur with water that appears blue because it is reflecting the sky light. A polarizing filter may also be used to eliminate unwanted reflections in water.

Exposure for a fully lighted landscape can be based on a reflected-light reading from the overall scene, an incident-light reading, or the simple rule of f/16 at 1/film speed. Bright or reflective scenes—snow, beach, or those scenes with large areas of sky or water—will require one to two f-stops less exposure. On a cloudy-bright day exposure must be increased by about one f-stop. As a landscape is an essentially unchanging subject, it is practical to take several pictures at various exposures to assure good results.

Terrain features establish the basic composition of a landscape photograph: long rolling hills are seldom framed vertically, or a waterfall horizontally. Two other major factors in composition are the position of the horizon and the camera elevation. If the sky or cloud

formations are a major element in the scene, the horizon line may be kept low in the picture to let them dominate; if the terrain is of major importance, including more of it forces the horizon higher or even completely out of the frame. An elevated camera position looking downward across the landscape, provides a maplike view that emphasizes the expanse of the scene. A ground location with the camera at average eye level gives the greatest sense of being in the scene and can concentrate attention on closer rather than more distant features. It also permits near-far size and distance comparisons that can be exaggerated by use of a wide-angle lens. Placing the camera at ground level is seldom effective for a horizontal line of view because foreground objects block so much in the middle ground and distance. However, an upward angle of view can dramatize tall features such as trees, cliffs, and waterfalls.

Most landscape photography is done with a normal-focal-length lens because this produces the most natural-looking perspective. A wide-angle lens can provide greater scope without apparent perspective distortion if there are no major foreground objects; otherwise, the foreground is rendered at a greater scale than middle-ground and distant features, an effect that is sometimes quite appropriate. Long-focal-length lenses make it possible to visually leap over the foreground to frame a more distant view. The apparent crowding of perspective these lenses produce can be effective in emphasizing the density of a distant forest or the toothlike progression of jagged peaks.

The most effective landscape photographs generally are those which acknowledge the beauty and grandeur of nature in a straightforward manner and use technique to reveal scale, color, and detail in a way that gives the viewer a sense of actually looking at the scene. Techniques that exaggerate or distort space, color, detail, or other factors tend to produce pictures that say, "Look at what has been done to this landscape," rather than, "Look at what this landscape is." Such pictures are about the nature of the photographer, not about Nature.

See also: DISTORTION; NATURALISTIC PHOTOGRAPHY; PERSPECTIVE; PICTORIAL PHOTOGRAPHY/PICTORIALISM.
Color photographs: pp. C-29, C-30.

Lange, Dorothea

American; 1895–1965
As a member of the Farm Security Administration (FSA) photographic unit

Lange, Dorothea. "Migrant Mother" (Destitute Pea Pickers. Mother of 7. 32 years old—1936). Library of Congress.

Lange began to photograph people in their social contexts on the streets of San Francisco. She was the subject of an Oakland, California, exhibition. In 1934 a critical article about Lange written by Willard Van Dyke appeared in *Camera Craft*.

With Paul Taylor (whom she later married) Lange began work for the California Rural Rehabilitation Administration in 1935. The example set by their efforts was partly responsible for the creation of the photographic unit of the Federal Resettlement Administration later that year. Lange photographed with the RA/FSA from 1935 to 1942. She was awarded a Guggenheim Fellowship in 1941 for "photographic study of the American social scene," a project she was prevented from completing by the United States' entry into World War II. Lange worked for the U.S. War Relocation Agency in San Francisco in 1942, and for the Office of War Information, San Francisco, from 1943 to 1945. Many of her photographs from this time were lost in transit.

Poor health forced Lange to remain inactive for several years until 1950–1951 when she conducted seminars and participated in photographic conferences. In 1954–1955 she was a staff photographer with *Life* magazine. She worked again as a freelance photographer from 1958 to 1965, accompanying her husband on U.S. aid assignments in Asia, South America, and the Middle East. She died of cancer in Marin County, California, in 1965, just before the opening of her major retrospective exhibition at the Museum of Modern Art in New York City.

Lange was placed on the Honor Roll of the American Society of Magazine Photographers in 1963. She was honored with solo exhibitions at the San Francisco Museum of Art (1960), the Museum of Modern Art (1966), the Oakland Art Museum (1960, 1966, 1971, and 1978), and the Victoria and Albert Museum in London (1973). Her work has been included in important group shows, including *6 Women Photographers*, the *Family of Man*, and *The Bitter Years: FSA Photographers 1935–1941* at the Museum of Modern Art; *Photography in the Twentieth Century* at the National Gallery of Canada in Ottawa; and *Women of Photography* at the San Francisco Museum of Art. Her presentation *The American Country Woman* was the most popular exhibit ever distributed by the U.S. Information Agency. Lange's archive was donated to the Oakland Museum.

See also: DOCUMENTARY PHOTOGRAPHY; FARM SECURITY ADMINISTRATION.

under Roy Stryker, Dorothea Lange photographed migrant workers, sharecroppers, tenant farmers, and other victims of the Depression in 22 states, primarily in the South and West, between 1935 and 1942. Her "Migrant Mother" (1936) is one of the classic images of the period.

Lange was born Dorothea Margaretta Nutzhorn in Hoboken, New Jersey, of German descent. As a young girl she was stricken with polio, which left her with a lifelong limp which she believed heightened her sensitivity to the sufferings of others. She attended grade school in New York City's Lower East Side and the Training School for Teachers also in New York.

In 1914 Lange visited the Fifth Avenue portrait studio of Arnold Genthe; he gave her her first camera and encouraged her photographic work during the next year. In 1917–1918 Lange studied at Columbia University with the pictorial photographer Clarence White. Later in 1918 she became employed as a photo-finisher in San Francisco, where she worked as a freelance photographer and operated her own studio from 1919 to 1940, at which time she established a studio in Berkeley, California. In 1932, after a decade as a studio portraitist,

Langenheim, Friedrich
German; 1809–1879
Langenheim, Wilhelm
German; 1807–1874

The Langenheim brothers emigrated separately to the U.S. in the 1830s, but by 1840 were together in Philadelphia where they established a daguerreotype studio. Their success was almost immediate, perhaps aided by the first Voigtlander-Petzval portrait camera in the U.S., a gift from their brother-in-law, who was a son of the founder of the Voigtlander firm. Their skill as portraitists brought them as subjects John Tyler, Henry Clay, Lewis Cass, Andrew Jackson, Martin van Buren, John J. Audubon, and other celebrities. Alert to novelty, technical achievement, and publicity, they achieved all three in a five-plate daguerreotype panorama of Niagara Falls in 1845; copies were presented to President James Polk, Queen Victoria, L. J. M. Daguerre, and various princes of Germany.

An attempt to monopolize paper photography led to near financial disaster. In 1849 the Langenheims contracted for exclusive U.S. rights to Talbot's calotype process, expecting to recover the $6000 fee by selling licenses. They sold none, and although they had paid Talbot two-thirds of the price before failure was obvious, were unable to break the contract. American photographers used the paper negative process without concern for Talbot's patent, and in 1851 turned immediately to the far superior collodion process. The Langenheims survived with their introduction of glass magic lantern slides, patented as Hyalotypes, in 1849, and subsequently with the introduction of stereographs. They became dominant in the production of stereo paper prints mounted on cards and stereo glass slides in the 1850s, and maintained a major position in American photography until their deaths some 20 years later.

Lantern Slide

A lantern slide is a positive transparency made or mounted on glass for projection. The term originated in the 19th c. when projectors were called magic lanterns. There were several slide formats then. Today black-and-white *projection slide plates* are available in 2″ × 2″ (for use in standard 35mm slide projectors), 3¼″ × 4″, and 6.5″ × 9cm (2½″ × 3½″) sizes. A glass slide is thick, heavy, and fragile, but in formats larger than 35mm it is essential to insure the image flatness in the projector that produces overall sharpness on the screen.

Lartigue, Jacques-Henri
French; 1894–

Photographing for his own innocent pleasure the varied day-to-day activities of his family and friends, Jacques-Henri Lartigue, a child prodigy of the camera, captured the excitements and fragile beauties of La Belle Epoque at the beginning of the century with a striking freshness and authenticity. Richard Avedon has called Lartigue "the most deceptively simple and penetrating photographer in the history . . . of that art."

Lartigue was born into an upper-middle-class family in Courbevoie, near Paris. He began to photograph at age seven when he received his first camera, a large 13 × 18cm affair on a wooden tripod, from his father, an amateur photographer himself. As accompaniment to his photographs, Lartigue kept a diary, illustrated with sketches, in which information regarding the photos was recorded. Upon receiving his first camera, he wrote: "Now I will be able to make portraits of everything . . . *everything*. I know very well that many, many things are going to ask me to have their pictures taken, and I will take them all!" But Lartigue took few posed photographs; his concern lay with seizing the moment as it was speeding by. Ladies of fashion in the Bois de Boulogne, bicycle and early auto races, glider planes and kites were all seen with an instinctive spontaneity and exuberance unimaginable in an older, more sophisticated photographer. For Lartigue was influenced by no one and his pictures existed for his private amusement and that of his family. The world he recorded soon vanished with the arrival of World War I. Lartigue was able to document the end of the old world and the beginning of the new.

In addition to his black-and-white stills and muted autochromes, Lartigue made several short films in 1913 and 1914. The following year he attended the Académie Julian where he studied under J.-P. Laurens and made his first oil painting. After armed service during the war, Lartigue lost his youthful passion for photography and devoted himself to painting. It is as a painter that he has made his reputation, though he has continued to photograph sporadically, including a series of images of films-in-progress by directors such as Abel Gance, François Truffaut, and Claude Renoir. While his paintings were on display in galleries in New York and Paris, including a major exhibition at Galérie Charpentier in 1939, Lartigue's photographs were closeted. After the publication of a selection of his photographs in *Life* in 1962, the first public exhibition of these images took place at the Museum of Modern Art in New York in 1963.

Since then a number of books of his photographs have been published and further shows mounted at Photokina, Cologne; the Photographers' Gallery, London; the Neikrug and Witkin galleries, New York; the Museum of Decorative Arts, Paris; and ICP. In 1979 he donated his entire work to the French government.

Photograph: p. 290.

Laser

A laser is a high-efficiency source of light that is monochromatic (single wavelength, or color), coherent (completely in phase), and collimated (having parallel ray paths). Its output is a beam that may be no more than 0.05° (1 milliradian) wide and that can be focused with a depth precision of up to one-quarter of its own wavelength. The light intensity can vary over an extreme range. Very high power lasers are used for precision drilling of diamonds and hardened metals; lesser power beams are used as scalpels in retinal surgery, to remove wavelength-thick samples for spectrography and chromatography, and to cut stacks of cloth several inches thick precisely to pattern in the garment industry. Lasers at non-destructive power levels are used for illumination in holography, schlieren photography, and high-speed photography at pulse rates of a few nanoseconds (billionths of a second) or single exposures of a few picoseconds (trillionths of a second). Laser scanners are used for color analysis of photographic images, and for conversion of images to digital form. Laser interferometers for optical testing and precision alignment can detect variations of a quarter-wavelength; laser flow meters and seismographs can detect movement as slow as 0.01 in. (0.25mm) per second, or position shifts of only 0.000,001 in. (0.000,025mm). In surveying, a laser beam can provide an undeviating line of sight for miles over inaccessible terrain. Using target reflectors, radarlike (pulse-and-return) distance ranging can be accomplished at night or in any weather conditions over vast distances. The distance to the moon has been measured with an accuracy of ±1 ft. (0.3m); satellite-borne lasers have measured earth contours with equal accuracy.

The first practical laser was constructed in 1960. Its name is an acronym for the principle of operation: *light amplification by stimulated emission of radiation*. The laser principle is as follows. Most substances exist at a low level (ground state) of energy within their molecular structures. Certain substances can be raised to a higher (excited) energy level when bombarded or stimulated with energy from an external source. At a certain excitement level, some atoms or molecules give off a photon (quantum) of energy; this occurs at a particular frequency, depending upon the substance and the intensity of the stimulating energy. Released photons may collide with partially excited particles, exciting them to the photon-emission level as well. If the emitted photons are not allowed to escape but are confined within the substance, a stimulus interaction occurs that builds the photon store with ever-increasing intensity. The quantum mechanics of this action produces photons of exactly the same frequency, or wavelength, and vibrating precisely in phase with one another. Thus, the energy is both monochromatic and coherent. In a laser, control mechanisms provide for release of the energy at a selected intensity.

A laser consists of a resonant cavity containing a substance that will lase (emit photons) at a certain frequency or frequencies, and associated stimulus and control components. The lasing frequency corresponds to a visible wavelength in most cases, but some lasers can emit infrared or ultraviolet energy. The lasing substance may be a solid, a mixture of gases (a helium-neon laser is most often used for holography), or a liquid. A typical solid laser consists of a cylindrical rod of material a few inches long; however, there are also solid-state lasers constructed like a transistor, with a layer of lasing material sandwiched between two electroconductive plates. Gas and liquid lasers are sealed glass or quartz tubes of lasing substances. Photon confinement for purposes of amplification is achieved by mirror-coating the ends of a rod or tube, or by placing it between external mirrors, so that light is reflected back and forth along the length of the laser. The mirror at one end is partially transmissive and will allow light above a certain level of intensity to pass. A shutter at one end controls the output. In a low-power laser the shutter is a simple opaque device. With high-power lasers and in high-speed applications, a more sophisticated shutter such as a Kerr cell is used. The stimulus energy may be light, high voltage electricity, or very high frequency electromagnetic energy. In the first laser it was supplied by a stroboscopic gas-discharge (electronic flash) tube coiled around a rod of solid lasing material. Electrical energy may be applied by induction through plates or coils around the laser tube, or by elec-

trodes in contact with the lasing substance. Laser output can be continuous, or pulsed. Pulsing can be controlled by the stimulating energy, by resonance characteristics of the lasing material, or by the shutter; pulse rates of up to several million per second are possible. While high-power lasers are large, expensive devices, low-power lasers about the size of a standard flashlight are available.

Two major developments in laser technology have enormous potential. One is the tunable laser, which can be adjusted to emit light at any of several distinct wavelengths. The other comprises techniques to modulate and otherwise control the light beam with communication signals in essentially the same way that energy at radio and television frequencies is controlled. The characteristics of a laser beam make it virtually impervious to interference (e.g., static, video snow); it can travel great distances without the need for relay stations; and its higher frequency allows thousands of times more information to be transmitted within a much smaller bandwidth in the electromagnetic energy spectrum.
See also: HOLOGRAPHY; LIGHT; VIDEO IMAGING/RECORDING; WAVELENGTH.

Latensification

Latent-image intensification, or *latensification*, is the treating of a film after exposure to increase the effective speed so that greater image density will be produced upon development. The intensification is achieved by many of the same methods used for hypersensitizing an emulsion. The difference is that hypersensitizing, carried out before exposure, creates latent exposure specks that function like the sensitivity specks in the emulsion; thus, there are more locations for exposure to be registered as a latent image. Latensification acts to increase the strength of the latent image wherever it has been registered. Although both treatments could in theory be used to achieve a greater increase in film speed, in practice excessive fog would result because an undue number of unexposed halide cyrstals would be brought to a developable state.

A weak flashing exposure to a white or gray surface after the main exposure produces a basic kind of latensification that is most noticeable in the dark areas of an image. An overall effect is produced by exposing the film to a very weak (7½-watt) dark-green safelight at a distance of at least 6 ft (1.8m) for 5 to 60 seconds; fast emulsions require much less time than slow emulsions. Simple chemical hypersensitization can be achieved by soaking the film for up to

five minutes before development in a solution of 0.5 percent each of sodium bisulfite and sodium sulfite, or a 1.5 percent solution of hydrogen peroxide; the treated emulsion must be washed for about five minutes before being placed in the developer. Any method of latensification must be tested for a given situation because its effect will vary with the speed of the emulsion and the brightness range of the subject. At most, a 3× to 4× increase in speed—equivalent to 1½ to 2 *f*-stops of exposure—can be expected, and the effect may well be less.
See also: FLASHING; HYPERSENSITIZING; LATENT IMAGE.

Latent Image

The invisible record of the effect of exposure in an emulsion is known as a latent image (Latin: *latens* = hidden). When the exposing energy has been focused by a lens, the record is an image that can subsequently be made visible by the chemical process of development; non-image exposure develops to an overall density called fog. According to the generally accepted Gurney-Mott theory, a latent image is produced when atoms of silver form at sensitivity specks on the surface of silver-halide crystals affected by the exposing energy. The exposure effect may also be recorded by silver atoms forming at points of structural imperfection (kink sites) inside the crystals. Under some circumstances this internal latent image can be developed to recover a visible image when the surface-formed image has been destroyed. In certain emulsions (e.g., that used in Kodak Instant Print film) the entire latent image effect is recorded within the crystals rather than on the surface; it is effectively trapped there, and development reduces the unexposed crystals to silver, forming a direct positive image instead of a negative. In conventional emulsions at least four atoms of silver must form for a halide crystal to become developable. This requires the energy from four quanta (photons) of light, but as little as one quantum of higher-wavelength energy such as x-rays. Somewhat more exposure is required to insure that the latent image in a crystal will not dissipate. With normal full-strength exposure, the latent image formed in a black-and-white film will remain developable for several years; any loss will occur in the least-exposed (i.e., shadow) areas. The latent image in a color film is more fugitive. Largely because exposure is divided among three layers of emulsion, the amount of exposure received by any given halide crystal in an image area may be much less than in a single-layer emulsion. For this reason, color materials should be processed as soon as possible after exposure to obtain optimum quality. Above-normal temperatures accelerate latent-image deterioration in all emulsions, as does high humidity. Cold, even freezing, is an excellent preservative of the latent image. Exposed films recovered after half a century in arctic conditions have produced images with little loss of quality when developed.

See also: DEVELOPMENT; FOG/ FOGGING; GURNEY-MOTT THEORY.

Lateral Chromatic Aberration

See: ABERRATIONS OF LENSES.

Latitude

The degree to which exposure of a subject can be varied without exceeding the useful exposure limits of a film is the film's latitude. The term is often used to mean the *exposure range* of a film: the difference in *f*-stops between an exposure that produces the minimum printable density and one that produces the maximum printable density. Most black-and-white films have an exposure range of 10 or more *f*-stops, color negative films about 8 stops, and transparency films about 5 stops. A more meaningful use of the term latitude relates the film exposure range to the subject brightness range. If both are 10 stops, for example, there is no latitude (i.e., leeway, or margin of error) for exposure variation. If less than proper exposure is given, the darkest areas will not be recorded; if more exposure is given, the brightest areas will be too dense to be anything other than featureless white in the final image. When the subject brightness range is less—say 7 stops with a 10 stop film—there is a latitude of 3 stops. That is, in addition to the minimum adequate exposure, it is possible to give up to 3 *f*-stops more exposure without exceeding the highlight exposure limit of the film. Film speeds are set so that a meter reading will indicate near-minimum exposure of a subject, because excess exposure produces excess density—visible as graininess—upon development. In practical terms this means that any latitude in a given situation will be on the side of increased rather than reduced exposure. The exposure range of a film, and thus the potential latitude, can be increased by hypersensitizing the emulsion, or by reducing development of a black-and-white negative film. The second procedure will reduce contrast in the image.

See also: BRIGHTNESS RANGE; GRAIN/ GRAININESS/GRANULARITY; HYPERSENSITIZING.

Laughlin, Clarence John

American; 1905–

Clarence John Laughlin is an extraordinarily prolific American surrealist photographer who has consistently produced disturbing and hauntingly beautiful images since the late 1930s. He has combined still-lifes, abstractions, architectural photos, and multiple exposures in an entirely original, romantic-mystical synthesis which has influenced the last few generations of photographers and Jerry Uelsmann in particular.

Laughlin writes, "I did not start out as a photographer but, instead, as a writer. Whether for good or ill, this fact has inspired and colored many of my concepts . . . . Through photography I have also tried to tie together and further my active interests in painting, in poetry, in psychology, and in architecture. Whatever value my photography has, it is *only* because of these other interests."

Laughlin was born in Lake Charles, Louisiana. He lived on a plantation near New Iberia, and has spent most of his life since 1910 in New Orleans. He attended high school for one year in 1918. Obliged to support his family upon the death of his father, he worked at a variety of jobs between 1924 and 1935.

Laughlin's early interests were with the writings of Baudelaire, Rimbaud, and the French Symbolists, who inspired him to write prose poems and stories. He began to photograph in 1934, influenced by the work of Alfred Stieglitz, Paul Strand, Edward Weston, Man Ray, and Eugène Atget. His first major project was the documentation of New Orleans architecture, privately and as a Civil Service photographer for the United States Engineer Corps in New Orleans from 1936 to 1941.

Laughlin's first one-man show was held at the Isaac Delgado Museum, New Orleans, in 1936. His New Orleans architectural work was exhibited in 1940 at the Julien Levy Gallery, New York, along with photographs by Atget of Paris.

In 1940–1941 Laughlin did fashion photography for *Vogue* in New York. During World War II, he first worked for the Photography Department of the National Archives, then served in the United States Army Signal Corps Photographic Unit in Long Island City, New York, and with the U.S. Office of Strategic Services, where he specialized in color photography.

Laughlin has earned his living since 1946 as a freelance photographer of contemporary architecture. His book of photographs of Southern plantation mansions, *Ghosts Along the Mississippi*, was published in 1948. It has since been reprinted 20 times.

Since 1948 Laughlin has lectured throughout the country on photographic aesthetics and American Victorian architecture, which he has documented extensively in Chicago, Milwaukee, St. Louis, San Francisco, and elsewhere. His photographs have appeared in *Harper's Bazaar, American Heritage, Architectural Review, Life, Du, Aperture, Look,* and *Art News* among other publications.

Since 1936 Laughlin has been the subject of over 200 one-man shows, including exhibitions at the Museum of Contemporary Art, Chicago; the Smithsonian Institution, Washington, D.C.; the Los Angeles County Museum; and George Eastman House, Rochester, N.Y. A major retrospective of 229 photographs was held at the Philadelphia Museum of Art in 1973.

Laughlin was named an Associate of Research at the University of Louisville in 1968, and has been the subject of an Aperture monograph. Since 1974 he has concentrated on prose writing and the care of his enormous library of fantasy literature. A large portion of his body of over 17,000 sheet-film negatives was donated to the University of Louisville Archives in 1970.

Leader

An extra length of motion-picture film or video tape known as a leader is attached to the beginning (head) and end (tail) of a reel to permit threading and alignment in projectors and other equipment. The head leader is usually marked with a series of descending numbers or other symbols to indicate the number of seconds remaining before the first frame of picture arrives in the projector gate. The last few seconds of a motion-picture head leader are usually opaque black so that the lens path to the screen can be unblocked at the last moment without a bright glare or visually distracting material being visible before the picture appears. Leaders also serve as a wrapping to protect the outer layers of the picture section of film and tape wound on reels.

Le Gray, Gustave

French; 1820–1882

Gustave Le Gray is famous for his pastoral landscapes, seascapes, and architectural views, and as an early experimenter with combination printing. Among his most significant works were seascapes made from two negatives—one of the body of water, the second of clouds—because materials of the time could not record both with the same exposure.

Le Gray was born in Villiers-le-Bel, France. He was a student of the painters Picot and Delaroche in the 1840s. His fellow-pupils in the Delaroche studio included Charles Nègre, Henri Le Secq, and Roger Fenton. Unable to support his family as a painter, Le Gray turned to photography. He opened a portrait studio in the Madeleine district of Paris in 1848, in the same building as the Bisson brothers. He met with little success as a

Laughlin, Clarence. "A Haunting Gaze. A strange remoteness, dream-like impassivity. This face looks into an unseen region, a lovely eye staring out of some timeless world, although surrounded by the imprints of time, in the dress and on the wall. One side of her face is covered by an exquisitely beautiful shadowmask; on the other, her eye pierces the dark web of the veil. And the mystery of her gaze lingers on, to haunt us forever." (1941). Permanent collection, ICP, New York.

portraitist and soon turned to architectural views and landscapes.

Le Gray was an influential teacher of photography whose students included Nègre, Maxime Du Camp, and Le Secq. He was the author of *A Practical Treatise on Photography* (1850) and many other pamphlets on photographic techniques. Le Gray invented the dry waxed-paper negative process, and was an early experimenter with collodion techniques.

Le Gray photographed significant national sites and monuments for the French Committee of Historical Monuments, working with Le Secq, Hippolyte Bayard, and Edouard Baldus, among others. He documented military life at the Châlons camp, including the visit of Napoleon III in 1858, and the Palermo barricades.

In 1850 Le Gray was the first photographer included in the graphic arts section of the Salon des Beaux-Arts. He was awarded a first-place medal at the Exposition Universelle of 1855, "bearing witness to his success in all branches of photography." He exhibited throughout Europe: in Paris (1855, 1857, 1859, 1867), Amsterdam (1862), Brussels (1856), Edinburgh (1857), London (1856, 1857, 1858, 1861), and Marseilles (1861).

Of his own work Le Gray wrote, "The future of photography does not lie in the cheapness but in the quality of a picture . . . .For my part, it is my wish that photography, rather than falling into the domain of an industry or of commerce, might remain in that of art."

Le Gray was forced by financial difficulties to close his studio in 1859. He traveled to Palermo and other cities where he photographed occasionally. He was reported to have worked as a professor of drawing and painting in Cairo in 1865. He died in Cairo about 1882 after a fall from a horse.

See also: WAXED PAPER PROCESS.

Leica

The Leica camera, invented by Oscar Barnack and marketed from 1924 to the present by the German optical firm of Ernst Leitz, was the major factor in the popularization and growth of 35mm

The Leica (*Leitz camera*) came about as a result of Barnack's need for a compact, portable camera to be used for test exposures in cinematography. Barnack built a small cine camera, the design of which led to an even smaller model for still photography, using a 24 × 36mm frame, double the size of the standard cine format. The 1913 Leica prototype, or Ur-Leica, had no viewfinder; a fixed, 50mm *f*/3.5 anastigmat lens; and a non-self-capping shutter, which required that the front element of the lens be covered during film advance so as not to fog the emulsion. In spite of these limitations, Barnack's employer recognized the potential of the camera and decided to market an improved version. Production began in 1924 with a model having a self-capping shutter, coupled film advance and shutter cocking mechanisms, and various internal improvements. The camera was an almost instant success, and gained international acclaim very quickly.

Subsequent Leicas were equipped with a lens-coupled rangefinder for focusing, and the capability of interchanging lenses. Various special-purpose models also were constructed. By the advent of World War II, the camera had become the working tool of many photographers, including André Kertész, and Henri Cartier-Bresson, both of whom claimed that the Leica afforded a new mode of photographic seeing. This sentiment was echoed by numerous other photographers. The Leica became one of the tools used to record the war from both sides of the conflict, and in the post-war years established itself as the camera of choice for journalists and photographic artists alike.

The extremely quiet shutter, inconspicuous size, and excellent optical quality of its lenses made the Leica capable of recording scenes unobserved. Its precision and wide range of matched accessories made it a camera of unequalled versatility until the rise of the 35mm single-lens reflex camera in the 1960s.

The Leica has gone through many incarnations since its inception. Recent models have included through-the-lens exposure metering and other convenience features, but the basic concept of making an extremely compact, highly precise rangefinder camera remains the same. Since 1976, Leitz has also produced a series of single-lens reflex cameras.

The Leica reputation is so high that a mystique has developed around the name; collectors pay premium prices for old models and even for such things as out-of-print Leica literature. Even less-than-rare Leicas command high prices in used-camera stores because of their remarkable solidity and overall quality.

See also: BARNACK, OSCAR; CAMERA; LEITZ, ERNST.

Leitz, Ernst (I)
German; 1843–1920
Leitz, Ernst (II)
German; 1871–1956

In the decade from 1870 to 1880, Ernst Leitz (I) transformed a small optical shop in Wetzlar, Germany, into one of the world's most important manufacturers of microscopes and scientific optical instruments, surpassed only by the Carl Zeiss Optical Works in Jena. Leitz's company has maintained a major position in the manufacture of scientific instruments since that time, and in the 20th c. also originated modern 35mm photography with the introduction of the Leica camera and associated equipment.

After his schooling, Ernst Leitz was first apprenticed to a German manufacturer of laboratory apparatus and industrial machinery, then worked in Switzerland, learning precision production methods in the manufacture of electric clocks and telegraph instruments. In 1865 Leitz moved to Wetzlar to work for Friedrich Belthle in manufacturing microscopes, binoculars, and telescope eyepieces. Ten years earlier, Belthle had

Le Gray, Gustave. "Napoleon III with his officers" (1857). Smithsonian Institution.

become owner of an optical instrument shop established in 1849 by Carl Kellner (1826–1855), who at the age of 21 had invented an optically corrected ("orthoscopic") eyepiece that greatly improved the quality of the image in field glasses and telescopes. Within a year of going to Wetzlar, Leitz became a full partner in the business. He became sole owner on Belthle's death in 1869, and issued the first list of precision optical instruments produced under the Leitz name in 1870.

By the end of the century the Leitz company had grown from one room to several small buildings, with more than 250 employees and a cumulative production record of 50,000 microscopes and a similar number of binoculars and scientific instruments. The first Leitz photographic instruments were introduced in 1882—accessories for photomicrography, produced by Leitz's eldest son, Ludwig, who supervised several aspects of the company's operations.

Ernst Leitz (II) rose to a major role in the company soon after the accidental death of Ludwig in 1898. He coordinated expansion of the business and the manufacturing facilities, becoming a partner with his father in 1906 and head of the business on his father's death in 1920. Ernst (II) placed great emphasis on practical research and development as precursors to introducing new products. He added industrial optical measuring instruments to the Leitz line early in this century. It was he who brought Oskar Barnack to the company, encouraged Barnack's experimentation from 1913 onward with a small-format still camera, and who decided in 1924 to begin commercial production of Barnack's inven-

tion, the Leica camera. In 1926 the Leitz company produced the first 35mm projector, which accepted both slides and film strips, and in 1933 the first autofocus enlarger. Leica cameras, lenses, and accessories established standards of small-format precision manufacture and performance that were unequaled in photography until well after World War II.

A sales office that eventually became E. Leitz, U.S.A. was established in New York City in 1892. The family-owned company became a public limited corporation in 1920. The sons of Ernst (II)—Ernst III, Ludwig, and Gunther—became directors of various parts of the company from 1930 onward. After World War II, the Leitz glass research laboratory was established in Germany (1949), and an assembly and optical production plant was established at Midland, Ontario, Canada (1952). The latter facility became a major producer of lenses and in 1961 developed the first lens designed solely for underwater photography. A separate line of *Elcan* (for E. Leitz, Canada) photographic equipment was also produced there. In subsequent decades Leitz established a camera production facility in Portugal, entered into co-production with Minolta Camera Corp. of Japan, and became associated with the Wild Corporation, a Swiss manufacturer of scientific equipment.

See also: BARNACK, OSKAR; LEICA; ZEISS.

Lenses

A lens is composed of optical-quality glass or plastic shaped so as to bend light rays to form an image. Light rays refract, or bend, when they pass from one transparent medium to another. The shape, thickness, and density of the lens material determine how light passing through is bent. A simple convex lens was first used in the sixteenth century camera obscura to form a relatively sharp image. A convex lens is curved on one or both sides so that it is thickest in the middle. This shape allows the lens to gather light rays originating at a point on one side of the lens and bend them toward each other on the other side. When the light rays originate from a point at infinity, they converge, or focus at a distance equal to the *focal length* of the lens. A lens that converges light rays to form a *real image*—one that is visible on a flat surface such as film—is called a positive lens. A negative lens—one with a concave center shape—diverges or spreads light rays so they cannot be projected onto a flat surface. It forms a *virtual image*, which becomes visible only when viewed with a positive lens. A *simple lens*, comprised of only one shaped element, is found only in inexpensive snapshot cameras. Most camera lenses today are *compound*, or made of several elements that work together to form an image. A compound lens uses elements of different shape, thickness, and density to minimize aberrations. Aberrations are optical imperfections that cause the lens to form a less-than-perfect image.

One of the earliest single-element lenses was the Wollaston meniscus of 1812. It was superseded by the two-element design of Chevalier in 1829. Chevalier combined a positive crown glass with a weaker negative flint glass to improve image quality by a slight color correction. In 1840, Petzval developed a completely different design with a fast $f/3.6$ aperture. The next step in lens evolution came with the symmetrical design. Two elements or groups of equal power but opposite sign (positive, negative) are symmetrically placed on opposite sides of a stop, or diaphragm. Different lens designs continued to evolve because of specific photographic needs. Most modern lenses are of the anastigmat form. This is an arrangement of positive and negative elements that is well corrected for chromatic and spherical aberration, coma, astigmatism, field curvature, and distortion. The anastigmat design is derived from the early symmetrical and Cooke Triplet designs.

Normal Lenses. Basic categories of lens types are: normal, wide-angle, telephoto, and long focus. A normal lens has a focal length that is approximately equal to the diagonal measurement of the film area it covers. This generally corresponds to the normal field of view of the human eye, about 50 degrees. The relative size and shape of objects photographed with a normal lens therefore appear normal to the eye. For the 35mm format camera, a normal lens ranges in focal length from 40mm to 55mm. Correspondingly, a normal focal length for the larger 2¼" format would be approximately 80mm. A large-format 4" × 5" camera would require at least a 135mm lens. A large-format camera has perspective controls that move the lens off the central axis of the film. A normal lens for large format may be required to form a circular image greater than the actual film size. A longer-than-normal focal length of 210mm would cover the 4" × 5" format and allow for vertical and horizontal displacement off the central axis.

Wide-Angle Lenses. A wide-angle lens covers a field of view of approximately 90 degrees. Corresponding focal length for the 35mm format is 20mm. Wide-angle lenses may be of either symmetrical or retrofocus design. The retrofocus, or inverted telephoto design has greater distance between the rear of the lens and the film plane than its actual focal length. This allows space for camera viewing devices such as a reflex mirror in the SLR. Semi-wide-angle lenses of 65 to 75 degrees also are commonly referred to as wide-angle lenses. Despite their narrower field of view, they provide similar advantages in use as wide-angle lenses of 90 degrees. Wide-angle lenses are particularly useful for interior photography. The photographer may use a wide-angle lens to view a large part of the room from a close distance. A normal lens would require a greater camera-to-subject distance to produce the same size image. The wide-angle lens is also useful in photographing large subjects such as buildings and landscapes from a close distance.

Long-focus and telephoto lenses. Telephoto and long-focus lenses produce a magnified image size in comparison to a normal lens used at the same camera position. Their field of view is correspondingly narrower than the standard 50 degrees. Long-focus lenses are of normal optical design and thus have a physical length proportional to their focal length. Telephoto lens design achieves long focal length with much shorter physical length and a shorter lens-to-film distance than a normal design of the same focal length. When extra extension is required, as in close-up photography, a telephoto lens will require less extension than a normal-design lens of the same focal length. To achieve compactness and light weight, long lenses for the 35mm format are telephoto designs ranging from 75mm to 350mm. Extremely long lenses extend the range to 2000mm. Telescopes with even greater magnification may be attached to some 35mm cameras for surveillance or astrophotography. Long-focal-length lenses are commonly used for portraiture, and for such subjects or wildlife and distant scenery. In some situations, physical obstacles may also prevent a close camera-to-subject distance. Long lenses visually span the distance to bring the subject close or allow catching a candid moment without disturbing the subject.

Special-purpose lenses. Soft-focus, macro, supplementary, process, enlarging, mirror, and zoom lenses are just a few of many special-purpose lenses. These lenses cover a wide range of focal lengths and may utilize a basic, modified, or unusual optical design.

A soft-focus lens is used mainly in portraiture and romanticized illustration. A macro lens yields a high-quality image at life-size magnifications and larger. A supplementary close-up lens is fitted in front of a standard lens to provide limited close focusing. Process and enlarging lenses are highly corrected for all aberrations and used for reproduction. Both exhibit exceptionally high color correction. A mirror lens, typically used with a 35mm or medium-format camera, utilizes refracting glass lenses and reflecting mirror surfaces to produce an image. Focal lengths range from 250mm to 2000mm. An all-glass lens of comparable focal length would be physically much longer, heavier, and generally have a smaller maximum aperture. A zoom lens varies focal length—and thus angle of view and image magnification—by changing the relative position of its lens elements.

Computers play a significant role in creating modern optical designs. They speed complex calculations and handle the great number of variables more efficiently than the human mathematician. Recent improvements in lens coating and application of new types of optical glass also contribute to the improved quality and wide variety of modern lenses. Lens like devices are also constructed of fiber optic material. Electromagnetic lenses are used to focus electron beams in television equipment, electron microscopes, and similar devices.

See also: ABERRATIONS OF LENSES; ANASTIGMAT; ANGLE OF VIEW; APLANAT; APOCHROMAT; ASPHERIC LENS; BACK FOCUS; CONDENSER; COVERING POWER; DAGOR LENS; DEPTH OF FIELD; DEPTH OF FOCUS; DIOPTER; FIBER OPTICS; FIELD LENS; FOCUSING; FRESNEL

LENS; JENA GLASS; MENISCUS; MIRROR LENS; OPTICS; PETZVAL, JOSEPH; PORTRAIT LENS; PROCESS CAMERA/LENS; SUPPLEMENTARY LENS; TESSAR LENS; ZOOM LENS.

Lenticular Systems

The image from a camera lens can be re-imaged onto an emulsion as a series of minute points or lines by a lenticular screen; this procedure has been the basis of both color and stereoscopic processes in photography. A lenticular screen consists of a transparent material, usually plastic, embossed with a pattern of tiny lens segments—lenticules. The pattern may consist of cylindrical lens sections, forming a series of parallel ridges, 1600 or more to the inch. Or it may consist of a grid of spherical lenticules—lens dots, in effect—as closely spaced. The idea of preparing a film with an integral lenticular screen was first proposed by Gabriel Lippmann in 1908. Some films have the optical pattern embossed on the base, other in a plastic layer applied on top of the emulsion. When the film is in the camera with the lenticular surface facing the lens, each lenticule sees a different point or strip of the image from a unique angle and re-images it as a distinct element on the emulsion. Thus, each image element represents a single element of the subject.

The method of using a lenticular black-and-white film for additive-color photography was described by Rodolphe Berthon in 1909. A filter divided into three primary-color (red, green, and blue) bands is used at the camera lens. Light from each subject point strikes the entire surface of the lens and so strikes the entire surface of the filter. In each band, only the wavelengths corresponding to that filter color are transmitted, which performs the three-color analysis necessary for color reproduction. The lenticule corresponding to that subject point forms distinct records on the emulsion of the amount of light from each filter band. The emulsion is reversal processed to form a black-and-white transparency with densities corresponding to the variations in the exposing light. When projected back through a matching lens-and-filter arrangement, the light from all the lenticules is colored and focused into a full-color image. This procedure is simpler than processes that use a color screen of minute filter elements at the film plane because the banded filter is easier and cheaper to manufacture, and because there is no need to register a screen with the processed image. Lenticular color systems attracted great interest early in the 20th

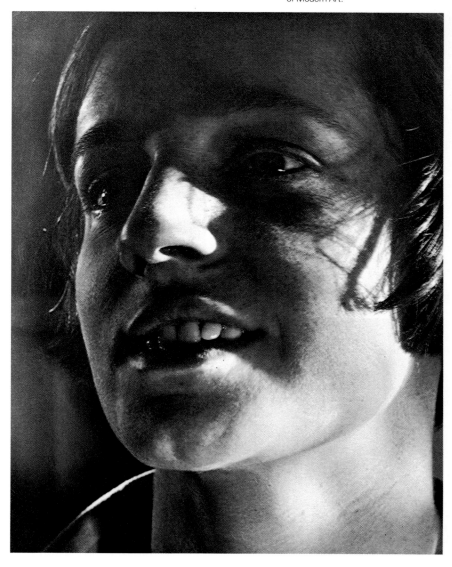

c., and during the 1920s fully one-third of all patents in color photography were for lenticular devices or processes. One of the most successful was the Keller-Dorian process, which formed the basis of an amateur color motion-picture process called Kodacolor (unrelated to the present-day negative color film).

Lenticular stereoscopic systems rely on the fact that each lenticule sees the images from the two—or, in the newest version, four—camera lenses at distinct angles and forms distinct images of them on the emulsion. Thus the processed image is composed of alternating or interlaced right and left image elements. In viewing, the optical characteristics of the lenticules let the left eye see only left-lens image elements and the right eye see only right-lens image elements. The lenticules are sufficiently fine and spaced closely enough so that the eyes blend the images into a three-dimensional impression in which the screen pattern is essentially invisible. This basic system has been adopted for interlaced images printed by halftone reproduction. An embossed plastic coating is applied after printing; if it is slightly out of register, a correspondingly slight change in the viewing angle—made automatically by the person holding the image—corrects the situation. Postcards, display posters, and even magazine illustrations have been produced in this way.

See also: ADDITIVE COLOR SYNTHESIS; IMAGE DISSECTION; KELLER-DORIAN PROCESS; STEREOSCOPIC PHOTOGRAPHY.

Lerski, Helmar
Swiss; 1871–1956

Helmar Lerski became known in the 1930s for his full-frame close-up portraiture in a highly personal style. Often photographing in daylight, with the sun

Le Secq, Henri. "Hotel de Ville de Molcheim" (1851); salt print from calotype negative. Smithsonian Institution.

behind the sitter's head, he employed unorthodox lighting techniques, including numerous mirrors, to achieve dramatic highlights and shadows.

Curt Glaser wrote in 1931: "Helmar Lerski believes that the photographer's medium cannot by its nature be anything but light. He uses light to model the features of a human face, to make it speak in a particular way. . . . He allows light to play upon salient forms so that the whole surface becomes lively and the expressive, plastic image of a human countenance comes into view."

Lerski was born in Strasbourg, France, but was raised in Zurich, Switzerland. In 1893 he came to the United States where he worked as an actor in German theaters throughout the country. His career in photography began in 1911, when he was 40 years old, after his wife, a professional photographer, taught him basic photographic techniques. At the convention of the Photographers' Association of America in St. Louis two years later, Lerski received encouragement from the noted Hamburg portraitist Rudolph Duhrkoop.

In 1914 Lerski taught photography at the University of Texas, Austin. He worked as a cameraman on major films at the UFA film studios in Berlin from 1915 to 1929, then turned again to portrait photography. Lerski's work was included in the *Film und Foto* exhibition in Stuttgart in 1929. A selection of his portraits, *Kopfe des Alltags* (*Everyday Heads*) was published in 1931.

From 1931 to 1948 Lerski made documentary films and photographed in Palestine; his work in this period included a major series of 175 portraits of

one man, *Transformation Through Light*. Lerski returned to Zurich in 1948 and died there eight years later. A collection of his photographs was acquired in 1960 by George Eastman House, Rochester, N.Y.

Le Secq, Henri
French; 1818–1882
Henri Le Secq, known for his documentation of cathedrals, was one of a small group of fine architectural photographers in France in the 1850s. During his brief career as a photographer, Le Secq preserved on wax-paper negatives the medieval and ancient monuments and other treasures threatened by modernization. His images are memorable for their dramatic use of shadow. He was responsible for one of the first books of photographic illustrations published in France, *Amiens: A Collection of Photographs*.

Le Secq was born Jean-Louis-Henri Le Secq Destournelles in Paris. He studied painting in the studios of the sculptor Pradier, Granger, and Paul Delaroche, and became a minor painter of genre scenes, exhibiting regularly in the Paris Salon until his death.

Le Secq received instruction in photography from Gustave Le Gray and Charles Nègre in 1848–1849. He made views of the cathedral of Amiens in 1850, and the following year he began to make views of sites and monuments of Champagne, Alsace-Lorraine, and other regions as one of the five photographers (Bayard, Le Gray, Mestral, Baldus, and Le Secq) in the Mission Héliographiques of the Comité des Monuments Historiques. In 1852 Le Secq documented the

cathedrals of Chartres, Strasbourg, and Riems. He returned to many of the sites to photograph sculptural details and architectural ornaments.

Le Secq's views of Paris were included in the albums of Blanquart-Evrard from 1849 to 1853. He was concerned with documenting the city's obscure and forgotten structures as well as the major monuments, and he photographed many demolitions-in-progress. Le Secq is also credited with a series of poetic still-lifes, landscapes, and photographs of works of art. He was the subject of a striking portrait (in which he is surrounded by the gargoyles atop Notre Dame Cathedral) taken by his friend Nègre in 1853.

Le Secq's work was exhibited in London in 1851 and in Paris and Amsterdam in 1855. In 1851 he was a founding member of the Societé Héliographique, the world's first association of photographers. His photographs are in the collections of the Biblioteque Nationale and the Musee des Arts Decoratifs in Paris and the George Eastman House in Rochester, New York.

Le Secq abandoned photography in about 1856 to pursue his career as a painter and other interests, including an enormous collection of antiquarian forged ironwork. He died in his native Paris in 1882.
See also: WAXED-PAPER PROCESS.

Lester, Henry M.
American; 1899–1974
A prolific technical innovator, Henry Lester is known equally for his pioneering work as a scientific and industrial photographer and as a leading American photographic publisher, author, and editor.

A Polish-born immigrant, Lester was one of America's earliest professional 35mm photographers, using Leica cameras, starting in 1930, to solve the specialized needs of medical, scientific, and technical researchers in both private and governmental fields. From his base in New York he worked all over the U.S.

Ultimately Lester's work grew to include photomicrography, motion pictures of all types, and high-speed photographic motion picture research. He continually broke new ground and helped pave the way for a great number of today's technical photographers.

In 1935 Lester formed the photographic publishing firm of Morgan & Lester with Willard D. Morgan, issuing the first edition of the *Leica Manual*, a leading guide for 35mm photographers all over the world in a sequence of 15 editions that still continues. At Morgan & Lester he went on to publish many of the world's leading informational books on photography for the next few decades.

In 1939 the firm started publishing Henry Lester's *Photo-Lab Index*, which quickly came to be known as "the photographer's bible." A vast compilation of photographic facts and data, the Index was issued annually and brought up to date quarterly. It provided photographers, darkroom workers, and researchers with unified information on all the latest changes in films, developers, lighting, filters, and the thousands of other facts needed in a constantly expanding photo era. Other landmark books published under Henry Lester's editorial stewardship included the *Leica Annual, Miniature Camera Work, Graphic Graflex Photography*, the *Stereo Realist Manual*, and the original *Ansel Adams Basic Photo Series*, commencing in 1948.

In his photographic work, Lester covered so wide a range of subjects that many people were not aware of his extraordinary reach. *Life* magazine, in its first month of existence in 1936, commissioned him to photograph a flea circus, for which he built his own close-up equipment, there being none available at the time. Also in the early 1930s he did available-light theatrical photography for *Stage* magazine, producing remarkable images in the era before fast films and push-processing. Very quickly he became known as a photographer who could "solve anything."

From the 1930s on he did groundbreaking medical and surgical photography, in both still and motion pictures. Many of the operating-room techniques he originated were used extensively by still photographers and motion-picture and TV cameramen. Well known in New York at Columbia Medical Center, Mt. Sinai Hospital, Sloan-Kettering Memorial Cancer Hospital, and other health institutions, Lester made research films that were prizewinners. As early as 1934, *Movie Makers* magazine selected his film *Thyroidectomy* as one of the ten best films of the year. One of Lester's most notable medical-film achievements was the recording of eye surgery in collaboration with the noted Spanish surgeon Dr. Ramon Castroviejo, the originator of corneal transplant surgery. Lester's films of transplant techniques instructed surgeons all over the world.

In the latter part of his career Henry Lester was especially noted for his work in high-speed motion-picture photography. Much of this material was made for private and industrial clients and is not available to the public. Of his public high-speed movies, some of the most

Levitt, Helen. Untitled, New York (ca. 1954). Courtesy Helen Levitt.

spectacular are films of hummingbirds in flight, the drone fly in flight, and the strike of a rattlesnake, made in collaboration with the Bronx Zoo in New York. Taken at speeds up to 3,000 frames per second, these movies slow down the action to "super slow motion" when viewed on the screen.

Always active in the photographic community, Henry Lester was a founder of the Miniature Camera Club of New York, the Society of Photographic Engineers, and the Circle of Confusion, as well as a member of the Society of Motion Picture and Television Engineers. He was a Fellow of the Photographic

Society of America, the Royal Photographic Society of Great Britain, the Biological Photographic Association, and others.

Levitt, Helen

American; 1918–

Helen Levitt's work consists primarily of dynamic and lyrical photographs of the spontaneous social life of New York City streets. Since the late 1930s she has photographed in a straightforward style, in black-and-white and in color, often returning to the same neighborhoods. Her concerns are with the unforeseen, fleeting gestures that occur when the brief and graceful coming-together of people constitutes an event. A large proportion of her preserved moments of evanescent configurations has focused on the lives of children, their fantasies and games. Her films made in collaboration with the writer James Agee have won world acclaim.

Levitt was born in New York City. She was inspired by the work of Henri Cartier-Bresson to begin photographing with a 35mm camera. Her first images were of children in the streets of Harlem in 1936. In 1938–1939 she studied with Walker Evans, who became her friend and mentor, and at whose studio she met Agee. Evans later wrote: "Levitt's work was one of Agee's great loves; and in turn, Agee's own magnificent eye was part of her early training." Evans, Agee, and Levitt shared a deep desire for the most direct artistic expressions of feeling.

In 1941 Levitt traveled to Mexico where she again photographed children at play. She was given a solo exhibition, *Children: Photographs of Helen Levitt*, at the Museum of Modern Art, New York, in 1943. She began to publish regularly in such periodicals as *Fortune*, *Harper's Bazaar*, *Cue*, and *Time*.

Levitt was a Museum of Modern Art Photography Fellow in 1946. Her collaborations with Agee produced a book, *A Way of Seeing* (written in 1946 but unpublished until 1965), and two films, *The Quiet One* (1949) and *In the Street* (1952), which won awards at the Venice and Edinburgh Film Festivals. She exhibited at the New York Camera Club in 1948.

Levitt photographed very little during the 1950s because of ill-health and her career as a film director and editor. She had a joint show with Frederick Sommer at the Chicago Institute of Design in 1952. In 1956–1957 she studied art at the Art Students League, New York.

She was awarded a Guggenheim Fellowship in 1959 for a study of the techniques of color photography; the grant was renewed in 1960. Shortly after her poetic street-documentary color slides from this period were shown at the Museum of Modern Art in 1963, they were stolen and never recovered. For the next several years, Levitt again did little photographic work.

She returned to street photography in 1971. A continuous color slide projection of this new work was exhibited at the Museum of Modern Art in 1974. Levitt was a National Endowment for the Arts Photography Fellow in 1976. She continues to live and work in New York.

Liberman, Alexander

American; 1912–

Alexander Liberman has been acclaimed for his work during the last 40 years as art director of *Vogue* magazine and editorial director of Condé Nast Publications, and as a photographer of distinction in his own right. As an editor working with the world's top fashion and commercial photographers, he has shaped the practice of photography around the world. His own work includes a major body of portraits of artists—including Picasso, Matisse, Ernst, Dali, and Giacometti—photographed in their studios.

Liberman was born in Kiev, Russia. He was educated in England and Paris and attended the Sorbonne, where he studied philosophy and mathematics from 1927 to 1930. In 1931 Liberman studied painting with the Cubist André Lhote, and in 1931–1932 he studied architecture with Auguste Perret at the Ecole Speciale d'Archi. He attended the Ecole des Beaux-Arts in 1932–1933.

Liberman's career began as a design assistant to A.M. Cassandre in Paris in 1931–1932. From 1933 to 1936 he was art director and managing editor of *Vu* magazine. He was the recipient of a Gold Medal for Design at the Paris Exposition Internationale in 1937. In 1941, after service in the French Army, Liberman began work for *Vogue* in New York City, and he acted as a layout artist and art director until 1944. From 1944 to 1961 he was art director of Condé Nast Publications, and since 1962 he has been their editorial director. In recent years Liberman has given his energies to painting and large-scale sculpture.

In 1980 Liberman received a Doctor of Fine Arts degree from the Rhode Island Institute of Design. His photographs, paintings, and sculpture have been included in group shows around the world. Solo exhibitions of his work have been held at the Museum of Modern Art in New York City (1959), the Musée des Arts Décoratifs in Paris (1961), the Corcoran Gallery in Washington, D.C. (1970), and the Storm King Art Center in Mountainville, New York (1978).

Light

Light is radiant energy with wavelengths from about 400 to 700 nanometers (nm) in the electromagnetic spectrum. It is unique in being detectable by the eye, and it is the mediating agency by which an object is seen. Light is produced by the movement of electrons and ions in nuclear reaction (e.g., sunlight), combustion (flames), electrical flow through a filament (tungsten lamp), electrical discharge through a gas (flash tube, lightning), excitation (fluorescence), and chemical reaction (phosphorescence).

Light from natural sources and almost all artificial sources is *incoherent*: it is composed of a mixture of wavelengths with random phase relationships, and radiates in all directions from the source unless its path is shaped by reflectors or lenses. *Coherent* light is composed of matching wavelengths that are precisely in phase; i.e., that vibrate in unison so that the energy level of each wave is exactly the same as all others at every instant. Such light is highly directional. A laser produces collimated coherent light. *Collimated* light consists of wavelengths all travelling parallel paths, such as sunlight or light from a source effectively at infinity. Both coherent and incoherent light can be collimated. Like all electromagnetic energy, light travels at about 186,000 miles (300,000km) per second in space. It travels in straight lines through a given medium, but over vast distances its path is affected by gravitational pull. When it encounters a different medium, the path of light may be refracted (bent), reflected (bounced), diffused (scattered), or blocked by absorption. A beam of light can be dispersed or diffracted—spread—to reveal its constituent wavelengths. The different effects of various wavelengths on the eye—or the different responses of the eye to various wavelengths—are identified as colors. The optical behavior of light, as above, indicates that it has a wave nature. Its interaction with substances, causing photochemical reactions, indicates that it has a particle, or quantum, nature. A photon contains one quantum of energy; although energy increases as wavelength grows shorter, the range of light wavelengths is sufficiently narrow that all photons of light have essentially the same amount of energy. Whenever light encounters a substance that is not completely transparent and colorless, some photons give up their energy; this may be evidenced by the production of heat or by a chemical reaction, and usually by both. In the reaction called photographic exposure at least four photons of light are required to create the change in a silver-halide crystal that forms a stable latent image.

When considered as illumination, light is measured in terms of the intensity of the source, the amount of light falling onto a surface (illuminance), and the amount of light reflected or emitted by a surface (luminance). The wavelength composition of light from a continuous-spectrum source is expressed as color temperature. Exposure calculations and the selection of emulsions and filters are based on these factors. The expressive character of light is generally described by two sets of adjectives: direct, specific, hard; and indirect, general, diffuse, soft. The terms *cold* and *warm* refer to subjective qualities commonly associated with discernible bluishness or reddishness, respectively, of the light. The role of light from various sources in a photographic situation is described by such functional terms as frontlight; backlight; rim or edge light; eye, hair, or clothes light; and the like.

See also: COLOR; COLOR TEMPERATURE; DIFFRACTION; DISPERSION; LIGHT UNITS; REFLECTANCE/REFLECTION; REFRACTION; SPECTRUM; VISION; WAVELENGTH.

Light Box

Two kinds of light boxes are used in photography. One is a device for direct viewing of transparencies and negatives by transmitted light; the other is a device for shadowless lighting of small objects. A viewing box usually consists of a sheet of translucent white plastic placed over a box containing two or more fluorescent tubes spaced to produce uniform brightness over the entire area of the plastic. The interior of the box is painted white to aid in light distribution; the ends or sides must have ventilation holes. For viewing color transparencies, tubes should be used that produce light with an equivalent color temperature of 5000–5500K and with a color rendering index (CRI) of at least 90. Ordinary "daylight" fluorescent tubes do not meet these specifications and can produce inaccurate color impressions. A light box can be used as an illuminator for copying negatives and transparencies if the area surrounding the image is masked off to prevent flare in the camera lens. A small light box equipped with a safelight filter is convenient for inspecting negatives for printing in a darkroom where white light cannot be used freely, for example when two or more people are working in the same area. An open light box with tubes around the inner edges at the top can illuminate a subject placed in the center without creating shadows. The tubes should be masked from direct lens view; if they have individual switches, soft directional lighting can be produced by using only two or three at a time. Objects placed on a sheet of clear glass or plastic over the box opening can be lighted independently while the lighted interior of the box provides a white background bright enough to wash out any shadows falling on it.

Lighting

In photography light is the illumination by which a subject becomes visible and photographable. *Lighting* consists of illumination that is controlled and arranged to reveal various aspects and qualities of the subject in the most expressive or communicative way. Lighting has three major functions. The first is to model the subject—that is, to reveal the shape, volume, surface contours, and texture of the objects in the scene. The second function is to define the space in the scene by making the objects visually distinct from one another and their surroundings (background); clearly delineating the ground plane—the surface on which the objects rest—is an important part of this function. The third function of lighting is to contribute to that intangible emotional quality of a photograph called mood.

As discussed in the entry on light sources, there is a wide array of bulbs and instruments for use in lighting. Outdoors in daylight there is one major source: the sun or the open sky. In that situation lighting technique largely consists of orienting the subject to the source for best effect, and perhaps using reflectors or supplemental light such as electronic flash to fill in (lighten) dark, shadowed areas.

Kinds of light. Whatever sources are used, they are arranged to provide specific kinds of illumination; these are key light, fill light, backlight, special-purpose light, and base and background light.

The key light is the brightest frontal light; it is often specific light, such as that supplied by a spotlight or a direct, undiffused flash unit. However, in portraiture and much color photography a diffuse "bounce" light, as from an umbrella reflector, is frequently used as the key light. The angle of the key light establishes the modeling of the subject. A common position for the key light source is 45 degrees to one side of the camera and 45 degrees above the lens-subject axis. This throws both horizontal and vertical variations in subject contour into highlight-and-shadow relief. As the key light is moved closer to the camera, modeling is diminished; as it is moved farther away, to strike the subject from an angle closer to 90 degrees, the relief, especially that of surface texture, is heightened.

The key light creates shadows that are dark and sharply defined in direct proportion to how "hard" (specific) the key light is. In many cases, and almost always with color films, the shadows are too dark to register detail with normal exposure. Fill light is directed into the shadows from the other side of the camera from the key light to lighten them somewhat. Fill light is usually softer (more diffused) than the key light, and it is always less intense (if it were equally as bright, modeling would be destroyed). It is often supplied by a reflector positioned to pick up spill light from an intense backlight source; this is especially common outdoors when the sun is used as a backlight. Fill-light intensity may be from one-half to one-eighth as bright as the key light or even less, depending on the effect desired. The ratio between key- and fill-light intensities is called the *lighting ratio*, or illuminance ratio, and is measured by incident-light meter readings or by reflected-light meter readings from a neutral, single-tone surface such as a gray card or white card. (Readings taken directly from the subject measure the brightness, or luminance ratio; they may not match the lighting-ratio readings because of variations in subject reflectivity.) The ratio is measured by a reading of the fill light alone—with the key light turned off or the meter shadowed from it—and a reading of the combined effect of the fill and the key lights. The second reading accounts for the brightness of those subject areas, such as flat frontal planes, in which the two kinds of illumination overlap. The ratio may be expressed in the number of f-stops difference between the two readings, or in terms of equivalent units of light, with the fill light taken as one unit. Thus, if the key light is twice as bright as the fill light, the lighting ratio is 1:3. It is not 1:2 because the lights add together in the overlap areas. If the key light is four times (two f-stops) brighter than the fill light, the lighting ratio is 1:5. In portraiture, fashion photography, and similar applications, a lighting ratio no greater than 1:5 is suitable for color films or 1:9 for black-and-white films. For other kinds of subjects or dramatic effects, higher lighting ratios may be suitable.

The backlight serves to outline the subject edges, thereby giving the subject increased visual separation from the background. This is especially important when the subject and background have essentially the same tone or color. The backlight is specific light aimed directly at the subject from above or to one side, but from out of the camera's field of view. It must be at least twice as intense as the key light, or its effect is likely to be invisible. In outdoor photography with color film it is common to use the sun as a backlight to avoid harsh shadows and extreme contrast on the front of the subject. Reflectors or flash provide the frontal illumination.

Special-purpose light is any light added to enhance a particular subject quality or to solve a specific problem. It may be a top light used to create highlights in dark hair, or an eye light aimed to create a tiny reflection (catchlight) in the subject's eyes, or a clothes light used to increase the brightness of a very dark suit or dress. Special-purpose light is carefully controlled with barndoors, baffles, snoots, and other devices so that the light falls on a specific area and does not interfere with the modeling or overall lighting balance.

Base light is general, overall illumination used to raise the brightness of the entire scene to a minimum level. It is more commonly used in motion-picture and television lighting than in still photography, but it may be required for high-key pictures, or when working in dark surroundings or in open spaces with no nearby reflective walls and ceilings. If required, base lighting is established first, with banks of floodlights or diffused electronic flash to give even illumination in all parts of the scene. The key and other lights are then added, with intensities greater than the base light.

Background light is illumination specifically directed at the background and ground plane; insofar as possible, it does not fall on the main subject. It may be highly specific, picking out some background objects and details and throwing others into shadow, or it may illuminate everything equally. Often a cookie (patterned baffle) is used in front of the background light source to produce varying shadows on an otherwise plain background. If sufficiently bright, the background light can wash out shadows cast by the subject.

The mood created by lighting is influenced by the overall brightness level, by the relative hardness or softness of the light, and in color photography by the color balance or visible color of the light. A brightly lighted subject or scene has a different expressive appearance than one that is dark. The crisp delineation of textures, shadows, and highlights produced by hard, specific light creates a very different feeling from that produced by soft, diffused light, which smooths and blends small variations in a flattering way. For true rendition of the subject in color photography, the color balance of the light must match that of the film emulsion. If necessary, balance can be achieved by filtering the light sources or, if the sources are all of the same type, the camera lens. Light-film mismatches may purposely be used to achieve an overall warm, yellow-gold effect (daylight film with tungsten illumination) or a cold, bluish tone (tungsten film with electro-nic flash or daylight). Colored light sources produce many kinds of mood variations according to the nature of the subject and the general emotional associations of the color used. Most often colored light is used for background illumination, and light of proper color balance is used for subject illumination so as not to distort the subject's appearance.

See also: BOUNCE LIGHT; BRIGHTNESS RANGE; BROAD LIGHTING; COLOR BALANCE; FLASH FILL; FLAT LIGHTING; HIGH KEY; LIGHT; LIGHT SOURCES; LOW KEY; MODELING; MODELING LIGHT; MULTIPLE FLASH; NARROW LIGHTING; PAINTING WITH LIGHT; REFLECTORS; RIM LIGHT; SHADOWLESS LIGHTING; SILHOUETTE; UMBRELLA LIGHTING.

Lightning, Photographing

Lightning provides striking images when photographed under favorable conditions; the major problem is its unpredictable occurrence at any moment during a storm. To allow for this, the camera is aimed toward the oncoming storm and the shutter locked open on the "B" or "T" setting; a tripod or other unmoving support is necessary to avoid blurred images. Either color or black-and-white film may be used, and one or more flashes may be recorded on the same frame before advancing the film. The lens should be set at infinity focus, but because of the intense brightness of lightning the aperture setting is not critical. A wide aperture provides a thicker line of stick or "bolt" lightning than a smaller aperture; sheet lightning seldom provides dramatic pictures of itself.

Lightning is most clearly visible at night, and the dark sky avoids the exposure problems of leaving the shutter open that daylight would cause. If there is significant glow in the sky or at ground level—as from the lights of buildings—the lens should be blocked or the shutter closed between exposure attempts. Prolonged exposure to faint sky light after a lightning bolt has been recorded may create "black lightning" in the final image, a complete tone reversal of the brightest exposed portion, also called the "Clayden effect."

A protected camera position is necessary if the storm is in the immediate vicinity; however, metallic structures, tall trees, and other prominent features tend to be the focus of lightning and are not safe locations.

Light Sources

Any source of illumination, from the sun to a match, can be used for photography, although the light produced by some sources is not suitable for color films, and the intensity of some light may be so low that inconveniently long exposures are required. Light sources specifically intended for photographic use are bulbs and instruments that produce light with sufficient intensity to be usable with almost all films, and with a color balance that can be adjusted, if necessary, by simple filtration.

There are three major types of photographic artificial-light sources: continuous-output, momentary (flash), and intermittent (pulsed light). For each kind of source there are instruments that emit specific, focusable beams of light (spotlights), and others that diffuse light over a broad area (floodlights). Most photographic light sources produce illumination of a particular color balance, specified as a color temperature. There are three standard color temperatures corresponding to the balance of the three types of color film emulsions: 3200K (tungsten, Type B films), 3400K (Type A film), and 5500K (daylight-type film). All are usable with panchromatic black-and-white films; daylight-balance illumination is best with orthochromatic (red-blind) films.

Continuous light sources are fluorescent tubes, conventional tungsten-filament bulbs, and tungsten-halogen bulbs or so-called quartz lights. Fluorescent tubes are seldom used because they are difficult to control and their color balance is unsuitable for color films, as explained in the entry on fluorescent-light photography. Photographic tungsten-filament bulbs are called photofloods and photo lights. They are similar to standard household bulbs, but they have a much higher output at one of the standard color temperatures; this is achieved at the expense of a much shorter life. Most such bulbs must be used in a reflector or spotlight housing; some have built-in reflectors and lens-pattern front surfaces. They variously have screw, bayonet, and pin-type bases. Tungsten-halogen bulbs produce about 25 percent more light than photofloods that have the same power consumption. The quartz bulbs have a much longer working life, and their light does not drop in color temperature over the life of the bulb, as is the case with photofloods and photo lights. Tungsten-halogen bulbs have pin-type or other plug-in connectors and must be used in appropriate spot or flood housings. Most slide projectors use small quartz lights with self-contained reflectors. Continuous light sources operate on standard 110/220 ac voltage; some quartz lights can also be operated from rechargeable battery packs.

Continuous light allows the photographer to see the effect of the illumination without the need for test shots, and it is readily measured with standard exposure meters. However, continuous light creates constant glare and heat that may affect the subject. Tungsten-halogen lamps in particular emit a potentially dangerous amount of heat; at close range they can quickly melt, scorch, or ignite many materials, or they can cause severe burns.

There are two kinds of momentary light sources: flashbulbs and electronic flash tubes. Flashbulbs are almost obsolete, having been replaced by electronic flash in even very simple cameras. They are most commonly supplied as 4-bulb flashcubes, or as strips or bars of up to 12 miniature bulbs. Large, individual disposable flashbulbs are also available, but now they are used primarily for special purposes in industrial, technical, and similar kinds of photography. Electronic flash tubes are used in built-in camera flash units, in portable units with self-contained reflectors and battery power packs, and in studio units with interchangeable reflectors and high-output ac/dc power supplies. Flash units generally are more compact and of lighter weight, and they have greater light output than continuous light sources of equal or greater power consumption. Flash illumination does not build up heat or glare on the subject. It has a daylight color balance, and it can be brief enough to freeze movement sharply well beyond the limit of the fastest shutter speeds.

Although initially more expensive than comparable continuous light sources, electronic flash equipment is more versatile and has much longer life; flash tubes provide tens of thousands of flashes before needing replacement. The primary disadvantage of flash is that its effect cannot be judged by eye. Although flash units can be equipped with continuous-output modeling lights to aid in estimating the effect, only a test shot can give an accurate indication. Determining exposure may also be more difficult with flash units than with continuous light. That is not the case with a single automatic flash unit, but with nonautomatic portable and studio units and in multiple-flash setups exposure must be calculated from guide numbers or equivalent data or must be determined with a specialized flash exposure meter.

Intermittent light sources emit pulses of illumination at regular rates ranging from two or three to several hundred or thousand times per second. The most common such source is a stroboscope, a kind of repeating electronic flash unit used for high-speed and motion-study photography and for special effects. Pulsed xenon light sources are used in process cameras, automatic printers, high-output motion-picture projectors, and other equipment that requires intense, daylight-balance illumination. Most intermittent light sources have special-purpose applications. Other specialized light sources with photographic applications include lasers, fiber-optic devices, microscope illuminators, and ultraviolet- and infrared-emitting tubes and bulbs. Often equipment with an internal light source is adapted for lighting use—e.g., a slide projector used as a spotlight, or a motion-picture projector used as a kind of stroboscope.

A great many accessories are available to adjust and control the output of light sources. These include reflectors, diffusers, and filters; barndoors and other adjustable baffles; snoots (chimneylike hoods that shape a light beam); and constant-voltage transformers and dimmers. Specialized light sources or lighting setups may also require timers, remote-control switches, and similar special-purpose devices.

See also: AUTOMATIC FLASH; ELECTRONIC FLASH; FLASH; FLUORESCENT-LIGHT PHOTOGRAPHY; LIGHTING; MODELING LIGHT; MULTIPLE FLASH; PHOTOFLOOD BULB; QUARTZ LIGHT; REFLECTORS; SPOTLIGHT; STROBOSCOPE; TUNGSTEN BULB; XENON ARC LAMP.

Light Units

A great number of units are used to measure various aspects of light for many different applications. Only those of reasonably common photographic usefulness are defined here.

The intensity of a light source is expressed in *candela* (cd) or *candlepower* (cp). The radiant energy or luminous flux emitted by a given source is measured in *lumens* (lm). A one-candela or one-candlepower source emits 12.6 lumens. As the luminous flux is radiated outward, it spreads over a larger area as it gets farther from the source; thus, the amount arriving at any one point on the area decreases with distance, as expressed in the inverse square law. For photographic purposes the significant factor is the illumination falling onto a surface—the incident light, or *illuminance*. Illuminance is measured in terms of the lumens falling on a square unit of area: lumens per square foot (lm/ft^2) = *footcandles* (fc); lumens per square meter ($1m/m^2$) = *lux* (lx). The amount of light reflected from the surface (or emitted by a radiant surface) depends on the illuminance and the reflection or diffusion factor of the surface. Reflected light or surface brightness is called *luminance*. It is commonly measured in *candelas per square meter* (cd/m^2) (a unit also called the *nit*), or in *candles per square foot* (c/ft^2). Other measures of luminance are the *lambert* (lumens per square centimeter), *footlambert* (lumens per square foot), and *apostilb* (lumens per square meter). All these units deal with aspects of what is commonly called brightness, a subjective impression of intensity.

The total quantity of light received or emitted is the product of intensity and a time factor. For example, exposure is a matter of how bright the light is and how long it strikes an emulsion. The total quantity of light received by a surface is a factor of illuminance and time. It is measured in *meter-candle seconds* (mcs), *footcandle-seconds* (fcs), or *watt-seconds (Joules) per cm^2*. Light sources that do not have continuous output are measured in terms of luminous flux versus time. The units are *lumen-seconds* (lmsec), *candlepower-seconds* (cps), or *watt-seconds* (w/s), also called *Joules* (J). The accompanying tables show how to convert units for a given factor.

See also: INVERSE SQUARE LAW; JOULE.

CONVERTING LIGHT UNITS

Unit	× Factor	= Unit
Source Intensity; Luminous Flux		
Candlepower	12.6	Lumens
Candlepower	0.02	Watts*
Lumens	0.08	Candlepower
Lumens	0.0015	Watts*
Watts	54	Candlepower*
Watts	680	Lumens*
Illuminance; Incident Light		
Footcandles (lm/ft^2)	10.75	Lux (meter-candela; lm/m^2)
Lux	0.09	Footcandles
Luminance; Reflected Light; Surface Brightness		
Candles/ft^2	10.75	Candles/m^2 (nit)
Candles/ft^2	3.14	Lumens/ft^2 (footlambert)
Candles/m^2 (nit)	0.09	Candles/ft^2
Candles/m^2	0.28	Lumens/ft^2 (footlambert)
Footlambert	10.75	Lumens/m^2 (apostilb)
Light Quantity Received		
Meter-candle sec.	0.09	Footcandle-sec.
Footcandle-sec.	10.75	Meter-candle sec.

Light Quantity Emitted

Lumen-seconds	0.08	Candlepower-sec.
Lumen-sec.	0.0015	Watt-sec. (Joules)*
Candlepower-sec.	12.6	Lumen-sec.
Candlepower-sec.	0.0059	Watt-sec. (Joules)*
Watt-sec. (Joules)	680	Lumen-sec.*
Watt-sec.	54	Candlepower-sec.*

*These conversions are approximations for the broad-wavelength band light normally used for photography.

INCIDENT LIGHT: APPROXIMATE ILLUMINANCE EQUIVALENTS

Footcandles	Lux
1	11
2	22
4	44
8	85
16	170
32	345
65	700
130	1,400
260	2,800
500	5,400
1,000	10,750
2,000	21,500
4,000	43,000
7,200*	77,500*
8,000	86,000
16,000	172,000
32,000	34,400

*Average illuminance of sunlighted subject, upon which *f/16 @ 1/film speed* exposure estimation is based; see the article on exposure.

Line Image

In the graphic arts and photomechanical reproduction, a line image is one that consists of only two tones, neither of which varies in intensity or color. One tone is the background (e.g., white paper or clear film); the other depicts the image shapes in a single, solid density. The shapes may be lines, or large or small areas of tone, but their intensity is everywhere the same. A line image is distinct from a continuous tone image, in which tones and colors do vary, and from a halftone image, which imitates continuous tone effects in reproduction.

A line image is produced by photographing a subject, artwork, or other material directly on a lith film, a very high contrast film that produces only maximum density or no density, with no intermediate tones. The material being photographed may itself be line art or line copy such as an ink drawing, a single-color chart or plan, or printed letters. If the material or subject has tone variations, the lith film registers a certain part of the tonal range as a single density and does not register the rest. The result is the greatest possible simplification of subject variations: only differences in form remain.

Line images are used primarily to reproduce drawings, diagrams, text, and similar elements in books, magazines, and newspapers. In photography, line images may be an intermediate of a final stage of many special effects. Although prepared on black-and-white film, the image can be printed with any single color ink, or color filter.

See also: CONTINUOUS TONE IMAGE; HALFTONE PROCESSES; HIGH CONTRAST MATERIALS; LITH FILMS/PAPERS.

Linked Ring

The Brotherhood of the Linked Ring was the first organization formed to advance artistic photography as an independent expressive medium whose works were to be exhibited and evaluated on their own terms, not on how closely or successfully they imitated painting, etching, and other media. It was founded in London in May 1892 by Alfred Maskell, H. P. Robinson, and several other photographers who were dissatisfied with the exhibition policies of the Royal Photographic Society (RPS). They particularly objected to three practices: (1) lumping all kinds of photography together on a basis of equal importance, (2) using painters, sculptors, and other non-photographers to jury the art photography entries, and (3) awarding prizes at several levels, down to honorable mention, in various fine art categories (Landscape; Portrait; Still Life; etc.) on the assumption that one image could be artistically better than all others. The primary purpose of the Linked Ring was to establish an alternate art photography exhibition, The Photographic Salon. The first presentation, in 1893, was directed by J. Craig Annan and Frederick H. Evans; no medals were awarded. The Ring had no officers or council of directors; it was a loose confederation of artist photographers who elected others throughout the world to membership solely on the basis of the artistic quality of their work. The serious and high-minded ideals of the Ring were echoed in the founding of the Photo-Club de Paris in 1894 by Robert Demachy and other French Pictorialists, and by similar salons in Belgium, Germany, Austria, and other countries. Alfred Stieglitz was elected a member of the Linked Ring in 1894. Many of the photographers who became part of the Photo-Secession under his leadership just after the turn of the century also were elected to the Ring. The Photo-Secession itself became an affiliated organization and eventually submitted work that so dominated the Photographic Salon of 1908 that the Ring dissolved with dissension over whether or not the Salon should be restricted exclusively or primarily to the work of English photographers. The Salon was subsequently re-established as the London Photographic Salon by several of the dissident members.

See also: PHOTO-SECESSION; PICTORIAL PHOTOGRAPHY/PICTORIALISM; ROBINSON, HENRY PEACH; STIEGLITZ, ALFRED.

Lippmann Process

A method of recording full-color images by means of interference between wavelengths, without the use of dyes or colorants, was invented by Gabriel Lippmann in 1891. A grainless, highly transparent panchromatic emulsion coated on a glass plate is laid in contact with the flawless mirror surface created by a layer of mercury. The image is focused through the glass plate. Light passes through the emulsion and is reflected by the mercury mirror; reflection shifts its phase to some degree, so that it interferes with succeeding wavelengths in the emulsion. Some wavelengths cancel one another completely; others create various degrees of mutual reinforcement and these intensities create a latent-image exposure. The developed interference pattern varies in density and in wavelength selectivity. The image is viewed by placing the emulsion against a mirror and shining light into it. The recorded pattern interferes with the reflected light, allowing only those wavelengths that correspond to the original colors to be transmitted, so that a natural color image is seen. The viewing angle is critical, and the emulsion is at least 100,000 times slower than that of ordinary films; as a result, the process has had only scientific investigation and application. Lippmann also originated, in 1908, the first lenticular system to produce stereographic images.

See also: INTERFERENCE; LENTICULAR SYSTEMS.

Lissitzky, El

Russian; 1890–1941

El Lissitzky, a Russian avant-garde artist, envisioned an art that could not be

contained by the easel, the studio, or the museum. Whether he worked on book design, architecture, posters, advertisements, or exhibition spaces, he perceived art's task as that of social reconstruction. Rather than produce precious objects for the few, Lissitzky believed, it was the artist's duty to harness all the resources of technology to liberate and elevate the sensibility of the masses. Lissitzky seldom worked in a single medium, but mixed media freely and dynamically in an attempt to produce a modern, energetic mode of expression. Thus, his use of photography centered on the creation of photomontages for billboards, magazines, pamphlets, and posters. Composed on Constructivist/Suprematist principles, his montages were almost all devoted to communicating socialist messages and ideals in an enthusiastic manner. They represent some of the most effective marriages of typography and photoimages produced in the 1920s and 1930s, the peak period of photomontage production. They are free of the self-conscious concern with being "art" that characterizes the work of Moholy-Nagy, Herbert Bayer, Man Ray, and others, and their positive tone and intent is the opposite of the brilliantly effective viciousness of the anti-Nazi montages of John Heartfield.

Born in Russia, and trained at Vitebsk in engineering and architecture, in 1917 Lissitzky joined the circle of Marc Chagall and a number of other Jewish graphic-artist illustrators in Kiev. He proved to be an innovative lithographer with a long rolled-scroll illustration for *The Legend of Prague* and a series of nine illustrated children's books. In 1918 Lissitzky joined the faculty of the Vitebsk Art Labor Cooperative—of which Chagall was director—as a professor of architecture and the graphic arts. As supervisor of the lithography studio he produced the book *On New System in Art* by the Suprematist painter Kasimir Malevich, who had taken over leadership of the school in 1919, and became a disciple of Malevich.

At this time Lissitzky began a series of "proun" constructions—three-dimensional paintings that combined elements of contemporary geometric abstraction with perspectival illusions. A marriage of Dada and de Stijl, the proun paintings represented to Lissitzky "interchange stations from painting to architecture"; they were meant to transcend the earthbound pragmatism of the blueprints, diagrams, charts, tables, and other means by which utopian futures previously had been planned.

Lissitzky's fervent belief that Russian society required a new world of abstract shapes and colors was shaken by his discovery that the Russian people neither appreciated nor understood his efforts. In 1922 he went to Berlin to be represented and to assist in the organization of the mammoth exhibition "Erst Russiche Kunstausstellung" (First [of the Communist regime] Russian Art Exhibition). Posters, billboards, brochures, and photo-composite displays for this exhibition represent his first major use of photoimages.

During this period, Lissitzky met and married Sophie Küppers, who came to play a crucial role as an assistant and collaborator. In Switzerland from 1924 to 1926 for treatment of tuberculosis, he gave up painting and turned to producing architectural plans that could bring in the new society he envisioned. His utopian optimism that design can permanently expand consciousness is shared by few designers today.

Returning to Russia, Lissitzky began concentrating on photomontages in 1927. Like the Dadaists, who believed that photomontage was an artmaking tool uniquely in touch with the times, Lissitzky hoped to attain maximum force of expressivity through simultaneous use of photographs, slogans, press cuttings, lines, planes, and colors. Along with Man Ray and Moholy-Nagy, he hoped that the next phase would be "photowriting" directly on unexposed film.

By 1930 Lissitzky was actively producing catalogs and brochures in which he skillfully collocated text and reproduction, and boldly employed formal contrasts and foreshortening. A key outlet for his talents was the propaganda magazine *USSR in Construction* published in Moscow from 1932 to 1938. He died after a long illness.

List, Herbert

German; 1903–1975

Günter Metken coined the term "Fotografia Metafisica" to describe Herbert List's photographs. Inspired and influenced by the Surrealists, List found many of his ideas and visions realized in the paintings of Giorgio de Chirico, Max Ernst, and Salvador Dali. He sought to "capture the magic of images, hoping to reveal their hidden spirit," and spoke of "the secret marriages between table and chair, or glass and bottle."

List was born and educated in Hamburg and continued to live there until he was obliged to leave Germany in 1936. The son of a coffee importer, List apprenticed in the business in the early 1920s, studied commerce, and joined the family firm of List and Heineken in 1925. During the course of his business, he traveled to the coffee-growing countries of Brazil, Guatemala, San Salvador, and Costa Rica, then to the United States (1926–1928). Between 1928 and 1936 List progressed to a partnership in the firm. During this time he participated in the cultural life of Hamburg. A stylish young man, he moved in affluent, unconventional circles of artists, performers, and the intelligentsia.

List liked to see himself as an amateur, but was obliged to earn his living as a professional photographer in Paris in 1937. He took his first photographs (of the city of Hamburg) in 1930, following some technical instruction from Andreas Feininger, who introduced him to the newly developed twin-lens reflex camera. In Paris, his fashion photographs followed the slightly Surrealistic style of Durst, Horst, and Cecil Beaton: the arrangement of models in tableaux, with mirrors, veils, and cultural props like busts and statues. His photographs appeared in *Vogue*, *Verve*, and *Harper's Bazaar*. In 1937–1938 he traveled to Greece with George Hoyningen-Huene, where he photographed and planned publication of *Licht über Hellas* (Munich, 1953). His photographs of fallen neo-classical sculpture amongst the debris of the destroyed city of Munich date from his return to Germany after the war's end (1945–1946). He worked for the magazine *Du* (1945–1960), photographing portrait and travel subjects. List stopped taking photographs in the early 1960s, devoting himself instead to his collection of Italian old master drawings.

Literature of Photography

The literature of photography is vast, for since the medium's invention, practitioners, scientists, social critics, and artists have all sought to convey their understanding of its importance in print.
Technique and Theory. Technical works on photography (as opposed to those written on the inventions that led up to it) begin with François Arago's *Rapport sur le Daguerréotype* (1839) and Daguerre's first manual on his method, *Historique et description des procédés du Daguerréotype et du Diorama* (1839), as well as William Henry Fox Talbot's "Some Account of the Art of Photogenic Drawing" (1839). Thereafter, treatises on daguerreotypy, calotypy, collodion-on-glass, and film have appeared frequently and in great number; Ansel Adams's popular *Basic Photo Series* is only the most recent example of this genre.

Publications on optical and color theory have been as important to the development of photography as the practical manuals; Hermann Vogel's *The Chemistry of Light and Photography* (1875) and Moritz von Rohr's *Theorie und Geschichte des photographische Objektivs* (1899) are classics, respectively, of photochemical and lens theory, while Charles Cros's *Solution générale du problème de la photographie des couleurs* (1869), A. and L. Ducos du Hauron's *Traité pratique de photographie des couleurs* (1878), Hermann Vogel's *Die Photographie farbiger Gegenstande in den richtigen Tonverhältnissen* (1885), L. P. Clerc's *La Photographie des couleurs* (1898), A. Lumière and son's *Autochrome Plates: instructions for their use* (1904), and Victor Cremier's *La Photographie des couleurs par les placques autochromes* (1911) are the most significant early texts on color photography.
Criticism and History. Photography's critics have written on the medium's impact since its invention in 1839. William Henry Fox Talbot, in his serial publication *The Pencil of Nature* (1844–1846), foresaw many of the ways in which photography would profoundly alter society. A decade later, Charles Baudelaire, writing in Paris, quoted early enthusiasts less optimistically: " 'Since Photography gives us every guarantee of exactitude that we could desire [they really believe that, the mad fools!], then Photography and Art are the same thing.' From that moment our squalid society rushed, Narcissus to a man, to gaze at its trivial image on a scrap of metal."

More recently, photography has been viewed by critics as a democratizer and trivializer of the once-unique art object (Walter Benjamin, "A Short History of Photography," 1931, and "The Work of Art in the Age of Mechanical Reproduction," 1936), and as a substitute for first-hand experience (Susan Sontag, *On Photography*, 1977).

Photography's historians began their work almost as soon as Daguerre's and Talbot's inventions were announced: Nicéphore Niépce's son, Isidore, published his *Historique de la découverte improprement nommée Daguerréotype* in 1841. The most useful standard works today are Josef Maria Eder's *Geschichte der Photographie* (4th ed., 1932), which, though dated, contains more on the technical evolution of photography than any other history; Helmut Gernsheim's *The History of Photography from the camera obscura to the beginning of the modern era* (1969), an immense work that is particularly useful on 19th-c. English and German photography; and Beaumont Newhall's *The History of Photography* (1982) and its companion volume of primary source readings, *Photography: Essays and Images* (1980).
Photography as Art. As photography has become accepted as an art medium, more and more photographers have presented their work in book form similar to the monographs of the art press. Fox Talbot's *The Pencil of Nature* must be counted as the first such volume, for besides its philosophical speculations, it also includes 24 tipped-in calotypes. Both French and English photographers of the 1850s published their work in book form, although they did not present it as art. To find again a conscious identification of photography as art in a book form, we must look to Peter Henry Emerson's *Life and Landscape of the Norfolk Broads* (1886), which was followed by several other volumes containing handsome pictorial plates.

By the turn of the century, Alfred Stieglitz's privately financed labor of love, *Camera Work*, was providing art photography's growing audience with gravure reproductions of Photo-Secessionist and historical images that rivaled the originals in quality. When *Camera Work* ended in 1917 after fifty issues, art photography in print lost its handsomest vehicle. Stieglitz's circle of camera artists—Strand, Steichen, White, Käsebier—survived in print through the popular photo press until a new commitment to high-quality art reproductions arose in the 1950s. Since then publications by, in particular, the French firm Robert Delpire, the German firm Schirmer/Mosel, and the American firm Aperture have ensured photographers of their representation in the literature of photography.
See also: APPENDIX: BIBLIOGRAPHY; BOOKS, PHOTOGRAPHIC; COLOR PHOTOGRAPHY—HISTORY; HISTORY OF PHOTOGRAPHY.

Lith Films and Papers

The very high-contrast materials used for graphic arts applications and photomechanical reproduction are known as lith films and papers; the name is an abbreviation of the term *lithographic*, or *photolithographic*. When processed in their associated developers, their response to exposure is to produce either maximum density or none at all. Middle-

tones are not distinctively recorded, but register with the same density as the shadows or the highlights, depending on their relative brightness. This is precisely the kind of response required to make halftone dot images and produce other kinds of screened images. The break point between those brightnesses that are recorded and those that are not can be adjusted by choice of material and to some degree by exposure and processing. Some materials produce limited middletones when processed in ordinary full-range developers; this technique has been used primarily for artistic effect.
See also: HIGH-CONTRAST MATERIALS.

Lithography

Lithography is a graphic reproduction process based on the fact that oil and water repel one another. The name, which means "stone writing" (or drawing), describes the original process, invented by Alois Senefelder circa 1794, in which a slab of Bavarian limestone was used as a printing surface. Today stone lithography is used almost exclusively as a direct art medium. Modern commercial reproduction of photographs, illustrations, and graphic and fine art images employs photolithography with metal, plastic, or paper-surface offset printing plates.

Lithography is a planographic process: the inked image areas are on the same level as the uninked, nonprinting areas. It is thus distinct from relief or raised-image processes (e.g., letterpress) and intaglio or incised-image processes. A limestone slab of appropriate size and desired texture is ground flat on one surface and thoroughly cleaned. The image is drawn directly on the stone with a lithographic crayon or with an oily or soapy ink; alternatively the drawing is made on special paper which is then pressed against a heated stone surface to transfer the image. Direct-stone illustration requires drawing the image reversed left for right so that it will be printed properly. Most artists prefer the transfer method because it does not require reversed drawing.

Oil from the drawing penetrates the stone so it becomes receptive to printing ink in the image areas but will repel water there. The image is treated to prevent spreading, and the stone surface is dampened so that it will repel ink in all nonimage areas; then the drawing is cleaned off. The stone is inked with a roller and the excess removed with a scraper blade; ink remains only in those areas made receptive by the original drawing. For printing, paper is laid face down on the stone which then passes through a roller-pressure or sliding-bed press. The stone must be re-inked for each impression. Multi-color images usually require a separate stone for each color and a means of laying the paper in proper register for successive printings. In some cases a single stone may be inked with different colors in selected areas.

Lithography directly reproduces the energy of the artist's original line; in addition it can produce a range of tones from complete saturation through the lightest pastel, and can accurately simulate the character of drawing in pen, pencil, crayon, or brush. It was used as a direct art medium by 19th c. artists as diverse as Toulouse-Lautrec, Goya, Daumier, Currier and Ives, and many others, and is used by many fine-art printmakers today.
See also: INTAGLIO PROCESS; PHOTOENGRAVING; PHOTOGRAVURE; PHOTOLITHOGRAPHY; OFFSET PRINTING.

Little Galleries of the Photo-Secession

The gallery operated by Alfred Stieglitz, in rented rooms at 291 Fifth Avenue, New York City, was first known as the Little Galleries of the Photo-Secession. The opening exhibit in 1905 consisted of 100 prints by members of the Photo-Secession. In the following two years exhibitions included work by Robert Demachy, E. J. C. Puyo, Gertrude Käsebier, Clarence H. White, David Octavius Hill, J. Craig Annan, Edward Steichen, Heinrich Kuehn, Baron A. de Meyer, Alvin Langdon Coburn, and many other leading American and European pictorial photographers. The restrained style of presentation established a new standard for the exhibition of photographs in the U.S. The gallery closed because of financial pressures in the spring of 1908, but reopened in the fall of that year under the name "291" in the adjoining building.
See also: Photographers cited; GALLERIES, PHOTOGRAPHY; PHOTO-SECESSION; PICTORIAL PHOTOGRAPHY/PICTORIALISM; STIEGLITZ, ALFRED; 291.

Long Focus

The term *long focus* refers to focal length and is commonly used to distinguish a long-focal-length lens of conventional optical design from one of telephoto design.
See also: FOCAL LENGTH; LENSES.

Long Shot

In motion pictures and television, an overall view of the subject or scene that has been—or appears to have been—taken from a distance is a long shot. The term is a relative one: a long shot may show a single figure from head to toe, a football field, or a broad landscape. Closer views are called medium shots and closeups. The usual function of a long shot is to establish for the viewer the physical location of major elements in the scene and the dominant angle of view. When, in the course of action shown in closer views, major changes of position occur, it is common to show a re-establishing shot—another long shot—to reorient the viewer.

Lorant, Stefan

American; 1901–
Stefan Lorant is regarded as the first major editor of modern photojournalism.

Born and educated in Budapest, Lorant left Hungary in the fall of 1919, after the collapse of the Béla Kun government which led to the beginning of fascism in that country. Helped by Franz Kafka to find a job in Czechoslovakia, he played the violin in a movie house orchestra before moving on to Vienna, where he became a film cameraman, scriptwriter, and director. His first film, *The Life of Mozart*, established him as one of the leading cameramen in Europe. He was then 19 years old. In Vienna and in Berlin he made 14 films, some of which he wrote, directed, and photographed.

In 1925, after mastering the German language, Lorant left filmmaking and began to write articles for various Berlin newspapers (*Berliner Zeitung am Mittag, Morgenpost,* and others). He became assistant editor of *Das Magazin,* which became a huge success, and in 1926 was hired as editor of the *Ufa Magazin* (later *Film Magazin*). During those years he also edited the Sunday magazine of the *Berliner Borsen Courier*—the *Bilder Courier* (Picture Courier)—and became Berlin editor of the *Münchner Illustrierte Presse.* In 1928 he was appointed chief editor of the Munich weekly, which under his editorship became the first modern photojournalistic paper in Europe.

When the Nazis took over Bavaria in March 1933, Lorant was taken into "protective custody" and was imprisoned for most of the year. Released through the intervention of the Hungarian government, he returned to Budapest where he edited the Sunday Magazine of the *Pesti Napló.* After completing his book *I was Hitler's Prisoner,* based on his prison diary, in 1934 he took the manuscript to London where it was published the next year.

Lorant arrived in London barely fluent in English, but he soon became editor of Odham's *Weekly Illustrated*, the first popular illustrated paper in England, and the model for the famous picture magazines founded in the 1930s: *Life, Look, Vu,* and others.

In 1937 he founded *Pocket Publications* in London and brought out a pocket magazine, *Lilliput,* which became a phenomenal success. A year later he sold his publishing company to Edward Hulton, who was ready to finance the publication of an illustrated paper under Lorant's guidance. Thus *Picture Post* came into being, with Lorant as its editor-in-chief. In a short time the paper had a circulation of 1,750,000.

Lorant left England for the United States in 1940. There, he published many books with text and illustrations on American history (*The Glorious Burden,* the history of the American Presidency; *The New World,* the first pictures of America; *Pittsburgh,* the story of an American city). His pictorial volumes on Abraham Lincoln, Theodore Roosevelt, and Franklin D. Roosevelt introduced a new genre, that of the picture biography.

After receiving an honorary doctor's degree from Knox College in 1958, Lorant entered Harvard University to work for a graduate degree. He received his M.A. in 1961. His book *Sieg Heil,* published in 1974, is an illustrated history of Germany from Bismarck and the foundation of the German Reich until the death of Hitler and the end of the Third Reich.

Since 1980 Lorant has been working on his autobiography, *I Lived Six Lives,* about his careers in six countries: Hungary, Czechoslovakia, Austria, Germany, England, and America.
See also: PHOTOJOURNALISM.

Loupe

A loupe is a viewing lens used directly in front of the eye to focus greatly magnified images at very close range. Photographers use loupes to inspect sharpness and image detail in negatives, transparencies, and small-format contact proof sheets, and as an aid in focusing the image on the ground glass of large-format view cameras. The quality of a loupe may range from a simple uncorrected plastic lens to a flat-field achromat. Some designs incorporate a transparent or lighted supporting base to allow examination of opaque or dark objects; an open base allows retouching and spotting. Technical loupes for machinists, pressmen, and others often include a reticle (comparison scale) for taking measurements, thread counts, or similar data directly from the magnified image. Such scales are especially useful in scientific and technical photography, inspecting photographically derived devices such as printed circuits, and similar applications. The approximate magnification of a loupe can be determined by dividing 10 in. (250mm), the minimum focusing distance of the average eye, by the focal length of the loupe in inches or millimeters, as appropriate. This is especially helpful when using an ordinary camera lens as a substitute loupe; the lens must be set at its infinity focusing position for this purpose.

Low Key

The term low key describes a subject or an image in which dark tones, black, and dark grays are predominant. The dark tones occur throughout the picture or scene; they appear richer, and the differences among them are more apparent, if there are also some accents of light tones or white. Although dim light conditions give a low-key visual appearance to many subjects, this is partly because the eye's ability to perceive color decreases as subject brightness drops. A successful low-key photograph requires a genuinely low-key subject, with sufficient illumination to permit full exposure of the dark tones without prolonged exposure times. Strong, direct light may create problems of glaring highlights and deep shadows that obscure differences between neighboring dark tones. An incident-light meter reading of the illumination on the subject, or a reflected-light meter reading from a standard gray card will provide accurate exposure indications. A reflected-light reading taken directly from the subject will suggest overexposure, because exposure meters are calibrated to a middle-gray standard, but the major subject tones are darker grays. Such a reading should be adjusted downward, for the equivalent of one to two-and-a-half *f*-stops less exposure. Underexposing a full-tonal-range subject will not produce a low-key effect, but will submerge the darkest tones into a featureless black and make the highlight appear muddy in a print. A negative of a low key subject can be given limited additional exposure in printing to emphasize its qualities, but it is not possible to produce a convincing low-key image by "printing down" (overexposing) from a negative of a normal-range subject.
See also: BRIGHTNESS RANGE; CONTRAST; EXPOSURE; EXPOSURE METERS; GRAY CARD; HIGH KEY.

Lumen

See: LIGHT UNITS.

Lumière, Auguste
French; 1862–1954
Lumière, Louis
French; 1864–1948

The Lumière brothers were prolific scientists and astute manufacturers. They made direct practical use of the information in many of the hundreds of scientific papers they produced, they introduced landmark inventions in photography, and they presented the best of their inventions in a way that stimulated public interest and acceptance. Their father, Antoine, founded the company of Lumière and Sons to manufacture photographic gelatin dry plates in Lyons in 1882. The following year the company offered its first film, a collodion stripping film invented by Georges Balagny, but real growth occurred only after 1887 when the brothers expanded the factory to produce roll films and printing papers.

The Lumières' research work produced notable advances in the chemistry of development and led them to investigate the problem of photography in color. They were the among the most successful investigators and developers of the Lippmann interference color process, and in 1892 they exhibited projected Lippmann images. This was followed by two assembly color processes. In one, bleach-out exposure and processing of subtractive-color stripping emulsions produced positives that were assembled in register. In the other, gelatin reliefs on celluloid bases were prepared from separation negatives, then individually dyed and assembled to form a composite color image. The innovations in these procedures were primarily in the chemical processes involved, not in the fundamental process, but they led to recognition of the need for a single-plate single-exposure method of color photography to be a commercially successful venture. Their triumph in this area was the Autochrome plate, which was introduced in 1907 after the invention of a panchromatic emulsion made accurate translation of colors possible.

A second major invention of the Lumières was the first commercially successful celluloid-film motion picture camera-projector. This device, the *cinématographe,* was introduced in December 1895 and was used for scheduled public showings of motion pictures on a regular basis well before the similar inventions of Edison, Friese-Greene, and other pioneers. Constructed by Jules

Carpentier, the cinématographe introduced the use of a clawlike device to provide the required intermittent pulldown movement of perforated 35mm celluloid film (manufactured by the Lumières); it was copied in almost every subsequent motion picture camera and projector.

Other notable Lumière inventions included the Photorama, a 360° panoramic projector using 70mm film introduced at the Paris International Exhibition of 1900, and an anaglyphic (overlapping color image) stereoscopic motion-picture system introduced in 1935. Auguste Lumière devoted the latter part of his life to biological and physiological research at the Lumière Clinic, which he founded in Paris. Louis continued his lifelong research in photographically related subjects.
See also: AUTOCHROME; COLOR PHOTOGRAPHY—HISTORY; LIPPMANN PROCESS.

Luminance

The measured brightness of a surface that is reflecting or transmitting light, or that is self-luminous, is called luminance. The distinction between luminance and brightness is that of objective measurement. Brightness is a subjective impression influenced by the color of the light and the adaptation of the eye to a particular situation. Luminance is a measurement made with a photometer. The international standard for such measurements is candelas per square meter, expressed as so many *nits*. When the brightness range of a subject is measured on a comparative basis with an exposure meter, the result is properly termed the luminance range. The measured brightness of the light falling onto a surface—i.e., the incident light—is called *illuminance*.
See also: BRIGHTNESS RANGE; CANDLE/CANDELA/CANDLEPOWER; LIGHT UNITS; PHOTOMETER/PHOTOMETRY.

Lux

See: LIGHT UNITS.

Lynes, George Platt

American; 1907–1955
George Platt Lynes was famous during his lifetime for his technically virtuosic commercial and portrait photography for *Harper's Bazaar, Vogue,* and other popular magazines, but the images for which he is now highly regarded are Surrealist-inspired homoerotic nudes and mythological studies.

Lynes was born in East Orange, New

Lynes, George Platt. "Portrait of Jean Cocteau" (n.d.). Courtesy Russell Lynes; collection Museum of Modern Art, New York.

Jersey, the son of a clergyman. He was educated at private schools and numbered among his friends Lincoln Kirstein, who became one of the major art patrons in the U.S. in this century. In 1925, on his first trip to Europe, Lynes encountered such luminaries in the arts as Gertrude Stein, Jean Cocteau, and Glenway Wescott, all of whom he later photographed.

After a brief period at Yale University, Lynes opened a bookshop in 1929. He published booklets of the writings of Stein, Hemingway, and others, illustrated by Cocteau and Pavel Tchelitchew. He took up photography at this time and soon exhibited his portraiture in the bookshop gallery.

In 1931 Lynes met and was encouraged by Julien Levy, with whom he collaborated on a series of Surrealist-influenced still-lifes. Work by Lynes was included in the seminal *Surréalisme* exhibition at the Julien Levy Gallery in

1932 and he was given a one-man show by Levy later that year.

Lynes opened a portrait studio in New York City in 1933 and quickly became known for his portraits and fashion photographs. His work began to appear in a variety of magazines and he acted as official photographer to Lincoln Kirstein's American Ballet Company, documenting George Balanchine's productions until the early 1940s.

A second solo exhibition at the Levy Gallery was held in 1934. Two years later Lynes's work was included in the Museum of Modern Art's *Dada and Surrealism* exhibition in New York. Over 200 of Lynes's portraits and other photographs were shown at the Pierre Matisse Gallery in 1941.

Lynes moved to California in 1945 to become director of *Vogue's* Hollywood studios. He made many portraits of film stars at this time but found this work debilitating. He returned to New York after three years and spent the remainder of his life doing fashion photography and continuing his personal work. Lynes was unable to exhibit most of this creative work during his lifetime for fear that its homoerotic qualities would endanger his career. He destroyed a large portion of these photographs, and few of the remainder were made public until two decades after his death. His studies of the male nude now command extremely high prices.

Lynes was the subject of a major retrospective at the Art Institute of Chicago in 1960. A monograph, *George Platt Lynes: Photographs 1931–1955*, was published in 1981.

Lyons, Nathan

American; 1930–

Nathan Lyons has been one of America's most important curators and photographic editors for 25 years. He was associated with George Eastman House, Rochester, N.Y., from 1957 to 1969. In 1963 he was a founding member and first Chairman of the Society for Photographic Education. He was the founder and Director of the Visual Studies Workshop, Rochester, in 1969. He has lectured, conducted workshops, and curated shows at museums and universities across the country, and has edited many important books and catalogs. In recent years, his own photography has gained wider recognition.

Lyons was born in Jamaica, New York. He became interested in photography in 1946 while still in high school. In 1947–1948 he studied architectural drafting. He attended Alfred State Technical Institute, Alfred, N.Y., where he majored in business administration, from 1948 to 1950, then changed his studies to philosophy and creative writing. Later that year he enlisted in the U.S. Air Force where he served in photo-intelligence and as a staff newswriter and public relations photographer until 1954. Lyons resumed his studies at Alfred University and worked as a freelance photographer. He received a B.A. in 1957 and began his long association with George Eastman House.

In the next decade Lyons worked at Eastman House as Director of Information, Assistant Editor of *Image* magazine, Editor of Publications, Assistant Director, Director of the Office of Extension Activities, and Associate Director and Curator of Photography.

He organized and published catalog essays on many significant exhibitions including *Seven Contemporary Photographers*, a traveling exhibition (1959); *Masterpieces of Photography* for the American Federation of the Arts (1961); *Photography 1840–1915* for the AFA (1962); *Spectrum* for AFA (1963); *Contemporary Photographers from the George Eastman House Collection 1900–1964* for the New York World's Fair (1964); *Aaron Siskind, Photographer*, a

retrospective (1965); *Toward a Social Landscape* (1966); *Contemporary Photography Since 1950* for the New York State Council on the Arts (1967); *Photography in the Twentieth Century* for the National Gallery of Canada (1967); *Persistence of Vision* (1967); and *Vision and Expression* (1969).

In 1966 Lyons became the editor of the "Contemporary Photographers Series" for Horizon Press and the "Modern Photography Series" for Prentice-Hall Publishers. He left George Eastman House in 1969 to found and direct the Photographic Studio Workshop (later Visual Studies Workshop). He has organized traveling exhibitions for the VSW on Ken Josephson, Les Krims, Ralph Eugene Meatyard, Tony Ray-Jones, Todd Walker, and many more. He became a trustee of the Center of the Eye, Aspen, Colorado, and was appointed full Professor at the State University of New York, Buffalo, in 1970.

Lyons has been Editor of *Afterimage* since 1972. He has been a member or advisor of numerous organizations including the New York State Foundation for the Arts, the National Endowment for the Arts, the New York State Council on the Arts, and New York Governor Carey's Task Force on the Arts. He has lectured and conducted workshops at most of the country's major universities including Cornell University, Rhode Island School of Design, Art Institute of Chicago, and Cooper Union.

M

Mackie Line

A Mackie line, one type of edge effect in negative development, is a line of unusual contrast along the border between a heavily exposed image area and a less exposed area. Unused developer in the less exposed area diffuses across the border to develop extra density at the edge; simultaneously, development byproducts that have a restraining effect diffuse in the other direction to reduce the amount of density produced on the less exposed side of the border. The result in a print is heightened edge brightness in the more exposed area, surrounded by a black or very dark-tone line. A Mackie line forms readily between two clearly defined areas of distinctly different tone when an image is solarized, but it can also occur with normal exposure; it can be emphasized by letting the film lie emulsion-side-up in the developer, with little or no agitation. Some modern film and developer combinations are designed to produce Mackie lines around fine detail as a means of increasing acutance.

See also: ACUTANCE; AGITATION; EDGE EFFECTS; SOLARIZATION.

MacPherson, Robert

Scottish; 1811–1872

Robert MacPherson made his name in photographic circles with poetic architectural views in Italy during the 1850s and 1860s. MacPherson studied medicine in Edinburgh from 1831 to 1835 but did not receive a degree. He moved to Rome, perhaps for reasons of health, about 1840, and enjoyed a brief career as a competent painter and art dealer. He became known as a connoisseur of art, and his home became a center of British literary and artistic life in Rome. Among his close friends was Lord Thackeray.

MacPherson first turned his hand to photography in 1851. Within several years his picturesque views of Roman classical sites were in great demand among tourists.

MacPherson took up the collodio-albumen process in 1856 in order to work with dry glass-plate negatives ranging from 12″ × 16″ to 18″ × 22″ in size. He traveled and photographed in Assisi, Perugia, Gubbio, Tivoli, the Falls of Terni, and other areas of Italy as well as in his beloved Rome. In 1863 he published a guidebook to the Vatican, illustrated with his photographs of over 300 pieces of sculpture.

MacPherson was an active member of the Scottish Photography Society. His work was acclaimed at exhibitions in London and Edinburgh. A major exhibition of over 400 of his photographs was mounted at the London Architectural Photography Association in 1862. By 1863 MacPherson offered for sale over 300 architectural and landscape views. He died in Rome in 1872.

See also: ALINARI; PONTI, CARLO.
Photograph: p. 316.

Macrophotography

Properly defined, macrophotography refers to the making of very large photographs such as photomurals. However, established common usage gives the term the same meaning as photomacrography: the recording of images that on the film are the same size or larger than the subject. With that meaning, macrophotography occupies a middle position in the range of techniques for taking pictures at closer than normal distances. Close-up photography records images that range from about one-tenth the size of the subject (0.1×) to the same or life size (1.0× or 1:1). Macrophotography produces images from 1.0× up to a theoretical limit of about 50×, but there are factors that limit the maximum image size to much less than that in practice. Photomicrography produces images from about 10× up to 200× or so; it is distinguished by the fact that the pictures are taken through a compound microscope, whereas the other two techniques use conventional lenses and accessories. (Microphotography deals with making images at extreme reductions.)

In order to obtain macro-range images the lens must be placed a greater than normal distance from the film; this is usually accomplished by inserting an extension tube or a bellows between the lens and the camera body. The normal distance is the lens position when focused at infinity. When the desired macro-image size is expressed as magnification, M, and the lens focal length as F, the additional extension required beyond the infinity-focus position can be calculated:

$$\text{Extension} = F \times M$$

Thus, for a life-size image (M = 1.0×), extension equal to the focal length of the lens is required. This formula makes practical limitations on magnification readily apparent. To attempt 50× magnification with a 2-inch (50mm) lens would require 100 inches of extension, or some 8⅓ feet; it would also require just over 11 f-stops additional exposure. If an arbitrary but wholly practical limit is taken of 12-inch extension with a 35mm camera, the maximum magnification (calculated M = Ext. ÷ F) is 6× with a 2-inch lens. Shorter focal lengths produce greater maximum magnifications: a 1-inch (25mm) lens yields 12×, and a ⅝-inch (15mm) lens yields approximately 20×.

Ordinary photographic lenses can produce satisfactory results with almost any camera that provides or accepts suitable extension. For example, a lens for a 35mm camera can be used on a 4″ × 5″ view camera. Camera lenses perform best in macrophotography when used in reverse position, with the rear element facing the subject. This is because they are designed for the rear-element distance to be smaller than the front-element distance. In macrophotography the lens-subject distance is equal to or less than the lens-film distance. Enlarger lenses and lenses for 16mm motion-picture cameras are highly corrected and give good results in this application. The highest quality images are produced by special short-focal-length macro lenses.

MacPherson, Robert. "Porta San Lorenzo" (n.d.); albumen. Collection, Museum of Modern Art, New York.

They are corrected for use at very close distances and high magnifications. They have no focusing adjustment, so they must be used with a bellows. (So-called macro-focusing lenses for normal and close-up use are misnamed and do not produce exceptional results in the true macro range.)

Four operating factors are of special importance in macrophotography: rigidity; focusing and depth of field; lighting; and exposure.

Any slight vibration of the camera or the subject will be magnified to the same degree as the image. The camera and bellows in particular must be rigidly supported; often a supplementary flat bed of wood is constructed to support the camera and extensions. A cable release avoids vibration from direct finger pressure on the shutter control; a reflex-viewing mirror should be released well before the shutter is activated, if possible. Outdoors the camera and subject must be protected from air currents.

Focusing requires through-the-lens viewing, as provided by a single-lens reflex camera or a view camera. The extreme lens extension makes the viewing image very dim; a fine-texture viewing screen and a magnifier are very helpful in seeing focus accurately. Once the extension required for a desired magnification has been established, it is easiest to focus by moving the subject or by moving the entire camera-lens assembly as a whole. Moving only the lens changes the magnification and often requires major repositioning of the other elements. At high magnifications depth of field is minimal, often no more than a few sixteenths or thirty-seconds of an inch. This is an unavoidable condition. It is not practical to close the lens to a very small f-stop because that increases the significant problem of exposure compensation, and because diffraction can actually degrade rather than improve sharpness. Camera and enlarging lenses generally produce their best overall sharpness at a middle aperture; true macro lenses are corrected for maximum sharpness at their largest apertures.

Ordinary photographic lighting instruments are too broad for most macrophotography, and existing light is almost always too dim. Suitable light sources include small-reflector electronic flash units and bare-bulb units; an electronic flash ring light that encircles the lens; high-intensity, miniature reading lamps; and light sources designed for use with microscopes. Lighting is often difficult to position because the frontal working distance (lens-subject distance) is so slight. Using a lens of greater focal length will provide more working room at a given magnification, but it will also require increased extension. Mirrors and reflectors are important lighting aids. The heat produced by continuous-light sources used at close distances may present a danger for the subject.

Extreme lens extension reduces the image brightness in the camera and requires significant exposure compensation. A through-the-lens meter reading will accurately indicate the required exposure in most cases. The exposure indicated by an incident-light reading at the subject (if it is possible to get a meter into position) must be adjusted. The exposure increase factor (E_I) can be calculated from the magnification, or from the lens-film distance (v) and the lens focal length (F) as follows:

$$E_I = (M + 1)^2$$
$$E_I = (v \div F)^2$$

The exposure time must be multiplied by this factor, or the lens aperture opened an equivalent number of f-stops. Additional compensation will probably be required for reciprocity effect. With some lenses the first formula may have to be adjusted for pupil magnification, as explained in the entry on magnification. In the second formula, v is measured from the rear nodal point of the lens as explained in the entry on optics.
See also: BELLOWS EXTENSION FACTOR; CLOSE-UP PHOTOGRAPHY; DIFFRACTION; MAGNIFICATION; MICROPHOTOGRAPHY; OPTICS; PHOTOMICROGRAPHY; RECIPROCITY; SCALE.

Maddox, Richard Leach
English; 1816–1902
R. L. Maddox was the inventor of the first practical formula for a gelatin-silver-halide emulsion. A physician and avid amateur photographer, Maddox wanted to be free of the equipment and cumbersome procedures of the wet plate process; equally important, he wanted to find a substitute for collodion because the alcohol and ether fumes it gave off seriously aggravated a chronic illness he had. As early as 1847 others had experimented with sensitized gelatin as a coating for glass plates, but they found it difficult to keep the gelatin from dissolving during processing, or to produce an emulsion that was not several times less sensitive than existing materials. Maddox published a brief description of his emulsion, which had about the same speed as collodion wet plates, in 1871; he pointed out that much improvement on his idea could be made, and left the formula without restrictions so that others would be free to experiment.

In 1873 John Burgess marketed the first prepared liquid gelatin emulsion with which photographers could coat their own plates, and a few months later he offered prepared gelatin dry plates, the first of their kind. Neither product was commercially successful, but a dried, prepared emulsion called *pellicle*, produced by Richard Kennett in 1874, was immediately successful, largely because he inadvertently had found a way (high-temperature "ripening") to significantly increase the speed of the emulsion during manufacture. Photographers dissolved the pellicle, which kept indefinitely in a dry state, in water and coated their own plates ahead of time as needed. Kennett also offered prepared dry plates, but large-scale manufacture of such plates did not begin until 1876 in England. By that time Maddox's original formula had been extensively revised and improved.
See also: DRY PLATES; EMULSION; GELATIN.

Magic Lantern
In the 19th c. transparency (slide) projectors were popularly called magic lanterns. Hand-painted glass slides were used before the invention of photography, but were replaced first by albumen and then collodion glass plates, which often were also hand-colored before being varnished for protection. Light sources were variously a built-in kerosene or illuminating-gas lamp, acetylene, limelight, or arc light, depending on the size of the lantern and the facilities where it was used. Magic lanterns ranged from toys to powerful theater projectors; those that were not toys used 3¼″ × 4¼″ or 4″ × 5″ glass plates. Magic lantern presentations were extremely popular features of community and church meetings, lectures, Chautauqua programs, and similar functions. Various adaptations of the magic lantern with shutters and rapid image changing, such as the zoopraxiscope, provided audiences late in the 19th c. with the world's first projected motion pictures.
See also: HYALOTYPE; ZOOPRAXISCOPE.

Magnetic Image Recording
Visual images can be recorded on a magnetically manipulable material in much the same way that audio is recorded. The fundamental principle of such recording is the fact that every electrical field has an accompanying magnetic field. When a sound or an image is converted into a varying electrical signal, the magnetic field varies in a corresponding manner. Recording is accomplished by applying the electrical signal to an electromagnetic "head." In most equipment the head is stationary and the recording material (plastic tape with a surface coating of metallic oxide particles) moves past at a constant speed. Alternatively, the head moves across a revolving coated disk in a manner similar to direct-disk phonograph recording. The varying magnetic field produced by the recording head arranges the metallic particles in the coating in a unique pattern. During playback, the recorded pattern induces variations in the weak magnetic field around a pickup head. These variations are converted to an electrical signal that is amplified and used to reproduce the original image. The greatest fidelity can be achieved by converting an image to digital signals and recording these on the magnetic medium. This system is now used in audio magnetic recording; its potential in video recording is just being explored.

At the present time, all practical magnetic image recording and playback involves a moving tape or a scanning signal that moves across the image area, no matter whether the image involves a moving or a still subject. A charge-coupled device consisting of a mosaic of photosensitive solid-state elements can translate a still image into a corresponding fixed magnetic pattern, but pickup and playback problems have not been solved. It is likely that this basic principle will be developed first for applications such as snapshots. Whether it has potential for high-quality images or sophisticated applications has not been determined. A drawback of magnetically recorded images is their susceptibility to distortion or destruction by accidental exposure to random external magnetic fields. This has not been a major problem in the field of audio recordings, but

it severely limits the use of the medium for safe long-term preservation of the recorded information.
See also: DIGITAL IMAGES.

Magnification

Magnification is the ratio between the size of an object in its image on film and its actual physical size, expressed *image: object*, or I/0. When values are given, the smaller of the two is made equal to 1. In most photographs the image is smaller than the object, so the ratio or fraction takes the form of, say, 1:5 or 1/5. If the division is carried through it is common to add a multiplication sign to indicate that the answer is an expression of scale, not an actual measurement: $1/5 = 0.2\times$. A magnification or scale of less than 1 is in fact an optical reduction; at 1:1 ($1\times$) reproduction is exactly life-size; a scale greater than 1 (e.g., 3:1 or $3\times$) is a true magnification and the image is in the realm of macrophotography or, at about $20\times$ and larger, photomicrography.

With a view camera it is possible to measure the image size of a subject dimension on the viewing screen, or the image of a reference scale such as a card with a one-inch line placed temporarily at the subject position. Then, *magnification = image measurement ÷ object (or scale) dimension*. With a small-format camera one dimension of the viewing screen can be taken as the image size, and the visible amount of a ruler placed at the subject, as the object size. For example, the short dimension of a 35mm camera screen is 1 in.; if 2 in. of the ruler can be seen across this dimension, the magnification is $1 \div 2 = 0.5\times$.

Magnification can also be determined from the lens-to-film and lens-to-subject distances (image distance and object distance, respectively) and the lens focal length. The image and object distances can be measured from the diaphragm of normal-focal-length and symmetrical-design lenses, or from a position halfway between the nodal points of wide-angle and telephoto-design lenses. The methods of calculating magnification are:

(1) Image distance ÷ Object distance
(2) (Image distance − Focal length) ÷ Focal length
(3) Focal length ÷ (Object distance − Focal length)

Method (1) is more accurate than the others for wide-angle and telephoto lenses.

A magnification (M) greater than 1:3 ($0.3\times$) may need exposure compensation unless a meter reading is taken through the camera lens. The required exposure increase factor equals $(M + 1)^2$. If the pupil magnification (P) of the lens is outside the range of 0.9 to 1.2, it must be taken into account. For a lens used in normal position, the exposure-increase factor equals $[(M \div P) + 1]^2$. When a lens is used in reversed position for increased close-up sharpness, the calculation is $[(M \times P) + 1]^2$.

In an enlarged print, the final scale of the image is equal to the magnification on the negative multiplied by the degree of enlargement. For example, a $0.25\times$ (1:4) image enlarged ten times has a print scale of $0.25 \times 10 = 2.5\times$.
See also: MACROPHOTOGRAPHY; OPTICS; PHOTOMICROGRAPHY; PUPIL MAGNIFICATION; REDUCTION, OPTICAL; SCALE.

Magnum Photos

The photographic agency Magnum Photos was founded in Paris in 1946 by Henri Cartier-Bresson, Robert Capa, David ("Chim") Seymour, George Rod-Rodger and Bill Vandivert; a New York office was opened the following year. Magnum became the preeminent photographic agency, for the quality of its members' work was unequaled. It was the first cooperative photo agency. The working photographers who comprised the membership chose the editors and staff and set policy on how work would be represented and sold. They shared the agency's profits in proportion to the contributions their work made. Magnum's membership has included a significant number of the leading photojournalists of the past three decades. Today, the organizational scheme is somewhat modified, and the work of some younger photographers—Magnum associates—is represented on a commission basis.

Mannes, Leopold Damrosch

American; 1899–1964
Leopold Mannes and Leopold Godowsky were co-inventors of Kodachrome film and processing. Mannes's training at Harvard was in musicology and physics, and he taught music composition and theory in New York City in the 1920s while doing fundamental research and obtaining basic patents in color processes with Godowsky. In 1930 they joined the Kodak Research Laboratories in Rochester, New York, to concentrate on developing practical monopack color materials and processes. Mannes left Kodak in 1939 to become co-director, and later president, of the Mannes College of Music, founded in 1916 by his parents. He rejoined Kodak for research work during World War II, but returned to the College afterward.
See also: COLOR PHOTOGRAPHY—HISTORY; GODOWSKY, LEOPOLD; KODACHROME.

Man Ray

See: RAY, MAN.

Mantz, Werner

German; 1901–1983
A masterful photographer of architecture, Werner Mantz devoted his talents to his subject and the needs of his clients, refusing to claim credit for interpretation or to indulge in overt self-expression. "Sun and clouds often make more of the picture than I do" was more than a modest admission, it was the foundation of his approach to the medium. Mantz despised every form of photography that claimed to produce its own artistic reality independent of the inherent qualities of the subject itself. His main goal was to produce perfect documents that satisfied the leading architects who employed his services. The clarity with which he perceived the essential characteristics of buildings, and the precision with which he recorded them, raised what were intended as functional photographs to the level of art.

Born in Cologne, Mantz bought his first camera, a Kodak Brownie, at the age of 14. In the next five years he used it and more sophisticated successors to enthusiastically explore the old sections of Cologne and the surrounding region. During this period he came to realize that architecture in all its variety was a subject of ever-increasing fascination for him. In 1920–1921 he studied photography at the Bavarian Educational and Research Institute in Munich, and a year later established himself as a freelance photographer at his parents' home in Cologne. He obtained various assignments to reproduce works of art and to make portraits of local prominent persons.

Mantz's first major architectural assignment came in 1927 when Cologne's leading architect, Wilhelm Riphahn, commissioned him to photograph the newly built suburbs of the city. The photographs he produced were the foundation of his professional success. Other assignments followed throughout Europe, but his most famous works were produced in a series of commissions from Riphahn.

In 1932 Mantz had his first exhibition at the Museum for Decorative Art in Cologne. He maintained a studio there, but in the same year moved to nearby Maastricht, The Netherlands, where he opened a second studio. In 1937–1938 he

Mantz, Werner. Untitled (n.d.). Sotheby, New York.

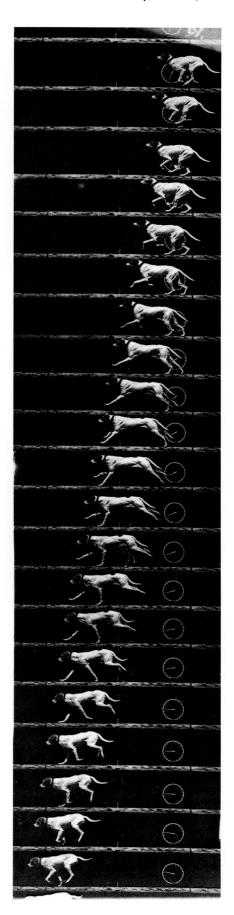

worked for the state mines of the province of Limburg and created a second important body of work of industrial architecture and landscapes. The Cologne studio was closed in 1938 and Mantz remained in Holland. He had begun "spontaneous" portraiture of children with the opening of the Maastricht studio, and was successful from the beginning. He continued with portraiture in Holland after World War II until his retirement in 1971.

Marey, Etienne Jules

French; 1830–1904

A physiologist, Marey became fascinated with the problem of analyzing how insects, birds, animals, and humans move. He created several methods of obtaining time and motion recordings by means of mechanical or pneumatic devices attached directly to the subject that activated a pen resting on a band of moving paper. In 1881 Marey was host in Paris to Eadweard Muybridge, whose still photographs and demonstrations with the zoopraxiscope convinced Marey of the value of photography for his work. He invented a number of repeating-shutter cameras, most of which recorded a series of images on a single plate, allowing the flow of the movement to be analyzed. His various devices were the foundation of a number of motion-picture, slow-motion, and high-speed cameras and projectors developed and commercially exploited by others. His sequence pictures were at least as valu-

Marey, Etienne-Jules. "Chrono Photography," Marey's first (late 19th c.). Courtesy David Eisendrath.

able, and as influential, as those of Muybridge in establishing the modern techniques of physiological movement analysis. They had even wider impact, serving as the impulse for works of art such as Marcel Duchamp's famous cubist-futurist painting of 1912, "Nude Descending a Staircase." The Marey Institute, founded in Paris a few years before his death, carried Marey's work forward, particularly with early developments in high-speed photography under the direction of Dr. Lucien Bull.

See also: GUN CAMERA; MOTION STUDY AND ANALYSIS; MUYBRIDGE, EADWEARD; HIGH-SPEED PHOTOGRAPHY; SLOW MOTION PHOTOGRAPHY; SEQUENCE PHOTOGRAPHY; ZOOPRAXISCOPE.

Martinez, Romeo E.

Mexican; 1912–

Romeo Martinez was a vital influence on the development of contemporary photography, particularly as editor-in-chief from 1950 to 1968 of *Camera* magazine, an international journal published in Switzerland by C.J. Bucher in French, German, and English editions. In 1933, Martinez began working in illustrated journalism and was soon contributing to *Le Monde Illustré, Vu,* and *Regards.* He was quick to recognize the potential of photojournalism as a force of communication and information. He had met Henri Cartier-Bresson and Robert Capa during the Spanish Civil War and through these relationships, was instrumental in promoting the Magnum photo agency.

Throughout his years at *Camera,* Martinez was, for the most part, the sole contributor of articles and criticism. The reputation he gained at *Camera,* and contacts established by extensive travel, enabled him to publish the work of an exceptionally wide range of photographers. Quality was his standard. He recognized no limitation in terms of content, age, or nationality. His understanding of the photographic medium and his passionate interest in the work and the lives of photographers earned him their friendship and confidence. The magazine was an early showcase for the work of such photographers as Berenice Abbott, Bill Brandt, Robert Doisneau, Elliott Erwitt, Florence Henri, André Kertész, William Klein, and Marc Riboud.

After collaborating in the 1948/1949 *Exposition Internationale de Photographie* in Lucerne, Martinez founded and directed, from 1957 to 1965, the Venice *Mostra Biennale Fotografiche.* The photo-archive at the Bibliothèque Publique d'Information was begun at his instigation. In 1971, Martinez was made a consultant at Beaubourg. He is a member of the Council of Administrators of the Société Française de la Photographie, the Salon de la Photo, and Photokina and an associate of the Deutsche Gesellschaft für Photographie.

More recently Martinez has published a monograph on Eugène Atget and curated the series *Bibliothek der Photographie* (English: *Photography: Men and Movements*). Recently he has edited a series of about 70 monographs on great photographers, published by Editore Fabri, Milan, in Italian. The series will soon be published in other languages as well.

Marville, Charles

French; 1816–1879

Charles Marville was a prolific early French photographer who documented the architecture of Paris before the radical changes made by Napoleon III and Baron Haussmann. He was known as the first official photographer of the city of Paris.

Little is known of Marville's life. He was born in Paris and worked as a painter, engraver, and illustrator in the 1840s before learning the rudiments of photography around 1850. His first landscapes and architectural photographs appeared in 1851 in the albums published by Blanquart-Evrard. Marville was then 35.

For nearly 20 years, beginning in 1852, Marville methodically documented the old streets, architectural monuments, and parks of Paris. He photographed the old structures, their demolitions, and the new constructions. In addition to his Paris work, Marville traveled and photographed in Algeria, the Rhineland, and throughout France, specializing in country scenes and landscapes. In 1856 he was one of three photographers to document the baptism of the Prince Imperial at Notre Dame Cathedral. For many years he was the official photographer of works of art for the Louvre.

During his career Marville worked with calotype and collodion processes and salt and albumen printing techniques. He also made several technical innovations, including a portable negative-holder that allowed photographers to take several pictures in succession, and a technique for photography on cloth. In order to emphasize the textures of the streets and buildings he often deliberately photographed in the rain.

Marville's work was consistently praised for its precision and balance. Nadar wrote, "Only Marville (a painter yet!), with the remarkable photographs he did for the Paris Archives, could be considered their [the Bisson brothers] equal."

Marville operated several Paris studios during his career. He exhibited regularly but was not an active member of the French photographic societies. His work was included in the Paris Universal Exhibitions of 1867 and 1878, and in exhibitions in London (1862) and Vienna (1873). He was awarded a medal at the London exhibition and received the Grande Médaille d'Or of Italy.

Marville died in Paris in 1879, leaving a large collection of his photographs to various Paris institutions.

Masking

Masking is the technique of combining an auxiliary copy of an image with the original negative or positive transparency in order to adjust contrast and tone or color rendition in a print, duplicate, or reproduction. A mask is a same-size, low-contrast copy on film. It may be either a black-and-white silver image or a dye image, and it usually is slightly unsharp. The unsharpness makes registration with the original easier, and

Image Enhancement. NASA, "Rings of Saturn" (1981). Courtesy NASA.

Impressionistic Photography. Edward Alenius, "Colorful Roses" (n.d.); multiple gum print. Smithsonian Institution.

Industrial Photography. Dick Luria, Untitled (1981). © Dick Luria.

Industrial Photography. Allan Weitz, "Hess Refinery" (1979). © Allan Weitz.

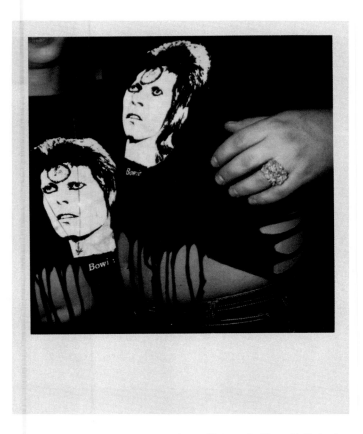

Instant Photography. Sharon Smith, two images from "New York Night Life" series (1980). © Sharon Smith.

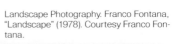

Kror e, Hermann. "Höhnstein" (n.d.). Courtesy Agfa Historama Museum.

Landscape Photography. Franco Fontana, "Landscape" (1978). Courtesy Franco Fontana.

Landscape Photography. Joel Sternfeld, "Near Lake Powell, Arizona" (1979). © Joel Sternfeld; courtesy Daniel Wolf, Inc., New York.

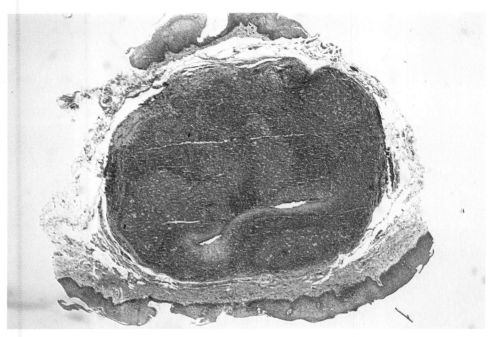

Medical Photography. Leonard Lessen, "Lymphoid epithelial cyst," 8.5 × original magnification. Courtesy Leonard Lessen.

Medical Photography. Jonathan Goell, Untitled (1983). These Thallium-201 images, taken before and after exercise, may warn of future cardiovascular disorders. © Jonathan Goell.

Meyerowitz, Joel. "Red Interior. Provincetown" (1977) © Joel Meyerowitz.

actually improves sharpness in the final image by emphasizing edge contrast. A mask functions by adding density to a particular segment of the image-density range, usually either the highlights or the shadows; full-range, equal-density masks and middletone masks are less commonly used. A mask may be either negative or positive to match or oppose the original image densities as required. Adding a negative highlight mask—one with only highlight densities—to a negative original when making a print increases overall contrast because highlight exposure is blocked more than when only the original negative is used. Adding a negative shadow mask to a negative original can lessen overall contrast by holding back exposure so that those areas do not print so darkly. More importantly, it may improve dark area visibility with an exposure that prints middletones and highlights properly, by preventing shadow areas from being so heavily exposed that they merge in featureless black. A negative-positive mask-original combination reduces contrast because the densities in the affected area work in opposition to each other. A common application of this technique is in making reversal prints or direct duplicates from a color transparency. When a negative highlight mask is registered with the positive transparency, exposing light is held back in those areas. That makes it possible to give full exposure for the middletones and shadows without loss of color saturation or detail in the highlights. Masking is widely used to adjust contrast and color balance in making separation negatives and positives for photomechanical reproduction. It is also a valuable technique in scientific and technical photography to improve the sharpness and clarity of details in selected areas of an image.

Matte; Matte Box

A matte-surface print or projection screen has a slightly textured surface that diffuses light to a limited degree. A matte screen provides an image of acceptable brightness over the widest seating area for an audience, but the average brightness is lower than that produced by other screen surfaces. A matte surface print avoids glare and fingermarks, and is easy to spot or retouch, but its tonal scale is less than that of a glossy-surface paper. That is because the matte surface scatters light from the bright areas of the image, reducing the amount that is directed to the viewer. Some of the light is scattered into dark tone areas, reducing their effective density. To achieve images of matching contrast, a higher-contrast negative is required to make a print on matte paper than on glossy paper.

The special-effects device called a matte box is placed in front of a camera lens to hold various opaque mattes (or masks) that block portions of the image. The mask may produce a shaped image, such as a heart or a keyhole, or it may be used with a reverse, matching mask to create a composite image. For example, a subject can be shown on both sides of a scene by making a double exposure with masks that block equal but opposite portions of the image. Similarly, a center-insert combined image can be produced by using a mask with an opaque center to photograph the background or surrounding image, and a mask with a clear center that blocks off the outer area for the second (insert) exposure. Most matte boxes also accept filters and other special-effect devices, which may be used individually or in combination with masks.
See also: COMBINATION IMAGES; SCREENS, PROJECTION; SPECIAL EFFECTS.

Maxwell, James Clerk

Scottish; 1831–1879
Maxwell's brilliant career included formulation of the laws of electromagnetic energy and the kinetic theory of gases, investigations of the movements of the rings of Saturn, fundamental discoveries as to the nature of light and color, and creation of the Cavendish Laboratory at Cambridge in 1871. The importance to modern science of his theoretical work on energy is considered equal to that of Newton and Einstein.

Of particular importance to photography is his work in light and color, which was carried out in the 1850s and 1860s. Working from Faraday's discoveries in electricity and those of Gauss in magnetism, he discovered the interrelationship of the fields of these two kinds of energy. When research confirmed his theory that the combined energy is propagated at the speed of light, he deduced the electromagnetic nature of light waves and showed that light is only a small portion of the entire energy spectrum. His studies of the refraction and reflection of light were expanded upon by von Helmholtz, as were his confirmations of Thomas Young's color theory. Maxwell devised the familiar triangle diagram to illustrate the theory of three-color additive synthesis and created the Maxwell disk—a circle divided into wedge-shaped segments of various colors that blend into a combined color effect when whirled before the eyes because of the persistence of vision.

In 1861 Maxwell produced the first full-color image by photographic means. He had a plaid ribbon photographed separately on black-and-white plates through red, green, and blue filters. Positive transparencies from these plates were projected separately through the same filters. When the images were registered with one another, the picture burst into color. The demonstration before the Royal Society should not have worked, because the collodion emulsion on the plates was not sensitive to red or green. However, the dyes creating these colors in the ribbon also reflected some ultraviolet wavelengths, to which the plates were sensitive, which produced sufficient exposure for the effect to occur.
See also: ADDITIVE COLOR SYNTHESIS; COLOR; COLOR PHOTOGRAPHY—HISTORY; GAUSS, KARL F.; HELMHOLTZ, H. L. F. VON; SPECTRUM; YOUNG, THOMAS.

Mayall, John Jabez Edwin

American; 1810–1901
A lecturer in chemistry in Philadelphia, Mayall opened a daguerreotype studio there in 1842, operating under the name "Professor Highschool." In 1846 he sold out to his partner, Marcus A. Root, and moved to London, where he worked briefly for the leading portraitist, Antoine Claudet. Within a year Mayall opened his own studio in the Strand. His success was immediate; his skill in portraiture was supported by technical excellence and a lively sense of the unusual and interesting. He specialized in full-plate (6½″ × 8½″ [16.7 × 21.9cm]) and larger daguerreotypes, and astonished the public with an exhibition plate measuring 15″ × 24″ (38.5 × 61.5cm). He made story series illustrating sentimental poems, historical themes, and a 10-plate sequence of The Lord's Prayer. He introduced "crayon pictures"—vignette images—to England, and in 1855 he patented the *ivorytype,* a method of printing photographs on artificial ivory. He launched the carte-de-visite craze in England in 1860 with publication of a 14-carte album of the royal family. His individual cartes of Queen Victoria and Prince Albert sold in the tens of thousands in the first year, and he was besieged with customers. His studio, then in Regent Street, produced as many as 500,000 cartes a year, along with stereo views, full-size portraits, landscapes, and illustrative images.

Mayall was active in photographic affairs, helping to establish several organizations. He was also the first to try (unsuccessfully) to obtain recognition

and reward for Frederick Scott Archer, inventor of the collodion process, which every photographer used. In the early 1880s his establishment in Bond Street was one of the first in England to take portraits by electric light. At his death at age 91 he was mayor of Brighton.

See also: ARCHER, FREDERICK SCOTT; CARTE-DE-VISITE; CLAUDET, A. F. J.; CRAYON PICTURES; IVORYTYPE.

Mayer, Grace

American

Grace Mayer was born and educated in Manhattan. In 1931, she became curator of New York iconography at the Museum of the City of New York, where she remained until 1959. She then moved to the Museum of Modern Art, where she continues as curator in the department of photographs.

In her work with New York iconography, Mayer appreciated the value of photographs from a historical standpoint and included them in such early mixed-media exhibitions as Parades and Processions, 1936; The Statue of Liberty, 1936–1937; Dining in Old New York, 1937; and Philip Hone's New York, 1940. Mayer also organized the exhibition of Berenice Abbott's photographs for the WPA-funded project Changing New York, 1937. In 1942 Percy C. Byron donated over 5000 prints and negatives of Byron Company's early New York views to the museum. Recognizing the unique aspect of this archive, Mayer based her book, *Once Upon a City* (New York, 1958), on the Byron Collection. Later the firm of Gottscho-Schleisner donated over 3000 negatives to the Museum of the City of New York following a 1956 exhibition of their architectural photographs. Mayer was also instrumental in acquiring the donation of Jacob Riis's glass plate negatives from Roger William Riis for the museum.

In 1957–1958, Mayer, in conjunction with Edward Steichen, organized the *Photographers Look at New York* exhibition at the Museum of Modern Art. In her work at the Museum Mayer developed a close friendship with Steichen, and in 1961 she organized the retrospective exhibition *Steichen the Photographer.*

From 1962 to 1968, Mayer curated the Edward Steichen Archive for the museum; she is currently writing Steichen's biography.

McCullin, Donald

British; 1935–

Throughout the 1960s and 1970s Donald McCullin made painfully moving images

of chaos and violence, and death and destruction around the world. His photographs, in the tradition of Robert Capa and W. Eugene Smith, are brutally powerful yet compassionate attempts to come to terms with human suffering.

McCullin was born to a working-class family in London, where he studied painting at Hammersmith School of Arts and Crafts from 1948 to 1950 on a Trade Arts Scholarship. Forced to leave school because of the death of his father, McCullin was employed by British Railways and Larkins Cartoon Studios. From 1953 to 1955 he served with the

Royal Air Force in the Middle East and Mediterranean as a photographic assistant in aerial-reconnaissance printing. He then returned to Larkins, where he remained until 1961 when he began work as a freelance photojournalist primarily for *The Observer.* Since 1964 McCullin has been a staff photographer for *The Sunday Times.*

McCullin's first published story (1959) concerned a British youth gang of which he was a member. His breakthrough story as a photojournalist reported on the construction of the Berlin Wall in 1961. Since that time he has

Meatyard, Ralph. Untitled (ca. 1962–65).
Courtesy Madeline and Christopher Meatyard; permanent collection, ICP, New York.

traveled throughout the world photographing major stories in the Congo, Cambodia and Vietnam, Biafra, India and Pakistan, the Sahara, and Northern Ireland. His photographs have been published in most of the world's leading periodicals, including *Time, Life,* and *Der Spiegel.* His book *The Destruction Business* (1971), revised and expanded as *Is Anyone Taking Any Notice?* (1973), is a passionate protest against contemporary acceptance of violence and devastation throughout the world.

McCullin has been a member of Magnum Photo Agency since 1967. He is the recipient of many awards, including the Warsaw Gold Medal for Photography (1964), the World Press Photographers Award (1965), and the Special Achievement Award from the American Society of Magazine Photographers (1974). His work has been included in group shows at Photokina in Cologne, the Israel Museum in Jerusalem, and the Victoria and Albert Museum in London. He has been the subject of one-man shows at the Victoria and Albert Museum and at ICP in New York City.

Meatyard, Ralph Eugene

American; 1925–1972

Ralph Eugene Meatyard spent the last two decades of his life in Lexington, Kentucky, making his living as an optician, photographing mostly on weekends. Yet in the time snatched here and there, he was able to create a large number of haunting, enigmatic images. Meatyard's photographs present a world of somnambulistic mystery, a realm of disquieting intimations. Children appear as masked figures in decrepit rooms, enacting inscrutable dramas or charades. In every image there is something askew. Max Kozloff called Meatyard "a still-life artist whose subjects unaccountably take off in slow, slight ways."

Intriguingly, Meatyard was born in Normal, Illinois. He did not begin to photograph until 1950 when he moved to Kentucky after service in the U.S. Navy, studies at Williams College and Illinois Wesleyan University, and an optician apprenticeship in Chicago. In 1954, he studied with the art historian and photographer Van Deren Coke. In the same year he joined both the Lexington Camera Club and the Photographic Society of America (in whose salon he first exhibited his work). His photographs were shown with those of Ansel Adams, Aaron Siskind, Harry Callahan and other modern masters in an exhibition curated by Coke in 1956. That summer Meatyard attended a photography workshop in Indiana where he worked with Henry Holmes Smith and Minor White. In 1957 Meatyard shared an exhibition with Coke at A Photographer's Gallery in New York City. His first one-man show was held at Tulane University in 1959, the year in which a Meatyard portfolio was published in *Aperture* with an accompanying text by Coke. Meatyard was included by Beaumont Newhall in the "New Talent in Photography U.S.A." section of *Art in America* in 1961. During 1967–1970 he collaborated with the writer Wendell Berry on work which resulted in the book *The Unforeseen Wilderness.* Berry wrote of Meatyard's images: "These pictures invite us to live on the verge of surprise, where fear accompanies delight." It was fitting that some of Meatyard's best work was accompanied by written texts, for he was an avid reader, deeply influenced by modernist literature. The works of Pound, Gertrude Stein, and William Carlos Williams were especially important to him. He was influenced as well by painters such as Cézanne and Ensor.

In 1970 Meatyard learned that he had cancer. He continued to photograph, creating the major series of Lucybelle Crater images based on a story of Gertrude Stein's. He died in Lexington in May, 1972.

Medical Photography

Medical photography comprises a wide range of photographic and quasi-photographic techniques. Medical photographs may be specialized records such as opthalmic images (pictures within the interior of the eye) and records of fiber-optic endoscopy (images produced inside a subject's gastro-intestinal tract). On the other hand, they may be as routine as before-and-after pictures of the removal of a skin lesion, or a copy of an x-ray of a fractured toe. Clinical photography refers principally to pictures made of the body and used for diagnosis, explanation, or evaluation of treatment. Biomedical photographs often employ close-up techniques. Common subjects include bacteriological cultures, gross specimens, and tissue specimens. Certain specialized areas—notably radiography (x-ray photography)—are usually classified separately.

Medical photographs are essentially factual records produced for future reference or comparison. As such, they must be accurate in color and perspective (subject proportions) and as uniformly sharp as possible.

On a relatively small hospital or clinic staff the professional medical photographer is apt to be called upon to cope with an uncommonly wide variety of techniques. Larger facilities may employ specialists, particularly for video, opthalmic, endoscopic, and similar records. Quite often physicians in private practice become quite skilled themselves as photographers for general record purposes.

As with many other specialized branches of photography, the medical photographer must have a summary knowledge of the specialty itself. At the very minimum this includes a working knowledge of common medical terminology, basic anatomy, and fundamental medical procedure. To simplify physician-photographer communication, schematic outlines of the body are sometimes employed. The doctor outlines the parts of the body he wants photographed and adds whatever notes are appropriate.

The photographer also needs to have a general understanding of the subject's condition to be aware of physical limitations and special handling requirements. In clinical photography the subject is first and foremost a patient and a human being, not a condition or an assignment. A camera manner very much akin to the physician's bedside manner often is called for. Clinical photography requires that a release be signed for the protection of both the patient and the institution. Hospitals often include such a document as part of the normal admitting process, especially when surgery is indicated. The photographer must check this before proceeding, because he or she, as well as the institution, may be held legally accountable should this detail be overlooked. There are two general types of releases. The more common type restricts the use of pictures to medical purposes. The other allows for commercial usage, as in the promotion of medicines or drugs.

A major use of photography is in the operating theater. The pictures taken may be external stills, internal stills, or motion pictures. The external still photograph shows what an exposed area was like. For example, before-and-after external pictures may be made of the incised area of a properly sutured wound or pictures may be taken to identify a particular problem. Internal photographs also depict situations and results; they are usually made with the aid of an endoscope. Motion pictures or video record the procedures used. As with all other personnel and equipment, the photographer must be surgically garbed, and all photographic equipment must be sterilized. Because oxygen and other combustible gases are often used during surgery, all equipment—especially flash units and film motor drives—must be tested to ensure that they do not generate electrical sparks.

A surgical photographer is, in effect, part of the operating team and must acquaint himself or herself with the procedure and discuss with the surgeon when pictures are likely to be needed. It is the surgical photographer's responsibility to produce an accurate and graphically clear set of pictures or film.

The type of equipment used in medical photography varies with the application. Frequently 35mm cameras are employed in the operating theater and elsewhere, both because they are convenient and because many accept a large number of accessories. As important is the type of lighting equipment. In surgery electronic flash units are favored because they do not emit a significant amount of heat and can be battery powered. In general, lighting in medical photography should reveal and accurately portray the characteristics of the particular pathology being illustrated. The characteristics of the subject may dictate specialized lighting techniques. For example, lighting may emphasize texture or penetrate a cavity, or even reveal special characteristics by the use of infrared or ultraviolet light sources.

A number of special techniques are often used in medical photography. Some clinical and nearly all biomedical photography is done from at or near the beginning of the close-up range (one-tenth life size) to hundreds of times life size via photomicrography. Gross specimens, either preserved or newly removed, are commonly recorded. The simplest method is to standardize the photographic procedure in a setup similar to a vertical copy stand with the camera mounted above the specimen stage.

Many of the specialized techniques used in medical photography are discussed in the entries listed in the cross-references. Special training programs in medical photography are offered by some large clinics and medical centers or hospitals in major cities and by a number of university medical schools. Manufacturers of specialized equipment such as endoscopes and electron microscopes periodically offer workshops, and seminars are frequently offered by medical photographers, physicians, and manufacturers at medical and scientific conventions.

See also: BIOLOGICAL PHOTOGRAPHY; CLINICAL PHOTOGRAPHY; ENDOSCOPE; ELECTRON MICROSCOPE, MICROGRAPHY; FLUOROGRAPHY; INFRARED PHOTOGRAPHY; MACROPHOTOGRAPHY; PHOTOMICROGRAPHY; ULTRAVIOLET AND FLUORESCENCE PHOTOGRAPHY; X-RAY PHOTOGRAPHY.
Color photograph: p. C-31.

Mees, Charles Edward Kenneth

English; 1882–1960

Mees's career as a scientist and research administrator shaped the scientific understanding and development of photography throughout the first half of the 20th c. His earliest work, in England, built upon the research of Hurter and Driffield, the founders of sensitometry. Together with Samuel E. Sheppard he expanded and extended the field of sensitometry, laying the groundwork for and pointing out the directions in which almost all photographic research and development has proceeded. This culminated in 1907 in the publication of Mees and Sheppard's book *Investigations in the Theory of the Photographic Process*, which immediately became and has remained one of the classic references of photographic science.

Under Mees's scientific direction from 1907–1913, the firm of Wratten and Wainwright became England's leading producer of panchromatic and special-purpose emulsions and filters. Eastman Kodak Co. purchased the firm in 1913 as part of an agreement that brought Mees to the United States to establish the Kodak Research Laboratory in Rochester, New York. Virtually every Kodak product and scientific advance in the following 40 years was the result of Mees's own work or of research he approved and administered with a staff that grew from 20 to more than 1000. He instituted the publication of research bulletins, journals, and practical instruction manuals. In 1942 he published *The Theory of the Photographic Process*, compiled from his own work and that of the leading photographic scientists of the time. Currently in its fourth edition (edited by T. H. James), it is the standard reference in the field.

Mees was also a principal figure in the establishment of the International Museum of Photography at George Eastman House in Rochester and served as the first chairman of the board of the institution.

See also: DRIFFIELD, VERO CHARLES; HURTER, FERDINAND; SENSITOMETRY.

Megascope

The early enlarger introduced by Adolphe Bertsch for making prints from the 2¼-inch-square glass negatives produced by his "automatic" (i.e., fixed-focus) camera was called the megascope. It was a telescoping brass tube with a slot to receive the plate and a lens to focus the projected image. The tube fitted through a hole in a lighttight window shutter and had an adjustable mirror on the outer end to reflect light through the plate. A negative could be projected onto printing paper, but the very slow speed of papers made it more practical to contact print a negative to get a positive image on glass. This was then projected onto a larger glass plate to get an enlarged negative from which the final-size print could be made by contact exposure. The name *megascope* was also applied to early forms of opaque projectors, sometimes called aphengescopes.

Megatype

Originally, the term *megatype* referred to an enlarged image made by the megascope of Adolphe Bertsch; then, by extension, it briefly referred, in European usage, to any enlargement.
See also: MEGASCOPE.

Melainotype

For a short time after their 1857 commercial introduction in the U.S., ferrotypes (tinytypes) were called melainotypes. Apparently this term was also used in Europe to mean ambrotypes as well as ferrotypes. The name reflects the fact that a black background (Greek: *melas* = black) was required for the images to appear positive.
See also: AMBROTYPE; FERROTYPE.

Melanograph

The melanograph was a variant of the ambrotype and ferrotype, in which black paper (Greek: *melas* = black) was used as a support for the collodion emulsion rather than glass or sheet iron. The process was independently invented in the U.S. in 1853 and in England in 1854. The melanograph was also called the atrograph (Latin: *ater* = black).
See also: AMBROTYPE; FERROTYPE.

Meniscus Lens

The meniscus lens is a single-element lens in which both sides are curved in the same direction, but have different radii (i.e., originate from different centers of curvature; a concavo-convex lens). It is the type of lens used in most eyeglasses, and can be either positive (converging) or negative (diverging—thicker at the edges than the center). A meniscus lens is used alone only in the simplest, low-quality cameras. A small-aperture stop can make some correction of its coma and astigmatism, but it possesses other aberrations in a high degree. However, meniscus elements have been used to good effect in some compound lens designs of high quality.
See also: ABERRATIONS OF LENSES; LENSES.

Meter

See: EXPOSURE METERS; METRIC SYSTEM.

Meter Candle

See: LIGHT UNITS.

Metric System

Three units form the basis of the metric system, the system of weights and measures used for all scientific work, and for industrial and domestic purposes throughout the world except in the U.S. and a few technologically undeveloped countries. These units comprise the *MKS System:* the *meter* of length, the *kilogram* of mass (weight), and the *second* of time. Today the units are defined by atomic standards or fundamental properties of a few stable elements. Units in the scientific *Systeme Internationale* (SI units) derive from the MKS system. The earlier *CGS System,* based on the centimeter, gram, and second, has been largely abandoned because, although its units are direct fractions of MKS units, they make measurements too small for practical general use. In the metric system all subdivisions and multiples of length and mass are powers of 10 of the basic units, and units of area and volume are derived from them. Time is similarly subdivided by fractional powers of 10, although longer periods are measured in minutes and hours rather than decimal multiples of the second. Examples of fractional units and multiples include:

millimeter	=	1/1000 (0.001) meter
centimeter	=	1/100 (0.01) meter
kilometer	=	1000 meters
gram	=	1/1000 (0.001) kilogram
are	=	100 square meters
liter	=	volume contained in a cube 1/10 meter on each edge
milliliter	=	1/1000 (0.001) liter

The relative sizes of fractional and multiple units are indicated by a prefix, as shown in the accompanying table. Because all are factors of 10, conversion from one unit to another can be accomplished by shifting the decimal point an appropriate number of places right or left. Calculations with actual measurements are also simplified because of the decimal base of the system. Conversions between the metric and customary U.S. systems are given in the entry on weights and measures.

The metric system was first adopted in France, in 1799, and by most other major countries in the next few decades. It was made a legal alternative system in the U.S. in 1866. In the mid-20th c. congressional action authorized a 10-year changeover period to the metric system in the U.S., but the conversion has not been actively pursued. In part this is because of the enormous investment in stored information (data base) and in-

METRIC (SI) UNIT PREFIXES

Multiples and Fractions			Prefix	Symbol/Abbreviation
1,000,000,000,000	=	10^{12}	tera-	T
1,000,000,000	=	10^{9}	giga-	G
1,000,000	=	10^{6}	mega-	M
1,000	=	10^{3}	kilo-	k
100	=	10^{2}	hecto-	h
10	=	10^{1}	deka-	da
0.1	=	10^{-1}	deci-	d
0.01	=	10^{-2}	centi-	c
0.001	=	10^{-3}	milli-	m
0.000 001	=	10^{-6}	micro-	u
0.000 000 001	=	10^{-9}	nano-*	n
0.000 000 000 001	=	10^{-12}	pico-	p
0.000 000 000 000 001	=	10^{-15}	femto-	f
0.000 000 000 000 000 001	=	10^{-18}	atto-	a

*Formerly *millimicro-*, which is no longer used.

dustrial capacity based on the U.S. customary system. It is also because of psychosocial resistance to change on the part of the general public and institutions such as school systems. The growth of international distribution of manufactured goods is probably the strongest long-term pressure for eventual conversion. The trend is particularly noticeable in the size designations and measurements used for photographic materials and equipment.

See also: WEIGHTS AND MEASURES.

Metzker, Ray

American; 1931–

For the past two decades Ray Metzker has questioned the nature of the photographic image and photographic "reality," experimenting with multiple-image constructions of great technical virtuosity. Disenchanted with the aesthetics of the single image, he has explored the possibilities of juxtaposition, repetition, and superimposition of near-abstract, tonally rich images in large sculptural works. His manipulation of subjects ranging from the urban environment to nudes to architectural details has created striking and baffling graphic images from familiar materials.

Metzker was born and raised in Milwaukee, Wisconsin, and began to photograph at the age of 14. He studied art at Beloit College, where he received a B.F.A. degree in 1953. Metzker worked briefly as an assistant in a commercial and portrait studio before serving in Korea with the United States Army from 1954 to 1956.

Metzker received an M.S. degree in photography from the Institute of Design, Illinois Institute of Technology, where he studied under Harry Callahan, Frederick Sommer, and Aaron Siskind from 1956 to 1959. He has been a freelance photographer since that time. In 1962 Metzker became Instructor of photography at the Philadelphia College of Art, and was named Professor of Photography in 1978. He has also taught at the University of New Mexico in Albuquerque and the Rhode Island School of Design in Providence.

Metzker was the recipient of two Guggenheim Fellowships for Photography in 1966 and 1979 and was awarded a Photography Fellowship from the National Endowment for the Arts in 1974. He has been honored by one-man shows at the Museum of Modern Art in New York City (1967), the Art Institute of Chicago (1959), Picture Gallery in Zurich (1976), ICP in New York City (1978), the Center for Creative Photography in Chicago (1979), and several shows at Light Gallery in New York

City. His photographs have been included in group shows such as *New Photography USA* (1970) and *Mirrors and Windows: American Photography Since 1960* (1978) at the Museum of Modern Art in New York City; *Photography in the Twentieth Century* (1967) at the National Gallery of Canada in Ottawa; and *Seven Contemporary Photographers* (1961) and *Photography and Mid-Century* (1959) at George Eastman House in Rochester, New York. Metzker's recent work includes a series "Pictus Interruptus," in which unidentifiable objects in the foreground obstruct the viewer's reading of the subject.

Meyerowitz, Joel

American; 1938–

Since the late 1970s Joel Meyerowitz has created a significant body of color landscape photographs which explore the delicacies of changing light and atmospheric conditions of particular sites.

Meyerowitz was born in New York City. From 1956 to 1959 he studied painting and medical illustration at Ohio State University in Columbus where he received a B.F.A. degree. In the early 1960s Meyerowitz worked as an advertising art director and designer in New York. He became a photographer in 1962 after working on an advertising

Michals, Duane. "Magritte" (1965). Courtesy Duane Michals.

assignment with Robert Frank. Meyerowitz's early work was in black-and-white street photography, but he soon became one of the pioneers of artistic color street photography. Since 1976 he has worked producing color landscapes with large-format cameras. His book of photographs of Cape Cod, entitled *Cape Light* (1978), was published to great acclaim and was followed by *St. Louis and the Arch* (1981). His recent work includes photographs of redheads and other portraiture, as well as the book *Wildflowers* (1983).

Meyerowitz was Adjunct Professor of Photography at Cooper Union in New York City from 1971 to 1979. He has been Associate Professor of Photography at Princeton University in New Jersey since 1977.

Meyerowitz was named Photographer of the Year by the Friends of Photography, Carmel, California, in 1981. He has been the recipient of numerous grants, including two Guggenheim Fellowships (1970 and 1978), a New York State Council on the Arts C.A.P.S. grant (1976), and grants from the National Endowment for the Arts and the National Endowment for the Humanities (1978). His work has been included in group shows at the Museum of Modern Art in New York City, the Corcoran Gallery in Washington, D.C., and ICP in New York City. He has been honored with solo exhibitions at George Eastman House in Rochester, New York, the Museum of Fine Arts in Boston, the Museum of Modern Art, the Akron Art Institute in Ohio, and the Witkin Gallery in New York City.

Color photograph: p. C-32.

Michals, Duane

American; 1932–

Duane Michals has been successful as a commercial photographer and artist of personal vision for many years. He became known primarily for his tightly structured sequences of black-and-white photographs depicting altered realities and mysterious dramas. These works have been influential upon younger photographers since the late 1960s.

Michals was born in McKeesport, Pennyslvania, and had early interests in drawing and poetry. He studied at the Carnegie Institute in Pittsburgh, the University of Denver (where he recieved a B.A.), and Parsons School of Design, and was a lieutenant in the U.S. Army before becoming an art director for *Dance Magazine* and *Time*.

He did not begin to photograph until 1958, while visiting the Soviet Union as a tourist. Among his first important works was a series of unpeopled urban environments (hallways, laundromats, restaurants and lobbies), influenced by Atget, called "Empty New York." His first major exhibition was *Toward a Social Landscape* in which his work was shown with that of other influential photographers of the 1960s and 1970s: Lee Friedlander, Garry Winogrand, Bruce Davidson, and Danny Lyon.

Michals's later, better-known works have been influenced by Zen Buddhism and in particular by the Surrealist art of René Magritte, whom Michals came to know very well and to photograph many times. Michals has said, "Magritte was the first person who graphically challenged my preconceived notions about reality . . . . What I look for in my own work and in other people's is not something aesthetically satisfying but something to jar my sensibilities."

Michals's images consist of erotic, humorous, sometimes violent personal fantasies which occur in ordinary settings. They are staged events documentarily viewed and recorded in sequences, like the key frames in a motion picture. The simplest means are employed in the photography of each *mise-en-scène;* he uses natural light and no extraordinary technical equipment. Mundane and fantastic elements have equal weight. Blurred and superimposed images are regularly used to suggest the spiritual, ghostly quality of the stories and characters and to emphasize the importance of the unseen.

In 1974 Michals began to caption sequences in longhand, making the literary narrative elements of his work explicit. Recent work has involved his painting directly on areas of the photographic print.

Michals's photographs have been seen in numerous shows and in books, where his sequences may perhaps be seen to best advantage. He was the subject of a one-man show at the Museum of Modern Art, New York, in 1970 and has exhibited at many galleries including Light Gallery and Sidney Janis Gallery.

Microfiche

A microfiche is a sheet of film containing microphotographic transparency images in a standard arrangement of columns and rows. A microfiche is one of the most convenient means of storing and handling large numbers of related images—e.g., pages of documents—in permanent, non-magnetic form. When inserted into a viewer-reader, a microfiche need be shifted only a few inches vertically or horizontally to locate any one of up to 300 black-and-white or 98 full-color images, depending on the format used. A strip of 35mm or 16mm film containing the same images cannot be advanced or rewound as quickly or with as little physical handling. Microfiche are readily duplicated in large numbers by contact printing from a master negative. Their flat, rectangular shapes are easy to file, enclose in notebooks, and mail. The most common standard size of microfiche is 105 × 148mm (approximately 4″ × 6″), but both larger and smaller sizes are used and reduction ratios vary according to the application. Standard reductions are 24 and 48 times smaller than the original. Ultramicrofiche equipment uses reductions of 150–200 times, or more, to record up to 3200 black-and-white images on a standard 4″ × 6″ film, or 1000 images on a 3″ × 5″ film. Higher storage densities can be obtained with computer-controlled camera and retrieval systems.

See also: MICROPHOTOGRAPHY.

Microphotography

Microphotography, or microfilming, consists of making reduced-size images for purposes of information storage, photofabrication, and similar applications. (Photomicrography deals with magnified images obtained by means of a microscope.) In almost all applications, the original material is two-dimensional (e.g., documents, drawings, diagrams, photographs) of any size; the micrographic image may be from ten to several thousand times smaller.

Some of the first experimental microphotographs were made in 1853 by J.B. Dancer. Early practical applications included the Pigeon Post during the siege of Paris in 1870, and mid-19th c. novelty photo-jewelry items called Stanhopes. The modern micrographics industry began early in the 20th c. and has grown steadily. The major microforms used for information storage and retrieval are: *microfilms*, strips of 35mm or 16mm film carrying frame-by-frame microimages, much like a motion-picture film; *microfiche,* film transparencies in standard sizes from about 3″ × 5″ to 4″ × 6″ (7.6 × 12.7cm to 10 × 15cm), bearing an array of negative or positive images in a pattern of rows and columns; and *microcards,* positive images on opaque sheets in the same sizes and arrangements as microfiche.

Originally, only very high-contrast black-and-white film had sufficiently fine grain and high resolving power to record microphotographs. Today, suitable panchromatic and color films are available, extending the range of micrographics to continuous-tone and color original material. Large-scale duplication of micrographic originals is usually accomplished with non-silver rapid access diazo or vesicular materials. These provide extremely high resolution at costs three to ten times less than equivalent silver-emulsion duplicating films. Perhaps the most unusual non-silver material used for microphotography is photochromic glass. Under stringently controlled conditions of temperature and exposing radiation (commonly ultraviolet at the imaging stage, although infrared or visible wavelengths may be used), extremely high resolution is achieved as the glass changes color to record an image. The process can be reversed to permit corrections if required; a silver-film copy is made for printing purposes. Although the photochromic process was an important step in the de-velopment of ultra-fiche—permitting reductions of 200× as early as 1962—it is economocially suitable only for very large scale applications such as found in government, the military, and major industries.

In conventional microfilming, optical image reduction is achieved with ultra-high quality apochromatic lenses and planetary or rotary cameras. A planetary camera is similar to a copy stand, and accepts hand-fed material on a sheet-by-sheet basis. In a rotary camera, the film and the original material flows through in continuous movement at a recording rate of up to several thousand images per hour. Microfiche and microcards take more time than microfilms because the film must be shifted repeatedly to register the images in the required pattern. In some cases extreme reductions are obtained by first making an image at an intermediate degree of reduction, then re-imaging that image to the final size. Non-optical reduction is achieved by direct exposure using a laser or electron beam guided by signals derived from photoscanning of the original material. This method is used for film storage of digital data, and in photofabrication of ultraminiature parts such as integrated circuits and computer chips. Laser beams are also used to record holographic and videodisc microimages. The degree of reduction possible with videodiscs is limited by the relatively low resolving power of television screens on which playback must be displayed. High-resolution television, now under development, offers greatly increased potential for videodisc micrographics.

See also: DANCER, J.B.; DIAZO; DIGITAL IMAGES; MICROFICHE; PIGEON POST; PHOTOFABRICATION; SCANNER, FLYING SPOT; STANHOPE; VESICULAR MATERIALS.

Microscope

See: ELECTRON MICROGRAPHY; PHOTO-MICROGRAPHY; SOLAR MICROSCOPE.

Mili, Gjon

American; 1904–1984

Trained as an engineer and self-taught in photography, Gjon Mili was the first to use electronic flash and stroboscopic light to create photographs that had more than scientific interest. Since the late 1930s his pictures of dance, athletics, and musical and theatrical performances have astonished and delighted millions of viewers, revealing the beautiful intricacy and graceful flow of movement too rapid or too complex for the eye to discern. His portraits of artists, musi-cians, and other notables are less visually spectacular, but equally masterful.

Born in Albania in 1904, Mili emigrated to the United States at the age of 19. He took a degree in electrical engineering at the Massachusetts Institute of Technology, where he came to know Harold Edgerton, developer of the gas discharge (electronic flash) tube and the modern stroboscope. For 10 years, until 1938, Mili worked for Westinghouse Electric Company as a lighting research engineer. There he developed improved tungsten filament designs for projection and photographic lamps, and lighting equipment for color photography. Photographic experimentation in conjunction with Edgerton during these years produced a number of stunning stop-action and stroboscopic images that brought him to the attention of the editors of the fledgling *Life* magazine.

In 1939 Mili became a freelance photographer working for *Life*. In the course of more than four decades literally thousands of his pictures were published. At first the images were spectacular action images, including a photographic tour de force: a re-creation of Marcel Duchamps's painting *Nude Descending a Staircase*, which had been inspired by the late 19th c. action-sequence photographs of E. J. Marey. Later for *Life* he photographed Picasso, Pablo Casals, Sean O'Casey, Nazi war criminal Adolf Eichmann, Duke Ellington, Billie Holiday, and countless athletes, dancers, and world celebrities. From the mid-1940s on Mili also made films of artists (Raoul Dufy, Picasso, Salvador Dali), musicians (Ellington, Casals, Dave Brubeck), photographers (Alfred Eisenstaedt, Henri Cartier-Bresson), and others.

Late in his career Mili produced outstanding interpretive photographs of sculpture and architecture and a sensitive investigation of his family heritage. A major retrospective of his work in 1980 at the International Center of Photography in New York City revealed the range of his achievement and emphasized the fact that he is the one who has formed our contemporary visual understanding of movement, both in the direct example of his pictures and in the influence his work has had on all action photographers who have come after him. His book *Photographs and Recollections* (1980) was a summary of his fifty years of work in photography.

Mired

Mired is the acronym for *micro-* (i.e., one-millionth) *reciprocal degree,* a unit of value derived from the color tempera-

Mili, Gjon. "Nude Descending Staircase"
(1942). Courtesy Gjon Mili.

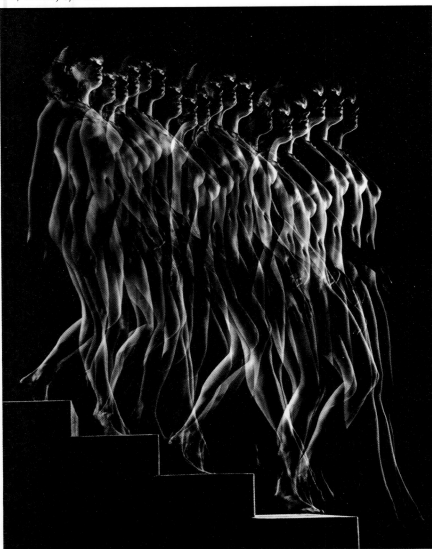

by some manufacturers of filters and color temperature meters, largely because it reduces the ratings to one- and two-digit numbers, which are easier to fit on dials, charts, and calculators. The decamired unit is ten times larger than the mired; that is:

$$DMV = MV \div 10$$

See also: COLOR BALANCE; COLOR TEMPERATURE.

Mirror

The image formed by a plane (flat-surface) mirror is a virtual image, one that cannot be cast on a screen but that must be focused by a lens—e.g., the eye or a camera—to be seen. The angle at which the image is reflected is equal to the angle of incidence of light rays from the subject on the mirror surface. The subject in the mirror image is reversed left-for-right and appears to be located behind the mirror a distance equal to the actual subject distance in front of the mirror. To focus the mirror image most accurately, a camera lens must be set for the total distance from camera to mirror to subject; the magnification of the subject on the film will be proportional to this distance. With an ordinary rear-surfaced mirror, focusing on the mirror distance rather than the total subject distance increases the clarity of the secondary image reflected from the front glass surface. Because the glass image is polarized by reflection, but the primary metal-surface image is not, using a polarizer in front of the camera lens can screen out the double image, but at the expense of an additional *f*-stop of exposure. To avoid double images, front-surface mirrors are used in most camera reflex-viewing systems, in mirror lenses and precision optical instruments, and in holography and other kinds of specialized photography. Front-surface coatings are extremely delicate; they must not be touched with the fingers and should be cleaned only by blowing off or by light dusting with a very soft brush.

Curved mirrors have distinctive effects. Concave mirrors reflect parallel light rays to a focus, forming a real image. The image is located on the same side of the mirror as the subject; with a spherical mirror it is located halfway between the center of the mirror and the center of curvature of the sphere. When used to reflect light onto a subject, a concave mirror concentrates the illumination in a kind of spotlight effect. Convex mirrors form virtual images with the subject a greater apparent distance (and therefore reduced in size) behind the mirror than its actual distance in front of the mirror.

ture of light. The mired value (MV) of illumination is equal to 1,000,000 divided by the color temperature of the light; for example, the mired value of 5500K light is 182. The mired value system makes it possible to rate the effect various filters have on the color balance of light. Equal changes in color temperature do not create changes that appear visually equal; however, equal changes in mired value do create equal visual changes. For example, a 500K change from 2500K to 3000K makes a more noticeable difference in the light than a change from 5500K to 6000K. But a change of 50MV from 357MV to 307MV (2800K to 3255K) looks to be the same degree of change as the 50MV shift from 182MV to 132MV (5500K to 7575K). Filters used to adjust color temperature are assigned *mired shift values*. Warming filters (amber, yellowish, reddish) have

positive (+) shift values: they raise the mired value of light passing through, which lowers its color temperature (because the mired is a reciprocal unit). Cooling filters (bluish) have negative (−) shift values, which lower the mired value of transmitted light, raising its color temperature (i.e., increasing the proportion of blue wavelengths). A filter with a given shift value will produce an equal degree of visual change in light of any color temperature. Some manufacturers offer tables or graphs to simplify the choice of filters to accomplish a desired change in color temperature. However, it is relatively easy to calculate the mired values of the original light and the desired light to determine how much + or − shift is required. Any filters or combinations of filters whose shift values total the required shift may be used. A related unit, the *decamired* (DM), is used

A number of special purpose mirrors are used in photographic equipment. Half-silvered mirrors are used as beam splitters in a variety of viewing, projection, and lighting set-ups. Diathermic mirrors are heat filters; they reflect light, but transmit a significant portion of accompanying heat energy on a path away from that of the image. Dichroic mirrors reflect only certain wavelengths of light, canceling others by interference among reflections within thin-layer surface coatings.

See also: BEAM SPLITTER; DICHROIC FILTER; MIRROR LENS.

Mirror Camera

A camera in which the major image-forming component is a mirror, or a series of mirrors, rather than a lens, is a mirror camera. The first such camera was patented by Alexander Wolcott in 1840 in the U.S. It was constructed by Henry Fitz, and had been anticipated by the suggestion to use a mirror in place of a lens, made by a Scottish physician, Dr. Andrew Fyfe, in 1839. The Wolcott camera was a wooden box about 8 inches (20cm) square and 15 inches (38cm) long. One end could be raised to admit light; a concave metal mirror at the other end reflected an image back toward the opening, onto a small daguerreotype plate mounted on a movable pedestal about 7 inches (18cm) in front of the mirror. The focus was first adjusted by using an unsensitized plate and looking through an opening in the top of the camera. This arrangement produced an unreversed image and exposures short enough to make portraiture practical, but it was limited to a plate about 2″ × 2½″ (5 × 6.3cm). The Wolcott camera was used in the first portrait studios, notably those of John William Draper and Samuel F. B. Morse in New York, and Richard Beard in London.

In modern photography, the Schmidt camera is widely used for astronomical work. It is a catadioptric reflecting telescope built to accept films or plates at the focal plane. Various mirror cameras are used in high-speed photography. One such camera has a rotating mirror that can reflect images onto a stationary film at rates of several million exposures a second. A mirror drum camera has a many-faceted reflective cylinder that rotates to direct a series of images from the lens system onto a circular band of film that is rotating at a synchronous speed. Devices such as mirror lenses and endoscopes convert conventional cameras into what are essentially mirror cameras, as do specialized set-ups for surveillance,

hazardous-area, and scientific and technical photography.

See also: ENDOSCOPE; HIGH-SPEED PHOTOGRAPHY; MIRROR LENS; SCHMIDT CAMERA; TELESCOPE; WOLCOTT, ALEXANDER S.

Mirror Lens

In a mirror lens optical system, mirror elements fold a long light path into a short distance, and lens elements correct aberrations and increase magnification. The result is a very long focal length in a lens of much shorter physical length than that of an equivalent telephoto lens. A typical 500mm (19¹¹⁄₁₆″) focal-length mirror lens is only 92mm (3⁹⁄₁₆″) long, and a 300mm (11⅞″) mirror lens is only 73mm (2⅞″) long. In order to achieve usable maximum apertures (e.g., $f/5.6$ to $f/8$), mirror lenses have diameters one and one-half to three times greater than those of equivalent telephoto lenses. However, given their short barrel length, mirror lenses are reasonably compact and easy to handle. They are primarily made for use with 35mm cameras and are based on a catadioptric design first produced for astronomical telescopes.

Light enters the lens through an aberration-correcting front element. It is reflected by a concave mirror at the rear of the lens barrel on a converging path to a second, much smaller mirror on the central axis of the lens, close to the front. The small mirror reflects the light toward the rear where it passes through other lens elements and a hole in the center of the primary mirror to be focused on the film. The hole does not affect the lens coverage nor the sharpness of the focused image, but causes out-of-focus highlights to have a characteristic ring- or doughnutlike shape. A mirror lens does not have an iris diaphragm because that would increase the overall diameter to an unwieldy size or would interfere with the camera mounting mechanism at the rear. Instead, light transmission is controlled by inserting neutral density filters at the rear of the lens where the image path is quite narrow—filters to cover the large front diameter would be prohibitively expensive. Color filters may also be used at the rear. With a fast film it is possible to hand-hold a camera with a mirror lens to photograph subjects in bright sunlight. However, to obtain the best quality images, the camera-lens combination should be firmly supported by a tripod, the mirror of a reflex-viewing system should be pre-released if possible, and the shutter should be operated with a cable release. These techniques will

minimize vibration effects, which are greatly magnified by very long-focal-length lenses.

See also: CATADIOPTRIC AND CATOPTRIC LENSES; TELESCOPE.

Mixed-Media Images

Mixed-media images are created by combining materials and techniques from two or more of the graphic arts, fine arts, and crafts. The intent is to achieve a more varied, complex, or subtle expressiveness than is possible using only one medium. A very basic sort of mixed-media imagery is a photograph or a series of photographs carrying a hand-written legend or narrative, such as some of the sequences of Duane Michals. Other fundamental examples are photographs that have been altered with overpainting or hand-applied colors for expressive effect. Assemblages of photographic and non-photographic elements have been produced by artists from the early 1920s. Robert Rauschenberg, Andy Warhol, and other painters and printmakers have made extensive use of photographic and photomechanical images in conjunction with painted, drawn, etched, engraved, and screen-printed elements. Especially since the 1960s, the borders between various two-dimensional image-making techniques have been erased with bold experiment and creative "misuse" of materials.

Marriages of two- and three-dimensional media have been equally as innovative in this period. Naomi Savage has used the materials and techniques of photomechanical platemaking and photofabrication to create deep reliefs with photo-image elements. Bea Nettle, Betty Kuhn, and others have altered photographic images with needlepoint, applied clothwork, woven elements, and other techniques of the fabric arts. Many sculptors have pasted photographs onto their constructions, or applied emulsion and printed the image directly on the surface. Catherine Jansen has created photo-peopled environments, such as a bedroom of real furnishings with images of the inhabitants printed on the dresser mirror, television screen, bedsheets, and framed wall hangings. Sculptors have also used photo images as the basis for shaping their materials by carving, sandblasting, slump-melting, and a variety of chemical-etch procedures. Others have stuffed or inflated constructions composed of photo-printed flexible materials, creating, for example, a giant pillowlike toothbrush with photographically real bristles.

Electronic and computer manipulation of images produces other kinds of media mixing. A projected image may be made to vary with changing aspects of accompanying music or the movements of a dancer. Image tones, shapes, and colors can be altered and elements of many different images combined in a hard-copy printout on a great variety of materials, from paper to fabrics, plastics, metals, and veneers.

The integration of photographic elements with performance art is a further extension of mixed-media presentation. Depending on the degree of importance of the photo elements, from background to central focus of the action, such presentations may be performances with visual elements, or visual images with live-action elements.

See also: ARTISTS AND PHOTOGRAPHY; CERAMIC PROCESSES; ENAMEL PROCESSES; GLASS, PHOTOGRAPHS ON; HYALOGRAPH; MULTI-MEDIA PRESENTATIONS; PAINTING AND PHOTOGRAPHY; PHOTOSCULPTURE; RELIEF IMAGES.

Color photograph p. C-33.

Mixing Photographic Solutions

It is an easy task to mix photographic solutions when chemical formulas premixed in powder or liquid form are used. The chemicals are simply mixed with the proper amount of water to make a stock solution. In some cases, this solution is used at full strength and subsequently replenished. In other cases the solution is further diluted for limited or one-time use. At times, however, there is a need to use a special formula or to modify a standard one. In these instances, the formula must be prepared from its separate chemical components—a process that requires each ingredient to be measured accurately and mixed into the solution carefully and in proper sequence.

Photographic solutions must be mixed and stored in containers made of appropriate materials; otherwise, a chemical reaction may occur that contaminates the solution. Glass, stainless steel, polyethylene, and hard rubber are materials commonly used. Containers must be kept scrupulously clean to insure solution purity. It is also important that stirrers be made of hard plastic, hard rubber, or stainless steel. Absorbent materials, such as wood or flexible rubber, will absorb chemicals and contaminate the solutions.

Ordinary tap water is usually adequate for mixing chemicals. When sediment, rust, or other foreign matter is present in the water, filtration can eliminate it. If precipitates appear during the mixing process, filtration should also be used when pouring the solution into its storage container. Distilled water, which can be used if a serious problem exists in the water supply, is often desirable for solutions such as developers, which are the most susceptible to contamination.

When chemicals are mixed, the water must be brought to the temperature specified in the formula or instructions. In the case of some powdered developers, this temperature will be as high as 125°F (50°C), and if the water temperature is too low, the powder may not dissolve properly. Dry chemicals must be poured into the water slowly. This facilitates the dissolving process and helps to prevent chemical dust from escaping into the air and creating a safety or contamination hazard. Continuous stirring prevents clumping of chemicals at the bottom of the container, but overly vigorous stirring brings too much air into the solution and promotes oxidation, which is particularly injurious to developers.

It is customary to pour the chemical into two-thirds of the required amount of water, and then to add more water to bring the solution to the correct level. The final addition of water is less than a third, since the dissolved chemical itself adds to the volume of the solution. With prepackaged dry chemicals, the entire package should be used. The various ingredients are not likely to be distributed evenly throughout the powder; thus, even if half a package is precisely measured out, the solution will not have the correct consistency.

When mixing a solution for which the chemicals have not been pre-packaged, add the chemicals in the order called for in the formula. Otherwise, some chemicals may not dissolve properly or may react undesirably with each other. When preparing such solutions, it is not advisable to pour a powdered chemical directly onto a scale. Instead, the chemical should be placed on a piece of paper, such as filter paper, to make it easier to handle and to avoid contamination.

The mixing area should be well-ventilated and the chemicals handled carefully to prevent the breathing of fumes or dust. No chemicals should come into contact with the eyes, and concentrates and dry chemicals should not come into contact with the skin. People with sensitive skin may require rubber gloves. Warning labels should be scrupulously observed. Acid should always be poured into water, not water into acid. Concentrated acid should be diluted before being poured into an alkaline solution, and it should be poured slowly and stirred continuously. Strong alkalis such as sodium and potassium hydroxides should be dissolved separately in cold water; a glass container is not advisable since they generate a great deal of heat. Chemical spills should be cleaned up promptly and thoroughly.

mks System

The meter-kilogram-second system of measurement.
See: METRIC SYSTEM; WEIGHTS AND MEASURES.

Model, Lisette

Austrian; 1906–1983

Born to a wealthy Viennese family before World War I, Lisette Model was privately tutored; it was perhaps in consequence that her thought avoided conventional habits, following instead her own mixture of intelligent observation and intuition. "I am not a visual person," she once stated; her photographs refute this.

As a young girl Lisette Model became a protégée of the composer Arnold Schoenberg, and worked toward a musical career. She got into photography by chance. In Paris in the mid-1930s she met on the street a composer she knew, a refugee from Nazi Germany. When she said she had begun to paint, he told her she was crazy: a war was coming and she'd better learn something that could support her. Her sister Olga was working for a photographer, which prompted Model to learn developing and printing as a trade she could fall back on. To get exposed film to practice with, she began to photograph people she saw around her—the poor, the rich, anyone with enough visible character. The vitality of these people and their sometimes grotesque appearance animated the pictures and lent them power. This was a new kind of photograph.

In 1937 she and her husband, the painter Evsa Model, came to New York for a short visit that lasted a lifetime. They came with money, but in 1940 this began to run out. Looking for work, Model answered an ad from the newspaper *PM* for a darkroom worker, and brought prints to show her skill. *PM*'s photo columnist, Ralph Steiner, was impressed and shocked. Instead of hiring her for the darkroom, the paper published a portfolio of her work under the title "Why France Fell"—a context that Model never accepted.

The *PM* portfolio attracted the attention of Alexey Brodovitch, art director of *Harper's Bazaar*, and Model began to photograph for that magazine, working in New York much as she had worked in Paris. Her pictures began to be shown in art museums.

About 1950, her friend Berenice Abbott persuaded Model to start teaching photography at the New School for Social Research in New York. She taught there and at many workshops for the remainder of her life.

Lisette Model's work has a projective force: often the people in her pictures seem to bulge forward out of the print instead of receding. It is an involved and passionate photography. Recent shows of her work include *Photographs by Lisette Model*, at the Focus Gallery, San Francisco (1973); *Lisette Model Photographs*, at the Sander Gallery, Washington, D.C. (1976); *Lisette Model: Photographs*, at the Vision Gallery, Boston (1979). An Aperture monograph on her work was published in 1979.
Photograph: p. 314.

Modeling

Modeling is the effect of light in revealing the three-dimensional characteristics of an object. Light that strikes the front of an object from an angle produces highlights and shadows that model its contours. Similarly, modeling of fine surface details reveals texture. The light must strike the object from an angle. Head-on frontlight is flat; that is, it does not produce modeling because all parts of the object receive equal illumination. Light from behind the object outlines its shape, but does not reveal form (volume) or texture because the portion facing the camera or observer is unilluminated. Light from directly to one side or from directly overhead may produce some modeling, or it may simply produce a flat pattern of light and dark shapes.

Modeling can be observed and adjusted by moving the main light source to various positions, or by changing the orientation of the object in relation to a fixed source such as the sun. A common modeling arrangement is called architectural lighting. It is produced by a main light source positioned 45 degrees to one side and 45 degrees above the lens-object axis. This position reveals lateral variations of form and texture as well as those which run vertically. An intense, specific (direct or hard) light provides the greatest degree of modeling, but it may require that fill light be added to the shadowed areas to prevent their looking like flat, black "holes" in the object. As light is progressively diffused (made softer), its modeling effect diminishes.
See also: LIGHTING.

Modeling Light

A modeling light is a relatively low-output continuous light source (usually a tungsten bulb) built into or attached to an electronic flash head. It allows the photographer to see the highlight and shadow, or modeling, effect that the flash will produce. This permits setting up a lighting arrangement without having to take repeated test shots to check the effect. In multiple-flash setups, if the modeling lights are all equally proportional to the output of their associated flash heads, lighting ratios can be established on the basis of incident-light meter readings taken from the modeling lights. In most equipment the flash output is so much greater than that of the modeling light that it is not necessary to turn off the modeling light during an exposure. The flash washes out its slight effect on color balance, and it does not add enough illumination to require an exposure adjustment.
See also: LIGHTING; MULTIPLE FLASH.

Models

Professional modeling has become one of the highest-paid and most glamorous pursuits related to commercial photography. Models are used daily to advertise everything from high-fashion clothing to cleaning fluid, and many professional photographers would find it impossible to make a living without the constant supply of ideal faces, figures, and hands provided by modeling agencies.

Established models command fees well beyond the reach of the amateur or beginning illustrative photographer. However, an aspiring commercial photographer living in a large urban area such as New York, London, or Chicago can obtain, usually free of charge, the services of all but the best-known models through a system known as "testing." Young models recently having embarked on their careers are constantly in search of new photographs. Through their agencies or individually they often will agree to pose for photographers in exchange for finished pictures from the session. The successful model "test" not only can provide the model with added images for his or her portfolio, but it also might bring the photographer to the attention of others.

In order to be considered seriously for testing, the photographer already should have produced a technically strong, visually interesting portfolio of pictures that have a direct bearing on the kind of work the model normally does. A good portfolio of people's hands will not go a long way in a high-fashion modeling agency, for example. The models for this "entry" portfolio can be obtained from local dance schools, fashion-art institutions, or colleges. For the photographer in search of figure-study models or attractive faces for portraiture and the like, these institutions might supply all of the talent needed. Art schools are another excellent source for models; most of them employ men and women as models for figure drawing and photography classes on a regular basis and can provide the interested photographer with a list of people who will pose for a nominal fee.

Whether the model is a professional or an amateur, a model release should be obtained by the photographer for any pictures that might be published. Model-release forms are required by all publications; they are available in variously worded forms from photographic stores and stationery shops. A typically worded model release form is reproduced below; the "valuable consideration" mentioned in the release can be any amount of money of $1.00 or more, or if so stated on the release, it can be a photograph or photographs from the shooting.

Models, Scale and Miniature

Scale models and miniature constructions are often used in still photographs and motion pictures for reasons of economy, especially when they are to serve merely as backgrounds. They are less expensive to produce and require much

---

MODEL RELEASE

Date ———————

For valuable consideration, I hereby irrevocably consent to and authorize the use and reproduction by you, or anyone authorized by you, of any and all photographs which you have this day taken of me, negative or positive, proofs of which are hereto attached, for any purpose whatsoever, without further compensation to me. All negatives and positives, together with the prints, shall constitute your property, solely and completely.

Signature ————————————————————
(Model or parent/guardian)

Address ————————————————————

Witnessed by ————————————————————

less studio space than full-size settings. With careful attention in construction, perspective can be forced so as to make it appear that a scene of great scope is included within the field of view. When photographing full-size foreground subjects against a miniature background, the primary problem is finding the camera, subject, and background positions (distances from one another) that make the change in scale seem continuous—i.e., that create a realistic sense of perspective. This problem can be eased by using foreground framing elements at the bottom of the picture or by choosing a relatively low angle of view so that the ground plane leading back to the model cannot be seen. The direction of foreground and background light must correspond, and it helps to use light of a general quality on the model while the main subject is in more specific illumination. The overall effect can first be judged by viewing through the camera lens, but can only be fully evaluated by making test shots—the effect produced in a two-dimensional image is somewhat different from what even a single eye sees. Instant-print films make trial shots easy, but they must be taken through the lens that will actually record the image, not through that of an auxillary camera. Such tests can be used to examine perspective, lighting, depth of field, contrast, color balance, and exposure. Neutral density filtration may be required to match the speed of the test film to that of the film to be used so that the camera settings will be identical.

Photographing a model as the primary subject so as to make it appear realistically full-sized is technically more difficult. However, this is a common requirement in architectural and advertising still photography and in special-effects motion-picture photography. The model must be constructed of materials whose textures retain a realistic appearance when magnified many times; for example, a strip of cloth painted to simulate a concrete sidewalk must not reveal the pattern of its weave in an enlarged close-up. Unless a simulated aerial view is desired, it must be possible to obtain a viewpoint at scale height within the model. In some cases this can be achieved by aiming down into an angled mirror appropriately placed in the model, or by using an inverted periscope or an endoscope. The actual height is determined by the scale of the model. In an architectural model the viewpoint is commonly taken as the equivalent of 6 ft., approximately the height of the average person. If the model scale is 1:10, everything is reproduced one-tenth of actual size, so the equivalent scale height

for the camera viewpoint is one-tenth of 6 ft., or 7 in. The apparent viewing distance must be similarly reduced to scale. If a building in the 1:10 model is to appear as it would look full-size from a distance of 30 ft., the actual camera viewpoint must be 30 ÷ 10, or 3, ft. from the model building. It is commonly necessary to use a supplementary lens or a wide-angle lens to obtain relatively realistic perspective at scale distances. Small lens apertures are required to obtain as much depth of field as possible, because it decreases drastically as the lens gets close to the subject. Camera angles that include objects that block the distant background ease the problem of sharpness in depth.

See also: ENDOSCOPE; PERSPECTIVE; SCALE.

Modotti, Tina

Mexican; 1896–1942

Until recently Tina Modotti's reputation was based on her personal association with Edward Weston, for whom she modeled during the 1920s. However, her sharply focused portraits, still-lifes, and abstract compositions, made in Mexico contemporaneously, show her to have been an accomplished photographer in her own right. Modotti's work combines a sophisticated sense of design with socially and politically oriented subject matter. Her images of the Mexican working classes and Mexican artifacts became powerful revolutionary emblems.

Assunta Adelaide Luigia Modotti was born in Undine, Italy. She was educated at schools in Italy and Austria. From 1908 to 1913 she worked in an Undine textile factory. Joining her father in San Francisco, she worked in a silk factory from 1913 to 1914 and as a freelance dressmaker from 1914 to 1917.

Modotti married poet and painter Roubaix (Robo) de l'Abrie Richey in 1917. She worked as an actress in several Hollywood films in 1920 and 1921 and began to model and study photography in San Francisco with Edward Weston at that time. Modotti's husband died in Mexico City in 1922. She and Weston had an intimate relationship of mutual influence, working together regularly from 1922 to 1930 in San Francisco and in Mexico, where they had studios in Tacubaya and Mexico City.

Modotti became a revolutionary activist in the early 1920s and developed strong ties with members of the Mexican Artists Union group, including Manuel Alvarez Bravo, Diego Rivera, Charlot, Orozco, and Siqueiros. She became a member of the Mexican Communist

Party in 1927. She was a contributing editor and photographer for *Mexican Folkways* magazine from 1927 to 1930, photographing murals and other works of art.

Modotti began an affair with Cuban revolutionary Julio Antonio Mella in 1928. She was accused but found innocent of complicity in his murder in 1929. The following year she was accused of complicity in the assassination attempt on the life of Pascual Ortiz Rubio, President of Mexico, and was deported. She continued to photograph in exile in Berlin in 1930. She became a member of the Union GmbH press photographers association and published photographs in *Der Arbeiter-Fotograf.* She abandoned photography for political activism while in Moscow from 1931 to 1934 working for Soviet International Red Aid.

Modotti moved to France in 1934 and worked in Madrid and Valencia, Spain, from 1935 to 1938. She was a reporter for the Republican newspaper *Ayuda* and worked for revolutionary movements and the International Red Cross from 1936 to 1938. She returned to Mexico City under an alias in 1939, photographed, traveled, and continued her political work until her death of an apparent heart attack in 1942.

Modotti's work has received deserved attention in recent years after a long period of neglect. Her photographs were included in the *Women of Photography* touring exhibition of 1975, and she was the subject of a two-woman show with the painter Frida Kahlo in 1982–1983 in London and New York City. She has been honored by one-woman shows at the Museum of Modern Art in New York City (1977), Festival Internazionale delle Donne in Arezzo, Italy (1978), and the Museum of Fine Arts in Lodz, Poland (1980).

Photograph: p. 334.

Moholy-Nagy, László

Hungarian; 1895–1946

Although Moholy-Nagy never referred to himself as a photographer, and indeed made relatively few photographs throughout his life, he was nonetheless a crucial figure in modern photography and a powerful propagandist for its importance among the visual arts. Among the first to make photograms (contemporaneously with Man Ray and Christian Schad), Moholy additionally pioneered what he termed the "New Vision" photography, a radical, formalist, machine-age notion of photography which he successfully transplanted to America with his founding of the New

Bauhaus, which became the Chicago Institute of Design.

Born in southern Hungary, Moholy-Nagy entered the University of Budapest as a law student in 1913. With the outbreak of World War I the following year, he was conscripted into the Austro-Hungarian Army. Severely wounded in 1917, during his convalescence Moholy made drawings, watercolors, and helped to establish a literary revue to which he contributed. With the defeat of the Hungarian Soviet Republic in 1919, Moholy—then a Marxist—was compelled to flee the country, initially to Vienna, and later that year to Berlin. In Berlin, a veritable cauldron of avant-garde production and activity, Moholy became associated with the Russian and Hungarian Futurist circle, the Berlin Dadaists, and the Russian Constructivists, notably El Lissitzky. In 1922, in collaboration with his first wife Lucia, he produced his first photograms. The following spring he became director of the metal workshop at the Weimar Bauhaus and for the next five years produced the major body of his photographic work as well as drawings, sculptures, constructions, and design projects. In keeping with the precepts of Constructivism and other art currents, his photographs featured unusual viewpoints, e.g., worm's-eye views, bird's-eye views, suppressed horizons, and diagonal compositions. At the same time, working with other members of the Bauhaus staff, he made designs for theatre, ballet, and other spectacles. In 1924 he published *Painting, Photography, Film* as part of the Bauhaus Books series of which he was the editor. After the Bauhaus was forced to relocate to Dessau due to political attacks, Moholy remained on staff for another two years. In 1928, however, along with Walter Gropius and Herbert Bayer, Moholy left the Bauhaus and moved to Berlin. There, he occupied himself with numerous projects: the publication of his book *From Material to Architecture,* exhibition and stage design, participation in and organization of a large part of the seminal exhibition *Film und Foto* held in Stuttgart in 1929, the making of experimental films, and extensive lecturing.

With the rise of Nazism, Moholy fled Germany in 1934, emigrating first to Amsterdam, and later—with the support of Sir Herbert Read—to London. There he took on various commercial assignments, produced several photographically illustrated books, and designed lighting effects for the science fiction film *The Shape of Things to Come,* which were, however, never used. Through the assistance of Walter Gropius—now settled in the U.S.—Moholy was invited by a consortium of Chicago businessmen to direct a new design school. The New Bauhaus, as Moholy named it, lasted but a year, and in 1938, was forced to close down. By 1939, however, Moholy and some of the former staff were able to open a new school—The School of Design—with the financial support of Walter Paepcke of the American Container Corp. Transplanting the theoretical and pedagogical concepts of the Bauhaus, Moholy was able to introduce new notions of photographic practice as well as to establish a precedent for the teaching of photography on a graduate level. His last book, *Vision in Motion,* appeared shortly after his death from leukemia.

Modotti, Tina. "Number 28: Marionette" (1926). Collection, Museum of Modern Art, New York.

Mcholy-Nagy, Laszlo. "Photogram" (1922). Smithsonian Institut on.

because the developing and fixing compounds can interact to produce excessive fog. A monobath is not suitable for general photographic use because it produces more graininess and less effective emulsion speed than conventional processing. It is also temperature sensitive: high temperature delays fixing and produces high contrast; low temperature delays development and produces low contrast; however, these effects cannot be utilized for contrast control in the way that normal development can be adjusted. There is no universal monobath; to get the best quality, monobath ingredients must be selected and proportioned for a particular type of emulsion. In spite of these limitations, a monobath is valuable for quick exposure tests or equipment checks, for processing under difficult field conditions, and for rapid access and other special-purpose applications.

Monochromatic

The adjective monochromatic indicates illumination of a single color, as produced by a strongly filtered or selectively emissive light source. It also refers to an image composed of colors that are all variants of one basic hue or of a group of very closely related hues, such as browns tans, and deep yellows.

Monorail Camera

A view camera in which the components are mounted on a single tube or rod rather than on a flat bed is called a monorail camera. The rail may be circular, triangular, or square in cross section, and may have grooves or a toothed track along its length to guide the components. The monorail design permits either the front (lens) or the rear (film) standard, or both, to be moved freely to adjust the bellows extension. Some rails can have lengths added to accommodate supplementary bellows or other accessories requiring additional lens-to-film distance. A camera of this type must be supported on a tripod. A tripod coupling block shifts along the rail so the point of balance can be adjusted as required.
See also: CAMERA MOVEMENTS; VIEW CAMERA.

Montage

A montage is an assemblage of image elements selected for their specific visual content and arranged to make a single visual statement. It differs from a composite image produced by combination printing in that the elements are physically cut out, arranged, and pasted in

Moiré

The visible interference pattern produced when two unidentical, closely spaced line or dot patterns are superimposed out of register is known as moiré. Because the spacings do not match, at some places the elements in both patterns are close enough to merge visually into a solid; at other places the elements are aligned one above the other so the spaces between them are visible. The result is a repeat pattern of circles, squares, lines, or other visible elements not present in either of the individual patterns. Moiré occurs most readily between two regular patterns, as when a halftone dot image is rephotographed through another halftone screen, or when the screen pattern angles are not sufficiently different among a set of

separation images made for photo-mechanical reproduction. Moiré can also occur when a special-effect or texture screen used in front of the camera or enlarger lens interferes with an irregular subject pattern such as that of dappled leaves, or a regular pattern such as that of bricks in a distant wall or fabric texture in a close-up.

Monobath

The one-step negative processing solution known as monobath contains both developing agents and a fixing compound. The developing agents must act rapidly to develop a sufficient amount of image density before the fixer has dissolved all the halides. A significant amount of restrainer must be included

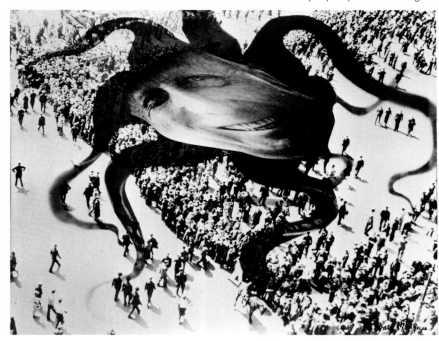

place rather than being optically combined. *Collage* is a kind of montage generally distinguished by a purely artistic—and usually abstract—intent and a less finished or less precise technique in which irregular shapes, torn edges, elements without image content (e.g., scraps of cloth, pieces of newspaper), and the like are used freely. Montage creates a unified image in which technique is somewhat more concealed, and in which elements are chosen for their image content rather than their physical characteristics. Thus, montage is likely to be more concerned with an explicit "message" than collage. Montage may have a purely communicative intent, as in the assembly of aerial photographs into an overall image of an area or the combining of the individual sections of a multi-exposure panoramic photograph. Montage may also have artistic intent. The term *photomontage* was first used by German Dada artists in the early 1920s to identify works in which multiple photo elements were joined with type and other graphic devices (German: *montage* = mounting, fitting, assembly). Among the most outstanding and most effective productions of the 1920s and 1930s were the social comment, anti-Nazi montages of John Heartfield. Non-Dada artists such as Moholy-Nagy explored the genre, using drawn, diagrammatic elements to link photo images, and combining paste-up with photogram techniques. And, inevitably, photomontage was used for commercial illustration and advertising, much of which was trivial because it was self-consciously avant-garde. Today montage is an established artistic and illustrative technique used with many degrees of sophistication and success.

In an artistically intended montage the image characteristics of the elements, the treatment of edges, and other factors of technique are matters of expressive choice. When a montage is to be an informative image construction—a "seamless whole" such as an aerial mosaic or a panorama—certain technical requirements are important. The individual photographs must match in contrast, image color, graininess, perspective, depth of field, scale, direction of light within the image, and similar factors. They should be printed on single-weight paper to minimize thickness where elements overlap; edges can cast revealing shadows or create a highlight line under directional lighting. In a montage that is to be displayed directly (rather than rephotographed after construction) it is not practical to cut two overlapping pieces and discard the waste in order to butt their edges together for a single

thickness. In a short time expansion and contraction of the emulsion will cause some seams to open and become visible. Overlapping assembly insures that there is image beneath each edge so that slight movement is not revealed. The top piece must be cut cleanly, preferably not in a straight line; the cut should coincide with well-defined edges in the image if possible. The thickness of the top piece must be reduced by scraping, sanding, or tearing away some paper from the back along the edge; this is a delicate operation often best done before the final trim cut is made from the face of the image. A temporary montage—one that is to be rephotographed to obtain a master negative or positive—is most easily assembled with rubber cement because edge cleanup is easy with a pure rubber eraser or a fingertip, and because solvent can be used to free an element for repositioning without affecting the image. However, sulfur compounds in rubber cement will eventually attack photographic images, so a permanent montage should be assembled with a gum-arabic solution (true stationer's mucilage) or a polyvinyl acetate (household liquid white) glue thinned with water. When the assembly is dry, edges can be further concealed and blended-in with spotting colors and various retouching techniques.

See also: COLLAGE; COMPOSITE PHOTOGRAPHS; MULTI-IMAGE TECHNIQUES.

Moon Photography

Like most other objects illuminated by direct sunlight, the moon is photograph-

able with ordinary equipment and standard color or black-and-white films. When the moon is included with lighted earth subjects (e.g., a landscape at twilight), proper exposure for those subjects will also usually record the moon properly. When the moon is photographed alone in the sky, exposure must be estimated or based on experience, for few exposure meters take in a small enough area to read the moon's brightness accurately. The familiar $f/16$ rule for estimating exposure of sunlighted subjects is based on the fact that their average reflectance is about 18 percent. However, the moon reflects a little less than half that much, 7 or 8 percent, so the rule must be adjusted for one f-stop more exposure: $f/11$ at 1/film speed. Thus, with an ISO 125/22° film, exposure would be $f/11$ at 1/125 sec. The moon's brightness is reduced by haze, mist, and other atmospheric conditions, so additional pictures should be taken with increased exposures. A tripod is useful in most cases, and essential if a long-focal-length lens is used. The lens focus should be set at infinity.

Although the moon often seems quite large when viewed directly, it is disappointingly small in pictures taken with a normal-focal-length lens. A long-telephoto lens, mirror lens, or small telescope will provide significantly larger images. The diameter of the moon's image on the film can be calculated as follows:

Image size = Lens focal length ÷ 110

For example, with a 50mm (2 inch) lens,

Morgan, Barbara. "Martha Graham: Letter to the World (Kick)" (1940). Courtesy Barbara Morgan.

the image size on 35mm film would be 0.45mm, or a little less than 1/50 inch. But with a 500mm lens, it would be 10 times larger.

There are three ways to include a large moon image in a picture of an earth subject such as a tree silhouetted against the sky. The first is to use an appropriately long focal-length lens and take up a camera position at the distance that gives the desired composition. This is a limited method because there must be a clear view of the subject from the required distance, and the moon actually must move into the desired position. The second method is to photograph the subject at a convenient distance with a normal lens and then change to a long-focal-length lens to photograph the moon separately in a double exposure. This permits adjusting the moon's position in the picture, but the subject's location in the frame must be carefully noted to avoid unintentional superimposure of the two elements. The exposures may be taken days apart if it is possible to rewind or reload the film to place the first

exposure in the camera's film gate accurately.

The third method offers the greatest control and variety. It is to photograph the subject and the moon separately and to combine the images later. Slides can be sandwiched in a single mount. Prints can be made by sandwiching two negatives, or by combination printing: separate exposures on the same paper through the two negatives. The latter method permits placing the moon wherever desired and adjusting its size by raising or lowering the enlarger head from the position at which the first image was printed.
See also: ECLIPSE PHOTOGRAPHY; EXPOSURE; MOONLIGHT; SUN PHOTOGRAPHY; TELESCOPE.

Moonlight

The illumination called moonlight is in fact light from the sun reflected off the surface of the moon. Because of the low reflectivity of the moon, the light intensity is about 7 percent that of direct

sunlight. In the earth environment, clouds and atmospheric scattering and absorption may reduce the light intensity even more. Photographs are possible by moonlight, but a tripod is required to ensure sharp images during the long exposures required. Either color or black-and-white film can be used, and exposure must include some adjustment for reciprocity effect.
See also: DAYLIGHT; MOON PHOTOGRAPHY; RECIPROCITY.

Mordant

A mordant is a compound that combines with a dye—either chemically or by absorption—to fix the dye in place so that it cannot migrate or bleed within the dyed medium. Some mordants cause the visible color to precipate as they react with dye compounds that are colorless in an unmordanted state. The receiving emulsion in the dye transfer process must be mordanted before the dyed image matrices are placed in contact with it.

The permanent, insoluble compound formed when a mordant reacts with a soluble dye is called a *lake*.

Morgan, Barbara

American; 1900–

Barbara Morgan's photographs of dancers and children have brought her her greatest acclaim. But she has worked in photomontage, figurative, and abstract modes with equal skill, evidencing an abiding concern with rhythm, motion, and dynamism.

Morgan was born Barbara Brooks Johnson in Buffalo, Kansas, and grew up on a peach farm in southern California. She painted from early childhood and studied art from 1919 to 1923 at UCLA. During college she began exhibiting paintings and woodcuts in West Coast art societies. She studied puppetry and stage lighting informally.

Morgan taught art at San Fernando High School in 1923–1924. She married the photographer and writer Willard Morgan the following year. From 1925 to 1930 she taught design, woodcut, and landscape at UCLA. In 1926 she was convinced of the artistic possibilities of photography by Edward Weston.

Morgan and her husband spent their summers in the Southwest, where she painted and photographed the desert and cliff ruins. Her dance photography began when she was able to record Hopi, Zuñi, and other American Indian dances and rituals with a Leica.

In 1930 the Morgans moved to New York City, and she established a painting and lithography studio the next year. She continued to exhibit paintings, including a one-woman show at the Mellon Gallery in Philadelphia. She turned to photography as her principal medium in 1935 when her family responsibilities left her insufficient time for painting. Her first works were in photomontage, influenced by the work of Moholy-Nagy. She photographed and exhibited a wide variety of subjects (children, light drawings and photomontages of New York City) for the next several years.

Morgan was attracted to modern dance by a performance of Martha Graham's dance company in 1935. She was struck by the similarity of the dances to those she had documented in the Southwest. For the next five years, she photographed Graham and her dancers regularly in her studio, where she was able to control lighting and isolate individual gestures. She believed that dance photography required careful previsualization. Morgan's photographs of Graham were published in 1941 in a volume for which she received the American Institute of Graphic Arts Trade Book Clinic Award. She went on to photograph a large number of dancers including José Limón, Erick Hawkins, Anna Sokolow, and Merce Cunningham.

Morgan performed various functions on photographic publishing projects from 1935 to 1972, first for Morgan and Lester, and then for Morgan and Morgan Publishers. She made an archaelogical trip to Crete, Greece, Spain, Italy, France, and England in 1959. Her husband Willard died in 1967.

In 1970 Morgan was elected a Fellow of the Philadelphia Museum of Art. She received a grant from the National Endowment for the Arts in 1975 and participated in the *Women in Photography* exhibition at the San Francisco Museum of Art. In 1978 she was the recipient of an Honorary Doctorate of Fine Arts from Marquette University.

Barbara Morgan has lectured and conducted seminars throughout the country. She has had one-woman shows at the Pasadena Art Museum; the Institute of American Indian Art, Santa Fe; the Museum of Modern Art, New York; and George Eastman House. An Aperture monograph on her work was published in 1964. *Barbara Morgan: Monograph* was issued by Morgan and Morgan in 1972.

Photograph: p. 337.

Morris, Wright

American; 1910–

Wright Morris has been known primarily as a writer of fiction until recent years, when his photographs and unique "photo-texts" of rural and small-town midwestern American life in the 1930s and 1940s have gained recognition. Both his writings and photographs show a marked concern with the commonplace, with formal elegance and precision. Whereas his fiction contains many well-drawn characters, his photos are almost solely of utensils, artifacts, and unpeopled environments. Morris writes, "It is my feeling that the absence of people in my photographs enhances their presence in the structures and artifacts. The people absent from the photographs are explicitly present in the text in my photo-text books, where verbal images enhance those that are visual."

Morris was born in Central City, Nebraska. He moved with his father to Omaha, and then to Chicago, Illinois, as a young boy. He attended Lakeview High School, Chicago, from 1925 to 1928; Crane College, Chicago in 1929–1930; and Pomona College, Claremont, California, from 1930 to 1933. He has been a writer and photographer since 1934.

On a cross-country trip, moving to Connecticut in 1938, Morris encountered his major photographic subject: "I saw the American landscape crowded with ruins I wanted to salvage. The Depression created a world of objects toward which I felt affectionate and possessive. I . . . believed myself chosen to record this history before it was gone."

In 1939, Morris began to link his prose and his photographs, working on a photo-text, *The Inhabitants*. A Guggenheim Fellowship in Photography in 1942 helped him to complete the project, which was published in 1946. In 1947 Morris received a second Guggenheim for work on *The Home Place*, a photo-text which was published the following year.

Morris made most of his lasting images between 1938 and 1947. For the next 20 years, he concentrated on his novels, but did continue to photograph. His plan to photograph in Mexico on a third Guggenheim in 1954 fell through as he became immersed in fiction-writing. His third photo-text, *God's Country and My People*, did not appear until 1968. It contained many of his early photographs accompanied by new and different texts. Morris published a book of color photographs, *Love Affair: A Venetian Journal*, in 1972. His *Photographs and Words*, in which he wrote of the origin and development of his work with photo-texts, was published in 1982 by the Friends of Photography. He writes, "Through writing, through the effort to visualize, I became a photographer, and through my experience as a photographer I became more of a writer."

Morris has exhibited at the New School for Social Research, New York (1940); the Prakapas Gallery, New York (1976, 1977); and the Witkin Gallery, New York (1980, 1981). He has been the recipient of numerous awards and grants including a National Book Award, a National Institute of Arts and Letters Award, and two American Book Awards, in addition to his three Guggenheim Fellowships.

He was awarded Honorary Doctorates from Westminster College, Missouri, and the University of Nebraska, Lincoln (1968), and from Pomona College (1973). He was Honorary Fellow of the Modern Language Association in 1975 and Senior Fellow of the National Endowment for the Humanities in 1976. He is a member of the National Institute of Arts and Letters and the American Academy of Arts and Sciences.

Morris retired from his position as a teacher of creative writing at San Francisco State University in 1975.

Morris, Wright. "Powerhouse and Palmtree"
(1940). Courtesy Wright Morris.

Morse, Samuel Finley Breese

American; 1791–1872
Morse is best known, particularly in the
U.S., as the inventor of the electric telegraph, although in this he was preceded
by Karl Friedrich Gauss and Sir Charles
Wheatstone, among others. Of more importance, his dot-dash code was adopted
for all systems throughout the world and
remains the universal code for manually
operated radiotelegraph communication.

Morse's early training and first career
was as a painter. Landscapes were his
preferred subject, but only with portraits
could he earn a somewhat uncertain living, supplemented by a position at New
York University. It was his artistic background coupled with his interest as an
inventor that led him to request a private showing of L. J. M. Daguerre's
invention—the world's first photographs—in March 1839, when Morse
was in Paris during a trip intended
to arouse foreign interest and investment in the telegraph. A letter from

Morse written the next month describing
the amazing fidelity of the daguerreotypes he saw became the first published account of photography in the
U.S. It was during a reciprocal visit to
Morse's hotel for a demonstration of the
telegraph that Daguerre's theater, the
Diorama, burned to the ground.

Upon his return to New York, Morse
made some of the earliest daguerreotypes in the U.S., but his results were
surpassed by those of a fellow university
professor, John Draper, who succeeded
in obtaining the first extant portrait in
this country. Anxious to secure a more
substantial income, Morse established a
portrait studio with Draper in mid-1840
after Alexander Wolcott, inventor of
the mirror daguerreotype camera, refused Morse's partnership offer. The
studio prospered briefly, and when
Draper chose to devote himself to his
work in teaching chemistry, Morse
moved it from the University to a location on Nassau street. Morse gave in-

struction in the daguerreotype process to
a number of aspirants, including Edward
H. Anthony, Albert Southworth, and
Mathew Brady, all of whom became important American photographers.

In 1842 Morse devoted himself to
finding support for his telegraph system;
its success took several years, but even-
tually earned him a fortune.
See also: ANTHONY, E. & H. T.; BRADY,
MATHEW; DAGUERRE, L. J. M.; DRAPER,
JOHN WILLIAM; GAUSS, KARL F.; SOUTH-
WORTH, ALBERT; WHEATSTONE, SIR
CHARLES; WOLCOTT, ALEXANDER S.

Mosaic Systems

In mosaic systems patterns (mosaics) of
tiny primary-color (red, green, blue) elements are used to produce positive images; the full range of image colors is
created by additive synthesis. The image
must be formed by light passing through
such a mosaic, and it must be viewed
with light passing through an identical

mosaic. In photographic systems the intensity of the light is modulated by a positive black-and-white transparency image formed through the mosaic. The mosaic may be composed of a random arrangement of color elements, as in autochrome plates, or it may be a precise, regular pattern, as in Dufay, Finlay, Joly, and other screen processes. The mosaic technique has been tried for motion pictures, but the enlargement created by projection has made the mosaic pattern objectionably noticeable; in addition, the mosaic absorbs much more light than the chromogenic images of subtractive color materials. Color television screens are composed of a regular mosaic of red, green, and blue phosphor elements.

See also: ADDITIVE COLOR SYNTHESIS; AUTOCHROME PROCESS; CHROMOGENIC DEVELOPMENT; DUFAY COLOR; FINLAYCOLOR PROCESS; JOLY, JOHN; SCREEN PROCESSES.

Motion Pictures

Devices for blending a series of still images (drawings) into apparent motion (e.g., the *phenakistiscope)* were invented in the 1820s and 1830s. The first commercially successful machine using a continuous band of transparent film was the Edison *kinetoscope* of 1891, a one-person peep-show device. In basic concept and operation it had been preceded by E. J. Marey's *chronophotographe,* devised for the specialized purpose of motion study and analysis. The Lumiere brothers created the first regular public exhibitions of motion pictures projected from continuous rolls of celluloid film in 1895 with their *cinématographe.* Similar machines also using perforated film and an intermittent movement that stopped each frame momentarily at the instant it was projected were invented almost simultaneously by William Friese-Greene and Birt Acres in England, and by C. L. Jenkins (Edison *vitascope*) and W. K. L. Dickson (*biograph*) in the U.S. Although mechanisms have been vastly improved, the principles of photographic motion pictures have not changed since that time.

Motion pictures are possible because of the visual response popularly known as the persistence of vision: after a visual stimulus is removed, it takes from 1/10 second to 1/14 second for affected receptor cells in the retina to return to a neutral, no-output state. When stimuli such as successive images occur at a more rapid rate, one image has not completely "disappeared" on the retina before another appears, with the result that they seem blended or continuous. Early

devices such as the kinetoscope operated at a rate of 30 to 40 images per second, but it was soon recognized that this used unnecessary amounts of film. A rate of 16 images per second produced the desired fusion so that motion looked continuous, although a momentary drop in intensity was perceptible, giving rise to the descriptive term *the flickers.* The solution to this problem was to equip projectors with triple-bladed shutters, so that, although the camera and projector actually operated at 16 frames per second, each frame was flashed 3 times on the screen, for an effective rate of 48 impressions per second, eliminating the flicker. When sound was added to motion pictures at the end of the 1920s, it was discovered that the camera and projector had to operate at a faster speed for undistorted sound quality. A rate of 24 frames per second became standard, and double-bladed shutters or the equivalent were used on projectors to maintain the flicker-free 48 images per second viewing standard. When, in the 1950s, magnetically recorded sound was made available for motion-picture formats smaller than 35mm, the slower standard speed was advanced to 18 frames per second in order to synchronize with recording and playback standards of existing tape equipment.

The standard 35mm film width and a nominal frame size of 18 × 24mm were established by pragmatic decisions in the early development of motion-picture equipment; subsequent 16mm and 8mm formats were subdivisions of this standard. The Super 8 format, introduced for amateurs in the 1960s when 16mm began to become a professional-quality medium, was simply a larger frame size with different perforation spacing on 8mm film. Wide-screen motion-picture production after World War II led to the introduction of 65 and 70mm film with a variety of frame sizes, according to the system that was used. The introduction of sound, in 1927–28, required a slight decrease in the 35mm frame size to make room for the sound track; magnetic sound tracks (*sound stripes*) on 16mm and smaller formats became available in the late 1950s. It is not possible to place the sound pickup head exactly at the picture gate of a projector. For this

reason, a given sound on the track is physically several frames ahead of the picture to which it corresponds, so that the pickup can be located to play the sound at the instant the frame is being projected. This separation and other standard characteristics are as the accompanying chart indicates.

Motion-Picture Production. Commercial television production developed, from the late 1940s without a capability for prerecording a presentation. Consequently several cameras were used to view action from various viewpoints, and a presentation was created by electronically switching among them to obtain the required shot as the action was performed only once, at the time of presentation. This is exactly the opposite of motion pictures, which are only a prerecorded medium; "live" or real-time presentation of the action is not possible. The production technique that evolved from the beginning of the 20th c., as such pioneers as Edwin S. Porter and D. W. Griffith showed how to tell stories with sequences of varied views, centered on using a single camera. Now, as then, the camera is repositioned, the lighting adjusted, and the action repeated for each different view required. Only with mass action and scenes of spectacular destruction or other unrepeatable action are two or more cameras commonly used to record the scene simultaneously.

Each separate recording, or shot, begins and ends with a board or *slate* held briefly in front of the lens to provide an identifying number. A synchronized starting point to match the picture with the sound, which is recorded separately on magnetic tape, is provided by a scissorslike set of sticks that produce an audible "clap" as they are snapped shut in front of the lens, or by a built-in system that simultaneously produces a flash of light on the film and a "beep" on the tape. Shots are not necessarily photographed in the sequence in which they appear in the finished presentation; instead, they are photographed according to the dictates of economics and logistics. In many cases, all shots involving a particular performer or setting will be taken together, say in two or three days of work, even though these shots are to

	Camera Frame Size	No. Frames per Foot	No. Perforations per Frame	Sound-Picture Separation (Frames)
35mm	16 × 22mm	16	4	20 (0)*
16mm	7.5 × 10.3mm	40	2	26 (0) 28 (M)*
Super 8	4 × 5.6mm	72	1	22 (0) 18 (M)
8mm	3.7 × 4.9mm	80	2	56 (M)

*0, Optical track; M, Magnetic track.

Motion-Study Analysis. Philip Leonian, "Tennis Player" (1982). © 1982 Philip Leonian.

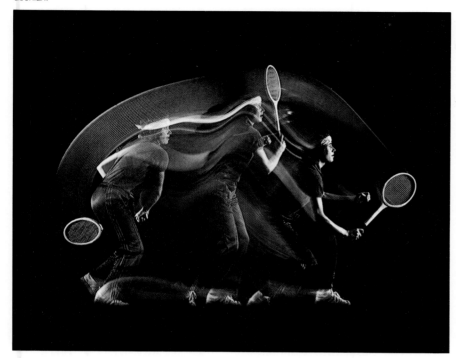

be used throughout the finished film and the schedule includes several weeks of photography.

Although each day's photography is processed immediately and sample prints—*rushes*—are reviewed to evaluate quality and to detect errors, the major construction process, called *editing*, does not begin until after all photography has been completed. Editing is carried out with prints made from duplicate negatives or with videotape copies, to protect the original negative. The best versions of the various shots are assembled in order to create a workprint. This is revised several times in a series of *fine cuts* in which shots are trimmed to length, arranged, rearranged, substituted, and variously combined until the most effective visual sequence is achieved. Then the sound recordings and the master negative, or an equivalent, are cut, trimmed, and arranged in corresponding sequence. Matching numbers or other identifying symbols or signals on all film and tape copies make it possible to *conform* the original material to the approved edited version with a minimum of difficulty. Music, sound effects, additional dialogue or narration, visual special effects, and similar elements are added in later phases of post-production work. Finally a composite negative is created from which release prints are made for distribution.

The production sequence described applies to motion pictures that are entirely staged. News, documentary, and special event photography does not involve re-enactment, alternate versions, and leisurely editing. The action in films of that sort is photographed as it happens, as best the camera operator can get it. As many additional shots of related and incidental elements are taken as possible; they are used in editing to cover gaps of missed or unusable action and to add variety and interest to the presentation.

See also: CUT; CUTAWAY; DISSOLVE; EDITING; FADE-IN/FADE-OUT; LONG SHOT; PANNING; TELEVISION.

Motion Study and Analysis

The ability of photography to freeze rapid movement in a sharp image taken in a fraction of a second was convincingly demonstrated in 1851 by W. H. F. Talbot. Many experimenters in the 1860s pointed out that it would be possible—if plates were sensitive enough—to take a rapid sequence of such pictures for use in a motion-integrating viewing device such as the phenakistiscope. But, in fact, such sequences were made at the time only by posing each stage of the action for an exposure on the order of one to three seconds or longer. Oliver Wendell Holmes was the first to indicate the value of photographs for analyzing how various movements were actually made. In 1861 he reported noticing in stereographs of street scenes that pedestrians were often accidentally caught in midstride. He collected a great number of such views and made drawings of details of walking, eventually obtaining a kind of animator's sequence chart of the movements of the knee, ankle, and foot, which he used in his work at that time: improving the design of articulated artificial limbs for Civil War amputees. These and related developments were all preliminary to the taking of photographs specifically for the purpose of studying and analyzing how a particular movement progressed or was accomplished, first the movement of humans and animals, later that of mechanical devices and machines.

The earliest significant motion-study sequences were trotting and galloping horse studies done by Eadweard Muybridge in 1872 and 1877–78 for Governor Leland Stanford of California. These, and an astronomical sequence of the transit of Venus by P. J. C. Janssen in 1874, established one mode of photographic motion analysis—single images on separate plates (later sheets of film, and still later frames on a continuous strip of film), or images sufficiently separated on a single plate so that the details of each recorded stage are clearly visible, with no overlapping of adjacent images in the sequence. Janssen's method used the forerunner of a number of gun cameras, with a slowly revolving plate and shutter operated by clockwork. Muybridge used a line of separate cameras whose shutters were released either by strings that were broken as the animal moved past, or by electromagnets activated when the metal wheel of a racing sulky passed over pairs of bare wires laid across the track. In his most extensive movement studies, at the University of Pennsylvania in 1884–85, Muybridge used three batteries of cameras, usually arranged to give a direct side view, a three-quarter frontal or a head-on view, and a similar angled view from behind. Each battery consisted of 12 film chambers with individual lenses and electrically controlled shutters. A complex plugboard and multiple-contact rotating disk switch permitted firing any selection of shutters simultaneously in a sequence and at intervals to suit the movement being recorded.

The other mode of early motion study with still photography was developed by E. J. Marey beginning in 1882. This consisted of a sequence of closely spaced images on a single plate or frame in which overlapping was common, but which revealed the continuous flow aspect of movement that was virtually impossible to discern by the separate-image technique. Marey's revolving-disk gun cameras achieved higher speeds and much shorter intervals than Muybridge's method, and his *chronophotographe,* using a continuous band of sensitized paper or film, achieved rates of up to 200 exposures per second; it was the direct predecessor of the motion-picture camera.

Prior to the advent of television and computer technology, motion study and analysis in the 20th c. developed along three main lines:

(1) Still or motion-picture sequences recorded by pulsed or intermittent illumination. This method originated in the 1880s with Ernst Mach and Ottomar Anschutz, both of whom used rapid electric-spark sequences to photograph bullet and projectile trajectories. (Anschutz also used a rapid-firing single camera and multiple camera batteries to photograph animals and birds in motion.) Pulsed-light photography as carried out today dates from the 1930s, when electronic flash tube stroboscope was invented by Harold Edgerton.

(2) Time-lapse photography, in which exposures taken at equally spaced, relatively lengthy intervals can be examined individually or compared by superimposition, or can be projected at normal motion-picture rates to reveal the flow of movement otherwise too slow to be detected by the eye.

(3) High-speed motion-picture sequences projected at normal speed, providing slow-motion presentation of rapid action, or still or streak sequences taken on continuous strips of film by similar techniques for image-by-image inspection.

All of these approaches are widely used today and are continually being refined and improved. They are paralleled by video-disk or tape-recording methods, with playback on equipment that permits various slow-motion rates or freeze-frame viewing, and some degree of accelerated-motion viewing. Image digitization and computer processing of material obtained by any of these methods permits integration, analysis, and presentation of movement and of derived data in a great number of ways, including translation into animated diagrams or other graphic forms. This capability extends the realm of motion study and analysis from determining what did happen to determining what would happen if a specified variation occurred; this aspect of the field is in its infancy.

See also: ANSCHUTZ, OTTOMAR; DIGITAL IMAGES; GUN CAMERA; HIGH-SPEED PHOTOGRAPHY; MAREY, ETIENNE JULES; MUYBRIDGE, EADWEARD; SLOW-MOTION PHOTOGRAPHY; STREAK CAMERA; STROBOSCOPIC PHOTOGRAPHY; TIME-LAPSE PHOTOGRAPHY.

Mounting Photographs

Photographic prints are often attached to stiff backing material to give them physical protection, to provide a handling area around the image, to hold the image flat, and to place the picture within a plain, non-distracting background. Prints must be mounted if they are to be hung unframed or if they have an overmat (a sheet of covering material with a window for the image area). They should also be mounted if they are to be framed, in order to keep the image from slipping out of position and to keep the photographic paper from sagging or buckling against the cover glass.

A wide variety of mounting materials may be used. The most common is cardboard with a surface layer of finished smooth or textured paper; it is commonly supplied as art or photographic mounting board. Composition hardboard, wood, smooth-surface plastic foam board, hard plastic, and metal are also widely used. A 100-percent acid-free (so-called museum or archival) mounting board is the best choice for long-term protection from chemical contamination that can cause staining or fading. Wood, hardboard, foam board, and plastics are more likely to react with the image at some future time; metal will not. These materials are often required for display of very large prints (e.g., 20″ × 30″ [51.3 × 76.9cm] and larger) because they can be braced or fastened to prevent warping and bending. Photographic emulsions expand and contract with changes in humidity and can exert a powerful pull on mounting material.

The print may be temporarily or permanently attached to the mounting board. Temporary attachment is preferred when the picture is to have an overmat, with or without additional framing. The two most common methods of temporary attachment are folded-paper corners that adhere to the mounting board into which the print corners can be slipped, and paper or cloth tabs that are adhered to the back edge of the print and then adhered to the mounting board. In both cases the print must have borders beyond the image area. Permanent attachment is accomplished with adhesive materials and usually fastens the entire back surface, not just the edges or corners, of the print to the mount. Rubber cement is widely used with expendable prints because cleanup is easy and because the print can be removed from the mount by means of a solvent. However, rubber cement and other solvent cements will react with images on fiber-base papers and cause staining. How soon this will occur depends on the chemical nature of the solvent and temperature and humidity conditions; in any case, the print is lost, even if it is subsequently removed from the mount. Prints on resin-coated papers resist solvent-staining to a much greater degree, and solvent adhesives may be used freely (as long as they do not attack the resin coating itself) because such papers do not have long-term permanence. Water-base adhesives such as plain wheat paste or thinned household white glue are widely used for wet-mounting large prints. They must be used with care to avoid getting adhesive on the face of the print, but they give good results with fiber-base papers and cardboard, hardboard, or wood.

Dry mounting is the preferred method of permanent attachment. It is accomplished by sandwiching a thin sheet of adhesive material between the print and the mounting board. So-called cold-mount tissue is adhered by pressure with a hand burnisher or by means of a set of rollers. (Some cold-mount materials permit later removal without damage to the print.) The long-term chemical safety of this method has not been demonstrated. Classic dry mounting uses heat-activated tissue. The tissue is tacked to the back of the print in three or four places with a hot iron—a household iron or a special tacking iron may be used. The print then is turned face up and the tissue is trimmed to the print edges. If the print has borders to be removed, the cut is made through the face of the print, simultaneously trimming both to exactly the same size. Next the print and its tissue are centered as desired on the mounting board. With the print held firmly in place, one corner is lifted and the corner of the dry-mounting tissue is tacked to the backing board; this is repeated with a second corner. The face of the print then is protected with a sheet of clean paper, and the sandwich is placed in a heated dry-mounting press. Instructions with the dry-mounting tissue indicate the proper time and temperature for various print papers. An electric household iron can also be used. The heat melts the shellac adhesive of the tissue, fusing the print to the mounting board. If a print is to be flush mounted (i.e., with no borders of print paper or mounting board), it is adhered with its borders on, and then print and mount are trimmed at the same time. The cut edges are usually blackened afterward.

See also: FILING AND STORING PHOTOGRAPHS; FRAMING.

M–Q Developer

An M-Q developer is one that contains the developing agents metol (*N*-methyl-*p*-aminophenol sulfate) and hydroquinone (*p*-dihydroxybenzene; quinol), whose individual values in development

Mulas, Ugo. "Homage to Niépce" (1970).
Courtesy Lanfranco Colombo, Milan.

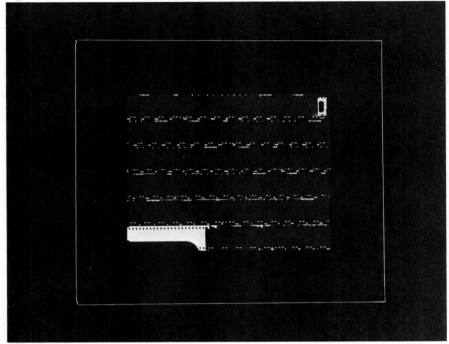

were discovered in 1890 and 1891, respectively. Formulas using this combination of agents comprise the largest and most versatile class of general-purpose developers for both films and papers. The most widely used black-and-white developers—Kodak D-76 developer for films, and D-72 or Dektol developer for papers—are M-Q formulas. Metol and hydroquinone exhibit a very high degree of superadditivity when combined, and development characteristics can be altered significantly by changing their ratio, as well as the proportion of the activator—usually sodium carbonate. In general, increasing the proportion of metol produces lower contrast. M-Q developers characteristically produce medium to fine grain and low fog, and have moderately short developing times, long working life, and good storage and replenishment characteristics.

See also: ACTIVATOR/ACCELERATOR; P-Q DEVELOPER; REPLENISHER; SUPERADDITIVITY.

MTF: Modulation Transfer Function

The resolving power of a lens or an emulsion—its ability to image fine, closely spaced details clearly—is affected by the spread function as the spacing between details gets narrower. Because of image spreading, at some point the fringe densities of adjacent details begin to overlap, reducing the difference (the contrast) between the details themselves and the space between them. As the spacing gets closer the overlapping becomes stronger and the contrast is progressively reduced until it is no longer possible to distinguish details from spaces. In some cases the overlap density becomes greater than that of either detail and an apparent reversal (a phase shift) occurs, producing spurious resolution. This interaction of resolving power and contrast is examined with a test target composed of bar-space pairs of continually decreasing width—i.e., of increasing spatial frequency. The rate of change in width corresponds to a sine wave function, which facilitates obtaining readings with electronic instruments and analyzing results mathematically. A graph of contrast versus spacing across the target—each pair representing a different equivalent number of lines per millimeter—is called a *contrast transfer graph*. When the target image is scanned electronically and the contrast represented as a waveform of changing amplitude—i.e., a modulated waveform—the graph representing the amplitude peaks is called the *modulation transfer function*. If a phase shift has occurred and is factored into the analysis, the graph is called the *optical transfer function*. These analyses of performance will be different for each aperture setting of a lens, and will be different between the center and edges of a lens. A published MTF curve is usually based on central area readings, where lens correction is best, and may represent best single-aperture performance or an average of performance at all apertures. Lens readings are commonly taken by a photocell behind a slit in the plane of the aerial image behind the lens; the target is moved across the field of view to obtain the various readings. Emulsion MTF readings are obtained by contact-exposing the target on the emulsion and subsequently scanning the processed image with a microdensitometer.

Standard tests for resolving power use a simpler set-up and furnish perfectly adequate information for many purposes. The MTF system of testing—with sinusoidal test objects, careful control of input/output relationships, and final readouts made by electronic instruments (rather than by eye)—furnishes a highly precise evaluation of photographic performance. It is of particular value in evaluating complete photographic systems including the lens, film, processing and prints, or projected images.

See also: RESOLVING POWER; SINE WAVE TARGET; SPREAD FUNCTION.

Mulas, Ugo

Italian; 1928–1973

Mulas was self-taught in photography, and after a short period of doing social reportage he expanded his professional activity, working in various fields such as stage, fashion, industrial photography, and magazine reportage. But he became well known above all for his photographs of artists and their works, an activity he started at the time of the 1954 Venice Biennale when he was appointed official photographer, a position he maintained until 1968.

After concentrating on Biennale artists, such as Smith, Giacometti, Ernst, and Fautrier, Mulas became interested in the New York avant-garde art scene, and particularly in those artists grouped around the Castelli and Solomon galleries. In 1967, he published *New York: The Art Scene*, for which he made portraits of many leading American contemporary artists in their working and living environment: Noland, Lichtenstein, Dine, Rauschenberg, Warhol, Johns, Stella, Duchamp, and Oldenburg. Back in Italy he made portraits of other famous artists, including De Chirico, Carra, Melotti, Fontana, Pomodoro, Calder. In those years, he also produced two large but rather conventional reportages on New York City and the U.S.S.R.

By the late 1960s Mulas became increasingly weary of "photographing other people's art," and not surprisingly the most challenging part of his work was produced after 1970. That year he started working on a series of conceptual photographs he called "Verifiche." They were meant to investigate, or "verify," the photographic medium itself—the process by which pictures come into being, the evolution of the medium, and above all the full extent of its pretended objectivity. Mulas thought that first of all the photographer should have a clear idea of the field of vision he wants to explore through his camera lenses; then the picture will create itself, or better "the material itself becomes the picture." To understand this mechanism Mulas made a conscientious study of all the basic elements of his own craft: the negative, optics, enlargement, exposure, the development of the negative, lighting, and finally the photographer (also considered an element of his craft) through self-portraiture. Mulas's approach had nothing to do with the mere learning of a technique or a trade; rather, this was a careful and meaningful re-appropriation of the medium by a professional and an artist wishing "to touch with my hands the sensation of operations I have repeated a hundred times a day for many years."

Mulas came to the conclusion that as long as the photographer consciously and precisely delimits his own field of vision, he is able to produce exactly what he wants: in the hands of the artist, the camera ceases to be a blind machine and becomes instead a truly controlled and creative instrument.

Multi-Image Techniques

Photographs composed of repetitions of a single image or of several different images can be created in the camera, in the darkroom, or in the post-processing stages of print finishing and presentation. Such photographs may be produced primarily for graphic effect or to attract attention, or for factual, polemic, or artistic communication. In any case, the intent is to present a more varied and complex message than can be carried by a single image. The major techniques by which multi-image photographs are produced are described briefly here; they are discussed further in the entries listed in the cross-references.

The basic in-camera technique for creating a multi-image photograph is multiple exposure. Repeat exposures made by means of the camera or lens shutter must be individually reduced so as not to create overexposure if there is significant overlapping of the images. A slotted or segmented shutter, such as used in some motion-study cameras, will produce multiple images as it revolves or slides past the lens or film. Repeated firings of a flash unit, or use of a stroboscope, will provide multiple exposures while the camera shutter remains open.

In these techniques either the subject or the camera must move to avoid image build-up at a single point on the film. Images can be separated in a series of exposures on a single frame by means of a set of two or more mattes, each of which exposes one part of the frame; the matte is changed to uncover a fresh portion of the film with each exposure.

Multiple images can be recorded in a single exposure by placing a multi-faceted prism attachment in front of the camera lens; by photographing an array of mirror pieces, either randomly scattered to break up a single image, or fixed in place to reflect subjects from several directions; or by aiming the lens into a V-shaped or triangular open-ended tube of mirrors that produces kaleidoscopic reflections.

Darkroom techniques for multi-image photographs generally consist of making multiple exposures on one piece of paper through a single negative or a series of negatives, moving the paper each time to achieve the desired arrangement. It is also possible to sandwich two negatives and print them with a single exposure. Ribbed glass, lenticular lens screens, and other optical devices can be used beneath the lens or against the paper surface to multiply the image. Printing masks can be used to cover and uncover various portions of the paper in much the same way that camera mattes are used.

Post-processing techniques include making montage and collage arrangements pasted in place, and assemblages of transparencies and print elements laminated together or mounted in a common material. The major presentation techniques are the projection of sandwiched transparencies, projection through image-multiplying optical devices such as prism attachments, and the use of multiple projectors to throw images on a common screen area.

Images can also be multiplied and combined in highly diverse ways by means of electronic (video) systems and by computer manipulation of digitized images.

See also: COLLAGE; COMPOSITE PHOTO-GRAPHS; DIGITAL IMAGES; LAMINATED IMAGES; MATTE/MATTE BOX; MIXED-MEDIA IMAGES; MONTAGE; MOTION STUDY AND ANALYSIS; MULTIPLE EXPOSURE/MULTIPLE PRINTING; STROBOSCOPIC PHOTOGRAPHY; VORTOGRAPH.

Color photograph: p. C-34.

Multimedia Presentations

A multimedia production combines two or more audio-visual media (e.g., slides, motion pictures, video) with other techniques such as live dramatic action or

dance to form a composite presentation. These elements are integrated so that they interact with and complement one another to form a unified whole; they do not simply follow after one another in a first-that, now-this manner. Multimedia presentations may be staged productions presented to an audience gathered for the purpose, or they may be self-contained, automatically repeating presentations that attract the attention of a passing audience. Presentations of both kinds are widely used to introduce new products and generate interest or publicity at press and sales conferences, expositions, and trade fairs; in programs and dynamic displays at museums and public institutions; and at concerts, celebrations, and special events for entertainment purposes. Multimedia techniques are also sometimes employed in the aesthetic events generally called performance art.

The foundation of most informational multimedia productions is multiple slide projection, to which motion pictures and, often, live action are the most common additional elements. From two to a dozen or more projectors of various types may be used; the projectors commonly are arranged to project their pictures side-by-side in some cases and into the same area in other cases. The screen(s) may be equipped to roll up out of the way during portions of the presentation, or they may be incorporated into scenery used for live-action segments. The projectors commonly are interconnected with remote-control dissolve/special-effect units, which in turn are controlled by cue signals recorded on one track of an accompanying sound/music tape, or in complex productions by a program stored in a minicomputer. The program may also control stage lighting, microphone switching, and the activation of many other elements.

While a simple multimedia presentation can be the work of one or two people, production of a major presentation can be equally as complex as staging a musical comedy or making a motion picture. The personnel required often include writers, graphic and scenic designers, photographers, editors, directors, performers, musicians, costume and makeup specialists, audio and video engineers, lighting specialists, a variety of technicians and assistants, and an overall coordinator, called a producer. Such a production begins with a full script, or at the very least a detailed storyboard, which is revised as experimentation and rehearsal reveal more effective or more efficient ways to achieve the desired effects.

A major photographic concern in

Multiple Exposure. Jerry Uelsmann, untitled (1971). © Jerry Uelsmann; permanent collection, ICP, New York.

related to its adjoining sprocket holes in the same alignment. The processed film is mounted in matching pin-register slide mounts so that alignment is maintained from image to image throughout projection. Photography of graphic material and copying of other photographs is commonly accomplished on a motion-picture animation stand using a precision 35mm still camera, or a single-frame motion-picture camera that has been adapted to produce full-frame 35mm images rather than standard motion-picture frames, which are equivalent to 35mm half-frame size. Multimedia slides are also produced by means of computer graphic systems, which can produce a wide variety of special effects unattainable by direct photography.

See also: AUDIO-VISUAL; ANIMATION; PROJECTION; REGISTRATION OF IMAGES; SPECIAL EFFECTS.

Multiple Exposure; Multiple Printing

The technique of multiple exposure records several images on a single sheet or frame of film. The same subject may be imaged several times, or different subjects may be combined. Multiple printing is the process of making repeat exposures of a single negative on one sheet of paper. A related technique, combination printing, exposes a number of different negatives onto one sheet of paper.

One approach to camera multiple exposure with a single subject is to keep the shutter open while a stroboscope produces light pulses or a series of flash units fires in succession. It is also possible to rotate an auxillary shutter—an opaque disk with an open segment—in front of the lens. In order for the multiple images to be somewhat separated on the film with these techniques, there must be movement: of the subject, the camera, a zoom lens, or any combination of these.

A second, more common approach to multiple exposure is to operate the shutter for each exposure. With 35mm and roll-film cameras this requires recocking the shutter without advancing the film. Some cameras have a built-in multiple-exposure feature. In other cameras it is possible to activate the rewind release to prevent film movement while operating the thumb lever to cock the shutter. If the various subjects have dark areas, it may be possible to compose each so that there is no overlapping of significant bright areas among the images. In that case each image receives normal exposure. With a view camera the position of each subject can be marked on the view-

multimedia production is the compatibility of all images in quality and in registration. Image quality is a matter of equal sharpness, exposure, and color balance. This is especially important with images that are shown simultaneously or that blend into one another. Sharpness and exposure are matters of using high-quality equipment and meticulous technique; color balance is controlled primarily by using only one kind of film of the same emulsion batch for all photography and by careful attention to light balancing and filtration. Precise registration is required so that images will align or superimpose accurately on the screen.

A common technique in multimedia production is to have three or four matching images form a continuous wide-screen picture, or for a number of images to follow one another in rapid succession in exactly the same place; this is impossible without proper registration.

Registration is achieved by using a camera with a ruled grid on the viewing screen so that images may be framed with repeatable precision. The camera must also have an internal pin-registration system that engages the sprocket holes after the film has been advanced and ensures that every image is

ing glass or on an overlay to achieve precise composition. If middletone and highlight areas do overlap among the various images, their exposure effects will be added together on the film. To avoid overexposure, each subject must receive only a proportion of the total exposure. This is determined by dividing the normal exposure for one image by the total number of exposures to be made, and giving each only that partial amount. With an automatic-exposure-control camera the same thing can be accomplished by multiplying the film speed by the total number of exposures and resetting the meter to that speed.

The overlapping exposure effect is also a problem in multiple printing, where it will create excessive darkness (in films, overexposed areas are too light in the final print or slide). Proper balance of printing exposure is relatively easy to establish by means of test strips and sample prints. The more significant problem is achieving a controlled degree of image overlap and separation. This requires some means of graduated registration so that the paper can be shifted a certain amount, or the lens can be moved (as with a camera zoom lens), between exposures.

See also: COMBINATION IMAGES; MULTI-IMAGE TECHNIQUES.

Multiple Flash

Lighting arrangements that require two or more light sources are often made with electronic flash units rather than with continuous sources such as quartz lights or photofloods. Using flash avoids heat and glare that may affect the subject, it permits the use of daylight-type color film, and it permits subject movement without the need for a fast shutter speed to get unblurred images.

The desired arrangement is set up just as it would be with continuous-source lighting instruments. Setup is made easier by equipping the units with low-output continuous modeling lights so the effect can be seen; otherwise, test shots are necessary. A particular balance, or lighting ratio, is established by setting the variable-output controls, if the units are so equipped, or by varying the flash-to-subject distance of each unit as required. The latter method begins by establishing the position of the key light unit and calculating the *f*-stop that will be used for exposure. The required difference in brightness of each additional unit then is determined in terms of *f*-stops (e.g., a fill-light unit might be one stop less bright, a backlight one stop brighter). Using the guide number of each unit for the film speed in use, the

Munkacsi, Martin. "Zuschauer" (n.d.). Collection, Museum of Modern Art, New York.

distance the unit must be placed from the subject can be calculated easily. The output of flash units can also be reduced with diffusers or neutral density filters.

Automatic flash units should be set for manual operation in multiple-flash setups, or their output will be affected by the light from the other units. In order for all units to fire simultaneously, they must be connected to the main unit with sync cords; in turn the main light is connected to the camera shutter. A less cumbersome method is to equip all but the key light unit with a *slave trigger*. This is an instantaneous-reaction photo-electric switch that reacts to the flash of the main unit and causes its own unit to fire; no interconnecting wires are required. Some auxiliary flash units are supplied with built-in slaves. There are also slaves that can be triggered by infrared or radio signals; these are useful in very bright ambient light conditions over long distances, or where flash units used by other photographers might cause unwanted triggering.

See also: FLASH; GUIDE NUMBER; LIGHTING; MODELING-LIGHT; SLAVE UNIT.

Munkacsi, Martin

American; 1896–1963

Martin Munkacsi was a celebrated fashion photographer in the 1930s and 1940s. He rose to prominence through a zestful and inventive approach and distinctive personal style that was unfettered by the stale conventions of the day.

In his work for *Harper's Bazaar* he was more concerned with conveying moods and emotions than with the careful delineation of clothes and accessories. He was particularly skillful at depicting movement in a manner which appeared entirely spontaneous, and he is therefore rightfully credited for having introduced realism into fashion photography.

In fact, the ideas Munkacsi introduced into fashion photography had been his stock-in-trade as a photo-reporter in Berlin. There he had absorbed the lessons of the New Objectivity school, characterized by dramatic angles, strong diagonals, and bold patterns. He advised would-be photographers to "pick unexpected angles. Lie down on your back, climb ladders."

Munkacsi was born in Kolozsvar, Hungary, in 1896, and left home on several occasions as a young boy. In 1912 he arrived in Budapest, where he wrote poetry for magazines and newspapers and began to report on sports for the magazine *Az Est*. In 1921 he also began to photograph sports for the magazine, demonstrating a sense of timing and drama. In 1927 he arrived in Berlin and almost immediately received a three-year contract with the Ullstein Press. He contributed regularly to the *Berliner Illustrirte Zeitung* (sometimes also under a ficticious name), *Die Dame*, *Koralle*, *UHU*, and other Ullstein publications. During the Berlin years he traveled widely on assignment, once by zeppelin to America.

In 1934 Munkacsi took advantage of Carmel Snow's offer to work at *Harper's Bazaar*. In extending the invitation Snow defied her publisher's orders, but by 1940 her instinct had proved correct: Munkacsi was an unqualified success; by his own reckoning he was earning more than $100,000 a year. He was fond of quipping, "A picture isn't worth a thousand words, it's worth a thousand bucks!" The influence of the spontaneity and out-of-the-studio settings of his best work was extensive. Richard Avedon in particular has acknowledged poring over Munkacsi's pictures as a youth.

In 1943 Munkacsi suffered a heart attack and was forced to cut back on his professional work, but took the opportunity to begin a semi-autobiographical novel. *Fool's Apprentice* was published in 1945. In 1951 he published a book of his nudes, with a cover design by Alexei Brodovitch. In 1963 Munkacsi died of a heart attack.

During his lifetime, Munkacsi's work was never shown in a one-man exhibition, although there were a few group exhibitions, one of which was held at the Museum of Modern Art in 1937. A full retrospective of his work, including a sizable representation of his Hungarian and German photography, was held at the International Center of Photography in New York in 1978. A monograph, *Style in Motion*, edited by Nancy White and John Esten, with an introductory essay by William A. Ewing and forewords by Richard Avedon and Henri Cartier-Bresson, appeared in 1979.

Munsell System

The Munsell system is the standard U.S. system for specifying the color of pigments and other opaque colorants. It is objective in that standard colors are supplied, each classified by a numerical rating of its characteristics. It is a subjective system in that colors are identified by visual matching and the intervals between standard color variations are chosen to appear visually equal.

Colors in the Munsell system are classified according to a combination of three attributes: hue, value, and chroma. The color of a sample is called its hue. There are five principle hues—red (R), yellow (Y), green (G), blue (B), and purple (P)—and five intermediate hues—red-yellow (RY), yellow-green (YG), green-blue (GB), blue-purple (BP), and purple-red (PR)—located exactly halfway between the principle hues. Additional hues are located between the principle and intermediate hues, for a total of about 100. The system allows for the addition of new hues as distinct colorants are developed. The value of a color is its visual brightness as compared to a gray scale of equal visual steps from black (1) to white (9). Chroma is the saturation of a color, its relative purity or freedom from white, black, or gray. Chroma runs from 0, colorless, to a maximum of 16; not all hues require 16 steps to reach full saturation.

The Munsell system is sometimes represented as a three-dimensional model called a "Munsell Color Solid," an asymmetrical sphere containing all the color samples. The north-south axis is the value scale, 1 (black) being the south pole. The east-west axis is the chroma scale. Far east on a particular plane represents a fully saturated sample; the center is neutral gray and far west is the complementary fully saturated color. The various hues are represented laterally around the circumference of the orb. In practice, the plane of each hue becomes a color chart with samples of each possible combination of value and chroma arrayed according to the scales. The system is also widely available as the *Munsell Book of Color*.

For simplified identification of an individual sample, Munsell patches are coded according to their hue, value, and chroma as (H V/C). For example, a 5B 7/4 has a hue of 5 blue, a value of 7, and a chroma of 4; in common language it might be described as a baby blue. These codings are now cross-referenced with the CIE system for objective correlation with equivalent colors of light.

It is important to note that the spacings of the patches are based on appearance only. Thus, the number 5 gray patch of the value scale, representing middle gray, reflects 18 percent of the incident light—not 50 percent. The reason is simply that the eye sees shades of gray roughly in terms of doubling reflectances (e.g., 1, 2, 4, 9, 18 percent, etc.). The Munsell system is important photographically because of this. For example, averaging exposure meters are commonly calibrated to respond to a middle gray representing a reflectivity of 18 percent. The limits of the system are confined to what can be produced by inks, dyes, or pigments on paper, cloth, or other opaque materials. It is most useful to printers, manufacturers, and painters.

See also: CIE COLOR SYSTEM; COLOR; COLORIMETRY.

Murals

Photographic murals are used primarily for architectural decoration and for advertising and exhibition display purposes. Images for display murals are selected on the basis of the message to be conveyed or other function to be performed, for example to indicate the location and subject matter of a particular section of an exhibition. Images for decorative murals must meet other criteria, the most important of which is that their content and tones or colors must be suitable to the location. An energetic or graphically bold image with bright, assertive colors might be suitable for an airline terminal or bank lobby, but not for a library or hospital waiting room. An image that will interest passersby in a public place is not necessarily one that will be suitable in an office where it is seen by the same workers every day throughout the day. In interior, furnished locations a mural must harmonize with the style and colors of the furnishings, which may be a matter of its exerting an influence on the choice of what is placed there.

The complexity and scale of the image are also important. A mural running the length of a 10-foot-wide (3-meter-wide) passageway cannot be seen in its entirety, and so it must have a kind of running composition that presents a series of interesting views at various points along the way. In such a situation viewers will be only 2 to 8 feet (0.6 to 2.5 meters) from the mural, so very large-scale shapes or huge areas of color will not be grasped visually. In contrast to this, a mural seen across the distance of a large building lobby must have shapes, colors, and an overall composition suitable to its being seen as a single image, and those elements must carry effectively across the distance. Scale considerations are equally as important in room-size murals. Excessive scale will make an image seem to crowd the space and threaten to overwhelm the inhabitants.

In general, murals are about 4' × 6' (1.2 × 1.8m) or larger and are composed of two or more sections joined together. (Smaller prints are essentially just big enlargements.) Most murals are produced by specially equipped commercial laboratories. In limited sizes they can be produced, with difficulty, by hand methods in a well-equipped darkroom of sufficient size. An enlarger capable of projecting an image of the size required for each section must be rigidly mounted and equipped with a lens that does not exhibit falloff in sharpness or illumination at the edges of its field. When the original image is in a small format, best results are obtained by making a 4" × 5" intermediate negative from which the image is printed. The board to which the paper is tacked or taped must be absolutely parallel with the negative plane. At mural-size magnifications any misalignment will produce noticeable unsharpness in part of the image. Exposure is determined by tests with small patches of paper placed at various points within the image field. Ordinary enlarging paper is supplied in widths up to 40 inches (1 meter); special mural paper on reinforced single-weight stock is supplied in widths from 42 to 54 inches (1.1 to 1.4 meters) in long rolls. The paper should have a matte, tweed, or similar surface. A glossy surface will produce glare and reflections when the mural is in place, will show fingermarks and abrasions clearly, and will resist the spotting and retouching that are always necessary after the mural has been assembled.

The major problem is processing. If there is suitable space, the paper can be laid on the floor and solutions sponged or swabbed on. Smaller lengths can be seesawed through troughs of solution—almost always a two-person operation at least. Thoroughly washing large sheets and drying them without rippling, uneven shrinkage, or tearing are particularly difficult to accomplish. A rack or frame over a bathtub or floor drain and a garden hose offer a method of washing. Drying can be accomplished by hanging the sheets edgewise tacked to battens or clipped to lengths of wire. Each section must be exposed with plenty of overlap image area at the edges to permit this kind of handling and to ease the problems of matching in final assembly.

The mural is assembled in the same manner as a giant-scale photomontage, with straight-cut overlaps pasted together and the edges retouched. Assembly should be made on the final backing material—usually composition hardboard reinforced with a backing frame to resist the pull of the print. Wet-paste mounting is the only suitable hand method, but it requires experience. Final mounting may best be left to a professional framer. Retouching and spotting are done after mounting is completed. *See also:* MONTAGE.

Muray, Nickolas

American; 1892–1965

Nickolas Muray became famous for his witty and graceful portraits of the 1920s and for creating the pre-World War II glamour style of photographing Hollywood stars. Important figures of the artistic, literary, musical, and theatrical worlds were captured, often in their trademark poses, by his camera. Muray was known as a perfectionist in the studio and darkroom, and in every area of his photographic work: advertising, fashion, and dance photography in addition to his portraiture. Among Muray's

Muray, Nicolas. "Babe Ruth [George Herman Ruth]" (1927). Courtesy Mimi Muray; collection, Museum of Modern Art, New York.

sitters were the dancers Ruth St. Denis and Martha Graham; the writers Eugene O'Neill, D.H. Lawrence, and F. Scott Fitzgerald; the film stars Marlene Dietrich, Lillian Gish, and Gloria Swanson; Presidents Coolidge, Hoover, and Franklin Roosevelt; and several hundred other well-known figures including Babe Ruth and Claude Monet.

Muray was born in Szeged, Hungary, and raised in Budapest from the age of two. He studied fundamentals of photography, photoengraving, and lithography at the Budapest Graphic Arts School from 1904 to 1908. In 1908–1909 he worked as a journeyman engraver in Germany and Hungary, receiving an International Engravers Certificate. Muray did further study in color photoengraving and filter making at the Berlin State Technical School from 1909 to 1911. He worked as a photoengraver in Berlin with Ullstein Publishers from 1911 to

1913, at which time he emigrated to the United States.

Muray worked as a color-separation printer in Brooklyn, N.Y., from 1913 to 1916, and for Condé Nast Publications in New York and Chicago as a color-print processor from 1916 to 1921. His career as a photographer began in 1920, after receiving encouragement from Pirie MacDonald. Muray worked mainly as a portraitist at first, then in advertising, fashion, and commercial photography on a freelance basis, operating his own studio until his death in 1965. His work appeared regularly in *Vogue*, the *New York Times*, *Vanity Fair*, *Dance* magazine and *Harper's Bazaar*. He was under contract for several years to *Ladies' Home Journal* and *McCall's*.

Muray was also active as a fencing master, competing in the Olympic Games of 1928, 1932, and 1936, and as a judge in the Tokyo Olympics of 1964.

During World War II he served as a flight lieutenant in the United States Civil Air Patrol.

Among the highlights of Muray's later career was an eight-month photographic trip around the world with the Wenner-Gren Foundation for Anthropological Research.

Muray's work was exhibited in group shows including *The Twenties Revisited* at the Gallery of Modern Art, New York, in 1965; *Fleeting Gestures: Dance Photographs* at ICP, New York, the Photographers' Gallery, London, and Venice '79 in 1979; and *Amerika Fotografie 1920–1940* at Kunsthaus, Zurich, in 1979. His *Celebrity Portraits of the Twenties and Thirties* was reissued in 1978.

Museums and Collections

In the broadest sense, photographic collections are of two categories: documentary and aesthetic. The documentary image records a fact that is generally historical (scientific, sociological, political, and so on). The aesthetic image is concerned with issues of artistic tradition and innovation, for photographic composition and content have long been in discourse with the media of painting, lithography, and engraving. Though it is true that documentary images often succeed aesthetically and that aesthetic picture-taking frequently captures documentary information, these two categories are useful determinants of a collection's orientation and strength.

There are over 200 American museums and collections that include photographs of every kind, and a cursory survey abroad from Australia to Yugoslavia, Venezuela to Norway, accounts for 120 more. The history of European collecting began in France when the Cabinet des Estampes (now the Département des Estampes et de la Photographie, which to the present day collects an estimated 5,000 photographs annually), became the despository of photographs in 1851, when a law required that a copy of each print offered for sale be sent there. At the same time, the Société Héliographique was founded; and in London, a group of photographs was shown at the Great Exhibition in the Crystal Palace. In 1853, the Photographic Society of Great Britain (now the Royal Photographic Society) was established. Meanwhile in Paris, the Société Française de la Photographie was founded by several enthusiasts and practitioners of the new art, including Hippolyte Bayard, the Bisson frères, Louis-Désiré Blanquart-Evrard, Gustave Le Gray, and Charles Nègre. Two years later, they inaugurated a museum

that remains a splendid archive of early photographic work, with over 15,000 prints, negatives, and daguerreotypes. The United States, though relatively backward in matters of culture in the mid 19th c., began gathering photographs on a national scale even earlier than the Europeans. As early as 1846, the Library of Congress commenced its collecting when the Copyright Deposit Law demanded a copy of each "book, map, chart, musical composition, print, cut, or engraving." Thus was started the largest of America's photographic holdings. The Library of Congress now has in excess of 10 million photographs in 800 distinct collections that exemplify documentary photography.

The Library of Congress collection is notable for a diversity that seems to represent the photographic enterprise as a whole, with the various challenges this has created for the curator. The vast realm of subjects collected here, from the first architectural photographs of Washington, D.C., to images of the Crimean War to pictures of the Middle East in the 19th c. and Erwin Evan Smith's record of cowboy life, indicates the catholicity of the camera eye, the potentially infinite substantiations of phenomena as visual artifacts, the repetition of photomechanical image-making, and the consequent difficulties in selecting a manageable image-repertoire for collecting. The Smithsonian Institution's Division of Photographic History at the National Museum of American History in Washington, D.C., the Humanities Research Center (formed around the Gernsheim collection) at the University of Texas in Austin, and the International Museum of Photography at the George Eastman House in Rochester, New York, are the other major collections that have the facilities to encompass the gargantuan body of photography. For example, the Smithsonian holds the encyclopedic Underwood and Underwood Illustration Studios collection. Its 8,000 stereo and 13,000 glass and film negatives document the fields of agriculture, anthropology, art, archeology, biology, botany, costumes, cultual history, entomology, manufacturing, military and naval history, mineral sciences, musical instruments, sports, and transportation. Beyond this range of documentary work, the four museums mentioned above have wide selections of aesthetic images and the most considerable holdings of photographic apparatus, which trace the history of the technology of photography.

The great array of aesthetic imagery is equally a subject of interest. The San Francisco Museum of Modern Art has

built its collection of 20th-c. photographs as a complement to its collection of the century's painting and sculpture, emphasizing photography's stylistic dependence on earlier media. One of the most celebrated collections, that of the Museum of Modern Art in New York, includes such influences while fully examining the autonomous developments of photographic vision. Since its inception in 1929, this museum has been a center for the most advanced aesthetic work.

The Art Institute of Chicago, the University of Arizona's Center for Creative photography, and the University of New Mexico's Art Museum are other institutions with extensive generalist collections. Becuse of photography's wide range of subjects and styles it is more common for collections to specialize in one or more aspects of the medium; period, geographical area, subject, school, and individual photographer are the categories around which collections are often built. Examples of such specialized collections are the collection of 19th c. photographs at the Boston Museum of Fine Arts; the collection of Western photography at the Amon Carter Museum in Fort Worth, Texas; the collection of local images, and the archive of the work of Clarence John Laughlin at the University of Louisville's Photographic Archives; the 20th c. collection, the regional collection, and the collection of German photographs of the 1920s and 1930s at the New Orleans Museum of Art; the 19th c. collection and the holding of Alfred Stieglitz's work at the Metropolitan Museum of Art in New York; the selection of 20th c. photography, including many photographs by Stieglitz, at the Philadelphia Museum of Art; and the 19th and 20th c. aesthetic photographs, Western landscapes, and theatrical, literary, and political portraits at the Art Museum and the Firestone Library of Princeton University.

Institutions where other significant collections are located include the New York Public Library, the Sheldon Memorial Art Gallery at the University of Nebraska, the Exchange National Bank in Chicago, the Friends of Photography in Carmel, California, the Carpenter Center for Visual Arts and the Fogg Art Museum at Harvard University, the International Center of Photography in New York, the Museum of the City of New York, and the New York Historical Society.

There are substantial photographic archives in many countries of the world. The following list indicates the wide international distribution of such collections; it is far from being a complete listing. Volumes listed in the bibliography under "Collections," "History," and "Reference" provide more nearly complete listings of museums and collections, with addresses, and listings of galleries as well.

National Gallery of Canada, Ottawa; McCord Museum, Montreal; National Film Board of Canada, Ottawa; Casa de las Americanas, Havana; Consejo Mexicano de Fotografia, Mexico City; Museu de Arte Moderna, Rio de Janeiro; Museo de Bellas Artes, Caracas; Osterreichisches Fotomuseum, Bad Ischl, Austria; Provinciaal Museum voor Kunstambachten, Antwerp; National Gallery, Prague; Royal Library, Copenhagen; National Portrait Gallery, London; Victoria and Albert Museum, London; National Museum of Photography, Bath; Finska Fotograpfiska Museet, Helsinki; Fondation Nationale de la Photographie, Lyons; Musée d'Orsay, Paris; Centre George Pompidou, Paris; Musée Nicephore Niepce, Chalonsur-Saône, France; Museum Folkwang, Essen; Museum für Kunst and Gewerbe, Hambuɟ3; Rheinisches Landes Museum, Bonn; Museum der Photographie, Dresden; Hungarian Photographic Archives, Budapest; Gallery of Photography, Dublin; Israel Museum, Jerusalem; Museo del Cinema, Turin; Fotografijos Musiejus, Siauliai, Lithuania; Stedelijk Museum, Amsterdam; Preus Fotomuseum, Horten, Norway; Museum Sztuki, Lodz, Poland; Museu Nacional de Arte Antiga, Lisbon; U.S.S.R. Central State Archives of Cinema and Photodocuments, Krasnogorsk, Moscow Region; TASS Agency Collection, Moscow; U.S.S.R. Central State Archives of Literature and Art, Moscow; Museum of Photographic Art, Moscow; Rhodes National Gallery, Salisbury, Zimbabwe; Nehru Memorial Museum and Library, Bombay; Victoria Memorial, Calcutta; City Palace, Jaipur; the archives of the various Indian States; The National Library, Singapore; The National Archives, Singapore; National Museum of Modern Art, Tokyo; Nippon University Photography Department; Osaka University of Arts; Tokyo Institute of Polytechnics; Australian National Gallery, Canberra; Geelong Art Gallery, Geelong, Victoria; Australian Centre for Photography, Sydney, New South Wales; National Gallery of Victoria, Melbourne, Victoria; National Gallery, Wellington, New Zealand.

See also: CONSERVATION OF PHOTOGRAPHS; GALLERIES; HISTORY OF PHOTOGRAPHY; PICTURE LIBRARIES/ AGENCIES.

Mutoscope

An early 1890s motion-picture viewing machine, the Mutoscope was based on

Muybridge, Eadweard. "16 Frames of Race Horse Galloping" (1883–87); photolithograph. Library of Congress.

the flip-book principle of rapidly riffling a motion sequence of still pictures before the eyes. The action was photographed on a continuous strip of celluloid negative film in the *mutograph*, one of the earliest motion-picture cameras. Several hundred frame-by-frame paper prints were individually mounted on flexible cards arranged in a circular stack around a central hub. As a crank in the machine was turned, each picture was retained briefly in front of the viewing hood by a spring-lever before pressure from the cards behind caused it to flip down, out of the way, revealing the next picture. Governing gears limited the rate to the 16–18 images-per-second minimum necessary for the visual fusion of motion, no matter how rapidly the crank was turned. As the original coin-operated peepshow machine, the Mutoscope was one of the first successful commercial exploitations of motion pictures. Like its rival, the Kinetoscope, it was limited to one viewer at a time and found it greatest market in penny arcades and similar installations. Although popular up to about 1910, in the long run it could not compete with group-audience projection machines such as the zoopraxiscope, vitascope, or the Biograph, also made by the American Mutoscope Company. Small mutoscopes were made for the home, but they were much bulkier and far more expensive than novelties such as the praxinoscope and zoetrope, and thus were not particularly successful.

See also: KINETOSCOPE; MOTION PIC-

TURES; PRAXINOSCOPE; VITASCOPE; ZOETROPE; ZOOPRAXISCOPE.

Muybridge, Eadweard

British; 1830–1904

Eadweard Muybridge was the most significant contributor to the early study of human and animal locomotion. His extensive studies and inventions were acknowledged by such pioneers of motion pictures as E. J. Marey, the Lumière brothers, and Thomas Edison.

Muybridge was born Edward James Muggeridge at Kingston-on-the-Thames, England, in 1830. (He adopted early in life the Saxon spelling of his name.) He attended school in Kingston, and worked in his family's stationery and papermaking business in London. He was employed by the London Printing and Publishing Co. and came to the U.S. in 1852 as their representative. In San Francisco he learned photography from daguerreotypist Silas Selleck in the early 1860s, and worked for Carleton E. Watkins, the major West Coast scenic photographer, before striking out on his own. He made photographic surveys for the firm of Thomas Houseworth and worked for the U.S. War Department documenting areas of the West Coast.

Muybridge first gained recognition in 1867 for a prizewinning series of dramatic Yosemite views. The following year, he was the official photographer with the American military presence in recently-purchased Alaska. He took over 2000 photographs of the American Far West between 1868 and 1873.

Mydans, Carl. "Earthquake, Fukui, Japan" (1948). Carl Mydans, LIFE Magazine, © 1948 Time Inc.

In 1872 Muybridge was enlisted by Leland Stanford to settle a wager regarding the position of a trotting horse's legs. Using the fastest shutter available, Muybridge was able to provide only the faintest image. He was more successful five years later when, employing a battery of cameras with mechanically tripped shutters, he showed clearly the stages of the horse's movement: at top speed, a trotting horse had all four hooves off the ground simultaneously, and in a different configuration from that of a galloping horse.

In the interim between these two studies, Muybridge photographed ruins and Indian village life in Central America. He had left the U.S. after killing his wife's lover. Though acquitted at trial, he did not return to the U.S. until 1877.

Muybridge concentrated his efforts on studies of the motion of animals and human models. His work in stop-action series photography soon led to his invention of the "zoopraxiscope," a primitive motion-picture machine which recreated movement by displaying individual photographs in rapid succession. This machine was demonstrated privately in America as early as 1879, and at public gatherings in Europe over the next two years. Muybridge demonstrated and lectured on his work at the Royal Institution and Royal Academy, London, in 1882 and in major American cities in 1883.

Thomas Eakins, who painted motion subjects, helped arrange for Muybridge to work at the University of Pennsylvania, Philadelphia. Muybridge's major accomplishments date from his three-year stay there, during which he was able to improve his techniques. In 1887 his most important work, *Animal Locomotion,* was published in 11 volumes. It contained over 100,000 photographs taken between 1872 and 1885.

Muybridge lectured at "Zoopraxographical Hall" at the World's Columbian Exposition of 1893 in Chicago. He returned to England in 1894 and did little photography in his last years. His book *The Human Figure in Motion* was published in 1901. He died three years later at his native Kingston-on-the-Thames.
See also: MOTION STUDY AND ANALYSIS; ZOOPRAXISCOPE.

Mydans, Carl

American; 1907–
Carl Mydans prepared himself from an early age for his lifelong involvement with journalism, whether it was to be with words or with photographs. Born and raised in Boston, he earned a B.S. degree from the Boston University school of Journalism in 1930. Mydans's career as a journalist began with free-lance work for the Boston *Globe* and the Boston *Post.* He continued as a staff writer for the *American Banker,* a New York Wall Street daily.

In 1931 Mydans acquired a 35mm camera and entered the world of photo-journalism, becoming one of a new breed of reporter: those who know how to handle the typewriter and the camera alike. Observant by nature, Mydans was now able to translate into the visual what was sometimes difficult to describe with words alone.

He obtained his first important photographic assignment in 1935 after he had joined what was to become the Farm Security Administration (FSA). He began work as a photographer under the leadership of Roy Stryker, who assigned Mydans to document the cotton industry in the South. Besides recording the facts of that industry, Mydans photographed compassionately the lives of those who suffered, the dispossessed and the exploited, setting a pattern to be followed by many other photographers who worked for the FSA.

Mydans's stay with the FSA was brief. In 1936 he was hired as one of the four photographers to help launch *Life* magazine; he remained an active staff photographer until the magazine closed in 1972. Those 36 years, during which he covered major news events in the United States, Europe, and Asia, were the most important years in his career.

During World War II, Mydans photographed England preparing for attack, Italy under Mussolini, the Finnish campaign against Russia, Belgian refugees streaming into France, and France at war in 1940 and again in 1944 during the advance of the 5th U.S. Army. Between 1940 and 1944, Mydans and his wife Shelley, a former *Life* researcher, were in Asia, first covering Chungking in its stand against the Japanese bombings, then in Burma, Malaya, and the Philippines. In the Philippines they were both captured by the Japanese and imprisoned for 21 months. They were released to U.S. authorities in exchange for Japanese prisoners.

In 1944, after a short time in Europe, Mydans was assigned to General MacArthur's command in the Pacific, during the reconquest of the Philippines. At the war's end, Mydans was chief of the *Time-Life* news bureau in Tokyo for four years; he went on to cover the war in Korea, then was stationed for several years in England, and for a year and a half in Moscow.

After *Life* ceased to exist, Mydans continued his work as a photojournalist, handling assignments from *Time, Fortune, Smithsonian Magazine,* and many other publications. He published several books, one co-authored by his wife, and in 1951 he was the recipient of the *U.S. Camera* Gold Achievement Award.

Nègre, Charles. "Henri Le Secq at Notre Dame Cathedral, Paris" (1851); calotype. Smithsonian Institution.

N-O

Nadar (Gaspard-Félix Tournachon)

French; 1820–1910

Nadar must be ranked not only among the greatest photographers of the 19th c., but as one of the great personalities of his age. Caricaturist, journalist, novelist, balloonist, propagandist for heavier-than-air flight, friend of almost every notable French writer, artist, journalist, and socialist of the Second Empire (many of whom he photographed), Nadar was a paragon of enthusiasm, energy, and productivity.

The son of a printer, Nadar was born in Paris and attended a lycée in Versailles. In 1838, the family moved to their native Lyon where, after the death of his father, Nadar began his journalistic career by writing drama criticism for a Lyonnais newspaper. Within a few years Nadar returned to Paris and embraced enthusiastically the poor but spirited world of Second Republic bohemia. In his memoirs written 60 years later, Nadar listed among his various jobs of this period poacher, smuggler, clerk, peat seller, and secretary. It was, however, journalism that became increasingly his means of support, and throughout his life he continued regularly to produce a stream of essays, reviews, short stories, articles, and books. During the 1840s Nadar wrote for numerous revues and newspapers, punctuated in 1848 by his enlistment in the Polish Legion—a feckless band of Polish exiles and French sympathizers who set out to liberate Poland—only to be arrested in Germany and sent back to France.

By the end of the 1840s, he had taken up caricature, which he produced for humorous journals, signing his work " Nadar." After a brief stint in debtor's prison and a subsequent trip to London to visit the Great Exhibition, Nadar launched the project he called the Panthéon Nadar, a planned series of lithographic caricatures illustrating the 1000 most prominent personalities of the day. It is possible that the Panthéon project led Nadar to take photographs as aids to making the caricatures, but by 1854 he had set up his younger brother Adrian Tournachon as a photographer. Shortly thereafter, Nadar himself set up a studio on the roof of the house he shared with his mother and divided his time between his brother's studio and his own. As Nadar's photographic fortunes prospered, his brother's appear to have been eclipsed. In fact, Nadar initiated a lawsuit to prevent Adrian from using the name Nadar commercially. By 1860, Nadar had opened a new, sumptuously appointed studio on the Boulevard des Capucines, a building that had earlier provided space for the photographic studios of Gustave Le Gray and the Bisson Frères. Emblazoned across the front was the signature "Nadar" (he had a natural gift for publicity and self-promotion) and to his studio flocked the stellar lights of French arts and letters.

Although Nadar remained a photographic entrepreneur for most of his long life, his passion for the medium and his experimentation with it lasted a scant 10 years. It was during that initial period that he made the first photographs with artificial light, descending into the sewers and the catacombs of Paris with magnesium flares. These forays took place in 1861. The magisterial portraits he produced from the mid-1850s through the mid-1860s are notable for their ability to convey the sitter's personality, the ease and naturalness of the pose, and the clear but subtly orchestrated lighting. Nadar typically chose three-quarter views, often hiding the hands so that the full force of the portrait was conveyed by the face, the expression, and the position of the seated body.

By 1863, Nadar's capacity for boundless enthusiasm had shifted to the then visionary idea of heavier-than-air flight. His studio became the official headquarters of "The Society for the Encouragement of Aerial Locomotion by Means of Heavier than Air Machines," with Nadar as president and Jules Verne as secretary. To publicize the idea, Nadar launched a funding drive which subsidized his giant hot-air balloon, "Le Géant." It was in fact from a hot-air balloon that Nadar had made in 1858 the first aerial photographs. In 1870, during

Nadar. "George Sand" (n.d.). Woodburytype. Collection, Museum of Modern Art, New York.

the siege of Paris, Nadar also used a balloon to bring out the mail from the beleaguered city. Ruined financially in 1871, Nadar gave up the studio on the Boulevard des Capucines and more or less turned over the running of the business to his son Paul, who became a fairly successful commercial portraitist. Although Nadar's interest in photography waned, he remained actively involved with the Parisian art world and in 1874, the First Impressionist Exhibition was held in his studio. Four years later, he helped organize a large exhibition of the work of the caricaturist Honoré Daumier, a close friend who had died penniless. His last photographic innovation was the development of a photo interview with the centenarian scientist Michel Chevreul, "The Art of Living for 100 Years," which was photographed by his son Paul and published in the *Journal Illustré*.

See also: CARJAT, ETIENNE; PHOTO-JOURNALISM; PORTRAITURE.

Narrow Lighting

In the portrait lighting technique called narrow, or short, lighting, with the subject's face seen in three-quarter view (rather than head-on or in full profile), the key light falls on the narrow part of the face farthest from the lens. The broad plane of the face closest to the lens is in shadow; its relative visibility is determined by the strength of the fill light. Narrow lighting is the most common portrait arrangement with average faces because it reveals facial structure more clearly than broad lighting. It also tends to make round or plump faces look narrower.

See also: BROAD LIGHTING.

Naturalistic Photography

The doctrine of Naturalistic Photography championed by Peter Henry Emerson in the 1880s and 1890s was the first forceful statement of what is now called the *straight* approach to photography as a conscious aesthetic attitude. It was a reaction in direct opposition to the artificiality and triteness that had enveloped Pictorialism and dominated photographic salons and exhibitions throughout the world. Naturalistic Photography, or Naturalism, advocated a return to a direct experience of nature, which meant photographing natural subjects in their natural surroundings. The intent of Emerson and those who followed him in great number was to produce artistic images. Their final results are, to contemporary eyes, more nearly similar to than different from the images of Pictorialist photographers, but the attitudes and working methods were different. To partisans of both schools, those differences were critical. As in naturalistic painting of the 19th c., the aim of Naturalistic Photography was the direct recording of the effects of nature on the eye. This demanded that the subject be real, not artificially arranged or contrived, and that technique be straightforward; any manipulation to add or subtract effect could only tamper with the truth (= beauty) of the image and consequently undermine its artistic worth. The aim of Pictorialism was not recording but imitating the effects of nature on the eye, by whatever straight or—much more commonly—manipulative techniques were necessary. Like romanticism in painting, this approach emphasized emotion, sentimentality, and nostalgia for a graceful, ennobling past that in fact never existed; it elevated commonplace ideas to the level of universal truths and idealized the supposed simplicity and purity of rustic life. In sum, the subject and the photographer's experience were imaginary in Pictorialism, real in Naturalism.

See also: EMERSON, PETER HENRY; IMPRESSIONISTIC PHOTOGRAPHY; "NATURALISTIC PHOTOGRAPHY"; PICTORIAL PHOTOGRAPHY/PICTORIALISM; ROBINSON, HENRY PEACH.

"Naturalistic Photography"

The first edition of the book *Naturalistic Photography*, published in 1889, was the major salvo in P. H. Emerson's energetic war with Pictorialism in photography. Of the several books he produced, it was the only extended statement of his doctrine of the naturalistic approach, and the only textbook of technique. The first third discussed his understanding of art theory and argued that the greatest art in all ages had resulted from a direct reaction to and recording of the effects of nature; that contrivance and artificiality led away from, not toward, true art. The middle section of the book discussed the selection and use of photographic equipment and materials, and the virtues of straight printing. The final portion discussed principles of composition and true (i.e., unmanipulated) artistic effect. The book was unillustrated, but his volume of photogravures, *Pictures of East Anglian Life,* published the year before, was intended to be a companion volume to the text. The advice and instruction Emerson gave was highly opinionated, but it did much to counteract the attitudes of Pictorialism embodied in H. P. Robinson's very popular book, *Pictorial Effect in Photography.* A second edition of Emerson's text appeared in 1890. Eight years later, Emerson astounded his followers by announcing in a funereal pamphlet, "The Death of Naturalistic Photography," his new conviction that photography could not be a true art. The third, and final, edition of his text, published in 1899, reflected this reversal. The summary chapter, "Photography—A Pictorial Art," was changed to "Photography—Not Art." There Emerson explained, without great clarity, that he had mistaken the potential of machine-made art—photographs—for the far greater and more sublime potential of true fine art: painting. It was his last book on photography.

See also: EMERSON, PETER HENRY; NATURALISTIC PHOTOGRAPHY; "PICTORIAL EFFECT IN PHOTOGRAPHY"; PICTORIAL PHOTOGRAPHY/PICTORIALISM; ROBINSON, HENRY PEACH.

Natural-Light Photography

In general, natural-light photographs are pictures made by daylight: direct or reflected sunlight, open or overcast sky light, or some combination of these sources. Photography by moonlight—entirely natural illumination, being reflected sunlight—is commonly included in the category of available- or existing-light photography because of the low intensity of the light.

The sun's relatively constant level of illumination from about two hours after sunrise to two hours before sunset allows for a generalized exposure calculation for all general-purpose films: correct exposure for a subject frontlighted by sun and skylight is a shutter speed of 1/Film speed at *f*/16; the arithmetic daylight film speed is used. For example, exposure with an ISO 125/22° film would be 1/125 sec. at *f*/16. Any equivalent exposure, such as 1/250 sec. at *f*/11, or 1/60 sec. at *f*/22, would also be correct.

This general rule can be adapted for other natural light conditions, as follows:

Condition	Exposure (1/Film speed at)
Highly reflective surroundings (snow; sand; open water)	*f*/22
Hazy sun (soft shadows)	*f*/11
Cloudy bright (no shadows)	*f*/8
Heavy overcast	*f*/5.6–*f*/8
Open shade (full sun, but subject in skylighted area only)	*f*/5.6

More precise exposure determinations can be made for black-and-white film by taking reflected-light brightness-range readings. Exposure for color film should be determined by an incident-light meter reading, or a reflected-light reading from a key highlight value such as skin tone.

Natural light is essentially uncontrollable. Its effect can be adjusted by changing the subject or camera position, or both. The major problems with direct sunlight are harsh, unpleasant shadows and extreme contrast. Using a reflector or fill-in flash to illuminate shadow areas can reduce these problems to an acceptable level. Often it is effective to position the subject so that the sun is a backlight, and reflectors or flash illuminate the side facing the camera. Extremely diffuse light, such as that of a cloudy bright or overcast day or in open shade, provides few highlights and little modeling or delineation of texture. One solution is to use flash as the main light and let the natural light act to fill in the shadows.

Because they have high inherent contrast, slow-speed films are not necessarily the best choice in bright, direct natural-light conditions. A medium-speed film (e.g., ISO 64/19° to ISO 125/22°) will give better results. A neutral density filter can be used to photograph at a slower shutter speed or a larger aperture, if desired. A No. 1A skylight filter is recommended for use with color film in natural light, especially in open shade, to avoid excess bluishness from open sky illumination. An ultraviolet-absorbing filter will prevent excess bluishness in color pictures of distant landscapes; a light or medium yellow filter serves a similar function in black-and-white photography.

See also: BRIGHTNESS RANGE; DAYLIGHT; FLASH FILL; MOONLIGHT.

Nature Photography

Nature is an immensely popular photographic subject among amateurs; it also is a major subject in professional photography for both commercial and scientific purposes. Illustrative photographers produce nature pictures for use in posters, travel brochures, and many other kinds of publications; for decorative use; and for backgrounds in studio photography. Scientists and field workers in a number of the natural sciences and related fields depend on photography as a major tool of record and investigation. These fields include biology, botany, geology, ecology, wildlife management, and others. Nature is considered to be all things that live and grow on the earth, and their environments, with the exception of human beings. Landscape and underwater photography commonly are discussed as separate categories, although they are indeed part of nature photography. Thus, the subject matter in nature is trees, plants, flowers, lichens, and mosses; and animals, birds, and insects, and the ponds, thickets, soil, nests, burrows, and other places in which they live.

Early development. The first images in photography were nature photographs, although not in the sense of subjects shown in their natural habitat. About 1800 Thomas Wedgwood and Humphry Davy obtained impermanent silhouette images (photograms) of leaves, shells, nuts, and other objects placed in contact with sensitized materials. W. H. F. Talbot secured far more detailed—and permanent—images of botanical specimens by a similar technique in 1835 and after, in the course of inventing the paper negative-positive (calotype) process. In the next few years, Talbot and several others also recorded images of natural subjects projected by a microscope.

Although there are some extant landscape, flower, and similar pictures from the daguerreotype and calotype era of the 1840s, their number is small. Comparatively few nature pictures were taken because photographic materials were only blue-sensitive, with the result that reddish or greenish objects were generally recorded too dark and without significant differentiation. Toning or hand-coloring were sometimes used to surmount the problem in some degree. During the succeeding wet-plate period (ca. 1851–1885), nature photographs began to become common, especially after the introduction in the 1870s of orthochromatic plates, which were both blue- and green-sensitive. Factual records of natural scenes and details were made with great visual power by Timothy H. O'Sullivan, William Henry Jackson, and many other expedition photographers from the 1860s onward. Simultaneously, nature pictures of great pictorial beauty were photographed in a straightforward style by masters such as the Bisson *frères,* Carleton E. Watkins, and Eadweard J. Muybridge.

In the 1880s and 1890s art photographers of the Pictorialist and Naturalist schools made nature pictures largely in imitation of paintings. At the same time the straightforward approach was used by others with the newly available, faster dry plates and hand cameras to record living creatures in their natural surroundings. Action sequence pictures of animals and birds—notably a series on nesting storks—taken by Ottomar Anschutz at this time are landmarks in the development of nature photography.

The introduction of color and panchromatic emulsions in the first decade of the 20th c.. gave great impetus to nature photography because subjects could now be recorded in natural color or translated into intensely realistic black-and-white images. Since the 1920s the masters of photographing the natural scene have included Edward Weston, Ansel Adams, Eliot Porter, William Garnett, and Paul Caponigro. Outstanding pictures of animals, birds, insects, and other living subjects have been produced by Andreas Feininger, Nina Leen, John Dominis, Roger Tory Peterson, Maitland Edey, and Stephen Dalton, among others. Underwater nature photography has been epitomized in the work of Douglas Faulkner, and scientific photography in the work of Roman Visniac, David Scharf, and Lennart Nilsson. Such listings of course cannot be all-inclusive; they indicate only a few leading photographers.

Techniques. Nature photography is field photography, which puts a premium on lightweight, versatile equipment. A 35mm or medium-format single-lens reflex camera is the almost universal standard, because it is compact, holds enough film for several exposures, and accepts a wide range of lenses and accessories. Daylight type color film is most widely used because exposures are either by daylight or electronic flash, and because color is a characteristic of major importance with most subjects. Black-and-white films are used when possible, often for reasons of economy, but their use has declined significantly since the introduction of color films with speeds of ISO 650/29° to ISO 1000/31°. Infrared-sensitive film and suitable flash is employed for some kinds of work at night or in caves and similar locations when it is important not to disturb the subject.

A great deal of nature photography is carried out at either a very great distance from or a very close distance to the subject. Because many animals and birds cannot be approached closely, a long-focal length lens is essential. A focal length from 12 in. to 20 in. (300mm to 500mm) is the most common choice; the effective focal length can be doubled or tripled by use of a 2× or 3× tele-extender between the lens and the camera. A long lens requires substantial support—a chestpod or gunstock mount when hand-holding the camera or when following a bird in flight or an animal in motion, and a tripod whenever possible. A hand-held spot-reading (1° to 2° area) exposure meter is very useful for long-distance photography.

Close-range photography is facilitated with a so-called macro-focusing lens, which typically produces images up to one-half life size. However, extension tubes or an accessory bellows are necessary with any lens to get into the true macro range of images: life-size and larger. This kind of photography can produce fascinating pictures, but it involves significant problems of focusing, exposure, and depth of field, as discussed in the entry on macrophotography. Electronic flash commonly is required for adequate illumination in macro-range pictures.

Middle-distance pictures—those in which an image of useful size can be obtained with a normal-focal-length or moderate-telephoto lens—are often desirable, but are difficult to obtain with living creatures. Very long-focal-length lenses have a narrow field of view and shallow depth of field and present an apparently compressed perspective that may not reveal the subject as clearly as desired. Normal-lens pictures have a normal-looking perspective and generally provide the most realistic reproduction of a subject or a scene. Middle-distance wildlife pictures commonly are obtained in one of two ways: by means of a blind that matches the surroundings and conceals the photographer, or by means of a camera operated by remote control. A zoom lens is very useful when working from a blind. A remote camera and flash may be triggered by the photographer, who watches through binoculars, using wired or radio-signal devices, or by the subject, who trips the shutter by moving across a selected spot or by taking food from a baited switch.

A responsible nature photographer is constantly aware of the fact that his or her function is to observe and record nature, not to destroy it. Often branches or other obstacles must be removed from the line of view. It is best to tie branches out of the way; otherwise, they should be cut off cleanly at an appropriate point (a book on pruning is a good guide to the fundamentals). The person who breaks branches or uproots plants is a vandal, not a photographer. In close-up work it often is possible to place a cloth or card behind a subject to provide a plain background, rather than disturbing the natural elements. (Cards are also useful to direct light toward the subject and to protect a subject from breezes. A sheet of transparent plastic provides breeze protection without blocking any light.) Logs or rocks ought to be disturbed as little as possible; they are habitats for creatures within or beneath them. Similar concern should be exercised in getting to and from a site and in moving about while there—without care, a great deal inadvertently can be trampled underfoot. On a large scale Nature is a combination of vigorous forces; on a small scale the life forms of nature exist in a delicate balance, and the major unbalancing force is the action of human beings. The nature photographer tries to maintain the balance.

See also: ADAMS, ANSEL; BIOLOGICAL PHOTOGRAPHY; GEOLOGICAL PHOTOGRAPHY; LANDSCAPE PHOTOGRAPHY; MACROPHOTOGRAPHY; PORTER, ELIOT; UNDERWATER PHOTOGRAPHY.

Negative Prints

A print in which the tones or colors are the opposite of their normal values is produced by exposing the paper to a positive rather than a negative image. The simplest way to obtain a black-and-white positive for printing is to copy a negative, as in a slide copier, using negative film, or to contact print it on film. Copying a color negative is complicated by the integral masking color in such films; its effect can be neutralized by filtration.

A negative print can also be obtained by loading paper in place of film in a camera, by printing a negative onto direct positive (reversal) paper, or by using another print on single-weight paper as a negative for contact printing. Waxing the back of the positive print increases its light transmission and subdues the shadow image of the fibers in the paper base; resin-coated papers cannot be used in this way.

A negative image on color film without masking colors can be obtained by photographing a subject, slide, or print on transparency film, but processing the film in color negative processing solutions.

See also: COPYING PHOTOGRAPHS; DUPLICATE IMAGES.
Color photograph: p. C-34.

Negatives

Negatives are images on film in which the tonal values or colors are the oppo-

site of those in the subject to which the film was exposed. Thus, the thinnest (most transparent) areas of the negative correspond to the darkest areas of the subject, and the thickest or densest (most opaque) image areas correspond to the brightest subject areas. In conventional black-and-white films, the negative image is composed of silver particles; in chromogenic (dye-forming) color and black-and-white films, the image is composed of dye compounds that replace the silver during processing. The reversed tonality of the image is clearly visible in black-and-white negatives. The complementary color values in a color negative are difficult to discern because all such films incorporate corrective masking that gives them an overall orange-brown or pinkish-tan cast. The masking improves their printing characteristics.

The range of density gradations of a negative is called contrast. The thinnest (shadow) densities are determined by exposure; too little exposure will fail to register those parts of the subject. With most black-and-white films, contrast in the brighter areas can be adjusted to some degree by varying development. Negative contrast in chromogenic films cannot be controlled by processing variations.

Negative materials differ in speed (light sensitivity), graininess, contrast, and color or spectral sensitivity. In general, graininess increases and contrast decreases as speed increases; color or spectral sensitivity is independent of speed.

The function of a negative is to be a master image or matrix for obtaining multiple positive images of the subject. A positive is made by passing light through a negative onto the emulsion of a printing paper or another piece of film. The negative may be in contact (emulsion to emulsion) with the printing material, or the image may be projected, as by an enlarger. In some cases a negative is used as the finished image for special effects or expressive purposes, or because the information contained in the picture is more easily perceived in reverse tonalities.

See also: BLACK-AND-WHITE MATERIALS; COLOR MATERIALS; NEGATIVE PRINTS.

Nègre, Charles

French; 1820–1880

Charles Nègre was a versatile photographer of the mid-19th c., accomplished and prominent in his day. He was one of the first to photograph genre scenes of everyday life. Using a fast lens he had designed, Nègre was able to photograph the movements of people in the streets and markets of Paris. In addition to his images of working-class tradespeople, he was known for his views of the town and cathedral of Chartres. His images of Provence, *Le Midi de la France,* constitute the first portrait of the totality of a region.

Nègre was born in Grasse, France. A student of Ingres and Paul Delaroche, he came to photography by way of painting. He began making daguerreotypes of his paintings in 1844 and continued to paint, but soon saw the merits of photography as an art form itself. He was awarded a gold medal for painting at the Salon of 1851. Three of his works were purchased by Napoleon III.

Nègre studied the waxed-paper process with Gustave Le Gray and began photographing in earnest in 1851. His first exhibition of photographs was held that year at the Société Héliographique. His large (20½″ × 29″) paper negatives of Chartres date from this time as well. In 1852 he taught at the Ecole Supérieure du Commerce in Paris and began his extensive work in the south of France. Nègre photographed the seaports, landscapes, ancient and medieval monuments, and country folk to create a rich portrait of the region's past and present.

Nègre was commissioned in 1860 by Napoleon III to document the new Vincennes Imperial Asylum for disabled workmen. He made extraordinary photographs under poor conditions of the personnel and patients in their daily routines.

Nègre experimented with various photographic processes including photogravure, collodion, and photogalvanographic techniques. He received many awards and commissions between 1855 and 1861, when ill health forced him to retire to Nice. He spent his last years making portraits and views for tourists. He died in Grasse in 1880.

Neue Sachlichkeit

The term *Neue Sachlichkeit,* German for New Realism or New Objectivity, was first applied to the work of German painters who in the 1920s turned away from Expressionism to a contemporary realism in style. It was extended to the work of photographers who similarly rejected the Pictorialism that had dominated the salons for more than three decades, and looked to the real world, directly seen and recorded without artifice, as the source of artistically valid images. The leader in this new style was the German photographer Albert Renger-Patzsch, whose work—beginning about 1922—exerted as strong an influence in Europe to establish straight photography as an aesthetic approach as did the work of Paul Strand and Edward Weston in the U.S., both of whom arrived independently at the same kind of vision, and at the same time.
See also: LINKED RING; PHOTO-SECESSION; PICTORIAL PHOTOGRAPHY/PICTORIALISM; RENGER-PATZSCH, ALBERT.

Neutral Density

Density in a filter, negative, or transparency is called *neutral* if it affects all visible wavelengths equally so that the transmitted light is reduced in intensity but its color balance is unaffected. Neutral density filters have a grayish appearance; they are used for exposure control—for example, with a fast film when the lens aperture cannot be closed down far enough to properly expose a subject in very bright light—or with a mirror lens, which does not have an iris diaphragm for light control. They also may be used to permit setting the lens at a large aperture for shallow depth of field without producing overexposure. Neutral density filters are graded in actual density values; each 0.1 increase in value indicates a decrease in light transmission equivalent to one-third of an f-stop. Thus, ND 0.3, ND 0.6, and ND 3.0 filters produce exposure reductions of one, two, and ten f-stops, respectively. Two or more filters can be combined for a greater value, e.g., ND 0.3 + ND 0.6 = ND 0.9.

In subtractive color printing, neutral density is produced when all three filter colors—cyan, magenta, and yellow—are used simultaneously. This is undesirable because it reduces exposure without creating any color correction in the image. The amount of neutral density is equal to the common density among the filters—i.e., the least single-color density—and it can always be eliminated. For example, in a filter pack composed of 5Y + 15M + 35C, 0.5 density of each color is canceled in effectiveness by the same amount of the other two colors. The pack can be simplified by subtracting the common amount from each color. The new pack, (0Y) + 10M + 25C, has the same color effect as the original pack but transmits 1⅔ f-stops (= 0.5 ND) more light.
See also: COLOR BALANCE; DEPTH OF FIELD; SUBTRACTIVE COLOR SYNTHESIS.

New Bauhaus

A professional school of art and design founded by László Moholy-Nagy in Chicago in 1937, the New Bauhaus incorporated the curriculum and methods he and others had developed at the Bauhaus in Germany from 1919 to 1932 under the leadership of Walter Gropius and Mies van der Rohe. The school was closed after the first year because of financial problems of its sponsor, the Association of Arts and Industries. Moholy-Nagy revived it independently as the School of Design in 1938; it subsequently became the Chicago Institute of Design and, in 1950, was incorporated into the Illinois Institute of Technology. Faculty members of particular significance in photography have included Herbert Bayer, Gyorgy Kepes, Harry Callahan, and Aaron Siskind.
See also: BAUHAUS; CALLAHAN, HARRY; KEPES, GYORGY; MOHOLY-NAGY, LASZLO; SISKIND, AARON.

Newhall, Beaumont

American; 1908–
Both a historian and a photographer, Beaumont Newhall is known better for his work in the history of photography than as a practicing photographer. He is particularly famous as the founding director of the department of photography at the Museum of Modern Art and as the curator and director of the International Museum of Photography at the George Eastman House during that institution's formative era. Born in Lynn, Massachusetts, and educated at Harvard University in art history, Newhall has been the recipient of numerous honorary degrees and awards from the Guggenheim Foundation, the Royal Photographic Society and most recently, the German Photographic Society, from which he received the Cultural Prize. His extensive research has resulted in a bibliography of over 600 titles including *Airborne Camera, Latent Image: The Discovery of Photography, The Daguerreotype in America,* and five editions of *The History of Photography.*

Newhall began his museum career as assistant in the department of decorative arts at the Metropolitan Museum of Art in New York, moving from that institution to become the librarian and then the curator of photography at the Museum of Modern Art. In 1937 he wrote the catalog for the first survey exhibition of photography, *Photography 1839–1937.* In 1948 he became the curator at the George Eastman House and served from 1958 to 1971 as the director of that institution. Not only the author of the classic text on the subject, but also the teacher of a majority of those educated in the history of photography, Newhall is an Honorary Fellow of the Royal Photographic Society, an Honorary Master of the Photographers' Society of America, a corresponding member of the German Photographic Society, and a Fellow of the American Academy of Arts and Sciences, as well as an advisor for most of the photographic research produced in the United States and abroad. Newhall resides in Santa Fe and teaches at the University of New Mexico in Albuquerque.
See also: HISTORY OF PHOTOGRAPHY.

Newman, Arnold

American; 1918–
Arnold Newman has worked in a variety of photographic fields, but he is most famous for his environmental portraits of artists in which the setting and surrounding objects symbolize or comment upon the sitter's vocation. His work consistently has emphasized strong composition in his intimate glimpses of prominent personalities whose ranks include Picasso, Stravinsky, Stieglitz, O'Keefe, Dali, Ernst, Eisenhower, John F. Kennedy, Nixon, Duchamp, and Cocteau.

Newman was born in New York City, the son of a clothing manufacturer. He attended public schools in Atlantic City, New Jersey, and Miami Beach, Florida. He studied art on a scholarship to the University of Miami in 1937–1938. Forced by the Depression to give up his desire to become a painter, in 1939 Newman took a position in Philadelphia with a chain of photography studios that specialized in quick, inexpensive portraits. Also in Philadelphia he maintained his association with a group of photography students who had studied under Alexey Brodovitch at the Philadelphia School of Industrial Arts.

Newman, Arnold. "David Hockney" (1978).
Courtesy Arnold Newman.

the world: at the Museum of Modern Art and the Metropolitan Museum both in New York City, George Eastman House in Rochester, New York, and the Smithsonian Institution in Washington, D.C. He has been the subject of solo exhibitions at the Camera Club of New York (1951), the Art Institute of Chicago (1953), and Light Gallery, New York (1972, 1974, 1977, 1980), among others. In 1979 he was commissioned by the National Portrait Gallery, London, to do a series of 50 photographs for the exhibition *The Great British;* Newman subsequently published the photographs as a book of the same title. Among his other works are *One Mind's Eye: The Portraits and Other Photographs of Arnold Newman* (1974) and *Artists: Portraits from Four Decades* (1980).

News Photography

News photography deals with events and the individuals or personalities involved in events. The subject matter of news photography has momentary importance (e.g., a landslide, a building dedication, a race result), whereas the subject matter of documentary photography is ongoing conditions that affect human or animal living patterns, or the ecological balance of the planet. News photography is part of photojournalism, which includes hard news (events of immediate political, economic, or social impact), feature news (subjects of cultural significance, human interest, or general lifestyle), and some kinds of documentary reportage. News photography may also be classified in terms of spot news—single pictures that report an event—and picture stories in which a series of images comprises a more fully developed report.

The essence of a news photograph is that it is relevant, emphatic, and timely. Relevant photographs deal with the most significant aspects of the subject; they are factual and accurate, and they indicate the importance of things relative to one another and to the overall event. Photographs are emphatic when they are sharp, well exposed, graphically bold, and composed to make the main subject immediately apparent. Photographs are timely when they show things of immediate import or interest.

News photographs are produced by staff photographers of news agencies, newspapers, magazines, and television organizations; by "stringers" who have contracts or agreements with particular outlets but are paid only for work accepted; and by freelance photographers. Staff photographers often work in conjunction with a writer, re-

From 1939 to 1941 he managed a West Palm Beach, Florida, studio and pursued abstract and documentary photography experiments.

Newman returned to New York in 1941. He received encouragement from Alfred Stieglitz, Ansel Adams, and Beaumont Newhall at this time, and he was given a two-man show (with Ben Rose) at the A.D. Gallery in New York City. He began his environmental portraiture soon thereafter, concentrating primarily on portraits of artists. He operated the Newman Portrait Studio in Miami Beach from 1942 to 1945. Since 1946 he has owned and operated Arnold Newman Studios, Inc. in New York City.

Newman rapidly became a successful freelance commercial and portrait photographer, publishing regularly in *Look, Life, Time, Esquire, Fortune, Harper's Bazaar, Holiday, Travel and Leisure,* and *Town and Country.* At *Harper's Bazaar* he worked closely with art director Alexey Brodovitch. In 1947 Newman photographed the first of many *Life* covers he was to produce. He has traveled and photographed widely throughout the United States, Europe, and the Middle East.

Since 1965 Newman has been Advisor on Photography to the Israel Museum in Jerusalem. He has been Visiting Professor of Photography at Cooper Union in New York since 1975, and he was awarded an honorary doctorate from the University of Miami in 1981.

Newman has been the recipient of numerous awards, including a Photokina Award (1951), a Gold Medal at the Venice Biennale (1963), and a Life Achievement Award from the American Society of Magazine Photographers (1975). His work has been included in one-man and group shows throughout

porter, or correspondent, and the report filed with the publication or broadcast station is an integrated, collaborative product. Most still news photographs are taken with 35mm cameras, often equipped with zoom lenses and electronic flash units; the majority of still photographs are taken in black-and-white. Television news photography is recorded with lightweight videotape cameras equipped with zoom lenses, high-output continuous light sources (usually quartz lights), and built-in or attached microphones. All television news recording is in color.

Whatever their medium and equipment, news photographers constantly are faced with two major logistical problems: getting to the event in time to take significant pictures, and getting the pictures to the publication or station before they have lost significance. This is a very demanding area of photography.
See also: DOCUMENTARY PHOTOGRAPHY; PHOTOJOURNALISM; PRESS PHOTOGRAPHY.

Newton, Helmut

Australian; 1920–

Helmut Newton's photographs are made for the primary purpose of fashion illustration. Their theme of aggressive sexuality in opulent settings is regarded by some as an underlying element of social criticism, and by others as fetishism or blatant exploitation of women. In the lavish surroundings associated with the upper class and *grand luxe* hotels, nudes are shown in situations of strongly implied sexual tension, lesbianism, or physical menace; they are women both aggressive and daring one to dominate them. An air of self-assured decadence is pervasive.

Born in Germany and educated in German and American schools in Berlin, Newton apprenticed to the fashion and theater photographer Eva from 1936 to 1940. Upon emigrating to Australia, he served in the army from 1940 to 1945, then began working as a freelance photographer in Sydney and married a photographer/actress. Beginning in 1958 he became a contributor to such publications as *Jardin des Modes, Elle, Queen, Playboy,* and *Nova.* Now a resident of Paris, his images of erotic fantasies are frequent inclusions in the French and American editions of *Vogue,* and in *Stern.* Although his photographs are in an illustrative tradition developed by Baron de Meyer, Edward Steichen, and Irving Penn, Newton has added eroticism and an almost ever-present element of voyeurism.

News Photography. Thomas Howard, "Execution of Ruth Snyder" (1928). Courtesy The Daily News, New York.

Newton's work is widely published. He is the recipient of the Tokyo Art Directors Club's Best Photography Award in 1976, the American Institute of Graphic Arts Award in 1978, and the German Art Directors Club's Gold Medal in 1978 and 1979. He has exhibited in both group and individual exhibitions in Amsterdam, Geneva, London, Paris, Los Angeles, and New York. Newton's work is in the collections of the Bibliothèque Nationale, Paris; the Fashion Institute of Technology, New York; the George Eastman House, Rochester; and the Museum of Modern Art, New York. His photographs are included in major treatments of contemporary fashion illustration and nude photography. Newton is the author of *White Women/Femmes Secrètes* (1976) and *Sleepless Nights/Nuits Blanches* (1978), among other publications.
See also: EROTIC PHOTOGRAPHY.

Newton's Rings

Newton's rings are a pattern of concentric light and dark or rainbow-colored lines in an image. They may appear in enlarged prints or in projected slide images. The pattern is caused by the interference of light wavelengths around the point at which one part of the film base touches the glass in a negative carrier or a slide mount. In an enlarger they can be avoided by using a glassless negative carrier or, with large-format films, by inserting a paper mask to provide separation between the glass and the film base. In slide projection newton's rings can be eliminated by using glassless slide mounts, by using anti-newton-ring textured glass on the film-base side, by inserting a separator mask, or by giving the glass an imperceptible dusting with talcum or "platemaker's powder," available from graphic arts suppliers.
See also: INTERFERENCE.

Newton, Helmut. "Girl, construction site" (n.d.). Courtesy Helmut Newton/Xavier Moreau Inc., New York.

NiCad Batteries

NiCad batteries are direct-current dry cells composed of nickel and cadmium elements and an electrolyte. They are widely used as a power supply for portable flash units and a variety of camera accessories because they are rechargeable. Ordinary alkaline-manganese dry batteries may deliver more initial working life before exhaustion—typically 1½ to 2 times more flashes in a small flash unit—but then they must be discarded. Aside from the repeated expense of replacement, this makes it necessary to always have sufficient fresh batteries on hand. Nickel-cadmium batteries are more expensive, but may be recharged hundreds of times, even after having been left uncharged for a period of time. In flash units they provide faster recycling times than alkaline-manganese batteries. Many small flash units have built-in recharging circuitry and non-removable NiCad cells. Others have removable cells that are recharged in an accessory unit. This makes it possible to have one set of cells charging while another is in use, so that photography can continue with minimum delay when the set in use must be changed. Nickel-cadmium batteries have a rated output of 1.2 to 1.25 volts d.c., while alkaline-manganese batteries are rated at 1.5 volts. This difference may cause some equipment to operate less efficiently if NiCad cells are substituted where alkaline-manganese batteries were originally used. The equipment instructions usually state whether substitution is possible or advisable.

Niépce, Joseph Nicéphore

French; 1765–1833

The first permanent recordings by chemical means of images in the camera obscura were made by Joseph Nicéphore Niépce in 1824 and 1826. He may be called the inventor of photography in that he demonstrated the possibility of obtaining camera-made images; however, his method was unrelated to the first practical photographic processes of Daguerre and Talbot which appeared almost 15 years later. According to correspondence, Niépce and his brother Claude (1763–1828) first experimented along this line, using paper sensitized with silver compounds, in 1793 while both were engineers in French military service; the results were apparently unsuccessful. Experimentation was resumed in 1813–1814 by Joseph Nicéphore in an effort to invent an improved method of preparing plates for lithographic printing, a process that was introduced in France with great success. By this time Claude was in England attempting to promote commercial development of the *pyréolophore*, an internal combustion engine for boats that the brothers had patented in 1807.

Nicéphore's efforts with silver-sensitized materials produced reverse-tone (negative) images, but they could not be made permanent (fixed). By 1822 he had turned to using a coating of bitumen on a glass plate to copy engravings on paper that was oiled to make it transparent; a contact printing exposure was made by sunlight. In 1824 he began coating metal plates in a similar manner, and in 1826 he obtained what he deemed his first success, this time using a coated pewter plate in a camera obscura. This image of the courtyard of his house at Gras in Chalon-sur-Saone, Burgundy, is the world's first permanent photograph. Niépce called his various methods *heliography*.

During a visit to England in 1827 Niépce failed to find support for his metal-plate process because he insisted on keeping the details secret. For this same reason he was denied the opportunity to present the process before the Royal Society, whose rules demanded full disclosure in the interests of advancing scientific knowledge. Returning to

France, Niépce was contacted by L. J. M. Daguerre, who had been experimenting unsuccessfully with camera-obscura recording. In December 1829 Niépce and Daguerre formed a partnership to develop a perfected camera-image process. Niépce then turned to using silver-coated copper plates which he covered with bitumen to produce an image as in his basic heliography. He carried the process further by exposing the developed plate to iodine fumes, which darkened the bare silver portions representing the dark areas of the image. Using alcohol, he then dissolved the hardened bitumen in the middletone and highlight areas, revealing bright silver to represent those parts of the picture. After Niépce's death in 1833, Daguerre discovered how to sensitize a silver plate with iodine fumes and how to produce a direct positive image without the use of a bitumen coating. Upon Niépce's death the partnership was extended to his son, Isidore (1805–1868), but by the time Daguerre's final process was made public in 1839, Niépce had been forgotten,

and his family received only a token payment for his contributions.

See also: DAGUERRE, L. J. M.; DAGUERRE-OTYPE; HELIOGRAPHY; NIÉPCE DE SAINT-VICTOR, CLAUDE FELIX ABEL; TALBOT, WILLIAM HENRY FOX.

Niépce de Saint-Victor, Claude Félix Abel

French; 1805–1870

A cousin of Joseph Nicéphore Niépce, who first recorded a permanent image in the camera obscura, Claude Félix Abel Niépce invented the albumen-on-glass process in 1848. In 1859 he experimented with printing on paper sensitized with uranium nitrate, a method demonstrated three or four years earlier in England by C. J. Burnett, who also first demonstrated platinum printing. In 1867 Niépce showed an improved version of Becquerel's heliochromy—direct recording of colors on specially treated daguerreotype plates—but was unable to make the images permanent. His most significant contribution was the heliogravure

process for halftone reproduction of photographs, which he invented in 1855.

See also: ALBUMEN PROCESSES; BECQUEREL, A.E.; COLOR PHOTOGRAPHY—HISTORY; HELIOGRAVURE; NIÉPCE, JOSEPH NICÉPHORE.

Niépceotype

The name *niépceotype* was applied to the bitumen process by which Nicéphore Niépce obtained the first permanent contact-print copies of engravings and made the first permanent camera photograph; the term was also sometimes applied to the albumen-on-glass process of Abel Niépce de Saint-Victor. The term is in fact spurious, having been coined well after Nicéphore's death, on the pattern by which the daguerreotype, talbotype, and other 19th c. processes were named. It is inaccurate and its use is improper; Nicéphore Niépce called his process *heliography*.

Night Photography

Photography outdoors at night commonly is confronted with one of two problems: either the entire scene is dim and has overall low contrast, or parts of the scene are brightly lighted while others are very dark, producing unusually high contrast. While these problems can be overcome by adding light (usually electronic flash) the night mood is captured best by using existing light.

Fast black-and-white and color films with speeds up to ISO 1000/31° or better make dim-light night photography relatively easy. When used with fast lenses, the fastest films make it possible to photograph almost anything that can be seen, and in many cases this can be done while hand-holding the camera. Slower films require time exposures with the camera mounted on a tripod or other solid support. Exposure often is difficult to determine because the subject may not reflect enough light to affect even the most sensitive meters. It may be possible to obtain a usable reflected-light reading by placing a white card or paper at the subject position; the exposure time indicated by the meter from such a reading should be multiplied by five, or the aperture setting should be increased two-and-a-half f-stops.

Illumination falling on a scene from a full moon is about five f-stops less bright than sunlight would be, but almost always it is reduced further by atmospheric factors, and the subject reflects only a small portion of that. Thus, a moonlighted subject requires the equivalent of at least ten f-stops more exposure than if it were in sunlight; this demands a time exposure, to which further compensation for reciprocity must be added. The low contrast of dim-light scenes can be improved by increased development of black-and-white films; color reversal films can also be push-processed for some improvement, but color negative films cannot.

High-contrast night scenes result when some subjects are in areas lighted by streetlamps, signs, shop windows, headlights, and other sources. Generally the choice must be either to expose and develop normally for the lighted subjects, letting dark areas go, or to expose for dark-area detail and attempt to keep the bright areas printable by significantly reducing development. The latter technique is suitable only with black-and-white films.

Electronic flash can be used outdoors at night either as a supplementary light to fill-in shadow areas, or as the main source of illumination. If flash is used in a manual mode and exposure is determined by guide number, a guide number three-quarters to one-half of the normal number should be used. This is because the normal guide number is calculated

for interior conditions where some light is reflected from walls and ceilings. A large area can be illuminated with a single unit by the technique called *painting with light,* described separately.

In addition to a tripod, the most essential accessory for night photography is a small flashlight so that meter readings, camera settings, and other details can be seen. Placed at the subject position, the flashlight also can serve as a bright point on which to focus.
See also: AVAILABLE-LIGHT PHOTOGRAPHY; PAINTING WITH LIGHT; PUSHING/ PUSH PROCESSING; RECIPROCITY.

Nilsson, Lennart

Swedish; 1922–
Lennart Nilsson is perhaps the world's most famous microbiological and medical photographer. Working closely with medical experts, he has used the most advanced photographic techniques— including much equipment of his own design, electron microscopes, and fiber optics—to magnify objects to over 70,000 times their normal size. His books, *A Child Is Born* (1965, concerning the development of the human embryo from fertilization to birth), and *Behold Man* (1973, photographs of the inner world of the human body), brought before the general public color-tinted microscopic views never seen before.

Nilsson was born and educated in Strangnas, near Stockholm, Sweden, the son of a railroad worker and amateur photographer. A naturalist from an early age, he began to photograph as a boy of 12, encouraged by his father and by an uncle who operated a professional photography studio. Originally a free-lance press photographer, Nilsson began in the early 1950s to make close-ups of organisms. In the late 1950s he began a long association with *Life* magazine where, in addition to his scientific studies on the heart, brain, eye, ear and other human organs, he published many popular photo-essays on such diverse subjects as a polar bear and her cub, the lives of ants, everyday life in Sweden, deep sea organisms, and the filmmaking of Ingmar Bergman.

Nilsson has worked for the World Health Organization and is a member of the Swedish Medical Association. He has been the recipient of numerous honors in his homeland and awards including the Photographer of the Year Award from the University of Missouri School of Journalism (1965), the Picture of the Year Award from the National Press Photographers' Association (1965), an American Heart Association Medal

(1968), the Europhot Prize (1970), and the Hasselblad Prize (1981).

A major exhibition of his work was held at the Museum of Modern Art, Stockholm, in 1973, and he has been the subject of countless touring exhibitions both in the United States and throughout the world. He continues to live and work in Stockholm.

Nodal Point
See: OPTICS.

Nojima, Yasuzo

Japanese; 1889–1964
Yasuzo Nojima was a seminal artist, patron, and photographer in the establishment of Japanese modern art. Born in Urawa, just outside the newly established (1868) capital of Tokyo, to a wealthy, well-connected family (his father was president of the Nakai Bank), Nojima began to study painting and photography at Keio University in 1905, a time of great artistic ferment.

The challenge taken up during the Meiji period (1868–1912) was for Japan to reverse some 400 years of almost total cultural isolation and inward-directed development, in order to assimilate international culture and become an active force in the modern world. In the arts this brought traditionalists and conservatives into conflict with those who embraced all that was new from the outside world; this included the conflict between tradition and modernism in Western art. There was strong resistance to avant-garde movements within traditional Japanese art forms, and an attendant failure by many to recognize the artistic potential of photography or the merits of its achievements in the West. In Western photography a similar situation existed in the conflict between Pictorialism, derived from the conventions of 19th-c. painting, and straight or purist photography. This too was imported into Japan.

Yasuzo Nojima came to maturity at the height of this artistic turmoil. He embraced the new medium of photography, and although he first took up Pictorialist themes and techniques (e.g., the gum bichromate process), he came to use them in accord with an emerging new Pictorial aesthetic in Japan. At the same time, he drew upon his family's wealth to become a patron for those individual artists who dissociated themselve from traditionalism and who were to establish the foundations of modern Japanese art.

Nojima's early work, from about 1905 to 1917, was shown largely within the context of the Tokyo Photography

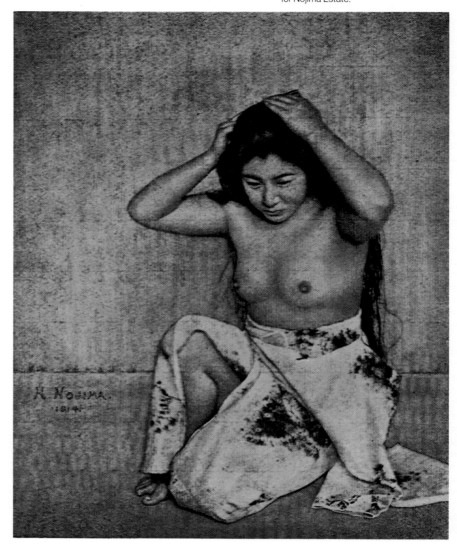

Nojima, Yazuso. "Seated nude combing her hair" (1914); gum print. Courtesy Toshiro Fujii for Nojima Estate.

Study Group (Tokyo Shashin Kenkyu Kai) and the Photography Critics Group (Shashin Hinpyo Kai). The majority of these photographs were done in gum bichromate; they are marked by soft-focus subjectivity beautifully rendered by Nojima's impeccable skill in printing.

The most productive and important phase of Nojima's career took place between 1915 and 1933. He quietly shed the self-consciously artistic approach and painterly legacy of his early gum prints, and began working with directness and remarkable precision in the rich, deep-toned monochromes of bromoil. The new photographs attempted to direct the viewer beneath the picture surface to an experience of the deep, inner response Nojima felt with his three principal subjects: nudes, portraits, and still-lifes. About 1931 he began making gelatin-silver prints to achieve an even more direct statement.

Nojima's powerful artistic development in this period shared deeply in the initial response of Japanese artists to post-Impressionism and other contemporary developments. Nojima was an early collector of Picasso, Braque, Maillol, and other Western artists in addition to many modern Japanese painters. He frequently exhibited these and other promising young artists in private salons in his home. For one year between 1919 and 1920, he opened a commercial gallery, Kabutoya Gado, in Tokyo, and supported the work of individuals representing the new art societies. Nojima also developed a serious interest in the modern reemergence of Japanese traditional arts which had foundered during the Meiji period. Nojima patronized a variety of artisans who were, 30 years later, named Living National Treasures (*ningen kokuho*). He was also an avid student of Noh singing (*utai*), and drew contemplative strength from Japan's past which frequently survives as "living traditions" in the present day.

Nojima's attention to contemporary needs saw him develop two seminal gallery/studios in Tokyo for photography: the Mikasa Shashinkan (1915–1920), Nonomiya Shashinkan (1920–ca. 1943). He was also a founding member of photography sections within the art societies, and of several photography organizations. Nojima remained open to change, and at the height of his career in 1932–1933 he published the journal *Koga* (*Light Pictures*). The articles and reproductions in *Koga* introduced the international developments of the "New Vision," and the work of a new generation of Japanese professional photographers.

The new generation had the way opened for them in many respects by Nojima's widespread efforts and earnest contributions. The "new objectivity" and "new materialism" expounded through *Koga* merged with reportage, and a social documentary spirit began to emerge. But artistic development was lost as Japan progressed from Asian expansionism toward world war. It is understandable that Nojima retired from the forefront of his campaign for photography and the establishment of Japanese modern art. His extant works produced in the early 1940s are chiefly experiments with the haunting reversals of photograms. The work Nojima did in his later years remains largely unseen, although he remained active in post-war photo societies.

Normal Lens

A camera lens whose focal length is approximately equal to the diagonal measurement of the rectangular format it is intended to cover is called a normal lens.

See: ANGLE OF VIEW; COVERING POWER; LENSES.

Notch Code

Most sheet films carry an identification coded as a series of notches. Each kind of film has a unique pattern of rectangular, V-shaped, or circular notches cut into the edge, near the corner of one narrow end. The notches are about ⅛ in. deep and the pattern up to about ¾ in. long. Each manufacturer has a distinct notch code system. The notches also help to identify the emulsion side of the film, an especially helpful feature when film holders are being loaded in total darkness or by touch in a changing bag. When the sheet is held so that the narrow, notched end is at the top and the notches are at the right-hand corner, the emulsion is facing up, toward the photographer.

Notman, William

Canadian; 1826–1891

Born in Scotland, William McFarlane Notman settled in Montreal and became noted for commercial portraits, tableaux, and composite montages of Canadian life made in his studios. He was active from the mid-1850s and established studios in Montreal, Ottawa, Toronto, and Halifax, Nova Scotia. He also formed the Notman Photographic Company in the United States with studios in New York and Boston.

The foundation of Notman's enterprise was portrait photography. From the beginning, his clientele included Canada's leaders—people of means, accomplishment, and power—as well as the general public. His studios produced popular cartes-de-visite that depicted the collective portraits of indigenous Indians, hunters, trappers, and foreign dignitaries who had settled in Canada. For his group portraits of sledge and hunting parties, Notman created elaborate settings to simulate the great outdoors.

Another innovation of the Notman Studios was the creation of hand-painted composite montages. Sketches were made of the whole composition; then models were photographed in the desired pose and scale. Several small prints were made, cut out, and combined on a sheet of cardboard. Backgrounds and additional details were then drawn by hand on the collage and the entire composition was finally rephotographed and printed. The resulting albumen prints were frequently hand-colored, as were many of the Notman Studios' more conventially posed portraits.

During his lifetime, Notman received wide recognition. In 1861 Queen Victoria named him "Photographer to the Queen." He was invited to exhibit at numerous world's fairs, and was placed in charge of all photography at the United States Centennial Exposition in Philadelphia. After his death in 1891, the firm was managed with continued success and acclaim by his sons, William McFarlane and Charles F. Notman. The Notman archive is at the McCord Library, McGill University, Montreal.

Nude Photography

The nude figure appeared as a subject in photography almost immediately after the invention of the medium. In some cases the purpose was unambiguously prurient: photographic pornography is as old as the daguerreotype. But the nude, as a venerable subject in painting and sculpture, is considered to involve much more than the simple portrayal of

Notman. "Blackfoot brave with pony" (ca. 1885). Collection, Museum of Modern Art, New York.

the naked human body. It is through the idealizing aesthetic conventions of art that the naked is transformed into the nude. During the 19th c., it was firmly maintained by traditional artists that photography's inherent realism precluded the possibility of an artistic photographic nude. But to the extent that photography has continued to aspire to the status of art, the nude has remained a challenging subject to ambitious camera artists. The delicate figure studies of Imogen Cunningham, the startling Surrealist concoctions of Man Ray, and the sculptural renderings of Edward Weston all testify to the variety and vitality of this genre.

The early 19th c. witnessed the eclipse of the male nude as a traditional art subject: thus the majority of the photographs devoted to the artistic nude portray the female figure. As in painting, it was considered objectionable to represent female body hair; this taboo re-

mained in force until past the mid-20th c. Photographers of the last century, when treating the female nude, typically resorted to the expedients of a bit of strategically placed drapery or to the retoucher's art. Another element of the code that served to distinguish the "acceptable" nude was the convention that the nude be presented as a type, and not as an individual. This, it was frequently argued, photography could not accomplish. In one of the first notable instances of nudity in a publicly exhibited photograph, Oscar J. Rejlander's allegorical composition "The Two Ways of Life" (1857), half-clad figures personify various vices. But the faces of the models who posed for the camera are concealed in different ways, partially to preserve the reputations of the models and partially to insure that the figures remained allowably nonspecific. Although the picture was exhibited on at least one occasion with a drape covering

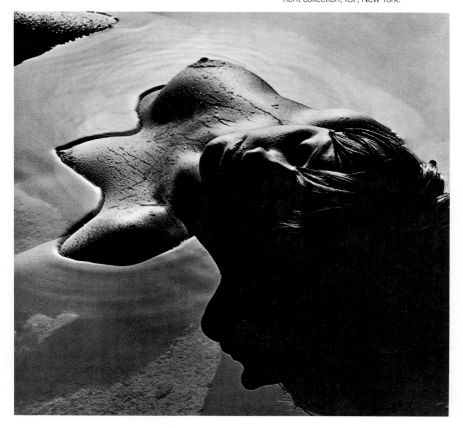

the more questionable half of the composition, the fact that it was subsequently purchased by the British Royal Family suggests that it fully met Victorian standards of decency.

There existed an important exception to these aesthetic stratagems: photographic figure studies that were prepared especially for the use of artists. Here there was no pretense that the women depicted were anything other than paid models arranged in standard academic poses. Because such photographs were much less expensive for a painter or sculptor than hiring a live model for a prolonged sitting, there grew up, especially in France, a thriving market for what were called "académies." The celebrated French painter Eugène Delacroix himself commissioned (and possibly made) a number of such photographic studies, and employed them for sketches and paintings. In the early 1850s the French lithographer Vallou de Villeneuve, who earlier had won notoriety for his erotic lithographs, was responsible for a large group of photographic studies of nude and semi-draped figures; these were intended for the use of artists as well as for the appreciation of a more general audience. The use of such photographic shortcuts by painters and sculptors in the 19th c. remained, by and large, a professional secret. It was considered harmful to an artist's reputation to admit that photographs, not sheer inspiration, were the sources of his imagery.

In addition to the 19th-c. depiction of the unclothed human figure in artistic nude photography, academic studies, and, surreptitiously, in pornography, mention should be made of its use in scientific and physiological studies. In Eadweard Muybridge's monumental *Animal Locomotion* (1887), sequential photographs of nude and partly clothed subjects analyzed the mechanics of human movement, along with motion studies of horses and other animals. The results proved of enormous value to artists concerned with the realistic portrayal of the human figure in motion. The American painter Thomas Eakins, who himself used the camera to record nude studies for his paintings, became so fascinated by photographic motion analysis that he carried out several such experiments of his own.

This straightforward, informational approach to the representation of human form had little in common with that of the artistically inclined Pictorialist photographers who came to prominence at the end of the 19th c. It was primarily through the idealized, soft-focus images of the Pictorialists that the nude became

a generally accepted photographic subject. Photographers like Robert Demachy, Frank Eugene, and Clarence White looked for new inspiration in painting, and adopted techniques like the delicate platinum print or the vigorous gum bichromate print to lend their works the richness of older art media. "Impressionistically" rendered treatments of the nude became standard offerings at the international salons of Pictorial photography. Among the most enduring works of this kind are those by the young Edward Steichen, such as "Dawn Flowers" and "In Memoriam," made in the early years of this century. Unfortunately, the vast majority of Pictorialist photographers who continued working in this style eventually lapsed into imitative, reptitious imagery. The major exception was F. Holland Day, an eccentric Bostonian who continued to produce soft-focus, outdoor studies of the male nude which maintained a high level of originality.

The first sign of a more direct manner of representing the nude emerged in a female torso study by Alfred Stieglitz and Clarence White, published in the Photo-Secession journal *Camera Work* in 1909. Its soft focus and stylized pose were unquestionably Pictorialist. But the frontal exposure of the body, and the tight framing that crops the torso, pro-

duce a powerful sense of physical immediacy that heightens the sensuous appreciation of the body's tactile qualities—an effect that depends on direct photographic perception, not painterly idealization. This hint of a shift in attitude predicts the change that would take place in Stieglitz's own work in the next decades as he moved away from Pictorialism toward a sharp-focus, "straight" approach. Stieglitz's success in presenting the nude via straight photographic techniques can be judged by his extraordinary series of nude studies of his wife, the painter Georgia O'Keefe, during the 1920s and 1930s.

The same evolution from Pictorial to straight photography marks the work of two other important photographers, Imogen Cunningham and Edward Weston. Each produced highly acclaimed nude studies in the Pictorial style for over a decade before beginning, in the 1920s, to experiment with the straight approach. Each, too, favored the device of revealing, closely cropped sections of the human body, seen in such a way that they suggested near-abstract arrangements of shapes and forms. Weston especially, in his best-known nudes, achieved a sculptural quality that has come to be widely imitated.

In Europe during the 1920s and 1930s, treatments of the nude were much more likely to be influenced by Surrealist art. The Surrealists' fascination with the psychological theories of Sigmund Freud helped insure that the erotic aspect of the nude would be emphasized in their photographs. Indeed, Surrealists like Man Ray became notorious for the ease with which they mingled elements of the classic nude with erotic imagery and even pornography in their work. In the classic vein, Man Ray's solarized figure studies, as well as his other technical experiments in this genre, have become landmarks in 20th-c. nude photography.

The Surrealist attitude has strongly influenced several other important photographers of the nude. In the 1930s Paul Outerbridge, Jr., utilized his mastery of the intricate carbro color printing technique to produce a series of disturbing, fetishized nudes—for example, a nude torso with metal-fingered gloves pressed into her flesh. André Kertész, in the early 1920s, was responsible for an impressive *Distortions* series that showed the human form as reflected by an undulating fun-house mirror. These images were alternatively humorous, graceful, and grotesque, but never abandoned the sense of warm, substantial human flesh. In the 1950s, the Englishman Bill Brandt employed extremely wide-angle lenses and high-contrast printing to transform the human body into a dazzling variety of abstract sculptural forms. Finally, Man Ray's experiments in solarization and chemical manipulation have been extended, since the 1960s, in the photographs of Todd Walker, who frequently situates his models in unusual "artificial environments" fashioned in his studio.

In recent decades the classic nude has survived notably in the work of Irving Penn, who in 1949–1951 produced a group of monumental nude studies whose statuesque forms seem to have been cut from blocks of marble. In a much more personal vein, Harry Callahan's photographs of his wife Eleanor convey an impression of intimacy and tenderness perhaps unmatched in the field of nude photography.

Currently there exists a greater diversity of approaches to nude photography than ever before. The range encompasses the use of the nude in fashion photography by Helmut Newton and Guy Bourdin, the commercial exploitation of the subject in various men's magazines, as well as its enduring presence in art photography. Particularly in Europe, the use of the nude in advertising photography has long since ceased to raise eyebrows.

Until very recently, nude photography has been dominated almost exclusively by representations of the female body. The male nude in photography is only now beginning to find public acceptance. In the last decade a number of younger photographers, both male and female—including Robert Mapplethorpe, Peter Hujar, Marsha Burns, and Jacqueline Livingston—have begun to seriously explore this aspect of nude photography.

See also: ABSTRACT PHOTOGRAPHY; ARTISTS AND PHOTOGRAPHY; ART OF PHOTOGRAPHY; EROTIC PHOTOGRAPHY; FANTASY IN PHOTOGRAPHY; MOTION STUDY AND ANALYSIS; NATURALISTIC PHOTOGRAPHY; PAINTING AND PHOTOGRAPHY; PICTORIAL PHOTOGRAPHY/PICTORIALISM.
Color photographs: pp. C-35, C-36.

Numerical Aperture (NA)

Numerical aperture is a means of specifying the relative aperture of a microscope lens (objective), from which resolving power can also be determined. The usual scheme of *f*-numbers cannot be used with microscope objectives for two reasons: (1) Because of the very close distance from the objective to the subject (specimen), the angle between a light ray entering the lens at the center, along the axis, and a ray entering the outermost edge of the lens becomes a significant factor in light transmission. Subject distances are 100 or more times greater in ordinary photography, making this angle so small that it has no effect. (2) In ordinary photography both the subject and the lens surface are in the air. In microscopy the specimen may be exposed to the air, or may be immersed in a drop of water, oil, epoxy, or other transparent medium; in addition, the surface of the objective lens may be touching the medium. Each of these media has a different refractive index, and this too affects light transmission. The numerical aperture (NA) is calculated by multiplying the sine of the most extreme light ray angle (as in 1 above) by the refractive index of the medium (2 above). The specifications for a microscope objective state the NA for a designated medium.

When the NA is known, the relative *f*-value for the objective in a given application can be determined by: $f = 1 \div 2NA$. This *f*-value can be used to calculate exposure if photomicrography is to be carried out. The maximum possible value in air-to-air situations, including those for ordinary camera lenses, is $f/0.5$; however, the greater refractive indices of some specimen media make it possible to have a relative value of $f/0.3$ in some microscopy. Because the function of microscopy is to examine very fine details, the resolving power of an objective is a factor of importance. The resolving power (R) can be calculated from the NA and the wavelength of the specimen illumination by: $R = Wavelength \div 2NA$. In the case of white light, a mid-spectrum wavelength value is used.

See also: PHOTOMICROGRAPHY; RESOLVING POWER.

Objective

In a compound lens or optical system (e.g., microscope, telescope) the objective is the lens or element facing the subject. It receives the light from the subject and forms an image which it passes to the film or the eyepiece of the optical system. In a reflecting telescope or a catoptric lens, the objective is a concave, front-surface mirror.

See also: LENSES; MIRROR LENS; TELESCOPE.

Offset Printing

Offset printing is the most widely used method for the photomechanical reproduction of text and illustrations. It differs from other methods in that the plate carrying the pattern of the material to be printed never touches the paper surface that receives the image. Instead, it transfers (offsets) the inked pattern to an intermediate surface which subsequently comes in contact with the paper to print the image. This procedure has a number of advantages. It generally creates cleaner impressions than direct letterpress or gravure printing; it permits printing on a wide variety of papers and surfaces from a single plate; it requires less time to make a composite plate of text and illustrations and less time to set up the press; and it minimizes plate wear so that inexpensive materials (paper, plastic) can be used for short-run plates, and very long runs from plates of standard materials (zinc, copper) are possible without a decrease in quality.

The offset printing technique can be used with letterpress (relief) and gravure (intaglio) plates, but the lithographic process is most commonly employed. Once it has been exposed to the material to be printed and processed, the lithographic plate chemically maintains the definition between the image and non-image areas by using the separating properties of oil and water. The image areas of the plate are made grease receptive so that they will capture the oil-base ink; the non-image areas are made water receptive so that they will repel the ink. The plate is mounted on a revolving cylinder for use. Rollers apply continuous streams of water and ink to the surface of the plate as it revolves. The ink pattern picked up by the image areas is transferred to a smooth rubber blanket on the offset cylinder that revolves in contact with the plate cylinder. Paper passing between the offset cylinder and a third cylinder, the pressure cylinder, receives the image from the offset blanket. The plate is reinked and the image transferred with every revolution.

An offset press that takes single sheets of precut paper is called a sheet-fed press; one that accepts long rolls of paper is called a web press. In multiple-color printing there is a separate plate and offset roller for each color of ink. The paper passes in a continuous path from one roller to the next. The major problems in setting up for multiple-color offset reproduction are adjusting roller pressure so that each color prints with equal density, and aligning the plates so that all impressions print exactly in register.

See also: LITHOGRAPHY; PHOTOMECHANICAL REPRODUCTION.

Oil Coloring

The use of photographic oils and conventional oil pigments to add color to black-and-white photographs gives the photographer complete control over the hues in the image. Colors and tints can be applied to simulate the original tones of the scene, or completely false, incongruous colors can be applied for expressive effect. In this method, details of the printed photographic image are incorporated in the final result; in the process called *oil printing*, described in a separate entry, colors are applied to an otherwise colorless relief image.

The materials needed for successful oil coloring include a set of photo oils or painter's oil pigments that are appropriate to the scene or to the outcome desired; cotton swabs on wooden sticks; a container of extender, which allows the thinning of oils without diluting their intensity; some photo-oil thinner for mixing and diluting colors when desired (turpentine can be used, as in oil painting, but it leaves a tacky residue that attracts dust particles); a drawing board or other tilted working surface; and a test print on which to try colors before applying them to the final print. Unlike watercolors, which must be applied in diluted form and built up, oils are applied thickly to the area being colored and then wiped off gently in a circular motion with cotton until the desired hue is produced.

For a natural effect the tenets of oil painting should be observed. Shadows invariably contain some color—the folds of a white shirt in a photograph made outdoors might look more realistic if a small amount of blue were added to them, for example. Large areas of color such as green fields of foliage will look more natural if hints of brown, red, and yellow are added.

Small areas of color can be added with a No. 00 brush or a thin, pointed stick wrapped in cotton. In order to avoid unwanted spreading of colors when the excess is wiped off, areas of the print can be masked with thinned rubber cement (liquid frisket) which can be peeled off later. Rubber cement should not be put on areas that have already been colored. The cement also is useful for protecting the borders of matted or mounted prints while they are being worked on.

Oils take a reasonably long time to dry, especially if they have been thinned with turpentine. Care must be taken not to touch painted print surfaces for at least 24 hours. To avoid accidental smearing, it is best to work from the top of the print down. Once dry, a colored print can be dry mounted, provided the print surface is protected with a sheet of cellophane or other nonporous, smooth material.

See also: OIL PRINTS; PAINTING ON PHOTOGRAPHS.

Oil Prints

Oil prints were hand-colored photographic images produced by a variant bichromate process. They were introduced in England in 1904 by G. E. H. Rawlins. Paper coated with plain colorless gelatin was sensitized with a bichromate solution and dried. It was contact-exposed under a negative, which hardened the gelatin completely in the shadows and to various degrees in the middletones. When washed to remove the unused sensitizer, the unhardened middletone and highlight areas absorbed water. Printing was done by dabbing and stippling on various oily inks. The dry areas absorbed the oil colors, but the wet, swollen areas rejected them. The print could be dried for permanence in this state, or the oil image could be transferred to another sheet in a press and the gelatin image re-inked for further copies. The bromoil process was an improved and more widely used method of oil printing.

See also: BICHROMATE PROCESSES; BROMOIL PROCESS.

Opacity

The degree to which a translucent or semitransparent material blocks the transmission of light is called its opacity. It is the ratio between the intensity of the original, incident light and the intensity of the transmitted light, expressed I_O/I_T. For convenience in graphing characteristic curves and otherwise handling the data, opacity (O) is usually expressed as its logarithm; in that form it is called density. Thus, $\text{Log } O = D$. The opposite counterpart of opacity is *transparency* (T); the two factors are reciprocal: $T = 1/O$, and $O = 1/T$.

See also: DENSITOMETRY; SENSITOMETRY; TRANSMISSION.

Optics

The scientific investigation of light is divided into three areas. Physical optics deals with the fundamental nature and properties of light. Physiological optics deals with the role of light in vision. Geometrical optics deals with the behavior of light as it is affected by lenses, mirrors, prisms, and other devices that produce refraction, reflection, dispersion, diffraction, and similar effects. The discussion here is concerned with some geometric optical principles of camera lenses and with some practical calculations for determining various factors in the formation of photographic images.

A camera lens is a compound positive or converging optical system, one that can form a real image that is visible when it falls on a plane surface (e.g., film, focusing screen). A lens has three inherent sets of optical reference (Fig. 1): focal points, nodal or principal points, and principal planes. When parallel light rays (from infinity, or in practice from an object at least 1000 yards or 915 meters away) enter the front of the lens (with any internal focusing adjustment set to infinity), they converge on the other side at the rear focal point, *FP2;* this is where the film must be located for an infinity focus setting. If parallel light rays enter the rear of the lens, they will similarly converge on the other side at the front focal point, *FP1.* Of more practical concern, if an object is located at *FP1* (or closer), light rays from it will emerge in parallel (or diverging) paths; i.e., there will be no real, focused image. The nodal, principal, or Gauss points *N1, N2* lie equal distances to the rear of *FP1* and to the front of *FP2;* the distance is equal to the focal length of the lens. The principal planes *P1, P2* pass through the nodal points, perpendicular to the lens axis. The principal points or planes are of significance because image and object distances for various calculations must be measured from them. With normal-focal-length lenses for most cameras and with lenses of symmetrical

Mixed-Media Images. Pierre Cordier,
"Chemigram 4/10/77 IV Detail" (1977)
© Pierre Cordier.

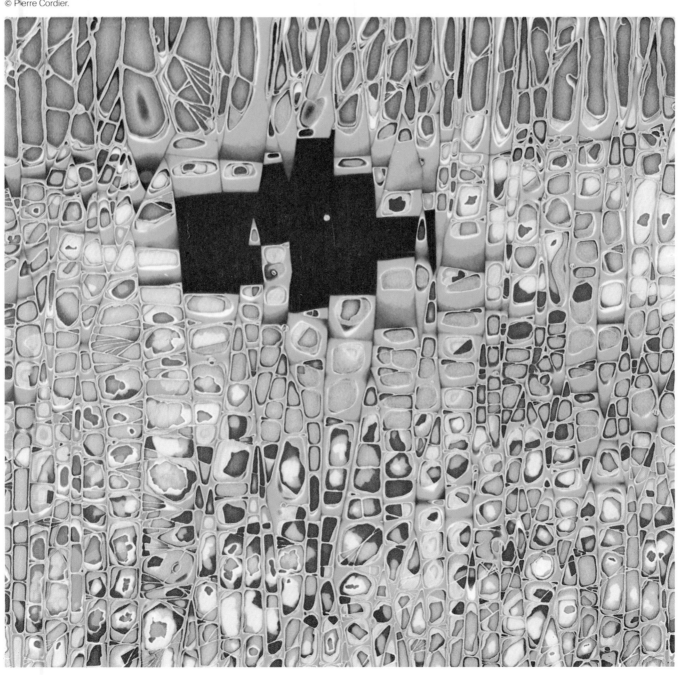

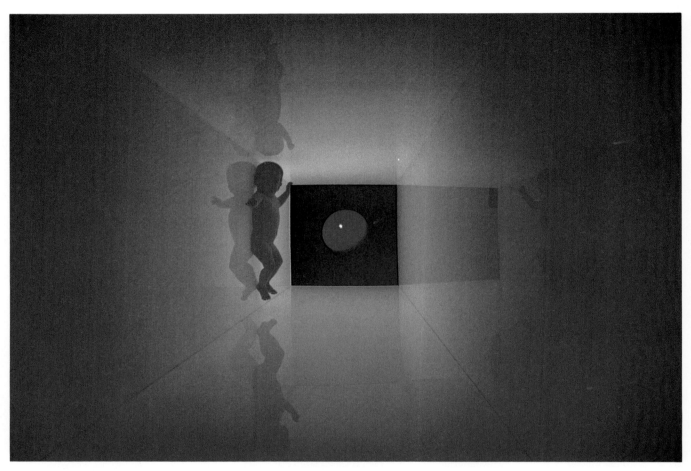

Multi-Image Techniques. Pete Turner, Untitled (1974). © Pete Turner.

Negative Prints. Edward Steichen, "Experiment in Negative Color" (ca. 1940); dye transfer. Permanent collection, ICP, New York.

Nude Photography. Dennis Manarchy, "Two
Nudes" (1978). © Dennis Manarchy.

Nude Photography. Lucien Clergue, "Eve is Black, #16, Death Valley" (1981). Courtesy Lucien Clergue.

Optics

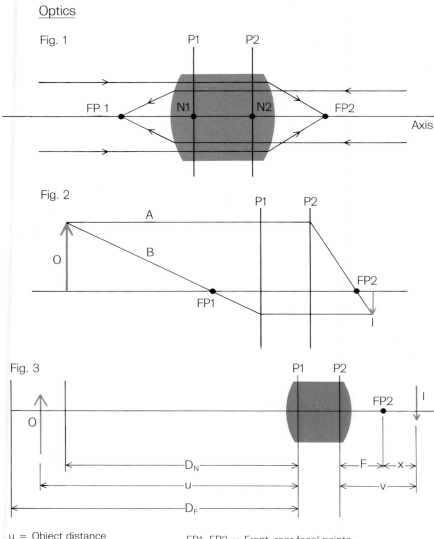

Fig. 1

Fig. 2

Fig. 3

u = Object distance
D_N = Near limit of depth of field
D_F = Far limit of depth of field
O = Object height or width
P1 = Front principal plane
P2 = Rear principal plane

FP1, FP2 = Front, rear focal points
N1, N2 = Front, rear nodal points
F = Focal length of lens
x = Lens extension for image of object not at infinity
v = Image distance (= F for object at infinity)
I = Image height or width

the lens axis (this is a matter of graphical simplification; the picture might well be composed differently through the viewfinder). From the top of the object, line *A* is drawn parallel to the lens axis until it encounters *P2*; then it is drawn downward through *FP2* and continued as shown. From the top of the object a second line, *B*, is drawn through *FP1* until it encounters *P1*; then it is projected parallel to the axis until it meets *A*. Finally, the image line *I* is drawn perpendicular from the axis to the meeting point of *A* and *B*. The image size is equal to the length of *I*; the image location behind the lens is the distance *P2* to *I*.

Calculations. The graphical method has limited application in practical situations because accurate scaling of object size and distance makes the lens and image representations extremely small. In addition, it is time-consuming and subject to inaccuracies of technique. It is easier, and more accurate, to make simple calculations—perhaps with the aid of a pocket calculator—as shown in the following formulas. It is only necessary to decide what factor is wanted, and to identify the factors that are known or can immediately be determined. Then the known values can be substituted in the appropriate formula chosen from the several listed for each factor. Fig. 3 identifies the symbols used in the formulas.

Basic Relationship:

$$\frac{1}{F} = \frac{1}{u} + \frac{1}{v}$$

Focal Length (from *P2*):

$$F = \frac{vu}{v+u} = \frac{v}{M+1} = \frac{uM}{M+1}$$

Lens Movement or Extension (beyond infinity-focus position):

$$x = \frac{vF}{u} = \frac{F^2}{u-F} = FM = uM-F$$

Object Distance (from *P1*):

$$u = \frac{vF}{v-F} = \frac{vO}{I} = \frac{v}{M} = \frac{F(M+1)}{M} = \frac{WF}{N}$$

Image Distance (from *P2*):

$$v = \frac{uF}{u-F} = uM = F(M+1) = F+x$$

Object Size (height or width):

$$O = \frac{I}{M} = \frac{Iu}{v} = \frac{I(u-F)}{F}$$

Image Size (height or width):

$$I = OM = \frac{Ov}{u} = \frac{FO}{u-F} = \frac{Ox}{F}$$

design, it is sufficient to measure from the position of the diaphragm because it is usually located midway between the principal planes. But with wide-angle and telephoto lenses the planes must be located and used for reference. A practical method of location is as follows: The lens is mounted in normal position, and an object at infinity is focused. A measurement forward, from the image plane, equal to the marked focal length of the lens locates *N2-P2*; in a telephoto lens this point may fall in front of the lens, in which case its distance from the front edge of the lens barrel should be noted for reference purposes. Then the lens is reversed and focused on an object at infinity. A focal-length measurement

from the image plane locates *N1-P1*; again, if it falls outside the physical body of the lens its position from a reference point should be noted.

A fundamental question of practical optical planning is: For an object of a particular size and distance (closer than infinity), where will the focused image lie and how big will it be with a lens of a given focal length? The classic graphical method of locating the image is shown in Fig. 2; it requires drawing all factors precisely to scale, beginning with the positions of *FP1* and *FP2* on the lens axis and the locations of *P1* and *P2*. Next, the scaled distance to the object is measured from *P1*, and the height of the object *O* is marked, with one end of *O* located on

Field Covered (height or width):
[N = negative dimension]
$$W = \frac{N}{M} = \frac{Nu}{F}$$

Magnification (image size relative to object size):
$$M = \frac{I}{O} = \frac{v}{u} = \frac{v-F}{F} = \frac{F}{u-F}$$

Reduction (inverse of magnification):
$$R = \frac{O}{I} = \frac{u}{v} = \frac{F}{v-F} = \frac{u-F}{F}$$

Hyperfocal Distance (for depth of field calculations): Use F equal to normal-focal-length lens for medium and small formats, but equal to focal length of lens actually to be used for large formats:
$$H = \frac{1000F}{f\#}$$

Depth of Field:
$$D_N = \frac{Hu}{H+(u-F)} \qquad D_F = \frac{Hu}{H-(u-F)}$$

See also: ABERRATIONS OF LENSES; BACK FOCUS; CHEMICAL FOCUS; COVERING POWER; DEPTH OF FIELD; DEPTH OF FOCUS; DIOPTER; DISPERSION; DISTORTION; f-NUMBER/f-STOP; FIBER OPTICS; FIELD LENS; HYPERFOCAL DISTANCE; JENA GLASS; LENSES; LIGHT; LONG FOCUS; MIRROR LENS; MTF: MODULATION TRANSFER FUNCTION; NUMERICAL APERTURE; PRISMS; REDUCTION, OPTICAL; REFLECTANCE/REFLECTION; REFRACTION; SUPPLEMENTARY LENS; VISION; ZOOM LENS.

Orthochromatic

The adjective orthochromatic (or simply ortho) designates an emulsion sensitive to ultraviolet, blue, green, and some yellow wavelengths—a "red blind" emulsion. Compared to the blue-sensitivity of most 19th c. materials, this kind of emulsion produced a corrected translation of colors into gray tones (Greek *ortho* = straight, true, correct; *khroma* = color). The basic principle by which an ordinary (i.e., UV- and blue-sensitive) emulsion can be made sensitive to green, called dye sensitization, was discovered by H. W. Vogel in 1873. The first such gelatin dry plates were produced in France in 1882, where they were called "isochromatic" (Greek *isos* = equal). An improved orthochromatic gelatin emulsion was produced by J. M. Eder in 1884. Many graphic arts materials (e.g., lith films) and most black-and-white printing papers have ortho emulsions, which permits them to be handled freely under red safelight.
See also: DYE SENSITIZATION; VOGEL, H.

Ortiz-Echagüé, José. "Sermon in the Village" (n.d.). Royal Photographic Society, Bath, England.

Ortiz-Echagüe, José

Spanish; 1886–1980

José Ortiz-Echagüe can be considered the most outstanding Spanish photographer. He studied at the Academy of Military Engineering in Guadalajara from 1903 to 1909, and army service and engineering enterprises, especially aeronautics, were his lifelong profession. Photography, in which he was self-taught from the age of 12, was a pastime for him as for many other pictorialists who followed the aesthetic trends recorded in the annual European publication *Photograms of the Year.* An amateur in the truest sense, Ortiz-Echagüe produced photographs devoted to the Spanish people—their traditions and religious life, their landscapes and historical sites—in which an ethnographic, geographic, and archeological concern was added to the artistic.

From an ideological point of view, his idealized vision of Iberian types paralleled the spirit of the so-called "Generation of '98," a group of intellectuals who tried to rediscover and extol the "grandeur" of the Spanish past embodied its glorious history and culture.

With the exception of photographs he took in North Africa (most of them be-tween 1909 and 1915, and his masterpiece "Siroco en el Sahara" made in 1964), his work is compiled in a tetralogy of books: *España, tipos y trajes* (1933, previously published in Germany in 1930 as *Spanische Köpfe*); *España, Pueblos y paisajes* (1938); *España, mística* (1943); and *España, castillos y alcáceres* (1956). These books were all self-published. The first one was printed in 12 editions and sold more than 70,000 copies. His exhibition prints were made by his own "direct-carbon" variation of the Fresson process, an early non-transfer method similar to the Artigue process. Some plates in his books came from these artistic prints, but most of them were made from conventional gelatin-silver prints.

Ortiz-Echagüe was the most prominent and active of a number of accomplished photographers unknown outside Spain, including Pla Janini, Campañá, Vilatobà, and Conde de la Ventosa.
See also: ARTIGUE PROCESS; CARBON PROCESSES.

Ostwald System

The Ostwald system is a method of color specification based on the subjective re-

O'Sullivan, Timothy. "Field where General Reynolds fell, Gettysburg" (1863). National Archives

sponse of a viewer to even spacing among physical samples. The system is based on additive amounts of white, black, and color such that the sum adds up to one (i.e., W + B + C = 1).

The Ostwald system commonly is displayed as either a color solid taking the shape of a double cone or as an atlas. The solid is arranged so that variations of each hue (or color) are shown as an equilateral triangle turned so that the base is a vertical line. The vertical axis represents the gray scale with white located at the top and black at the bottom. It also is the physical center of the solid. Color saturation of a hue increases the farther from the vertical axis a patch is located. The purest sample able to be produced then is located at the vertex at the side. Mixtures of white, black, and color are shown as small triangles within the overall figure.

The geometry of the solid is such that the lines of color patches parallel to the line formed between the top (white) and side (color) vertex all have equal black content. They are referred to as *isotones*. In the samples closer to the color vertex the white content is lessened while the color content is increased. The line of patches parallel to the line formed between the bottom (black) and color vertex all have equal amounts of white and are called *isotints*. Patches on a line parallel to the vertical axis all have a constant color content and are denoted *isochromes*. Since the Ostwald system presents the variations of each hue within a regular shape, there is an equivalent position for each additive mixture of white, black, and color among the differ-

ent hues. Patches occupying similar positions from hue to hue are said to be *isovalent*. In the *Color Harmony Manual*, the Ostwald system atlas, the samples are made of pigment applied to a cellulose-acetate base. Thus, each patch has a glossy side and a matte side.

One value of Ostwald color description is its correlation to nature, which often forms colors as isotints or isotones. The principal disadvantage is in the relative inflexibility of the system. When research develops a more saturated ink, for example, the entire triangle for that hue must be reconstructed. A second drawback lies in the coding. Unlike the Munsell system, the identification of samples in the Ostwald system does not relate them to the common language of color.

See also: CIE COLOR SYSTEM; COLOR; COLORIMETRY; MUNSELL SYSTEM.

O'Sullivan, Timothy Henry

American; 1840–1882

Although little is known of the life of Timothy O'Sullivan, in the course of a career that covered barely two decades he produced one of the major bodies of photographic work in 19th c. America. Born in Staten Island in 1840, by 1860 he was working in Mathew Brady's New York photographic portrait studio, which then was headed by Alexander Gardner.

During the Civil War O'Sullivan and Gardner were Brady's most important field photographers until 1862, when Gardner set up his own Washington, D.C. gallery and launched field units to

photograph the war. O'Sullivan joined Gardner and photographed the aftermath of battles such as Bull Run, Gettysburg, and Appomattox using the wet-plate (collodion) process that he was to utilize throughout his career. Many of his powerful photographs of the ruins of war and the devastation of the battlefield were issued as stereo views and were included in two folio volumes published by Gardner under the title *Photographic Sketchbook of the War.*

In 1867 O'Sullivan went west to work as official photographer for the U.S. Government Fortieth Parallel Survey, one of the many commissioned by either the government or railroad companies to describe and map the vast, uncharted expanses west of the Mississippi—in this case an area including the proposed route of the Central Pacific Railway. The area, 900 miles long and 100 miles wide, reached from Virginia City (Nevada) to Denver City in the Utah Territory. During this first expedition O'Sullivan photographed the interior of the Comstock Lode mine using magnesium flares; these are among the earliest known photographs of mine interiors. For the next two years, constantly on the move and undergoing considerable hardship in the field, O'Sullivan produced hundreds of mammoth (20″ × 24″ [51.3 × 61.5cm] and larger) glass plates of which Weston J. Naef has written, "... for O'Sullivan a photograph was equally an image chosen and organized by the artist and a specimen of preexisting physical fact recorded by the technician. The perfectly balanced tension between these subjective and objective concerns is a central characteristic of his work."

In 1869 O'Sullivan went as photographer with the Darien Survey, an expedition to determine possible routes for a canal across the isthmus of Panama. He seems to have taken relatively few photographs there, perhaps as a result of climatic conditions and dense jungle growth. Two years later O'Sullivan returned to the west, this time employed by the Geological Surveys West of the One Hundredth Meridian. He photographed in Nevada, in Owens Valley and Death Valley (where the intense heat caused his chemicals to boil inside his darkroom tent), in Colorado (where the party ascended the Colorado River through the Grand Canyon), and in Utah (where he apparently produced only stereographic views).

In 1873 O'Sullivan led his own expedition to the Southwest, photographing the Canyon de Chelly—producing one of his best-known images of the huge cliff overhanging the site of an ancient, abandoned pueblo—and the Zuñi Pueblo, New Mexico. The following year he again worked in the Southwest, this time documenting the Indians in their natural environment in pictures remarkable for their lack of sentimentality and "noble savage" attitude and for their respect for Indian culture. At the end of the 1875 expedition he returned east, where in 1882 at the age of 42 he died of tuberculosis.

See also: BRADY, MATHEW; GARDNER, ALEXANDER.

Outerbridge, Paul Jr.

American; 1896–1958

Paul Outerbridge enjoyed a long and varied career as a photographer. His early work, influenced by Paul Strand, consisted primarily of still-life abstractions of ordinary objects such as cups, light bulbs, milk bottles, machine parts, and eggs. He became a fashion and commercial photographer when his work attracted the attention of national and international magazines. He was especially acclaimed for his work in color. Finally, he produced a series of erotic and fetishistic nudes in color, few of which he was able to exhibit or publish during his lifetime.

Outerbridge was born into a wealthy family in New York City. He attended private schools, studied anatomy, drawing, and aesthetics at the Art Students League, and began his career as an illustrator and theatrical designer. He joined the Canadian Royal Flying Corps in 1917, but was discharged after a few months' time, following an accident. He subsequently enlisted in the U.S. Army where he gained his first photographic experience documenting materials in a lumber camp.

In 1921, he enrolled in the Clarence H. White School of Photography and started his serious photographic work, shooting still-lifes and nudes with large-format cameras. He insisted upon using only the finest platinum paper, an indication of the perfectionism which was to be a hallmark of his entire oeuvre. His first published picture appeared in *Vogue* in 1922, the year he also became acquainted with Alfred Stieglitz and began sculpture studies with Alexander Archipenko.

By 1924 Outerbridge had taken on many commercial accounts. His work appeared in *Vanity Fair, Harper's Bazaar,* and other periodicals. He desired total control of lighting and design, often employing preliminary sketches, and made the most meticulous adjustments to achieve his elegant textures and tones.

Outerbridge traveled to London in 1925. He was made an honorary member of the Royal Photographic Society but declined the Society's offer to give him a one-man show. He went on to Paris where he was to live for the next several years. He soon became a prominent member of the avant-garde artistic community, becoming friendly with Man Ray, Marcel Duchamp, and Berenice Abbott, and meeting such important artists as Brancusi, Picasso, Stravinsky, and Picabia. He began his serious study of eroticism, decadence, and fetishism during this time.

In May 1925, Outerbridge began photographing for *Paris Vogue,* working with Edward Steichen. Three months later he began his own freelance business. A large and expensive studio he opened with a partner closed within a year. Outerbridge worked briefly with film director G. W. Pabst in Berlin and acted as set advisor for the film *Variety.*

In 1929 Outerbridge returned to New York and set up a country studio where he began to do challenging work in carbro color photography. Achieving mastery quickly, he became a successful commercial color photographer and worked in earnest on his color nude studies.

During the 1930s and 1940s, Outerbridge shot many covers for *House Beautiful,* some of which were included by Beaumont Newhall in *The History of Photography* exhibition at the Museum of Modern Art, New York, in 1937. Outerbridge published his classic book, *Photography in Color,* in 1940.

In 1943 he moved to Hollywood and then to Laguna Beach, California, where he opened a small portrait studio but lived in virtual retirement. He closed the studio in 1945 to work in the fashion industry in an administrative position. In the late 1940s and early 1950s he traveled and contributed photo-stories to various magazines. He wrote a monthly column for *U.S. Camera* in 1955.

A one-man show of his work was held at the Smithsonian Institution in 1959, a year after his death, but his reputation waned until the mid-1970s when several books and exhibitions brought him back to the public eye. Recent shows have been mounted at the Corcoran Gallery, Washington, D.C.; the Center for Visual Arts at Illinois State University; and the G. Ray Hawkins Gallery, Los Angeles.

Overdevelopment

Overdevelopment produces excessive contrast in a negative, often accompanied by fog. All the exposed halide crystals are quickly developed in the shadow areas of the image, but there are more exposed crystals than required for good contrast in the middletones and highlights. When development is unnecessarily prolonged, excess density is produced in these areas; because the density increases in proportion to the exposure received, both local and overall contrast is increased. It is common for an unprintable amount of density to be produced in the brightest areas, which makes them featureless white in a print. Excess density also produces increased graininess. During prolonged development, a significant number of unexposed halides are also developed throughout the emulsion. The effect of this nonimage density (fog) is masked by heavy image densities, but it noticeably reduces contrast and obscures details in the less dense shadow areas.

See also: CONTRAST; DEVELOPMENT; FOG; GRAININESS.

Color photograph: p. C-37.

Overexposure

Any exposure greater than necessary for optimum image quality is called overexposure. With black-and-white negative films, optimum exposure is usually the minimum possible exposure, one that registers the darkest subject tones on the toe of the characteristic curve. Greater exposure produces more density throughout the image. This is likely to be visible as increased graininess because it causes all tones to be registered farther up on the characteristic curve. This can produce exaggerated tone separation (local contrast) in the shadow areas of the image.

Medium-speed and fast negative films have sufficient latitude for the brightness range of most subjects to produce acceptable images with up to two or three *f*-stops overexposure. Beyond that point, graininess and compressed (reduced-contrast) highlights begin to reduce image quality noticeably. The brightest subject areas may produce an unprintable amount of density, even with normal development. Extreme overexposure—on the order of 1000 times (10 *f*-stops) or more—may produce the tone reversal called solarization. Overexposure of color slide film produces faint, washed-out (desaturated) colors and blank white highlights.

See also: BRIGHTNESS RANGE; DENSITY; EXPOSURE; LATITUDE.

Overhead Projector

In an overhead projector, the material to be projected lies facing upward on a horizontal stage; a mirror- or prism-and-lens arrangement above the stage projects the image horizontally onto a wall or vertical screen. The stage is usually large enough to accommodate an open book and material of similar size; the standard transparency size is 9″ × 9″. In some models it is possible to reach into the stage to write, draw, or point out details on the material being projected. The most versatile overhead projectors (epidiascopes) accept both transparent and opaque materials; others accept only one kind of material.

Oxidation-Reduction

The fundamental chemical reaction in development of a silver halide emulsion and in other processing procedures is simultaneous oxidation and reduction. As a developing agent reduces exposed halides to metallic silver, it oxidizes. Some bleaching solutions function by oxidizing the silver in the image into silver halides (which may subsequently be redeveloped, or be dissolved out by fixing) and simultaneously reducing the bleach compounds.

The actions of oxidation and reduction are inseparable. In reduction, a compound accepts positive charges, reducing its electronegative character by balancing or neutralizing some or all of its electron charges; another compound must be present to supply the necessary positive charges, thus shifting its own electrobalance in a more negative direction, the process called oxidation.

See also: CHEMISTRY OF PHOTOGRAPHY.

Ozalid Process

The Ozalid process, commonly called brownline or blackline, is a commercial diazo process introduced in 1922 for copying plans and drawings. Because it was a completely dry process and produced positive (i.e., dark lines on a light background) copies, it rapidly replaced the blueprint process. The Ozalid paper surface contains diazo and dye coupling compounds. Exposure destroys the dye-forming capability; only those parts shadowed under the lines of the original drawing are protected. Ammonia fumes cause the positive line image to form; the lines are dark brown-black and the paper has a slight purplish-gray tone. Other Ozalid-type materials are manufactured for photolithography and related reproduction processes.

See also: BLUEPRINT; DIAZO PROCESS.

Ozotype and Ozobrome Processes

Ozotype was a pigment process introduced by Thomas Manly in 1899; it was a kind of carbon printing. A sheet with a bichromate-sensitized gelatin emulsion (or, in the Gum Ozotype, a gum arabic emulsion) was contact-exposed under a negative. It was then squeegeed face-to-face with a pigmented carbon tissue that had been soaked in a dilute solution of hydroquinone and acetic acid. Chemical reaction with the exposed bichromate tanned (hardened) the carbon emulsion in proportion to the degree of exposure. The sheets were then separated and the unhardened pigment areas washed away, leaving the tanned areas to form the image. Manly's Ozobrome process of 1905 was an improvement that used a bromide print—which could be made by enlarging—in place of the bichromated sheet. It was marketed in 1907 as the carbro process.

See also: CARBON PROCESSES; CARBRO PROCESS.

P

Painting and Photography

The long and fascinating interaction between photography and the older medium of painting has only in the last few decades begun to be seriously investigated. For centuries before the advent of photography itself, artists had made regular use of the camera obscura as an aid to more accurate rendering in painting. When it was announced in 1839 that Daguerre had devised a technique to fix the camera's images permanently, the distress felt by painters was sounded in the despairing words of the French artist Paul Delaroche: "From today, painting is dead." And indeed, one of the earliest consequences of the introduction of photography was to drive out of business those painters who specialized in the production of miniature portraits; unable to compete with photography's speed, accuracy, and relatively low cost, many of these painters ended as photographers themselves.

During the 1840s and 1850s, when public enthusiasm for the new medium was especially great, a number of young, academically trained painters began to explore the visual potential of photography. While some photographers—Charles Nègre, Gustave Le Gray, and Henri Le Secq among others—applied photography to such traditional themes as landscape or still life, they considered the conventions of painting only as guides to be judiciously reinterpreted in light of photography's

own inherent visual qualities. Likewise, the Scottish painter D.O. Hill, by freely adapting his knowledge of portraiture to the practice of calotype photography, won lasting renown for the portraits he produced in the 1840s with Robert Adamson—photographs that would be remembered long after his paintings were forgotten.

Although many 19th c. painters violently condemned photography as a mechanical, lifeless medium, few were averse to using photographic studies as models for their paintings. Photographs of foreign landscapes, historical architecture, regional costumes, and nude figures posed in academic postures were frequently consulted, offering painters a time-saving shortcut that only a handful were able to completely resist. Partially in consequence, realistic painting from the 1850s on began to incorporate new effects of detail and accuracy that imparted a decidedly photographic look to many works. Such blatant mimicry of photography by painters was loudly denounced in 1859 by the French poet and art critic Charles Baudelaire, who warned of the demise of poetic feeling in painting and condemned photography as the "refuge of all failed painters with too little talent."

But aside from such instances of outright copying, painting in the late 19th c. was affected by the spread of photography in more subtle ways. With remark-

able ease, photography lent itself to forms of picturemaking that differed radically from the conventions long established in painting—for example, the use of unusually high or low vantage points, abrupt croppings, wide-angled perspectives, and the unexpected overlappings of visual forms. By the 1870s, a few innovative painters like Edgar Degas began to explore these new pictorial devices as a means of expanding the formal vocabulary of painting. Degas introduced dramatic perspectives in his paintings of the 1860s and 1870s, and showed how the cutting off of forms by the edges of the picture frame could be used to great visual effect. These provided classic examples of the intelligent adaptation by painters of visual possibilities suggested by the photograph.

By the 1880s, the arrival of stop-motion photography opened up a new visual world previously inaccessible to the unaided eye. Using sequential photographs, Eadweard Muybridge demonstrated conclusively that artists' traditional ways of portraying human and animal movement were in error. Similarly, the French physiologist-photographer E.J. Marey was able to present the flow pattern as well as the stages of a complex motion—running or jumping, for example—in analytic detail. But aside from their immediate impact on the artistic rendering of movement, such photographs eventually had a more important effect: they suggested to artists new visual techniques for conveying, in a more abstract sense, the idea or the feeling of movement. In the years just before World War I, Anton Bragaglia attempted to realize futurist images photographically, while painters such as Marcel Duchamp looked back to photographs like Marey's not so much for their realism as for their ability to evoke an altogether different kind of pictorial reality.

Especially in Europe, the years following World War I saw a far-reaching reexamination of the relation between painting and photography. In a period when the dawning age of technology was thought to promise a modern utopia, many young painters turned with heightened interest to the medium which represented a technological approach to image-making. For iconoclastic Dada artists like Kurt Schwitters and Francis Picabia, photography seemed about to render easel painting obsolete, a vestige of the pre-industrial past. Strikingly similar views were voiced during the 1920s by such revolutionary Russian artists as Alexander Rodchenko and El Lissitsky, who hailed photography as a means to overthrow antiquated habits of seeing, and as a way to behold the world with modern eyes. By the late 1920s, ideas such as these had found a place in the program of the influential German design school, the Bauhaus. There, one-time painters like László Moholy-Nagy and Herbert Bayer encouraged their students to explore all aspects of the new medium through photograms, photomontage, and abstract photography. While their experiments came to a virtual halt with the beginning of World War II, the transplantation of the Bauhaus program to the United States ensured that the intermingling of photography and painting would continue during the postwar years.

In recent decades, as photography has increasingly come to be accepted as a fine art, a number of painters have begun to actively explore the similarities and differences that exist between the painted and the photographic image. Most notable in this area are the efforts of the Photorealist painters to surpass photography in the realistic representation of the visual world. Chuck Close's portraits, Richard Estes's cityscapes, and Audrey Flack's still-life paintings all seek to attain, through the use of detail, color, and large scale, a vividness and immediacy beyond that of the most convincing photograph. Other painters, such as Robert Rauschenberg, have incorporated photographically derived images into their paintings, as if to acknowledge the important place occupied by the photograph in the modern visual vocabulary. Predictably, some artists and critics have lamented the attention accorded to photography in recent years; one critic, invoking Baudelaire, has spoken of the "remorseless decline in artistic taste" that has accompanied photography's rise. But as signalled by the surging number of painters, sculptors, and other artists currently making use of photography in some way—either in their own artworks or as an independent print-making medium—few contemporary artists are inclined to underestimate the value or importance of photography as an image-making system. Today, more than ever, painting and photography seem inextricably entwined.

The previous discussion has concentrated on the influence of photography on painting. While the influence of painting on various styles of photographic expression has been more widely noticed, most photographic efforts along "artistic" lines have been highly imitative. This is particularly apparent in the pictures of O.G. Rejlander, H.P. Robinson, and their followers in the "high art" Pictorialist movement from the 1860s through the turn of the century. Art photography successively passed through imitations of Impressionism, Surrealism, Cubism, and a number of other movements, as discussed in various other entries. For the most part photographers have been far less successful in integrating painterly influences into truly original modes of expression than the painters who have assimilated photographic revelations and contributions to visual knowledge.

See also: ABSTRACT PHOTOGRAPHY; ALLEGORICAL PHOTOGRAPHS; ARTISTS AND PHOTOGRAPHY; ART PHOTOGRAPHY; BAUHAUS; CONCEPTUAL PHOTOGRAPHY; FANTASY IN PHOTOGRAPHY; GENRE PHOTOGRAPHY; IMPRESSIONISTIC PHOTOGRAPHY; MONTAGE; MULTIMEDIA PRESENTATIONS; NATURALISTIC PHOTOGRAPHY; PHOTOREALISM; PHOTOSCULPTURE; PICTORIAL PHOTOGRAPHY/PICTORIALISM; SEQUENCES; SUBJECTIVE PHOTOGRAPHY; SURREALISM IN PHOTOGRAPHY.

Painting on Photographs

The hand-coloring of black-and-white photographs has been practiced since the days of the daguerreotype. Skillful use of oils, watercolors, dyes, or acrylics can produce visual effects that are uniquely attractive and bear little resemblance to the results obtained with color films.

The most common method of painting on photographs is that which allows the detail and texture of an original black-and-white image to show through the hues applied. The easiest method of applying transparent color is to use specially designed photo oils, placing them in the appropriate areas of the print with cotton swabs or small balls of cotton, and then wiping away the excess. Watercolors will also allow the colorist to apply transparent shades, although this technique demands more skill. Watercolors should be applied to a print surface that first has been treated with a dilute ammonia solution; this removes any grease left on the print by handling.

The colors should be applied in highly dilute form, the appropriate hue and density being built up with repeated applications. Watercolors and some dyes can leave a dull finish and therefore are best used with semi-matte or matte-surface prints. For extremely fine work use of an airbrush is recommended, especially if large areas are to be colored in an even wash of color. For a natural effect shadows should be colored in a slightly warmer hue than is desired for the final result; the grays of the black-and-white print tend to cool down colors somewhat.

Food-coloring dyes dissolved in water can be used in the same manner as watercolors. Special dyes for coloring and painting on photographs are available in sheet form. These are best for small areas, where a brush can be used. Color is picked up with a dampened brush. Acrylic colors can be used with some success, provided they are first thinned with either a matte- or gloss-acrylic medium, depending on the print surface and the result desired. Acrylics can be used directly if the colorist desires an impasto effect, although the opacity of the result will hide the detail of the photograph. In such cases the photograph essentially is used as a guide for the final result. Photographs can also be colored with washable or permanent felt-tip markers.
See also: OIL COLORING; OIL PRINTS.
Color photographs: pp. C-38, C-39.

Painting with Light

Painting with light is a technique of using a single portable light source to illuminate a very large area or a physically complex subject so that it can be photographed. The technique often is used to illuminate a building facade at night or a dimly-lighted interior—especially one of considerable depth. It also is used to obtain pictures of a subject such as an automobile engine without shadows that create confusing patterns and obscure some parts.

Painting with light may be accomplished with a continuous light source such as a quartz light or a photoflood, or with a flash unit. The basic technique is simply to open the camera shutter for a time exposure and to continuously move the light over the subject area by area until each portion has been "painted" with an equal amount of illumination. A flash unit is fired repeatedly while aimed at various areas to achieve the same result. Equal illumination is achieved by moving to keep the light source the same distance from each area during the time it is being lighted. If this is not possible with some areas (e.g., the ceiling of a building lobby), the continuous light must be painted there for a longer time, or the flash unit must be fired several times.

With a continuous light source the basic exposure is determined by an incident- or reflected-light meter reading. An f-stop that requires a time of at least two or three seconds should be chosen; otherwise it is difficult to equalize the painting of each area. Exposure with a flash unit is determined by using the guide number to find the proper flash-subject distance for the f-stop to be used, or by consulting the distance-range scale of an automatic flash unit. With either kind of light source each area must receive the same exposure.

While painting with light is a simple technique, certain precautions are important. If painting cannot be done from the camera position, two people are needed—one to handle the light source, and the other to block the lens when the light is being repositioned so that an exposure from the ambient light is not picked up. It is not advisable to repeatedly open and close the shutter because of the danger of moving the camera. The light source must be in an opaque holder or reflector and must never be turned so that its light can be seen directly by the lens; otherwise glare or flare will be recorded. The lighting instrument and the person handling it must never be positioned between the lens and the area being illuminated, or a silhouette will be recorded. Coverage must be planned so that the edges of the various areas blend without excessive overlap, which would cause strips of overexposure, and without separation, which would cause dark strips of underexposure. Coverage is easy to see with a continuous light source, but it is more difficult to estimate with a flash unit. Trial runs recorded on instant film are very helpful. Shadowless lighting is achieved by making sure that each part of the subject is lighted from at least two opposing angles, taking care to avoid overexposure.

See also: LIGHTING; SHADOWLESS LIGHTING.

Palladiotype

The palladiotype is a variant of the platinum print process. Palladium papers were introduced about 1916 because the cost of platinum—expensive from the start—had increased more than 500 percent from 1878 when the platinotype was introduced. Palladium became prohibitively expensive in the early 1920s, and manufacture of all such materials ended.

See also: PLATINOTYPE.

Panchromatic

The adjective panchromatic designates an emulsion that has essentially equal sensitivity to all visible wavelengths (Greek: *pan* = all). Almost all general-purpose black-and-white films and color films and papers have panchromatic emulsions. Black-and-white papers commonly have orthochromatic (red-blind) emulsions, but those especially designed for true gray-tone translation of images from color negatives have panchromatic emulsions. The ordinary ultraviolet- and blue-sensitivity of a silver halide emulsion is extended to the green and red portions of the visible spectrum by dye sensitization during manufacture. A number of compounds for green sensitization were identified in the 1880s and 1890s; red sensitizers were discovered by I. G. Farben chemists in Germany in 1905. The first photographic plates with panchromatic emulsions were produced a year later, in England, by Wratten and Wainwright.

See also: DYE SENSITIZATION; ORTHOCHROMATIC; WRATTEN, F. C. L.

Panning

The camera movement in which a stationary camera pivots left or right to follow a moving subject or to scan the scene, is called *panning*. The term is used primarily with reference to television and motion-picture cameras. A camera may also pan up or down, but the term *tilting* is preferred to distinguish the vertical from the horizontal movement.

See also: CAMERA MOVEMENTS.

Panoramic Photography

Panoramic photographs cover horizontal fields of view from about 180° to a full 360°. They may be produced with special lenses or cameras, or by a panning-sequence technique with ordinary equipment. Some fisheye lenses have angles of view of more than 200°, but they produce significant distortion. Special panoramic cameras can produce distortion-free images over fixed or adjustable fields. In one type of camera, the film is held in a curved plane while a motor drive pivots the lens from left to right. A vertical slit shutter that moves with the lens ensures that only a narrow central portion of the image, directly on the lens axis, falls on the film; in this way the film is progressively exposed without image smear or flare and overexposure. In another type of panoramic camera, the lens is fixed, but the entire camera body is mounted on a rotating platform. Inside, the film moves past a slit image at a speed that matches the platform rotation.

Panoramic photographs can be taken with an ordinary reflex-viewing or view camera on successive frames or sheets of film by swinging the camera after each exposure to get a series of views with a slight amount of overlap coverage (about 5°) at the edges. Prints of these views are laid out with their overlaps matched so that two adjacent prints can be trimmed with a single cut; this allows them to be edge-butted in final mounting for a continuous image of uniform thickness. The cut is made along the least noticeable path—e.g., along the edge of a building or the trunk of a tree. High-quality results with this technique involve several factors. The camera must be absolutely level on the horizontal plane in all directions (i.e., N-S and E-W); otherwise, it will tilt progressively up or down from exposure to exposure. A circular bubble-centering level is valuable for this purpose. The camera should be swung—panned—the same distance each time; a protractorlike indexing device on the tripod head—which can be improvised—is helpful. The camera should be mounted so that it pivots directly under the rear nodal point of the lens, or as nearly so as possible, so that the perspective is the same in each segment of the overall view. Exposure may have to be adjusted if the brightness is very different in some parts of the scene. Progressive exposure corrections in half-stop steps will insure that areas of continuous tone and brightness, such as sky, are not so different in adjoining segments that they can not be matched with normal burning-in or dodging during printing.

See also: FISHEYE LENS; OPTICS.
Color photographs: pp. C-39, C-40-41.

Pantograph

The pantograph is a device for drawing copies of an original at enlarged or reduced scale. It consists of two jointed arms pegged together to form a pivoted double-X. At each side the end of one arm is fixed in place while the other arm is movable. Tracing over a drawing with a stylus attached to one arm causes the other arm, fitted with a pen or pencil, to move in a duplicate pattern. Changing the points at which the two arms are pegged together changes the scale of the duplicate drawing. The pre-photographic technique called *physionotrace*, invented by G. L. Chrétien, was produced by means of a pantograph.

Paper Negative Process

See: CALOTYPE; SALT PAPER PROCESS; WAXED PAPER PROCESS.

Paper Positive Process

See: BAYARD, HIPPOLYTE; DIRECT POSITIVE.

Papers, Photographic

The papers used for making photographic prints all have a similar basic construction, but they have major differences in physical and image characteristics and in application. Papers generally are classified as enlarging or contact-printing papers, and as black-and-white, color negative, or color reversal (print from a positive transparency) papers. There are also black-and-white direct positive (reversal) papers and a number of other special papers.

A photographic paper consists of a base material with a white or near-white surface that is coated with one or more emulsion layers. Conventional papers have a fiber paper base; resin-coated papers have a paper base that is coated with plastic on both sides to make it non-absorbent. A few "papers" have entirely plastic base material. The thickness of the base material is classified according to weight: light-, single-, medium-, or double-weight. Lightweight paper can be folded without emulsion cracking. Double-weight papers are highly resistant to distortion or tearing when wet, and to rippling or curling when dry. Almost all resin-coated papers are of medium weight. Papers are supplied in a great number of standard sizes from 2½″ × 2½″ to 30″ × 40″ (6.4 × 6.4cm to 77 × 102.6cm). Certain standard widths are also supplied in rolls up to 500 ft. (152.4m) long, primarily for use in automatic printing and processing machines.

Paper emulsions have various surface textures. Glossy, smooth lustre, semimatte, and matte are the major textures; others include silk, tweed, pearl, and crystal—all with a noticeable texture characteristic. A glossy surface produces maximum image contrast or color saturation because it scatters viewing light the least; however, it also is the most highly reflective and most clearly reveals surface effects such as fingermarks and scratches. The tint of the paper surface beneath the emulsion determines the color of image highlights; it is usually pure white, buff, or ivory, but novelty papers with pastels or strong colors are also available. The image tone in black-and-white papers may be warm (brownish), neutral, or cool (bluish), depending on the chemical composition of the emulsion, and the expressive effect of this coloration must be taken into account in selecting a paper. (Image color or can be changed by toning after processing.) Color papers differ somewhat in the "palette" of their colors, some having an overall warm or red bias throughout their range, and others having a green or blue bias; this is a subtle difference, most noticeable in side-by-side comparisons.

Paper emulsions also differ in speed, spectral sensitivity, and contrast. Contact-printing papers are much slower (less light-sensitive) than enlarging papers, some of which are available in normal speed and "rapid" emulsions; the latter require one-third to one-half as much exposure as those of normal speed. The speed of a particular paper varies with its contrast grade, becoming slower as contrast increases. There is a speed rating system for black-and-white papers similar to that for films; however, it is little used because negatives vary so much that it is simpler to determine exposure by means of test strips or enlarging-meter readings. Spectral sensitivity refers to the color sensitivity of the emulsion. Color papers have full or panchromatic spectral sensitivity, as do special black-and-white papers intended for making prints from color negatives. Black-and-white papers are sensitive only to blue (contact and lith papers) or blue and green (enlarging papers); this affects their relative speeds and determines what kind of safelight illumination can be used with them. Color papers are supplied in a single, normal grade of contrast; black-and-white papers are supplied in several grades usually numbered from 0 (least contrast) to 5 (greatest contrast). Contrast refers to the number of equal gray-scale steps an emulsion produces in the range from paper-base white to maximum image black. As contrast increases, fewer steps are produced at greater equal intervals. Some papers have a variable or selective contrast emulsion; its response is varied by using different degrees of yellow or magenta filtration during exposure.

Most photographic papers are processed in solutions similar to those used for conventional film processing; however, some use diffusion transfer processing in which the print paper receives a positive image from a sheet exposed to the negative or slide being printed. The newest diffusion transfer papers have greatly simplified the techniques of color printing. Most color papers create an image by forming dyes in three different emulsion layers during processing; dye destruction papers begin with a full density of dye in each layer, and processing removes the unneeded amount. Black-and-white papers for rapid processing by the activation (and activation-stabilization) process have developing agents as well as light-sensitive silver halides in their emulsions. Some black-and-white papers have printing-out emulsions that produce an image solely by the action of light, without development; these include high-contrast instrument-recording papers, and continuous-tone papers primarily used for proof prints of portraits.

Special-purpose papers and related print materials, in addition to those mentioned, include rolls of extra-width paper used for photomurals; papers with translucent bases for day/night display by reflected and transmitted light; high-contrast papers for phototypesetting and computer graphic printouts; and sensitized fabrics, glass, plastic, and metal with continuous-tone emulsions for image reproduction or high-contrast emulsions for photofabrication and similar applications.

See also: BLACK-AND-WHITE MATERIALS; COLOR MATERIALS; CONTRAST; DYE DESTRUCTION PROCESS; EMULSION; FERROTYPING; LITH FILMS/PAPERS; PRINTING, BLACK-AND-WHITE; PRINTING, COLOR; PRINTING-OUT PAPER; RAPID PROCESSING; SAFELIGHT; STABILIZATION PROCESS; VARIABLE-CONTRAST MATERIALS.

Parallax

A discrepancy in the field of coverage between two views of a subject seen from different viewpoints is called parallax. In photography the error created by parallax is sometimes a problem at close subject distances when the camera's viewing system does not look directly through the exposing lens. In rangefinder and twin-lens reflex cameras the viewing system is located above the camera lens one to two-and-a-half inches and thus has a different line of view. In some rangefinder systems it is also offset to the side slightly. If a subject at a close distance is framed to just fit inside the top edge of the viewing frame, it may be cut off on the film because the camera lens looks straight forward from a lower position. The usual device for avoiding this parallax error is a set of reference marks in the viewfinder that indicate the close-distance top cutoff line. The reference marks commonly are fixed, but in some rangefinders they shift as the camera lens is focused. While insuring corrected framing of the main subject, this system cannot reveal the differences in foreground-background overlapping as seen along the two lines of view; only through-the-lens viewing can show accurately what overlap will be recorded on the film.

Parallax Stereogram

A parallax stereogram is a stereoscopic print or transparency composed of very narrow alternating strips of the images taken by the left and the right camera lenses. This array is covered by an opaque grating with matching slits. The grating is slightly above the image strips so that at normal viewing distance the right eye can see only right-lens strips through the slits and, from its slightly different angle of view, the left eye can see only left-lens strips. The brain fuses the two images into a three-dimensional impression of the subject photographed. A similar, and more versatile, system uses a lenticular screen instead of a grating.
See also: LENTICULAR SYSTEMS; STEREOSCOPIC PHOTOGRPHY.

Parfocal, Parfocus Lens

See: ZOOM LENS.

Parkes, Alexander

English; 1813–1890
A significant contributor to the growth of metallurgy, and especially electroplating, in the 19th c., Parkes is better known as a founder of the plastics industry, particularly for his economically practical methods of molding a cellulose nitrate compound, xylonite, into useful objects. His interest in photography produced a method of making collodion stripping plates, patented in 1856; in the patent he also suggested the possibility of creating a flexible emulsion support from layers of collodion. In 1861 he patented *Parkesine,* an improved form of xylonite, which was the first form of modern celluloid. It was subsequently improved for photographic use by J. W. Hyatt and John Carbutt in 1888.
See also: CARBUTT, JOHN; CELLULOID; STRIPPING FILM.

Parks, Gordon

American; 1912–
Gordon Parks, born in Fort Scott, Kansas, worked as a piano-player, busboy, dining-car waiter, and semi-professional basketball player. He first worked as a photographer under Roy Stryker in the Farm Security Administration (1942–1943) and again for Standard Oil Company of New Jersey (1945–1948). In 1949 he became a member of the staff of *Life* magazine.

Regarded as a major photojournalist, Parks has also earned considerable distinction as a writer, poet, novelist, composer, and filmmaker. He produced, directed, and wrote the script and music for the film based on his novel *The Learning Tree,* and directed the films *Shaft, Shaft's Big Score,* and *Leadbelly.* In his early years he also photographed high fashion and beautiful color still lifes.

It could not have been easy to be the first recognized black professional photographer in America. Whatever the difficulties, Parks was successfully able to overcome the slights and anger to do the job. Many of his memorable essays for *Life* dealt with the Black Revolution of the 1960s: "The Black Muslims" (1963), "The Death of Malcolm X" (1965), "On the Death of Martin Luther King, Jr." (1968), "The Black Panthers and the Police" (1970), and "Papa Rage: A Visit with Eldridge Cleaver" (1970). His style in these essays is more direct than poetic, more realistic than sentimental. The photographs are not those of a hard-hitting news reporter but the work of an objective observer; they are gentle in their compassion.

Parks, Gordon. "Muhammad Ali" (ca. 1965). Courtesy Gordon Parks; permanent collection, ICP, New York.

Parks's extraordinary essay on Flavio da Silva, a poverty-stricken Brazilian boy whom Parks found dying in the notorious slums above Rio de Janeiro in 1961, is an unforgettable story. The photographs and diary of his three-month stay with Flavio and his family touched off a chain of events that went to the heart of journalism. Parks became very attached to Flavio, and was more than an objective reporter. He made it possible for Flavio to receive the medical attention needed to survive the illness and early death that was predicted for him. Parks was not able to document poverty and despair without becoming involved in the lives of the people he photographed.

There are many other aspects to Parks's work. In 1981 he opened an exhibition of large prints that combined photography and oil painting. They are colorful and graphic and show a yearning for the abstract. His current projects include a novel based on the life of the painter J.M.W. Turner.

In addition to other citations, in 1972 Gordon Parks received the coveted Spingarn Medal, the highest award presented by the NAACP. He also is the recipient of 14 honorary degrees.

Pellicle

A pellicle is a thin skin or filmlike surface layer. Pellicles of collodion bearing microphotographs of messages were stripped from glass plates and transported by the Pigeon Post during the Siege of Paris, 1870–1871. The first successful gelatin dry emulsion was marketed in 1876 as R. Kennett's Sensitized Gelatino Pellicle. Photographers dissolved it in warm water in order to coat their own glass plates. The sense of a photographic emulsion being a pellicle is present in the Spanish *pelicula* and Italian *pellicola*, meaning "film." A pellicle is also the thin partially reflecting coating used for some beam splitters and other kinds of semitransparent mirrors.

"Pencil of Nature, The"

The first book with true photographic illustrations was *The Pencil of Nature*, published by W. H. F. Talbot in 1844–1846. It is a landmark for being the first book about the applications of photography, and even more so for being illustrated with actual photographs— calotypes— printed by Nikolaas Henneman and his assistants from Talbot's paper negatives and pasted in by hand. Two books with photographically derived illustrations had previously appeared: *Excursions daguerriennes:*

vues et monuments les plus remarquables du globe, published in Paris in 1840—1842 by N. P. Lerebours, had engravings copied from daguerreotypes as well as some illustrations made directly from engraved daguerreotypes; *Paris et ses environs reproduits par le daguerreotype*, published in 1840, was illustrated with lithographs based on daguerreotypes.

Talbot's book had photography as its subject. The introduction traced his invention of the negative-positive process of photography. Twenty-four succeeding sections illustrated and briefly discussed present and future possible applications of this new medium, including artistic expression, various documentary uses, scientific illustration, recording and duplicating works of art, and aiding study and teaching. One section even anticipated photography by the invisible illumination of "chemical rays"— ultraviolet and infrared.

The book was published by subscription, and appeared in six installments. Just under 300 copies were produced; 24 are known to exist today, several of which are incomplete.

See also: BOOKS, PHOTOGRAPHIC; CALOTYPE; HENNEMAN, NIKOLAAS; TALBOT, W. H. F.

Penn, Irving

American; 1917–

Born in New Jersey, Irving Penn studied design at the Philadelphia Museum School, where he became a student of Alexey Brodovitch. In 1937, the year before he graduated, several of his drawings were published by *Harper's Bazaar*. From 1940 to 1941, he worked for the art and advertising director of Saks Fifth Avenue, and the following year he spent in Mexico painting, a medium he subsequently abandoned. Returning to New York, Penn was hired by *Vogue* magazine, first to create ideas for cover illustrations, then to photograph covers as well as editorial illustrations for the interior of the magazine. Working closely with Alexander Liberman, Penn developed a highly stylized, graphically compelling form of fashion photography which did much to define post-war notions of feminine chic and glamour. In his fashion and portrait photography, Penn favored the use of a neutral backdrop of gray or white seamless paper, or alternatively, the use of constructed architectural sets which created striking effects with oblique, diving diagonals and upward-tipped perspectives. Penn also created numerous still-life compositions for the magazine: carefully orchestrated assemblages of food or objects characterized by a play of three-

dimensional and two-dimensional forms. In 1953 Penn opened his own commercial studio and almost immediately became one of the most influential and successful advertising photographers in the world.

Eschewing any notions of naturalism, spontaneity, or chance, Penn has always favored the rigidly controlled, formal conditions of the studio. Thus, even when photographing North African nomads, New Guinea tribesman, Peruvian Indians, or Hell's Angels, Penn contrived portable studios that permitted much the same degree of elegant and structured lighting and composition that he used to photograph fashion models and socialites.

In addition to his fashion and commercial work, Penn has produced a body of art photography. Using platinum and other precious-metal processes, Penn has photographed urban detritus (cigarette butts, crumpled wrappers, etc.), the torsos of plump artists' models, and most recently, still lifes of skulls, bones, and construction materials. While the subject matter represents the antithesis of his fashion and commercial work, as does the use of artisanal printing processes produced in numbered editions, both bodies of work reveal the same preoccupation: balance of form and carefully calibrated composition, with nuances of light and tone, presenting a subject that is emotionally neutral or kept always at emotional and psychological arm's-length.

Pentaprism

See: PRISMS; VIEWING AND FOCUSING SYSTEMS.

Percentage Solution

A percentage solution is one containing a specified strength of a chemical compound. The percentage strength is calculated from the weight or volume of the compound and the total volume of the solution. In the U.S. customary system, the compound is measured in solid or fluid ounces, and the solution in fluid ounces. In the metric system, the compound is measured in grams (solid) or milliliters (liquid), and the solution in milliliters. The calculation is:

$$\text{Percent strength} = \frac{\text{Compound measurement}}{\text{Solution volume}} \times 100$$

Thus, each of the following is a 25 percent solution: 25 oz. in 100 oz. of solution; 250g in 1000ml of solution; 2.5ml in 10ml of solution.

A percentage solution is prepared by adding the required measurement of the compound to about two-thirds the final volume of water. After the compound is completely dissolved or mixed in, water is added to make up the final amount.

This procedure takes into account the volume of the compound itself.

A percentage solution provides a way to measure out a very small amount of a compound, one that cannot be accurately measured directly. For example, a

Penn, Irving. "Mother and daughter, Cuzco, Peru" (1948). Courtesy *Vogue,* © 1949, 1977, by Condé-Nast Publications Inc.; collection, Museum of Modern Art, New York.

1 percent solution of silver iodide contains 1 oz. of iodide per 100 oz. of solution (or 10g per 1000ml). A fractional amount of the solution contains a proportionate fractional amount of the iodide. Taking 1 oz. of the solution effectively measures out 0.01 oz. of the iodide (10ml of solution contains 0.1g). A solution containing more than one ingredient has a percentage strength of each. A developer composed of 7.5g of metol and 100g of sodium sulfite in water to make one liter (1000ml) can be described as a solution of 0.75 percent metol and 10 percent sodium sulfite in water. Formulas are sometimes written in percentage terms in general photographic literature, leaving the reader free to determine specific amounts for whatever final volume is desired.

See also: MIXING PHOTOGRAPHIC SOLUTIONS.

Perforations

The rectangular holes regularly spaced along one or both edges of various films permit advancing the film with precise spacing from frame to frame and, in motor-driven equipment, at a constant speed. These perforations also avoid repeated pulling on the entire length of the film that could cause tearing or scratches by cinching the film tighter and tighter on the supply and take-up spools. Most unperforated roll films have a backing paper to absorb the pull and to act as cushioning between the layers on the spools. All motion-picture films are perforated, and 35mm still film has the same perforations along each edge as 35mm positive motion-picture film. There are 64 perforations per foot, or 8 for each full-size 35mm still frame (4 per frame in 35mm half-frame and standard motion-picture formats). Still camera 70mm film does not have the same perforations as that for motion-picture cameras; it is also available unperforated. Cartridge (126 and 110) films have one perforation per frame, along one edge of the film.

See also: FORMAT.

Periodicals

See: APPENDIX.

Perspective

The impression of depth separation or distance between elements in a visual image is called perspective. It produces a sense of space extending from the frontal plane of the picture into the visual distance. If the image is large enough to fill the visual field of the viewer, the space seems to extend forward from the picture plane, surrounding the viewer. Classical discussions of perspective, involving vanishing points, central viewpoint, horizon, and similar considerations serve admirably for producing diagrams and for constructing perspective in a drawing or painting. They are of little use in photography because perspective is not constructed in a photograph, it is obtained as a given condition, a consequence of using a particular lens from a particular standpoint.

Certain factors provide clues that some picture elements are more distant than others. One is overlapping—a shape that blocks part of another shape from view is the closer of the two. A second is aerial perspective, the graying of tone or color and the obscuring of detail that increases with distance and is caused by haze, smoke, dust, and other atmospheric particles. Its effect is increased in outdoor photographs by the additional exposure effect of ultraviolet in the atmosphere, unless a UV-absorbing filter is used. The most important factor in perspective is the visually diminished size of distant objects and the apparent convergence of parallel lines. These are two aspects of the same effect—the differences in magnification that correspond to differences in distance from the lens.

The role of magnification. A typical situation will serve to illustrate the role of magnification in perspective. Consider two people—A and B—of the same height, standing so that B is 10 ft. beyond A's position. If a camera is placed 10 ft. from A, it is 20 ft. from B. In normal-range (i.e., not close-up) photography, magnification varies directly with distance. B is twice as far as A, so B's image is one-half the size of A's image on the film. If the camera is moved to 5 ft from A, it is 15 ft. from B. The distance ratio is now 5:15 = 1:3, and B looks one-third the size of A. As a result of their visual experience humans "know" that smaller size means greater distance, so the picture at this position seems to have greater depth or more forceful perspective than the picture at the first position. If the camera then is moved to a position 50 ft. from A, it is 60 ft. from B; in the picture, B appears to be five-sixths the size of A, or nearly the same, and the depth between them appears reduced. All objects in a picture are similarly magnified in proportion to their distances from the lens. Thus, details on the ground plane are magnified in progressively lesser degrees as they are more distant, providing a continuous rate of visual change that adds to the perspective effect. In the same way, the separation between parallel lines such as the edges of a sidewalk, or the tops and bottoms of a line of fence posts, is magnified in decreasing amounts as the distance increases. The decreasing separation makes them appear to converge at the point where the eye or the lens can no longer resolve them individually.

These effects occur no matter what focal length of lens is used. At the starting point of the example situation, B looks one-half the size of A. If a wide-angle lens is used, a great deal is taken in, and A may not appear particularly large in the overall view, but B is half A's size. If a telephoto lens is used instead, the angle of view is narrower, so a much smaller view is taken in and A looks larger, but B remains half A's size because their relative distances from the lens have not changed. The same is true for all other lenses. If a matching area is taken from the center of all the pictures and enlarged so that A is the same size in each sample, B will be correspondingly the same size—half that of A. Thus: *from any given camera position all lenses produce the same perspective.* This does not appear true in looking at photographs because viewing distance tends to remain constant.

Seeing true perspective. For the eye to see true perspective in a photograph, it must view a contact print from a negative or a transparency from a distance equal to the focal length of the lens used to take the picture. If a two-inch (50mm) lens is used to make a picture on 35mm film, a contact image or slide must be viewed from two inches for the perspective to appear normal; if a six-inch (150mm) lens is used, the contact print must be viewed from six inches. If the image is enlarged, the viewing distance must be multiplied by the enlargement factor. The image from the two-inch lens, if enlarged 10 times, must be viewed from $2'' \times 10 = 20''$ for the perspective to appear normal, and the image from the six-inch lens in a similar enlargement from $6'' \times 10 = 60''$. But viewing distance seldom varies according to focal length and enlargement. Normal viewing or "reading" distance for prints that can be held in the hand is about 12 inches. The two-inch lens image on 35mm film enlarged six times (to about $6'' \times 9''$) would look normal at this distance. But a similar enlargement from the six-inch lens image would be seen from too close a distance; and an enlargement of an image from a one-inch (25mm) lens would be seen from too far a distance. As a result the perspective in these other prints would appear distorted. Too great a viewing distance exaggerates the depth or perspective effect of the image (so-called wide-angle lens depth distortion); too small a viewing distance diminishes the depth effect (telephoto lens depth "compression").

Peterhans, Walter. "Still Life" (ca. 1928–32). Courtesy Sander Gallery, Silver Spring, MD; collection, Museum of Modern Art, New York.

The fact that viewing distance tends to remain constant and that therefore the apparent perspective will vary, leads to using various focal-length lenses for expressive rather than literal visual effect. *See also:* DISTORTION; MAGNIFICATION. Color photographs: pp. C-41, C-42.

Perutz, Otto

German; 1847–1922

A chemist, Perutz began photographic manufacturing with a line of gelatin dry plates in Munich in 1880. Four years later he was one of the first to produce orthochromatic plates sensitized to green light with eosin, discovered by H. W. Vogel, using an emulsion formulated by J. B. Obernetter. The Perchromo plate, introduced in 1904, was an early—and imperfect—attempt to produce a panchromatic plate on a commercial basis.

The Perutz firm was one of the first in Europe to introduce systematic testing as a means of quality control in photographic manufacturing and to create a research laboratory to develop new materials. In the first half of the 20th c. Perutz products grew to cover a wide spectrum of black-and-white and color films and plates for general use and for scientific, medical, x-ray, aerial, and other specialized kinds of photography. *See also:* DRY PLATES; DYE SENSITIZATION.

Peterhans, Walter

American; 1897–1960

Walter Peterhans was an influential proponent of the New Objectivity (Neue Sachlichkeit) and a teacher of photography and the visual arts in Weimar Germany and the United States. His highly original vision was responsible for extraordinary still-life juxtapositions in a surrealist vein, emphasizing abstract textures. Mies van der Rohe has written: "In 1930, when I took over the German Bauhaus in Dessau, Walter Peterhans was head of the Department of Photography. There I became acquainted with his painstaking work with the students and the great discipline he taught and demanded of them. Not only was he a photographer second to none, but a strong personality with a broad education in many fields. . . ."

Peterhans, the son of the director of Zeiss-Ikon Company, Dresden, was born in Frankfurt am Main, Germany, and photographed from an early age. He attended school in Dresden until 1916 and served in the German Army from 1916 to 1919. He continued his studies at the Munich Technical School in 1920–1921, at the University of Gottingen (where he studied mathematics, philosophy, and art history) from 1921 to 1923, and at Leipzig's State Academy of Printing and Graphic Art (where he studied photographic reproduction techniques) in 1925–1926. He received a master's degree in photography at Weimar in 1926.

Peterhans worked as a freelance industrial and portrait photographer and teacher of photography in his own studio in Berlin from 1927 to 1929. He established and was head of the Department of Photography at the Dessau Bauhaus and at Mies van der Rohe's Bauhaus Institute in Berlin from 1929 to 1933. In 1934–1935 he was an instructor of photography at the Reimann-Haring School, Berlin, and he worked again as a freelance industrial photographer in Berlin from 1935 to 1938, when he abandoned photography.

Peterhans emigrated to the United States the same year. He taught classes in visual awareness and art history as a professor in the Department of Architecture at the Illinois Institute of Technology, Chicago until his death in 1960. In addition to his permanent position, Peterhans was a guest lecturer and teacher in the United States and West Germany on several occasions and was research associate in philosophy and instructor of photography at the University of Chicago from 1945 to 1957. He died in Stetten, Baden-Wurttemburg, in 1960, while a guest professor at the Academy of Fine Arts, Hamburg.

Peterhans's photographs have been exhibited in group shows including *Film und Foto* in Stuttgart in 1929; *Modern European Photography* at Julien Levy

Gallery, New York, in 1932; *Neue Sachlichkeit and German Realism of the Twenties* at the Hayward Gallery, London, in 1978; *Avant-Garde Photography in Germany 1919–1939* at the San Francisco Museum of Modern Art and ICP, New York, in 1980; and *Germany: The New Vision* at the Fraenkel Gallery, San Francisco, in 1981. He was honored by a retrospective at Sander Gallery, Washington, D.C., in 1978.
See also: BAUHAUS; NEUE SACHLICHKEIT; NEW BAUHAUS.

Petzval, Josef Max

Hungarian; 1807–1891

A mathematician whose adult career was in Vienna, in 1840 Petzval designed the first lens specifically intended for photographic use, and indeed the first lens with element spacings and surface curvatures mathematically calculated before grinding operations were begun. He was assisted in the complex and tedious calculations—only pencil-and-paper methods were available—by a team of mathematically trained members of an artillery section of the Austro-Hungarian army.

The Petzval lens of 1840 was additionally a landmark because it could be used at full aperture, $f/3.6$, which was some 16 times (4 f-stops) faster than the $f/14$ (later $f/12$) Chevalier lens supplied with Giroux daguerreotype cameras. This increase alone made portraiture possible; when coupled with the Goddard method of increasing the speed of daguerreotype plates, it made portraiture commercially practical. The lens was far superior to the Wolcott mirror camera used for the earliest portraits, because it was at least 2 stops faster, but more importantly because it could cover a full $6\frac{1}{2}'' \times 8\frac{1}{2}''$ daguerreotype plate, while the Wolcott camera was limited to about a $2'' \times 2''$ plate. The Petzval portrait lens was well corrected for all aberrations except astigmatism and curvature of field; however, only the center of the field was used, so these effects were minimized. In any event, the fall-off in definition in outer areas of the field was not particularly disturbing in a portrait, where all attention is on the face, and even created a pleasing softness of the hair, costume, and background.

The lens was manufactured by the firm of Voigtlander beginning late in 1840; by 1862, 10,000 such lenses had been produced by Voigtlander alone, and the design had been copied by every lens maker in the world under descriptions such as "Petzval Type," "Vienna Portrait," and "German (Austrian) System." The original design had a 6 inch (15cm) focal length, which is shorter than what is considered normal for a full-plate format (diagonal = $10\frac{5}{8}$ in.), but as only the center of the field was used, the camera could be placed far enough away to prevent noticeable distortion of the subject's features. The original lens was featured in a unique, tubular "spyglasslike" camera produced by Voigtlander in 1841, and was subsequently produced in other focal lengths for use with standard cameras. Most portrait lenses of the 19th and early 20th c. followed its innovative symmetrical design, because it provided speed along with a pleasing softening of field. Today the speed it produces with simplicity of design is utilized in medium- and small-format motion-picture and slide-projection lenses, where it is practical to use only the relatively well-corrected center portion of the field.

Petzval's later career produced other lens designs (none as notable as his first) and significant contributions to methods of mathematical lens calculation—particularly the Petzval sum, which is a method of predicting the degree and power or direction (concave/convex) of curvature of field from the number of elements in a lens and their cumulative index of refraction.
See also: ABERRATIONS OF LENSES; MIRROR CAMERA; LENSES; OPTICS.

pH

The acidity or alkalinity of a water-based solution is rated on a scale of pH values from 0 (most strongly acid) to 14 (most strongly alkaline); the neutral point is 7.0, the pH value of pure water. Relative acidity is proportional to the concentration of hydrogen ions in a solution; the pH numbers are negative logarithms of this concentration. Being logarithms, each change of 1 in pH value represents a change of 10× in solution strength; e.g., a solution of pH 7.5 is 10 times more alkaline than one of pH 6.5.

Developers are alkaline solutions and must have pH values above 7.0 to be active; acid solutions such as stop baths and fixers have pH values below 7.0. Compounds called buffers are incorporated in some formulas to maintain the pH value of a solution very close to a particular level as the solution is used.

Phantom View

In a phantom, ghost, or "x-ray" view, the interior structure or components of an object can be seen through its outer covering, as if the exterior were partially transparent. The effect is produced on transparency film by a simple double exposure with and without the object cover in place. Both the camera and the object must be locked in place, and the total exposure must be divided between the two views. In most cases the interior (uncovered) view requires more than half the total exposure so that details can be clearly seen. It is common to make tests with instant print film to establish correct exposure balance. To avoid confusing shadows, the interior view may be illuminated by a "painting with light" technique.

A phantom view may also be produced by photographing the two views separately on negative film. They are then sandwiched to make a print in a single exposure, or used separately to make a combination (double-exposure) print. The second technique allows the greatest control of the visual balance between the two views.
See also: EXPLODED VIEWS; PAINTING WITH LIGHT.

Phenakistiscope

The phenakistiscope is an animation viewing device invented in 1831 by the British physician Peter Mark Roget (later compiler of the original *Thesaurus of English Words and Phrases*). In one version two disks mounted on a horizontal shaft were held in front of the eye. The nearest disk had a series of slits around the circumference that permitted intermittent glimpses of a matching series of movement-sequence drawings on the second disk when the two were rotated; at sufficient speed the drawings seemed to blend into continuous movement. In a simpler version the drawings were on the back side of the slotted disk and were seen by looking through the slits at the images reflected in a mirror. The basic principle of the phenakistiscope was most successfully used by Eadweard Muybridge in his zoopraxiscope projector.
See also: ANIMATION; ZOOPRAXISCOPE.

Phenidone

See: ILFORD; P-Q DEVELOPER.

Phosphorescence

When excited by energy of invisible wavelengths, some materials respond by radiating a visible glow called phosphorescence. Materials that exhibit phosphorescence continue to glow after the exciting energy has been removed. The period of after-glow grows shorter as the temperature of the phosphorescing material rises; in addition, phosphorescence can be quenched by external in-

frared radiation. Materials that cease to glow as soon as the exciting energy is removed are said to exhibit fluorescence.
See also: INFRARED PHOTOGRAPHY; ULTRAVIOLET AND FLUORESCENCE PHOTOGRAPHY.

Photochemical Reaction

A chemical change caused by the action of radiant energy, especially light, is a photochemical reaction.
See: CHEMISTRY OF PHOTOGRAPHY; LATENT IMAGE.

Photo-Drawing

See: BLEACH-OUT PROCESS.

Photoengraving

Originally the term photoengraving specifically referred to various processes in which an engraving needle was moved over the surface of an appropriate plate, incising a pattern of ink-retaining lines in direct reproduction of a photographic master image. Such processes now use laser, electron, or ion beams guided by computer programs that may or may not be derived from photographic master images. In any case, they are not called photoengraving, and they are used primarily in the production of things such as electronic microchips, rather than in the reproduction of visual images.

Today, "photoengraving" refers to any of the procedures in photomechanical reproduction by which a chemically etched printing plate is prepared. Its most accurate reference is to the preparation of photogravure plates, in which an intaglio image is produced, but it also applies to the production of letterpress (relief) and lithographic (planographic) plates. All three processes depend upon exposing a resist-coated plate (or a separate resist tissue that later is adhered to a plate) to a master paste-up or film transparency of the type and illustrations to be reproduced. (Continuous-tone illustrations must be copied through a halftone screen at some stage before final plate exposure.) The resist then is treated to remove the non-image portions so that chemical treatment can affect the plate directly in the image areas. After the resist is removed, the plate can be inked for printing.
See also: CONTINUOUS-TONE IMAGE; HALFTONE PROCESSES; PHOTOMECHANICAL REPRODUCTION; PHOTORESIST.

Photofabrication

Photofabrication is a photographically controlled method of creating a relief metal image on the surface of plastic, glass, or another metal. Its uses include the manufacture of printed circuits and computer chips. The photoresist is the key to photofabrication. A photoresist is an organic resin used to form a stencil pattern that controls formation of the photofabricated object.

Whether the surface is ultimately to be etched, plated, or electroformed, it is prepared in basically the same way. The pattern that is to constitute the finished product is drawn or pieced together from cutout elements on a scale up to several hundred times its final size. Extreme care is taken to ensure that the dimensions of the pattern are exactly according to specification. The completed artwork then is photographically reduced to actual size, often in two or more steps if the reduction is to microscale. The result is a high-contrast line-copy transparency.

The transparency next is sandwiched together with a photoresist-coated material. The sandwich is exposed to highly actinic light for a relatively lengthy exposure. With a negative photoresist the exposed areas harden, while the unexposed areas remain soluble. The opposite is true of a positive resist. In some cases metal material has a resist on both sides and is simultaneously exposed through exactly matching transparencies placed in contact with the top and bottom surfaces. After exposure the resist-coated surfaces are treated with an appropriate solvent to remove the unhardened areas of the resist. The result is that the underlying material is selectively uncovered for further treatment according to the pattern of the original artwork.

The prepared material now may be fabricated in a number of ways, including chemical milling, etching, plating, and electroforming. In chemical milling a double-coated plate is immersed in an acid or other corrosive solution that dissolves away the exposed metal from both sides, leaving an object composed of metal ribs in a partial or full lacework form. Etching is a similar process with a material having a surface layer of metal (beneath the resist). Exposed areas are eaten away, leaving a pattern such as a so-called printed circuit. After treatment the hardened resist is removed from these objects.

In electroplating a thin layer of metal may be deposited on the relief pattern of the resist, which remains as a support; it may be deposited within the spaces of the relief pattern, which is subsequently removed; or the relief may be removed after an etching or other treatment so that metal may be deposited on the previously protected areas. Similarly, in electroforming metal may be shaped over the resist relief, or into an intaglio pattern that is etched in the substrate material before the resist pattern is removed.

The most recent advances in photofabrication use direct exposure or etching by laser or electron beams guided by a computer program that is derived from a photographic master image or pattern. The precision of such methods has never previously been approached; it makes possible microelectronic chips in which literally thousands of components and circuit connections are contained on a surface less than ¼ in. (6.4mm) square.
See also: PHOTORESIST.

Photofinish Photography

In close finishes between racing horses, runners, automobiles, or other competitors, an objective record such as a photograph is needed to judge the winner accurately; the record is also useful in settling immediate or subsequent disputes. Various timing devices such as a photoelectric beam can trip a shutter to take a picture at the exact instant the winner reaches the finish line, but the second- and third-place finishers may or may not be within the camera view at that time; even if they are in view, their places may change by the time they reach the finish. The problem of obtaining accurately comprehensive race-finish photographs is solved by a kind of slit or streak camera called a photofinish camera. Its view of the track is restricted to just a narrow strip exactly at the finish line; this is accomplished by a fixed slit-shutter behind the lens. The slit is about 0.01 in. (0.25mm) wide, and the film in the camera moves past the slit so that there is new emulsion to record each new detail as the racers cross the finish line. The camera begins operating when the leader reaches a particular point on the straightaway leading to the finish and continues operating until all competitors who are to be placed have crossed the line. Because the image size is a reduction, the film movement can be proportionately reduced from the actual racing speed. It is impossible to get an exact match every time, so some records show elongated figures because the film is moved a bit faster to insure that all details will be adequately separated—a film travel of one to two in. per second is adequate for animal and foot races. The film is unperforated 35mm black-and-white film. It shows the image from the camera viewpoint and a parallel image from a mirror 180° opposite the camera position on the other side of the finish line. This insures that a finisher partly blocked from one view can be seen from the other. The film also records date and timing data, and a series of alignment marks along both edges. Because every point in the picture represents the view exactly at the finish line at a different moment, placing a straightedge across the picture between any two matching marks shows the situation at the finish line at that instant. This makes it possible to judge close finishes for second, third, or other places as well as to determine the first-place finisher.

Cameras using conventional film have associated rapid-processing setups that can produce a negative in less than 5 seconds, and a print in another 10 seconds. Some cameras use instant-print film in a moving holder. Most racetracks now also have parallel video recording equipment to get instant replay of the finish for judging. The replay can be in slow motion, frame by frame, if required. This makes rapid processing of the film unnecessary, but the film record is completed because it is far more permanent than the signals on a magnetic tape.

See also: MOTION STUDY AND ANALYSIS; RAPID PROCESSING; STREAK CAMERA.

Photoflood Bulb

A photoflood is a high-efficiency tungsten light bulb that produces as much light as an ordinary bulb of three times greater wattage. However, this output is obtained at the expense of working life:

Photoflood	Wattage	Average Life
No. 1	250	4 hrs.
No. 2	500	8 hrs.
No. 4	1000	10 hrs.

White frosted photoflood bulbs produce light with a color temperature of 3400K; light from blue-frosted bulbs has a color temperature of 4800K.

See also: COLOR TEMPERATURE.

Photogalvanography

One of the earliest methods of obtaining a printing plate from a photograph was photogalvanography. Invented by Paul Pretsch in 1854 and commercially introduced in England, the method produced results superior to W. H. F. Talbot's *photoglyphy*, patented two years earlier. In photogalvanography, a bichromated gelatin coating on a glass plate was exposed under a positive transparency.

When soaked in cold water, the bichromate salts dissolved out, and the unexposed shadow and middletone areas swelled in slight relief; the exposed portions did not. The swollen areas were made to reticulate during drying, producing a pattern of fine lines—as in a collotype—that served as the halftone element required for ink reproduction. A mold taken in a plastic material (gutta-percha) from the gelatin relief image was used to prepare a copper printing plate by electrotyping procedures; this was filled from behind with type metal to strengthen it for printing. It took about six weeks to produce a plate, which usually needed some hand correction to improve details, but several plates could be made at once and each plate gave far more copies than other methods. By the standards of the time, the inked reproductions were of excellent quality.

See also: COLLOTYPE; PHOTOGLYPHY; PRETSCH, PAUL.

Photogenic Drawing

Photogenic drawing was W. H. F. Talbot's original process, by which he at first obtained photograms and contact-print copies of objects and drawings, using paper sensitized with salt and silver nitrate solutions. By 1835 he was also able to use this paper to record images in the camera obscura. *Photogenic drawing* specifies the process that relied on a printing-out exposure for both camera negatives and for prints. Talbot's improved process, which developed the negative image (but still printed-out the positive), was called the *calotype*.

See also: CALOTYPE; SALT-PAPER PROCESS; TALBOT, W. H. F.

Photoglyphy

Photoglyphy was a steel-plate photoengraving process (Greek: *gluphe* = carving, engraving) first patented in 1852 by W. H. F. Talbot, and in improved form in 1858. In both versions a bichromated gelatin coating on the plate was exposed under a positive transparency and then washed to dissolve away the gelatin in the shadow areas and parts of the middletones. Gelatin hardened by exposure remained on the plate and acted as a resist that controlled the area and depth of the etching produced at first by a solution of platinum chloride, later by a solution of ferric chloride, which was more efficient.

To obtain the halftone dot pattern necessary for ink reproduction, Talbot first used a piece of black mesh cloth as a screen between the transparency and the gelatin coating during exposure. The results were only partially successful because the dots formed in dark areas were too weak to hold the ink properly. In the 1858 process, exposure was made without a screen. After the gelatin was "developed," the surface was dusted with aquatint resin and the plate heated to fuse the resin particles in place. This procedure resulted in a random dot pattern of the required strength. After etching, the surface was cleaned and inked for printing. A copper plate could also be used when only short printing runs were planned. A later process, the Woodbury-type, was called *photoglyptie* in France, where it was introduced in 1867. Its method was entirely different from photoglyphy, in spite of the similarity of names.

See also: AQUATINT; BICHROMATE PROCESSES; PHOTOGALVANOGRAPHY; TALBOT, W. H. F.; WOODBURYGRAVURE/ WOODBURYTYPE.

Photogram

A photogram is cameraless image created by placing two- or three-dimensional objects on photographic film or paper and exposing the arrangement to light. The developed image shows no exposure effect where opaque objects touched the emulsion; tones where translucent objects were placed and where partial shadowing occurred under solid objects not completely touching the surface; and maximum exposure in areas that were completely uncovered. The early inventors of photography all began experimenting by placing objects on sensitized material—the first, in about 1799, were apparently Thomas Wedgwood and Humphry Davy.

The use of the photogram technique to create abstract images began about 1918 with Christian Schad, and soon thereafter with Man Ray and László Moholy-Nagy. The current use of the term *photogram* to mean primarily that kind of image began at that time, although it sometimes also refers to cartoonlike and other trivial arrangements. In the mid-19th c. there were some advocates of the use of *photogram* as the noun naming the finished product, as against *to photograph* as the verb for the activity by which it was made. The usage did not take hold, but one annual publication of all kinds of photographs retained the title *Photograms of the Year* well into the 20th c.

See also: MOHOLY-NAGY, LASZLO; RAY, MAN; SCHADOGRAPH; WEDGWOOD, THOMAS.

Color photograph: p. C-43.

Photogrammetry

Photogrammetry is the branch of photography concerned with making measurements from pictures. Historically photogrammetry has been a function of aerial photography and still is used primarily for surveying and map making. Recent technological advances have resulted in applications which include underwater mapping and medical research.

In theory aerial photogrammetry is quite straightforward. An aircraft flies a straight course at an exact altitude over the area to be measured. At predetermined intervals based on altitude, ground speed, and lens focal length, vertical (i.e., straight down) pictures are made. This produces a neat, easily interpreted aerial survey. For map making a scale of distance is determined simply by dividing the altitude by the lens focal length. Therefore, at 1000 ft. (305m) with a 12 in. lens (300mm), the scale would be 1:1000. Thus, two buildings appearing 5¼ in. (13.5cm) apart on the negative would actually be situated 5250 ft. (1.5km), or almost exactly 1 mile, apart. Moreover, by timing the interval between frames so that an overlapping mosaic is created, stereographic images may be produced. These allow the photogrammetrist to measure the height of objects on the ground.

From a practical standpoint the situation is significantly more complex. To begin with, the theory assumes absolutely accurate navigation, which is not ordinarily the case. Altimeters are meant to be piloting aids, not precise scientific tools, and therefore scale, which is based on altitude, usually must be determined with the assistance of a ground surveying team. Also, even experienced pilots must contend with thermal drafts and side winds, both of which produce some deviation from what should be an arrow-straight line. Additional complications are caused by the surface contours of the earth. Radar and laser-beam systems are used to control the flight and minimize the effects of these variables, and to record fiducial data on the film to aid in correcting the measurements made during interpretation. Stereoplotting and various projection devices also help in interpretation.

Typically, a rigid body, fixed-focus aerial camera with a 6 in. (150mm) or longer focal-length lens is employed to produce square-format images on film 9 in. (225mm) or 5 in. (125mm) wide. Long rolls of film are used to eliminate the necessity of reloading in the air. Both conventional and infrared-sensitive black-and-white and color films are used according to the kind of data sought. The most modern equipment uses direct laser- or electron-beam exposure of film guided by data derived from laser scanning of the area surveyed or of the camera image of the area. Film exposure may be accomplished by on-board equipment, or the scanning data may be electronically relayed to ground-station equipment. This latter method is used for photogrammetry with images obtained by orbiting satellites.

See also: AERIAL PHOTOGRAPHY; PHOTOINTERPRETATION; SURVEILLANCE PHOTOGRAPHY.

Photogravure

The most faithful method for the photomechanical reproduction of photographs, photogravure originated in W. H. F. Talbot's *photoglyphy* of 1858, and the modern procedure in the 1879 and 1895 processes of Karel Klič. A bichromate-sensitized gelatin stripping emulsion or carbon tissue is exposed to a screened positive image and transferred to a copper printing plate. It is washed with warm water to dissolve away unhardened portions, leaving the various densities hardened by exposure to act as a resist in the middletone and highlight areas. When etched in ferric chloride solutions of various strengths, pits—corresponding to the "holes" in the gravure screen—are created with depths in inverse proportion to the amount of resist in each area. When the resist is cleaned off and the plate is inked, these pits hold various densities of ink according to their depths. Thus the printed reproduction has deep blacks and various gray tones because the densities of ink deposited on the paper vary and modulate the light in much the same way as do the densities of the original image. Other methods of reproduction deposit a single of density of ink in dots of various sizes; the tonal differences are an optical illusion dependent upon how much paper shows through the ink dots in each area.

Hand-pulled photogravure reproductions—rather than automatic press copies—were favored by photographers such as P. H. Emerson, A. L. Coburn, Alfred Steiglitz (they were used in *Camera Work* and other periodicals he edited), and Paul Strand (for his *Mexican Portfolio*), because they so faithfully imitated the appearance of photographs printed on matte surface papers. In the hand-pulled process, a screen often is not used; instead, the plate is given an aquatint grain before the resist—exposed to an unscreened positive—is transferred. This produces a random pattern in the ink-retaining pits, in contrast to the regular pattern of a gravure screen.

Photogravure plates are used for both black-and-white and color reproductions. For press runs of any size, the copper plate is electroplated with steel to give it durability.

See also: HALFTONE PROCESSES; KLIČ, KAREL; PHOTOGLYPHY; PHOTOMECHANICAL REPRODUCTION.

Photointerpretation

Photointerpretation is the specialized reading of aerial photographs, particularly those taken from a vertical angle. It is an essential skill because objects photographed from directly above are often unrecognizable to the untrained eye. Often considerable information can be gleaned simply from the size and shape of the shadow cast by an object. The greatest degree of recognizability is obtained when the image is oriented with shadows pointing toward the bottom of the frame; then objects seem to rise in relief above the ground surface. If the picture is turned so that shadows project toward the top, a visual illusion often occurs that makes the objects appear to be holes in the ground.

When possible, pairs of overlapping aerial photographs are combined in a stereoplotter to produce a three-dimensional image, even from vertical pictures. Objects completely unidentifiable in two dimensions frequently become readily apparent in three. The photointerpreter must be thoroughly conversant with the problems of determining scale in an aerial image, which is a fundamental of photogrammetry. In some military applications in which speed is essential, the interpreter may be required to work from the negative. Photointerpretation also is used in conjunction with scientific fields such as geology, archaeology, and geography.

See also: AERIAL PHOTOGRAPHY; PHOTOGRAMMETRY.

Photojournalism

Photojournalism is a broad category that includes news, war, feature, and documentary photography. Today television and satellite communication has taken over the major function of journalistic still photographs in the first half of the 20th c.—that of immediate reportage. Nevertheless, still photographs are used more extensively than ever before in newspapers and magazines because they add information and give a story dramatic psychological impact. The most haunting images of war and disaster are those produced by still photog-

raphers. They have long-term effect because the viewer, not the medium, determines how much time is spent with an image, and because periodicals and books have long lives and repeated readership. More so than ever before photojournalism deals with the effects and significance of events, while the electronic media report the bare facts of the events.

Historical development. Modern photojournalism began to emerge as a distinctive mode of communication in the 1920s, but its origins lie in the mid-19th c. The Crimean War photographs (1855) of Roger Fenton, and those of the U.S. Civil War (1861–1865) by Mathew Brady's photographers, are generally considered the first major reportage-documentary use of the medium. The Civil War pictures in particular have journalistic significance because they were widely reproduced (by hand-engraving methods) in periodicals of the time. But these were primarily single pictures of individuals and of things before or after the event ostensibly being reported. This was largely because technical limitations (cumbersome equipment, exposures of 1/30 sec. or longer, the need for on-the-spot proc-

essing) did not permit direct coverage. More fundamentally, these pictures (and almost all such pictures for several decades) were used to follow a text, that is, to illustrate what was written. The essence of photojournalism, on the other hand, is that the photographs establish the story—the text follows the line of development established by the pictures, not the reverse. The "illustrative" reservations also holds for early social documentary work often cited as the foundation of photojournalism, such as John Thompson's photographs for the book *Street Life in London* (1877) and Jacob Riis's pictures taken to support his newspaper reports and books (ca. 1880–1910). The first example of a journalistic picture story is probably a famous interview conducted in 1886 by the retired photographer Nadar with Michel Chevreul, a French scientist, at his 100th birthday. The pictures, taken by Nadar's son Paul, appeared as a series and were keyed to Chevreul's replies to the questions, as transcribed by a stenographer. Again, however, the pictures served to illustrate rather than to lead the development of the story. Nevertheless, these early efforts and many that followed laid the foundation for the truly visual mode

of reporting that appeared after World War I.

The evolution was slow for technical as well as cultural reasons. Photojournalism almost by definition is intended for mass-audience publications, primarily magazines and newspapers. The first direct reproduction of a photograph in a newspaper using a mechanical halftone process—without hand-copying or engraving—was in 1880, when the New York *Daily Graphic* published a picture of shanties erected by the destitute on the fringes of Central Park. In the long run, it is the process, rather than the content of this picture, that is significant in the development of photojournalism. From the 1850s onward, illustrated periodicals became common, some with circulations of 100,000, throughout the world, but all relied on hand-work processes for their illustrations. Improvements in halftone processes in the 1880s and 1890s expanded the use of photographs and began to bring a new veracity to periodical illustrations. The first all-photographic illustrated magazine, the *Illustrated American*, was introduced in 1890 (it could not obtain sufficient material to maintain its character). By about 1915 most major newspapers regularly used line- or dot-halftones in their pages and issued a pictorial supplement each week of photographs reproduced by the higher quality rotogravure (rotary press gravure) process in brown ink—a pictorial convention, not a technical necessity. The news pictures tended to be arranged or posed; "artistic" studies such as landscapes were a staple; and most often the pictures with the most spontaneity were snapshots submitted by amateurs and chosen for human interest or novelty of subject matter. Even during World War I the journalistic content of pictures in these sections was slight, largely because of extreme censorship conditions in the field on both sides. Pictures came primarily from military sources, civilian photographers were seldom allowed near the actual fighting or the scenes of defeat, and censorship on the home fronts was doubly cautious. In addition, professional quality equipment and materials were relatively slow, amateur cameras capable of "instantaneous" (about 1/40 sec.) exposures notwithstanding. The two miniature hand cameras that revolutionized journalistic photography did not appear until the mid-1920's. They were the Ermanox, with an astonishingly fast $f/2$ (later $f/1.8$) lens and a $4\frac{1}{2} \times 6$cm (approx. $1\frac{3}{4}'' \times 2\frac{1}{4}''$) image; and the Leica, which took 36 exposures on a single load of 35mm film. Used with films developed during the next decade, they made hand-held available light photography a practicality, and became an extension of the photographer's eye, permitting an immediacy of response and an unobtrusive manner of working that brought a new sense of spontaneity and intimacy to journalistic photographs.

In the 1920s, Germany had more illustrated periodicals, with greater circulation, than any other country. This, and the fact that many of the editors were aggressively imaginative in their ideas for stories, attracted photographers who were anxious to try the new and the difficult in reportage, and who were encouraged to do so. Erich Salomon, pioneer of unobtrusive and secret coverage of court trials and of conferences at the League of Nations, was the first modern photojournalist. Others included Willi Ruge, Walter Bosshard, Umbo (Otto Umbehr), Martin Munkacsi, Wolfgang Weber, Tim and Georg Gidal, Felix Man, Kurt Hübschmann (K. Hutton), Alfred Eisenstaedt, André Kertész, and the editor Stefan Lorant. Though photographers followed their lead, illustrated periodicals in Paris, London, New York, and other cities trailed well behind the editorial

innovations of *Berliner Illustrirte, Münchner Illustrierte Presse, Arbeiter Illustrierte Zeitung* (AIZ—Worker's Illustrated Newspaper), and at least a dozen more German publications.

The German lead ended abruptly in 1933 when Adolf Hitler and the Nazi party seized control. Within a year or two most of the innovative editors and photographers were in France with *Vu*, in England with the *Weekly Illustrated* or the soon-to-be-created *Picture Post*. They were in Switzerland, Holland, and the U.S. as well, where their work inspired and aided a new group of like-minded photographers: Henri Cartier-Bresson, Werner Bischof, Robert Capa, Margaret Bourke-White, Peter Stackpole, and many more. The availability of photographers like Eisenstaedt in the U.S. directly influenced Henry Luce to launch *Life* magazine in 1936, and Gardner Cowles to introduce *Look* the following year. These publications rapidly became the most sophisticated and renowned newsmagazines in the history of photojournalism, and they were the training ground for the next generation: W. Eugene Smith, David Douglas Duncan, Gjon Mili, Lisa Larsen, George Silk, Philippe Halsman, Eliot Elisofon, Ernst Haas, John Dominis, Carl Mydans—to name less than one-tenth of those whose work has defined the nature of modern photojournalism.

Photojournalistic practice. Photojournalism evolved after World War I as some news photographers came to feel that their job was to be the reporter, the primary storyteller, rather than an illustrative assistant to a writer. From that time, the best photojournalists have realized that their task is more than a simple, uninvolved recording of people and events. The essence of photojournalism is that there is a story to be told factually, visually, and compellingly. That requires a varied collection of skills; it also requires energy, intuition, and keen judgement. The story may be told in a single picture taken at the "decisive moment" that characterizes an entire scene. Or, it may require a series of pictures to cover the variety and complexity of the subject fairly and effectively. In either case, consistent journalistic success is seldom a matter of luck, it is the result of hard work and careful preparation. Undeniably, some pictures are the result of being in the right place at the right time. But the photojournalist who has researched the subject and who has considered the potential stories to be found and the kind of pictures that will tell them, is the one most likely to correctly anticipate where the right place will be, and when the right time will be.

Ideas for photojournalistic assignments sometimes originate with the photographer. More often they come from an editor who outlines and develops the idea with the photographer. It is unusual for specific pictures to be called for. Instead, when possible the editorial approach and the major statement of the story are established, along with the potential length and the amount of accompanying text. These factors are subject to change, especially with current events (as compared with feature stories), for it is not always possible to anticipate what things will be like or how they will develop. The photographer's task is to adapt to the realities of the situation and get a story that is appropriate to the intent of the assignment.

All photojournalistic stories involve both pictures and text. It is very useful for the photographer to know ahead of time what the balance is likely to be. Some stories are primarily told in pictures, with the text limited to captions. In others the pictures serve to illustrate an extended text. In still other stories the text and pictures are essentially self-sufficient essays that reinforce but do not necessarily depend on one another. In some cases the photojournalist is also the reporter. In other cases he or she is teamed with a writer. Each of these situations will affect what the photographer notices and decides is important and the number and kind of pictures he or she takes.

Each image of a sequence or picture story must be made with regard to the neighboring pictures, although the final sizes and juxtapositions are usually determined by an editor. The sequence is analogous to a motion-picture short subject. One generally brief event is portrayed. The picture sequence usually develops chronologically with an identifiable beginning, middle, and end. A picture story is longer, composed of several sequences. Like a major segment of a motion picture, there may be an establishing shot that provides a reference point or context for other, more detailed pictures.

Depending on the nature of the story and the photographer's working methods, the coverage may be shot as things are found, or it may be directed and constructed. The found story is most likely to be a news event. It emphasizes the photographer's ability as hunter, able to anticipate the subject's development and sense the critical instants of which to release the shutter. The directed approach is more appropriate to feature stories, where arranging things for greater interest and visual effect will not affect the truth or accuracy of the report. With either approach a real event is being recorded, and the pictures should not violate the standards of objectivity that imposes.

The equipment and films of the photojournalist are those most appropriate to the assignment. More often than not, coverage is recorded with 35mm cameras supported by an electronic flash unit and a variety of lenses and accessories. The demands of travel and shooting on location make photojournalists concentrate on versatile equipment and multi-purpose accessories so as to keep the equipment kit to a minimum. Getting along with standard cameras and lenses is preferable to struggling with the precise but limited functions of specialized equipment, and it is far better to give over space to extra film rather than an extra lens if a choice must be made. *See also:* DOCUMENTARY PHOTOGRAPHY; NEWS PHOTOGRAPHY; PRESS PHOTOGRAPHY.

Color photograph: p. C-44.

Photo League
See: FILM AND PHOTO LEAGUE.

Photolithography
The original method of lithography was based on a hand-drawn image made directly on a printing stone or transferred from a sheet of drawing paper. The modern method, photolithography, uses a photographic method to copy an image of any sort onto a grained aluminum or zinc plate for commercial, high-volume reproduction, or onto a plastic-coated paper "plate" for short runs. The basic lithographic principle of the repulsion of oil and water is still used.

The plate has a coating of a light-sensitive colloid (bichromated gelatin). It is exposed to a film negative of the material to be reproduced, or with a positive-working coating, to the material itself; in either case continuous-tone visual images must first be converted to screened (halftone) form. Exposure hardens the coating; unexposed areas dissolve away when the plate is treated with a solvent (often water). For printing the plate is dampened and then inked. The hardened colloid areas, which make up the composite image, do not absorb the water but do retain the ink; the exposed non-image metal or plastic areas of the plate are moist on the surface and repel the ink. The image is printed by direct contact of the plate with the paper or more commonly by the offset process.

Almost all commercial printing is now accomplished by offset lithography. *See also:* HALFTONE PROCESSES; LITHOGRAPHY; OFFSET PRINTING.

Photomacrography
See: MACROPHOTOGRAPHY.

Photomechanical Reproduction
The various methods by which text and illustrations are reproduced in ink from photographically prepared printing plates are embraced by the general term photomechanical reproduction. There are three major kinds of such reproduction: (1) relief or letterpress, in which the ink-bearing areas of the plate rise above the surrounding areas (this was the first method of printing invented); (2) intaglio or gravure, in which the ink bearing areas are cut below the surface of the plate; and (3) planography or lithography, in which the inked and uninked areas are on the same level. Serigraphy or fabric screen stencil printing sometimes is also included as a method of photomechanical reproduction.

A plate is prepared from a high-contrast black-and-white photographic negative or positive transparency of the material to be reproduced. Continuous-tone illustrations must be in the form of screened halftone images on the film. In some cases both the text (type) and the illustrations are photographed through a screen. Better quality is achieved by photographing type and single-tone illustrations as line images, without a screen. This film is then stripped up (assembled) with screened film images of multiple-tone illustrations to form the composite master film to which the plate is exposed. When multicolored text or illustrations are to be printed, separate films are required to make individual plates for each of the colors to be printed. Full-color reproduction commonly uses four inks: the subtractive colors cyan (process blue), magenta (process red), yellow, plus black. After exposure to the master film, a plate is processed to produce the appropriate ink-retaining characteristics in all image areas.

A plate or stencil prepared by any of the various photomechanical methods may be printed by direct contact with the paper or other receiving surface. However, most modern printing is accomplished by offsetting the inked image onto a rubber-surface roller which in turn transfers the ink to the paper. This provides the fastest, cleanest reproduction and the longest plate life.

The newest methods of reproduction include jet printing, in which ink is sprayed in letter and image patterns onto the paper through microscopic holes in a master plate, and beam printing, in which a laser or electron beam scans a sensitized paper that forms an image directly upon exposure, without subsequent processing. These methods do not involve plate making; they are controlled by computer programs which work with data derived from converting the text and illustrations to digital form. *See also:* CONTINUOUS TONE IMAGE; DIGITAL IMAGES; FLEXOGRAPHY; GRAPHIC ARTS PHOTOGRAPHY; HALFTONE PROCESSES; LINE IMAGE; LITH FILMS/PAPERS; OFFSET PRINTING; PHOTOENGRAVING; PHOTOGRAVURE; PHOTOLITHOGRAPHY; SCREENED NEGATIVES AND PRINTS; STRIPPING FILM; SUBTRACTIVE COLOR SYNTHESIS.

Photometer; Photometry
A photometer is a device for measuring illumination by means of visual comparison, or by means that are equivalent, such as photocells filtered to approximate the wavelength sensitivity of the eye. Photographic exposure meters are simple special-purpose photometers; some have been designed on the visual comparison principle. In a visual photometer, a surface illuminated by the light to be measured (test light) is compared with a surface illuminated by a standard or reference light of known intensity. An adjustment is made until the two surfaces are visually the same; the intensity of the test light can then be calculated from the degree of adjustment required. The earliest instruments—such as the Bunsen grease spot photometer—and several today operate by moving the reference light toward or away from its surface to achieve a match; the light measurement is calculated by the inverse square law, using the distances of both lights from their surfaces. Other photometers operate by moving a graduated neutral density filter in front of the reference light, or by polarizing both lights oppositely and rotating a polarizer until they match. A flicker photometer permits measurement of two colored lights. The test light and the reference light are continuously alternated at a high rate on a single surface. Above a certain rate the eye no longer sees color differences, but a single color that flickers. An adjustment by distance or graduated filter is then made until the flicker disappears. Specialized photometers include densitometers, colorimeters, glossmeters (to measure the specular reflection, or relative "shininess" of a surface), and a variety of scientific instruments such as

spectrophotometers and atomic absorption photometers.

Photometry. The science of the accurate measurement of light—and by extension other radiant energy—principally in terms of those characteristics that relate to the illumination of a surface is called photometry. Other aspects of light measurement and analysis—e.g., spectral analysis—have an overlapping relationship with photometry. Photometric measurements are made in terms of standard light units, and those dealing with surface illumination operate with three fundamental laws regarding a point source of light:

1. *Inverse square law.* Illuminance (E) at a given point on a surface is equal to the intensity (I) of the light source divided by the square of the distance (d) from the source to the illuminated point:

$$E = I \div d^2$$

The relationship between distance and illuminance is inverse: as one increases, the other decreases. Distance and intensity must be expressed in related units; i.e., feet and footcandles; meters and lux; or centimeters and lumens.

2. *Cosine law.* The inverse square law holds generally for light striking a surface perpendicularly. If the light source is at an angle to the surface, the illuminance is proportional to the cosine of the angle (Cos A) between the light path to a given point and the normal (perpendicular) at that point on the surface:

$$E = (I \div d^2) \times Cos\ A.$$

3. *Cosine-cubed law.* When a source is perpendicular to a surface, some light strikes head-on, but the light at the edges of the area illuminated strikes at an angle. The illuminance of the head-on light is calculated by the inverse square law. The illuminance at the edges is proportional to the cube of the cosine of the angle between the light path and the surface being illuminated:

$$E = (I \div d^2) \times Cos\ A^3$$

Here, *d* is the perpendicular distance from the source to the center of the area covered.

See also: COLORIMETRY; EXPOSURE METERS; INVERSE SQUARE LAW; LIGHT; LIGHT UNITS.

Photomezzotint

In hand engraving, a mezzotint is produced by engraving a random pattern of closely spaced, crisscrossing lines over the entire surface of the plate to create thousands of tiny ink-retaining pits; middletones and highlights are created by cutting, scraping, and burnishing away the pits in various degrees. In photomezzotint an equivalent tonal effect is achieved by copying an image through a glass screen etched with an overall random grain pattern, rather than the precise column-and-row dot pattern of an ordinary halftone screen. The screened image is used to prepare a photoengraving plate. A screen with a pattern of parallel wavy or undulating lines is also sometimes called a photomezzotint screen. Line width in the reproduction varies with exposure through the screen, just as dot size varies with a halftone dot screen.

In 1865, Joseph Swan patented a nonengraving process he called Photomezzotint. It was almost identical with the Woodburytype, and produced carbon relief images without the need for hand preparation and transfer of every print. A master gelatin relief image was prepared and electroplated with copper. The copper shell was stripped off and served as a mold for carbon-pigmented gelatin. When the gelatin had set sufficiently, it could be transferred to the final support in a press. Several molds could be made from one master image so as to produce multiple prints simultaneously.

See also: CARBON PROCESSES; HALFTONE PROCESSES; WOODBURYTYPE/WOODBURYGRAVURE.

Photomicrography

Photomicrography is the technique of recording highly magnified images by means of a compound microscope used in conjunction with a camera. Magnifications range from about 5× to a useful limit of 1200× to 2000×. Higher magnifications are possible, but they are "empty" because the resolution of fine details is not increased; thus, although bigger, the image contains no additional information. Professional units reach magnifications up to about 30×. Lower magnifications (1× to 10×) are commonly obtained by so-called *macrophotography* or, more accurately, photomacrography. (*Microphotography* consists of making images at extreme degrees of reduction rather than magnification, for example as in microfilming.) The most extreme magnifications (100,000×) are obtained not with light, but with electron beams, as explained in the entry on electron micrography.

Microscope. A compound microscope is so named because it uses two or more steps of optical magnification to produce an image. (A simple magnifier, such as a reading glass or a loupe, has only one step of magnification.) The microscope, in all but the least expensive models, is built with modular components. The interchangeability of components permits the instrument to be adapted to the requirements of different types of subjects. From the bottom upward, a typical modular microscope has the following components: the microscope stand, to which the other components are affixed; a light source, or a mirror to reflect an external light source; a stage to support the microscope slide, with a condenser below to help direct light for transmission illumination to the subject. The magnifying section of the microscope consists of a body tube with objective lenses at the bottom and an eyepiece on top; and a photographic device, either built in or attached.

The objective is a critical element in the microscope system. Primary magnification is produced by the objective, a high-quality lens used at the stage end of the tube. The image produced by the objective is picked up and further magnified by the eyepiece at the opposite end of the tube. Image quality depends on the quality of the objective; later stages and other factors (eyepiece, projection relay lens or camera lens, adjustment of illumination system, vibration) may degrade the image, but cannot improve it. Objectives are short-focal-length lenses, about 40mm (4×) to 1.7mm (100×) covering the most widely used ranges. They are classed according to degree of correction (mainly spherical and color correction), magnification, numerical aperture (NA)—a measure of resolving power—and whether they are used "dry" (in air) or immersed in another medium such as water, glycerin, or a particular immersion oil. Standard objectives are designed for use with white light transmitted by a transparent or semi-transparent specimen. For the highest quality in specialized work, objectives are specifically designed for use with fluorescent light, polarized light, incident or frontal illumination, and with uncovered specimens. Some specialized objectives must be used in conjunction with a special condenser. An example is phase contrast micrography, a system that permits living, unstained micro-organisms which would normally be too transparent in bright-field illumination to be readily seen and photographed. This technique employs existing differences in the refractive index of various parts of the subject. By introducing phase shifts it produces contrast that differentiates the subject structures and separates them from the background.

The degree of correction (color and spherical) of an objective is one of three categories of increasing quality: achromatic (two-color corrected objectives, used widely); semi-apochromatic (fluorite); and apochromatic (three-color corrected). Apochromatic objectives are required for the most critical scientific work. The marking "PL," or the prefix "plan" (e.g., Plan Apo 20), indicates a flat field objective that maintains resolution to the edges of the image; this is highly desirable in an objective for photomicrography. As magnification increases, numerical aperture increases while focal length and working distance (the distance between the tip of the objective and the slide) decrease. For instance, in a current planachromat series, the $4\times$ objective has a numerical aperture of 0.10 with a focal length of 40mm and a working distance of 14mm. A $100\times$ oil-immersion objective has a numerical aperture of 1.25 with a focal length of about 2mm and a working distance of 0.2mm. The limits of useful magnification may be calculated as $100\times$ the numerical aperture. The magnification seen in the microscope eyepiece is indicated by:

Objective Eyepiece
magnifying $\times$ magnifying
power   power

With objectives commonly in the range $2\times$ to $100\times$, and eyepieces in the range of $5\times$ to $15\times$, the resultant visual magnification is from $10\times$ to $1500\times$. The final magnification on film varies with the photographic device used to record the image.

Photographic methods. While a camera with a fixed focus or non-interchangeable lens set at infinity focus is capable of making an image of limited quality of the central portion of the microscope field, a much higher quality image is achieved through use of a camera with a removable lens. With the camera acting primarily as a film transport, and possibly shutter, it is the microscope which is responsible for the basic quality of the final image recorded. Therefore, to achieve the full resolution of the system, the use of critical microscopy is an important preliminary to the photographic process. Attention to details such as the proper use of Kohler illumination is necessary.

To couple the camera to the microscope, a connecting tube is used. It serves to exclude ambient light, hold the camera central to the optical pathway, and rigidly attach it to the microscope to minimize vibration. Its most important function is to position the film plane at the proper distance from the eyepoint. With an infinity-focused camera the lens should be at the eyepoint. With the lens removed—the better arrangement, particularly with a single-lens reflex camera—the film plane should be above the eyepoint at the position where the focus in the viewfinder agrees with the focus of the microscope. This is achieved by first focusing the microscope visually, then moving the camera into position so that the sharpest image is seen in the viewfinder, without touching the microscope adjustment. When the two are locked together in this alignment, they are "parfocal." If this is not the case, adjusting the microscope focus in order to focus an image on the film plane introduces aberrations and degrades resolution. Connecting (adapter) tubes that fit various cameras are available from microscope manufacturers.

A single-lens reflex camera is the most adaptable for photomicrography. It should permit the mirror to be moved out of the image path before the shutter is released, because the common focal plane shutter is a deadly source of vibration in photomicrography. Through-the-lens viewing and focusing are difficult because the image is dim, and because the coarse texture of the typical viewing screen interferes with seeing details. A clear glass screen permits sharp focusing. An optimal arrangement is a single-lens reflex camera with a removable focusing hood and interchangeable viewing screen. A good choice is a clear glass focusing screen with grid lines viewed through a $6\times$ magnifying focusing finder with a diopter adjustment to correct for individual eyesight. A more sophisticated arrangement uses a special eyepiece camera, sometimes called a micro-attachment camera. This consists of a camera body and coupling tube especially designed for a particular model of microscope. The tube has a beam splitter that divides the image between a viewing eyepiece and the film plane to furnish accurate aerial image focusing, and a low-vibration leaf shutter. There are also photomicroscopes, precision instruments that combine visual and photographic systems in a permanent vertical or horizontal configuration; they are made in formats from 35mm to $4'' \times 5''$.

The majority of photomicrographs are made by means of light projected from below and transmitted by the specimen; some microscopes also permit incident (frontal reflected) illumination of very dense or opaque specimens. In black-and-white photomicrography, the light is usually passed through a green filter when an achromatic objective is used. This ensures maximum sharpness by screening out all wavelengths except those for which the lens is most highly corrected. In color photography, the light source must match the color balance of the film used. For example, a tungsten light source, commonly 2800°K, requires an 82B correction filter for use with Type B Tungsten color film. Polarized light, infrared, or ultraviolet wavelengths may also be used with appropriate filters or films for specialized images.

See also: BRIGHT-FIELD ILLUMINATION; DARK-FIELD ILLUMINATION; ELECTRON MICROGRAPHY; MACROPHOTOGRAPHY; MICROPHOTOGRAPHY; SOLAR MICROSCOPE.

Color photograph: p. C-45.

Photomontage
See: COLLAGE; MONTAGE.

Photomural
See: MURALS.

Photo-Paintings
See: OIL COLORING; OIL PRINTS; PAINTING ON PHOTOGRAPHS; PHOTOREALISM.

Photorealism

Photorealism (also known as superrealism or Hyperrealism) is a movement in painting that began in the 1970s, and which is noted for its use of photographs as models from which to prepare large, meticulously detailed canvases. Its advent marked another stage in the rivalry between painting and photography.

It has often been argued that the invention of photography enabled painters to set aside the pursuit of realistic representation and begin to explore various kinds of abstraction. But photorealist painters seemed to take a peculiar delight in producing paintings that looked even more realistic than the sharpest photograph. With the extensive and precise use of the airbrush, the painter's brushstrokes are all but eliminated, thus effacing the "hand" of the artist in favor of a uniform surface recalling that of the photograph. Because they initially seem machinelike and impersonal, and because they frequently mimic the perspective relations produced only by a photographic lens, photorealist paintings acknowledge that photography, not painting, has become the basis for the way of seeing that most people today consider natural. Such work, however, seems to argue that even the reality of the photograph can be significantly heightened by the artist.

With some photorealist paintings—such as the portraits of Chuck Close or the cityscapes of Richard Estes—a photograph or a projected color slide indeed serves as the model for the artist. In other cases, however, even if photography is not used in the making of the work, the end result nevertheless imitates the effect of photographic seeing. Such is the effect conveyed by the nudes of Philip Pearlstein, for example, which feature lenslike perspective distortions and eccentric croppings, or the highlighted still-lifes of Janet Fish.

The various picture-making strategies employed by photorealist painters serve to raise questions concerning the assumptions commonly made about the ways that painting and photography ought to look. By heightening the apparent reality of the painted image, these artists create a stubborn tension between the viewer's intellectual knowledge that he is looking at a handmade object, and the visual "evidence" that identifies it as a photograph.
See also: ARTIST AND PHOTOGRAPHY; PAINTING AND PHOTOGRAPHY.

Photoresist

A photoresist is an exposure-sensitive protective layer over the surface of a metal, glass, or plastic plate (substrate). Photographic methods are used to remove portions of the resist, which bares selected areas of the plate for further processes such as chemical etching. This general procedure is the key to a number of graphic arts processes, to manufacturing procedures for microelectronic devices such as printed circuits and integrated circuit "chips," and to other kinds of photofabrication.

Basic materials may be manufactured with a resist layer, or the resist may be coated on a suitable substrate as required. In normal-scale operations a high-contrast transparency of the desired finished pattern is placed emulsion-side-down on the resist and a contact exposure is made with a highly actinic light source (i.e., one rich in ultraviolet wavelengths). Micro-scale operations may use transparency patterns reduced from the original several hundred or even thousand times, but more precise exposure is now obtained with a laser or electron beam that is guided by computer control over the surface of the resist.

In a negative resist the exposed areas are polymerized, or hardened, by the exposing energy. When the plate is treated with a solvent, the softer, unexposed areas wash away. In a positive resist the action is the opposite. The re-

sist is hard to begin with, and exposure causes the affected portions to become soluble so that subsequently they can be washed away. In either case the substrate is uncovered in the pattern required so that it can be etched, milled, electroplated, or otherwise treated to form a relief or an intaglio copy of the pattern. *See also:* PHOTOENGRAVING; PHOTOFABRICATION.

Photosculpture

Techniques for translating camera images into a solid, three-dimensional representation of a subject, originated in the mid-19th c. Today laser-computer systems that provide reproductions at any scale, with accuracy of 0.001 in. (0.025mm) or better, have applications far beyond creating portrait sculpture. They are used to make master molds from one-of-a-kind scale models in industry, to generate operational instructions for robot machines, to produce reproductions of living organs and organisms for analysis and study, to create solid models from two-dimensional plans and drawings, to directly control the operation of duplicating machines, and to inspect, compare, accept, or reject the duplicates produced.

Photographic techniques such as bas-relief, stereoscopic photography, and holography produce an illusion of sculptural reality in or from a flat image. Other techniques deform a flat image into a relief. In one method, shapes cut from cardboard are stacked to form a positive mold. A wet print on thin, matte-surface paper (to prevent surface cracking) is pressed into shape over the mold and held in place to dry in that form. In another method, the print is mounted on a thin sheet of soft metal such as lead foil that can pushed into relief from behind. These techniques are all approximations; true photosculpture produces a free-standing solid object derived from two-dimension photographic images.

Early methods. The first photosculpture system was patented in France in 1860, by François Willeme. The subject sat on a raised platform surrounded by a circle of 24 cameras placed at 15° intervals; the cameras operated simultaneously to record 24 angular views in a single moment of exposure, about four seconds long. A print of each view was mounted on thick cardboard and the figure carefully cut out to provide a template for tracing with a pantograph stylus. The duplicating arm of the pantograph was fitted with a blade that shaved a lump of clay in the pattern traced. As each suc-

cessive template was traced, the clay was turned 15° so that full shaping was obtained. After the last cutting, the clay was smoothed and blended by hand and then used to prepare a mold in which castings could be made in plaster or molten metal.

Several systems created in the 1920s and 1930s relied on a light pattern projected onto the subject to provide guidance for successive operations. The pattern was variously a spiral, parallel bars of light, or a single narrow stripe. The regularity of the pattern was distorted by the contours of the subject surfaces on which it fell. The distortions were recorded in 50 to 150 or more separate exposures, each taken from a different angle. In a typical setup, the subject was on a platform that revolved full circle in a few seconds as a modified motion picture camera recorded the changing patterns in rapid single-frame operation. The processed light patterns were traced with optical devices that controlled engraving or carving tools, or that cut a series of profiles in cardboard; these were laminated with thickness pieces into layered solid form. Hand shaping and blending completed the figure, from which a mold was made.

Modern photosculpture. The most sophisticated method of photosculpture is today's Solid Photography ^{SM} system. In portrait sculpture, a battery of eight cameras surrounds the subject, which is illuminated with a stripe-and-shadow pattern from four sides, as if it were in the center of a cube. The cameras use 35mm black-and-white film, and the eight views are obtained in less than a second. (Video cameras and tape recording, or direct video processing without recording, can also be used.) When processed, the negatives are optically scanned and the light-pattern distortions automatically supplied to a computer. The computer cross-compares data from all the views to determine how far left-right, up-down, and in-out each point on the subject surface was, in comparison to corresponding points on the reference surfaces of the surrounding imaginary cube. From this, a set of instructions is generated to operate automatic milling machines with multiple cutters. Like many-fingered lathes, these machines shape a block of soft plastic material into an exact reproduction of the subject at any programmed reduction or enlargement in size. The final reproduction can be finish-coated, or can be used to create a mold for casting with a variety of materials.
See also: BAS-RELIEF IMAGES; HOLOGRAPHY; PANTOGRAPH; STEREOSCOPIC PHOTOGRAPHY.

Photo-Secession

The Photo-Secession was an informal organization of pictorial photographers, primarily American, formed by Alfred Stieglitz early in 1902 as the core of an exhibition at the National Arts Club in New York City. Barely a concept at first, it became the worldwide focal point for the finest artistic photography in the first decade of the 20th c. The spirit of the group was the same as that which guided the Linked Ring in England, the Photo-Club de Paris, the Secessionist movement in German art, and similar organizations. Stieglitz stated its aim: ". . . loosely to hold together those Americans devoted to pictorial photography in their endeavor to compel its recognition, not as the handmaiden of art, but as a distinctive medium of individual expression." Founding members of the Photo-Secession included Edward Steichen, Clarence White, Gertrude Käsebier, Alvin Langdon Coburn, Frank Eugene, Annie Brigman, Alice Boughton, and Joseph T. Keiley. Others, including several European photographers, subsequently became members. The group showed work together and individually throughout the world, and at the Little Galleries of the Photo-Secession—later "291"—founded by Stieglitz in New York. The organization dissolved in 1910 after a final exhibition at the Albright Art Gallery in Buffalo, New York.

See also: LINKED RING; LITTLE GALLERIES OF THE PHOTO SECESSION; PICTORIAL PHOTOGRAPHY/PICTORIALISM; STIEGLITZ, ALFRED.

Photosilkscreen Process

See: SILKSCREEN PRINTING.

Photostat

Photostat® is a patented commercial photocopying process. It produces high-contrast paper images most commonly used in making scaled layouts (dummies, mechanicals) for photomechanical reproduction. A Photostat camera can produce enlargements and reductions of up to several hundred percent, so an exact-size image can be used in the layout. Exposure is made on a paper material that produces an image on a receiving sheet in one-step diffusion transfer processing. Both positive-acting and negative-acting materials are available so that either negative or positive originals can be reproduced. The Photostat process is widely used because it is far faster and many times less expensive than copy photography with conventional transparent films and gelatin-emulsion printing

papers. However, Photostat materials are orthochromatic and produce very high-contrast images that are suitable for direct reproduction only of line originals; continuous-tone and color differences are not distinguished in the copy. For the most part, Photostats are used in layouts to indicate the size, placement, and identification of images that will be stripped into the master film from which a printing plate is made.

The Photostat process has been so widely used that the name often is applied casually to a number of similar reproduction processes used for the same purposes. Photostats are also used to obtain enlarged or reduced copies of documents and other material for direct use. Now same-size copies most often are produced on xerographic copiers some of which also can make limited enlargements and reductions.

See also: DIFFUSION TRANSFER PROCESS; PHOTOMECHANICAL REPRODUCTION; XEROGRAPHY.

Phototransmission

Instantaneous transmission of a photograph can be achieved by an ordinary television system, but the low resolution of the final image limits its usefulness. Until the advent of modern digital image techniques, high quality wire or broadcast transmission had been based on principles established by Alexander Bain in 1842 and elaborated by others in many ways in the 1860s, 1880s, and continuously since the 1920s. A major development occurred in the 1920s when the invention of the electronic vacuum tube (since replaced by the transistor) made it possible to amplify a varying signal and use it to modulate another (carrier) signal. Prior to that time, signal-no signal or dot-dash encoding was used. Almost all facsimile systems operate in the same way. An original image is scanned by a pin-point beam of light—a laser beam in the most modern equipment—that is reflected or, in the case of a transparency, transmitted to a photocell. Scanning may be accomplished by the beam's traversing a rotating cylinder on which the original picture is mounted, or by its being deflected across the surface of a stationary picture. The output of the photocell varies as the light it receives is varied by the tones or colors of the picture. This output is suitably amplified and transmitted by cable (phototelegraphy; wirephoto) or used to modulate a broadcast signal (radiophoto). The process is reversed by receiving equipment to vary a light beam that exposes photographic material in a synchronized scanning pattern. A direct im-

age can be obtained without processing on electrosensitive paper: the received signal is not converted to light, but applied as a varying electrical current to the paper surface, which darkens in proportion to the current strength at each point. The image quality obtained this way is markedly inferior to that produced by photographic receiving materials.

The highest quality, fastest, and most versatile transmission is now achieved with digital image techniques. The system is almost completely error- and distortion-free, but the equipment is many times more expensive than earlier systems. The image is scanned at high speed with a light beam or electronic beam, and the varying output translated into digital form that can then be relayed to receiving equipment by any data transmission link.

See also: DIGITAL IMAGES; RESOLVING POWER; TELEVISION.

Phototypesetting

Phototypesetting is the process of producing columns or pages of text by photographic means rather than by hand-assembling individual letters of metal type or preparing a matrix in which hot-type metal is cast. It is now the major method by which type is set. The phototype reproductions are pasted-up with reproductions of other elements, such as illustrations, to form "mechanicals" which represent the pages of a book, magazine, newspaper, or similar end product. The mechanicals are then photographed to produce master films from which the printing plates are made.

Historically, type has been set mechanically, a procedure that suffers from several drawbacks. Each different character size requires a separate piece of type, or master stamp. Where type is physically assembled letter by letter, hundreds of pieces of each character in each size have to be stocked so as not to run out of letters after setting a few pages. In a publication using several type sizes and styles, both the logistics and the expense of this method are restrictive. Even mechanical typesetting with 20th-c. machinery that casts each letter as required is relatively slow.

Phototypesetting solves these problems. Basically, the font (or type source) is a negative film image of each character, symbol, and integer which may be used. The chosen character is positioned in front of the photographic typesetting paper or film. A system of lenses and prisms focuses the character image onto the receiving material. By optically altering the image, the type size may be enlarged or reduced within considerable limits. Thus, for each type style only a single source may be required to produce all sizes. Exposure is usually made with a high-speed flash. The receiving material is stabilization-process photographic paper or, in some cases, lith film. By mounting the negative font on a rotary disk and using electronic accessories, exposures can be made faster than an operator can enter instructions via a typewriter-like keyboard. One solution is to have the operator's output punched onto paper tape which then is used to produce input signals at the required speed. That way two or more operators can simultaneously prepare material for a single phototypesetting machine.

Sophisticated, contemporary phototypesetters use computer-controlled character generators to display type on a CRT (cathode-ray tube) display. Editing may be done efficiently and inexpensively at this point. The approved page then can either be fed directly to the phototypesetter or magnetically stored for later batch entry. In practice, this system eliminates the necessity of separately projecting and exposing each character or line of type; the entire page is exposed as a unit.

Phototypesetting is essentially an optical process which utilizes a rather small negative. Dust and dirt are liable to degrade the quality of the image produced. Consequently, the highest standards of cleanliness are mandatory. Also, for consistently high quality, strict processing controls must be maintained for the receiving material.

See also: PHOTOMECHANICAL REPRODUCTION.

Physical Development

Conventional photographic chemical development produces an image by reducing exposed silver halide crystals to metallic silver; all the metal in the final image is supplied by the emulsion. In physical development the image-forming silver is supplied by silver nitrate in the developer; the emulsion supplies only the fractional amount of silver produced by latent image formation during exposure, and perhaps a bit more produced by chemical action during the course of physical development. Physical development occurs when silver is deposited on the image silver specks in the emulsion; it is a kind of intensification in which the developer silverplates the trace (latent) image. The result is almost grainless because the image-forming grains produced by development are not directly related to the original size of the emulsion crystals, but to the specks that are

built upon. Physical development can be used to rescue an image that has mistakenly been put into a fixing solution instead of a developer. Although all the halides are dissolved by this error, the latent image silver specks remain to serve as points for the physical deposition of silver.

Physical development was used for collodion wet plate processing. It occurs in monobath processing, and it produces the positive image in black-and-white diffusion transfer (instant photography) films. Although valuable for certain scientific purposes, and for photofabrication of printed circuits with some photoresists, it is not particularly useful for general photography for a number of reasons. Physical development requires one to four f-stops—or more— additional exposure to ensure that there is sufficient silver on which to build an image; this is effectively a reduction in emulsion speed. Panchromatic films may not respond because some sensitizing compounds used in such emulsions block physical development. Physical developers are difficult to compound accurately so as to avoid unwanted side effects. They must be mixed and used under scrupulously clean conditions; they have a shelf life of a few hours at most; and they permit only one-time use.

See also: CHEMISTRY OF PHOTOGRAPHY; DEVELOPMENT; DIFFUSION TRANSFER PROCESS; INTENSIFICATION; MONOBATH.

Physiogram

A physiogram is a photographic light tracing that shows the path of a moving light source suspended as a pendulum. The exposure may be recorded directly on a piece of uncovered film, or by means of a camera with the shutter locked open for a time exposure. The most interesting patterns are generally obtained from a position directly beneath the pendulum center, but some multi-cord hangings produce interesting patterns from a horizontal view. The most clearly defined traces are produced by a small bare bulb. A flashlight with the lens and reflector removed is a good source because the bulb is small and there is no electrical cord that might damp the pendulum swing. A flashlight of the size that uses two or more D cells has sufficient weight to provide a long period of motion. The surroundings must be completely dark to prevent overall exposure of the film. Either black-and-white or color film may be used. A color filter at the film or lens produces a stronger effect than a colored

light source; the filter can be banded or varicolored, or it can be changed during the recording for additional effect. Simple circle and ellipse patterns are produced by the uninterrupted swing of a single-cord pendulum. Eccentric wobbles can be created by tapping the cord at some midway point after the pendulum has started swinging. More complex patterns are obtained with V, Y, and three-, four-, or five-cord arrangements. Multicord arrangements not all tied to the same central point produce intricate variations, as does attaching one or more cords to a spring at their tie-off points. *See also:* TRICKS.

"Pictorial Effect in Photography"

The book in which Henry Peach Robinson first stated the tenets of Pictorialism was titled *Pictorial Effect in Photography*. Pictorialism is a stylistic mode of photographic expression that is considered to begin with Robinson's picture "Fading Away," created in 1858, and O. G. Rejlander's "The Two Paths of Life" of the year before. The book justified the attitude that the aesthetic standards of photography were the same as those of painting, and by direct statement as well as implication it maintained that artistic photography was more nearly true art in proportion to how faithfully it imitated painting. A formally trained painter and accepted academician, Robinson was benevolently condescending to his assumed audience: well-meaning but aesthetically uneducated photographers to whom he would give artistic understanding and "Hints on Composition and Chiaroscuro"—the subtitle of his book. First published in 1869, the book was extremely popular with artistically aspiring but basically imitative photographers; it went through several editions until after the turn of the century.

The first statement of art theory in photography—and soundly based on the unimaginative mid-19th c. standards of England's Royal Academy of the Arts— in the long run the book did immense damage by laying down laws (Robinson's word, along with "principles") for the selection of artistically acceptable themes and subjects, and for the composition of pictures. Further, it taught that a photograph should be composed as a painter composes a picture, by selecting, arranging, rejecting, and rearranging elements to produce a pleasing result. This was to be done not by sensitive seeing and perceptive selection of viewpoint in regard to a natural subject, but if necessary by assembling models, props, and costumes, and by combination printing, montage paste-up, and

Pictorialism. Annie W. Brigman, "Soul of a Blasted Pine" (1907). Collection, the Metropolitan Museum of Art, New York.

similar techniques. The artificiality this attitude fostered dominated, and undermined, artistic photography for decades. Its first effective opposition appeared in the person of Peter Henry Emerson and his doctrine of Naturalistic Photography, and later in the work of Alfred Stieglitz.

See also: COMPOSITE PHOTOGRAPHS; EMERSON, PETER HENRY; NATURALISTIC PHOTOGRAPHY; PICTORIAL PHOTOGRAPHY/PICTORIALISM; REJLANDER, OSCAR; ROBINSON, HENRY PEACH; STIEGLITZ, ALFRED.

Pictorial Photography; Pictorialism

The terms "Pictorialism" and "Pictorialist" came into wide usage within photographic circles in the last decade of the 19th c., and were applied to artistic photography in several modes. Pictorialism became the general term for art photography, which included, often in mixed or hybrid forms, genre studies, work in a naturalistic style influenced by Peter Henry Emerson, and soft-focus, impressionistic photography.

Pictorialist aesthetics may be said to stress formal and atmospheric effects of the image over the subject matter, so that composition and tonal values become the most important elements of the photograph. At the same time, Pictorialists considered photography as a tool or means to achieve desired aesthetic effects. Highly elaborate and controlled printing processes became characteristic of Pictorialist work.

The Pictorialist movement was preceded by the "high art" photography of O.G. Rejlander and H.P. Robinson in the late 1850s. Their work, like that of subsequent Pictorialists, was deeply influenced by contemporary fashions in painting, yet they attempted to gain recognition of photography as a form equal to the other visual arts.

The United States and Great Britain were the main centers of Pictorialism, though there were significant Pictorialist groups around the world, usually as the core of a salon. Pictorialist impulses are recognizable among the first generation of photographers in the 1840s, but the Pictorialist movement did not crystallize until the last decade of the century.

The 1880s saw both a blossoming of amateur photography and a reaction against the work of the prevailing "high art" photographers. The early ideas of Emerson, though later repudiated by him, were widely promulgated and fostered a new naturalism. In 1883, three significant events occurred: the Hamburg Exhibition of Pictorial Photography, the

founding of the Paris Photo-Club, and the organization of the London Photographic Salon. Pictorialist work began to receive attention during the next decade, at exhibitions throughout Europe. Pictorialism quickly became the dominant mode of amateur photography around the world.

The Linked Ring Brotherhood, consisting of Pictorialists who had seceded from the Royal Photographic Society, was founded in London in 1892. The Linked Ring continued to have an inestimable influence upon Pictorialist practice until its collapse in 1910. Nearly all the leading Pictorialist photographers were members, including J. Craig Annan, Alvin Coburn, F. Holland Day, Frederick Evans, Gertrude Käsebier, Alfred Stieglitz, Edward Steichen, and Clarence White.

A significant technical advance, the development and perfection of the gum bichromate process, was achieved by 1895, and was employed by many Pictorialist photographers. The influence of the paintings of Turner, Whistler, Degas, Monet, and of Japanese artists became prevalent, and much of Pictorialist output was devoted to slavish imitation of the subjects, composition, and surface effects of painting.

In 1897, Alfred Stieglitz, who was to become the most important proponent of American Pictorialism, was named editor of *Camera Notes,* the journal of the Camera Club of New York. The First Philadelphia Salon, including work by Clarence White, Steichen, and other

Pictorialists, was held in 1898. Two years later, F. Holland Day's *New School of American Photography,* an exhibition of 400 prints by such Pictorialists as White, Steichen, and Coburn, was mounted at the Royal Photographic Society Galleries. The exhibition traveled to Paris in 1901.

In 1902, the Photo-Secession, the American equivalent of the Linked Ring, was founded in New York. With Stieglitz as its guiding light, the Photo-Secession became the most important force in the American photographic community. Frank Eugene, Gertrude Käsebier, Joseph Kieley, Edward Steichen, Annie Brigman, Frances B. Johnston, Alvin Coburn, Clarence White, and Stieglitz were among its members.

Camera Work, the organ of the Photo-Secession, under the editorship of Stieglitz, was founded in 1903. For 15 years *Camera Work* reproduced the work of the leading Pictorialists. The Little Galleries of the Photo-Secession, where many Pictorialist photographers were exhibited, were opened at 291 Fifth Avenue, New York, in 1905. In Great Britain, the International Society of Pictorialist Photographers was founded in 1903.

Perhaps the seminal retrospective exhibition of the European and American Pictorialist tradition, *The International Exhibition of Photography,* organized by Stieglitz, was held at the Albright Gallery, Buffalo, N.Y., in 1910. But by this time, the Pictorialists were embroiled in divisive internal disputes. The Linked Ring dissolved, and the Photo-Secession began to fade in significance.

Pictorialist aesthetics underwent a vital transformation in the first decades of the century, with the assimilation of contemporary avant-garde painting (Cézanne, the Cubists, etc.). Pictorialism was gradually replaced by a new, hard-edged "straight" photography. Several members of the Photo-Secession (Steichen, Paul Strand, and even Stieglitz himself) were transitional figures.

In 1915, Coburn, Käsebier, and White founded the Pictorial Photographers of America. Two years later, the final issue of *Camera Work* appeared and the 291 gallery closed.

The major Pictorialist photographers continued to produce and exhibit fine work, some for many years, but Pictorialism was considered finished as an art movement by the mid-1920s. An enlightening, if indecisive, debate between "the last of the Pictorialists," William Mortensen, and the *f*/64 Group took place in the pages of *Camera Craft* in the early 1930s. Pictorialist attitudes and methods have dominated much of portrait photography and virtually all of illustrative photography throughout the 20th c., differing in style from decade to decade, but consistent in a concern with the beauty of the constructed (rather than discovered) image and with idealization of the subject. In the 1970s, a renewed interest in Pictorialist aesthetics and techniques appeared among young photographers, a trend that continues to this day.

See also: ABSTRACT PHOTOGRAPHY; ART OF PHOTOGRAPHY; EMERSON, P. H.; FANTASY IN PHOTOGRAPHY; LINKED RING; NATURALISTIC PHOTOGRAPHY; PAINTING AND PHOTOGRAPHY; PHOTOSECESSION; ROBINSON, H. P.; SALON PHOTOGRAPHY; STIEGLITZ, ALFRED.

Picture Agencies and Libraries

Picture agencies or libraries, also known as stock agencies and commercial archives, deal in the rights to reproduce pictures. They serve as a source of visual materials for publishers, advertisers, manufacturers, and others who have need of illustrations. Clients turn to picture agencies rather than hiring a photographer for a number of reasons of which economy, immediacy, and range of choice are the most important. Unlike galleries, which sell photographs outright, picture agencies loan a picture to a client and charge a fee for the right to reproduce it. Because a picture potentially has a great many such "sales," the fee is generally much less than it would cost

to have the photograph made. Agencies have their pictures on file and can supply them without delay, a factor of considerable importance to newspapers, magazines, and others who work with frequent deadlines and short lead-times. Agencies also offer immense scope and variety. Their files may contain hundreds of pictures in a given subject-matter area, including photographs from all over the world and reaching back to the earliest decades of photography. Some agencies—often self-styled as "archives"—include engravings, photographs of paintings, and similar images that increase the variety of their material and may extend the time reach to the earliest examples of visual images.

Agencies differ according to the concentration of their holdings. A few giant picture agencies cover an encyclopedic range of subjects and have hundreds of thousands of pictures available. Others cover a narrower range of related areas, or specialize in a single subject such as sports/athletics or current news. Some agencies deal only in color pictures (almost entirely 35mm slides and larger-format transparencies); others stock black-and-white and color prints and slides. The degree of organization and automation ranges from computerized storage and retrieval with videotape copies used for searching (viewing and selection), to file cabinets of prints and slides in plastic storage sheets which are examined by hand. Some small agencies keep little-used semi-historical materials in cardboard boxes or manila envelopes, and looking for pictures is much like searching the shelves of a used-book store.

Picture agencies provide for the selection of photographs in two ways. Almost all agencies provide a search service to find specific images or to make a selection of possible choices according to want lists submitted by clients. Some agencies also permit outside picture researchers working for potential clients to examine the files and select pictures. This greatly complicates the task of keeping pictures properly filed and protecting them from excessive handling. In some cases limited access is offered, or duplicate search files, microfilms, or videotapes are maintained to protect originals from damage, misfiling, or loss.

Pictures are submitted to clients on approval. There are generally three types of fees charged to the client for the agency service: a search fee, a holding fee, and a reproduction or use fee. The search fee covers the cost of the agency's selecting pictures for the client; it is often waived if the fees for the pictures used exceed a certain minimum amount.

In some cases a fee is charged to allow an outside researcher to make the selection. A holding fee is charged if unchosen pictures are retained by the client beyond a stated approval period (usually 15 to 30 days), or if selected pictures are not returned promptly after use. In the case of publications, the use period is sufficient to allow halftone negatives or color separations to be made. There is a charge for lost or damaged pictures—moderate in the case of prints, which are replaceable, but quite high in the case of original slides and transparencies because they are unique images and their potential income from subsequent use is lost.

The major fee is the use fee. It varies with the nature of the intended use, the circulation of the publication or the number of copies in a book printing, the number of uses permitted, and the relative exclusivity of use. Fees are considerably higher for commercial use—as in advertising or as part of a product to be sold (e.g., calendar, postcard, or greeting card)—than for educational or public-service use (e.g., a textbook or informational brochure). The fee also may vary according to whether the picture will appear on an outside front or back cover, an inside cover, or within the body of a publication, and whether it will be reproduced at quarter-page size or less, or at half-page size or larger. Fees are higher for large-circulation or large-edition publications than for small ones, and for multiple use (as in successive issues of a periodical, or variant editions of a book—original, abridged, foreign language, etc.). Most pictures are leased for one-time use. Exclusivity is a matter of the area and the length of time for which the client has non-competitive use of a picture. The basic fee covers reproduction only in the U.S. and in a single language of publication. Increased fees are charged for various degrees of additional international and multi-language use, although the foreign-only fee may be less than the U.S. fee. Most agencies routinely protect clients by not reselling an image for a period of up to 90 or 180 days after its expected publication, nor to a similar kind of client (e.g., two calendar manufacturers) for a longer period. This is seldom the case with contemporary news pictures. If the client wants exclusive use of a picture for a significant time, the fee is much higher in order to compensate the agency for loss of potential income from other sales. This is often the case with pictures used in advertisements or as illustrations on product packaging.

An agency typically retains from 40 to 70 percent of the reproduction fee; the remainder goes to the photographer. The agency's share must cover the costs of editors/researchers, bookkeepers and accountants, classification and filing specialists, and clerical personnel. These functions may be encompassed by two or three people in a small agency or by a very large staff in a major organization. The agency must also bear the costs of keeping a sufficient quantity of prints in good condition in the files; mailing/shipping and insurance; and—in the case of an agency open to outside researchers—maintaining the business in a readily accessible location. The photographer is free to travel, live, and work in an out-of-the-way or very low-overhead location, and to spend little or no time or expense in making sales contacts, showing pictures, and doing a variety of other "non-visual" activities.

A photographer arranges to be represented by an agency by submitting a sizable selection of work for consideration. It must be technically excellent and appropriate to the range of subjects stocked by the agency. A few agencies buy pictures outright for their files, and many will buy an unusual picture that has high sales potential. However, most agencies are interested in photographers who can supply a significant amount of more than competent work with relative frequency. They are interested in photographers who photograph unusual subjects and in unusual locations, or those who photograph familiar subjects in fresh but straightforward ways. There is little need for highly manipulated and special-effect pictures; most clients need illustrations, not decorations. There is a constant need for pictures that are up to date. Styles in dress, hair, automobiles, and many other factors of contemporary life change rapidly, making pictures look out of date for at least 20 years before they begin to be interesting as semi-historical representations of a decade or an era.

A few agencies ask photographers to supply prints (which should be made with at least half-inch borders all around for handling protection); most require negatives so that they can make fresh prints as required without delay. Agencies also require original color slides and transparencies; duplicates may be made for use in the search and reference files, but originals are demanded by clients so as to obtain the best possible reproduction quality. (Photographers who want copies of their color work for themselves learn to make at least two exposures of everything.) Photographers must also supply caption information for every picture. At the very least this encompasses date, location, and subject matter. The more unusual the subject is, the more additional information is required. Frequently pictures supplied with comprehensive information sell better than those with only minimal data.

A few agencies are divisions of a major organization such as a news agency or a picture-magazine publisher. Their files are composed of pictures made by staff photographers or by freelance photographers working on assignment. A very small number of agencies are cooperatives owned by the photographers whose work they stock; the outstanding example is Magnum Associates. Most picture agencies are independent businesses. Their common contract with a photographer is a consignment sales agreement, although photographers of proven productivity and salability may receive a retainer or have a drawing account. The photographer generally is restrained from selling duplicate or similar work independently or to other agencies, but he or she is free to place elsewhere pictures of subjects that the agency does not handle.

See also: FREELANCE PHOTOGRAPHY; MAGNUM; MUSEUMS AND COLLECTIONS; PROFESSIONAL PHOTOGRAPHY; RIGHTS AND PERMISSIONS; SELLING PHOTOGRAPHS.

Pigeon Post

The Siege of Paris in the winter of 1870–1871, during the Franco-German war, saw one of the first practical applications of microphotography in the so-called Pigeon Post. Government headquarters had moved out of Paris with the advance of German troops. After Paris was blockaded but still unoccupied by the enemy, messages were sent into the city by photographing them in very reduced size onto collodion plates about 2″ × 2½″; several messages were recorded on each plate. The processed collodion was stripped off the glass support and the resulting pellicles attached to carrier pigeons that flew freely over the barricades. When received, the pellicles were projected in a magic lantern and the messages copied by clerks for delivery in normally legible size. Sir John Herschel had pointed out the potential value of microphotography for document handling almost two decades earlier. The Siege of Paris also saw the first human-attended air mail service, conducted by balloon by the photographer Nadar and a few other ballooning enthusiasts.

See also: HERSCHEL, J. W.; MICROPHOTOGRAPHY.

Pigment Processes

From about 1860 to 1910 a great many processes were invented for printing photographic images in pigments rather than silver or other metals; interest in several such processes has been renewed in the past two decades. Most pigment processes were variations of a few fundamental methods. They were created for a number of reasons:

1. Images in pigment are essentially permanent; they are not susceptible to fading, discoloration, and the various kinds of deterioration that are relatively common with silver prints.

2. Pigment materials were far less expensive than metal-image materials that had a high permanency, such as platinum and palladium papers.

3. Pigments offered a wide range of image colors—including neutral black—other than the red-brown or dark purple-black of 19th c. print papers.

4. Pigment processes could form colored images directly, without requiring the artistic skill that hand coloring and overpainting called for.

5. Some processes permitted a great deal of alteration and manipulation so that imitations of paintings, etchings, pastel drawings, and other media could be produced, completely concealing the photographic origins of the image if desired.

The pigments were variously particles of lampblack (carbon) and colored compounds of a similar nature; painters' dry and wet (water soluble) pigments; oil paints; oil-based inks such as those used in lithography; and particles of metallic and mineral compounds. Almost all pigment processes use one of two basic methods. In one, the pigment is part of the emulsion of the print material. Exposure to a negative fixes pigment corresponding to a positive image in place; processing dissolves, washes away, or otherwise removes the unnecessary pigment. Most carbon and bichromate processes are of this sort.

In the other method, exposure makes an unpigmented emulsion or surface receptive so that it will retain pigment dusted or printed on, transferred by pressure, or attracted by chemical action, static electrical charge, or some other force. The bromoil process and xerography are examples of this approach.

See also: ARTIGUE PROCESS; AUTOTYPE; BICHROMATE PROCESSES; BROMOIL PROCESS; CARBON PROCESSES; CARBRO PROCESS; ELECTROPHOTOGRAPHIC; GUM BICHROMATE PROCESS; OIL PRINTS; OZOBROME PROCESS/OZOTYPE; PALLADIOTYPE; PLATINOTYPE; TRANSFER PROCESSES; XEROGRAPHY.

Pincushion Distortion

See: ABERRATIONS OF LENSES; DISTORTION.

Pinhole Photography. Ruth Thorne-Thomsen, "Expedition series" (1979); toned silver print from paper negative. © Ruth Thorne-Thomsen; courtesy Marcuse Pfeifer Gallery, New York.

Pinhole Camera

A pinhole camera is the most basic image-forming device because it requires no lens, mirror, or other optical component. Instead a small hole lets light enter a dark container to form an inverted image of the outside scene. This is the foundation of the device known to Leonardo da Vinci and other artists from before the Renaissance to the 19th c. as the *camera obscura,* the direct predecessor of the photographic camera.

The pinhole camera forms an image based on the principle that light rays travel in straight lines. When light rays reflected from a subject encounter a wall or plate with a small hole, rays from every point on the subject strike every part of the obstructing surface, but those striking the hole arrive at a unique angle from each point. The hole acts as a kind of one-opening sieve. A light ray approaching from a particular angle passes through and encounters a surface on the other side, such as a film emulsion, at just one point. Other rays, approaching from other angles, similarly fall on distinct points of the film surface. Thus, there is a one-to-one correspondence between points at which the light rays originate at the subject and points they illuminate on the film; the result is an image of the subject.

The image formed by a pinhole has a number of important characteristics. (1) It is quite dim, because the hole passes only a very small amount of the light from each subject point. (2) It is not precisely sharp because no physical hole can be limited to the diameter of a single ray of light. Thus, the hole passes a small bundle of light rays that originate at each point but that are spreading apart as they travel, with the result that the image of their origin point that they form is actually a small circle. The larger the hole and the farther the image plane is from the hole, the less sharp is the image. Diffraction limits how small the hole can be made to improve rather than degrade sharpness. (3) Whatever the degree of sharpness, it is the same throughout the image for objects at all distances from the pinhole. That is, the image has universal depth of field. (4) The angle of view is determined by the distance of the receiving surface, or image plane, from the pinhole. (In theory the size of the hole is also a determining factor, but the difference in pinhole diameters is so slight as to be negligible.) As the receiving surface is moved closer to the hole, the angle of view increases. The angle is defined by lines projected from the pinhole to the edges of the receiving surface. When projected through the hole, the lines show the angular field of view. The effective focal length of the hole is equal to the distance straight back to the image, measured along a line that is perpendicular to the receiving surface.

A pinhole camera is easy to construct or improvise. A lighttight can or box painted black inside can be fitted with a pinhole at one end or side, or a pinhole plate can be used in place of a lens on a conventional camera. A pinhole can be made in a piece of shim metal with a sharp awl, or by drilling with a needle through a piece of stiff aluminum foil temporarily sandwiched between two pieces of cardboard for support. The pinhole piece then is taped to a "lens board" of stiff cardboard or wood, with the pinhole centered in a larger hole in the board, and the lens board is fastened in place in the camera. A flap of opaque tape over the pinhole can act as a shutter. The camera must be loaded in a darkroom; either film or printing paper can be taped opposite the pinhole inside the camera.

Exposure must be determined by trial, but the approximate f-number of the pinhole can be calculated as follows:

$$f/no. = \frac{\text{Pinhole-film distance}}{} \div \frac{\text{Pinhole diameter}}{}$$

For example, at a 4 in. (101.6mm) distance, the f-value of a pinhole 0.025 in. (0.635mm) in diameter is $f/160$. A reading taken with a reflected-light exposure meter can suggest a starting point for a series of test exposures. If the meter f-number scale does reach the required value, it can be extended on the basis that f-numbers double at every other step in the sequence (e.g., the values following $f/16$ and $f/22$ are $f/32$ and $f/45$) and that each higher value requires twice as long an exposure as the preceding value. The exposure time arrived at by this mathematical approach should be at least doubled to compensate for reciprocity effect. On this basis, using an $f/160$ pinhole at about a 4 in. (10.16cm) focal length with ISO 125/22° film, exposure of a subject in bright sun would be 2 to 4 seconds. Obviously the camera must be placed on a firm support so that it cannot move during the exposure.

See also: CAMERA OBSCURA; DIFFRACTION; RECIPROCITY.

Color photograph: p. C-45.

Pin-up Photography

See: GLAMOUR PHOTOGRAPHY; EROTIC PHOTOGRAPHY.

Pizzighelli Process

The so-called Pizzighelli process was a variant of the platinotype in which the image printed-out completely, whereas in the basic platinum process it printed-out partially during exposure and was completed by development. The process was invented in 1882 by Guiseppe Pizzighelli—who, with J. M. Eder, had produced the first developing-out gelatin chloride paper—and Baron von Hubl, inventor of the multiple gum print process.

See also: PLATINOTYPE.

Platinotype

The platinum printing process was patented in England by William Willis in 1873 but was not marketed—in improved form—until 1879 under the name Platinotype. The potential use of platinum compounds in photographic printing had been demonstrated two decades earlier. It is by far the most beautiful of the iron printing processes and—for artist-photographers such as P. H. Emerson, Frederick H. Evans, A. L. Coburn, and many others—more beautiful than silver printing processes as well. The image has the surface texture of the paper used, because the paper is sensitized directly, not coated over with a layer of gelatin. The tonal scale is very long, with a basic image color ranging from delicate silvery-gray to a tinge of rose-brown. Although it does not produce the deep, rich black of a silver emulsion—partly because of the matte surface texture—the tonal effects are far more subtle. In addition, the platinum image is the most permanent of all metal images in photography; it is chemically inert, and so will last without change as long as the paper that supports it.

Platinum-process papers were manufactured until about World War I, when the cost of platinum had risen so high that they became unaffordable. Palladium papers were introduced in 1916; they produced almost identical results, but also became too expensive to manufacture profitably within a decade.

Present use. Today a few photographers (e.g., Irving Penn, George Tice) have revived the platinum process, preparing paper themselves to make exhibition prints. Paper is sensitized with a solution containing principally potassium chloroplatinite (or sodium chloropalladite) and ferric oxalate. Contact exposure under a long-scale negative to sunlight or ultraviolet reduces the oxalate from the ferric to the ferrous state, in which form it can reduce the platinite to metal. This occurs when the developer, a saturated solution of potassium oxalate, dissolves the ferrous salts; thus the platinum image is formed in proportion to the exposure received in each area. Image tone can be adjusted from warm brown-black to cool blue-black by developer temperature and chemical additives; it can be toned to green, olive, red, or deeper black with uranium nitrate or gold chloride solutions. Control of local areas can be achieved by glycerin development. The developed image is cleared of an overall yellowish color produced during development by successive baths of very dilute hydrochloric acid; it is then washed and dried.

See also: GLYCERIN DEVELOPMENT; IRON PRINTING PROCESSES.

Playertype

The first practical copying process to use reflex exposure was invented by J. Hart Player in 1896; the image produced was called a playertype. A high-contrast original such as a printed document or ink drawing was placed face-to-face in contact with high-contrast photographic paper. Exposure was through the back of the photo paper; the white parts of the original document reflected the light, producing twice as much exposure in those areas. Development yielded a negative that was used to make positive copies, again by a contact printing exposure through the back of the photo paper. This was a normal negative-positive exposure, because only the clear parts of the negative—corresponding to the image or information parts of the original—transmitted the light.

See also: REFLEX COPYING.

Plumbe, John Jr.

American; 1809–1857

One of the most successful of the first American daguerreotypists, Plumbe began in 1840 with a Boston portrait studio he called the National Daguerrian Gallery. His immediate success led to an expansion that within five years totalled fourteen studios in Boston, Albany, Saratoga Springs, New York City, Philadelphia, Baltimore, Washington, Louisville, New Orleans, St. Louis, and his birthplace, Dubuque, Iowa. Alert to the appeal of novelty, he purchased one of the first patents for coloring daguerreotypes so as to introduce tinted portraits at his Boston studio in 1843. His Philadelphia studio produced Plumbeotypes—enlarged hand-drawn lithographic copies of scenic and portrait daguerreotypes. In 1845 he began recording government figures and the buildings of Washington, D.C.; surviving daguerreotypes are the earliest photographs of the city. In 1847 Plumbe's business collapsed and he sold off his studios in bankruptcy. By 1849 he

Outerbridge, Paul Jr. "Female nude with snake" (1938); Carbro color print. Courtesy G. Ray Hawkins Gallery, Los Angeles.

Painting on Photographs. Ann Rhoney,
"Glass Table" (1980). © Ann Rhoney; courtesy Daniel Wolf Inc., New York.

Painting on Photographs. Allan Weitz,
"Amusements," from Coney Island series
(1977). © Allan Weitz.

Panoramic Photography. Jim Dow, "Veteran's
Stadium, Philadelphia" (1981). © Jim Dow;
courtesy Freidus/Ordover Gallery, New York.

Panoramic Photography. Jerry Dantzic,
"Ninilchik, Kenai Peninsula, Alaska" (1981).
Courtesy Jerry Dantzic.

Perspective. Ruth Orkin, "Balloon over Central Park," from a series of photographs taken from the same vantage point (1971). © Ruth Orkin.

Perspective. Pete Turner, "Road Song" (1967). © Pete Turner.

Perspective. John Pfahl, "Triangle, Bermuda," from Altered Landscapes series (1975). © 1982 John Pfahl; courtesy Freidus/Ordover Gallery, New York.

Photogram. Malekeh Nayiny, "The Fool," part of a series on the Tarot (1983). © Malekeh Nayiny.

Photogram. John Herschel, "Algae" (1842); cyanotype photogram. Private collection, Paris.

Photojournalism. Susan Meiselas, "Mano Blanca" (White Hand), symbol of the death squad, left on the victim's door, El Salvador (1980). Susan Meiselas/Magnum.

was in California speculating unsuccessfully on the future development of the railroad. He committed suicide in 1857.

Poitevin, Alphonse Louis

French; 1819–1882
A chemist and civil engineer, Poitevin experimented widely and invented a number of fundamental photographic processes. In the 1840s he devised various ways to electroplate daguerreotypes for use as printing plates. In 1850 he produced a primitive dry plate in which he formed silver iodide on the surface of a gelatin coating on a glass plate. (In a practical emulsion the light-sensitive compounds must be formed within the gelatin solution before coating.) The plate was of limited use because it was very slow, the surface was delicate, and the gelatin was likely to dissolve during processing. His major achievements dealt with the light sensitivity of coatings treated with potassium bichromate. In 1855 he invented the first carbon process, and in 1860 the collotype process, which he called photolithography. He also invented a method for direct lithographic reproduction of photographs from stones treated with a light-sensitive coating.
See also: BICHROMATE PROCESSES; CARBON PROCESSES; COLLOTYPE; ELECTROTYPE; PHOTOLITHOGRAPHY.

Polarized Light

Light is normally composed of energy vibrating in all directions at right angles to the direction the light waves are traveling. When light is polarized, the vibration is only—or predominantly—in one plane at right angles to the direction of travel. If seen head-on, the planes of vibration of unpolarized light radiate out from the center like lines pointing to all the minutes on the face of a clock; the vibration of polarized light is in a plane that joins two points directly opposite one another—e.g., 1 o'clock and 7 o'clock. When light is *plane polarized,* the plane of polarization maintains a constant flat angle along the direction of travel. When light is *circularly polarized,* the plane rotates in a spiral pattern along the line of travel.

Light becomes polarized by reflection from smooth, polished surfaces such as glass, plastic, polished wood, lacquered or varnished surfaces, and water. Light is not polarized by reflection from metal surfaces or from paints or other coatings that are composed of a suspension of metallic particles. Reflection from a matte surface destroys whatever polarization light may have. Polarization by

reflection from smooth surfaces is seldom total; a significant portion remains unpolarized, which makes it possible to use a polarizer to select either component of the reflected light for transmission. This is the principle of glare and reflection control with a polarizer. Light is also polarized by passage through certain crystalline minerals and liquids, and through artificial materials composed of aligned anisotropic crystals, such as Polaroid® plastic sheets. Substances that polarize light by transmission are said to be *birefringent.* Light from the open blue sky is polarized by atmospheric scattering. Maximum polarization is observed at right angles to the path of the direct sunlight; it diminishes from directly overhead to the horizon.
See also: POLARIZER.

Polarizer

The device used to polarize light in photography is usually a gray-brown filterlike plastic or glass screen called a polarizer. It is placed in front of a light source or, much more commonly, in front of the camera lens. Most polarizers have an index mark on the edge or are mounted in an indexing rim so they can quickly be set to any desired orientation. The variable degree to which a polarizer blocks unpolarized light and transmits the polarized component can be seen directly as it is rotated in front of the eye or the camera lens.

A polarizer is most often employed to reduce reflections from nonmetallic surfaces, and to improve color saturation by screening out scattered glare light in a scene. The color of open blue sky can be deepened by using a polarizer when the direct sunlight comes from an angle to one side of the line of view. The basic exposure compensation factor with a polarizer is $2.5\times$ ($1\frac{1}{3}$ f-stops); some built-in camera metering systems will give accurate readings only through a circularly polarizing screen. Two polarizers used together will transmit a varying amount of light as one is rotated in relation to the other; when their axes of polarization are at 90°, all light is blocked. Opposed polarizers are the basis of special-purpose high-speed shutters such as Kerr and Kappa cells and the Faraday shutter. Some variable-color filters consist of a two-color component and a polarizer. As the polarizer is rotated it increases the transmission of one color and decreases transmission of the other.

In copying and the photography of glossy-surfaced objects, maximum glare control can be obtained by using polarizers at the light sources as well as in

front of the camera lens. The procedure is to place a screen in front of the main light and then to rotate the lens polarizer until reflected glare is eliminated. Then screens are added to the other light sources, one at a time, and rotated until no glare is seen through the lens; no previously adjusted polarizer is changed as each new screen is adjusted. Only one light at a time is turned on so that the adjustment can be clearly seen.
See also: GLARE AND REFLECTIONS; KERR CELL; POLARIZED LIGHT.

Polaroid Photography

See: DIFFUSION TRANSFER PROCESS; INSTANT PHOTOGRAPHY.

Police Photography

Law enforcement agencies use a variety of photographic techniques to aid in the generation of evidence. Pictures are widely accepted by judges and juries as proof that a suspect was at a particular place at a given time. The individual may be pictured on a scene by surveillance techniques, or fingerprints may be recorded to demonstrate a past visit. Evidence photographs also include the environment around a crime scene, pictures showing areas of personal injury, and analytical and comparison photographs. To be useful in a court of law, they should have a straightforward perspective, be unretouched, and be well documented from negative through print.
See also: CRIME PHOTOGRAPHY; FINGERPRINT PHOTOGRAPHY; FORENSIC PHOTOGRAPHY; SURVEILLANCE PHOTOGRAPHY.

Pollack, Peter

American; 1909–1978
A historian and curator of photography, Peter Pollack established the photography department of the Art Institute of Chicago (AIC) and served as Curator of Photography there from 1945 to 1957. During that time he became one of the first museum photography curators to mount exhibitions of contemporary photographic work as a legitimate art form. Among the photographers whose work he exhibited were Brassaï, Henri Cartier-Bresson, Aaron Siskind, and Harry Callahan.

Pollack was born in Wing, North Dakota, and grew up in Chicago. He attended the University of Chicago, the AIC, and was a student of Laszlo Moholy-Nagy at the New Bauhaus in Chicago. He was director of the Chicago Artists Group Gallery (1936–1939), and

Director of the South Side Community Art Center (1939–1943) under the Federal Arts Project. Following service as field director for the American Red Cross in the Middle East during World War II, Pollack began his long association with the Art Institute of Chicago.

After leaving Chicago in 1957, Pollack served as a private consultant to museums throughout the country, including the Guggenheim Museum, New York; the Worcester (Massachusetts) Art Museum; the Archives of American Art; the Detroit Institute of the Arts; and the Cincinnati Museum. He served as Director of the American Federation of the Arts from 1962 to 1964. In 1964 he was appointed honorary curator of photography at the Worcester Art Museum and was instrumental in making important additions to that museum's collection.

Pollack was editor of facsimile photographic books for Amphoto (American Photographic Book Company), and was director of photography for original editions of world-famous photographers published by Harry N. Abrams. He was the author of *The Picture History of Photograpy* (1958; rev. ed., 1970; concise ed., 1977), and many articles on photographic subjects for *Art News, Modern Photography, Popular Photography,* the *Journal of American Art, Life, Look,* the *Encyclopaedia Britannica,* and the *Encyclopedia Judaica.* He published a second book, *Understanding Primitive Art,* in 1968. Pollack appeared as a guest lecturer at major universities throughout the country, speaking on photography and on painting (especially the works of Van Gogh and Cézanne).

Pollack was director of the "World of Ancient Gold" exhibition at the 1964 New York World's Fair, and was given one-man exhibitions of his own work at the Overseas Press Club and the Worcester Art Museum (1972); the University of Iowa and the University of Indiana at Evansville (1973); and the Illinois Arts Council (1974). Following his death in Sarasota, Florida, in 1978, the Worcester Art Museum held a memorial exhibition in his honor consisting of photographs from its collection.
See also: NEW BAUHAUS.

Ponti, Carlo

Italian
Carlo Ponti was a Venetian optical-instrument maker and architectural photographer active from 1858 to 1875. He is best known for his views of Venice, Padua, and Verona published in a series of albums under the title "Ricordo di Venezia." Each album contained twenty 10¼″ × 14″ views to which other Venetian photographers including Antonio Perini, Giuseppe Coen, and later Naya, contributed.

Ponti made large glass-plate collodion negatives and albumen contact prints of the interiors and exteriors of palaces and churches. He also recorded the backwater canals and scenic corners of Venice and closeups of the Greek bronze horses at the Basilica di San Marco. In the early 1860s, he made a group of documentary portraits of "picturesque Venetian street characters," not with sociological concern, but rather for sale to tourists. He posed many of his subjects in his studio while attempting to retain a naturalistic effect.

In 1860 Ponti invented the Megalethoscope (or Alethoscope), a large magnifying device through which a viewer could see a photograph or drawing. The name literally means "an instrument for enlarging the view." The illusion of day or night could be achieved with this device by manipulating the light falling on the image from the top or rear. The photographic views were made as double-image albumen prints, usually with a daytime scene on one side and a nighttime view on the other. They were frequently hand-colored. When viewed with reflected light, the daytime picture would appear and with rear light, the second picture would become visible.

When Venice was relinquished by Austria after the Seven-Weeks War in 1866, Ponti was appointed optician to King Victor Emmanuel II.

Ponti, Carlo. "Bragozrio Baria di Pescatori" (n.d.). Collection, Museum of Modern Art, New York.

Ponton, Mungo

Scottish; 1801–1880
In early 1839, while experimenting with Talbot's photogenic drawing process (contact copies of engravings and objects placed on sensitized paper), Ponton discovered that potassium bichromate was light sensitive. As described in his published account, he brushed a water solution of bichromate—which has an orange-yellow color—on paper and dried it in the dark. He exposed it to sunlight with an object placed on the paper. The areas affected by the light did not dissolve during subsequent washing, but the unexposed coating under the object did. The result was a white silhouette on an orange background—a photogram, in modern terms. Ponton pointed out that this method was much simpler and cheaper than Talbot's silver-sensitizing solution, but he did not develop the process. That remained for A. L. Poitevin, Talbot, J. W. Swan, and others to do after 1850. Ponton's discovery was the basis for a great number of non-silver photographic processes and most photomechanical reproduction processes of the 19th c.
See also: BICHROMATE PROCESSES; CARBON PROCESSES; PHOTOGALVANOGRAPHY; PHOTOGLYPHY; PHOTOLITHOGRAPHY; SWAN, J. W.; TALBOT, W. H. F.

P. O. P.

See: PRINTING-OUT PAPER.

Pornographic Photography

See: EROTIC PHOTOGRAPHY.

Porter, Eliot

American; 1901–

Eliot Porter is one of the best-known nature photographer-writers of our time. His work is significant both as art and science. He has developed new methods of photographing wild animals, birds, and insects using long-distance lenses, flash, and shutters. He has given us our most intimate and detailed look at the activities of wild creatures.

The son of a wealthy Chicago architect and the brother of the painter Fairfield Porter, Eliot Porter was born in Winnetka, Illinois. He began to photograph birds and landscapes as a boy of 13 on Great Spruce Head Island, Maine, the summer home of his family, and won an Eastman Kodak prize at age 16. Porter graduated from Harvard Engineering School in 1924, and from Harvard Medical School in 1929. He taught and did research there in biochemistry and bacteriology for the next 10 years.

In 1930, Porter acquired a Leica camera and began to photograph a wide variety of subjects in his spare time. In 1933 he was profoundly impressed by the work of Ansel Adams, whom he met soon thereafter. The following year he showed his work to Alfred Stieglitz in New York and received both approval and encouragement. He began photographing with a large-format camera in 1935, and in 1936 exhibited at Delphic Studio, New York. In 1937 he began his serious recording of the lives of birds.

Porter was given a show at An American Place in 1938–1939, the last exhibition of another photographer Stieglitz mounted. Porter exhibited landscapes, New England village scenes, and a few photographs of birds. At the close of the show, Stieglitz uncharacteristically wrote Porter: ". . . I must thank you for having given me the opportunity to live with your spirit in the form of those photographs that for three weeks were on our walls. . . . Some of your photographs are the first I have ever seen which made me feel 'there is my own spirit,' quite an unbelievable experience for someone like myself."

Encouraged by Adams and Stieglitz, and influenced by the work of Paul Strand, Porter devoted himself to photography full-time from 1939 on. He started to work in color in 1940 and made his own separation negatives and dye transfer prints in order to control color values. He was given a one-man show at the Art Museum of Santa Fe the same year; with his wife he settled in New Mexico after the war, during which he worked in the Radiation Laboratory at MIT.

Porter received a Guggenheim Fellowship in 1941 to photograph birds in their natural habitats and exhibited *Birds in Color* at the Museum of Modern Art, New York, in 1943. His Guggenheim was renewed in 1946.

In addition to countless exhibitions and publication in magazines, Porter has published almost 20 books, including *In Wilderness Is the Preservation of the World* (1962), and *All Under Heaven: The Chinese World* (1982). His was the first one-man show of color photographs held at the Metropolitan Museum of Art (1979).

Color photograph: p. C-46.

Portrait Lens; Portrait Attachment

A *portrait lens* is one specifically designed to provide a (usually variable) degree of soft focus, on the convention that the function of a portrait is to flatter the subject, and that a certain softening of facial details is flattering. In some portrait lenses—as in the first, the Petzval lens of 1840—the softness results from aberrations only partially corrected, or left uncorrected. The degree of softness increases outward from the center of the field, and diminishes somewhat as smaller apertures are used. Other portrait lenses provide varying degrees of softness as one component is shifted in relation to the others, or as different screens, each with a pattern of different-sized holes, are inserted in the barrel. The center of each screen is completely open, and the effect varies with the aperture setting. A portrait lens usually has a focal length 1½ to 2 times that of the normal lens for the format in use. This provides a larger image, especially in head-and-shoulder compositions, from a distance that avoids unpleasant distortion of the subject's features.

A *portrait attachment* is a positive supplementary lens used in front of a normal camera lens. It permits focusing at a close enough distance to essentially fill a small- or medium-format frame with a head-and-shoulders view. However, the closer camera position creates distortion, a fact seldom pointed out in the descriptions of such devices. *See also:* DISTORTION; PORTRAITURE; SUPPLEMENTARY LENS.

Portraiture

Today portraits are taken with all kinds of equipment. Small-format cameras are commonly used for informal portraits both in natural light and with portable electronic flash. Medium- and large-format cameras are most often used for studio portraits. Generally a lens approximately 1½ to 2 times the normal focal length is preferred to minimize distortion of facial features. In black-and-white photography a medium-speed film is usually chosen for its moderate contrast characteristics.

For studio portraiture a film with a retouching surface on the emulsion or base, or both, is used to make corrective work easier. Today, light sources are more frequently soft (diffused) than hard and direct, and lighting ratios seldom exceed 3:1 unless an interpretive or dramatic effect is sought. Papers with semi-matte surfaces and a slightly warm base tint and image tone are used for most prints. Textured papers, hand coloring, rich framing, and similar finishing touches are common with studio portraits, but inappropriate for other kinds of portraits unless used with great restraint.

Nineteenth-century portraiture. Historically, the first photographic processes announced in 1839—the daguerreotype in France and the calotype in Britain—required exposures too lengthy to make commercial portraiture immediately practical. Within a short period, however, technical improvements overcame this difficulty and brought about an explosive growth in photographic portraiture, which became the foundation of all photographic commerce and industry. The traditional practice of the miniature hand-painted portrait was virtually eliminated, and many former portrait painters joined the ranks of portrait photographers. By the middle of the 1840s, thriving photographic portrait studios existed in every major city of Europe and America.

The daguerreotype was the most widely employed portrait medium through the 1840s. Characterized by small format, a highly reflective silver surface, and precise detail, daguerreotypes were usually mounted behind glass in elaborate cases. The other major photographic process of the 1840s, the calotype, which utilized a paper negative to produce a paper print, was considered inferior to the daguerreotype for portraiture because of the graininess and diffusion of the resulting image. It was the calotype, however, which was used to produce the remarkable series of portraits by David Octavius Hill and Robert Adamson in Scotland in the mid-1840s. Hill, a painter, intended the photographs to serve as aids in the preparation of a large group-portrait painting. But Hill's mastery of lighting effects and the largely unaffected poses in which he placed his subjects rendered these the most successful of early attempts at portrait photography. While Hill's paintings have been forgotten, his calotype portraits are still acclaimed as masterworks.

Portraiture. Berenice Abbott, "James Joyce" (1928). © 1983 Berenice Abbott.

In the 1850s both the daguerreotype and the calotype were replaced for portraiture by prints from wet collodion-on-glass negatives. These combined the daguerreotype's clarity of detail with calotype's ability to yield unlimited positive prints. The most eminent practitioner of wet-collodion portraiture in the 1850s and 1860s was Félix Nadar, who founded his own successful commercial studio in Paris and who was responsible for a remarkable series of portraits of the leading writers, artists, and musicians of the era. Many of these figures were Nadar's friends and acquaintances, and he photographed them with affection and sympathy.

In 1854 the French photographer Disdéri's invention of the carte-de-visite format set the stage for a quantum leap in the volume of photographic portraiture. By reducing the size of the portrait photograph to roughly 2½" by 4" (6.35 × 10.16cm)—small enough to be pasted onto a calling card—Disdéri was able to increase the number of exposures that could be made on one standard-sized glass negative. The price of the portrait could thereby be reduced dramatically. The popularity of these photographic card portraits was enormous among the middle and upper classes, and helped call into existence a vast photographic industry to provide the portrait studios with chemicals, paper, and equipment.

In addition to his technical innovation, Disdéri pioneered the idea of what today is known as the celebrity portrait. He arranged to photograph well-known writers, statesmen, theatrical personalities—even emperor Napoleon III—and to prepare huge editions of these portraits to sell to a curious public throughout Europe. Such portraits of leading contemporary figures were often pasted into albums and collected along with portraits of family and friends. In addition, although he was not the first to do so, Disdéri popularized the use of studio props such as pillars, extravagant draperies, and emblems of the sitter's occupation. These remained the common mark of the studio portrait until well into the 20th c.

Aside from the spectacular growth in professional portrait photography, art photographers turned to portraiture as a subject to explore in its own right. The most original of these artistically inclined 19th-c. amateur portraitists was Julia Margaret Cameron, whose soft-focus, intimate presentations of the eminent scientists and men of letters of Victorian England rank among the greatest of photographic portraits.

Early twentieth-century portraiture. Cameron's example was known to a number of the outstanding portraitists who emerged from the Pictorialist and Photo-Secession movements around 1900. The young Edward Steichen's portraits of artists and literary figures such as the sculptor Rodin and the playwright George Bernard Shaw were thought at the time to represent the summit of photographic portraiture. Shrouded in shadow, with the subject's features emerging in a dramatic burst of light, Steichen's portraits created an atmosphere of mystery and glamour around their sitters. During the years before World War I, the American photographer Alvin Langdon Coburn, working in England, also produced a series of striking soft-focus portraits of leading literary and artistic personalities. Collected in his book *Men of Mark* (1913), Coburn's portraits of figures such as the novelist Henry James and the poet W.B. Yeats reflect his own fascination with the creative imagination.

Considered in the broadest sense, portraits such as those made by Steichen and Coburn represent a continuation and refinement of Disdéri's celebrity portraiture. The public's interest in such photographs has to do largely with curiosity about those who have become celebrated for their power, prestige, beauty, or glamour. After World War I this kind of portraiture found a home in new magazines such as *Vanity Fair* and *Vogue*. Throughout the 1920s and 1930s, these publications regularly presented the work of Steichen, Cecil Beaton, and Horst P. Horst, and similar photographers.

Recent trends. In the early 1940s, Philippe Halsman in New York and Yousuf Karsh in Canada each began to achieve great success making studio portraits of celebrities for a variety of publications; both also did private portraiture. Though Karsh's portraits tend to have a monumental quality while Halsman's are more direct, the two photographers

Portraiture. Mike Disfarmer. "Homer Eakers, Loy Neighbors, and Julius Eakers, brothers-in-law" (1945). Permanent collection, ICP, New York.

quality small-format cameras and first widely shown in photojournalistic magazines. In such pictures the sitter is posed in surroundings that convey a distinct impression of his or her occupation or interests in life. In the post-war period, Arnold Newman raised this approach to new heights in his large-format portraits of artists; for example, his portrait of the abstract painter Piet Mondrian is placed in a setting that calls to mind the characteristic look of the artist's work.

A notable trend in the portraiture of the last two decades is what might be called the "anti-glamour" portrait. In the 1960s, the former fashion photographer Diane Arbus introduced this approach in her uncompromising portraits of social misfits and outlaws, portraits in which her subjects seemed willing to show themselves at their most vulnerable. During the same years, the fashion photographer and celebrity portraitist Richard Avedon, too, produced a series of highly unconventional portraits of members of the American cultural and political elite. Avedon's portraits appear to strip away his subjects' public faces and reveal less appealing aspects of their characters.

In much the same way that the miniature portrait painting was replaced by the daguerreotype, so the local portrait studio has in recent years been threatened by the popularization of Polaroid and other instant photography technologies. While the formal portrait is likely to remain a permanent tradition within art photography, the most revolutionary aspect of today's photographic portraiture is certainly the ease with which virtually everyone can obtain inexpensive photographic likenesses of themselves, their family, or their friends.

See also: PHOTOGRAPHERS CITED; SELF-PORTRAIT.

Positive

A positive image is one in which the relative brightnesses or colors of various areas correspond directly to those of the original subject. The use of this term and its opposite, "negative," to describe the two visible states of a photographic image was suggested in 1840 by Sir John Herschel. A positive relief or matrix, as required for various pigment or transfer processes, is one in which portions of the recording substance (e.g., gelatin) are raised above the plane of the supporting surface in direct proportion to the various subject brightnesses. Confusingly, a negative relief or matrix may be one in which negative-corresponding areas are raised above a surface, or one in which

shared the feeling that the active psychological influence of the photographer upon the portrait subject in the course of the sitting was of great importance.

In contrast to the type of portraiture that focuses on the exceptional individual, another more recent approach concentrates instead on what might be called the "social type." The most remarkable example, perhaps, of this concept of portraiture is the work of the German photographer August Sander. Between 1918 and 1934, Sander developed an encyclopedic documentation consisting of portraits of individuals drawn from every level of society. While today it seems possible to glimpse in Sander's searching, sometimes accusa-

tory portraits a foreshadowing of the darkness of the Nazi period. Sander insisted that his purpose was not to criticize his subjects, but to record their roles in social history, as reflected in their faces. A comparable treatment of the same idea, carried out on a much smaller scale, can be seen in the work produced by the American portraitist Michael Disfarmer in the years 1939–1946. The anguish and uncertainty of the World War II years mark the faces and even the physical gestures of the men and women who came to Disfarmer's Arkansas studio.

A pre-World War II innovation in portraiture was the "environmental portrait," made possible by professional

Portraiture. Scavullo, "Louise Nevelson" (1981). Courtesy Scavullo.

positive-corresponding areas are hollowed out in depth below the surface plane.
See also: PIGMENT PROCESSES; RELIEF IMAGES; TRANSFER PROCESSES.

Posterization

A poster is commonly composed of flat areas of tone and color having a single value, with no variation. Photographic posterization is the process of imitating this effect by translating a continuous-tone image into a range of only three or four tone steps. Thus in a three-tone posterization, the gradations in the first one-third of the continuous tone scale are represented by one tone; those in the middle third by another tone; and those in the last third step by a third tone. The effect with a suitable image is one of graphic boldness and simplicity, but the maximum effective number of tonal steps from a photographic original is five; beyond that, the final image is increasingly seen as continuous tone.

Tonal separations are made on a high-contrast graphic arts (lith) film, one for each tonal step. For a final black-and-white image, only tone-separation negatives are required; they must be made from a continuous-tone positive image, either a print or a transparency. If a transparency must be made from a black-and-white negative as an intermediate step, it should have a full tonal range but slightly greater than normal contrast. If the positive image to be posterized is in black-and-white, an orthochromatic high-contrast film can be used; if in color, a panchromatic high-contrast film must be used. It must be possible to register the negatives accurately over the final print paper. This is relatively easy in contact printing up to about 11″ × 14″. Larger posterizations are made by projecting smaller-format negatives, but registration is more difficult in enlarging. A stepped-exposure test strip is made on the high-contrast film from the positive to determine exposures for making the negatives. The following examples are for a three-tone posterization.

One negative receives an exposure that registers only the highlights; the middletones and shadow areas are underexposed and thus fail to register on the high-contrast film. A second negative receives an exposure that registers middletones and highlights (which will be over-exposed and blocked up), but not shadows. The third exposure registers the shadows properly, blocking up the other areas of the image. A print is made starting with the shadow-tone negative, using an exposure that prints the tone as a light gray. The middletone separation is registered and given the same exposure. Then the highlight separation is registered and given the same exposure. The additive effect of exposure in the previous areas makes the shadows darkest, the middle tones a lighter single tone, and the highlights the lightest single tone.

Color posterization requires a set of tone-separation negatives and a matching set of positives. Negatives obtained from an original continuous-tone positive image are contact-printed on high contrast film to obtain the positives. If the original image was a negative, the first tone separations are positives; they are contact-printed on high-contrast film to produce negatives. Color is obtained by filtering the exposing light; any colors may be used, and the filters changed for each exposure. The exposure at each step must be full exposure; there is no additive effect as in black-and-white posterization, because the separation positives are used to protect previously exposed areas. The first exposure is through the shadow negative, which is self-blocking in the middletones and highlights. The second exposure is through the middletone negative plus the shadow-area positive, which blocks the already-exposed shadow areas. The third exposure is through the highlight negative plus the middletone positive, which blocks both the shadows and the middletone areas already printed. Three-tone separation is usually the practical maximum in color posterization; the ability to change both colors and exposures in the various steps makes a great number of variations possible.
See also: CONTRAST; LITH FILMS/PAPERS; SPECIAL EFFECTS; TONE-LINE PROCESS.

Postvisualization

A composite photograph created by sandwiching, multiple printing, or various montage techniques may not be visualized by the photographer until after pictures containing all the elements eventually used have been taken. The process of examining completed photographs as potential sources of material for composite images, and of building mental images of possible combinations, is called *postvisualization*. The term originated with the contemporary American photographer Jerry N. Uelsmann, in whose work this procedure is fundamental. It is meant to distinguish the kind of perception required from that of *previsualization* of the final image before the camera is used, usually for a single picture done in a straightforward, realistic style.
See also: COLLAGE; COMPOSITE PHOTOGRAPHS; MONTAGE; MULTI-IMAGE TECHNIQUES; MULTIPLE EXPOSURES/PRINTING; PREVISUALIZATION; UELSMANN, J.

P-Q Developer

A developer in which the developing agent Phenidone (1-phenyl-3-pyrazolidone) is used in combination with the agent hydroquinone (*p*-dihydroxybenzene; quinol) is called a P-Q developer. Phenidone is a proprietary product of Ilford, Ltd. The basic compound was first produced in 1890 but its properties as a developing agent were not discovered until 1940, and it was not produced in quantity for photographic use until 1951. Phenidone has the same developing characteristics as metol, but it is much more active. When substituted for metol in a formula combination with hydroquinone (M-Q developer), only about one-tenth as much Phenidone as the specified amount of metol is required. A substitution is recommended for people who have a dermatitis reaction (so-called metol poisoning) to contact with metol solutions; Phenidone is not known to cause such reactions. In addition, hydroquinone reacts with development byproducts to regenerate Phenidone as a developer is used, producing very long solution life at a constant level of activity. The superadditivity of the two developing agents is like that of the metol-hydroquinone combination and can be adjusted to produce desired characteristics by varying the proportion of each in the formula.
Preventing fog. Phenidone does not respond to the restraining effect of potassium bromide in a solution, or to the bromide accumulation that occurs with use. This fact and the high activity rate of the compound can result in fog (excess non-image density) in negatives, especially with high-speed, thick emulsion films. To prevent fog, an inorganic restrainer such as benzotriazole, which does affect Phenidone, is added to P-Q formulas for such films. Formulas for P-Q fine-grain (slow film) developers and for paper developers generally do not require the additional restrainer. Phenidone dissolves best in water at a much higher temperature than is considered safe (to avoid chemical breakdown) for most other developer ingredients. The usual procedure is to dissolve the required quantity of Phenidone separately in a small amount of hot—e.g., 175°F (79°C)—water; the amount of water should be enough so that no more than a ten percent solution is formed. This is then added to the larger quantity of cooler water (typically 125°F, or 52°C) used for the other ingredients.
See also: DEVELOPING AGENT; FOG/FOGGING; M-Q DEVELOPER; PERCENTAGE SOLUTION; RESTRAINER; SUPERADDITIVITY.

Praxinoscope

The praxinoscope was an improved zoetrope for viewing animation, invented in 1877 by Emile Reynaud. Movement-sequence drawings mounted on the inner wall of a revolving circular drum faced the center, where they were reflected by a many-sided drum that revolved in the opposite direction. The inner drum had as many mirrored facets as there were drawings. The spectator looked through a mask that restricted the view to the area occupied by a single mirror. As the images jumped into view in rapid succession, an illusion of continuous movement was created. If a projection lens was placed in the viewing position, the images could be thrown on a screen, but it was difficult to illuminate the drawings sufficiently for more than a dim image, and impossible to eliminate flickering and blurring of the image on the screen. The name, from Greek roots, means "action viewer."
See also: ANIMATION; ZOETROPE.

Pre-Raphaelite Movement

The allegorical style of the early works of Julia Margaret Cameron and that of many Pictorialists was a direct photographic expression of the themes, attitudes, and styles of the painters and poets who composed the Pre-Raphaelite Brotherhood. Founded in 1848, this group rejected the materialistic standards and the elevation of science and industry that marked 19th c. England and the emotional Romanticism that marked much art of the period. They called for a return to the simplicity, naiveté, purity of color, and clarity of detail they perceived in the work of Italian painters before Raphael. The original members—Dante Gabriel Rossetti, Wm. Holman Hunt, and John Everett Millais—were joined by Edward Burne-Jones, George Frederick Watts, William Morris, and several others. Although the group disbanded in 1853, the attitudes persisted in their work and in such activities as the Arts and Crafts Movement fostered by Morris. All of the leading Pre-Raphaelites were close friends of the Cameron family and influenced Mrs. Cameron's development by direct instruction as well as by appreciative critical comment. Nearly all were portrait subjects for her at one time or another.
See also: CAMERON, JULIA MARGARET; PICTORIAL PHOTOGRAPHY/PICTORIALISM.

Preservation of Photographs

See: ARCHIVAL PROCESSING; CONSERVATION OF PHOTOGRAPHS; FILING AND STORING PHOTOGRAPHS.

Preservative

Developers and fixers include an ingredient that prolongs their storage and working lives by protecting the active agents from deterioration. In most formulas the preservative ingredient is sodium sulfite, but it functions differently in the two kinds of solutions. When a developing agent dissolves in water, it can be oxidized by oxygen contained in dissolved air in the water; oxidation is accelerated if the solution is alkaline, which is the case as soon as the activator is added when preparing a developer. In addition, a developing agent oxidizes during developer storage and use as the surface of the solution is exposed to air, and it oxidizes during use when it reduces exposed halides to produce a visible image. The oxidation byproducts can cause increasingly rapid oxidation of the remaining developing agent. Sodium sulfite greatly retards oxidation by the air, and it combines with oxidation byproducts during development so they cannot promote developing agent breakdown. The result is an extended working life.

A fixing solution must be somewhat acidic to neutralize any alkaline developer carried in by the emulsion, and to permit the fixing agent to work effectively. However, acid attacks the fixing agent, precipitating colloidal sulfur that can lodge in the emulsion, degrading image contrast and clarity. Sodium sulfite in the solution combines with the sulfur to form the fixing agent sodium thiosulfate, thus protecting the image and extending the life of the fixer. Toners and various other solutions may also incorporate preservatives. A few drops of acid added to gelatin or gum arabic solutions preserves their lives by preventing the growth of fungus or molds that feed on those substances.

See also: ACTIVATOR, ACCELERATOR; CHEMISTRY OF PHOTOGRAPHY; DEVELOPING AGENT; FIXING; OXIDATION-REDUCTION.

Press Camera

A press camera is a medium- to large-format folding hand camera. The design derives from portable glass-plate cameras of the late 19th c. The first model specifically called a press camera was offered in about 1910 for use by newspaper photographers, who required a compact, rugged camera that produced relatively large negatives. It became standard equipment for news photographers until finally supplanted in the 1960s by 35mm and medium-format roll-film cameras. The best-known press camera in the U.S. was the Speed Graphic, introduced in 1912 and produced in formats from $2\frac{1}{4} \times 3\frac{1}{4}$ to 5×7 for more than 60 years.

A typical press camera consists of a boxlike frame 2 to 4 in. (5.1 to 10.2cm) deep. One side of the box is hinged at the bottom and drops to a horizontal position to form a bed for the lens standard and bellows, which move out along tracks in the bed for focusing. The lens standard permits limited rise, shift, swing, and tilt movements. The bed can be dropped to an angle below horizontal to obtain a fall movement; however, the primary purpose of this position is to move the front edge of the bed out of the field of view of a wide-angle lens. Lenses are interchangeable and have built-in shutters; some cameras also have a focal-plane shutter. The back of the camera is a hooded ground-glass screen that permits viewing and focusing. The screen is spring-mounted and is displaced as sheet film holders are inserted. In some cameras the screen can be removed so that a roll-film adapter can be mounted. Focusing can also be achieved by means of a coupled rangefinder mounted on one side of the frame. A pop-up wire frame on top of the camera allows the picture to be composed when the viewing screen is blocked by a film holder. Both the lens and the focal-plane shutters synchronize with flash units.

The press camera evolved into the so-called technical hand camera, of which several models are manufactured today. This design offers more extensive lens movements, extension tracks so the lens can be extended for close-up photography or to permit use of longer-focal-length lenses, and some degree of back movement.

See also: CAMERA; CAMERA MOVEMENTS.

Press Photography

Press photography, or the making of pictures for periodical publications, can be divided into three fundamental categories, each of which at times overlaps the other: "spot" or breaking news photography, feature photography, and photojournalism.

The breaking news photographer is responsible for making visual records of newsworthy events as they occur. News photographers usually work as staff members of their publications, and they are often dispatched with the reporters covering the story or event. Many times the breaking news photographer cannot be on the scene as an event unfolds, and he or she is left to record the aftermath; many of the photographs that depict moments of unexpected drama or disaster and that are published in newspapers and magazines are made by amateurs who were by chance on the scene as the event occurred. In most cases, however, the events are of an ongoing or more predictable nature, and the news photographer must provide his or her publication with images that clearly and powerfully depict the event and complement the reportage, and that are arresting enough visually to make the reader want to read the story. Except in extremely important or dramatic cases, breaking news is illustrated with a single photograph per story.

Feature photography, of the type found in Sunday supplements and magazine sections of newspapers, allows the photographer to plan a series of pictures that are used to illustrate a more extensive treatment of some event. Features can range from the domestic to the dramatic; photographers are often called in from outside the publication by virtue of their specialization in the area being written about. For example, still-life and food photographers are assigned to articles about eating in restaurants or about the daily activity of a vineyard; architectural photographers may be called upon to make pictures of a new or historic building; war photographers or photojournalists are asked to submit or make pictures depicting a battle in the news; and so on. More general features

usually are photographed by staff photographers with a special interest in or photographic knowledge of the topic being discussed.

Photojournalism is the extended photographic treatment of a specific newsworthy topic. Instead of making photographs to augment a text, the photojournalist must carry the story, along with its editorial slant, in the photographs he or she makes. The text in this case acts as a complement to the pictures. Many photojournalistic essays are initiated by the photographer and then proposed to the publication.

Rising printing costs and, in the U.S., loss of advertising revenues to television have considerably reduced the number of publications making extensive use of photoessays such as those done by W. Eugene Smith, Margaret Bourke-White, and a number of other photojournalists who became well known through the pages of magazines such as *Life* and *Look*. However, markets for the work of photojournalists still exist; many of them work through picture agencies rather than for specific publications.

The press photographer must be ready to respond immediately to the situation at hand; there is seldom the time or opportunity to arrange lights or make adjustments to the scene. If the photographic assignment is one of reportage, it often requires the use of existing light. Fast films and lenses, 35mm cameras (often with motorized film advance), and electronic flash are the working tools of most press photographers.

See also: DOCUMENTARY PHOTOGRAPHY; NEWS PHOTOGRAPHY; PHOTOJOURNALISM.

Pretsch, Paul

Austrian; 1808–1873

Trained in printing and engraving, Pretsch eventually became assistant to the director of the Austrian Imperial Printing Office. In the early 1850s he developed a method of making printing plates directly from photographs. He resigned his position and went to England, where he patented the process under the name *photogalvanography*. He set up a printing company to exploit his invention commercially, with Roger Fenton as chief photographer and photographic manager. Their first publication, issued in parts in 1856–1857, was *Photographic Art Treasures, or Nature and Art Illustrated by Art and Nature*. It consisted of landscapes, still lifes, and architectural views by leading English photographers, and photographic reproductions of paintings and sculptures. It was the first book produced by photoengraving, and the quality of its reproductions amazed the public. These illustrations and others were also offered as individual prints suitable for framing or preservation in an album or portfolio.

Pretsch's company did not succeed commercially, largely because it was bitterly opposed by William Henry Fox Talbot, who claimed that the process violated his patented *photoglyphy*. There was in fact no violation, but Pretsch was unprepared for the expense and effort of what seemed to him an uncertain court battle. He dissolved the company and returned to Austria in 1863. The lapsed patent was subsequently exploited in a modified form by Pretsch's assistant, Campbell Dallas, as the *dallastype*.
See also: PHOTOGALVANOGRAPHY; PHOTOGLYPHY; TALBOT, W. H. F.

Previsualization

Many photographers—especially photographers working in black and white—find that they can create a mental image of a desired final print as they are examining a subject before photographing it. This act of *previsualization* results from an integration of thoroughly mastered technique with a perception of the unique qualities of the subject and an understanding of the print qualities that will convey this perception with the greatest expressive power. The objective problems of technique are primarily those of selecting exposure, development, and printing to produce the clarity and emphasis of tone and detail that the photographer's subjective response to the subject calls for. The faculty of previsualization evolves only from direct experience with the materials and processes of the medium and from involved concern with effective use of its expressive potential. The term arose in the writings and work of Edward Weston and Ansel Adams. It has been used by photographers working in a great many styles, but its fundamental application is to artistically intended work done in a straightforward, unmanipulated, realistic manner.
See also: POSTVISUALIZATION.

Primary Colors

See: ADDITIVE COLOR SYNTHESIS; COLOR.

Primoli, Count Giuseppe Napoleone

Italian; 1851–1927
Giuseppe Primoli and his younger brother, Luigi (1858–1925), were typical of the gentlemen photographers of their day: talented amateurs with the financial means to indulge a hobby without regard for its expense. Of the two, the work of Giuseppe, who only began to take pictures at the age of 38, was by far the most extensive and interesting. Of his more than 30,000 photographs, about 13,000 have survived, preserved at the Fondazione Primoli in Rome. They include portraits of French and Italian aristocracy and pictures of major social and cultural events from 1888 onwards. With immense energy, Primoli pursued subjects and situations to which most professionals had little or no access, and recorded them with a technical skill and visual talent superior to that of most of his amateur and professional contemporaries.

Count Giuseppe Primoli was born into a noble family from the Marches in central Italy, a direct descendant on his mother's side of the Bonapartes. The family moved to France when Napoleon III became emperor, and were part of the highest levels of Parisian social and cultural life. Primoli, more a boulevardier than a political figure, was an habitué of the most fashionable salon in Paris, conducted by his aunt, Princess Mathilde Bonaparte. There he met, and arranged to photograph, Charles Gounod, Alexandre Dumas fils, Guy de Maupassant, Théophile Gautier, the Goncourt brothers, and many other leading writers, artists, and social figures of the late 19th c.

Primoli was perhaps the world's first press photographer before that profession even came into being, for his social standing got him a front-row position at all the major events of his time and he recorded them avidly with his camera: Thomas Edison at the Eiffel Tower at the time of the Universal Exhibition; the wedding of the Italian Crown Prince in 1888; May Day parades with red flags aflutter; chained convicts being marched off to prison; performances at the French Consérvatoire, and of *Parsifal* at Bayreuth. His Italian street scenes were full of life, his takeoffs on the serious "art" pictures of amateurs humorous, and many of his portraits of celebrities such as Sarah Bernhardt, Eleanora Duse, and Annie Oakley, creatively unconventional.

Most of what is known of Primoli's life and work is contained in Lamberto Vitali's book, *Un Fotografo Fin de Siècle, il Conte Primoli*. There, and in the picture files at the Primoli Foundation, is evidence that his style heralded a kind of photography that would be used brilliantly in the 20th c. by such as Jacques-Henri Lartigue and Henri Cartier-Bresson. It is one of the regrettable caprices of time and history that his work is so little known.
Photograph: p. 374.

Primuline Process

The first practical process of printing diazo images used the dye Primuline yellow; it was invented in the U.S. in 1890, by A. Green, C. F. Cross, and R. Bevan. The light sensitivity of diazo compounds had been reported in 1881 by French chemists, and experimental diazo printing had been demonstrated in 1885. In the 1890 process, fabric was impregnated with primuline solution and treated with nitrous acid, which converted the primuline to a diazo compound. Exposure to sunlight under a line image destroyed the dye-forming potential in exposed areas. A selection of alkaline solutions permitted developing the unexposed lines to red, orange, purple, black, or brown. The original process was not sensitive enough to print from continuous tone or halftone images, or to give unmuddied images on paper.
See also: DIAZO PROCESSES.

Printed Circuits

Printed circuits are layouts, often highly miniaturized, of electrical connections among components on the surface of a plaque or chip of insulating material. Originally the circuits actually were printed with an electrically-conductive ink. The printing plate was prepared by photocopying procedures from a large-scale master inked pattern. Although still called printed circuits, most such devices now are not produced with inks, but with photoresists and a variety of photofabrication procedures. They are relatively simple to design, fast to produce, uniformly high in quality, and far more troublefree than wired circuits. They also permit a degree of miniaturization impossible to obtain with wiring.
See also: PHOTOFABRICATION; PHOTORESIST.

Print Finishing

The term print finishing encompasses techniques for changing the appearance of a print after chemical processing, and for displaying the print.

With glossy fiber-base papers, print finishing begins with the drying technique used. If these papers are dried on drying racks or in blotting paper, they will have a smooth finish, but one without the glazed look seen on prints intended for commercial reproduction. If a high-gloss look is desired, it must be given to the print through ferrotyping, which consists of drying the print against chrome-plated metal. Resin-coated papers, whether for black-and-white or color printing, dry naturally to a high-gloss finish.

In some cases a print curls somewhat during drying. This is much more likely to happen with fiber-base papers. If the print is to be matted or dry-mounted, this is not much of a problem. Otherwise, the print can be dried between sheets of weighted-down blotting paper. If an already dry print has too much of a curl, the back of the print can be dampened and the print can be dried again while weighted down, or it can be soaked in a commercially available print-flattening solution and dried. Some prints will have small white marks caused by dust or other materials on the negative during printing. These are eliminated by a technique called spotting—the addition of a colored dye to make the spots blend into the image. Sometimes there are black spots on a print. These can be removed by an etching knife, and the resulting white spot can then be spotted.

Dyes and other coloring materials can be used for retouching a print. Retouching can produce a variety of effects. It can conceal defects, give more natural-looking tone or coloration, or give an artificial, painted look to the image. At one time retouching with oil colors was often used to color black-and-white portraits. Colors are often added to prints for artistic or graphic purposes—to achieve surrealistic effects, for example. In such cases almost anything from conventional retouching colors to felt-tipped pens can be used to obtain the desired results.

Various products are available to add a texture effect to a print after the processing stage. These include lacquers or other liquid or gelatin substances that can be sprayed or spread onto a print. Brushes, palette knives, or texture rollers can be used with these materials to give the print the desired look. Prints are also sometimes lacquered (with lacquers designed for photographic purposes) for protection.

Prints are often dry- or wet-mounted or matted for exhibition purposes. Dry-mounting consists of using a mounting tissue to attach a print to a mounting board. In some cases, heat must be applied (as with a dry-mounting press) to make the print adhere. In other cases it is sufficient simply to apply pressure. Wet-mounting is done with liquid pastes or glues or spray-on adhesives. In matting, the print is attached to a backing board which then is covered with another board that has a cutout opening the size of the print. Matted or unmatted prints may also be framed in many ways.
See also: DRYING FILMS AND PRINTS; FERROTYPING; FRAMING; MOUNTING PHOTOGRAPHS; PAINTING ON PHOTOGRAPHS; RETOUCHING; SPOTTING.

Printing, Black-and-White

Making a high-quality print from a black-and-white negative (or from a color negative on black-and-white paper with a special panchromatic emulsion) involves an interaction between technique and subjective evaluation of the results at various steps in the process. The techniques of contact printing and enlarging, and related procedures, are discussed in the entries listed as cross-references; some general considerations are discussed here.

An image commonly is chosen for printing from examination of a contact sheet or other proof print. On a properly made proof sheet, images that have been misexposed or misdeveloped will be distinct from other images by being too light, being too dark, or having very abnormal contrast. Unless the content is of great importance, such images should be rejected. If they must be considered, the negatives should be examined to evaluate whether special treatment such as reduction or intensification might make them more easily printable. The negatives of images that seem slightly out of focus should also be examined. Sometimes the unsharpness results from the negative not being in complete contact with the paper when the proof is made; this is frequently the case when a contact sheet is made without removing the film strips from transparent plastic sleeves in which they are stored.

Once an image is selected for printing, a sample print is made using a paper contrast grade and an exposure determined by test strips or an enlarging-meter reading. The print should be at the intended degree of enlargement, should show the entire image area, and should be made with a single exposure, without burning-in or dodging.

Careful evaluation of this first print can decide—or begin to decide—several important factors. The darker tones indicate whether there is proper contrast. If they are muddy or are merged in a single tone, higher contrast is needed. The lighter tones reveal whether the print received too much or too little exposure, by being too dark or too light, respectively. If the exposure is about right, the brightest highlight areas will indicate whether burning-in is required to produce traces of detail or tone. If either contrast or exposure, or both, seems wrong, it must be adjusted before the other basic factors can be evaluated meaningfully. Test strips made on different grades of paper to determine contrast are equally as useful as those made to determine exposure. Exposure test strips at this stage, or more probably at later stages, are also valuable in determining the timing of burning-in and dodging that may be required in various areas.

In addition to contrast and exposure, the first print should be examined in terms of its size; it may become clear that a larger or smaller image would be more effective. Finally, this print can be used to determine whether cropping might improve the composition. Although many photographers crop enlargements by observing the negative image projected on the paper easel, only a positive image makes it possible to evaluate the effect on composition of variations in background tones, or to judge the subtle differences that often result from moving an edge slightly closer to or farther from the main subject.

The subsequent steps in printing consist of making a series of prints, each of which incorporates the changes and improvements indicated by close examination of the previous attempt, until the desired final result is obtained. The same general process is followed when unusual or manipulated rather than straightforward printing techniques are used. However, evaluation is often more difficult because the expressive effect of experimental variations in technique can be judged only by making different prints and comparing them. In making a solarized (Sabattier effect) print, for example, basic exposure, development time, developer dilution, and the intensity and length of re-exposure all may be varied. The range of combinations can be enormous. Only methodical, carefully recorded procedures will make it possible to arrive at a controlled rather than an accidental final result.

The conventional processing steps—development, stop bath, fixing, and washing—may be followed by special treatments that affect the image. The most common of these is toning, which may alter the color of the image, or may provide long-term (archival) protection with little or no visible effect. The procedures of drying, spotting or retouching, and mounting, matting, and framing, are considered part of the supplementary process called *print finishing*.
See also: ARCHIVAL PROCESSING; BLACK-AND-WHITE PROCESSING; BURNING-IN; CONTACT PRINTING; CONTRAST; DODGING; DRYING FILMS AND PRINTS; ENLARGING: PAPERS, PHOTO-

GRAPHIC; PRINT FINISHING; PRINT QUALITY; PROCESSING FILMS AND PRINTS; PROOF PRINTS; TONE REPRODUCTION; WASHING.

Printing, Color

Modern materials and processes make it as easy to produce prints from color negatives or transparencies as it is to produce them from black-and-white negatives. Color printing differs primarily from black-and-white printing in that filters are used during exposure to adjust the color balance of the image, and some materials require more solutions and processing steps. Color printing is also slower than black-and-white printing, because image development requires more time and because some papers must be dried before the color qualities of the image can be evaluated accurately.

There are four kinds of materials and processes for making direct color prints.

1. *Negative paper*, which is exposed to a color negative and processed in developer, stop bath, and bleach-fix solutions.

2. *Reversal paper*, which is exposed to a positive color transparency and processed in first developer, stop bath, second (color) developer, bleach-fix, and stabilizer solutions.

3. *Dye-destruction (silver-bleach) paper*, which is exposed to a color transparency and processed in developer, bleach, and fix solutions.

4. *Diffusion transfer films*, which are exposed to a color negative or transparency (a different type of film in each case), soaked in an activator solution, and laminated with a print paper until the image has transferred.

There is also one major indirect color printing method: the *dye transfer process*. It is indirect because the print paper is not exposed to a color image. Instead, black-and-white separation negatives are made from the color negative or transparency. These are used to make gelatin-relief matrix images which absorb dyes and transfer them to the final print sheet.

Because direct-printing color materials are sensitive to all colors of light, printing and processing must be carried out in total darkness for optimum results. A few materials can be handled for a limited time under a very weak safelight fitted with a dark-brown filter. Processing can be carried out with trays, motor-driven drums, or tubes. Some tubes have lighttight caps so they can be used in full light once the paper has been loaded in, and some are agitated by motors rather than by hand. Processing

is generally carried out at temperatures in the 80–100°F (approximately 27–38°C) range. At the 68–70°F (20–21°C) temperature used for black-and-white processing, color development takes from 11 to 20 minutes or more. Diffusion transfer materials require a light-tight soaking container and laminating rollers.

Color print materials can be exposed either additively or subtractively. In additive color printing exposures are made through red, green, and blue filters. Most color printing is done by subtractive exposure using cyan, magenta, and yellow filters. These filters are placed in the path of white light from a single source to adjust its color balance according to the requirements of the image being printed. A maximum of two subtractive filters are used at any one time; if all three colors are used, whatever density they have in common adds up to neutral density, which reduces the light intensity without altering its color balance. Enlargers designed for subtractive color printing have built-in dichroic filters to color the light. The density of each color can be set by a dial or other control. Other enlargers can be used by inserting color filters in the lamphouse or beneath the lens. Color printing (CP) filters of acetate are used along with a heat-absorbing glass in the lamphouse. Gelatin color-correction (CC) filters are used in front of the lens. CP filters do not have sufficient optical quality to be used in the image path; CC filters are too heat-sensitive to be used in the lamphouse. The color and degree of filtration required is determined from the basic recommendations given by the paper manufacturer and by test prints. Color imbalance in a print is the result of an excess of one or two primary colors; it is corrected by adjusting the printing filtration to remove those colors. In negative-positive printing a color is removed from a print by adding the same color to the filter pack or by subtracting the complementary color. This procedure works because the colors in the negative are the opposites of those in the positive image. In reversal color printing a color is removed from a print by subtracting that color from the filter pack or by adding the complementary color.

Detailed instructions for color printing are given in a number of manuals and darkroom handbooks (see Appendix) and in the instructions supplied with sets of processing chemicals. Two accessories are especially valuable in making color printing simple and easy. One is a filter grid or similar device placed over the print paper for a test print exposure. It helps to determine both the exposure

time and the filtration required for a good quality print. The other accessory is a print evaluation kit, consisting of a set of CC filters through which a sample print is viewed and instructions for determining how to adjust the printing filtration to correct any color deficiencies in the print.

See also: ADDITIVE COLOR PRINTING; COLOR; COLOR MATERIALS; DIFFUSION TRANSFER PROCESS; DYE DESTRUCTION PROCESS; DYE TRANSFER PROCESS; REVERSAL MATERIALS AND PROCESSING; SUBTRACTIVE COLOR SYNTHESIS.

Printing-Out Paper (P.O.P.)

During most of the 19th c., photographers developed negatives and positive glass-plate transparencies, but made prints on papers that produced an image solely by the action of exposure, without need for a chemical solution. This procedure, called *printing-out*, was both necessary and practical. Until the last decade of the century, few papers were sensitive enough to be exposed by common artificial light sources (kerosene and gas lamps); sunlight was required, and printing exposures were long enough that clock timing was not necessary. Instead, the image was inspected from time to time to see how the printing-out was proceeding; thus, prints seldom had to be discarded because of underexposure. Contact-printing frames had two-section locking backs; one section could be opened and the paper peeled back from the negative while the other section remained locked to keep the negative and print paper clamped together in register. In commercial photo-printing establishments printing-out papers eliminated the need for extensive darkroom facilities, and they permitted using relatively unskilled help who had only to load and unload the frames, and fix and wash the prints.

The image color of printing-out paper was a rather unpleasant purplish red-brown; it could be toned to a purple-black after fixing. Portrait photographers submitted proofs to customers on unfixed printing-out paper that would darken completely in a week or two. This prevented a customer's keeping the proofs as "good enough," and not ordering finished prints. Only one or two portrait-proof printing-out papers are available today. They were supplanted by developing-out papers for most kinds of photography at the beginning of the 20th c. Some high-speed, very high contrast printing-out papers are now used to record instrument traces and displays, but they have no general-purpose applications.

Print Quality

Evaluation of photographic print quality is a matter of evaluating the total expressive effectiveness of a great many tangible and intangible factors. It is relatively easy, and quite common, to speak of print quality only in terms of objective technical factors. These include contrast, tonal richness or color saturation, sharpness, balance or evenness of exposure, and freedom from flaws such as dust spots, fingermarks, and scratches. Without question these are of fundamental importance; a print that is not technically excellent can never be a high-quality print. But quality is also a matter of how well the elements of a print fulfill the expressive intent of the photographer. Thus, there is a subjective aspect of print quality that has to do with whether the tone or color scale used is the most effective or appropriate; whether the size of the image, the tint of the paper base, and the emulsion surface or texture are the best expressive choice; and similar considerations. Although these are physical factors, their relation to print quality is a matter of their effect on what is communicated.

To a straight, or purist photographer, a fine print is most often one in which there is a full range of tones from black to white (or an equivalent color range), sharpness throughout, and fully rendered detail in shadows and highlights as well as in middletone areas, all adding up to an intense impression of realism. To a more expressionistically oriented photographer, the highest quality print may require a range of only a few tones or colors, perhaps of an exaggerated or distorted character (e.g., negative; solarized) or that have no direct relationship to original subject values, creating an effect that is far from realistic but is no less intense than that of the straight print. Again, a pictorial photographer may regard a fine print as one that achieves a highly painterly effect, with an illusionistic imitation of brushstrokes or other physical characteristics as well as of color qualities.

No matter what the diversity of their expressive aims may be, photographers generally agree that high print quality first and foremost requires clarity. Assuming that camera angle, framing, composition, and other factors of visual selection and arrangement are as desired, expressive clarity in a print begins with tonality. Tones or colors that are not fully rendered cannot be the most expressive. This does not mean that there must be a full scale, or that all tones must have maximum saturation. Low-key and high-key pictures require quite limited tonal scales, but each tone must be clear-ly rendered. Over- or underexposure of negative or print cannot produce these ranges, they simply blur and mix tones unclearly. Even when a musician slurs a passage to blend the effect, the sound of each note is distinct. Similarly, photographic tones must be distinct. To print an image of muddy conditions requires individual tones that render each of the different values of mud, not a muddy (weak, undifferentiated) mixture of tones. The analogy holds for subtle effects, such as pastels or faint traces of gray tone that make highlights seem to glow. A musician achieves a delicate effect by playing very quietly, not by playing weakly; a photographer achieves a delicate effect by using materials and techniques that produce tonal values that are convincingly "quiet," not simply visually weak.

Factors that control tonal clarity. The three factors that control tonal clarity are focus, exposure, and processing; they may be supplemented by the use of filters or by the choice of paper contrast grade, but they are fundamental. Various aspects of tonal clarity are discussed more fully in the entries on tone/tonality and on tone reproduction. Briefly, the major considerations are these:

An out-of-focus image has degraded tones because details are blurred together so that their values mix. This is a critical factor in enlarging: the grain of the image must be sharply focused onto the paper emulsion so that the maximum amount of information recorded by the negative is transferred to the positive. Using a focusing magnifier, and setting the enlarger lens for its optimum sharpness (usually two or three f-stops less than wide open) are important. Over- or underexposure of a negative loses highlight or shadow values, respectively, and shifts other tones up or down the scale. The photographer may choose to do this deliberately. Overexposure of a print crowds dark tones together and makes other tones look muddy because they are too dark. Underexposure of a print crowds the lightest tones into featureless white and makes other tones look weak and insubstantial. Improper processing also loses tones or gives them weak or unconvincing values. While paper contrast grade and printing techniques such as burning-in and dodging can be used for expressive control to achieve a high-quality print, that is not the case with a poor negative. Then such techniques must be used simply to get a printable image; there is no leeway in which to use them creatively.

From the first steps in making a picture through printing and finishing, the most important factors in obtaining high print quality are the following:

Solid camera support, best-quality lens, precise focusing — every precaution against unwanted lack of sharpness is important.

Largest film format possible — both tonality and sharpness are affected by enlargement. The loss is slight in many cases, but it is minimized by keeping the degree of enlargement required as small as possible.

Accurate exposure to record tones or colors in the desired way — what is not recorded on the negative cannot be reproduced in the print. Accurately calibrated meters and shutters, and knowledgeable use of filters are important at this stage.

Fresh film and processing solutions; accurate temperature measurement and control; accurate timing; consistent, repeatable processing techniques.

Clean, dust-free film drying and printing conditions.

Vibration-free enlarger mounting; highest-quality lens; even illumination of enlarger field; parallel alignment of negative stage, lens board, and paper easel; voltage control for constant brightness during exposure.

Fresh paper and solutions; accurate exposure tests; optimum processing; careful washing and drying—protective toning, as for archival processing, generally enriches the tonal quality of black-and-white prints.

Careful spotting of dust specks and other minute imperfections; appropriate trimming and mounting.

The craft aspects of photography—using the best-quality materials and equipment, and using proper techniques with meticulous care—are one part of achieving the best quality, and in fact the easiest part. The more difficult part is learning to see what true print quality is and to evaluate one's own work objectively. This is a matter of studying the prints of as many photographers as possible, comparing their qualities, and putting one's own efforts up against them. The first step is to learn to look beyond subject matter, to look with an eye that asks, "What is being shown here, and how well?" Informed, critical seeing develops slowly, over a long period of time. It requires patience and conscious effort to develop, and results in a constant desire to do more, more effectively, each time one makes a print. *See also:* ARCHIVAL PROCESSING; CONTRAST; TONE REPRODUCTION; TONE, TONALITY.

Prisms (SLR). Image (F) is laterally reversed but upright as reflected from mirror behind lens up to viewing screen. Reflection from slanted faces of prism roof keeps image upright but presents it laterally corrected to eyepiece.

Prisms

Pentaprism in Single-Lens Reflex Viewing System

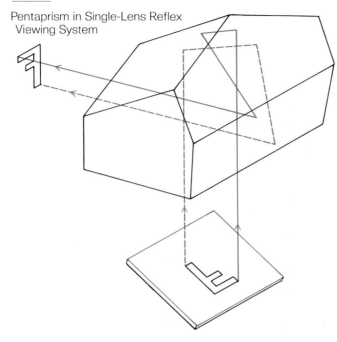

Prisms

A prism is a reflecting and refracting device composed of a solid block of optical glass or plastic with two or more flat surfaces. The angular relationships of the surfaces, or faces, of a prism determine its optical action. When a band of white light is directed into a triangular prism at less than the critical angle, it emerges dispersed into a spectrum display of its constituent wavelengths. At the critical angle or greater, the light is reflected without dispersion. Some prisms have one or more silvered faces so as to reflect light from the entire range of acceptance angles. Prisms are used in place of mirrors in many optical devices because, being solid, the angle between reflecting surfaces is unchangeable, even with the roughest handling. In binoculars and camera viewing systems, prisms are used to shorten the optical path to provide compactness without affecting focal length, and to provide images that are laterally or vertically corrected, or both. Prisms that are partially transmitting and partially reflective are used to combine or divide optical paths in rangefinders, photometers, densitometers, beam splitters, and similar devices. Two of the most common photographic uses of prisms are shown in the diagrams.

See also: BEAM SPLITTER; DISPERSION; INCIDENCE, ANGLE OF; MIRROR; REFLECTANCE/REFLECTION; REFRACTION.

Process Camera; Process Lens

A *process camera* is a precision copying camera used to make continuous-tone and screened negatives and positives for photomechanical reproduction. It consists of a copyboard, lensboard, bellows, and film chamber. These are interconnected by drive mechanisms that move them to the necessary positions when a control indicator is set to any given percentage size of reproduction. Copyboard lighting units may also be interconnected and automatically positioned

to maintain a constant image brightness at the film plane at all reproduction scales. The smallest film or plate size is 8″ × 10″ (20.3 × 25.4cm) or 16″ × 20″ (40.6 × 50.8cm), and may be 48″ × 48″ (121.9 × 121.9cm) or larger. Film is held flat by a vacuum back, or by a glass pressure plate over its face. In some designs the film chamber is an opening in a darkroom wall; this permits loading and unloading film without the need for cumbersome holders with giant darkslides. Other camera models have a vertical construction, like a typical copy stand or motion-picture animation stand. There is provision for inserting a halftone screen in front of the film, and rotating it to various angles to avoid moiré in multiple-plate reproduction. Exposure is controlled by a series of fixed-aperture Waterhouse stop plates, or by a precision iris diaphragm marked in degrees or aperture diameters rather than *f*-numbers. The actual exposure is made by an automatic timer or, more commonly, by an integrating meter and control system; both arrangements turn the copyboard lights on and off as required.

The *process lens* used with such a camera is an apochromat (three-color corrected) for maximum sharpness and flatness of field. It is corrected for use over a reproduction range of about 0.25× to 10× or more. The lensboard and standard, and all other camera components, are massive to resist the slightest vibration. They are machined to extreme tolerances to maintain precise alignment over years of use.

See also: APOCHROMAT; INTEGRATING METER; PHOTOMECHANICAL REPRODUCTION; VACUUM BACK/VACUUM EASEL; WATERHOUSE STOP.

Process Colors

Most photomechanical reproduction color processes achieve their effects by printing various amounts of three standard colors of ink, plus black. The colors are those that are the basis of subtractive color: cyan, magenta, and yellow. The first two are often referred to as "process blue," and "process red," a usage that is well understood within the printing industry but often confusing to outsiders. The color absorption and reflection characteristics of process color inks are defined in national and international standards. Some ink and printing concerns define other key or reference colors by specified mixes of two or three process colors; these are sometimes—inaccurately—also called process colors.

See also: PHOTOMECHANICAL REPRODUCTION; SUBTRACTIVE COLOR SYNTHESIS.

Rangefinder

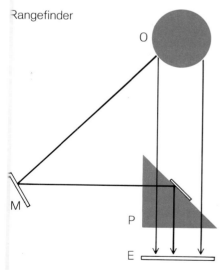

Prisms (Rangefinder). Prism, P. passes direct rays from object, O, but reflective center section shows image from mirror, M, which moves as lens is focused at various distances. When the images match in eyepiece, E, lens is sharply focused on object.

Processing Films and Prints

Photographic processing is accomplished in two stages. In the first the latent image of the exposed film emerges in the form of a negative, in which the light and dark areas of the original scene are reversed. In the second stage the negative is turned into a positive image, in which the light and dark areas again correspond to the scene as it was photographed. With black-and-white and color negative film the positive image is produced as a print on printing paper which has been exposed with an enlarger or contact printer. When color reversal film (used for slides) is processed, the negative image is turned into a positive on the film itself, although a print subsequently can be made if desired.

Black-and-White Film. The processing of conventional black-and-white films is comparatively simple. With roll film complete darkness is required only to load the film into daylight developing tanks. The processing itself then can be performed with room lights on. In addition, the working temperature required for the chemical baths is generally easy to maintain. The standard recommended temperature is 68°F (20°C), although a certain amount of latitude is permitted.

In the developing solution the exposed silver halide particles in the film emulsion are reduced to metallic silver in the shades of gray and black that compose the negative image. Control over development is based on giving the film the length of development appropriate for the solution temperature. During development, and during each subsequent chemical treatment, there must be an adequate amount of agitation to ensure uniform chemical activity.

Development is followed by a stop-bath treatment or water rinse to stop the action of the developer. The stop bath is a weak acid solution which neutralizes the alkalinity of the developer. A water rinse can be adequate when long development times make precise control less critical. However, a stop bath is more effective in quickly arresting development and in preventing contamination of the fixer.

At this point there are still unreduced, and thus light-sensitive, silver halides in the emulsion. They must be eliminated if the image is to be permanent, and this is accomplished by the fixing bath. After the halides are dissolved by the fixer, the film can be exposed to light without any further change in the image. For film processing it is advisable that a fixer with a hardening agent be used for protection of the delicate emulsion.

For the image to be truly permanent, the chemical residues from processing must be washed away. Washing is much quicker and more effective if a washing aid (also known as a hypo eliminator) is used prior to the wash period. As a last step before drying, the film is often treated with a wetting agent to prevent water spots.

Chromogenic black-and-white films produce a negative image composed of a dye rather than metallic silver. In this respect they are similar to color negative films, and they are processed in the same manner. Printing procedures are the same as for other black-and-white films.

Black-and-White Prints. Black-and-white print processing is quite straightforward. Tray processing is a simple matter, since all of the steps can be performed with the use of an appropriately filtered safelight. Black-and-white printing papers each have optimum development times which do not change as long as the developing solution is within a few degrees of the usually recommended 68 to 70°F (20 to 21°C).

It is important to use a stop bath after development to stop development and to prolong the life of the fixer. A water rinse should not be used for prints. The time required for proper fixing is much shorter for resin-coated papers than for fiber-base papers. With the latter, adequate fixing is more difficult to achieve, and two fixing baths are often employed to ensure that a sufficient amount of fresh fixer is acting upon the emulsion. For prints a non-hardening fixer is often desirable. A hardening agent can impede the effect of toners and spotting dye, and it can increase the wash time for fiber-base papers.

Since resin-coated papers resist water absorption, the washing process is simple and a washing aid is not needed. A wash period of 5 minutes, or even less, is sufficient if the print receives an adequate flow of fresh water. Fiber-base papers must be washed much more carefully, and a washing-aid treatment is essential. Resin-coated papers dry quickly without curling and thus can be dried on any clean, dry surface. Fiber-base papers can be dried with heat dryers, with blotting paper, or on drying racks. Racks provide the least risk of contamination if they are kept clean. Because of their coating, resin-coated papers should not be heat dried.

Color Films. Color film processing requires special care in maintaining the correct temperature, which is commonly higher than in black-and-white processing, and in timing the length of each chemical treatment. Color roll films can be processed in the same kind of daylight tanks used for black-and-white films. The actual number of steps required for processing color film depends on the particular process being used. In all cases agitation instructions must be followed carefully.

The emulsion of both color negative and color reversal film contains silver halides and color-coupling agents. Development of color negative film reduces the exposed halides to darkened silver, and at the same time it acts on the couplers to produce image dyes.

After development the film is bleached to remove the silver. The negative image then consists of the superimposed dyes in the emulsion layers. The film is washed, fixed (in some systems the bleaching and fixing are combined in one treatment), and washed again. In most cases a stabilizing treatment is given to protect the dye colors from deterioration. The final negative often has an orange-brown color, which is actually a mask to facilitate proper color rendition in printing.

The first development of color reversal film also produces a darkened silver negative image, but the dyes are not yet released. After this initial development the film is given a reversal bath which has the effect of exposing, or "fogging," the unexposed silver halides and developing them to form a positive silver image and an accompanying color dye image. The film is treated with a conditioner so that the silver images can be converted to silver salts in the bleaching that follows. After fixing, these salts are washed away along with other chemical residues. The dyes are stabilized as the last step before drying.

Color prints. Color prints can be processed in trays, but they commonly are processed in cylindrical tubes. Thus, once the tube has been loaded, processing can be accomplished with the lights on. Proper agitation is critical, and in most cases relatively high chemical temperatures must be maintained.

When a color negative is printed, development of the printing paper produces a black-and-white image and releases a color dye in three layers, just as with color film. Development is followed by a stop-bath treatment (this step is omitted in some processing systems). The subsequent steps are a bleach-fix treatment, which leaves only the color image, and the final wash.

There are two basic systems for processing prints made from color transparencies. The conventional method is a reversal process which includes a first developer, stop bath, color developer, bleach-fix, and stabilizer, with frequent wash periods required between the various steps. The dye-destruction process has fewer steps. The emulsion of the paper contain fully-formed dyes. The print is developed once, then rinsed and bleached to remove the portions of the dyes not needed for the image. The print then is fixed and given a final wash.

There are also two major special processing methods. Diffusion transfer processing is used for instant films and for some color printing materials. Activation and activation-stabilization processing are used for rapid processing of black-and-white prints. Both processes require special films or papers and specialized cameras or processors.

See also: ARCHIVAL PROCESSING; BLACK-AND-WHITE PROCESSING; BLACK-AND-WHITE MATERIALS; COLOR MATERIALS; DEVELOPMENT; DIFFUSION TRANSFER PROCESS; DYE DESTRUCTION PROCESS; FILMS; FIXING; PAPERS, PHOTOGRAPHIC; PRINTING, BLACK-AND-WHITE; PRINTING, COLOR; RAPID PROCESSING; STABILIZATION PROCESS; STOP BATH.

Processing for Permanence

See: ARCHIVAL PROCESSING.

Product Photography

Photographs in which manufactured products are the main subject are used in advertisements, catalogs, brochures, instruction manuals, and similar publications. They are also used in posters and point-of-sale display materials, and on packages to show what is contained within. Informational applications require clear, straightforward product photographs that show the color, shape, materials, and construction of the item; these are often called "nuts and bolts" or "needle and thread" pictures. Advertising and sales applications generally require photographs that enhance the appearance of the product; that dramatize it (a "glamour shot"); or that show it in a context that suggests the tangible or intangible benefits it offers. "Benefit" pictures often show the product in use.

Product photography is most often done in the studio, where lighting and other important factors can be totally controlled. Some pictures showing a product in the environment in which it is used—e.g., a motorboat—must be taken on location, but the vast majority, whether of a truck or a computer microchip, are taken in the studio, often with a great deal of effort to create a setting that appears to be on location. The photographer commonly works from a layout supplied by an art director if the picture is more than just a simple recording of a single item against a plain background. The layout may be any-

thing from a rough sketch to a highly detailed color drawing, or a "comp" (comprehensive presentation) that shows how the illustration will be integrated with text material or other elements. With products of medium and small size, the basic task is one of still-life photography, with the composition or arrangement designed for the camera's point of view. The most common equipment is a 4″ × 5″ or larger format view camera. The large film size provides a high quality image for reproduction, especially in the case of color transparencies, and one that is easy to retouch if necessary. The camera adjustments offer maximum control over distortion, depth of field, and related factors.

Lighting. While creating a setting for a product and building the desired composition are often time-consuming, the most important factor in product photography is lighting. The quality and direction of the light define form, texture, and volume, reveal color, and may create mood in the picture. Distinctly different techniques are required for glassware, for highly reflective items such as silverware and chrome-plated appliances, and for products made of a variety of other materials. The problem of lighting an arrangement of several products is far more complex than that of lighting one, especially if they have different characteristics (e.g., an arrangement of wineglasses, fruit, bread, and silverware). Many successful product photographers, while skilled in several areas, are specialists with one category of product such as food, tools and hardware, or glassware. This is quite natural, for although the picture ideas may be different, the basic technical problems in photographing jars and bottles, for example, are the same whether they contain perfume, hair tonic, soft drinks, or pickles.

All kinds of light sources are used for product photography. Continuous-output instruments make it easy to see the effect produced without the need for test shots; electronic flash is essential with perishable products such as ice cream, to avoid the effects of accumulated heat. Frontal lighting ratios are relatively low, usually no more more than 4:1, to obtain an image with the best contrast characteristics for reproduction; a strong backlight is common to emphasize the edges of the product and separate it distinctly from the background. Catalogs and instruction manuals often require special-technique pictures such as silhouettes, backgroundless or shadowless views, exploded views, or phantom views. The cross-reference entries will provide information about various

techniques that are particularly useful in product photography.

See also: ADVERTISING PHOTOGRAPHY; BACKGROUNDS; CLOSE-UP PHOTOGRAPHY; EXPLODED VIEWS; GLARE AND REFLECTIONS; GLASS, PHOTOGRAPHING; LIGHTING; PAINTING WITH LIGHT; PHANTOM VIEW; SHADOWLESS LIGHTING; SILHOUETTE; STILL LIFE PHOTOGRAPHY; STUDIO PHOTOGRAPHY; TENT LIGHTING; TEXTURE; UMBRELLA LIGHTING.

Color photograph: p. C-47.

Professional Photography

By definition, professional photography is the business of making photographic images as a main source of income. Usually professional photographers work for specific clients. Staff photographers make their pictures on a more or less exclusive basis for a specific organization or agency which sometimes owns the publication rights of the pictures made. A number of magazines and newspapers have their own photographic staffs.

Freelance photographers work for clients of their choosing on a per-assignment basis and often retain ownership of their photographs; the client may be given first-time or limited-use rights to the photographs. The main advantage of freelance photography is that the photographer may work for more than one client during any given period; the disadvantage lies in the lack of a guaranteed income. Many publications and corporations make extensive use of freelance photographers, as do picture and press agencies.

By far the largest group of professionals are those who are self-employed either as freelance workers or as specialists in various fields such as commercial illustration, portraiture, child and wedding photography, architectural photography, and the like. In the U.S. any photographer can operate as a professional in almost all locations, subject only to ordinary state and local business regulations. Government agencies at various levels often require certification by examination or approved training for staff photographers. In many other parts of the world, especially in Europe, a photographic business may be operated only by a fully licensed professional; in some cases employees of such businesses must also be certified at certain levels of training or competence.

See also: FREELANCE PHOTOGRAPHY.

Programmed Exposure

See: AUTOMATIC EXPOSURE CONTROL.

Projection

The presentation of still or moving photographic images by projection permits viewing by groups of up to several hundred people. Under proper conditions—a darkened room with no stray light falling on the screen—the projected image of a transparency can have a much greater brightness range and longer tonal or color scale than can be obtained with a print. Modern control devices used with two or more projectors permit continuous presentation of still images from slides with no unnecessary blank-screen intervals, and with dynamic visual linkages such as superimposures, dissolves, and fade-out fade-in transitions. Overhead projectors permit use of opaque as well as transparent materials, and make it possible to alter the image by drawing, writing, or inserting or removing elements while it is being shown.

Good projection technique calls for the equipment and screen to be set up, aligned, and focused, and the volume of accompanying sound to be set, before the arrival of the audience. Whenever possible the projector(s) should be located behind the last row of the audience. Equipment that produces significant operating noise should be placed in a separate booth or at least isolated as much as possible with sound-absorbing screens. For informational presentations with words and numbers included in some images, the most distant audience member ought to be no farther from the screen that eight times the height (8H) of the projected image. This distance can be extended up to 14H if the written material is above minimum size (*see* VISUAL AIDS) or if the presentation is entirely pictorial, especially if it is primarily entertaining in content.

Viewing Area. The width of the audience area will be determined by the screen surface characteristics. The major limiting factor is the fall-off in image brightness for viewing positions to either side of the projection axis. This can be checked with a reflected-light exposure meter that permits spot (small area) readings; a telephoto lens on a camera with a built-in meter provides this capability. Readings should be taken with no film in the projector, from a middle audience distance on the projection axis and from various side angles. The side viewing limits are the points at which the reading is one-half to two-thirds of an *f*-stop less than the center reading. (A difference of a full *f*-stop represents a 50 percent loss of image brightness, which is too much under almost all conditions.) When two projectors are to be used independently on two screens placed side-by-side, the greatest amount of useful audience area is obtained by angling the screens slightly so that the right-hand projector is aimed directly at the left-hand screen, and the left-hand projector at the right-hand screen.

Projection distance. The projector-to-screen distance required for a desired image size with a given focal length projector lens can be determined from the image *magnification.* Conversely, the lens focal length required for a given image size and projection distance also can be determined.

$$\text{Magnification} = \frac{\text{Projected image}}{\text{dimension}}$$

÷ Corresponding dimension of original image (slide, film frame, overhead transparency or opaque)

Screen distance = Focal length × (Magnification + 1)

Focal length = Screen distance ÷ (Magnification + 1)

Note that, like an enlarger, a projector is the reverse of a camera. When applying standard lens-image-extension optical formulas to a projection situation, the screen distance is the image distance, and the lens-to-film distance is the object distance.

In addition to proper setup, effective projection requires that the room be adequately ventilated yet protected from extraneous sound, that the lighting be easily controlled, and that spare bulbs and other emergency items be at hand. Above all, the presentation material must be interesting, properly sequenced, and technically well produced.

See also: AUDIO-VISUAL; FILMSTRIPS; FRONT PROJECTION; MULTI-MEDIA PRESENTATIONS; OVERHEAD PROJECTOR; PROJECTORS; REAR PROJECTION; SCREENS, PROJECTION; VISUAL AIDS.

Projection Printing

See: ENLARGING.

Projectors

Projectors for small- and medium-format images accept only appropriately mounted individual slides or, with an adapter, filmstrips. Light from the projector lamp is collected by a condenser lens system to provide uniform brightness across the area of the projection gate. The light path commonly incorporates a heat filter or a cold mirror, or both, to protect the image being projected. Slides are moved in and out of the projection gate by gravity or by a variety of push-pull mechanisms. The slides are loaded in circular or rectangular trays that hold up to 120 images, or in stacks or clips of up to 40 images. Many projectors block the light path during a slide change so that the image is not seen to move on the screen, and so that the audience is not dazzled by white light on a blank screen after every image. Projector lenses are available in a number of focal lengths and moderate zoom ranges to accommodate various screen distances and sizes. Projectors that accept plug-in remote control of slide changing and focusing can also be connected to multiple-projector dissolve and sequence control systems, random-access slide selectors, and slide-sound synchronizing equipment.

Large-format still projectors may accept transparent or opaque materials, or both, as described in the entry on overhead projectors.

See also: FILMSTRIPS; OVERHEAD PROJECTOR; SCREENS, PROJECTION.

Proof Prints

Uncorrected, single-exposure sample prints are called proofs. Most proofs are contact prints; for file and record purposes it is common to print all exposures of one roll of film on a single sheet of 8″ × 10″ paper (8½″ × 11″ paper is required to accommodate all the images of a 36-exposure length of 35mm film). Sheet film negatives are similarly proofed in groups, as far as possible. With small-format films an enlarged proof sheet offers the convenience of bigger images for inspection and evaluation. This is produced by placing several strips of negatives together in the double-glass carrier of a large-format enlarger and projecting them simultaneously onto a single sheet of paper. The preferred proof exposure for properly exposed and developed negatives is one that just prints the maximum black tone through the clear borders or frame lines around the images. This permits all image densities to register as lighter-than-black tones. However if a negative has been underexposed, a reduced proof exposure may be required to avoid printing some image details as maximum black. Conversely, images with heavy densities (from negative overexposure/overdevelopment) may require more proof exposure to print details that otherwise would remain paper-white.

On a contact sheet of mixed images, it is sometimes possible to group the film strips for two or more different exposures; otherwise the best overall exposure is given for the majority of the images, and difficult frames are reprinted separately to be stapled or taped in place on the sheet.

Portrait proofs may be uncorrected contact prints or enlargements; in any case they are usually cropped or trimmed to eliminate the film borders and other distracting details before they are submitted to the customer.

Proofs of three- or four-color photomechanical reproductions are prepared by making separate exposures from the separation negatives on transparent cyan, magenta, and yellow diazo materials; these are assembled in register to provide some indication of color quality. Another kind of photomechanical proofing material uses wipe-on liquid emulsions that are exposed and processed in register, one after another, on a single sheet of base material.

Psychic Photography

See: SPIRIT PHOTOGRAPHY.

Pupil Magnification

A lens has two pupils: the *entrance pupil* is the effective diameter of the bundle of light rays striking the front of the lens; the *exit pupil* is the diameter of the image-forming bundle emerging from the rear of the lens. These pupils are equal, or nearly so, in most normal focal-length lenses and lenses of symmetrical optical design; they are not equal in telephoto and wide-angle lenses. The difference can be seen clearly by setting the diaphragm to a medium *f*-stop and sighting through the lens towards a light-colored surface from each end in turn. The diameter of each pupil seen in this way can be measured by holding a scale across the lens.

The ratio between the two pupils may affect exposure. Known as the pupil (or pupillary) magnification, P, this ratio is calculated:

$$P = \frac{\text{Exit pupil}}{\text{diameter}} \div \frac{\text{Entrance pupil}}{\text{diameter}}$$

When the two pupils are not essentially equal, the effective brightness of the image is affected. This is not a significant factor in normal-range photography, but in close-up and macrophotography when P is less than 0.9 or greater than 1.2, it must be taken into account when using magnification (M) as a basis for determining exposure compensation; the method is given in the entry on magnification. A through-the-lens metering system automatically makes the required compensation unless the light reduction is too great to obtain a meter reading.

Pushing; Push Processing

Pushing is the technique of exposing a film at a higher than normal speed rating (exposure index). This is most often done in order to photograph at marginal light levels, or to use a smaller aperture or a faster shutter speed than normal conditions allow. The practical effect of pushing is that the film is underexposed, and underexposure causes reduced contrast. *Push processing* is extended development of a pushed film to restore the density and contrast in middletones and highlights that would be lost by normal development of the underexposed image.

Pushing will fail to register detail in the darkest parts of the subject and will produce lower contrast in those dark tones that are registered; these are inescapable consequences of underexposure. Push processing is primarily suitable for low-contrast (short brightness range) subjects; it will produce excessive density and contrast or blocked highlights with subjects of normal or high contrast. It will also produce increased graininess and reduced tone quality. Push-processed color images also commonly show some degree of color shift.

Color reversal (slide, transparency) films and silver-image black-and-white negative films can be pushed to good effect; color negative films cannot. Chromogenic black-and-white films (i.e., those which are processed like color negative films) produce different degrees of contrast with different amounts of exposure; processing cannot be altered without adverse effect.

Black-and-white negative films can be pushed one to two *f*-stops with suitable low-contrast subjects; that is, they can be rated at two to four times the normal ISO speed. Medium- and high-speed films can be pushed to good effect; slow-speed films produce poor results. Black-and-white push processing consists of extending development time 25 to 50 percent with normal developers. More than 50 percent extra development will produce significant amounts of image-degrading density and fog. Fine-grain developers should not be used for push processing.

Color reversal films can be pushed effectively, and in fact they show a true increase in film speed, because the shadow areas of the scene are recorded as the densest part of the image, not the least dense as in negative films. There is a useful latitude between normal shadow density and the maximum density that a reversal film can produce. The result of intentional underexposure is an overall increase in density, which can be partially corrected by increased first development. Almost all color reversal films are processed in Kodak E-6 solutions or the equivalent. Push processing for a film that has been pushed one *f*-stop generally requires 2 minutes additional time in the first developer; a film that has been pushed two *f*-stops requires about 5½ minutes additional first development. Many processing laboratories offer one- and two-stop push processing of E-6 type reversal films at additional cost. Kodachrome film processing is far more complex; only a few laboratories offer push processing of Kodachrome, and those only at very high cost.

See also: BLACK-AND-WHITE PROCESSING; CONTRAST; REVERSAL PROCESSING.

Q-R

Q-Factor

The Callier effect describes the difference in the amount of light lost to scattering and absorption in a negative (or other material, such as a filter) according to whether the light falling on the negative is specular (parallel ray paths) or diffuse (random, many-direction paths). The loss is greatest with specular light because scattering can only direct light out of the parallel paths, whereas with diffuse light as much is scattered into effective paths as is scattered out. With either kind of light, the amount of scattering increases with density, grain or particle size, and emulsion or layer thickness. The ratio between the two degrees of scattering, measured as specular and diffuse density, is called the *Callier coefficient,* the *Q-factor,* or simply Q. It provides an objective measurement of the light-scattering power of the area or material examined, and is calculated:

$$Q = \frac{\text{Specular density}}{} \div \frac{\text{Diffuse density}}{}$$

The specular density is measured with a densitometer cell that collects only transmitted light traveling in the same direction as the parallel incident light rays. Diffuse density is measured with a cell that collects transmitted light traveling in all directions.
See also: CALLIER EFFECT; DENSITY.

Quadrant Diagram

The various stages in photographic tone reproduction—from original subject through emulsion images to the final visual image—can be plotted on a four-part graph called a quadrant diagram, that relates their characteristic or equivalent reproduction curves. This graphical method was invented by Lloyd A. Jones in 1920. Each of the first three quadrants of the diagram show how the subject or its image is recorded at one stage, and how that becomes the source of exposure for the next stage. The illustration shows typical black-and-white negative and print tone reproduction. The labels on the axes pertain only to their adjacent quadrant and are located to give the least interference with the graph drawings. "Brightnesses" (i.e., luminances), "exposure," and "density" are all logarithmic units.

Quadrant 1 at the lower right shows subject brightnesses along the bottom axis. Three example values are projected upward to the solid line that represents the brightnesses of all the subject values in the image that the lens projects onto the film. Flare adds brightness in the shadow areas, so the actual optical image curve differs from an ideal, nonflare curve (broken line). Turning the diagram so that Quadrant 1 is in the lower left-hand corner, the optical image brightnesses become the exposures falling on the film.

The toe and straight-line portions of the characteristic curve of the film are shown in Quadrant 2, aligned so that the minimum subject brightness is recorded as the first printable negative density. Projections of the example subject brightnesses to the film curve show the densities that record them. Turning the diagram back to normal position, the negative densities in Quadrant 2 become exposure values projected onto the characteristic curve of the print paper, shown in Quadrant 3. Projections show what print density represents each of the sample values. Finally, in Quadrant 4 horizontal projections from the print curve intersect vertical projections from the optical image curve (Quadrant 1) to produce the tone reproduction curve. If the camera image were free of flare and the negative and paper characteristics were perfectly matched, this curve would be a straight line (broken line in graph). The shape of the curve shows the actual relationship of values in the final image.

The quadrant diagram method is also used to analyze reproduction in a positive transparency (slide); reproduction of a movie or slide image by a given projector and screen combination; and by extension, various aspects of photomechanical reproduction.
See also: CHARACTERISTIC CURVE; CONTRAST; JONES, LLOYD AMCILE; TONE REPRODUCTION.

Quadrant Diagram

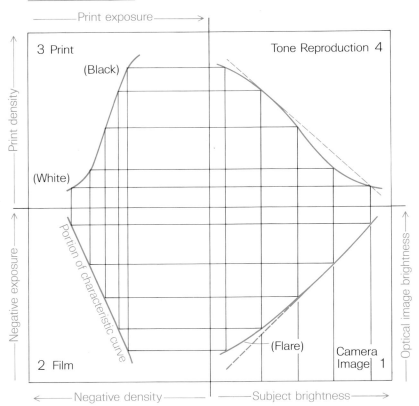

Quartz Light

A tungsten bulb with halogen (iodine or bromine) vapor in the gas surrounding the filament can provide 25–30 percent more light at a constant color temperature for up to twice as long as a conventional tungsten bulb. This efficiency is produced by the halogen, which prevents tungsten evaporated by the heated filament during operation from being deposited on the walls of the surrounding glass envelope; instead, it helps to redeposit the tungsten on the filament. For this to occur the vapor temperature must be kept very high, which is accomplished by using a small envelope to reduce the interior volume. When such bulbs were first manufactured, quartz was the best available material with the necessary heat resistance; hence the general name, quartz light. Today various kinds of high-temperature glass are used instead of quartz, but the name persists. The preferred term is tungsten halogen bulb.
See also: LIGHT SOURCES.

Quinol; Quinone

Quinol is an alternate chemical name for the developing agent hydroquinone; other names are hydrochinon; paradihydroxybenzene; and 1:4-benzenediol.

Formula: $C_6H_4(OH)_2$. The photographic use of hydroquinone was discovered by William Abney in 1880; it is now one of the most widely used developing agents. Used alone, with sufficient activation, it is rapid acting and produces good contrast in well-exposed areas (i.e., highlights and bright middletones), but does not produce good detail in lightly exposed areas (shadows). It is most often combined with metol or Phenidone, which produce excellent shadow area development, to form general-purpose developers with a wide range of characteristics.

Quinone is sometimes improperly used to mean hydroquinone. It is in fact a compound formed when hydroquinone oxidizes. If left uncombined in the developer it would promote rapid oxidation of the remaining hydroquinone, significantly shortening the developer life. The preservative sodium sulfite combines with quinone as it is formed to prevent this.
See also: DEVELOPING AGENT; M-Q DEVELOPER; P-Q DEVELOPER; SUPERADDITIVITY.

Rack-and-Pinion Focusing

This method of adjusting the extension between the lens board and camera back is most commonly used with a bellows-type camera. Movement is achieved by a toothed wheel (pinion gear) that travels along a matching track (the rack).
See: FOCUSING; VIEWING AND FOCUSING SYSTEMS.

Radiography

See: X-RAY PHOTOGRAPHY.

Rangefinder

A rangefinder is a device that measures the camera-to-subject distance for accurate focusing. In rangefinder-equipped cameras the rangefinder is coupled to the lens focusing mechanism so that both are adjusted simultaneously. There are two kinds of rangefinder—active and passive. An active rangefinder emits a pulse or beam of energy and determines subject distance by measuring the time it takes to receive a reflected echo, or by sensing the angle at which the echo is received. Active rangefinders that emit either infrared or ultrasonic signals currently are used in some automatic-focusing cameras.

A passive rangefinder operates with the light reflected by the subject. The type used on all manual-focusing cameras allows the photographer to see the subject and visually determine when the sharp-focus adjustment has been achieved. The simplest such device is used in the center portion of some reflex viewing screens. It consists of two prism wedges set side by side at opposing angles. When the lens is out of focus, the portion of the image falling across the wedges is discontinuous, or one portion is blank. When the lens is in focus, the image is fully visible and intact.

The kind of coupled rangefinder used with cameras that do not have a reflex viewing system employs mirrors or prisms to present two images of the subject in the viewfinder. One is a fixed image seen directly along the lens axis; the other is an image from a movable mirror located to one side so as to view the subject from an angle. This angle must change with the subject distance. When the lens is out of focus, the movable mirror is at the wrong angle so that its image is out of register with the fixed image. Adjusting the lens focus control also moves the mirror; when the two images are perfectly aligned, the lens is focused at the subject distance. Either of two methods is used to show image alignment. In a *coincident-image* rangefinder a portion of the movable image is superimposed on the fixed image. When the lens is out of focus, that portion of the subject is shown as a double image. In a *split-image* rangefinder part of the fixed image is blocked off and the movable image appears in its place. When the lens is out of focus, the movable image is shifted to one side or the other, with the result that there is a break in what should be continuous lines in the image. The clarity of these two methods varies with subject characteristics; for example, split-image focusing is difficult with a subject that has no sharply defined edges or lines, such as sand dunes or a scene in mist or haze.

At one time a projection rangefinder, the Focuspot, was offered for use in dim light conditions where optical focusing was difficult or impossible. It applied the two-image principle in reverse by using the rangefinder optical system to project two pencil beams of light onto the subject, one fixed and the other movable. Changing the lens focus shifted the movable beam; when both beams hit the same spot, the lens was focused at that distance.

See also: AUTOMATIC FOCUSING; FOCUSING; VIEWING AND FOCUSING SYSTEMS.

Rapid Processing

Many needs for immediate access to a photographic image can be met with diffusion-transfer instant photography films. When other films are used, black-and-white film processing can be reduced to at least one-quarter of the usual time and print processing to less than one minute. Hand-processing of conventional color materials cannot be accelerated appreciably; automatic processors already operate at near minimum times to avoid excessive swelling and softening of gelatin emulsions in the processing solutions. Rapid processing produces acceptable images with different contrast and greater graininess than normal processing would produce; in no case will rapid processing provide the best possible image quality.

Typical nonmachine rapid film processing can produce a black-and-white negative in about five minutes, using elevated temperatures and highly active solutions. Most modern general-purpose films can be processed at up to 75°F (24°C) if all solutions are at the same temperature to avoid reticulation, and if the emulsion is handled very carefully. Some special-purpose instrumentation and rapid-access films can be processed at 85°F (29°C) or higher without the need to first treat the emulsion in a hardening solution. Development takes 2½ to 4 minutes, depending on the emulsion, stop bath 10 seconds, and rapid fixer 1 to 2 minutes. After a quick

rinse, surface water can be squeegeed off and the wet negative placed in a glassless carrier for immediate enlarging. Rapid drying before printing can be achieved with warm forced air, or by soaking the film in a solution of 4 parts ethyl or isopropyl (not methyl) alcohol to 1 part water. The alcohol displaces water in the emulsion and subsequently evaporates faster. An unfixed (to avoid paper contamination) negative can be contact-printed onto wet paper immediately after the stop bath and a quick rinse, but it must be discarded afterward.

Rapid hand-processing of prints is achieved with waterproof (resin-coated) paper and concentrated solutions. Development takes 1 minute, stop bath 10 seconds, and rapid fixer 1–2 minutes. Maximum speed is obtained with a stabilization or activation processor and a print paper that has a developing agent incorporated in the emulsion. The stabilization process, described in a separate entry, operates at a rate of one inch per second and delivers a damp-dry print with temporary image stability (typically a minimum of a few weeks); the print can be conventionally fixed and washed for permanence at a later time. An activation processor takes about 14 seconds to pass an exposed waterproof paper through an activating solution, which causes the image to develop, and through a stop bath. This is followed by high-temperature surface spray of concentrated fixer, a spray rinse, and infrared drying. A fixed and dried print is delivered in 55–60 seconds. Special-purpose rapid film and print processors are used for photofinish, medical, and other applications. Some diffusion-transfer large format materials substantially reduce the time required for color printing from a slide or a negative.

See also: DIFFUSION TRANSFER PROCESS; STABILIZATION PROCESS.

Ray, Man

American; 1890–1976

A tireless experimenter with photographic techniques who participated in the Cubist, Dadaist, and Surrealist art movements, Man Ray created a new photographic art which emphasized chance effects and surprising juxtapositions. Unconcerned with "craft," he employed solarization, grain enlargement, and cameraless prints (photograms)—which he called "Rayographs"—made by placing objects directly on photographic paper and exposing them to the light. Man Ray was, with Moholy-Nagy, the most significant maker of cameraless photographs in the 1920s and 1930s.

As a painter, sculptor, and filmmaker,

as well as a photographer, Man Ray brought his diverse techniques to bear upon one another in the attempt to create "disturbing objects." His life and art spoke of freedom, pleasure, and the desire for extended awareness and means of expression. His work has been a significant influence on Bill Brandt and Berenice Abbott (both of whom studied with and assisted him), and more recent photographers using multi-media techniques.

Man Ray was given that name by his family when he was 15, and wished to be known only by that name. He was born in Philadelphia, and later moved with his family to New York City where he attended the Academy of Fine Arts and the Ferrer School. He had an early desire to become a painter, studied architectural drawing and engineering, and began his career as a graphic designer and typographer.

In 1910 he met Alfred Stieglitz at the 291 gallery and became acquainted with the work of important modern artists Stieglitz exhibited. Man Ray took early portraits in a style influenced by Stieglitz as well.

He was given a one-man show of paintings at Charles Daniel's gallery in New York in 1915. The same year he met Marcel Duchamp who encouraged his making assemblages and collages. Around 1920 he began photographing his paintings for record purposes, but soon started to explore the photographic medium for its own sake. He became a member of New York's proto-Dada group about this time along with Duchamp, Francis Picabia, and others.

Man Ray moved to Paris in 1921 where he made his living as a professional fashion and portrait photographer while pursuing more creative work on the side. He became internationally famous as the photographer of Parisian artists between the wars. He made portraits of the entire intellectual elite: Breton, Joyce, Eliot, Schoenberg, Matisse, Ernst, Artaud, Stein, Brancusi, and Hemingway, to name a few.

Soon after his arrival in Paris, Ray made his first Rayograph. He participated in the first international Dada show held in Paris, was a member of the Surrealist movement from 1924, and exhibited at the first Surrealist show in Paris in 1925. In 1932, his work appeared in the major Surrealist exhibition at New York's Julien Levy Gallery. He was included in the Museum of Modern Art's *Fantastic Art, Dada and Surrealism* show in 1935.

Ray fled Paris before the Nazi occupation in 1940 and settled in Hollywood where he continued to work and teach for the next 10 years. Photography took second place to painting for the rest of his career, although he experimented with color photography in the late 1950s and early 1960s.

He returned to Paris in 1951 and remained there until his death in 1976.

Man Ray received the Gold Medal at the Photography Biennale, Venice, in 1961, and the German Photographic Society Cultural Award in 1966. He was the subject of major retrospectives at the Bibliothèque Nationale, Paris (1962), the Los Angeles County Museum (1966), and a European traveling show in 1971–1972. A monumental show of over 300 photographs, paintings, and objects was held at the Centre Georges Pompidou, Paris, in 1982.

Rayleigh, Lord (John William Strutt)

English; 1842–1919

England's leading physicist for much of his career, Rayleigh succeeded James Clerk Maxwell as director of the Cavendish Laboratory, and made it one of the world's outstanding research centers. He developed the electromagnetic theory of light advanced by Maxwell; explained how the primary scattering of light in the atmosphere produced the blue color of the sky and polarized sunlight; investigated color vision; and devised mathematical methods for analyzing the effects of prisms and diffraction gratings on light and for determining the resolving power of diffraction-limited optical systems. His range covered all of physics. He made discoveries and original contributions in all areas, especially in sound, electromagnetism, wave theory, and electricity, in which he devised fundamental units for measuring current, resistance, and voltage. In 1904 he received the Nobel prize in physics for measuring the density of the atmosphere and, along with the chemistry Nobelist Sir William Ramsay, for the discovery of a new class of elements consisting of argon and related inert gases.

RC Paper

See: RESIN-COATED PAPERS.

Rear Projection

A slide or motion picture may be projected onto a translucent screen and viewed from the opposite side. Once widely used to produce background images for studio photography, rear projection is now primarily used in portable display projection units, and in situations where equipment must be concealed or made inaccessible to the audience. In studio photography, rear projection has several drawbacks. There must be extra room behind the screen for the projector throw. The screen reduces image brightness, the image has a central hot spot, and brightness and definition fall off rapidly toward the edges. Spill light on the front of the screen washes out the projected image, and elements too close to the screen may cast revealing shadows.

There are a number of ways in which these disadvantages can be minimized, and rear projection is still used for backgrounds in a significant amount of motion-picture photography. For still photography, front projection is far more versatile and avoids all these disadvantages.

See also: BACKGROUNDS; FRONT PROJECTION.

Ray, Man. "Nue de dos [Juliet]" (ca. 1946). Sotheby, New York.

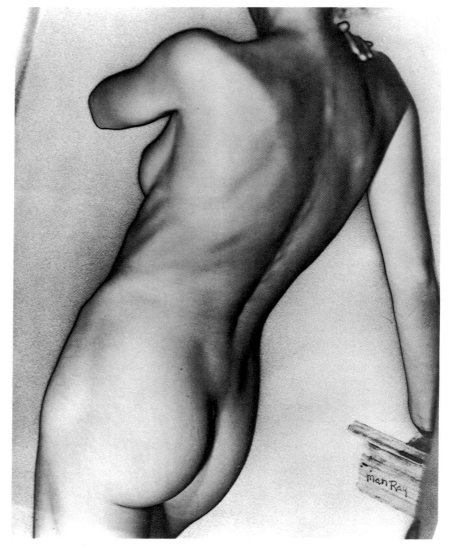

Reciprocity

Most photographic materials make equal responses to a wide range of reciprocal exposures—those that give equal amounts of exposure because their time and light quantity factors are equivalent although different. For example, $f/8$ at 1/125 sec., $f/11$ at 1/60 sec., and $f/5.6$ at 1/250 sec. are reciprocal, or equal, exposure settings. Compared to the first exposure, the second reduces the light by one-half but doubles the time; the third doubles the light, but halves the time. However, beyond a certain point—one that varies according to conditions and the emulsion used—there is a failure of reciprocity. Although the emulsion receives an exposure that is mathematically equal to another, it does not respond to create a latent image of equivalent strength or permanence. This *reciprocity effect* most often occurs with long exposures to low intensity light. Color films

other than those with type L (long-exposure) emulsions may exhibit reciprocity effect with exposures of 1/10 sec. or longer. Some black-and-white films show the effect at 1 sec., most begin to show it with 10 sec. and longer exposures. Many manufacturers publish reciprocity compensation data for their films. In color, additional exposure and perhaps some corrective filtration is required; in black-and-white, increased exposure and perhaps increased development is required. The reciprocity effect can also occur with extremely short exposures and very bright light. Sufficient conditions seldom arise in ordinary photographic situations, but they may be encountered in high-speed and stroboscopic photography.
See also: EXPOSURE; LATENT IMAGE.

Red Eye

In some color pictures taken by electronic flash the eyes of a human or animal have red pupils instead of black; in black-and-white pictures the pupils appear light gray or white. This "red-eye" effect is caused by the reflection of light from a layer of blood vessels on the inner surface of the eye. It occurs when the flash unit is close to the lens axis and the subject is looking directly at the camera. It is most likely to occur in dimly lighted surroundings because there the pupils open to adapt. The effect is avoided by locating the flash unit at least six inches above the lens, or off to one side; by viewing the subject from a slight angle, or having the subject look a bit to one side; and by raising the ambient light level so the pupils will close to a significant degree.

Redevelopment

A developed silver image may be treated in a bleaching solution that converts the silver into colorless silver halides or other compounds and then be redeveloped to produce an image with different tone, color, or contrast characteristics that those of the first image. This is the basis of a number of toning and intensifying procedures. The first image must be fixed and washed before bleaching so that no originally unused halides are present during redevelopment to produce unwanted density or spurious image effects. The term *redevelopment* is also sometimes used—inaccurately—for the positive-image development step in reversal processing. This is properly called second or reversal (or positive) development, because the bleached negative first image is not redeveloped—the originally unde-

veloped halides that correspond to the positive aspect of the image are developed for the first time.

Reducer; Reduction

A reducer is a chemical solution that removes silver or dye density from an image. It may increase the overall transparency of an image for printing or projection, or it may change the contrast of the image; in some cases it does both. In color retouching, certain reducing bleaches selectively attack cyan, magenta, or yellow dyes; other bleaches attack all three dyes simultaneously. Reducers are more often used to alter the printing characteristics of black-and-white negatives. There are three classes:

1. A *subtractive* (or cutting) reducer removes equal amounts of density from all areas; it is especially useful with an overexposed but normally developed negative, or one that has been fogged.

2. A *proportional* reducer removes equal proportions or percentages of density from all areas; its effect is to reduce contrast, and it is useful with an overdeveloped image of a subject of normal brightness range.

3. A *superproportional* reducer removes greater proportions of density in relation to increasing density in the negative; thus it removes a considerable amount in the highlights and little in the shadows, an action that is useful with an overdeveloped image of a contrasty subject.

The most common reducer is Farmer's reducer. For subtractive negative reduction a small amount of a 7.5 percent solution of potassium ferricyanide is mixed with four times as much of a 24 percent solution of plain hypo (sodium thiosulfate) just before use. This is diluted with five times as much water and a thoroughly washed negative is immersed in the solution immediately. For proportional reduction the negative is soaked for two or three minutes in a 0.75 percent ferricyanide solution and then transferred to a 20 percent hypo solution. Prints may be treated the same way, or the two-step method may be used by swabbing the ferricyanide solution into selected areas of the image. Other reducers use stronger bleaching agents than potassium ferricyanide, followed by hypo or other solutions to remove the dissolved silver compounds. Reduction may be carried out in white light and its effect judged by visual inspection from time to time; the change is usually too gradual to be appreciable when looking constantly at the image. All materials must be thoroughly

washed after reduction to remove all traces of hypo or other chemicals.
See also: INTENSIFICATION.

Reduction, Optical

Except in macrophotography and photomicrography (which produce images that are life-size or larger), the images recorded on film are reductions of the actual object (subject) sizes. The image scale is often given as a fractional magnification—e.g., $\frac{1}{3}\times$ or $0.33\times$—but in some cases it is more convenient to express the scale in terms of the degree of reduction, R. For one thing, this procedure eliminates a fraction or a decimal in making calculations. Reduction can be determined in the following ways:

$$R = \text{Object size} \div \text{Image size}$$

$$R = \frac{\text{Lens-to-object}}{\text{distance}} \div \frac{\text{Lens-to-film}}{\text{distance}}$$

Reduction is the reciprocal of magnification (M), so it can be calculated by $1 \div M$ or by inverting any formula for calculating magnification. Reduction varies directly with lens-to-object distance; thus, if the distance doubles, the reduction factor also doubles. When the reduction factor is known, the image size can be calculated:

$$I = \text{Object size} \div R$$

In document or data storage, photofabrication of miniature circuits, and other applications of microphotography, image reductions of several hundred or even thousand times are common. This may be accomplished in two steps, the first reduction being a factor of 10 to 100, after which the processed image is rephotographed at a further degree of reduction.
See also: MAGNIFICATION; MICROPHOTOGRAPHY; OPTICS; SCALE.

Reflectance; Reflection

Reflectance is a measure of the degree to which a surface reflects light; it is the ratio:

Reflected light $\div$ Incident light.

In practice, the reflectance of a material is determined in comparison to the amount of light reflected by a reference surface. This surface is pure white (reflects all wavelengths equally) and is a virtually perfect diffuse reflector (absorbs less than 3 percent of the light and reflects essentially equal amounts is all directions over a 180° solid angle).

The reference surface is illuminated from a 45° angle and the reflected light measured head-on, from a 90° angle to the surface. Then the sample material is illuminated and the light measured in the same way. The *reflectance* (R) or reflectance factor (R_F or p) is then:

$$R = \frac{\text{Sample light}}{\text{measurement}} \div \frac{\text{Reference light}}{\text{measurement}}$$

The *reflection,* or percent reflectance, of the surface is:

$$\%R = R \times 100$$

Absorptance (A) is the reciprocal of reflectance:

$$A = 1 \div R$$

In the case of a transparent or translucent material, some light is reflected, some absorbed, and some transmitted. If the total amount of incident light is taken as 1.0, these three factors account for it in what is called the RAT (Reflectance-Absorptance-Transmittance) Law:

$$R + A + T = 1.0$$

Thus, if two factors are known, the third can be calculated. (When percentages are used, Reflection + Absorption + Transmission = 100.)

The densities of a print are measured by the reflectance method. A reflection densitometer shines a light of known intensity onto a selected spot from a 45° angle and a photocell measures the reflected light from 90° angle. The readout is *reflection density*, D_R, which is the logarithm of the absorptance; thus:

$$D_R = \text{Log } A, \text{ or Log } 1 \div R$$

A single reading measures density in a given area of a black-and-white print; separate readings through red, green, and blue filters are required with a color print.

Reflection. Reflection from most surfaces is *diffuse reflection*, in which a significant portion of the light is reflected in many different directions. A highly polished smooth surface produces *specular* (mirrorlike) *reflection*—most of the light is reflected at an angle opposite but equal to the angle of incidence. The image visible in specular reflection is reversed left-for-right each time it is reflected; thus, an image relayed by an odd number of reflecting surfaces is reversed, while one relayed by an even number of reflecting surfaces is properly oriented. Neutral surfaces (whites, grays) reflect all colors equally; colored surfaces exhibit chromatic reflection in which some wavelengths are more completely reflected than others.
See also: DENSITOMETRY; INCIDENCE, ANGLE OF; MIRROR; TRANSMISSION.

Reflectors

Photographic reflectors are of two types—those placed directly around a light bulb or flash tube to concentrate all the illumination in the same direction, and those used separately to redirect the illumination emitted by one or more light sources. While many light sources have built-in reflectors, accessory reflectors are widely used with studio flash heads and screw-type bulbs such as photofloods. These reflectors generally are made of aluminum with a satin (matte) or polished inner surface; they screw on or otherwise attach to the socket that holds the light source. Accessory reflectors have three types of curvature: spherical, parabolic, and elliptical; they are made in various standard diameters as measured across the open side. When the bulb or flash tube is positioned properly in the focus of the reflector's curvature, a spherical reflector forms a diverging beam of light, a parabolic reflector forms a parallel beam, and an elliptical reflector forms a converging beam. Spherical reflectors are used as floodlights; elliptical and parabolic reflectors are more nearly spotlight in effect. The quality of the light from a satin-surface reflector is softer than that from a polished reflector. The light can be softened and spread by placing a diffuser in front of the reflector. Clips for diffusing screens or filters usually hold them a few inches in front of the reflector, leaving a gap for heat to escape. Large, shallow reflectors with equally spaced sockets for several bulbs are called pans or broads. They are often constructed of wood that is covered with metal and painted white, and measure 2′ × 3′ (0.6 × 0.9m) or larger. They are used to throw an even, general light over a large area, much as a skylight or large window would.

Separate reflectors usually are flat cards or boards with white, silver, or gold surfaces. The metallic surfaces may be paint, crinkled foil, or sheet metal; a gold surface has a warming effect with color film, and a silver surface has a cooling color effect. Reflectors of this sort range from about 2′ × 2′ (0.6 × 0.6m) up to studio flats 4′ × 8′ (1.2 × 2.4m) or larger. Portable reflectors often fold in the middle for easy carrying and so they can be free-standing in a V-shape. They are placed to pick up spill light from a light source and direct it to the subject. For example, when the sun is used as a backlight in outdoor photography, one or more reflectors can provide the necessary frontal lighting. By varying the distance and using different surfaces, key and fill light effects can be created. Reflectors can also be improvised from a piece of cloth such as a white shirt or from an open magazine or newspaper. In the studio, light sources are often directed at large flat reflectors rather than at the subject to obtain diffuse illumination. A special white or silver fabric reflector is often used with small flash units; it folds like an umbrella and may be opened to a curved or a completely flat profile. Hard light effects can be obtained by using mirrors as reflectors; convex and concave mirrors respectively diverge and converge the light beam without diffusing it.
See also: LIGHT SOURCES; LIGHTING; UMBRELLA LIGHTING.

Reflex Copying

Reflex photocopying reproduces printed documents and high-contrast line originals without using a lens system. High-contrast copy paper is placed with its emulsion side in contact with the face of the document. The exposing light is directed through the back of the copy paper; it is absorbed by the black ink of the document, but reflected back by the white areas. The light intensity is such that the slow-speed copy paper is affected only in the areas receiving the double or reflex exposure. Development produces a negative image from which positive copies can be made.

Most office reflex copying machines use diffusion transfer materials to avoid separate negative and positive processing steps. The negative diffusion transfer paper is placed face-to-face with the document and passed through the exposure section of the machine. Then the exposed sheet is fed with a sheet of receiving (print) paper through rollers that coat the exposed surface with an activator and press the two sheets together, face-to-face. As the negative develops in one sheet, the unused silver diffuses to the other sheet and develops as the corresponding positive image. The sheets are peeled apart after 30 to 60 seconds and the negative discarded; no further processing is required.

The first reflex-copying method, the Playertype, was invented in 1896; it used developing-out, not diffusion transfer, papers.
See also: DIFFUSION TRANSFER PROCESS; PLAYERTYPE.

Reflex Viewing

Camera viewing systems may use fixed or movable mirrors or other reflective devices to direct an image to the viewing screen or eyepiece. This permits continuous viewing up to and during (or immediately after) the moment of exposure. In a *twin-lens reflex* camera a fixed mirror relays the image from a viewing lens to a ground-glass or similar screen. This lens matches the focal length of the film-exposure lens mounted just below, but it may have a larger maximum aperture to provide the brightest possible viewing image, and it does not need to be so highly corrected for aberrations. The two lenses are interconnected so that they focus with a single control. This kind of system is quiet and vibration-free because it does not involve a moving mirror, but at close distances there may be parallax error in the viewing caused by the separation between the two lenses.

In a *single-lens reflex* (SLR) camera, a mirror located in front of the film plane reflects the image to a screen or relay prism. When the shutter release is pushed, the mirror flips out of the way just before the shutter opens for the exposure. Almost all 35mm SLR cameras have instant-return mirrors so that viewing resumes as soon as the shutter closes. In some medium- and large-format SLR cameras the mirror remains out of the viewing path until the shutter is cocked again. A few cameras have used a fixed-position beam splitter in front of the film. While this eliminates vibration and provides absolutely uninterrupted viewing, it divides the light so that neither the viewing nor the exposing image has maximum possible brightness.

A reflex mirror can be used with a view camera to provide an uninverted image for composing and focusing the picture. It is placed behind the camera to reflect the focusing screen image upward; most such accessories have hoods to shield the image from stray light. As with all such cameras, through-the-lens viewing is lost as soon as a film holder is inserted. Motion-picture cameras may provide continuous reflex through-the-lens viewing in two ways. Some lenses—especially zoom lenses—incorporate a fixed beam-splitting prism to provide an image to the eyepiece; with other lenses a reflecting shutter can provide reflex viewing. The shutter is a revolving disk with an open segment that allows light to pass during a portion of each revolution. The opaque portion of the disk is mirror-coated on the side facing the lens; the disk is mounted at a slight angle in front of the film gate, or has a conical shape that slopes away from the center. Whenever the film is blocked, the shutter reflects the lens image to a prism-and-eyepiece viewing system.

See also: BEAM SPLITTER; PARALLAX; PRISMS; ZOOM LENS.

Refraction

Refraction is a change of direction in the path traveled by a light wave; it occurs at the border between two transparent media of different densities. Energy such as light travels about 186,000 miles (300,000km) per second in a vacuum and nearly as fast in air. When it enters a more dense medium (e.g., glass; water), its speed is slowed somewhat; when it emerges, its original speed is resumed. If the energy crosses the border between the two media at an angle, its direction as well as its speed changes. This is because wave fronts have breadth, so that in angular travel one corner crosses the border and changes its rate of travel before other points across the wave front. Going into a more dense medium, the leading corner slows and begins to drag, causing the wave front to wheel in that direction. Coming out into a less dense medium, the leading corner picks up speed while the trailing corner drags, causing a wheeling movement in the other direction. This change of direction, called refraction, is the basis of lens construction. If the two borders of the intermediate medium—e.g., the two sides of a piece of glass—are parallel, the angle at which a light ray enters (angle of incidence) and the angle at which it emerges will be equal; the two paths will be offset but parallel. The angles are measured between the ray path and the normal—a reference line perpendicular to the surface at the point the ray crosses it. Lens elements have curved surfaces, so the entrance and exit paths are almost never parallel. However, refraction is always toward the normal upon entering a more dense medium, and away from the normal upon emerging into a less dense medium.

Various types of glass exert different degrees of refraction on light rays; that is, they have different bending powers. The measure of this power is the *refractive index* of the glass. It is the ratio between the sine of the angle in the less dense medium and the sine of the angle in the more dense medium—again, as measured between the ray path and the normal at the point of transition. Thus, for a ray entering the glass from the air, the refractive index is:

Sin Angle of   ÷   Sin Angle of
incidence   refraction
                           (interior angle).

For a ray emerging from glass into the air, it is:

Sin Angle of   ÷   Sin Angle of
emergence   (interior) incidence.

When light passes from one glass to another, the measure is:

Refractive index   ÷   Refractive index
  of glass #1   of glass #2.

A given type of glass does not have the same refractive index for all wavelengths of light. In general, shorter (bluish) wavelengths are refracted more than longer (reddish) wavelengths. There is a progressive degree of change in refraction across the spectrum, with the result that white light is spread into a rainbow of its constituent colors, an action called *dispersion*. A major design concern in correcting chromatic aberrations in lenses is to select types of glass and shape their surfaces so that the dispersive characteristics of various elements cancel one another.

See also: ABERRATIONS OF LENSES; DISPERSION; LENSES; OPTICS; SPECTRUM; WAVELENGTH.

Refraction. Refractive Index
at (1) = Sin I ÷ Sin R
at (2) = Sin E ÷ Sin I

Refraction

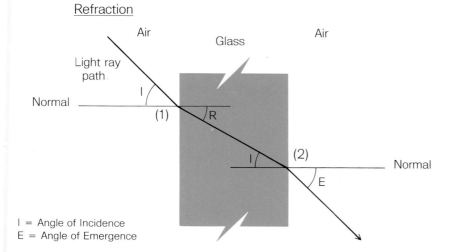

I = Angle of Incidence
E = Angle of Emergence

Regeneration

Some bleach solutions used in color processing can be chemically treated after partial exhaustion to regenerate their working strengths. This action breaks down the by-products of exhaustion and restores a solution to its original composition. Regeneration is distinct from replenishment, which adds compounds to replace those used up but does not dispose of accumulated by-products. Removing silver from a used fixer or bleach-fix solution is not true regeneration, because fixing and pH-balancing compounds must also be added to restore working activity.

See also: pH; REPLENISHER.

Registration of Images

Various photographic and photomechanical printing processes rely on superimposing different versions of the same image—e.g., successive printings from the cyan, yellow, and magenta matrices in the dye transfer process. Corresponding details in all the images must be registered in precisely the same position, otherwise the final image will be unsharp and colors will show muddiness and edge fringing. Either of two devices—edge guides or register pegs—is commonly used to insure positive registration in photographic transfer, photosilkscreen, and similar processes. Edge guides are wood, plastic, or even cardboard strips secured along one side and the top of the printing easel or surface. The successive images, trimmed to have exactly matching borders, are butted snugly against the guides to position them accurately. Register pegs are somewhat more secure than edge guides because they engage matching holes punched in the borders of the various images, so there is little chance that the

image can slip out of register during printing. Two pegs, usually located at the top edge of the printing area, are sufficient for most work.

Initial registration. Before use, the processed images—e.g., separation negatives, or lightly dyed transfer matrices—are assembled on a light box and registered visually. As each is correctly positioned it is temporarily taped to those below to maintain its alignment. It is common to photograph registration marks along with the subject to assist in this process. The marks are typically circle-and-cross symbols, small checkerboard patterns, or an improvised set of X-marks; they are placed along two edges, outside the primary image area. The registered images are edge-trimmed or punched simultaneously, while still taped together; then they are separated for use. If there is not sufficient border area for punching, auxiliary pieces of scrap film or celluloid are first taped on.

In motion-picture photography and in some kinds of precision slide photography the location of the image area in relation to the film's sprocket holes must be consistent, as must be the spacing between frames. Registration pins at the film gate of the camera engage the sprocket holes to control these factors. Slides photographed in a pin-register camera are mounted in matching pin mounts to insure that every image is similarly centered and will not shift during use. This is especially important in multiple-projector presentations in which images may be superimposed, or must be precisely positioned in relation to one another on the screen.

Rejlander, Oscar Gustave
British; 1813–1875

Oscar Gustave Rejlander, called by E. Y.

Jones "the Father of Art Photography," was an early exponent of photography as an art in itself who became famous as the originator of multiple-print composite photographs of complex theatrical and literary allegories on moral subjects. He was one of the first experimenters with double exposure and photomontage techniques in an effort to expand the expressive capabilities of photography, and did significant work in character portrait and child studies.

Rejlander is believed to have been born in Sweden, probably the son of a Swedish army officer. He studied painting at the Academy of Rome and worked as a portraitist, lithographer, and copyist. He later moved to England where he lived in Lincoln and Wolverhampton. At the Great Exhibition in Hyde Park of 1851 he was impressed by the daguerreotypes on display. He received a single afternoon's instruction in photography from Nikolaas Henneman in London in 1853. Although inadequately prepared, he opened a Wolverhampton photographic portrait studio and began work in portraiture and genre scenes. He made portraits of his students (Lewis Carroll, Alfred Lord Tennyson, and Gustave Doré among others), and supplied useful photographic studies to painters. He made a habit of writing humorous captions for his posed scenes.

In order to surmount technical difficulties with the slow wet-collodion process, Rejlander experimented with laborious and time-consuming techniques of cut-and-paste assemblage and of printing from several negatives onto a single sheet of photographic paper.

His first combination print was exhibited in 1855. He was elected to the Photographic Society, London, the following year. His reputation was established in 1857 when he unveiled "The Two Ways of Life (Industry and Dissipation)" at the Manchester Art Treasures Exhibition. This 31″ × 16″ work modeled after Raphael's "Disputa" ("The School of Athens") employed 30 negatives printed on two sheets of paper and created a storm of controversy over Rejlander's techniques and his use of nudes. Several prints of the photograph were made, one of which was purchased by Queen Victoria.

Rejlander moved his studio to London in 1862. He had given up composite printing to concentrate on portraiture, landscapes, and studies of emotions (used as illustrations for a book by Charles Darwin in 1872). He had some success when one of his emotional studies became a popular seller but he died in poverty in Clapham, England, in 1875.

Registration of Images

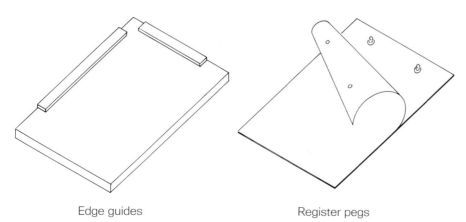

Edge guides   Register pegs

Rejlander, Oscar. "Two Ways of Life" (1857).
Royal Photographic Society, Bath, England.

A major exhibition of 400 prints was held in London in 1889. Peter Henry Emerson wrote at that time that Rejlander was "decidedly no genius, no artist, vain, sentimental, theatrical, but at the same time tremendously enthusiastic, energetically experimental, and best of all, self-sacrificing."
See also: HENNEMAN, NIKOLAAS; PICTORIAL PHOTOGRAPHY/PICTORIALISM.

Relative Aperture

The *f*-number or *f*-stop setting of a lens is its relative aperture, so-called because it is an expression of the effective entrance diameter (entrance pupil) of the aperture relative to the focal length of the lens.
See also: *f*-NUMBER/*f*-STOP; PUPIL MAGNIFICATION.

Relief Images

An image in which the visual elements protrude above the supporting material is a relief image. The opposite, one in which the elements are cut down into the supporting material, is an intaglio image. Many transfer and pigment processes rely on reliefs to carry or receive the colorant that makes the image visible. Most such reliefs are produced with a gelatin emulsion that has been sensitized with potassium bichromate and exposed in contact with a negative or a positive transparency. The gelatin is hardened in proportion to the amount of exposure

received. The image is "developed" in warm water, which dissolves away the unexposed gelatin, leaving the other areas in relief. Some processes for etching photographs on glass or metal produce relief images. Photomechanical reproduction by letterpress uses relief engraving plates. A visual illusion of relief is produced in the bas-relief method of making a photographic print.
See also: ETCH-BLEACH PROCESS.

Rembrandt Lighting

In the portrait lighting effect known as Rembrandt lighting, important parts of the subject (e.g., face, hands) are picked out by bright light, while other portions and the surroundings are suffused with shadow. The dark areas are not simply blank, but permit object contours and key details to be seen in a subdued luminous glow. The effect is achieved by establishing sufficient overall base light for the shadow areas to register properly, and then adding somewhat diffused spotlighting to illuminate the major areas. The effect derives its name from the use of light in a great many paintings, especially self-portraits, by the 17th c. master Rembrandt Harmenzoon van Rijn (1606–1669).
See also: LIGHTING; PORTRAITURE.

Rem-Jet Backing

Certain films are coated on the back with a removable jet-black anti-halation layer.

This rem-jet backing is composed of carbon particles suspended in gelatin; it has virtually perfect anti-halation characteristics, and anti-static properties. Films intended only for automatic machine processing have rem-jet backings; these include Kodachrome film and a number of professional motion-picture negative and print films. The backing is removed during the first step of machine processing. Some films for specialized astronomical photography—where the slightest degree of halation could be significant—also have rem-jet backings. Removal of the backing by manual methods, as for home processing, is not practical with color films because it must be done by safelight to insure that removal is complete and to guard against damaging the film during handling. The backing from a short length of black-and-white film can be removed with cotton soaked in methyl or ethyl alcohol; this must be done before development, under appropriate safelighting. Larger quantities of film can be soaked several minutes in a developing prebath consisting of 1.5 percent borax and 10 percent sodium sulfate in water. Cotton is used to wipe off the coating while the film is in this bath. The carbon particles do not dissolve, so the film must be thoroughly rinsed in running water to make sure no carbon remains on the back or, more particularly, becomes lodged in the soft emulsion. Great care in handling is required.
See also: ANTI-HALATION LAYER.

Remote Control

Photographic equipment can be operated from a distance by direct or indirect methods of remote control. Direct methods involve physical connection between the operator and the equipment; e.g., a six-foot cable release, or an electrical circuit. Indirect methods transmit control signals through the air. Today most indirect methods rely on miniature radio transmitter-receiver links or on pulses of infrared energy. The essence of true remote control is that operation occurs or begins only by decision and action of the photographer. Many automatic control devices operate unattended equipment, but do not provide independent go/no go decisions at any time; instead, they are preset to operate at a given time or under given conditions. There are three general classes of automatic controls:

1. *Timers,* from built-in self-timer shutter releases in cameras to interval (time-lapse) and similar accessory units; they are spring- or electrically powered.

2. *Event triggers,* such as a trip wire, a photocell ("electric eye"), or a sound-activated switch.

3. *Condition responders,* equipped with sensors that detect a particular degree (or change) of pressure, temperature, movement, or other variable in environment or state.

Renger-Patzsch, Albert

German; 1897–1966

Albert Renger-Patzsch was a major figure of the Neue Sachlichkeit (New Objectivity) movement of the 1920s and early 1930s. His images, often taken close up or from unusual angles, employed even, overall lighting to achieve the greatest descriptive accuracy. His subjects, ranging from machinery and architectural details to plants, were photographed with a constant eye for design and precise texture, making natural forms and man-made objects analogous. He believed that photography "appears to be more suited to do justice to an object than to express artistic individuality." His book *The World Is Beautiful* (1928), with a text by Carl George Heise, presented 100 of his crisp images of industrial forms and became perhaps the most influential book of the New Objectivity.

Born in Wurzburg, Germany, Renger-Patzsch spent his youth in Essen and Thuringen. The son of an amateur photographer, he started to photograph as a teenager. He attended Classical Grammar School in Sondeshausen and the Kreuzschule in Dresden. After service in the German Army between 1916 and 1918, he studied chemistry at Technische Hochschule in Dresden from 1919 to 1921.

Renger-Patzsch was director of the photography department archive of the Folkwang Publishing House in Hagen from 1921 to 1924. During 1923 he served as head of the Visual Propaganda Department of the Central Office for Home Affairs in Berlin. After working as a bookseller, merchant, and bookkeeper, he became a freelance documentary and press photographer, working in Bad Harzburg and Essen from 1925 to 1933. He was instructor and head of the department of Pictorial Photography at the Folkwangschule in Essen in 1933–1934, at which time he began to devote himself to personal creative work.

During World War II Renger-Patzsch acted as a war correspondent. His studio and its contents, including over 18,000 negatives, were destroyed in a bombing raid in 1944. From 1944 to his death in 1966 Renger-Patzsch lived in Wamel bei Soest, concentrating primarily on landscape photography.

Renger-Patzsch was a member of the Gesellschaft Deutsche Lichtbilbner from 1964 to 1966. He was the recipient of numerous prizes, including the David Octavius Hill Medal of the GDL (1957), the Culture Prize of the Deutsche

Renger-Patsch, Albert. "Chambered Nautilus" (ca. 1925–28). Courtesy Galerie Wilde, Cologne; permanent collection, ICP, New York.

Gesellschaft für Photographie (1960), and a Gold Medal from the Photographische Gesellschaft in Vienna (1961).

He was honored by one-man shows throughout Germany, at Sander Gallery in Washington, D.C., and at Prakapas Gallery and Sonnabend Gallery in New York City. Group shows included *Film and Foto* in Stuttgart, and *Avant-Garde Photography in Germany* at the San Francisco Museum of Modern Art and the International Center of Photography in New York City.

See also: NEUE SACHLICHKEIT.

Repeating Back

A repeating back is a movable back or film holder, usually on a view camera, that accepts film at least twice the size of the picture format and can be shifted between exposures to permit recording more than one image—e.g., four 4″ × 5″ images on one 8″ × 10″ sheet of film. It is used for some kinds of portrait work, and to obtain multiple original negatives for high-volume production of duplicate images. Exposing film in a repeating back also permits simultaneous multiple-image processing with equipment that accepts only one size of film.

See also: STEP-AND-REPEAT.

Replenisher

A solution added periodically to a processing solution to replace chemicals consumed during use is called a replenisher. The replenisher maintains the chemical activity of the working solution so that consistent results are obtained, and it replaces the volume of solution carried out in the emulsion of films. In high-volume commercial processing laboratories, replenishment of all solutions permits uninterrupted operation at a constant speed and is far more economical than replacing huge amounts of partially exhausted solutions. In the medium and small darkroom, only replenishment of film developer is practical; it is easier and cheaper to replace stop and fix solutions entirely, as necessary. Developer working solutions prepared by diluting a concentrate or stock solution with an equal or greater volume of water (i.e., 1:1, 1:3 dilutions, etc.) should not be replenished because they are essentially completely exhausted during one-time use. This is also true of print developers, which deteriorate rapidly because the large surface area exposed to the air in an open tray promotes oxidation.

Replenisher chemical composition differs from that of the original developer. During development, developing agents and activator are consumed, while additional amounts of potassium bromide—which acts as a restrainer—are generated as a by-product. To compensate for this, a replenisher has no restrainer but has a high percentage strength of the other ingredients in order to overcome the effect of the additional restrainer as well as to replace the exhausted chemicals. In practical use, the amount of restrainer required is often based on the amount of emulsion processed. Typically, ¾ to 1 oz. (22 to 30ml) of replenisher is added for each 80 square in. (516 sq. cm) of emulsion processed—the equivalent of one 36-exposure roll of 35mm film, or one 8″ × 10″ film sheet. Some used developer is removed from the tank, the proper amount of replenishers added, and then developer replaced as necessary to return to the original volume; excess used developer is discarded. Replenishment can be repeated until the total volume added equals the original volume of developer; then the developer should be entirely discarded and a fresh solution prepared.

Reproduction Ratio

The relation between the size of an object in an image and its actual physical size indicates the reproduction ratio or scale of the image. The ratio is always stated *image size: object size,* and the smaller of the two made equal to 1. Thus, if an object 8 in. tall is recorded as an image 2 in. high, the reproduction ratio is (2:8 =) 1:4. A ratio of 1:1 is same-size, or life-size reproduction.

In macrophotography and photomicrography the image is larger than the object, so reproduction ratios take the form 2:1, 10:1, 30:1, etc. When a print is made by enlargement, the image size must be multiplied by the enlargement factor to determine the final reproduction ratio. For example, if a 1:4 negative image is enlarged eight times, the reproduction ratio in the print is (8:4 =) 2:1, or twice life-size. When the reproduction ratio is divided through —e.g., 1:4 = 1 ÷ 4 = 0.25—the result is called the image magnification.

See also: MAGNIFICATION; REDUCTION, OPTICAL; SCALE.

Reproduction Rights and Fees

Reproduction rights are given by a photographer or his or her legal representative (e.g., agent) to clients who wish to publish or otherwise reproduce pictures taken by the photographer. The rights must be extended in a written agreement that specifies the pictures involved, identifies the particular rights and the period for which they are extended, and indicates the payment to be received by the photographer. The agreement may not be legally valid in the U.S. if there is not specified payment of at least one dollar or "other valuable consideration." Assigning rights does not transfer copyright to the client unless that is specified. The rights usually are limited by time or number of uses, geographic area, or other stipulations. The major usage classes are first-time or first publication, one-time, and all rights. Typical restrictions include first magazine rights within (time period); one-time North American rights; and world rights, excluding (areas or countries).

A photographer must examine carefully an agreement drawn up by a client and should guard against assigning more than he or she is being reasonably paid for. An agreement that assigns world rights to: "(client) and/or his or her assignees, licensees. . ." gives the client permission to resell the rights anywhere to anyone during the period of the agreement. If the client is being granted world rights only for use in English language publications, or only in his own publications, that must be specified. A freelance photographer should seek legal advice in having a standard agreement form drawn up, and he or she should make note of the various kinds of rights that may be assigned and what they encompass.

Most publications have established policies regarding the rights they expect to obtain from staff and non-staff photographers. If the photographer is on staff, the usual arrangement is a "work for hire" basis—the publication pays the photographer a salary for making pictures which become the property of the publication and can be used at the publication's discretion. Such arrangements are spelled out in the employment contract between the photographer and the publication. Occasionally the publication will agree to retain publication rights only for the images they choose from the shooting, allowing the photographer to use the remainder of the photographs for his or her own purposes. Most photographers who work for magazines or other periodicals on a freelance, per-assignment basis are paid a shooting fee rather than a retainer or a salary; they generally are required to sign a contractual agreement giving the publication first-time usage rights for the pictures selected from the shooting. In this arrangement the photographer usually retains copyright of the photographs.

Photographs solicited from a photographer's personal work usually are sold with the understanding that the publisher is given *one-time* usage rights (the photographs in this case might have been published elsewhere before). Since publications and books are copyrighted by the publisher, the photographer should make sure that all personal photographs submitted for publication are copyright-marked before they appear in print so as to avoid any potential legal problems regarding ownership.

Photographers working under contract for news agencies often make arrangements whereby the agency owns extensive reproduction rights and sometimes has copyright of the pictures made on assignment. Usually the agency will acknowledge the photographer by giving him or her credit for the pictures when they are published.

Fees for reproduction vary widely. Small magazines and newspapers often pay as little as $30 for one-time reproduction rights of black-and-white photographs; magazines with large circulation, especially those with international distribution, can offer many times that amount for one-time use of a photograph. In most cases full-page reproduction and cover use command substantially higher fees than internal or smaller-size reproduction.

While there is no standardized fee schedule for reproduction of photographs, organizations such as ASMP (The American Society of Photographers in Communications, previously known as the American Society of Magazine Photographers) publish a practices and fees guideline. This type of publication gives suggested fee schedules for various types of assignments and reproduction arrangements, and it can be quite useful to the photographer in search of a basis from which to negotiate fees with a prospective client. The suggested fees are usually open to discussion outside major market areas and with small-business clients.

See also: COPYRIGHT; RIGHTS AND PERMISSIONS; SELLING PHOTOGRAPHS.

Resin-Coated Papers

The fiber base material of many photographic print papers is coated on both sides with a plastic resin. The coating on the side beneath the emulsion typically contains white pigment to form a background for the image; the coating on the back side is usually transparent. The resin prevents the paper base from absorbing processing solutions or wash water; only fibers at the edges, where the paper was trimmed to size during manufacture, are exposed, and their absorption is minimal. The result is a short washing time—a maximum of four minutes in most cases—with an accompanying economy of water, because only the emulsion contains chemicals that must

be flushed out, and a shorter drying time. The term *RC Paper* is a registered product designation of Eastman Kodak Co.; the generic terms for such papers are *resin-coated* and *water-resistant*.

Resolving Power

The ability of a lens and a film, individually or together, to produce distinct images of fine, closely spaced details is called resolving power or resolution. Factors that affect resolving power are sharpness and freedom from aberrations of the optical components, the relative graininess of the emulsion, the contrast of the subject details and the contrast characteristics of the emulsion, and the degree of light scattering throughout the system. Good quality modern lenses generally have greater resolving power than film emulsions and so—assuming all surfaces are clean and free of defects—they are seldom the limiting factor. A slow, fine-grain emulsion has greater resolving power than a faster emulsion with larger grains. The fine-grain emulsion has greater acutance, which produces sharper outlines of the details, and higher contrast, which increases their visibility; in addition, the emulsion is thinner and so produces less internal light scattering (irradiation) that tends to blur distinctions between details. In a thicker emulsion, irradiation and other spread-function factors degrade edge delineation and cause spurious density to build up in the spaces between details. This density reduces the contrast between details and background, making them more difficult to distinguish. Similarly, light scattered by the lens (flare) or by particles in the air inside and outside the camera will reduce contrast. Overexposure and overdevelopment each can produce excess density that will increase light scattering in an emulsion, again reducing edge sharpness and contrast, and thus resolving power.

Contrast is important when resolving power is evaluated visually, because increased contrast produces increased visibility, other things being equal. The resolving power of a lens is evaluated by examining the aerial image of a test target (i.e., it is intercepted in the air, not viewed on a ground glass or other screen). It is measured at various apertures because it is usually poorest at the maximum aperture and best at a medium aperture; at the smallest apertures it may be degraded by diffraction. The resolving power of an emulsion is evaluated by examining test target images produced by contact exposure, or by exposure through an optical system of known quality. The most common test target

consists of groups of alternating black bars and white spaces of equal thickness in a given group. The spacing decreases from group to group, representing finer, more closely spaced details. Test targets for color resolution have red-, green-, and blue-bar groups of each size. When a target is imaged from a distance equal to a specified multiple of the focal length of the lens in use, numbers with each group permit translating the spacing directly to number of lines per millimeter, the standard measurement of resolving power. The image is examined with a low-power microscope to determine the smallest group in which distinct bars and spaces can be distinguished. This group establishes the resolving power of the lens or the emulsion. It is common to use several targets placed throughout the lens field in order to compare edge and outer zone resolution with on-axis resolution, where a lens is most highly corrected.

White-and-black resolution bar charts have a contrast ratio of 1000:1 and are used to measure maximum resolving power; typical quality levels of film resolution are given in the accompanying table. The contrast of details in average subjects is much lower, and consequently lower resolving power is likely to be encountered in actual photographic situations. Because of this, some film manufacturers provide resolving power data for both high-contrast (1000:1) and low-contrast (about 1.5 or 2:1) targets. Low-contrast resolution with black-and-white films is typically one-half to one-third of high-contrast resolution. The relationship between resolving power and its effect on the contrast of details in the image may be evaluated with a test chart composed of constantly decreasing bar-space widths; the resulting measurement is called the modulation transfer function.

See also: DIFFRACTION; IRRADIATION; MTF (MODULATION TRANSFER FUNCTION); SPREAD FUNCTION.

TYPICAL FILM RESOLVING POWER

Lines/mm (1000:1 target)	Quality Level
50 or less	Low
65–90	Medium
100–140	High
150–200	Very high
250–500	Extremely high

Restoring Photographs

Positive and negative images that are faded, stained, cracked, torn, scratched, or dirty often can be restored to obtain

Restoring Photographs. Photographer unknown. An old, faded photograph from Birmingham, Alabama (ca. 1908), recently restored to its original clarity and detail using a new autoradiographic process. Utilizing minute amounts of radioactive materials, the process can bring out details in some films that were underexposed by as much as 80–90 percent. NASA.

an image of greatly improved quality. Although it may not be possible to equal the original quality, the results frequently justify the care and effort required, especially with images of highly unusual content or of special value. In some cases the original can be restored, but that is delicate work, and the risk to unique materials must be considered carefully. A safer course is to make a copy of the damaged original and to work on that. The restored copy is then photographed to obtain a negative for final printing. A slight loss of quality is involved, but the original is not endangered.

Prints, glass plates, and films can be cleaned with a gentle rewashing. Prints must be handled with great care when wet, because the fibers are likely to have lost strength and resiliency as they have dried out over several decades. Most 19th c. papers are thinner than those of today, and they are more susceptible to tearing. Some materials may also be cleaned by sponging gently over the surface with cotton dampened in a 50-50 solution of distilled water and denatured alcohol. This method should be tested on a tiny, unimportant part of the image to make sure it has no adverse effects;

alcohol can dissolve some coatings or base materials. Ambrotypes (collodion positives on glass with a black backing) often can be restored by washing them and replacing the backing; if the backing is lacquer, it can be scraped off and black cloth substituted. Daguerreotypes (positive images on silver plates) must never be touched, rubbed, or brushed on the surface; the image is extremely fragile. They can be cleaned by soaking them in distilled water or in a thiourea and phosphoric acid solution, but the latter method should be researched carefully before being attempted.

Prints that have faded commonly have a yellowish-brown color. Copying them through a deep-blue filter on orthochromatic or panchromatic film often will obtain a negative of near-normal contrast that then can be printed by normal methods. Stains on prints seldom can be removed safely, but they can be eliminated in a copy negative on panchromatic film by photographing through a filter of the same color as but of greater strength than the stain—e.g., a medium- or deep-green filter for a light-green stain.

Some negative stains may be removed

by treatment in a fresh hardening fixer, followed by thorough washing; this treatment will remove milky-gray splotches that are the evidence of incomplete original fixing. The emulsion of a negative on a cracked glass plate sometimes can be transferred to a new glass support. This is more feasible with a collodion-coated plate than with a gelatin-coated plate, but it is a delicate operation and requires research. It is better to fasten the pieces in proper alignment on a larger piece of glass using tape only at the edges, outside of the image area. This is then printed, and the print is spotted or retouched to eliminate the crack marks. Retouching a copy print is also the best way to deal with negative scratches.

Torn prints sometimes can be repaired by gently realigning the adjoining segments and using a moist flour paste to glue them together on an adequate support; the temperature required for heat-set adhesives such as dry mounting tissue may endanger old papers and emulsions. In general, retouching and other physical work should not be carried out on an original unless it is considered expendable if something should go wrong. In any case, a damaged original should be copied before handiwork of any sort is attempted on it so that the image will not be lost even if the original is destroyed. A good copy negative should be fully exposed to ensure recording all dark-area detail and developed to a bit less than normal contrast to ensure that all light-area detail is printable. Contrast can be restored by proper choice of paper grade in making a print.

Except for basic cleaning, professional restorers work on originals only if the plate or print itself is a valued antique or art object. In most cases, they instead use the full arsenal of copying techniques; retouching; and chemical treatments such as reduction, intensification, and toning on a copy print or duplicate negative. Not only does this eliminate the anxiety involved in handling originals, but it also permits use of contemporary techniques and chemicals on modern materials which are likely to be chemically compatible, thereby creating predictable effects.
See also: COPYING PHOTOGRAPHS; DUPLICATE IMAGES; RETOUCHING; SPOTTING.

Restrainer

Developing agents attack the exposed silver halide crystals in an emulsion with relatively high efficiency; they also attack unexposed halides somewhat less efficiently, producing non-image density called fog. Most developers contain one or more restraining ingredients to slow the rate of development so that by the time the image is completely produced, the amount of fog developed has no significant effect on image quality. The most common restrainer is potassium bromide. During film development additional bromide builds up in the solution as the silver bromide crystals are reduced to metallic silver; this slows the rate of development progressively with repeated use. A replenisher adds sufficient quantities of developing agents and other ingredients to overcome this bromide buildup and maintain constant developing times over an extended period of use. The developing agent Phenidone is not restrained by potassium bromide or similar compounds. Instead an inorganic compound such as benzotriazole must be added to the formula to control fog production by the Phenidone.
See also: ANTI-FOGGANT; DEVELOPMENT; FOG/FOGGING.

Reticulation

Film reticulation is the wrinkling of the emulsion into a weblike pattern of tiny lines. The pattern is random, without the size uniformity of graininess, and it is much more visible than a grain pattern. Reticulation is caused by excessive swelling of the softened wet gelatin at some point during processing. When the gelatin dries it cannot evaporate the water evenly and return to its previous uniformly flat state; instead it shrinks to a dimpled surface which in extreme cases may develop cracks along the dimple ridges. The primary cause of reticulation is elevated solution temperature—75°F (24°C) or higher for most films. It is aggravated if the following solution or wash water is cooler; a drop of 5°F (3°C) is sufficient to reticulate some emulsions. In some cases slight reticulation can be eliminated by soaking the film in ethyl alcohol diluted in a 1:5 ratio with water; this must be done before the emulsion has dried.

Normally considered a flaw because it interferes with image details and destroys the uniformity of areas of continuous tone, reticulation is sometimes purposely created for the graphic character of the texture effect it produces. Typical methods include warm developer followed by cold stop bath, warm fixer followed by cold wash water, or warm fixer followed by freezing before washing. In the collotype process, reticulation is used to create a kind of halftone rendition in shadow areas and middletones in the ink reproduction.

Retouching

Retouching is the process of correcting flaws and deficiencies in a negative or positive image by adding, subtracting, or concealing tone (density), color, and details. Retouching is distinguished from related procedures by its corrective purpose. Hand-coloring, painting, or drawing on photographs and similar techniques are part of the intended procedure. They are part of the construction of the image, not its correction.

A variety of techniques are used to retouch negatives, prints, and transparencies. The most basic procedure is using a fine-tip brush and appropriate dyes to conceal white dust spots and similar non-image elements in a print; the technique is described in the entry on spotting. Prints intended only for reproduction are often corrected by airbrushing with opaque paints to conceal unwanted backgrounds, smooth out wrinkles, eliminate glare or add highlights, and otherwise alter the image. This kind of retouching is common with pictures taken as catalog and advertising illustrations.

In addition to commercial illustrations, the greatest amount of print retouching is for portraits. Most portraits are printed on non-glossy surface papers, and retouching is done with special pencils available in black, white, and a variety of colors. The shadow lines in creases or wrinkles are lightened to match the surrounding tone, stray hairs are concealed, a beard shadow is eliminated, highlights are added to the eyes, reflections in eyeglasses are toned down or eliminated, and many other corrections are made. The technique calls for slow, careful work with soft pencils the lead or color deposits of which are frequently smoothed and blended with a fingertip or a tuft of cotton. Very dark flaws such as skin spots or a black spot from a pinhole in the negative often are etched away carefully with a pointed knife of scalpel-like sharpness, and the treated area is spotted-in with color. Larger areas may also be rubbed gently with pumice on a cotton wad to remove tone by abrasion, or they may be given local chemical treatment, as with a reducer. A thin frisket solution (highly diluted rubber cement) first may be painted on other areas to protect them during chemical retouching; it is easily peeled off or removed with a pure rubber "pick-up" eraser.

The most delicate, and difficult, retouching is direct work on a negative or transparency. The film, usually no smaller than 4″ × 5″, is placed on a light box so that changes in silver or dye density can be seen clearly. Color negatives are seldom retouched because of the difficulty of evaluating changes in the different dye layers of the emulsion as seen through the integral orange-brown masking color in such films. It is easier and more accurate to retouch a print from the negative and photograph that to obtain a corrected copy negative. Black-and-white negatives are retouched by abrasion or local chemical reduction to remove density from selected areas; this will cause those areas to print darker. Pencil or brush-and-dye work is used to add density so that treated areas or details will print lighter. The film must have "tooth," an invisible surface roughness, to retain pencil and brush deposits. Several films intended primarily for portrait use are manufactured with a tooth on the base side, or on both the base and emulsion sides. Other films can be painted with a clear retouching ground to give them the required surface. Wrinkles, folds, hairlines, and similar elements are corrected by adding density at the most transparent point (which would print darkest) and working outward to blend with the surrounding density. Brushwork is achieved with a stippling movement, or by dragging the tip of the brush in short, irregular strokes over an area, creating little "worms" of dye that blend together.

Color transparency retouching is the most difficult of all such procedures. It is accomplished with various bleaching solutions that affect only one dye layer at a time and dye solutions that are used to add color. The work demands excellent color vision and an artist's skill and taste in adding or removing color and evaluating the effect as the work progresses. Transparency retouching is offered by only a relatively few specialists among professional retouchers, and it is extremely expensive.

See also: RESTORING PHOTOGRAPHS; SPOTTING.

Color photographs: pp. C-48, C-49.

Retrofocus Lens

This is a lens of inverted (reversed) telephoto design; i.e., one having a greater back focus than its focal length, usually a wide-angle lens.

See: BACK FOCUS; LENSES.

Reversal Materials and Processing

Reversal photographic materials produce a positive image directly from exposure to a subject or another positive image by means of two-step development; no intermediate negative printing step is required. Reversal materials are technically distinct from direct positive materials, which produce positive-to-positive results with only one development step; however, the term direct positive is often used for both kinds of materials. The most common reversal materials are slide films and larger format transparency films, and papers for making prints from slides and transparencies. Many 16mm and smaller motion-picture films also have reversal emulsions.

The reversal process is based on the fact that once the negative image recorded by exposure has been developed, the remaining undeveloped silver halides in the emulsion represent the positive aspect of the image. The procedure is to eliminate the negative and develop the positive. The positive image halides can be made developable by reexposing the emulsion to white light, or by using a developer with a fogging agent, which has the same effect. Typical black-and-white reversal processing is as follows:

1. Negative image is developed.
2. Negative image is bleached to a colorless state.
3. Positive image is produced by (a) white-light exposure followed by a normal developer, or (b) by a fogging developer.
4. The emulsion is fixed, to remove the bleached negative compounds, washed, and dried.

In black-and-white processing the negative must be bleached in step 2 so that it will not interfere with reexposure and—even if a fogging developer is used instead—because it cannot be bleached later without also affecting the positive image. In color reversal processing that is not the case. A fogging developer is used to develop the silver positive image and simultaneously produce the color dye image; it does not matter that the negative image silver is present. Bleaching of both the negative and positive silver images takes place in a single step, after the positive development; then the emulsion is fixed. In some processes these two final steps are combined by using a bleach-fix, or "blix" solution, followed by washing and drying.

See also: DIRECT POSITIVE; ETCH-BLEACH PROCESS.

Reverse Angle; Reverse Shot

In motion pictures and television camera work, a reverse angle shot is one taken from a viewpoint approximately 180° opposite that of the preceding shot. A typical use of this technique is to alternately show the faces of two people engaged in conversation. In continuous recording with two cameras, the reverse angle must be less than 180° so that neither camera is within the field of view of the other. With a single camera the usual procedure is to record the entire scene or action from one angle, then reposition the camera to the desired reverse angle and record the scene a second time; the alternation between the two views is achieved by subsequent editing. The trick effect in which normal action progresses backward is called a *reverse-action shot*.

Revolving Back

Some medium-format and most large-format cameras have backs that revolve so that a rectangular film format can be used either horizontally or vertically. The most versatile backs revolve a full 360° and can be locked at any intermediate position. This permits intentionally tilted composition if desired, or permits correcting for a camera that is not level from side to side so that subject lines are made parallel to the film edges.

Riboud, Marc

French; 1923–

Associated with Magnum Photo Agency for 25 years, Marc Riboud has created visually complex, lyrical, and discerning images throughout the world. He is best known, however, for his attention to detail in his black-and-white and color photographs of life in Communist China before and after the Cultural Revolution of the 1960s. Sinologist Orville Schell has written, "Not since the late 1940s, when Henri Cartier-Bresson photographed China poised on the edge of communist takeover, has anyone portrayed the Chinese with such mastery."

Riboud was born in Lyons where he attended secondary schools. After service with the French Army and Resistance from 1943 to 1945, when he was awarded the Croix de Guerre, he studied engineering at the Ecole Centrale in Lyons from 1945 to 1948. Upon receiving his degree, he worked as an industrial engineer until 1952 when he began to photograph. He became a Paris-based freelance photographer the following year and was invited to join Magnum by his mentor, Cartier-Bresson, and Robert Capa. He was associated with the agency in Paris and New York as a member (1953–1979), vice-president (1958–1975), president (1975–1976), and chairman of the board (1976–1977).

Riboud worked on the film *Around the World in 80 Days* in 1956 and has himself traveled widely in the Far East, Turkey, Iran, Afghanistan, Russia, and the Congo.

Riboud is the recipient of numerous awards, including two awards from the Overseas Press Club in New York. He has published several important books, including *Three Banners of China* (1966), *The Face of North Viet Nam* (1972), and *Visions of China* (1980).

He has been the subject of one-man traveling exhibitions originating at Asia House, the Photographers Gallery, and ICP in New York. His work has been included in group shows at the Metropolitan Museum in New York, the Israel Museum in Jerusalem, and the Massachusetts Institute of Technology in Cambridge, Massachusetts. His photographs have appeared in mass-circulation newspapers and magazines throughout the world.

Photograph: p. 418.

Rights and Permissions

The photographer's right to make pictures in public places is largely taken for granted in most non-authoritarian countries. Elsewhere the photographer might be restricted severely by regulations that establish "appropriate" or permissible subject matter and location. For example, in certain nations unauthorized photography of seemingly innocuous subjects such as industrial buildings and train movements is illegal and may be regarded as espionage. Even in democratic societies making pictures near military or strategically sensitive installations is a restricted or forbidden activity.

Generally speaking, the photographer is subject to the same rules and regulations as the ordinary citizen. While there may be no specific ordinance forbidding photography on the street, there are laws governing the obstruction of traffic, creation of a public nuisance, or posing a hazard to passers-by. Any or all of these regulations can be violated by the tripod-laden photographer who unheedingly blocks the flow of pedestrian or vehicular movement.

Private or municipal museums, churches, and parks commonly have their own regulations governing photography. Some museums allow picture-taking as long as a tripod or flash is not used; others require the payment of a nominal fee. In a number of cases official permission is required beforehand. The photographer should find out in advance if written permission is needed and if any restriction exists regarding the kind of equipment he or she is allowed to use. The photographer should also find out whether or not the regulations are variable. Many museums allow the use of tripods or flash equipment in non-peak times, but ban their use when the museum is crowded.

There are usually few regulations regarding photography in parks. Those which do exist regard the use of models, elaborate lighting, and any other equipment normally associated with commercial photography. In most cases permission to do photography of this sort can be obtained easily from the municipality, provided the photographer makes an advance request in writing.

A photographer making pictures on privately owned land without the owner's permission is guilty of trespassing; prior permission must always be obtained. Even in publicly acessible areas such as streets, common sense and courtesy should prevail. Regardless of the photographer's right to make pictures in public places, insisting on getting the picture over the subject's objections can result in an altercation and possible injury to the photographer and his or her equipment. Often professional news photographers and photojournalists run this risk as part of their occupation; however, it is a rare situation when the risk is justified for the non-professional. In the same regard, the photographer should heed police lines and stay out of the way of firefighters, medical personnel, and other emergency workers.

With few exceptions, the right to make photographs in no way guarantees the photographer's right to publish them without specific permission from the subject; this is true even for a photo-

Riis, Jacob. "An ancient woman lodger in Eldridge Street Police Station" (ca. 1890). Museum of the City of New York.

graph of a private individual in a public place. Such permission should be obtained at the time of the shooting in the form of a model release or an equivalent signed document.

See also: COPYRIGHT; MODELS; REPRODUCTION RIGHTS AND FEES; SELLING PHOTOGRAPHS.

Riis, Jacob A.

American; 1849–1914

America's first journalist-photographer, in fact a muckraker with a camera, Jacob Riis was known at the turn of the century as the "Emancipator of the Slums" because of his work on behalf of the urban poor. His brutal documentation of sweatshops, disease-ridden tenements, and overcrowded schools aroused public indignation and helped effect significant reform in housing, education, and child-labor laws.

Riis was self-taught. His photographs, taken over a 10-year period, were made without artistic intent, yet they deeply influenced the course of American documentary photography. Riis wrote: "I came to take up photography . . . not exactly as a pastime. It was never that for me. I had to use it, and beyond that I never went." The camera was a weapon of propaganda he wielded in his fight to ameliorate the living conditions of countless underprivileged people who would have remained unseen if not for his passionate social concern.

Riis was born in Ribe, Denmark, the third in a family of 15 children (one of them adopted). In opposition to his

father's wishes, he was a carpenter's apprentice in Copenhagen from 1866 to 1870, when he emigrated to the United States.

Riis lived in poverty in New York City for some time before he found a job with a news bureau in 1873. He became a police reporter for the New York *Tribune* and the Associated Press in 1877. Horrified by the squalor of immigrant life, he began a series of exposés on slum conditions on New York's Lower East Side. In 1884 he was responsible for the establishment of the Tenement House Commission.

In 1888 he left the *Tribune* for the *Evening Sun* and began work on his book *How the Other Half Lives*. Riis was among the first photographers to use flash powder, which enabled him to photograph interiors and exteriors of the slums at night. He worked at first with two assistants but soon found it necessary to take his photographs himself. Primarily a writer, he wanted pictures to document and authenticate his reports, and to supply the vividness that would ensure attention.

Sections of *How the Other Half Lives* appeared in *Scribner's* magazine in December 1889. The full-length book attracted immediate attention upon publication some months later and was reprinted several times. It had a powerful and lasting effect on movements for many kinds of social reform.

For the next 25 years Riis continued to write and lecture extensively on the problems of the poor. He published over a dozen books, including his autobiography, *The Making of an American* (1901), and many articles. He became known as "the father of the small parks movement" after his success in creating a park in the infamous Mulberry Bend section of lower Manhattan. Following a decade of heart trouble, Riis died in Barre, Massachusetts, at the age of 65.

Riis's photographs fell into obscurity for many years until Alexander Alland was able to find and salvage them in the early 1940s. Riis's son presented 412 4″ × 5″ glass negatives, by Riis and his assistants, to the Museum of the City of New York in 1946. A major exhibition of prints from these negatives was held at the Museum in 1947. Riis's home in Richmond Hill, New York, was designated a National Historical Landmark in 1971.

See also: DOCUMENTARY PHOTOGRAPHY.

Rim Light

Rim light is a bright outline of illumination around the edges of an object. It is created by placing an intense light source behind and aimed at the object. The light is diffracted at the edges, creating greater intensity there than in the spill light farther outside. The light source is blocked from the lens view by the object. It may be a spotlight, electronic flash unit, bare photoflood bulb, or reflector floodlight. The effect varies with the area and intensity of the source; a broad source produces a softer, halo-like glow. The spreading of the light can be emphasized by smoke or dust in the air or by use of a diffusion filter at the camera lens. The background should be dark, and frontlight must be added if subject details are to be seen. The rim light must be at least twice as bright as the total front illumination, or its effect will be washed out.

A similar effect, edge light, is produced by directing light at the subject from light sources positioned behind but outside the camera range at the sides and above—a kind of surrounding backlight. Edge light does not create the luminous glow that is characteristic of rim light, but it is more effective in separating a subject from a lighted background.

See also: BACKLIGHT; LIGHTING; SIDE LIGHT.

Ring-around

Controlled variations in exposure, development, filtration, and other factors can be compared by means of a ring-around. Variant images are arranged in a ring or box pattern around a central "normal" image made without varia-

Ring-around. (A) Ring-around for variations in film exposure and development. (B) Ring-around for variations in color printing filtration; figures indicate density added or subtracted.

Ring-around

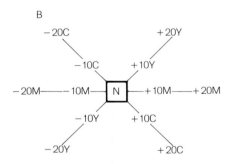

UE UD	UE ND	UE OD
NE UD	NE ND	NE OD
OE UD	OE ND	OE OD

U = Under-   E = Exposure
O = Over-   D = Development
N = Normal

tions. The procedure is equally valuable in examining negatives, prints, and transparencies. Most commonly, a standard ring-around is prepared for use in identifying the characteristics or faults of later images by comparison. A ring-around is also a revealing way to explore the results obtainable with a new material, solution, or processing/printing procedure. The accompanying diagrams show two typical ring-around patterns.

N = Normal filtration
C = Cyan
M = Magenta
Y = Yellow

Rise and Fall

See: CAMERA MOVEMENTS.

Robertson, James

See: BEATO, FELICE.

Robinson, Henry Peach

British; 1830–1901

Henry Peach Robinson was a leading "high art" pictorial photographer in the last half of the 19th c. Deeply influenced by the work of O. G. Rejlander, he produced many combination prints after 1857. He was known as "the high-priest of photographic picture-making by rule and combination." In Robinson's work, every picture tells a story. In imitation of the popular painting of his time, he assembled his photographs from different negatives, concentrating on strictly posed and composed narrative scenes. His later work was almost entirely of peopled, picturesque landscapes and he disclaimed his early opinions about the value of combination prints.

Robinson was born in Ludlow, Shropshire, England. He worked in a Leamington bookshop while studying art and contributing articles and sketches to various periodicals. He had diverse interests in painting, etching, sculpture, and literature, and continued to sketch and paint all his life. Acceptance of his paintings by the Royal Academy led to an arrogant assumption of authority in his later pronouncements on art in photography.

Robinson became interested in photography at the Great Exhibition of 1851. He opened a portrait studio in Leamington Span in 1857, the year of Rejlander's controversial "Two Ways of Life." Robinson made his first composite print the following year. Called "Fading Away," it depicted a dying girl surrounded by her relatives and was made from five different negatives. Upon seeing this work, Prince Albert agreed to buy one of each of Robinson's pictorial photographs. Robinson became the champion of pictorialism, and in the 1880s and 1890s did artistic battle-royal with P. H. Emerson, leader of the naturalist school.

Robinson exhibited annually at the Photographic Society, London, and throughout Great Britain and Europe. He won over 100 competition awards during his career of 40 years, for combination prints and his later, more conventional work.

Robinson moved to London in 1864 when ill-health forced him to sell his studio. He worked in partnership with N. K. Cherrill in Turnbridge Wells from 1868. After a temporary retirement in 1875, he built "Great Hall Studio," completed in 1878. He retired from business in 1888.

Robinson published regularly in photographic journals, promoting and developing his aesthetics. He was the author of the most widely read photographic textbooks of his day. His most influential books included *Pictorial Effect in Photography* (1869), *Picture Making by Photography* (1889), and *Art Photography* (1890).

Robinson was a founding member of the Linked Ring in 1892, and was made an Honorary Fellow of the Royal Photographic Society in 1900, a year before his death.

See also: EMERSON, PETER HENRY; NATURALISTIC PHOTOGRAPHY; "PICTORIAL EFFECT IN PHOTOGRAPHY"; PICTORIAL PHOTOGRAPHY/PICTORIALISM.

Rodchenko, Alexander

Russian; 1891–1956

Alexander Rodchenko, one of the most versatile Constructivist and Productivist artists to emerge after the Russian Revolution, worked as a painter and graphic designer before turning to photomontage and photography. His photography was socially engaged, formally innovative, and opposed to a painterly aesthetic. Concerned with the need for analytical-documentary photo series, he often shot his subjects from odd angles—usually high above or below—to shock the viewer and to postpone recognition. He wrote: "One has to take several different shots of a subject, from different points of view and in different situations, as if one examined it in the round rather than looked through the same key-hole again and again."

Rodchenko was born in St. Petersburg, Russia. He moved with his family to Kazan, in eastern Russia, in 1902. He studied at the Kazan School of Art under Nikolai Feshin and Georgii Medvedev, and at the Stroganov Institute in Moscow. He made his first abstract drawings, influenced by the Suprematism of Malevich, in 1915. The following year, he participated in "The Store" exhibition organized by Vladimir Tatlin, who was another formative influence in his development as an artist.

Rodchenko was appointed Director of the Museum Bureau and Purchasing Fund by the Bolshevik Government in 1920. He was responsible for the reorganization of art schools and museums. He taught from 1920 to 1930 at the Higher Technical-Artistic Studios (Vkhutemas/Vkhutein).

In 1921 he became a member of the Productivist group, which advocated the incorporation of art into everyday life. He gave up painting in order to concentrate on graphic design for posters, books, and films. He was deeply influenced by the ideas and practice of the filmmaker Dziga Vertov, with whom he worked intensively in 1922.

Impressed by the photomontage of the German Dadaists, Rodchenko began his own experiments in the medium, first employing found images in 1923, and from 1924 on shooting his own photographs as well. His first published photomontage illustrated Mayakovsky's poem, "About This," in 1923.

From 1923 to 1928 Rodchenko collaborated closely with Mayakovsky (of whom he took several striking portraits) on the design and layout of *LEF* and *Novy LEF,* the publications of Constructivist artists. Many of his photographs appeared in or were used as covers for these journals. His images eliminated unnecessary detail, emphasized dynamic diagonal composition, and were concerned with the placement and movement of objects in space.

Throughout the 1920s Rodchenko's work was abstract often to the point of being non-figurative. In the 1930s, with the changing Party guidelines governing artistic practice, he concentrated on sports photography and images of parades and other choreographed movements.

Rodchenko joined the October circle of artists in 1928 but was expelled three years later for "formalism." He returned to painting in the late 1930s, stopped photographing in 1942, and produced abstract expressionist works in the 1940s. He continued to organize photography exhibitions for the government during these years. He died in Moscow in 1956.

In recent years Rodchenko's work has been the subject of renewed interest. His work has been included in exhibitions at the Hirshhorn Museum, Washington, D.C., and the Guggenheim Museum, New York. A show of 50 prints was held in 1976 in Milan and Rome.

Robinson, Henry Peach. "Fading Away" (1858). Royal Photographic Society, Bath, England.

Rodger, George

British; 1908–

Documenting and recording have been George Rodger's main aims throughout his life. In his early days, photography was for him nothing more than a supplement to his writings, an additional means of expression. As time went on, his written captions and notes became a valued addition to his photographs.

Rodger was born and schooled in England. In the late 1920s he toured the world twice as a merchant seaman, then worked as a laborer in a variety of jobs in the U.S. until 1936, when he returned to England. Like so many others who became photojournalists in the 1930s, Rodger was a self-taught photographer. For a few years he worked for the BBC and, until 1939, with the Black Star photo agency in London. At the outbreak of World War II he became a war correspondent for *Life* and was on the staff of that magazine from 1945 to 1947.

As a war correspondent for *Life,* he trekked 75,000 miles across Africa and the Sahara, the Middle East, and India. This incredible journey took nearly two years and many of its struggles were published in *Life* in August 1942. It was a feat no one had ever accomplished before under so many adverse conditions, continuously coping with local conditions, people of all types, the weather and, more often than not, lack of adequate food and water. After this odyssey, Rodger continued to photograph other war assignments for *Life.* He was sent to Europe and to Burma, and became the magazine's most traveled correspondent, having covered in all more than 150,000 miles.

Once the war ended, Rodger flatly re-

Rodchenko, Alexander. "At the telephone" (1928). Collection, Museum of Modern Art, New York.

fused to be associated with anything showing conflicts between peoples. He had seen the horrors of war at too-close range and wanted to devote his time to more peaceful subjects. His chief aim was to promote more understanding for people in general and especially for those people who could not speak up for themselves. In 1947, having become a founding member of Magnum Photos, Rodger established himself in Africa. There he photographed the vanishing wildlife and the last remaining primitive tribes. He photographed these people in their own environment, highlighting their customs and their ceremonies. His soft-spoken attitude and his ability to become totally absorbed in the lives of his subjects brought him total acceptance.

Some of Rodger's African photographs can be seen in his book *Le Village des Noubas*, published in Paris in 1955. His return to Africa at age 70 to photograph the Masai resulted in an exhibition, *Masai Moran*, that toured England and France.

Rolleiflex

A number of twin-lens reflex (TLR) cameras were introduced toward the end of the 19th c., but by about 1910 the design had almost disappeared. It was reintroduced in 1928 as the Rolleiflex, designed and produced in Germany by Franke and Heidecke. The Rolleiflex created a great wave of popularity for

the TLR, and was widely imitated. The original model had a 75 or 80mm $f/4.5$—soon $f/3.8$—taking lens and an $f/3.0$ viewing lens; it took 2¼"-square (6 × 6cm) pictures on 117-size roll film. Its all-metal construction was an innovation for this kind of camera. The Rolleiflex Standard, introduced in 1932, used the more widely available 120-size film and replaced the film-advance knob with a crank, a feature that became standard with almost every TLR camera. A later innovation coupled shutter cocking and automatic frame-by-frame stopping to the crank movement. Various models introduced from the 1930s through the 1950s included the 4 × 4cm Rolleiflex for 127 film; a model with insert masks to change from the square format to various rectangular formats; a model that used 35mm film; the Tele-Rolleiflex with 135mm lenses; and the Rolleicord, a less versatile, more economical version of the basic camera. For more than four decades the Rolleiflex set the standards and introduced the features that other TLR cameras imitated; it is no longer manufactured.
See also: CAMERA; TWIN-LENS CAMERA.

Roll Film

Unsprocketed film for still photography supplied in lengths of up to about six ft. on camera-loading spools is called roll film, as distinct from film lengths supplied in cassettes (e.g., 35mm film) or cartridges (e.g., 110, 126 films). Most roll films have a continuous but separate opaque paper backing attached to the leading end of the film by tape. This backing permits daylight-loading and helps prevent abrasions between the layers as the film is rolled onto the takeup spool. In some cameras a small red plastic window reveals numbers printed on the backing paper by which exposures are counted. In order to contain the extra length of 220 size film (twice as long as 120 film, the most common roll size) on standard spools, only a short length of backing paper is attached at each end to protect the film from light when it is rolled up on a spool. The first successful celluloid-base roll films were introduced by the Eastman Co. in 1889, to replace the paper-base films used in the original Kodak camera; daylight-loading spools with backing paper were introduced in 1895.

Rothstein, Arthur
American; 1915–
Arthur Rothstein has been a leading American photojournalist since the 1930s when he was a member of the

Rodger, George. "Dinkas, Sudan" (n.d.).
George Rodger/Magnum.

photographic teams of the Resettlement and Farm Security Administrations under Roy Stryker. His photographs of the Dustbowl and other areas of rural America are perhaps the best known of his prolific career, which is noted for craftsmanship and succinct wit.

Rothstein was born and educated in New York City. He attended Stuyvesant High School from 1929 to 1932, and Columbia University where he received his B.A. in 1935 after studying under Stryker. A photographic hobbyist as a young man in high school, Rothstein was a founder of the Columbia University Camera Club and photography editor of *The Columbian.*

In a style influenced by Walker Evans and Ben Shahn, Rothstein worked for Stryker with the RA/FSA from 1935 to 1940 photographing throughout the U.S. He was a *Look* photographer in 1940–1941. With the outbreak of the war, he worked as a picture editor for

the U.S. Office of War Information in New York from 1941 to 1943 and served as a photo officer with the U.S. Army Signal Corps in India, Burma, and China from 1943 to 1946.

Upon his discharge from the Army, Rothstein worked briefly photographing in China for the United Nations Relief and Rehabilitation Administration. He became technical director of photography for *Look,* eventually becoming Director of Photography, a position which he held until 1971.

In 1971–1972 Rothstein was editor of the American Society of Magazine Photographers' *Infinity* magazine, and a Visual Aids Consultant to the U.S. Environmental Protection Agency and the American Iron and Steel Institute in Washington, D.C. He has been director of photography for *Parade* magazine since that time.

Rothstein was a founding member of the ASMP in 1941 and president of Pho-

tographic Administrators in New York from 1961 to 1963. He was an instructor at the Graduate School of Journalism, Columbia University from 1961 to 1970. He has published more than half a dozen books on photojournalistic and technical subjects and was the developer of the Xograph lenticular-print 3-D process.

Rothstein is the recipient of numerous awards, including a National Press Photographers Association Award (1963) and an International Award from the Photographic Society of America (1968). He was named a Fellow of the Photographic Historical Society of New York in 1979.

Rothstein's work has been included in group exhibitions at the Museum of Modern Art in New York, the Victoria and Albert Museum in London, the National Gallery of Canada in Ottawa, and others. He has been the subject of one-man shows at George Eastman House in Rochester, New York (1956 and 1976), the Smithsonian Institution in Washington, D.C. (1963), Photokina in Cologne (1966), Rizzoli Gallery in New York (1980), and Prakapas Gallery in New York (1978).

See also: FARM SECURITY ADMINISTRATION; LENTICULAR SYSTEMS.

Royal Photographic Society (RPS)

The Photographic Society of London was founded in 1853, largely through the efforts of Roger Fenton, several members of the Calotype Club—the first, and an informal, English organization devoted to photography—and a number of scientists. The first president was Sir Charles Eastlake; Fenton was honorary secretary; and the vice-presidents were Sir Charles Wheatstone, Sir William Newton, and Earl Somers. In 1874 the organization became the Photographic Society of Great Britain. It became the Royal Photographic Society in 1894 by act of Queen Victoria who, with her husband Prince Albert, had been an interested observer of the growth of the medium. The Society has consistently encouraged scientific activity in photography and has published journals reporting progress and achievement. Since 1878 it has awarded an annual Progress Medal for outstanding publication or achievement; the first medal was awarded to Sir William Abney. In the course of time the great majority of those who have made notable technical advances in photography have been Associates or Fellows of the Society. Its support and recognition of the communicative and expressive uses of photography has also been constant, but conservative to the point of being reac-

Rothstein, Arthur. "Girl at Gee's Bend, Alabama" (1937). Courtesy Arthur Rothstein; Library of Congress.

tionary. The RPS is the oldest extant photographic organization in the world. *See also:* APPENDIX.

RPS

See: ROYAL PHOTOGRAPHIC SOCIETY.

Rudolph, Paul

German; 1858–1935

A brilliant optical mathematician, Rudolph's first major lens design utilized the Jena glasses produced by Abbe and Schott to create an innovative, asymmetrical, unconvertible doublet anastigmat lens first manufactured by Carl Zeiss in 1890. Derivatives of this design were known as Protar lenses; they provided normal fields of view at wide apertures without astigmatism or curvature of field, and provided wider corrected fields at smaller apertures. Rudolph's masterpiece was the triplet Tessar design of 1902, produced in many different series, and even today the basis of many wide-aperture designs for small-format lenses. He was one of the first (in 1896) to produce a perfected lens, the Planar, using basic Gauss design principles. His later work for the firm of Hugo Meyer Optics produced the Plasmat and, in 1920, Double-Plasmat designs. Many aspects of modern camera lens design derive from innovations he introduced or first perfected.

See also: ABBE, ERNST; ANASTIGMAT; JENA GLASS; ZEISS, CARL.

S

Sabattier Effect

Partial reversal of a black-and-white or color image caused by exposing it to light during development is called the Sabattier effect; the final image contains both positive and negative tonalities or colors. Discovered by French scientist Armand Sabattier in 1862, this effect has been used expressively by many photographers, one of the first and most successful being Man Ray. The effect is often incorrectly called solarization, or more accurately "darkroom solarization." The results are generally more dramatic with negatives than with prints, but the principle is the same.

Procedure. Development starts normally, producing significant density along with desensitizing by-products first in the most heavily exposed areas—the highlight portions of a negative, the shadow areas of a print. When the image is momentarily flashed with light, these areas are thus protected, but the originally less exposed and consequently less dense areas are affected. As development is completed in the dark, the flashed areas now build to densities far greater than they would originally have achieved, with the result that their printing value or visual appearance is reversed. The reexposing light may be white, or colored, for special effects with color materials. The degree of effect depends upon when the reexposure occurs and its strength. The sooner the image is flashed and the stronger the light (or the longer it is left on), the greater the reversal in the final image. Reexposure time is a matter of seconds, not minutes. Results are not entirely predictable, but can be brought under some control by repeated experimentation with a constant light-to-image distance, and careful notation of reexposure timing and duration. A definite demarcation, the Mackie line, is produced at the boundary between reversed and unreversed areas; it will print as a distinct black line from a Sabattier-effect negative, but may be unnoticeable in prints given Sabattier treatment.

Safelight

A low-wattage light that is filtered to provide darkroom illumination that will not fog (expose) printing papers or film is known as a safelight. A safelight is used primarily for printing and enlarging rather than for film processing. This is because all color films and most black-and-white films are panchromatic—sensitive to all colors in the spectrum—and so must be processed in total darkness. (A very brief exposure to a dim, dark-green safelight is sometimes possible in order to inspect the progress of black-and-white film development, but it is not possible to use safelight illumination throughout panchromatic film processing.) Many graphic-arts lith films have orthochromatic (red-blind) emulsions; these can be handled and processed under red safelight illumination.

Black-and-white contact printing and enlarging papers are sensitive to blue light and some portion of the green part of the spectrum. It is therefore possible to use a safelight that filters out these wavelengths. A light-amber filter generally is suitable for all papers; a greenish-yellow filter is often recommended if only contact printing papers are to be used. A red filter also is suitable for both kinds of paper, but it provides less illumination than the other filters.

Color reversal papers, used to make prints from slides, must be handled and processed in total darkness. Color negative papers, and panchromatic papers used to make black-and-white prints from color negatives, generally may be handled under a deep-amber filter for no more than 1½ minutes total exposure.

A variety of hanging, wall-mount, and table-top safelights are available; most accept interchangeable filters and screw-in tungsten bulbs. A safelight aimed directly at a work area must be kept at least 4 ft. (1.1m) from the level at which materials will be handled. A 7½-watt bulb is the maximum for most color safelighting, and a 15-watt bulb is maximum for black and white. If the safelight is positioned to reflect off a wall or ceiling, a 15-watt bulb may be used for color, and a 25-watt bulb for black-and-white. Tubular safelight filters that slip over low-output fluorescent tubes are also available. Some high-intensity safelights contain a sodium-vapor tube that emits a very narrow-wavelength yellowish light to which the eye is quite sensitive but black-and-white paper emulsions are not. Such safelights are used for reflected rather than direct illumination and have adjustable filters for use with some color papers. While providing the greatest amount of working illumination, they are the most expensive kind of safelight.

A single safelight is often sufficient in a small darkroom; otherwise, it is convenient to have one or more safelights in both the printing and the processing areas. Many enlarging timers have a socket for a safelight connection. They turn off a tungsten-bulb safelight whenever the enlarger light is on. This limits safelight exposure of the paper and makes it easier to see the projected image for focusing and printing operations such as burning-in and dodging.

Testing. An important factor is whether or not a safelight is in fact safe. If the light is too bright or if the filter is the wrong type or faded, papers can receive unwanted exposure called *fogging*. This may not be visible in the borders of a print, but it can add to the exposure in the highlight areas of the image to produce veiling—a contrast-reducing trace of gray tone. A simple test can be conducted by making a print of an image with a sizable area of even highlight tone or simply by giving a piece of paper the minimum exposure required to produce a trace of tone. The paper must be handled and exposed with the safelight turned off. It then is placed face up on a work surface, and all but a small strip is covered with a piece of opaque cardboard. The safelight is turned on. After 3 minutes the card is shifted to expose an additional strip; it is shifted again at intervals of 2, 2, and 1 minute, leaving a strip of the unexposed portion covered during the last minute. This produces segments with 8, 5, 3, 1, and 0 minutes of safelight exposure. The paper is processed and examined to see if there is any variation in tonality. If fogging is revealed by a visible change, the test shows for how many minutes the safelight is safe. A minimum of five minutes safe time is required to allow for loading the easel, making an exposure, and processing a print to the point that it is put in the fixing bath. An unsafe condition may require changing to a lower wattage bulb, moving the safelight farther away or using it for reflected rather than direct illumination, or replacing the filter. Safelight filters fade with age, so periodic retesting is advisable.

See also: INSPECTION DEVELOPMENT.

Safety Film

Film with a base of cellulose acetate or triacetate, or with a polyester base, is called safety film because the base material will not decompose and ignite spontaneously, and will not independently sustain a flame. The first celluloid material used as a film base, cellulose nitrate, was highly flammable and decomposed during prolonged storage. Safety-base films for still photography were introduced early in the 20th c.; their use in motion pictures did not become universal until several decades later.

See also: CELLULOID.

Salomon, Erich. "French Foreign Minister Aristide Briand addressing the League of Nations" (n.d.). Courtesy Bildarchive, Berlin; permanent collection, ICP, New York.

Salomon, Erich

German; 1886–1944

Erich Salomon was among the first photographers to use a miniature camera to take unposed, unguarded photographs of politicians and high society celebrities. The London *Graphic* coined the term "candid camera" for his work. Known for his clever means of avoiding detection in situations where photography was prohibited—he hid his camera in his hat, a valise, a potted plant, used silent shutters and cable releases—Salomon's journalistic "spy work" earned him a number of nicknames: "The Houdini of Photography," "Master of Indiscretion," and "Invisible Cameraman."

Salomon was born the son of a wealthy Jewish banker in Berlin, Germany. He had early interests in zoology and carpentry but studied mechanical engineering and law at Rostock University, Munich. He received a doctorate of law in 1913. Taken as a prisoner-of-war at the Battle of the Marne, the multilingual Salomon acted as an interpreter from 1914 to 1918. The inflationary post-war period forced him to take a number of jobs before he found more regular employment in the publicity department of the Ullstein publishing house in 1925.

Salomon began to photograph in 1927 using an Ermanox, an innovative small camera with a fast (*f*/2, later *f*/1.8) lens that allowed him to shoot indoors without flash. (He switched to a Leica in 1932.) He soon got a series of scoops using his inconspicuous camera and ingenuity, and began his career in earnest

in 1928. He would work for little more than a decade.

Salomon photographed diplomats at the League of Nations conferences and became a documenter of political and cultural events. His work was published regularly in the *Berliner Illustrirte Zeitung* and other leading mass-circulation periodicals of the day.

Photographing in Geneva, Paris, and London, Salomon established a style of informal glimpses of important figures which has influenced the entire course of photojournalism.

In 1930 he traveled to the United States where he photographed Marlene Dietrich, William Randolph Hearst, and Herbert Hoover, among others. His book, *Famous Contemporaries in Off-Guard Moments,* was published to acclaim in 1931.

In 1932 Salomon fled Germany to live in The Hague, Netherlands. He continued to work in England, France, and Switzerland until 1940 when the Netherlands were occupied by the Nazis. Salomon, his wife, and one of their sons were imprisoned at Scheveningen, then deported to Theresienstadt, Czechoslovakia, in 1943. They were killed at Auschwitz in 1944.

Exhibitions of Salomon's work have been held at major museums and galleries including the Royal Photographic Society, London; the International Museum of Photography at George Eastman House; Photokina; and ICP.

Salon Photography

Photography salons—international exhibitions of the work of artistically inclined photographers—played an important role in the growth of the art photography movement in the 1890s. Photography salons, modeled directly upon the painting salons that had been held regularly throughout Europe since the 18th c., had been held in Britain and France as early as the 1850s. Featuring works selected by a prominent jury and open to the public, these painting salons were responsible for bringing a vast popular audience to contemporary art. By exhibiting regularly in such salons, artists could hope to attract commissions from both private and official patrons. The earliest photography salons sought to accomplish these same ends, and thus to conclusively demonstrate the legitimacy of artistic photography.

In 1891, as the Pictorial movement in photography was just beginning to attract attention, the Vienna Salon attempted to apply more rigorous standards to the selection of works to be exhibited. A jury of 11 painters examined over 4,000 photographs and selected 600 to be hung; these included works by such venerable photographers as Henry Peach Robinson and such promising newcomers as Alfred Stieglitz. The Vienna Salon marked the first attempt to assemble the most outstanding photographic work from around the world without the prizes and awards that had lent earlier salons an openly competitive atmosphere; instead, its object was to advance the cause of artistic photography as a whole, rather than the reputations of a few individual photographers.

This precedent of exhibiting photographs chosen strictly on the basis of aesthetic rather than technical merit was followed in the Photographic Salon organized in 1893 by the Linked Ring group in Britain. Prizes and medals were omitted, commercial sponsors were excluded, and the submission of work by professionals was discouraged. Because of the international interest in the kind of Pictorial photography encouraged by the Photographic Salon, similar exhibitions on a yearly basis were quickly organized in France, Germany, and the U.S. These annual salons allowed photographers to follow the progress of Pictorial photography closely, and contributed to a feeling of international camaraderie among artistic amateurs of many nations.

The importance of the salons was linked directly to that of Pictorial photography, and did not outlive the Pictorialist movement. By 1910, various "secession" groups such as Stieglitz's Photo-Secession had moved far beyond the Pictorial aesthetic, but the audience for this new work was considerably diminished. While international photography salons continue to be held annually by Pictorial photographers in Europe, America, and Japan, their impact on contemporary art photography and commercial photography is minimal.

See also: ART PHOTOGRAPHY; LINKED RING; PHOTO-SECESSION; PICTORIAL PHOTOGRAPHY/PICTORIALISM.

Salt Paper Process

Because light-sensitive silver halide crystals are salts of silver, any method that prepares them directly on a paper surface—rather than in a coating of gelatin or a similar substance—can be called a salt paper process. However, the term is most often used to designate the process in which common salt, sodium chloride (NaCl), is used. As such, the term is a synonym for the calotype process invented by W. H. F. Talbot, but salt—or salted—paper was also the basis of the direct positive process of Hippolyte Bayard, and the waxed paper process of Gustave LeGray.

In essence, the process consists of impregnating the surface of paper with a solution of salt dissolved in water. This is accomplished by brushing or swabbing the solution on, or by floating the paper on the surface of a tray of solution. After the paper is dried, it is swabbed with, or floated on, a silver nitrate solution. A chemical reaction occurs, forming light-sensitive silver chloride on the surface of the paper. This is a slow, high-contrast compound that can produce an image either by printing-out exposure, or by a shorter exposure and subsequent development. The equivalent speed of salt paper is less than ISO/ASA 1; the process has no practical application today.

See also: CALOTYPE; DIRECT POSITIVE; WAXED PAPER PROCESS.

Salzmann, Auguste

French; 1824–1872

Auguste Salzmann's photographic work is limited to the projects he undertook in the Middle East between 1854 and 1865. Like many other aspiring young artists of the French Second Empire, Salzmann undertook a Middle-Eastern tour in his youth (1850–1851), returning several years later with a commission from the French Ministry of Public Instruction to photograph the remaining monuments of the Crusades erected by the Knights of the Order of St. John in Jerusalem, Rhodes, Kos, Cyprus, and Crete. While undertaking this commission, Salzmann also photographed monuments of disputed attribution for Louis T. Caignart de Saulcy, an archaeologist who believed that he had found artifacts dating from the ancient Kingdom of Judah in Jerusalem.

With over 200 paper negatives, Salzmann returned to Paris in mid-1854. His work was published by Blanquart-Evrard in a three-volume album of salt-paper prints: *Jérusalem, époques judaïque, romaine, chrétienne, arabe, explorations photographiques* (1854). The volumes were reissued in 1856 by Gide and Baudry as *Jerusalem, vues et monuments de la ville sainte de l'époque judaïque au present.*

Salzmann returned to the Middle East in 1863 to join one of de Saulcy's expeditions; his *Bijoux phénéciens* was published later that year. The photographs he made as a pictorial record of archaeological excavations on Rhodes (1858–1865) were published after his death as *Nécropole de Camirros* (1875).

Unlike the prints of other mid-century Western travelers in the Near and Middle East, which clearly documented their subjects from distances that made context and scale clear, Salzmann's images avoided such references, thus producing an effect where formal elements appeared more important than informational ones.

Photograph: p. 444.

Sander, August

German; 1876–1964

August Sander's most famous photographs are portraits of the German people, social types of all classes and occupations, taken for a vast documentary archive project of his own conception. Sander attempted to make "natural portraits that show the subjects in an environment corresponding to their own individuality." Of Sander's work, Thomas Mann wrote in 1929: "This collection of photographs, as finely delineated as they are unpretentious, is a treasure-trove for the student and lover of physiognomy and provides an excellent opportunity to explore the occupational and class-structured imprints on humanity." These images, part of a monumental series Sander called "Man in the Twentieth Century," were abhorred by the Nazis and banned in the 1930s.

Sander was born in Herdorf, near Cologne, Germany, the son of a mining carpenter. The young Sander began an apprenticeship as a miner in 1889. He received a 13 × 18cm camera from an uncle in 1892, built a darkroom, and began to photograph in his spare time. After military service, he toured Germany as a commercial photographer specializing in architectural and industrial photos. In 1901 he was employed by

Salzmann, August. "Absolom's Tomb, Valley of Kidron, Jerusalem" (1854). Canadian Centre for Architecture, Montreal.

Late that year he showed 60 photographs from the "Man in the Twentieth Century" series in the Cologne Kunstverein exhibition. This show led to an agreement with the publisher Kurt Wolff to issue books covering the entire project. The first of these volumes, *Face of Our Time,* appeared in 1929 with an introduction by Alfred Doblin.

Sander delivered a series of highly popular radio lectures on "The Nature and Development of Photography" in 1931. The rise of Hitler began to affect his work about this time. His son Erich joined the Socialist Worker's Party and anti-Nazi movement in 1933; he was jailed for treason in 1934 and died in prison 10 years later. At the same time (1933–1934) five books of Sander's "German Land, German People" series were published. They met with immediate disapproval by the Nazi authorities and he was forced to cease work on "Man in the Twentieth Century." His *Face of Our Time* was seized, the plates destroyed, and negatives confiscated by the Ministry of Culture.

Sander began a series of Rhineland landscapes and nature studies in 1935 on which he worked for the rest of his life. During World War II he made prints of pre-war photographs for families of men who had died or were missing in action. He began some work on "Man in the Twentieth Century" once more. His studio was destroyed by bombing, but thousands of negatives were salvaged. Tragically, the same negatives were destroyed by looters in 1946. Despite these setbacks, Sander continued to work on a variety of special projects and books.

In 1951 Sander's work was mounted at the first exhibition at Photokina. His documentation of pre-war Cologne was bought by the city the same year. A number of his photographs were selected by Edward Steichen in 1952 for inclusion in the *Family of Man* show of 1955.

Sander was named an honorary member of the German Photographic Society in 1958 and was given a one-man show by that body the following year. He received the Order of Merit of the Federal Republic of Germany in 1960. Sander suffered a stroke in late 1963 and died in Cologne some months later.

Sander has been honored by major shows at the Museum of Modern Art, New York, and at the International Center of Photography. His work has influenced countless other photographers in recent years, from Walker Evans to Robert Frank and Diane Arbus.
Photograph: p. 440.

the Photographic Studio Graf in Linz, Austria. He and a partner bought this concern the following year and renamed it Studio Sander and Stuckenberg. Two years later he bought out his partner and started the August Sander Studio for Pictorial Arts of Photography and Painting.

Sander was awarded a gold medal and Cross of Honor at the Paris Exposition of 1904, the first of hundreds of such awards he would receive in his career. He began at this time to experiment with color photography and his work in this field was soon acquired by the Leipzig Museum. In 1906 Sander's first one-man exhibition, of 100 prints, was held at the Landhaus Pavilon in Linz.

After selling his studio in Linz, Sander moved his family to Trier and then to Lindenthall, a suburb of Cologne. While photographing peasants in nearby Westerwald, Sander originated his life-project, "Man in the Twentieth Century." His intention was to document the entire German people. While pursuing this work, he continued to photograph industrial and architectural subjects to make his living.

Sander served in the German Army during World War I but continued to photograph. He began teaching apprentices and other students in 1919.

In 1927 Sander traveled to Sardinia to photograph the people and landscapes. This was his only trip outside Germany.

Satellite Photography

See: SPACE PHOTOGRAPHY.

Satire in Photography. Burk Uzzle, "Memorial Day" (1982). © Burk Uzzle.

Satire in Photography

Satire's particular targets are human vice, folly, and absurdity masquerading as virtue, wisdom, or other forms of superiority. Photography's ability to capture moments when such poses are clearly exposed made it a powerful new weapon in satire's arsenal. Photography could also be used, in fictionalized or composite images, to make a satirical point by bringing together revealing discrepancies.

In the 19th c., photography was itself more often the target of satire than the medium of its expression. In 1839, the year Daguerre announced his invention, Theodore Maurisset's lithograph "Daguerreotypomania" made fun of the countless Parisians who had taken up what was expected to be a short-lived fad. An 1840 lithograph by Gerard Fontallard ridiculed the long exposures required by early photography. He showed the photographer taking a long nap while the camera made the exposure, over the title "The talent lies in sleeping." And in 1858, when the French photographer Nadar succeeded in taking photographs from a balloon, he was good-naturedly mocked by the artist Daumier, who portrayed Nadar aloft over Paris, "raising photography to the heights of art."

The first such satire to issue from within the ranks of photography was apparently the 1855 book *Photographic Pleasures—Popularly Portrayed with Pen and Pencil*, by Cuthbert Bede. Lewis Carroll, the author of *Alice in Wonderland* and himself a talented amateur photographer, in 1857 satirized the difficulties of early photography in "Hiawatha Photographing," a poem patterned on Longfellow's earlier verse. Carroll made fun of sitters who refused to sit still in his lines on a matron

. . . Holding in her hand a bouquet
Rather larger than a cabbage.
All the while that she was sitting,
Still the lady chattered, chattered,
Like a monkey in the forest.
"Am I sitting still?" she asked him.
"Is my face enough in profile?
Shall I hold the bouquet higher?
Will it come into the picture?"
And the picture failed completely.

Since the 1920s as artists and photographers have begun to expand the medium's expressive capacities in many directions, satire has come to play a recognized role in photography. In the last 60 years photographic satire has usually been directed against three targets: political or social conditions, the conventions of art, and the conventions of photography itself.

No photographic satire has been more slashing than the anti-Nazi photomontages of John Heartfield in the late 1920s and early 1930s. Heartfield described himself not as an artist but as an "engineer," whose intention was not so much self-expression but the transformation of photographs he found in the German mass media to a political end. By cutting up and rearranging these images, Heartfield gave them a biting new meaning. His 1934 montage titled "German Natural History: Metamorphosis," made after the Nazi seizure of power, showed the ineffective politicians of the previous years as caterpillars curled up in their cocoons, while Hitler had burst out of his and spread ominous wings. Because of this and other montages published on the covers of the anti-Nazi magazine AIZ, Heartfield was eventually forced to flee Germany.

An example of a more recent use of photography as a medium of social satire is Les Krims's *The Deerslayers* (1972). While his title calls up images of heroic pioneers hunting game in the wilderness, Krims's photographs present typical suburbanites posing proudly next to the deer carcasses strapped to their shiny automobiles. The visual effect is one of immediate incongruity, and implicit criticism.

In the 1920s, the irreverence that the European Dada artists had directed against traditional art after World War I began also to be expressed through photography. The German Dadaist Raoul Haussmann, in a well-known photomontage, depicted the art critic as an anachronistic figure who used his pencil as a lance. In France, Man Ray satirized 19th-c. classical art by pasting onto the nude back of Kiki, his favorite model, two f-script cutouts resembling the sound holes of a stringed instrument; he called the picture "Ingres's Violin," in mocking tribute to the 19th-c. painter of academic nudes. André Kertész in 1926 took a playful swipe at the angular conventions of cubist art in his photograph "Satiric Dancer," which showed a jazz dancer sprawled on a couch in a pose which mimicked a nearby cubist statuette as well as a cubist print on the wall. In a similar vein, Edward Weston's "Civil Defense" of 1942 gives an unexpected twist to the painterly tradition of the reclining nude by showing the model on a couch wearing only a gas mask.

In recent years, as art photography has begun to display its own variety of pomposity and convention, it has become a frequent target of satiric attack. The tendency to hero-worship successful photographers gave rise, in the mid-1970s, to Larry Sultan and Mike Mandel's production of a set of humorous bubble gum trading cards featuring the likenesses of Ansel Adams, Brett Weston, and a number of other prominent photographers. In 1979, in their exhibition *Evidence*, Sultan and Mandel satirically commented on the recent trend on the part of museum curators to analyze documentary photographs as formal compositions. Selecting anonymous 8" × 10" glossies from a number of government files, they carefully matted and framed the photographs and hung them in a gallery. The result was a barbed commentary on the aura of prestige that a formal showing lends to practically any photography.

Much photographic satire is not biting

or antagonistic, but tends toward gentle irony or amused tolerance. The humorous social observation of Kertész, Brassaï, and others in the 1920s and 1930s was echoed in the post-World War II period in marvelous appreciations of the absurd by Robert Doisneau, Elliot Erwitt, and Burk Uzzle, and with more penetration and implied criticism by Charles Gatewood and especially Garry Winogrand, all of whom have generated a stream of imitators. There is brilliant covert satire in some of the mid-career work of Richard Avedon, especially in images of the Generals of the Daughters of the American Revolution, the teenage singing idols the Everly Brothers, the British author Somerset Maugham, and the American Nazi leader George Lincoln Rockwell. These are far more incisive and far less grotesque than 1940s critical images by Weegee; they are more individually specific than images by Diane Arbus who, like Garry Winogrand, found satiric material in simply photographing the middle-class putting forth its "best face" with unconscious, blind smugness. Les Krims has taken this kind of comment into the realm of surrealism with devastating effect.

Since the 1960s, a number of photographers have satirized Western peoples' inability to separate their self-images from those foisted upon them by advertising and media manipulation. Robert Heinecken has blended media images with "real" photographs to make the point vividly. A great deal of fashion and advertising photography has pretended to satirize modern psychological intensity, but in the work of Guy Bourdin, Rebecca Blake, Chris von Wagenvoord, and Helmut Newton—all of whose pictures go well beyond the mere camp exploitation of the themes they take up—satiric content is often submerged by implicit (and frequently explicit) expression of the perverse, sexually exploitative, and bestial.
See also: BEDE, CUTHBERT; FANTASY IN PHOTOGRAPHY; SURREALISM IN PHOTOGRAPHY

Sayce, B. J.

English; 1837–1895
Together with a fellow amateur photographer, W. B. Bolton (1848–1899), Sayce invented the first true emulsion in photography—a coating for glass plates that contained silver halides and required no separate sensitization, as did all other processes of the time. Sayce and Bolton published their invention in 1864 and began to manufacture it commercially three years later. It consisted of collodion with silver bromide and tannin. The tannin kept the pores of the collo-

dion open so it could be allowed to dry and still be usable; the silver bromide was more light sensitive than the silver iodide used in the wet-plate collodion process, which helped limit the loss of speed that drying the plate produced. The potential convenience for photographers was enormous. They could buy the liquid emulsion, coat their plates a few hours before use, photograph in the field without all the sensitizing and processing paraphernalia required for the wet-plate process, and develop the plates in the darkroom. Although this was the first practical dry-plate process, it was not widely adopted, perhaps because it was two or three *f*-stops less sensitive to light than the wet plate. In the 1870s Bolton marketed a dry pellicle version of the emulsion—chips of sensitized collodion that the photographer dissolved in alcohol in order to coat a plate. Both versions of this collodion-bromide emulsion enjoyed moderate commercial success, but only with the invention of the gelatin emulsion did the dry plate become dominant in photography.
See also: DRY PLATES; WET-PLATE PROCESS.

Scale

The relationship between the size of an object in an image and its actual size is called the object scale. In looking at photographs a general sense of scale is obtained by unconsciously comparing various elements in an image with other elements of a known or average size. A common technique for this purpose is to include a person in an overall landscape or architectural view to provide a scale reference. More precisely, scale is determined by a measured comparison of image size and the object size. When expressed on a relative basis, with the smaller of the two factors set equal to 1, scale is also called the *reproduction ratio*. The image factor is always given first. Thus, if the actual measurements reduce to 1:3, the image is one-third the size of the object, while a ratio of 5:1 indicates that the image is five times larger than lifesize, or object size. When such ratios are divided through, the resultant scale factor is also called *magnification* and is commonly written with a multiplication sign to indicate that the object size must be multiplied by the factor; e.g., 1:3 = 0.3X, and 5:1 = 5X.

In scientific and technical photography a precise scale reference is recorded along with the image. In close-up and macrophotography an inch or millimeter scale is placed at the subject plane. In normal-distance views—e.g., in archaeological site recordings—a reference bar marked with alternating light

and dark sections six inches or ten centimeters long is included. Any such scale must be at the same distance from the lens as the object for which it serves as a reference. If the object stretches away from the camera, the scale must be laid parallel in similar orientation so that its markings are imaged with the same changes in magnification as corresponding portions of the object. In precision aerial photography, altitude and angle data are automatically recorded alongside each exposure so that scale throughout the image can be calculated.
See also: DISTORTION; MAGNIFICATION; PERSPECTIVE; REDUCTION, OPTICAL; REPRODUCTION RATIO.

Scaling

Scaling is the procedure of taking or printing a photograph to exact size, or of determining the degree of enlargement or reduction required so that an image will be reproduced at a desired size. The term also may mean the process of determining the actual sizes of objects from measurements taken of their sizes in photographs.
Photography to scale. Taking a photograph at a particular scale is most often required with transparency films; negative films permit adjusting the image size by enlargement or reduction during printing. In large-format photography it is relatively easy to photograph to scale because the image size can be measured directly on the viewing screen. Adjustments in lens-to-subject distance control the image size; critical focusing is

Scaling

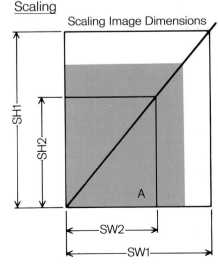

A = Original image size with projected diagonal
Enlargement: SW1 = Desired scale width
SH1 = Equivalent scale height
Reduction: SH2 = Desired scale height
SW2 = Equivalent scale width

accomplished by moving the camera back, if possible, so as not to change the image size. In medium- and small-format photography it is not common to record images at a specific scale because it is easier to obtain a required size accurately during printing, projection, or reproduction. If photographing to scale is necessary, a preferred method is to compute the relative magnification factor of the desired image, and to establish the required setup by means of a ruler placed at the subject position, the method is described in the entry on magnification.

Printing to scale. Sized prints are set up by measuring the projected image and adjusting the enlarger until the required size is achieved. Because object edges may be difficult to discern, accurate measurement is more easily achieved by temporarily replacing the negative with a piece of film or plastic marked with an I-shaped line exactly one in. (or cm) long. The necessary degree of enlargement is determined, and the enlarger adjusted until the sharply focused image of the line is that size; then the negative is put in place of the scale device. For example, if the negative image is ½ in. long and a 6 in. image is desired, the enlargement factor is 12; the enlarger is adjusted to make the projected one-in. reference line 12 in. long.

Scaling. Determining the actual dimensions an image will have at a different scale is necessary in order to draw accurate layouts, cut mat openings, and accomplish similar tasks. Dimensions are also required to calculate scale as an equivalent percentage. A graphic arts circular slide rule simplifies dimension work. One actual image dimension is set opposite the desired scale dimension; the other scale dimension is then found opposite the other image dimension. This kind of device also indicates the equivalent percentage of the new scale.

Dimensions can also be determined by a graphical method, as diagrammed. A diagonal is drawn between opposite corners of the image—or of the cropped area to be used from a larger picture—and extended as necessary; a tracing paper overlay, or a same-size rectangle drawn on a separate sheet is used to protect the image. Starting at the corner where the diagonal originates, the desired dimension of the scaled image is measured off along the corresponding edge of the original. Then, measuring up (or across) to the diagonal gives the other scale dimension. The method can be used to size both enlargements and reductions.

Percent scale. When images are to be copied or separations made for photo-mechanical reproduction, it is necessary to express the desired size as a percentage of the original because the controls of the special cameras used for this kind of work are marked in percentages. A copy made at 100 percent is exactly the same size as the original; reductions are percentages less than 100, enlargements more than 100. The percentage reproduction (%R) is calculated from the actual image size along one dimension and the desired scale size of the same dimension:

$$\%R = (\text{Scale size} \div \text{Actual size}) \times 100$$

For example, if an image 8 in. wide is to be reproduced 24 in. wide, the percent reproduction is $(24 \div 8) \times 100 = 300\%$. Similarly, an 4 in. tall image copied to a 3 in. height has a percent reproduction of $(3 \div 4) \times 100 = 75\%$.

Scaling the actual size of objects from measurements taken from the image usually requires that a reference scale be recorded with the image.

See also: MAGNIFICATION; REDUCTION, OPTICAL; SCALE.

Scanner, Flying-Spot

A flying-spot scanner is an image analysis and reconstruction device. It consists of a laser beam focused into a tiny spot of light that moves over the area of the image in a pattern called a raster. In television, micro-photofabrication, and certain other applications an electron beam is used rather than a light beam. The raster is commonly a rectangular or square field composed of a succession of lines traced from left to right; the beam jumps back, or retraces, to the left to start each new line (right-left, or vertical, scanning is also possible). The raster may also be circular, created by a continuous scanning path that spirals toward the center, or helical, created by a straight-line trace along the length of an image on a revolving cylinder.

Image analysis is performed by photo- (or electron) receptors that take repeated readings of the changes in the scanning beam intensity caused by density or color variations in the image. With films, readings are taken from the transmitted light; with images on opaque materials they are taken from the reflected light. Each reading represents one image point or picture element, called a pixel. Color images are analyzed by separate scanning beams of red, green, and blue light, or by a separate white light beam that, after encountering the image, is directed by a three-way beam splitter to receptors fitted with red, green, and blue filters.

The receptor output is an analog electrical signal that can be used for immediate or delayed reconstruction of the image. In immediate reconstruction it may be used to modulate a light beam or electron beam that is synchronously scanning over a photosensitive material. This method is used for direct, camera-less production of color separations for use in photomechanical reproduction and for direct-etch photofabrication. The signal may also be transmitted to distant equipment for image reproduction there. In general, if the image is to be transmitted or stored, the signals are converted from analog to digital form; this makes them essentially error-free and safe from distortion by spurious interference signals. This is essential in obtaining images from satellite-borne equipment and for storing scientific image data. In digital form the image can be improved (enhanced) by computer processing before reproduction, if required. The precision, color purity, and intensity of laser beams have increased the speed and quality of scanner images many times beyond that previously attained with conventional light beams. They have also extended the applications of image scanning to areas that were impractical or even impossible less than a decade ago.

See also: DIGITAL IMAGES; ELECTRON IMAGING; IMAGE ENHANCEMENT; LASER; PHOTOFABRICATION; PHOTO-TRANSMISSION; SPACE PHOTOGRAPHY.

Schadograph

The use of the photogram technique to produce abstract images apparently originated with Christian Schad, a German painter who was a member of the Dada group of artists in Zurich, Switzerland. His first collages of this sort were produced in 1918 by placing scraps of paper and other translucent and transparent flat materials on film or photographic paper, exposing them to light, and developing the image. Tristan Tzara, self-appointed publicist for the group, coined the punning designation "Schadograph."

See also: PHOTOGRAM.

Scheele, Carl Wilhelm

Swedish; 1742–1786

A chemist and apothecary, Scheele accomplished an astonishing amount of research and discovery before his death at the age of 44. He discovered oxygen, chlorine, manganese, baryta, hydrogen sulfide, and at least two dozen other compounds. (In the 20th c. baryta was used as the pure white layer under the emulsion of photographic printing

paper.) His greatest work was experimentation with oxygen, but his contribution to photography lies in his investigation of silver chloride. Following observations of the effect of light on silver compounds by Johann Schulze and others, in 1777 Scheele discovered that silver chloride was reduced to metallic silver by light, and that ammonia would dissolve away the unreduced chloride, leaving the metallic grains formed by the light action. He also discovered that when the spectrum created by a prism from white light was directed onto silver chloride, reduction took place at the blue-violet end most rapidly, and even more rapidly just beyond the visible violet. He deduced that there were invisible rays there and named them "chemical rays"; today they are called ultraviolet rays. All early experimenters in photography drew upon his information about silver chloride, but missed the significance of ammonia as a potential fixing agent. It was a half century after his death before the first practical photographic process appeared.
See also: HERSCHEL, SIR JOHN; SCHULZE, JOHANN HEINRICH; WEDGWOOD, THOMAS.

Scheimpflug Condition

The optical condition in which the planes of the object (subject), lens, and image intersect at a common point is called the Scheimpflug condition. Its primary practical application is in the use of camera movements to insure that a desired subject plane is in sharp focus. It is especially useful when the depth of field produced by normal camera settings is not sufficient.

The Scheimpflug condition is achieved by tilting/swinging the camera lens board or the film holder; a combination of the two movements is commonly used to avoid acute camera angles or extreme positions of camera components that might cause vignetting or image cutoff. Although this technique produces maximum sharpness over a desired area, it also produces distortion because the film (image) plane must be placed out of parallel with the subject plane to achieve the condition.
See also: CAMERA MOVEMENTS; DEPTH OF FIELD; DISTORTION; VIGNETTING.

Scheiner Speed

See: SPEED OF MATERIALS.

Schlieren Photography

Density differences in air and gases are invisible to the eye but can be recorded as patterns of light and dark or colored bands by schlieren photography (German: *schlieren* = [optical] streaks, striations). Density differences are caused by radiated heat—even as little as that rising from the fingertips—differentials in pressure, the flow of air or gas around an object, the movement of an object through the medium, and other factors. Different gases at the same temperature and pressure have distinct densities that can be detected when they flow in currents one through another because each density has a different power of refraction. Schlieren photography—which must be carried out in a controlled environment—uses a strong backlight focused by condensers into parallel rays passing through the medium. Horizontal knife edges located before and after the condenser system act as a kind of diaphragm to block light from one half of the recorded field. If there are no density differences, the light is uniform; if there are density differences, some light is refracted into the light field or into the dark field. Reinforcement and cancellation produced by the refractions create banded patterns corresponding to the flow currents and density differences in the medium. In most setups a lensless camera or simply a film holder can be used because the system is self-focusing. If the knife edge nearest the film is replaced with a filter composed of color bands, the streaks are recorded in distinguishing colors as well as brightness differences. Schlieren photographs are

used to analyze heat flow; the design of missiles, projectiles, and supersonic aircraft; air pollution; combustion, heating, and cooling; and related phenomena.
See also: REFRACTION.

Schmidt Camera

A Schmidt camera is a specialized reflecting telescope used for astronomical photography and other applications where a very wide aperture (as much as $f/0.7$) is required in conjunction with a relatively wide field of view and long focal length. Its ancestor is the mirror camera of Alexander Wolcott, used in the earliest daguerreotype portrait studios. The camera invented by Bernhard Schmidt in 1930 is a catadioptric system in which a concave spherical mirror focuses an image onto film mounted on a convex spherical surface located at the focal point of the mirror. A corrector plate at the aperture (tube mouth) of the camera—a distance equal to the center of curvature of the mirror—is a glass lens element with one aspheric face that is convex in the center and slightly concave near the edges. This plate corrects the spherical aberration induced by the mirror's shape, which is used because it is free of the coma and astigmatism produced by the parabolic mirrors of most reflecting telescopes and mirror lenses. In addition, front-surface mirrors—unlike glass lens elements—are free of chromatic aberration.

Scheimpflug Condition

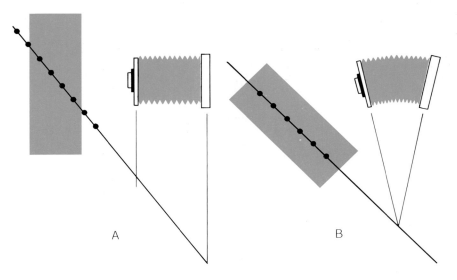

A = Some subject details fall outside maximum depth of field obtained at normal camera settings.

B = Scheimpflug condition: lens and film moved to intersect subject plane at common point so all details are sharp.

Photomicrography. John W. Alexanders,
"Zinc Acetate" 33 × original magnification
(1981). © John W. Alexanders.

Pinhole Photography. John Calvelli, Untitled
(n.d.). © John Calvelli.

Product Photography. Ralph Chandler, "Emerging Motorcycle" (1980). © Ralph Chandler.

Push Processing. David Fairman, "Manhattan" (n.d.). © 1983 David Fairman, London.

Retouching. Before and After—Master-Charge advertisement. Retouching by Vincent Musilli, New York.

Retouching. Before and After—
Revlon ad. Retouching by Sandra Sutton,
Sutton Studio, New York; courtesy Revlon.

Sculpture, Photography of. Vic Kranz, "Totem Pole—3 exposures to show 3 sides" (n.d.). Smithsonian Institution.

Schulthess, Emil. "Swiss Panorama" (1982).
Courtesy Emil Schulthess.

Self-Portrait. David Lebe, "Self-Portrait, Philadelphia" (1981); hand-colored gelatin silver
print. © David Lebe; courtesy Marcuse
Pfeifer Gallery, New York.

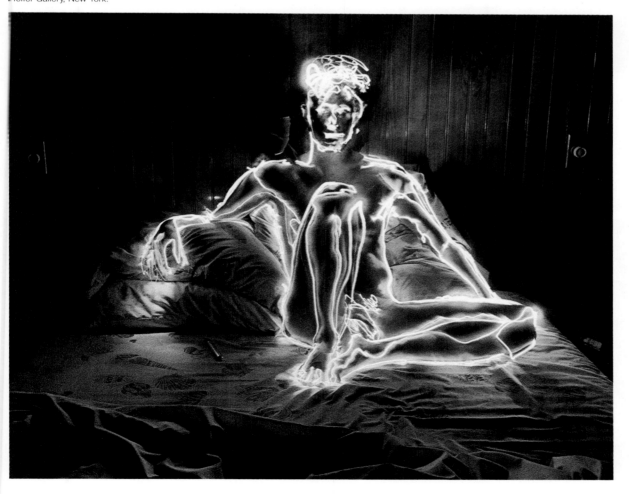

Space Photography. Using a slightly modified Hasselblad loaded with stock Ektachrome 64, astronaut Karol J. Bobko
photographed crewmember Donald H.
Peterson inspecting the aft bulkhead aboard
the earth-orbiting space shuttle Challenger
(early 1980s). Courtesy NASA.

Special Effects. Pierre Cordier, "Homage to
Marey" (1975); chemigram. © Pierre Cordier.

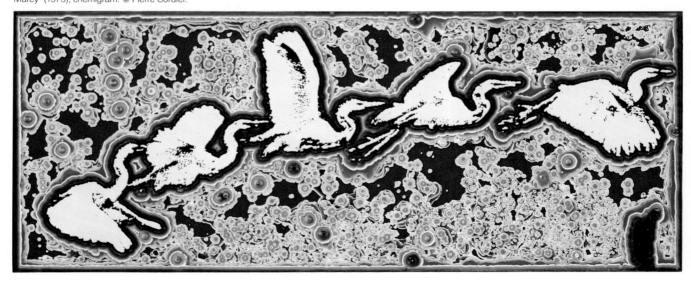

The Maksutov-Bowers 1944 adaptation of the Schmidt camera uses a large meniscus lens—which is much easier and cheaper to produce—in place of the aspheric corrector. The Cassegrain-Schmidt design uses a plane mirror in front of the concave objective mirror to reflect the image through a hole in the center of the objective to a film plane outside the rear of the instrument; a field-flattening lens is located directly in front of the film. The various Schmidt camera configurations provide images that are essentially totally corrected and that have brightnesses unobtainable with other systems.

See also: CATADIOPTRIC AND CATOPTRIC LENSES; MENISCUS; MIRROR CAMERA; MIRROR LENS; TELESCOPE.

Schulthess, Emil

Swiss; 1913–

For 30 years, Emil Schulthess has combined the role of photojournalist with that of travel, nature, aerial, and popular scientific photographer to create color panoramas around the world. From his first photo-story concerning the daily transit of the sun, to his recent aerial photographs, Schulthess has overcome enormous technical difficulties, designing special lenses, printing with multiple negatives, inventing new techniques, to present his viewers with novel visual information and metaphors. He is famous for the care he has lavished over every stage of the publication of his images.

Schulthess was born and raised in Zurich. Following secondary school, he was a graphics apprentice to Alex Walter Diggelmann from 1928 to 1932. He then studied photography with Hans Finsler at Zurich's Art Trades School, and art in Paris at the Académie de la Grande Chaumière.

Schulthess was a freelance graphic artist in Zurich from 1932 to 1936. From 1937 to 1941 he was employed by Conzett and Huber Publishers, Zurich, as a graphic designer. He was associated with *Du* magazine as an art director, picture editor, and photographer from 1941 to 1957, when he began his career as a freelance photographer, writer, and art director. During the past 25 years he has worked primarily for Artemis Publishers, Zurich. He was a member of the Swiss Army Reserves from 1940 to 1966.

Schulthess has published numerous books for which he was designer and printing supervisor, including *Africa* (1959), *Antarctica* (1960), *The Amazon* (1962), *China* (1966), *Soviet Union* (1971), *Midnight Sun* (1973), *New York* (1978), and *Swiss Panorama* (1982).

Schulthess is the recipient of numerous honors including *U.S. Camera* Awards in 1959 and 1967; the Annual Award from the American Society of Magazine Photographers in 1958; the Prix Nadar, France, in 1960; the Culture Prize of the Deutsche Gesellschaft für Photographie in 1964; and the Goldene Blende Award, Stuttgart, in 1972.

Schulthess's work has been exhibited in group shows including *Photography in the Fine Arts* at the Metropolitan Museum of Art, New York, in 1961; *Photographie in der Scheweiz von 1840 bis Heute* traveling exhibition originating at Kunsthaus, Zurich, in 1974; and *Stiftung für die Photographie* at Kunsthaus, Zurich, in 1981. Among the solo exhibitions of Schulthess's photographs were: *Africa* at the American Museum of Natural History, New York, in 1958; *Africa–The Amazon–Antarctica* at the Smithsonian Institution, Washington, D.C., in 1965; *China* at Galerie Form, Zurich, in 1966; and *Unspoiled Nature*, American and European traveling exhibition, 1972–1975.

Color photographs: pp. C-50-51.

Schulze, Johann Heinrich

German; 1687–1744

In 1725 Schulze made the key discovery that some 110 years later made possible the invention of photography: the action of light, not heat, causes certain compounds of silver to darken. He had mixed nitric acid with a solution of chalk precipitate in water; the solution also contained a small amount of silver, which reacted with the acid to form silver nitrate. Schulze was unaware of this additional reaction, but was surprised to see that the side of the bottle struck by the sun's rays coming through a window darkened, while the shadowed side did not. Experimentation led him to observe that white substances other than chalk could be used; that heating the acid-and-silver solution caused no darkening, but that both direct and reflected light did; and that letters or designs cut out of paper and pasted on a bottle of solution left white silhouettes of themselves when peeled away after exposure—a kind of photogram in liquid. He recorded and published these observations, but it remained for others to put the information to practical use.

See also: DAGUERRE, L. J. M.; SCHEELE, C.W.; TALBOT, W.H. FOX; WEDGWOOD, THOMAS.

Schwarzschild, Karl

German; 1873–1916

An astronomer, Schwarzschild became concerned with the problem of reciprocity failure in the very long time exposures common to astronomical photography. He attempted to find a mathematical means for predicting how much exposure compensation would be required for any given weak light intensity and long exposure. His results, published in 1899 and refined by a co-worker in 1913, had application only to certain kinds of emulsions and a limited range of conditions. The problem is still unsolved except on the basis of data derived from trial-and-error testing. The term "Schwarzschild effect" is sometimes used in Europe to mean the failure of reciprocity.

See also: RECIPROCITY.

Scientific and Technical Photography

From its very beginnings, photography has been an indispensable tool of scientific and technical investigation. It is the primary means for observing the invisible—those details and events that cannot be seen directly because they are too small or too vast, too distant, too rapid or too slow moving, or because they are hidden within a larger structure, or are not revealed by those wavelengths to which the eye is sensitive. Photography is also the primary means of recording the physical aspects of processes and events that cannot be expressed adequately by the shorthand of scientific or technical notation. The visual records are documentation. They may also be sources of new information, gleaned from close inspection and analysis, or from comparison with other records, as in astronomical photographs taken at intervals, or pictures of an eroding land formation. The unique and selective response characteristics of various emulsions allow photography to be used as a tool of direct analysis, especially with regard to the wavelength composition of emitted or transmitted energy, as in spectrography.

The specialized equipment, materials, and techniques developed for scientific photography range from the simplicity of a pinhole aperture and a prism, to the enormous complexity of computer-directed equipment on earth and in space. Electron micrography has made the infinitesimally small—even the individual atom—visible. Photogrammetry from space has provided maps of earth areas far beyond the scope of conventional aerial photography, and with immensely better resolution of detail and degree of accuracy. High-speed photography has made it possible to view events lasting a billionth of a second or less, while time-lapse photography has revealed the flow of processes that take from hours to years to be completed. Astronomical photography has spanned distances so vast they are measured by time (light years) rather than linear units; the advent of space platform astronomy has extended the distance/time range of vision enormously. Structure, composition, and process have been imaged at all levels from the submicroscopic to the supermacroscopic, both by optical magnification/reduction, and by the specialized illumination provided by x-rays, ultraviolet, and infrared energy. Nonvisible characteristics and events—sound patterns, heat emanation, magnetic fields—have also been translated into visible equivalents to be recorded photographically.

Today, photography is a tool that the scientist, researcher, engineer, biochemist, surveyor, doctor, and all other specialists cannot do without. Scientific photography encompasses more areas and requires technical knowledge and expertise far beyond that required for any other kind of photography. The range and technical applications of scientific photography are discussed in the entries listed as cross-references; many will lead to additional entries related to scientific and technical photography.

Historical development. It was inevitable that photography would be used scientifically from the beginning. The first experimenters and inventors were amateur or, as in the case of W. H. F. Talbot, professional scientists. Upon its invention, photography was regarded as a technical astonishment—even a miracle—and those first attracted to it were of a scientific bent, interested in experimenting, testing, and exploring the nature and capabilities of the new medium. The tasks they set for it, the subjects that came to mind, were those of their professional fields: optics, physics, mechanics, botany, astronomy, and the like; the portraitists and artists came later.

The following chronology lists some of the landmarks in the scientific and technical use of photography. In most cases several individuals achieved the same thing at about the same time; the events listed are generally recognized to be the first instances of major significance in their respective areas, even though earlier results may have been recorded. The list is intended to show the broad framework of development; it is not all-inclusive.

1835 Botanical specimens recorded by contact exposure (photograms)— W. H. F. Talbot, England

[1839 Daguerreotype process made public]

1839 Photomicrographs on paper with solar microscope—J. B. Reade, England

1840 Photomicrographs: on daguerreotype plate, by sunlight—C. L. Chevalier, France
  by limelight (oxy-hydrogen)— L. L. B. Ibbetson, England
  by gas light—J. B. Dancer, England

1840 Medical photography: photomicrographs of bones, teeth— A. Donné, France

1840 Astronomy: daguerreotype of moon—J. W. Draper, U.S.

1840 Physics: daguerreotype of spectrum of sunlight—J. W. Draper, U.S.

[1841 Talbotype (calotype) paper negative/positive process made public]

1844 Photomicrographs by electric (carbon arc) light—J. B. L. Foucault, France

1845 Astronomy: daguerreotypes of sun's disk—H. Fizeau and J. B. L. Foucault, France

[1851 Collodion "wet plate" process introduced)

1851 Microphotographs (extremely reduced images) on wet plate—J. B. Dancer, England

1851 Motion-stopping photograph by electric spark illumination—W.H. F. Talbot, England

1851 Photographs for the physiological analysis of sub-normal individuals—M. Baillarger, France; of psychologically disturbed and insane individuals—H. W. Diamond, England.

1852 Photographs for comparative (before–after) records of medical treatment—H. W. Berend, Germany

1852 Photographic methods of surveying introduced (patented in advanced form, photogrammetry, 1861)—A. Laussedat, France

1856–1858 Aerial photographs from balloon—Nadar, France

1856 Underwater photography with unmanned submersible camera— W. Thompson, England

1861 Medical stereophotographs— J. Ganz, Switzerland

1862 Photographs of larynx by means of endoscope—J. N. Germak

1866 Underwater photography with manned camera in diving bell— M. Bazin, France

1867 Photothermographs and photobarographs—Royal Meteorological Society, England

[1871 Gelatin emulsion for dry plates introduced]

1873 Map-making based on aerial photographs from captive balloons patented—U.S.

1874 Timed-sequence astronomical photographs (transit of Venus across sun, Auckland Islands)—P. J. C. Janssen, France; H. Krone, Germany

1872–1885 Motion study and analysis sequence photographs by means of multiple cameras—E. J. Muybridge, U.S.

1882–1894 Chronophotography: motion study and analysis by means of single camera—E. J. Marey, France

1882 Photographic and physiometric system for identifying criminals— A. Bertillon, France

1884 Photographs of projectiles in flight by means of electric spark illumination—E. Mach, Germany

1885 Photographs of retina of living subject—W. T. Jackman and J. D. Webster

1887 Aerial photographs from kites—A. Batut, Belgium

1888 Time-lapse and stroboscopic photographs—E. Mach, Germany

1888 Photographs from a rocket— A. Denise, France

1891 Anaglyphs, 3-D photographs using color discrimination (red-green) for visual separation—L. Ducos du Hauron, France

1893 Underwater photography with hand camera, artificial light (magnesium ribbon)—L. Boutan, France

1894 Slow-motion photography—E. J. Marey, France

1895 Radiographs by means of just-discovered x-rays—W. K. Roentgen, Germany

1897 Stereo-radiographs—M. Levy-Dorn, Germany

1893 Photographs by extreme ultraviolet illumination—V. Schumann, Germany

1898 Photographs of interior of stomach of living subject—H. Lange and H. Meltzing, Germany

1900 Systematic meteorological photography from kites—U.S. government observatories

[1906 Panchromatic plates commercially produced—Wratten and Wainwright, England]

1906 X-ray motion pictures of living subjects—M. Levy-Dorn, Germany

1909 Discovery of nuclear particle tracks in photographic emulsion— O. Mügge

1909 Photographs from manned, heavier-than-air craft—A. Maurisse, France

1912 Radiographs of x-ray diffraction by solids (crystals), foundation of solid-state physics—M. T. F. von

Laue, W. Friedrich, and P. Knipping, Germany

1912 X-ray spectrography—K. M. G. Siegbahn, Germany

1912 Photographs of nuclear particle trails in cloud chamber—C. T. R. Wilson, England

1917 X-ray radiographs for industrial inspection, analysis—Woolwich Arsenal, England

1919 Photographs by infrared illumination—E. Q. Adams and H. L. Haller

1921 X-ray tomography of living subjects—A. Bocage

1925 Electric discharge in rare gas for photographic illumination of extremely fast movement (forerunner of electronic flash)—A. and L. Séguin, France

1926 Microphotographs of 1/1000 life size and smaller on newly invented grainless emulsion—E. Goldberg

1930 Photographs of sun's corona by means of coronagraph, precision device to obscure body of sun—B. Lyot, France

1931 Transmission electron microscope invented; first commercial model available, 1939–Germany, U.S.

1935 Scanning electron microscope demonstrated; first commercial model available, 1965–Germany, U.S.

1938 Systematic microcopying of documents for storage introduced—England

1940 Fabrication of aircraft parts by means of phototemplates—G. L. Martin Co., U.S.

1950 Atoms (of barium) imaged by field electron microscope—E. W. Muller, Germany

1952 Photographs of nuclear particle trails in bubble chamber—D. Glaser

1958–1959 Photographs outside earth's atmosphere—U.S., U.S.S.R.

1959 Photographs of dark side of moon—U.S.S.R.

1960–1961 Laser; 3-D holographic recordings

1964 Closeup photographs of surface of moon returned to earth—U.S.

For the most part, our perspective is not yet great enough to identify the most significant developments of the last two decades on a year-by-year basis. The most productive innovations and achievements include digital image processes, image enhancement, space imaging systems, improved electron microscopy at the atomic level, and processing of equivalent images from non-visual sensing systems such as nuclear magnetic resonance scanners.

See also: ARCHAEOLOGICAL PHOTOGRAPHY; ASTROPHOTOGRAPHY; BIOLOGICAL PHOTOGRAPHY; BUBBLE CHAMBER PHOTOGRAPHY; CLINICAL PHOTOGRAPHY; DIFFRACTION PHOTOGRAPHS; DIGITAL IMAGES; ECLIPSE PHOTOGRAPHY; ELECTRON MICROSCOPE/MICROSCOPY; EXPEDITION PHOTOGRAPHY; FLOW PHOTOGRAPHY; FLUOROGRAPHY; GEOLOGICAL PHOTOGRAPHY; HEAT RECORDING; HIGH-SPEED PHOTOGRAPHY; INDUSTRIAL PHOTOGRAPHY; INFRARED PHOTOGRAPHY; MACROPHOTOGRAPHY; MEDICAL PHOTOGRAPHY; MICROPHOTOGRAPHY; MOTION STUDY AND ANALYSIS; PHOTOFABRICATION; PHOTOGRAMMETRY, AERIAL; PHOTOMICROGRAPHY; SCHLIEREN PHOTOGRAPHY; SLOW-MOTION; SPACE PHOTOGRAPHY; SPECTROGRAPHY/SPECTROSCOPE; STEREOSCOPIC PHOTOGRAPHY; STOP-MOTION PHOTOGRAPHY; STREAK CAMERA; STROBOSCOPIC PHOTOGRAPHY; THERMOGRAPHY; TIME-LAPSE PHOTOGRAPHY; TOMOGRAPHY; ULTRAVIOLET AND FLUORESCENCE PHOTOGRAPHY; WEATHER PHOTOGRAPHY; X-RAY PHOTOGRAPHY.

Scioptric Lens

In the 17th c. some rooms fitted as camera obscuras used a rotating scioptric or "ox-eye" lens to obtain an effective field of view much wider than that provided by a fixed lens. The lens body was a wooden ball mounted in a socket or collar in one wall or in a window shutter. The ball was hollowed out from one side to the other and had a simple lens element in the opening on each side. Together the elements produced a shorter focal length and thus a wider field than either provided separately. The field could be extended further by rotating the ball in its socket, much as the eye of an ox or cow rolls to cover a very wide area.

See also: CAMERA OBSCURA.

Screen, Halftone

A number of different types of optical grid patterns, called halftone screens, are used to convert a continuous-tone image into a dot pattern suitable for photomechanical reproduction. The most common type is a *cross-line screen*, invented by F. E. Ives in 1885 (a later improved version is called a Levy screen, after its inventor). Two sheets of glass are engraved with equally spaced, parallel fine lines. The lines are filled with black pigment, and the sheets are cemented face-to-face with the lines crossing at right angles to produce dots at their intersections of identical size and spacing. Screens are made with line frequencies from 55 to 400 lines per inch. Coarse line screens are used to prepare images for printing on soft, absorbent paper such as newsprint, which allows the ink impression of each dot to spread a bit. Higher-quality reproduction on smooth-surface or coated papers is achieved with 133-line or finer screens. The screen is used in front of the lith film in a process camera when the image to be reproduced is photographed at the required size for reproduction. The screen is separated slightly from the film so that light in the very brightest parts of the image can "bleed" into the shadows of the dots, reducing their size or washing them out completely. Dot sizes in other areas similarly vary according to the image brightnesses there. The dot size in a particular part of a screened image or printed reproduction is described in terms of a percentage value. A full-size dot covers 100 percent of its area; a 50-percent dot covers half its area. Traces of tone in highlight areas commonly are represented by dots from 1 to 5 percent in size.

A halftone *contact-screen* consists of a dot pattern reproduced on a sheet of film. Each dot is graduated in density, being opaque in the center and fading out to its edges. This produces the same kind of dot variation in proportion to image brightness, but allows the screen to be used in direct contact with the lith film. The dot pattern is magenta for screening black-and-white originals; this allows controlling the contrast of the screened image by means of yellow and magenta filters. A gray dot pattern is used for making screen exposures from color originals.

The regular dot pattern may interfere with a pronounced pattern of detail in an image, producing moiré; this frequently occurs when a screened image is re-screened for reproduction. Moiré can be avoided by use of a halftone screen with a random grain or dot pattern, called a metzograph screen. A similar result is obtained with a mezzograph screen, which consists of parallel, wavy lines. Other special-purpose screens have diamond-shaped, elliptical, or round dots rather than squares.

See also: IVES, FREDERIC EUGENE; HALFTONE PROCESSES; MOIRÉ; SCREENED NEGATIVES AND PRINTS.

Screened Negatives and Prints

Photomechanical reproduction requires that continuous-tone images be broken up into a pattern of discrete dots; this is accomplished by copying the image through a halftone screen. A screened image on film is required for subsequent exposure of the printing plate; it may be a negative or a positive, depending on the reproduction process to be used. The screened film is combined (stripped up) with the film record of the type and other line (single-tone) material to be printed to form the film master from which the plate is made. The stripping-up procedure allows original images of various sizes to used; the screened copy is simply photographed at the degree of enlargement or reduction required for the final reproduction size. When multicolor images are to be reproduced, screened separations are required. These are screened copies made through red, green, and blue filters on separate pieces of film. The screen must be rotated 30 degrees after each exposure to avoid moiré when the inked patterns are printed in register on top of one another.

A screened print, often called a *velox*, is used to avoid the stripping process in making the master plate negative. The screened print is pasted into position on the final layout (mechanical) along with the type reproductions and other elements so that they can be copied together in a single line, or unscreened, exposure. This procedure requires that all elements be final size, for an enlarged or reduced line copy would change the value of the dot pattern in the screened print.

See also: HALFTONE PROCESSES; PHOTO-MECHANICAL REPRODUCTION; SCREEN, HALFTONE; SEPARATION NEGATIVES/POSITIVES; VELOX.

Screen Processes

A great many methods of recording or reproducing images depend on breaking the image into minute dot or line elements. Most methods use an optical or a physical screen in the image path to form the elements. An optical screen refracts or reflects the light rays of the image into dots or lines. It may be a fly's-eye lens array, a lenticular surface, or a sheet of fiber optic segments. A physical screen may consist of opaque elements, as in a halftone dot or line screen, or it may consist of red, green, and blue filter elements. Primary-color filter screens have been the basis of a great number of additive color systems that require only a single sheet of black-and-white film to record the image (other additive color systems have required three sheets of film, one for each primary-color record). The color screen principle was first described by Ducos du Hauron in 1862 and patented in 1868. However, emulsions of the time did not have sufficient spectral sensitivity, and the first practical color screen process, invented by John Joly, did not appear until 1896.

Color screen processes. A color screen process works as follows. For photographic reproduction a subject can be analyzed and recorded in terms of its primary-color components. This can be done on separate films, each photographed through a different filter or—as in modern films—on separate emulsion layers on a single base, each of which is effectively sensitive to only one primary color. Alternatively, the entire three-color analysis can be recorded on a single emulsion by providing minute red, green, and blue filter groups over the whole area of the image; that is what the color screen does. For a full-color image, each detail must be color analyzed. The resolving power of the human eye at normal reading distance is 0.01 in., so the three-color filter group for each detail must be no larger than this in order for the screen pattern not to be visible. (It must be many times smaller if the image is to be projected, a difficulty that has limited the success of projection color-screen processes.) The screen provides an array of filter groups either as parallel lines (line screen), 300 or more per in., or as a mosaic of randomly positioned particles of irregular shape, or a precise pattern of squares, triangles, or diamonds created by crisscrossing the filter lines at various angles. Exposure is made through the screen onto a panchromatic (black-and-white) emulsion. At each point, the wavelengths making up the color of the detail imaged there register proportionate exposures. For example, a magenta detail produces equal exposures through its red and blue elements, but nothing through the green. An orange detail registers twice as much exposure through its red element as through its green, and nothing through its blue element. All other details are similarly recorded. The film is reversal-processed to produce a black-and-white transparency that transmits light at each point in direct proportion to the exposure there. When viewed through a matching screen placed in exact register with the image, each filter element passes to the eye an equivalent amount of light of the same color that it originally passed to the film. The eye blends signals into a full-color image.

Early Processes. From 1895 to the early 1930s more than a hundred color screen processes were invented; the most successful, described in separate entries, were the Autochrome, Dufaycolor, Finlaycolor, and Joly color processes. Other processes that enjoyed success included Krayn and Omnicolor (1907), Aurora and Dioptichrome (1909), Leto and Paget (1913), Agfa Color (1916), and Lignose Natural Color (1926). The earliest processes used a separate screen that was placed in front of the film for exposure, and again in front of the processed film for viewing. This had the advantage of allowing a choice of film emulsions but presented the problem of re-registering the screen after the image was processed. In some systems the camera screen was a glass plate but the viewing screens were on celluloid to limit the cost, bulk, and weight of the final image. Most systems managed to produce screens that were exact duplicates in element spacing, but none could guarantee that the film the photographer chose to use would not change dimensions slightly during processing, making screen registration imprecise or even impossible. Integral-screen materials solved the registration problem by having an emulsion coated directly over a screen on a glass or celluloid base. This restricted the choice of emulsion and presented the manufacturing problem of insuring that the dyed screen elements would be protected from processing solutions.

All screen processes required long exposures because primary-color filters absorb up to two-thirds of the light falling on them. Compared to a direct black-and-white exposure on the same emulsion, a color screen exposure typically had to be 16 to 250 times (four to eight *f*-stops) greater. Similarly, the viewing screen typically passed only one-sixth to one-ninth of the light, making many images look subdued or simply too dark. Modern technology has eased some of these problems significantly, but there is only one kind of additive color screen process material currently produced: 35mm self-processing transparency film with an integral screen.

See also: ADDITIVE COLOR SYNTHESIS; AUTOCHROME PROCESS; COLOR PHOTOGRAPHY—HISTORY; DUCOS DU HAURON, L.; DUFAYCOLOR; FINLAYCOLOR PROCESS; IMAGE DISSECTION; JOLY, JOHN; LENTICULAR SYSTEMS; SCREENED NEGATIVES/PRINTS.

Screens, Projection

Portable and roll-up projection screens are usually square so that vertical- and horizontal-format images can be shown without adjustment. Permanent screens for motion-picture or multi-media presentations are commonly rectangles corresponding to the most extreme format that may be used; many have adjustable side borders to adapt the screen to various aspect ratios. When speakers are located behind a permanent screen, the material is usually perforated with an overall pattern of holes about ⅛" in diameter to transmit the sound; the holes are not distinguishable at normal viewing distances. Opaque screens for front projection have white or metallic surfaces. A matte white surface provides uniform illumination across a wider field—up to 45 degrees to each side of the screen edge—but with less overall brightness than other surfaces. A beaded screen—a white surface coated with minute glass or plastic beads that act as lenses—provides a considerably brighter image up to about 25° on each side, but the illumination falls off considerably beyond that. Aluminized-surface screens are noncollapsible and are generally used in semipermanent installation, although small sizes are portable. They provide greater image brightness over about the same area as beaded screens, but the image is more easily degraded by stray light. Lenticular screens have metallic or nonmetallic ribbed surfaces that produce the greatest image brightness over a field of intermediate width. The ribbing, which is invisible at normal distances, acts as cylindrical mirrors or lenses to confine the image light to the viewing area with very little scatter, and is quite effective in preventing stray light originating outside the viewing area from degrading image contrast or color. High-efficiency screens with specially designed lenticular surfaces are used for the front projection of backgrounds in studio photography. Rear projection screens are made of translucent, neutral-color material. They produce less image brightness than front-surface screens, and suffer severe edge falloff in large sizes. However, they are very useful in small, self-contained projection units, and in permanent installations where they can be protected from stray frontal light.

See also: FRONT PROJECTION; PROJECTION; REAR PROJECTION.

Sculpture, Photography of

Sculpture consists of material that has been shaped, formed, or assembled by the hand of the artist. Successful photography of sculpture must reveal the nature of the material (color, texture, and other physical qualities); the three-dimensional aspects of the object (or grouping) and its relative size or scale; and, if appropriate, evidences of the artist's working process (e.g., chisel or saw marks in stone or wood, finger marks in wax or clay, welding or forge burns on metal). In addition, a successful photograph must show the sculpture from a point of view that reveals its aesthetic character, or from one of the many aspects of a piece created to be approached from more than one direction. Finally, many sculptures are created to define the ground plane on which they stand (or over which they hang) and to articulate the volume of space around them. A successful photograph may also show this environmental interaction.

To accomplish all these things equally well in a single image is far from easy. Rendering the physical aspects of a sculpture draws on techniques used for product illustration. Capturing the personality of the piece is most like a problem in portraiture. Showing its environmental effect is often like a problem in architectural photography. Lighting reveals color and defines texture, form, and space. Angle of view and lighting create a sense of specific personality. Camera position (distance, height, angle) reveals environment and influences the sense of the scale of the piece.

Distortion and scale are two factors of major importance in photographing sculpture. As in portraiture, distorted proportions create a seriously false representation, and the solution is the same: use of a longer-than-normal focal-length lens so as to keep the camera at a distance that avoids foreshortening of those portions of the subject nearest the lens. Scale is particularly difficult to indicate visually without including one or more objects of known average size for comparison (e.g., a person, a park bench). In a full environmental picture of a sculpture, that is both possible and natural looking. However, when a piece is photographed in the studio—for a catalog illustration, for example—or when it is small or is not intended to play an environmental role, including other elements in the picture would be both inappropriate and distracting.

Two factors influence the sense of scale in a sculpture photograph: camera height and clarity of texture. A high camera angle, looking down at the piece, tends to diminish its scale; it is a viewpoint that says, in effect, you, the viewer, are bigger than this, the sculpture. A low camera position, looking up at the sculpture, tends to suggest the opposite. This is something of a simplification, because a high camera position may be necessary to show that a sculpture is in fact quite sizable and extends over a large area, but particularly in the case of single-object sculptures, camera height can influence scale. If fine details of texture are clearly defined, the viewer makes an unconscious judgment that says, "In order to see this kind of detail (e.g., the grain of wood), I would have to be about such-and-such a distance from this, so its size must be about . . . ," and thereby gets a rough estimate of scale. Similarly, if texture is unperceivable, the viewer assumes a more distant viewpoint and receives a different impression of the scale of the piece. Like camera height, texture supplies only approximations of scale and is a highly subjective visual factor. The size of a sculpture is the one item of data that most often has to be communicated in a caption accompanying a photograph.

Underlying all the decisions that must be made in photographing a sculpture is the photographer's understanding of the piece and his or her intent. The function of a sculpture photograph is to *show* a work of art, not to be a work of art (or virtuoso performance) itself. The photographer's primary task is to study the piece to sense what its unique properties are and what the intent of the artist was, and then to find the viewpoint and use the techniques that show this most clearly so that the viewer can have as direct an experience of the piece as possible. Thus, the role of photography is to be invisible so as to make the sculpture more visible in the ways that achieve true visual communication. If the sculptor intended his or her work to be dramatic, that must be shown. However, it is not shown faithfully by dramatizing the photograph with special techniques. It is possible to create drama, graphic impact, or other visual effects with extreme lighting, filters, unusual films, and a variety of devices and materials. But doing so is an act of interpretation, not communication. The picture then speaks more of the photographer's work than the sculptor's, and whatever the picture's other interest may be, it becomes meaningless as a photograph of sculpture.

See also: ART, PHOTOGRAPHY OF; DISTORTION.

Color photograph: p. C-50.

Selective Contrast

This is an alternate term for so-called variable contrast black-and-white printing papers.

See: PAPERS, PHOTOGRAPHIC; VARIABLE CONTRAST MATERIALS.

Selenium Treatment

A dilute solution of selenium toner may be used to enhance the tonality of black-and-white prints or to promote the greater longevity of prints made on fiber-base papers.

Preservation is achieved by the reaction of the selenium with the silver in the print. The result is a stable compound that is resistant to the effects of gases in the environment as well as to contamination by chemicals in materials that may come into contact with the print.

When selenium is used for toning, the

desired result often is not a real change in image color, but rather a slightly cooler tonality with a deepening and intensification of the dark areas. The toning imparts a slight purplish quality.

For subtle tonal enhancement effects and for print preservation, the toner can be combined with the washing aid. A basic formula is 7 oz. of toner concentrate with one gallon of working solution of washing aid. For best results, 2½ oz. of sodium metaborate is added. A great deal of control over the toning process can also be maintained by using a dilution of one part concentrate and 12 parts water to treat the print. The print should then be given a washing aid treatment before the final wash for maximum print permanence. Dilutions of 1:9 or 1:3 are used for more pronounced effects. In the washing aid/toner combination and in the 1:12 dilution, tonal changes will begin to show in three to five minutes. Highly dilute selenium treatment of black-and-white negatives has both a protective and an intensifying effect.

See also: ARCHIVAL PROCESSING; INTENSIFICATION; TONER/TONING.

Self-Portrait

A photographic self-portrait is obtained by aiming the camera at one's image in a mirror, or by sitting in front of the camera at a prefocused point and releasing the shutter with a long cable release, self-timer, or similar device. With the latter method it is helpful to place a mirror at the camera position to aid in establishing one's position and expression.

The tradition of rendering one's own likeness was well-established in painting for several centuries before the invention of photography. Artists such as Michelangelo and Dürer are known to have included their own likenesses in larger group compositions, and Rembrandt was responsible for a series of revealing self-portraits that reflected his own changing self-awareness as he grew older. The first photographic self-portrait was apparently taken by Hippolyte Bayard in 1840—a staged rendition of himself as a corpse laid out in a morgue, supposedly a suicide drowned in protest against the French government's neglect of his own photographic inventions at the same time that Daguerre was being rewarded. While hardly a self-portrait in the classic sense, Bayard's fictionalized self-portrayal looks forward to the use of the self-portrait by contemporary photographers as a means of psychological disclosure.

True self-portraits are relatively rare in 19th-c. photography. One notable exception is the French portraitist Nadar's self-portrait from the 1850s, showing himself with casually crossed arms, glancing coolly to one side: a convincing specimen of the natural superiority of the artist. A somewhat different approach was used by Eadweard Muybridge in the 1880s. While carrying out his famous sequential photographs of a variety of human activities, he served as his own nude model for a series depicting an "aging ex-athlete" climbing an incline.

With the advent of the Pictorial movement in photography in the 1890s, a number of art photographers began to appear in their own elaborately conceived compositions. The California Photo-Secessionist Annie Brigman photographed herself nude amid dramatic landscape scenery. In 1898 the flamboyant Bostonian F. Holland Day went so far as to portray himself as Christ on the Cross, attracting outraged criticism as a result.

The use of the self-portrait as a means of projecting visions of one's own self-image can be seen in three different self-likenesses by Edward Steichen. In a self-portrait of 1901, the young Steichen presented himself as a painter with brush and palette, wrapped in a dark cloak and revealed in a dramatic light. By 1920, when he had committed himself entirely to photography, he pictured himself in an open-collared work shirt next to his studio camera, standing in clear, even light. In 1936, after his success as a portrait and fashion photographer in New York, Steichen showed himself posed with casual elegance in a sleek suit, illuminated by blazing studio lights. Together, these three self-portraits show three different facets of a complex, many-sided personality.

In the 1920s, with the growing interest in the writings of Sigmund Freud, photographic self-portraits began to display more concern with mirroring the workings of the psyche. In a 1925 self-portrait by Paul Outerbridge, Jr., for example, the photographer used a double-exposure technique to present himself as a ghostly apparition before a crumbling wall, perhaps reflecting Outerbridge's own sense of insubstantiality as a floating presence who does not affect the reality of his surroundings. A similar dreamlike logic is evident in a striking 1932 self-portrait by the Bauhaus photographer Herbert Bayer, in which he portrays himself in wide-eyed astonishment before a mirror as he dismantles (with the help of photomontage) a section of his own arm.

The fascination of many Surrealist photographers with the new technolog-ical age prompted many of them to depict themselves as appendages of the camera itself. An example is a self-image by Man Ray which shows the photographer's own tightly cropped face in high contrast beneath an overlying grid—as the image might appear on the ground glass of a view-camera. Similarly, in a 1930 self-portrait by the German photographer Umbo, the shadow of the camera held between the photographer and the sun causes a camera-shaped mask to obscure his features altogether, implying that the photographer has been effaced by the machine.

In the years since World War II artistic photographers have turned increasingly away from photography's traditional concern with mirroring social reality, producing instead images which are more personal and introspective. This trend has been reflected in the increasing use of the self-portrait as a photographic theme. Jerry N. Uelsmann, for example, has made an almost annual series of self-portraits since the 1960s, conveying his changing sense of himself and his work. The most humorous, made in 1964, shows him sitting facing himself in the bathtub, with and without a beard and glasses. Its title, "Double Self-Portrait: Homage to Robinson and Rejlander," pays tribute to the 19th-c. originators of combination printing, the technique which Uelsmann has revived and applied so effectively.

One of the most extensive uses of self-portraiture by a single photographer is found in Lee Friedlander's book *Self-Portrait* (1970). Friedlander's presence is captured in shadows, mirrors, and other reflections in crowded urban scenes. The photographer shifts between self-revelation and ironic evasion, sometimes seemingly mocking himself, as when he photographs his image reflected in a plate-glass window on which is stencilled, "American Temporaries—Male Division."

Current self-portraiture is less likely to deal simply with the physical appearance of the subjects than with the cultural and psychological pressures that make them who they are. In Cindy Sherman's recent series of self-portraits, she assumes the roles of the different types of women she finds presented in the mass media. Her own attitude toward these stereotypes swings back and forth between affection and criticism. Judith Golden, working with similar concerns, has made fascinating self-portraits in which she juxtaposes her own features with those of women found on glossy magazine covers.

The contemporary range of approaches to the self-portrait is vast. A valuable survey of current work in self-portraiture can be found in *Self-Portrayal*, edited by James Alinder (1979).

See also: PORTRAITURE.

Color photograph: p. C-51.

Self-timer

A self-timer is a delayed shutter release mechanism built into many small- and medium-format cameras; auxiliary timers that screw into the shutter cable-release socket are also available. Most self-timers are set by a lever or dial for a delay of from two to ten seconds; some timers provide significantly greater delays. A few built-in timers can be set accurately for a specific number of seconds, but most permit only approximate settings up to the maximum. A timer has its own release button. Some timers have a blinking light or emit a beeping sound that increases in rate as the delay nears an end. A self-timer allows the photographer to leave the camera unattended in order to get into the picture or to attend to last-second details in the setup. In some single-lens reflex cameras the mirror is released when the timer is activated. This is useful in close-up and precision work because any vibration caused by the mirror movement can be dissipated during the delay before the shutter is released.

Selling Photographs

The market for photographs, both artistic and utilitarian, is large and varied. In addition to advertising and commercial illustration, businesses need record photographs of their facilities, activities, and personnel; community groups, social organizations, schools, and societies require photographs of their members and activities; few publications are without photographic illustrations; and many businesses and private individuals purchase photographs for display or collect them as artistic and financial investments.

There are two aspects of the sale of a photograph. One is the transfer of ownership of a physical object, the print or transparency. The other is granting the right for a particular use of the image. As discussed in the entry on reproduction rights, a sales agreement must state specifically what is being transferred to the buyer so that the photographer will not lose rights inadvertently; additional factors regarding ownership of photographs are discussed in the entry on copyright. The photographer must also be extremely careful not to sell rights he or she does not own. For example, a portrait assignment involves the client's hiring the photographer's services, but ultimately results in the sale of one or more photographs to the client. Although the photographer legally owns the negatives of these photographs, he or she does not own the right to publish the picture, sell copies of it to other parties, or give others permission to use the picture. (e.g., in advertisements). Only if the sales agreement with the client specifically gives these rights to the photographer can any other such use be made of the pictures. That is seldom the case in personal portraiture, but is usually the case when professional models are used; the wording of model releases reflects that fact.

Work offered for sale on any basis should be technically excellent, with the possible exception of a picture of a news event of such importance that the immediate interest value of the picture makes any level of quality acceptable. The entries on freelance photography and on picture agencies and libraries discuss many of the considerations in selecting and preparing photographs to be offered for sale.

Many photographers who do not sell photographs individually or through their own studios and who do not place pictures with an agency may rely on a personal agent or sales representative ("rep") to show their work, deliver pictures, and handle all the details of selling. The agent receives a percentage of all sales, ranging from 10 to 40 percent or higher, depending on the reputation and business contacts of the agent, the career level of the photographer, and the amount of money involved. The advantage of this kind of arrangement is that it lets both the photographer and the agent concentrate on the area in which each is a specialist. The result is usually greater output of better quality and more frequent sales at higher prices.

See also: COPYRIGHT; FREELANCE PHOTOGRAPHY; MODELS; PICTURE LIBRARIES/AGENCIES; PROFESSIONAL PHOTOGRAPHY; REPRODUCTION RIGHTS AND FEES; RIGHTS AND PERMISSIONS.

Sensitivity

The ability of materials to respond to image-forming or image-revealing energy is called photographic sensitivity. Image-forming energy includes visible, ultraviolet, and infrared wavelengths; image-revealing energy is generally composed of much shorter wavelengths, such as x-rays that produce shadow or differential transmission images of objects. Materials may also be sensitive to heat and electrical energy, reacting with visible change although not forming images of photographic clarity or detail. Colloidal substances such as gelatin and gum arabic solutions can be sensitized to ultraviolet by various bichromate compounds that "harden" them to a high degree of insolubility upon exposure.

There are two aspects to the sensitivity of photographic silver halide emulsions: speed, and wavelength or spectral sensitivity; both are established during manufacture. Silver halide crystals have a fundamental spectral sensitivity to blue and ultraviolet wavelengths; they are also sensitive to shorter wavelengths but the normal background intensity of x-rays and similar energy does not affect halide image-recording properties. Sensitivity to green, yellow, red, and infrared wavelengths is achieved by adding sensitizers to produce orthochromatic, panchromatic, or infrared-sensitive emulsions. Speed—the readiness with which halides respond to exposing energy—is primarily related to crystal size. Larger crystals have more surface area to intercept photons, and more sensitivity specks where the effect of exposure is registered, than smaller crystals. As a result, they can more easily collect enough energy to form a latent image under dim light conditions. Film speed can to some degree be altered by desensitization and hypersensitization. Latensification, push processing, and similar post-exposure precedures may produce some change in the effective response, but do not in fact affect the actual speed with which the emulsion recorded the exposure. Similarly, filters alter the effective spectral sensitivity of an emulsion by limiting the wavelengths that pass to it, but they do not alter the actual spectral sensitivity.

See also: DESENSITIZING; DYE SENSITIZATION; HYPERSENSITIZING; LATENSIFICATION; LATENT IMAGE; SPEED OF MATERIALS.

Sensitizer

A sensitizer is a compound that makes another compound or substance responsive to the effects of exposing energy, or that increases a basic degree of responsivity. Optical or *spectral sensitizers* extend the range of wavelengths to which a substance responds; the most important examples are the dye compounds used to extend silver halide sensitivity to the orthochromatic, panchromatic, and infrared ranges. *Chemical sensitizers* combine with a substance to form a new compound that is exposure-sensitive; this is the basis of bichromate sensitization, which is fundamental to many relief and transfer processes. The term *sen-*

sitizer is also used loosely to mean a solution containing light-sensitive compounds that is coated onto a material to prepare it for image recording; e.g., a fabric sensitizer.

See also: BICHROMATE PROCESSES; DYE SENSITIZATION; ORTHOCHROMATIC; PANCHROMATIC; RELIEF IMAGES; TRANSFER PROCESSES.

Sensitometry

The scientific study of the response of photographic materials to exposure and development is called sensitometry. In the narrowest sense it is the process of obtaining accurate numerical expression or quantification of emulsion response. That was the foundation laid in the work of Hurter and Driffield in the last three decades of the 19th c. Today sensitometry has much greater scope because of the number of factors involved in investigating emulsions with precision, and because of the wide application of the information obtained. Major aspects of sensitometry include photometry and spectroanalysis in calibrating light sources used for test exposures; the basic procedure of giving emulsions controlled, repeatable series of exposures; emulsion and developer chemistry to obtain controlled processing; densitometry in measuring and otherwise investigating results; and spectrography in analyzing spectral sensitivity.

Sensitometry investigates not only the exposure effect of light, but of infrared, ultraviolet, x-ray, and other energy as well. The fundamental findings of sensitometry are embodied in the characteristic curve plotted from the results of each exposure-development test. From this come speed and contrast ratings, measurement of exposure range and latitude, fog and solarization data, analysis of the response balance among the layers of color emulsions, information on the effects of development variations, and other data. Microdensitometer readings provide information on spread function, edge effects, acutance, granularity, and various image structure factors. Readings by other instruments evaluate resolving power and modulation transfer function. Wedge spectrograms show relative sensitivity to each wavelength in the exposing energy. (These applications and areas of investigation are discussed in separate entries throughout the Encyclopedia).

The information obtained about an emulsion is used to control its manufacture and to provide instruction for its most effective use and processing. Similar information is used to design new emulsions, developers, and other processing solutions, and to test the effect of various processing techniques. In practical applications, sensitometric measurements are used to monitor processing and control reproduction in studios, commercial laboratories, and printing and engraving plants. Comparison of emulsion response obtained with a standard, expected, or predicted response allows manufacturers to evaluate shutters, light meters, flash units, and other equipment.

Separation Negatives/Positives

In all processes in which a full-color image is reproduced by a combination of subtractive color (cyan, magenta, yellow) dyes or inks, each reproduction color must be printed from a separate version of the image. These *separations* are made by photographing the original color image or subject individually through primary color (red, green, blue) filters, or by means of a laser, as explained in the entry on scanners. The separations are made on black-and-white film, and may be negative or positive images depending upon the process to be used. If halftone reproduction is planned, the separations may be made through an appropriate dot or line screen, or they may be copied through a screen at a later step. The filters analyze the subject color composition in terms of its primary color components. The image recorded through the red filter becomes the master for preparing the matrix or plate that prints the cyan dye or ink. The green-filter or green-record image is the master for the magenta printer. The blue-record image is the master for the yellow printer. In four-color photomechanical reproduction—the most common ink process—a fourth separation is made through a yellow filter to prepare a moderate-density black ink printer. This is used to achieve richer blacks and shadow detail than the subtractive colors can produce in combination.

See also: ADDITIVE COLOR SYNTHESIS; PHOTOMECHANICAL REPRODUCTION; SUBTRACTIVE COLOR SYNTHESIS; SCANNER, FLYING-SPOT.

Sequence Camera

Some kinds of time-lapse and high-speed photography are achieved with a sequence camera—a camera that, when triggered, automatically makes a predetermined number of exposures at predetermined intervals. The camera may be activated by direct manual action, by remote control, or by an automatic triggering device. Marey, Muybridge, and Anschutz were among the first to invent and use such cameras for motion study and analysis. Their equipment included riflelike cameras (Marey), and batteries of cameras that operated in succession (Muybridge). Today most sequence cameras are highly sophisticated variants of precision motion-picture cameras. However, a motorized film advance makes sequence photography of a sort quite practical with many modern 35mm still cameras. The shutter release may be operated manually, or by means of a suitable interval timer.

See also: ANSCHUTZ, OTTOMAR; GUN CAMERA; HIGH-SPEED PHOTOGRAPHY; MAREY, ETIENNE JULES: MOTION STUDY AND ANALYSIS; MUYBRIDGE, EADWEARD; TIME-LAPSE PHOTOGRAPHY.

Sequences

Sequence photography is the making of a series of images placed together in a specific order so as to convey a visual message or pictorial effect that cannot be expressed with a single photograph. The word *sequence* in this case implies the picturing of an action or event as it progresses through chronologically linked stages; a series of pictures presented together as one piece—e.g., a triptych—in which the individual images have no chronological connection is not considered a sequence.

Sequential image-making is used for both expressive and applied scientific purposes. Sequential time-lapse photography is used to study the rate of growth of flowers and other plants, for example. It is also employed by urban planners and industrial engineers to study the flow of traffic or the efficiency of assembly-line installations. The individual photographs in these cases are made from a fixed location at prescribed intervals, and then presented together in order to examine the flow of objects or events under study.

The most celebrated and historically significant photographic sequences were made by Eadweard Muybridge using as his subjects horses, other animals, and human beings in motion. His work in the 1870s and 1880s and that of his contemporary, E. J. Marey, greatly expanded the scientific understanding of movement and completely changed the way movement was depicted in paintings and drawings.

Story-telling sequences have been made since the middle of the 19th c. Many early sequences were simply retellings of fairy tales and similar stories or illustrations of popular song lyrics and poems; most have had little more depth than the average comic book.

Portrait of Harry Torczyner, 1981

Sequences. Duane Michals, "Portrait of Harry Torczyner" (1981). Courtesy Duane Michals.

However, since the 1960s some photographic artists have developed the sequence as a mode of serious aesthetic expression. The best known of these is Duane Michals, many of whose works involve the depiction of events as they unfold within a certain span of time. The use of sequential flow allows Michals full control over the visual and narrative tensions exerted on the viewer, thereby increasing the overall impact of his sometimes Freudian, often surreal images.
See also: MICHALS, DUANE; MOTION STUDY AND ANALYSIS; MUYBRIDGE, EADWEARD; TIME-LAPSE PHOTOGRAPHY.

Series-Parallel Circuit

The life of incandescent bulbs such as photofloods can be extended by operating them in pairs in a circuit that can be switched between series and parallel connection to the voltage supply. The series circuit is used during setup and adjustment. It divides the voltage be-

tween the two bulbs so they operate at a lower intensity and consequently at a lower temperature; this prolongs filament life and makes the situation more

Series-Parallel Circuit

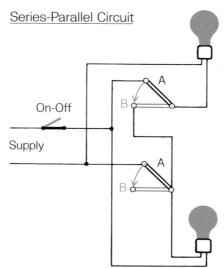

A-A = Parallel circuit; full-power
B-B = Series circuit; divided power
On-Off switch is optional

comfortable for any live subjects. Switching to the parallel circuit operates both bulbs at full intensity for taking meter readings and making exposures. The diagram shows a typical circuit using a double-pole, double-throw switch. Some switches of this sort have an intermediate off position; otherwise an On-Off switch can be included in the hot side of the supply line.

Seymour, David ("Chim")

American; 1911–1956
David Seymour was a noted photojournalist for 20 years, a founder of the Magnum Photo Agency, and its president at the time of his tragic death.

He was born David Syzmin (the surname was the source of his nickname "Chim") in Warsaw, the son of a publisher of Hebrew and Yiddish books. His family spent the years of World War I in Russia and returned to Warsaw in 1919.

Seymour trained to be a concert pianist but turned, as a young man, to graphics and photography. He studied at the Leipzig Academy for Graphic Arts and further at the Sorbonne in 1931. A liberal and anti-fascist, he became a free-lance photographer and pioneer photo-journalist, specializing in documentation of left-wing political movements,in 1933. He shared a Paris darkroom with his friends Henri Cartier-Bresson and Robert Capa, and traveled throughout France and to North Africa and Czechoslovakia.

In 1936 Seymour began reporting on the Spanish Civil War, particularly the effects of the aerial bombardment on civilians and children. He received international recognition when his photographs appeared in *Life* in 1938.

The following year, Seymour covered the voyage of Loyalist Spanish refugees to Mexico. With the outbreak of World War II, he crossed from Mexico to the United States and made his way to New York City where he worked as a darkroom technician until his enlistment in the U.S. armed forces. He worked in photo reconnaissance and interpretation until the end of the war and became an American citizen at that time.

For the next several years, Seymour documented the effects of the war on children throughout Europe for UNESCO. He photographed Italian cities and the countryside, and worked on a book about the Vatican, among other projects. He reported on the Israeli fight for independence and the emergence of Israel.

Seymour joined with Cartier-Bresson, Capa, and others to form Magnum in 1947. He became its president in 1954 when Capa was killed in Indochina. While covering the Suez conflict in 1956, Seymour himself was killed by Egyptian gunfire.

The following year, a major traveling show, "Chim's Children," originated at the Art Institute of Chicago. Seymour was named to the Honor Roll of the Overseas Press Club in 1958.

Shadowless Lighting

Shadowless lighting is of two types, that which creates no shadows on or within the subject, and that which creates no shadows on the background or ground plane. Shadowless subject lighting is used when the subject itself is flat (as in copy photography), when the flat pattern aspect of the subject's tones or colors is to be emphasized, or when the subject is highly reflective. It is created by using broad, diffused light sources placed at equal angles (usually 45 degrees) on either side of the camera, or by surrounding the subject with a "tent" of translucent white material and lighting it evenly from the outside. The latter tech-

Seymour, David ("Chim"). "Terezka, a disturbed child in an orphanage. The scrawls on the blackboard are her drawing of 'home.'" Poland (1948). David Seymour/Magnum; Permanent collection, ICP, New York.

nique commonly is used with highly reflective objects such as jewelry and silverware. Shadowless lighting does not model the three-dimensional form of a subject or reveal surface texture, and therefore it has limited use in most commercial photography and portraiture.

Shadowless background lighting produces an image of the subject fully lighted and three-dimensionally modeled, surrounded by a single, even tone, usually white or black. If a black surround is acceptable, it is relatively easy to put black velvet or similar highly light-absorbent material beneath and behind the subject and arrange the lighting as desired. This works well with small subjects, but is not always practical or economical on a large scale. When a white or colored background is required, it is often possible to keep the background at a distance and arrange the subject lighting so that all shadows fall on the ground

plane. If it is possible to frame the picture to cut off the lower portion of the subject and the ground plane, the problem is solved. If the entire subject must be shown, three techniques are possible. One is to fasten the subject to a sheet of glass that is supported vertically or horizontally (with the camera above) far enough from the background so that the shadows fall out of camera range. The lens takes in a view within the edges of the glass, and a black curtain conceals the camera and tripod to avoid reflections. A second technique is to place the subject

Sheeler, Charles. "Wheels" (1939). Collection, Museum of Modern Art, New York.

on a continuous sweep of white paper or plastic material that curves up behind to form a background. This is flooded with enough light from above and behind the subject (so as not to wash out the effect of the frontal light on the subject) to erase any shadows. The third technique is to place the subject on a similar sweep of translucent material supported below by a sheet of glass and rising up behind. Light directed through this material from below and behind washes out all shadows without affecting the subject illumination.

It is also possible to eliminate shadows around a subject by hand-bleaching those areas of a print, or by air-brushing the background to a uniform tone and copying the image to get a final negative. Retouching to remove shadows is not always possible with color transparencies (which must be in large format to permit such work) and is very expensive when it is possible.

See also: EXPLODED VIEWS; LIGHTING; SILHOUETTE; TENT LIGHTING.

Sharpness

The subjective impression of accurate focus and the clarity of details in an image is called sharpness. Like brightness, it is not a measurable quantity. The factors of acutance and resolving power contribute to the impression of sharpness and can be objectively measured. However, the influence of contrast, certain color characteristics, and subject matter cannot be directly measured. In general, of two essentially identical prints most observers will choose the one with greater contrast as being the sharper, even though the prints may have equal acutance and resolving power. In some cases the choice is made in spite of the fact that these factors are objectively greater in the lower-contrast print. Similarly, an image with greater color purity or saturation is often identified as having greater sharpness. Familiar subject matter is often seen as being rendered sharper than unfamiliar, perhaps because it is given less searching attention. The matter of familiarity also

may underline the phenomenon of different viewers assigning different sharpness ratings to the same image.

See also: ACUTANCE; BRIGHTNESS RANGE; RESOLVING POWER.

Sheeler, Charles

American, 1883–1965
Charles Sheeler was known primarily as a Precisionist painter of American urban and industrial scenes, but he was a significant figure for many years in the field of architectural photography. He produced memorable series of images of the Ford Motor Company plant at River Rouge, Michigan, and of Chartres Cathedral, as well as abstractions of common objects and cityscapes. Influenced by Cubism, his photographs are characterized by a fine sharpness of texture and complex structural balances.

Sheeler was born in Philadelphia, Pennsylvania. He studied applied design at the Philadelphia School of Industrial Art (1900–1903) and painting with William Merritt Chase at the Pennyslvania Academy of Fine Arts (1903–1906), where he was a friend and classmate of Morton Schamberg.

Sheeler began to photograph as a student. To earn a living and support his painting he worked as an architectural photographer beginning in 1912. The following year he exhibited six paintings at the Armory Show. He turned to photographing works of art for museums, dealers, and collectors in 1914. He made studies of architectural details of houses and barns in Doylestown, Pennsylvania, for several years.

Sheeler's work was appreciated early on by Alfred Stieglitz. On his visits to New York from his Doylestown home, Sheeler became friendly with Stieglitz and Edward Steichen, and was a member of the Arensberg artistic circle.

He was awarded the first and fourth prizes at the John Wanamaker Photography Exhibition in 1918. The same year, he exhibited with Paul Strand and Schamberg and was given a one-man show at Maurice de Zaya's Modern Gallery in New York City.

Sheeler moved to New York in 1919. He met and collaborated with Strand on a film, *Mannahatta*, a hymn to the urban metropolis, in 1921. He began at this time to photograph the city from unusual perspectives to emphasize abstract geometric forms. He also made a series of experiments with double exposures. In 1922 he met Edward Weston who called Sheeler's work "the finest architectural photography I have seen." In 1923 Sheeler was hired by Edward Steichen at Condé Nast Publications as a fashion and portrait photographer for *Vogue* and *Vanity Fair*. He did little painting during the next decade.

Sheeler's most famous photographic work was done in six weeks in 1927 when he photographed the Ford plant at River Rouge. In later years, these images, among the most powerful industrial landscapes of the first half of the century, would continue to influence Sheeler's paintings.

After resigning from Condé Nast in 1929, Sheeler traveled to Europe and photographed a significant series on Chartres Cathedral. He began concentrating on his work as a painter from 1932 on, but continued to make important photographs. In 1935–1936 he photographed at Williamsburg, Virginia, and used these photos as studies for paintings. From 1942 to 1945 he was staff photographer of artwork for the Metropolitan Museum of Art, New York, and in 1950–1951 photographed major buildings in Manhattan.

Sheeler suffered a stroke in 1959 which

left him unable to photograph or paint. His work was exhibited widely both before and after his death in 1965. He was the subject of retrospectives at the Museum of Modern Art, New York (1939), the Walker Art Center, Minneapolis (1952), UCLA (1954), the Allentown Art Museum, Pennsylvania (1961), the National Collection of Fine Arts, Smithsonian Institution, Washington, D.C. (1968), and the Museum of Art, Pennsylvania State University (1974).

Sheet Film

See: FILMS.

Short Focus

A lens with a focal length shorter than the diagonal measurement of the rectangular format it is intended to cover is referred to as a short-focus lens. Properly, it identifies lenses of this sort not of retrofocus or inverted telephoto design, but it is often used to mean a wide-angle lens in general.
See: LENSES; OPTICS.

Short Lighting

See: NARROW LIGHTING.

Shutter

A shutter is the mechanism in a camera or lens that controls the length of time that film is exposed to light. Early cameras had no need for shutters; the lens cap simply was removed and replaced to expose slow glass plates for the required several seconds or minutes. As faster emulsions evolved, a more accurate means of regulating exposure time was needed and by the 1880s shutters were in common use. Modern shutters are complex devices that can accurately expose film for a fraction of a second; some 35mm cameras have shutters that provide exposures as brief as 1/4000 sec. Shorter exposures generally are achieved by shutterless means such as electronic flash, as explained in the entry on high-speed photography.

The early shutter was a separate accessory attached in front of or behind the lens. Today's shutter is integrated into the lens assembly or camera body. Three basic modern shutter designs are revolving disk or sector, diaphragm or leaf, and focal-plane or curtain.

The common sector shutter is a plate with a hole. It is spring-driven and moves through an arc over the lens opening. This type of shutter generally has one true speed setting which may be

from 1/15 sec. to 1/50 sec. and is sometimes marked *I* (instantaneous). A second setting, *B* (brief) or *T* (time), allows for long exposures. Most sector shutters and some simple leaf shutters are everset, or self-tensioning: after the shutter is released, the spring mechanism resets itself for the next exposure. Sector shutters usually are located behind the lens; leaf shutters often are located between the lens elements.

The leaf shutter has a number of overlapping metal or plastic blades much like an iris diaphragm; the blades open and close by means of a complex spring tension system. The blades pivot at their outer edges and open from the center to allow light rays to pass through. The tension of the drive spring governs the shortest exposure time (fastest speed), usually 1/500 sec. A gear escapement mechanism similar to that found in a watch controls slower speeds that commonly extend to one full second. Some leaf shutters for large-format cameras are accessories that are located behind the lens, allowing for lens interchangeability. Most leaf shutters and all focal-plane shutters in small- and medium-format cameras are tensioned when the film is advanced in the camera. Large-format lens shutters usually are not interlinked with the film transport mechanism.

The modern focal-plane shutter has two blinds, or curtains, that are driven horizontally or vertically across the film plane by a spring-wound mechanism. The curtains are adjusted to create slits of various widths to produce different exposure times. As the first curtain travels across the film plane, the emulsion is exposed to light. The second curtain follows after a specific time delay and forms the end of the slit. When the shutter is cocked, the curtains travel together back to the starting position with a self-capping effect. This allows the camera to accept interchangeable lenses while the film chamber remains light-tight. The exposure time, or shutter speed, is determined by the width of the slit between the curtains and the rate at which they travel. The shutter curtains are constructed of thin, black, rubber-coated cloth or thin, flexible metal such as titanium foil. The vertical-travel small-format shutter design uses several metal blades connected to two sets of arms. The arms are spring-driven and controlled by an escapement timing mechanism as in horizontal-travel shutters. In a camera with a rectangular (rather than square) picture format, a vertical shutter travels across the shorter dimension of the frame. This permits a faster speed for flash synchronization than the more common horizontal des gn, as well as a faster maximum speed. To correct this, most leaf shutters synchronize at all speeds with electronic flash, but have a maximum speed of 1/500 sec.

Shutter speeds are set manually by means of a dial on most cameras and lenses, or electronically by internal meter-coupled circuitry. Like *f*-stops, shutter-speed settings differ by a factor of two, so exposure is doubled or halved at each step. The international standard speed progression is 1 sec., 1/2, 1/4, 1/8, 1/15, 1/30, 1/60, 1/125, 1/250, 1/500, 1/1000, 1/2000 sec. Some shutters have faster or slower speeds; electronically governed shutters may produce intermediate speeds such as 1/28 or 1/340 sec., even though the speed indicated on the setting dial or in the camera viewfinder is the nearest speed in the standard series.

The use of electronic components to control the timing of shutter speeds has become commonplace in the modern shutter. Electronics may also link other functions such as lens aperture control and exposure metering to the shutter. In an electronic shutter the mechanism itself may be spring driven, but the timing mechanism consists of electronic circuitry. When current flows from the camera battery through an electromagnetic switch, the shutter opens. A resistor regulates the current flow to a capacitor. Speed timing is related to the charging time of the capacitor. When the capacitor is charged to a given value, a control circuit shuts off the current and the shutter closes. Electronic timing controls may extend the slow speed range of the mechanical shutter from 1 second to as much as several minutes.

An electromagnetic shutter has shutter blades that are driven by powerful magnets instead of springs. Because the shutter blades are the only moving parts, this design is virtually vibration free in operation. Electromagnetic shutters are used in scientific and industrial photographic systems.

A shutter may be operated by direct pressure on the release trigger, through a self-timing mechanism, or through an extension such as a plunger cable, pneumatic bulb, or a remote release triggered by radio or infrared signals. An electromagnetic release, not to be confused with the shutter mechanism itself, uses a solenoid rather than a mechanical linkage to trip the shutter. The electromagnetic release requires much less pressure than a mechanical device; this minimizes possible camera vibration. Delayed release may be achieved with a built-in or accessory self-timer. Automatically controlled shutters are discussed in the entry on automatic exposure control.
See also: AUTOMATIC EXPOSURE CONTROL; "B" SHUTTER SETTING; CAMERA; HIGH-SPEED PHOTOGRAPHY; SELF-TIMER; "T" SHUTTER SETTING.

Sidelight

Sidelight strikes the subject from a direction at right angles to the camera-subject axis. It produces maximum separation between highlighted and shadow areas and is used primarily as fill light rather than main light. In portrait photography sidelight used as the key light illuminates half of the subject's face and produces an effect known as hatchet lighting. This effect is used rarely because it is generally unflattering, but it can hide facial defects, narrow a broad nose, or produce melodramatic contrast. Sidelight provides maximum clarity of surface texture and detail; it is often used in product photography to emphasize these aspects of the subject.
See also: LIGHTING.

Siegel, Arthur Sidney

American; 1913–1978
One of László Moholy-Nagy's first American students at the New Bauhaus School in Chicago, Arthur Siegel went on to head the Department of Photography after the school was reorganized as the Institute of Design. Under Siegel's direction, the Institute built one of the most impressive photography programs in the country.

Siegel's teaching philosophy and personal/professional work were strongly influenced by Moholy. In search of what was uniquely photographic about light-sensitive images, Siegel pioneered the expressive use of 35mm color photography and explored the plastic and expressive possibilities of photograms, combination prints, and Polaroid SX-70 prints. Moving back and forth between freelance commercial work and teaching, Siegel applied the technical and aesthetic solutions he had learned under Moholy to industrial and corporate commissions, editorial work for magazines, and to teaching. The program he developed at the Institute of Design employed Harry Callahan, Aaron Siskind, Art Sinsabaugh, Joseph Jachna, Frederick Sommer, and other well-known modernist photographers.

In 1963, Siegel began preparing the images for his *Chicago's Famous Buildings* (University of Chicago Press, 1965), which established his eminence as an architectural photographer. Thereafter, he returned to teaching full-time (1967) at the Institute. He died in 1978.
Photograph: p. 462.

Silhouette

The term *silhouette* has two meanings in photography: a black, detailless shape seen against a lighted background, or—in photomechanical reproduction—a fully-detailed object shape seen against the white background of the page. The first definition refers to the photographic equivalent of the black paper cutouts first popularized (although not invented) in the 1760s by Etienne de Silhouette, a French government official, whose skill in reproducing object shapes and profiles by the freehand use of scissors was remarkable. The major photographic method of producing silhouettes is to place the subject in front of a fully-lighted background and to keep frontal light off the subject. Exposure is made for the background, with the result that the subject is underexposed. The background must be a minimum of two *f*-stops brighter than the subject with reversal film, or three *f*-stops brigther with negative film, to obtain the effect. Outdoors the open sky, a sunset scene, or bright snow, sand, or water provide suitable backgrounds for silhouettes. The subject must be in a shaded location, or the sun must be behind the subject. A silhouette can also be created by illuminating the subject with a single, intense light beam, such as that of a spotlight or a slide projector, and photographing the hard-edged shadow this produces. The shadow can be thrown on an opaque white surface and photographed from the same side as the subject. Or, it can be projected onto translucent material and photographed from the opposite side. Using colored light or a colored filter over the camera lens gives the subject a colored background.

The photomechanical-reproduction silhouette commonly is created by painting out (opaqueing) the unwanted background around the subject on the halftone negative. This kind of image also can be produced in the camera in two ways. One is to place the subject on a translucent light-table–background setup that washes out all shadows. The transilluminated background should be at least two *f*-stops brighter than the subject. The second technique is to photograph the fully-lighted subject on continuous-tone film. Then without moving the camera or the subject, a second exposure is made on high-contrast lith film with the background fully lighted but no light whatsoever on the subject. The background is overex-

posed so that it will be totally opaque on the negative, but transparent where the subject was located. This serves as a printing mask; it is sandwiched in register with the continuous-tone negative of the subject and blocks all background exposure when a print is made.

See also: SHADOWLESS LIGHTING.

Silkscreen Printing

Serigraphy—popularly called silkscreen printing—is a reproduction process that uses a fabric screen as a stencil through which ink is forced to print an image. In the photosilkscreen process the stencil is prepared by photographic methods. Originally silk was used for the screen because it had a very fine mesh and stood up well to repeated use; today synthetic fibers or metal screens are used. Silkscreening can be done by hand methods or commercially by rapid-printing machinery. It is widely adaptable and can print on a great variety of materials and shapes. In addition to art prints, posters, and other flat image reproductions, it is used to print drapery fabrics and clothing; beverage containers, bottles, and other such products; signs and notices; and many other kinds of objects.

To prepare a photosilkscreen stencil, a high-contrast film positive is required with the image at final reproduction size. If the original image is a negative, it is enlarged onto high-contrast lith film. If the original is a positive or a three-dimensional subject, it is photographed on either continuous-tone or lith film to get a negative, and this is contact-printed or enlarged onto a second piece of lith film to produce the required positive. If some approximation of continuous tone is desired in the final image, the positive must be prepared from a continuous-tone negative and a halftone screen, which is placed in contact with the positive film during exposure. It is also possible to use an auto-dot film for the positive, one that has a pre-exposed dot pattern that appears when the film is developed.

The screen, stretched taut on an open printing frame, is coated with a photosensitive solution or transparent adhesive film and is allowed to dry. It then is exposed in contact with the film positive to a highly actinic light source such as an arc lamp or ultraviolet lamp, or the sun. Exposure makes the coating insoluble in those areas struck by light; the other areas dissolve away when the screen is washed with water or a suitable solvent. The result is a negative stencil. When dry, pinholes and other imperfections in the stencil are filled in. Then the stencil is clamped in place on the material to be printed. Ink, applied to the screen in a bead outside the image area, is drawn across the stencil with a squeegee blade or a roller (brayer). The pressure of the blade forces the ink through the screen in the unblocked areas, printing the image. In hand-printing, ink also can be applied with a stiff stenciling brush.

See also: SCREEN PROCESSES; HALFTONE PROCESSES.

Silver; Silver Halide

The metallic element silver—chemical symbol, Ag—has unequaled heat and electrical conductivity, and reflectivity to light. It is easily malleable, ductile, insoluble in most acids and water, and readily forms amalgamlike combinations with a number of other metals. Widely used in industry, its great value in photography is the light sensitivity of silver-halogen salts (halides), and especially the degree to which a very small amount of exposure to light enables them to produce proportionately vast amounts of silver. The trace of silver produced by exposure is multiplied up to 100 billion times by the chemical amplification called development.

Silver halides. Silver forms crystalline compounds with the halogens: chlorine, bromine, iodine, and fluorine. Silver fluoride has no photographic application, but the others are all used. The halides become developable (reducible to silver) after only slight exposure, or they will darken and reduce under prolonged exposure to light without further chemical action. Halide crystals are insoluble in water, but soluble in sodium or ammonium thiosulfate (used as fixers); silver chloride is most readily soluble, silver iodide least so. Silver chloride and silver bromide are used individually or in combination in paper emulsions. The chloride produces a blue-black tone, the bromide a brown image tone, although the tones can be varied somewhat by the choice of developer; used together they produce neutral black tones. Silver chloride has the least sensitivity to light of the three halides. Silver bromide has much greater sensitivity and therefore is the principal ingredient of film emulsions. Silver iodide is used only in small amounts, primarily to increase the speed of film emulsions.

See also: BROMIDE PAPER; CHEMISTRY OF PHOTOGRAPHY; CHLORIDE PAPER; CHLORO-BROMIDE PAPER; DEVELOPMENT; EMULSION.

Silver-Dye Bleach Process

See: DYE-DESTRUCTION PROCESS.

Silver Recovery

Dissolved silver accumulates in photographic bleach and fix solutions, and to a lesser degree in wash water. All of the silver is removed from color materials during processing, a significant portion during most black-and-white processing. Scrap film and paper, unprocessed or processed (black-and-white), also contain silver. The potential value of this silver is many thousands of dollars a year for large processing facilities. Depending on market conditions it can also be significant for a studio producing as little as 40–50 gallons (150–190 liters) of fully used fixer or bleach a year. Recovery of silver from scrap materials is practical only for a specialist and only in great volume but silver recovery from processing solutions can be worthwhile on an individual basis.

Recovery methods. Large volumes of solution are most efficiently handled by electrolytic processors; small volumes with metallic replacement cartridges. Units using replacement cartridges are available commercially at moderate cost. A typical unit is essentially a 5-gallon or larger plastic container that acts as a temporary holding tank before used solution flows to a drain or other disposal facility. The solution comes in contact with the steel wool (iron wire) filling of a cartridge insert. The iron dissolves into the solution, replacing the silver, which precipitates out and collects as a sludge at the bottom of the container. The cartridge must be replaced periodically because the steel wool is consumed; the silver sludge can be sold to a metal recovery concern. Some recovery units are sold or leased with a sludge-handling agreement, others offer guidelines and suggestions for making local arrangements. Aside from potential economic return, silver recovery may be desirable or necessary to meet local code restrictions on discharging wastes into municipal sewer systems.

See also: DISPOSAL OF PHOTOGRAPHIC WASTES.

Sine Wave (Sinusoidal) Target

Test objects or targets composed of elements that change in a smooth progression—derived from the formula that generates a sine wave graph—are used to measure the imaging performance of a lens or emulsion in terms of modulation transfer function (MTF). The best-known sinusoidal MTF target is composed of alternating bars and spaces; the width of each bar-space pair differs from the preceding pair in accord with the sine wave function. This produces a constant decrease in the equiva-

lent lines-per-millimeter spacing, with a regularity analogous to a continuous tone change. The spacing decreases well beyond the resolving power limits of lenses and emulsions so that cut-off frequencies can be identified along with other image transfer characteristics. Other sinusoidal targets have repeating elements that individually vary in size, shape, or density according to the sine functions. Their images are scanned across the field by a fine slit to discover variations and distortions.

See also: MTF/MODULATION TRANSFER FUNCTION; RESOLVING POWER.

Sine Wave Target

Sinsabaugh, Art

American; 1924–1983
Beginning in the early 1960s, Art Sinsabaugh developed a strikingly new way of seeing in his long-horizontal rural and urban landscapes. Focusing primarily on Midwestern scenes, using a 12″ × 20″ view camera invented for banquet photography, he made contact prints noted for their exquisite detail and frieze-like compositions. Of Sinsabaugh's Chicago photographs, John Szarkowski has writ-

ten: "Sinsabaugh photographed the great prairie city—America's exemplary city—as no living city had been photographed. He photographed it not as a participant and partisan, but as an archaeologist: with fascination, disinterested sympathy, and aesthetic detachment."

Arthur Reeder Sinsabaugh was born in Irvington, New Jersey. He began photographing as a young boy, first with an 8mm, $9.95 Univex movie camera, then with a Brownie. As a high-school student, he worked for a department-store photography studio and as a Junior Photographer for the United States War Department. He served as a photographer in the United States Army Air Corps in the U.S. and the Far East from 1943 to 1946. From 1946 to 1949 he attended the Chicago Institute of Design (where he received a B.S. degree), studying under Arthur Siegel, László Moholy-Nagy, and Harry Callahan. He began to work as a freelance photographer in 1945, in Chicago and Champaign-Urbana, Illinois.

Sinsabaugh was instructor of photography at the Institute of Design from 1949 to 1952, and head of the evening program from 1952 to 1959. In 1959 he was named associate professor, then professor of art at the University of Illinois, Urbana. As head of the Photography/Cinematography Department he started an undergraduate and graduate program. He also founded the Visual Research Laboratory and was co-director for several years.

Sinsabaugh served as a photography, printing, and graphic design consultant to various advertising and industrial concerns. He was commissioned by the Plan Commission of the city of Chicago to make a series of photographic studies in 1963–1965, and later received a similar commission from the city of Baltimore. Sinsabaugh returned for graduate studies

at the Institute of Design in 1964, and received an M.S. degree in 1967. In addition to his permanent teaching positions, he also taught at the University of Oregon, the University of New Hampshire, Williams College, and the School of the Art Institute of Chicago. He was appointed an Associate Member of the University of Illinois Center for Advanced Studies in 1972-1973. He was a founding member of the Society for Photographic Education and was the recipient of numerous honors including: *Art in America's* New Talent Award in 1962; Society of Typographic Arts Awards in 1964, 1965, and 1966; Art Directors' Club of Indiana Award in 1964; Art Directors' Club of Los Angeles in 1964; Illinois Arts Council Award in 1966; and a Graham Foundation Award in 1966. Sinsabaugh was the recipient of a Guggenheim Fellowship in 1969, a National Endowment for the Arts Photography Fellowship 1976, and a Nettie Marie Jones Fellowship in 1983.

Sinsabaugh's last work included landscapes of the American Southwest, New England, and Britain in addition to his trademark Midwestern scenes. He had also experimented with small (2″ × 5″ [5 × 12.7cm]) color prints of similar subjects.

Sinsabaugh's work has been exhibited in group shows at the Museum of Modern Art, New York, in 1963, 1971 and 1978; at the National Gallery of Canada, Ottawa, in 1967; and at Photographers' Gallery, London, in 1977. He was honored with one-man shows at St. Mary's College, Notre Dame, Indiana, in 1959; at the Art Institute of Chicago in 1963; at the Underground Gallery, New York, in 1970; at the Museum of Modern Art, New York, in 1978; and at the Daniel Wolf Gallery, New York, in 1980. The Sinsabaugh Archive is deposited at the Indiana University Art Museum, Bloomington. Sinsabaugh published two

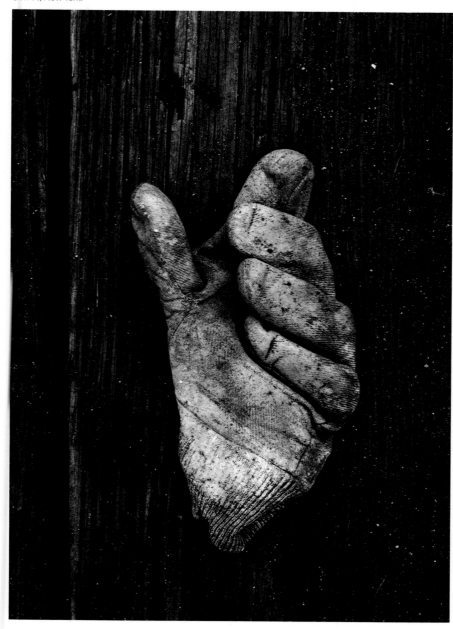

Siskind, Aaron. "Glcucester" (1944). Courtesy Aaron Siskind; collection, Museum of Modern Art, New York.

Siskind's subsequent relationship with the Egan Gallery, a major center in the development of Abstract Expressionism in painting, both broadened and consolidated his concern with formal and abstract qualities in image making. His first major one-man show of abstract photographs was at the Egan in 1947. The following year he met Harry Callahan, who brought him to the Institute of Design (New Bauhaus) in Chicago in 1950 to teach photography. In 1961 Siskind became head of the Department of Photography at the Institute, and in 1963 he was one of the founding members of the Society for Photographic Education (SPE).

For well over 40 years Siskind has been an influential photographer and teacher. The decisive shift in his work from the socially-oriented documentary form championed by the Film and Photo League to a highly modernistic belief in the photograph as "a new object to be contemplated for its own meaning and its own beauty" is one of the benchmarks in the evolution of mid-20th c. art photography. Paralleling comparable developments in American painting, Siskind turned from the kind of subjects exemplified by projects in the 1936–1941 period such as the Harlem Document, "Dead End: The Bowery," and "Portrait of a Tenement," to photographs in which, as he described it, "subject matter as such ceased to be of primary importance."

As Siskind abandoned documentary subject matter, he eliminated from his images perspective and the illusion of volume and depth in space; the photograph was no longer a transcription of a social reality, but rather was a surface to be inscribed. His subject matter became isolated objects, peeling paint, weather-stained stone, portions of letters on signs, and other fragments seen for their formal characteristics rather than for their commonplace reality. Siskind wrote in 1950: ". . . first and foremost I accept the flat picture surface as the primary frame of reference of the picture. The experience itself may be described as one of total absorption in the object. But the object serves only a personal need and the requirements of the picture. . . ."

See also: FILM AND PHOTO LEAGUE; NEW BAUHAUS.

Sizes of Materials

The standard dimensions in which films and papers are supplied may also be used to designate an image format, or the reverse may be true, but seldom is one an accurate measurement of the other. For example, a 4″ × 5″ camera uses sheet film

books of landscapes and a portfolio of photographs.
See also: NEW BAUHAUS.

Siskind, Aaron

American; 1903–
A New York City English teacher, Aaron Siskind first became interested in photography in 1930 and shortly thereafter joined the Film and Photo League. He left the League in 1933, but was persuaded to rejoin three years later; he became quite active, organizing the Feature Group within the League and directing group projects such as the Harlem Document. However, almost from the beginning a certain dissonance existed between the documentary and social-

political goals of the League and Siskind's emerging preoccupation with formal and aesthetic concerns. This conflict in approach and expressive style surfaced decisively when Siskind's photographs of Tabernacle City—a Methodist camp meeting community established in the 1830s on Martha's Vineyard—were exhibited in 1941. Several League members sharply criticized Siskind's interest in the folk-art aspects of the community architecture as formalism, and accused him of devoting the documentary approach to a subject of little or no social importance. In response Siskind left the League for good and thereafter worked in an increasingly abstract, personal, and contemplative mode.

of those dimensions, but the maximum image area is 3¾″ × 4¾″. Similarly, none of the formats recorded on 35mm film has an actual image dimension of 35mm. The numbers designating roll film sizes have no direct relation to film width: 120, 220, and 620 films are all 2⁷⁄₁₆ in. wide and are used for a variety of image formats, all of which are nominally 2¼ in. one dimension but are likely to be closer to 2⅛ in. Roll film designations and actual film sizes are the same around the world. Sheet films and papers are cut to inch sizes in the U.S., but to metric sizes in Europe and Asia (as well as to inch sizes for export to the U.S.). The slight differences in paper sizes make little difference, except perhaps with high volume automatic printing equipment. Sheet film cameras of a particular format accept film holders of universal outer dimensions, but the film retaining lips and the dark-slide openings differ for inch- and metric-size films. All films and papers are manufactured in continuous wide rolls and later trimmed to size. A great many sizes that were used at some point in the development of photography have been abandoned. Current standard U.S. sizes for general-purpose photographic materials are given in the table. Special-purpose materials may have other sizes; e.g., most films for aerial photography are supplied in 5 in. and 9½ in. widths. Most enlarging papers are additionally supplied in rolls from 200 to 500 feet long, in widths from 5 in. to 50 in. for use in automatic equipment.

STANDARD SIZES OF U.S. PHOTOGRAPHIC MATERIALS

Sheet Films and Papers (Dimensions)	Still Photography Films in Rolls, Cassettes, Cartridges (Size Designation)
2¼″ × 3¼″	110
3¼″ × 4¼″	126
4″ × 5″	127
9 × 12cm	135 (35mm)
5″ × 7″	116/616
8″ × 10″	120/220/620
8¼ × 11″	828
10″ × 10″	70mm
10″ × 12″	
11″ × 14″	
14″ × 17″	
30 × 40cm	
16″ × 20″	
20″ × 24″	
24″ × 30″	
30″ × 40″	

Note: Not all materials are manufactured in all sizes.

Sky Filter

A sky filter is used in outdoor photography to reduce the intensity of illumination from the sky without affecting the ground portion of the picture to any significant extent. The filter is graduated from zero density at the bottom or center to maximum density at the top. Filters that reduce the sky exposure by one, two, or three stops are available; the scene is exposed at normal camera settings, without any compensation for the filter. Sky filters for black-and-white photography are usually yellow; those for color photography are of neutral density (gray), or various special-effect colors.
See also: FILTERS; NEUTRAL DENSITY.

Skylight Filter

A skylight (No. 1A) filter is colorless or a pale salmon or pinkish color; it absorbs ultraviolet wavelengths and a slight amount of blue light. It is used without exposure compensation in color photography to reduce excess bluishness (caused by both ultraviolet and blue exposure) in distant portions of landscapes, in locations lighted by the open sky but shielded from the direct sun (open shade), and under overcast conditions. It has no significant effect on black-and-white films.
See also: FILTERS.

Slave Unit

A flash unit that is triggered by the operation of another, master, unit is called a slave. It may be connected by a cable to the master unit or, more commonly, may be controlled by a sensor cell. A wide variety of sensor devices, called slave switches or triggers, is available for use with any flash unit. Most triggers respond to light from the master flash, others react to infrared signals; the response is immediate so that all units fire simultaneously. Some flash units have built-in slave triggers and can be used either as masters or slaves. Cordless slaves with self-contained power supplies permit multiple-flash lighting setups without the hazard of wires to be tripped over. They also ease the problem of concealing units within the scene when large areas must be lighted.
See also: FLASH; MULTIPLE FLASH.

Slide

A positive transparency in a mount suitable for projection is called a slide. The term is also commonly used to refer to a small-format transparency whether mounted or not. A *dark slide* is the opaque, insertable blind that protects film in an accessory film holder or removable camera back.

Slide Presentation

Effective slide presentation is a matter of content as well as technique, whether the slides are being projected for an audience or are being offered for direct consideration by an art director, picture editor, or client. Except perhaps for a family showing—where the interest of a picture's subject may outweigh any of its faults—slides for presentation first should be edited rigorously to eliminate those which are improperly exposed, unsharp, poorly composed, or otherwise weak. Next they should be edited to eliminate those which are inappropriate to the intent of the presentation; this includes all duplicates and near duplicates. Only the best pictures should be retained, and two or more pictures of the same subject should be kept only if they are different in significant ways and are of equal interest and quality. Finally, the slides should be grouped or sequenced. A presentation with a narrative thread, such as an informational talk or the story of a trip, has an obvious sequence. The task then is to arrange the pictures within each topic or section in the most effective or interesting order. There should be visual variety, with frequent close-ups or single-element pictures used for emphasis, and broad, overall views primarily used as introductory images from section to section. Slides to be submitted as a kind of portfolio illustrating the scope of a photographer's work should be grouped by subject matter or style. Portraits, landscapes, fashion and product photographs, and sports pictures should not be intermingled, but should be collected into separate groups. If major differences in style or technique were used for various pictures within a group, they should be separated accordingly. For example, straight portraits should be separated from those in which colored light on the subject and special-effect filters were used to create unusual images.

The factors that go into effective slide projection are discussed in the entries on projection and screens. Portfolio presentation of slides differs somewhat according to whether the photographer is attempting to sell the pictures themselves or trying to sell his or her services. Pictures submitted for sale generally are placed in flexible plastic sheets with individual pockets for several mounted slides or transparencies; the number differs according to format. This protects them, avoids spilling and excessive handling, and allows many to be seen at a time by placing the sheet on a light box. The plastic permits marking selections with a crayon or china marker without actually marking the slide, and it allows identifying data written on the mounts to be seen. The pockets permit easy removal of those finally selected.

Slides used to promote the sale of services commonly are placed in a formal framing sheet that gives them a more impressive appearance. This is a stiff cardboard that is black on the face and has a series of openings exactly the size of the image area of the format used. Each slide slips in retaining slots on the back of the card, and its mount is completely hidden from the other side. The black color of the face allows the colors of the images to be seen with the greatest richness, especially when the sheet is placed on a light box. A "services" presentation may also be made by placing the slides in a standard tray so the client or the photographer can project them. In some cases it is effective to make the presentation by means of a compact, self-contained rear projection outfit that closes up into a small suitcase.

See also: PROJECTION; PROJECTORS; REAR PROJECTION; SCREENS, PROJECTION; SELLING PHOTOGRAPHS.

Slow-Motion Photography

The illusion of slow motion usually is created in motion pictures by photographing action at a greater number of frames per second (fps) than the intended projection rate. For example, action photographed at 72 fps, three times the standard projection rate of 24 fps, will take three times longer than normal on the screen, giving the appearance of slow, continuous movement. A similar effect is produced by using a slower projection speed with action photographed normally, but this is not practical when a presentation also includes action that should be seen at normal speed. A kind of false slow motion is created by step printing. When a print is made, every second or third frame is printed twice, which effectively doubles the length of a scene, or increases it by one third, respectively. The illusion of smooth, continuous movement may be lost with this technique. Video slow motion is produced by slowing the playback scanning rate, or by the electronic equivalent of step printing, in which every second or third frame is scanned twice at a normal rate.

Slow motion is often used dramatically for dreamlike or fantasy action, for comic effect, or to emphasize the flow and beauty of movement, such as that of a dancer. "Hidden" slow motion is used to smooth out visual bumps and jerks recorded when walking with a handheld camera or using it on a moving, vibrating vehicle or helicopter. A speed a few frames faster than normal, say 32 fps, often can conceal a significant amount of extraneous camera movement without being noticeable to an audience. Action in reduced-scale models, for instance the bursting of a miniature dam, commonly is photographed in slow motion so that it will take time on the screen equivalent to that of the full-scale event.

Slow motion is also widely used for informational purposes such as analyzing an athlete's performance, observing a machine in motion, or studying the evolution of an explosion. Much of this kind of photography is done with modified or specialized cameras operating at speeds from 100 to several thousand frames per second.

See also: HIGH-SPEED PHOTOGRAPHY; MODELS, SCALE AND MINIATURE; MOTION STUDY AND ANALYSIS; STOP-MOTION PHOTOGRAPHY; TIME-LAPSE PHOTOGRAPHY.

SLR (Single-Lens Reflex) Camera

The single-lens camera design in which a mirror reflects the image upward to a viewing screen was used in camera obscuras as early as 1676, more than a century and a half before the introduction of photography. The earliest adaptations for photographic use placed the mirror outside the rear of the camera to reflect the image of the focusing screen; both mirror and screen had to be removed to attach the plate holder. The Sutton camera of 1861, with bellows focusing and an internal mirror that was manually moved up out of the image path after focusing, was the first true single-lens reflex (SLR) camera.

From the 1880s to about 1915 a great many designs were produced using plates or films from 2¼" × 3¼" to 6" × 8"; most had an automatic mirror movement activated by the shutter release. By far the most successful of the SLRs in the U.S. was the Graflex, manufactured by Folmer and Schwing in many standard sizes and special-purpose models. Roll-film SLR cameras were introduced in the 1920s, all patterned after box or folding pocket camera designs. The basic shape now associated with 35mm SLR cameras first appeared in the Exacta Model B of 1935, which used 127 roll film. A year later the Kine Exakta introduced a new spelling of the camera name and the first use of 35mm film in an SLR. However, a long-focus lens with an integral reflex-viewer that attached in front of a 35mm Leica body had been offered in 1933. A single control to simultaneously advance the film, cock the shutter, and return the mirror to its viewing position was first incorporated in the Primarflex camera of 1935. The Contax S of 1949 was the first 35mm SLR to use a pentaprism above the viewing screen to provide an image that was not only upright, but properly oriented left-for-right. The pentaprism idea had originally been suggested in the 19th c., and previously had been used in a few roll film SLRs. The instant-return mirror was introduced in the Asahi Pentax camera in 1957, giving SLR photographers essentially continuous viewing of the subject. The Hasselblad camera, which established the design of modern medium-format SLR cameras, was introduced in 1948. The past two decades have seen little change in basic SLR design, but vast improvements in interior mechanisms. These include automatic exposure control, electromagnetically governed shutters, automatic coupling with dedicated electronic flash, and automatic focusing.

See also: CAMERA; CAMERA OBSCURA; REFLEX VIEWING.

Smith, Adolphe

English; dates unknown

In 1877 Adolphe Smith Headingly and the photographer John Thompson published the first of 12 monthly installments of their book *Street Life in London.* Smith, who did not use his last name professionally, was a reporter and writer deeply concerned with the condition of the working class and of those who eked out a living on the streets. His book was patterned after Henry Mayhew's monumental *London Labour and London Poor* of the 1850s, the first objective study to call attention to the plight of the bulk of the city's population. Twenty-five years later, conditions were no better, a situation Smith and Thompson wanted to bring to public attention in the hope of arousing concern and perhaps even action. Each installment was devoted to one kind of street person or occupation with interviews and observations by Smith and photographs by Thompson.

Mayhew's book had been illustrated with woodcuts and wood engravings, some based on daguerreotypes. Smith's book had Woodburytypes—the finest direct reproduction possible—of 36 of Thompson's photographs. Their intent was to achieve a compellingly real statement, as they explained in the introduction: "... we... have sought to portray these harder phases of life, bringing to bear the precision of photography in illustration of our subject. The unquestionable accuracy of this testimony will enable us to present true types of the London Poor and shield us from the accusation of either underrating or exaggerating individual peculiarities of appearance." The book is the first instance of photographic social documentation in print.

See also: DOCUMENTARY PHOTOGRAPHY; THOMPSON, JOHN; WOODBURY-GRAVURE/WOODBURYTYPE.

Smith, W. Eugene

American; 1918–1978

W. Eugene Smith, one of America's most acclaimed photojournalists for more than three decades, was highly respected for his compassionate images and uncompromising positions concerning craftsmanship and the social responsibilities of the photographer. From his early work as a combat photographer to his photoessay on Minamata, Japan, in the early 1970s, Smith advocated the photographer's right to direct editorial control over the layout of images, captions, and text for publication and exhibition. He was known to study his subjects in painstaking detail before shooting a single frame. He wrote, "I am constantly torn between the attitude of the conscientious journalist who is a recorder and interpreter of the facts and of the creative artist who often is necessarily at poetic odds with the literal facts."

Smith was born and educated in Wichita, Kansas, where he attended Catholic elementary and high schools from 1924 to 1935. After making his first photographs between 1933 and 1935, encouraged by Wichita press photographer Frank Noel, Smith contributed occasional photographs to local newspapers. His earliest admiration was for the work of Martin Munkacsi.

The distortion in newspaper accounts of his father's suicide left Smith with lasting doubts concerning the role and standards of American journalism. He resolved to pursue photojournalism, but to apply the highest standards to his own practice.

Smith studied photography on a scholarship to the University of Notre Dame, Indiana, in 1936–1937. The following year he became a *Newsweek* staff photographer in New York. In 1938–1939 he worked as a freelance photographer for the Black Star Agency, publishing photographs in *Life, Collier's, Harper's Bazaar,* and other periodicals before becoming a staff photographer with *Life* from 1939 to 1941.

From 1942 to 1944 Smith was a war

correspondent in the Pacific theater for *Popular Photography* and other Ziff-Davis publications. In 1944 he returned to *Life* as a correspondent-photographer. Smith was badly wounded at Okinawa in 1945. After a long recuperation he worked for *Life* between 1947 and 1954. His first photograph upon his recovery was one of his most famous: "A Walk to Paradise Garden," an image of his two children, which was the final photograph in *The Family of Man* exhibition and book. Working for *Life,* Smith published many significant stories, including "The Country Doctor," "Nurse Midwife,' "Spanish Village," and a profile of Albert Schweitzer as a medical missionary to lepers in Africa.

Smith resigned from *Life* and became a member of Magnum Photo Agency in 1955. During the next three years he

contributed photoessays to *Life, Sports Illustrated, Popular Photography,* and other periodicals, including a major photographic documentation of the city of Pittsburgh. In 1956 he was commissioned by the American Institute of Architects to photograph contemporary American architecture in color.

From 1959 to 1977 Smith worked as a freelance photographer for *Life,* Hitachi Company, and other clients. His last major story, concerning the mercury poisoning of the fishing village of Minamata, Japan, was completed in the early 1970s and contained several of his most moving images. Smith died in 1978.

Smith was the recipient of Guggenheim Fellowships in 1956, 1957, and 1968. He was voted one of the world's ten greatest photographers in a *Popular Photography* poll of 1958. He received an Honor Award from the American

Society of Magazine Photographers and an award from the University of Miami, Florida, in 1959. In 1971 he was honored with an award from the National Endowment for the Arts.

Smith taught intermittently at schools throughout the country, including the New School for Social Research and the School of Visual Arts, New York, and the University of Arizona, Tucson.

Smith's work was exhibited in group shows, including *The Family of Man* at the Museum of Modern Art in New York City, *Photography in the Twentieth Century* at the National Gallery of Canada in Ottawa, *Photography in America* at the Whitney Museum in New York, and *Photography in the 50s* at the International Center of Photography. He was the subject of one-man shows at the Museum of Modern Art, ICP, George Eastman House, in Rochester, New York, and the Witkin Gallery in New York City. A major retrospective of 640 prints was held at the Jewish Museum in New York City. The W. Eugene Smith Archive is housed at the Center for Creative Photography in Tucson.

Snapshot

A snapshot is a casual photograph taken for purposes of immediate personal record or pleasure, usually with a handheld camera and with little concern for the formal values of visual images. It is the equivalent in intent and function of a brief note jotted in an informal diary. The term was coined in 1860 by Sir John Herschel, who foresaw such pictures—taken as impulsively as a hunter snaps off a reaction shot when there is no time to aim—some two decades before technical developments made them possible.
See also: SNAPSHOT AESTHETIC.

Snapshot Aesthetic

The snapshot aesthetic is based on the conviction that the "naive" use of the medium is the source of those qualities which define the unique characteristics of expression and art in photography. Snapshots as such are not considered art. Rather, the basic expressive nature of photography is defined as springing from the photographer's ability—unique among visual artists—to record his immediate perceptions and reactions without particular technical skills or reliance on visual conventions. This kind of photography did not become possible until the advent of roll film and the hand camera in the late 1880s, and was a mode adopted almost exclusively by amateurs for several decades. Thus, according to this aesthetic, it is in the amateur product, snapshots, that the nature of photographic art is to be found. The idea of a photographic snapshot aesthetic received a great deal of attention among photographers and critics in the 1960s and 1970s. In the hands of artists like Lee Friedlander and Garry Winogrand, the use of seemingly random framing, harsh flash lighting, and banal subject matter became the key to a particular approach to art photography. The Museum of Modern Art and its director of photography, John Szarkowski, paid particular attention in a number of exhibitions to photography of this type.

The amateur snapshot itself was made possible in the 1880s by a combination of three technical innovations: faster emulsions which could capture some movement sharply; the replacement of glass plates by roll film which could be sent through the mail for processing by the manufacturer; and the introduction of the push-button handheld camera, which enabled even children to take pictures. Indeed, one of the photographers now viewed as an important forerunner of the snapshot aesthetic, Jacques-Henri Lartigue, took his most delightful and audacious photographs between the ages of seven and twelve in Paris at the turn of the century.

In the early 1900s the snapshot, and amateur snapshot photographers, were looked down upon by professional photographers—who faulted the snapshot's lack of technical accomplishment—and by amateurs with artistic yearnings, who equated beauty with the standards of painting. Members of such art-photography organizations as the Linked Ring and the Photo-Secession sought to place themselves at the greatest possible distance from what the snapshot represented: the passage of the power of picture-making from a small elite to the entire public. Even when important modernist photographers like Alfred Stieglitz, Edward Weston, and Paul Strand broke with the tradition of art photography imitating painting, they continued to separate their own work—sharply focused, deliberately composed, and meticulously printed—from that of the mass of everyday snapshooters. Steiglitz, however, pioneered in demonstrating that a hand camera—so-called amateur equipment—could be used to produce art photographs: the crucial factor was the photographer, not the camera.

In the early 1930s, young photographers such as Walker Evans, disturbed by what they felt was the pretentiousness of much of the art photography of the day, began to reconsider the alternative forms of photography such as the documentary and the snapshot. Evans's photographs of people in the streets of New York aspired to the casualness and matter-of-factness of the snapshot, and its feeling of being an immediate response to the immediately seen. That these photographs looked nothing at all like the works of Stieglitz and his followers was part of their attraction. While Evans ultimately chose to work primarily in the documentary mode with a large view camera, his earliest photographs with a handheld camera mark the appearance in America of a fully conscious snapshot aesthetic.

In Europe during the 1920s and 1930s, a number of photographers experimented with images that borrowed from the snapshot's unexpected croppings, skewed perspectives, and haphazard composition. In the Soviet Union in the 1920s, artist-photographers such as Alexander Rodchenko produced images in which tipped horizons, seemingly random compositions, unconventional viewpoints, and blurred movements all pointed to a familiarity with the typical "accidents" of amateur snapshot photography. In the same years, the Hungarian André Kertész began photographing informal, spontaneous events in a style combining human warmth and gentle wit; the precedent for Kertész's attention to the undramatic, everyday aspects of human life can be found in the snapshot. And while nothing could seem farther from the typical amateur snapshot than the intricate precision and striking formal arrangement of Henri Cartier-Bresson's photographs, his famous insistence on the "decisive moment" can be seen as a sophisticated variation on the snapshot principle of an unpremeditated response to an immediate event.

In the 1950s, two photographers emerged who took elements of the snapshot look and used them to fashion distinctive, highly personal idioms. The Swiss-born Robert Frank, who emigrated to America after World War II, used the "unfinished" appearance of the snapshot to convey his response to the United States of the 1950s in his book *The Americans*. Although many critics derided his photographs as incompetent because of his frequent use of blur, tilt, and out-of-focus techniques, in Frank's case these devices were purposely and effectively employed to convey his impression of America as a land of transient people and haphazard events. In the same years, the American photographer William Klein, who had trained as a painter in Paris after World War II, produced a series of photographic books dealing with the world's great cities—

New York, Rome, Tokyo, and Moscow. In his photographs Klein went even farther than Frank in making use of the amateur's "mistakes" for his own expressive purposes. Grainy, overexposed, blurred, and out of focus, Klein's images manage to suggest the tumult and chaos of modern urban life.

By the 1960s, with the arrival on the scene of photographers like Lee Friedlander and Garry Winogrand—both of whom began their careers as magazine photographers—the idea of a full-blown "snapshot aesthetic" began to receive attention in art photography circles. Both at first were regarded as photographers of the "social landscape," and considered to be following in the footsteps of the FSA and other social documentary photography. But their photographs quickly turned away from straightforward social documentation toward experimentation with the expressive effects of the snapshot look. Friedlander produced many urban photographs that seemed to have no clearly defined center of interest: window frames and lampposts bisected his images, fragments of human figures were lopped off at the edge of the frame, indecipherable accumulations of visual detail purposely induced disorientation in the viewer. Winogrand made photographs that looked like "grab shots" on city streets, and from moving cars. Such images might have attracted little attention but for the persuasive critical writings of John Szarkowski of the Museum of Modern Art, who found in them the glimmer of a new kind of photographic art, one not beholden to the traditions of painting. In books like *The Photographer's Eye* (1966), Szarkowski argued that the most inventive photographs were often those that seemed unconventional or accidental, and thus escaped from the bounds of traditional art. Seen in this light, a snapshot might seem more formally provocative than a Stieglitz.

The followers of Friedlander and Winogrand carried the snapshot aesthetic into many different areas. Joel Meyerowitz, in the early 1970s, produced a series of color photographs on the streets of New York that expressed a vivid sense of that city's anarchic energy. Larry Fink, photographing for several years at fashionable parties in New York and Washington, made images that seemed like accidental exposures capturing uneasy moments of confrontation. Nancy Rexroth, using a toy camera with a plastic lens, fashioned hazy, indistinct photographs that suggested memories of a long-lost childhood. And Nicholas Nixon in the early 1980s demonstrated that the snapshot look could be attained

even with an 8″ × 10″ view-camera, as evidenced in his informal portraits of groups of children. The banality of snapshot color quality as well as its subject matter was projected as a mode of formal expression in the work of William Eggleston, introduced to the museum-going public in 1976.

One of the most valuable surveys of recent work in the snapshot vein is *The Snapshot* (1974), edited by Jonathan Green, which includes examples of the work of Frank, Winogrand, Rexroth, and many others.

See also: ART OF PHOTOGRAPHY; CONCEPTUAL PHOTOGRAPHY; DOCUMENTARY PHOTOGRAPHY; PICTORIAL PHOTOGRAPHY/PICTORIALISM; SNAPSHOT; SOCIAL LANDSCAPE.

Snoot

A snoot is a device used to form illumination from a spotlight or flash unit into a small, shaped beam. There are two kinds of snoot. One is a metallic cone open at both ends; the wider opening is fitted over the front of the light source, and the narrower end is directed toward the subject. The other kind is a flat, opaque plate that fits over the face of the lighting instrument. A hole in the center of the plate is extended by a chimneylike

tube. The diameter, length, and shape of the tube define the size and shape of the light beam. Snoots are painted black inside to prevent stray reflections.

A snoot allows light to be directed precisely to a very small area of the subject. Instruments with snoots are often used for hair lights and eye lights in portraiture, and to create spotlight pools of illumination in product and small-object photography. A snoot also makes it much easier to aim a light source from behind the subject toward the camera without spilling illumination into the lens.

See also: LIGHTING; LIGHT SOURCES.

Social Landscape

Social Landscape is a term first used in 1966 to describe the work of a group of young photographers—including Bruce Davidson, Lee Friedlander, and Danny Lyon—then beginning to attract wide attention. Coined by Nathan Lyons, who organized an early exhibition featuring their work, Social Landscape indicated a shifting of concern from portraying the natural landscape to showing people in their created environment. Unlike social documentary photographers, these photographers of the Social Landscape were less interested in criticizing

Social Landscape. Danny Lyon, "Llanito, New Mexico" (1970). Courtesy Danny Lyon permanent collection, ICP, New York.

social ills than in exploring the ephemeral, everyday aspects of modern social life. Like Robert Frank, whose 1950s photographs of the American scene were an important precedent, the Social Landscape photographers of the 1960s produced images marked by a deceptively artless style, an underlying tone of ironic detachment, and an absence of moralizing.

Such photographs were also frequently described as "street photography," since the photographers typically worked quickly and unobtrusively with 35mm cameras on city streets. The means used to convey a sense of the seemingly random occurrences that give the urban social environment its peculiar flavor included techniques borrowed from the vocabulary of the snapshot: seemingly haphazard framing, chance configurations of people and objects, and ambiguity of the meaning of the actions pictured. Garry Winogrand has come to exemplify this approach, partially because in much of his work he pushes this "snapshot" strategy to an extreme. Other photographers took a more considered approach to subject selection and picture organization.

In 1967, the year after the introduction of the idea of the Social Landscape in photography, two major exhibitions gave wider currency to this approach. The Brandeis University show *12 Photographers of the American Social Landscape* gave a clear indication of the range of young photographers working in this direction. Probably more important, however, was the exhibition *New Documents* at the Museum of Modern Art, which included the work of Friedlander,

Winogrand, and Diane Arbus. In his introduction to their photographs, MOMA director of photography John Szarkowski pointed out that the intention of these photographers lay not primarily in making a social statement, but in using public spaces to make provocative, adventurous, innovative photographs. This attitude toward the aims of photography proved enormously influential among a great many photographers during the 1970s.

Other photographers whose work has at one time or another been considered to involve the idea of the Social Landscape include Henry Wessel, Jr., Bill Zulpo-Dane, Joel Meyerowitz, Mark Cohen, Tod Papageorge, Anthony Hernandez, Burk Uzzle, and John Gossage.
See also: ART PHOTOGRAPHY; SNAPSHOT AESTHETIC.

Societies and Associations, Photographic

See: APPENDIX.

Soft Focus

Soft focus occurs when some rays from each point at the focused (subject) distance are brought to focus at the image (film) plane, but other rays from the same points are not. The result is a kind of halo definition area for each detail rather than a specific definition point. The effect creates a gentle, controlled degree of indistinctness that is commonly used to flatter, romanticize, or glamorize subjects. Soft focus is produced by lenses that have uncorrected spherical abberation. Portrait lenses in particular are

often purposely made this way, usually with some means to vary the degree to which focus is softened. Soft focus can also be produced by placing diffusing material in front of the camera lens. Soft focus is not achieved simply by throwing a lens out of focus, even to a slight degree. In that case, no rays from the points of principal concern in the subject are brought to a focus; the result is more visually confusing than with true soft focus, and the degradation of tone or color is greater.
See also: ABERRATIONS OF LENSES; PORTRAIT LENS/ATTACHMENT.

Solarization

The partial reversal of tone in a photographic image caused by vast overexposure—on the order of 1000 to 10,000 times normal—is called solarization. Historically a common problem associated with emulsions sensitive only to blue light, true solarization occurs rarely in modern emulsions. More commonly, the Sabattier effect is used today to create a similar reversal.

Although some present-day commercial materials such as x-ray film show a tendency to solarization, most do not because they have anti-halation backings that help limit the effects of overexposure. When solarization is desired, a specially made emulsion is necessary for full effect. Most often, solarization is encountered as a result of accidentally including an extremely bright light source in the picture area. When this happens, the light will reproduce as black or very dark gray rather than white.

Solarization was first noticed in daguerreotypes, in the 1840s. The blue-sensitive surface of daguerreotype plates required substantial exposure to record the small amounts of blue light reflected by red, green, and mixed-color objects. When sufficient light had struck the plate to record those areas, blue areas such as sky and white materials in the blue-rich sunlight had become solarized. This accounts for the semi-negative appearance of many of the earliest daguerreotypes. Unskilled portrait photographers of that era frequently overexposed their plates, causing white shirt fronts to register as blue-gray; they were contemptuously dismissed as "blue bosom boys" by their more professional colleagues.

Although many theories have been put forth to explain solarization, the phenomenon is still not completely understood.
See also: ANTI-HALATION LAYER; SABATTIER EFFECT.

Solarization. Carlotta Corpron, "Solarized Calla Lilies" (1948). © Carlotta Corpron; permanent collection, ICP, New York.

Solar Microscope

Early microscopy was limited by the weak intensity of, and the difficulty of controlling, artificial light sources of the time—candles, and kerosene or gas lamps. The solar microscope, invented in 1740, reflected sunlight to the specimen stage, making it possible to examine relatively thick-sliced or semitransparent samples by transmitted light. A smoked-glass filter could be inserted in the microscope tube to protect the user's eye, but this reduced the visibility of specimen details. The great advantage of the solar microscope was that the intensity of sunlight made it possible to use a long focal-length eyepiece and project the image at full brightness onto a piece of paper or a wall several inches away. The projected image was easy to trace to obtain drawings at magnifications of typically 10× to 20× with much greater accuracy than provided by

freehand drawing based on direct viewing. When photography was invented, it occurred to several scientists to substitute sensitized material for the drawing paper in order to record images directly. Those using the solar microscope to capture the first enlarged photographic images included Humphry Davy in 1802; Thomas Young, who recorded the first image of Newton's rings; W. H. F. Talbot in 1835 and 1837; and Hippolyte Bayard in 1839. Images recorded before 1839 were short-lived because no adequate method of fixing them for photographic permanency was known.

Solio Paper

In 1892, Eastman Kodak Co. introduced Solio Paper, probably the most successful printing-out paper ever produced for amateur use. A gelatin-emulsion chloride paper that was progressively im-

proved, it remained available in some countries until the late 1960s, at least two decades after manufacture of almost all other such papers had ended.
See also: CHLORIDE PAPER; PRINTING-OUT PAPER.

Solubility; Solutions

See: MIXING PHOTOGRAPHIC SOLUTIONS.

Sommer, Frederick

American; 1905–
Sommer may fairly be said to represent the ideal of the photographer's photographer. Neither as well known as many of the other acknowledged masters of art photography, nor as prolific, Sommer is nonetheless considered one of the very great living photographers. Working throughout the entire spectrum of photography, with an authentically surrealist sensibility, Sommer has produced a body of work which is as disturbing as it is exquisite. Typically, his photographs require long periods of preparation, nowhere more so than in his manufactured objects and collages which he then photographs. It was not until 1956 that his first major portfolio of photographs was published, and six years later that the first monograph on his work appeared.

Born in Angri, Italy, Frederick Sommer lived from 1913 to 1930 with his family in Brazil, where he returned to practice as a landscape architect and city planner after receiving an M.A. in Landscape Architecture from Cornell University in 1927. Sommer contracted tuberculosis and was forced to abandon his career, but his interest in art, philosophy, and aesthetics blossomed during his convalescence in the American Southwest, which became his permanent home. Continuing to paint and draw, Sommer began to photograph seriously soon after a series of meetings with Alfred Stieglitz in 1935. Influential, too, was his exposure to the work of Paul Strand and Edward Weston during the same period. His earliest photographs were taken in Arizona, where he had settled with his wife Frances in 1930. They include some of his most famous photographs: unsettling studies of animal entrails and dried carcasses, and startling images of the desert landscape with suppressed horizons and confusing spatial configurations. In the early 1940s, Sommer met two artists who were also to influence his work, the Precisionist painter and photographer Charles Sheeler, and even more importantly, the Surrealist artist Max Ernst. Both men en-

Sommer, Frederick. "Circumnavigation of the Blood" (1950). Courtesy Frederick Sommer; collection, Museum of Modern Art, New York.

couraged Sommer's interest in exploring the shared problems of different media. Sommer would later say, "It is with the sensitized surface rather than with photography itself, that I am concerned." Consistent with such a notion has been Sommer's experimental and systematic exploration of a range of photographic practices: cameraless negatives, clichés-verre, smoke-on-glass, paint-on-cellophane, cut-paper images, and—outside of the range of photography altogether—musical notation as art.

Sommer's first one-man show of photographs was held at the Santa Barbara Museum of Art, California, in 1946. This was followed by a larger exhibit, one of the series *Diogenes with a Camera*, at the Museum of Modern Art, New York, in 1952.

Throughout the last three decades, Sommer has traveled widely and taught photography at many institutions including Prescott College, Arizona; the San Francisco Art Institute; Princeton University; and the Rhode Island School of Design. In 1974 he received a Guggenheim Fellowship. He has also written

a number of suggestive papers on aesthetics and pictorial logic.

The Center for Creative Photography at the University of Arizona established an extensive archive of Sommer's work in 1975 and a major retrospective was held at the International Center of Photography in 1981.

Southworth, Albert Sands
American; 1811–1894
Hawes, Josiah Johnson
American; 1808–1901

Southworth and Hawes were the most internationally prestigious American daguerreotype portraitists during the 1840s and 1850s. In partnership for nearly 20 years, they made thousands of sensitive, direct, and detailed portraits, and views of Boston and Niagara Falls. Among the cultural elite who were their sitters were Daniel Webster, Ralph Waldo Emerson, Henry W. Longfellow, John Quincy Adams, Jenny Lind, Lola Montez, Harriet Beecher Stowe, Oliver Wendell Holmes, and Charles Goodyear.

Southworth wrote, "The whole character of the sitter is to be read at first sight. . . and it is required of and should be the aim of the artist-photographer to produce in the likeness the best possible character and finest expression of which that particular face or figure could ever have been capable. But in the result there is to be no departure from truth in the delineation and representation of beauty, and expression, and character."

Hawes was born in East Sudbury, Massachusetts. While a carpenter's apprentice, he began to paint miniature portraits. He worked as an itinerant portrait painter and lecturer on electricity from 1829 to 1841. In 1840 he attended Daguerre's American agent's lectures on daguerreotype in Boston. Hawes gave up painting to make daguerreotypes the following year.

Southworth was born in West Fairlee, Vermont. He attended Bradford Academy, and Phillips Academy, Andover, Massachusetts, from 1833 to 1835. After working briefly as a teacher, he opened a drugstore in Capotville, Massachusettes, in 1839. Like Hawes, he

Southworth, Albert and Hawes, Josiah. "Daniel Webster" (1851); daguerreotype. Metropolitan Museum of Art, New York.

attended lectures on the daguerreotype in Boston in 1840. He traveled to New York soon after to study daguerretoypy with his former roommate, Joseph Pinnell. Southworth and Pinnell trained with Samuel Morse and returned to Capotville where they opened a portrait studio. In 1841 they moved their studio to Boston.

Southworth and Hawes became partners when Pinnell left the studio in 1843. Southworth traveled to California during the Gold Rush in 1849 but continued to photograph (primarily views of San Francisco) until he returned to the Boston studio in 1851. Southworth and Hawes photographed intensively for the next decade. Throughout this time, they never ceased experimenting with new methods to improve their work. They introduced the "crayon picture," or vignette portrait to photography, and a variety of other innovations in technique. At the same time, Southworth invented and patented technical equipment including the Grand Parlour Stereoscope which won several awards. After dissolution of the partnership in 1862, Southworth studied and lectured on the applications of photography to graphology. Hawes continued to operate a Boston studio until his death in 1901.

In 1976, *The Spirit of Fact: The Daguerreotypes of Southworth and Hawes, 1843–1862* was published by David Godine Publishers and George Eastman House.

See also: CRAYON PICTURES.

Space Photography

This is a general term used to denote all photography or quasi-photographic imagery originating from an artificial satellite or from a spacecraft, notably the U.S. Space Shuttle. While the limits of current technology are screened from the public because of the need for defense security, it has been noted that the image of a single person can be resolved from an earth orbit satellite. This level of photographic capability, along with the vast array of photographic data that have been derived from space flight, has evolved since the initial U.S. Mercury manned satellite was orbited in 1962. At that time it was the widespread opinion of cartographers, geologists, and other interested scientists that photographs from space probably would not be clear enough to be useful. They could not have predicted the rapid advancement in lens designs and electronic sensing systems. Most important, no one was yet aware of the spectacular strides that were about to be made in computer technology. Digital image sensing and processing

techniques are undoubtedly the underpinning that have transformed the multitude of images from space into a usable condition. Four broad but distinct categories of space photography may be identified: (1) photography aboard the Space Shuttle, (2) earth orbit satellite images of earth, (3) earth orbit satellite astronomy, and (4) deep space probe images. Of the four, the latter three are entirely remote controlled.

Space-shuttle photography. All flights of the Space Shuttle carry both 35mm and 2¼″ square format cameras for use by the astronauts in documentation. Cameras used inside the module are similar to those sold to the public. For extravehicular photography, the camera is placed in a thermal bag for protection from temperatures of −15° to 100°F with oversized and simplified controls for ease of operation. The hyperfocal dis-

tance, for example, is located by a click stop on the focusing tab. At this setting, with the standard 35mm lens (a shorter focal length lens is used as normal in space due to limited subject-to-camera distances), and commonly used *f*-stops, objects from about 5¾ ft. (1.75m) to infinity are sharply focused without the need for visual reference. An ordinary color transparency emulsion coated on a thin base to allow 72 frames to be loaded into a standard cassette is used. The film is advanced automatically via a motor drive. Photographs made by the astronauts, as well as those made by many nonclassified satellites, are available to the public at NASA's extensive picture library in Washington, D.C.

Satellite photography. In terms of sheer volume of images produced, satellite photography of earth is by far the largest area. In turn it may be subdivided into three parts—earth survey and resources, meteorological, and military reconnaissance. The current generation of earth resources satellites is the Landsat series begun in 1970. Although now inoperative Landsats I, II, and III each mapped the entire earth every 18 days in a mosaic of 30,000 pictures. To convert such an overwhelming abundance of images to a coherent set of pictures by conventional photographic means would have been an impossible burden. Consequently the camera and film were replaced by what is called a multispectral scanner (MSS). In this type of system the area of the earth imaged is sensed by a flying spot scanner (or similar device) that records the scene in binary code in a raster pattern pixel (or smallest resolvable picture unit) by pixel. Records are made in both visible and infrared wavelengths simultaneously. The information is stored aboard the satellite until it can be conveniently radio transmitted to a ground receiving station. From there it is sent via ground wire to NASA's data center in South Dakota for computer processing. Landsat IV, the present earth resources orbiting satellite (EROS), is the most sophisticated of the series. The MSS aboard it is capable of distinguishing a tonal scale of 256/1 (as opposed to 64:1 previously). This quadrupling of fineness in the recorded tones provides significantly greater ability for scientists to note variations in light reflection from the earth's surface. In addition, the increased capability and broadened spectral sensitivity of the new MSS allow it to produce thematic maps. These are maps that, in effect, concentrate on a particular geologic concern such as glacial flow or forest distribution. Aside from the research benefits produced by Landsat, a variety of practical values have been derived as well, including major oil discoveries and substantially improved agricultural yields.

Meteorology. Improvements in the accuracy and timeliness of weather predictions were and continue to be of prime importance in space photography, conducted by the National Oceanographic and Atmospheric Administration (NOAA). At present, the third generation of meteorological satellites consists of NOAA A through NOAA F (only A, B and C have actually been launched as of this writing). The sophisticated radar imaging systems allow recording of meteorological conditions even when the satellite is over the dark side of the earth. In combination with digital recording and transmission this means weather maps can be generated and disseminated to local forecasters with unprecedented speed. This is a crucial consideration in a

scientific discipline that considers information more than 24 hours old of archival value only. NASA also maintains a Geostationary Operational Environmental Satellite series in high (about 35,000km) earth orbit that is capable of keeping a virtually continuous check on large developing storm systems such as hurricanes.

Military. The most advanced digital imaging systems have been reserved for the military's exclusive use aboard the new KH-11 Keyhole series of reconnaissance satellites. In part the KH-11 series augment the DEW (distant early-warning) radar line across Canada and Alaska. They are capable of spotting an ICBM from the time it is launched. Also, in part, this series provides photographic evidence of compliance with armament control treaties. Besides having access to NOAA satellite data, the Air Force also operates a series of meteorological satellites. All Defense Department satellite photography is based on digital imaging techniques.

Astronomical. For many years astronomers have been aware that some types of stellar observations simply could not be made from the earth's surface due to the interference of the atmosphere. The most spectacular observational platform launched to date is the International Ultraviolet Explorer (IUE). Placed in orbit in 1978, the IUE is a 17.7in. (45cm), $f/15$, axis-stabilized, reflecting telescope. At the focal plane it is a spectrograph, thus making it capable of rendering the spectral emission content of quasars, the most distant objects known to man. Even shorter wavelength phenomena in the x-ray and gamma-ray range are studied aboard the High Energy Astronomical Observatory (HEAO). From this series, neutron stars, binary stars, and black holes may be investigated. Further information is expected from the launch of the Gamma Ray Observatory in the late 1980s. In 1983 NASA, in conjunction with the European Space Agency, launched the Space Telescope aboard the Space Shuttle. It is expected to be a long-lived instrument that the shuttle will service periodically. The primary reflecting mirror is 7.8 ft. (2.4 m.) in diameter with a relative aperture of $f/24$. Wavelengths from 115nm to 1mm will be observed. While instruments of substantially larger size exist on earth, the absence of atmospheric disturbance will allow the space telescope to form images of objects $10\times$ fainter than previously possible. Initially the images will be shared among two cameras, two spectrographs, and one photometer.

There have been several deep space

probes, some of which have returned spectacular photographs. As with the newer earth orbit satellites, they use electronic imaging and transmission systems and computer control. Typically a probe has a high resolution scanner that can be filtered to produce color images and a low resolution backup scanner in case of failure. The image data are encoded and stored temporarily until optimum transmission conditions are encountered. The Goldstone Tracking Station receives the data and transfers them to the Deep Space Network at the Jet Propulsion Laboratory in California where they are processed.

See also: ASTROPHOTOGRAPHY; DIGITAL IMAGES; PHOTOGRAMMETRY, AERIAL; SCANNER, FLYING SPOT; WEATHER PHOTOGRAPHY.

Color photograph: p. C-52.

Spark Photography

A high-voltage electric spark dissipates a great amount of energy as a proportional amount of light in an instant as brief as 1/200,000 sec. The first demonstration of motion-stopping photography by means of spark illumination was made in 1851 by W. H. F. Talbot, who recorded a sharp image of a newspaper page mounted on a rapidly revolving wheel, illuminated by the discharge from a wet-cell spark discharge circuit built by Michael Faraday. The first significant applications of spark photography were made by Ernst Mach in the mid-1880s and Sir Charles Boys in the following decade. Both men photographed bullets in flight.

In many applications, spark illumination has been replaced by very high speed electronic flash, but it is still used in some ballistics work and in certain kinds of schlieren photography. Most spark photography consists of lensless shadow or refraction images because a great deal of the actinic (photo-effective) output of an electrical spark is in the ultraviolet range absorbed or blocked by ordinary optical glass.

See also: SCHLIEREN PHOTOGRAPHY; TALBOT, WILLIAM HENRY FOX.

Special Effects

Photographic special effects transform normal, "straight" images into pictures that could not be achieved without photographic manipulation. The special effect can be as simple as adding fog to a photograph taken on a clear, sunny day, or as complex as simulating an automobile in orbit around the earth. Special effects can be accomplished in the camera or by darkroom manipulation.

Some of the major techniques are mentioned here; the cross-references list many more, but do not include antique and non-standard processes, which are often used for special effects.

Effects with lens attachments. Filters offer a simple method for achieving special effects. With color film, strongly colored filters will transform an ordinary scene or subject by overriding the natural colors. Colored filters also are available in half-color, half-clear form to enable color to be added to part of the scene without affecting the rest of the photograph. Fog filters simulate various fog densities when none exist. Diffusion filters give a soft-focus effect with normal, sharp-focusing lenses. For a graduated effect, diffusion and fog filters are manufactured with clear centers and increasing diffusion or fog out to the edges. Diffraction filters break up specular white light into a variety of rainbow patterns such as streaks of color from the light source, circles of prismatic color surrounding the light, or spokes of color.

Multi-image effects can be obtained in a single exposure by use of prism lenses that attach to the front of the camera lens. The pattern produced depends on the number and arrangement of the prism facets. Some prism attachments will simulate the effect of a stroboscopic exposure of a moving subject when in fact no motion occurred.

In-camera special effects. Multiple images and superimposition of images can be achieved through multiple-exposure techniques. Basically, multiple exposure is accomplished by deliberately exposing a single frame of film more than once. Depending on the subjects used and the backgrounds chosen, the final effect can resemble a montage or multi-image photograph.

Multiple images also can be accomplished with a matte box. A matte box resembles a bellows lens shade; it is placed in front of the camera lens and allows masking attachments to be added for multiple imagery or shaped images. Multiple exposures can be made on a single frame of film without superimposing images or being restricted to special backgrounds.

Another in-camera special effect is the intentional blurring of images. This is accomplished by using a slow shutter speed and moving the camera during the exposure; the camera may be moved in a circular motion, moved in a random pattern, or panned in the direction opposite to subject movement. A zoom lens may be shifted during exposure to produce an effect of the subject rushing toward or away from the viewer.

Special effects with film. Unusual types of film emulsions are another source of special effects. High-contrast lith films will produce negatives that contain only highlight and shadows, with all the middle tones dropped out. Infrared color and black-and-white films will yield unnatural tones and colors from ordinary subjects. High-speed surveillance films produce images with pronounced grain structure and low contrast.

Darkroom special effects. Darkroom manipulation allows many effects to be created from photographs already taken. Many of the special effects that are accomplished with filters on the camera lens can be achieved in the darkroom using filters over the enlarging lens. Fog, diffusion, and similar devices can be used when making black-and-white or color prints. Colored filters are usable for changing the overall color tonality of color prints.

Superimposed images are created by placing two or more negatives in the enlarger at the same time, or by multiple exposures from one or more negatives used separately. The latter method offers more control of composition, as the images combined can be of any size or arranged anywhere on the enlarging paper.

A negative print, in which tones or colors are the opposite of their normal appearance, is achieved by printing from a positive rather than a negative film image.

Texture—such as burlap, silk, and brush-stroke—can be added to photographic prints through the use of texture screens that are laid on top of the enlarging paper or are sandwiched with the negative in the enlarger. Another method of adding texture to a negative is by reticulation, the intentional cracking of the emulsion layer of the film. The effect varies, but it resembles a cracked or stippled surface. A bas-relief three-dimensional effect is accomplished by printing from a sandwich in which positive and negative versions of the same image are positioned slightly out of register. The Sabattier effect, or darkroom solarization, combines positive and negative tones in a single image; it is accomplished by briefly flashing a print or negative with white light while it is developing.

See also: BAS-RELIEF IMAGES; BLEACH-OUT PROCESS; COLLAGE; COMPOSITE PHOTOGRAPHS; DISTORTION; ETCH-BLEACH PROCESS; EXPLODED VIEWS; FILTERS; FRONT PROJECTION; HIGH-CONTRAST IMAGE; HIGH KEY; INFRARED PHOTOGRAPHY; LOW KEY; MATTE/MATTE BOX; MIXED-MEDIA IMAGES; MONTAGE; MULTI-IMAGE TECHNIQUES; MULTIPLE EXPOSURE/MULTIPLE PRINTING; NEGATIVE PRINTS; PAINTING ON PHOTOGRAPHS; PAINTING WITH LIGHT; PANORAMIC PHOTOGRAPHY; PHOTOGRAM; POSTERIZATION; RETOUCHING; SABATTIER EFFECT; SHADOWLESS LIGHTING; SILHOUETTE; SOFT FOCUS; STAR SCREEN/FILTER; STROBOSCOPIC PHOTOGRAPHY; TEXTURE; TONE-LINE PROCESS; TONER/TONING; ULTRAVIOLET AND FLUORESCENCE PHOTOGRAPHY; VIGNETTE.
Color photograph: p. C-52.

Specific Gravity

Specific gravity (SG) is the ratio between the density of a given solution and the density of pure water at a reference temperature—39.2°F (4°C) for scientific work, 60°F (15.6°C) for the more common Baume SG scale. The density of a solution increases with the weight of chemicals dissolved in it.

Specific gravity is often specified for various acid baths used in photogravure etching, and for alkali solutions such as diluted ammonia, used in some photographic processes. Some chemicals are supplied in solutions of particular specific gravity. A hydrometer—a device familiar as an automobile battery tester—can be used to measure the specific gravity of such solutions. The hydrometer has a weighted floating bob with a calibrated upright stem; the bob floats at a higher level—as indicated by the stem calibrations—as the density of the solution increases. Other measuring devices are also available, but most are special-application indicators.

Spectral Sensitivity

The ability of a substance, sensory organ, or device to respond to electromagnetic radiation is called spectral sensitivity; the range of sensitivity is defined by the shortest and longest wavelength that produce a response—e.g., the spectral sensitivity of the human eye extends from about 700 to 400 nanometers (nm), the range of wavelengths called light. The degree of sensitivity is seldom the same at all wavelengths and so must be separately measured or compared at those wavelengths of primary interest; in photography this is accomplished by making a wedge spectrogram.

The silver halides used in photographic emulsions are fundamentally sensitive to blue, blue-violet, and near ultraviolet wavelengths, a range from about 500 to 300nm. Sensitivity in the remaining visible part of the spectrum is produced by coating the halide crystals with light-reactive dye compounds.

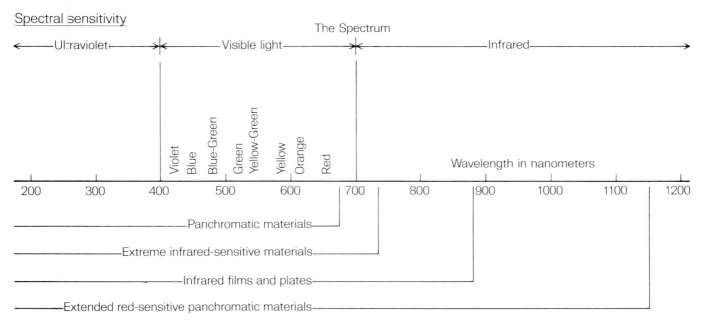

Spectral Sensitivity. Different types of photographic materials, as well as sensory organs and mechanical measuring devices, respond to different ranges of electromagnetic radiation, as measured in nanometers. The range to which something responds is its spectral sensitivity. The spectral sensitivity of the human eye is between 400 and 700nm, the area of the spectrum designated as visible light.

Green-sensitive dyes extend response to about 600nm (orthochromatic response); red-sensitive dyes extend it to about 650nm (panchromatic response) for ordinary films, and about 720nm for some technical films. Additional sensitizers can extend sensitivity into the near infrared, usually to about 900nm but special emulsions can be sensitized as far as 1400nm. At the shorter end of the spectrum, optical glass absorbs ultraviolet wavelengths shorter than 320nm, but crystalline quartz lenses can be used to about 280nm. Silver halides are sensitive to the entire range of energy beyond the near ultraviolet, but at about 210nm wavelengths are increasingly absorbed by the gelatin of an emulsion. In order to utilize the spectral sensitivity of halides for x-ray and gamma ray recording, emulsions must be specially prepared with a minimum thickness of gelatin and with the halide crystals concentrated at the surface.

See also: DYE SENSITIZATION; INFRARED PHOTOGRAPHY; SPECTRUM; ULTRAVIOLET AND FLUORESCENCE PHOTOGRAPHY; WAVELENGTH; WEDGE SPECTROGRAM; X-RAY PHOTOGRAPHY.

Spectrography; Spectroscopy

Many substances can be analyzed from the way they transmit, emit, or respond to various wavelengths in the electromagnetic energy spectrum. This analysis is performed most accurately by using a spectrograph or a spectroscope to disperse (spread or separate) light and other energy from a sample of the substance into its various wavelengths. Spectrography consists of making a photographic record, called a spectrogram, of the wavelength pattern; spectroscopy consists of making direct visual examination of the pattern.

A common method of spectral analysis is to burn a sample and disperse the light it produces. Various chemical elements emit unique "fingerprint" patterns of wavelengths which are revealed in the dispersed pattern. This technique can be used to determine the chemical composition of solids, liquids, or gases with a speed and accuracy obtainable with almost no other method. Wavelength-emissive bodies can be analyzed in a similar manner. This is the means by which astronomers determine the composition and temperature of stars, with analysis extended beyond the visible wavelengths into the ultraviolet and infrared.

Spectrography has two direct applications in photography. One is the analysis of the spectral sensitivity of emulsions, achieved by projecting a dispersed spectrum of white light onto a sample and measuring the exposure effect of each wavelength; this is explained further in the entry on the wedge spectrogram. The second application is determining the absorption-transmission characteristics of color filters by observing which white-light wavelengths are not transmitted, and the intensity of each wavelength that is transmitted.

A spectrograph consists of five major elements: a variable-width slit, a collimating lens, a dispersion device, a focusing lens, and a recording medium (i.e., film). The light-admitting slit is comprised of two adjustable metal jaws. The jaws are machined extremely accurately so that a slit a few thousandths of an inch wide can be formed to admit a precise amount of light in a single plane. The collimating lens transmits the light from the slit and focuses it onto the dispersing device. Both the collimating and the focusing lenses must be free of chromatic aberration.

The dispersing device is the key to the spectrograph because it forms the spectrum to be observed. A number of devices and materials are used, depending on the application and the portion of the electromagnetic spectrum being observed. For observations in the visible range a 60-degree glass prism normally is used. The kind of glass is selected for its ability to widely separate the individual colors. The major advantage of a glass prism is that it transmits substantially all of the light incident upon it. Thus, relatively weak light sources can be recorded. The main disadvantage within the visible range is that a prism does not disperse light evenly. The longer wavelengths are spread out over a wider area than are the shorter wavelengths. The result in a spectrogram is that red and orange bands appear abnormally wide, and blue and cyan bands appear compressed. When an evenly dispersed spectrum is important, a diffraction grating is used. This kind of grating is a flat piece of optical-quality glass upon which thousands of parallel lines per inch have been etched. The ridges of these lines cause an interference pattern that, evenly disperses light. However, because of the interference patterns the light cannot be imaged as sharply as with a prism. Also, a diffraction grating only affects a fraction of the light it transmits, and so the image it produces is relatively dim.

After being dispersed, the light passes through a second lens which focuses the spectrum pattern onto the recording emulsion. In general, an emulsion is

throughout the spectrum, differing only in wavelength and its inversely related characteristic, frequency. Long wavelengths are produced by electrical current running through wires, such as radio antennas; progressively shorter wavelengths are produced by molecular and atomic motion, by the movements of charges within atoms (light), and by action within the nuclei of atoms (gamma rays). This energy consists of related electrical and magnetic fields that vary together in intensity and travel in straight lines at a speed in space of 186,000 miles (300,000km) per second.

low, and red visible wavelengths, and into a part of the infrared portion of the spectrum.

See also: DIFFRACTION GRATING; DISPERSION; LIGHT; PRISMS; SPECTRAL SENSITIVITY; VISION; WAVELENGTH.

Speed of Materials

The relative sensitivity of various film emulsions is expressed in a numerical rating of "speed" derived by procedures adopted by the International Standards Organization (ISO). The procedures are the same as those previously used for American (ASA), British (BSI), Japanese

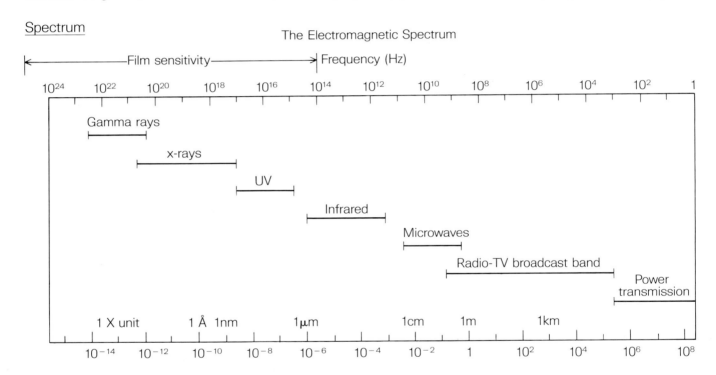

Spectrum

The Electromagnetic Spectrum

chosen which is most sensitive to the area of the spectrum being investigated. When the composition of the light source is known, a relatively high-contrast (and thus fine grain) emulsion may be chosen to emphasize small changes in intensity. When an unknown sample is being analyzed, a lower contrast but faster emulsion makes it easier to obtain a usable exposure.

See also: DIFFRACTION GRATING; DISPERSION; SPECTRUM; WEDGE SPECTROGRAM.

Spectrum

Electromagnetic energy constitutes a vast range, or spectrum, from electrical power waves hundreds of kilometers long to cosmic rays with wavelengths only one-millionth of one-billionth of a meter long. This energy is the same

The energy is put to practical use according to the degree to which various wavelengths can be generated, transmitted, modulated, focused, reflected, absorbed, and otherwise controlled. Substances and organisms have different degrees of sensitivity and response to various portions of the spectrum energy. The human eye detects the small range from 700 to 400nm (one nm [nanometer] = one-billionth of a meter), the portion of the spectrum called light. When white light is dispersed into its constituent wavelengths by a prism or diffraction grating, the eye distinguishes the wavelengths as separate colors. Photographic materials have an inherent sensitivity to the blue wavelengths in the visible portion and to all shorter wavelengths in the spectrum; the sensitivity can be extended to the green, yel-

(JSA), and German (DIN) speeds. They apply to black-and-white panchromatic, color negative, and color reversal films of the type used for general photography. The exposure and processing criteria specified to establish speeds are the equivalent of exposure to a subject of full brightness range illuminated by white light, and development to a normal degree of contrast. Films without panchromatic sensitivity—e.g., orthochromatic graphic arts films—are not included in the ISO (ASA) speed system, but they may be assigned a similar *exposure index* for a specified illumination to guide in their use.

Calculating Speeds. Film speeds are calculated from the characteristic curves of samples exposed and processed according to the test criteria. A "speed exposure" is determined from the curve

Speed of Materials

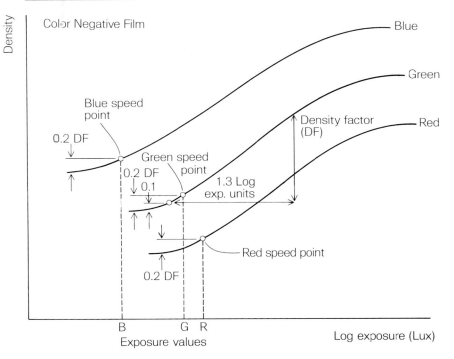

Color Negative Film

Density

Blue speed point

0.2 DF

Green speed point

0.2 DF

0.1

1.3 Log exp. units

Density factor (DF)

Blue

Green

Red

Red speed point

0.2 DF

B G R
Exposure values

Log exposure (Lux)

and its value in lux seconds (metercandle seconds) is mathematically manipulated with a constant to obtain the speed number. The constant simply insures that all speed numbers will be positive; otherwise a very slow emulsion might have a negative number as a rating. The answer obtained with the constant is rounded off to the nearest number in the standard series, as shown in the table. Two series are used, one arithmetic, the other logarithmic, and the speed rating for a film is written to indicate both, with a degree symbol marking the logarithmic speed—e.g., ISO 400/27°. In the arithmetic number series, a doubling of the number corresponds to twice as much sensitivity, so that a 400 speed film requires only half as much exposure as a 200 speed film (i.e., one f-stop or one shutter setting less). In the logarithmic series, an increase of 3 indicates a doubling of speed. The logarithmic speeds offer convenience in marking instruments and crowded scales, for the numbers 1–41 are equivalent to arithmetic speed numbers 1–10,000. As shown in the diagrams, film speeds are calculated as follows.

The speed of a black-and-white negative emulsion is taken from the characteristic curve of a sample processed to these criteria: an exposure 1.3 log units greater than that of the speed point exposure produces a density 0.8 greater than the speed point density, when the

speed point is located on the toe of the curve 0.1 above filmbase-plus-fog density. The speed exposure value is that of the speed point. Then:

$$\text{Arithmetic speed} = 0.8 \div \frac{\text{Speed}}{\text{exposure value}}$$

The speed of a color negative film is derived from the characteristic curves of all three emulsion layers, using the processing specified by the manufacturer. First, a density factor is obtained from the green-sensitive emulsion curve; it is the difference in density between a

point 0.1 above filmbase-plus-fog and the point on the straight line portion produced by 1.3 log units more exposure. The density factor is used to locate the speed point on each curve, at a density of 0.2 × Density factor above filmbase-plus-fog. The exposure values of these three points are averaged (added, then divided by 3) to obtain the speed exposure value. Then:

$$\text{Arithmetic speed} = 1 \div \frac{\text{Speed}}{\text{exposure value}}$$

The speed of a color reversal film is derived from the single curve produced

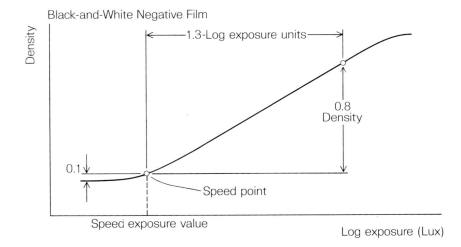

Black-and-White Negative Film

Density

1.3-Log exposure units

0.8 Density

0.1

Speed point

Speed exposure value

Log exposure (Lux)

Color Reversal Film

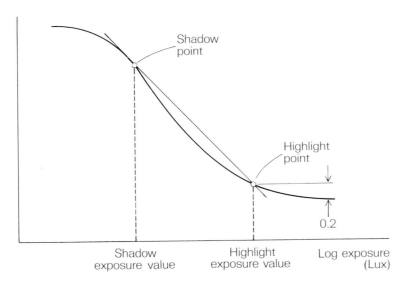

The logarithmic speed ratings are derived from the arithmetic speeds (A_s) as follows:

$$\text{Log speed} = (\text{Log}_{10} A_s \times 10) + 1$$

ISO FILM SPEEDS

Arithmetic	Logarithmic	Arithmetic	Logarithmic
3	6	200	24
4	7	250	25
5	8	320	26
6	9	400	27
8	10	500	28
10	11	650	29
12	12	800	30
16	13	1000	31
20	14	1250	32
25	15	1600	33
32	16	2000	34
40	17	2500	35
50	18	3200	36
64	19	4000	37
80	20	5000	38
100	21	6400	39
125	22	8000	40
160	23		

by exposure to a neutral gray scale and processed as specified by the manufacturer. Two speed points are located: a highlight point (minimum density) 0.2 above filmbase-plus-fog, and a shadow point where a line drawn from the highlight point is tangent to the shoulder of the curve, or at a density of 2.0, whichever is less. The speed exposure value is calculated from the exposures of these two points; it is the square root of the value produced by multiplying them together. Then:

$$\text{Arithmetic speed} = 8 \div \frac{\text{Speed}}{\text{exposure value}}$$

Speeds for black-and-white papers are derived from characteristic curves generated by reflection density readings. Each contrast grade has a different curve and thus a different speed; all papers are developed to maximum density. The speed point is located on the curve 0.6 above base-plus-fog density; the exposure of this point is the speed exposure value. Then:

$$\text{Paper speed} = 1000 \div \frac{\text{Speed}}{\text{exposure value}}$$

Some enlarging exposure meters are marked for paper speeds, but in general they are much less useful than film speeds.

See also: CHARACTERISTIC CURVE; DENSITOMETRY

Spherical Aberration

See: ABERRATIONS OF LENSES.

Spirit Photography

So-called "spirit" photographs purport to be visual records of ectoplasmic or other manifestations of persons in a state of existence equivalent to or "beyond" what is commonly defined as human death. Photographs of a similar kind, generally called psychic photographs, purport to show energy fields ("auras"), energy or personality extensions ("astral projections"), pre- or postcognitive mental images, or various other supranormal visual manifestations.

Black-and-White Paper

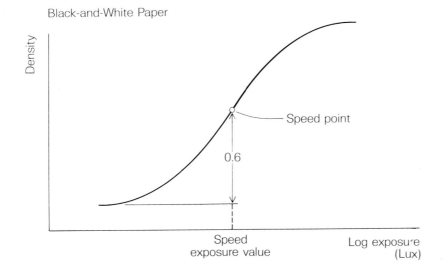

Spirit photographs were first "taken" in the 1860s, accompanying the rise of Spiritualism, a quasi-religious belief in a physical life after death. Such photographs apparently were first produced in 1863 by a Boston photographer, William Mumler. Although almost immediately demonstrated to be fraudulent images produced by double exposure or multiple printing, spirit photographs attracted a sizable audience of believers and were a commercially viable product into the 1920s. Present-day "psychic" photographs are almost equally as successful with an audience that has a predisposition to accept their claims to validity.

The acceptance of spirit and psychic photographs is a matter of subjective faith. No such images have been shown to be authentic by objective standards. The great majority of such photographs have been demonstrated to be outright or extremely probable frauds by experts in deception and photography such as Harry Houdini, Charles Reynolds, Jr., David B. Eisendrath, and James Randi. The least disputable fact about spirit photographs is that they represent the first major commercial application of the multiple-exposure technique.

Splicing

Splicing is the process of physically joining separate pieces of film, or audio or video tape. In motion pictures splicing may be accomplished with cement, tape, or heat-welding. The original procedure was to trim the pieces to be joined to proper overlapping lengths and scrape the emulsion from the overlap area of the underlying piece. A solvent adhesive was applied to this area, and the overlapping piece was pressed into place. The present-day technique for commercial workprints and amateur films is to trim the pieces so that their ends butt together, and then join them with transparent, sprocketed tape applied to one or both sides. Permanent commercial splicing is now accomplished with an ultrasonic heat device that fuses the butted ends together.

In photomechanical reproduction, film elements that make up a composite master image to which a printing plate is exposed are spliced or "stripped" together with tape. The various pieces are cut to butt together, and joins are made outside the information area of each piece.

Audio and video tapes can be physically spliced by applying a suitable adhesive tape to the base sides of the pieces being joined (tape on the recording side would block the sound or picture). Video tape cannot be imperceptibly joined within a picture sequence. The signal pattern is so complex that any physical interruption creates a rollover or other disturbance in the playback. Most commercial audio and video splicing is actually edit-recording. The two pieces are on separate playback equipment, and their synchronized output is combined on a separate recorder. Splicing is accomplished by electronically switching from one playback source to the other.

See also: EDITING.

Sports Photography

Meticulous preparation and planning are the hallmarks of successful sports photography. Although it is undoubtedly true that luck plays some role in getting exciting and timely sports pictures, repeated success is the result of awareness of a few general photographic techniques, thoughtful equipment and film selection, basic knowledge of the sport in question, and a finely honed innate sense of anticipation akin to that found in many photojournalists.

Until the post-World War II period, many sports photographers were photojournalists who sometimes covered sports events. In recent decades photographers specializing in sports coverage have emerged. Among them are Hy Peskin, George Silk, Mark Kaufmann, John Zimmerman, Rich Clarkson, Walter Loss Jr., and Neil Leifer.

Nearly all sports involve a certain amount of quick movement, particularly during crucial moments of play. Four factors primarily influence whether a subject will appear blurred or frozen: (1) subject-to-lens distance, (2) lens focal length, (3) subject speed, and (4) direction of motion. The farther the subject is from the camera, the slower is the shutter speed that will produce a sharp image; e.g., a skier frozen with 1/125 sec. at 100 ft. (30.5m) may be a total blur at 10 ft. (3m) from the camera. Focal length is directly proportional to appropriate speed, so that a 100mm lens requires a higher speed than a 50mm one. Less obviously, perhaps, a subject moving directly across the field-of-view requires the fastest speed. Movement diagonally toward or away from the camera may be photographed at speeds 1½ times as long and movement on the subject-to-lens axis at speeds twice as long. A sense of which range of shutter speeds is generally useful for a particular sport is best gained from practice, although tables and similar guides are available.

Often sports photographers will decide to include some degree of blur, especially in background areas, to give a symbolic feeling of motion. The most commonly employed technique is to pan with the subject. The photographer aims the camera at the subject well before the predetermined "shoot point" and moves it to keep the action in the frame. When the key moment arrives, the smooth camera motion blurs the background during exposure. After the shutter release, most photographers continue to pan briefly to guard against camera shake during exposure—a gesture similar to follow-through in swinging a bat.

In techniques like panning, and in many others, there is frequently no time to refocus as the subject moves or approaches the "shoot point." The solution is to zone focus; that is, to prefocus the camera lens for the range where the action is most likely to be at the desired picture moment. Clearly this is more appropriate to some sports than others; e.g., auto racing rather than soccer. Moreover, it places a premium on depth-of-field, which can conflict with high shutter speed requirements. Even so, it generally yields a high percentage of sharp pictures and is far easier to execute than the alternative—follow-focusing. Sometimes, however, the only way to make a picture of a completely unpredictable event is simply to follow a player until a timely moment presents itself. This demanding ability is achieved solely through considerable practice, and is greatly aided by a zoom lens.

In a wide variety of sports, focusing and framing difficulties can be minimized by studying the action before shooting to see if a pattern can be discerned. This allows a better guess as to where significant action will be occur next. In a sport like track, this is relatively simple, but even in tennis, for example, it may be possible to spot the tendency of a player to rush the net, thus setting up the chance of getting a spectacular shot of an overhead smash.

The drama of a sport is usually exemplified in just such pictures, but the experienced professional knows that many times the moments before and after a flurry of excitement can yield equally provocative images. For instance, the thrill of a stolen base is often pictured in the high-spiked, dirt-churning slide. However, the human interest of the event is also evidenced in the look of intense concentration on the runner's face as the pitcher winds up or the slump of dejection as the umpire calls him out. Even pictures of the reactions of fans can produce insightful photographs.

The 35mm single-lens reflex (SLR) camera is employed almost exclusively in sports photography for a number of reasons. The SLR does not suffer from parallax. The photographer sees the same image area through the viewfinder that will be recorded on the film. Also, SLR viewfinders display the image erect and laterally corrected; this makes following action relatively easy. Finally, many modern 35mm cameras are designed as systems that accept an array of accessories. The two most useful to the sports photographer are a motor drive (or power winder) and interchangeable lenses, especially telephoto lenses. Ultra-high-speed black-and-white film—ISO 2000/34° or more—and color negative film—ISO 1000/31°—substantially obviate the need for electronic flash, which is frequently discouraged because of its disturbing nature and which is useless beyond a moderate distance.

Baseball. In the professional leagues, the best vantage points are from the field-level seats between home plate and first base, and between third base and home plate. In particular the front row of a section helps avoid the nuisance of fans standing up in front of the lens. For most pictures a lens of 200mm or longer is necessary with the ideal being a 200–600 zoom. Amateur baseball officials are usually much more accommodating about allowing pictures to be made from anywhere but on the playing field. Photographers who move in close should remain alert to the sizzling line drive foul.

Football. This is similar to baseball in that the photographer's mobility is usually limited by the status of the game. The main difficulty is that key encounters are liable to take place anywhere on the field. Alertness is necessary. Lens choice will largely be determined by how close to the action the photographer can get.

Linear-action sports (track, swimming, horse racing, auto racing). Several difficulties are eliminated by knowing exactly where the athletes are going. Pictures of the entire group are best made shortly after the starting gun when the contestants are bunched together. Even photographs centering on a single individual are most effective when another person is included in the picture area to heighten the sense of competition. Turns are often the most exciting areas of a track. Especially in auto racing, the photographer should always position himself on the inside. If a racer loses control, he is unavoidably going outside.

Winter sports. Extreme cold weather found in snow areas can have a profound effect on camera performance. Effective techniques are discussed in the entry or winter photography.
Color photograph: p. C-53.

Spotlight

A spotlight is a lighting instrument that produces a well-defined, intense beam of light. It is most often used as a key light in photographic lighting setups. Its illumination produces bright highlights and sharp-edged shadows. The light in a spotlight is concentrated by a parabolic or elliptical mirrored reflector behind the bulb and is focused with a condenser- or Fresnel-type lens. In most instruments the bulb and reflector can be moved toward or away from the lens to adjust the spread of the beam. Some spotlights have built-in baffles that permit adjusting the shape of the beam.
See also: LIGHTING; LIGHT SOURCES.

Spotting

Spotting is the technique of adding colors to a print to conceal or eliminate white and light-colored lines and spots that are not part of the image. These imperfections usually are caused by dust, hair, or fingerprints on the negative when it is printed.

Concentrated liquid spotting dyes commonly are used for black-and-white prints. The dyes are available in warm (brownish), cold (bluish), and neutral tonalities; neutral is suitable for a great many papers. Liquid dyes are also available for color prints, but dry spotting colors are often easier to use and control.

In addition to the dye, a sable or camel-hair brush is required. It must form a fine point; a No. 0 or thinner brush is needed for small spots. Dyes commonly are diluted with water for use, but a 1-percent acetic acid solution may be required with glossy prints and those on resin-coated papers. The surfaces of these prints tend to resist the absorption of water-diluted dye. Dry colors also work best when diluted with an acetic acid solution. Black-and-white prints will accept spotting more readily if they have been processed in a plain, rather than a hardening, fixer.

The print to be spotted must be dry. It is placed on a clean, flat surface, and a light is positioned so that there is no surface glare and the area to be worked on is not shadowed by the brush or the photographer's hands. White cotton gloves or a piece of clean paper protect the print where the hands must rest on it. A few drops of dye are placed in a white saucer and diluted with water or acid solution. The strength of the diluted tone is tested on a scrap of print paper, or on the borders of the print if they are later to be trimmed off. The tone should be a bit lighter than required to blend the spot into its surroundings. The required tone is built up by repeated applications

of diluted dye to the spot. This provides maximum control for feathering the effect out at the edges of the spot. It also avoids the error of applying too much dye at first touch. Dyes can be mixed to adjust the color of the tone as required.

A stippling action is used, working outward from the center of a spot. If the brush deposits a drop of liquid, it should be blotted up immediately with a clean tissue. Touching a tissue to the side of the brush, above the dye depth, will remove excess liquid from the bristles. Hair lines and white scratches are spotted by breaking them up with dots of dye randomly spotted along their length. Some of the intervening white spots are dyed next, followed by the remaining sections. This technique imitates the way grain forms the image shapes and tones; trying to paint along the length of a line only calls attention to it. In each area only enough dye should be applied to make the spot or line blend with its surroundings to become invisible at normal viewing distance. The dye should penetrate the emulsion, not form a surface coating.

With dry spotting colors the brush is dipped into the acetic acid solution and then stroked across the dye cake. Some dry colors are supplied as a coating on a small card or sheet of plastic. Dry colors are applied in the same way as liquid colors—with a stippling movement, building up the required density gradually.

Retouching pencils sometimes can be used to eliminate small spots on prints. They are suitable for matte-surface papers, but leave a visible deposit on the surface of glossy papers.

Black spots are removed by etching them away with the point of a knife or razor blade, or by bleaching them with a single drop of iodine solution or a single crystal of potassium ferricyanide. This leaves a light-colored area that is then spotted with an appropriate dye.
See also: BLEACHING IMAGES; RETOUCHING.

Spread Function

Various factors cause a subject point not to be imaged by a lens or emulsion as a corresponding point of uniform brightness or density; instead, the image spreads over a minutely larger area, decreasing in brightness or density outward from the center. The *spread function* is the graph produced by microdensitometer readings taken across the width of the point. The spread function may also be measured across the border of a line in the image, the line being essentially a series of points.

Some spreading is caused by diffraction and aberrations in a lens; however, the primary cause is irradiation in an emulsion as the light strikes the halide crystals. Spreading may be emphasized or increased by various edge effects produced by development.

Spread function effects serve to limit resolving power because they add together between closely spaced lines or points, reducing the contrast and thus the visibility of details against the background density. The progressive nature of this effect is revealed by plotting the modulation transfer function of the lens or emulsion.

See also: DIFFRACTION; EDGE EFFECTS; IRRADIATION; MTF: MODULATION TRANSFER FUNCTION; RESOLVING POWER.

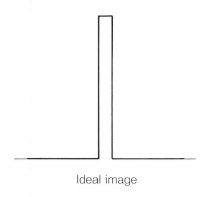

Spread Function

Ideal image

Actual image

Spy Camera

See: SURVEILLANCE PHOTOGRAPHY.

Stabilization Process

The stabilization process is a method of rapid-processing black-and-white prints. The images produced are temporarily stable, but they will deteriorate and fade if they are not subsequently fixed and washed in a conventional manner. A developed emulsion that is treated in a highly concentrated fixing solution but not washed is said to be stabilized: the fixer retained throughout the emulsion prevents unexposed and undeveloped silver halides from reacting with light striking the image. Depending on the amount of exposure to light, and the heat and humidity of storage conditions, the image will remain stable from a few weeks up to about two years.

Rapid processing that incorporates

this principle is in fact activation-stabilization processing. It is carried out in a simple processing machine and requires printing paper with a special emulsion. The emulsion contains crystals of developing agent as well as light-sensitive silver halide crystals. After exposure, it is fed into the machine, where it first passes between two rollers that coat the emulsion with a highly concentrated chemical activator that causes the developing agent in the emulsion to act immediately. The print passes directly to a second set of rollers that immerse it in the concentrated stabilizing solution. Processing proceeds at a feed-through rate of about 1 in. (25mm) per second. The print emerges damp-dry and air-dries completely in a few minutes. The image can be made permanent by treating the print in a fixing bath and washing

it in the normal manner. This can be done at any later time before the image has begun to fade.

A stabilized print remains chemically active and should be kept away from fixed and washed prints and films; its fixing compounds can contaminate them. Heat-mounting is not recommended because high temperatures will cause a yellow-brown stain.

See also: FIXING; RAPID PROCESSING.

Staining Developer

A staining film developer stains the gelatin in proportion to the amount of silver reduced to metallic form as the image develops. Its principal application today is to obtain maximum emulsion speed: the staining provides additional density in shadow areas, increasing the visibility of faint details. A secondary effect is to

limit contrast in images of subjects with extreme brightness ranges. Highlight areas produce large amounts of silver and a correspondly high degree of staining; however the large amount of stain actually retards silver development somewhat. The result may be lower contrast than would be produced by a normal developer.

The two most common stain developing agents are pyrogallic acid and pyrocatechin. In general, a formula with high alkalinity promotes the staining action that results as the developing agent oxidizes with use; the amount of sodium sulfite in the formula controls the degree of staining. Contemporary staining formulas for maximum emulsion speed frequently use a combination of pyro and metol, a normal developing agent that is most effective in shadow areas. The stain image produced is normally a yellowish or reddish brown. Although it may appear thin to the eye, it has significant opacity to the wavelengths in exposing light that affect print emulsions; there is no way to accurately judge by eye the effective printing density of a stain-image negative.

Skin stains produced by this kind of developer can be removed by acid fixer, citric acid solution, or lemon juice.

Stains

The majority of stains in photographic images are caused by exhausted processing solutions or by contamination from chemicals left in the material or encountered at a later time. The major precautions against stains are the use of fresh solutions, proper fixing and washing, and—especially important—proper procedures in filing and storing photographs. By-products in overused developer commonly cause brown stains; exhausted fixer will permit the light tones in the image eventually to discolor and darken, or may produce dichroic fog (a greenish or red-purple discoloration that is not truly a stain). Excess fixing compounds left in the emulsion will cause yellowish stains, which may appear immediately with heated drying or may develop at a much later time. Storage in contact with contaminated materials—including many low-quality kinds of paper, file folders, envelopes, and the like—can produce a variety of stains, as can excessive heat or humidity during storage.

Treating stains. If the negative still exists, a stained print can be discarded and a new print made. With important black-and-white prints the safest procedure is to make a copy negative on panchromatic film, using a filter the same color as the stain, but stronger—a deep yellow filter to counteract a lighter yellow stain, for example. If filtration is ineffective—as with multicolored stains—the image may be bleached back to silver halide and redeveloped in a standard low-sulfite-content developer; bleach-redevelopment toning solutions may also be used. These procedures are also effective with negatives. No unique, rare, or valuable image should be subjected to chemical treatment.

Chemical stains on clothing may be removed by a solution of 0.75 percent thiourea and citric acid in water, but a test is advisable to make sure the fabric color is not affected. Stains on the skin can be prevented by frequent rinsing in fresh acid fixer and by washing, or by rubbing with a slice of lemon or a few crystals of citric acid. Most stains in trays and tanks can be removed by a solution of 0.2 percent potassium permanganate and 0.4 percent sulfuric acid in water, followed by a neutralizing solution of 30 percent sodium sulfite and sodium bisulfite, and thorough washing. Commercial photographic stain remover concentrates are diluted for use on equipment; some can be diluted further for skin stains, but none should be used on prints or negatives.

See also: FILING AND STORING PHOTOGRAPHS; FIXING; FOG/FOGGING; TONER/TONING; WASHING.

Stanhope

In the 1860s a fad developed briefly for jewelry items composed of miniature photographs less than a quarter-inch in size mounted under a plano-convex magnifier called a Stanhope lens. Brooches, rings, earrings, tieclasps, cufflinks, and similar objects were produced. The popularity of tiny images led to the production of true microphotographs on collodion glass slides for viewing in a low-power microscope. Common usage extended the term Stanhope to these novelties as well.

See also: MICROPHOTOGRAPY.

Stannotype

The Woodburytype process, which produced permanent reproductions of photographs in pigmented gelatin images of exquisite quality, required hydraulic presses to form the image molds. To make the basic process feasible without the need for machinery, W. B. Woodbury patented the Stannotype process in 1879. A relief image, prepared by exposing bichromated gelatin under a positive transparency, was coated with tinfoil (Latin: *stannum* = tin); this formed the

shallow mold into which the pigmented gelatin was poured and then covered with paper. When the gelatin set, it adhered to the paper, which was lifted free and trimmed at the image edges. The mold image had to be reversed right-for-left so that the final image would be right-reading against the paper background.

See also: WOODBURYTYPE/WOODBURYGRAVURE.

Stars

See: ASTROPHOTOGRAPHY.

Star Screen; Star Filter

A fine-screen pattern of elements with sharp corners will diffract light in the image of a small, intense light source into starlike arms or rays. A ray is generated at each corner of the element shape; thus, a square produces a four-pointed star, a hexagon produces a six-pointed star. Commercial star screens or "star-effect filters" consist of crossing line patterns engraved or ruled on colorless glass or plastic. The screen is placed in front of the camera lens like a filter, and used without exposure compensation; it can be combined with colored filters or other special-effect filters. Some star screens have a diffraction-grating ruling so that the star rays of a white light source have a rainbowlike array of color. A star screen can be improvised from a piece of black fine-mesh material such as window screening.

See also: DIFFRACTION GRATING; FILTERS; SPECIAL EFFECTS.

Static

Flashes of static electricity occuring on the emulsion or base of a film can leave exposure traces that appear as dark treelike patterns or fuzzy-edged smudges. Static is most often produced in low humidity, especially in winter. It occurs when smooth film surfaces are pulled rapidly through the light-trap edges of a cassette, or when they rub together on a takeup spool, both in the camera and in the darkroom. Pulling a darkslide rapidly from a film holder also may generate static. A static spark is frequently produced when the tape that secures the paper backing to roll film is pulled off; this is seldom a problem because it is not within an image area.

Anti-static precautions include advancing or unrolling film slowly, maintaining normal humidity in studios and darkrooms, and touching cassettes, reels, and other equipment to a grounded point such as a water tap to discharge any accumulated static.

Uniform static electrical charges induced over the surface of a recording plate or a printing material are the basis of various electrophotographic processes.

See also: ELECTROPHOTOGRAPHIC PROCESSES.

Steichen, Edward
American; 1879–1973

Photographer and curator Edward Steichen was one of the most prominent and influential figures of 20th c. photography. During his long career he worked in a variety of styles in black-and-white and in color; his subjects ranged from portraits and landscapes, to fashion and advertising photography, to photography of dance and sculpture. His early work demonstrated a mastery of soft-focus Pictorialism, yet after the first World War he became a proponent of "straight" photography and the New Realism. Steichen's entire body of work is noted for a highly developed sense of design. As a curator at New York's Museum of Modern Art, for 15 years Steichen was responsible for many important exhibitions, including the *Family of Man.*

Steichen was born Eduard Jean Steichen in Luxembourg. His family came to the United States in 1881 and settled in Hancock, Michigan; in 1889 they moved to Milwaukee. Steichen's early interest in art was encouraged by his mother. He attended the 1893 World's Columbian Exposition in Chicago, where he was introduced to important contemporary works of art. At age 15 Steichen began a 4-year lithography apprenticeship at Milwaukee's American Fine Art Company. From 1894 to 1898 he worked under Richard Lorenz and Robert Schode at the Milwaukee Art Students League. He began to photograph in 1895, but continued to pursue his career as a painter for the next 20 years.

Steichen's photographs received their first public showing at the Second Philadelphia Salon in 1899. The following year (in which he became a naturalized American citizen), Steichen received encouragement from Clarence White, who prompted Alfred Stieglitz to purchase three Steichen prints.

While in Paris at this time Steichen was deeply impressed by the work of Rodin, of whose work and person he would create many extraordinary images. Thirty-five Steichen photographs were included in F. Holland Day's *The New School of American Photography* exhibition in London and Paris in 1901. Steichen was elected to the Linked Ring

Steichen, Edward. "Self portrait with brush and palette. Paris" (1901); pigment print. Art Institute of Chicago.

at this time. In 1902 he became a founding member of the Photo-Secession and designed the cover of its journal, *Camera Work,* in which his work often was reproduced in the coming years. Steichen's first one-man show of photographs and paintings was held at La Maison des Artistes in Paris the same year. In New York Steichen helped Stieglitz open the Little Galleries of the Photo-Secession ("291") at which Steichen exhibited regularly.

Steichen began experimenting with color photography in 1904 and was an early user of the Lumière Autochrome process. He returned to Paris in 1906 and was responsible for selecting work to be exhibited by Stieglitz in New York. Among the artists whose work he sent on were John Marin, Picasso,

Matisse, Brancusi, Cezanne, and Rodin.

In 1910 thirty-one Steichen photographs were exhibited at the International Exhibition of Pictorial Photography in Buffalo, which was curated by Stieglitz. The following year Steichen made his first fashion photographs, but he began devoting much of his time to painting. In 1913 Stieglitz wrote of the double issue of *Camera Work* devoted to Steichen's photographs: "Nothing I have ever done has given me quite so much satisfaction as finally sending this Number out into the world."

As commander of the photographic division of the Army Expeditionary Forces in World War I, Steichen became acquainted with aerial photography, which required a new precision. He became chief photographer for Condé

Nast Publications in 1923, publishing regularly in *Vogue* and *Vanity Fair* for the next 15 years, being based in New York. He was also employed as an advertising photographer by the J. Walter Thompson Agency. Among Steichen's sitters during these years were his brother-in-law Carl Sandburg, Greta Garbo, Charles Chaplin, Gloria Swanson, and H. L. Mencken. Steichen's relationship with Stieglitz was strained over issues concerning commercial and advertising work to which Stieglitz objected. Steichen believed that his fashion and other commercial photography could be raised to the level of art.

In 1938 Steichen retired from commercial photography. He became Director of the U.S. Naval Photographic Institute in 1945, was placed in command of all combat photography, and was discharged in 1946 with the rank of captain. During the war years Steichen organized the *Road to Victory* and *Power in the Pacific* exhibitions for the Museum of Modern Art in New York City. From 1947 to 1962 Steichen was director of the Department of Photography at the Museum. He did no photographic work of his own during these years, but was responsible for nearly 50 shows, including the *Family of Man* (for which he selected images from over two million photographs and which became the most popular exhibition in the history of photography as well as a best-selling book), *The Bitter Years,* and the *Diogenes with a Camera* series.

In 1961 Steichen was honored by a one-man show of his photographs at the Museum of Modern Art. The Edward Steichen Photography Center was established at the museum in 1964. In 1967 Steichen wrote, "Today I am no longer concerned with photography as an art form. I believe it is potentially the best medium for explaining man to himself and to his fellow man." Steichen died in West Redding, Connecticut, shortly before his 94th birthday.

Steichen was the recipient of countless awards, including the Chevalier of the Legion of Honor, France (1919), the Distinguished Service Citation from General Pershing (1919), a Distinguished Service Medal (1945), First Prize Eastman Kodak Competition (1903), Honorary Fellow of the Royal Photographic Society (1931), a Silver Medal "In Recognition of Distinguished Service to Advertising" (1937), Art Directors Club of New York Award (1945), *U.S. Camera* Achievement Award for "Most Outstanding Contribution to Photography by an Individual" (1949), German Prize for Cultural Achievement, Photographic Society of Germany (1960),

Honor Roll of the American Society of Magazine Photographers (1962), and the Presidential Medal of Freedom (1963).

Steichen's work was included in group shows around the world at galleries and museums in London, Paris, Berlin, New York, Chicago, and Philadelphia. He was honored with one-man shows at Photo-Secession Galleries (1908), the Baltimore Museum of Art (1938), the American Institute of Architects Headquarters in Washington, D.C. (1950), the Museum of Modern Art in New York City (1960, 1978), the Bibliothèque Nationale in Paris (1961), and George Eastman House in Rochester, New York (1979). He was the recipient of honorary degrees from the University of Wisconsin, the University of Hartford, and Wesleyan University.

See also: PHOTO-SECESSION; STIEGLITZ, ALFRED.

Steiner, Ralph

American; 1899–

Born in Cleveland, Ohio, Ralph Steiner was expected to go to work in his uncle's brewery, but escaped into photography instead while studying chemical engineering at Dartmouth. The technical studies were not wasted. Steiner has a scientific bent as well as a lyric visual one, and uses his knowledge of chemistry and physics to solve photographic problems. He has been a resourceful technical experimenter all his adult life.

After Dartmouth, Steiner studied in 1921 and 1922 at the Clarence H. White School of Photography in New York. It took Steiner some time to recover from the painting-oriented design instruction that dominated the curriculum. A guest lecture by Alfred Stieglitz disappointed Steiner, ultimately profitably, when it provided no formula for photographic creativity. After a year spent working in a photogravure plant, Steiner began to earn a living at advertising and magazine photography.

In the late 1920s he met Paul Strand in New York. Strand's prints were a revelation that left Steiner deeply dissatisfied with the commercial photography he was then doing. He dropped this work for the time to spend the summer at Yaddo, an artists' retreat near Saratoga Springs, New York, where he worked long hours daily to teach himself better craftsmanship "so I could call myself a photographer." Working in an 8 × 10 format he photographed "objects with texture," producing such well-known images as his Nehi sign pictures, his Ford car series, and his photograph of a rocking chair. Steiner's career has alternated between periods doing adver-

Steiner, Ralph. "Ford Front" (1929). Courtesy Ralph Steiner.

tising, public relations (Gypsy Rose Lee was one of his subjects), and editorial photography to accumulate funds, and periods spent making still photographs and films for himself. His second effort as a cinematographer, H_2O, is often cited as the second earliest American art film (after *Manhatta* by Paul Strand and Charles Sheeler). Steiner also made *Cafe Universal*, an improvised, semi-dramatic antiwar film based on drawings by George Grosz, cast with leading members of the Group Theater. His film on a New York City dump starred Elia Kazan in a largely improvised role. He and Paul Strand were hired by Pare Lorentz as the cameramen on *The Plow That Broke the Plains;* they directed much of that landmark documentary as well. With Willard Van Dyke, Strand shot and directed the documentary *The City,* which ran for a year at the New York World's Fair of 1939. In the late 1930s he worked as a picture editor on *PM,* and in advertising and public relations work. His optioning of the film rights to the biography of H.S. Maxim, an eccentric 19th c. inventor, led him to Hollywood where he spent four years as a writer/executive. On his glad return to New York, with an out-of-date portfolio, Walker Evans gave him photographic assignments for *Fortune.* In the 1960s Steiner finally began to be able to devote most of his time to his personal photography and cinematography. He moved to rural Vermont in 1963, spending summers on a Maine island, and his work since then includes many lyrical images from those landscapes, including trees, coastline hills, and wash on rural clotheslines.

Steinert, Otto. "View from Arc de Triomphe" (ca. 1950). Courtesy Museum Folkwang; International Museum of Photography at George Eastman House.

Many of Steiner's lyrical, sometimes gently satirical photographs can be seen as conveying, along with sophistication and concern, a sense of wonder about the 20th century which he entered at the age of one, and yet has been so much a part of.

Steiner's autobiography, *A Point of View*, was published in 1978. Among exhibitions of his work were a one-man show in 1949 at the Museum of Modern Art, New York, and exhibitions in 1981 at the Milwaukee Art Center (with Walker Evans) and at the Northlight Gallery in Tempe, Arizona (with Wright Morris).

Steinert, Otto

German; 1915–1978

As photographer, teacher, and exhibition organizer, Steinert was a catalytic force in the development of the concept of "subjective photography." He founded the avant-garde Fotoform group of photographers in 1949 with Peter Keetman, Toni Schneiders, Ludwig Windstosser, and Siegfried Lauterwasser and acted as its leader and spokesman. At the first Photokina in 1950, the photographs of the young Fotoform group had the effect of "an atom bomb in the compost heap of German photography," as one reviewer put it. Steinert made his name quickly in the medium and lost no time in doing away with outdated rules in order to devote himself to trends begun by Moholy-Nagy, Man Ray, Herbert Bayer, and other photographers of the 1920s New Vision movement. These trends had been undermined in 1933 by the rigid codes set up by Hitler's government, which made innovation in the arts almost impossible. Steinert aimed to revive the ideas of the New Vision photographers in his own photographs and teaching, and in the exhibitions he organized in the 1950s.

It was at the age of 32 that Otto Steinert started his photographic career. Previously he had studied medicine at the Charité Surgical Clinic in Berlin; he received his degree in 1939 and was a health officer in the German army until the end of World War II. Steinert was self-taught in photography, a life-long interest, but it was not until 1947 that he decided to pursue it as a profession, working as a successful portrait photographer in his native Saarbrucken. Steinert's photography covers a large range of techniques and subjects: photogram-montages in 1949; dramatically lighted and psychologically probing portraits of Nobel prizewinners and celebrated scientists; and "Metropolitan Man," fleeting images of people disappearing in motion on a city street.

At Saarbrucken in July 1951, Steinert designed the first important German exhibition of modern photography, *Subjektive Fotografie*, the movement of which he became leader. As he described the concept of subjective photography, "A new photographic style is one of the demands of our time. . . . Subjective photography for us means the framework embracing all aspects of individual photographic creation from the non-objective photogram to the profound and aesthetically satisfying reportage." J. A. Schmoll in his essay *Objective and Subjective Photography*, (*Otto Steinert, Subjektive Fotografie*, Bonn, 1952), speaks against the popularly held illusion that photography can be absolutely objective. He describes subjective photography thus, "The beginnings: conscious subjectivism in relation to the process of choice; technical procedure: exploitation of all limits and all variational processes with the aim of achieving formal objectivation, that is to say significant and harmonious photography." He quotes Werner Heisenberg's comments on newly made discoveries in atomic physics, "In our time we regard as belonging to the sphere of reality not only what we can see and touch but also what we think about it. These two notions cannot be separated as sharply as logical thinking will have it." In *Subjektive Fotografie 2*, held at the State School of Arts and Crafts, Saarbrucken, in winter 1954–1955, Steinert set forth an important analysis of the creative elements of photography and attempted to clarify the definition of subjective photography to avoid continued misinterpretation. *Subjektive Fotografie 3*, the last exhibition of this name, followed in 1958, though Steinert had doubts about staging it, since he felt the concept of subjective photography had been widely misunderstood.

The inspiring meetings, lectures, and discussions Steinert organized at the schools at Saarbrucken for photographers and students have become legendary. Steinert's achievements as a teacher are widely recognized. Anyone who aspired to become a progressive photographer attempted to become a student of his. He began teaching at Saarbrucken's newly opened Staatliche Schule für Kunst und Handwerk (1948–1951), then moved to the Werkkunstschule as director of the photography department (1952–1959) and was appointed professor there in 1954. After *Subjektive Fotografie 3*, Steinert was appointed professor and director of the department of photographs at Folkwangschule in Essen (1959–1978). In addition to his teaching work, he was occupied with organizing exhibitions on the history of photography at the Folkwang Museum, attached to the school (Founder/Curator, Photography Collection, Museum Folkwang, 1959–1978). He was a life member of the Deutsche Gesellschaft für Photographie, an honorary member of the Société Française de la Photographie, and president (1963–1974) of the Gesellschaft Deutscher Lichtbildner. He wrote numerous essays and articles on photographic aesthetics, technique, and history. Steinert died in Essen-Werden.
See also: SUBJECTIVE PHOTOGRAPHY.

Steinheil, Carl August von
German; 1801–1870
Steinheil, Hugo Adolph
German; 1832–1893
Carl August von Steinheil, a mathematician and astronomer, was perhaps the first person in Germany to take a photograph. With a colleague at the University of Munich, Franz von Kobell, Steinheil constructed a camera obscura and secured negatives on silver chloride paper in March or April 1839. Their work was inspired by a letter to the Academy of Sciences from William Henry Fox Talbot which included some mention of his calotype process. In September of that same year Steinheil constructed a daguerreotype camera and took pictures by that process shortly after it had been made public. In 1855 Steinheil established the optical works in Munich from which came some of the finest lenses of the 19th and 20th c. His son, Hugo Adolph, became principal designer and purchased the firm in 1866. Among the innovative designs of the first 50 years were the *Periscope* lens (1865), with a distortion-free 100-degree field of view; the *Aplanat* (1866), a design outstanding in its class until well into the 20th c.; a series of *Antiplanat* lenses (from 1881 on); the *f*/6.8 *Orthostigmat*, one of the earliest double anastigmats; and the *Unofocal* (1901), one of the fastest (*f*/4.5) early anastigmats.
See also: LENSES.

Step-and-Repeat
Multiple identical images can be registered on a single piece of photographic material by a step-and-repeat printer or camera. Each exposure is registered through an opening in a masking plate, then the material is shifted to bring a fresh area into the opening. Manually-operated repeating camera backs or step-and-repeat printing easels are frequently used in portrait studios. Automatic equipment is used in high-volume photofinishing plants, and in photomechanical reproduction plants to prepare printing plates for postage stamps, paper money, certificates, and other items of identical design that must be reproduced in vast numbers.
See also: REPEATING BACK.

Step Wedge
The density of a true optical wedge changes smoothly and continuously from minimum to maximum value. It is easier to produce and use a "wedge" composed of discrete steps, each of a single density, and differing from one another by an equal degree of change. A density progression of this sort is produced either by giving a photographic emulsion a series of exposures that increase equally, typically in half- or full-stop increments, or by building up layers of a material of a fundamental density. The second method produces a device in which the thickness increases in stairlike steps. A stepped scale, whether transparent or opaque (i.e., a transmission or a reflection scale) is properly called a tablet, to distinguish it from a continuous-gradient wedge.
See also: WEDGE, OPTICAL.

Stereoscope; Stereograph
Stereoscopic viewing devices must present a different image to each eye with no visible crossover or overlapping. Such devices, called stereoscopes, have used five fundamental methods: reflection by mirrors or prisms; refraction by lenses; blocking by a slotted grating; color filtration; and polarization. The images used in stereoscopes are called stereographs or stereograms.

Reflecting and refracting stereoscopes were first designed by Sir Charles Wheatstone in 1832 for use with hand-drawn designs. The reflecting stereoscope was immediately usable with the earliest forms of photography, invented a few years later. It consisted of a pair of mirrors in a 90° V-shape set pointing at the observer. Reversed images at the left and right were reflected by the mirrors—becoming unreversed in the process—each to the appropriate eye. This device places little limitation on the size of the images. Variations of the design are used today to view stereo x-ray images and—in an upright, prismatic version—with stereo prints made for aerial photogrammetry and photointerpretation.

The basic refracting stereoscope, introduced in its first practical form by Sir David Brewster in 1849, was by far the most widely used until the end of the popular stereograph era, about 1915. The best-known model, devised by Oliver Wendell Holmes in 1861, was a T-bar with a folding handle beneath. A hood at one end of the bar housed two short-focus spectacle or prism lenses; a crosspiece at the other end had wire clips to hold a card with 3″ × 3″ stereo photographs pasted on. A card with cutouts backed with tissue-paper diffusers was used with transparencies. The crosspiece could be moved toward or a way from the lens hood for focusing; an opaque divider extending from between the lenses prevented each eye from seeing the opposite image. Compact, enclosed refracting stereoscopes with focusing eyepieces were manufactured from the 1930s for use with slide stereographs made on modern transparency films. A ribbed-lens refracting stereo system that requires no separate viewer is described in the entry on lenticular systems. The slotted grating system is described in the entry on parallax stereograms.

Color-filter stereoscopes use anaglyph stereograms—overlapping images printed in two different colors, typically light red and light green. The observer looks through strong red and green filters. The right eye image, printed in green, is seen through the red filter, with the result that its tones look gray and black. The left eye image, in red, is not

Stereoscopic Photographs. Photographer unknown, "In a great pine forest, collecting turpentine, North Carolina" (n.d.). Private collection.

seen because the filter makes the white background red as well. But the left eye, looking through a green filter sees the red image in black and grays. The opposite, green image is made invisible by the green filter. This system has also been used for motion pictures.

A polarizing stereoscope is similar, but the viewing filters are colorless, opposed polarizers. The images are polarized in complementary fashion to be seen by one eye, but blocked from the other. This system has also been used with projected images and permits use of full-color stereo pairs in projection.

See also: LENTICULAR SYSTEMS; PARALLAX STEREOGRAM; STEREOSCOPIC PHOTOGRAPHY.

Stereoscopic Photography

The three-dimensional effect produced by stereoscopic photography requires separate views of a subject taken from viewpoints 2½ in. (63.5mm) apart, the average separation of the human eyes. This is most easily accomplished with a properly spaced twin-lens camera that has an interlocked double shutter to record two images simultaneously, side by side on the film, or interlaced with one another by a lenticular screen. It is also possible to use a single-lens camera and shift it left or right the necessary distance between successive exposures, but this technique is limited to subjects and scenes in which there is no movement. The normal stereo effect is seen beginning at a distance of about 5 ft. (1.5m) from the camera; at closer distances it appears exaggerated. The distance at which the effect ends—stereo infinity—ranges from 200 to 1500 ft. (about 60 to 460m), depending upon the viewer and upon a variety of depth clues in the scene. The angular difference between the two views that comprise a stereo pair is an important factor. Too great a separation between the picture-taking

viewpoints produces a hyperstereoscopic effect in which depth and the sizes of objects are exaggerated; it is especially noticeable in the foreground of the picture. Too little separation between viewpoints produces hypostereo—diminished depth and object size. Hyperstereo can also be produced by improper separation of the images in viewing. Pictures up to 2½ in. wide can be mounted in a simple viewer with the proper distance between their centers. Larger images will have more than 2½ in. between centers; they must be viewed in a stereoscope with a lens or prism system that compensates for the greater distance and presents them to the eyes with an apparent proper separation. (See the entry STEREOSCOPE for additional methods of viewing.)

Stereoscopic photography was attempted experimentally in the 1840s, but exposure and viewing with the daguerreotype process were difficult and cumbersome. However, with the adoption of the glass negative (wet plate) process, making twin exposures and twin prints became easy and practical. Stereo pictures enjoyed enormous popularity from about 1854 to 1880, and again from about 1890 to 1910. Literally millions of stereographs (prints on cards), stereo transparencies, and viewers were sold. Stereo photography on 35mm film was introduced in 1920, and on 120 roll film in 1925, although there had been many earlier roll film stereo cameras in other sizes. The most successful 35mm system was introduced with the Stereo Realist camera in 1945; its design was widely copied. Today only two stereo cameras are produced: a 120-size camera that produces the traditional two separate images, and a 35mm camera with

four lenses that uses lenticular interlacing. The first system requires an optical viewer, the second produces single prints that can be viewed directly without special equipment.

See also: BREWSTER, SIR DAVID; LENTICULAR SYSTEMS; PARALLAX STEREOGRAM; STEREOSCOPE; WHEATSTONE, SIR CHARLES.

Stieglitz, Alfred
American; 1864–1946
Had Alfred Stieglitz never taken a photograph in his life, he would still be numbered among the most significant influences in American cultural life in the period before the World War II. As editor of the now legendary magazine *Camera Work*, as proselytizer for the art of photography, and as director of the 291 gallery and, later, The Intimate Gallery and An American Place, Stieglitz was among the first to introduce the art of the European and American avant-garde to the American public while simultaneously championing, publishing, and exhibiting much of the best photography of the period. Nevertheless, it is Stieglitz's body of photographic work which has firmly established his place among 20th c. artists.

Stieglitz's career spanned more than 50 years and bridged 19th- and 20th-c. styles in photography. Born in Hoboken, New Jersey, Stieglitz studied mechanical engineering in Berlin, Germany. Even while an engineering student he was drawn to photography, and in the 1880s he traveled throughout Europe taking pictures. At the age of 24 he received first prize in a British photographic competition judged by P. H. Emerson, the first of the 150 medals he

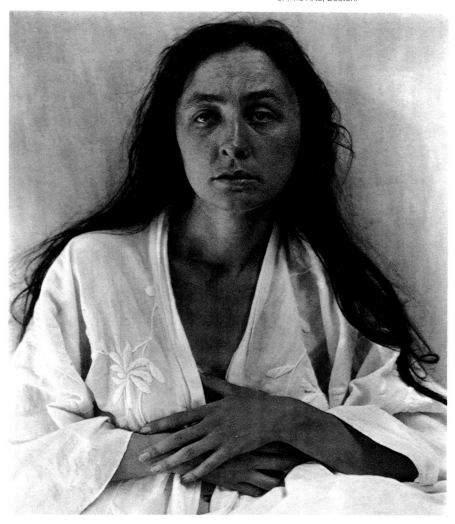

Stieglitz, Alfred. "Georgia O'Keeffe #34" (1918). Courtesy Georgia O'Keeffe; Museum of Fine Arts, Boston.

was to receive in his lifetime. In 1889 Stieglitz returned permanently to New York where he began exhibiting his own work extensively and writing on photography—predominantly on the movement now known as Pictorialism, whose influence pervaded his early work. Pictorialism had originated in France and England (where its major practitioners were loosely organized into a group called The Linked Ring, which conferred honorary membership on Stieglitz). When, in 1902, Stieglitz formed the Photo-Secession group and opened the first of his galleries, the American photographers he exhibited were more or less influenced by Pictorialist tenets. These included the application of Aestheticism and Symbolist styles borrowed from the fine arts, and the use of the gum bichromate and glycerin printing processes, soft focus, and retouching of the negative or positive to achieve painterly or graphic effects. In his own work Stieglitz soon came to reject retouching and other forms of manipulation, often choosing to photograph in rain, mist, or snow to create the desired softness of effect as well as to demonstrate that vision was more important than condition or equipment. Among Stieglitz's most celebrated photographs of this period are "Paula" (1889), "The Terminal" (1893), and "The Steerage" (1907).

In the same year that he established the Photo-Secession, Stieglitz began publishing the quarterly *Camera Work*, which continued until 1917 and featured hand-tipped photogravures, criticism, and reproductions of the work of vanguard artists. In 1908, Stieglitz began exhibiting painting and sculpture at his 291 gallery. Exhibitions included the works of Matisse, Cezanne, Rodin, Bracque, O'Keeffe (whom he was to marry in 1924), and primitive African artisans. His own work evolved progressively toward "pure" photography, a direction confirmed by his recognition of Paul Strand, whose photographs comprised the last two issues of *Camera Work*. Writing in 1922, Stieglitz stated: "My aim is increasingly to make my photographs look so much like photographs [i.e., rather than paintings, etchings, etc.] that unless one has *eyes* and *sees*, they won't be seen—and still everyone will never forget having once looked at them." That same year Stieglitz began his extended series of cloud photographs, which he termed "equivalents" and of which he wrote: "[They] are equivalents of my basic philosophy of life." Later he was to describe all his work as "equivalents"—a Symbolist notion which Stieglitz was effectively able to translate into photographic expression.

After the closing of 291 and the termination of *Camera Work*, Stieglitz opened the Intimate Gallery (1925–1929) and An American Place (1929 until his death in 1946), in which he exhibited principally painting, sculpture, and graphic work, and occasionally photography. His work of this later period includes portraits, hundreds of studies of Georgia O'Keeffe, photographs of Lake George (where Stieglitz summered), clouds, and New York City views.
See also: AN AMERICAN PLACE; CAMERA WORK; LINKED RING; LITTLE GALLERIES OF THE PHOTO-SECESSION; PHOTO-SECESSION; 291.

Still-Life Photography

A still-life photograph is not simply a picture of an inanimate subject or grouping—e.g., a rock, or a stack of books—that the photographer has discovered. It is a photograph of such subject matter carefully selected and arranged for pictorial effect by the photographer. This definition conforms to the major tradition of the still life developed in painting from the 15th c. onward and handed on to photography at the beginning of the 19th c. Some of the earliest extant photographs are still lifes (Daguerre, "Corner of the Artist's Studio," 1835; Bayard, "Statuettes," 1840)—most certainly because of the need for an unmoving subject—but the still life was little explored in photographs until an art movement (Pictorialism) was well established within the medium, toward the end of the century. A major factor in this slow development must have been the blue-sensitive response of photographic plates before the 1880s. The inability to translate reds and greens into monochromatic tones with any fidelity, or even differentiation, made the results artistically unappealing in most cases. Some outstanding efforts by Henri LeSecq and Adolphe Braun in the 1850s come close to surmounting this difficulty, but their still lifes are more accurately characterized as excellent indications of what might someday be possible than as artistic achievements in themselves. Orthochromatic (blue- and green-sensitive) materials and various single-color printing methods (e.g., carbon, gum bichromate) brought increased attention to the still life as a pictorial genre in the last two decades of the century, but it was not until the advent of panchromatic black-and-white emulsions and true full-color plates early in the 20th c. that significant numbers of such pictures were produced.

Originally pursued as an artistic exercise, still-life photography is most often seen today as a commercial undertaking, for it is the basis of product illustration, the very foundation of advertising photography. This application is discussed in the entries on product photography and advertising photography.

The challenge of the still life, whether undertaken for commercial or artistic purposes, is in creating a deliberate composition that has the desired expressive effect. Whereas the photographer's task with a "found" grouping of objects is to find the camera angle and distance that produce a satisfying composition, with a still life the task is to construct the picture from the lens point of view. The arrangement is built up element by element, and progress is checked repeatedly by viewing through the camera or by placing the eye directly in front of the lens position. The choice of elements, composition, and lighting are totally under the photographer's control. There is no need for psychological or emotional manipulation, as is often the case in working with living subjects, and the photographer can work alone, without distraction and at as deliberate a pace as desired. Because the formal factors of composition, lighting, and precise rendering of all detail are of major importance, most still-life photography is done with a large-format view camera. The direct viewing and the individual movements or adjustments offered by this kind of equipment increase the photographer's control over the formal aspects of the picture.

Many photographers attracted to still life work with mixed-media techniques that add diversity of concept and presentation to the diversity that still life permits in selecting and arranging subject elements. Among contemporary photographers who choose to produce artistic still lifes with purely photographic techniques, two are particularly outstanding: Irving Penn and Marie Cosindas. Penn's mastery of still life was evident from the beginning of his career,

in the late 1940s, in illustrations created for fashion magazines and later for advertising clients. In the 1970s and 1980s his noncommercial work has included two notable still-life series. One consists of full-color studies of elegant arrangements of exquisite crafted artificial flowers. The other consists of very large platinum prints of gutter detritus— candy wrappers, cigarette butts, crushed tin cans—raised by isolation, enlargement, and tonal simplification to the level of formal art objects. The still lifes of Maire Cosindas are complex arrangements of flowers, tapestries, and other multicolored, intricately patterned elements, recorded with rich saturation on Polaroid color materials. Although there are a number of masters of the commercial still life, and many of the "found" arrangement (especially in black-and-white), Penn and Cosindas have few rivals in the area of the constructed artistic still life.

See also: ADVERTISING PHOTOGRAPHY; COSINDAS, MARIE; PENN, IRVING; PRODUCT PHOTOGRAPHY.

Color photographs: pp. C-54, C-55.

Stock Solution

A photographic processing solution prepared in concentrated form is called a stock solution. The term is also sometimes applied to individual chemicals in concentrated liquid form. For use, a small quantity of the stock solution is diluted with a larger quantity of water to form a working-strength solution. The required dilution is specified with the amount of stock solution given as 1 (e.g., 1:5, 1+5, or 1 to 5). Because of its higher chemical concentration, a stock solution has a longer storage life than a working-strength solution.

When a processing solution is made up from formula, preparing a relatively large quantity of stock solution eliminates the need to go through the entire mixing procedure before each working session. Some developers and toners cannot be stored in final mixed form, but can be prepared in two or three stock solutions which keep various ingredients apart and which individually have good storage properties. Small quantities of each stock solution are mixed together and diluted to form a working solution just before use.

See also: MIXING PHOTOGRAPHIC SOLUTIONS; STORAGE OF MATERIALS AND SOLUTIONS.

Stop, Lens

See: ƒ-STOP, ƒ-NUMBER; DIAPHRAGM.

Stop Bath

A stop bath is a chemical solution used to halt the action of a developer on a print or film emulsion. The stop bath is usually acidic, and it achieves its effect in a few seconds by neutralizing the alkalinity of the developing solution. The stop bath helps to control development time precisely; it also prolongs the life of the fixing bath by helping prevent residual developer from reducing fixer acidity.

Acetic acid is used for most stop baths; it is supplied in two forms, glacial (99 percent concentration) and a 28 percent solution. The glacial form is extremely corrosive; it can be diluted to 28 percent strength as required by carefully stirring 3 parts of acid into 8 parts of water. (Water must not be poured into the concentrated acid.) A typical stop bath is prepared by diluting 28 percent acetic acid 1:21 with water. Some stop-bath concentrates are supplied with an indicator chemical that causes a diluted working solution to turn dark purple (which looks black under safelight) when the acidity drops below an effective level.

A stop bath can also be prepared with citric acid or potassium metabisulfite, both of which are supplied in dry crystalline form. A 2 percent solution of either in water is equally as effective as an acetic acid stop bath. The solution is prepared by dissolving ⅔ ounce of crystals in 32 ounces of water (or 20 grams in 1 liter of water).

See also: MIXING PHOTOGRAPHIC SOLUTIONS; PERCENTAGE SOLUTIONS.

Stop-Motion Photography

The single-frame exposure technique used with a motion-picture camera to record the stages of an animated sequence is called stop-motion photography. Some photographers use the term to mean only the photography of cutouts or three-dimensional objects, which are moved slightly, step-by-step, between exposures; the term "animation photography" then refers only to the photography of drawing. Time-lapse photography is also sometimes called stop-motion photography.

See also: ANIMATION; TIME-LAPSE PHOTOGRAPHY.

Storage of Materials and Solutions

Photographic materials and solutions must be stored correctly if they are to achieve their maximum useful life. For printing papers and films proper storage means protection from humidity and high temperatures as well as light. For chemical solutions air, bright light, and both excessively high and low temperatures can cause problems.

All photographic solutions have a limited shelf life that is longest when they are kept in full, tightly capped containers. Whenever solutions are kept in only partially full containers, the air that is present can accelerate deterioration of their effectiveness; developers are especially vulnerable to oxidation. Several precautions can be taken: containers of different sizes can be kept on hand so that a solution can be poured into a smaller container as its volume decreases; accordion-style or collapsible plastic containers can be used so that excess air can be squeezed out; marbles can be added to containers to displace the air. High-density plastic containers are best for storing photographic solutions; the soft plastic used in many household containers "breathes" to some extent, permitting air to reach the contents inside.

Chemicals can be protected from light by the use of amber or opaque storage containers and by storage in cabinets or closets. Temperature extremes must be avoided; a range of 65° to 75°F (18° to 24°C) is usually satisfactory and is easy to maintain. Very cool temperatures, especially below about 45°F (7°C) can cause crystallization, and very high temperatures can be detrimental as well.

Unused liquid concentrates tend to keep their effectiveness longer than stock solutions made from powdered chemicals. The chemicals used for color processing generally have a shorter shelf life than their black-and-white counterparts. All chemicals keep for only relatively short times if they are being used frequently. When solutions, especially those prepared from powders, have been kept in storage for long periods, the heavier chemicals may settle to the bottom. Thus, the contents should be stirred before the solution is used.

Printing papers are vulnerable to heat and humidity, as well as to fogging from extraneous light. Unopened packages of black-and-white printing paper that will be used soon can be stored in a dry area, preferably with the temperature at about 70°F (21°C) or lower. Color papers are even more likely to be affected by heat and humidity, which may cause changes in the paper, leading to erratic color rendition. Color paper should be used as soon as possible or refrigerated (even for short-term storage) at temperatures of 50°F (10°C) or lower. Even when refrigerated, color paper may undergo gradual emulsion changes. Thus, for longer-term storage freezing is required at temperatures as low as 0° to −10°F

(−18° to −23°C). Black-and-white papers also can be frozen for extended storage. Frozen materials generally retain full effectiveness well past their nominal expiration date. If a package of paper has been opened, a moisture barrier must be created before it can be frozen (or refrozen). This can be done by placing the box inside two plastic refrigerator bags which have the excess air squeezed out and are individually taped completely closed. Before it is used, refrigerated, or frozen paper must be allowed to stand at room temperature. Refrigerated paper requires a warm-up period of at least an hour; frozen paper must thaw for several hours. To prevent moisture condensation on cold paper, a sealed package must not be opened before warm-up or thawing has been completed.

Film, both black-and-white and color, can also be refrigerated or frozen if necessary. With black-and-white and amateur color films this is not critical if the film is to be used within a short period. However, professional color films can undergo shifts in color balance after a relatively short time, and they should be refrigerated or frozen if they are not to be used right away. As with papers, they should be in sealed packages or bags when refrigerated or frozen, and they must be given a sufficient thawing-out period before use.

The latent images of exposed film are also vulnerable to heat and humidity. If such film—especially color film—cannot be given immediate processing, it should be refrigerated or frozen, depending on the length of storage time required.

See also: FILING AND STORING PHOTO-GRAPHS; MIXING PHOTOGRAPHIC SOLUTIONS.

Story Board

The sequence of slide presentations and animated—or even live-action—motion pictures and television presentations is commonly worked out using rough sketches of principal images. During planning and revision, these sketches on individual slips of paper or index cards are temporarily pinned or taped to a story board—a visual-sequence display board that may cover a wall or may be only a few square feet in size. The story board display allows the visual flow to be scanned rapidly and directly, and permits rearrangements, additions, and deletions to be made easily. By extension, any process of making sketches or sample shots to develop a visual presentation is called storyboarding.

Strand, Paul

American; 1890–1976
Paul Strand, one of the towering figures of American 20th c. photography, was born in New York City, the only child of parents of Bohemian-Jewish descent. He first became interested in photography as a student at the Ethical Culture School under the influence of Lewis Hine. It was Hine who introduced Strand to Alfred Stieglitz and the Photo Secession Gallery in 1907. In the next few years Strand was exposed both to the new abstract painting and sculpture exhibited by Stieglitz—works by artists such as Picasso, Braque, and Brancusi—and also to the photography of such 19th c. masters as Hill and Adamson and Julia Margaret Cameron, and such contemporary photographers as Edward Steichen. Strand became a self-employed commercial photographer after graduation and a brief European trip. He began his own photographic work on the side, experimenting with soft-focus lenses, and generally working in a pictorialist style. During this period, he exhibited at both the New York Camera Club and the London Salon.

In the years 1915–1917, Stieglitz and Strand were in close contact. It becomes difficult to distinguish who influenced whom, but when at the end of this period Strand produced a body of sharp-focus work, including somewhat abstracted still-lifes of kitchen bowls and cityscapes, Steiglitz was prompt to recognize the breakthrough this work represented. The last two issues of *Camera Work* were devoted to the most recent work of Strand, and Stieglitz gave Strand a one-man show at the 291 gallery. In an essay he wrote in 1916 Stieglitz said: "Strand is a young man I have been watching for years . . . without doubt the only important photographer developed in this country since [Alvin Langdon] Coburn. . . . He has actually added some original vision to photography." Strand became known as an advocate of the new realism called "straight" photography.

After a brief stint as an Army Medical Corps x-ray technician in World War I, Strand was employed as a freelance motion-picture cameraman, photographing sports and medical films, and collaborating with Charles Sheeler on the short film *Mannahatta*. In 1925, Strand was one of the photographers represented in the *Seven Americans* exhibition at the Anderson Galleries, and in that year he began his renowned series of close-ups of vegetation and other natural forms.

The 1930s was a period of political concern and activism for Strand; he was an advisor to the Group Theatre in New

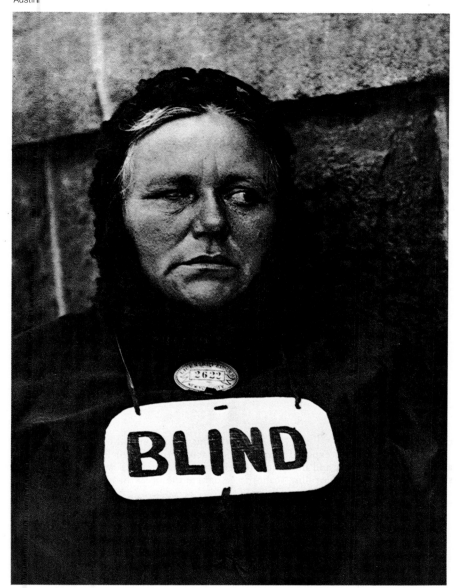

Strand, Paul. "Blind Woman" (ca. 1917); photogravure. Courtesy The Paul Strand Foundation Gernsheim Collection, Humanities Research Center, University of Texas at Austin

Honor Roll of the American Society of Magazine Photographers (1963), David Octavius Hill Medal (1967), Swedish Photographers Association and Swedish Film Archives Award (1970), and major retrospectives at the New York Metropolitan Museum of Art and the Los Angeles Country Museum (1973). His last years were spent working in close collaboration with his third wife, Hazel Kingsbury. He died after a long illness in 1976 at his home in Orgeval, France.

An impeccable printer whose photographs are typified by great richness and sensuousity of surface detail, Strand was one of the major forces of photographic modernism. Embracing a variety of subject matter in his work—landscapes, portraits, still-lifes, architecture, and abstraction—his photographic production was consistent in its concern for formal relationships, its respect for the subject depicted, and an innate classicism.

Streak Camera

In many phenomena and events, time is a dimension of at least equal importance to physical movement or change. High-speed, discrete-exposure cameras cannot provide a continuous time-dimension record because there are instants between exposures that are missed as the shutter operates or a stroboscope blinks. While gaps of a few thousandths or a millionth of a second are of no consequence in many events, they may miss critical information in explosions, electrical arcing, material rupture, machine operation, and other phenomena. In addition, very high speed shutter or stroboscope operation may not be sustainable for the duration of the event. A streak camera makes an unbroken time record, either on film that moves past the lens image without shutter or light interruption, or on stationary film that is swept with the image by a rotating mirror or prism. A plate with a slit, fixed in front of the film, allows only a very narrow portion of the image to register. The film or mirror moves fast enough so that whatever change occurs within the slit area of the image, each detail is recorded in succession at a new point on the emulsion; changes occuring only one-billionth of a second (one nanosecond) apart can be separated. From the known speed of film or image travel and the film area exposed, the timing of details and the speed of the event can be determined. A high-speed streak recording is not visually distinct—the technique is also called smear photography—and special equipment is needed to analyze and interpret the record. Slow speed

York, visited the Soviet Union (where he met Sergei Eisenstein and other key Russian avant-garde artists), worked on the film *The Plow that Broke the Plains* in the U.S., and was active as a producer for Frontier Films on many projects. During this period Strand also worked in Mexico and gathered images for his work *The Mexican Portofolio*, published with hand-pulled gravures in 1940. It was not until 1943 that Strand ceased his film production and returned to still photography full-time.

The Museum of Modern Art, New York, mounted its first full-scale retrospective of a contemporary photographer with the work of Strand in 1945. In 1946–1947 he collaborated with Nancy Newhall on the classic *Time in New England,* in which excerpts from various texts were joined with Strand's emblematic images of New England's artifacts, architecture, and regional attributes. In the 1950s and 1960s he traveled throughout France, Italy, Egypt, and Ghana, producing a series of photography books: *Un Paese* (1954), *Tir a 'Mhurain: Outer Hebrides* (1968), *Ghana: An African Portrait* (1976). He closely supervised the second printing of *The Mexican Portfolio* in 1967. In 1971, the Philadelphia Museum of Art honored Strand by organizing a major retrospective, and a two-volume monograph of his work from the years 1915–1968 was published by Aperture. He received numerous other awards and honors in the last two decades of his life:

streak recordings such as those made for photofinish photography do produce visually interpretable images.

See also: HIGH-SPEED PHOTOGRAPHY; PHOTOFINISH PHOTOGRAPHY.

Stripping Film

A stripping film or plate allows the image-bearing emulsion to be removed intact from the base material, usually for transfer to another, more substantial or transparent, support. The idea originated with the collodion (wet plate) process: to avoid carrying a large number of glass plates into the field, the photographer could strip the processed image off one plate and save it, in order to recoat the plate for further use. In fact, few photographers chose to do so because the procedure was not simple. The first major gelatin-emulsion stripping film was Eastman American Film. Intended to be rolled through the Eastman-Walker roller back (1885) or the No. 1 Kodak camera (1888), this film had a paper base for strength. In the final stages of processing, the paper was soaked off and the emulsion for each exposure was adhered to a glass plate for printing and storage.

A variety of transfer processes involve stripping, usually of a bichromated gelatin emulsion. Transfer to another support usually reverses the image right for left; often it is assembled in register with other stripped images for composite color effects. Stripping emulsions were used in many photomechanical reproduction applications up to about the mid-20th c. because they permitted using glass plates for flatness and rigidity during photography of very large format negatives and positives, and later removing the image for easy cutting, splicing, image reversal, and other operations. In the graphic arts today, "stripping" usually denotes the procedure of cutting and splicing a number of film elements to assemble the master negative or positive through which a printing plate is exposed.

See also: COLLODION PROCESS; PHOTOMECHANICAL REPRODUCTION; TRANSFER PROCESSES; WET PLATE PROCESS.

Stroboscope

The term stroboscope originally identified an interrupted-image viewing device invented by Simon von Stampfer in Vienna in 1832; today the term commonly means a light source that produces a pulsing illumination. The pulse rate is regular and may range from a very few to several thousand pulses per second. A continuous light source fitted with a rotating slotted shutter plate can produce intermittent illumination, but with greatly reduced intensity. A modern stroboscope with sufficient output for high-speed photography consists of a high-intensity gas discharge (i.e., electronic flash) tube and a rapid-cycling trigger circuit; the power is a.c. voltage converted to d.c. by appropriate circuitry in the unit. Some stroboscopes have a variable pulse rate. They are primarily used in high-speed photography to obtain a series of separate images of a very brief event, or to obtain an apparent still image of cyclic movement.

See also: HIGH-SPEED PHOTOGRAPHY; STROBOSCOPIC PHOTOGRAPHY.

Stroboscopic Photography

Photography of moving objects by repeated flashes or a pulsing light source called stroboscopic photography, was first achieved by Ernst Mach, who photographed the flight of bullets and other projectiles shortly before 1900. Modern stroboscopy dates from the development of the high-intensity, gas discharge tube (electronic flash) stroboscope by Harold Edgerton in the early 1930s. Two effects are possible in stroboscopic photography. The first is a single image of an apparently still subject that in fact was moving too rapidly for exposure by a single flash. This can be achieved with a subject that repeatedly cycles through a given location, such as a rapidly spinning flywheel or a reciprocating crank. When the stroboscope rate is synchronized with the rate of movement, a pulse of light is emitted each time the part reaches exactly the same point in its cycle. Visually it appears to be motionless because the eye fuses the multiple impressions into a single continuous image. The apparently still image also can be photographed directly with a conventional camera. The second stroboscopic effect is a series of separate images of a moving subject, each produced by one pulse of light. If the movement is across the field of view, the separation of the images on a stationary film depends on the speed of the subject and the pulse rate of the light. For a given pulse rate, the faster the subject moves the greater the displacement between images on the film. Slow rates are used for multiple-image illustrative photography and for motion studies of dancers, athletes, and similar subjects. Separated images of very high speed subjects are achieved with a correspondingly high pulse rate and moving film. The film is pulled continuously through the camera gate; there is no need for intermittent movement or for a shutter, as in a motion-picture camera, because each light pulse is so brief that no relative movement occurs during the exposure. Rates equivalent to hundreds of thousands of frames per second are possible with this technique. The limiting factors are how much film can be loaded and how fast it can be moved without damage or overheating, and how long the stroboscope can be operated without overheating.

See also: EDGERTON, HAROLD E.; HIGH-SPEED PHOTOGRAPHY; MOTION STUDY AND ANALYSIS; STROBOSCOPE.

Struss, Karl

American; 1886–1981

Pictorial photographer and cinematographer Karl Struss was born in New York City and began making photographs in about 1896 while still in high school. In 1908, he enrolled in a photography class taught by Clarence White at Columbia University's Teacher's College. Through White, Struss became acquainted with the Photo-Secessionists. In the summer of 1909, Struss toured Europe, taking with him two Century cameras, a Goerz Dagor lens, and the Struss Pictorial Lens, a soft-focus lens of his own invention.

In 1910, Struss visited the 291 gallery in New York and met Alfred Stieglitz, who selected 12 of Struss's hand-coated platinum prints for exhibition in the Albright Art Gallery show in Buffalo. Steiglitz also published Struss's work in *Camera Work* in 1912, the same year that Struss became a member of the Photo-Secession and took over White's photography course at Columbia's Teacher's College.

Struss's first major commercial commission was for some photographic illustrations in Bermuda in 1914; later that year he established a professional studio in New York City. Between 1914 and 1917, he did portraiture, advertising illustration, and commercial work. His photographic illustrations appeared in such magazines as *Harper's Bazaar, Vanity Fair,* and *Vogue.* Struss also did publicity for the Metropolitan Opera House, photographed Nijinsky, and filmed the influential dancer and teacher, Adolph Böhm. Also in 1914, Struss began to offer his Struss Pictorial Lens for sale. Among the purchasers were several cinematographers and his former mentor, Clarence White.

In 1916, with White and Edward Weston, Struss became one of the founders of the Pictorial Photographers in America. Struss's soft-focus landscapes, atmospheric cityscapes, and studies of New York's bridges at night were very much in keeping with the aesthetic of this group. His work regularly appeared in Pictorialist exhibitions of the period and he won numerous prizes and honorable mentions for images made between 1910 and 1915, the period of his strongest work.

During World War I, Struss entered the military and did some infrared aerial photography to detect camouflaged sites and to penetrate fog. After the war, he went directly to Hollywood to become a cinematographer. He began to work with Alvin Wyckoff as a still photographer for Cecile B. DeMille, then, in 1919, became DeMille's cinematographer. Struss continued to show his still photography in exhibitions through the 1930s. His principal still work after World War I consisted of theatrical portraits and movie stills.

Edward Weston made a series of portraits of Struss in 1923 and the two served together as judges several times at the Los Angeles Camera Pictorialist's international photo salons. In 1924 Struss traveled to Italy with director Christy Cabanne to shoot *Ben-Hur* for Louis B. Mayer. Struss's most significant contribution to that film was a special effect created with various color filters and panchromatic film to show the miraculous healing of lepers. He also photographed Frederick March in the 1931 version of *Dr. Jekyll and Mr. Hyde* using similar filtering techniques for the transformation special effects. In 1927 Struss and his co-cinematographer, Charles Rosher, won the first Academy Award for cinematography for their work on F. W. Murnan's *Sunrise,* one of the recognized classics of the silent era.

Struss continued working as a leading cinematographer for films and then for television commercials until 1970, when he retired from a 51-year career.
Color photograph: p. C-56.

Stryker, Roy Emerson

American; 1893–1975
Trained as an economist at Columbia University in the 1920s and interested in social problems from an early age, Roy Stryker, as chief of the New Deal's Farm Security Administration (FSA) photography project from 1935 to 1943, encouraged the careers of many talented young photographers and built up an unmatched photographic legacy documenting America in the 1930s.

The FSA (originally named Resettlement Administration), initiated by Rexford Tugwell—a member of Franklin Roosevelt's Brains Trust, and Stryker's mentor at Columbia—provided rehabilitation loans and resettlement opportu-

nities to farmers impoverished by drought, soil erosion, and the effects of the Great Depression. Building on the documentary tradition established by the work of Jacob Riis and Lewis Hine, Stryker instituted a photographic survey of life in rural and small-town America to publicize the hard conditions then current and the government's innovative projects for relieving them. Though not a photographer himself, Stryker's boyhood farm background and his longstanding interest in visual communication enabled him to develop and to direct an outstanding team of photographers sent into agricultural areas of the country on individual assignment. Some, such as Walker Evans, Ben Shahn, and Dorothea Lange, quickly made their reputations, and others, such as Carl Mydans, Russell Lee, and Gordon Parks, gained prominence as photojournalists somewhat later.

It was Stryker's particular talent not only to choose and encourage promising photographers who could make the kind of straightforward documents necessary to convey the government's reformist message, but also to establish an extensive network of contacts among book and magazine publishers that ensured that FSA photographs, which came to number 270,000, were widely used. By the late 1930s, FSA photographs had appeared in countless books and magazines, including the newly founded mass circulation pictorial magazines such as *Look* and *Life,* and project photographs had been exhibited in museums and galleries including the Museum of Modern Art in New York and at the 1939 World's Fair in New York City.

With the outbreak of World War II in 1941, the photographic unit was absorbed by the Office of War Information, and turned to the production of more positive images of America aimed to boost American morale and to aid the Allied cause abroad. In 1943 Congress voted to reorganize rural assistance programs and to disband the FSA. Turning to corporate public relations, Stryker organized and directed a large-scale documentary project, using several former FSA photographers as well as others including Elliott Erwitt and Lisette Model, for Standard Oil of New Jersey during the years 1943 to 1950. In later years, Stryker served as a consultant to companies including Jones & Laughlin Steel. Some 170,000 FSA prints and negatives are now held at the Library of Congress, and prints are available to the public for a small fee. Collections of Stryker's papers, including extensive correspondence with FSA photographers, are held at the University of

Louisville and at the Archives of American Art. Prints and negatives from the Standard Oil and Jones & Laughlin projects are held by those companies. Aspects of his life and contributions are documented in several books, notably *In this Proud Land* (Stryker and Nancy Wood, 1973), *A Vision Shared* (Hank O'Neal, 1976), and *Roy Stryker: U.S.A., 1943–1950 (The Standard Oil [NJ] Photography Project)* (Steven W. Plattner, ed., 1983).
See also: DOCUMENTARY PHOTOGRAPHY; FARM SECURITY ADMINISTRATION.

Studio Photography

Working in a studio offers a photographer the greatest degree of control over the factors involved in making many kinds of pictures. Working on location takes advantage of real settings, but the photographer may encounter adverse weather, interruptions, insufficient electrical power, the need for extra film or an accessory that was left behind, or any of hundreds of other difficulties and unforeseen problems. Particularly in formal portraiture and commercial (advertising, product, fashion) photography, the advantage of working in controlled conditions is so great that photographers are willing to spend considerable effort and money to obtain props, build sets, arrange projected backgrounds, and otherwise create a seemingly real location.

Perhaps the single greatest advantage of studio photography is control over lighting. The color and reflectivity of the ceiling and walls are known, as is the capacity of the electrical system and the location of outlets. A studio photographer acquires a great variety of lighting equipment that can be used flexibly for many different setups, and that provides known effects and results. The sense of confidence this imparts frees the photographer to concentrate on the expressive aspects of a picture and makes it easier for him or her to experiment with new subjects and picture ideas. It also makes is possible for the photographer to work efficiently with a minimum cost in time and in materials used for testing.

A studio also permits the photographer to work in a psychologically controlled environment. It becomes possible to create an atmosphere that will help a portrait subject or a model project a desired emotional mood. It allows a rapport to develop between photographer and subject without distraction, and provides a sense of privacy when that is important. In the case of a still life or a particularly intricate setup, the studio setting allows the photographer to concentrate entirely on the job at hand. The psychological and technical factors offer such great advantages in achieving high-quality results that the vast majority of illustrative and portrait photographers choose to work only in the studio.

See also: ADVERTISING PHOTOGRAPHY; PORTRAITURE; PRODUCT PHOTOGRAPHY.

Color photograph: p. C-57.

Style

Style comprises the factors that make up a distinctive or characteristic manner of expression. In photography those factors include choice of subject, the way in which the subject is viewed, and the manner in which the print or transparency is made. True style arises from the way in which a particular individual uses these factors in an extended body of work. Style is not an element that is added to the handling of a picture, except in an effort to be fashionable, to conform to the mode of the times—and that is something defined by the work of others. In fact, a great deal of so-called style in photography consists of making pictures in the manner of pictures already made, in conscious or unconscious imitation of the work of one or more other photographers. This is a natural, even inevitable, part of learning and growth, but it is not evidence of style in any meaningful sense; rather it is evidence of mannerism and fashion.

When, for cultural or imitative reasons, many individuals adopt the same approach, a style of a given period or genre can be identified (although it may not be recognized at the time of its development). Thus it is possible to identify the daguerreotype portrait style, for example, or 19th-c. Pictorialism, in broad terms, without reference to individuals. Similarly, in a broad sense one can speak of a photographer's having a documentary, or an advertising, or a portrait style, or some similar kind of style. This is a convenient way of making major classifications, but it gives no significant indication of the individual character of a photographer's work. There is a wide variety of styles in each of these areas. The documentary styles of Jacob Riis, Dorothea Lange, and W. Eugene Smith are very different. So are the advertising or fashion styles of Richard Avedon, Irving Penn, and Hiro, or the portrait styles of Julia Margaret Cameron, Yousuf Karsh, Arnold Newman, August Sander, and Man Ray. Art photography is a progression of styles: pictorial, purist, surrealist, abstract, conceptual, snapshot aesthetic, mixed-media . . . the list is potentially endless, and the difficulty of separating subjective and objective factors in style is apparent. Thus, when used meaningfully, the term *style* almost always specifies or implies, "the style of so-and-so" or of a particular, recognized mode of expression.

Although true style—i.e., that other than design or technique mannerism—may be present in every picture of a photographer's work, it cannot originally be defined or identified from examination of a single picture. (When an individual's style is known, it is of course possible to see whether a particular picture contains the qualities that identify the style). Style is the aspect of expression that links a group of pictures. It emerges or becomes apparent because the photographer had a consistent way of seeing a particular kind of subject, a similar reaction in each instance, and a preferred manner of presenting the subject or communicating the reaction. Further, the composite effect of these factors is distinguishable from that of other photographers dealing with the same kind of subject. That is, the pictures are recognizably more like one another than like those of anyone else.

Individual style develops slowly, as the result of a photographer's both consciously and intuitively discovering and refining the ways of expressing what he or she finds it most interesting or necessary to say in pictures. The evolutionary nature of style is difficult to discern at times. A developing uniqueness in the work of an advertising or fashion photographer, for example, may be masked by more obvious surface changes made from the commercial necessity to keep up with the taste of the times. Frequent, rapid shifts are more likely to be evidence of technical virtuosity than of true style. When a major change in a photographer's style becomes apparent, the evidences of change-in-progress that preceded it may go unnoticed until the entire body of work is seen in hindsight. The difference is dramatic between the rampant pictorialism and salon aesthetic of Edward Weston's first 15 years in photography and the straight or purist mode of his mature work. The shift is generally dated from his first trip to Mexico, in 1923, but it is clearly emerging in photographs of steel factories taken the year before—as Weston was well aware—and in other pictures, such as an uncompromisingly direct closeup of a nude breast made in 1920. Similarly, the mature, antiglamour portraits of Richard Avedon are vastly different from earlier celebrity portraits that were an outgrowth of his fashion work in the 1950s. The brutal directness of the late work is often regarded as originating in pictures of Alexey Brodovitch and of Avedon's father, both terminally ill, taken in 1969 and the early 1970s. But the statement here is evident in work throughout the preceding decade, perhaps most compellingly in "all-masks-gone" pictures of Dorothy Parker and Marilyn Monroe, both of which communicate a sense of being at the end of experience rather than midway in a journey.

Photographers do not necessarily change style in the course of their development, some continue in the same mode. This is the case with Irving Penn, for example, whose late-career still lifes are direct descendants of his early work, although far more austerely elegant, and whose portraits of tribespeople (*Worlds in a Small Room* series), workers (*Small Trades in London, Paris, and New York*), and celebrities reveal a consistent psychological distance and preoccupation with formal picture values across three or more decades.

For every photographer who develops a recognizably individual style there are thousands who do not. Amateurs, technicians, and others who use photography for essentially souvenir and record-keeping purposes are unconcerned with style. Many photographers are content to adopt the style of someone else, finding it congenial, convenient, and satisfactory. Those photographers who do develop a true style, and whose work influences that of others, are concerned with effective, meaningful expression. They achieve powerful communication by learning to do things in their own ways, not the way of someone else—and by knowing the difference.

See also: ABSTRACT PHOTOGRAPHY; ARTISTS AND PHOTOGRAPHY; ART OF PHOTOGRAPHY; DOCUMENTARY PHOTOGRAPHY; FANTASY IN PHOTOGRAPHY; GENRE PHOTOGRAPHY; GLAMOUR PHOTOGRAPHY; IMPRESSIONISTIC PHOTOGRAPHY: KITSCH PHOTOGRAPHY; NEUE SACHLICHKEIT; PAINTING AND PHOTOGRAPHY; PHOTOREALISM; PICTORIAL PHOTOGRAPHY/PICTORIALISM; PORTRAITURE; SATIRE IN PHOTOGRAPHY; SNAPSHOT AESTHETIC; SOCIAL LANDSCAPE; SUBJECTIVE PHOTOGRAPHY; SURREALISM IN PHOTOGRAPHY.

Subjective Photography

Photography is often felt, even by photographers themselves, to be essentially a technique for obtaining objective, factual records of the visual world. But in the last 60 years, it has gradually been accepted that a photograph can express something more than a simple visual record. A number of photographers, believing that photography could not become a fully mature medium until it was applied to exploring the interior world of the psyche as well, have developed a variety of approaches to *subjective photography*. At least one great photographer, Alfred Stieglitz, and two influential photographer-teachers, Minor White and Otto Steinert, have pioneered in this area. Stieglitz was responsible for introducing to photography the idea of the *equivalent*—the photograph that serves as a metaphor for the photographer's inner state. White expanded on the notion of the equivalent, and encouraged his students to use photography as a means of spiritual self-examination. Steinert, working along somewhat different lines, sought to promote the use of the widest possible variety of expressive techniques in photography, in the hope of contributing through photography to greater mutual human understanding.

Stieglitz, the founder of the Photo-Secession movement in 1902 and one of the leading figures in American art photography, came to the concept of the equivalent only in the 1920s. After an exhibition of his portraits had been criticized because his sitters all seemed to have fallen under Stieglitz's mesmerizing spell, he resolved to show what he could do with the simplest natural subject—clouds. He intended to show that the power of successful photographs did not depend on special subject matter, but on the photographer's special sensitivity to subjects that could be available to anyone. Stieglitz at first called his cloud photographs "Songs of the Sky," because he hoped that they would suggest qualities of tone, harmony, and melody to the viewer. Printed as small black-and-white images, they showed an incredible array of different moods of the sky: some were quiet, some agitated; some were melancholy, some exalted. Later he hit upon the terms "equivalents" to describe them—to drive home the point that they should be seen not just as clouds, but as visual metaphors equivalent to his own feelings at the moment he made the photographs. He wrote, "All my photographs are equivalents of my basic philosophy of life. All art is but a picture of certain basic relationships; an *equivalent* of the artist's most profound experience of life." For Stieglitz, then, the "straight," unmanipulated photograph could be used as a metaphor for the photographer's most profound thoughts and passions.

In the late 1940s Minor White began to employ Stieglitz's theory of the equivalent in order to demonstrate the subjective, emotional content of photographic images. Very interested in Zen and other Eastern philosophies, he believed that photography, if properly practiced, might lead the photographer to "those rarified moments when psychology, art, science, and religion overlap in one outward manifestation." White advised his students to begin with a blank, receptive state of mind, and rely on their intuition to lead them to subjects that might result in "equivalent" photographs. Like Stieglitz, he favored a "straight" approach to subjects drawn from nature—especially materials in a constant state of flux like water, ice, and clouds. Doorways of all kinds also figured prominently in White's own photographs—a reference, perhaps, to the mystical opening of the "doors of perception." He felt, too, that photographs like these, when studied in a state of intense awareness, should be able to lead the viewer into a transcendent, visionary state. While critics have objected that White's approach amounted to using photographs as a Rorschach blot to stimulate fantasies, his spiritual/mystical version of the equivalent idea has continued to be reflected in the work of such accomplished photographers as Paul Caponigro and Walter Chappell. Many of White's own photographs are collected in his book *Mirrors, Messages, Manifestations* (1969).

In Europe, the idea of "subjective photography" is especially associated with the name of Dr. Otto Steinert, who, at the end of World War II, left his medical practice to teach photography at the Saarbrucken School of Arts and Crafts in Germany. In an attempt to revive the heritage of the "new vision" photography of the prewar era (such as that of Moholy-Nagy and Man Ray), Steinert encouraged a rebirth of creative photography among his students and contemporaries. He called for the exploration of the creative possibilities of all the aspects of the photographic process; his students produced pictures that ranged from "straight" photographs of reflections in pools and close-ups of tree bark and machine parts, to blurred images of birds in flight or dancers photographed in slow exposures. Photograms and montages were also regularly produced by Steinert's followers, whom he organized in 1950 as the "Fotoform" group. Their work, and the work of other photographers sympathetic to Steinert's ideas, were shown in three large *Subjektive Photografie* exhibitions between 1951 and 1958. According to Steinert, subjective photography "embraces all areas of personal photographic creation from the abstract photogram to the psychologically profound and visually composed reportage." Such ideas helped to prepare the way for today's widespread photographic experimentation in Europe.

See also: ABSTRACT PHOTOGRAPHY; ART PHOTOGRAPHY; CONCEPTUAL PHOTOGRAPHY; FANTASY IN PHOTOGRAPHY; IMPRESSIONISTIC PHOTOGRAPHY; NEUE SACHLICHKEIT; STEINERT, OTTO; SURREALISM IN PHOTOGRAPHY.
Color photograph: p. C-57.

Subtractive Color Synthesis

Paints, dyes, inks, and natural colorants create color by absorbing some wavelengths of light and reflecting or transmitting others. This subtractive action is the basis of photographic filters, almost all films and color papers, and photomechanical reproduction in color.

White light is composed of all visible wavelengths, which can be divided into three primary-color bands, red, green, and blue. A colorant that absorbs one wavelength band has the combined color of the other two; it is the complement of the color it subtracts from white light. Thus:

Primary Color Absorbed	Primary Colors Unaffected	Combined Color of the Subtractive Complementary
Red	Blue, Green	Cyan
Green	Blue, Red	Magenta
Blue	Red, Green	Yellow

The complementary colors are the control colors of subtractive color synthesis; thus, the dyes in color filters and emulsions, and the inks (process colors) used in photomechanical reproduction are cyan, magenta, and yellow. A single complementary produces its own color. In full strength it has maximum saturation; in lesser strength its color is desaturated, because the primary amount it does not absorb combines with the other two to produce a certain proportion of white that mixes with the total color effect. Two complementaries in equal strengths produce a primary color because each absorbs a primary—e.g., magenta and yellow absorb green and blue, respectively, leaving red to be seen. Combinations of unequal subtractive strengths produce intermediate colors from white light: full-strength yellow absorbs all blue, half-strength magenta subracts half the green; the remaining green combines with the unaffected red to produce orange. A combination of all three complementaries produces black (full strengths) or gray (lesser equal strengths) because all colors are subtracted. In color filtration this produces neutral density, which reduces exposure without affecting color balance; it can always be eliminated without changing the color control effect of the filtration by subtracting equal amounts of each color from the filter pack.

Primary-color lights can be additively mixed to produce colors, but primary-color dyes, inks, or filters do not permit selective color control by subtractive action because each absorbs the other two primaries equally. Thus, using a red dye to subtract blue also subtracts green, which may not be desirable, or perhaps not in equal degree. Using any two primary dyes together subtracts all colors of light. The complementary colors permit subtractive control of each of the three primaries individually; like additive synthesis, this corresponds with the three-color theory of vision.

See also: ADDITIVE COLOR SYNTHESIS; COLOR; COLOR MATERIALS; NEUTRAL DENSITY; PROCESS COLORS.

Sudek, Josef

Czechoslovak; 1896–1976

Josef Sudek, National Artist of Czechoslovakia, "the poet of Prague," was his country's most famous photographer. He enjoyed a long career and published many books. Although his style moved from Pictorialism through Impressionism to experimental functional compositions, his subjects were constant: poetic landscapes and still-lifes, scenes of the city of Prague, and views from his window. Mainly concerned with tonal value and gradation, he was among the most lyrical of photographers.

Sudek was born in Kolin, Bohemia. As a young man he was apprenticed to a bookbinder and began to photograph as an amateur in 1913. He was inducted into the Army in 1915 and served on the Italian front, where he was badly wounded and lost his right arm. During three years spent in hospitals after his injury, Sudek decided to become a photographer. He joined the Prague Club for Amateur Photographers in 1920, and studied formally with Karel Novack at the State School of Graphic Art in Prague in 1922–1923. He was influenced early on by the work of the American photographer Clarence White in particular.

Sudek worked from 1922 to 1927 on a series of photographs of disabled soldiers in Veterans' Hospitals. In 1924 he and his close friend and ally Jaromir Funke were founding members of the

Sudek, Josef. "Still life" (ca. 1950). Permanent collection, ICP, New York.

avant-garde Czech Photographic Society, dedicated to photography as a documentary medium.

From 1924 to 1928, Sudek photographed the renovation of St. Vitus Cathedral and produced a series of "Contrasts" juxtaposing workmen's tools with the surrounding architectural grandeur. He was awarded the title "Official Photographer of the City of Prague" for this work. In 1926 he took a trip to Belgium and revisited the Italian sites he had known in the war. After this journey he was never to leave Czechoslovakia again.

Sudek started his own photographic business in 1928 and took on a wide variety of commercial and portrait assignments while continuing his personal work. His first one-man show took place in 1933 at the Druzstevni Prace Gallery, and he exhibited with Moholy-Nagy, Man Ray, John Heartfield, and Alexander Rodchenko at the International Photography Exhibition in Prague in 1936.

Sudek discovered the almost magical quality of tone and detail in large-format contact prints in 1940 and immediately switched to that medium. "From that day on, I never made another enlargement." The war years led Sudek to reevaluate his work. He worked on his series of "Windows" and "Magic Garden" images (the latter extending into the 1960s).

In 1960 a major tribute, *Sudek in the Arts,* exhibited work by 22 artists who had known or been influenced by him. A year later he was the first photographer to receive the "Artist of Merit" award from the Czech government. One-man shows were held in both Prague and Brno in 1966, the year Sudek was given the "Order of Work" award. The 1970s saw the development of a new series of images of tangled string, torn paper, and other scraps called "Labyrinths," still-lifes meant to remember and evoke the photographer's friends.

On Sudek's 75th birthday, a one-man show opened in New York at the studio of Sonja Bullaty and Angelo Lomeo. Numerous other exhibitions followed in the next several years at Neikrug Gallery, Light Gallery, George Eastman House, and again in Prague and Brno. Sudek died in September 1976. He was the subject the following year of a retrospective at the International Center of Photography in New York, and of exhibitions throughout Europe. Of his own work Sudek stated: "I believe that photography loves banal objects. . . . I like to tell stories about the life of inanimate objects, to relate something mysterious. . . . If you take photography seriously you must also get interested in another art form. For me it is music. This listening to music shows up in my work like a reflection in a mirror. . . . I have no particular leaning toward. . . the all-too-clearly defined; I prefer the living, the vital, and life is very different from geometry; simplified security has no place in life."

Sun Photography

The center of our solar system is the only stellar body near enough to the earth to be seen as an extended object. At the sun's average distance of 93,000,000 miles (150,000,000km), its 865,000-mile (1,395,161km) diameter is sufficient to be magnified easily and thus studied photographically in considerable detail. Moreover, sun photography is one branch of astrophotography that does not necessarily require large quantities of highly specialized and expensive equipment to yield spectacular results. Usually the sun is pictured directly only for scientific purposes, at sunrise and sunset for pictorial effect, and during the relatively rare occurrences of solar eclipse for both reasons.

Photographing the sun must be done only with an understanding of its extreme and potentially hazardous brightness. The sun as seen from the earth is hundreds of billions of times brighter than the brightest star. Such intense light is capable of causing blindness or retinal damage, for the eye lens can act in the same way that a magnifying glass can ignite a piece of paper on a clear day. One should never look directly at the sun with unprotected eyes when it is more than a few degrees above the horizon. Similarly, an unfiltered camera lens must not be aimed directly at the sun; the intense light can burn a hole in a shutter curtain very quickly.

Suitable filtration can overcome these problems, but adequate screening for the camera and film is not necessarily safe for the human eye. For example, a 5.0 neutral density (ND) filter reduces the intensity of light 10,000×. This brings the sun's radiation approximately into the exposure range of most contemporary films. If a 5.0 ND filter is not readily available, two or more filters of lesser density may be sandwiched together to achieve the required total strength. Thus, the camera may be aimed directly toward the sun safely, although not for extended periods. Even so, it is still dangerous to look through the viewfinder of the camera, because the filtration does not affect infrared wavelengths. Many panchromatic emulsions are not sensitive to infrared and therefore do not require protection; the eye does. Authorities usually suggest exposing two strips of medium-speed black-and-white silver-emulsion film to full daylight and developing them for maximum density. Sandwiched together they produce a safe, usable eye screen. The dyes used in sunglasses, color film, and chromogenic black-and-white film do not absorb infrared radiation.

Almost any type of camera may be used for sun photography, particularly if it is equipped with a means of manually overriding exposure settings. Coupled automatic meters are often inaccurate during partial phases of solar eclipses. The most important consideration is lens selection. The sun is one of the few celestial bodies that are not seen as a point source of light. It has dimension and therefore can be magnified on the film. The common rule of thumb is that the sun's image on the film is equal to the focal length of the primary lens divided by 110. Thus, a 200mm lens would produce an image slightly under 2mm (1/12in.) in diameter. The diameter of the sun on the film is enlarged easily and inexpensively by adding tele-extenders to the primary lens. A 2× extender would double the image size, for example. Enlargement of the negative in a print or projection of a slide will further increase the image size. For higher quality pictures or large magnifications, the camera may be fitted to a telescope or binoculars. Some manufacturers produce instruments of significant power designed specifically to be adapted directly to the 35mm camera. Whatever system is used, it should be supported securely. For short exposures with simple equipment a tripod will suffice; long exposures may require a means of compensating for the earth's rotation.

A total solar eclipse occurs when the photographer is directly in the shadow of the moon; that is, the moon is exactly between the sun and the observer. Even though this exact set of conditions, referred to as totality, lasts only a few moments, the partial phases take about an hour before and an hour after totality. This presents a marvelous and relatively simple opportunity for a multiple exposure showing the progression of an eclipse. A "normal" lens (i.e., 50mm in a 35mm format) has a field of view of about 45 degrees. The sun traverses about 15 degrees per hour. Thus, the entire eclipse can be seen on a single frame of film.

The most spectacular visual events occur immediately before, during, and just after totality. Bailey's Beads is a phenomenon which lasts only seconds, but is well worth waiting for. Just before and after totality the sun shines through the valleys of the moon, producing an intermittent effect commonly described as beads. Judicious adjustment of the exposure setting will yield the well-known, if difficult to capture, "diamond ring" effect of a large bright spot flanked on each side by arcs of smaller spots.

Because the sun and the moon are seen from earth as about the same size, at the moments of totality the disc of the sun is hidden, but its atmosphere, or corona, is visible. Brightness levels vary radically between the inner corona and the streamers of escaping gases which extend thousands of miles out from the sun. Thus, a decision must be made about which is to be recorded on the film. Approximate exposure settings are published by several sources; all are greatly dependent on the clarity of the earth's atmosphere, and bracketing is a wise precaution when time permits. Artificial eclipses may be produced for scientific investigation via a coronagraph—a type of telescope which blots out the disc of the sun. Local university or museum observatories are good sources for specific information about solar events and photographic techniques and exposure data.

The sun is often used as a richly romantic background at sunrise and sunset. When it is near the horizon, there is little danger to eyes or equipment. Considerable care should be taken to clean all glass surfaces to avoid flare. Due to increased dispersion of the shorter wavelengths of visible light as the sun nears the horizon, it appears to glow increasingly redder. Some correction for accurate color temperature matching with a daylight-balanced film may be necessary, although many photographers welcome the added pictorial warmth. Sunrise/sunset exposure may be based on a meter reading of the lighted sky, but not of the sun itself; additional reduced exposures are useful to achieve more pronounced color.

Highly specialized photographs of the sun's disc are made by scientists to study its interior structure. Often these are done by a scanning spectrograph, which displays the quantity of a single element (e.g., hydrogen) present in various areas. *See also:* ECLIPSE PHOTOGRAPHY; MOON PHOTOGRAPHY.

Color photographs: pp. C-58, C-59.

Superadditivity

When certain developing agents are combined in a single formula, they produce greater density in a given time than the simple total of the effects they produce when used separately; this synergistic action is called superadditivity. For example, if agent A separately produces 0.2 density, and agent B produces 0.5 density, their simple additive effect is 0.7 density. However, in a combined solution their superadditivity may produce many times more density than that. (It is assumed that identical exposures and development times are used in all three cases.)

Superadditivity was first noted in 1900 by Heinrich Lüppo-Cramer, a German photographic scientist who discovered that a combination of metol and gallic acid produced faster development than metol alone, and gallic acid alone had almost no effect. Superadditivity is the basis of the great number of developer formulas that combine hydroquinone with metol or Phenidone, and of most other combined formulas. *See also:* DEVELOPING AGENT; DEVELOPMENT; M-Q DEVELOPER; P-Q DEVELOPER.

Superimposure

A superimposure is a combination of two pictures in which details of one image show through the other. In still and motion-picture photography superimposure is achieved by double exposure in the camera or in printing, or by printing from two negatives sandwiched together. In television it is achieved by transmitting or recording two pictures simultaneously. Superimposure is the simplest means of adding subtitles, names, and similar matter to a background picture. It can also combine images for dramatic or emotional effect. Each image must be relatively detailless and of a contrasting tone or color in those areas where important details of the other image occur. *See also:* INSERT.

Superrealism

See: PHOTOREALISM.

Supplementary Lens

A simple (one- or cemented two-element) lens used in combination with another, prime, lens to reduce or increase its focal length is called a supplementary lens. Supplementary lenses are rated by power, expressed in diopters; the power is the reciprocal of the focal length (FL) in meters:

$$\text{Power} = 1 \div \text{FL}$$

A lens with a positive (+) power shortens the focal length of a prime lens, making it possible to focus subjects at a closer than normal distance to obtain larger images. Positive supplementary lenses are sometimes called close-up or portrait attachments; they are useful with fixed-focus cameras, and with lenses that have insufficient close-focusing limits. When the prime (i.e., camera) lens is focused at infinity, the plane of sharp focus is at a distance equal to the focal length of the supplementary lens, measured from the face of the supplementary. Most fixed-focus camera lenses are set to their hyperfocal distance; the following formula gives the supplementary-focus distance; it can also be used when adjustable camera lenses are focused at distances other than infinity:

$$\text{Actual focus} = (u \times \text{SFL}) \div (u + \text{SFL})$$

where *u* is the distance setting of the camera lens focus, and *SFL* is the focal length of the supplementary lens. Both factors must be measured in the same units; SFL can be determined as follows:

For *u* in	SFL		
Meters	1	÷	
Centimeters	100	÷	
Millimeters	1000	÷	Supplementary
Feet	3.3	÷	lens power
Inches	39	÷	

A supplementary lens with a negative (−) power increases the focal length of a prime lens, for greater magnification from a fixed distance. It requires being able to increase the lens-to-film distance to achieve any focus whatsoever. The focal length of the combination can be approximately calculated from the powers:

$$\frac{\text{Combined}}{\text{power}} = \frac{\text{Camera lens}}{\text{power}} - \frac{\text{Supplementary}}{\text{lens power}}$$

It is necessary to first convert the camera lens focal length to power (1000 ÷ FL in mm), and the negative sign of the supplementary lens power is ignored. The combined power can be converted to a focal length by using it in place of supplementary lens power in the SFL conversion table above.

For reasonable image definition, the camera lens must be set to a medium or small aperture. A single-element meniscus supplementary lens should be mounted as close to the front surface of the camera lens as possible, with the convex side facing the subject. *See also:* CLOSE-UP PHOTOGRAPHY; DIOPTER; FOCAL LENGTH; MENISCUS; OPTICS.

Surface Development

In some kinds of photography—especially in scientific and technical applications—obtaining maximum resolving power with a minimum of edge effects is more important than obtaining normal contrast or maximum density. This is achieved by surface development, which affects only the exposed halide crystals at the surface of the film or plate emulsion. Those at greater depths are left undeveloped because that is where irradiation, halation, and other factors contributing to the emulsion spread factor have an effect. A surface developer contains a developing agent with a very short induction period; it begins reducing exposed halides as soon as it comes in contact with them, developing the image from the top down as it penetrates the emulsion. Stopping development short insures that only the surface image is produced. Phenidone, metol, para-aminophenol and other rapid-acting agents are used for surface development. Most normal developers have a longer induction period so that they soak deeper into the emulsion before any significant amount of development takes place. Hydroquinone is the agent commonly included to produce development in depth. *See also:* DEVELOPING AGENT; DEVELOPMENT; EDGE EFFECTS; HALATION; IRRADIATION; RESOLVING POWER; SPREAD FUNCTION.

Surrealism in Photography

Photography has frequently been nourished and given new life by de-

Surrealism in Photography. Bill Brandt, Untitled, from *Perspecitve of Nude* (ca. 1957). Courtesy Bill Brandt.

velopments in painting and the fine arts; the influence of the Surrealist movement on photography is a compelling case in point. Surrealism as an artistic approach emerged in Europe at the end of World War I (and, in large measure, as a reaction to that war) and remained a vital style until the beginning of the World War II. While it was never a truly unified movement, the works of art that have become identified as Surrealist displayed a number of shared concerns, most important among them a revolutionary philosophical and sociopolitical consciousness.

Certain that accepted reality is itself a human-invented fantasy, in structure as well as in content, the Surrealists created works that attempted to uproot and review this reality at a much deeper level than did other forms of fantastic art. The plausibility of various alternative realities and combinations thereof was

shown, ranging from microscopic and hallucinatory perceptions and the constructs of the Freudian unconscious, to mathematically conceived extradimensional universes. By exhibiting in public their paradoxical, often shocking images, the Surrealists hoped to jolt viewers out of their traditional habits of thought and behavior. Salvador Dali, the painter whose images of limp clocks scattered in a dreamscape are among the best-known of Surrealist works, declared that the Surrealist aim was to "systematize confusion and contribute to the total discrediting of the real world."

The camera's ability to record scenes and objects with unrelenting fidelity made it, paradoxically, an important tool for Surrealist expression. Because of the conflict between the popular belief in the inherent "truth" of the photographic image and the reality that the photo-

graph can be manipulated or altered in any number of ways, photography became an ideal medium with which to undermine commonly held ideas about the "true nature" of things.

The American-born Man Ray was one of the first Surrealists to use photography in an extensive way. Working in Paris, he pioneered in the use of cameraless photograms (which he called "rayograms"), solarization, and other manipulations to challenge the very idea of what a photograph should look like. In his solarized nudes and his more shockingly erotic photographs, he sought to call into question the traditional ways in which the art had represented the human form.

Among the most prominent Surrealist photographers was Raoul Ubac, who began to work with the camera in 1936, at Man Ray's prompting. His photographs included combination prints that recall the contradictory perspectives of the Surrealist painter De Chirico, as well as a number of "straight" images that make use of multiple mirror reflections.

The Hungarian-born photographer Brassaï was another major figure in French Surrealist circles. Best known for his photographs of Parisian night life in the 1930s, he was often called upon to furnish portraits and other photographic illustrations for Surrealist publications like *Minotaure*. Important here was his idea of the "found" object: a commonplace item that becomes mysterious when isolated and photographed in close-up.

Other important French Surrealist photographers were Roger Parry, Maurice Tabard, and Pierre Boucher. Tabard's photographs combined positive and negative images, projected shadows, and geometric lighting to situate his subjects in dreamlike surroundings. Boucher made a number of straight as well as montage photographs using the sky as a backdrop for subjects who appeared to be suspended in mid-air.

Because many of the Surrealist photographers—in particular Man Ray—were officially employed by fashion magazines as studio photographers, Surrealist visual ideas were quickly passed along to fashion photography in the 1930s. Frequently this involved no more than photographing fashion models in studio sets modeled after Surrealist paintings, but innovative work in the Surrealist vein was done by photographers such as Erwin Blumenfeld, Anton Bruehl, André Durst, and Peter Rose-Pulham. Man Ray, for example, photographed a model in a bare studio seated in a wheelbarrow; Blumenfeld used solarization to convey a freakish look to a photograph of a woman modeling a new hat.

The British photographer Bill Brandt studied briefly with Man Ray in 1929–1930, and elements of Surrealism have continued to appear from time to time in his work—most notably in his high-contrast, distorted nudes and in his gloomy landscapes. The mood of claustrophobia and potential menace that marks much of Brandt's work can be traced to the Surrealist quest for visual equivalents of unconscious states.

The foremost American exponent of Surrealism in photography is Frederick Sommer. Sommer's attachment to Surrealism undoubtedly owes much to his friendship with the painter Max Ernst, one of the founding fathers of the movement. Sommer's preference for shocking or eccentric subjects—such as an amputated foot he found in the Arizona desert—and his depiction of the desert landscape as a confusion of hallucinatory detail, testify to his continuing exploration of the Surrealist point of view.

The visual language of Surrealism has now become a familiar part of advertising and other commercial photography, a conventional strategy for gaining the viewer's attention. Among the recent art photographers who have continued to investigate the possibilities of Surrealism are Jerry Uelsmann, Duane Michals, Ralph Gibson, Les Krims, and Arthur Tress.

See also: ARTISTS AND PHOTOGRAPHY; FANTASY IN PHOTOGRAPHY; PAINTING AND PHOTOGRAPHY.

Surveillance Photography

Conventional photographic surveillance consists of the close, often systematic observation and recording of a person, persons, or place. It is usually a function of criminal or espionage investigations although the basic techniques may be applied to other kinds of photography. (Military and related surveillance of the earth's surface is described in the entry on space photography.) Surveillance photography is different from candid photography, which simply attempts to capture people as they normally are. Surveillance implies the existence of an ulterior, and concealed, observation purpose.

The photographer begins by visiting the surveillance scene and deciding whether to be physically present or to install automatic or remote control equipment. Which basic approach is desirable depends in large part on the situation. Unmanned camera setups are inflexible, fixed, and relatively expensive, but they are infinitely patient. However, when the camera is operated actively,

there is the opportunity to react to a developing situation and revise camera position, lens choice, exposure setting, and other factors as necessary.

A critical factor in approaching a scene for active surveillance is not to disturb or alert the subject. Misdirection is a common ploy. There is no reason why a surveillant (photographer) should not openly carry a camera in an area where cameras are common. He needs only to avoid bringing attention to himself. Usually the camera is not pointed at the subject for more than a second or two. When it is physically possible to view a scene unobstructedly from a considerable distance, a long subject-to-camera separation is an uncomplicated and safe solution to secrecy. Covert activity can also be concealed by using a rolled-up newspaper or hollowed out loaf of bread to hide a camera, but such gambits are used more often in adventure movies than reality.

Equipment. For most purposes, a 35mm single-lens reflex camera with adjustable shutter speeds and capable of accepting interchangeable lenses is highly desirable. In certain situations smaller or subminiature cameras might be preferred, but it should be noted that in all circumstances the quality of the negative must be high enough to establish the identity of the subject. With an extraordinarily tiny film format, this means the subject has to be kept relatively large in the viewfinder, thus limiting the number of camera positions available to the surveillant. A tripod may be a nuisance, but it can be invaluable especially with long focal length lenses from a fixed position. Although most surveillance photography is done by available light, additional illumination in the infrared region is occasionally practicable. In addition to a normal focal length lens, a longer one (sometimes very substantially longer) will likely be called for; all of these should be as fast as possible.

Film. Similarly, the film of choice is the fastest one consistent with adequate negative quality. This allows a motion-freezing high shutter speed and small aperture for maximum depth-of-field to be used. Some very high speed recording films have extended red sensitivity. This matches well with best exposure of Caucasian skin tone. Also useful in dim lighting situations is infrared film. This film is sensitive to wavelengths of electromagnetic energy beyond the visible spectrum. An infrared light source or filter (such as a Wratten #87) over a standard source, and high-speed infrared sensitive film will allow a subject to be recorded even in complete darkness. In practice, a faint deep red glow can be

seen, but only when looked at directly.

Two fairly exotic techniques permit continuous observation of a subject with nearly no light of any sort: sniper or surveillance scopes and image intensifiers or amplifiers. Sniper scopes obtain an infrared image that is converted electronically to a visible one and then displayed on a screen. An arrangement can be made whereby the subject can be photographed directly from the sniper scope image or the scope can be simply used as a locator for a conventional camera and lens. Image intensifiers are also electronic devices. They sense whatever light is reflected from a subject and amplify it thousands of times. The intensified image is then recorded conventionally. Image intensifiers are effective in extremely low light levels.

The photographer is apt to use equipment that does not require his presence when a fixed scene is going to be observed over a substantial amount of time. Such is the case in bank surveillance, where cameras may record at constant intervals even when no particular threat is imminent.

Planning and maintenance. Prior to installation of equipment, a plan is devised that assures all necessary camera angles are covered for identification of subjects. The lighting is checked and possibly adjusted; equipment is mounted and controls are set. The photographer then leaves the scene, to return only to change film or perform maintenance. When surveillance is to take place over a long time and lighting levels are likely to change, an automatic exposure control system is called for. Obviously a large load of film is required for a setup like this to be valuable and for this reason modified motion picture cameras are often used.

To further lengthen the time between visits to a surveillance scene, cameras are commonly operated intermittently. For example, an exposure may be made every two seconds or only once in ten minutes. A motor driven camera is connected to an intervalometer that trips the shutter at a preselected rate. In this time-lapse technique, real-time occurrences can be condensed dramatically.

Even with intermittent recording, film may be used up at an economically disastrous pace. Surveillance over an extended period where the relevant activity is expected to be relatively brief frequently makes use of a triggering device. The same sort of electric eye system that opens supermarket doors for shoppers can easily be connected to a camera. When infrared wavelengths are used for the sensor, the mechanism can be virtually undetectable, even at night. Highly secret facilities may use a number of more sophisticated devices. Vibration detectors sense the motion of footsteps across a room. Audio detectors are, in effect, microphones that are set to react to sound above a certain decibel level. Ultrasonic detectors fill an enclosed space with sound waves beyond the audible range and react whenever the standing pattern is broken, e.g., whenever someone enters the room. The reality of modern surveillance technology is that there are virtually no locations or conditions that prevent pictures being taken without knowledge of the subject. See also: FORENSIC PHOTOGRAPY; INFRARED PHOTOGRAPHY; REMOTE CONTROL; SPACE PHOTOGRAPY.

Swan, Sir Joseph Wilson
English; 1828–1914
A prolific inventor with more than 60 patents to his name, J. W. Swan was trained as a chemist and entered into partnership with a chemical supplier, John Mawson. The firm was soon engaged in manufacturing photographic materials, many of them invented or improved by Swan. These included the first commercially practical carbon process in 1864, later known as the Autotype; the photomezzotint process, based on an electrotype mold taken from a carbon-tissue relief image; rapid gelatin dry plates; the first automatic emulsion-coating machine for dry plate manufacture; a greatly improved bromide paper; and a number of other materials. Swan discovered and developed the process of "ripening" an emulsion at a high temperature to increase its speed—a procedure stumbled upon but not recognized by others. As early as 1865 he proposed photographing a screen of lines or dots to break an image into elements suitable for halftone reproduction. The procedure was not adopted until 1879 when he patented a parallel-line screen and a technique of turning it halfway through the copying exposure to create square dots formed by the line images crossing at right angles.

Swan is widely known outside photography as the inventor of the carbon-filament incandescent electric light bulb, which he demonstrated in 1860, some 20 years before Thomas Edison, and began manufacturing in the late 1870s. Swan's priority was upheld in patent infringement suits in the 1880s and Edison entered into partnership with him in England. Swan also invented one of the first synthetic fabric processes, a method of making artificial silk, based on his research to produce filaments for electric light bulbs.

See also: AUTOTYPE; CARBON PROCESSES; ELECTROTYPE; HALFTONE PROCESSES; PHOTOMEZZOTINT.

Swings and Tilts
See: CAMERA MOVEMENTS.

Symmetrical Lens
See: LENSES.

Synchronization
Synchronization refers to the timing relationship between the action of a camera or lens shutter and the firing of a flash unit. The flash fires when shutter contacts complete an electrical circuit. In some shutters that moment can be timed for proper exposure with flashbulbs or with electronic flash either by means of a selector lever, or by separate sockets for a synchronizing cord from the flash unit. Synchronization for flashbulbs is marked M (for medium peak); that for electronic flash is marked X. Because an M-class flashbulb takes about 17 milliseconds to reach peak output, with M synchronization the circuit closes just before the shutter opens. Electronic flash peaks instantaneously; therefore, X synchronization does not close the circuit until just after the shutter opens. Flashbulbs are obsolete for most photography, so much equipment no longer has the M sync option; only X synchronization is provided.

With electronic flash the shutter must be fully open before the unit fires, or part of the picture will be blocked. Synchronization is not a problem with lenses that have built-in (leaf) shutters, because the shutter must open fully at all speeds, and flash can be used at any setting. However, in cameras with focal-plane shutters—the majority of 35mm cameras—that is not the case. The shutter is composed of two blinds which uncover the film by moving in sequence across the focal plane. The effective shutter speed is determined by the gap between the blinds. At the higher speeds the film is never entirely uncovered at any one moment; instead a narrow slit moves across the focal-plane, making it impossible for the very short duration of electronic flash to illuminate the entire frame. In cameras with focal-plane shutters that travel horizontally, shutter speeds above 1/60 sec. cannot be synchronized with electronic flash because of this. With shutters that travel vertically, the fastest sync speed is 1/125 sec. On most cameras the maximum sync speed is distinctively marked in color or with a lighting bolt symbol or a small "X." All slower shutter speeds assure flash synchronization, but may allow the ambient light to add unwanted exposure or, with

moving subjects, create ghosting.

Dedicated camera-flash combinations automatically set the proper shutter speed on the camera when the flash is connected and return to the auto-exposure or manually set shutter speed when the flash is removed. When more than one flash unit is used, synchronized firing is achieved by interconnecting the extra units with the one connected to the camera, or by equipping them with wireless slave triggers that respond to the camera flash.
See also: AUTOMATIC FLASH; GHOSTING; FLASH.

Szarkowski, Thaddeus John
American, 1925–
John Szarkowski followed Edward Steichen in 1962 as Director of Photography at the Museum of Modern Art. He has arranged exhibitions and written numerous works in an attempt to establish criteria inherent to the medium of photography. In 1966 he published *The Photographer's Eye*, in 1973 *Looking at Photographs*, and in 1978 *Mirrors and Windows, American Photography since 1960*. The most controversial photography exhibition of the 1970s was William Eggleston's color show at the Museum of Modern Art and the subsequent publication of the *Guide* which included an extended introduction to the photographer's work by Szarkowski.

A practicing photographer himself, Szarkowski was educated in art history at the University of Wisconsin. Professor John Kienitz noted his interest in photography and suggested that he examine the work of Walker Evans. After graduation, Szarkowski served in the United States Army from 1945 to 1946, worked as a staff photographer at the Walker Art Center in Minneapolis, and taught art history and photography at the Albright Art School in Buffalo. The recipient of a Guggenheim Fellowship in 1954 to complete a photographic project on the architecture of Louis Sullivan, Szarkowski published *The Idea of Louis Sullivan* in 1956. He also produced a book titled *The Face of Minnesota* in 1958.

Concerned with the relationship between fine and vernacular photography, Szarkowski established the snapshot aesthetic with his 1967 show *New Documents*, which included the work of Diane Arbus, Garry Winogrand, and Lee Friedlander. Szarkowski is more interested in the formal qualities of the image than in the intent of the photographer. He does not address the issue of whether or not photography is art, but rather of "what photographs look like [and] why they look that way."

Tabard, Maurice. Untitled [Two men] (1930).
Collection, Museum of Modern Art, New
York.

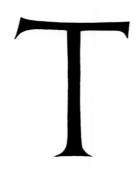

Tabard, Maurice

French; 1897–1984

Maurice Tabard was highly regarded as an experimental photographer in Paris between the wars and as an advertising and fashion photographer for international magazines after World War II. The few remaining early Tabard photographs—photograms and solarizations—give evidence of ingenious artistic experimentation with the simplest technical means. Although Tabard's portraits and life studies in a surrealist mode stretched the boundaries of the medium while maintaining formal assurance, no books of his photographs have been published and he was critically neglected until the late 1970s.

Tabard, the son of a silk manufacturer, was born in Lyons, where he studied violin from 1903 to 1913, and fabric design in his father's plant until 1918. Tabard emigrated to New York that same year, abandoning his early interest in painting to study photography at the New York Institute of Photography. In 1922 he became an assistant photographer associated with Bachrach Studios—one of the most prominent portrait concerns—first in Baltimore, then in Cincinnati and Washington, D.C. He remained with Bachrach until 1928, when he returned to France.

In the following decade Tabard worked on a freelance basis as a fashion, advertising, and portrait photographer for magazines. His most innovative work appeared at this time in such periodicals as *Vu, Arts et Métiers Graphiques, L'Art Vivant, Photographie,* and *Jardin des Modes.* Tabard held a number of other positions during these years as well, working as a darkroom assistant for publishing and motion-picture concerns, and as a still and motion-picture photographer for both commercial and government newsreel bureaus.

Tabard spent the years during World War II as a freelance photographer in the south of France. His entire negative archive was lost during the Nazi occupation of Paris. From 1946 to 1948 he traveled and photographed in England and Scotland as a staff photographer with *Harper's Bazaar,* under the editorship of Carmel Snow. He worked for Alexey Brodovitch in the United States from 1948 to 1950, and during 1948–1949 for Paul Linwood Gittings Studio, New York. He was an instructor of photography at the Winona School for Professional Photographers in Indiana in 1950.

Tabard worked as a freelance photographer based in Paris from 1950, publishing work regularly in *Paris-Match, Elle, Marie-Claire,* and other periodicals. At the time of his death Tabard had been retired for many years, living in Paris and in the South of France.

Tabard work has been exhibited in group shows including *Film und Foto* in Stuttgart in 1929; *Surréalisme* and *Modern European Photography* at the Julien Levy Gallery, New York, in 1932; *Paris—Berlin 1900–1933* at the Centre Georges Pompidou, Paris, in 1978; and *La Photographie Française 1925–1940* at Zabriskie Galleries in Paris and New York in 1978. He has been the subject of one-man shows at the Galerie de la Pléiade, Paris, in 1933; the Professional Photographers' Association of America, Chicago, in 1948; Marlborough Gallery, New York, in 1976; Sander Gallery, Washington, D.C., in 1977 and 1981; and at the Institute Française, Cologne, in 1979.

See also: FANTASY IN PHOTOGRAPHY; SURREALISM IN PHOTOGRAPHY.

Tachyscope

See: ZOETROPE.

Talbot, William Henry Fox

British; 1800–1877

William Henry Fox Talbot, scholar, scientist, and photographic pioneer, was the discoverer of the negative-positive process of photography in the late 1830s. He was also the author and publisher of the first book to use photographs as illustrations.

Talbot's earliest experiments led to "photogenic drawings" made by placing objects on paper sensitized with silver chloride and exposing them to the light. By 1841 Talbot had invented and patented the calotype process. He was

among the few early practitioners who foresaw the wide range of uses of photography.

Talbot's distinguished career in science began when he was elected to the Royal Astronomical Society while a student of classics and mathematics at Trinity College in Cambridge, where he received his M.A. degree in 1825. In 1832 he became a Fellow of the Royal Society, a group of British scientists, on the basis of a series of mathematical papers. He served in Parliament in 1833–1834.

Unsatisfied with the results he obtained sketching with a camera lucida while on a trip through Italy in 1833, Talbot was inspired to attempt to permanently fix an image on paper. He soon began his serious photographic experiments which resulted in photogenic drawings. He made his first paper negative image in 1835. Talbot's other scientific pursuits left him little time for photographic work. It was not until four years after his successful experiments with negatives, immediately upon the announcement of Daguerre's invention, that Talbot exhibited his photographs and lectured on his experiments at the Royal Society. He considerably improved his original process in 1840 to create the camera obscura process he patented the next year under the name *calotype*. Talbot's discoveries may be said to have surpassed Daguerre's because the negative-positive process permitted the duplication of prints from a single negative, while daguerreotypes were unique direct-positive images on metal plates.

In 1843 Talbot started the first printing house for the mass-production of photographic prints. The following year he published *The Pencil of Nature*, the first photographically illustrated book, which included Talbot's images of sculpture and drawing and views of Oxford and Paris. He continued to develop new photographic techniques for the next several years and to wage court battles against all photographic innovations, claiming they infringed on his various patents. In the final landmark suit in 1854, the jury concluded that Talbot was the true inventor of the negative-positive process, but that subsequent inventions, especially the wet-collodion process, were not covered by the calotype patent. The effect was to free photography in England from a virtual stranglehold.

Talbot's last years were devoted to various scientific studies and the decipherment of Assyrian cuneiform inscriptions. He was awarded the Grand Medal of Honor by an international jury at the Universal Exposition of Paris in 1855. He received an honorary degree from the University of Edinburgh in 1864 and became an Honorary Member of the Photographic Society of London in 1874. He died at his home, Lacock Abbey, in 1877 while writing a history of his photographic inventions.

See also: CALOTYPE; CAMERA LUCIDA; CAMERA OBSCURA; DAGUERRE, L. J. M.; HENNEMAN, NIKOLAAS; HERSCHEL, SIR JOHN; HISTORY OF PHOTOGRAPHY; "PENCIL OF NATURE, THE"; PHOTOGENIC DRAWING; SALT-PAPER PROCESS.

Talbotype

When, in 1841, William Henry Fox Talbot patented his calotype process—the first negative-positive process in photography—it became known as the Talbotype. The name was coined on the model of "daguerreotype," for Talbot's friends urged him that an Englishman could without conceit commemorate his own name in his own invention at least as justifiably as any Frenchman.

See also: CALOTYPE; DAGUERRE, L. J. M.; DAGUERREOTYPE; TALBOT, W. H. F.

Tanks

The containers (tanks) used to hold films and chemicals during processing are of two basic types: cylindrical "daylight" tanks used for processing roll film and deep rectangular tanks used for sheet films.

Daylight tanks are so named because they have lighttight lids which enable them to be used with room lights on. They make film processing much easier, because the only time complete darkness is required is when the film is being loaded into the tank. With daylight tanks a darkroom is not necessary; the required loading operation can be done with a changing bag, if necessary. Daylight tanks are made of plastic or stainless steel, and most have spiral reels onto which the film is wound. They are made in various sizes to accomodate anywhere from two to ten reels.

With stainless steel tanks and reels the film is attached to a clip on the reel core and wound outward into the grooves. This is a process that requires a degree of practice to master, since it must be performed in total darkness. Some manufacturers provide loading devices which facilitate the procedure. All-plastic tanks are generally "self-loading," which means that once the end of the film has been inserted at the outer rim, it is drawn into the grooves as the reel flanges are rotated.

Most stainless steel and many plastic tanks have leakproof lids. These permit inverting the tanks for agitation. Some plastic tanks have a center rod which is turned to provide agitation.

Rectangular or "deep," tanks come in various sizes to accept sheet film holders, and roll film reels on spindles or in an open-frame basket. They are made of stainless steel, plastic, or hard rubber, and have lids that either float on top of the chemicals or fit over the top of the tank. Since floating lids rest directly on the chemical solutions, they help prevent oxidation between developing sessions.

Stainless steel tanks are the easiest to clean, and tanks should be kept scrupulously clean when not in use. Because stainless steel is an excellent conductor of heat, such tanks are the best choice when a water bath is used for temperature control.

See also: DRUM AND TUBE PROCESSING.

Tanning Developer

In photography, tanning is the action of hardening the gelatin in a relatively soluble emulsion to make it insoluble. A tanning developer produces this action in the course of developing a silver halide image; the degree of tanning is directly proportional to the amount of silver developed in each area. In most cases, the silver image is bleached and fixed out, and the unhardened gelatin dissolved away, leaving a relief image. Matrix films used in the dye-transfer process, and films for certain other transfer and relief processes allow either enlarging or contact exposures: they require tanning development of their silver halide emulsions. Nonsilver bichromated emulsions are tanned by the action of exposure alone, but are not sensitive enough for enlarging. Certain bleaches and other solutions can also produce a tanning action.

See also: BICHROMATE PROCESSES; DYE TRANSFER PROCESS; GELATIN; RELIEF IMAGES; TRANSFER PROCESSES.

Teaching Photography

See: EDUCATION, PHOTOGRAPHIC.

Technical Camera

A technical camera is a versatile, folding flat-bed camera usually accepting sheet film up to 4″ × 5″ and 2¼″ wide roll film. It is intended primarily for use outside the studio for applications such as industrial, scientific, landscape, and architectural photography. The design derives from the press camera and includes some view-camera features. Contemporary models frequently have interchangeable backs to allow changing film formats, and a flat bed which provides triple bellows extension for images up to twice life size. Viewing may be either through a ground glass at the rear of the body or through a rangefinder located on top. Technical cameras differ from studio view cameras in having more limited movements, particularly at the film plane. They are of a size and design that allows them to be hand-held easily as well as used on a tripod.

See also: CAMERA; PRESS CAMERA.

Technicolor

Originally a two-color motion-picture process introduced in 1915, Technicolor achieved dominance in the 1930s when it became a three-color subtractive process with prints made by imbibition, the basis of the dye-transfer procedure. The first film in the new process was Walt Disney's *Flowers and Trees*, produced in 1932. For some 20 years, a bulky camera was used to accommodate beam splitters and filters that made simultaneous separation negatives directly on a bipack (two-emulsion) film and a monopack film.

In 1953 the system changed to what it essentially remains today, using conventional cameras and integral tripack color negative film from which separation negatives are made in a subsequent step. For printing, reliefs are made on matrix films from the separation negatives. These are individually dyed cyan, magenta, and yellow and placed in contact with the receiving (print film) emulsion to transfer the color. The print film emulsion also carries a moderate density silver image to add definition and richness, especially in shadow details and blacks. The crux of the process is the need to repeat precise registration three times for each frame (the average-length film has more than 130,000 frames), because any deviation is magnified at least 100 times upon projection.

See also: DYE-TRANSFER PROCESS; MOTION PICTURES; SEPARATION NEGATIVES; SUBTRACTIVE COLOR SYNTHESIS.

Telephotography

Telephotography involves the use of lenses with a focal length about 1½ times or more longer than the diagonal of the film format for which they are designed. Variously called telephoto, long-focus, and simply "long," such lenses are used extensively for wildlife photography, portraiture, surveillance, sports photography, and many other applications.

The difference between long-focus and telephoto lenses is one of optical construction; they produce the same visual effects. The physical differences are of more practical importance. Telephoto lenses are generally more compact and lighter weight than long-focus lenses of equal focal length, which makes them easier to carry and use in almost all situations. The word telephoto is commonly used, somewhat inaccurately, to mean either kind of lens.

Long-focal-length lenses offer greater-than-normal subject magnification and a narrower-than-normal angle of view. The "tele-power" of a lens indicates the increase in magnification it produces as compared to the image produced by a normal-focal-length lens at the same subject distance. It is indicated by the ratio between the two focal lengths. Thus, in 35mm photography a 4-in. (100mm) lens is twice as long as the normal 2-in. (50mm) lens and produces twice as much magnification (its tele-power is 2×). Similarly, a 6-in. (150mm) lens tele-power is 3×. The narrower angle of view cannot be calculated from the focal-length ratio, but the width or height of the field covered is inversely proportional. That is, a 2× long lens covers half the field of a normal lens, and a 3× lens covers one third of the field. Of course, the area covered is projected to fill the entire frame of the format in each case.

Moderate telephoto lenses, those up to about 2×, are extremely useful for portraiture and journalistic work. They are relatively light and portable, allow the photographer to maintain a comfortable working distance from the subject, and generally allow the camera to be hand held. They produce a normal-looking perspective without the distortion of subject proportions that often results from using a shorter lens close enough to get the same image size. The shallower depth of field they produce at a given *f*-stop, compared to shorter lenses, helps make the subject stand out from a confusing or unimportant background.

Long and extra-long telephoto lenses, from about 2.5× to 10×, produce signficantly less depth of field and noticeably flattened perspective as the focal length increases. Lenses of about 4× are used extensively in travel, sports photography, and some kinds of illustrative photography, such as fashion, to obtain large images of subjects well separated from their surroundings. Long and extra-long lenses require the use of a tripod or other support in most cases, and have a smaller maximum aperture than shorter-focal-length lenses. They require extreme care in focusing because of the shallow depth of field, and even the slightest vibration has serious effects because of the high degree of magnification. In the moderate-focal-length range, telephoto zoom lenses are becoming

widely used for medium- and small-format photography. In very long focal lengths, mirror-design lenses often are used with these formats.
See also: DISTORTION; LENSES; MIRROR LENS; PERSPECTIVE; WIDE-ANGLE PHOTOGRAPHY; ZOOM LENS.

Telephoto Lens

A lens in which the front element groups have a positive (converging) power and the rear element groups a negative (diverging) power, so as to achieve a focal length significantly longer than the back focus is called a telephoto lens.
See: BACK FOCUS; LENSES; OPTICS.

Telescope

A telescope is an optical instrument used to obtain magnified images of subjects at extreme distances; the images may be viewed directly, or recorded photographically. The principal light-gathering and image-forming component of a telescope is called the objective. In a *refracting* telescope the objective is a lens element or element group; in a *reflecting* telescope it is a concave, front-surface mirror. The image from the objective passes to an eyepiece lens group. The magnifying power of a telescope is determined by the ratio:

$$\frac{\text{Objective}}{\text{focal length}} \div \frac{\text{Eyepiece}}{\text{focal length}}$$

Changing to a shorter focal-length eyepiece produces greater power; many telescopes permit this. The simplest statement of telescope specifications is magnification and objective diameter—e.g., 30 × 60 specifies a telescope that mangnifies a subject in the field of view 30 times and has an objective 60mm in diameter. More comprehensive specifications give objective focal length and diameter, aperture, and the power produced by various eyepieces. The aperture or basic *f*-value—equivalent to the speed of a lens—is:

$$\frac{\text{Objective}}{\text{focal length}} \div \frac{\text{Objective}}{\text{diameter}}$$

A reflecting telescope generally has a wider aperture, and therefore produces a brighter image than a refracting telescope of the same power because it is much easier and less expensive to produce large-diameter, highly corrected (for aberrations) mirrors than lenses. Reflecting telescopes of *f*/1 and even wider apertures have been produced. A major limitation on the size of a refracting objective lens is the plastic nature of

glass. The element must be supported only by the edges in order not to interfere with the image, but the weight of a large-diameter element can cause it to sag in the center, changing its optical characteristics. In addition, a large mass of glass contracts and expands to a significant degree with temperature changes.

Refracting (Galilean) telescopes are primarily used for terrestrial observation. With reasonable diameters they are relatively compact, have internal focusing for subjects at various distances, and provide an erect (right side up) image. Some use internal prisms to obtain long optical length within limited physical length—spotting scopes, monoculars, and binoculars are usually of this design. However, as refracting focal length (and thus basic magnification) increases, the field of view and the image brightness rapidly decrease. Beyond about 40× the usefulness of a refracting telescope is severely restricted by loss of brightness and by magnification of external factors such as vibration and the optical distortion of heat waves.

Reflecting telescopes can achieve wide fields of view and relatively great image brightness at almost any focal length. They are preferred for astronomical observation because of the large apertures possible, and because mirrors are essentially free of chromatic aberration: color fringing would make it very difficult to obtain precise measurements from the images of distant points of light. Because astronomical subjects are at such great distances, reflecting telescopes are designed with infinity focus and do not have internal focusing for closer distances. However, the eyepieces do focus for various viewing setups and for differences in observers' eyesight. Whether or not the image is erect depends upon system design; it is not a matter of importance in most astronomical work. In the basic (Newtonian) reflector telescope, the image formed by the concave objective mirror is directed by a small plane mirror in the center of the tube to an eyepiece at the side, near the aperture end. In more compact reflecting designs, the secondary mirror directs the image back through a hole in the center of the objective to an eyepiece directly behind the telescope. This provides easier viewing and camera-coupling in many situations; in addition, the folded optical path provides focal-length increase without additional physical length. The secondary mirror is either convex (Cassegrainian design) or—to provide an erect image—concave (Gregorian design). Improved versions of these instruments include glass lens

Telescopes

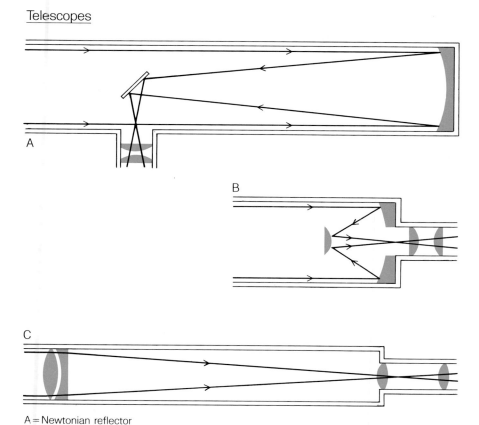

A = Newtonian reflector
B = Cassegrainian design
C = Galilean straight-tube refractor

plates at the tube opening that correct various aberrations without affecting magnification or aperture. The Cassegrainian catadioptric (lens-mirror) configuration is the basis of the very long focal-length mirror lenses used in photography today. A highly specialized catadioptric telescope is the Schmidt camera and its derivatives, in which the film may be located inside the telescope tube itself.

A camera can be combined with a telescope to record images in four ways.

1. *Eyepiece-plus-camera lens.* The camera lens is focused at infinity and is joined to the telescope eyepiece by an accessory coupling tube. This method produces the least image brightness and—because of the number of glass elements involved—probably the greatest number of aberrations.
2. *Eyepiece projection.* The camera lens is removed and the camera is mounted so the eyepiece image is focused directly on the film.
3. *Prime focus.* The eyepiece and camera lens are both removed, and the image from the objective is focused directly on the film. This method produces the brightest image with the fewest

aberrations, but eyepiece projection and negative-lens projection produce greater magnification.

4. *Negative-lens projection.* The eyepiece is replaced with a Barlow lens, a negative lens group that increases the effective focal length of the objective; the image is focused directly onto the film, without use of the camera lens.

Camera and telescope manufacturers supply accessories and adapters to make these combinations, and provide data for determining the changes in focal length, aperture, and magnification that each produces.
See also: CATADIOPTRIC AND CATOPTRIC LENSES; MIRROR; MIRROR LENSES; SCHMIDT CAMERA.

Television

The wireless transmission of moving or still pictures and accompanying sound by means of electromagnetic (radio) waves was first demonstrated in 1926 by J. L. Baird in England, and C. F. Jenkins in the United States. Their systems were severely limited in image brightness and resolving power because they relied on mechanical methods of scanning a picture to divide it into elements for trans-

mission. An electronic system patented in the U.S. in 1928 by V. K. Zworykin became the basis of all modern television. A small amount of scheduled telecasting was done on a local basis in the late 1930s in London, New York, and a few other major cities. Mass production of television receivers, establishment of large numbers of local stations, and the growth of networks began after World War II, in 1946. A system of color television that was compatible with existing black-and-white receivers was approved in the U.S. in 1953. The first intercontinental television transmission by means of a satellite microwave relay link was made in July 1962.

Image Transmission. The essence of present-day television is electron-beam scanning of the picture focused on the face of a cathode-ray image tube to develop signals that vary according to the brightness and color characteristics of the image. In a receiving set, these signals vary the strength of an electron beam that scans the face of a cathode-ray tube to create a matching image. Scanning proceeds in a series of lines traced left to right, from top to bottom of the picture; the scanned area is called a raster. From the right end of each line, the scanning beam retraces to the left side without generating a signal. In the U.S., the picture area is scanned in 525 lines, of which 480 are actually used for picture formation. Foreign systems use 405- or 625-line scanning patterns. High-resolution television systems now under development use scanning patterns of 1100 lines or more to achieve image quality approaching that of a 35mm color slide projected to the same picture size.

Scanning is divided into two fields that together form one frame, analogous to a motion-picture frame. The first field scans the odd-numbered lines, the second field the even-numbered lines. This interlaced pattern provides a constant image brightness and is carried out at a rate that allows the persistence of vision to blend successive frames into smoothly continuous motion. In the U.S., the rate is 30 frames, comprising 60 fields, per second. This corresponds to the 60 Hz frequency of domestic a.c. power in order to help synchronize scanning in all cameras and all receivers concerned with the same transmission. In Europe, a 25-frame, 50-field scanning rate corresponds to the 50 Hz frequency of the power in most countries.

In a color television camera the lens image is focused through a beam-splitter system onto the faces of three image tubes individually fitted with a red, green, or blue filter. Of various types of camera tubes, the image orthicon and the vidicon have been most widely used. The various image brightnesses on the photosensitive tube face cause proportional changes in the electron emission or the conductivity/resistance of an associated grid; these changes modify the output derived by the scanning electron beam. The scanning signals for the three tubes represent additive color coding of the image. They are processed with the sound signals from other equipment and various timing and control signals to form the composite signal that is transmitted. Broadcast transmission is limited to the line of sight distance—about 45 to 60 miles—between transmitting and receiving antennas because, unlike radio signals, energy at television frequencies does not follow the curvature of the earth but travels in straight lines. (Satellite broadcasting covers a much greater range, but the large receiving antenna needed is expensive for the individual viewer.) Each transmitter broadcasts on an assigned channel or band of frequencies 6000 KHz wide (voice radio channels are only about 5 KHz wide). In the very-high-frequency (VHF) range of the electromagnetic spectrum, from 54–216 MHz, there are 12 channels, numbered 2–13 (there is no broadcast channel 1). In the ultra-high-frequency (UHF) range, 470–890 MHz, there are 70 channels, numbered from 20 upward.

Nonbroadcast transmission is possible by cable connection to the origination point, a rapidly growing system in the U.S. The number of channels available by cable is essentially limited only by the number of selector positions built into the receiver. Video signals can also be recorded on magnetic tape or on disks for direct playback at the receiver.

The receiver (or video player) separates the timing component of the incoming signal and uses it to establish synchronization. The audio signal is processed and amplified for the speaker system. The video signal is separated into its three color components, which are used to vary three electron beams that scan the picture tube (kinescope) face in unison. The tube face is coated with a mosaic of red, green, and blue phosphor dots that glow with a brightness corresponding to the variations in their individual scanning beams. A shadow mask—an opaque plate with a pattern of minute holes—covers the mosaic and, by parallax with the positions of the electron guns, ensures that each beam goes only to the dot of its corresponding color at every point on the screen. The full-color image viewed on the other side of the tube is produced by additive color synthesis.

Production. Sports events and news and discussion programs are commonly telecast live, as they happen; almost all other presentations are prerecorded on videotape. However, the basic production procedures are the same. The action is viewed continuously from different viewpoints by two or more cameras; sound is picked up by an appropriate number of microphones. A small viewing screen in each camera shows the operator the picture obtained; earphones communicate the sound. An indicator light shows when the camera's picture is actually being used; at other times the operator can adjust the zoom lens, refocus, reposition the camera, and perform other adjustments in preparation for the next shot. The pictures from all cameras—and those from slide, film, videotape and disk equipment—are fed to a switching panel in a control room. There, all pictures are seen on separate monitors, and the one chosen for use is also seen on the output or line monitor. The switching panel permits cuts, dissolves, superimposures, inserts, and other transitions and combinations of pictures. A technical director operates the switching panel and coordinates technicians who monitor and adjust the electronic performance of each camera. Other technicians process the audio portion of the presentation. A director decides which picture and sound is to be put on the line—i.e., actually broadcast or recorded—at each moment and calls for the changes as necessary. Instructions to camera personnel, stage managers, projection operators, announcers, and others outside the control room are relayed by an earphone communication system.

Some recorded productions are made as if they were live broadcasts, with the line picture going to a single recorder. Others are created by recording the output of each camera on a separate tape and subsequently editing to select and assemble the desired elements. The process is similar to that use in motion pictures except that the tapes are not physically cut and spliced together. Instead, the selected portions are rerecorded in order on a single tape.

See also: ADDITIVE COLOR SYNTHESIS; BAIRD, JOHN LOGIE; BEAM SPLITTER; CUT; DISSOLVE; EDITING; INSERT; MAGNETIC IMAGE RECORDING; MOTION PICTURES; VIDEO IMAGING AND RECORDING; ZWORYKIN, VLADIMIR.

Television, Photographing

The image on a television set can be photographed in black-and-white or color using an ISO 200/24° or 400/27° film (faster or slower films can also be used, but proper exposure settings may be difficult to make with some cameras). For color pictures a daylight-type color film will give more pleasing results than a tungsten-type film. The television picture should be adjusted, and the photograph should be taken with the room lights turned off so that stray light will not degrade the image and so that the edges of the TV set around the picture will be black. The contrast of a black-and-white TV picture must be set a bit lower than for normal viewing to ensure that detail is visible in both the highlight and shadow areas. A color picture should be adjusted for the most pleasing visual quality.

Exposure is determined by a reflected-light meter reading of the image on the TV screen. Because the image is formed at the rate of 30 frames per second, a slow shutter speed must be used to record a picture of uniform brightness (too fast a speed will record a dark band across the image). A speed of 1/30 sec. or slower is suitable with a between-the-lens leaf shutter; for technical reasons a speed of 1/8 sec. or slower is required with a focal-plane shutter. Typical exposures with an ISO 400/27° film are 1/30 sec. at $f/4$ (leaf shutter) or 1/8 sec. at $f/8$ (focal-plane shutter). Speeds this slow require that the camera be mounted on a tripod or other firm support and that the picture be taken at a moment when there is no movement in the TV image; otherwise, the picture may be blurred. Television images have limited sharpness and resolving power, so pictures taken from the screen will not look as crisp as direct photographs of a subject. If color pictures look too green-blue, a CC40R (red) filter will improve results by enhancing the reds. The exposure meter reading should be taken through the filter.

See also: TELEVISION.

Temperature Control

Because development is a highly temperature-sensitive process, temperature control is a factor of major importance in photographic processing. A variation of 1°F (0.6°C) can produce noticeable changes in black-and-white film development, as can a variation of only 0.5°F (0.3°C) in color development. Some developers are effectively inoperative below 60°F (15.6°C); at elevated temperatures almost all developers produce fog and increased graininess in films, and have very short working lives. Other stages of processing—especially of color materials—are also temperature-sensitive, although to a lesser degree. Keeping all solutions and wash water within a few degrees of the same temperature is important in film processing to avoid possible reticulation of the gelatin emulsion.

Effective temperature control in the darkroom begins with at least one accurate thermometer for solutions and another to indicate the ambient temperature. In black-and-white processing it is often relatively easy to maintain a room temperature of 68–70°F (20–21°C) so that solutions can be used without special attention. However, that is not always possible when external conditions are particularly cold or hot, and it is impractical when color processes that operate in the 80–100°F range are used. In addition, ambient temperature control is not effective for quickly bringing newly mixed solutions, or large quantities of stored solutions, to operating temperature. Adding cold water or ice to a solution dilutes its chemical strength; heating a container directly is likely to change the chemical composition of the solution. Moderate quantities of solution can be brought to working temperature by placing a plastic or metal container filled with ice or hot water in the tray or tank and stirring the solution to help distribute the temperature effect. Large quantities of solution in tanks are more easily warmed with immersion heating elements, or by a surrounding hot or cold water bath, which in turn may be kept at temperature by a thermostatically controlled immersion heater. A high-temperature water jacket is the most effective means of keeping containers of color-processing solutions precisely at the required temperature. A jacket of running water direct from a mixing valve or sink faucet is both wasteful and expensive in terms of water and the energy used to heat the water; a self-contained recirculation arrangement is preferable. Commercial units are available, but it is also reasonably simple to construct one using a large tank or plastic tub, and a circulating pump and heating element of the type used for aquariums. Pumping the water into a small container where the heating element is located and pumping it back into the larger water-jacket tank is the most effective arrangement. When cooling rather than heating is required, it is possible to pump the water through a hose that is coiled through a container of cold water or ice. The solution containers in the water jacket should be immersed as far as possible in the tempered water; a retaining cover may be required to keep them from bobbing and floating. Metal containers transmit temperature changes more efficiently than glass or plastic containers.

See also: MIXING PHOTOGRAPHIC SOLUTIONS; RETICULATION; THERMOMETER.

Temperature Scales

There are a number of systems for measuring heat in evenly spaced degrees. The three scales commonly used in photography are the Fahrenheit, Celsius, and Kelvin; the first two appear on most thermometers. The common scale in the United States is the Fahrenheit, on which the freezing point of water is 32°, and the boiling point is 212°. The Celsius scale (sometimes called centigrade, from its 100-degree range) is used throughout most of the rest of the world. The freezing point of water is equal to 0° Celsius, the boiling point to 100°. To avoid mistakes, the initial of the scale in use is commonly written following the temperature figures; e.g., 68°F (20°C). Conversion from one scale to the other is accomplished by simple arithmetic. To convert from Celsius to Fahrenheit, multiply the degrees Celsius by $\frac{9}{5}$ and add 32 to the product. To convert from Fahrenheit to Celsius, subtract 32 from the Fahrenheit reading and multiply the remainder by $\frac{5}{9}$.

The Kelvin scale indicates absolute temperature, the standard in scientific work. Total lack of heat—the point at which all molecular activity ceases—is 0K or absolute zero, equivalent to −273.15°C. (The units of measurement are Kelvins, not degrees; the ° symbol is not used in Kelvin readings.) To convert from Celsius to Kelvin, add 273 to the Celsius reading; subtract 273 to convert from Kelvin to Celsius.

The color temperature of a continuous light source is the Kelvin temperature to which a black body would have to be heated to emit light of the same wavelength composition.

See also: BLACK BODY; COLOR TEMPERATURE; THERMOMETER.

Tent Lighting

Highly reflective polished and metallic objects often present photographic lighting problems. The mirrorlike surfaces of silver, coins, jewelry, chrome-plated products, and similar items reflect whatever they see. Lighting such objects with direct specular or diffused light creates glaring highlights and distracting reflections. Tent lighting prevents these unwanted effects by enveloping the object with a white, evenly illuminated environment. The object is fully illuminated without glare, and the reflective quality of its surface is preserved.

A tent is constructed of translucent material such as thin drawing paper or white or frosted plastic sheeting. Small objects such as rings, watches, and coins are placed in a cone-shaped tent. The camera lens looks down through the open top or through an opening cut in one side. Larger objects are placed in tents of appropriate size fashioned from wire frames covered with translucent material. An opening is cut for the camera lens. The tent is lighted from outside with broad, diffused light sources. Its sides transmit the light as a bright, even glow all around the object.

If an object does not have to be tented on all sides, a partial tent of more opaque white material can be constructed. Light directed into the tent through its various openings is bounced by the inner surfaces of the tent material onto the object. The lights must be positioned carefully so that they are not directly reflected by the object, and the object must be oriented so as not to reflect the camera or other things outside the tent.

In some cases tent lighting creates too many white reflections or gives the subject a uniform, featureless appearance. This can be corrected by strips of black paper placed inside the tent so that their reflections define the shape and contours of the object.

See also: GLARE AND REFLECTIONS; LIGHTING; PRODUCT PHOTOGRAPHY.

Tessar Lens

The Tessar lens, designed in 1902 by Paul Rudolph and E. Wandersleb for Zeiss, introduced the use of a cemented doublet as the rear component of a triple anastigmat. First made with an aperture of $f/5.5$ it was far better corrected than any lens of comparable speed. It became the fundamental design for a great number of variations, permitting wide fields at up to $f/3.5$, and normal fields to about $f/2.8$. It remains the most widely used design for $f/3.5$–4.5 lenses for cameras from 35mm to the largest formats.

See also: ANASTIGMAT; LENSES; RUDOLPH, PAUL.

Testing Materials and Solutions

User-testing of photographic materials and solutions serves to establish or confirm performance characteristics, and to determine whether they are in usable condition. Most testing of these factors is on a comparative basis to provide objective answers to questions such as: How does this compare to the behavior of known fresh material, or to established (or assumed) normal procedure? The essence of testing is to make controlled, repeatable changes from the norm and to keep records of what is done so that a particular effect can accurately be related to its cause. The degree of variation must be meaningful. Negative films show significant (i.e., printable) image differences with full *f*-stop exposure changes, reversal (slide) films with half-stop changes. Exposure and filtration tests are comparable only if the subject and lighting, and the processing, are identical for all images. Various films can be compared meaningfully only after exposure tests have established their individual effective speeds; then each can be accurately exposed to the same range of sample subjects. The performance characteristics of solutions (e.g., developers, bleaches, toners) or procedures are evaluated by treating one image in normal fashion, and identical images in variant ways.

The usability of materials is tested by comparison with fresh materials, e.g., to determine how much contrast is lost or fog is produced—if any—by outdated film or paper. Used or old solutions can be compared with the performance of freshly mixed solutions, or they can be checked with various test liquids. Most testing methods produce a precipitate or a color change in the sample to indicate exhaustion beyond the point of usability. Unfortunately, there is no way to tell how much material passed through an exhausted stop bath, fixer, or clearing bath before it was discovered, although reasonably frequent testing can keep the doubt to a minimum. Solutions that incorporate indicator chemicals are self-testing because they reveal their loss of effectiveness as soon as it occurs.

The most important tests are for proper fixing and adequate washing because, more than any other factors, they have a direct effect on image permanency. Many books on photographic processing (*see* Appendix) include procedures and formulas for testing materials and solutions.
See also: INDICATOR CHEMICAL; SAFELIGHT.

Test Strip

A test strip is a sample exposure series used to determine exposure in enlarging or contact printing. In black-and-white printing the common procedure is to use less than a full sheet of paper and to position it in the most important area of the image. When exposure is begun, the paper is progressively covered with an opaque card in steps of, say, 5, 10, 15, 20, and 25 seconds cumulative exposure. The test strip must be taped or otherwise held in place so it will not move as the covering card is shifted. When an image is composed of important areas with significant differences in brightness, it is often easier to use a series of narrow strips of paper. Each strip is laid in the same position so as to cross several of the important areas, and each is given a different exposure. This procedure takes longer, but potentially yields more information. The *f*-stop and exposure time should be pencilled on the back of each strip immediately after it is exposed. When processed, test strips show the effects of the various exposures. In the multiple-strip procedure the most-exposed strips may give some indication of what various degrees of burning-in might produce in the brightest image area, and the least-exposed strips may show what dodging can do in the darkest areas.

In color printing it is common to use the multiple-strip method, but to vary exposure by changing the enlarging lens *f*-stop setting rather than the exposure time. This permits using the recommended optimum exposure time for the paper in order to avoid possible color shifts from reciprocity effects.
See also: PRINTING, BLACK-AND-WHITE; PRINTING, COLOR; RECIPROCITY.

Texture

Texture consists of the small surface variations that are a distinctive physical characteristic of a particular substance or material. An optical sense of texture in a photographic image may be recorded from the subject or added as a special effect. A physical texture is achieved by printing on paper or cloth with a distinctive surface, or by treating the surface of the print after the image has been produced.

The texture of a material is revealed most clearly by a light that skims or rakes across the surface at a low angle. Direct specific light (rather than diffused light) throws the surface variations into visual relief so the true texture can be photographed. An illusion of texture can be created by printing the image through a patterned screen, either a contact screen that is placed directly on the paper during exposure, or an enlarging screen that is sandwiched with the negative being printed. Such screens are available commercially in a wide variety of textures (e.g., burlap, stone, etched lines, wood grain, linen), or they can made by photographing textured surfaces on high-contrast black-and-white film.

Intentional reticulation of a negative will produce a visible texturelike pattern when the image is printed. A more subtle effect is achieved by using photographic grain as a texture pattern. A grain screen can be obtained by overexposing a very fast black-and-white film to a neutral gray or other plain surface and developing it in a high-energy high-contrast developer. This can be used as a sandwich, or it can be enlarged onto high-contrast film to obtain a contact screen. The integral grain pattern of the image itself can be used by processing the film for maximum graininess and then greatly enlarging the picture.

Physical texture is obtained most easily by printing on a paper with a silk, tweed, linen, or other emulsion surface. There are also photo-sensitized linen and canvas which impart their own texture to an image, and liquid emulsions that can be painted on any textured material. Print surfaces can be textured after processing with pressure rollers that have embossed patterns, or by spraying the print with any of a variety of commercial lacquers which can be textured while soft or which dry and crack in a manner similar to varnish on an antique painting. The "varnish" effect sometimes is used with an image printed on photo canvas or linen to heighten the impression that the picture is a painting rather than a photograph.
See also: RETICULATION; SPECIAL EFFECTS.

Theatrical and Dance Photography

Theatrical and dance photographs have in common the task of communicating a sense of specific performance, whether they were taken in the theater or in the studio, and whether they include the ensemble or concentrate on one or two individuals. (Nonperformance photographs that deal with the personalities of individual performers are efforts in portraiture or glamour photography, and are discussed in those entries.) While the conditions under which such photographs are taken call for similar equipment and techniques, communicative aims and problems differ according to the art being recorded and the purposes to which the photographs will be put. Pictures for direct publicity such as lobby display generally must show what the audience can expect to see inside; thus, they are sharp and clearly detailed as to faces, sets, costumes, and moments that actually occur during the performance. Pictures for more general publicity such as newspaper ads and posters may be far less specific and be designed to quickly convey an idea of the overall character of a presentation—e.g., comedy, tragedy, classical, popular, avant-garde. Pictures

Sports Photography. Tony Tomsic, "Bill Johnson, Olympic Skiing Champion, Sarajevo" (1984). Tony Tomsic/ SPORTS ILLUSTRATED.

Still-Life Photography. Leslie Gill, "New York Tribune" (1949). Collection of Frances McLaughlin-Gill. © 1983.

Still-Life Photography. Ralph Chandler, "Tomatoes and Basil" (1980). © Ralph Chandler.

Struss, Karl. "Boardwalk, Long Island" (1910); autochrome. Collection, Stephen White Gallery, Los Angeles.

Studio Photography. Michel Tcherevkoff,
"Keds Tennis" (n.d.). © 1981 Michel
Tcherevkoff, Photography; Sarah Oliphant,
Backgrounds.

Subjective Photography. Deborah Turbeville,
"Loretta de Lorenzo," Paris (1978). © Deborah Turbeville, Paris.

Subtractive Color Synthesis

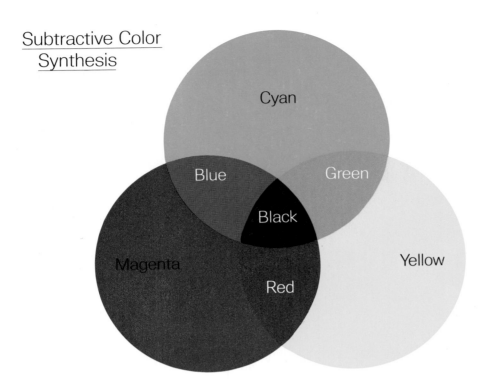

Cyan

Blue   Green

Black

Magenta

Yellow

Red

Subtractive Color Synthesis. Depending on the nature of the cyan, yellow, magenta materials, the intersections represent equal-strength overlapping of filters or transparent dyes, equal mixes of opaque dyes or pigments, or equal interlacings of halftone dots. The illuminant is white light in all cases.

Sun Photography. Cheryl Rossum, "Corrida, Nîmes" (1972). © Cheryl Rossum

Sun Photography. Wyatt Kash, "Arctic Midnight" (1976). © Wyatt Kash.

Theatrical and Dance Photography. George Hoyningen-Huene, "Josephine Baker" (ca. 1930). Courtesy Horst P. Horst.

taken for the photographer's own purposes (e.g., exhibition; a book) rather than those of the performers may be highly interpretative and deal with a subjective response rather than an objective representation of the performance.

Early development. Since the mid-19th c., performers of all kinds have been both willing and favored subjects for portrait photographers. Daguerreotypes of Jenny Lind by Mathew Brady (1850) and Lola Montez by Southworth and Hawes (1851), and albumen prints of Sarah Bernhardt by Nadar (ca. 1860)—and many images of lesser known performers by other photographers—were the forerunners of a great tide of such pictures that reached especially notable high points in the work of Nickolas Murray and Edward Steichen for *Vanity Fair* in the 1920s, and the work of Richard Avedon since the 1950s. Few photographers have matched Avedon's ability to produce pictures that epitomize a performer's public image as well as other pictures that reveal the private individual with great, even shocking, clarity (e.g., his pictures of Marilyn Monroe).

Today's ubiquitous 5″ × 7″ or 8″ × 10″ glossy print—distributed by every established and would-be performer to agents, news media, and fans in great numbers—originated in the carte-de-visite era of the 1860s and 1870s. Popular performers ordered these inexpensive small images in quantity, usually to be sold in the theater lobby. Photographers often gave free sittings and prints to well-known personalities in return for the right to sell their pictures from the studio. Actors and operatic performers were usually photographed in costume and makeup for their current or most famous roles, while variety performers included their juggling clubs, unicycles, or other props, and dancers were shown in appropriately graceful or energetic poses. In every major American and European city, certain studios became dominant in this area; in New York the leading studios were those of Napoleon Sarony, J. M. Mora, and B. J. Falk, each of which photographed many thousands of performers in a period extending past the turn of the century. The carte-de-visite gave way to the larger cabinet-size picture, which in turn gave way to enlarged images on gelatin emulsion papers in the 20th c. The professional and public demand for such pictures grew steadily, finally to be serviced largely by mass-production studios turning out a standardized image based on Hollywood glamour techniques of the 1930s.

On-stage pictures apparently originated about the turn of the century. They originally were made to add interest to portraits of stars as well as to call attention to specific productions. At first only operas, classic plays, and productions with a major star were photographed with any frequency, usually by a prestige studio such as that of Joseph Byron or a specialist such as the White studios in New York. In the 1920s, introduction of the photographically illustrated program created a need for performance photographs (taken during dress rehearsals or photo calls) as well as cast portraits for almost every production. In the same decade, the work of scenic and lighting designers began to be recognized as a creative contribution, and the practice of photographing the sets and lighting effects of major productions was initiated. Today, it is common practice to document all aspects of a production in photographs.

These developments were paralleled in the motion picture industry by still photographers who had three functions: to get apparent in-production action pictures for publicity purposes (frame enlargements from the movie itself had limited quality); to make accurate production records so that details could be matched when reshooting or other re-creations were necessary; and to provide publicity portraits and (usually fictional) "at home" human interest pictures of the stars. No one photographer performed all those functions for a given production.

Aside from their role as a production medium, motion pictures (and now video recording) have been used to document the actual dynamics of a performance, something beyond the capabilities of still photography. Especially since the addition of sound (after 1928) and full color (after the mid-1930s) to motion pictures, a complete record of a production has been possible. This is of extreme importance in the case of dance (for which various systems of written notation have been devised), mime, circus performance, and other presentations for which a script either is not prepared or cannot serve as any meaningful description of what was done.

Characteristics and practice. There is an even more fundamental difference between theatrical and dance photography. A theatrical presentation such as a play creates its effects primarily through the power of words and the psychological projection of emotion. The photographic task is to find the tableau (or individual pose) and facial expressions that can stand as a visual equivalent or summation of the dramatic point at that moment (e.g., denunciation; triumph; exaltation). Dance is the direct physical expression of emotion; it is intended to be experienced visually by the audience and therefore can be photographed directly, not in terms of equivalent images. The dance photographer's primary problems are to develop such a feeling for music and movement that he or she can release the shutter precisely at on expressive moment, and can decide whether to record it as a sharply frozen peak of movement, or as an expressive blur that conveys the sense of movement in space and time. Other kinds of performances pose similar problems between these two expressive extremes. Musicians and singers, for example, must be shown in essentially equivalent moments because their art is not in itself visual; jugglers or acrobats can, like dancers, be recorded directly at key physical moments of performance.

Except for journalistic coverage of an event, very little theatrical or dance photography is done during an actual performance. The photographer's moving about and the use of flash is too disturbing to the performers and the audience; remaining in an unobtrusive spot and working with available light is too restrictive for the photographer to obtain the best results. Most successful photographs are taken at special "photo calls" in the theatre or in the rehearsal or photographic studio, at which those parts of the performance selected for photographing are repeated as necessary until the desired results are obtained. When the setting must be included—especially in group shots and large-area views—the actual performance lighting

in the theater is used; it is not practical or necessary for the photographer to bring equipment to light the stage. In close shots, and in studio work the photographer is much more likely to use electronic flash—often direct flash for dramatic theatrical effects, and bounced (reflected) light to cover a large area with a minimum of shadow problems for dance action.

A medium- or large-format camera is used for good image quality, the choice depending on how mobile the photographer must be and on personal preference. Medium-speed films are common for theatrical pictures because it is easy to have the actors pose briefly at the crucial moment; this allows using apertures that provide good depth of field even with existing lighting. Fast films are common for photographing dance action by existing light because they permit the use of fast shutter speeds; because of their superior grain and contrast characteristics, medium-speed films are preferred when electronic flash is used to freeze movement. When peak moments are photographed, surprisingly slow shutter speeds (e.g., 1/60, 1/30 sec.) often may be used to capture dance. As in much sports action, each peak of extension, carry, or turn results in a momentary stop in the dancer's movement; proper timing releases the shutter at that instant. Normal focal-length lenses are used to maintain a normal perspective in most theatrical photographs; wide-angle lenses are common for dance photography to obtain increased depth of field and a visual emphasis of space, however very close foreground figures are avoided to prevent distortion. Long focal-length lenses are used primarily for special emphasis or detail shots, or to reach out from offstage positions during actual performances. The shallow depth of field of long lenses is seldom an advantage in this kind of work.

Dance photographs with expressively blurred movement are taken either with a slow shutter speed, which blurs the dancer's form, or by panning the camera with the action, which blurs the background; the former technique is the most common.

Among the most successful theatrical and dance photographers in the United State in the past several decades are Barbara Morgan (studies of Martha Graham in the 1940s and 1950s), Martha Swope, Herbert Migdoll, Alexey Brodovitch, and Jack Mitchell.

See also: ACTION PHOTOGRAPHY; GLAMOUR PHOTOGRAPHY; PORTRAITURE.

Color photograph: p. C-60.

Thermography

The term thermography originally referred to certain direct-heat imaging methods used in the printing industries and the duplication of documents. Its contemporary meaning most often refers to the varied state-of-the-art systems which sense nonvisible infrared radiation and/or heat, and use electronic image conversion to produce a visible image (indirect heat imaging). Such images can be photographed conveniently with conventional camera and film systems to give sensitive, noncontact (often remote) heat readings for science, industry, and medicine.

Scanning thermographs, easily produced on-site or in the studio by small portable units, have found many applications. In a typical unit, infrared radiation—which the subject emits in proportion to its temperature—passes through an infrared-transmitting lens and falls on a motor-driven scanning mirror. The varying intensities of infrared radiation are reflected onto a pyroelectric detector. Other electronic components use the detector output to modulate a light source which is directed by a beam splitter to a second mirror that scans the focused beam across the recording photographic material. Portable industrial thermography units, designed for specific ranges, check temperatures from $-40°$ to $5450°F$ ($-40°$ to $3010°C$) in monitoring production procedures. In another application, a scanner mounted in a special van recorded the thermograms of all 2,460 homes and businesses in a town as part of a federally assisted energy conservation project. The results of this pioneering effort of 1979 were photos that showed how much heat loss each building had, and just where the loss occurred. Similar surveys have been conducted with airborne equipment to determine relative heat loss through roofs, skylights, and chimneys.

The recent use of thermography in medicine has included many noteworthy applications. By sensing temperature variations in particular parts of the body, it is capable of providing valuable diagnostic information. The thermographs are displayed on a color TV screen with specific pseudo-colors to indicate particular temperature ranges; the display includes a calibrated reference scale complete with digital readout indications. In dermatology, for example, thermography can determine the depth and scope of severe burns, thereby preventing delays in treatment. In carcinoma of the breast, it is valuable in the early identification of high-risk patients, and in monitoring developments after surgery. In cerebrovascular disease, it can show the location of carotid obstruction and allows follow-up monitoring of post-surgical stroke patients without the use of invasive dye injections, radiation, or anesthesia. In addition to medicine, applications for thermography continue to grow in many areas.

See also: HEAT RECORDING; INFRARED PHOTOGRAPHY; REFLEX COPYING; XEROGRAPHY.

Thermometer

Temperature-indicating instruments for photographic use require a range of about 40–140°F (10-60°C) for maximum usefulness in mixing solutions and controlling processes in both color and black-and-white. An accuracy of ± 1°F (0.6°C) is sufficient for black-and-white work, ± 0.5°F (0.3°C) for color work. The most common type of thermometer is a glass tube filled with mercury or colored alcohol; a mercury-filled thermometer is the more accurate. Precision increases with the length of the tube because degree or fractional-degree markings can be more clearly separated. A thermometer with markings engraved directly on the tube is preferable to one with markings on an attached card or plate, which can slip out of alignment. A dial-type thermometer provides greater readibility than a glass tube instrument—an important factor under safelight conditions. It consists of a bimetallic coil attached to a metal sensing stem; expansion and contraction of the coil move a needle across a scale. Maximum visibility is provided by an electronic thermometer that displays the temperature digitally on a panel of light-emitting diodes or liquid crystals. However, it requires shelf space for the display unit and is limited by the length of the cord connected to the thermoelectric probe that is inserted into the solution.

It is convenient to have several thermometers in a darkroom. Only one need be of great precision and accuracy; the others can be calibrated to it by means of comparative readings in a common solution and their deviations marked. Inexpensive thermometers tend to lose accuracy in time, and so should be recalibrated periodically. The persistence of the Fahrenheit scale in the U.S., and the wide availability of chemicals and materials from the rest of the world, where the Celsius scale is used, make it convenient to have thermometers marked with both scales.

See also: TEMPERATURE CONTROL; TEMPERATURE SCALES.

Thérond, Roger

French; 1924–

Roger Thérond has been one of the world's most influential photographic editors, primarily associated with *Paris Match,* for 30 years.

Thérond was born in Sète (Hérault), France. He attended the Còllege de Sète, and is a graduate of the Faculty of Letters, Montpellier. He worked as a reporter from 1945 to 1950 for such publications as *L'Ecran Français* and *Samedi Soir.* In 1950 he became Editor-in-Chief of *Paris Match,* and was its Editorial Director from 1962 to 1968. Since 1968 he has been associated with Publications Fillipachi in a variety of roles. In addition to his work for *Paris Match,* Thérond has been an associate or advisory editor for many other publications including *Photo, Ski Magazine, Son Magazine,* and *L'Express.* Thérond has been General Director and Editor-in-Chief of *Paris Match* since 1976.

35mm Photography

Introduced between 1910 and 1925 were more than a dozen cameras that took still pictures on sprocketed 35mm film of the type that had been invented for motion-picture use just before the turn of the century. Most of these cameras took pictures the same size as the standard motion-picture format (18 × 24mm); their film capacities ranged from 25 to 400 exposures. None was particularly successful for a variety of reasons. Films were extremely slow by today's standards, and they showed very noticeable graininess in prints enlarged only to about 6″ × 9″ (15 × 23cm). Electric-light enlargers for home use were relatively crude devices, more homes had gas illumination than electricity, and commercial processing and printing facilities were equipped for larger roll and sheet film formats. In addition, tourism ceased during World War I, and that eliminated the major need for a small, lightweight, multiple-exposure camera.

The modern era of 35mm photography began in 1925 with the introduction of the Leica camera, which was designed by Oskar Barnack and manufactured in Germany by Ernst Leitz Optical Works. In the next few years Leicas sold in the thousands and established the standards of the medium: precision manufacture, interchangeable lenses, a coupled range/viewfinder, an ever-growing range of accessories that made the camera body the center of an entire photographic system, and the standard frame size of 24 × 36mm. The Kodak Retina camera of 1936 introduced the folding "pocket"

design to the 35mm format; it was copied by a number of other manufacturers, but survived only until the early 1950s. The single-lens reflex design that is now the world-wide standard in 35mm photography was also introduced in 1936 in the Kine Exakta (a still camera; "kine" alluded to the origins of the film size).

Until the 1950s, 35mm photography was referred to as "miniature" or "minifilm" photography, because it was the smallest standard format. Sheet film sizes of 2¼″ × 3¼″ and larger were considered "professional" formats; roll films were for amateur use. These were gross generalizations. In fact, 35mm cameras—primarily Leicas and Contaxes—were used professionally in the 1930s by photojournalists such as Peter Stackpole and a few others on the staff of *Life* magazine, Henri Cartier-Bresson, André Kertész, one or two of the Farm Security Administration photographers, and a number of others. The format became firmly established during World War II with the work of Robert Capa, W. Eugene Smith, David Douglas Duncan, and a great many lesser-known combat photographers and photojournalists.

The current widespread popularity of 35mm photography began in the 1950s with the Nikon and Pentax cameras, the first in a continuing series of high-quality and highly sophisticated cameras designed and manufactured in Japan. Although more pictures may be taken annually with cartridge, disk, and instant snapshot cameras, nothing rivals the widespread use of the 35mm format by both amateur and professional photographers. Efforts to improve the performance of the format have led to new optical glass formulas and computer-generated lens designs, automatic exposure control, automatic focusing, dedicated and automatic flash units, and films with speed and grain characteristics believed unattainable only a generation ago. No photographic format has found so many applications, from recording the most demanding scientific images to masterpieces of human communication in social documentary and artistic photographs. No other format can make such a valid claim to being the truly universal mode of photography.

See also: BARNACK, OSKAR; CAMERA; LEICA; SLR/SINGLE-LENS REFLEX CAMERA.

Thompson (Thomson); John

Scottish; 1837–1921

John Thompson was a significant figure in the early social documentary photography of London and the Far East who

Thomson, John. "Street groups, Kiu-Kiang" (ca. 1874); collotype. Collection, Museum of Modern Art, New York.

made portraits, landscapes, and architectural and travel views, attempting to present a frank and accurate description of social worlds few people had encountered. His best photographs are both beautifully composed and rich in social detail. Of his extensive series of images of Chinese life he wrote: "...the faithfulness of such pictures affords the nearest approach that can be made towards placing the reader actually before the scene which is represented."

Thompson was born in Edinburgh, Scotland. He studied chemistry at the University of Edinburgh in the late 1850s and began photographing in the early 1860s. In 1862 he traveled and photographed in Ceylon. Returning to Scotland, he made a series of architectural views before traveling in the Far East between 1865 and the early 1870s. During these years, five of which he spent in China, Thompson published several books of his images in Edinburgh and London, including photographs of Cambodia, Hong Kong, and China. His four-volume *Illustrations of China and Its People* appeared in 1873–1874.

In the mid-1870s Thompson photographed and published images of working-class and poor people in the streets of London. His *Street Life in London*, with a text by Adolphe Smith, was a classic work of social reform illustrated with photographs.

In 1878–1879 Thompson traveled and photographed in Cyprus after the English takeover. He began operating a London portrait studio in 1880 and wrote and published extensively on photographic subjects until the turn of the century. He was the English translator of Gaston Tissandier's *History and Handbook of Photography*.

Thompson was elected a Fellow of the Royal Geographical Society in 1866 and instructed its members in photography for over 50 years. He died in London at age 83.

See also: DOCUMENTARY PHOTOGRAPHY; SMITH, ADOLPHE.

3-D Photography

See: STEREOSCOPIC PHOTOGRAPHY.

Threshold

The threshold of an emulsion is the point at which exposure first produces a measurable amount of density above filmbase-plus-fog density—i.e., the minimum exposure point. At one time the threshold was used to determine film speed. This system was not particularly accurate because a just-measurable density may well not be sufficient to print as a tone distinguishable from maximum black. Thus, although the threshold is of interest in film sensitometry, it has no significance in practical photographic applications.

See also: DENSITY; SENSITOMETRY; SPEED OF MATERIALS.

Tilts and Swings

See: CAMERA MOVEMENTS.

Time Exposure

An exposure longer than the slowest speed setting of a shutter, or in general longer than one second, is a time exposure. Some shutters have a "T" setting for time exposures: operating the shutter release once opens the shutter, operating it a second time closes the shutter. Other shutters have a "B" setting, at which the control must be held in the operating position to keep the shutter open for the required period of time; a locking cable release is commonly used for this purpose. The camera must be on a tripod or other unmoving support throughout the exposure to avoid a blurred image. A time exposure can be used to eliminate traffic and other moving elements in a scene by repeatedly blocking the lens before they come into the field of view and unblocking it when they have passed, until the unblocked time totals the required amount. It is not practical to repeatedly open and close the shutter with this technique because of the danger of moving the camera each time the shutter is recocked. A time exposure indicated by a meter reading is likely to be too short because of the reciprocity effect. Film manufacturers offer general guidelines, but practical tests are a more accurate way to determine the actual exposure required. Otherwise, additional exposures two, four, and eight times greater than the meter indication should be made.

See also: RECIPROCITY.

Time-Lapse Photography

Time-lapse photography consists of making single-frame motion-picture exposures at regular intervals in order to make a time-condensed record of a slow, continuous process. The camera remains in a fixed position, and exposures usually are made automatically by an interval-timer control system. The intervals may be a few seconds long, or minutes, hours, or even days long, according to the rate of change in the subject. When the film is projected at normal speed, the action progresses at a much greater than normal rate, allowing the overall flow of the process to be seen. Substances melting, weathering or fading, plant growth, building construction, and erosion are typical of the processes that have been investigated with time-lapse photography.

See also: HIGH-SPEED PHOTOGRAPHY; SLOW-MOTION PHOTOGRAPHY; STOP-MOTION PHOTOGRAPHY.

Timer

Timing devices for photographic use are two types, reference and control. Reference timers are simply clocking devices that indicate how much time has elapsed or—in those that can be set to count down to zero—how much time remains. The primary requirements for reference timers are visibility—especially in darkroom conditions—and time units small enough for the task; e.g., minute indications are sufficient for fixing and washing, second indications are necessary for developing. Timers with lighted faces or numerals can be covered with a safelight filter if necessary. An audible signal that indicates the end of a measured period is a convenient feature. A timer with an audible beat is required for operations in total darkness. A metronome set to 30 or 60 beats per second is a useful expedient so long as the photographer is not likely to be distracted and lose count.

Control timers operate equipment. They include built-in camera self-timers, interval timers for time-lapse photography, and electrical switching timers such as those used to control printing exposures. Spring-powered timers are less expensive than those with electronic circuits, but also less accurate and generally less versatile. Accuracy in spring-powered units decreases with age, and may not be uniform across the setting range. For example, the interval measured at a 30-second setting may not be the same as the total of three operations at a 10-second setting. Most electronic timers provide uniform accuracy across the range, and can be reset with a repeatable precision greater than that possible with other kinds of timers.

Time-Temperature Development

Accurate and consistent results in developing films and prints are attained by controlling the temperature of the developing solution and the length of development with proper agitation. This regulation of time and temperature is critical in certain types of processing. Color films, chromogenic black-and-white films, and much color print developing requires specific time-temperature combinations that can be altered only within very narrow limits, if at all. There is a somewhat wider latitude in the development of black-and-white films and printing papers. Development is usually ended quickly and precisely by immersing the emulsion in an acidic stop bath.

In processing black-and-white films the length of development is based on the temperature of the developing solution. A standard working temperature is 68°F (20°C), but somewhat higher or lower temperatures (with appropriately shorter or longer developing times) can be equally as effective. Extremely short developing times should be avoided when possible, since they make precise control over the degree of development more difficult to maintain. The effective temperature range for developers is commonly from 65 to 75°F (18 to 24°C). Film processing instructions usually include charts showing the adjusted times at various temperatures.

Black-and-white print development is based on an optimum length of development, which varies according to the type of paper used, but is usually 1½ or 2 minutes. The temperature recommendation is 68 to 70°F (20 to 21°C).

Mistakes in the exposure of black-and-white films can sometimes be partially compensated by varying the standard developing time for a given temperature. Reduced development can help offset overexposure, and extended development can sometimes salvage underexposed film

See also: BLACK-AND-WHITE PROCESSING; DEVELOPMENT; INSPECTION DEVELOPMENT; STOP BATH.

Tinting

See: PAINTING ON PHOTOGRAPHS; TONER/TONING.

Tomography

In a medical x-ray (radiograph) taken from a fixed position, an internal organ may be obscured by the shadow images of other organs in front of or behind it. Tomography reduces this effect by spreading the unwanted images over a large area of the film so that the obscuring density at any point is greatly reduced. This is achieved by moving the x-ray tube during exposure in an arc centered on the point of interest. The film holder, on the other side of the subject, moves simultaneously in the opposite direction. This keeps the central point in relative sharp focus, but blurs the images of objects at other depths. The accuracy of the technique and the clarity of the image is greatest in computer-assisted tomography, or CAT-scan recording.
See also: X-RAY PHOTOGRAPHY.

Tone; Tonality

In black-and-white photography tone and tonality are aesthetic qualities related to the reflection densities in prints—the whole range of black, gray, and white tones—and to their interrelationships, not as measured, but as seen and felt. There is no precise definition for either term.

The ranges of brightness of the things we see and photograph seldom can be reproduced accurately in photographs, but usually must be compressed to fit within the much shorter light-to-dark scales of printing papers. The maximum range attainable in prints seems to be about 1:250, where white gives off 250 times as much light as the paper's deepest black; however, few actual prints have a reflectance range beyond about 1:100 and 1:50 or so is more usual. Because the eye sees differences among dark tones poorly, as compared to the perception of differences among light and middle tones, it is hard to tell a 1:200 print from a 1:100 or 1:50 print by eye judgment unless the prints are seen together and compared directly. Visually these are small differences. Each print seen alone appears to have a full range of tones from pure white to solid black.

Besides the compression of scale in photographs, there is distortion at both the light and the dark ends of the tonal scale. Contrast within the lightest and darkest tones of photographs is typically much lower than in the intermediate gray tones. Given reasonably good exposure and processing of the negatives, the grays generally take care of themselves. The art of tonality is to use the tones in the shrunken and distorted scale eloquently so that they convey to the viewer not only adequate middle tones, but a sense of brilliance and luminosity in the light tones and depth and transparency in the dark tones.

It is simple to represent subjects with short brightness ranges in lively, clearly separated tones by developing the negative to comparatively high contrast and printing on a normal-contrast paper, or by developing the film normally and printing on a contrasty paper. This expands the light-gray to dark-gray range of the subject to fill the white to black scale of the paper, amplifying tonal differences in the middle range and showing them almost in normal contrast in the light and dark tones. This gives an impression of tonal vitality. However, that approach fails when the subject's brightness range exceeds the paper's reflection-density range. The light or dark tones, or both, then fall beyond the paper's range and are seen in the print as blank white and featureless black. No matter how well the grays are rendered in such a print, the viewer is frustrated by seeing only blank paper where he or she looks for the picture's light details and only blackness where he or she looks for its dark details. This is a common problem. There is a simple technical solution, which is to expose the film to the point at which the negative renders the subject's dark tones in nearly normal contrast, and to avoid overdeveloping the film, which would make highlights in the subject too dense in the negative to register clearly on the printing paper at a print exposure that renders the other tones well. One approach to achieving these results is the *zone system* of black-and-white photography.

What photographers need most if they are to achieve good tonality consistently is a developed sense of tone acquired through time and work. Then handling tone well is easy: the necessary decisions have become intuitive and are less a matter of measurement and calculation and more one of recognition and response. *See also:* BRIGHTNESS RANGE; CONTRAST; TONE REPRODUCTION; ZONE SYSTEM.

Tone-Line Process

The tone-line process converts a continuous-tone image into a kind of photographic line drawing. The process requires a negative image and a corresponding positive image on separate pieces of film. The images have opposite densities—where one is dense the other is thin. When placed together they can produce an image in which all tonal gradations are eliminated but the edges of objects appear as lines.

The negative and the film positive made from it must be the size of the final image because a contact exposure technique is used. They should have nearly equal density ranges in order to be mutually masking (light-blocking) in all areas. The two images are sandwiched and taped together in exact register with the films placed back-to-back; this separates the images by the thickness of two film bases. The sandwich is placed on the emulsion of a sheet of high-contrast film in a contact printing frame or a printing easel. Exposure is made with as near a point light source as possible; e.g., an unfrosted high-intensity bulb. The light source must be above and 45° to the side of the center of the image. The best results are obtained with the frame or easel secured to a turntable that can revolve during exposure at 50–60 rpm. Alternatively, the light can be moved continuously around the frame in a circle at a constant distance and angle. Because of the separation between the images, the angled light can penetrate past the edges of the object shapes but is blocked by the density of the tonal areas. The processed result is a black-line image on clear film that can be used to print a white line image on paper. Or, it can be

copied on a second piece of film to obtain a negative for printing black-line images. The use of color film or paper and colored light sources produces variant image renditions.
See also: BAS-RELIEF IMAGES; ETCH-BLEACH PROCESS.

Tone Reproduction

Visual tones are brightness differences, without regard for color differences. A fundamental problem in photography is producing a final image with brightness differences that seem to correspond accurately—or with the desired degree of expressiveness—to those of the original subject. Two factors complicate this problem. First, the overall brightness range obtainable with photographic materials does not match the range of an average subject. Negatives and print papers have narrower, more compressed ranges; positive transparencies have expanded ranges when projected. Second, it is in fact impossible for the eye to

disregard color in evaluating brightness. The eye is more sensitive to green-yellow light than to red or blue light. Panchromatic film emulsions have reasonably well equalized color response, but the eye sees longer red wavelengths than many emulsions record, while most film emulsions have a greater sensitivity to blue. In addition, all emulsions are sensitive to ultraviolet—which the eye cannot see—and register it as additional exposure, most commonly in association with the visible blue. Further, the color response of exposure meter cells does not exactly match that of either the eye or film emulsions. In practical terms, this means that in order for a black-and-white print to seem realistic or "true," greenish and yellowish subject areas must be rendered as somewhat lighter tones—compared to the tones representing predominantly blue and red subject areas—than measurement with an exposure meter might suggest. This fact is reflected in the common recommendation that a

No. 8 yellow filter be used in daylight, or a No. 11 light yellow-green filter in tungsten light, to obtain gray-tone translations with a panchromatic film that closely match the visual brightnesses of subject colors. Black-and-white tone translation or reproduction of specific colors can be controlled to some extent with other filters. The operating principle is that a filter absorbs light opposite to its own color. This effectively increases the exposure effect of light of the filter's own color on the negative, with the result that corresponding subject areas look lighter in the print. Conversely, a subject area can be reproduced as a darker than normal tone by photographing it through a filter of opposite (complementary) color. The limitations are that only colors of one primary-color group (i.e., reddish, greenish, or bluish) can be controlled at a time, and that other colors may be changed to an unwanted degree.

The relationship of brightness range to tone reproduction is primarily a matter of the inherent characteristics of the materials used. The recordable brightness range of an average subject in daylight is about 160:1, or 7¼ f-stops, measured from a dark area that is to be represented in the print by the first tone discernible above maximum black, to a diffuse highlight—a fully-lighted white area with a nonglossy surface. The overall brightness range is even greater in most cases because there are darker subject areas that will register as no tone (maximum black), and specular highlights—direct light sources in the picture and reflections of light sources on metallic, glass, and similar surfaces—that will register as no tone at the opposite end of the scale (pure paper base white).

Flare in modern lenses and cameras is slight, but even a small amount is sufficient to reduce the brightness range of the optical image falling on the film by about one f-stop, to 80:1. The highlight and middletone brightness relationships are not affected, but flare reduces the proportional differences among the darkest areas; visually they are less distinctly different because their local range has been compressed.

The greatest compression occurs in the negative as a result of the way image brightnesses are recorded as densities. To obtain optimum quality, the negative should receive the minimum possible exposure; greater exposure unnecessarily increases density, which produces increased graininess and reduced resolving power, and may exaggerate dark-tone separation in a print. However, minimum exposure records the compressed

dark areas on the toe of the film's characteristic curve where various brightness differences produce only slight degrees of density difference; thus the dark areas are compressed further. Middletones and highlights are compressed to a much smaller degree, and they are compressed equally, so their proportional relationships are not distorted as are those of the dark areas. The amount of compression that takes place on the straight-line portion of the characteristic curve—where the lighter areas are recorded—can be controlled somewhat by development. Determining how much compression is required—or how much expansion with a short-brightness-range subject—and developing the film accordingly is the basis of the *zone* system of tone control. The overall printable density range of a negative intended for a condenser enlarger is about 0.80, for a diffusion enlarger about 1.05. When light is projected through the negative, the densities become areas of various brightness exposing the print paper. In a properly exposed and developed negative, all the tones of the 160:1 (7¼ f-stops) subject are represented, but greatly compressed, especially in the dark areas. The equivalent brightness range of the condenser enlarger negative is about 6.5:1 (2⅔ f-stops), and of the diffusion enlarger negative about 12:1 (3½ f-stops).

The emulsion of a print paper has response characteristics that compensate for the tonal compression in the negative. The toe of the paper's characteristic curve is very steep, so it separates the dark tones in much greater proportion to their negative densities than it does the middletones and highlights. The effect is to restore the balance among the brightnesses so that they seem to correspond to those of the original subject. In fact there is still some compression in the darkest areas and in the brightest diffuse highlight area. And the overall brightness range is less than that of the subject because viewing light intensity and print paper reflectivity cannot equal the original conditions. In a typical full-range black-and-white print on a glossy surface paper, the 160:1 subject range is represented by a 64:1 (6 f-stops) brightness range of printed tones; maximum emulsion black and pure paper white at either end of the scale extend the range to about 115:1 (6¾ f-stops), however there is no visual information (texture, detail, or form) contained in these extremes.

Tone reproduction in color prints can be analyzed in a similar manner, but the psychological aspect of color perception makes objective measurements much

more difficult. The brightness range of a color print will be reduced to a greater degree because color dye densities and reflectivities are less than those of a silver image on a glossy surface paper. Tone reproduction analysis can be extended to photomechanical reproduction as well, where the major limiting factor is the further reduction of the brightness range produced by printing ink absorptance and the characteristics of the papers used.

The brightness- and density-range relationships involved in tone reproduction can be graphically presented in a quadrant diagram, described in a separate entry. This method can be used for photographic and photomechanical printing, slide and motion-picture projection, and a variety of other applications.

See also: BRIGHTNESS RANGE; CONTRAST; QUADRANT DIAGRAM; TONE/TONALITY; ZONE SYSTEM.

Toner; Toning

Toning is the process of altering the color of a black-and-white photographic image. There are three methods of affecting image color: by development, by replacing the silver image with inorganic compounds, and by dyeing the image.

Papers with silver chloride emulsions produce warmer tones during normal development than silver bromide papers. The length of development and the chemical composition of the developer both affect image tone, however control during development is the most limited of the toning methods. Using various inorganic compounds to replace the silver in a fully developed and fixed image allows a greater variation of image color. This is achieved by converting the silver compounds in the emulsion chemically with such toners as sulfur, iron, gold, selenium, and other metallic compounds. The image color is primarily determined by the toning compound. Many toners produce a wide range of results depending on the solution concentration, the length of time the image is in the solution, and the type of emulsion. Some toning processes act directly on the silver image; in others the image is first bleached to a colorless state and then redeveloped in a toning solution. Dye toning may be used for a wider range of colors. The image is converted to silver ferrocyanide, which is a mordant, and then placed in a dye solution. Dye is deposited in the emulsion in proportion to the density of the ferrocyanide image. Colors can be varied by mixing dyes or by immersing the image in consecutive baths of different colors.

Many of the compounds used for toning are very toxic; rubber gloves and efficient ventilation are essential.
See also: MORDANT.

Tournachon, Gaspard Felix
See: NADAR.

Transfer Function
See: MTF (MODULATION TRANSFER FUNCTION).

Transfer Processes
A wide variety of photographic printing processes have been developed that involve the transfer of an image from one emulsion or support to another. The reasons for making a transfer include achieving left-right reversal; forming an image in compounds that are more permanent or have different tonal or color characteristics than silver; placing an image on a support that could not be photographically exposed or processed; building a composite effect such as full-color reproduction; and achieving rapid, automatic processing. The last of these is the most common today; it is encountered in diffusion transfer films used for instant photography and in self-processing color print materials for darkroom use. The earliest transfer method was to strip a collodion positive from its glass plate and adhere it to another material such as porcelain, wood, leather, or metal. Various carbon processes involve transferring image-forming pigment to a new support; others, such as the bromoil process, transfer ink or oil paint images. The dye transfer process is self-descriptive. Some electrostatic processes transfer the image as a charge pattern that then attracts compounds that make the image visible.
See also: BROLOID PROCESS; CARBON PROCESSES; CARBRO PROCESS; CERAMIC PROCESS; DIFFUSION TRANSFER PROCESS; DYE TRANSFER PROCESS; ELECTROPHOTOGRAPHIC PROCESSES; ENAMEL PROCESS; FLEXOGRAPHY; GLASS, PHOTOGRAPHS ON; IVORYTYPE; OZOBROME PROCESS, OZOTYPE; TECHNICOLOR; TRICHROME CARBRO PROCESS; WOODBURYTYPE/WOODBURYGRAVURE; XEROGRAPHY.

Transmission
The percentage measurement of the ability of a transparent or translucent material to pass light is called transmission; it is determined from the ratio of transmitted light to incident light. The simple arithmetic result of this ratio is *trans-mittance* or *transparency;* when multiplied by 100 to produce a percentage, it is transmission, or *percent transmission.* The reciprocal of transmittance or transparency is *opacity.* Thus, if Incident light = 10, and Transmitted light = 5:

$$\text{Transmittance; Transparency} = 5 \div 10 = 0.5$$

$$\text{Percent Transmission} = (5 \div 10) \times 100 = 50\%$$

$$\text{Opacity} = 1 \div (5 \div 10) = 1 \div 0.5 = 2$$

See also: DENSITOMETRY; OPACITY.

Transparency
Any positive image on a film or clear glass base is called a transparency. The term commonly means an image not suitably mounted for projection—i.e., not a slide—and is sometimes used to distinguish a medium- or large-format image from one made on 35mm film. A positive image on a translucent white base intended for viewing by rear illumination is called a transmission print. Transparency as a measure of light passing power is discussed in the entry on transmission.

Transparency Materials
Although any film can be reversal processed, or can be exposed to a negative and normally processed to produce a positive image, the result is not likely to have optimum quality. Transparency materials are specific designed to produce a positive image on a transparent base. They generally have thin, fine grain emulsions so as not to produce excess density, which would reduce the brightness of the transmitted light and produce increased graininess, especially upon projection.

The great majority of transparency materials are color films in which the positive image is produced by reversal processing. A few black-and-white films are also designed for reversal processing to obtain monochrome transparencies directly from camera exposure. Special films are available to make medium- and large-format transparencies and 35mm slides from color negatives. Other color and black-and-white films have a translucent white base for rear illumination so their images can be seen as transparencies without the need for a viewer or projector. Certain black-and-white graphic arts films produce a positive image from exposure to a positive with one-step (i.e., not reversal) development. These can also be used to produce transparencies for use in overhead projectors. Other overhead projection materials on transparent bases generally have diazo or other nonsilver emulsions.
See also: DIAZO PROCESSES; DIRECT POSITIVE; REVERSAL MATERIALS/PROCESSING.

Travel Photography
Travel for pleasure or business invariably provides the photographer with a fresh source of subject matter; even those who do not consider photography an ongoing pastime will rarely travel without some sort of camera to record the places seen on their journeys. Travel pictures have been immensely popular since the beginnings of photography, although it was not until the end of the 19th c. that most travelers could take pictures for themselves. The realism of photographs essentially transports the viewer to the place shown. Thus the pictures provide a way to return to someplace visited, or to go somewhere never gone before. This vicarious experience helps satisfy the curiosity most people have about renowned, exotic, or distant places, people, and customs.

Early travel photography. For most of the 19th c. travel pictures, like all other kinds, were taken almost exclusively by experimenters and professionals. During the 1840s, the calotype (paper negative process) was used by traveling photographers much more extensively than the daguerreotype, primarily because the materials could be prepared for use ahead of time (especially with the waxed-paper process) rather than on the spot, and because multiple prints could be made, whereas the daguerreotype was a single-image process. A daguerreotype had to be copied as a hand-engraving for subsequent reproduction, but paper prints could be produced in quantity from a negative and hand-pasted into a book or album. That was the procedure used with great success by L. D. Blanquart-Evrard to publish pictures by Maxime Du Camp, Gustave Le Gray, and a number of other traveling photographers in the 1850s.

In spite of the cumbersome equipment and materials of the collodion (wet plate) process, the vastly improved quality offered by its glass negative, compared to a paper negative, led to its being used all over the world. Expedition photographers, mountaineers, balloonists, explorers, as well as photographer traveling for culture or pleasure produced an enormous volume of work from 1851 to about 1885 using the wet plate. Alpine views by the Bisson *frères;* the Crimea by Roger Fenton; the Middle East and India by Felice Beato and James Robertson, among others; Asia by John

Thompson; Panama by Timothy H. O'Sullivan; the American West by a great number of photographers—these are only a few of the major achievements of the period. Almost all such pictures were produced for commercial distribution. They were sold as individual prints, and in album and portfolio sets. They were reproduced as magic lantern slides to illustrate travel lecturers, which rapidly gained an immense popularity that extends to the present day. Packets of carte-de-visite views sold in the hundreds of thousands in the 1860s and 1870s at favorite tourist spots everywhere, the forerunner of commercially produced slide sets and picture postcards now offered in the same places. Sets of stereographs of people and places all over the world sold in the millions in the last quarter of the century. The professional photographer's task was made easier with the introduction of the gelatin dry plate in the early 1880s, while the public's appetite for travel photographs did not lessen.

The Kodak camera, introduced in 1888, made it both possible and easy for everyone to become his or her own travel photographer. Then, as now, taking travel and vacation pictures was the major reason amateurs gave for buying a camera. Professional travel photography has taken advantage of the improvements in equipment and films to grow and improve enormously in the 20th c.; amateur travel photography has grown at an even greater rate. The audience for travel pictures of all kinds has never been larger; making such pictures has never been easier.

Taking travel pictures. Professional travel photographers of necessity carry a substantial amount of equipment with them; many amateurs and hobbyists make the mistake of assuming that an important or distant journey requires more or different equipment than would be used in more domestic picture taking. Such is rarely the case; the most effective travel photographs are made when the equipment used is so familiar as to be an extension of the hand and eye. Few vacation or travel picture-making opportunities require more than the following: The camera the traveler feels most comfortable using; a fast, standard focal-length lens for most picture taking; a short telephoto lens for impromptu portraiture and candid street photography from a discreet distance; and a moderately wide-angle lens for scenic panoramas and work in close quarters. The three lenses can be replaced by a zoom lens, of which many excellent examples are available at reasonably moderate cost.

The basic travel outfit should also include the following items: extra batteries for the camera; a sensitive, well-made hand-held light meter (optional if the camera has a built-in meter); a lightweight but sturdy compact tripod; a small electronic flash unit; lens tissue; and as much film as can be comfortably carried, unless there is some assurance that fresh film can be bought along the way. It is best to take a plentiful supply of a preferred film. In some cases film of the same brand but manufactured abroad produces different results; this is especially true of color transparency films. Film imported from the United State for sale may cost twice as much, or more, than that of domestic manufacture.

The amount of film allowed into certain countries is controlled by local laws; these should be checked beforehand through the tourist board or consulate of the intended destination. Photographers on assignment are usually given a dispensation from the regulations by most governments; a similar waiver of the rules often can be obtained by writing or paying a visit to the commission in charge and presenting oneself as a "serious amateur" or artist.

Local laws and customs. Before making an excursion into a foreign land, the traveling photographer should make him- or herself aware of the local culture and customs. In many places outside of Western culture, photography of people is considered a gross invasion of privacy, and might even be deemed against established religious or social customs. It is better to be forewarned than to find oneself at the center of hostile attention.

Certain countries have severe restrictions placed on photographers. The photography of trains, police and military personnel, and even industrial installations is an imprisonable offence in a number of Eastern Block countries, for example. Even in such democracies as France and Great Britain, photographing law enforcement and military personnel is forbidden in certain circumstances.

The traveler should not leave home without taking along the original receipts for all cameras and lenses; in lieu of these, a special customs registration form can be obtained at the point of departure. This documentation shows that the equipment was not bought while traveling and thus is not subject to duty on return.

Film. The proper choice of film speed and type depends much on the personal taste of the user, and on the kinds of subjects to be photographed. Users of black-and-white film will find chromogenic films extremely useful in travel; they have great exposure latitude, allowing for substantial over- and underexposure while still providing eminently printable negatives. Such chromogenic films are processed like color negative films, but yield a black-and-white image.

If the location traveled to is a scenic one and color pictures are needed, a slow- or medium-speed transparency film will provide the richest color saturation and finest detail. Transparency films have very limited exposure latitude; consequently, care must be taken in measuring exposure. "Bracketing" of exposures by taking the picture first at the indicated settings, then two others, at ½ stop more and less than the indicated exposure, is recommended; all three transparencies will be usable in the vast majority of cases, but one of them usually will have the most pleasing combination of color richness and detail. Transparency films can be used for direct projection of the image, or can be used for making prints. A more direct route to color prints is via color negative films, which have slightly more exposure latitude, but at the cost of some loss in fine-grain characteristics and detail rendition. Indoor photography and evening scenes will require the use of faster films: Color films are now available with a speed of ISO 1000/31°—fast enough for most available light and nighttime situations the traveler is likely to encounter.

Sometimes, photographers traveling for the first time to a new or exotic locale become too enthusiastic about recording the sights they are confronted with; better pictures will be obtained if time is first taken to become familiar with the environment. A stroll or bus ride through the locale will allow the photographer to discover the most likely places for meaningful photographs, and at the same time offers an opportunity to appreciate the spot with the eyes directly, rather than through the lens.

In some resorts and other locations frequented by tourists, the local inhabitants expect payment for posing, whether or not they are asked to at the time the pictures are being made. Being aware of this at the outset might help avoid unnecessary embarrassment or unpleasantness. The travel agent is a good source of information about such matters. Should a likely looking subject refuse to be photographed when asked, the picture, out of simple courtesy, should not be taken.

Many places of photographic interest, such as museums and churches, have their own rules about what can and cannot be photographed. In some cases, photography is allowed as long as a tripod is not used; in others, tripods are allowed, but flash is not. Usually such rules are posted in plain sight, and written in a number of languages.

Camera equipment should always be hand-carried aboard vehicles and aircraft, both for its protection from damage and to avoid theft or loss. Airports pose radiation problems for both exposed and unexposed films. Some security x-ray machines are more powerful than others; low-energy radiation can be guarded against by special bags lined with lead foil, available at most camera shops. These bags are useless against high-energy x-ray machines, and all efforts should be made to have camera gear and film inspected by hand. In most cases, security personnel will comply with a courteous request for this service. The effects of the radiation are cumulative; one exposure may not cause any visible effect on the film, but two or more exposures will often cause fogging. One way to avoid this problem on an extended trip involving a number of flights is to mail the film home by insured post. Before taking this step, however, the traveler should be sure that the local postal service has a reliable reputation.

Color photograph: p. C-61.

Triacetate Film

Film with a base material of cellulose triacetate or a related compound is called "safety film" because it is nonflammable. All films now have safety bases.
See also: CELLULOID; SAFETY FILM.

Trichrome Carbro Process

A method of producing color images by assembling registered layers of subtractive color images in carbon pigments was first demonstrated by Ducos du Hauron in 1868. But only after the monochrome carbro process had brought the freedom to use enlarging to produce the basic image at any size was a full-color carbon process perfected, in the 1900s: trichrome or three-color carbro. Separation negatives are made from the original subject or color image; from these a matched set of black-and-white bromide prints is made. The prints are placed in contact with suitably prepared cyan, magenta, and yellow carbon tissues for image-hardening transfer to occur. Then the carbon face of each tissue is pressed against a temporary plastic support sheet and the backing paper stripped away for development, which washes away the unhardened areas of gelatin. Next, the carbon images are transferred one at a time to an intermediate assembly sheet or, in the single-transfer procedure, to a base sheet. The first image is laid down and its plastic support stripped away. The second is registered over it and the plastic removed, then the third. In double transfer, this assemblage is then transferred to the final support. Materials are available on a very limited basis, and the handling is more delicate but no less involved than in the dye-transfer process.
See also: CARBRO PROCESS; DUCOS DU HAURON, L.; DYE-TRANSFER PROCESS; SUBTRACTIVE COLOR SYNTHESIS.

Tricks

Trick photography consists of the techniques used to create "impossible" images—those in which elements are combined or visual effects are produced that could not be seen and straightforwardly photographed in the normal world. Often the term trick photography is limited to those techniques which produce the desired effect in the camera without darkroom manipulation or subsequent alteration of the image. In that case tricks are accomplished by means of filters, prisms, mirrors, mattes, lighting, special lenses and films, multiple exposure, camera movement, and similar devices and techniques. In the broader sense of image manipulation at any stage, trick photography draws on the methods described in the entry on special effects and those listed in the cross-references with that entry.

The term *tricks* also refers to tricks of the trade—those techniques used to enhance a subject or to overcome problems in relatively straightfoward photography. They include things such as using concealed clothespins to improve the fit of a garment on a model, using dulling spray to eliminate a glaring highlight, using colored light in a specific area to heighten subject color there, and aiming the lens into a suspended mirror to get an apparent overhead camera position. Problem-solving tricks of this sort arise from trial-and-error experimentation as well as from sudden inspiration; they tend to be passed on verbally among photographers and assistants as part of the largely unwritten lore of the medium. Such subterfuges are legitimate as long as they do not falsify what is being said by the photograph. Otherwise, they become lies and, in the case of commercial illustration, may violate truth-in-advertising regulations. For example, it is possible to use a blowtorch to brown the skin of a partly roasted turkey; this avoids the shrinkage, skin rippling or splitting, and uneven browning that may result from full roasting, and it provides a visually more ideal result. That is perfectly acceptable in an advertising picture in which the turkey is part of the overall setting, such as one that says "our crystal and china make a holiday table setting of great beauty." However, it is a false representation in a picture that is meant to illustrate the idea "our oven produces perfect roasting." The photographer has a moral as well as legal responsibility to avoid deliberate falsification in what viewers will assume is a factual representation.
See also: SPECIAL EFFECTS.

Tricolor Filters

Tricolor filters are matched sets of deep primary red, green, and blue filters. They are used to photograph separation negatives and positives, and to make additive color prints by the three-exposure method. Filters for separation photography have slightly different transmission characteristics from those used for color printing.
See also: ADDITIVE COLOR PRINTING; SEPARATION NEGATIVES/POSITIVE.

Triplet

A lens composed of three separate elements or element groups.
See: LENSES.

Tripod

A tripod is the most common form of camera support. It is used to avoid blur due to camera shake at slow shutter speeds, to support equipment that is too bulky or heavy to be hand held, to keep the camera exactly in place for precise focusing and picture composition, and to permit releasing the shutter from a distance. Tripods range in size from pocket or tabletop models only a few inches tall to those which extend 10 feet or more and are sturdy enough for equipment weighing over 100 pounds. Whatever their size, the basic construction is the same: three telescoping legs hinged to a plate to which the camera attaches, usually with a screw that threads into a socket on the camera body. The top plate often has a spirit level to assist in setting the camera vertically and horizontally, and controls that allow the camera to be panned left or right and tilted up or down. An accessory panhead also can be attached to any tripod to accomplish the same movements. Some tripods are constructed with a center column that moves in a collar to which the three legs are attached. The column can be extended vertically for extra height or to make fine adjustments once the basic setup has been established. In some models the center column can be inverted to support the camera close to the ground. The basic camera height is established by extending the legs and spreading the feet to the required position. A tripod usually is set up with one leg pointing toward the subject so that the photographer can stand comfortably within the V of the other two legs. However, on slopes or stairs the tripod is oriented with two legs on the downhill side for stability. On uneven terrain the three legs may be extended to different lengths in order to achieve a level setup.

Lightweight tripods can be used in a variety of other ways to help support the camera. The telescoped legs can be spread to brace against a wall or door, or they can be turned to rest against the photographer's shoulders and chest. Grouped together, they can be placed under the arm or against one shoulder like a gunstock. Extended in a group, they form a monopod for use where crowding and traffic would make spreading the feet dangerous. This arrangement also permits extending the camera into the air to look over the heads of a crowd or to get a high-angle view; the shutter is released by a self-timer or a cable release.
See also: CAMERA SUPPORTS.

Tropical Photography

The high humidity and intense heat of tropical conditions can be very damaging to photographic equipment and materials; the natural light in the tropics creates problems of excessive contrast. Constant attention to careful procedures and frequent cleaning of equipment can overcome the difficulties of tropical photography and help produce high-quality pictures.

Heat rapidly ages films and papers; humidity accelerates this process and promotes the growth of fungi that thrive on the gelatin of emulsions. Such materials should be kept in sealed containers along with packages of dessicant (silica gel drying agent), which will absorb humidity from the air that gets in whenever the container is opened. Containers used outdoors should be white to reflect heat, and they should be kept in shaded locations at all times. Foil wrappings should not be opened until just before the material is used. Prints, and slides even more so, must be kept in low-humidity conditions or they quickly will become spotted with fungi or mildew.

Camera bags, bellows, lens and meter cases, carrying straps, and similar items are highly susceptible to mildew and fungi. Plastic materials are less susceptible to direct attack than leather and cloth, but all containers can collect moist dust in crevices that will be a breeding ground for unwanted growths. Containers should be wiped clean, vacuumed, and sun-dried frequently; fresh packets of dessicant should be placed inside after every cleaning.

The combination of heat and humidity can cause metals to corrode or oxidize rapidly both in cameras and inside lenses. Some fungi also thrive on the materials used for lens element coatings. Frequent cleaning, use of protective caps on the camera body and both ends of lenses, and keeping equipment as cool as possible are the best protective measures. Special care must be taken not to leave perspiration on glass and metal parts when handling equipment; skin oils and traces of salt can quickly etch or corrode glass as well as metal. A skylight or UV-absorbing filter will offer lens protection during use. Some photographers use amphibious cameras of the self-contained type designed for beach and underwater use. These have plastic-coated bodies and controls, and rubber or plastic gaskets around all openings to seal out moisture. The choice of lenses and focusing capabilities is limited, and most are available only in 35mm format. However, they will continue to function in conditions of constant humidity and hard usage long after conventional equipment has succumbed.

Exposure in tropical conditions is determined in the same ways as elsewhere and in fact is no different. However, the high contrast created by the bright, intense light and the resulting hard, dark shadows make it difficult to estimate exposure accurately by eye. In addition, the extreme brightness (contrast) range of subjects in direct tropical sun is difficult to record, especially with color films. Fill-in flash or reflectors are essential, and the subject should be turned so that the sun is a backlight. Whenever possible direct sun should be avoided by moving the subject into open shade; the reflected light level in shade frequently is quite high, but the contrast is well within normal range.

Films must be protected after exposure with as much care as before exposure, and they should be processed promptly. The latent image can deteriorate rapidly from the effects of heat and humidity. Processing in an air-conditioned humidity-controlled darkroom poses few problems if the film is given time to adjust before being loaded onto reels or into hangers. In warm, humid darkrooms a hardening prebath before the developer and a hardening fixer are essential to protect the emulsion. The temperatures of all solutions must be within a few degrees of one another to avoid reticulation. Drying is likely to be slow in high humidity, and the emulsion will remain susceptible to dust and handling damage for a long time. Only constant care will avoid film and print damage.
See also: HARDENER; TEMPERATURE CONTROL.

"T" Shutter Setting
See: TIME EXPOSURE.

T-stop

A T-stop is a lens calibration similar to an *f*-stop. The *f*-number system of lens aperture settings is based on the relationship between the effective aperture opening and the lens focal length. Mathematically, all lenses set to the same *f*-number transmit the same amount of light. This is true in a practical sense for motion-picture and still photography in black-and-white, and for still photography in color. In fact, lenses of various designs transmit slightly different amounts of light at the same *f*-number because of differences in the number of elements, the physical distances the light travels, internal flare, and similar factors. These differences may be apparent in color motion pictures when shots of the same subject taken with different lenses (i.e., normal, wide-angle, and telephoto) are intercut with one another. To insure absolutely matching exposures, such lenses may be calibrated in T-stops based on settings that transmit exactly the same amount of light, regardless of whether their aperture-focal length ratios match mathematically. T-stop values are calculated:

$$T \text{ No.} = (FL \div \text{Effective aperture}) \times \sqrt{T}\text{ransmittance}$$

where *FL* is lens focal length, *Effective aperture* is the entrance pupil diameter, and *Transmittance* is the ratio of the light—measured in lumens—at the exit pupil to the light at the entrance pupil.
See also: *f*-NUMBER; LIGHT UNITS; PUPIL MAGNIFICATION.

TTL (Through-the-lens)

The greatest precision of framing and alignment is provided by a camera that allows the photographer to view the subject directly through the lens that will form the image on the film. In general, sheet film cameras have a screen at the film plane for direct TTL viewing, but this is obscured when the film holder is inserted in the camera. Roll-film and 35mm cameras with TTL viewing use a mirror-prism system to reflect the image to a screen or eyepiece, as described in the entry on reflex viewing. The image in TTL viewing is never as bright as that of a rangefinder or direct-frame system because the light is reduced by the maximum aperture of the lens (generally used for at least initial framing and focusing) and by the screen on which the image is seen. With lenses that do not have automatic diaphragms—virtually all view and press camera lenses—image brightness is greatly reduced when the lens is closed to working aperture, making it very difficult to see any focus shift or change in alignment that might occur.

Through-the-lens exposure metering offers great accuracy if the picture area covered by the meter is sufficiently precise or significant. Large- or full-area coverage readings are useful only when the subject has a truly average distribution of light and dark elements; otherwise small-area or spot readings are required. A TTL reading automatically compensates for the effect of extra lens extension in close-up and macrophotography, and for the effect of most color balancing filters used in color photography. Meter readings taken through stronger filters, such as those used for special effects and for black-and-white photography, may not be accurate because of differences in the spectral sensitivity of the meter cell and the film emulsion.

See also: REFLEX VIEWING.

Tube Processing

See: DRUM AND TUBE PROCESSING.

Tungsten Bulb

Tungsten-filament light bulbs are used in photography for subject illumination, projection, and enlarging exposures. All have glass envelopes filled with an inert gas that prolongs filament life by displacing oxygen-rich air. Some bulbs also contain a halogen to further extend filament life with increased intensity and to maintain the color temperature of the output over the life of the bulb. Non-halogen bulbs for photographic illumination generally have a frosted, pear-shape (PS) glass envelope and a medium screw base, like household bulbs; some have blue glass. Those most used for photography are described in the entry on photoflood bulbs. Screw-base PS enlarger bulbs have a special white interior coating to insure uniform light distribu-

tion; typical specifications are given in the accompanying table. Screw-base bulbs in a conical shape with an interior reflective coating are designated R and may further be distinguished as spotlight (RSP) and floodlight (RFL) bulbs. Those of high intensity for photographic use are often called movie lights; typical specifications are included in the table.

Typical Photographic Tungsten Bulb Specifications

Screw-Base Enlarging Bulbs

No	Watts	Avg. Life*	Approx. Color Temp.*
211	75	100 hrs	2950K
212	150	100	2950K
300	150	100	3100K
300C	300	20	3200K
301	300	100	3125K
302	500	100	3150K

Reflector Flood (RFL) Bulbs

ANSI Code	Watts	Avg. Life*	Approx. Color Temp.*
DAN	200	4 hrs	3400K
EBR	375	4	3400K
BEP	300	4	3400K
DXH	375	15	3200K
BFA	375	4	3400K
DWD	300	2000	2800K
DXC	500	6	3400K

*At 118 volts

Tungsten-halogen lamps have a variety of small tubular shapes; those for projection commonly have a surrounding reflector. These bulbs have contact pins at the rear, bottom, or at either end; their construction is described in the entry on quartz lights.

Non-halogen tungsten projection bulbs have clear glass envelopes in a vertical tubular shape with contacts at the bottom end. The base may have short, protruding side contacts (bayonet type), or bottom pins or contacts. Many bulbs have a keyed base pin or a flange or collar at the shoulder of the base to insure that the filament is precisely positioned behind the image gate of a projector.

See also: PHOTOFLOOD BULB; QUARTZ LIGHT.

Tungsten-Halogen Bulb

See: QUARTZ LIGHT; TUNGSTEN BULB.

Twin-Lens Camera

A camera with two lenses of matched focal length, one to form an image on the film, the other for reflex viewing via a

mirror and ground glass is called a twin-lens camera. The lenses are mounted on a common board that moves back and forth to adjust the focus of both simultaneously. The viewing lens is often of greater maximum aperture than the image lens, to provide as bright an image as possible for viewing; however it does not have to be of as high quality as the image lens, nor does it require a diaphragm or shutter. A twin-lens camera is essentially composed of two lighttight compartments, with a viewing section above an image-recording section that accepts medium-format roll film. Because there is no mirror movement, viewing is continuous throughout exposure and there is less vibration than with a single-lens reflex camera of equivalent size. The twin-lens camera has two major drawbacks: the viewing system produces significant parallax with subjects at close range, and both lenses must be changed when a different focal length is desired. Few cameras offer twin-lens interchangeability; in those that do, the entire lensboard must be replaced with another carrying different lenses—a solution that is both awkward and expensive. Some special-purpose cameras have twin lenses, most notably stereoscopic cameras; these require matched image-quality lenses with duplicate diaphragms and synchronized shutters.

See also: PARALLAX; REFLEX VIEWING; SINGLE LENS REFLEX CAMERA.

Two-Bath Development

Negative contrast can be limited by development carried out in two separate solutions. In water bath development the first solution is normal developer, the second plain water. More commonly a split developer is used: the first bath contains developing agents, preservative, and restrainer, but no activator, which is the major ingredient of the second bath. The film or print is soaked in the first bath for up to three minutes, by which time the emulsion has absorbed the maximum amount of solution; little or no development takes place during this time. It is then transferred to the second bath, where the activator enables development to occur. The process is self-limiting because the developing agents absorbed by the emulsion are rapidly exhausted in the most exposed areas but continue to work until later exhaustion in the less exposed areas; thus it is virtually impossible to overdevelop the image. The material must not be returned to the first bath without thorough washing; otherwise activator will be carried into the first bath and it will become a working developer rather than a prebath.

Although two-bath development will limit contrast, and is especially useful with seriously overexposed negatives for that reason, it does not permit a range of contrast control, as do variations in time, temperature, and agitation in normal single-bath development. Almost any developer can be prepared from formula for two-bath use by not adding activator to the first bath. The activator is mixed at four to eight times normal strength (to allow repeated use) as the second bath. Time and temperature are not critical with this technique. A minimum of three minutes in each bath is required, but longer times will do no harm; any temperature within a reasonable range—55–75°F (13–24°C)—may be used so long as both baths are the same. Development is followed by normal stop bath, fixing, and washing procedures.
See also; DEVELOPMENT; WATER-BATH DEVELOPMENT.

Two-Color Photography

All practical photographic color systems are based on three-color synthesis to create an image that reproduces the full range of subject colors with a high degree of accuracy. The synthesis is either additive, using red, green, and blue, or subtractive, using cyan, magenta, and yellow. Limited success has also been achieved using only two colors to synthesize all or most others. In a subtractive mode the two colors are orange and a near-cyan. Color reproduction is quite acceptable with subjects having little significant blue content, but cyan and orange cannot produce a blue free of a large amount of green, or in many cases a blue that is even distinguishable from

green. The first subtractive-color amateur movie films, introduced in the 1920s, used two-color synthesis. Reproduction of interior scenes, illuminated with blue-deficient incandescent light, was reasonably good. Outdoor scenes including blue sky, or blue sky and foliage, had a strong green cast, as did scenes photographed in open shade lighted by the blue sky. Two-color photomechanical reproduction with cyan and orange, plus a gray printer derived from the cyan separation, produces better results, but again only with subject matter of slight blue content.

Two-color additive photographic images have most successfully been produced by E. H. Land and his associates. The method involves two black-and-white positive transparencies of a full-color subject. Both images are recorded on panchromatic film, one through a deep primary green filter, the other through a deep primary red filter. The green-record positive is projected with white light, the red-record positive with white light and a matching red filter. When the images are brought into exact register on the screen, a full-color reproduction of the subject is seen in most cases. If the red filter is used with the other image, reversed color is seen. As neither image is actually in color, this is perhaps more accurately termed two-stimulus rather than two-color photography. The process by which the eye perceives a full color range in this situation is not completely understood. However, it has been shown that the key factor is the wavelength difference between the two images. The red record is a long wavelength image, the green record a short wavelength image. So long as the exposing light of the two records is separated by about 100 nanometers,

the same result can be achieved with filters that pass light at other parts of the spectrum. The mechanism is incorporated in the *retinex* theory of vision, and is an area of active investigation.
See also: ADDITIVE COLOR SYNTHESIS; COLOR MATERIALS; LAND EDWIN H.; SUBTRACTIVE COLOR SYNTHESIS; VISION.

291

The Little Galleries of the Photo-Secession, founded in 1905 by Alfred Stieglitz, were located at 291 Fifth Avenue, New York City, in parlor floor (first floor above ground level) rooms of the same building in which Edward Steichen had a studio. In 1908, a rent increase forced the gallery to close. It was able to reopen later that year in similar rooms in the adjoining building, 293 Fifth Avenue. The two buildings shared a common entrance, so the move was in fact just across the hall. The gallery had become known simply as "291" among its regular patrons; Stieglitz chose this as the new name because it signified a change, but maintained a continuity of identification. The first exhibit in the new rooms showed work by members of the Photo-Secession; the final exhibit, in April/May 1917, showed watercolors, drawings, and oil paintings by Georgia O'Keeffe. Much of the historical importance of 291 lay in its presentation of avant-garde European painters and sculptors like Auguste Rodin, Paul Cézanne, Pablo Picasso, and Constantine Brancusi to the American public, in addition to exhibitions of American and European photographers.
See also: LITTLE GALLERIES OF THE PHOTO-SECESSION; PHOTO-SECESSION; STIEGLITZ, ALFRED.

Uelsmann, Jerry. "Small Woods Where I Met
Myself" (1967). Courtesy Jerry Uelsmann;
Collection, Museum of Modern Art, New
York.

U-V

Uelsmann, Jerry N.

American; 1934–

Jerry Uelsmann has been a fantasist and explorer of the boundaries of the photographic medium for over 25 years. He has experimented with complex multiple prints, negative imagery, and other techniques in elaborating a personal mythology the elements of which include nudes, floating trees, clouds, reflections in bodies of water, details of plants; his work emphasizes the ambiguities of space and scale. He has been a prominent spokesman for "post-visualization"—that is, "the willingness on the part of the photographer to revisualize the final image at any point in the entire photographic process."

Uelsmann was born in Detroit, Michigan, and developed an interest in photography as a high-school student. He graduated in the first four-year B.F.A. degree program in photography at the Rochester Institute of Technology in 1957, and published his first image in *Photography Annual* of that year. Ralph Hattersley and Minor White were his major influences as teachers. Continuing his studies in audio-visual communications, art history, and design, he worked under Henry Holmes Smith at Indiana University, where he received a M.F.A. degree in 1960.

For the next four years Uelsmann was Instructor of Art at the University of Florida, Gainesville (where he has continued to teach) on a faculty which included Van Deren Coke. In 1964 Uelsmann was a founding member of the Society for Photographic Education. He was elected to the Board of Directors of the Society two years later.

Uelsmann's first one-man exhibition, of 103 photographs, was held at the Jacksonville Art Museum in Jacksonville, Florida, in 1963. The following year his first important portfolio of work appeared in *Contemporary Photographer.*

He began to use the darkroom as a "visual research lab" in 1965. In 1966 he was appointed Associate Professor of Art. A major one-man show at the Museum of Modern Art in New York City was mounted by John Szarkowski in 1967. Uelsmann was awarded a Guggenheim Fellowship for "Experiments in Multiple Printing Techniques in Photography" the same year. In 1968 he began an extensive lecture tour and printmaking demonstration at schools including the Rhode Island School of Design, MIT, and the Art Institute of Chicago. *Aperture* published a major essay by William E. Parker on his work at this time.

In 1969 Uelsmann was named Professor of Art and began teaching under the auspices of the Friends of Photography. He was cited for Special Recognition by the American Society of Magazine Photographers in 1970. Two years later he received a National Endowment for the Arts Fellowship. He was made a Fellow of the Royal Photographic Society of Great Britain in 1973, the year an entire issue of *Aperture* was devoted to his work with an essay by Peter Bunnell.

Uelsmann was appointed Graduate Research Professor at the University of Florida in 1974. He has been the recipient of a Certificate of Merit from the Society of Publication Designers and a Certificate of Excellence from the American Institute of Graphic Arts.

In addition to the exhibitions mentioned, retrospectives of Uelsmann's work have been held at the Philadelphia Museum of Art, the San Francisco Museum of Art, and the Witkin Gallery in New York City. In a 1981 report by *American Photographer,* Uelsmann's work was named one of the ten most collected in the country.

See also: ABSTRACT PHOTOGRAPHY; FANTASY IN PHOTOGRAPHY; SURREALISM IN PHOTOGRAPHY.

Photograph: p. 526.

Ultra-miniature Camera

When 35mm still photography was introduced the format became known as "miniature," in contrast to the medium- and large-formats in common use. An ultra-miniature camera is thus one using a format smaller than 35mm. More specifically, the term refers to a still camera that is physically about the size of a matchbox, and that uses 16mm or smaller film. So-called spy cameras, and disk cameras using film 2–3 in. or less in diameter are representative ultra-miniature cameras. Although they are often mechanically and electronically highly sophisticated devices, such cameras have limited usefulness.

See also: DISK CAMERAS.

Ultraviolet and Fluorescence Photography

Ultraviolet energy occupies the range just beyond the blue-violet end of the visible spectrum, from about 400 to 10 nanometers in wavelength. All photographic silver halide emulsions are sensitive to ultraviolet (UV), and the optical glass used in camera lenses readily passes long-wave UV of about 400 to 320nm (special quartz lenses are required to transmit shorter-wavelength UV). In ordinary outdoor photography it is common to use a haze, skylight, or other UV-absorbing filter to avoid the grayish or bluish effect in scenic views caused by excess exposure from the ultraviolet. However, although invisible to the eye, ultraviolet energy has important uses as a photographic illuminant, particularly for investigating properties of materials that are not revealed by light or infrared radiation. There are two methods of photographing by ultraviolet. One is to exclude light from the lens and directly record only the ultraviolet energy reflected or transmitted by the subject. The other is to record the visible wavelengths various materials emit when they are stimulated by ultraviolet.

UV Photography. Direct UV photography is used to examine documents for suspected alteration or forgery, to investigate the underlayers of paintings, to copy faded or burned materials, to examine subsurface skin conditions, and to investigate unstained microscopic specimens. In each of these cases, and similar applications, material bleached out, covered over, or otherwise not visible may reflect or transmit ultraviolet to a different degree than the surrounding material; this causes a difference of exposure, making the situation visible upon development. The photographic technique is simple and direct. The subject is illuminated with UV-rich energy, as produced by the sun, sunlamps, "blacklight" fluorescent tubes, or electronic flash (bare-tube flash with a temporary aluminum reflector provides more UV than a sealed-lens flash unit). The camera lens is fitted with a filter such as a No. 18A that excludes visible light and transmits only long-wave UV. A slow film is preferred because of its inherently high contrast—UV images have low contrast—or high-contrast development of a medium- or high-speed film. Black-

and-white film is used because direct UV does not have color differences. Exposure must be established by testing.

Fluorescence photography. The second, indirect, method of UV photography depends upon the fact that many substances will absorb short-wavelength, invisible energy and in response emit longer wavelengths within the visible range; thus they glow with colors that are distinctly different from their ordinary colors revealed by reflected light. This phenomenon is called *fluorescence* if it occurs only while the exciting energy (i.e., the UV) is being absorbed; it is called *phosphorescence* if the light emission continues after the exciting energy has been removed or turned off. The colors emitted differ according to the nature of the material and so can reveal differences among substances that are visually the same.

Fluorescence photography is used for many of the same applications as direct UV photography, and for biomedical research; chemical analysis; geological and mineralogical investigation; and analysis of dyes, inks, and other colorants. The bizarre color effects produced by many ordinary materials such as clothing, cosmetics, costume jewelry, and household objects have been used in illustrative photographs for advertising, record albums, posters, and similar purposes. Because the effect is within the visible range, ordinary color film can be used and exposure determined by a direct meter reading of the subject. The surroundings must be completely dark so that only the fluorescence is seen. The subject is illuminated with UV-only sources, either "blacklight" tubes or other sources fitted with UV-transmission screens (such as No. 18A filters). The camera lens is fitted with a UV-blocking filter so that only the visible colored light emitted by the subject will be registered on the film. A No. 2B filter provides efficient UV absorbtion with no significant effect on visible wavelengths.

See also: INFRARED PHOTOGRAPHY; SPECTRUM.

Umbo (Otto Umbehr)

German; 1902–1980

As a photographer, Otto Umbehr—Umbo—is remembered for his innovativeness and his originality. He is considered one of the pioneers of modern photojournalism. At the Bauhaus (1912–1923) he studied under Johannes Ittens, Walter Gropius, Wassily Kandinsky, and Paul Klee. A refreshingly versatile artist, Umbo experimented with political and social photomontage, collage, the

use of multiple exposure, unusual perspective and cropping, x-ray film (which did not produce halftones), and the fisheye camera. Before his enrollment in Itten's preparatory course at the Bauhaus, Umbehr (he adopted the name Umbo in 1924) worked as a coal miner, a potter, and as an actor with a traveling theater group. On leaving the Bauhaus, he moved to Berlin and worked there as a clown, housepainter, film-poster designer, and film assistant (production assistant to Kurt Bernhardt, camera assistant to Walter Ruttman). In 1926 Umbo's father gave him a 13 × 18cm 5" × 7") studio camera. Paul Citroen, a friend from the Bauhaus, built him a darkroom. By 1927 Umbo was making his first portraits of the actresses and newsworthy personalities of the day. These pictures provided his entry to the rapidly developing field of photojournalism.

The Dephot (Deutsche Photodienst) agency, founded by Simon Guttman, was the first cooperative of photojournalists. It was founded at the end of 1928 with Guttman as literary manager and director, Felix H. Man as director of press photography, and Umbo as studio director as well as photojournalist. Umbo was considered the most versatile photographer at the agency; he specialized in photoreportage and in writing about film, theater, and dance. Other photographers in the agency were Harald Lechenperg, Andreas Feininger, Fritz Goro, Hans Reinke, Werner Colnitz, Robert Capa, and Kurt Hutton. Umbo's photographs, noted for their strength of form and composition as well as their feeling for the subject, appeared in the publications *Berliner Illustrirte Zeitung, Münchner Illustrierte Presse, Uhu, Scherl's Magazin, Dame, Neue Linie,* and *Koralle.* His work was also reproduced in publications about photography, *Es Kommt de Neue Fotograf* (Werner Graff, Berlin, 1929), *Foto-Auge: 76 Fotos der Zeit* (Franz Roh, Stuttgart, 1929), and the photographic annuals published by *Arts et Métiers Graphiques.* His photographs were exhibited in *Film und Foto,* Stuttgart, 1929. The Dephot agency was dissolved in 1933 as an indirect result of the strictures of the Hitler regime. Umbo continued to work in Berlin as a freelance photojournalist, undertaking one assignment in North Africa (1941), another in Italy (1942). In the last years of the war he became a driver in the German army (1943–1945). His studio in Berlin, with all his photographs and negatives, was destroyed in 1945.

In the postwar period, until his death in 1980, Umbo lived in Hanover, work-

Umbo. "Mannequin: Legs and Slippers" (ca. 1928). Rudolph Kicken Gallery, Cologne.

ing as a freelance photographer, photojournalist, and teacher. He contributed to *Picture Post, Quick,* and *Der Spiegel* and traveled to the United States in 1952. He was instructor in photography at the *Landesversehrtenberufsschule,* Bad Pyrmont (1957–1974); *Werkkunstschule,* Hanover; and *Werkkunstschule,* Hildesheim (1965–1974). A retrospective of Umbo's 1925–1933 photographs was held at Galerie Spectrum in Kunstmuseum, Hanover, in 1979; and a large exhibition of his work, and Herbert Bayer's, was shown at the Centre Georges Pompidou, Paris, in 1981. *See also:* PHOTOJOURNALISM.

Umbrella Lighting

A photographic umbrella is a collapsible fabric reflector constructed in the same manner as a conventional umbrella. It may be circular in shape and open to one or more degrees of parabolic curvature, or it may be square and open to a relatively flat surface. The umbrella's light weight and collapsibility make it easy to use on location and mount on a lightweight stand. The light source, either a continuous-output instrument or electronic flash, is mounted on the stand or clipped onto the umbrella shaft and aimed into its center. The umbrella is positioned to reflect the light onto the subject, or with translucent fabric it may be turned to transmit diffused light. The concentration of the light can be adjusted somewhat by sliding the instrument along the shaft closer to or farther from the center of curvature. The quality of the light is determined by the umbrella position and its fabric. A thin, white fabric produces softer, less intense light than fabric with a reflective silver or gold surface. Gold and light-blue fabrics are used to shift the color temperature of the light somewhat for a warming or cooling effect, but not with the accuracy provided by filters. Fabrics of other colors may be used for special effects; some umbrellas permit the fabric to be removed easily and replaced with another. An umbrella produces less light than is obtained by aiming the light source directly at the subject. Depending on the shape, size, and reflectivity of the fabric, the light loss commonly is between 1½ and 3 *f*-stops.
See also: LIGHTING; LIGHT SOURCES; REFLECTORS.

Underdevelopment

Underdevelopment most often occurs when the length of development is too short or when the developer temperature is too low. It will also occur when the

developer is too highly diluted or near exhaustion.

Underdevelopment of a negative affects the highlight and middle-tone densities. The negative looks thin (transparent) because these areas do not reach sufficient density. Shadow areas may appear normal because their development is quickly completed and is usually finished even when other areas are underdeveloped. (Shadow detail is a key to distinguishing underdevelopment from underexposure, which produces little or no shadow density.) A print from an underexposed negative is too dark and lacks contrast; if exposure is adjusted to obtain a lighter print, tones

will be weak and washed-out. Underdeveloped slide film produces an image that is too dark throughout. A print that is properly exposed to a normal negative but is underdeveloped has a muddy look, with a lack of rich tonality or color.

Underdevelopment is much more likely to be a problem in film processing than in printing, because there are more variables and because even slight differences produce noticeable changes in the image. If correctly exposed negatives are consistently too thin with standard development procedures, the developing time can be increased experimentally until the desired negative density is achieved. Printing papers should always be given the full recommended development. *See also;* DEVELOPMENT; UNDER-EXPOSURE.

Underexposure

Any exposure that fails to register subject tones or details with sufficient density to print or be visible with the desired strength is an underexposure. In general, underexposure of a negative or reversal film produces a final image (print or slide) that is too dark; an underexposed print from a normal negative looks pale and weak. The darkest areas in a subject are the most affected by underexposure; they fail to register in a way that is distinguishable in the final image.

An exposure that does not register dark area detail is not necessarily underexposure. If the intent is to merge all dark areas into black for graphic effect, or if it is to reduce exposure in order to retain highlight detail of major importance, the exposure given is proper exposure, not underexposure, no matter what average standards may suggest.
See also: EXPOSURE; OVEREXPOSURE.

Underwater Photography

History. As early as 1855, photographers were attempting to take pictures underwater. During the Crimean War (1853–1856), William Bauer, a German inventor, made unsuccessful attempts to take pictures through the portholes of a submarine he had built for the Russian navy. In 1856, William Thompson, an Englishman, made a marginally successful photograph of seaweed and sand in the waters near Weymouth, England, using a camera in a watertight box. Ten years later, Ernest Bazin, a French photographer, tried repeatedly but unsuccessfully to make pictures from diving bells. Success also eluded Eadweard Muybridge in the 1870s when he attempted underwater photography using a camera in a watertight container in the San Francisco Bay.

It was not until 1893 that the first successful underwater photographs were made. Louis Boutan, a French scientist who had learned diving in order to study mollusks, made pictures of swimmers, marine animals, and the underwater terrain in the Bay of Bayuls in southern France. Boutan has rightly been referred to as the father of underwater photography because his work at the end of the 19th c. established principles that are still valid today.

Underwater cinematography became practical in the early part of the 20th c. with the invention of a device by Jack Williamson, an American journalist, photographer, and writer. The device

consisted of a long tube with a sphere at the submerged end which held the camera and crew. The top of the tube was attached to a surface support vessel which supplied air and electrical power to the equipment and personnel below. The device was shortly made obsolete by improved housings for motion picture equipment, but Williamson proved it was possible to make commercial films on the ocean floor. He worked on the first motion picture adaptation of Jules Verne's *20,000 Leagues Under the Sea* and on several other films with similar themes.

During the 1920s and 1930s, underwater photography began to be popularized in magazines, books, and films. In 1927, the first underwater color still photographs were published in *National Geographic* magazine. The photographs were made on Autochrome plates by Dr. William Longly, an ichthyologist, and Charles Martin, a photographer for the magazine. During the late 1930s, the German photographer Hans Hass gained a worldwide reputation through his underwater films, lectures, and books.

Recent decades have seen a great expansion in the field of underwater photography and cinematography, perhaps first stimulated by the development of the Aqualung regulator in the 1940s. In the 1950s such photographers as Jerry Greenberg, Walter Starck II, and Flip Schulke designed and built much of their own equipment to take advantage of the new developments in diving equipment. Luis Marden provided photographic coverage of Jacques Cousteau's activities in the Red Sea and Indian Ocean for *National Geographic;* when Cousteau's book and movie *The Silent World* appeared, they vastly increased public interest in the undersea environment. Marden's underwater natural history work was followed by that of Bates Littlehales and Emory Kristof, and later, William Curtsinger, Ron and Valerie Taylor, and David and Anne Doubilet. Al Giddings, like Cousteau, went from still photography to cinematography. In contrast, Douglas Faulkner continues to use a twin-lens reflex camera in a camera housing developed by Hans Hass over 30 years ago. Other noted underwater photographers are Werner Braun, Flip Nicklan, Koji Nakamura, Carl Roessler, and the late Ron Church.

The range of underwater photography has been extended by such sophisticated tools and technologies as wet and dry suits, portable air compressors, waterproof strobe lights, mixed-gas diving, deep submersibles, and underwater habitats for extended stays below. Many

advances in underwater camera housings permit closeup and wide-angle single-lens reflex photography of anything from feeding coral to whales. Faster color film with greater color saturation greatly extended the range of underwater photographic possibilities, for even with flash illumination, water absorbs light rapidly.

With the simplification of diving equipment in the late 1940s and the introduction of a self-contained underwater camera for amateur photographers in 1959 (Calypso/Nikonos), more people began taking pictures underwater. Today, there are approximately 5 million skindivers around the world, many of whom take pictures underwater as part of their hobby.

Equipment and environment. Although a number of self-contained, waterproof cameras now exist, the basic photographic equipment used today is not greatly different from that used by Louis Boutan and other pioneers. Many photographers, professional and amateur, rely on waterproof housings to protect their "in-air" cameras from the underwater environment. Today, it is possible to buy housings for almost every type of camera made—including disk, instant-film, and video cameras.

Self-contained underwater cameras and housings are made to withstand the corrosive effects of seawater; regular exposure to sand, shocks, and sun; and most important, the increased pressure underwater. The materials used for underwater photographic equipment include cast aluminum, stainless steel, and various recently developed plastics.

In addition to a housing for an in-air camera or a self-contained underwater camera, a flash unit is almost essential for good underwater photographs. Without auxiliary lighting, all color photographs—except those taken within 10 ft (3m) of the surface—will have an overall blue or green cast depending on the color of the water in which they are taken. The water acts as a filter and selectively absorbs various wavelengths from sunlight as depth increases; at 60 ft (20m), almost all colors except blue have been absorbed.

In addition to absorption, three other factors affect the quality and quantity of the light that will reach film in an underwater camera: reflection, refraction, and scattering. During the two hours before and the two hours after noon, underwater light penetration is greatest. At other times, when the sun is closer to the horizon, most of its light is reflected off the water's surface. When the water is choppy, large amounts of light never penetrate the depths because it is reflected by the many small surfaces created by the wind and waves.

Refraction, the bending of light rays as they pass from one medium to another, also alters the amount of sunlight that penetrates the water. When the sun is overhead, the least amount of light-ray bending takes place, but as the sun approaches the horizon, the rays are bent more and more. The light must travel farther to reach a particular depth, and this reduces its intensity.

Scattering also reduces the intensity of natural light at a given depth. Light rays are scattered by the suspended debris and microscopic organisms found in all bodies of water. Light passing through a heavy concentration of such particles will be reduced and diffused by scattering. Suspended particles also affect underwater flash photography because light reflected toward the camera—called backscatter—can create bright pinpoints that degrade colors and contrast and may obscure the subject.

The combined effects of absorption, reflection, refraction, and scattering can degrade images even in water that is very clear. They can be minimized by photographing when the sun is high in the sky and by reducing the camera-to-subject distance. To obtain a close subject distance, most underwater photographs are made either with wide-angle lenses or with close-up equipment. Normal and long-focal-length lenses simply do not render very good results because their minimum focusing distance is often too great for optimum photography. The clearest and sharpest photographs are made when the camera-to-subject distance is only 20 to 25 percent of the total distance one can see underwater.

Deep-sea photography. Most sport diving is done within 130 ft (40m) of the surface; the practical limit for diving and using air as the breathing medium is about 225 ft (68m). Since most photographic equipment available for more than shallow-water snapshots is pressure-tested to about 300 ft (90m), it is more than adequate for general-purpose underwater photography. When photographs have to be made at greater depths, special equipment is required. Manned submarines with special air-gas breathing mixes can be used to about 10,000 ft (3050m), but beyond those depths, remote-controlled devices are used to get the camera equipment to the depths needed. Most deep-sea photography is done as part of ocean mapping programs, mineral exploration, or biological research. In such applications, photographs are regularly made miles below the surface. The devices that take the cameras to these depths include

Union Case. Smithsonian Institution.

remote-control submersibles, sleds towed at a greater depth behind a surface or underwater vessel, and untethered "boomerang" equipment that is released at the surface, travels to the ocean floor, makes a photograph, and returns to the surface. Stationary devices that remain at depth in one location to record the changes in the surrounding scene over a period of time are also used in oceanographic research.

Future development. As with other specialized areas of photography, miniaturization and electronic imaging are changing the equipment used for shallow and deep-sea underwater photography. Diver-held equipment is being changed by many of the developments that swept 35mm still photography equipment in the late 1970s. Self-contained, fully automatic 35mm single-lens reflex underwater cameras will soon be introduced, followed closely by self-contained video equipment. Deep-sea equipment will increasingly depend on video digital image methods and on image enhancement. Developments in high-resolution video will greatly improve the quality and thus the information content of images returned by unmanned equipment at greater and greater depths.

See also: BOUTAN, LOUIS; DIGITAL IMAGES.

Union Case

A Union case was a molded, booklike case for a daguerreotype or ambrotype,

patented in the United States by Samuel Peck in 1854. It was the first significant commercial use of thermoplastic molding, a process that permitted mass production of a durable case with intricate designs on both covers at low cost; the substance used was a mixture of sawdust and shellac. The Union case immediately supplanted wood-and-leatherette and other cases that required some degree of hand assembly; they were imported into England and Europe, but were manufactured and most widely used in the United States. The molded relief designs were variously pictorial, classical, and symbolic (e.g., the American eagle). Designs were easily changed by making a new set of molds, and it is possible to approximately date a case by consulting catalogs and advertisements announcing the introduction of a new design. This is an unreliable way to date the image within, however, because it was common practice to transfer the plate from a damaged original case (leatherette scuffed easily and had a relatively short life as hinging, for example) to a new case of later manufacture. Union cases are a specialty area of photographic collecting today.

See also: AMBROTYPE; COLLECTING PHOTOGRAPHICA; DAGUERREOTYPE.

U.S.; Uniform System

Before the *f*-number system of designating lens aperture settings was universally adopted, many diaphragms were calibrated by the U.S., or Uniform System of settings. Like *f*-stops, each U.S. setting changed the exposure by a factor of two (i.e., doubled or halved the exposure). The first setting, marked U.S. 1, provided an effective aperture having a diameter one-fourth of the focal length; in the *f*-number system, the equivalent setting is *f*/4. This base was established because few lenses at the time had a wider maximum aperture, and those that did produced poor image quality at the wider settings. Because each successive setting halved the exposure (i.e., ½, ¼, ⅛, etc.), the successive U.S. numbers indicated the degree of change; thus:

U.S. 1 = *f*/4	U.S. 32 = *f*/22
U.S. 2 = *f*/5.6	U.S. 64 = *f*/45
U.S. 4 = *f*/8	U.S. 128 = *f*/90
U.S. 8 = *f*/11	U.S. 256 = *f*/90
U.S. 16 = *f*/16	U.S. 512 = *f*/128

See also: *f*-NUMBER/*f*-STOP.

Vacuum Back; Vacuum Easel

The most efficient film holders (camera backs) and printing-paper easels for large- and very-large-format work hold materials in place by means of a vacuum. Such devices consist of a thin, hollow chamber with a flat surface that is perforated with an overall pattern of holes or channels. A suction pump is connected to the chamber by means of a flexible hose so as not to transmit vibration. When the pump operates, it pulls air from inside the chamber, and outside air rushes through the perforated surface to replace it. When a piece of film or paper is laid over the holes, the pressure of the outside air forces it flat against the surface. Efficiency is increased by placing a mask around the material to cover unused holes.

Vacuum backs are an essential part of graphic-arts process cameras, in which sheets of film up to 30″ × 40″ (76.9 × 102.6cm) or larger must be held absolutely flat. Factors of weight, dust, and reflections make it impossible to use a sheet of glass inside the camera to hold the film. A vacuum back also ensures perfect contact at all points between a film-type halftone screen and the lith film being exposed. Accessory vacuum backs are also available for large-format view cameras to prevent the film from sagging or buckling out of the focal plane.

Vacuum easels are similarly used to hold large-format printing papers flat, and to ensure intimate contact between negative and paper in contact printing.

They are widely used in photofabrication and in other industrial, technical, and scientific applications of photography.

Van Der Zee, James

American; 1886–1983

In a career of more than 70 years as a professional photographer, James Van Der Zee produced thousands of pictures which form the greatest single record of middle-class black Americans—an achievement that was hardly known outside his own community until the last 15 years of his life, but which then brought him world-wide recognition.

Born in Lenox, Massachusetts, Van Der Zee became interested in photography at the age of 14 when he bought a rudimentary camera and darkroom outfit by mail order. For the next several years in his spare time he photographed the people around him, first at home and school, then in Phoebus, Virginia, where he befriended the teachers and pupils of the Whittier Preparatory School, and finally in New York City, where he supported himself by doing odd jobs and playing the violin in small dance orchestras. His professional photographic career began in 1914, when he got a job as a darkroom assistant for a small department store in Newark, New Jersey. Within two years he opened his first photographic studio, Guaranty Photos, in Harlem. The studio moved to various locations in Harlem, finally becoming permanently established from 1943 to 1969 as the GGG Studio at 272 Lenox Avenue.

During these years the people of Harlem passed before his camera: proud parents, children, clergymen, newlyweds, lodge members, politicians, entertainers. Van Der Zee photographed Harlem during its renaissance, which saw the rise of black writers such as Countee Cullen and Langston Hughes; religious leaders such as Adam Clayton Powell, Sr., and Father Divine; musicians such as James P. Johnson and Duke Ellington; and activists such as Marcus P. Garvey, founder of the Back-to-Africa movement. However, the great majority of Van Der Zee's subjects were not celebrities; they were the middle-class families who made up the community of Harlem.

Van Der Zee's record of these people in studio and location portraits, individually and in lodge, sports club, and social groups, is warm, gentle, and understanding. He loved people and worked to include that feeling in every picture. Van Der Zee's style was basically a romantic one. His subjects' poses

were formal, often before backgrounds he had painted himself, and lighting was soft and expressive. A photograph of a young woman during World War I might have had an image of the sweetheart or husband in her thoughts—away in the service—printed in. Similarly, a funeral photograph—a tradition that lasted in Harlem well into the 1930s—might have had an image of the deceased, drawn from Van Der Zee's files of years before, printed in above the scene. Other pictures were straightforward studies of people proud of their achievements who came to be recorded in their finest clothes and uniforms.

Van Der Zee's view of the real Harlem was seldom, if ever, seen by the rest of America until it formed a major portion of the exhibition *Harlem On My Mind* at the Metropolitan Museum of Art in New York City in 1967. Despite extreme reverses, dispossession, and neglect, Van Der Zee was still active, and the main body of his work—some 75,000 glass plates, negatives, and prints, most of them clearly signed and dated—was intact. Recognition followed immediately. At the age of 81 he received the ASMP Photographer's Award, and in the following year, 1970, he was awarded Life Fellowship at the Metropolitan Museum of Art, which purchased a number of his pictures for their collection. Other awards followed: the Living Legacy Award, presented by President Carter at the White House in 1979; the Pierre Toussaint award for outstanding service to humanity presented by Cardinal Cooke at St. Patrick's Cathedral in 1978; and many others.

James Van Der Zee died in 1983 at the age of 97 while in Washington, D.C. to receive an honorary Doctorate of Arts from Howard University.

Van Dyke, Willard

American; 1906–

Williard Van Dyke, known primarily for his work in documentary filmmaking, was first a still photographer and has now returned to that medium. One of the founders of Group *f*/64, Van Dyke was Edward Weston's first apprentice in 1929. In the early 1930s he left California for New York with the intention of influencing social reform through the medium of film. As a cameraman on *The River*, Van Dyke began a distinguished career which included coproducing with Ralph Steiner the classic film *The City*, as well as the social documentaries *Valleytown* and *The Bridge*.

Self-taught in photography, Van Dyke was born in Denver, Colorado, and

Van Der Zee, James. "Couple in Raccoon Coats" (1932). Courtesy James Van Der Zee Estate.

attended the University of California. During World War II, he was a producer for the OWI Overseas Motion Picture Bureau, making the official government film on the founding of the United Nations, titled *San Francisco,* in 1945. From 1946 to 1965 he worked in the field of television under sponsorship from the Carnegie, Ford, and Rockefeller foundations. His films have won many major awards; *Skyscraper,* produced in collaboration with Shirley Clarke, took two prizes at the Venice Film Festival for a total of eight international awards.

Van Dyke was appointed Director of the Department of Film at the Museum of Modern Art, New York, in 1965, and served at that post until his retirement in 1972. He was the chairman of the faculty at the first cinema session of the Salzburg Seminar in 1969, and taught from 1972–1977 at the State University of New York at Purchase. He now teaches at the University of New Mexico, Albuquerque, and lives in Santa Fe, New Mexico,

continuing his career in still photography.

Vandyke Process

The Vandyke or brown-print, is an iron printing process, the most fundamental version of the kallitype. It was named for the rich brown tones characteristic of some work of the 17th c. Flemish painter Anthony Vandyke (or Van Dyck). The process requires a long scale negative (density range about 1.8) for best results, and contact exposure by sunlight or ultraviolet radiation. The Vandyke sensitizer is composed of equal amounts of three solutions that must be prepared separately before being combined in order: (1) a 27 percent solution of ferric ammonium citrate; (2) a 4.5 percent solution of tartaric acid; (3) an 11.5 percent solution of silver nitrate. The sensitizer is brushed liberally over paper or cloth, which is dried in the dark. Contact exposure is extended until middletones

print out full visibility. The image is "developed" in running water for about one minute, and fixed in a 5 percent plain hypo solution; prolonged fixing lightens the image. Thorough washing after fixing is required; the image tone can be intensified or modified with a gold chloride solution.
See also: IRON PRINTING PROCESSES; KALLITYPE.

Variable Contrast Developers

A number of black-and-white print developers have claimed to produce significant contrast variations in a single (normal) contrast grade of paper. Most such formulas have relied primarily on increased dilution or the addition of a restrainer to progressively reduce contrast. At one time the Beers variable-contrast formula was effective with silver-rich contact printing papers. Most modern enlarging papers show little or no response to such formulas. However, some photographers use various proportions of a standard developer and a very soft-working "portrait" or warm-tone developer to vary the contrast of certain bromide enlarging papers. The degree of variation is not great, but may be expressively useful. Typical combinations of stock (full strength) developer solutions and water are given in the table.

Contrast control in black-and-white film development is achieved first by choice of developer, then by varying the time of development and, perhaps, the agitation. Contrast is not effectively variable in color processing.
See also: CONTRAST; DEVELOPMENT.

Contrast Control Developer

Normal Developer*	Soft Developer*	Water	
			Highest
8 parts	+ 0 parts	+ 0 parts	contrast
4	+ 0	+ 4	
3	+ 1	+ 4	
2	+ 2	+ 4	
1	+ 3	+ 4	
0	+ 4	+ 4	Lowest contrast

*Full strength stock solution

Variable Contrast Materials

Certain black-and-white printing papers are coated with an emulsion that produces different degrees of contrast depending upon the color of the exposing light; they are variously known as variable contrast, multiple-grade, or selective-contrast papers. The emulsion is constructed of two layers: a high-contrast layer sensitive to blue light, and a low-contrast layer sensitive to green light. Various yellow (blue-absorbing) and magenta (green-absorbing) filters are used to control which layer is most affected by exposure. Using a filter of intermediate color and strength permits both layers to receive part of the exposure, producing an intermediate degree of contrast. It is also possible to print one portion of an image with light passing through a low-contrast filter, and another portion with high-contrast filtered light. Although the filters are numbered, they have no direct relationship to the numbers used with graded contrast papers. The range available with most variable contrast papers is a bit less than four graded paper steps. The primary advantage of variable contrast papers is economy: it is only necessary to stock one paper, rather than a

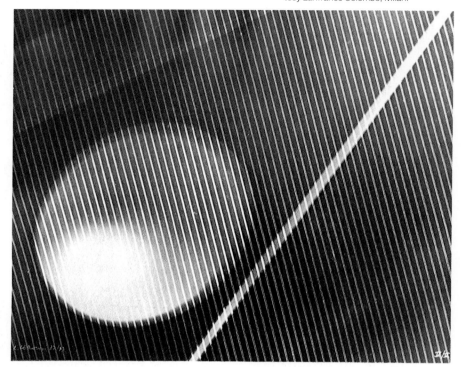

Veronesi, Luigi. "Fotogramma" (1937). Courtesy Lanfranco Colombo, Milan.

supply of each contrast grade that might be needed.

Varifocus Lens

Like a zoom lens, a varifocus—or varifocal—lens can be shifted over a continuous range of focal lengths. Unlike a zoom lens, a varifocus lens does not maintain sharp focus; it must be refocused at each new setting. Although less convenient for rapid, continuous photography, a varifocus lens is more economical than a zoom lens and may offer better correction of aberrations throughout its range.
See also: ZOOM LENS.

Velox

Introduced as a gaslight-exposure, developing-out contact paper in 1893, Velox paper has been used for most of the 20th c. by amateurs and mass-processing labs to print black-and-white snapshots. The name *Velox* is a product trademark of Eastman Kodak Co., which now offers the paper in four contrast grades of contact-speed emulsion, and a single unicontrast grade of an enlarging speed emulsion for automatic printing equipment. Because the paper is widely used for the purpose, the term *velox* is often used generically in the graphic arts to mean a halftone (i.e., screened) positive print on paper. Such prints, made to final size, are often used when mechanicals—the final assembly of

type and picture reproductions—are prepared for photomechanical reproduction in black-and-white. This procedure avoids the time and expense of having the photograph separately screened and stripped by hand into the master negative from which the printing plate is made.
See also: GASLIGHT PAPER; SCREENED NEGATIVES/PRINTS.

Veronesi, Luigi

Italian; 1908–
Luigi Veronesi is best known in his country as a painter, but his contribution to the development of Italian photography is invaluable. For over 50 years his faith in the expressive possibilities of the photographic medium has remained unshaken and he has refused to draw a line between photography and the so-called nobler arts, as so many artists and art critics do in his own country.

Veronesi studied art, painting, and graphics in Milan. His first one-man exhibition, held in that city in 1934, presented abstract paintings and mixed-media-and-photogram images. Veronesi's personal contacts with the contemporary European art scene, particularly with protagonists of the avant-garde such as Vantongerloo and Moholy-Nagy, greatly influenced his cultural formation. Even in his earliest works, Veronesi has been involved principally in formal, non-figurative exploration in both painting and photography.

His interest in photography dates from the late 1920s, his work being directed towards a non-documentary illustration of reality through the technique of the photogram—pictures obtained without a camera, by the direct action of light on photographic paper or undeveloped film. As the artist himself explained: "In the majority of cases the photogram forms part of that metaphysical or abstract orientation that has influenced and conditioned so much of all modern art. In the photogram, objects rediscover their primordial expression; we can see them beyond their actual shape, in pictures that are not apparent to us and yet are true, and that change instantaneously at the movement of the least glimmer of light."

In the 1930s, Milan was a unique center in the Italian art world; not surprisingly, many extremely original interdisciplinary projects using photography were created there during those years, not so much by professional photographers as by painters, movie directors, and architects. While others like Albe Steiner, Bruno Munari, or Remo Muratore used the same techniques for advertising or graphic design, from 1939 Veronesi used the photogram to design experimental abstract films.

In the post-war years Veronesi began using microphotography to explore the formal analogies between the "landscape" revealed by the microscope and his photograms—which he had begun producing in color with startling results. His style and technique have stayed constant and highly recognizable over the years, at the same time retaining their freshness and originality.
See also: PHOTOGRAM.

Vesicular Images and Emulsions

A vesicular image is composed of microscopic bubbles embedded in an emulsion. When viewed by reflected light (with a black backing if the image is in a transparent film emulsion) the areas composed of bubbles scatter the light and appear brighter, forming a positive image. When the image is projected with light passing straight through, as in an enlarger or slide projector, the scattered light is lost and the image appears negative. However, if the illumination strikes the film from an angle, the projected image can be made to look positive.

Vesicular emulsions produce high-contrast images with very high resolving power: 300 to 500 lines per mm in some films. They require no wet processing; exposure and heat are sufficient to form a permanent image. The emulsion consists of colorless diazo compounds in a ther-

moplastic layer. Exposure causes the diazo compounds to break down, liberating nitrogen. Development immediately afterward by heat softens the emulsion slightly and allows the gas to form bubbles that are held in place as the emulsion cools. Fixing is by further overall exposure that breaks down the unused diazo compounds; without heat, the liberated nitrogen diffuses out of the emulsion. Because of their contrast and resolution characteristics, such films are used to make copies of microphotographic records, x-rays, and similar images.
See also: DIAZO PROCESSES; KALVAR PROCESS.

Video Imaging and Recording

Video systems convert moving images and sound into electrical signals. These signals can be transmitted, recorded, altered, or enhanced electronically and then reconverted and displayed on a TV or projection screen. There are two major recording media: magnetic tape and laser-beam disk.

The video camera is the basic component in a video imaging system. Like any camera, it uses lenses to focus light reflected from the subject. However, it does not carry film; instead it focuses the image onto a camera tube or charge-coupled device (sensor).

The vidicon is a commonly used type of camera tube. Although there are other tubes that operate at lower light levels or meet the higher quality standards needed in broadcast TV, all the tubes work on similar principles. The light image from the camera's lens is focused onto a target plate at the head of the vidicon tube. The front of the plate is transparent, and the image falls on a photo-conductive coating on the back of the plate. This coating changes its electrical resistance when exposed to light. The light parts of the image decrease the resistance of the part of the plate they fall on, while the dark parts of the image increase the resistance of their portions of the plate. A cathode at the rear of the tube generates a stream of electrons that are magnetically focused into a beam which scans the target plate in a rapid series of horizontal sweeps. Electrons that pass through the dark parts (the high-resistance portions of the plate) lose energy, and the loss is measured by an electrically conductive coating on the other side of the plate. Electrons passing through the light parts of the image (the low-resistance portions of the plate) gain energy, and their higher voltage is registered on the appropriate part of the plate.

The electron beam scans the entire im-

age area in a precisely controlled pattern. In this fashion a video signal that describes the image area's lights and darks in terms of higher and lower voltages is created. A picture tube of a TV set can recreate the original image essentially by reversing the process of the camera tube. Designed to accurately repeat the scanning pattern of the camera's cathode gun, the TV's electronic beam uses the video-signal information of high and low voltage to faithfully render the image on the TV's phosphorescent screen .

Integrated circuit (IC) technology has been used to develop a solid-state light-sensitive IC chip that eventually may replace the relatively bulky and delicate camera tube. Called charge-coupled devices (CCDs), these imaging sensors use less energy, give off less heat, and outlast conventional tubes.

Whether it uses a tube or CCD sensor, the camera must create video signals that conform to one of the several agreed-upon standardizations. In order for the signal to be correctly displayed on a TV screen or recorded on a video recorder, all the equipment must operate as a synchronized system and use a compatible standard for the formulation of the video signal. Although electronic devices that will make equipment with differing standards compatible are available, most video equipment is used with its own standardized components.

The most typical basic components are a camera, recorder, and monitor. Many cameras carry a miniaturized TV monitor that is used as a viewfinder and can also display images from the recorder. In addition, a number of manufacturers are developing "cam-recorders." These advanced systems offer a camera and recorder in one compact, portable unit. At the present time most cameras must physically be connected to a recorder by cables. This allows power-supply components to be located outside the camera to keep it small and lightweight, and provide the easiest way to synchronize the units. However, some professional systems transmit their video signals from the camera by microwaves to a remote recorder tuned to pick them up or relay them to a broadcast station.

Video tape recorders are often classified by the width of tape they employ . Systems that use a 1 in. (25mm) wide tape are now the accepted standard of quality in TV broadcasting. Yet electronic enhancement and miniaturization have encouraged the use of ¾ in. (1.9mm), ½ in. (1.3mm), and even ¼ in. (0.67mm) tapes for home and other non-critical use. Just as with audio tape recorders, the improvements in tape cassettes are quickly eliminating the need for reel-to-reel equipment. Small-format tape systems have gained significant acceptance in broadcasting since the introduction of the time-base corrector. This computer processor improves the quality and usefulness of the smaller formats. Home-format tape recorders use one of two systems: VHS (video home system) or Beta. They differ in cassette size, operating speed, and recording pattern on the tape. Their components and tapes are not interchangeable.

Video tape is essentially a polyester-based ribbon with a coating of magnetic particles of iron-oxide or chromium-dioxide. The magnetic recording heads on the video recorder inscribe the video and audio signal onto the tape. Since it is electronically represented, the image is not optically visible on the tape. As with ordinary audio tape, the signal can be erased and the tape reused. However, there is a practical limit to the number of times the same piece of tape can be recorded on or played back before the image quality begins to suffer. There are a variety of grades of tape, differing primarily in the nature of their magnetic coating. Better grades are longer lasting and produce a somewhat better image due to their superior ability to accept the video signal. All video tapes are capable of recording black-and-white or color images; this capability is determined by the camera and recorder.

Originally, the editing of video tape was achieved by physically cutting the tape at the points desired and gluing or taping the pieces together. This crude and time-consuming process usually created a visible, although momentary, disturbance ("glitch") in the image during playback. Modern editing is done electronically with the use of at least two video tape playbacks and control equipment that switches between them without loss of synchronization (the cause of glitches) to record their combined output on a final tape; no physical cutting or splicing is required. Computers commonly are used to program the editing sequence, and they can mix in material from a variety of sources. Often multiple cameras and pretaped and filmed materials are all integrated onto a master tape by a technical director at a single control console. Although these editing and switching techniques are becoming more accessible to the home or amateur video tape user, they are usually employed by broadcast professionals.

Some relatively inexpensive equipment capable of amplifying, enhancing, and correcting poorly recorded video tape images is beginning to reach the home user. These devices can automatically monitor and electronically adjust the video signal generated by cameras and recorded on tape.

The newest system of recording places signals on or in the metallic coating of a plastic disk that is much like a long-playing audio record. Some disks are permanent and can be prepared only by a manufacturers' master equipment; other can be recorded, erased, and rerecorded with portable or home equipment, much like video tape. This system has great potential for non-broadcast applications such as document and image storage and retrieval, home entertainment, and the equivalent of home movie-making. Laser-recorded images are not subject to accidental erasure or distortion from spurious magnetic fields, as taped images are, and the quality of the playback image is not affected by dirt or scratches on the hard plastic protective coating over the metal recording layer. The disk is also easier to handle, file, and store than a tape cassette.
See also: EDITING; MAGNETIC IMAGE RECORDING; TELEVISION.

View Camera

A view camera is a medium- to large-format camera composed of four major components: (1) a front standard that accepts a lens mounting board, (2) a bellows that connects the front standard to (3) a rear standard that accepts sheet-film holders and roll-film adapters, and (4) a bed or rail that supports the front and rear standards. Viewing is directly through the lens by means of a ground-glass (or equivalent) screen in the back. The screen is displaced when a film holder is inserted. Focusing is accomplished by moving the front and back standards toward or away from one another along the bed or rail; in some cameras only the front standard moves for focusing. The bellows must allow a lens to be positioned a distance equal to its own focal length in order to focus at infinity and to be extended farther to focus closer objects. (Additional extension from the infinity-focus position equal to only one-fourth the lens focal length will allow it to focus on an object five focal lengths away, the point at which exposure compensation for the additional extension becomes necessary.) Some cameras accept extra-long bellows for use with very long focal-length lenses, or a bag bellows that squashes outward to allow the front standard to be brought very close to the rear standard for focusing with short-focal-length wide-angle lenses.

View camera formats range from 2¼″ × 3 ¼″ to 20″ × 30″; the 4″ × 5″ and 8″ × 10″ formats are by far the most widely used. Many models permit changing from one format to another by means of interchangeable parts that attach to the basic front and rear standard or supporting rail. The view-camera design is extremely versatile for the wide range of lenses and film holders it can accept, and especially because the front and back have independent movements, or adjustments, that offer an unusual degree of control over framing, sharpness, and linear distortion or perspective. There are a number of variant designs, including the field camera, in which the flat bed folds up in front of the lens board, after the bellows has been collapsed completely, to a size and shape that is easily carried.
See also: BELLOWS; CAMERA; CAMERA MOVEMENTS: MONORAIL CAMERA; TECHNICAL CAMERA.

Viewing and Focusing Systems

Camera viewing systems vary from very simple independent wire frames to complex designs combining reflex viewing and automatic focusing. The basic function of a viewing system is to permit accurate composition and full use of the film area. Simple *wire-frame* finders allow the user to approximate the area viewed by the camera lens. They are often combined with a rear peep sight as on a rifle. Also known as a sports finder, the simple frame is useful when following fast action. A *direct optical* finder utilizes a front negative lens and a rear positive lens as an eyepiece. The direct optical finder is generally more accurate in defining the image area than the frame finder. The *albada* finder outlines the image area with a white line that appears suspended in the air. This effect is created by the reflection of a frame line painted or etched on a small piece of plain glass in the finder. The modern *bright-line* finder combines the optical viewfinder with an improved albada design. At close distances viewing parallax becomes apparent. This is often compensated in simple viewfinders by a small device that tilts the viewfinder to "see" the same area that the lens does. In more sophisticated viewfinder, cameras, fame lines move to correct for parallax.

A *rangefinder focusing* system is coupled to the lens in some cameras to measure precise distance from the subject. Without some focusing system the user must visually estimate distance and preset a distance on the lens scale. Some lenses use a zone focus method that relies on the depth-of-field properties of that particular focal length. The most direct viewing and focusing method is *ground-glass* viewing. A ground-glass

screen is illuminated by the lens when placed in the image path. The modern view camera operates on this direct through-the-lens viewing principle. Focusing is possible, but the image appears dim, upside down, and reversed from the left to right. *Reflex* viewing systems incorporate a mirror within the camera that reflects the image from the lens onto a ground glass. The image is no longer upside down, but must be seen from above. Eye-level viewing is accomplished by the addition of a right-angle mirror or glass prism above the ground glass. The *single-lens reflex* system views directly through the camera lens. During exposure the mirror is swung out of the light path. A *twin-lens reflex* camera uses one lens to take the picture and a second lens of equal focal length for viewing. Parallax error occurs here and may be corrected through several methods. Ground-glass focusing is aided by specially designed screens that improve image brightness and may have a split-image or microprism surface etched on them. Automatic focusing systems use visible light or infrared rays, or sound waves (sonar).
See also: AUTOMATIC FOCUSING; FOCUSING; GROUND GLASS; PARALLAX; RANGEFINDER; SLR: SINGLE-LENS REFLEX CAMERA; TWIN-LENS CAMERA.

Viewing Filter

It is extremely difficult to visualize accurately the shades of gray in which subject colors will be represented in a black-and-white print. It is also often difficult to visualize local contrast because certain colors seem brighter to the eye than others that objectively—i.e., in terms of film exposure—are equally as bright. A gray-amber or purplish-gray viewing filter erases color differences so that a subject can be seen in its relative brightnesses much as it will be recorded by panchromatic film. Held in front of the eye, such a filter is particularly valuable for evaluating contrast to determine whether lighting adjustments are required, such as adding light to shadow areas. With experience it is possible to relate the filtered image to equivalent print tones.

Viewpoint

Camera viewpoint—the angle and distance from which the subject is seen—affects the expressive quality of an image as well as more objective factors such as perspective and distortion. The function of viewpoint is to show selected aspects and qualities of the subject with the greatest clarity. Distance (for a given

lens focal length) determines the image size and thus the visibility of many details. Angle shows certain parts of the subject and conceals others, and it determines the background against which the subject is seen. A head-on view at eye level tends to emphasize symmetry and two-dimensional shape. A view from an angle to one side can increase the sense of three-dimensionality by showing two sides (e.g., face and end of a box) or, with elevation, three sides (top of the box as well).

In expressive terms, a head-on view is relatively neutral; an angled view suggests some degree of comment or interpretation. A very low or high angle can eliminate the horizon line from the field of view; a high angle also can emphasize the layout or locations of elements, like a map or plan drawing. Looking down on a subject tends to diminish or deemphasize it; looking up from a relatively close distance suggests exaggerated importance—the subject begins to be monumentalized. In the broadest sense, viewpoint establishes the fundamental relationships in the image; factors such as focus, tonality, color, and brightness or darkness refine and extend the effect of that basic statement.

See also: ANGLE OF VIEW; COMPOSITION; DISTORTION; PERSPECTIVE.

Vignette

In a vignette image the subject is shown in a soft-edged area that seems to float in the overall rectangle of the format; the surrounding area has no tonal variety or detail. A vignette is produced by photographing or printing through an opaque mask with a hole—usually an oval or a circle—in the center. In photographing a vignette, the mask is placed close enough to the lens to throw the edges of the hole completely out of focus. A fully lighted white or light-colored mask produces a light surrounding; a black mask produces a dark surrounding.

In printing, a vignette mask is kept moving during the exposure to insure that the edges of the printed area are diffused. A single exposure produces a white surrounding. A dark surrounding is created by removing the negative after the first exposure through the vignette mask and dodging (shading) the exposed central area while exposing the rest of the paper to white light. The dodging tool must be about the same size as the exposed area and held close to the paper surface so that spill light cannot degrade the image.

See also: CRAYON PICTURES.

Vignetting

An unintended curved cut-off of the corners—and in some cases the edges—of an image is called vignetting. It may be produced by a lens with a circle of coverage smaller than the format in use, or by a lens shade or filter ring that cuts into the field of view. It occurs in a view camera when the lens board or camera back is shifted, raised, or lowered so far that one end of the film is outside the circle of coverage. It is also caused by a lens mount that extends too far behind the rear element and cuts off angular rays to the corners of a format. The corners of the focusing screen in a view camera are commonly cut away so this can be inspected. If the diaphragm opening cannot be completely seen through the open corner (it will be an ellipse because of the oblique angle of view), the image will be vignetted; in some cases using a smaller aperture will solve the problem.

Vignetting may also result from underexposure at the edges, rather than from actual blocking of the image. The diagonal distance from the center of the lens to the corners of a film is much greater than the straight line distance to the center of the film. In very wide angle lenses the diagonal distance is so great that the light intensity is reduced enough to produce noticeably less exposure. Some fisheye lenses are supplied with a neutral density filter that is graduated outward from the center to no density at the edges so as to equalize exposure across the image area.
See also: CAMERA MOVEMENTS; COVERING POWER.

Vishniac, Roman

American; 1897–
Roman Vishniac's importance in photography is twofold: he photographed the lives of Eastern European Jews in the years just prior to the Holocaust, and he has made significant contributions to the development of the art of photomicrography.

Born in Pavlovsk, in Czarist Russia, to a well-to-do Jewish family, Vishniac became interested in photography as a very young boy. He took his first photograph through a microscope in 1906. In 1920 he received a doctorate in zoology from Shayavsky University and an M.D. from Moscow University. He fled post-Revolutionary Russia the same year and settled in Berlin, where he studied microbiology, endocrinology, and optics, as well as Far Eastern art (for which he was denied a doctorate on religious grounds) from 1928 to 1933.

Hitler's rise to power and the spread of anti-Semitism prompted Vishniac to begin to document the Jewish ghettos of

Vishniac, Roman. "Grandfather and Grand-
daughter" (1937). Courtesy Roman Vishniac;
collection, Museum of Modern Art, New
York.

Poland, Hungary, and Czechoslovakia. Nearly all the people he photographed and filmed died in the next decade.

Vishniac was interned as a stateless person in a French concentration camp for three months in 1940, but he managed to make his way to the United States in 1941. Upon arrival, he started a portrait studio which he operated until 1950. He became an American citizen in 1946. During these years Vishniac continued his experiments with photomicrography and time-lapse cinemamicrography. He gave up portraiture in 1950 to become a professional freelance photomicrographer specializing in photographing small animals, plants, and insect life. During the 1950s he developed a system of rationalistic philosophy which drew upon his scientific and artistic studies.

Vishniac was named to the American Society of Magazine Photographers Honor Roll in 1956 for "showing mankind the beauty of the world it cannot see." He was appointed Research Associate at the Albert Einstein College of Medicine in 1957 and Professor of Biological Education at Yeshiva University in 1961. He has taught at many other universities, including Fordham and the Rhode Island School of Design. From 1961 to 1964 he received grants from the National Science Foundation to produce the *Living Biology* film series.

Vishniac has lectured widely on numerous topics in the sciences, arts, and humanities. His major exhibitions include shows at the Louvre in 1939, the Jewish Museum in 1971, and a traveling show organized by ICP in 1972–1973. In addition to his still photography work he has made seven films. In recent years he has devoted himself to writing an autobiography.

Vision

Vision is the response of the eye and the brain to energy wavelengths from about 400 to 700 nanometers (nm)—the visible portion of the electromagnetic spectrum. Vision is not simply the physiological response of the eye to variations of intensity (brightness) or wavelength (color). It includes identification of the sensations in the eye with corresponding aspects of external objects; thus, vision includes recognition and interpretation, which assign meaning to the sensations generated in the eye. Those sensations are caused by the various ways elements within the field of view reflect, absorb, transmit, or emit light. They reveal the visual aspects of the elements, which include brightness, color, shape (edge form or outline), contour (surface form), texture, size, and location. Some of these aspects are also perceptible by other senses—e.g., texture is perceptible by touch. Memory of previous sensory experience also influences the brain's interpretation of eye responses, but eye response is the only direct physiological aspect of vision.

The Eye. The eye is the body's only

organ of external sense perception that is directly connected to the brain, by the optic nerve. The eye is nearly spherical, surrounded by a tough, whitish membrane the sclera. The front central portion of the sclera, called the cornea, is transparent, so as to admit light. It covers an anterior chamber filled with watery fluid, the aqueous humor, directly in front of the iris and the lens.

The iris is a circular structure of distinctively colored muscle fibers that involuntarily open or close in response to the brightness being received, in order to regulate the amount of light that enters the eye. The iris opening, the pupil, varies in diameter from about 3/8″ to 1/16″ (9.5 to 1.5.mm), but is never completely closed. The lens, directly behind the iris, is transparent and flexible; ciliary muscles attached to its outer edge change its shape to help focus at various distances.

The cornea, which bulges outward, provides the primary refraction of light rays toward the center of the eye, while the lens provides critical focusing. The image passes through the interior chamber, filled with a transparent, jellylike substance called the vitreous humor, and falls on the retina, a thin membrane that contains some 130 million light-sensitive receptor cells distinguished by their shapes as rods or cones. The cones are responsive to bright light and to differences in color. They are concentrated in a central region of the retina called the macula, and especially within the fovea, a tiny area of the macula directly on the lens axis. The fovea cones provide the sharpest image signals, and the signals in which color is most accurately distinguished. Rod cells are concentrated outside the macula. They are at least 1000 times more light-sensitive than cones but have no color discrimination, with the result that things can be seen at night or in very dim light, but only in shades of gray; they are not seen as sharply because there are no rods in the fovea.

The rods and cones are connected by intermediary cells to the optic nerve, which is attached at one small point to the retina. The optic nerves from the two eyes meet at a point called the chiasma, where various nerve paths cross, and then separate to go to opposite sides of the brain. The crossover network in the chiasma causes all impressions from the right half of the field of view in both eyes to go to the left side of the brain; all impressions from the left half of both fields of view go to the right side of the brain. This separation is apparently essential for depth perception and stereoscopic (three-dimensional) vision, and for the perception of some kinds of movement.

Vision
The Eye

Iris

Lens

Cornea

Anterior chamber (filled with aqueous humor)

Ciliary muscle (focuses the lens)

Retina

Vitreous cavity (filled with vitreous humor)

Fovea

Optic nerve

Seeing. Each eye takes in a field of view about 140° vertically and 150° horizontally; the fields overlap so that the total horizontal angel is about 180°. Accurate color vision occurs in about a 10° area in the center of each eye's field, corresponding to the macula area on the retina, and a sharp image is perceived within the central 2° area that falls on the fovea. Thus, when the eye is held fixed on a certain point, sharpness and color discrimination fall off rapidly toward the outer regions of the visual field. A person is seldom aware of this because the eyes, moving in unison, are constantly scanning the field in a series of leaps called saccades. Each saccade ends in a fixation—however brief—on a particular point, and the image of that point falls on the fovea. The ciliary muscles automatically adjust the lens shape to focus the image sharply at each fixation, a response called accommodation. In this way an overall impression of sharpness is built up. However, it is impossible for the eye to produce a single image with equal sharpness throughout in the way that a camera lens with great depth of field can .

Energy in the light rays falling on the retinal cells causes a momentary chemical breakdown of compounds in the cells—iodopsin in the cones, and rhodopsin or so-called visual purple in the rods. This breakdown generates the signals transmitted by the intermediary cells and the optic nerves to the brain. Even when the gaze is fixed on one point, involuntary slight movement shifts the image so that no rod or cone remains in a constant state of chemical discharge; otherwise the signals would stop and the image, or some portion of it, would disappear. A retinal image persists for about 1/4 sec. if light is flashed on and off or is otherwise interrupted. This "persistence of vision" makes motion pictures possible.

Exactly how the brain processes the signals from the optic nerves is not known; it is assumed to be one of the most complex and delicately precise processes of the human body, especially when the viewer and the subject are both in motion and the light intensities, as from a dappled leaf-and-sunlight pattern, are varying rapidly.

Color Vision. The cones are individually very sensitive to wavelengths of just one primary color—red, green, or blue—and only slightly sensitive to wavelengths of the other two colors. According to the classic Young-Helmholtz theory of color vision, the brain adds together the signals produced by the various kinds of cones to arrive at a composite color perception. If only red-sensitive cones are producing signals, the perception is red. If red- and green-sensitive cones are producing equal signals, the perception is yellow. However, if the red signal is stronger than the green, the perception is an orange, or if the green signal is stronger than the red, the perception is a lime green or chartreuse. The eye can be made to see any particular color by presenting it with appropriate proportions of one or more of the primary colors. Interestingly, the particular red, green, and blue wavelengths used do not matter so long as they are sufficiently different from one another. Whether the Young-

Helmholtz theory is the true explanation of color vision is not known, but it is operationally valid, as shown by a vast amount of experimental testing and by the fact that it forms the basis of all color photography and photomechanical reproduction in color. Another theory—

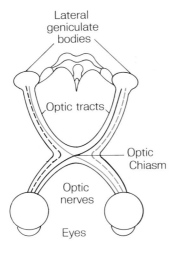

Lateral geniculate bodies

Optic tracts

Optic Chiasm

Optic nerves

Eyes

The Optic System

originated by Ewald Hering in the 19th c.—holds that color coding occurs in the nerve networks beyond the cones, and that what the cones distinguish are differences in the ratio between longer (reddish) and shorter (bluish) wavelengths in each part of the image. Research by Edwin H. Land and his associates along this line has produced full-color images using a mixture of white light and only a single primary color; this is discussed in the entry on two-color photography.

See also: DEPTH OF FIELD; DISTORTION; HELMHOLTZ, H.L.F.; MOTION PICTURES; PERSPECTIVE; STEREOSCOPIC PHOTOGRAPHY; TWO-COLOR PHOTOGRAPHY; YOUNG, THOMAS.

Visual Aids

Photographically produced illustrative materials for lectures, demonstrations, and similar presentations, called visual aids, include transparencies (slides, overhead projector materials, filmstrips, movies) and opaque images (prints, charts, diagrams). Whatever the subject matter, certain principles govern the selection or production of materials that

will communicate effectively. The most important considerations are the following.

Relevancy. The image must be related directly to the matter being covered at the moment. An audience cannot grasp aural information and puzzle out the significance of visual material simultaneously. A blank screen or easel is preferable to one with an image of only marginal importance.

Simplicity. Too much information at one time overloads the audience's ability to understand. Aural and visual material must make the same point simultaneously, not different points. In written visual material, five lines of reading matter is a maximum. Lists and tables of greater length should have the key items spotlighted, or otherwise made distinctive. Pictorial images also require simplicity, both in number of elements and in tonality or color.

Clarity. Shape, color, and size all affect visibility or legibility. Bold, regular shapes (e.g., sans-serif letters; stylized shapes in diagrams) that contrast well with the background can be seen at a good distance if they are large enough. Standard guidelines call for a projected area height (usable screen height) no smaller than one-eighth the maximum viewing distance, and a projected element or letter height no smaller than $1/25$ the height of the projected area. Opaque materials must meet the same standards.

See also: AUDIOVISUAL.

Visual Focus

The point or plane behind a lens at which visible wavelengths converge to form a sharp image is called the visual focus. Unless a lens is also specifically corrected for ultraviolet or infrared wavelengths, these may not focus at the same plane. Ultraviolet rays come to a focus closer to the lens than the visible rays, so the lens must be shifted slightly closer to the film—as if focusing on a more distant object —in order to record a sharp image. In the early 19th c., before they were identified, ultraviolet rays were called chemical rays, and the point at which they focused was called the chemical focus of a lens. Infrared rays come to a focus farther behind the lens than the visible rays, so the lens needs to be shifted slightly farther from the film. Some lenses have an infrared-focus reference mark next to the infinity mark on their focusing scales. The distance between the two mark shows an average correction when using infrared film and filtering out all or most of the visible wavelengths (if they are not filtered out, the visual focus is more important).

When visual focus is established, the focusing control is turned just that much in the direction that extends the lens farther from the film (i.e., focuses it on a closer object). In general, the amount of correction in lens extension for either kind of wavelength is equal to about 0.25 percent of the lens focal length. That is difficult to judge accurately; using a small f-stop to increase depth of field, and making test shots are more useful precautions.

Vitascope

Thomas Edison introduced the first commercially successful celluloid film motion-picture projector in the United States, the Vitascope, in 1896. It was, in fact, an improved version of the Phantoscope invented three years earlier by C. F. Jenkins. The right to the invention were sold to Edison by Thomas Armat, a financial backer of Jenkins.

See also: KINETOSCOPE; ZOOPRAXISCOPE.

Vogel, Hermann Wilhelm

German, 1834–1898

A brilliant chemist, in 1864 Vogel was named the first professor of photography at what was to become the Berlin Institute of Technology, where some 20 years later one of his students would be Alfred Stieglitz. In 1867 he published his *Handbook of Photography*, which was one of the leading texts for the remainder of the century. He was active in organizing photographic societies and publishing a photographic journal. In 1873 he made a discovery that shaped the entire development of photography—the fact that certain dyes extended the response of blue-sensitive collodion plates into the green region of the wavelengths of light. From this and subsequent research came improved sensitizers and eventually the entire field of dye sensitization of emulsions, without which panchromatic and color photography would be impossible. In 1884 Vogel devised the first true orthochromatic gelatin-silver dry plate in collaboration with Johann Obernetter; it was manufactured by the firm of Otto Perutz in Munich. Vogel's research enabled chemists who had studied under him to produce the first panchromatic emulsions early in the 20th c.

See also: DYE SENSITIZATION.

Voigtlander, Peter Wilhelm Friedrich

Austrian, 1812–1878

The instrument manufacturing firm of Voigtlander, established in Vienna in 1756, began manufacturing lenses in 1815. By 1840 its director was Peter

Vroman, Adam Clark. "Hairdressing" (1901). California Museum of Photography, Setzer-Alexander/Friends of Photography Collection.

Wilhelm, who supported the work of Professor Joseph Petzval in creating a revolutionary lens—the first specifically designed for photography. Voigtlander manufactured the lens, which with its speed of *f*/3.6 made photographic portraiture a practicality, and an accompanying camera of his own design featuring all-metal tubular construction. The firm grew throughout the 19th and 20th c., producing both cameras and lenses that were extremely popular. It continues today as part of a European consortium of photographic manufacturers.

See also: PETZVAL, JOSEPH.

Vortograph

Alvin Langdon Coburn gave the name vortograph to his photographs made with a kaleidoscopelike arrangement of mirrors around the camera lens. These images, made in 1917, were the first nonrepresentational abstract photographs. The name was derived from Vorticism, a British art movement somewhat related to Futurism and Cubism, led by Wyndham Lewis and Ezra Pound. Coburn's rationale for these images was that a photograph is in fact simply a pattern of various shapes and shades of gray; this, not the illusionary realism of the image, is what actually evokes response. Therefore it should be possible, and artistically valid, to create aesthetic response with patterns that do not represent identifiable objects but exist only to reveal their own, intrinsically abstract, qualities.

See also: ABSTRACT PHOTOGRAPHY; COBURN, ALVIN LANGDON.

Vroman, Adam Clark

American; 1856–1916

Adam Clark Vroman is noted for photographs of Indians in the American Southwest taken between 1895 and 1904. Born in Illinois, he worked as a railroad agent until the age of 36, then traveled west in 1892 for the sake of his wife's health. He settled in Pasadena, California and opened a bookshop in 1894 that continues to bear his name. His wife soon died. The following year, after having witnessed the Hopi snake ceremony, which impressed him greatly, he began to document the life and ritual practices of the Southwestern Indians.

A fine-book collector, merchant, amateur archeologist, historian of the American Southwest, and noted collector of Japanese netsuke and Indian arti-

facts, Vroman's interest in photography was more ethnological than aesthetic. His portraits of tribal groups and individuals, his views of populated villages built along the crests of mesas, and his records of craft and ceremonial activities are unpretentious. He made no attempt to romanticize or to hide the mixture of traditional crafts with the manufactured household items and clothing that were beginning to be appropriated into the culture at that time. His photographs were direct, respectful, and honest, free of the "noble savage" and pictorialist attitudes that distorted the work of his highly touted contemporary, Edwin S. Curtis.

His photographs were made with large glass-plate negatives, processed in his own darkroom, and meticulously contact printed on both platinum and silver-emulsion papers by exposure to the sun on the roof of his Pasadena apartment building.

In addition to his continued interest in the Hopi snake ceremony, Vroman photographed Navajo hogans; pueblos of the Zuñi, Laguna, and Acoma tribes; and the missions of Southern and Northern California. He visited all three Hopi mesas in 1900, photographing their snake and flute ceremonies. The following year he joined the Museum-Gates Expedition and photographed archeological digs in Navajo country, and made many photographs of the Navajos and a series of photographs of Yosemite Valley and the small Indian colony there. He continued to photograph the Hopi and Navajo people until 1904. After that time, he extended his travels to Asia, Canada, the East Coast, and Europe, but his photographs during this period were primarily of a tourist nature. Vroman made his last photographs on a trip to Cape Cod in 1914 and died in California in 1916.

Vroman did not exhibit his photographs, nor did he join the Los Angeles Camera Club formed in 1900, presumably because he did not consider himself an artist. Shortly before his death, Vroman donated his collection of books pertaining to California and the Pacific Southwest to the Pasadena Public Library; included were $10,000 for the maintainance of the collection and several albums of photographs, "many of which," he wrote, "I have taken myself."

Weston, Brett. "Monterrey Pine and Fog" (1962). Courtesy Brett Weston.

Warm Tone

The tones in a black-and-white print may be neutral grays, or they may have a slight color cast. Those with a brownish or reddish cast are said to be warm tones, in contrast to neutral or blue-black tones. Warm tone papers have chlorobromide emulsions; the warmth increases with the proportion of silver bromide in the emulsion. The paper base is often a buff or cream color to complement the image tone. Such papers are usually supplied in a limited range of contrast—grades 2, 3, and 4—in part because a warm tone image requires a slightly softer negative than a colder tone paper, and because the tonality is seldom chosen for subjects with contrasts at either extreme (i.e., that might require grade 1 or 5 paper). The most common subject for a warm tone image is a portrait. Warm tone developers have a high proportion of hydroquinone—in combination with metol or Phenidone in most formulas—and of potassium bromide; they are used at relatively high dilutions so as to be slow working. Warm tones can also be produced by toning a processed image with a brown, sepia, or very dilute red toner.
See also: CHLOROBROMIDE PAPER; TONER/TONING.

Warnerke, Leon (Vladislav Malakhovski)
British; 1837–1900
Hungarian-born Leon Warnerke was the inventor of several important pieces of photographic equipment. After working as a civil engineer in Czarist Russia, Warnerke established a private photographic laboratory in London in 1870. During the next 15 years he was responsible for the invention of a sensitometer and actinometer, and a compact roller slide for using rolls of paper-base film in large-format cameras. Warnerke won a prize in Belgium in 1873 for the best dry-plate process, and discovered the tanning action of pyrogallic acid on gelatin emulsions in 1881. He was awarded the Progress Medal of the Royal Photographic Society in 1882. He patented negative paper coated on both sides in 1885, and experimented with Steinbach (semitransparent) paper as a support for sensitive film. Warnerke opened a second photographic factory in St. Petersburg. From 1889 he worked with the silver chloride process. He died in Geneva in 1900.

War Photography
War photography is the branch of photojournalism that depicts combat and its immediate aftermath in both physical and human terms. The war photographer acts as a surrogate for viewers, expertly witnessing events far too dangerous for most people. As a group, war photographers have served to inform world audiences about the harsh realities of war. The first significant war photographs still in existence today were made by Roger Fenton in the Crimea in 1855. At the beginning of the 1860s, Mathew Brady's staff and others produced an exhaustive record of the U.S. Civil War. While the wet collodion process employed in that period required exposures far too long to capture the battlefield action, they still produced an unrelentingly straightforward documentation of the reality of life in armed conflict.

The tradition established over a hundred years ago continues today. War pictures are expected to be relevant, emphatic, and timely. Editors and viewers press these issues to the point where photographers often place themselves in positions of considerable physical danger for the sake of a picture. In the Vietnam conflict, improved transmission techniques resulted in a continuing flow of still, motion-picture, and video images of battles that had barely ended. Throughout combat the photographer is expected both to take the pictures and to note what each picture is about. Nowhere is the art of captioning practiced under more difficult circumstances. Good data provide key information that identifies the time, the place, the event recorded, and something of the event's significance. The best captions do this in no more than two or three sentences.

Possibly the most important equipment requirement is that everything be absolutely reliable and sturdy and easily carried. There is simply no opportunity for reshoots, nor is there any way to coddle finicky cameras. A sturdy 35mm camera, a spare camera body, and whatever lenses and film can be carried conveniently constitute the entire equipment list of most war photographers. A long-focal-length lens is a must.

Not every photographer is suited to a combat role. A freedom from fear for personal safety and a passionate desire to picture critical moments are traits that the best war photographers have displayed repeatedly. As a consequence many fine photographers, including Robert Capa and Larry Burrows, have been killed in action. Their legacy is an informed public in the highest journalistic tradition.

See also: DOCUMENTARY PHOTOGRAPHY; PHOTOJOURNALISM.
Color photograph: p. C-63.

Washing

Films and prints must be washed properly after processing to ensure that they will be free from chemical contamination; otherwise, some form of image deterioration, such as fading or staining, ultimately will occur. The keys to proper washing are continuous and even water circulation and enough complete water changes to eliminate residual chemicals. The effectiveness of washing can be increased by the use of a washing aid. This is a chemical solution that converts the fixing by-products in the film or paper into a form that dissolves more readily in the wash water. The usual procedure is to rinse the film or print for 1 to 2 minutes in plain water, treat for 2 to 5 minutes in the washing-aid solution, and then proceed with washing. Various washing aids are available commercially. As explained in the entry on archival processing, the latest research indicates that standards for washing times and procedures for maximum image permanence may have to be revised. The recommendations given here are the minimum safe requirements in any case. If standards for archival processing are revised, that information will be well publicized by film and paper manufacturers.

Roll films are often washed while they are still on reels in the developing tank. However, simply allowing water to splash onto the film is not sufficient. A preferable method is to run a hose from the faucet through the center of the film reels to carry the water to the bottom of the tank. The water then will flow up through the coiled film and over the top of the tank. This kind of water flow is used in many commercially available film washing devices.

The required wash time for black-

War Photography. Alexander Gardner, "Home of a Rebel Sharpshooter" (1863). National Archives.

and-white films is generally 20 to 30 minutes. However, a washing-aid treatment after fixing will cut the wash time in half. Even when a washing aid is used, the wash time should be at least 10 minutes, which is more than is usually stated in instruction sheets. A washing aid should not be used with color films; their wash times are determined by the particular developing process used. An alternative wash method for black-and-white films is to fill the developing tank with fresh water, agitate briefly (five inversions, for example), and pour the water out. This fill-and-dump procedure is repeated 20 times, or 10 times if a washing aid is used.

Sheet film generally is washed in a deep tank while the film is still in its processing holders. Either a continuous water flow from the bottom of the tank or the fill-and-dump procedure can be used effectively. In the latter method the film holders are moved up and down in the water to achieve agitation, which helps flush chemical-laden water out of the emulsion. Some vertical-style print washers can also accommodate sheet film. After washing, both sheet and roll films are often treated in a wetting-agent solution to promote trouble-free drying.

Print washing is simple when resincoated (RC) paper is used, because chemicals are not absorbed into the paper base. Usually a 2- to 4-minute wash is sufficient to dissolve the chemicals out of the emulsion. Such papers must not be over-washed, nor allowed to soak in a water holding bath; therefore,

they should be washed immediately after the fixing bath. A tray method of washing is easy and efficient. The print is agitated in a tray of water for about 1 minute, the water is replaced with fresh, and the procedure is repeated throughout the recommended manufacturer's wash time. A washing aid is not recommended or required with prints on resincoated papers.

Careful washing of fiber-base papers is required to ensure elimination of absorbed chemicals, especially from the base material; the washing method thus is quite important. One of the simplest systems is a tray-and-siphon setup that keeps water continuously circulating and draining. The commercially available siphon connects to the faucet by a hose and clips over the edge of the tray, which should be at least one size larger than the prints being washed (e.g., an 11″ × 14″ tray for 8″ × 10″ prints). The siphon directs a forceful flow of fresh water into the tray at an upper level and continuously removes chemical-laden water from a lower level. Other effective systems include water turbulators and rotary washers that force the water and prints to circulate and usually provide bottom drainage to remove dissolved chemicals. In all methods prints must frequently be turned over by hand and kept separated, or areas where prints touched or were in very close proximity will be incompletely washed.

Vertical washers use compartments or racks to keep prints separated; they are recommended for achieving archival

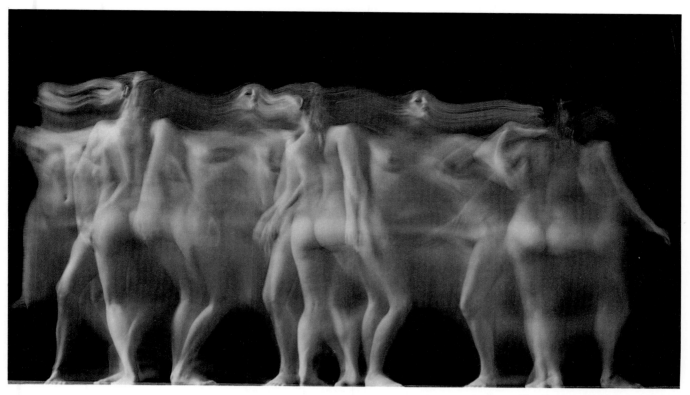

Time Exposure. Phillip Leonian, "Nude in Motion" (1978). © 1980 Phillip Leonian.

Travel Photography. Jay Maisel, "Reflections, Isfahan, Iran" (1971). © 1984 Jay Maisel.

Underwater Photography. Douglas Faulkner,
"Silver crinoid and red sea-whips." (n.d.). ©
Douglas Faulkner.

LIGHT ABSORPTION BY WATER

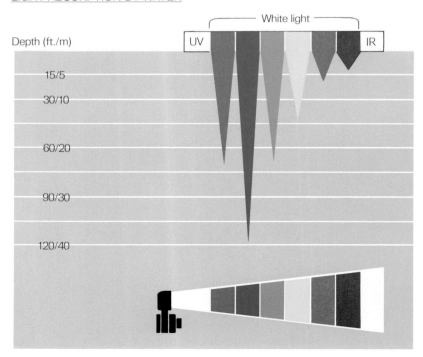

Underwater Photography. Water acts as a
filter to the white light coming from the sun,
selectively absorbing greater amounts of
color with increasing depth. The clearer the
water, the less rapid the filtration, but reds
are effectively lost by 20 feet, yellows by 40
feet, and greens and purples by 70 feet;
only blues persist to any considerable
depth.

War Photography. Tim Page, "Ambush—
Vietnam" (1965). © 1983 Tim Page.

Winter Subjects. Paul Bereswill, "Winter Fence" (n.d.). © Paul Bereswill.

permanence with black-and-white prints. At their best, vertical washers are extremely effective, but some do not permit an even water flow. Another sophisticated washing device is the drum washer; the print is inserted into a cage-like cylinder which rotates, subjecting the print to constant movement within the wash water.

Any of the washing methods effective for fiber-base papers is also suitable for RC papers, although some are more elaborate than is really required for the shorter wash times.

For fiber-base papers a washing aid is essential to keep the wash time within reasonable limits. However, wash times should be longer than the minimums called for in washing-aid instructions. Single-weight papers should be washed for at least 20 minutes and double-weight papers for 40 minutes. An hour or more may be required for archival permanence.

Wash-water temperatures for both films and prints should be kept consistent with the other processing temperatures. Cold-water washing is very inefficient, and a large temperature change can cause reticulation, especially of film emulsions. If the wash water cannot be brought to within a few degrees of the chemical solutions, the films or prints should gradually be brought to the temperature of the wash water. This can be done with a series of intermediate 1-minute water baths, each of which is about 3 degrees closer to the wash temperature.

So-called hypo-test solutions are available for both films and prints to test the effectiveness of washing procedures. A drop of solution is placed on the border of a print or on a blank part of a film roll for 1 minute and then rinsed off. The color of any remaining stain will indicate whether residual fixer has been eliminated effectively.

See also: ARCHIVAL PROCESSING; DRYING FILMS AND PRINTS; FIXING; WETTING AGENT.

Wash-Off Relief Process

The Eastman Kodak Co. introduced the wash-off relief process in the 1930s for printing full-color images from gelatin relief matrices prepared by exposure to separation negatives. The matrices were used to transfer subtractive color (cyan, magenta, yellow) dyes to a receiving emulsion. The relief was produced by treating the exposed and developed matrix film in a tanning bleach that dissolved the silver image and hardened the gelatin in the image areas proportionately. The unhardened gelatin was then washed away with warm water, leaving a positive relief to subsequently be dyed for transfer. The dye-transfer process is the modern, improved version of this procedure.

See also: DYE-TRANSFER PROCESS; TANNING DEVELOPER.

Water

In virtually all photographic solutions, the solvent is water, and water is required for washing films and prints. In general, water that is safe for drinking is suitable for photographic use. However, water may contain dissolved gases or fine particles that go unnoticed in drinking but can affect solution performance; this is more often a problem with water taken from a well or spring than from a municipal supply. Air dissolved in water promotes developer oxidation even as the solution stands in storage. Water drawn through a no-splash aerator on a faucet has extra air mixed in and is not suitable. Letting water stand in an open container for at least an hour before mixing a solution permits dissolved air and other gases to evaporate. Boiling the water gently drives off air and gases, and some dissolved chemicals, more rapidly. Distilled water is purest, but is seldom required. A pragmatic test is to prepare two batches of developer, one with ordinary water the other with distilled water, and process identically exposed films. If the results show no significant differences, there is no need to use distilled water. However, stock solutions of silver, gold, or platinum/palladium compounds should be prepared with distilled water; their ingredients are so expensive that every precaution should be taken. Very soft water can cause excessive swelling of gelatin and in particular should not be used for washing negatives, if possible; otherwise a hardening bath can help protect the emulsion. Water with a high degree of alkalinity—as found in much of the southwestern United States—may increase developer activity. The comparison test with a distilled water developer will indicate any problem; development time can be reduced accordingly, or the amount of activator can be reduced in solutions mixed from formula. Excess alkalinity can also shorten the life of a fixer; adding a small amount of boric acid will correct the situation. Extremely hard water contains excess calcium, and perhaps magnesium compounds. It should be boiled before use in mixing a developer. Such water may leave a powdery white deposit on emulsions upon drying. This can be avoided by giving the film a final rinse in water to which a few drops of acetic acid have been added before hanging it to dry.

Particles of foreign matter in water are more likely to be a problem than chemical impurity. Filtration before mixing a solution (and again before use if necessary) is the best correction. Activated charcoal filters remove dissolved gases, but are not particle filters; in fact, many of those sold for household use inadvertently add particles to the water. If a charcoal filter is used, it should be followed by a particle filter. Particles in the wash water can cause the greatest damage because they may cause scratches when the emulsion is wiped free of excess water, or may become embedded in the emulsion as it dries. A final rinse in a container of double-filtered water will avoid the problem.

Sea water can be used to wash films and prints on fiber base papers, but they must be given a final bath for at least five minutes in fresh water to remove all traces of salt. There is no point in using sea water with resin-coated papers because they require only four minutes total washing time.

See also: MIXING PHOTOGRAPHIC SOLUTIONS; WASHING; WATER CONSERVATION.

Water-Bath Development

Water-bath development is a simple two-bath procedure used with black-and-white materials to reduce overall contrast and achieve improved rendition of details at the lesser-density end of the tonal scale: shadow areas in a negative, highlight areas in a print. Two trays of solution are required, one of normal strength developer, the other of plain water. The negative or print is agitated vigorously in the developer for about two minutes, long enough for the emulsion to absorb as much developer as possible. It is then immediately drained and transferred carefully to lie emulsion-side-up in the water bath. Developer is quickly exhausted in the heavily exposed areas of the emulsion, but continues to work in the less exposed areas. The water bath must not be agitated during use, otherwise developer will be washed out of all areas and the effect of differential local development will be lost. Developer is exhausted in all areas in about four minutes; the film or print may be returned to the developer and the process repeated several times until the desired image contrast and detail are achieved. Films must be treated in total darkness and the effect briefly inspected by a safelight only after about two-thirds of normal development time has elapsed; prints may be observed under safelight

illumination throughout development. When the image is satisfactory, processing is completed with the usual stop bath, fixing, and washing.
See also: CONTRAST; INSPECTION DEVELOPMENT; TWO-BATH DEVELOPMENT.

Water Conservation

The cost of water is a major expense for photographic processing laboratories and professional studios; it can also be significant for home darkrooms that are used frequently. Aside from cost, the need to reduce water consumption is an important ecological concern. Continuous-flow automatic equipment presents the greatest consumption problem; certain conservation practices effective at that level can also be applied by individuals. A water bath used to keep solutions in tanks or other containers at temperature should be created by equipment that recirculates the same water; such a set-up can easily be improvised on a small scale with an aquarium pump and an immersion heating element. A system that uses a continous flow of hot water from the supply line wastes both the water and the energy used to heat it.

The greatest amount of water—65 to 85 per cent of that used for photography—is used for washing films and prints. Consumption can be greatly reduced by treating emulsions in a washing aid that effectively neutralizes the hypo and makes it more readily soluble in water, and by making prints on resin-coated papers whenever possible because they require no more than four minutes washing.
See also: WASHING; WATER.

Waterhouse Stop

John Waterhouse, a Scot, patented in 1858 the idea of using insertable thin metal plates to control the effective aperture of a lens. Each plate in a set had a different size hole in the center; the area of the holes changed in a progression that halved or doubled the amount of light passing through at each step. The plates were inserted in a slot in the lens barrel, or placed in front of or behind the lens. The best image quality was obtained with the first method. The Waterhouse stop was supplanted by the built-in iris diaphragm about 1900.
See also: DIAPHRAGM; *f*-NUMBER/*f*-STOP.

Waterproof and Water-Resistant Papers

Print papers in which the base material has been coated on both sides with a plastic resin do not absorb water, except for a fractional amount at the cut edges of the paper. They require less washing and dry much more rapidly than conventional, fiber base papers, and thus are widely used where speed and economy of processing are of major importance.
See also: RESIN-COATED PAPERS.

Watkins, Carleton E.

American; 1829–1916
In the last third of the 19th c. Carleton Watkins was known as one of America's foremost landscape photographers, primarily for his artistic panoramas of Yosemite and other wilderness areas. He made his reputation at a time when the competition included figures such as Timothy O'Sullivan, Eadweard Muybridge, and William Henry Jackson. Watkins photographed throughout the West on field expeditions, carrying huge cameras and other equipment. He also

Watkins, Carleton E. "Arbutus Menziesii Pursh, California" (1880-1885); albumen. Collection, Museum of Modern Art, New York.

made many memorable images of the rapid development of San Francisco.

Watkins was born in Oneonta, New York. He journeyed to California at the time of the Gold Rush, settling in Sacramento, where he worked as a carpenter. He moved to San Francisco in 1853, taking employment as a department-store clerk, and became acquainted with photography in 1854 at the studio of Robert Vance, for whom he worked in daguerreotype and wet-collodion processes. He began to record life in the Bay area at this time. From 1855 to 1861 he extensively photographed the New Idea and New Almaden mines and the Mission Santa Clara. In 1859 he made views of the Mariposa-Bear Valley for James Hutchings.

Watkins began his first series of Yosemite views with stereoscopic and specially constructed mammoth-view cameras in 1861. Oliver Wendell Holmes praised his stereographs in 1863 as "a perfection of art which compares with the finest European work." Watkins continued to photograph Yosemite for the next several years. He worked privately and on the geological surveys of Josiah D. Whitney (1866) and Clarence King (1867).

In 1867 Watkins renamed his San Francisco studio "Yosemite Art Gallery." He photographed extensively in Oregon, traveling with landscape painter William Keith in 1867–1868. He was awarded a medal for landscape at the Paris Exposition of 1868. For the United States Geological Survey he photographed the Mount Shasta and Mount Lassen area in 1870, and, in 1871, the North Bloomfield Gravel Mines in Nevada Country, California. He exhibited at the Vienna International Exposition of 1873 with O'Sullivan and Muybridge.

In a financial panic in the mid-1870s Watkins lost control of his gallery and many negatives. Much of the next decade was spent in an attempt to remake his lost work. He photographed in many of the exact locations he had visited earlier.

Watkins photographed Comstock Lode and Virginia City, Nevada, in 1876 and along the Southern Pacific rail lines to Tucson, Arizona, in 1880. During the next decade he photographed the Golden Gate and Feather River land claims and acted as manager of the gallery he had once owned .

In the early 1890s, after photographing in the Pacific Northwest and around Bakersfield, California, Watkins began to lose his eyesight and his work was curtailed. He was completely blind by 1906, at which time he lost his studio and the greater part of his negatives in the San Francisco earthquake and fire. He was committed to the California State Hospital for the Insane in 1910; he died there six years later.

Watt-Second

See: JOULE.

Wavelength

Electromagnetic energy consists of fields that continuously build to a maximum strength of one polarity, diminish, build to a maximum of the opposite polarity, and repeat the cycle. This repetitive action is a wave pattern. The energy travels at approximately 186,000 miles (300,000 km) per second, so a measurable distance is covered in the time it takes to complete one cycle. That distance is the *wavelength* of the energy, one of the characteristics by which energy is distinguished or identified. The measurement is made between the beginning and ending points of a cycle, or between corresponding points of the same polarity of two successive cycles. In the visible portion of the energy spectrum, the wavelengths of light are only a few hundred billionths of a meter long; the unit of measurement is the nanometer (nm), one billionth (10^{-9}) of a meter. Each color in the visible spectrum has a distinctive wavelength, from 700nm for one of the deepest reds, to 400nm for a deep violet.

Because wavelength is a factor of distance and speed, it can be related to time. The shorter the wavelength, the greater the number of cycles that occur in a given period. The time measurement of energy is called *frequency*. It is a count of the number of cycles per second, expressed in Hertz (Hz): one Hertz equals one cycle or one wavelength per second. Frequency and wavelength are inversely related; as wavelength gets shorter, frequency increases. In the visible spectrum, 700nm energy has a frequency of about ten thousand billion (10^{13}) Hz, and 400nm energy a frequency of about one trillion billion (10^{21}) Hz. The numbers are so vast that wavelength rather than frequency is generally used to identify energy in this range.

Wavelengths that vary in unison, reaching peaks of the same polarity at the same instant, are said to be in phase, or coherent. Perfect coherence can be achieved only by energy of exactly the same wavelength and frequency, such as that emitted by a laser. Most light is composed of a mixture of wavelengths with random phase relationships, and so is incoherent.

See also: LASER; LIGHT; METRIC SYSTEM; SPECTRUM.

Waxed Paper Process

In 1851 Gustave Le Gray, a French photographer, invented a greatly improved paper negative process called the waxed paper process. Calotype negatives were commonly waxed on the back to

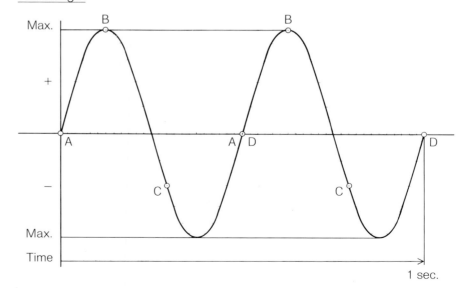

Wavelength

Wavelength = distance between two corresponding points: A–A; B–B; C–C.

   A–A and D–D are one cycle each; the indicated time is 1 second; therefore, Frequency = 2 Hz.

make them highly translucent for printing, but this was done after the negative was processed and dried. Le Gray waxed the paper before it was coated and sensitized. This filled in the fibers and pores far more effectively than post-process waxing, and kept the light-sensitive compounds from soaking into the paper fibers. His coating solution included a thin starch, and later albumen, to make the halide crystals adhere to the waxed surface. The paper was sensitized by floating it on a solution of silver nitrate. Paper could be prepared several days before use, and developed—in a gallic acid solution—several days after exposure. The calotype offered no such leeway, although it produced an image in a much shorter developing time. The tonal quality and detail obtained with the waxed paper process was vastly superior to that of the calotype, and nearly equal to that obtainable with glass plates. The convenience of dry materials and beforehand preparation caused many French photographers, especially those who traveled, to use the process well after the collodion wet plate process had become established.
See also: CALOTYPE; LE GRAY, GUSTAVE.

Waxing Prints

The tonal depth of images on matte or semimatte papers can be increased by waxing the surface; this treatment also serves to protect the surface from handling. The wax must be colorless, and must not yellow with age. Only paste or spray wax prepared with no solvents or additives can be used successfully. A very thin coat is applied with a soft pad or by spraying from a distance of about 18 inches. If the print has previously been mounted, the mounting board must be protected from the wax. When the wax is completely dry it is buffed by hand to a smooth, even surface, using a soft lintless cloth . A second coat can be added immediately or later, if desired; fingermarks and other minor surface impressions can be buffed out with care as necessary. The matte effect of the paper surface is greatly reduced or eliminated completely, but the result is not as mirrorlike as the surface of a glossy paper.

Weather Photography

Pictures made of the state of the atmosphere may range from larger-than-life images of individual snow flakes or raindrops, to ultrawide views of the earth which show extensive cloud formations and high and low pressure fronts. While most weather photography is very technically oriented, many atmospheric phenomena may also make impressively beautiful pictorial images.

The bulk of weather photography is used in support of meteorological forecasting efforts. Today most pictorial data is received from a series of Television and Infra-Red Observation Satellites (TIROS) which carry high-sensitivity video cameras equipped with both narrow and wide-angle lenses. Although TIROS orbit at altitudes of several hundred miles, their motion around the earth is so rapid that picture exposure times must be limited to a fraction of a second. It is of particular importance for accurate mapping that the lenses used be as free of radial distortion as is possible. Because some residual distortion is always present, each lens is tested prior to installation. Data on the aberrations of each lens are stored in National Oceanographic and Atmospheric Administration (NOAA) computers so that subsequent pictures can be corrected automatically. After a satellite has attained a precise orbit, the cameras are turned on. Normally a sequence of images is produced which is translated on board the satellite to a digitized form. This then can be transmitted easily to earth via radio waves. The data are fed directly to NOAA computers which take into account satellite position, camera angle, and lens distortion to make the now familiar photographs of the atmosphere complete with longitude and latitude lines.

Time is of the essence in forecasting. Consequently, every effort is made to disseminate the images to meteorologists around the country without delay via the latest laser transmission techniques. As a rule, information over 24 hours old is of historical value only.

Techniques for photographing weather phenomena from the earth's surface for pictorial purposes are relatively straightforward. Cloud formations are revealed most clearly by sidelighting or backlighting. A polarizer is the best means of making white clouds stand out against a blue sky with color film. Yellow, orange, red, or green filters produce increased cloud-sky tonal separation in black-and-white pictures. Filters have little use with storm clouds and overcast skies. Falling rain is most clearly seen when sidelighted against a dark background; including the ground or other surface on which the rain is falling makes it more apparent. Dripping or ice-laden limbs and foliage are most brilliant when backlighted. Fog and falling snow seem most dense when frontlighted, as by flash at the camera position. Tornado funnels, "dust devils," and similar phenomena can be photographed directly, but personal safety should be the primary concern. Lightning cannot be predicted; it requires leaving the shutter open on a tripod-mounted camera until one or more flashes have occurred. In severe weather (e.g., driving rain, dust storm, freezing cold) equipment must be protected. Sheltered locations, waterproof housings such as those used for underwater photography, plastic bags, and colorless (e.g., UV-absorbing or skylight) filters are the major protective measures.

See also: LIGHTNING, PHOTO-GRAPHING; SPACE PHOTOGRAPHY; SUN PHOTOGRAPHY; WINTER PHOTOGRAPHY.

Wedding Photography

Wedding photography imposes serious responsibilities on a photographer and poses a number of special problems. Marriage is the major event in the lives of most couples, so pictures of the event have enormous emotional value to those involved. The photographs taken must meet their expectations both in technical quality and in content, and they must be obtained in a way that does not create misunderstanding or give offense. The latter requirement is important and difficult. The weeks before a wedding are a very busy time for the bride. A great deal of tact is required to determine exactly what kind of coverage is desired, to set a price and execute a contract, and to schedule the photography. Even more tact is required in directing people, preventing interruptions, and dealing with problems during the actual shooting sessions.

In addition to photographs of the ceremony and the reception, wedding coverage may include showers, rehearsals, the groom's party, preparations at home, and studio portraits. The minimum number of formal poses and their content should be established, as should informal but posed pictures (e.g., bride feeding the first bite of cake to the groom) and candid pictures (primarily at rehearsals and the reception). The number and size of the prints to be delivered and whether they are to be in an album, framed, matted, or loose must also be determined. Locations (home, church, reception hall) must be looked over to see what problems and opportunities they present. It is especially important to determine whether pictures may be taken inside a church or temple. If that is permitted, the next considerations are whether they may be taken during the progress of the ceremony or only immediately before and after, and whether flash may be used. Photography has become an accepted part of weddings, but it is also a distracting activity, and many families and members of the clergy have strong feelings about what is permissible.

Some formal studio portraits may be scheduled in the days before or after the ceremony. Typical coverage on the day of the wedding usually begins in the bride's home, showing the bride at her dressing table, the bride with her parents and other family members and with her bridesmaids and maid of honor, the family leaving home, and the bride's father helping her into the car. The coverage continues chronologically into the church or synagogue with photographs of the bridegroom and best man waiting, the interior, entry of the bride, the group at the altar, the exchange of rings, bride and groom kissing, the receiving line, exiting the church or synagogue as rice is thrown, and the newlyweds in their car. Various posed pictures may also be taken after the ceremony. They include the bride and the groom individually and together, the full bridal party, the bride and all bridesmaids, the groom and ushers, the bride's parents, the groom's parents, and other formal group and individual portraits.

At the reception candid photographs are taken of the bride and groom entering the hall, the best man toasting the couple, the party at the head table, the wedding cake, the bride and groom cutting the cake, the bride and her father dancing, the bridegroom dancing with the bride's mother, a general view of everyone dancing, other photographs of relatives and guests, and the bride and groom leaving. The coverage may involve more or a great deal less than this, depending on the size of the wedding and the choice of the participants.

Almost all wedding photography is done with color negative film because many prints of at least some of the pictures usually are desired. Black-and-white prints can be made from color negatives if they are required. Studio photography is done with large-format films, but location pictures, especially on the day of the wedding, most often are taken with medium-format (120/220 or 70mm) roll film This provides very good quality prints at reasonable cost and lets the photographers use hand-held equipment with a minimum amount of time spent reloading. Outdoor photography is usually by natural light with electronic flash fill, and interior photographs are usually taken with portable electronic flash. This minimizes exposure problems and permits the use of daylight-type color film in all situations. Processing and printing are most often done by one of the many commercial laboratories that provide special wedding packages of various print assortments. The photographer sees to the processing and delivers the pictures.

Wedge, Optical

A piece of glass or other transparent optical material that changes continuously in density from zero at one end to a maximum opacity at the other end is called an optical wedge. The first such device, the Goldberg wedge introduced in 1910, actually had a wedge-shaped density component. It was formed by placing two slightly separated glass plates on an incline and filling the space between with black-dyed gelatin. The liquid gelatin flowed to a level, producing a full thickness at the low end of the incline and tapering to nothing at the high end. After the dyed gelatin had set, the glass-and-wedge sandwich was shifted and the remaining space filled with clear gelatin so that the thickness, and thus the refractive index, was the same at all points. Today, optical wedges are more often produced by grinding a block of black glass or optical plastic to a wedge and matching it with an opposing, transparent wedge of the same material to obtain uniform thickness. Another kind of optical wedge consists of a photographic emulsion that changes continuously in density; although not physically a wedge, its effect on light is the same.

An optical wedge is used as an exposure control device in sensitometry; light passing through is reduced in intensity so that it produces a true continuous-tone exposure on an emulsion. The density range of an optical wedge is from 0 to 5.0 or 6.0. The degree of density change in a properly made wedge is the same for equal intervals; this is expressed as the *wedge constant:* the density change per centimeter of length. For example, a wedge with a constant of 0.2 increases that much in density every centimeter, moving toward the densest end. When the density at any one point is calibrated, the density at any other print can be calculated by measurement. A simplified optical wedge is the *step wedge,* or step tablet, which does not vary continuously but is divided into a series of steps, each of a single density. Usually each step changes light transmission by the equivalent of one-half f-stop or a full f-stop, making calibration of the response range of photographic emulsions easy to accomplish.
See also: STEP WEDGE; WEDGE SPECTROGRAM.

Wedge Spectrogram

A *spectrogram* is a photographic record of the wavelength composition of a sam-

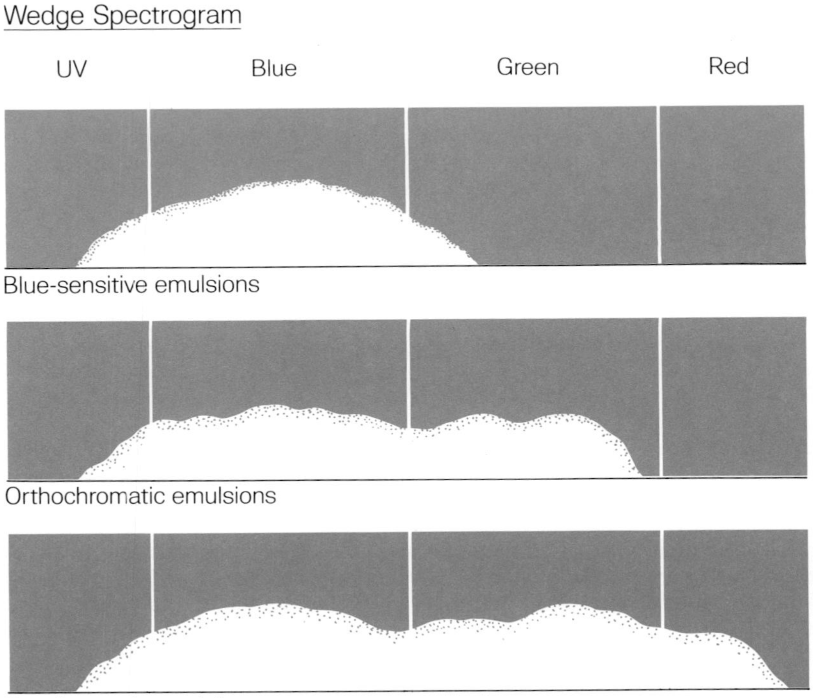

Wedge Spectrogram

UV   Blue   Green   Red

Blue-sensitive emulsions

Orthochromatic emulsions

Panchromatic emulsions

Weegee. "The Critic" (1943). Courtesy Marcuse Pfeifer Gallery, New York; collection, Center for Creative Photography, University of Arizona.

ple of light. It is made in a spectrograph, an instrument that uses a diffraction grating or a prism to spread or disperse the light into its separate wavelengths in a continuous display, usually from the shortest wavelengths at the left to the longest wavelengths at the right. This display is focused directly onto a film emulsion. A *wedge spectrogram* is used in sensitometry to determine the spectral sensitivity of an emulsion. The light is white light, which is composed of all wavelengths. In addition to being dispersed, it passes through an optical wedge graduated from no density at the bottom to maximum density at the top. Thus the light falling on the emulsion changes in wavelength left to right, and decreases in intensity from bottom to top. The more sensitive the emulsion is to a particular wavelength, the higher the exposure will register at that point. The resulting record is a direct graph of the sensitivity across the spectrum, with the line representing exposure cut-off varying up and down according to the sensitivity at each wavelength.

See also: DIFFRACTION GRATING; DISPERSION; PRISMS; SPECTROGRAPHY/ SPECTROSCOPE; WEDGE, OPTICAL.

Wedgwood, Thomas

English; 1771–1805

Thomas Wedgwood was the first to make documented attempts to record images in the camera obscura with light-sensitive material. Wedgwood's father, Josiah, was active in scientific investigations and in promoting the application of scientific knowledge to practical manufacturing technology, especially in the operations of the famous pottery works he had founded. One such advance was to use the camera obscura to obtain drawings of English architecture which were used to decorate a specially commissioned set of tableware.

Thomas Wedgwood became familiar with the use of the camera, and in the course of his tutoring and university studies in chemistry he also became familiar with a number of scientific notebooks and papers which his father had collected. Among these was the first account in English of Johann Schulze's discovery of the light sensitivity of calcium carbonate mixed with silver nitrate. It is almost certain that he also learned of the work of Jean Hellot in using a silver nitrate solution to write on paper, letting the action of the sun darken the writing, and of Giacomo Beccaria's discovery of the light sensitivity of silver chloride. All of this information was fundamental to conceiving the practical possibility of image-recording. Ironically, Wedgwood

and his co-experimenter, Humphry Davy (one of the most brilliant young chemists of the time), missed the discovery of Carl Wilhelm Scheele that ammonia destroyed the light-sensitivity of silver chloride. That information would have permitted the final result they could not achieve—that of making their images permanent.

The Wedgwood-Davy experiments began about 1799. They brushed paper with a silver nitrate solution, placed an object on the paper, and let the action of sunlight darken the surrounding area. The result was a photogram—a white silhouette of the object on a black background. Further experiments succeeded in capturing the veins of a leaf and the structure of an insect's wing. Davy discovered the greater sensitivity of silver chloride, and the fact that kid leather produced greater sensitivity than paper. Unknown to Wedgwood and Davy, this was because of the gallic acid present in tanned leather—the substance that W. H. F. Talbot was to use as a developer in the first negative-positive process, the calotype.

Wedgwood and Davy's attempts to record images in the camera obscura failed; they recognized that their materials were too insensitive for exposures of "moderate time." However, they did succeed in obtaining photograms of varied tonality by placing miniature paintings on glass over their sensitized paper and leather.

Davy published an account of their work in 1802, the first paper in the direct

history of photography: *An Account of a Method of Copying Paintings upon Glass and of Making Profiles* [photograms] *by the Agency of Light upon Nitrate of Silver. Invented by T. Wedgwood Esq. With Observations by H. Davy.* The report noted that once the object was removed from the sensitized material, sunlight would rapidly darken the unexposed areas, destroying the image. Images kept in the dark and examined only by candlelight lasted longer (because silver compounds are sensitive only to ultraviolet and blue wavelengths, a fact discovered by others a good deal later), but all were impermanent. That was a problem overcome 24 years later by Joseph Nicéphore Niépce, using a completely different method.

See also: CALOTYPE; CAMERA OBSCURA; DAVY, SIR HUMPHRY; HISTORY OF PHOTOGRAPHY; NIÉPCE, JOS. NICÉPHORE; PHOTOGRAM; SCHEELE, C. W.; SCHULZE, J. H.; TALBOT, W. H. F.

Weegee, (Arthur Fellig)

American; 1899–1968

Although Weegee photographed a wide panorama of urban life, the documentation of violent crimes, disasters, and their survivors and onlookers was Weegee's specialty. His work for New York City newspapers and photosyndicates in the 1930s and 1940s brought him international attention. His best-known images have a rawness and spontaneity rarely encountered.

Weegee was born Usher Fellig in

Zloczew, Austria (now in Poland). His name was changed to Arthur at Ellis Island when he came with his family to live on New York's Lower East Side in 1910. He quit school at age 14 to help support his family, working at odd jobs and as an itinerant street photographer and assistant to a commercial photographer.

Fellig had been a passport photographer for three years when he was hired in 1924 as a darkroom technician by Acme Newspictures (soon to become United Press International Photos). He left Acme in 1935 to freelance as a police beat photographer on the night shift. He used a standard 4″ × 5″ Speed Graphic camera with large-bulb flash to produce photographs that were published in nearly all of New York's papers over the next ten years. From 1940 to 1945 he was a staff photographer at *PM* magazine.

Fellig gained a reputation for knowing where disaster would strike next, hence the name "Weegee," a reference to the fortune-teller's Ouija board. He was aided in scooping competing photographers by carefully monitoring police- and fire-department radio dispatches. In 1938 he was the first photographer to obtain permission to install police radio equipment in his car.

Weegee had a gift for self-promotion which led to his stamping the backs of his prints with "Credit Photo: Weegee the Famous" in the early 1940s. He did not become truly famous, however, until the publication of his book, *Naked City*, the rights to which were bought by Hollywood for a film and television series. This book contained his crime photography and images of New York City's lonely and dispossessed. In addition to the hard-flash, frontal shots that were his trademark, he made photographs with infrared flash and film, which allowed him to work as unobtrusively as possible.

For several years from the mid-1940s on, Weegee abandoned crime photos and concentrated on advertising assignments for *Vogue, Holiday, Life, Look,* and *Fortune.* He lived in Hollywood from 1947 to 1952, working as a consultant and bit player in films. He began a series of photocaricatures and photodistortions of celebrities and politicians. This work was not greeted with the same enthusiasm *Naked City* had received, but Weegee continued his experiments. He completed several short films in the 1950s using kaleidoscopic lenses, mirrors, and other distorting techniques. A mass of contradictions, Weegee's praise at this time was reserved for Atget, Cartier-Bresson, and W. Eugene Smith.

Weegee published several other books, including *Naked Hollywood* and *Weegee by Weegee,* his autobiography. He lectured on his work throughout the United States, Europe, and the Soviet Union. He was a neglected figure at the time of his death.

Weegee was the subject of one-man shows at the Photo League in New York City (1944) and in Cologne (1962), and a major retrospective of his work was held at ICP in 1977.

Weights and Measures

Photographic measurements and formulas are given in most instructions and reference works either in the U. S. customary system, or in the metric system. Conversion factors between the two systems are given in the accompanying tables. Three factors are of importance in reading and interpreting measurements.

1. The abbreviation *g* or *gr* means *grains* in the U. S. customary system (437.5 grains = 1 ounce), and *grams* in the metric system (1000 grams = 1 kilogram). Both are units of mass, or weight. An inspection of the other abbreviations used in a formula or in instructions (e.g., *l*, liter; *ml*, milliliter; *oz*, ounce) will reveal which system is referred to.

2. Older metric system practice uses the unit *cc* (cubic centimeter) for liquid volumes less than one liter. Modern practice uses the unit *ml* (milliliter). The difference between them is insignificant for photographic purposes, so one may be taken for the other; e.g., 1000cc = 1000ml = 1 liter.

3. A quart and a liter are not equal volumes of liquid. Therefore it is not sufficient to convert only the weights and measures of formula dry ingredients from one system to another; the total liquid volumes must also be converted. The table of *compound conversions* simplifies quart/liter formula conversions.

Temperature conversions are given in the entry on temperature scales.
See also: METRIC SYSTEM.

Table I:

Decimal Equivalents of Inches and Feet

Inches		Decimal Inch		Millimeters
1/16	=	0.063	=	1.588
1/8	=	0.1250	=	3.1750
1/4	=	0.250	=	6.350
3/8	=	0.3750	=	9.5250
1/2	=	0.5000	=	12.700
5/8	=	0.6250	=	15.875
3/4	=	0.750	=	19.050
7/8	=	0.875	=	22.225
1	=	1.000	=	25.400

Decimal Foot		Decimal Inches		Centimeters
0.1	=	1.2	=	3.1
0.2	=	2.4	=	6.1
0.3	=	3.6	=	9.1
0.4	=	4.8	=	12.2
0.5	=	6.0	=	15.2
0.6	=	7.2	=	18.3
0.7	=	8.4	=	21.3
0.8	=	9.6	=	24.4
0.9	=	10.8	=	27.4
1.0	=	12.0	=	30.5

Decimal Inch		Millimeters
0.1	=	2.54
0.2	=	5.08
0.3	=	7.62
0.4	=	10.16
0.5	=	12.70
0.6	=	15.24
0.7	=	17.78
0.8	=	20.32
0.9	=	22.86
1.0	=	25.4

Inch		Decimal Foot
1	=	0.08
2	=	0.16
3	=	0.25
4	=	0.33
5	=	0.42
6	=	0.50
7	=	0.58
8	=	0.66
9	=	0.75
10	=	0.83
11	=	0.92
12	=	1.00

Table 2

Linear Conversion

cm (centimeters)

× 0.394	= inches
× 0.033	= feet
× 0.011	= yards
× 0.01	= meters

m (meters)

× 39.37	= inches
× 3.281	= feet
× 1.094	= yards
× 1000	= millimeters
× 100	= centimeters

in (inches)

÷ 12	= feet
× 0.0835	= feet
÷ 36	= yards
× 0.028	= yards
× 25.4	= millimeters
× 2.54	= centimeters
× 0.0254	= meters

ft (feet)

× 12	= inches
÷ 3	= yards
× 0.333	= yards
× 304.8	= millimeters
× 30.48	= centimeters
× 0.3048	= meters

yd (yards)

× 36	= inches
× 3	= feet
× 914.4	= millimeters
× 91.44	= centimeters
× 0.9144	= meters

Table 3:

Liquid Conversion

ml (millimeters)

× 0.0338	= ounces
× 0.0021	= pints
× 0.0010	= quarts
× 0.0010	= liters

l (liters)

× 33.814	= ounces
× 2.1133	= pints
× 1.0566	= quarts
× 0.2642	= gallons
× 1000.0	= milliliters

oz (ounces)

× 0.0625	= pints
× 0.0312	= quarts
× 0.0078	= gallons
× 29.573	= milliliters
× 0.0296	= liters

pt (pints)

× 16	= ounces
× 0.5	= quarts
× 0.125	= gallons
× 473.17	= milliliters
× 0.4731	= liters

qt (quarts)

× 32	= ounces
× 2	= pints
× 0.25	= gallons
× 946.35	= milliliters
× 0.9463	= liters

gal (gallons)

× 128	= ounces
× 8	= pints
× 4	= quarts
× 3785.4	= milliliters
× 3.7854	= liters

Table 4

Mass (Weight) Conversion

g (grams)

× 15.432	= grains

× 0.564	= drams
× 0.035	= ounces
× 0.002	= pounds
× 1000	= milligrams
× 0.001	= kilograms

kg (kilograms)

× 15432.4	= grains
× 564.383.	= drams
× 35.274	= ounces
× 2.2046	= pounds
× 1000	= grams

gr (grains)

× 0.365	= drams
× 0.0023	= ounces
× 0.00014	= pounds
× 64.799	= milligrams
× 0.0648	= grams
× 0.00006	= kilograms

oz (ounces)

× 437.5	= grains
× 16	= drams
× 0.0625	= pounds
× 28.349	= grams
× 0.02835	= kilograms

lb (pounds)

× 7000	= grains
× 256	= drams
× 16	= ounces
× 453.59	= grams
× 0.4536	= kilograms

Table 5

Compound Conversion of Formulas

Liquid Measure

Milliliters per liter	× 0.03	= fluid ounces per quart
Fluid ounces per quart	× 31.3	= milliliters per liter

Weight (Mass)

Grams per liter	× 14.6	= grains per quart
Grams per liter	× 0.03	= ounces per quart
Grams per liter	× 0.002	= pounds per quart
Grains per quart	× 0.07	= grams per liter
Ounces per quart	× 29.9	= grams per liter
Pounds per quart	× 479	= grams per liter

Weiner, Dan

American; 1919–1959

Dan Weiner believed that photography's noblest calling was communication about humanity.

Born in New York City, Weiner received his first camera, a 9 × 12cm Voightlander, at the age of 15; however, photography was not initially part of his life plans. His fervent desire to be a painter led to a confrontation with his father, an immigrant who found it difficult to support his family during the Depression. As a result, Weiner had to leave home to study painting, first at the Art Students' League in 1937, and then at the Pratt Institute in 1939.

While at Pratt, Weiner joined the Photo League, a group whose members were typically first-generation Americans and who aimed to document and socially reform their age through the camera. He was powerfully influenced by the work of Lewis Hine and Jacob Riis, and also by Dorothea Lange, Walker Evans, Ben Shahn, and others working for the Farm Security Administration. Rounding out his photographic education, he was introduced to the work of Ansel Adams, Edward Weston, Paul Strand, Berenice Abbott, Henri Cartier-Bresson, and Brassaï. His ambitions as a painter soon waned.

After concluding his studies at Pratt in 1940, Weiner taught at the Photo League, served as an assistant to the commercial photographer Valentino Savra, and opened his own advertising studio. From 1942 to 1946 he served in the U.S. Army Air Force, where he discovered the 35mm camera. It allowed him, for the first time, to eliminate the "paraphernalia of technique to the point where there would be no barriers between the initial vision and the logical, clean solution through the camera." After the war Weiner returned to his commercial studio in New York, but in 1949 he gave it up to devote himself full time to photojournalism.

Weiner considered himself fortunate to be one of a generation of photographers able to explore at close range central issues and human relationships of their time. Among his major stories were malnutrition in old-age homes; first communion in a primitive Italian village; and life in a fishing village where one family had lived for more than 100 years. One of the first documents published on the civil rights movement in America was Weiner's coverage for *Collier's* of the 1956 Montgomery, Alabama, bus boycott.

Weiner met Alan Paton in 1954 when *Collier's* commissioned them to do two articles on blacks in America. Their shared concerns and loathing of injustice led to the book *South Africa in Transition*.

In 1956, Weiner began traveling through Russia, Rumania, Czechoslova-

Weston, Brett
American; 1911–

Brett Weston became internationally famous at age 18, exhibiting at the landmark "Film und Foto" exhibition at Stuttgart, Germany, in 1929, where his work was hung with that of Edward Steichen, Berenice Abbott, Man Ray, Paul Outerbridge, and his father, Edward Weston. His black-and-white landscapes and nature studies of plants and rocks, noted for their precision and exquisite textures, have established him as one of the finest photographic printers in the world. He has lived for most of his life from the sale of his prints and portfolios, rarely taking on commercial assignments, traveling, dedicating himself to the deepening of his singular vision, and trying to achieve formal mastery. "Form," he has said, "is all through nature, riotous, sometimes explosive, a knowledge of it can be a dangerous thing: it is so easy to stylize and corrupt."

He was born Theodore Brett Weston, the second son of Edward Weston, in Los Angeles, California. He had early loves for drawing and carving and ended his formal schooling in the sixth grade. His first photographs were made with his father on a trip to Mexico in 1925.

Weston worked in his father's portrait studios in various cities in California for the next several years. He exhibited his first prints in 1927 at UCLA in an exhibition organized by Barbara Morgan. His first solo exhibition was held the same year at Jake Zeitlin's bookstore and gallery in Los Angeles. His first major one-man show took place at M. H. de Young Museum in San Francisco in 1932. Two years later he showed at New York's Julien Levy Gallery.

Weston worked for the Works Progress Administration in 1936 as a sculptor and photographer. He worked as a cameraman for 20th Century Fox war films and as a photographer for an aircraft factory before being drafted in 1943. He went through basic training three times before being stationed in New York with the Signal Corps. On his off-duty hours he began to photograph the city with an 8″ × 10″ view camera and an 11″ × 14″ camera which he would use for the next 20 years. He was discharged from the Army in 1946.

In 1947 Weston received a Guggenheim Fellowship to photograph along the East Coast. He returned to Carmel, California, where he lived for several years, assisting his ailing father with the printing of the *Edward Weston 50th Anniversary Portfolio* and his *Print Project*. His first book publication, *Brett Weston: Photographs*, containing

kia, and Poland, working extensively with interpreters, drivers, guides, factory owners, and engineers while trying to compile a portrait of the people and their industries. Much of this material, which Weiner hoped would become a book, was published in *Fortune*. In January 1959, he was killed in a plane crash while on assignment near Versailles, Kentucky.

Known primarily for work published in mass-audience publications, in 1953 an exhibition of Weiner's work originated at the Camera Club of New York and traveled to the George Eastman House and other major museums. In 1955, 1956, and 1959 he exhibited at the Limelight Gallery in New York City. In

1967 photography by Weiner and five other photojournalists constituted the book and international traveling exhibition *The Concerned Photographer* created by the International Fund for Concerned Photographers. It was in the tradition of the work of Weiner, David Seymour "Chim," Werner Bischof, René Burri, and Robert Capa that the International Center of Photography was established in 1974. *Dan Weiner*, an ICP Library of Photographers monograph, was published by Viking/Grossman in 1974.

See also: DOCUMENTARY PHOTOGRAPHY; PHOTOJOURNALISM.

twenty-eight 8″ × 10″ reproductions, appeared in 1956. Until this time he had published portfolios exclusively, the first, of images of San Francisco, in 1938.

During the 1960s Weston made numerous trips to Europe; Baja, California; Guatemala; and Mexico. He was a guest of the German government on a cultural exchange program in 1968 and exhibited throughout Germany. He began working with a small-format Rollei-Werkbund camera at this time.

Weston has been honored by over 100 one-man exhibitions, including shows at the Friends of Photography in Carmel, California, in 1970, the San Francisco Museum of Art, and the Museum of Modern Art in New York City. In 1973 he received a National Endowment for the Humanities grant to photograph Alaska. An Aperture monograph, *Brett Weston: Photographs From Five Decades*, was published in 1980.

Photograph: p. 542.

Weston, Edward

American; 1886–1958

Edward Weston is renowed as one of the grand masters of 20th c. photography. His legacy includes several thousand carefully composed, superbly printed photographs which have influenced photographers around the world for 50 years. Photographing natural landscapes and forms such as peppers, shells, and rocks, using large-format cameras and available light, Weston produced sensuously precise images raised to the level of poetry. The subtleties of tone and the sculptural formal design of his works have become the standards by which much later photographic practice has been judged. Ansel Adams has written: "Weston is, in the real sense, one of the few creative artists of today. He has recreated the matter-forms and forces of nature; he has made these forms eloquent of the fundamental unity of the world. His work illuminates man's inner journey toward perfection of the spirit."

Edward Henry Weston was born in Highland Park, Illinois, and raised in Chicago. He attended Oakland Grammar School and received his first camera, a Bull'sEye #2, from his father in 1902. He began photographing in his spare time in Chicago parks while working as an errand boy and salesman for Marshall Field and Company. In 1906 Weston traveled to California where he worked as a door-to-door portrait photographer. From 1908 to 1911 he attended the Illinois College of Photography, spending his summers in California working as a printer in photographic studios.

Weston operated his own portrait studio between 1911 and 1922 in Tropico, California. He became successful working in a soft-focus, Pictorial style, winning many salon and professional awards. After viewing an exhibition of modern art at the San Francisco World's Fair in 1915, Weston became more and more dissatisfied with his own work. By 1920 he was experimenting with semi-abstractions in a hard-edged style.

In 1922 Weston traveled to New York City, where he met Alfred Stieglitz, Paul Strand, and Charles Sheeler. His photographs of the ARMCO Steelworks in Ohio at this time marked a turning point in his career. These industrial photographs, similar to work by Sheeler, were true "straight" images: unpretentious, and true to the reality before the photographer. Weston later wrote, "the camera should be used for a recording of *life*, for rendering the very substance and quintessence of the *thing itself*, whether it be polished steel or palpitating flesh."

In 1923 Weston moved to Mexico City where he opened a studio with his apprentice and lover Tina Modotti, of whom he made important portraits and nude studies over several years. Through Modotti, who fast became an accomplished photographer in her own right, Weston became friendly with artists of the Mexican Renaissance including Rivera, Siqueiros, and Orozco, all of whom encouraged his new direction. In 1924 Weston abandoned the use of soft-focus techniques entirely and started his precise studies of natural forms. He returned to California permanently in 1926 and began the work for which he is most deservedly famous: natural-form close-ups, nudes, and landscapes.

Weston opened a San Francisco studio with his son Brett in 1928. The following year he moved to Carmel where he began photographing in the Point Lobos area. He organized with Edward Steichen the American section of the 1929 Stuttgart *Film und Foto* exhibition at this time. In 1932 Weston was a founding member of the *f*/64 group of purist photographers along with Ansel Adams, Willard Van Dyke, Imogen Cunningham, and Sonya Noskowiak. *The Art of Edward Weston*, a book of nearly 40 photographs, was published the same year.

Weston photographed for the WPA Federal Arts Project in New Mexico and California in 1933. He was the first recipient of a Guggenheim Fellowship for Photography in 1937, photographing extensively in the West and Southwest in 1937–1938. Two years later, he provided illustrations for an edition of Whitman's *Leaves of Grass* from photographs made in the South and East.

A major retrospective of 300 prints of Weston's work was held at the Museum of Modern Art, New York, in 1946. Weston began experiments with color photography the following year, and was the subject of a film, *The Photographer*, by Willard Van Dyke.

Weston's work of the late 1940s was hampered by Parkinson's disease. He took his last photographs in 1948 at Point Lobos. During the next 10 years of progressively incapacitating illness, Weston supervised the printing by his sons, Brett and Cole, of his life's work. His *Fiftieth Anniversary Portfolio* appeared in 1952. Three years later, eight sets of prints from 1000 Weston negatives were produced. Weston died in Carmel in 1958.

Weston was named an Honorary Member of the American Photographic Society in 1951, and was the recipient of numerous awards in all phases of his career. His work was exhibited in group shows around the world, including *Film und Foto*, Stuttgart (1929); *Group f/64*, San Francisco (1933); *The Photographer and the American Landscape*, Museum of Modern Art, New York (1963); *Photography in the Twentieth Century*, National Gallery of Canada, Ottawa (1967); and *Photography Rediscovered*, Whitney Museum, New York (1979). Weston was honored with solo exhibitions at the Los Angeles Country Museum (1927); the Museum of Modern Art, New York (1946 and 1975); the Musée d'Art Moderne, Paris (1950); the Metropolitan Museum of Art, New York (1970 and 1972); George Eastman House, Rochester, N.Y. (1966 and 1971); Witkin Gallery, New York (1969, 1975, 1977 and 1981); and the International Center of Photography, New York (1978). Weston's work has been the subject of numerous monographs and books. His *Daybooks 1923–1934*, daily photographic and biographical journals, were published in 1961 and 1966. A major biography by Ben Maddow was published in 1973.

Wet Plate Process

The collodion-on-glass negative process was commonly known as the wet plate process because the plate had to be exposed and completely processed before the collodion dried; in fact it was a damp or—given the adhesive quality of collodion—a "sticky plate" process. The basic method was published by Frederick Scott Archer in 1851. It was the first truly practical way to obtain permanent negatives or positives on glass, and the image produced by physical development was essentially grain-

Weston, Edward. "Pepper #30" (1930). Center for Creative Photography, University of Arizona.

less. Although inconvenient and cumbersome—the sticky surface caught dust and dirt, and an entire darkroom outfit had to be carried everywhere—its high quality and low cost led to its almost immediate success. The wet plate (and the related ambrotype and ferrotype) quickly made the daguerreotype and calotype obsolete; it remained dominant until gelatin dry plates were perfected in the mid-1880s. As practiced by most photographers, the wet collodion process had the following steps.

1. A glass plate was thoroughly cleaned with pumice and alcohol, and dried.

2. A small amount of iodized collodion (i.e., containing potassium iodide, and often potassium bromide as well) was poured in the center of the plate, held horizontally. The plate was tilted back and forth to flow the syrupy liquid evenly to the edges. When it had set just enough to adhere to the glass plate, the excess was poured back in the bottle.

3. The plate was immersed in a silver nitrate solution for sensitizing. A chemical reaction formed silver iodide (and silver bromide) crystals in the collodion.

4. The plate was transferred to the camera in a holder with a darkslide, and exposed—typically from 1 to 15 seconds, depending on the subject and light conditions. The photographer relied on experience and made sure not to underexpose.

5. The image was developed by inspection in a slightly acid solution of iron (ferrous) sulfate or oxalate, or pyrogallol. The photographer watched the highlight densities and stopped development when they were sufficiently strong; in this way the effects of overexposure were minimized.

6. The plate was fixed in hypo, washed, and dried.

The collodion emulsion was orthochromatic (red blind), so sensitizing and processing could be done by red safelight. Portable darkroom tents and tabletop hoods were usually made of red or orange canvas so as to transmit safe working illumination. The photographer had about 20 minutes to coat, expose, and process a plate under normal temperature conditions. In cold weather the collodion had to be warmed to pour out of the bottle, and working time was short; in hot weather it sometimes would not set sufficiently to stay on the plate. The finished negative was contact printed on albumen paper, or onto another glass plate to make a lantern slide. The ambrotype and ferrotype produced positive images directly.

See also: AMBROTYPE; ARCHER, FDK. SCOTT; COLLODION PROCESSES; FERROTYPE.

Wetting Agent

A wetting agent is a chemical that reduces the surface tension of water, with the result that the water does not have enough "skin strength" to form beads or drops on a smooth surface, but runs off freely. A very dilute solution of wetting agent commonly is used as a final rinse before a film is dried. After washing is complete, the film is placed in the wetting-agent solution without agitation for about one minute, and then removed, drained, and hung to dry. The water will run off, leaving only minute drops, if any at all, that will evaporate without leaving traces. (Large drops, common on untreated films, can leave spots of uneven density that create visible effects in a print.) The film surfaces must not be touched or wiped with a sponge or squeegee; that would destroy the effect of the wetting agent. There also must be no bubbles on the surface of the solution when the film is removed, for they will cling to the surface and leave drying marks. If bubbles do occur, they can be lifted or scraped off with a piece of clean paper, or plain water can be added until the solution overflows the container and they float over the edge.

Wetting agents are sold in concentrated form and must be highly diluted for use. Accurate measurement of the quantity needed to treat only one or two films is sometimes difficult; overdilution is preferable to under-, which may leave a scum on the film. A drop or two of wetting agent added to the water used for spotting or retouching may help dyes penetrate a print emulsion. There is no value in adding wetting agent to developers or other processing solutions or in using a wetting agent rinse after print washing.

See also: DRYING FILMS AND PRINTS; WASHING.

Wheatstone, Sir Charles

English, 1802–1875

In photography Wheatstone is known for his discovery of the stereoscopic effect in binocular vision, and for invention of both the reflecting (mirror) and refracting (lens) stereoscopes, which he reported to the Royal Society in 1838. His research established the concept of visual solidity, and in 1854 he demonstrated the role of stereoscopic vision in perspective using the pseudoscope—a device which transposed the right and left eye views—to produce inverted perspective. His investigations of light contributed to the theory of color vision and to the development of spectral analysis.

In 1837 Wheatstone and C. F. Cooke patented an electric telegraph system incorporating automatic transmitting and receiving equipment that used perforated paper tape and associated sensing needles. His rotating-mirror method of measuring the speed of electricity in wires was adapted in 1862 by J. B. L. Foucault for the first accurate (within 1 percent) measurement of the speed of light. Wheatstone's contributions to the theoretical understanding of electricity produced designs for more efficient dynamos; widespread application of Ohm's law relating current, voltage, and resistance; and the Wheatstone bridge for measuring resistance. His earliest work, which was in acoustics, confirmed and extended the work of predecessors, and as a by-product led to invention of the concertina, forerunner of the accordion.

See also: BREWSTER, SIR DAVID; STEREOSCOPIC; STEREOSCOPE PHOTOGRAPHY; VISION.

White, Clarence H.

American; 1871–1925

Clarence White is regarded as one of the turn-of-the-century's most influential Pictorial photographers and teachers of photography. Joseph Keiley sugggested in 1904 that White's work was "the best and most permanent produced in the first century of the application of photography to the production of original pictures." In 1966 Alvin Langdon Coburn called White "the most subtle and refined master photography has produced."

White was born in West Carlisle, Ohio. He lived there and in Newark, Ohio, until 1906. An early interest in painting was discouraged by his parents. Upon graduating from high school, White became a bookkeeper for a local grocery firm. He did not begin to photograph until 1893, the year of his honeymoon trip to the World's Columbian Exposition in Chicago. There he encountered first hand the works of major artists.

White's photographs were intimate studies of his family and friends, idyllic genre scenes, and melancholy portraits notable for their skillful use of natural light and quiet attention to detail. The photos were often shot in the early morning light because of White's work schedule. He exerted control over every phase of the photographic process, from costume design to the mounting and

White, Clarence. "The Ring Toss" (ca. 1899);
gum print. Library of Congress.

White, Minor. "Moon and Wall Encrustations" (1964). The Art Museum, Princeton University.

framing of his platinum prints. His work was influenced by Whistler, the early Impressionists, and Japanese art.

In 1898 White founded the Newark Camera Club, where he exhibited the work of many of America's finest photographers. The same year halftone reproductions of his photographs appeared in the national *Photographic Times.* He exhibited at the first Philadelphia Salon, and on a trip east met F. Holland Day and Alfred Stieglitz, both of whom were deeply impressed by his work. Stieglitz arranged for an exhibition of 122 of White's photographs at the New York Camera Club in 1899, and he regularly published White's images in *Camera Work,* an entire issue of which was devoted to him in 1908.

In 1900 White was elected to the Linked Ring, at whose Photographic Salon he had participated the previous year. He also participated in Day's *New School of American Photography* show in London at this time. White was a founding member of the Photo-Secession in 1902. In 1906 he exhibited with Gertrude Käsebier, with whom he had served on the jury for the Second Philadelphia Salon. He moved to New York City the same year, after spending two years as an itinerant photographer in the Midwest.

In 1907 White taught the first photography courses given at Columbia University. The next year he began teaching at the Brooklyn Institute of Arts and Sciences. He founded, with the painter Max Weber, a summer school of photography in Georgetown Island,

Maine, in 1910. Four years later he opened the Clarence H. White School of Photography in New York City. His pupils there included significant photographers such as Margaret Bourke-White, Doris Ulmann, Laura Gilpin, Ralph Steiner, Dorothea Lange, and Paul Outerbridge, Jr.

White was the first president of the Pictorial Photographers of America in 1916, following a break with Stieglitz in 1912. The two men eventually were reunited, but Stieglitz expressed disappointment with White's later work. Because of pressing financial obligations throughout his life, White was unable to devote himself to photography full-time. He did little creative work in his last years, which were burdened by a heavy teaching schedule. He died of a heart attack while on a tour with photography students in Mexico.

White was the subject of a Museum of Modern Art exhibition in New York City in 1971. His work is represented in most of the world's major collections of photography.
See also: LINKED RING; PHOTO-SECESSION; PICTORIAL PHOTOGRAPHY/ PICTORIALISM; STIEGLITZ, ALFRED.

White, Minor

American; 1908–1976
John Szarkowski has written, "Of those photographers who reached their creative maturity after the Second World War, none has been more influential than Minor White. . . . White's influence has depended not only on his own work

as a photographer but on his services as teacher, critic, publisher and house-mother for a large portion of the community of serious photographers."

White was known for his belief, influenced by Oriental philosophy, in the sacred and spiritual quality of photography. While his own work won him international acclaim, White devoted himself to bringing the work of countless other photographers before the public eye, and to achieving broad public recognition of photography as an art form.

White was born in Minneapolis, Minnesota. He attended public schools and became interested in photography as a young boy. He received a B.S. degree in botany, with a minor in English, from the University of Minnesota in 1933.

From 1933 to 1938 he worked as a hotel clerk in Portland, Oregon, where he was active in the Oregon Camera Club, photographing, exhibiting, and teaching. In 1939 he worked as a "creative photographer" for the Works Progress Administration photographing the Portland waterfront and iron-facade buildings. In 1940–1941 he taught photography and directed the La Grande Art Center in eastern Oregon. His first article, "When Is Photography Creative?," appeared in *American Photography* in 1943.

White participated in the *Image of Freedom* exhibition at the Museum of Modern Art in New York City in 1941. His first one-man exhibition was held at the Portland Art Museum in 1942.

From 1942 to 1945 White served in the United States Army Intelligence Corps. Unable to photograph regularly, he devoted much time to writing "Eight Lessons in Photography." He was baptized a Catholic by an Army chaplain in 1943. Zen, Gestalt psychology, and the teachings of G.I. Gurdjieff became other important spiritual influences in the course of his life.

After his discharge, White moved to New York City where he studied aesthetics under art historian Meyer Schapiro at Columbia University. He also worked with Beaumont and Nancy Newhall and as a photographer at the Museum of Modern Art, and he met Alfred Stieglitz, Edward Weston, and Paul Strand at this time.

White joined the photography faculty at the California School of Fine Arts, headed by Ansel Adams, in 1946. He developed close ties with Adams and Weston. Around this time he began to experiment with photographic sequences for wall exhibition.

With Adams, Dorothea Lange, the Newhalls, Barbara Morgan, and others, White founded *Aperture* quarterly, of which he was editor, in 1952. He directed the *How to Read a Photograph* exhibition at the San Francisco Museum of Art in 1953. The same year he joined the staff of George Eastman House in Rochester, New York, where he was curator of exhibitions for four years and editor of *Image* magazine in 1956–1957. Among the shows he directed during these years were *Camera Consciousness* (1954), *The Pictorial Image* (1955), and *Lyrical and Accurate* (1956). A large exhibition of his own work, *Sequence 13/ Return to the Bud*, was held at George Eastman House in 1959.

In 1955 White taught briefly at the Rochester Institute of Technology. He resigned as assistant curator of Eastman House and was appointed to the RIT faculty in 1956. At this time he began the influential workshops he would conduct throughout the country for the rest of his life.

In 1962 White was a founding member of the Society for Photographic Education. In 1965 he was made Visiting Professor in the Department of Architecture at MIT, where he continued to teach and organize exhibitions, including *Light[7]*. He was promoted to tenured professorship in 1969.

A major one-man traveling show of White's work originated at the Philadelphia Museum of Art in 1970. He was awarded a Guggenheim Fellowship the same year.

White retired from the faculty of MIT in 1974, but was appointed Senior Lecturer and became a Fellow of the MIT Council of Arts in 1975. He resigned as editor of *Aperture* the same year. His first major European traveling exhibition was also presented in 1975.

In 1976 White became a consulting editor of *Parabola* magazine and received an Honorary Doctorate of Fine Arts from the San Francisco Art Institute. He died of a heart attack in Boston in June, 1976. His archives are now in the Library of Princeton University.

White Light

Light composed of equal proportions of all visible wavelengths is white light. It is essentially the kind of light used in sensitometry to establish the spectral sensitivity of emulsions and the transmission characteristics of filters. The response of daylight type color film emulsion is balanced for the white light represented by average noon sunlight; it has a color temperature of 5500K.

The eye is a poor judge of white light because it accommodates (adapts automatically) to a memory of whiteness under widely varying conditions, with very different kinds of light. For example, when directly comparing incandescent light with daylight, the eye readily sees the yellow quality (blue deficiency) of the artificial light. But in a closed room or at night, it soon sees the same light as "pure" white. In addition, the eye can be made to see white by combinations of wavelengths that are neither continuous nor of relatively equal proportions across the spectrum. "White" fluorescent tubes emit discontinuous spectra of this sort, as revealed in color pictures taken by their light.

See also: COLOR; COLOR TEMPERATURE LIGHT; VISION.

Wide-angle Lens

A lens with an angle of view greater than about 45 degrees.

See: ANGLE OF VIEW; LENSES.

Wide-Angle Photography

The angle of view of wide-angle lens exceeds 45°, the approximate angle of view provided by the standard, or "normal," lens for any given film format. Within any format wide-angle lenses have shorter-than-normal focal lengths. Lenses of this type give smaller-than-normal image magnification with a consequent increase in subject coverage. The difference in magnification is directly proportional to the ratio of the focal lengths: a lens with half as much focal length as another produces half as much magnification. The increase in the field covered is inversely proportional: half as much focal length produces twice as wide a field; one-third as much focal length produces three times as wide a field.

Moderately wide-angle lenses are used in photojournalism and reportage, and in various other photographic situations in which pictures must be made in cramped surroundings. They are also useful for making photographs of large groups. Wide-angle lenses exhibit increased depth of field at any given aperture when compared with the normal focal length; this is especially useful in situations in which pictures are made rapidly and exact focus is sometimes difficult to achieve. The apparent perspective rendition given by these lenses is somewhat more exaggerated than normal, and this is most noticeable when the subject is close to the camera and is photographed obliquely. The perspective exaggeration contributes to distortion of vertical and spherical objects near the edges of the frame. This distortion becomes more and more obvious as the focal length of the lens becomes shorter, and increasing care must be taken to keep the camera level.

Extreme wide-angle lenses, taking in an angle of view up to 120° or so depending on their focal length, show extreme edge distortion, specially when the film plane of the camera is not parallel to the subject. Extreme wide-angle lenses have substantial depth of field even at wide apertures; in some cases the depth of field is so great that focusing becomes unnecessary. Lenses of this type are used in advertising illustration, in architectural photography, and as special-effects lenses by general photographers.

The widest view possible is given by fisheye lenses, which produce a 180-degree or greater angle of view. These lenses usually give a circular image and are purposely constructed to severely distort vertical and horizontal objects lying near the edges of the frame.

See also: DEPTH OF FIELD; DISTORTION; FISHEYE LENS; LENSES; PERSPECTIVE; TELEPHOTOGRAPHY.

Willis, William

English, 1841–1923

Willis, whose father invented the aniline process for copying plans and drawings, invented the platinum printing process in 1873, and subsequently the palladiotype process. He founded the Platinotype Company in England in 1878, and in the U.S. with Alfred Clements in 1879, to manufacture materials under a patent for an improved method. A major problem in manufacturing was obtaining 100 percent rag paper with no sizing, because the sizing compounds tended to react during processing to cloud the highlights of an image. The processes were greatly prized by artistic photographers such as Alfred Stieglitz, Peter Henry Emerson, and Frederick H. Evans for the delicate tonal scale they provided. Both processes became excessively expensive by World War I because platinum and palladium could be produced only by energy-intensive procedures; however, a small supply of materials was manufactured until the mid-1930s. Re-creations of the process today are entirely hand-crafted procedures by individual photographers.

See also: PLATINOTYPE.

Winogrand, Garry

American; 1928–1984

From the early 1960s on, Gary Winogrand's personal photojournalistic shots of disturbing, densely packed moments won him acclaim as an important chronicler of contemporary American life. Until recently he had worked exclusively with small-format cameras and available light to capture telling moments in a seemingly casual, "uncomposed" manner. His use of wide-angle lenses and tilted framing creates images both satirical and disturbing.

Winograd was born in New York City. He began photographing while in the United States Air Force in 1946–1947. He studied painting at City College of the City of New York in 1947 and painting and photography at Columbia University in New York City in 1948. In 1951 he attended Alexey Brodovitch's photojournalism class at the New School for Social Research in New York City. From 1952 to 1969 he worked as a freelance photojournalist and advertising photographer with the Pix Agency and Brackman Associates. His work was published regularly in *Sports Illustrated,* *Colliers,* and other national magazines.

Winograd's first one-man show was held at Image Gallery in New York City in 1960. One of several factors in the early 1960s powerfully affecting him and his work was the Cuban missile crisis of 1962. He photographed extensively for himself in New York City streets while making the rounds with his commercial work. Robert Frank joined Walker Evans as an important influence during this period. In 1963 Winograd had a solo exhibition at the Museum of Modern Art. He soon began a series of remarkable photographs in New York City zoos and the Coney Island Aquarium, published in his book *The Animals* (1969). Animals and humans in another human-made environment, the rodeo, were the subject of *Stock Photographs: Fort Worth Fat Stock Show and Rodeo* (1980).

Winograd was awarded a Guggenheim Fellowship in Photography in 1964, and he photographed extensively in California and the American Southwest for the next year.

In 1966 Winograd's work was exhibited with that of Lee Friedlander, Duane Michals, Bruce Davidson, and Danny Lyon in *Toward a Social Landscape* at George Eastman House in Rochester, New York. He showed the following year with Friedlander and Diane Arbus in the *New Documents* exhibition at the Museum of Modern Art.

Winograd received a second Guggenheim Fellowship in 1969. His work of the early 1970s was concerned with "the effect of the media on events." A major show of this work, called *Public Relations,* was held at the Museum of Modern Art in 1977.

Winograd received a grant from the New York State Council on the Arts in 1971. He was the recipient of an award from the National Endowment for the Arts in 1975 and a third Guggenheim Fellowship in 1979. He exhibited widely including shows at MIT (1978), the Santa Barbara Museum in California (1979), and Light Gallery in New York City (1975, 1976, 1979, and a major retrospective in 1981), and his work is many major collections. He taught at a number of schools, including the University of Texas, Austin, and the Art Institute of Chicago.

Winquist, Rolf

Swedish; 1910–1968

Rolf Winquist brought the era of Pictorialism in Sweden to a brilliant end and then went on to be one of the leading innovators and artists of "modern" photography.

After studying photography in Gothenburg from 1927–1931, Winquist alternated as advertising photographer and photographer on board the luxury cruiser *Kungsholm,* touring the world in

Winograd, Garry. "Fort Worth, Texas" (1974). Courtesy Garry Winograd; permanent collection, ICP, New York.

the winter season. Shortly before World War II these trips came to an end and he began a professional career as a portrait photographer. In 1939, he was invited to head and build up a new studio for portraits and advertising in Stockholm, known as Atelje Uggla. Under his guidance the studio soon became a leader in its field, and so it remained for three decades—Winquist was in charge until his death in 1968.

Winquist was a rare all-round master in photography. His everyday portrait work had elegance and style. His technique—in lighting, composition, printing—was faultless. He made thousands of wedding photographs, superb film star portraits, and (after the war) trend-setting fashion and advertising photographs. His work had a definite influence on professional photography in Sweden, and a number of that country's prominent contemporary photographers studied and worked with him over the years.

In addition to his daily professional work, Winquist was continuously active as a creative amateur, in the real sense of the word. He researched and learned to master many old techniques. His early personal work was clearly influenced by the Pictorialists. From the mid-1940s his work was hung in the major photo salons and exhibitions all over the world. He was invited to join the exclusive London Salon of Photography and the Cercle Royal d'études photographiques in Paris. He was elected a fellow of the Royal Photographic Society of Great Britain, and his photographs appeared in leading annals of Pictorialism.

In the early 1950s Winquist renounced his position in international art photography and turned to a straight, documentary approach, using 35mm cameras. His observations of summer life in England are the work of a photo-essayist with a warm human interest. He made a series of "street portraits" in Stockholm, and often used 35mm for studio portrait work as well. In his photographs from this period, artistic brilliance gives way to an intimate, poetic realism; his concerns are more with content than form. During the 1960s Winquist made many of his finest portraits, often of children and old people.

As social and political reportage became a prominent part of the photo scene in Sweden, Winquist instead became more involved in work of an experimental character, to a great extent in color. He made studies of plant fragments and experimented with multiple paper negative printing and the Sabattier effect. During the last months of his life,

he concentrated on close-up studies of garden flowers in bright colors.

Some 700 of Winquist's prints are housed at the Museum of Photography in Stockholm.

Winter Photography

Photographing in winter poses a special set of problems. Snow scenes are frequently underexposed, especially by automatic-exposure cameras, because they are so much brighter than the average subject for which exposure meters are calibrated. If the scene is predominantly snow-covered, the meter system will indicate an exposure that will record the snow darker than normal. To make the snow appear white, exposure must be increased by the equivalent of 1½ to 2½ f-stops with black-and-white and color negative films, but only about 1 f-stop with color transparency films, because their proper exposure is based on highlight values. If the scene is bright and there are significant shadows, the shadows may be rendered too light on black-and-white film. This is because the shadows reflect blue sky light, to which the film is more sensitive than the eye. A medium-yellow filter will record the shadows and the sky as nearer the tonal values the eye sees in the scene.

The high blue reflectivity of snow scenes also poses a problem with color films. The blue can be reduced somewhat by using a skylight 1B (pinkish) filter. Using a polarizer to deepen the blue of the sky is not recommended in this situation; it may cause an increase in the blueness of the snow and heighten the overall contrast rendition in the process.

Snow, fog, or other inclement winter weather offers an array of interesting photographic opportunities both during the day and at dusk or in the early morning hours. In most cases, cameras and lenses can be protected from moisture by a plastic bag with a hole in one side for the lens; the mouth of the bag is at the bottom. This arrangement is most effective with single-lens reflex cameras. The front surface of the lens can be kept from getting wet with a lenshood or an appropriate filter. If the weather is especially wet, a small underwater housing will protect the camera completely without adding an inordinate amount of bulk. Amphibious cameras are ideal for foul-weather photography.

Cold weather poses a hazard to cameras, lenses, and film, and to photographers as well. When the temperature is extremely low, frostbite of the extremities is a real possibility; layered clothing and some covering for the face

and head are extremely important, as is a well-made pair of insulated boots. Hands can be kept warm and flexible with a pair of hunter's or shooter's mittens. These have openings through which one or two fingers can be extended for releasing the shutter and making exposure adjustments.

Electronically governed equipment is notorious for failing in extremely cold weather. Extra batteries should be carried for cameras, light meters, and flash units, and they should be kept in an inside pocket so that the cold does not lower their effectiveness. Cameras can be kept warm by using a neck strap and letting them hang inside a coat or parka with the front element of the lens protruding. If the front of the lens is kept warm, exposed to extended use, and then placed back in a warm place, condensation can occur.

Cold weather makes photographic film brittle. It must be wound through the camera slowly so as to avoid breakage and the discharge of static electricity. Static will cause lightning-bolt or treelike exposure streaks across the emulsion which cannot be removed. Because of this, motorized film advance is not recommended in cold conditions. To avoid inadvertently tearing 35mm film out of its cassette at the end of a roll, most photographers do not expose the last two or three frames in very cold weather, but rewind the film slowly before they arrive at the end of the spool.

Breathing carelessly near the camera's eyepiece can cause fogging (condensation), making focusing difficult. The photographer should exhale away from the camera whenever possible. (In addition, metal camera parts that have been exposed to extreme cold for any length of time can be a hazard to the skin; metal conducts heat quickly, and therefore touching an extremely cold camera with the bare skin or lips can cause scorching.) Warm air will cause condensation on and in cold cameras and lenses. Cold equipment should be brought into warm indoor environments gradually, wrapped in a plastic bag; the condensation will form outside the bag rather than on the camera itself. Immediately taking the camera from an extremely warm room into very cold weather should also be avoided to prevent the risk of cracking the lens elements due to the sudden extreme change in temperature.

If extended use of the camera in cold weather is expected, it can be "winterized." Manufacturers and repair shops make use of special dry lubricants for this purpose. The standard lubricant used in cameras can become stiff in ex-

treme cold, causing the camera mechanisms to seize and rendering the equipment useless. The cost of replacing or removing the lubricant from a conventionally constructed camera may be prohibitive. It is far less expensive to buy a camera specially treated at the outset for extreme cold. Most major manufacturers make cold-proof cameras on a special-order basis, but this kind of equipment is necessary only if extended use in near-arctic conditions is expected. Under normal winter conditions in most parts of the world a mechanically governed camera will function properly.
Color photograph: p. C-64.

Witkacy (Stanislaw Ignacy Witkiewicz)

Polish; 1885–1939

The versatile Polish artist who signed his works in photography, painting, literature, and drama "Witkacy," was born in Warsaw, the son of the painter and critic Stanislaw Witkiewicz. With his father's encouragement and guidance, he started to paint at an early age, and soon thereafter to take photographs. His early snapshots of landscapes, such enthusiasms as steam locomotives, and objects of his immediate curiosity, served variously as souvenirs of trips and vacations and as preparatory notes for his paintings. From 1904 to 1910 he attended lectures at the Academy of Fine Arts in Cracow. His work of this period was influenced by the Young Poland modernist movement and by the paintings of Arnold Boecklin, Wladyslaw Slewinski, and Paul Gauguin.

As he matured artistically, Witkacy's youthful impulse to explore subjects of all kinds gave way to a concentration on portraiture, which for him was the attempt to penetrate human nature, whatever the medium of expression might be. Portraiture was his favorite, personally natural means of getting across ideas, defining reality, examining people, and—most of all—examining himself. The role of photography in this was simply to be a medium, one to be used without pretension, and one which possessed no inherent artistic qualities. "I consider," he wrote, "making a good, psychologically naturalistic portrait. . . no crime, providing, of course, the public is not being deluded into the belief that this is the very supreme art, with a capital A."

With this no-nonsense approach, Witkacy became an ardent and prolific photographer from 1905 onward. For the most part he took pictures of his father, himself, his sweethearts, and the bohemians of Zakopane, a fashionable

Witkacy. "Portrait of Father" (1912). Collection, Muzeum Sztuki Wlodzi, Poland.

holiday resort in the Tatra mountains, where he had taken landscapes as a boy. Beginning with beautifully refined, fully lighted, and classically composed portraits, he evolved to recording half-lit faces, and this led to an exploration of fragments—a mouth, eyes, brows, a nose. With an improvised extension tube he achieved a very tight framing which he used to explore what is most fundamental in human nature, revealed by a twist of the mouth, an expression in the eyes. He was looking for the very essence of human beings, an individual's identity and truth.

In 1914, after the death of his fiancee, Witkacy joined an expedition to Australia headed by the world-famous anthropologist Bronislaw Malinowski. Back in Poland at the outbreak of World War I, he saw army duty at the front near St. Petersburg and eventually became involved in the tide of the Russian October Revolution. In Russia, in 1915–1917, his quintuple portrait—one of a series of turning-point images in his career—was created. Decomposition of the subject was a major artistic concern of the times, especially in movements such as cubism and futurism. Witkacy's response was a "multiplication," a variety of treatments and representations of a single subject. The subject and model was Witkacy himself, who arranged and directed the pictures, but which were taken by his friend Jozef Glogowski. In this and later multiplications, Witkacy is seen as a clergyman, an artist, a Merry Andrew, a meditating sage, a prisoner, a man of the world, a bum, a judge, and other personae. He is always himself, but always made different by the situation, clothes, and, particularly, by the different faces he takes on.

The artistic point of this apparent clownery is what Witkacy called "Individual Being. . . the basic category of any form of being." We reveal ourselves by subtle aspects of what we are prompted to put on or show when challenged to express ourselves, he believed. "Only the lens," he wrote, "can provide an image capable of 'dragging up' from the bottom of our unconscious that need to substitute an object with something more than an imperfect replica, with a new object in itself, free from the circumstance of time. . . ."

In his multiplications, which became a major concern in his later career, Witkacy attempted a highly complex kind of psychological portraiture. Superficially the images seemed to involve playacting; fundamentally they revealed longings, fantasies, and self-images. In his diverse embodiments and transformations, deformations, splittings, and caricatures, Witkacy illustrated his own experience of his identity, or, more accurately, his identities. He simultaneously questioned the objectivity of photography (believing that every single image was both true and false in the most fundamental sense), and demonstrated its analytical function. His work is remarkable in the way that it translated philosophical, psychological, and artistic concepts into the visual idiom of form, shade, and line.

Witkacy died September 18, 1939, in Jeziora, Poland.
See also: PORTRAITURE; SELF-PORTRAIT.

Wolcott, Alexander Simon

American, 1804–1844
A manufacturer of dental equipment and instruments, Wolcott was informed of the daguerreotype process by his partner, John Johnson, in October 1840. His immediate interest led him to design a mirror camera to take photographs. His first attempts produced a positive image on one plate and a negative image of the same subject on another plate, the result of solarization from overexposure. A day later he succeeded in taking the first photographic portrait in the U. S., a profile view of Johnson on a plate only 3/8 in. (1cm) square. Rejecting an offer from Samuel F. B. Morse to become partners, Wolcott and Johnson opened the first photographic portrait studio in

the world in New York City in March 1840.

At the same time Wolcott patented an improved version of his mirror camera, incorporating an 8 in. (2.5cm) diameter mirror produced by their new associate, Henry Fitz, Jr., a telescope maker. Wolcott also patented a method of lighting that used large mirrors set outside the window of a studio to direct sunlight onto the sitter through a rack of bottles filled with a blue (copper sulfate) solution. The daguerreotype plate was sensitive only to blue and ultraviolet light; this large-scale filter arrangement removed the ultraviolet and most of the red and green rays, reducing both the heat and the intensity of the light for the increased comfort of the subject, who typically had to pose from two to five minutes. Johnson's father took the camera design to England, where a patent was obtained in June 1840. The rights were purchased by Richard Beard, who quickly established throughout England the world's largest chain of portrait studios.

In 1843 Wolcott and Johnson were in England to supervise establishment of a factory to manufacture the patented camera. They nearly perfected an albumen-on-glass process, some seven years before C. F. A. Niépce de Saint-Victor, and patented an enlarger—in fact an adjustable copying camera—to obtain large daguerreotype or calotype copies of the small (2″ × 2½″ [5.1 × 6.4cm]) plates used in the Wolcott camera. Wolcott contracted a fatal disease at this time and returned to the U.S., where he died a year later.
See also: ALBUMEN PROCESSES; BEARD, RICHARD; CALOTYPE; DAGUERREOTYPE; MIRROR CAMERA; MORSE, SAMUEL F.B.; NIÉPCE DE SAINT-VICTOR, C. F. A.

Wolfe, Louise Dahl

See: DAHL-WOLFE, LOUISE.

Wollaston, William Hyde

English, 1766–1828
Trained as a physician, Wollaston practiced for eleven years before devoting himself to research in astronomy, physics, physiology, and metallurgy. He was one of the first to make comparative measurements of the brightness of the sun and the moon and in 1800–1801 to investigate the darkening action of "chemical rays" (unidentified ultraviolet) in the spectrum of sunlight on silver chloride—research that was noted by Humphry Davy in reporting his experiments with Thomas Wedgwood in

their attempts to record camera obscura images.

In 1802 Wollaston discovered the spectral dark lines (Fraunhofer lines) that "fingerprint" the identity of a burning compound. In 1807 he invented the drawing device called the camera lucida, which was to impel William Henry Fox Talbot to invent a photographic process a quarter-century later. In 1812 he invented the meniscus lens, now the fundamental lens of eyeglasses. An improved version, consisting of a positive (biconvex) crown glass element cemented to a negative (biconcave) flint glass element was the first achromatic lens. It produced relatively flat field and, with a stop in front of it, reduced coma. Until the invention of the Petzval lens, it was the lens most suited for photography at the birth of the medium.

In 1827 Wollaston, a vice-president of the Royal Society, met with Joseph Nicéphore Niépce in England and apparently was involved in Niépce's failure to present his camera obscura recording process before the Society, an event that would have changed the history of the invention of photography. Wollaston made a fortune from the invention of a process to turn platinum into a practical, workable metal. In the course of this work he discovered the elements rhodium and palladium and the mineral named in his honor, Wollastonite.
See also: ABERRATIONS OF LENSES; ACHROMAT; CAMERA LUCIDA; MENISCUS; NIÉPCE, JOSEPH NICÉPHORE; PETZVAL, JOSEPH; PLATINOTYPE; TALBOT, W. H. F.; WEDGWOOD, THOMAS.

Women in Photography

Especially in the last half-century, women have been prominent in photography as in few other fields. While earlier periods saw the emergence of a number of women photographers of undeniable talent and accomplishment, these were mainly isolated exceptions; by and large, photography was regarded as a male occupation. Since the 1920s, however, as women have moved into increasingly important roles throughout society, a growing number of women have taken up photography as a profession and as a means of artistic self-expression. Today, women are among the leaders in such diverse areas as portraiture, photojournalism, fashion photography, documentary photography, advertising photography, and fine-arts photography.

In the 19th c. women were important to the development of photography in two very different ways. Commercial

establishments devoted to portraiture or the production of *cartes-de-visite* routinely employed women in secondary positions—as darkroom technicians, for example. In the first photographic printing concerns, Fox Talbot's establishment in Britain and Blanquart-Evrard's in France, most of the workers were, in fact, women. They were, however, paid considerably less than their male counterparts, and female proprietors of commercial studios or printing establishments were unheard of. In the 1880s, when the sudden boom in amateur photography caused a vast photofinishing industry to spring up, women were employed in large numbers. Photographs of Eastman Kodak's huge photo-processing operations during that period reveal that women made up the overwhelming majority of the work force.

A more discernible mark, however, was left on 19th c. photography by those well-to-do women amateur photographers who refused to be discouraged by the difficulty and unavoidable messiness of the early photographic processes. Independence and sometimes eccentricity of spirit characterized amateurs such as Lady Clementina Hawarden, whose genre studies and pictures of children were received with admiration when exhibited in the early 1860s. Amateur photographers were typically members of the upper middle class, and in no way dependent on photography as a source of livelihood; they could photograph primarily to please themselves. It was from this background that Julia Margaret Cameron, probably the most celebrated woman photographer of the 19th c. emerged. Cameron began her photographic career in the mid-1860s, when she was nearly 50 years old. A tireless and original worker, she divided her efforts among idealized portraits of children, costumed tableaux illustrating scenes from medieval legends, and astonishingly direct portraits of the poets, scientists, and other prominent figures who frequented her home. Her studies of such personalities as Henry Wadsworth Longfellow, Charles Darwin, and Sir John Herschel are today ranked among the most important photographic portraits ever made. Less well known are the photographs Cameron made in Ceylon after 1875, when she was in her sixties. In these she concentrated on Ceylonese women in marketplaces and other open-air environments.

Portraiture was the area that first attracted a sizeable number of women photographers. At the turn of the century, Gertrude Käsebier became one of the most prominent portraitists in New York, famous for her soft-focus, delicately-lighted portraits of female sitters. Subsequently Käsebier took her place as one of the leading members of the Photo-Secession group. A strong-willed personality, she eventually quarreled with the leader of that group, Alfred Stieglitz, and became a founder of the Pictorial Photographers of America.

Another well-known member of the Photo-Secession, the Californian Annie Brigman, produced a number of evocative soft-focus photographs in which she attempted to portray symbolic correspondances between the nude human figure and the natural landscape.

A portraitist who determined to take her camera outside the confines of the studio was Frances Benjamin Johnston, a well-known photographer in Washington, D.C., from the 1890s through the 1930s. Johnston was a pioneer in the emergence of photographic journalism, bringing back picture stories from the Pennsylvania coal fields for popular magazines, and photographing the U.S. fleet on a much-publicized round-the-world voyage. After completing frequent documentary commissions for the U.S. government, she turned to architectural photography, spending many years acquiring views of the architectural heritage of the American South.

Increasingly since the 1920s, women have moved into branches of photography once dominated exclusively by men.

In portraiture, Lotte Jacobi emerged in the late 1920s as an outstanding photographer of the artists, writers, and entertainers of Berlin. Forced to flee Germany by the Hitler regime, she reestablished herself as one of New York's leading portraitists. In Paris in the 1930s, Gisèle Freund won acclaim for her candid color portraits of literary personalities such as James Joyce and André Gide. In more recent years, the American photographer Marie Cosindas has produced a remarkable series of color portraits using the Polaroid process; warm and richly hued, these portraits testify to Cosindas's early training as a painter.

The importance of women in fashion photography dates from the 1930s. In 1936 Louise Dahl-Wolfe, who had previously trained as a painter, began to photograph for *Vogue* in New York. Using an 8″ × 10″ studio camera and the new Kodachrome film, she was responsible for many of the first successful color fashion photographs. During the same years, Toni Frissell helped introduce "snapshot" fashion photographs taken in outdoor locales to *Vogue*. Eventually seeking more exciting assignments, Frisell went on to photograph for *Sports Illustrated* for a number of years. Sarah Moon, a former model who took up photography in 1968, has become the leading practitioner of "impressionistic" fashion photography; her grainy, soft-focus color images lend an atmosphere of fantasy to the scenes that she portrays. Deborah Turbeville, a fashion editor turned photographer, also began to publish her work in the late 1960s in *Vogue*, *Harper's Bazaar*, and *Mademoiselle*. Turbeville's pale, monochromatic photographs spin a more ambiguous web of fantasy, and are apt to present models in unsettling, fictionalized settings.

In documentary photography, a number of important women have followed in the footsteps of Frances Benjamin Johnston. Berenice Abbott, one of the major documentary photographers of this century, was responsible for rescuing the negatives of the French documentarist Eugène Atget at the time of his death in 1927. Inspired by Atget's photographic record of the changing face of Paris, Abbott returned to New York and spent much of the 1930s engaged upon a similar documentation.

While Abbott relied primarily upon a large view-camera in her work, Dorothea Lange during the 1930s proved the value of the more easily manageable handheld camera in documentary work. One of the celebrated group of photographers employed by the federal Farm Security Administration during the Depression, Lange obtained remarkably candid, heartfelt images of Southern sharecroppers and migrants fleeing the desolation of the Dust Bowl. With her husband, the sociologist Paul Taylor, Lange was responsible for one of the most moving photographic books of the Depression era, *An American Exodus* (1939).

In the closely related field of photojournalism, the most renowned woman photographer of the 1930s and 1940s was Margaret Bourke-White. After establishing herself as *Fortune* magazine's star photographer, Bourke-White became one of *Life* magazine's original staff photographers in 1936. During World War II she served as one of the few women war correspondents, providing glimpses inside Stalin's Russia and horrific views of the Nazi concentration camps when they were opened at the war's end. She remained with *Life* until her retirement in the late 1950s, and was responsible for many of that magazine's most memorable photo-essays.

Two younger women photojournalists, Mary Ellen Mark and Susan Meiselas, have won wide recognition in the last decade. Mark, a member of the

Magnum agency, has photographed in Northern Ireland, produced a moving account of life inside a mental hospital (*Ward 81*, 1979), and, most recently, spent several months detailing the lives of a community of prostitutes in Bombay (*Falkland Road*, 1981). Meiselas, also a Magnum member, won attention with her first book, an unsentimental look at carnival strippers, in 1976. She confirmed her talent with her second book, *Nicaragua* (1981), a selection of vivid color reportage of the revolution in that Latin nation.

Women have come to play a more important role in fine-art photography than in perhaps any other branch of the medium. Margarethe Mather, who during the 1910s and 1920s was Edward Weston's partner in his Glendale, California, portrait studio, frequently exhibited her portraits, still lifes, and figure studies alongside his. Imogen Cunningham, one of the most eclectic and long-lived woman photographers, moved from Pictorial-style images of children and nudes to a "straight" approach in the 1920s. A founding member of the *f*/64 group along with Ansel Adams and Edward Weston, she produced sharp-focus studies of flowers and plants seen as strong graphic shapes, as well as a number of delicate nude studies. Italian-born Tina Modotti, who learned photography from Weston in Mexico in the 1920s, also produced a substantial body of work.

In Europe, too, a wave of talented female art photographers began to appear during the 1920s and 1930s. Germaine Krull, a freelance architectural photographer in Munich, produced an impressive portfolio of near-abstractions dealing with the contemporary uses of metals in architecture. Florence Henri, while studying at the Bauhaus in Germany, developed a provocative self-portrait technique that employed a series of mirror reflections. The European interest in photomontage and photograms was reflected in the work of Ilse Bing, a German who used these techniques to call attention to social and political conditions.

Barbara Morgan, a painter and photographer, became by the 1940s one of the foremost photographers of dance in the U.S. A master of flash photography techniques, her studies of dancers like Martha Graham, Merce Cunningham, and José Limòn remain classics of their kind. In addition, Morgan experimented successfully with multiple print and montage techniques, as well as a series of abstract light drawings.

Austrian-born Lisette Model, who emigrated to the U.S. in 1937, won distinction not only for her sharply etched, impromptu portraits of the extravagant characters she encountered; as a teacher at New York's New School for Social Research from the 1950s to the 1980s, she helped shape a great many young talents, including Diane Arbus. Originally a fashion photographer, Arbus shared Model's fascination with society's outcasts, and during the 1960s devoted her energies to assembling a group of powerful and disturbing portraits of the physically and mentally distressed. The 1972 exhibition of her photographs at the Museum of Modern Art, one year after her death by suicide, was judged one of the most important of the decade.

With the emergence of the feminist movement, a number of publications and exhibitions have sought to determine whether or not there exists a special "woman's way of seeing." The results suggest that there is not; the work of a modern formalist photographer like Jan Groover seems as cool and impersonal as similar work by her male counterparts. Women photographers do, however, seem more likely to involve themselves with work that explores the relation of women's self-images vis-à-vis their social roles. Most notable here have been the fictionalized "self-portraits" of Cindy Sherman, whose photographs present the female persona as a series of shifting roles and performances, and Irinia Ionesco, who has chosen to investigate the darker side of female sexuality.

In addition to the photographers mentioned above, many women have been influential in areas related to the display and publication of photographic art. Among them are Sue Davis, founder of the Photographers' Gallery in London; Helen Gee, founder of the Limelight Gallery in New York City; Grace Mayer, curator of the Edward Steichen Archive at the Museum of Modern Art, New York; Leni Riefenstahl, German filmmaker and photographer; and Carmel Snow, editor of *Harper's Bazaar* in its most innovative and influential years.

Woodbury, Walter Bentley

English; 1834–1885

At the age of fifteen Woodbury left England for gold mining in Australia. There in 1853 he became a professional photographer; he moved on to Java in 1859 and returned to England in 1863. For the remainder of his life he worked as an inventor, producing a variety of devices and processes, most of which were improvements or variations of projectors, viewers, and photomechanical reproduction methods. His two most important inventions were the Woodburytype and Stannotype reproduction processes.
See also: STANNOTYPE; WOODBURY-TYPE/WOODBURYGRAVURE.

Woodburytype; Woodburygravure

Unlike other methods of photomechanical reproduction, the Woodburytype achieved true continuous tone and such faithful reproduction that its images were virtually indistinguishable from original photographs. The process, invented in England in 1864 by Walter Woodbury, formed a final image in pigmented gelatin. It began with a bichromated gelatin emulsion exposed under a negative and processed to a positive relief image of extra hardness. The relief was placed with a sheet of lead in a hydraulic press that forced them together, forming the lead into a mold of the image; about six such molds could be taken from one relief. The mold was placed in a hand press and filled with liquid gelatin containing a black carbon or colored pigment; this was covered with a sheet of paper and the press was closed to squeeze them together and force the excess gelatin out around the edges. When the gelatin set, it adhered to the paper; its varying thicknesses formed the image tones, and the final drying reduced the relief to an almost flat surface. The paper was trimmed exactly at the image edges to eliminate the excess squeezed-out gelatin. It was either mounted and matted like a photograph or pasted-in as a book illustration. Because of their exquisite quality, Woodburytypes were used widely for fine book illustration, from about 1875 to 1900.

Woodburygravure. A process in which the gelatin image was adhered directly to the book page and the backing paper stripped off (the image having been formed in reverse) was called Woodburygravure. A simpler version that used tinfoil instead of lead to form the mold and required only a hand press, was called the Stannotype. The Woodburytype was eventually replaced by faster, more economical methods that printed reproductions directly on the book pages; none equaled the quality of its images.
See also: RELIEF IMAGES; STANNOTYPE; WOODBURY, W.B.

Wratten, Frederick Charles Luther

English; 1840–1926

Wratten invented the procedure of cutting ripened halide-carrying gelatin into "noodles" for washing and remelting in the manufacture of photographic emulsions. In 1878 he was co-founder of the firm Wratten and Wainwright, Ltd, one of the first manufacturers of gelatin dry plates. In 1906 the company became the first to produce true panchromatic plates on a commercial scale. C. E. K. Mees became scientific director of the company and insisted that it be purchased by Eastman Kodak Co. as a condition of his coming to the U.S. to create the Kodak Research Laboratories. The world-famous line of Wratten filters thus became part of the Kodak line. The numbers most commonly used today to identify filters (e.g., No. 25, red; No. 8, yellow; etc.) are Kodak Wratten filter numbers.

See also: DRY PLATES; EMULSION; MEES, CHARLES EDWARD KENNETH.

Writing on Films and Prints

It is frequently necessary to mark films and prints for identification, to indicate images to be printed or convey printing instructions, and to record various data. The most suitable areas for marking are the margins and the reverse side of prints, and the edges of film. If a mark must be made within the image area of a film, it should be made on the base rather than the emulsion side.

A number of common markers are suitable, the most readily available of which is the ordinary ball-point pen. Such pens work well on most surfaces except glossy papers and film bases. They leave a permanent mark, and most are reasonably fine-tipped, so they may be used in limited areas. Care should be taken when writing on the back of paper; too much pressure may crease the image on the front.

China markers ("grease pencils") commonly are used for temporary markings. They work well on all photographic surfaces and come in a variety of colors; orange and white stand out best on contact sheets. Their marks are removed easily with a soft, clean cloth and a drop of lighter fluid or film cleaner.

Felt-tip markers will write on some glossy surfaces, as well as on other surfaces if they use a "permanent" or "waterproof" solvent-based ink. Experimenting with a discarded piece of material is the only way to be sure. Special fine-tip pencils that will mark negatives are also available.

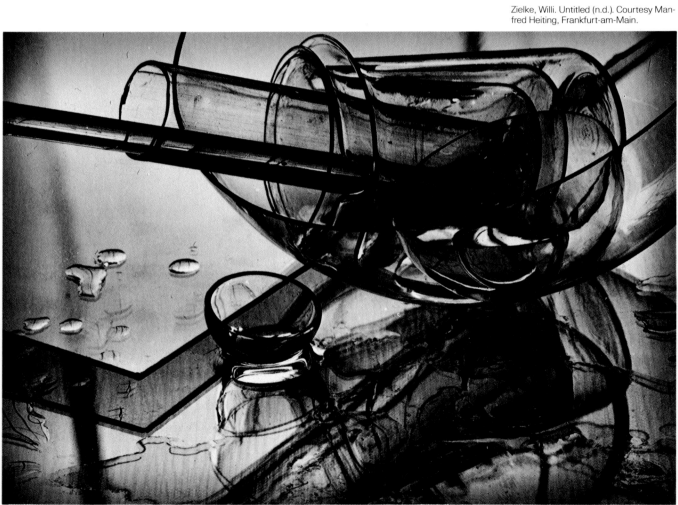

Zielke, Willi. Untitled (n.d.). Courtesy Manfred Heiting, Frankfurt-am-Main.

X-Y-Z

Xenon Arc Lamp

A discharge tube filled with pressurized xenon gas emits very high intensity white light when arcing is induced by high current electricity; a very small tube can produce a great amount of light. Continuous-discharge xenon tubes are used in long distance and high-intensity spotlights and projectors. Brief-discharge xenon tubes are used in electronic flash units; repeat-pulse tubes are used for illumination in process photography and in some motion-picture projectors.

Xerography

The most widely used electrophotographic process for reproducing images is xerography, invented in the U.S. in 1937 by Chester Carlson. It dominates the field of immediate document copying and has a great variety of other applications, from reproducing animation and architectural drawings to producing graphics directly from computer-controlled exposure. It is a dry process (Greek: *xeros* = dry) that uses a pattern of static electrical charges to temporarily register the image until it can be permanently recorded by a pigment (toner) fused to paper or another base such as celluloid. A typical xerographic copying machine functions in the following way.

1. The entire surface of a specially-coated revolving metal drum or continuous-loop belt is given a uniform charge of static electricity.

2. As the charged surface moves past the lighted document to be reproduced, the bright portions of the image destroy the static charge, leaving a pattern that matches the dark parts.

3. The drum or belt passes close to the surface of the copy paper and a corresponding pattern of static charges is formed on the paper surface.

4. A powdered toner is dusted or otherwise applied to the charged paper. The toner has an oppposite static charge and so is attracted to the dark areas of the image pattern but repelled by the light areas.

5. The paper passes a heating element that fuses the toner to the paper, making the image permanent.

The process is so rapid that some machines can produce 3000 or more black-and-white copies an hour. Variant methods use a liquid to carry the toner particles; it is sprayed on the paper and evaporates in drying. Other methods use a solvent rather than heat to fuse the image to the final support. Some machines eliminate the drum or belt and use a specially coated paper to receive the initial charge and exposure and then form the final image. Toners can be electrically charged to provide negative-to-positive copies rather than the common positive-to-positive images.

Color xerography requires three separate exposures and toner developments before the final image is fused. The first exposure, through a green filter, is treated with a magenta toner; the second, through a blue filter, with a yellow toner; the third, through a red filter, with a cyan toner. Some machines accept a projector so that color transparencies as well as opaque images can be copied. Exposure and toner controls permit some adjustment of color balance in the reproduction.

See also: CARLSON, CHESTER; ELECTROPHOTOGRAPHIC PROCESSES.

X-Ray Films and Plates

Radiographic materials for recording x-ray exposure have a plastic base that is coated on both sides with a silver halide emulsion. The double coating achieves increased density and contrast from a given amount of exposure because of the penetration of the exposing energy. This is important in limiting subject dosage, and limiting the power requirements of the equipment. The emulsions are relatively thick layers, to increase x-ray absorption, with large surface crystals, which have maximum sensitivity to exposure. X-ray films and plates are supplied in sealed envelopes or packets because the emulsion does not have to be uncovered to record an exposure. Direct x-ray emulsions are affected by the x-rays themselves. Screen x-ray emul-

sions are sandwiched between two sheets of material that emit energy the film can record when they are excited by x-rays. The sheets or screens may be coated with calcium or barium compounds that emit blue and ultraviolet wavelengths—to which all silver halide emulsions are sensitive—or they may be covered with thin metal foil that emits electrons that affect the emulsion along with the x-rays. Screen films require the least exposure and therefore are used for medical and dental radiography; direct films are used in industrial and physical science radiography. Ordinary films are used to photograph the visible images produced by x-rays in a fluoroscope.
See also: FLUOROGRAPHY; ULTRA-VIOLET AND FLUORESCENCE PHOTOG-RAPHY; X-RAYS; X-RAY PHOTOGRAPHY.

X-ray Photography

Because x-rays penetrate or are absorbed by virtually all materials, x-ray photographs—radiographs—are not reflected-energy images but shadow-graphs. That is, the subject is placed between the exposing energy (x-ray) source and the recording emulsion. The energy is focused into a narrow beam that is aimed at the subject area to be recorded, but unlike photography with light rays, the image-forming rays passing through the subject are not subsequently focused into a sharp image. The image recorded results from differing exposures created by the varying degrees of x-ray absorptance of the subject's material and internal structure. When organs, tissues, or other structural components have essentially the same x-ray transparency as surrounding material, they often can be made radiographically more visible by temporarily filling or treating them with an x-ray absorptive substance such as a barium sulfate solution, or various iodine solutions. Improved images of organs partly shadowed by others are obtained by a technique called *tomography,* in which the x-ray gun and the recording plate move during the exposure. Medical and dental radiographs are made with "soft" or comparatively long-wavelength x-rays at the lowest possible energy levels. Films sandwiched between phosphor screens are used to minimize the x-ray dosage required for exposure. Industrial radiographs use "hard," short-wavelength x-rays, or even gamma rays—which are unsafe for living subjects—and unscreened films. Exposing energy levels for industrial radiographs are typically many thousand or million kilovolts greater than those used for medical purposes. Indirect radiographs can also be

X-Ray Photography. Dr. Dain Tasker, "Flowers" (n.d.). Smithsonian Institution.

recorded by photographing the image created by x-rays on a fluoroscope screen.
See also: FLUOROGRAPHY; PHANTOM VIEW; TOMOGRAPHY; ULTRAVIOLET AND FLUOROSCENCE PHOTOGRAPHY; X-RAY FILMS AND PLATES; X-RAYS.

X-Rays

The electromagnetic energy between the ultraviolet and gamma ray portions of the spectrum is made up of wavelengths called x-rays. They were discovered in 1895 Wilhelm Roentgen and almost immediately applied to the medical examination of bone fractures. It is the ability of x-rays to penetrate a great many substances that is the basis of their most important applications. The shadow images they produce of internal structure are called radiographs or skia-graphs (Greek: *skia* = shadow). X-rays are produced when high-energy electrons pass near or through very strong electrical fields, or when various heavy

metals are bombarded by electrons. X-ray tubes use both methods to produce energy. Short-wavelength or "hard" x-rays of about 0.05 to 0.1nm are used for industrial radiography such as inspecting metal casting for internal flaws. "Soft" x-rays in the range of 10nm are used to investigate living tissue and similar substances.
See also; SPECTRUM; X-RAY FILMS AND PLATES; X-RAY PHOTOGRAPHY.

Young, Thomas
English; 1773–1829
A physician by profession, Young was also a fundamental researcher in physics and a key participant in deciphering the Egyptian hieroglyphics of the Rosetta stone. His first research identified accommodation in the human eye—the changing of lens shape to focus at various distances—and the aberration he named astigmatism. In 1801–1803 he revived the wave theory of light—in opposition to Newton's corpuscular, or

particle, theory, which had dominated for more than a century—and showed how simply it explained the phenomena of interference, diffraction, reflection, and refraction. In 1807 he advanced an explanation of color vision that von Helmholtz developed into the three-color theory that bears their names and that was first demonstrated by photographic means by J. C. Maxwell. Young established the modern concept of energy as physical force; made the first measurements of wavelength and of the size of molecules; investigated tidal phenomena; explained capillary action and the surface tension of liquids; and refined the mathematical analysis of the relation between stress and strain in a material by means of a coefficient of elasticity, now known as Young's Modulus.
See also: ABERRATIONS OF LENSES; COLOR; HELMHOTZ, HERMANN VON; LIGHT; MAXWELL, JAMES CLERK; VISION.

Young-Helmholtz Theory

See: HELMHOLTZ, HERMANN VON; VISION; YOUNG, THOMAS.

Zeiss, Carl

German; 1816–1888
Zeiss established a lens manufacturing concern at Jena in the mid-19th c. and sponsored the work of Ernst Abbé and Otto Schott in developing new optical glasses that were to revolutionize lens design and manufacture. Abbé became director of the concern upon the death of Zeiss. The chief Zeiss designer was Paul Rudolph, whose Tessar lens and other designs are still widely used in photography. The company's products included microscopes, telescopes, special-purpose lenses, cameras, and technical instruments. In 1926 a merger with Contessa-Nettel, Ica, Goerz, and Ernemann created the Zeiss Ikon organization. The Ikoflex, Contaflex, and Contax were three of the most popular cameras in the Zeiss line in the 1930s. Following World War II, a separate Carl Zeiss works was established at Oberkochen, West Germany, and the East German government rebuilt the plant at Jena.
See also: ABBE, ERNST; JENA GLASS; RUDOLPH, PAUL.

Zielke, Willy

German; 1902–
Willy Zielke was one of the European photographers who most enthusiastically welcomed the change in photography that began in the 1920s: a radical turning away from Pictorialism—"the warped photographic technique," in Zielke's

words—which had dominated art photography from the late 19th c.
Zielke was born in Lodz, the son of a businessman working in Russia. He studied at the School of Railways in Tashkent until 1921, when his family returned to Germany and he entered the Bavarian School of Photography in Munich. Although brought up on the tradition of academic Pictorialism, he broke free of its conventions and by 1923 had dedicated himself to photographic experimentation. In 1928 he became a professor of photography at the school, where he remained until 1936. In 1929 he showed for the first time his experimental photographs of glass objects at the Werkbund exhibition *Film und Foto* in Stuttgart.
The characteristics of glass especially interested Zielke at this time. He was taken with its ability to be transparent, translucent, or opaque according to how it was colored, polished, and lighted; he was fascinated as well by its ability to modulate light to create dimension and produce the entire range of the photographic gray scale. Although his still-lifes with glass were carefully arranged, they were not artificial. Common objects were included, and the viewpoint might be from any angle—the sides, above, below. The straight-on approach to the object was abandoned in the search for discovery through detail, and to deny a false reality. The aim was to say more by showing less, and thereby engage the viewer's imagination. Along with these objective still-lifes Zielke experimented with photograms, montages, and collages, giving them a fantastic dimension as he piled one reality on top of another. During the 1930s he also produced important bodies of portraiture and studies of the nude.
Zielke was an early adherent of the Neue Sachlichkeit (New Objectivity) movement, but was also among the first to disassociate himself from it as soon as it lost its original vitality, became a style rather than a genuine aesthetic stance, and degenerated into academicism through widespread imitation of superficial reality. As a result, Zielke's photographs changed: he created sequences in place of single images, and began to work with a reduced, more contrasty scale of grays for increased graphic impact.
Influenced by the radical experimentalism of Soviet avant-garde films, Zielke turned toward cinema in the 1930s. For him it was the logical marriage of photography and sequence. In his early films, of which the first was *Anton Nicklas* in 1931, the importance of each image is stressed, as in a sequence

of still photographs. He took up color photography in 1933, creating images that provoked much interest when published in *Das Deutsche Lichtbild*. At the same time he continued filmmaking and, although banned by the National Socialists (Nazis) in 1935, was asked to make the prologue for Leni Riefenstahl's film *Olympia: Test der Völker (Olympiad, 1936* in international release). From 1936 on, Zielke was no longer allowed to work professionally.
The end of World War II found Zielke working as a translator in the Babelsberg Studios. His main occupation in the postwar period was making industrial documentary films. Zielke lives in East Berlin.
See also: NEUE SACHLICHKEIT.
Photograph: p. 568.

Zoetrope

In the popular 19th c. animation viewing device called a zoetrope, a sequence of drawings on a paper band was mounted facing inward around the circumference of a metal drum about 12 in. in diameter. The viewer looked from the outside through a series of slits toward the drawings on the opposite inner wall of the drum. As the drum revolved, the slits provided intermittent glimpses of the drawings, which the eye blended into apparent continuous movement. A number of variations of the device were produced, including one by Anschutz that used stereoscopic sequence photographs. The name, derived from Greek, means "wheel of life." Related devices include the praxinoscope, phenakistiscope, and zoopraxiscope.
See also: ANIMATION; ANSCHUTZ, OTTOMAR; PHENAKISTISCOPE; PRAXINOSCOPE; ZOOPRAXISCOPE.

Zone Focusing

In some photographic situations there is no time to focus the lens without missing a shot. Zone focusing avoids this problem by presetting the focus to cover the range of most likely action. The photographer estimates where action will be centered, sets the lens focus to that distance, and chooses an *f*-stop that extends the depth of field sufficiently to cover the area in which the action might move, or first appear. Anything within that zone will appear acceptably sharp in the final image without further focus adjustment. The depth-of-field scale on a lens barrel or camera focus control shows the zone covered at each *f*-stop for any focused distance. The maximum depth of field at any *f*-stop is obtained by focusing at the hyperfocal distance for that aperture. This can be done quickly by setting the infinity (∞) symbol on the distance scale opposite the index mark for the *f*-stop to be used. The depth of field will extend from half the focused distance to infinity. In some cases the hyperfocal zone of focus will begin too far away to include the desired area; in that case a nearer, more limited zone must be chosen. Many simple cameras provide a kind of zone focusing with picture symbols on the focus control to indicate settings for close, near, middle-distance, and distant subjects.

See also: DEPTH OF FIELD; FOCUSING; HYPERFOCAL DISTANCE.

Zone System

The zone system was developed by Ansel Adams and Fred Archer as a means of explaining exposure and development control in black-and-white photography to students. It was formulated in the 1930s and has been continually expanded and refined; it is the foundation of much photographic instruction today.

A "zone" is a concept, not an area. It is the relationship of a particular subject brightness to the density it is represented by in a negative and the corresponding tone in a print. The gray scale of a full-range print contains tones that correspond to a range of ten zones, each equivalent to a one-stop difference in subject brightness and negative exposure. Zones are numbered from 0 to IX, using roman numerals to avoid confusion with *f*-numbers, shutter settings, film speeds, and other numbers in the photographic process. Zone 0 is represented by the maximum black tone obtainable in the print, Zone IX by pure paper-base white. Zone I is the first discernible gray-black tone, Zone VIII the last discernible almost-white tone; neither records textural detail. Zones II through VII do record subject details; this range corresponds to the seven-stop brightness range of an average full-scale subject. In Adams's latest revision, there are 11 zones. Zone X is pure white; Zone IX, is white with tone but no trace of texture.

The photographer uses an exposure meter to determine the brightness range of a subject, from the darkest area with important detail to the lightest area with detail. He or she previsualizes the desired print tonal range to represent the subject and then chooses exposure and development procedures to achieve the desired result. In order to do this, the photographer must have made tests to establish the "true" or effective working speed of the film, and to establish exactly what changes in development are required to expand a short-brightness-range subject to normal range, or to compact an extra-long-range subject to a scale that the print can reproduce. Then it is possible to determine the actual exposure to be given to the particular subject, and to know beforehand what kind of development this will require.

Several books and manuals devoted to the zone system (see Appendix) explain testing procedures, methods for determining exposure, and printing techniques. The value of the zone system is that it provides practical, step-by-step methods for putting densitometry and sensitometry to use without requiring scientific knowledge or instruments. It is a modern, ordered version of the 19th c. photographer's guideline: expose for the shadows and develop for the highlights.

See also: ADAMS, ANSEL; BRIGHTNESS RANGE; CONTRAST; DEVELOPMENT; EXPOSURE; GRAY SCALE; PREVISUALIZATION.

Zoo Photography

Zoos can provide a unique opportunity to photograph animals with safety and ease. Medium-size or large animals are by far the simplest to photograph; small, darting, nervous creatures are much more difficult. Furthermore, bears, primates, antelopes, etc., are often separated from the public with a moat arrangement rather than bars, thus simplifying the photographic situation. Some zoos also display certain types of birds in barless cages by controlling lighting levels. The viewer is in a darkened area, while the bird is in a brightly lighted area. In other areas bars and cages are a fact of life. If it is not possible to aim between bars, getting close to the bars (or cage mesh) with a long-focal-length lens will throw them grossly out of focus so that they create the least visual interference.

Whatever the subject may be, it is good practice to choose a spot and remain there for a while, especially if the animal is aware of the photographer. Many factors influence the choice of vantage point. An unimpeded view of the subject is essential, of course, but attention should also be paid to lighting, the traffic flow of other visitors, and the background. Often the best time to photograph animals is just before feeding time; they are usually most animated then.

With skittish animals it is a good idea to be quiet and move slowly. An alert pose can be elicited by making a sharp noise, but the opportunity may last only an instant, so the camera shutter should be ready for release. Enticing animals with food is sometimes effective but often inadvisable. While some zoos forbid feeding altogether, others sell bags of appropriate food. If the subject is fed, the camera lens should be protected. A surprising number of animals will give anything within range an exploratory lick.

Any reasonably quiet, small- or medium-format camera with a long-focal-length lens is suitable. A telephoto zoom lens is especially useful because it permits working at a wide range of subject distances. In general, tripods and flash are not a good idea. Even when zoos do not specifically forbid them, they tend to be clumsy and may frighten the animals.

Although the animals are the center of attraction, the people viewing the exhibits may be as interesting. Many photographers have found found it rewarding to keep an open mind about which subjects are the more exotic.

Zoom Lens

The focal length of a zoom, or *parfocal* lens can be varied over a continuous range; thus, from one camera position the angle of view (field coverage) and image magnification can be changed without having to stop shooting or to change lenses. Once focused at a particular distance, a zoom lens maintains focus at that distance as the focal length is changed. A *varifocus* lens also has an adjustable focal length, but must be refocused with each change. Focal length is changed by shifting the position of various elements inside the lens. Most zoom lenses for still photography have one-touch or two-touch controls. A one-touch zoom has a single collar or lever to control both focal length and focus; a two-touch zoom has separate controls. Zoom lenses for studio television and motion pictures have electrical controls, but those used on hand-held minicameras are usually manual zooms. As the focal length of a zoom lens changes, the *f*-value of the aperture also changes. In short-range zoom lenses the change is insignificant, but in long-range lenses exposure compensation may be required. Good quality zoom lenses automatically change the diaphragm opening to maintain a constant *f*-value (and thus a constant exposure) throughout the focal length range at any given aperture setting.

Zoom ratio. The range of a zoom lens is commonly expressed as the ratio between its long and short focal length settings; e.g., a 100-50mm zoom has a

2:1 zoom ratio. The ratio also expresses the magnification range of the lens: the example lens magnifies the image twice as much at the longest focal length as at the shortest. Zoom ratios for hand-held still cameras range from about 2:1 to 6:1, those for amateur movie and video cameras up to about 8:1. Television and motion-picture zoom lenses may have ratios of 20:1 or more.
See also: LENSES.

Zoopraxiscope

The zoopraxiscope was an animation projector invented by Eadweard Muybridge in 1879 and widely used by him in lectures to recreate the movement captured by his sequence still photographs taken for motion study and analysis. A large glass disk revolved through the focal plane of the projector lens, bringing a series of lantern slides of the sequence images into view one after another. An opaque shutter disk with a series of slits in its circumference also revolved behind the lens, synchronized so that each image was momentarily projected onto a screen but the in-between movement was blocked off. When operated at sufficient speed, the images blended into continuous movement; this was most effectively achieved by gearing the shutter disc to revolve at two to four times the rate of the image disc so that the eye received two or more impressions of each image before the next took its place. The illusion produced by this "life-action viewer" (the meaning of the Greek roots of its name) astonished and delighted audiences of the time. The zoopraxiscope utilized the basic principle of the phenakistiscope, which Muybridge improved so that the result could be observed by projection rather than direct viewing, and by more than just a few people at a time. It was in fact the first practical motion picture projector.
See also: MOTION PICTURES; MOTION STUDY AND ANALYSIS; MUYBRIDGE, EADWEARD; PHENAKISTISCOPE.

Zworykin, Vladimir Kosma
American; 1889–
Zworykin is the acknowledged inventor of the basic all-electronic system of television, as contrasted with systems that used mechanical scanning devices to dissect the image for transmission. Educated in Russia and France, he emigrated to the U.S. after World War I, becoming a citizen in 1924 and completing a Ph.D. in electrical engineering at the University of Pittsburg in 1926. He worked first for Westinghouse Corporation, and from 1929 on for Radio Corporation of America, where he eventually became vice-president and technical consultant. At RCA he was able to perfect the system he had first developed in 1923, based on the iconoscope camera tube and the kinescope picture tube, both of his own invention. His guidance of research and development made RCA dominant in the growth of television broadcasting. In 1939 he led a team that designed and built one of the first electron microscopes. In the latter part of his career before retirement he concentrated on the uses of electronics in medicine.
See also: ELECTRON MICROGRAPHY; TELEVISION.

Appendices

APPENDIX 1:

Biographical Supplement of Photographers

A

Aaland, Mikkel F. American; 1952– ; writer; photographer.
Abada, Alexander Russian; 1934– ; photojournalist.
Abbas Iranian; 1944– ; photojournalist.
Abercrombie, Thomas J. American; 1932– ; photojournalist, *National Geographic.*
Abramochkin, Yuri V. Russian; 1936– ; photojournalist.
Adal (Adal Maldonaldo) American, b. Puerto Rico; 1947– ; photographer.
Adam-Salomon, Antoine Samuel French; 1811–1881; photographer , portraits; sculptor.
Adams, Eddie American; 1933– ; photojournalist.
Adams, Robert American; 1937– ; photographer, urban landscapes, western America; writer.
Adelman, Robert American; 1930– ; photojournalist; author.
Aguado, Comte Olympe French; 1827–1894; photographer, carte-de-visite, landscapes.
Aigner, Lucien L. American, b. Hungary; 1901– ; photojournalist.
Akis, Aivar Russian; 1934– ; photojournalist.
Akiyama, Ryoji Japanese; 1942– ; photographer, social documentary; teacher.
Albuquerque, Francisco Brazilian; 1917– ;photographer, advertising.
Alinder, Jim American; 1941– ; photographer, scenes of everyday life; editor; teacher.
Allard, William Albert American; 1937– ; photojournalist, *National Geographic* staff.
Allen, Harvey (Harold) American; 1912– ; educator; photographer, documentary, architecture.
Almasy, Paul French, b. Hungary; 1906– ; photojournalist.

Ananin, Mikhail Russian; 1912– ; photojournalist, WW II.
Andrews, Mary Ellen American; 1937– ; photographer, contemporary urban society.
Andriesse, Emmy (Eugenie) Dutch; 1914–1953; photographer, artists' portraits.
Andujar, Claudia Brazilian; 1931– ; photographer, social documentary, anthropological.
Angel, Heather British; 1941– ; photographer, science, nature.
Angier, Roswell American; 1940– ; photographer, social documentary; teacher.
Apkalis, Ilmar Russian, 1931– ; photographer, social themes.
Arad, Shlomo Israeli, b. Poland; 1937– ; photographer.
Araki, Nobuyoshi Japanese; 1940– ; photographer, social documentary.
Araujo, Zeka Brazilian; 1946– ; photographer, documentary; editor.
Arita, Taiji Japanese; 1941– ; photographer, autobiographical portraits.
Armstrong-Jones, Anthony C.R. (see **Snowdon, Lord**).
Arnold, Eve American; 1913– ; photojournalist; author.
Atkins, Ollie American; 1916–1977; photojournalist, White House staff.
Attie, David Moses American; 1920–1983; photographer, multiple-image, photojournalism; teacher.
Atwood, Jane Evelyn American; 1947– ; photographer, social documentary.
Auerbach, Erich British, b. Bohemia; 1911–1977; photojournalist, musicians.
Ausloos, Paul Belgian; 1927– ; photographer, autobiographical still life; painter; educator.
Austen, Alice (Elizabeth) American; 1866–1952; photographer, social and domestic documentary.

Avison, David American; 1937– ; photographer, panoramas; teacher.

Azzi, Robert American; 1943– ; photojournalist; author.

B

Babbitt, Platt, D. American; (active) 1855–1878; photographer, daguerreotype, Niagara Falls.

Badger, Gerry (Gerald David) British; 1948– ; architect; photographer, landscapes; writer; teacher.

Baer, Morley American; 1916– ; photographer, landscapes, architecture.

Bailey, David British; 1938– ; photographer, fashion, personalities.

Bailey, Oscar W. American; 1925– ; photographer, social commentary.

Baird, Ken (Kenneth Winston) British; 1930– ; photographer, social documentary, landscape; educator.

Baldessari, John American; 1931– ; artist; photographer, social documentary; teacher.

Balodis, Leon Russian; 1939– ; photographer, social themes, portraits.

Baltauss, Richard French; 1946– ; photographer, portraits.

Baltz, Lewis American; 1945– ; photographer, industrial landscape, series.

Bar-Am, Micha Israeli, b. Germany; 1930– ; photojournalist.

Baranauskas, Marius Lithuanian; 1931– ; photojournalist.

Barbey, Bruno French; 1941– ; photojournalist, documentary, color.

Barboza, Anthony American; 1944– ; photographer, portraits, fashion, advertising.

Bareisis, Algimantas Lithuanian; 1940– ; photographer, documentary.

Barnard, George N. American; 1819–1902; photographer, American Civil War.

Barnbaum, Bruce American; 1943– ; photographer, landscapes, still life.

Barreto, Luiz Carlos Brazilian; 1929– ; photojournalist; film maker.

Barrow, Thomas F. American; 1938– ; photographer, urban landscape; designer; teacher.

Baruch, Ruth-Marion German; 1922– ; photographer, human condition; writer.

Batho, Claude French; 1935–1981; photographer, portraits, interiors.

Batho, John French; 1939– ; photographer, color, formalist.

Baum, Yngve Swedish; 1945– ; photographer, documentary; film maker.

Baumann, Horst H. German; 1934– ; photojournalist; graphic designer.

Bauret, Jean-Francois French; 1932– ; photographer, portraits, fashion, advertising.

Baz, Douglas Carl American; 1943– ; photographer, landscapes, architecture; teacher.

Beals, Jessie Tarbox Canadian; 1870–1942; photojournalist.

Beard, Peter Hill American; 1938– ; photographer, nature, Africa.

Becher, Bernhard German; 1931– ; photographer, industrial architecture, collaboration with Hilla Becher; teacher.

Becher, Hilla German; 1934– ; photographer, industrial architecture, collaboration with Bernhard Becher; teacher.

Beck, Maurice British; 1886–1960; photographer, portraits, fashion, theatre.

Bedford, Francis British; ca 1816–1894; photographer, picturesque landscapes, architectural views; lithographer.

Bedi, Mitter Indian; 1926– ; photographer, industrial landscapes.

Beebe, Morton American; 1934– ; photojournalist.

Beljaew, Alexander Russian; 1944– ; technician; photographer.

Bellia, Antonio Carlos Brazilian; 1940– ; photographer, documentary.

Bellmer, Hans German; 1902–1975; photographer, articulated doll-sculpture, surreal; sculptor; designer.

Bellocq, E(rnest) J(ames) American; 1873–1949; photographer, nudes, social documentary.

Ben Dov, Yaakov Israeli, b. Ukraine; 1882–1968; photographer, documentary, Israel film maker.

Benedict-Jones, Linda American; 1947– ; photographer, portraits, landscapes; teacher.

Bennett, Derek American; 1944– ; photographer, urban scenes.

Benson, Harry British; 1929– ; photojouranalist, *Life* staff.

Benson, Richard American; 1943– ; photographer, landscapes; master printer; teacher.

Benton-Harris, John; American; 1939– ; photographer, social scenes, England; teacher.

Beny, Roloff Canadian; 1924–1984; photographer, travel, color.

Berengo-Gardin, Gianni Italian; 1930– ; photographer, Venice, social documentary.

Berger, Paul Eric American; 1948– ; photographer, multiple-image, sequence; teacher.

Berko, Ferenc American, b. Hungary; 1916– ; photographer, nature, color; film maker.

Berman, Mieczyslaw Polish; 1903–1975; photographer, satirical photocollage.

Bernhard, Ruth American; 1905– ; photographer, nudes, still life.

Bernstein, Lou American; 1911– ; photographer, city streets, New York.

Berry, Ian British; 1934– ; photojournalist.

Berssenbrugge, Henri A. Dutch; 1873–1959; photographer, social scenes, pictorialist.

Besnyo, Eva Dutch, b. Hungary; 1910– ; photographer.

Beyer, Karol Polish; 1818–1877; photographer, portraits, cityscapes.

Bhedwar, Shapoor Indian; (active) 1885–1900; photographer.

Biermann, Aenne German; 1898–1933; photographer, nature, still life.

Bilzonis, Zigurd Russian; 1946– ; musician; photographer.

Binde, Gunar Latvian; 1933– ; photographer, nudes, portraits.

Bing, Ilse German; 1899– ; photographer, portraits, fashion, photo-essay; poet.

Bishop, Barry American; 1932– ; photographer, *National Geographic* staff; author; mountaineer.

Bishop, Michael American; 1946– ; photographer, surrealistic landscapes.

Bisilliat, Maureen British; 1931– ; photographer, documentary, ethnographic, Brazil.

Blair, Jonathan S. American; 1941– ; photojournalist, *National Geographic* staff.

Blake, Michael Irish; 1950– ; photographer, landscapes.

Blake, Rebecca American, b. Belgium; 1949– ; photographer, fashion.

Blakemore, John British; 1936– ; photographer, landscapes; teacher.

Blanco, Lazaro Mexican; 1938– ; photographer, social commentary; educator.

Blazer, Carel Dutch; 1911–1980; photographer, industrial, photo-murals; photojournalist; teacher.

Bloch, Ernest American, b. Switzerland; 1880–1959; composer; photographer.

Blomberg, Sven Swedish; 1920– ; painter; photographer, social documentary; author.

Blondeau, Barbara American; 1938–1974; photographer, strip-prints, photograms, cliche verre.

Blount, Arthur David Australian; 1951– ; photographer.

Blue, Patt American; 1945– ; photographer, social documentary.

Blumberg, Donald Robert American; 1935– ; photographer, experimental, socio-political.

Blumbergs, Janis Russian; 1947– ; television camera assistant; photographer.

Bodine, A. Aubrey American; 1906–1970; photographer, press, pictorialist.

Bohm, Dorothy German; 1924– ; photographer; educator.

Boltanski, Christian French; 1944– ; photographer, experimental, surrealistic themes.

Boltin, Lee American; 1917– ; photographer, artifacts.

Bonfils, Felix French; 1831–1885; photographer, views of Near East; traveler.

Bongé, Lyle American; 1929– ; photographer; teacher; sailor.

Boogaerts, Pierre Belgian; 1964– ; photographer, Manhattan skyline, color.

Bostelmann, Enrique Mexican; 1939– ; photographer, Mexican life, landscapes, formalist.

Boucher, Pierre French; 1908– ; photographer, nudes, leaping friends, advertising, photo montage; designer.

Boughton, Alice American; 1865–1943; photographer, portraits, children.

Bourdeau, Robert Canadian; 1931– ; photographer, landscapes.

Bowers, Harry American; 1938– ; photographer; teacher.

Brake, Brian New Zealander; 1927– ; photographer; photojournalist, landscapes, color.

Branca, Rio Brazilian; 1946– ; photojournalist.

Braun, Werner Israeli; 1918– ; photojournalist, underwater, aerial.

Brauns, Valdis Russian; 1945– ; photographer.

Brigman, Annie American; 1868–1950; photographer; pictorialist.

Brihat, Denis French; 1928– ; photographer, nature.

Brivlauks, Nikolai Russian; 1929– ; construction worker; photographer, social commentary.

Brook, John American; 1924– ; photographer, autobiographical, nature.

Brooks, Charlotte American; 1918– ; photojournalist.

Brooks, Ellen American; 1949– ; photographer, environmental installations; teacher.

Brown, Dean American; 1936–1973; photographer, landscapes, color.

Bruehl, Anton American, b. Australia; 1900– ; photographer, portraits, still life, color, advertising.

Brumfield, John American; 1934– ; teacher; photographer.

Bryson, John American; 1923– ; photojournalist.

Bubley, Esther American; 1921– ; photojournalist, children.

Buckley, Peter American; 1925– ; photographer, documentary.

Budnick, Dan American; 1933– ; photojournalist.

Buechel, Eugene S. J. German; 1874–1954; photographer, American Indians; priest; teacher.

Bujak, Adam Polish; 1942– ; photojournalist.

Bulgakovas, Zenonas Lithuanian; 1939– ; photographer, urban landscapes.

Bull, Clarence Sinclair American; 1895–1979; photographer, celebrity portraits.

Bullaty, Sonja American; (contemporary); photographer, landscapes, color, social commentary.

Bunnell, Peter C. American; 1937– ; teacher; curator; historian.

Burbosski, Oleg Russian; 1937– ; engineer; photographer, urban scenes.

Burchard, Jerry American; 1931– ; photographer, nocturnal city; teacher.

Burchfield, Jerry American; 1947– ; photographer, color.

Burden, Shirley C. American; 1908– ; photographer, photo-essay; author.

Burgin, Victor British; 1941– ; photographer, conceptual; teacher.

Burke, James American; 1915–1964; photojournalist, *Life* staff.

Burnett, David American; 1946– ; photojournalist.

Burns, Marsha American; 1945– ; photographer, social portraits.

Burns, Michael American; 1942– ; photographer, nudes, landscapes.

Burri, Rene Swiss; 1933– ; photojournalist; film maker.

Butler, George Tyssen British; 1943– ; photographer; writer; film producer/director.

Buttfield, Helen American; 1929– ; photographer; teacher.

Butyrin, Vitaly Russian; 1947– ; photographer, allegorical landscapes, photo montage.

C

Cagnoni, Romano Italian; 1935– ; photojournalist.

Callis, Jo Ann American; 1940– ; photographer, symbolic scenes, color.

Campana, Antoni Spanish; 1906– ; photographer, pictorialist.

Campbell, Bryn British; 1933– ; photographer; editor.

Cancellare, Frank American; 1910– ; press photographer.

Canovas, Antonio Spanish; 1862–1933; photographer, portraits.

Cantor, Fredrich American; 1944– ; photographer; teacher.

Caratini, Hector M. Mendez Puerto Rican; 1949– ; photographer, documentary, Puerto Rico.

Carey, Ellen American; 1952– ; photographer, altered prints, mixed-media.

Carmi, Boris Israeli, b. Russia; 1914– ; photographer.

Carmi, Lisetta Italian; 1924– ; photographer, human issues.

Carneiro, Dulce Brazilian; 1929– ; photographer, portraits, architecture, industry.

Carneiro, Luciano Brazilian; 1927– ; photojournalist.

Caron, Gilles French; 1939–1970; photojournalist.

Carroll, Lewis (Charles Lutwidge Dodgson) British; 1832–1898; writer; photographer, children; clergyman; mathematician.

Catala Pic, Pere Spanish; 1889–1971; photographer, experimental, photo montage, advertising.

Catany, Toni Spanish; 1942– ; photographer, still life.

Caujolle, Christian French; 1953– ; editor; curator.

Cavalli, Giuseppe Italian; 1904–1961; lawyer; photographer, surreal scenes.

Cazneaux, Harold (Pierce) Australian; 1878–1953; photographer, social scenes, Australia.

Centelles, Agusti Spanish; 1909– ; photojournalist, Spanish Civil War.

Chaiket, Arcadi Samoilovitch Russian; 1898– ; photojournalist.

Chamorro, Koldo Spanish; 1949– ; photojournalist.

Chamudes, Marcos Chilean; 1907– ; photojournalist.

Chappell, Walter American; 1925– ; photographer, nature.

Charbonnier, Jean-Philippe French; 1921– ; photographer, documentary; graphic artist.

Chargesheimer (Carl-Heinz Hargesheimer) German; 1924–1972; photographer, portraits; painter; sculptor.

Chiarenza, Carl American; 1935– ; photographer; author; educator.

Chintamon, Hurrychund Indian; (active) 1854–1875; photographer, portraits, painted photographs, field commissions.

Chochola, Vaclav Czechoslovakian; 1923– ; photographer, objets trouves, portrait.

Christenberry, William American; 1936– ; photographer, American south.

Citroen, Paul Dutch; 1896– ; painter; photographer, portraits.

Claass, Arnaud French; 1949– ; photographer, gardens, aerial perspective.

Claridge, John British; 1944– ; photographer, advertising.

Clark, Edward American; 1911– ; photojournalist, *Life* staff.

Clark, Larry American; 1943– ; photographer, social documentary; author.

Clarkson, Richard C. American; 1932– ; photojournalist, sports.

Clergue, Lucien French; 1934– ; photographer, nudes, landscapes.

Clift, William Brooks American; 1944– ; photographer, landscapes.

Clifford, Charles British; –1863; photographer, Crimean War, landscapes, architecture, art reproduction.

Cohen, Lynne Canadian, b. U.S.; 1944– ; photographer, urban interiors.

Cohen, Mark American; 1943– ; photographer, cropped figures.

Coke, Van Deren American; 1921– ; photographer; historian; curator.

Cole, Ernest South African; 1940– ; photojournalist.

Collier, John American; 1913– ; photographer, social documentary, anthropological.

Colp, Norman B. American; 1944– ; photographer.

Comesana, Eduardo Argentine; 1940– ; photojournalist.

Conant, Howell American; 1919– ; photojournalist, illustration, color.

Connor, Linda American; 1944– ; photographer, autobiographical, ancient architecture, wilderness.

Cooper, Ruffin Jr. American; 1942– ; photographer, color.

Cooper, Thomas Joshua American; 1946– ; photographer, landscapes; teacher.

Coplans, John American, b. Britain; 1920– ; photographer; critic; historian.

Cordier, Pierre Belgian; 1933– ; photographer, chemigrams.

Cornfield, James H. American; 1945– ; photographer.

Corpron, Carlotta M. American; 1901– ; photographer, light abstractions; teacher.

Corrales, Raul Cuban; 1925– ; photojournalist.

Corsini, Harold American; 1919– ; photographer, industry.

Costa, Joseph American; 1904– ; press photographer; educator.

Coster, Howard British; 1885–1959; photographer, portraits, South Africa.

Cowans, Adger W. American; 1936– ; photographer.

Cowherd, Barney American; 1922–1972; photojournalist.

Cowin, Eileen American; 1947– ; photographer; teacher.

Cox, Paul Australian, b. Holland; 1940– ; photojournalist; film maker.

Crane, Barbara Bachmann American; 1928– ; photographer; muralist; educator.

Crane, Ralph Swiss; 1913– ; photojournalist; *Life* staff.

Cranham, Gerry British; 1929– ; photojournalist, sports.

Cuallado, Gabriel Spanish; 1925– ; photographer, documentary.

Cumming, Robert H. American; 1943– ; photographer, conceptual; painter; sculptor; writer.

Curman, Carl Swedish; 1833–1913; photographer, landscapes, social scenes.

Curran, Darryl J. American; 1935– ; photographer, mixed media; teacher.

Current, William American; 1923– ; photographer, landscapes, nature.

Currie, David Garfield American; 1941– ; photographer; educator.

Curtsinger, William R. American; 1946– ; photographer, nature, whales.

Czeizing, Lajos Hungarian; 1922– ; photographer, landscapes, citycapes.

D

D'Alessandro, Robert American; 1942– ; photographer, satirical scenes, fanciful scenes.

Dalton, Stephen British; 1937– ; photographer, nature.

D'Amico, Alicia Argentinian; 1933– ; photographer, subjective themes.

Dabac, Petar Yugoslavian; 1942– ; photographer.

Dabac, Toso Yugoslavian; 1907–1970; photographer, social issues, pictorialist.

Dahlstroem, Jan-Haakan Swedish; 1947– ; photographer, social commentary.

Dale, Bruce American; 1938– ; photojournalist, *National Geographic* staff.

Dantzic, Jerry American; 1925; photographer, panoramas.

Danziger, Avery Coffey American; 1953– ; photographer, color.

D'Arazian, Arthur American, b. Armenia; 1914– ; photographer, industrial.

Darche, Jacques French; 1920–1965; photographer; graphic designer; illustrator.

Dater, Judy American; 1941– ; photographer, nudes, portraits.

Dauman, Henri French; 1933– ; photojournalist, advertising, illustration.

Davies, Bevan American; 1941– ; photographer, architecture.

Davies, George Christopher British; 1849–1922; photographer, nature, Norfolk broads.

Davies, John A. British; 1949– ; photographer, landscapes.

d'Avila, Antonio Carlos Brazilian; 1955– ; photographer, documentary; film maker.

Davis, Bob Australian; 1944– ; photojournalist, travel.

Davis, Margo Ann American; 1944– ; photographer, documentary; educator.

Deal, Joe American; 1947– ; photographer, changing environment.

Dean, Loomis American; 1917– ; photojournalist, circus, *Life* staff.

Dean, Nicholas American; 1933– ; photographer, New England landscapes, sailing vessels.

de Andrade, Alecio Brazilian; 1942– ; photojournalist.

Debabov, Dmitri Gueorguevitch Russian; 1901–1949; photojournalist.

De Boni, Jose Alberto Brazilian; 1951– ; photographer, documentary.

De Cock, Liliane American, b. Belgium; 1939– ; photographer, landscapes.

de Fenoyl, Pierre French; 1945– ; curator; writer; gallery director.

Dekkers, Ger Dutch; 1929– ; photographer, subjective landscapes.

Del Tin, Toni Italian; 1912– ; photographer, social themes.

Delamotte, Philip Henry British; 1821–1889; photographer, documentary, Crystal Palace.

Delano, Jack American; 1914– ; photographer, documentary, FSA; film maker.

de Lappa, William American; 1943– ; photographer, fabricated social scenes.

Delden, Jan Swedish; 1933– ; press photographer.

De Lekv na, Nicolas Spanish; 1913–1937; photographer, experimental, photo montage.

de Lory, Peter American; 1948– ; photographer; teacher.

Den Hollander, Paul Dutch; 1950– ; photographer, social landscapes.

Dena (Dinah Rubinstein) American, b. Finland; (contemporary); photographer, portaits, street scenes.

Denizart, Hugo Brazilian; 1946– ; photojournalist.

de Noijer, Paul Dutch; 1943– ; photographer.

Depardon, Raymond French; 1942– ; photojournalist; film maker.

Descamps, Bernard French; 1947– ; photographer.

Desfor, Max American; 1913– ; news photographer, *Associated Press*.

De Visser, John Dutch; 1930– ; photographer, documentary, Canada.

Diament, Rafail Russian; 1907– ; photojournalist; World War II.

Diamond, Hugh Welch British; 1809–1886; photographer, documentary, mental patients; physician.
Diamond, Paul American; 1942– ; photographer, peopled environments, fantasy.
Dias, Pavel Czechoslovakian; 1938– ; photographer, social themes.
Dibbets, Jan Dutch; 1941– ; photographer, abstract, sequential.
Di Biase, Michael American; 1925– ; photographer.
Dichaviciene, Valerija Lithuanian; 1930– ; librarian; photographer, portraits.
Dichavicius, Rimantas Lithuanian; 1937– ; photographer, nudes.
Dieuzaide, Jean French; 1921– ; photographer, color, various subject matter.
Disfarmer, Michael American; 1894–1959; photographer, social portraiture, Arkansas.
Disraeli, Robert American, b. Germany; 1905– ; photographer, social documentary.
Divola, John M. American; 1949– ; photographer, color; teacher.
Dixon, Henry American; 1820–1893; photographer, documentary.
Djordjevic, Miodrag Yugoslavian; 1919– ; photographer, social themes, experimental.
Dlubak, Zbigniew Polish; 1921– ; photographer, conceptual.
Dodgson, Charles Lutwidge (see **Carroll, Lewis**)
Doherty, Robert John American; 1924– ; museum director; teacher.
Dominis, John American; 1921– ; photojournalist, *Life* staff.
Donohue, Bonnie J. American; 1946– ; photographer, collage, multiple image; teacher; film maker.
Dorfman, Elsa American; 1937– ; photographer, portraits.
Dorr, Nell American; 1893– ; photographer, mother and child portraits.
Dorys, Benedykt Jersy Polish; 1901– ; photographer, portraits, street life.
Dotter, Earl American; 1943– ; photographer, social documentary.
Doubilet, David American; 1947– ; photographer, underwater.
Douglas, Ed American; 1943– ; photographer, conceptual; lecturer.
Drahos, Tom French, b. Czechoslovakia; 1947– ; photographer, fabricated interiors.
Draitschiow, Viktor Russian; 1957– ; photojournalist.
Dries, Antoon Belgian; 1910– ; photographer, familiar objects, abstract, series.
Driukow, German Russian; 1934– ; engineer; photographer, industrial landscapes.
Ducrot, Jerome French; 1935– ; photographer; publisher.
Dudkin, Anatoli Russian; 1935– ; actor; photographer, rural life.
Dupain, Max Australian; 1911– ; photographer, industrial architecture.
Durieu, Eugene (Jean-Louis-Marie) French; 1800–1874; photographer, nudes, astronomical studies.
Durst, Andre French; 1907–1949; photographer, fashion.
Dutton, Allen A. American; 1922– ; photographer, surreal photomontage.

E

Eagle, Arnold American; 1909– ; photographer; film maker.
Eakins, Thomas American; 1844–1916; painter; photographer, portraits, family and genre scenes, figure and motion studies.
Edinger, Claudio Brazilian; 1952– ; photographer, photo-essay.
Edgeworth, Anthony American; 1935– ; photographer, portraits, travel, fashion.
Edwards, Mark British; 1947– ; photographer, social issues.

Ehm, Josef Czechoslovakian; 1909– ; photographer, portraits, Prague; teacher.
Ehrhardt, Alfred German; 1901– ; photographer, marine still life, landscapes.
Eickemeyer, Rudolf Jr. American; 1862–1932; photographer, pictorialist.
Eleta, Sandra Panamanian; 1942– ; photographer, social portraiture.
Elisofon, Eliot American; 1911–1973; photographer, color, *Life* staff; painter.
Ellis, Rennie Australian; 1940– ; photographer, human issues.
Engman, Anders Swedish; 1933– ; photographer, social documentary.
Emmons, Chansonette Stanley American; 1858–1937; photographer, record of rural life, New England.
Engel, Morris American; 1918– ; photographer, documentary, New York City; film maker.
Enos, Chris American; 1944– ; photographer, still life, nature; teacher.
Eppridge, Bill American; 1938– ; photographer.
Epstein, Mitchell American; 1952– ; photographer, social landscapes, color; teacher.
Espada, Frank American; 1930– ; photojournalist.
Estabrook, Reed American; 1944– ; photographer, social landscapes; teacher.
Estrin, Mary Lloyd American; 1944– ; photographer, portraits.
Evans, Michael American; 1944– ; photojournalist, White House staff.
Ewald, Wendy Taylor American; (contemporary); photographer, portraits, anthropological; teacher.
Eyerman, J. R. American; 1906– ; photographer, *Life* staff.
Eymundsson, Sigufs Icelandic; 1837–1911; photographer, social scenes.

F

Faber, John American; 1918– ; photographer, industry; historian.
Facio, Sara Argentinian; 1932– ; photographer, contemporary society.
Faller, Marion American; 1941– ; photographer; teacher.
Farbman, N. R. American; 1907– ; photojournalist, *Life* staff.
Faucon, Bernard French; 1950– ; photographer, fabricated scenes.
Faulkner, Douglas American; 1937– ; photographer, color, underwater.
Faurer, Louis American; 1916– ; photographer, social documentary.
Featherstone, David American; 1945– ; photographer, landscapes, master printer; critic; arts administrator.
Fedorenko, Valery Russian; 1948– ; photographer.
Fein, Nat American; 1914– ; press photographer.
Feingersh, Ed American; 1924–1961; photojournalist.
Feldstein, Mark American; 1937– ; photographer, surreal landscapes, still life.
Fellman, Sandi (Sandra Lee) American; 1952– ; photographer, subjective still life; teacher.
Fener, Tamas Hungarian; 1938– ; photojournalist, performing arts.
Fenn, Albert American; 1912– ; photojournalist, *Life* staff.
Ferguson, Larry S. American; 1954– ; photographer, contemporary urban life; curator.
Fernandez, Benedict J. American; photojournalist; educator.

Fernandez, Jesse A. Cuban; 1925– ; photographer, social documentary.

Fichter, Robert W. American; 1939– ; photographer, subjective still life; teacher.

Fieger, Erwin German, b. Czechoslovakia; 1928– ; photographer, color photo essays, cities and countries.

Figueroa Flores, Gabriel Mexican; 1952– ; photographer.

Fink, Larry (Laurence) American; 1941– ; photographer, social documentary.

Filanow, Vladimir Russian; 1948– ; photographer, social commentary.

Fischer, Carl American; 1924– ; photographer; art director.

Fischer, Hal American; 1950– ; photographer, images and words; teacher; critic.

Fiske, George American; 1835–1918; photographer, landscapes, Yosemite.

Fitch, Steven Ralph American; 1949– ; photographer, highways, dusk, W. America.

Flaherty, Frances Hubbard American; ca. 1886–1972; photographer, documentary; lecturer.

Flaherty, Robert Joseph American; 1884–1951; photographer, exotic and primitive peoples; film maker.

Flick, Robbert Dutch; 1939– ; photographer, landscapes; teacher.

Flieg, Hans Gunter Brazilian, b. Germany; 1923– ; photographer, advertising, industry, architecture.

Flodin, Ferdinand Swedish; 1863–1935; photographer, portraits.

Flomen, Michael Canadian; 1952– ; photographer.

Fly, Buck (Camillus Sidney) American; 1849–1901; photographer, documentary, Tombstone, Arizona and environs.

Folberg, Neil H. American; 1950– ; photographer, color, landscapes.

Fontana, Franco Italian; 1933– ; photographer, color, landscapes.

Fontcuberta, Joan Spanish; 1955– ; photographer, writer.

Fonyat, Bina Brazilian; 1945– ; photographer, documentary, urban life.

Forman, Stanley American; 1945– ; press photographer.

Forsell, Jacob Swedish; 1942– ; press photographer.

Fox, Flo 1945– ; photographer, street people; stylist; teacher.

Fox, James British; 1935– ; photographer, documentary; editor.

Franck, Martine Belgian; 1938– ; photographer, documentary.

Frank, JoAnn L. American; 1947– ; photographer, interiors.

Franzen, Christian Spanish; 1864–1923; photographer, portraits.

Freed, Leonard American; 1929– ; photographer, documentary.

Freedman, Jill American; 1939– ; photographer, social issues; author.

Freeman, Roger American; 1945– ; photographer.

Freeman, Roland American; 1936– ; photographer, documentary.

Freund, Frank (David) American; 1937– ; photographer, master printer; teacher.

Fried, Larry American; 1926–1983; photographer.

Friedman, Benno American; 1945– ; photographer, altered prints.

Friedman, Endre Hungarian; 1934– ; photographer, social documentary.

Freixa, Ferran Spanish; 1950– ; photographer, subjective still life, formalist; graphic designer.

Frissell, Toni American; 1907– ; photographer, fashion, society.

Fujii, Hideki Japanese; 1934– ; photographer, fashion.

Fuka, Eva Czechoslovakian; (contemporary); photographer, collages.

Fukase, Masahisa Japanese; 1934– ; photographer, autobiographical themes, birds.

Fuller, John Charles American; 1937– ; photographer.

Fulton, Hamish British; 1946– ; photographer, conceptual themes; sculptor.

Fulton, Jack American; 1939– ; photographer, words and images, fanciful.

Fusco, Paul American; 1930– ; photojournalist, color, *Look* staff.

G

Gagliani, Oliver L. American; 1917– ; photographer, many genres; teacher.

Gagnon, Charles Canadian; 1934– ; painter; photographer, industrial landscapes; film maker.

Gallagher, Barrett American; 1913– ; photojournalist.

Ganor, Avi Israeli; 1950– ; photographer, advertising.

Garanin, Anatolij S. Russian; 1912– ; photographer, documentary, musicians, theatre.

Garcia, Alberto Schommer de la Pena Spanish; 1928– ; photographer, surreal images; film maker.

Gardner, George W. American; 1940– ; photojournalist.

Garo, J. H. American; 1870–1939; photographer, portraits.

Garrett, Wilbur E. American; 1930– ; photojournalist; editor.

Gatewood, Charles Robert American; 1942– ; photographer, urban life; educator.

Gatha, Ashvin Indian; 1941– ; photojournalist.

Gaumy, Jean French; 1948– ; photographer, social documentary.

Gautrand, Jean-Claude French; 1932– ; photojournalist; photohistorian.

Gazdar, Jehangir Indian; contemporary photographer, advertising, illustration.

Gedney, William American; 1932– ; photographer.

Gefter, Judith Michelman American; 1922– ; photographer, many genres.

Gehr, Herb (Edmund Bert Gerard) American, b. Germany; 1910–1983; photojournalist; film maker.

Gelpke, Andre German; 1947– ; photographer, surreal images.

Gende-Rote, Valeri Russian; 1926– ; photojournalist; engineer.

Gerlach, Monte H. American; 1950– ; photographer, social landscapes; teacher.

Gersh, Stephen B. American; 1942– ; photographer; teacher; consultant.

Gerster, Georg Swiss; 1928– ; photographer, aerial.

Gescheidt, Alfred American; 1926– ; photographer; humorist.

Ghirri, Luigi Italian; 1943– ; photographer, color, architectural environments.

Gianella, Victor Swiss; 1918– ; photographer, abstract.

Gibson, Tom Canadian, b. Scotland; 1930– ; photographer.

Gidal, Tim N. American/Israeli, b. Germany; 1909– ; photojournalist; historian.

Giedraitiene, Irena Lithuanian; 1935– ; architect; photographer, domestic subjects.

Gilbert, Douglas R. American; 1942– ; photographer, suburban landscapes; teacher.

Gilden, Bruce American; 1946– ; photographer, social scenes.

Giles, William B. American; 1934– ; photographer, portraits, large-format landscapes.

Gill, Leslie American; 1908–1958; photographer, fashion, advertising, portraits.

Gilpin, Henry B. American; 1922– ; photographer; teacher; peace officer.

Gioli, Paolo Italian; 1942– ; photographer, experimental; film maker.

Glass, Douglas British, b. New Zealand; 1901–1978; photographer, portraits; painter.

Gleizds, Janis Russian; 1924– ; photographer, female nudes.

Glinn, Burt American; 1925– ; photojournalist; author.

Gloaguen, Herve French; 1937– ; photographer, documentary.

Gnevashev, Igor Russian; 1941– ; photographer.

Gnisyuk, Mikola Russian; 1944– ; photographer, portraits.

Godes, Emili Spanish; 1895–1970; photographer, plant, still life, industrial.

Godfrey, Mark American; 1944– ; photojournalist.

Godwin, Fay British; 1931– ; photographer, British landscapes.

Gohlke, Frank William American; 1942– ; photographer, landscapes, American mid-west.
Goldbeck, E. O. (Eugene Omar) American; 1891– ; photographer, panoramic group portraits.
Goldblatt, David South African; 1930– ; photojournalist.
Golden, Judith American; 1934– ; photographer, self portraits; teacher.
Golubew, Saweli Lithuanian; 1935– ; photographer, seascapes.
Gonci, Sandor (Fruhoff) Hungarian; 1907– ; photographer, social scenes.
Goodman, Mark American; 1946– ; photographer, documentary, portraits.
Gordon, Jerome J. American; 1949– ; photographer, color, people in water.
Gordon, Morris American; 1908–1971; photojournalist.
Gorgoni, Gianfranco Italian; photographer, social documentary.
Gossage, John R. American; 1946– ; photographer, surreal gardens.
Goszleth, Istvan Hungarian; 1850–1913; photographer, portraits.
Gotlin, Curt Swedish; 1900– ; photographer; photohistorian; collector.
Gowin, Emmet American; 1941– ; photographer, social portraits, families.
Gowland, Peter American; 1916– ; photographer, nudes; film maker; camera designer.
Granirer, Martus American; 1933– ; photographer; teacher.
Grant, Allan American; 1920– ; photojournalist, *Life* staff.
Grazda, Edward American; 1947– ; photographer, documentary.
Grcevic, Mladen Yugoslav; 1918– ; photographer, human issues.
Grebnev, Victor Russian; 1907– ; photojournalist, World War II, sports.
Green, Jonathan W. American; 1939– ; photographer; educator; editor.
Greene, John B. French; 1832–1856; photographer, landscapes, architecture, Egypt, N. Africa.
Grehan, Farrell American; 1926– ; photographer, nature, color.
Greim, Michal Polish; 1828–1911; photographer, portraits, early reportage.
Griffin, Brian British; 1948– ; photographer, socio-political portraits.
Grignani, Franco Italian; 1908– ; photographer, experimental.
Groebli, Rene Swiss; 1927– ; photographer, social issues.
Groover, Jan American; 1943– ; photographer, formalist, color, still life.
Gros, H. F. Swiss; (active) 1869–1903; photographer, documentary, South Africa.
Grosvenor, Gilbert H. American; 1931–1975; photojournalist, *National Geographic* staff; editor.
Grosvenor, Melville B. American; 1901–1982; photojournalist, *National Geographic* staff; editor.
Gruen, John American; 1935– ; photographer, still life.
Gruyaert, Harry French; 1941– ; photojournalist, color, travel subjects.
Gudaitis, Pranas Lithuanian; 1948– ; painter; photographer, landscapes.
Gullers, Karl W. Swedish; 1916– ; photographer.
Gurney, Benjamin and Jeremiah American; (active) 1840–1871; photographers, daguerreotype, New York studio.
Gutierrez, Alberto Diaz Cuban; 1928– ; photojournalist, Fidel Castro; photographer, scientific, underwater.
Gutmann, John American, b. Germany; 1905– ; photographer, documentary; teacher.

H

Haar, Francis Hungarian; 1908– ; photographer; film maker.

Haas, Max Peter American; 1907–1966; photographer.
Hagel, Otto American, b. Germany; 1909–1973; photographer, human issues, *Life* staff.
Hagemeyer, Johan Dutch; 1884–1962; photographer, pictorialist; horticulturist.
Hahn, Betty American; 1940– ; photographer, mixed media.
Hajek-Halke, Heinz German; 1898– ; photographer, subjectivist.
Hajicek, James American; 1947– ; photographer, cyanotype landscapes.
Hak, Miroslav Czechoslovakian; 1911–1977; photographer.
Halevi, Marcus American; 1942– ; photojournalist, Alaska.
Hallman, Gary Lee American; 1940– ; photographer, large-format landscapes; teacher.
Halstead, Dirck American; 1936– ; photojournalist.
Hamilton, David British; 1933– ; photographer, portraits, adolescents, dance.
Hamilton, James American; 1946– ; photojournalist, portraits.
Hammarskiold, Hans Swedish; 1925– ; photographer, nature, still life, color.
Hammerbeck, Wanda Lee American; 1945– ; photographer.
Hammond, Mary Sayer American; 1946– ; photographer; teacher.
Hanabusa, Shinzo Japanese; 1937– ; photographer, documentary, children.
Harbutt, Charles American; 1935– ; photojournalist.
Harding, Goodwin Warner American; 1947– ; photographer.
Hardy, Bert British; 1913– ; photojournalist, *Picture Post* staff.
Hare, Chauncey American; 1934– ; photographer, social themes, western America.
Hare, Jimmy (James H.) British; 1856–1946; photojournalist.
Harissiadis, Dimitrios Greek; 1911– ; photographer, documentary.
Harris, David Israeli; 1929– ; photographer.
Harter, Donald Scott American; 1950– ; photographer; teacher.
Hartmann, Erich American; 1922– ; photographer, technology, laser.
Hartmann, Ilka Maria German; 1942– ; photographer, documentary.
Hartwig, Edward Polish; 1909– ; photographer, peopled landscapes, Poland.
Harvey, David Alan American; 1944– ; photojournalist, *National Geographic* staff.
Haskins, Sam South African; 1926– ; photographer, nudes.
Hassner, Rune Swedish; 1928– ; photographer; photohistorian; television producer.
Hattersley, Ralph Marshall Jr. American; 1921– ; photographer; writer; educator.
Haun, Declan American; 1937– ; photojournalist.
Hausmann, Raoul Austrian; 1886–1971; painter; sculptor; poet; photographer, Dadaist, photo montage.
Hausser, Robert German; 1924– ; photographer.
Haveman, Josepha Dutch; 1931– ; photographer; teacher.
Hawarden, Clementina Elphinstone British; 1822–1865; photographer, full length female portraits.
Haxton, David American; 1943– ; photographer, abstract sets, color; film maker.
Haya, Maria Eugenia Cuban; 1944– ; photographer; photohistorian, Cuban photography.
Haynes, Frank Jay American; 1853–1921; photographer, documentary, Yellowstone National Park.
Heartfield, John (Helmut Herzfelde) German; 1891–1968; photographer, Dadaist, political photomontage.
Heath, David Martin American; 1931– ; photographer, photo-essays, human conditions; teacher.
Heckel, Vilem Czechoslovakian; 1918–1970; photographer, mountains; mountaineer.
Hedges, Nick British; 1943– ; photographer, documentary, factory workers; teacher.

Hegg, Eric A. Swede; 1868–1948; photographer, topographical, Alaska.

Heinemann, Jurgen German; 1934– ; photojournalist.

Hellebrand, Nancy American; 1944– ; photographer, portraits.

Henderson, Nigel British; 1917– ; photographer, photograms, documentary, East London.

Henle, Fritz American, b. Germany; 1909– ; photographer, varied subject matter.

Hermansson, Jean Swedish; 1938– ; photographer, documentary.

Hernandez, Anthony American; 1947– ; photographer, social documentary.

Herraez Gomez, Fernando Spanish; 1948– ; photographer, documentary, cermonies.

Hers, Francois Belgian; 1943– ; photographer, documentary.

Hertzberg, Benjamin American; 1910– ; photographer, photo-essays, human condition.

Hesler, Alexander American; 1823–1895; photographer, daguerrotypist, Lincoln's portrait.

Heyman, Abigail American; 1942– ; photographer, documentary; author.

Heyman, Ken American; 1930– ; photojournalist; anthropology, social documentary.

Hidalgo, Francisco French; 1929– ; photographer, travel.

Higgins, Chester Jr. American; 1946– ; photojournalist.

Hill, Paul British; 1941– ; photographer; editor; educator.

Hillers, John K. German; 1843–1925; photographer, American Indians and Southwest.

Hilliard, John British; 1945– ; photographer, conceptual; sculptor; teacher.

Hinton, Alfred Horsley British; 1863–1906; photographer, pictorialist, landscapes.

Hirsch, Steven American; 1948– ; photographer, city streets.

Hirsch, Walter Swedish; 1935– ; photographer, domestic environment.

Hixon, Orval American; 1884– ; photographer, celebrity portraits.

Hlobeczy, Nicholas C. American; 1927– ; photographer.

Hoagland, John American; 1952–1983; photojournalist, E. Salvador.

Hockney, David British; 1937– ; painter; graphic artist; photographer.

Hoepffner, Marta German; 1912– ; photographer.

Hoepker, Thomas M. German; 1936– ; photojournalist; editor.

Hofer, Evelyn German; (contemporary); photographer, photo-essays, portraits.

Hoff, Charles American; 1906–1975; press photographer, sports.

Hoffman, Bernard American; 1913–1979; photojournalist, *Life* staff.

Holdt, Jacob Danish; 1947– ; photographer, documentary.

Holmes, Wendy American; 1946– ; photographer.

Holmgren, Robert Everett American; 1946– ; photographer, portraits.

Holub, Leo M. American; 1916– ; photographer, documentary; teacher.

Holzman, Marek Polish; 1919–1982; photographer, portraits, reportage.

Hopkins, Thurston British; 1913– ; photojournalist, *Picture Post* staff.

Horeis, William American; 1945– ; photographer.

Horvat, Frank Italian; 1928– ; photographer, fashion.

Hosking, Eric British; 1909– ; photographer, wildlife, birds.

House, Suda Kay American; 1951– ; photographer; teacher.

Howe, Graham Australian; 1950– ; photographer; curator; publisher.

Huang Xiang Chinese; 1903– ; photographer, landscapes.

Huet, Henri French, b. Vietnam; –1971; photojournalist.

Huffman, Laton Alton American; 1843–1931; photographer, American west.

Hujar, Peter American; 1934– ; photographer, portraits, nudes.

Hume, Sandy (Richard) American; 1946– ; photographer; teacher.

Hunter, Debora American; 1950– ; photographer, subjective portraits; teacher.

Hurley, (James Francis) Frank Australian; 1885–1962; photographer, documentary, travel; film maker; explorer.

Hurn, David British; 1934– ; photojournalist; educator.

Hurrell, George American; 1904– ; photographer, portraits, Hollywood celebrities.

Husebye, Terry L. American; 1945– ; photographer, landscapes.

Hutton (Hubschmann), Kurt British, b. Germany; 1893–1960; photojournalist, *Picture Post* staff.

Hyde, Philip American; 1921– ; photographer, landscapes.

Hyde, Scott American; 1926– ; photographer, color, offset lineographic prints.

I

Ichimura, Tetsuya Japanese; 1930– ; photographer.

Ickovic, Paul British; 1944– ; photographer, urban life.

Ignatovich, Boris Russian; 1899–1976; photographer, human issues.

Ikko (Ikko Narahara) Japanese; 1931– ; photographer, subjective landscapes.

Incandela, Gerald French; 1952– ; photographer, brushed-on developer.

Ingolfsson, Gudmunder Icelandic; 1946– ; photographer.

Inha, Into Konrad Finnish; 1865–1930; photographer, social documentary, anthropological.

Ionesco, Irena French; 1935– ; photographer, female portraits, interiors.

Ioss, Walter, Jr. American; 1943– ; photojournalist, sports.

Ishimoto, Yasuhiro Y. Japanese; 1921– ; photographer, American and Japanese cultures.

Ishiuci, Miyako Japanese; 1947– ; photographer, social documentary, domestic interiors.

Iturbide, Graciela Mexican; 1942– ; photographer, social portraits, Mexican Indians.

Ivanov, Vladimir Russian; 1926– ; photographer.

Ives, Frederick Eugene American; 1856–1937; inventor, half tone engraving process; photographer; printer.

J

Jachna, Joseph David American; 1935– ; photographer, nature; educator.

Jacobs, Mark American; 1951– ; photographer; writer.

Jacoby, Max German; 1919– ; photojournalist.

Jacot, Monique Swiss; 1934– ; photographer, documentary.

Jaffee, N. Jay American; 1921– ; photographer, social landscapes.

James, Christopher American; 1947– ; photographer, varied subject matter, hand enamelling; teacher.

Janini, Joaquim Pla Spanish; 1879–1970; photographer, pictorialist.

Jansen, Arno German; 1938– ; photographer, still life.

Jarché, James British; 1890–1965; press photographer.

Jaworskij, Stanislaw Russian; 1937– ; photographer, mother and child; engineer.

Jeager, Johannes Swedish; 1832–1908; photographer, portraits.

Jenshel, Len American; 1949– ; photographer, color, landscape.

Jodas, Miroslav Czechoslovakian; 1932– ; photographer, portraits, still life.

Joel, Yale American; 1919– ; photojournalist, *Life* staff.

Johansson, Lars Swedish; 1934– ; photographer, social documentary.

Johnson, Tore Yngve Swedish; 1928–1980; photojournalist.

Johnston, Frank B. American; 1904–1956; press photographer, *Philadelphia Inquirer*.

Johnston, J. Dudley British; 1868–1955; photographer, pictorialist, landscapes, cityscapes.

Jones-Griffiths, Philip British; 1936– ; photojournalist, *Sports Illustrated* and *Life* staffs; author.

Jones, Harold American; 1940– ; photographer; art administrator; educator.

Jones, Pirkle American; 1914– ; photographer, documentary, nature.

Jonsson, Sune Swedish; 1930– ; photographer, documentary; writer.

Jorge, Sergio Brazilian; 1937– ; photographer, advertising, fashion.

Josephson, Kenneth American; 1932– ; photographer, humorous subjects.

Joya, Mario Garcia Cuban; 1938– ; photographer, documentary.

Joyce, Paul British; 1940– ; photographer, panoramic landscapes; film and theatre director.

Jumonji, Bishin Japanese; 1947– ; photographer, humorous subjects.

Juskelis, Romas Russian; 1946– ; photographer, landscapes.

K

Kahn, Steve American; 1943– ; photographer.

Kalischer, Clemens Bavarian; 1921– ; photographer.

Kalisher, Simpson American; 1926– ; photographer, social documentary.

Kallay, Karoly Czechoslovakian; 1926– ; photographer, travel, fashion.

Kalvar, Richard American; 1944– ; photojournalist.

Kalvelis, Jonas Lithuanian; 1925– ; photographer, nature.

Kanaga, Consuelo American; 1894–1978; photographer, social issues.

Kane, Art American; 1925– ; photographer; art director.

Kantor, Tim American; 1932– ; photographer.

Kao Qifeng Chinese; active early 1900s; photojournalist.

Kaplan, Peter B. American; 1939– ; photographer, color, cityscapes, architecture.

Karales, James H. American; 1930– ; photojournalist, *Look* staff.

Karant, Barbara E. American; 1952– ; photographer, color, interiors; teacher.

Karsh, Malak Canadian, b. Armenia; 1908– ; photographer, portraits.

Karlsson, Stig T. Swedish; 1930– ; photographer, social documentary.

Kasten, Barbara American; 1936– ; photographer; teacher.

Katchian, Sonia Lebanese; 1947– ; photographer, social subjects.

Katsiff, Bruce F. American; 1945– ; photographer, documentary.

Kauffman, Mark American; 1922– ; photojournalist, *Sports Illustrated* and *Life* staffs.

Kawada, Kikuji Japanese; 1933– ; photographer.

Kazimierski, Daniel Canadian, b. Poland; 1949– ; photographer, social subjects.

Kearton, Cherry British; 1871–1940; photographer, documentary, wildlife.

Keegan, Marcia American; 1942– ; photographer, American west, color.

Keetman, Peter German; 1916– ; photographer.

Kehaya, Dorothy American; 1925– ; photographer, nature, color.

Keighley, Alexander British; 1861–1947; photographer, pictorialist.

Keiley, Joseph T. American; 1869–1914; lawyer; editor; photographer.

Kelley, Robert W. American; 1920– ; photojournalist, *Life* staff.

Kempe, Fritz (Max Kurt) German; 1909– ; photographer, portraits, photohistorian.

Kennedy, Clarence American; 1892–1972; photographer; art historian; teacher.

Kennerly, David Hume American; 1947– ; photojournalist, American presidency.

Kenyon, Colleen Frances American; 1951– ; photographer, portraits, self and sister; teacher.

Kenyon, Kathleen American; 1951– ; photographer, portraits, self and sister; teacher.

Kernan, Margot American; 1927– ; photographer; teacher.

Kernan, Sean American; 1942– ; photographer.

Kesting, Edmund German; 1892–1970; photographer, collages, montages.

Ketchum, Robert Glenn American; 1947– ; photographer, landscapes, nature; curator.

Kezys, Algimantas American, b. Lithuania; 1928– ; priest; photographer.

Khaldei, Yeugeni Russian; 1916– ; photojournalist, World War II.

Kharas, Rustom Indian; (contemporary); photographer, advertising.

Kiffl, Erika Austrian, b. Czechoslovakia; 1939– ; photographer, documentary.

Killip, Chris(topher) British; 1946– ; photographer, portraits, landscapes, Isle of Man.

Kimura, Ihei Japanese; 1901–1974; photographer, social subjects.

Kindermann, Helmmo R. American; 1947– ; photographer.

Kinsey, Darius Reynold American; 1869–1945; photographer, industrial, logging.

Kirkland, Wallace W. American, b. Jamaica; 1891–1979; photographer, nature, social documentary, *Life* staff.

Kirstel, Richard American; photographer, human condition; author.

Kitai, Kazuo Japanese; 1944– ; photographer, domestic interiors.

Klavins, Janis Russian; 1930– ; industrial designer; photographer.

Klein, Aart Dutch; 1909– ; photographer, documentary.

Klein, Erwin B. American; 1933–1974; photographer.

Klein, William American; 1928– ; photographer, documentary, fashion; film maker; author.

Kleins, Valts Russian; 1960– ; photographer.

Klipper, Stuart D. American; 1941– ; photographer, social landscapes; teacher.

Klosz, Gyorgy Hungarian; 1844–1913; photographer, urban scenes.

Knudsen, Knud Norwegian; 1832–1915; photographer, picturesque views, nature.

Koga, Mary American; 1920– ; photographer, documentary.

Kolko, Berenice American; 1905–1970; photographer, documentary, Mexico.

Koposov, Gennadi Russian; 1938– ; photojournalist.

Koppitz, Rudolf Austrian; –1936; photographer, portraits; educator.

Koreschkov, Valeri Belo-Russian; 1941– ; photojournalist.

Korniss, Peter Hungarian; 1937– ; photographer, dance, folklore.

Kosstromin, Sergej Russian; 1947– ; photographer, advertising.

Kowal, Cal American; 1944– ; photographer; teacher.

Kozloff, Max American; 1933– ; photographer, color, city streets; critic.

Kramer, Arnold American; 1944– ; photographer, social portraiture.

Krause, George American; 1937– ; photographer, surreal imagery.

Krementz, Jill American; 1940– ; photographer, portraits; author.

Krieger, Ignacy Polish; 1820–1889; photographer, portraits, cityscapes.

Krims, Les American; 1943– ; photographer, satirical subjects; author.

Kristof, Emory American; 1942– ; photographer, electronic images, *National Geographic* staff.
Kriz, Vilem American, b. Czechoslovakia; 1921– ; photographer, surreal still life.
Kroll, Eric David American; 1946– ; photographer, color, movement.
Kronengold, Eric Adolph American; 1935– ; photographer; teacher.
Kruse, Olney Brazilian; 1939– ; photographer, portraits.
Krzywoblocki, Aleksander Polish; 1901–1979; photographer, photomontage.
Krzyzanowski, Michel Dutch; 1949– ; photographer.
Kubota, Hiroji Japanese; 1939– ; photojournalist, color.
Kudoyarov, Boris Russian; 1903–1973; photojournalist.
Kuehn, Gernot American, b. Germany; 1940– ; photographer, documentary; film editor.
Kukojs, Robert Russian; 1949– ; engineer; photographer, portraits, landscapes.
Kumler, Kipton C. American; 1940– ; photographer, plants.
Kuncius, Algimantas Lithuanian; 1939– ; photojournalist.
Kurata, Seiji Japanese; 1945– ; photographer, documentary.
Kuscynskyj, Taras Czechoslovakian; 1932– ; photographer, portraits, nudes, fashion.
Kuus, Otto Russian; 1938– ; land surveyor; photographer, landscapes.
Kuwabara, Kineo Japanese; 1913– ; photographer, everyday life, Tokyo; author; teacher.
Kyiochi, Sawada Japanese; 1936–1970; photojournalist.

L

La Rosa, Fernando Peruvian; 1943– ; photographer, urban landscapes.
Labrot, Syl(vester Welch) American; 1929–1977; photographer, abstract, color; painter.
Laerka, Karl Swedish; 1892–1981; photographer, social documentary.
Laffont, Jean Pierre French; 1935– ; photojournalist.
Laizerovitz, Daniel Uruguayan; 1952– ; photographer, social documentary.
Lake, Suzy American; 1947– ; photographer, self portraits.
Lal, Priya Indian; (active) 1875–1910; photographer, studio portraits.
Lambert, Herbert British; 1881–1936; photographer, portraits; musician.
Lambeth, Michel Canadian; 1923–1977; photographer, social subjects; teacher.
Lambray, Maureen American; (contemporary); photographer; author.
Land-Weber, Ellen American; 1943– ; photographer.
Landweber, Victor American; 1943– ; photographer, social landscapes.
Lanker, Brian American; 1947– ; photojournalist.
Lang, Gerald American; 1939– ; photographer.
Lange, Vidie American; 1934– ; photographer, obsolete processes, photogravure.
Lanzano, Lou(is) American; 1947– ; photographer, spontaneous portraits.
Lapow, Harry American; 1909–1983; photographer; designer.
Larsen, Lisa American, b. Germany; 1925–1959; photojournalist, *Life* staff.
Larson, William American; 1942– ; photographer, domestic situations; educator.
Laschkow, Andrej Russian; 1946– ; psychiatrist; photographer.
Launois, John French; 1928– ; photojournalist.
Lazorik, Wayne Rod American; 1939– ; photographer; teacher.

Le Campion, Hubert French; 1934– ; photographer.
LeQuerrec, Guy French; 1941– ; photographer.
Lebeck, Robert German; 1929– ; photojournalist; collector; editor.
Lee, Russell American; 1903– ; photographer, documentary.
Leen, Nina American, b. Russia; (contemporary); photographer, *Life* staff.
Lees, David American, b. Italy; 1917– ; photojournalist.
Lehman, Yoram Israeli; 1939– ; photographer.
Leibovitz, Annie American; 1950– ; photojournalist, portraits.
Leifer, Neil American; 1942– ; photojournalist, sports.
Leipzig, Arthur American; 1918– ; photographer, documentary; educator.
Leonian, Leo American; photographer, color, movement.
Lenart, Branko Austrian, b. Yugoslavia; 1948– ; photographer, documentary.
Lennard, Elizabeth Anne American; 1953– ; photographer; film maker.
Lennard, Erica American; 1950– ; photographer, fashion.
Lengyel, Lajos Hungarian; 1904–1978; photographer, social realism, still life.
Leonard, Joanne American; 1940– ; photographer, interiors, household objects; teacher.
Leonardi, Cesare Italian; 1935– ; photographer; architect.
Leppikson, Harald Russian; 1933– ; photojournalist.
Lerner, Nathan Bernard American; 1913– ; photographer; educator.
Leroy, Catherine French; 1944– ; photojournalist.
Lessing, Erich Austrian; 1923– ; photojournalist.
Leverant, Robert American; 1939– ; photographer, landscapes; writer.
Levi, Hans Leopold American, b. Germany; 1935– ; photographer; educator.
Lewczynski, Jerzy Polish; 1924– ; photographer, sociological subjects.
Lewitt, Sol American; 1928– ; sculptor; photographer.
Libsohn, Sol American; 1914– ; photojournalist, teacher.
Lichsteiner, Rudolf Swiss; 1938– ; photographer, environment; teacher.
Liebling, Jerome American; 1924– ; photographer, documentary; educator; film maker.
Liftin, Joan American; 1935– ; photographer; editor.
Light, Ken American; 1951– ; photographer, social documentary; film maker.
Lindley, Daniel Allen Jr. American; 1933– ; teacher; photographer.
Lipskerov, Georgi Russian; 1896– ; photojournalist.
Livick, Stephen Canadian; 1945– ; photographer, documentary, Middle America.
Livingston, Jacqueline American; 1943– ; photographer, portraits; teacher.
Lleras, Camilo Colombian; 1949– ; photographer, self portraits.
Lloyd, Harvey American; 1926– ; photographer, color, landscapes; film maker.
Locke, Chris British; 1950– ; photographer, landscapes; teacher.
Lockwood, Lee American; 1932– ; photojournalist; author.
Loengard, John Borg American; 1934– ; photojournalist, *Life* staff; editor.
Lohse, Bernd German; 1911– ; photojournalist; writer.
Lokajski, Eugeniusz Polish; 1909–1944; photojournalist, Warsaw Uprising, World War II.
Lokuta, Donald Peter American; 1946– ; photographer; teacher.
Lomeo, Angelo American; 1921– ; photographer, landscapes, color.
Long, Chin-San Taiwanese; 1890– ; photographer, landscapes.
Longman, Eduardo Brazilian; 1952– ; photographer, documentary.

Lopez, Andy American; 1910– ; press photographer.
Lotar, Eli French; 1905–1969; photographer.
Lotti, Giorgio Italian; 1937– ; photojournalist, social documentary.
Lounema, Risto Finnish; 1939– ; photographer, landscapes.
Lown, Lynn American; 1947– ; photographer.
Luksenas, Antanas Lithuanian; 1948– ; photographer, landscapes.
Lundh, Peter P. Swedish; 1865–1943; photographer, social scenes.
Luskacova, Marketa British, b. Czechoslovakia; 1944– ; photographer, documentary, photo-essay.
Lux (Joan Pereferrer) Spanish; 1898–1974; photographer, social portraits.
Luthi, Urs Swiss; 1947– ; artist; autobiographical portraits.
Lyon, Danny American; 1942– ; photographer, social documentary.
Lyons, Joan American; 1937– ; photographer, self portraits, plants, various media.

M

MacAdams, Cynthia American; 1939– ; photographer, female portraits, female nudes; actress.
MacDonald, (Ian) Pirie American; 1867–1942; photographer, portraits.
MacGregor, Gregory Allen American; 1941– ; photographer, satirical subjects.
MacRae, Wendell Scott American; 1896–1980; photographer, documentary.
MacWeeney, Alen Brasil Irish; 1939– ; photographer, social themes, portraits.
Macijauskas, Aleksandras Lithuanian; 1938– ; photographer, social documentary.
Maddox, Richard Leach British; 1816–1902; photographer.
Maeda, Shinzo Japanese; 1922– ; photographer, landscapes.
Maestro, David Yugoslavian; 1927– ; photographer.
Maggs, Arnaud Canadian; 1926– ; photographer, social portraits.
Magnusson, Olafur Icelandic; 1889–1954; photographer.
Magritte, Rene (Francois Ghislain) Belgian; 1898–1967; printer; Surrealist; photographer.
Magubane, Peter South African; 1932– ; photojournalist.
Mahr, Mari Hungarian; 1941– ; photographer.
Maisel, Jay American; 1931– ; photographer.
Makarov, Alexandr Russian; 1936– ; photographer, ballet.
Makos, Christopher E. American; 1948– ; photographer, contemporary society.
Maldre, Mati German; 1947– ; photographer; teacher.
Malmberg, Hans Swedish; 1927–1977; photographer, documentary.
Maloney, Joe American; 1949– ; photographer, landscapes.
Malyshev, Vasili Russian; 1900– ; photographer, portraits.
Man, Felix H. British, b. Germany; 1893– ; photojournalist.
Mandel, Michael S. American; 1950– ; photographer.
Manning, Jack American; 1920– ; photojournalist.
Manos, Constantine American; 1934– ; photographer, social documentary.
Mante, Harald German; 1936– ; photographer, color; teacher.
Manzon, Jean French; 1915– ; photojournalist; film maker.
Mapplethorpe, Robert American; 1946– ; photographer, portraits, male nudes.
Marcus, Eli German; 1899–1977; photographer, theatre portraits, fashion, advertising; graphologist.
Marden, Luis American; 1913– ; photographer, underwater, *National Geographic* staff.

Margolies, John American; 1940– ; photographer, contemporary commercial architecture; lecturer; critic.
Margolis, Richard American; 1943– ; photographer, landscapes, gardens, lyrical.
Mark, Mary Ellen American; 1940– ; photojournalist, social documentary; teacher.
Maroon, Fred American; 1924– ; photojournalist.
Marotta, Tom French; 1943– ; photojournalist; author.
Marsden, Simon British; 1948– ; photographer, landscapes; teacher.
Martin, Charles American; (dates unknown); photographer, underwater, *National Geographic* staff.
Martin, Paul French; 1864–1944; photographer, Victorian life, Britain.
Martincek, Martin Czech; 1913– ; photographer, nature.
Martone, Michael American; 1941– ; photographer, autobiographical.
Mascaro, Cristiano Brazilian; 1944– ; photographer, documentary, architecture; teacher.
Masclet, Daniel French; 1892–1969; photographer, portraits; writer
Massar, Ivan American; 1924– ; photographer, industrial, documentary.
Mate, Olga Hungarian; 1878–1961; photographer, portraits, nudes.
Mather, Margrethe American; 1885–1952; photographer, portraits, still life, interiors.
Mathys, Max Swiss; 1933– ; photographer, nature, color.
Matta-Clark, Gordon American; 1945–1978; photographer; sculptor.
Matter, Herbert American, b. Switzerland; 1907– ; photographer; graphic designer.
Maurer, Neil American; 1941– ; photographer; teacher.
Max, John Canadian; 1936– ; photographer, social themes.
Mayall, John Jabez Edwin American; 1810–1901; photographer, daguerreotype portraits.
Mayes, Elaine American; 1938– ; photographer; film maker.
Mayne, Roger British; 1929– ; photographer, social documentary.
Mays, Buddy American; 1943– ; photographer, Southwest; author.
McAvoy, (Tom) Thomas Dowell American; 1905–1966; photojournalist, *Life* staff.
McBean, Angus British; 1904– ; photographer, celebrity portraits, theatre.
McBride, Will American; 1931– ; photographer, documentary.
McCombe, Leonard American, b. Britain; 1923– ; photojournalist, *Life* staff; film maker.
McCormack, Dan American; 1944– ; photographer; teacher.
McCormick, Ron British; 1947– ; photographer, documentary; gallery director; educator.
McCurdy, John Chang Korean; 1940– ; photographer.
McDarrah, Fred W. American; 1926– ; photojournalist, *Village Voice* staff.
McFarland, Lawrence Dean American; 1942– ; photographer; teacher.
McGowan, Kenneth American; 1940– ; photographer, social landscapes.
McMillan, Jerry American; 1936– ; photographer, photo-sculpture.
McPherson, Larry E. American; 1943– ; photographer, landscapes, nature.
McQuaid, Jim American; 1946– ; photographer; photo historian; teacher.
Meek, Richard A. American; 1923– ; photographer, *Sports Illustrated* and *Life* staffs.
Mehta, Ashvin Indian; 1931– ; photographer, seascapes.
Meiselas, Susan American; 1948– ; photojournalist; author.
Melnick, Philip Albert American; 1935– ; photographer, architectural details, interiors.
Menapace, John American; 1927– ; photographer; teacher.

Mendoza, Antonio Cuban; 1941– ; photographer, documentary, animals.

Merisio, Pepi (Giuseppe) Italian; 1931– ; photographer, rural life.

Merletti, Alejandro Spanish; 1860–1943; photographer, social documentary.

Mertin, Roger American; 1942– ; photographer, fantasy; teacher.

Mesch, Borg Swedish; 1870–1956; photographer, documentary.

Messina, John American; 1940– ; photographer; architect; teacher.

Metzner, Sheila American; 1939– ; photographer, portraits, color; art director.

Meyer, Pedro Mexican, b. Spain; 1935– ; photographer, social documentary; educator.

Michalik, Chester American; 1935– ; photographer, urban environment; teacher.

Michetti, Francesco Paolo Italian; 1851–1929; painter; photographer, documentary, rural life, social issues.

Midorikawa, Yoichi Japanese; 1915– ; photographer, landscapes, color.

Mieth, Hansel American, b. Germany; 1909– ; photojournalist, *Life* staff.

Mikhailovsky, Wilhelm Russian; 1942– ; photographer, montage.

Miki, Jun Japanese; 1919– ; photographer.

Mikolasch, Henryk Polish; 1876–1931; photographer, wildlife.

Millea, Tom American; 1944– ; photographer, nudes, landscapes.

Miller, Laurence Glenn American; 1948– ; photographer; teacher.

Miller, Lee American; 1906–1977; photographer, documentary, fashion; model; actress.

Miller, Wayne American; 1911– ; photojournalist; author.

Milmoe, James Oliver American; 1927– ; photographer.

Milon, Reuven Israeli; 1928– ; photographer.

Minick, Roger American; 1944– ; photographer, sociological, people and environment.

Minkkinen, Arno Rafael American, b. Finland; 1945– ; photographer, self portraits.

Miserachs, Xavier Spanish; 1937– ; photographer, documentary.

Misonne, Leonard Belgian; 1870–1943; photographer, pictorialist.

Misrach, Richard American; 1949– ; photographer, social landscapes, nocturnal scenes.

Mitchell, Julio American; 1942– ; photographer.

Mitchell, Margaretta K. American; 1935– ; photographer, portraits; teacher.

Mitchell, Michael Canadian; 1943– ; photographer, landscapes, portraits, color.

Miyatake, Toyo Japanese; 1895–1979; photographer, documentary, portraits.

Mobley, George American; 1935– ; photojournalist, *National Geographic* staff.

Moffat, Curtis American; 1887–1949; photographer, color, abstractions; designer.

Moholy, Lucia British, b. Austria; ca. 1900– ; photographer, portraits, architecture, documentary; art historian.

Mohr, Jean Swiss; 1925– ; photojournalist, social documentary.

Monserrat, Tomas Spanish; 1873–1944; photographer, social portraits.

Monti, Paolo Italian; 1908–1982; photographer, varied subject matter.

Moon, Sarah French; 1941– ; photographer, fashion, advertising.

Moore, Charles American; 1931– ; photojournalist, travel.

Moore, David Murray Australian; 1927– ; photographer, social documentary, industrial.

Moore, Raymond British; 1920– ; photographer; teacher.

Morath, Inge(borg) American, b. Austria; 1923– ; photographer, documentary.

Moreira, Carlos Brazilian; 1936– ; photographer, documentary; teacher.

Morey, Craig H. American; 1952– ; photographer; gallery director.

Morimoto, Hiromitsu Japanese; 1942– ; photographer.

Morinaga, Jun Japanese; 1937– ; photographer, water studies.

Moriyama, Daido Japanese; 1938– ; photographer, social documentary.

Morse, Ralph American; 1918– ; photojournalist, *Life* staff.

Mortensen, William American; 1897–1965; photographer, allegorical portraits, nudes.

Mott-Smith, John American; 1930– ; photographer.

Moulton, Rosalind Kimball American; 1941– ; photographer; teacher.

Mucha, Alphonse Marie Czechoslovakian; 1860–1939; graphic artist; painter; photographer, studies for painting.

Mudford, Grant Australian; 1944– ; photographer, landscapes, architecture.

Muehlen, Bernis von zur American; 1942– ; photographer; teacher.

Muench, David American; 1936– ; photographer, landscapes.

Muller-Phole, Andreas German; 1951– ; photographer; editor; teacher.

Murray, Joan American; 1927– ; critic; teacher; photographer.

Myers, Joan American; 1944– ; photographer.

N

Nachtwey, James American; 1948– ; photojournalist.

Nadar, Paul French; 1856–1939; photographer, portraits.

Nagarajan, T. S. Indian; 1932– ; photographer, chronicler, social change, India.

Nagatani, Patrick August American; 1945– ; photographer; teacher.

Naitoh, Masatoshi Japanese; 1938– ; photographer, documentary, Japanese folklore; chemist.

Nakagawa, Masaaki Japanese; 1943– ; photographer, nudes, subjective still life.

Nakamura, Masaya Japanese; 1926– ; photographer, nudes, fashion.

Namuth, Hans American, b. Germany; 1915– ; photographer, portraits, artists and writers.

Nappelbaum, Mikhail Salomonovitch Russian; 1869–1958; photographer, portraits.

Nash, Paul British; 1889–1946; painter; photographer.

Natali, Enrico American; 1933– ; photographer, social landscapes.

Navarro, Rafael Spanish; 1940– ; photographer, conceptual; critic.

Naya, Carlo Italian; –1873; photographer, views of Venice.

Neimanas, Joyce American; 1944– ; photographer, mixed media; teacher.

Nemeth, Jozsef Hungarian 1911– ; photographer.

Neto, Mario Cravo Brazilian; 1947– ; photographer, documentary; sculptor.

Nettles, Bea American; 1946– ; photographer, mixed media, autobiographical.

Neususs, Floris M. German; 1937– ; photographer, nudes, life-size silhouettes; teacher.

Newman, Marvin American; 1927– ; photojournalist, cityscapes.

Neyra, Jose Luis Mexican; 1930– ; photographer, social portraits.

Nicholls, Horace W. British; 1867–1941; photographer, documentary, English society, Boer War.

Niepce, Janine French; 1921– ; photographer.

Nilsson, Pal-Nils Swedish; 1929– ; photographer, nature, fashion, advertising; film maker, documentary.

Nixon, Nicholas American; 1947– ; photographer, family portraits.

Noggle, Anne American; 1922– ; photographer; teacher.

Nori, Claude French; 1949– ; writer; publisher.

North, Kenda American; 1951– ; photographer; teacher.
Noskowiak, Sonya American, b. Germany; 1900–1975; photographer, portraits, landscapes, still life.
Nothhelfer, Gabriele and Helmut German; 1945– ; photographers, social portraiture.
Noyes, Sandy American; 1941– ; photographer, landscapes, still life, interiors; teacher.
Nutting, Wallace American; 1861–1941; photographer, genre scenes, New England; clergyman.
Nykvist, Ralph Swedish; 1944– ; photographer, social documentary.

O

O'Brien, Michael American; 1950– ; photojournalist.
Ockenga, Starr American; 1938– ; photographer; teacher.
Oddner, Georg Swedish; 1923– ; photographer, documentary, travel, fashion.
Ohara, Ken T. Japanese; 1942– ; photographer.
Okamoto, Yoichi Robert American; 1915– ; photojournalist, U.S. presidency.
Okuhara, Tetsu American; 1940– ; photographer.
Ollman, Arthur American; 1947– ; photographer, urban environment; teacher.
Olsen, Lennart Swedish; 1925– ; photographer, architecture; film maker.
O'Neil, Michael American; 1946– ; photojournalist.
Ontanon, Paco Spanish; photographer, documentary.
Oorthuys, Cas Dutch; 1908–1975; photographer, documentary, industrial.
Opton, Suzanne American; 1945– ; photographer, autobiographical portraits; teacher.
Orkin, Ruth American; 1921– ; photographer, documentary, Central Park, New York; film maker.
Ornitz, Don American; 1920– ; photographer, female nudes.
Oron, Zvi Israeli, b. Poland; 1888–1980; photographer.
Ortiz Monasterio, Pablo Mexican; 1952– ; photographer.
Ostrovsky, Tzachi Israeli; 1945– ; photographer, human issues.
Owens, Bill (William Elmo) American; 1938– ; photographer, social documentary; author.

P

Pabel, Hilmar German; 1910– ; photojournalist.
Page, Homer American; 1918– ; photojournalist.
Page, Timothy John British; 1944– ; photojournalist, Vietnam War.
Pajunen, Timo Tallno Finnish; 1945– ; photographer; teacher.
Palfi, Marion American, b. Germany; 1907–1978; photographer, documentary, photo-essay.
Paolini, Ameris M. Brazilian; 1945– ; photographer, human condition.
Papageorge, Tod American; 1940– ; photographer, social landscapes; educator.
Parada, Esther American; 1938– ; photographer, mixed media.
Parker, Ann American; 1934– ; photographer, folk art, folk traditions; graphic artist.
Parker, Olivia American; 1941– ; photographer, still life.
Parkinson, Norman British; 1913– ; photographer, fashion, royal portraits.
Parks, Winfield American; 1932–1977; photojournalist, *National Geographic* staff.
Parr, Martin British; 1952– ; photographer, social documentary.
Parry, Roger French; 1905– ; photographer, female nudes, advertising.

Partridge, Rondal American; 1917– ; photographer, architecture, environment, advertising.
Patterson, Bruce American; 1950– ; photographer, altered landscapes.
Penow, Rjurik Russian; 1937– ; engineer; photographer.
Perres, Gilles French; 1946– ; photojournalist.
Perkis, Philip American; 1935– ; photographer, formalist landscapes.
Petersen, Anders Swedish; 1944– ; photographer, social documentary.
Petersen, K. Helmer Danish; 1947– ; photographer, abstract, color; author.
Petit, Pierre French; 1832–?; photographer, daguerreotype, portraits, documentary.
Petrusov, Georgii Russian; 1903–1971; photojournalist.
Peven, Michael D. American; 1949– ; photographer; teacher.
Pfahl, John American; 1939– ; photographer, altered landscapes.
Phillips, John American; 1914– ; photojournalist, *Life* staff; author.
Picker, Fred American; 1927– ; photographer, landscapes, portraits.
Pierce, Bill American; 1935– ; photojournalist.
Pilvelis, Algirdas Russian; 1944– ; photographer.
Pirotte, Julia Polish; 1911– ; photojournalist.
Pitkanen, Matti A. Finnish; 1930– ; photographer, documentary.
Pla Janini, Joaquin Spanish; 1879–1970; photographer, pictorialist.
Plachy, Sylvia American, b. Hungary; 1943– ; photojournalist, *Village Voice* staff.
Plossu, Bernard French; 1945– ; photographer, social documentary, travel subjects.
Plowden, David American; 1932– ; photographer, industrial landscapes.
Pocock, Philip Canadian; 1954– ; photographer, documentary.
Polak, Richard Dutch; 1870–1957; photographer.
Polk, Prentice H. American; 1898– ; photographer, social subjects.
Power, Mark American; 1937– ; photographer; teacher.
Pozherskis, R. Russian; 1951– ; engineer; photographer.
Prandi, Emanuele Italian; 1948– ; photographer, documentary.
Pratt, Charles American; 1926–1976; photographer, nature.
Prazuch, Weislaw Polish; 1925– ; photojournalist.
Pressma, Conrad J. American; 1944– ; photographer; gallery director; teacher.
Prince, Doug(las) American; 1943– ; photographer.
Pringle, Barry African; 1943– ; photographer; graphic designer.
Prokudin-Gorskii, Sergei Mikhailovich Russian; 1863–1943; photographer, documentary, Russian landscapes and architecture, color.
Prosek, Josef Czechoslovakian; 1923– ; photographer.
Purcell, Rosamond Wolff American; 1942– ; photographer, allegorical portraits.
Purina, Teiksma Russian; 1953– ; painting restorer; photographer.
Puyo, Charles French; 1857–1933; photographer, pictorialist.

Q

Qian Jinghua Chinese; (active) 1930s; photographer.

R

Rabinovitch, Mendel Brazilian; 1941– ; photographer, documentary; film maker.
Rachel, Vaughan American; 1933– ; photographer, domestic environment; teacher.

Rachmanow, Nikalaj Russian; 1932– ; photojournalist.
Ragazzini, Enzo Italian; 1934– ; photographer, documentary.
Raimond-Dityvon, Claude French; 1937– ; photographer, documentary.
Rajzik, Jaroslav Czechoslovakian; 1940– ; photographer, experimental light compositions.
Rakauskas, Romualdas Lithuanian; 1941– ; photojournalist; author.
Rankaitis, Susan Anne American; 1949– ; photographer, abstract; painter.
Ranney, Edward American; 1942– ; photographer, landscapes, archeological sites; teacher.
Rantoul, Talbot Neal American; 1946– ; photographer; teacher.
Rauschenberg, Robert American; 1925– ; painter; photographer.
Ravelle, Barbara Jo American; (contemporary); photographer.
Rawlings, John W. American; 1912– ; photographer, fashion, nudes.
Ray-Jones, Tony British; 1941–1972; photographer, English life.
Raymond, Lilo American, b. Germany; 1922– ; photographer, still life, interiors.
Rebot, Olivier French; 1949–1981; photojournalist, El Salvador.
Redkin, Mark Russian; 1908– ; photojournalist, World War II.
Regnault, Henri-Victor French; 1810–1878; physicist; photographer.
Reininger, Alon Israeli; 1947– ; photojournalist.
Renau, Josep Spanish; 1907–1982; photographer, socio-political photomontage.
Rentmeester, Co Dutch; 1936– ; photojournalist, *Life* staff.
Requillart, Bruno French; 1947– ; photographer.
Resnick, Marcia American; 1950– ; photographer, documentary portraits.
Ressler, Susan Rebecca American; 1949– ; photographer, documentary; teacher.
Reusens, Robert Belgian; 1909–1981; photographer, portraits, fashion, stage.
Reuter, John American; 1953– ; photographer, mixed media.
Rev, Miklos Hungarian; 1906– ; photojournalist; teacher.
Revesz, Tamas Hungarian; 1946– ; photojournalist.
Rexroth, Nancy Louise American; 1946– ; photographer, subjective landscapes, still life.
Reynolds, Charles Barton American; 1935– ; photographer, nature; editor; musician.
Ricciardi, Mirella Kenyan; 1933– ; photographer, documentary, Africa.
Rice, Leland David American; 1940– ; photographer, formalist, color.
Richards, Eugene American; 1944– ; photojournalist.
Rickerby, Arthur American; 1921–1972; photojournalist, sports, *Life* staff.
Riebesehl, Heinrich German; 1938– ; photographer, subjective documentary.
Riefenstahl, Leni German; 1902– ; film maker, documentary; photographer, social documentary.
Ries, Henry American, b. Germany; 1917– ; photojournalist.
Riise, John Norwegian; 1885–1978; photographer, portraits.
Riss, Murray American, b. Poland; 1940– ; photographer; teacher.
Robbins, LeRoy American; 1904– ; photographer, social documentary; film maker.
Roberts, Bruce Stuart American; 1930– ; photographer, human condition, American south; educator.
Roberts, Joseph Baylor American; 1902– ; photojournalist, *National Geographic* staff.
Roberts, Martha American; 1919– ; photographer, documentary, American south.
Robinson, David American; 1936– ; photographer, experimental, movement; teacher.
Roca, Francesc Catala Spanish; 1922– ; photographer, documentary.

Rodrigues, Antonio Carlos Brazilian; 1944– ; photographer, social documentary, photo-essay.
Roentgen, Wilhelm Conrad German; 1845–1923; physicist, discovered x-rays; teacher.
Rogovin, Milton American; 1909– ; photographer, social documentary.
Roiter, Fulvio Italian; 1926– ; photographer; author.
Roitz, Charles J. American; photographer; teacher.
Ronis, Willy French; 1910– ; photographer, social documentary, Paris.
Root, Marcus Aurelius American; 1808–1888; photographer, daguerreotype, Philadelphia studio.
Rose, Ben American; 1916–1980; photographer, advertising; editor.
Rose-Pulham, Peter British; 1910–1956; photographer, fashion, advertising; painter.
Rosenblum, Walter American; 1919– ; photographer, documentary.
Rosenthal, Joe American; 1911– ; photographer, social documentary.
Rosskam, Edwin American; 1903– ; photographer, social documentary.
Rosskam, Louise American; 1910– ; photographer, social documentary.
Rossler, Jaroslav Czechoslovakian; 1902– ; photographer, portraits, abstract compositions.
Rotkin, Charles American; 1916– ; photographer, social documentary, low altitude aerial.
Routh, Robert D. American; 1921– ; educator; photographer.
Rowe, William Henry American; 1946– ; photographer; teacher.
Rowell, Galen American; 1940– ; photographer, nature, color.
Rozumalski, Ted American; 1931– ; press photographer.
Rubenstein, Meridel American; 1948– ; photographer, biographical portraits; teacher.
Rubinstein, Eva American; 1933– ; photographer, portraits, documentary; teacher.
Rubinstein, Susan R. American; 1946– ; photographer; teacher.
Rubinger, David Israeli; 1924– ; photojournalist.
Ruohomaa, Kosti S. American; 1914–1961; photographer, marine seascapes, New England scenes.
Ruscha, Edward American; 1937– ; painter; photographer, Los Angeles architecture; author.
Russell, A(ndrew) J(oseph) American; 1830–1902; photographer, American west, Pacific railroad; painter.
Russo, Marialba Italian; 1947– ; photographer, anthropological subjects, rituals, rites, customs.
Rutledge, Don American; 1930– ; photojournalist.
Ryumkin, Yakov Russian; 1913– ; photojournalist.

S

Saakow, Alexander Russian; 1941– ; photographer.
Sage, Linn American; 1937– ; photographer, documentary.
Salgado, Sebastiao Brazilian; 1944– ; photojournalist.
Salzmann, Laurence American; 1944– ; photographer, documentary; film maker.
Samaras, Lucas American, b. Greece; 1936– ; artist; photographer, manipulated SX-70.
Sandels, Karl Swedish; 1906– ; press photographer.
Sanders, Norman American; 1927– ; photographer; printer.
Sanders, Walter German; 1897– ; photojournalist, *Life* staff.
Sankova, Galina Russian; 1904– ; photojournalist.
Sarony, Napoleon Canadian; 1821–1896; photographer, studio portraits, stage personalities.
Sarno, Dick American; 1904– ; press photographer; photo director, *Hearst* newspapers, American Broadcasting Company.

Saudek, Jan Czechoslovakian; 1935– ; photographer, portraits; factory worker.

Saur, Francoise French; 1949– ; photographer.

Savage, Charles Roscoe British; 1832–1909; photographer, western American scenes, Salt Lake City.

Savage, Naomi American; 1927– ; photographer, various genres.

Savin, Mikhail Russian; 1915– ; photojournalist.

Sawada, Kyoichi Japanese; (not known)–1970; photojournalist.

Sawatari, Hajime Japanese; 1940– ; photographer, nudes.

Sawyer, Charles M. American; 1941– ; photographer; writer.

Scavullo, Francesco American; 1929– ; photographer, portraits, fashion.

Schad, Christian German; 1894–1982; artist; photographer, Dadaist, schadographs.

Schaewen, Deidi Von German; 1941– ; photographer, walls.

Scharf, David American; 1942– ; photographer; scientist.

Schawinsky, Xanti (Alexander) American, b. Switzerland; 1904–1979; artist; photographer, experimental, portraits; educator.

Schegelmann, Sinowij Russian; 1940– ; surgeon; photographer.

Scheier, Peter German; 1906–1979; photographer, advertising, industry, architecture.

Scheler, Max German; photojournalist; editor.

Scherman, David American; 1916– ; photojournalist, *Life* staff, scenic; editor; writer.

Scherschel, Frank American; 1907–1981; photojournalist, *Life* staff.

Scherschel, Joe American; 1920– ; photographer, *National Geographic* staff.

Schlessinger, Peter M. American; 1946– ; photographer; educator.

Schmidt, Michael German; 1945– ; photographer, social documentary, Berlin.

Schneider, Martin American; 1926– ; photojournalist; environmentalist.

Schneiders, Toni German; 1920– ; photographer, urban landscapes, Subjectivist, Fotoform.

Schrager, Victor American; 1950– ; photographer, subjective still life; gallery director.

Schuh, Gotthard Swiss; 1897–1969; photographer, documentary, human concerns.

Schulke, Flip American; 1930– ; photojournalist, documentary, underwater; film maker.

Schulman, Sam American; 1906–1980; press photographer.

Schultz, Harald Brazilian; 1909–1966; photographer, documentary, ethnographic.

Schulze, John American; 1915– ; photographer; teacher.

Schurmann, Wilhelm German; 1946– ; photographer, architecture, portraits, still life.

Schutzer, Paul American; 1930–1967; photojournalist, *Life* staff.

Schwartz, Mark Coffey American; 1956– ; photographer, still life.

Schwerin, Ricarda Israeli, b. Germany; 1912– ; photographer.

Scianna, Ferdinando Italian; 1943– ; photojournalist.

Secchiaroli, Tazio Italian; 1925– ; photojournalist, celebrities.

Seed, Brian British; 1929– ; photojournalist.

Seed, Suzanne American; 1940– ; photographer, experimental techniques.

Seeley, George American; 1880–1955; photographer, pictorialist.

Segal, Patrick French; 1947– ; photojournalist; author.

Semak, Michael William Canadian; 1934– ; photographer, social issues; teacher.

Senn, Paul Swiss; 1901–1953; photojournalist; graphic designer.

Sexton, John American; 1953– ; photographer, nature; teacher.

Sha Fei Chinese; –1950; photojournalist.

Shagin, Ivan Russian; 1904– ; photojournalist.

Shahn, Ben American, b. Lithuania; 1898–1969; painter; photographer, documentary, FSA.

Shaikhet, Arkadi (Samoilovich) Russian; 1898–1959; photojournalist, human concerns.

Sharp, Vincent Canadian; 1937– ; photographer.

Shemtov, Igael Israeli; 1952– ; photographer; teacher.

Sheridan, Sonia Landy American; 1925– ; photographer; painter; teacher.

Sherman, Cindy American; contemporary photographer, self-portraits.

Shi Shaohua Chinese; (contemporary); photojournalist.

Shilinski, Michail Russian; 1950– ; photographer.

Shinoyama, Kishin Japanese; 1940– ; photographer, portraits, nudes, interiors.

Shirikawa, Yoshikazu Japanese; 1935– ; photographer, nature, landscapes, mountains.

Shishkin, Arkadii Russian; 1899– ; photographer, social documentary, farming.

Shook, M. Melissa American; 1939– ; photographer, autobiographical; teacher.

Shore, Stephen American; 1947– ; photographer, townscapes, color.

Shwachman, Irene American; 1915– ; photographer, social documentary, architecture; teacher.

Sichov, Vladimir Russian; 1945– ; photojournalist.

Sieff, Jeanloup French; 1933– ; photographer, fashion, nudes, landscapes.

Siegel, Adrian American; 1898–1978; musician; photographer, portraits, musicians, stage personalities.

Sievers, Ed American; 1932– ; photographer, social landscapes; teacher.

Sikora, Tomasz Polish; 1948– ; photographer.

Silk, George American; 1916– ; photojournalist, sports, color.

Silverstone, Marilyn American; 1929– ; photojournalist.

Silverthorne, Jeffrey Kim American; 1946– ; teacher; photographer.

Silvy, Camille French; (active) 1859–1869; photographer, studio portraits.

Simon, Michael American, b. Hungary; 1936– ; photographer; educator.

Singh, Raghubir Indian; 1942– ; photojournalist, color, Ganges.

Sisson, Robert American; 1923– ; photographer, science, nature, *National Geographic* staff.

Sisto, Ernie American; 1904– ; press photographer.

Sjostedt, Ulf Swedish; 1935– ; photographer; editor; author.

Skoff, Gail American; 1949– ; photographer, landscapes; teacher.

Skoglund, Sandy American; 1946– ; photographer, still life sets, fabricated scenes.

Skrebneski, Victor American; 1929– ; photographer, fashion, portraits.

Slavin, Neal American; 1941– ; photographer, group portraits, color.

Sloan-Theodore, Lynn American; 1945– ; photographer; teacher.

Small, Rena American; 1954– ; photographer; teacher.

Smelow, Boris Russian; 1951– ; photographer, still life, cityscapes.

Smith, Beuford American; 1939– ; photographer.

Smith, Bradley American; 1910– ; photographer, nature, landscapes; author.

Smith, Edwin British; 1912–1971; photographer, social documentary.

Smith, Henry Holmes American; 1909– ; photographer, experimental; educator.

Smith, J. Frederick American; 1917– ; photographer, fashion.

Smith, Keith A. American; 1938– ; photographer, male portraits; printmaker; teacher.

Smith, Luther American; 1950– ; photographer; teacher.

Smith, Michael A. American; 1942– ; photographer, landscapes.

Smith, Michael P. American; 1937– ; photographer, documentary.

Smokova-Vachova, Vera Czechoslovakian; 1940– ; photographer, nudes.
Smolan, Rick American; 1949– ; photojournalist.
Smoliansky, Gunnar Swedish; 1933– ; photographer, still life.
Smulders, Aivic Russian; 1940– ; photographer.
Snow, Michael Canadian; 1929– ; photographer; film maker.
Snowdon, Lord (Anthony Charles Robert Armstrong-Jones) British; 1930– ; photographer, social documentary; film maker; designer.
Snyder, Joel American; 1940– ; photographer; historian; curator.
Sochurek, Howard J. American; 1924– ; photojournalist, science, illustration, *Life* staff.
Solomon, Rosalind American; 1930– ; photographer, portraits, human condition, festivals.
Somoroff, Benjamin American; 1915–1984; photographer, still life, advertising.
Sonneman, Eve American; 1950– ; photographer, color, social still life.
Sonta, Virgilijus Lithuanian; 1952– ; engineer; photographer.
Soskin, Abraham Israeli, b. Russia; 1881–1963; photographer.
Sougez, Emmanuel French; 1889–1972; photographer, art and archaeology, still life; editor; art historian.
Soule, William Stinson American; 1836–1908; photographer, American Indians.
Spencer, Terence British; 1918– ; photojournalist.
Spender, Humphrey British; 1910– ; photographer, social documentary, *Picture Post* staff; painter; textile designer.
Spiegel, Ted American; photojournalist.
Splichal, Jan Czechoslovakian; 1929– ; photographer, photo montage.
Spuris, Egons Latvian; 1931– ; photographer.
Stackpole, Peter American; 1913– ; photojournalist, environment, underwater, *Life* staff.
Stage, John Lewis American; 1925– ; photographer, landscapes, personalities; editor.
Staller, Eric American; 1947– ; photographer, light-motion studies.
Staller, Jan Evan American; 1952– ; photographer, cityscapes, architecture.
Stanfield, James American; 1937– ; photojournalist, *National Geographic* staff.
Stankevic, Hubert Russian; 1928– ; photographer.
Stankevicius, Vytautas Lithuanian; 1942– ; photographer, advertising.
Stark, Ron American; 1944– ; photographer, still life, nudes.
Stecha, Pavel Czechoslovakian; 1944– ; photographer; teacher.
Steele-Perkins, Chris(topher) British; 1947– ; photojournalist, social documentary.
Steiger-Meister, Carla American; 1951– ; photographer, assemblage; teacher.
Stein, Fred American, b. Germany; 1909–1967; photojournalist.
Stein, Harvey American; 1941– ; photographer, photo essay; educator; author.
Steinberg, Vladimirovitch Jakob Russian; 1880–1942; photojournalist.
Sterenberg, Abraham Petrovitch Russian; 1894–1978; photographer, portraits, still life, landscapes.
Sterling, Joseph American; 1936– ; photographer, documentary, American adolescents.
Stern, Bert American; 1929– ; photographer, illustration, advertising.
Sternberger, Marcel American; 1899–1956; photographer, celebrity portraits.
Sternfeld, Joel Peter American; 1944– ; photographer, color, landscapes.
Stettner, Louis J. American; 1922– ; photographer, social documentary; writer.

Stewart, B. Anthony American; 1904–1977; photojournalist, *National Geographic* staff.
Stewart, James Arthur American; 1920– ; teacher; photographer.
Stiegler, Robert William American; 1938– ; photographer, teacher, film maker.
Stock, Dennis American; 1928– ; photographer, color; author; film maker.
Stoller, Ezra American; 1915– ; photographer, architecture.
Stone, Erika German; 1924– ; photojournalist.
Stone, John Benjamin British; 1836–1914; businessman; photographer, English manners and customs; politician.
Stoumen, Lou American; 1917– ; photographer, documentary, city streets.
Straukas, Vaclovas Lithuanian; 1923– ; photographer.
Strelisky, Lipot Hungarian; –1905; photographer, studio portraits, daguerreotype.
Strelow, Liselotte German; 1908–1981; photographer, portraits.
Stromholm, Christer Swedish; 1918– ; photographer, subjectivist, social studies.
Stromsten, Amy J. American; 1942– ; photographer, documentary; educator.
Stupakoff, Otto Brazilian; 1935– ; photographer, fashion, portraits.
Sturr, Edward Richard American; 1937– ; teacher; photographer.
Suda, Isser Japanese; 1940– ; photographer, social portraits.
Sudre, Jean-Pierre French; 1921– ; photographer, materiographies.
Sultan, Larry American; 1946– ; photographer; teacher.
Suna, Ilga Russian; 1931– ; designer; photographer.
Suprun, Alexander Russian; 1945– ; engineer; photographer.
Suschitzky, Wolf British, b. Austria; 1912– ; photographer, documentary, animals; cinematographer.
Sutcliffe, Frank Meadow British; 1853–1941; photographer, pictorialist, genre scenes, studio portraits; writer.
Sutkus, Antanas Lithuanian; 1939– ; photographer, portraits.
Swartz, Joel American; 1944– ; photographer; teacher; author.
Swedlund, Charles American; 1935– ; photographer; teacher.
Sykes, Homer Canadian; 1949– ; photographer, documentary, British customs.
Szabo, Stephen Lee American; 1940– ; photographer, landscapes; teacher.
Szasz, Suzanne American, b. Hungary; 1919– ; photographer, children.
Szczuka, Mieczyslaw Polish; 1898–1927; artist, constructivist; photographer, photomontage.
Szekessy, Karin German; 1939– ; photographer, nudes.
Szilasi, Gabor Canadian, b. Hungary; 1928– ; photographer, social portraiture, interiors.
Szubert, Awit Polish; 1837–1919; photographer, portraits, landscapes.

T

Taconis, Kryn Canadian, b. Holland; 1918–1979; photojournalist.
Tahara, Keiichi Japanese; 1951– ; photographer, windows.
Tas, Filip Belgian; 1918– ; photographer.
Tata, Sam Bejan Canadian, b. China; 1911– ; photojournalist, social documentary.
Tausk, Petr Czechoslovakian; 1927– ; photohistorian; author; photographer.
Taussig, H. Arthur American; 1941– ; teacher; photographer.
Taylor, Paul Schuster American; 1895– ; economist; photographer, field research document.
Teixeira, Evandro Salvadoran; 1935– ; photojournalist.

Tenneson, Joyce American; 1945– ; photographer, autobiographical.
Teres, Michael Jerome American; 1940– ; photographer; teacher.
Teske, Edmund American; 1911– ; photographer, fantasy portraits, landscapes; teacher.
Testa, Ron American; 1942– ; photographer.
Thomas, Lew American; 1932– ; photographer; publisher.
Thompson, Dody (Warren Weston) American; 1923– ; photographer; author.
Thorn-Thomsen, Ruth American; 1943– ; photographer; teacher.
Tice, George A. American; 1938– ; photographer, nature, master printer.
Till, Will South African; 1893–1971; photographer, landscapes.
Tischkowski, Pawel Russian; 1929– ; graphic designer; photographer.
Todd, Ronald James American; 1947– ; photographer, landscapes, figures, underwater.
Tomatsu, Shomei Japanese; 1930– ; photographer, social issues.
Tomiyama, Haruu Japanese; 1935– ; photojournalist.
Tonnies, Johan Goerg Heinrich Ludwig German; 1825–1903; porcelain painter; glass grinder; photographer, topographical studies.
Tooming, Peeter Estonian; 1939– ; photographer; cinematographer; journalist.
Torbert, Stephanie B. American; 1945– ; photographer.
Torosian, Michael Canadian; 1952– ; photographer, female portraits.
Toth, Istvan Hungarian; 1923– ; photographer.
Tourdjman, Georges French; 1935– ; photographer, illustration, fashion.
Traeger, Ronald American; 1937–1968; photographer.
Trager, Neil American; 1947– ; photographer; teacher.
Trager, Philip American; 1935– ; photographer, landscapes, architecture.
Trakhman, Mikhail Russian; 1918–1976; photojournalist, World War II.
Traub, Charles H. American; 1945– ; photographer, spontaneous portraits, social landscapes; teacher.
Traube, Alex American; 1945– ; photographer, autobiographical with text; teacher.
Treicis, Imant Russian; 1938– ; engineer; photographer.
Tress, Arthur American; 1940– ; photographer, surreal portraits, landscapes; author.
Tretick, Stanley American; 1921– ; photojournalist.
Trevor, Paul British; 1947– ; photographer.
Truax, Karen American; 1946– ; photographer; teacher.
Tsuchida, Hiromi Japanese; 1939– ; photographer, cultural documentary, Japan.
Tucker, Kay American; 1918– ; photographer, found objects.
Tucker, Nicolas British; 1948– ; photographer, portraits, nudes.
Tucker, Toba American; 1935– ; photographer, portaits.
Tuckerman, Jane American; 1947– ; photographer; teacher.
Tugalev, Leonid Russian; 1945– photographer.
Tuggener, Jakob Swiss; 1904– ; photographer, social scenes, industry.
Turbeville, Deborah American; 1937– ; photographer, fashion.
Turner, John B. New Zealander; 1943– ; teacher; editor; photographer.
Turner, Pete American; 1934– ; photographer, illustration.
Tweedy-Holmes, Karen American; 1942– ; photographer, varied subject matter; editor.
Tyomin, Viktor Russian; 1908– ; photojournalist.

U

Ueda, Shoji Japanese; 1913– ·; photographer; teacher.

Ulmann, Doris American; 1884–1934; photographer, portraits.
Underwood, Bert Elias American; 1862– ; news photographer; businessman, Underwood and Underwood.
Underwood, Elmer American; 1860–1947; news; photographer; businessman, Underwood and Underwood.
Unwalla, J. Indian; (contemporary); photographer, fashion, advertising.
Urban, Joao Aristeu Brazilian; 1943– ; photographer, social documentary.
Uribe, Jesus Sanchez Mexican; 1948– ; photographer.
Ustinov, Alexander Russian; 1909– ; photojournalist.
Uzlyan, Alexander Russian; 1908– ; photojournalist, World War II.
Uzzle, Burk American; 1938– ; photojournalist.

V

Vachon, John Felix American; 1914–1975; photojournalist, *Look* staff.
Vail, Roger American; 1945– ; photographer; teacher.
Vaitkevicius, Alvydas Lithuanian; 1942– ; engineer; photographer.
Van Dyke, Willard American; 1906– ; photogapher, portraits, nature, landscapes; film maker; teacher.
van Rheede van Oudtshoorn, Albert South African; 1894–1959; photographer, pictorialist, landscape, seascape; astronomer.
Van Vechten, Carl American; 1880–1964; photographer, portraits.
Van der Elsken, Eduard Dutch; 1925– ; photographer, social themes.
Verger, Pierre French; 1902– ; photographer, documentary, anthropological; author.
Vestal, David American; 1924– ; photographer; writer; teacher.
Vicente, Carlos Fadon Brazilian; 1945– ; photographer, photo-essay, urban environment.
Vilatoba, Joan Spanish; 1878–1954; photographer, pictorialist.
Villet, Grey American; 1927– ; photojournalist, *Life* staff.
Vishinath Indian; (active) 1875–1910; photographer, landscapes.
Vogt, Christian Swiss; 1946– ; photographer, subjective portraits, landscapes.
Von Gagern, Verena German; 1946– ; photographer.
Von Gloeden, Wilhelm German; 1856–1931; photographer, male nude; painter.
von Schaewen, Deidi German; 1941– ; photographer, documentary.
Von Wangenheim, Chris German; 1942–1981; photographer, fashion.

W

Wachstein, Alison Ehrlich American; 1947– ; photographer, social issues; author.
Wahlberg, Arne Swedish; 1905– ; photographer, portraits, advertising; teacher.
Waldman, Max American; 1919–1981; photographer, performing arts.
Walker, (Harold) Todd American; 1917– ; photographer, female nudes; teacher.
Walker, Hank American; 1922– ; photojournalist, *Life* staff.
Walker, Robert Canadian; 1945– ; photographer.
Walsh, John Australian; 1945– ; photographer, social documentary.
Warburg, J. C. (John Cimon) British; 1867–1931; photographer, pictorialist.
Ward, Fred American; 1935– ; photojournalist.

Warhol, Andy American; 1928– ; painter, photographic image; film maker; author.

Washburn, (Henry) Bradford, Jr. American; 1910– ; museum director; mountaineer; photographer, documentary, aerial, remote mountain regions.

Wasserman, Cary American; 1939– ; photographer, color.

Wassiljew, Juri Russian; 1939– ; engineer; photographer.

Wayman, Stanley American; 1927–1973; photojournalist, *Life* staff.

Webb, Alex American; 1952– ; photojournalist.

Webb, Todd American; 1905– ; photographer, social documentary.

Weber, Bruce American; 1946– ; photographer.

Wegman, William American; 1942– ; photographer, autobiographical, social commentary, humor.

Weiss, Murray American; 1926– ; photographer, social landscapes; teacher.

Weiss, Sabine French; 1924– ; photographer.

Wells, Lynton American; 1940– ; photographer, experimental, mixed media.

Wells-Witteman, Alisa American; 1929– ; photographer, autobiographical subjects.

Welpott, Jack American; 1923– ; photographer, social landscapes, industrial architecture, portraits; educator.

Welty, Eudora American; 1909– ; writer; photographer.

Wessel, Henry, Jr. American; 1942– ; photographer, social landscapes.

West, Edward American; 1949– ; photographer; teacher.

Whitmore, James American; 1926– ; photojournalist, *Life* staff.

Widmer, Gwen American; 1945– ; photographer; teacher.

Williams, Maynard Owen American; 1888–1963; photojournalist, *National Geographic* staff.

Williams, Stephen Guion American; 1941– ; photographer.

Wilse, Anders Beer Norwegian; 1865–1949; photographer, documentary.

Wilson, George Washington British; 1823–1893; photographer, studio portraits, landscapes, genre scenes; publisher.

Wilson, Marshall G. American; 1905– ; press photographer.

Wilson, Wallace American; 1947– ; photographer; teacher.

Windstrosser, Ludwig German; 1921– ; photographer, social documentary, industry.

Winningham, Geoff American; 1943– ; photographer, social documentary, Texas.

Wise, Kelly American; 1932– ; photographer, portraits; teacher; author.

Witkin, Joel-Peter American; 1939– ; photographer.

Witow, Vladimir Russian; 1936– ; chemical engineer; photographer.

Wittick, Ben (George Benjamin) American; 1845–1903; photographer, documentary, American Indians, railroad; ethnologist.

Wolcott, Marion Post American; 1910– ; photographer, documentary.

Wolff, Bernard Pierre American, b. France; 1930– ; photographer, urban landscapes, city streets; graphic designer.

Wolff, Paul American, b. Germany; 1887–1951; photojournalist; photographer, industry.

Wols (Alfred Orto Wolfgang Schulze) German; 1913–1951; photographer; painter.

Wood, Roger British, b. India; 1920– ; photographer, travel subjects, dance.

Worth, Don American; 1924– ; photographer, plants; teacher.

Wu Yinxian Chinese; 1900– ; photographer.

Y

Yamahata Yosuke Japanese; 1917–1956; photojournalist, Hiroshima.

Yamamura, Gasho Japanese; 1939– ; photographer.

Yavno, Max American; 1911– ; photographer, social documentary.

Yevzerikhin, Emmanuel Russian; 1911– ; photojournalist; lecturer.

Ylla (Camilla Koffler) American, b. Austria; 1911–1955; photographer, animals.

Yu Xunling Chinese; late 19th Century; photographer, imperial family portraits.

Z

Zelma, Georgij Russian; 1906– ; photojournalist, social documentary, Soviet Central Asia; filmmaker.

Zerkowitz, Adolf Spanish; 1894–1972; photographer, cityscape, urban landscape.

Zheng Jingkang Chinese; (active 1940s); photojournalist.

Zhou Yaoguang Chinese; (contemporary); photojournalist.

Zimmerman, John American; 1929– ; photojournalist.

Zimmerman, Philip B. American; 1951– ; photographer.

Ziziunas, Algimantas Lithuanian; 1940– ; photojournalist.

Zulpo–Dane, Bill American; 1938– ; photographer, social landscapes; teacher.

Zwart, Piet Dutch; 1885–1977; photographer, still life, advertising; architect; industrial designer; teacher.

Photographic Societies and Associations

The societies and associations listed below are concerned with various aspects of photography, its uses and applications. This selected list includes organizations which are likely to be of major interest to users of this Encyclopedia. Further listings may be found in directories of associations and societies, available in library reference departments, and in telephone directories and similar sources.

Advertising Photographers of America (APA)
118 E. 25th St., New York, NY 10010
Concerned with business practices and standards that improve the quality of advertising photography.

American Photographic Artisans Guild (APAG)
524 W. Shore Dr., Madison, WI 53715
Association of photographic color artists, retouchers, air brush artists, color correctors. laboratory technicians, receptionists, and professional photographers working for photographic businesses.

American Society of Magazine Photographers (ASMP)
[Former name of Society of Photographers in Communications. See that listing.]

American Society of Photographers (ASP)
P.O. Box 52836, Tulsa, OK 74158
Sponsors annual traveling exhibit of Masters' photographs (degrees awarded through Professional Photographers of America— see separate entry), and annual National Collegiate Youth Competition and Exhibit.

Architectural Photographers of America (APA)
% Gordon Schenck, Box 35203, Charlotte, NC 28235
Promotes understanding between photographers and architects, clients, builders, advertising agencies, and publishers through exchange of technical and aesthetic concepts.

Associated Photographers International (API)
Provides freelance and professional photographers with knowledge in all aspects of the field and acts as a collective voice for the freelance photographer; assists in locating markets, demonstrating professional techniques, and expanding creativity.

Association for Educational Communication and Technology
1136 Sixteenth St., NW, Washington, DC 20036
Specializes in the use of visual communications for classroom projects.

Association of Federal Photographers (AFP)
1213 Fern St., NW, Washington, DC 20012
Furthers the interests of federally employed photographers, photographic laboratory technicians, personnel in photographic supervisory positions, and related audiovisual specialists.

Association of International Photography Art Dealers (AIPAD)

60 E. 42nd St., New York, NY 10165

Members are galleries and private dealers working to promote high ethical standards, greater understanding of photography as art, and communication with the photographic community, and to encourage public support of art photography and increase the public's confidence in responsible photography dealers.

Association of Professional Color Laboratories (APCL)

3000 Picture Pl., Jackson, MI 49201

Establishes standards of quality and ethical business practice standards among professional laboratories working for professional photographers and individuals engaged in the manufacture, sale, and service of products and equipment for use in professional color laboratories.

Deutsche Gesellschaft für Photographie

Neumarkt 49, Cologne, West Germany

Evidence Photographers International Council (EPIC)

2040 Millburn Ave., Suite 306, Maplewood, NJ 07040

Aids in the worldwide advancement of forensic photography, assists in research and development of new techniques, enhances professional education, and informs members of new procedures.

Friends of Photography (FOP)

P.O. Box 500, Sunset Center, Carmel, CA 93921

Established to support and encourage serious, creative photography through the presentation, publication, and criticism of contemporary photographers' work.

International Congress on High-Speed Photography and Photonics (ICHSPP)

136 Garfield Ave., Janesville, WI 53545

Coordinates biennial congresses of international scope, publishes proceedings of each congress, and presents awards in high-speed photography and photonics.

International Fire Photographers Association (IFPA)

P.O. Box 201, Elmhurst, IL 60126

Promotes use of photography in the fire service and advances fire photography, and conducts courses on the use of visual aids and the preparation of public education programs.

International Museum Photographers Association (IMPA)

P.O. Box 30051, Bethesda Station, Washington, DC 20014

Auditing and accrediting body for individuals using photography as part of their job assignment in museums and similar institutions.

International Photo Optical Show Association (IPOSA)

1156 Ave. of the Americas, New York, NY 10036

Sponsors and produces photographic and video exhibitions which provide the opportunity for consumers to view a complete assortment of equipment, improve their skills, and increase their knowledge. Maintains a collection of over 1500 historical and contemporary photographs.

International Society for Photogrammetry

% Prof. Dr. Ing. L. Soliani, Instituto di Geodesia del Politechnico, Pza. Leonardo da Vinci 32, 20133 Milan, Italy

International Visual Literacy Association

National Center for Visual Literacy, Gallaudet College, Kendall Green, Washington, DC 20002

Emphasizes use of photography in teaching other subjects at all levels.

National Association of Photo Equipment Technicians (NAPET)

600 Mamaroneck Ave., Harrison, NY 10528

Develops cooperative programs for industry, government administrative agencies, and educational institutions and compiles detailed data on exports and imports of all types of photo products.

National Free Lance Photographers Association (NFLPA)

60 E. State St., Doylestown, PA 18901

Assists and cooperates with news media in obtaining photographs when regular coverage is unavailable and maintains photographic file from members for industry.

National Photographic Instructors Association

California State University Long Beach, Long Beach, CA 90840

Organization of high school and junior college instructors which emphasizes technical aspects of photography.

National Press Photographers Association (NPPA)

Box 1146, Durham, NC 27702

Association of professional news photographers and others whose occupation has a direct relationship with photo journalism, communication of news through photographic image through publication, television film, or theater screen.

North American Photonics Association (NAPhA)

% Joseph H. Owren, Marco Scientific, Inc., 1031H E. Duane Ave., Sunnyvale, CA 94086

Fosters programs designed to advance the technology of high-speed imagery in all areas of science and engineering.

Photo Marketing Association International (PMA)

3000 Picture Place, Jackson, MI 49201

Compiles statistics, offers placement service, and holds research programs for retailers of photographic equipment, film, and supplies and for firms developing and printing film.

Photographic Administrators, Inc. (PAI)
1150 Ave. of the Americas, New York, NY 10036
Activities concentrated mainly in New York City among persons associated with magazines, camera companies, and related businesses in executive or administrative capacities other than the taking of photographs or performing of darkroom work.

Photographic Industry Council (PIC)
% Frank S. Pallo, Eastman Kodak Co.,
343 State St., Rochester, NY 14650
Operates as a channel of communication and a clearinghouse for industry-wide projects; composed of societies and trade associations related to the photographic industry.

Photographic Manufacturers and Distributors Association (PMDA)
866 United Nations Plaza, New York, NY 10017
Composed of manufacturers, wholesalers, distributors, and importers of photographic equipment; sponsors a number of awards within the photographic industry.

Photographic Society of America (PSA)
2005 Walnut St., Philadelphia, PA 19103
Presents awards, maintains speakers bureau, and sponsors competitions for amateur, advanced amateur, and professional photographers, and camera clubs.

Pictorial Photographers of America (PPA)
% St. John's Lutheran Church, 83 Christopher St.,
New York, NY 10014
Purpose is to aid members in perfecting their photographic techniques through individual print and slide analysis, and field trips, for amateur and professional photographers.

Picture Agency Council of America (PACA)
% Joseph D. Barnell, Shostal Associates, 60 E. 42nd St.,
New York, NY 10165
Objectives are to unite the picture agencies of America into a cohesive organization and to foster common business and financial interests, to achieve uniformity in business practices, and to establish ethical business standards.

Professional Photographers of America (PPA)
1090 Executive Way, Des Plaines, IL 60018
Professional society of portrait, commercial, and industrial photographers which sponsors Winona School of Professional Photography and presents awards, maintains speakers bureau, and sponsors competitions.

Professional School Photographers of America (PSPA)
P.O. Box 220353, Charlotte, NC 28222
Encourages exchange of ideas and cooperation in overall promotion of photography among firms engaged in the photographing and/or processing of school photographs.

Royal Photographic Society of Great Britain (RPS)
National Center of Photography, The Octagon, Millson St.,
Bath BA1 1DN, England

Société Française de Photographie et de Cinématographie
9 Rue Montalembert, Paris VIIe, France

Society for Photographic Education (SPE)
Box 1651, FDR Post Office, New York, NY 10022
Organization of college photography instructors which emphasizes historical and esthetic aspects of photography.

Society of Photographers in Communications (ASMP)
[Formerly American Society of Magazine Photographers]
205 Lexington Ave., New York, NY 10016
Works to evolve trade practices for the photographer in the communications fields.

Society of Photographic Scientists and Engineers (SPSE)
7003 Kilworth Ln., Springfield, VA 22151
Organization of individuals who apply photography to science, engineering, and industry.

Society of Photo-Technologists (SPT)
International, professional society of camera repair technicians.

Society of Teachers of Professional Photography
[affiliate of Professional Photographers of America]
172 Marble Drive, Rochester, NY 14615
Organization of professional teachers of photography.

SPIE—International Society for Optical Engineering
P.O. Box 10, 405 Fieldston Rd., Bellingham, WA 98225
Technical society dedicated to advancing engineering and scientific applications of optical, electro-optical, fiber-optic, laser, and photographic instrumentation systems and technology.

Wedding Photographers International (WPI)
P.O. Box 545, Ben Franklin Station, Washington, DC 20044
Goals are to promote artistic and technical standards among wedding photographers and photographers employed at general photography.

United States Press and News Photographers Associations

Most major cities have local organizations of press and newspaper photographers. The listing below is by no means comprehensive:

American Racing Association, Westport, CT
Atlanta Press Photographers Association, Atlanta, GA
Boston Press Photographers Association, Inc., Boston, MA
California Press Photographers Association, Sacramento, CA
Chicago Press Photographers Association, Chicago, IL
Colorado Press Photographers Association, Denver, CO
Colorado-West Press Photographers Association, Delta, CO
Connecticut News Photographers Association, Bristol, CT
Copperstate Press Photographers Association, Tempe, AZ
Dakotas Press Photographers Association, Fargo, ND
Houston-Gulf Coast News Photographers Association, Houston, TX
Illinois Press Photographers Association, Evergreen Park, IL
Indiana News Photographers Association, Indianapolis, IN

Michigan Press Photographers Association, Grand Rapids, MI
Milwaukee Press Photographers Association, Cudahy, WI
Nebraska Press Photographers Association, Lincoln, NE
New Jersey Press Photographers Association, Lambertville, NJ
New York Press Photographers Association, New York, NY
Ohio News Photographers Association, Bowling Green, OH
Oklahoma News Photographers Association, Ada, OK
Pennsylvania Press Photographers Association, Lansdale, PA
Puget Sound Press Photographers Association, Bothell, WA
Rose City Press Photographers, Salem, OR
South Florida News Photographers Association, Miami, FL
United States Senate Press Photography Gallery, Washington, DC
Utah-Idaho Press Photographers Association, Salt Lake City, UT
White House News Photographers Association, Washington, DC

Bibliography

Bibliography

This bibliography lists works that provide an immediate supplement to the articles in the Encyclopedia, and especially works that include extensive bibliographies or reference lists of additional sources. Preference has been given to works that are currently in print, or to out of print works that are likely to be readily available in libraries. The bibliography places an emphasis on the history and the scientific/technical applications of photography because material in these areas is less likely to be easily located by the general reader than material in such areas as biography or picture-taking techniques. Space restrictions make it impossible to include biographies and autobiographies, collections of photographs by individuals or on specific subjects or themes, or handbooks and manuals on specific procedures or equipment. Indeed, simply to list one work for each individual for whom there is a biographical article in the Encyclopedia would have required more space than is available for the entire bibliography. Biographies, picture collections, and instructional works can easily be located by consulting the catalog of any major library under the name or the topic of interest. A second source is the annual *Subject Guide to Books in Print* (R. R. Bowker Company), available for use at libraries and many bookstores. The current *Subject Guide* lists nearly 3,000 books in some 100 "Photo-" categories, and perhaps 1,000 more books in related categories (e.g., "Astronomical Photography," "Cameras," "Color Photography"). The photography catalogs of the publishers listed below constitute a third source of additional titles.

The bibliography is divided into the following categories:

Art; Aesthetics; Criticism; Social Import
Basic Techniques; Facilities
Collections; Collecting; Preservation
Color
Early, Special, and Alternative Processes/Techniques
General Applications
History
Miscellaneous
Original Sources (Reprints, Facsimile Editions, Anthologies)
Periodicals
Reference
Scientific, Technical, and Specialized Applications
Theory, Science, and Principles

The *Color* category lists works on the history, theory, and techniques of that subject; for other subjects various works are generally listed in separate categories (e.g., *History; Original Sources;* and the techniques and applications categories). The *Periodicals* category includes publications for the amateur and photographic generalist, and a number of specialized scientific publications. The latter are included to help guide the reader who needs highly specialized information to appropriate sources. The same rationale accounts for the inclusion of certain advanced or very specialized works in the category on scientific and related applications of photography. Of selected foreign periodicals, only those with English texts or summaries are included. The *Miscellaneous* category lists works on the legal aspects of photography, on vision and perception, and on a number of other topics. The *Collections, etc.* category includes guides to and indexes of several major photographic collections. In each category, titles are listed alphabetically, without regard for initial articles ("The," "An," "A," etc.).

A great many publishers offer books that are collections of photographs, or a few titles related to photographers and photography. The following publishers issue the majority of books dealing with the art, techniques, history, and people of photography; their catalogs of photographic books are available at many libraries, or may be obtained directly. The primary sources of books on photographic equipment and techniques are Morgan and Morgan, H. P. Books, Focal Press, Amphoto/Watson-Guptill, Kodak, and Light Impressions Corporation.

Amphoto/Watson-Guptill Publishing Co., Inc., 1515 Broadway, New York, NY 10036.
Aperture, Inc., Elm Street, Millerton, NY 12546.
Arno Press, 3 Park Avenue, New York, NY 10016.
Dover Publications, Inc., 180 Varick Street, New York, NY 10014.
Focal Press, Inc., Butterworth Publishers, 10 Tower Office Park, Woburn, MA 01801.
Eastman Kodak Co., [Pub. No. L-5, Index to Kodak Information], Department 412-L, 343 State Street, Rochester, NY 14650.
H. P. Books, P.O. Box 5367, Tucson, AZ 85703.
Light Impressions Corp., Box 3012, Rochester, NY 14614.
Morgan and Morgan, Inc., 145 Palisades Street, Dobbs Ferry, NY 10522.
Prentice-Hall, Inc., Englewood Cliffs, NJ 07632.
Van Nostrand Reinhold Co., Inc., 135 West 50th Street, New York, NY 10020.

Art; Aesthetics; Criticism; Social Import
(See also: *History; Original Sources*)

Art and Photography. Rev. ed. Aaron Scharf. Hammondsworth, Middlesex, England: Penguin Books, Ltd., 1974.
The Art of Photography. Life Library of Photography. New York: Time-Life Books, Inc., 1982.
Avant-Garde Photography in Germany, 1901–1939. Van Deren Coke. New York: Pantheon Books, 1982.
Before Photography: Painting and the Invention of Photography. Peter Galassi. Museum of Modern Art. Boston: New York Graphic Society, 1981.
Camera Work: A Critical Anthology. Jonathan Green, ed. Millerton, NY: Aperture, 1973.
Circles of Confusion: Film Photography, Video; Texts 1968–1980. Hollis Frampton. Rochester, NY: Visual Studies Workshop Press, 1983.
Creative Photography: Aesthetic Trends, 1839–1960. Helmut Gernsheim. London: Faber and Faber, Ltd., 1962.
Counterparts: Form and Emotion in Photographs. Weston H. Naef. New York: Metropolitan Museum of Art, 1982.
Cubism and American Photography, 1910–1930. John Pultz and Catherine B. Scallen. Williamston, MA: Sterling and Francine Clark Art Institute, 1981.
Diana and Nikon: Essays on the Esthetic of Photography. Janet Malcolm. Boston: David R. Godine, 1980.
Family Photographs: Content, Meaning and Effect. Julia Hirsch. Oxford and New York: Oxford University Press, 1981.
The Grotesque in Photography. A. D. Coleman. New York: Summit Books, Simon and Schuster, 1977.
The Influence of Photography on American Landscape Painting, 1839–1880. Elizabeth Lindquist-Cock. New York: Garland Publishing Company, Inc., 1977.

Light Readings: A Photography Critic's Writings, 1968–1978. A. D. Coleman. New York: Oxford University Press, 1979.
Looking At Photographs. John Szarkowski. Museum of Modern Art. Boston: Little, Brown and Co., 1973.
Mirror Image: The Influence of the Daguerreotype on American Society. Richard Rudisill. Albuquerque: University of New Mexico Press, 1971.
On Photography. Susan Sontag. New York: Farrar, Straus and Giroux, 1977.
The Painter and the Photograph: From Delacroix to Warhol. Rev. ed. Van Deren Coke. Albuquerque: University of New Mexico Press, 1972.
The Photographer's Eye. John Szarkowski. Museum of Modern Art. Garden City, NY: Doubleday and Co., 1966.
Photography and Fascination. Max Kozloff. Danbury, NH: Addison House, 1979.
Photography and Society. Gisèle Freund. Trans. Richard Dunn et al. Boston: David R. Godine, 1980.
Photography As a Fine Art. Charles H. Caffin. [Reprint of 1901 ed.] Dobbs Ferry, NY: Morgan and Morgan, 1981.
Photomontage: Photography as Propaganda. Dawn Ades. New York: Pantheon Books, Random House, Inc., 1976.
Time in a Frame: Photography and the Nineteenth-Century Mind. Alan Thomas. New York: Schocken Books, Inc., 1977.
The Valiant Knights of Daguerre: Selected Critical Essays on Photography and Profiles of Photographic Pioneers by Sadakichi Hartmann. Harry W. Lawton, George Knox, eds. Berkeley: University of California Press, 1978.
Visual Communication and the Graphic Arts: Photographic Technologies in the Nineteenth Century. Estelle Jussim. New York: R. R. Bowker Co., 1974.

Basic Techniques; Facilities
(See also: *Color*)

The Art of Black and White Enlarging. David Vestal. New York: Harper and Row, 1984.
Basic Photography. New, rev., 4th ed. Michael Langford. London and Boston: Focal Press, 1978.
Basic Photography for the Graphic Arts. Kodak Publication No. Q-1. Rochester, NY: Eastman Kodak Co., 1982.
Black-and-White Darkroom Technique. Hubert C. Birnbaum. Kodak Publication No. KW-15. Rochester, NY: Eastman Kodak Co., 1981.
The Book of Close-Up Photography. Heather Angel. London: Ebury Press, 1983.
Building a Home Darkroom. Ray Miller. Kodak Publication No. KW-14. Rochester, NY: Eastman Kodak Co., 1981.
The Camera: The New Ansel Adams Photography Series, Book 1. Ansel Adams. Boston: New York Graphic Society, 1980.
The Craft of Photography. Rev. ed. David Vestal. New York: Harper and Row, 1978.
The Darkroom Book. Algis Balsys and Liliane DeCock Morgan, eds. Dobbs Ferry, NY: Morgan and Morgan, 1980.
The Darkroom Handbook: A Complete Guide to the Best Design, Construction, and Equipment. Updated ed. Dennis Curtin and Joe DeMaio. New York: Van Nostrand Reinhold Co., 1982.
Electronic Flash. Lester Lefkowitz. Kodak Publication No. KW-12. Rochester, NY: Eastman Kodak Co., 1981.
Exposure Manual. 4th ed. Jack F. Dunn and George L. Wakefield. Hertfordshire, England: Fountain Press, 1981.

Field Photography: Beginning and Advanced Techniques. Alfred A. Blaker. San Francisco: W. H. Freeman and Co., 1976.

Handbook for Contemporary Photography. 4th ed. Arnold H. Gassan. Rochester, NY: Light Impressions Corp., 1977.

The Manual of Close-Up Photography. Lester Lefkowitz. New York: Amphoto, 1979.

The Negative: The New Ansel Adams Photography Series, Book 2. Ansel Adams. Boston: New York Graphic Society, 1981.

Photography: Adapted from the LIFE Library of Photography. Barbara and John Upton, eds. New York: Little, Brown and Co., 1976.

Photolab Design. Kodak Publication No. K-13. Rochester, NY: Eastman Kodak Co., 1978.

The Print: The New Ansel Adams Photography Series, Book 3. Ansel Adams. Boston: New York Graphic Society, 1983.

Techniques of Photographic Lighting. New ed. Norm Kerr. New York: Watson-Guptill Publications, Inc., 1982.

Using Filters. Kodak Publication No. KW-13. Rochester, NY: Eastman Kodak Co., 1981.

View Camera Techniques. 4th ed. Leslie Stroebel. Boston: Focal Press, 1980.

Collections; Collecting; Preservation

America, 1935–1946: Guide and Subject Index to the Photographs of the Farm Security Administration and the Office of War Information. Teaneck, NJ: Somerset House, nd.

Archives and Manuscripts: Conservation. Mary Lynn Ritzenthaler. Basic Manual Series. Chicago: Society of American Archivists, 1983.

The Photograph Collector's Guide. Lee D. Witkin and Barbara London. New York: Little, Brown & Co., 1980.

A Bibliography of Photographic Processes, Their Conservation and Storage. Robert Deane. Canberra, Australia: Australian National Gallery, 1981.

Cameras, the Facts: A Collector's Guide 1957–1964. Focal editorial staff. London and Boston: Focal Press, 1982.

Caring for Photographs: Display, Storage, and Restoration. Life Library of Photography. New York: Time-Life Books, 1972.

A Century of Cameras. Rev. ed. Eaton S. Lothrop, Jr. Dobbs Ferry, NY: Morgan and Morgan, 1981.

Collection, Use and Care of Historical Photographs. Robert A. Weinstein and Larry Booth. Nashville. TN: American Association for State and Local History, 1977.

The Collector's Guide to Antique Cameras. Michel Auer. Wiltshire, England: Hilmarton Manor Press, 1981.

Directory of British Photographic Collections. John Wall. New York: Camera/Graphic Press, 1977.

Guide to Canadian Photographic Archives. Alain Clavet. Ottawa, Canada: Public Archives, Canada, 1979.

Guide to the Special Collections of Prints and Photographs in the Library of Congress. Paul Vanderbilt, ed. Washington, DC: Library of Congress, 1955.

Index to American Photographic Collections. James McQuaid and Paulette P. Wilson, eds. Boston: G. K. Hall and Co., 1982.

Jason Schneider on Camera Collecting. Books I and II. Jason Schneider. Des Moines, IA: Wallace-Homestead Book Co., 1976.

The Julien Levy Collection, Starting with Atget. Chicago: The Art Institute of Chicago, 1976.

The Life of a Photograph: Archival Processing, Matting, Framing and Storage. Laurence E. Keefe, Jr. and Dennis Inch. Boston: Focal Press, 1984.

The Photograph Collector's Resource Directory. Peter H. Falk, ed. New York: Photographic Arts Center, 1983.

Photographs of the Farm Security Administration: An Annotated Bibliography, 1930–1980. Penelope Dixon. New York: Garland Publishing, Inc., 1983.

Photography Galleries and Selected Museums: A Survey and International Directory. Max and Tina Lent. Venice, CA: The Garlic Press, 1978.

Photography Index: A Guide to Reproductions. Pamela Jeffcott Parry, comp. Westport, CT: Greenwood Press, Inc., 1980.

Photos at the Archives. Charles E. Magoon. New York: Macmillan Publishing Co., 1981.

Pictorial Americana: A Select List of Photographic Negatives in the Prints and Photographs Division of the Library of Congress. Washington, DC: Library of Congress, 1955.

Preservation of Photographs. Kodak Publication, No. F30. Rochester, NY: Eastman Kodak Co., 1979.

Storing, Handling, and Preserving Polaroid Photographs: A Guide. Cambridge, MA: Polaroid Corp., 1983.

World Photography Sources. David Bradshaw and Catherine Hahn. Flemington, NJ: Directories Publishing Co., Inc., 1983.

Color

Basic Color: An Interpretation of the Ostwald Color System. Egbert Jacobson. Chicago: Paul Theobald, 1948.

Basic Color for the Graphic Arts. Kodak Publication No. Q-7. Rochester, NY: Eastman Kodak Co., 1981.

The Basic Illustrated Color Darkroom Book. 2 vols. Bob Nadler. Englewood Cliffs, NJ: Prentice-Hall, Inc., 1982.

Color. Life Library of Photography. New York: Time-Life Books, 1970.

Color Essence and Logic. Rolf Kuehni. New York: Van Nostrand Reinhold, 1983.

Color Primer 1 and 2. New ed. Richard Zakia and Hollis N. Todd. Dobbs Ferry, NY: Morgan and Morgan, 1974.

The Color Print Book: A Survey of Contemporary Color Photographic Printmaking Methods. Arnold Gassan. Rochester, NY: Light Impressions Corp., 1980.

Color Printing Techniques. Vernon Iuppa and John Smallwood. Kodak Publication No. KW-16. Rochester, NY: Eastman Kodak Co., 1981.

Color Vision. Committee on Vision. Washington, DC: National Academy Press, 1973.

Colour Photography: The First Hundred Years, 1840–1940. Brian Coe. London: Ash and Grant, 1978.

Dye Transfer Made Easy. Mindy Beede. New York: Watson-Guptill Publications, Inc., 1981.

Eye, Film and Camera in Color Photography. Ralph M. Evans [1959]. Melbourne, FL: Robert E. Krieger Publishing Co., Inc., 1979.

A Grammar of Color. Albert H. Munsell. New York: Van Nostrand Reinhold Publishing Co., 1969.

History of Color Photography. 2d ed. Joseph S. Friedman. Introduction and appendix by Lloyd E. Varden. London: Focal Press, 1968.

History of Three-Color Photography. E. J. Wall [1925]. Boston: Focal Press, 1970.

Human Color Vision. New ed. Robert H. Boynton. New York: Holt, Rinehart and Winston, 1979.

Introduction to Color Photographic Processing. Kodak Publication No. J-3. Rochester, NY: Eastman Kodak Co., 1978.

Munsell Book of Color: Atlas of the Munsell Color System. [Various eds.]. Baltimore, MD: Munsell Color Co., Inc.

The Perception of Color. Ralph M. Evans. New York: John Wiley and Sons-Interscience, 1974.

The Principles of Harmony and Contrast of Colors and Their Application to the Arts. Michel E. Chevreul [1st ed., 1839]. Trans. [from the French] by Faber Birren. New York: Garland Publishing, 1977.

The Reproduction of Color in Photography, Printing and Television. 3d ed. R. W. G. Hunt. Hertfordshire, England: Fountain Press, 1975.

The Science of Color. Committee on Colorimetry. New York: Optical Society of America, 1963.

Early, Special, and Alternative Processes/Techniques
(See also: *History; Original Sources*)

The Albumen and Salted Paper Book: The History and Practice of Photographic Printing, 1840–1895. James Reilly. Rochester, NY: Light Impressions Corp., 1980.

Alternative Photographic Processes: A Resource Manual for the Artist, Photographer, Craftsperson. Kent E. Wade. Dobbs Ferry, NY: Morgan and Morgan, 1978.

The Ambrotype Old and New. Thomas Feldvebel. Rochester, NY: Graphic Arts Research Center, Rochester Institute of Technology, 1980.

Artistic Photographic Processes. Suda House. New York: Watson-Guptill Publications, Inc., 1981.

Bibliography of Photographic Processes in Use Before 1880: Their Materials, Processing, and Conservation. M. Susan Barger. Rochester, NY: Technical and Education Center for the Graphic Arts, Rochester Institute of Technology, 1980.

The Book of Special Effects Photography. Michael Langford. New York: Alfred A. Knopf, Random House, 1982.

Breaking the Rules: A Photo Media Cookbook. Bea Nettles. Rochester, NY: Inky Press Productions, Light Impressions Corp., 1977.

Cassell's Encyclopedia of Photography. Bernard E. Jones, ed. [Reprint of 1911 edition]. New York: Arno Press, 1974.

Cliché-Verre: Hand-drawn, Light-painted. Elizabeth Glassman and Marilyn F. Symmes. Detroit, MI: Detroit Institute of Arts, 1980.

Creative Darkroom Techniques. 3d rev. ed. Kodak Publication No. AG-18. Rochester, NY: Eastman Kodak Co., 1983.

A Guide to Early Photographic Processes. Brian Coe and Mark Haworth-Booth. London: Hurt Wood Press in association with the Victoria and Albert Museum, 1983.

The Gum Bichromate Book: Contemporary Methods for Photographic Printmaking. David Scopick. Rochester, NY: Light Impressions Corp., 1978.

History and Practice of Carbon Processes. Luis Nadeau. Fredericton, New Brunswick, Canada: Atelier Luis Nadeau, 1982.

How to Create Photographic Special Effects. Allan Horvath. Tucson, AZ: H. P. Publishing Co., 1979.

The Keepers of Light: A History and Working Guide to Early Photographic Processes. William Crawford. Dobbs Ferry, NY: Morgan and Morgan, 1979.

The Platinum Print. John Hafey and Tom Shillea. Rochester, NY: Rochester Institute of Technology, 1979.

Photo Art Processes. Nancy Howell-Koehler. Worcester, MA: Davis Publications, Inc., 1980.

General Applications

Advertising Photography. Allyn Salomon. New York: Watson-Guptill Publications, Inc., 1982.

The Book of Nature Photography. Heather Angel. London: Ebury Press, 1982.

Documentary Photography. Life Library of Photography. New York: Time-Life Books, Inc., 1971.

Fashion: Theory. Carol DiGrappa, ed. Rochester, NY: Lustrum Press, Light Impressions Corp., 1980.

Landscape: Theory. Carol DiGrappa, ed. Rochester, NY: Lustrum Press, Light Impressions Corp., 1980.

Photojournalism. Life Library of Photography. New York: Time-Life Books, Inc., 1971.

Professional Photographic Illustration Techniques. Kodak Publication No. O-16. Rochester, NY: Eastman Kodak Co., 1977.

Professional Portrait Techniques. Kodak Publication No. O-4. Rochester, NY: Eastman Kodak Co., 1980.

Special Problems. Life Library of Photography. New York: Time-Life Books, Inc., 1971.

History
(See also: *Collections etc.; Color; Early, Special, Alternative, etc.; Reference, Bibliographies; Original Sources*)

The American Daguerreotype. Floyd and Marian Rinhart. Athens, GA: University of Georgia Press, 1981.

The Art of French Calotype: With a Critical Dictionary of Photographers. André Jammes and Eugenia Parry Janis. Princeton, NJ: Princeton University Press, 1983.

The Birth of Photography: The Story of the Formative Years, 1800–1900. Brian Coe. London: Ash and Grant; New York: Taplinger Publishing Co., 1976.

The Camera Obscura, A Chronicle. John H. Hammond. Bristol, England: Adam Hilger Ltd., 1981.

Cameras: From Daguerreotype to Instant Pictures. Brian W. Coe. New York: Crown Publishers, Inc., 1978.

Canadian Photography: 1839–1920. Ralph Greenhill and Alfred Birrell. Toronto, Canada: The Coach House Press, 1979.

Cartes-de-Visite in Nineteenth Century Photography. William C. Darrah. Gettysburg, PA: W. C. Darrah, 1981.

A Century of Japanese Photography. Japan Photographers Association. New York: Pantheon Books, Random House Publishing Co., 1981.

The Century of Photography: Niépce to Atget, from the Collection of André Jammes. Chicago: The Art Institute of Chicago, 1977.

A Chronology of Photography. 2d rev. ed. Arnold Gassan. Rochester, NY: Light Impressions Corp., 1981.

From Dry Plates to Ektachrome Film: A Story of Photographic Research. C. E. Kenneth Mees. New York: Ziff-Davis Publishing Co., 1961.

The Frozen Image: Scandinavian Photography. New York: Abbeville Press, 1982.

The History of Fashion Photography. Nancy Hall-Duncan. International Museum of Photography at George Eastman House. New York: Alpine Book Co., Inc. 1979.

The History of Photography. Josef Maria Eder. Trans. from 1932 German ed. by Edward Epstean. New York: Dover Publications, Inc., 1978.

The History of Photography: From 1830 to the Present Day. Rev. and enlarged 5th ed. Beaumont Newhall. The Museum of Modern Art. Boston: New York Graphic Society, 1982.

The History of Photography: From the Camera Obscura to the Beginnings of the Modern Era, 1685–1914. Helmut and Alison Gernsheim. New York: McGraw-Hill Book Co., 1969.

History of Photography: India 1840–1880. G. Thomas. Bangalore, India: Andhra Pradesh State Akademi of Photography, 1981.

La historia de la fotografía en España desde sus origenes hasta 1900. Lee Fontanella. Madrid: Ediciones El Viso, 1981.

Mirrors and Windows: American Photography since 1960. John Szarkowski. New York: Museum of Modern Art, 1978.

Modern Photojournalism: Origin and Evolution, 1910–1933. Tim N. Gidal. Photography: Men and Movement series. New York: Macmillan Publishing Co., Inc., 1973.

The Origins of Photography. Helmut Gernsheim. London: Thames and Hudson, 1982.

The Photographic Heritage of the Middle East. Paul E. Chevedden. Malibu, CA: Undeno Publications, 1981.

Photography: A Concise History. Ian Jeffrey. London: Thames and Hudson, 1981.

Photography and Architecture, 1839–1939. Richard Pare. New York: Callaway Editions, 1982.

Photography and the American Scene: A Social History, 1839–1899. Robert Taft. [Original ed. 1938]. New York: Dover Publications, Inc., 1964.

Photography as Artistic Experiment: From Fox Talbot to Moholy-Nagy. W. Rotzler. Photography: Men and Movements series. New York: Amphoto, 1976.

Photography: Essays and Images; Illustrated Readings in the History of Photography. Beaumont Newhall, ed. Boston: New York Graphic Society, 1981.

Photography: History of an Art. Jean-Luc Daval. New York: Skira/Rizzoli International Publications, Inc., 1982.

Photography in America: the Formative Years, 1839–1900. William Welling. New York: Thomas Y. Crowell Company, 1978.

The Picture History of Photography. Rev. ed. Peter Pollack. New York: Harry N. Abrams, 1970.

Pioneer Photographers of Brazil, 1840–1920. Gilberto Ferrez and Weston J. Naef. The Center for Inter-American Relations and the American Federation of the Arts. Seattle, WA: University of Washington Press, 1976.

Reality Recorded: Early Documentary Photography. Gail Buckland. Boston: New York Graphic Society, 1974.

The Snapshot Photograph: The Rise of Popular Photography, 1888–1939. Brian Coe and Paul Gates. London: Ash and Grant, 1977.

The Truthful Lens: A Survey of the Photographically Illustrated Book, 1844–1914. Lucien Goldschmidt and Weston J. Naef. New York: The Grolier Club, 1980.

Women of Photography: An Historical Survey. Margery Mann. San Francisco: San Francisco Museum of Art, 1975.

The World of Stereographs. William C. Darrah. Gettysburg, PA: W. C. Darrah, 1977.

Miscellaneous

ASMP Professional Business Practices in Photography, 1982. Society of Photographers in Communication. New York: ASMP, 1982.

Bulletin of the New York Public Library. Vol. 80, Number 3; Spring 1977. [Photo-illustrated books]

Digital Image Processing. Gonzales and Wintz. Reading, MA: Addison-Wesley Publishing Co., 1977.

Eye and Brain: The Psychology of Seeing. R. L. Gregory. New York: McGraw-Hill Book Co., 1973.

Frontiers of Photography. Life Library of Photography. New York: Time-Life Books, Inc. 1971.

High-Voltage [Kirlian] Photography. 3d ed. H. S. Dakin. San Francisco: H. S. Dakin Co., 1978.

Images, Images, Images: The Book of Programmed Multi-Image Production. Rev. ed. Kodak Publication No. S12. Rochester, NY: Eastman Kodak Co., 1981.

Legal Guide for the Visual Artist. Tad Crawford. New York: Dutton, 1980.

1984 Photographer's Market: Where to Sell Your Photographs. Robert D. Lutz, ed. Cincinnati, OH: Writer's Digest Books, 1984.

Overexposure: Health Hazards in Photography. Susan Shaw. Carmel, CA: The Friends of Photography, 1983.

Perception and Photography. Richard D. Zakia. Rochester, NY: Light Impressions Corp., 1979.

Photography Marketplace, 3d ed. Fred W. McDarrah, ed. New York: The Photographic Arts Center.

Photography: What's the Law. Rev. ed. Robert M. Cavallo and Stuart Kahan. New York: Crown Publishers, Inc., 1979.

Stock Photo and Assignment Source Book, 2d ed. Fred W. McDarrah, ed. New York: The Photographic Arts Center, 1984.

Safe Handling of Photographic Chemicals. Kodak Publication No. J - 4. Rochester, NY: Eastman Kodak Co., 1979.

Selling Your Photography: The Complete Marketing, Business and Legal Guide. Arie Kopelman and Tad Crawford. New York: St. Martin's Press, 1980.

A Survey of Motion Picture, Still Photography, and Graphic Arts Instruction. Kodak Publication No. T-17. Rochester, NY: Eastman Kodak Co., 1981.

Visual Concepts for Photographers. Leslie Stroebel, Richard Zakia, Hollis Todd. Boston: Focal Press, 1980.

The World of Animation. Raul da Silva. Kodak Publication No. S-35. Rochester, NY: Eastman Kodak Co., 1979.

Original Sources (Reprints, facsimile editions, anthologies)
(See also: *Early, Special, Alternative Processes; History*)
[Original publication date in brackets]

The Art and Science of Photography. 23 selections from *On Photography: A Source Book of Photo History in Facsimile.* Beaumont Newhall, ed. Watkins Glen, NY: Century House, 1956.

The Camera Viewed: Writings in Twentieth Century Photography. Vol. 1, Before World War II. Vol. 2, After World War II. Penineh R. Petruck. New York: Dutton, 1979.

Dialogue with Photography. [Interviews with 21 master photographers of the mid-20th c.] Paul Hill and Thomas Cooper. New York: Farrar, Straus, Giroux, 1979.

The Ferrotype and How to Make It. Edward M. Estabrooke [1872]. Dobbs Ferry, NY: Morgan and Morgan, 1972.

An Historical and Descriptive Account of the Daguerreotype and the Diorama. Louis Jacques Mandé Daguerre [1839]. New York: Winter House Ltd., 1971.

The History and Practice of the Art of Photography. Henry H. Snelling [1849]. Dobbs Ferry, NY: Morgan and Morgan, 1970.

How the Other Half Lives: Studies Among the Tenements of New York. With 100 photographs from the Jacob A. Riis collection, the Museum of the City of New York. Jacob A. Riis [1890]. New York: Dover Publications, Inc., 1971.

Illustrated Catalogue of Photographic Equipments and Materials for Amateurs. E. & H. T. Anthony & Co. [1891]. Dobbs Ferry, NY: Morgan and Morgan, nd.

Interviews with [8] *Master Photographers.* James Danziger and Barnaby Conrad, III. New York: Paddington Press Ltd., 1977.

The Literature of Photography Series. Peter C. Bunnell and Robert A. Sobieszek, advisory eds. [Reprints of 62 books in English considered fundamental in recording the development of 19th c. and early 20th c. photography] New York: Arno Press, 1973.

Muybridge's Complete Animal and Human Locomotion: All

781 Plates from the 1887 *Animal Locomotion.* Eadweard Muybridge. Introduction by Anita Ventura Mozley. New York: Dover Publications, Inc., 1979.

Naturalistic Photography for Students of the Art. 3d ed. Including "The Death of Naturalistic Photography" [London, 1891]. Peter Henry Emerson [1899]. New York: Arno Press, 1973.

The Pencil of Nature. William Henry Fox Talbot [1844–1846]. New York: Da Capo Press, 1969.

Photographers on Photography. [Interviews with 13 contemporary photographers] Jerry C. LaPlante. New York: A Drake Publication, Sterling Publishing Co., 1979.

Photographers on Photography: A Critical Anthology [of essays, articles, etc. by leading photographers, 1886–1962]. Nathan Lyons, ed. Englewood Cliffs, NJ: Prentice-Hall, Inc., 1966.

The Photographic Researches of Ferdinand Hurter and Vero C Driffield. [A memorial volume published by the Royal Photographic Society, reprinting the published papers of the subjects, with a history of their early work and a bibliography of later work.] W. B. Ferguson, ed. [1920]. Dobbs Ferry, NY: Morgan and Morgan, 1974.

Photographic Sketchbook of the Civil War. Alexander Gardner [1866 ed.]. New York: Dover Publications, Inc., 1959.

Photographic Views of Sherman's Campaign. George N. Barnard [1866 ed.]. New York: Dover Publications, Inc., 1977.

Photography in Print: Writings from 1816 to the Present. [75 essays and excerpts]. Vicki Goldberg, ed. New York: Touchstone Books, Simon and Schuster, 1981.

Pictorial Effect in Photography. Henry Peach Robinson [1869]. Reprint. Pawlet, VT: Helios, 1971.

Russell's Civil War Photographs: 116 Historic Prints. Andrew J. Russell [ca. 1868]. New York: Dover Publications, Inc., 1982.

The Silver Sunbeam. John Towler [1864]. Dobbs Ferry, NY: Morgan and Morgan, 1969.

The Sources of Modern Photography. Peter C. Bunnell and Robert A. Sobieszek, advisory eds. [Reprints of 51 books in French, German, and English that reflect major technical and artistic developments from the pre-history of photography to the 1940s.] New York: Arno Press, 1979.

The Stereoscope: Its History, Theory, and Construction, Sir David Brewster [1856]. Dobbs Ferry, NY: Morgan and Morgan, 1971.

Street Life in London. Adolphe Smith and John Thompson [1877]. New York: Benjamin Blom, Inc., 1969.

Treatise on Heliochromy. Levi Hill [?1850]. State College, PA: Carnation Press, 1972.

Periodicals

[W: weekly; B-W: bi-weekly; M: monthly; B-M: bi-monthly; Q: quarterly]
The publications of various associations and societies may be distributed only to members, but frequently may be found in major libraries.

AAS Photo Bulletin [3 per year]. American Astronomical Society, 211 Space Science Building, University of Florida, Gainesville, FL 32611.

Afterimage [9 per year]. Visual Studies Workshop, 31 Prince Street, Rochester, NY 14607.

American Cinematographer: International Journal of Motion Picture Photography and Production Techniques [M]. American Society of Cinematographers, 1782 N. Orange Drive, Los Angeles, CA 90028.

American Photographer [M]. 1515 Broadway, New York, NY 10036.

Aperture [Q]. Aperture, Inc., Elm Street, Millerton, NY 12546.

Applied Optics [B-W]. Optical Society of America, Inc., American Institute of Physics, 335 E. 45th St., New York, NY 10017.

Audio-Visual Communications [M]. United Business Publications, Inc., 475 Park Avenue South, New York, New York 10016.

Australian Photography [M]. Globe Publishing Co. Ltd., 381 Pitt Street, Sydney, N.S.W. 2001 Australia.

British Journal of Photography [W]. Henry Greenwood and Co. Ltd., 28 Great James Street, London WC1N 3HL England.

Camera Lucida, The Journal of Photographic Criticism. P.O. Box 176, Sun Prairie, WI 53590.

Camerawork [B-M]. Half Moon Photography Workshop, 119-121 Roman Road, London E2 0QN England.

Camerawork Newsletter. San Francisco Camerawork, 70 Twelfth Street, San Francisco, CA 94103.

Canadian Photography [M]. Maclean-Hunter Ltd., Business Publication Div., 777 Bey Street, Toronto, Ontario M5W 1A7 Canada.

Creative Camera [M]. Coo Press Ltd., 19 Doughty Street, London WC1N 2P7 England.

Czechoslovak Photography [M; English summaries]. Panorama, Holkova 1, 12000 Praha Nove Mssto, Czechoslovakia.

Darkroom Photography [8 per year]. Sheptow Publishing Co., 609 Mission Street, San Francisco, CA 94105.

Exposure, Quarterly Journal of the Society for Photographic Education. P.O. Box 1651, FDR Post Office, New York, NY 10150.

Fotografie: Periodical for Cultural, Aesthetical and Technical Questions in Photography [M; English summaries]. VEB Fotokinoverlag Leipzig, Karl-Heine-Strasse 16, 7031 Leipzig, East Germany.

Fotomuveszet [Q; English summaries]. Lapkiado Vallalat, Lenin korut 9-11, 1073 Budapest, Hungary.

Functional Photography [B-M]. PTN Publishing Corp., 101 Crossways Park West, Woodbury, NY 11797.

History of Photography: An International Quarterly. 294 Materials Research Laboratory, University Park, PA 16802.

Image: Journal of Photography and Motion Pictures [Q]. International Museum of Photography at George Eastman House, 900 East Avenue, Rochester, NY 14607.

Imaging Science. Crane, Russak and Co., 3 East 44th Street, New York, NY 10017.

Indian Journal of Photography [M; English text]. 6/12-A Band Stand Area, Delhi 110009 India.

Industrial Photography [M]. United Business Publications, Inc., 475 Park Avenue South, New York, NY 10016.

Japan Camera Trade News [M; English text]. Genyosha Publications, Inc., 3-18-2 Shibuya, Shibuya-ku, Tokyo 150 Japan.

Journal of Applied Photographic Engineering [B-M]. Society of Photographic Scientists and Engineers [SPSE], 7003 Kilworth Lane, Springfield, VA 22151.

Journal of Evidence Photography. Evidence Photographers International Council, 24 East Main Street, Norwich, NY 13815.

Journal of Micrographics [B-M]. National Micrographics Association, 8728 Colesville Road, Silver Spring, MD 20910.

Journal of Photographic Science [B-M]. Royal Photographic Society of Great Britain, National Center of Photography, The Octagon, Millson Street, Bath BA1 1DN England.

Laser and Unconventional Optics Journal [B-M; English text]. European Abstracts Service, Box 12035, S-402 41, Goeteborg 12, Sweden.

Magazyn Fotograficzny Foto [M; English summaries]. Wydawnictwo "Arkady," Sienkiewicza 14, 00-950 Warsaw, Poland.
Modern Photography [M]. ABS Leisure Magazines, 825 Seventh Avenue, New York, NY 10019.
October: Quarterly Journal of Art, Theory, Criticism and Politics. MIT Press Journals, 28 Carleton Street, Cambridge, MA 02142.
Optical Engineering [B-M]. Society of Photo-Optical Instrumentation Engineers, 405 Fieldston Road, Box 10, Bellingham, WA 98227.
Optical Society of America Journal [M]. American Institute of Physics, 335 East 45th Street, New York, NY 10017.
Petersen's Photographic Magazine [M]. Petersen Publishing Co., 8490 Sunset Boulevard, Los Angeles, CA 90069.
Photo Canada [8 per year]. Maclean-Hunter Ltd., 777 Bay Street, Toronto, Ontario M5W 1A7 Canada.
Photo Communique [Q]. Fine Art Photography Publications Ltd., P.O. Box 129, Station M, Toronto, Ontario M6S 4T2 Canada.
Photogrammetric Engineering and Remote Sensing [M]. American Society of Photogrammetry, 105 North Virginia Avenue, Falls Church, VA 22046.
Photographer's Forum [Q]. 25 West Anapamu Street, Studio E, Santa Barbara, CA 93101.
Photographica [10 per year]. American Photographic Historical Society, P.O. Box 1775 Grand Central Station, New York, NY 10163.
Photographic Abstracts [B-M]. Royal Photographic Society of Great Britain, Scientific and Technical Group, 62 Chelmsford Road, Shenfield, Brentwood, Essex, England.
Photographic Journal [B-M]. Royal Photographic Society of Great Britain, National Center of Photography, The Octagon, Millson Street, Bath BA1 1DN England.
Photographiconservation [Q]. Technical and Education Center of the Graphic Arts, Rochester Institute of Technology, One Lomb Memorial Drive, Rochester, NY 14623.
Photographic Science and Engineering [B-M]. Society of Photographic Scientists and Engineers, 7003 Kilworth Lane, Springfield, VA 22151.
Photographic Trade News [B-W]. PTN Publishing Corporation, 101 Crossways Park West, Woodbury, NY 11797.
Photomethods [M]. Ziff-Davis Publishing Co., One Park Avenue, New York, NY 10016.
Picturescope: Quarterly Journal of the Picture Division. Special Libraries Association, P.O. Box 50119, F Street Station, Tariff Commission Building, Washington, DC 20004.
Popular Photography [M]. Ziff-Davis Publishing Co., One Park Avenue, New York, NY 10016.
The Print Collector's Newsletter [B-M]. 16 East 82nd Street, New York, NY 10028.
Print Letter [B-M; English text]. International Forum for Fine Art Photography, Zelgstrasse 14, P.O. Box 1343, CH-8036 Zurich, Switzerland.
The Professional Photographer [M]. Journal of the Professional Photographers of America, PPA Publications, Inc., 1090 Executive Way, Des Plaines, IL 60018.
PSA Journal [M]. Photography Society of America, Inc., 2005 Walnut Street, Philadelphia, PA 19103.
The Rangefinder [M]. 1312 Lincoln Boulevard, Box 1703, Santa Monica, CA 90406.
Reprographics [B-M]. Mass Media Publications, Inc., Box 969, West New York, NJ 07093.
SPIE Proceedings [50 per year]. Society of Photo-Optical Instrumentation Engineers, 405 Fieldston Road, Box 10, Bellingham, WA 98227.
Technical Photography [M]. PTN Publishing Corp., 101 Crossways Park West, Woodbury, NY 11797.

Reference

[Macmillan Biographical Encyclopedia of] Photographic Artists and Innovators. Turner Browne and Elaine Partnow, eds. New York: Macmillan Publishing Co., 1983.
Contemporary Photographers. George Walsh, Colin Naylor, Michael Held, eds. New York: St. Martin's Press, 1982.
Dictionary of Contemporary Photography. Leslie Stroebel and Hollis N. Todd. Dobbs Ferry, NY: Morgan and Morgan, 1974.
Dictionary of Photographic Technologies. D. A. Spencer, ed. Boston and London: Focal Press, 1973.
Dictionary of Photography in Three Languages: English, French, and German. A. S. H. Craeybeckx, ed. New York: Elsevier-North Holland Publishing Co., 1965.
Dictionnaire des Photographes. Carole Naggar. Paris: Editions du Seuil, 1982.
Die deutsche Photoliteratur: German Photographic Literature, 1839–1978; a Bibliography. Frank Heidtmann, Hans-Joachim Bresemann, Rolf H. Krauss, Munich: K. G. Saur, 1980.
Encyclopedia of Practical Photography. 14 vols. New York: Amphoto and Eastman Kodak Co., 1977.
Focal Encyclopedia of Photography. Desk ed. Leonard Gaunt and Paul Petzold, eds. London: Focal Press, 1980.
Illustrated Dictionary of Photography. D. Backhouse, C. Marsh, J. Tait, G. Wakefield. London: Fountain Press; Dobbs Ferry, NY: Morgan and Morgan, 1972.
International Glossary of Photographic Terms. [In English, German, Spanish, French, Italian, Dutch, Portugese and Spanish]. Kodak Publication NO. AA-12. Rochester, NY: Eastman Kodak Co., 1973.
International Lighting Vocabulary. 3d ed. International Committee on Illumination [ICI/CIE]. Paris: Commission International de l'Eclairage, 1970.
Library Catalog of the International Museum of Photography at the George Eastman House. Boston: G. K. Hall and Co., 1982.
Photographic Facts and Formulas. E. J. Wall and F. I. Jordan. Rev. and rewritten by John S. Carroll. New York: Amphoto, 1975.
Photographic Literature: An International Bibliographic Guide to General and Specialized Literature on Photography. Vol. 1, 1727–1960. Vol. 2, 1960–1970. Albert Boni, ed. Dobbs Ferry, NY: Morgan and Morgan, 1962 (v. 1); 1972 (v. 2).
Photography Books Index: A Subject Guide to Photo Anthologies. Martha Moss. Metuchen, NJ: Scarecrow Press, Grolier Pub. Co., 1980.
Photo-Lab Index. Lifetime looseleaf edition.[Updated with quarterly supplements.] Dobbs Ferry, NY: Morgan and Morgan.

Scientific, Technical and Specialized Applications

Amateur Photomicroscopy. M. I. Walker. London: Focal Press, 1972.
Applied Infrared Photography. Kodak Publication No. M-28. Rochester, NY: Eastman Kodak Co., 1981.
The Art and Science of Medical Radiography. 5th ed. James A. Morgan. St. Louis, MO: Catholic Health Association, 1977.
Basic Scientific Photography. Kodak Publication N-9. Rochester, NY: Eastman Kodak Co., 1978.
Basic Veterinary Field and Clinical Photography. Kodak Publication No. M3-715. Rochester, NY: Eastman Kodak Co., 1980.

Camera Techniques in Archaeology. V. M. Conlon. New York: St. Martin's Press, Inc., 1973.

Clinical Photography. Kodak Publication No. N-3. Rochester, NY: Eastman Kodak Co., 1972.

Close-up Photography and Photomacrography. Kodak Publication No. N-12. Rochester, NY: Eastman Kodak Co., 1977.

Electron Microscopy and Photography. Kodak Publication No. P-236. Rochester, NY: Eastman Kodak Co., 1973.

Electron Microscopy in Human Medicine. Vol. 1, Instrumentation and Techniques. Jan Vincents Johanenssen, ed. New York: McGraw-Hill Book Co., 1978.

Electrophotography, 2d ed. R. M. Schaffert. London and Boston: Focal Press, 1975.

Elements of Photogrammetry. Paul R. Wolf. New York: McGraw-Hill, 1974.

The Fundamentals of Radiography. 12th ed. Kodak Publication No. M1-18. Rochester, NY: Eastman Kodak Co., 1980.

A Guide to Medical Photography. Peter Hansell, ed. Baltimore: University Park Press, 1979.

Handbook for Scientific Photography. Alfred A. Blaker. San Francisco: W. H. Freeman and Co., 1977.

Handbook of Stroboscopy. Concord, MA: General Radio Corporation, 1966.

High-Speed Photography. Kodak Publication NO. G-44. Rochester, NY: Eastman Kodak Co., 1981.

Imaging Systems: Mechanisms and Applications of Established and New Photosensitive Processes. K. I. and R. E. Jacobson. New York: Halsted, 1976.

Interpretation of Aerial Photographs. 3d ed. Thomas E. Avery. Minneapolis: Burgess Publishing Co., 1977.

An Introduction to Radiographic Technique. Patricia A. Myers. New York: Praeger Publishers, Holt, Rinehart and Winston, 1980.

The Making and Evaluation of Holograms. Nils Abramson. New York: Academic Press, 1981.

Manual of Photogrammetry. 4th ed. Chester C. Slama, ed. Falls Church, VA: American Society of Photogrammetry, 1980.

Medical Infrared Photography. Kodak Publication N-1. Rochester, NY: Eastman Kodak Co., 1973.

Photochromism: Optical and Photographic Applications. George Henry Dorian and A. F. Wiebe. Boston: Focal Press, 1970.

Photographic Information Recording. Helmut Frieser. New York: Halsted Press, John Wiley and Sons, Inc., 1975.

Photographic Recording of High Speed Processes. Aleksandr S. Dubovik. Oxford and New York: Oxford University Press, 1968.

Photographic Surveillance Techniques for Law Enforcement Agencies. Kodak Publication No. M-8. Rochester, NY: Eastman Kodak Co., 1972.

Photographic Techniques in Scientific Research, 2 vols. J. Cruise and A. Newman, eds. New York: Academic Press, Inc., 1973 (v. 1); 1976 (v. 2).

Photography as a Tool. Life Library of Photography. New York: Time-Life Books, Inc., 1971.

Photography in Archaeological Research. Elmer Harp, Jr., ed. School of American Research Advanced Seminar Series. Albuquerque: University of New Mexico Press, 1975.

Photography Through the Microscope. Kodak Publication No. P-2. Rochester, NY: Eastman Kodak Co., 1980.

Photomicroscopy: A Comprehensive Treatise. 2 vols. R. P. Loveland. New York: John Wiley and Sons, 1970.

Practical Guide to Photometry. Measurement and Testing Guides Series. New York: Illuminating Engineering Society, nd.

Professional Techniques in Dental Photography. Kodak Publication No. M3-717. Rochester, NY: Eastman Kodak Co., 1980.

Schlieren Photography. Kodak Publication No. P-11. Rochester, NY: Eastman Kodak Co., 1981.

Techniques of Microphotography. Kodak Publication No. P-52. Rochester, NY: Eastman Kodak Co., 1981.

Thermal Imaging Techniques. Peter E. Glaser and Raymond F. Walker. New York: Plenum Publishing Corp., 1964.

Thermal Imaging Systems. J. M. Loyd ed. New York: Plenum Publishing Corp., 1975.

Ultraviolet and Fluorescence Photography. Kodak Publication No. M27. Rochester, NY: Eastman Kodak Co., 1974.

Understanding Holography. Michael Wenyon. New York: Arco Publishing Co., 1978.

Using Photography to Preserve Evidence. Kodak Publication No. M-2. Rochester, NY: Eastman Kodak Co., 1982.

Visual Anthropology: Photography as a Research Method. John Collier, Jr. New York: Holt, Rinehart and Winston, 1967.

Theory and Scientific Principles
(See also: *Color*)

Basic Chemistry of Photographic Processing, Parts 1 and 2. Kodak Publication No. Z23-ED. Rochester, NY: Eastman Kodak Co., 1979.

Electronic Flash, Strobe. Harold E. Edgerton. New York: McGraw-Hill Book Co., 1970.

Handbook of Photographic Science and Engineering. Woodlief Thomas, Jr., ed. Society of Photographic Scientists and Engineers. New York: John Wiley and Sons-Interscience, 1973.

Light and Film. Life Library of Photography. New York: Time-Life Books, Inc., 1971.

The Manual of Photography, 7th ed., rev. R. E. Jacobson, S. F. Ray, G. G. Attridge, N. R. Axford. Boston and London: Focal Press, 1978.

Modern Photographic Processing. 2 vols. Grant Haist. New York: John Wiley and Sons-Interscience, 1979.

Monobath Manual. Grant Haist. Dobbs Ferry, NY: Morgan and Morgan, 1966.

Photographic Chemistry in Black-and-White and Color Photography. Rev. ed. George T. Eaton. Dobbs Ferry, NY: Morgan and Morgan, 1981.

The Photographic Lens. H. M. Brandt. London: Focal Press, 1968.

The Photographic Lens. Sidney F. Ray. London and Boston: Focal Press, 1979.

Photographic Optics: Modern Approach to the Techniques of Definition. 15th rev. and enlarged ed. Arthur Cox. London and Boston: Focal Press, 1974.

Photographic Sensitometry: The Study of Tone Reproduction. Rev. ed. Hollis N. Todd and Richard Zakia. Dobbs Ferry, NY: Morgan and Morgan, 1981.

Photography Theory and Practice. L. P. Clerc. Completely rev. and enlarged. D. A. Spencer, ed. London: Focal Press, 1970.

Physical Optics in Photography. Georg Franke. Boston: Focal Press, 1966.

Processing Chemicals and Formulas [for black-and-white photography]. Kodak Publication No. J1. Rochester, NY: Eastman Kodak Co., 1977.

The Theory of the Photographic Process, 4th ed. T. H. James, ed. New York: Macmillan Publishing Co., 1977.

Color separation, printing, and binding by
Toppan Printing Co. (H.K.) Ltd., Hong Kong